Glencoe's Young Living
builds personal and management skills

Student Edition
EXPLORATORY FAMILY AND CONSUMER SCIENCES TEXT

Young Living
covers the areas of:

Personal Development

Relationships

Consumer Skills and Home Management

Foods and Nutrition

Clothing and Textiles

Over 250 activities highlighting *Teens Making a Difference, A Global View, Consumer Focus, Friends and Family,* and *Curriculum Connections* encourage discussion, promote critical thinking, and provide hands-on learning opportunities.

CUSTOMIZED FOR MIDDLE SCHOOL/ JUNIOR HIGH LEARNERS

Short, self-contained lessons can be used separately or sequentially, allowing you total flexibility in planning.

Engaging graphics and informative illustrations motivate students and provide content in a visually appealing format.

Side-bar features provide practical, how-to tips to guide students in managing their lives and making healthy, responsible decisions.

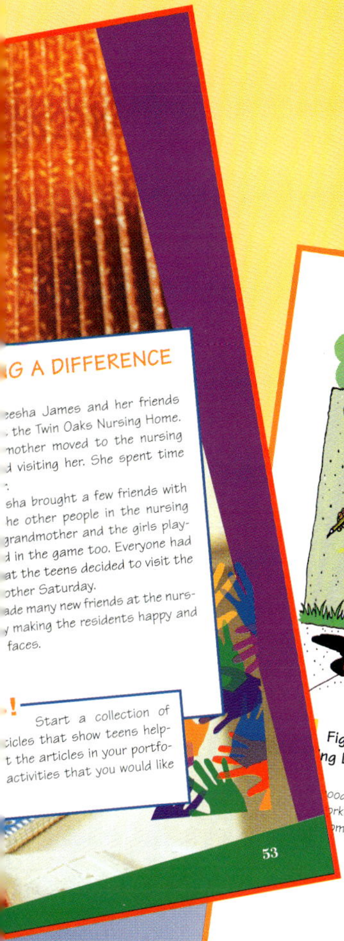
G A DIFFERENCE

...esha James and her friends ... the Twin Oaks Nursing Home. ...mother moved to the nursing ... visiting her. She spent time ...

...sha brought a few friends with ...he other people in the nursing ...grandmother and the girls play... ...in the game too. Everyone had ...at the teens decided to visit the ...other Saturday. ...ade many new friends at the nurs... ...making the residents happy and ...faces.

Start a collection of ...ticles that show teens help... ...t the articles in your portfo... ...activities that you would like

53

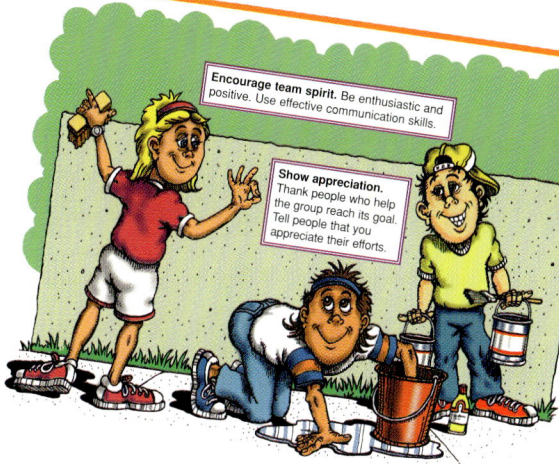

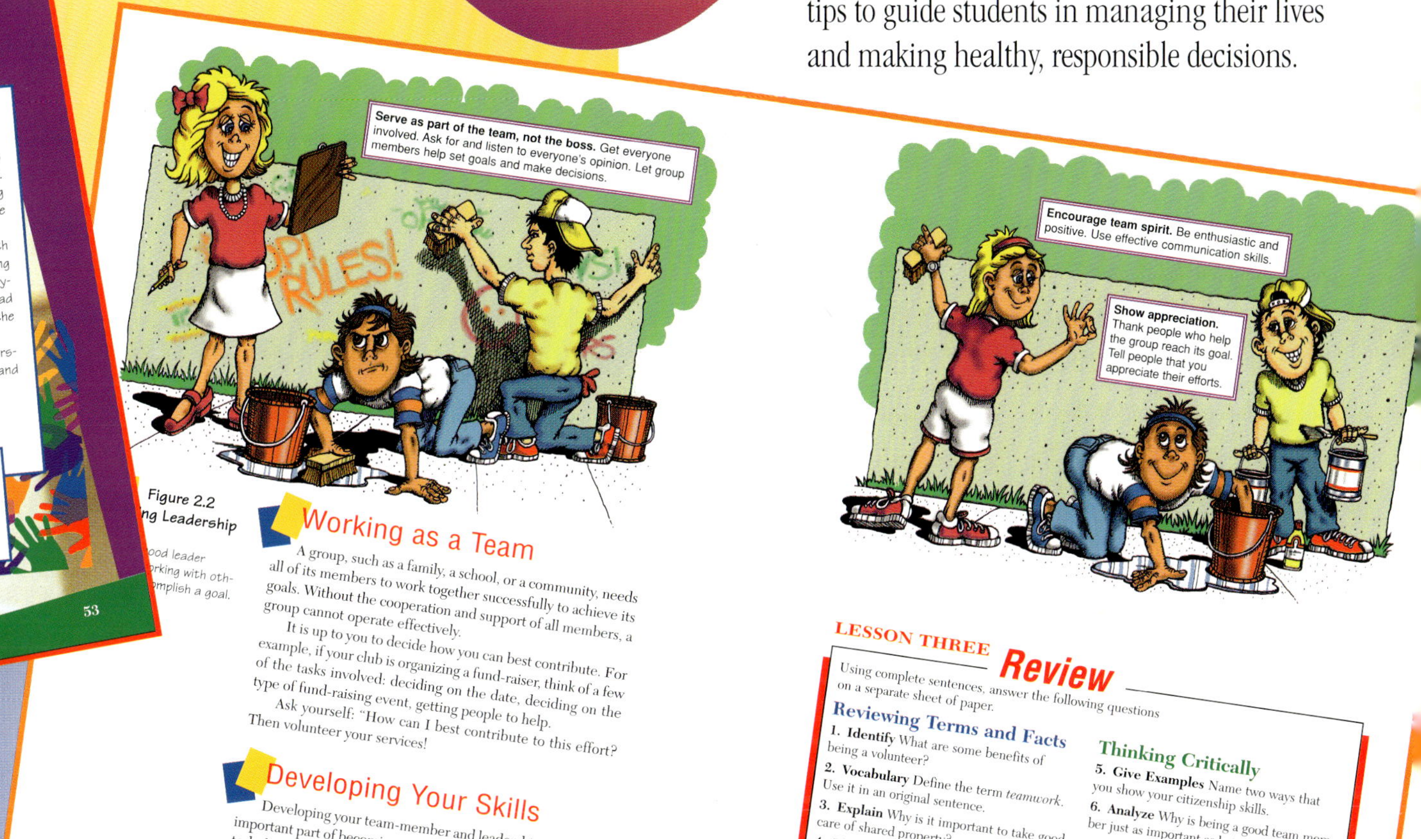

Serve as part of the team, not the boss. Get everyone involved. Ask for and listen to everyone's opinion. Let group members help set goals and make decisions.
Encourage team spirit. Be enthusiastic and positive. Use effective communication skills.
Show appreciation. Thank people who help the group reach its goal. Tell people that you appreciate their efforts.

Figure 2.2
...ng Leadership
...ood leader ...rking with oth... ...mplish a goal.

Working as a Team

A group, such as a family, a school, or a community, needs all of its members to work together successfully to achieve its goals. Without the cooperation and support of all members, a group cannot operate effectively.

It is up to you to decide how you can best contribute. For example, if your club is organizing a fund-raiser, think of a few of the tasks involved: deciding on the date, deciding on the type of fund-raising event, getting people to help.

Ask yourself: "How can I best contribute to this effort?" Then volunteer your services!

Developing Your Skills

Developing your team-member and leadership skil... important part of becoming an adult. When you u... to help others, you feel good about yoursel... ...ble experience.

40

LESSON THREE **Review**

Using complete sentences, answer the following questions on a separate sheet of paper.

Reviewing Terms and Facts

1. **Identify** What are some benefits of being a volunteer?
2. **Vocabulary** Define the term *teamwork*. Use it in an original sentence.
3. **Explain** Why is it important to take good care of shared property?
4. **Identify** List three ways to build leadership skills.

Thinking Critically

5. **Give Examples** Name two ways that you show your citizenship skills.
6. **Analyze** Why is being a good team member just as important as being a good leader?

Applying Concepts

7. Select a person whom you consider to be a leader. Write a list of the leadership qualities that you think the person has. Is this person a formal or informal leader? Write a list of guidelines that other people could use to develop leadership skills.

LESSON THREE: BEING A CITIZEN AND A LEADER 41

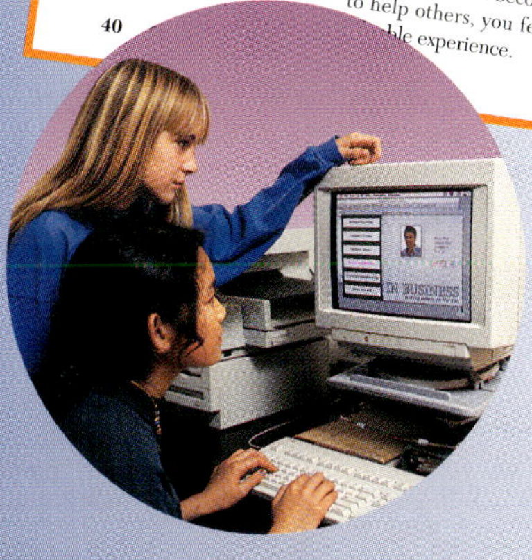

IN BUSINESS

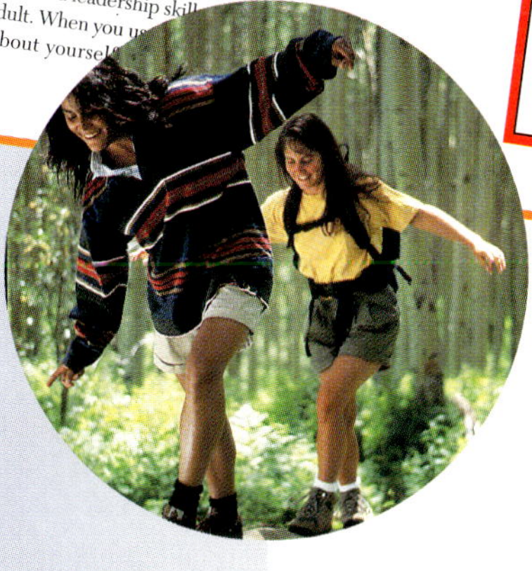

Teacher's Wraparound Edition

REDUCES PREPARATION TIME

NEW! Interleaf chapter planning pages list program resources for each lesson and provide culminating activities for Performance Assessment, Family and Community, and School to Work.

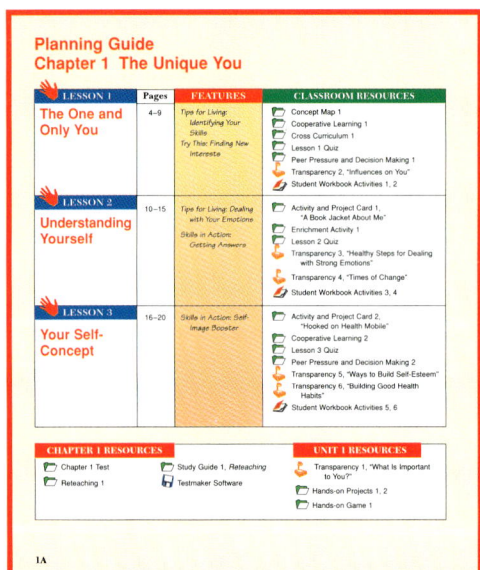

CHAPTER 1, LESSON 1

USING VISUALS
Have students study the illustration showing the factors that influence who they are in Figure 1.1. Ask volunteers to discuss the influence that makes them unique. Then have students create a drawing similar to the one shown. Their illustrations should picture themselves and the specific influences that help determine who they are. Display the illustrations on a bulletin board.

L1 Using Transparencies
Present Color Transparency 2, "Influences on You," in the TCR. Use this overhead visual to reinforce concepts from this lesson.

L2 Science
Explain to students that whether they have straight, wavy, or curly hair depends on the shape of their hair shafts. This trait is a result of heredity. An oval shaft causes wavy hair. A round shaft causes straight hair. A flat shaft causes curly hair. Have students use a magnifying glass or microscope to view a strand of their hair. Ask them to determine the shape of their hair shafts based on the shape of this hair strand. Ask students how their environment can change the inherited characteristics of their hair. (Humidity can cause hair to become curlier or straighten. Sunlight can lighten hair color. People can have their hair straightened, permed, or colored.)

L2 Social Studies Connection
Assign Cross-Curriculum Activity 1 in the TCR. Students research holidays from various cultures in this activity.

Figure 1.1 Influences on You
Many factors influence who you are. Which of these factors have influenced you the most?

Think about your interests, hobbies, and abilities. Some of them are **acquired,** or *learned from the people and things around you*. Perhaps your sister taught you how to skate. Maybe a friend sparked your interest in computers. These are examples of acquired skills or interests. Name three abilities that you have acquired or learned.

You have some characteristics that are influenced by both heredity and your environment. For example, body build may be inherited, but the athletic skill to play a particular sport is acquired.

Culture

Your culture also influences the person you become. **Culture** refers to *the ways of thinking, acting, dressing, and speaking shared by a group of people*. Cultures may be based

6   CHAPTER 1: THE UNIQUE YOU

TECHNOLOGY UPDATE

Crime investigators are recently starting using and ... to identify ... that there are trillions of different ways that the DNA molecule could be put together. Therefore, many people believe that it is highly unlikely that two people would be found with identical DNA molecules. Some critics, however, believe that techniques used to identify the patterns in DNA molecule are not absolutely reliable.

TIPS for living

IDENTIFYING YOUR SKILLS

Another name for an acquired ability is a skill. Everyone has skills. You might be good at playing soccer, or you might be a good listener. Identifying your skills gives you confidence to try new activities. Ask yourself the following questions.

- What activities do I most enjoy?
- What things seem easiest for me to learn?
- In what subjects do I get my best grades?
- What do my family and friends compliment me on?
- What tasks do my family and friends ask me to help them do?

on race, ethnic group, geographic location, or social class. You may not even think about your culture until you meet someone who speaks a different language at home or celebrates other holidays from yours.

Your culture may influence the food you eat or the holidays you celebrate. What might be some benefits of learning about other cultures?

Family Background

Your family has one of the strongest influences on the person you become. Are you an only child, or do you have brothers or sisters? Are you the oldest, the youngest, or in the middle? What activities do you do with family members? How important is spending time together with family members? These questions suggest some of the ways you are influenced by your family.

LESSON ONE: THE ONE AND ONLY YOU 7

MEETING STUDENT DIVERSITY

Cultural Perspectives Ask students to give examples of cultural groups, such as African Americans, Native Americans, Christians, Muslims, and so on. Point out that besides race, ethnicity, geographic location, or social class, cultures may also be based on occupations, religions, interests, or age. Have students determine all the cultural groups to which they belong. Emphasize that cultural differences add to the interesting diversity we experience every day.

CHAPTER 1, LESSON 1

TIPS for living
Allow students time to answer the questions that will help them identify their skills. Ask volunteers to name the skills they identified.

DID YOU KNOW
A simple strand of your hair can tell many things about who you are. Scientists can run tests on a strand of your hair to determine your age, gender, and race. Laboratory tests using strands of hair can also determine whether or not the person has been using certain types of drugs.

L2 Social Studies
Have students learn about the culture of another young person. Provide them with the addresses of organizations that connect young people from different countries who want to be pen pals. (World Pen Pals, 1690 Como Ave., St. Paul, MN 55108, or International Pen Friends, Box 65, Homecrest Station, Brooklyn, NY 11229; this organization has special services for the blind and permanently handicapped.) Encourage students to write letters to their pen pal describing their own culture and asking questions about their pen pal's culture.

L1 Discussing
Point out to students that their friends and peers also influence what kind of person they become. Ask students to give examples of ways their friends and peers influence them.

7

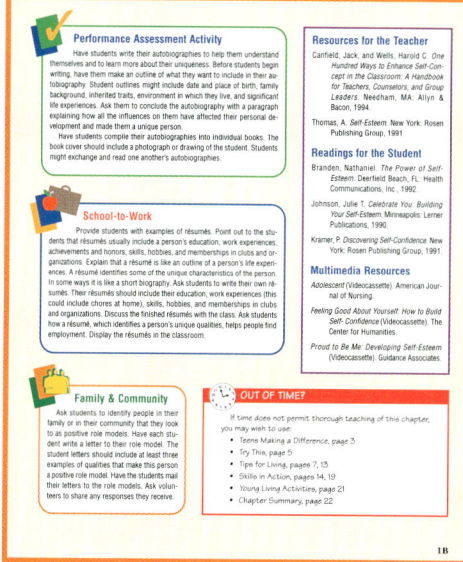

ORGANIZED FOR FLEXIBILITY

Multi-leveled teaching strategies help you guide students and adapt lessons to meet various learning styles and ability levels.

Offers solutions to accommodate diverse schedules and student interests.

Loads of suggestions and ideas that enable you to expand the lessons, effectively evaluate students' progress, keep the class lively and interesting, and reteach or expand your students' learning.

Teacher's Classroom Resources

ADDITIONAL MATERIALS FOR EFFECTIVE TEACHING

STUDENT WORKBOOK
Activity worksheets for each lesson reinforce content and strengthen basic academic skills. Study guides help ensure mastery of each chapter.

TEACHER'S CLASSROOM RESOURCES
The expanded teaching support materials include hundreds of resources all correlated at point-of-use in the Teacher's Wraparound Edition for convenient planning. You will find reproducible masters, games and exercises for reinforcing concepts and testing skills, projects and activities, and more. Supplements include:

Peer Pressure and Decision-Making Activities
Cooperative Learning Activities
Cross-Curriculum Activities
Lesson Plans
Concept Mapping Activities
Reteaching Activities
Enrichment Activities
Student Workbook
Hands-on Projects and Games
Activity and Project Cards
Food and Sewing Labs
Lesson Quizzes
Chapter Tests

Multimedia Components

Color Transparency Package

72 full color transparencies plus an activity booklet with teaching strategies for each transparency.

Testmaker Software

A databank of computerized test items allows you to construct your own tests, quizzes, and review sheets.

ABCNews InterActive™ Bar Code Correlation

A bar code correlation to the exceptional ABCNews InterActive™ Videodisc Series, *Understanding Ourselves,* provides further exploration of complex health issues for the following videodiscs:
Alcohol, Drugs and Substance Abuse, Food and Nutrition, Health: AIDS, Teenage Sexuality, Tobacco, and *Violence Prevention*

Professional Family and Consumer Sciences Series

Dealing with Sensitive Issues

Linking Home, School, and Community

Meeting the Special Needs of Students

Glencoe's Young Living
A Program for Building a Strong Foundation of Personal and Management Skills

Student Edition	0-02-642816-4
Teacher's Wraparound Edition	0-02-642817-2
Teacher's Classroom Resources	0-02-642819-9
Peer Pressure and Decision-Making Activites	0-02-642830-X
Cooperative Learning Activities	0-02-642829-6
Cross-Curriculum Activities	0-02-642828-8
Lesson Plans	0-02-642841-5
Concept Mapping Activities	0-02-642827-X
Reteaching Activities	0-02-642851-2
Enrichment Activities	0-02-642826-1
Student Workbook	0-02-642818-0
Student Workbook (TAE)	0-02-642820-2
Hands-on Projects and Games	0-02-642834-2
Activity and Project Cards	0-02-642839-3
Food and Sewing Labs	0-02-642833-4
Lesson Quizzes	0-02-642824-5
Chapter Tests	0-02-642825-3
Testmaker, Apple	0-02-642822-9
Testmaker, IBM	0-02-642823-7
Testmaker, Macintosh	0-02-642821-0
Color Transparency Package	0-02-642836-9
ABCNews InterActive™ Bar Code Correlation	0-02-642842-3

Professional Family and Consumer Sciences Series

Linking Home, School, and Community	0-02-642850-4
Meeting the Special Needs of Students	0-02-675461-4
Dealing with Sensitive Issues	0-02-642798-2

FCS 91264-4

GLENCOE
McGraw-Hill

For more information, contact your nearest regional office or call 1-800-334-7344

1. Northeast Region
Glencoe/McGraw-Hill
15 Trafalgar Square #201
Nashua, NH 03063-1968
Phone: 603-880-4701
Phone: 800-424-3451
Fax: 603-595-0204

2. Mid-Atlantic Region
Glencoe/McGraw-Hill
P.O. Box 458
Hightstown, NJ 08520-0458
Phone: 609-426-5560
Phone: 800-553-7515
Fax: 609-426-7063

3. Atlantic-Southeast Region
Glencoe/McGraw-Hill
Brookside Park
One Harbison Way, Suite 101
Columbia, SC 29212
Phone: 803-732-2365
Phone: 800-731-2365
Fax: 803-732-4582

4. Southeast Region
Glencoe/McGraw-Hill
6510 Jimmy Carter Boulevard
Norcross, GA 30071
Phone: 770-446-7493
Phone: 800-982-3992
Fax: 770-446-2356

5. Mid-America Region
Glencoe/McGraw-Hill
936 Eastwind Drive
Westerville, OH 43081
Phone: 614-890-1111
Phone: 800-848-1567
Fax: 614-899-4905

6. Great Lakes Region
Glencoe/McGraw-Hill
846 East Algonquin Road
Schaumburg, IL 60173
Phone: 708-397-8448
Phone: 800-762-4876
Fax: 708-397-9472

7. Mid-Continent Region
Glencoe/McGraw-Hill
846 East Algonquin Road
Schaumburg, IL 60173
Phone: 708-397-8448
Phone: 800-762-4876
Fax: 708-397-9472

8. Southwest Region
Glencoe/McGraw-Hill
320 Westway Place, Suite 550
Arlington, TX 76018
Phone: 817-784-2113
Phone: 800-828-5096
Fax: 817-784-2116

9. Texas Region
Glencoe/McGraw-Hill
320 Westway Place, Suite 550
Arlington, TX 76018
Phone: 817-784-2100
Phone: 800-828-5096
Fax: 817-784-2116

10. Western Region
Glencoe/McGraw-Hill
709 E. Riverpark Lane, Suite 150
Boise, ID 83706
Phone: 208-368-0300
Phone: 800-452-6126
Fax: 208-368-0303
Includes Alaska

11. California Region
Glencoe/McGraw-Hill
15319 Chatsworth Street
P. O. Box 9609
Mission Hills, CA 91346
Phone: 818-898-1391
Phone: 800-423-9534
Fax: 818-898-3864
Includes Hawaii

Glencoe Catholic School Region
Glencoe/McGraw-Hill
25 Crescent Street, 1st Floor
Stamford, CT 06906
Phone: 203-964-9109
Phone: 800-551-8766
Fax: 203-967-3108

Canada
McGraw-Hill Ryerson Ltd.
300 Water Street
Whitby, Ontario
L1N 9B6, Canada
Phone: 905-430-5088
Fax: 905-430-5194

International
The McGraw-Hill Companies
International Marketing
1221 Avenue of the Americas
28th Floor
New York, NY 10020
Phone: 212-512-3641
Fax: 212-512-2186

DoDDS and Pacific Territories
McGraw-Hill School
Publishing Company
600 Delran Parkway
Delran, NJ 08075
Phone: 609-764-4586
Fax: 609-764-4587

C 4/96

Young Living

SEVENTH EDITION

TEACHER'S WRAPAROUND EDITION

Teacher's Manual

GLENCOE
McGraw-Hill

New York, New York   Columbus, Ohio   Mission Hills, California   Peoria, Illinois

Teacher Reviewers

Joanne Furniss
Family and Consumer Sciences Educator
Glassboro Intermediate School
Glassboro, New Jersey

Debbie Harvey
Home Economics Teacher
Pleasanton Middle School
Pleasanton, California

Bonnie Jenuine
Home Economics Teacher
Carpinteria Middle School
Carpinteria, California

Brenda W. Owen
Life Skills Teacher
Morton Middle School
Lexington, Kentucky

Elaine S. Smith
Family and Consumer Sciences Educator
Department Chair
Stamford Central School
Stamford, New York

Glencoe/McGraw-Hill
A Division of The McGraw-Hill Companies

Copyright © 1997 by Glencoe/McGraw-Hill.
All rights reserved. Except as permitted under the United States Copyright Act, no part of this publication may be reproduced or distributed in any form or by any means, or stored in a database or retrieval system, without prior written permission from the publisher.

Send all inquiries to:
Glencoe/McGraw-Hill
15319 Chatsworth Street
P.O. Box 9609
Mission Hills, California 91346-9609

ISBN 0-02-642817-2 (Teacher's Wraparound Edition)
ISBN 0-02-642816-4 (Student Edition)

1 2 3 4 5 6 7 8 9   VHJ   02 01 00 99 98 97 96

Table of Contents

New Directions in Family and Consumer Sciences T4

Overview of *Young Living* T4

Inside the Student Text T6

Teacher's Wraparound Edition T10

Understanding the Teacher's Classroom Resources T13

Professional Notes T15

Course Presentation T19

New Directions in Family and Consumer Sciences

As a teacher in the field of Family and Consumer Sciences—or, as it has more commonly been known, Home Economics—you are aware of the many changes that have occurred in recent years. The lives of your students have become increasingly demanding and diverse. To succeed on their own, students need a strong foundation of personal and management skills.

Basic life management skills help students function and prosper as responsible teens and in their independent, postsecondary lives. Life management skills involve building self-esteem, making healthy decisions, using refusal skills, respecting cultural and ethnic differences, building teamwork, making wise consumer choices, managing stress, and more. As teens become adults, they also face the challenge of learning how to balance these skills with many other concerns and responsibilities, such as balancing the responsibilities of work and family.

Overview of *Young Living*

Welcome to the Seventh Edition of *Young Living*. In this revised and updated program, *Young Living* has been designed to meet the unique needs and characteristics of middle school and junior high students. Exciting new features and an expanded, activity-oriented program of components make *Young Living* an even more versatile tool for teaching and learning.

Young Living provides you with instructional flexibility. The varied-level activities, hands-on orientation, and practical coverage of material enable you to use the book in a variety of ways. Throughout the text, life-management, critical thinking, and decision-making skills are emphasized. At the same time students experience practical application of the basic skills—reading, writing, math, and science.

Young Living is an exploratory program that covers the comprehensive content of family and consumer sciences curriculum. This program encourages learning because of its outstanding visual appeal, its clear writing style, and its use of concrete examples. The shorter, concise lessons accommodate the attention spans of middle school/junior high students and help them grasp individual concepts. The use of infographics (teaching visuals that combine text and art, or text and photos) in every chapter also enables students to grasp various concepts and skills.

Young Living is based on several goals:

- **Provide a flexible instructional program.** The configuration and topic emphasis of the middle school/junior high family and consumer sciences program varies greatly from school district to school district. The *Young Living* program can easily be adapted to a 9-week, 18-week, or 36-week course. In addition, the program will accommodate a topical emphasis, such as life-management skills, relationships, or health and safety.

- **Develop an exploratory, comprehensive family and consumer sciences textbook.** For many students the middle school/junior high program is the only exposure that they will have to become familiar with family and consumer sciences content. The *Young Living* program enables family and consumer sciences teachers to provide experiences in all areas of family and consumer sciences content and to select lessons to fit their particular curriculum needs and emphasis. The short, concise lessons give students exposure to the scope of the family and consumer sciences curriculum, allowing them to survey the broad themes and topics of potential interest to them.
- **Create a program that includes a variety of learning experiences.** A wide range of skill levels exist in the middle school/junior high classroom. Therefore, *Young Living* provides a variety of learning experiences that include independent, group, and community experiences. *Young Living* strives for practical, activity-oriented lessons that appeal to the action-oriented characteristics of the young adolescent learner.
- **Promote self-esteem and responsibility.** As the middle school/junior high students move away from the comfort of the self-contained elementary classroom and struggle with self-identity and peer pressure, the need for a learning environment that enhances a positive self-concept is critical. The variety of activities in *Young Living* encourages a positive classroom environment. These activities visually reinforce the material, require cooperative work among students, and provide hands-on experiences, which increases the chances for success for all students.
- **Provide culminating, hands-on projects.** Each chapter offers culminating hands-on projects that integrate all learning and are appropriate for an activity-driven course.

In this Seventh Edition the basic goals and approaches of *Young Living* are carried out in a complete program for learning and teaching. The program includes:

- **Student Text.** This 576-page book introduces students to comprehensive family and consumer sciences principles and content.
- **Teacher's Wraparound Edition.** This version of the student text includes a special wraparound lesson plan format and special features. This puts teaching strategies and background information at your fingertips and references teaching resources at point of use.
- **Teacher's Classroom Resources.** This separate component includes reteaching, cooperative learning activities, hands-on projects, testing programs, and other educational resources.
- **Student Workbook.** The activities in this component help reinforce content and maximize students' learning.
- **Testmaker Software.** This computer program helps you vary and personalize tests quickly and easily.
- **Color Transparency Packet.** This packet includes 72 ready-to-use color transparencies, which are an effective way to introduce units and chapters, enhance lesson content, and stimulate classroom discussion.

Inside the Student Text

The *Young Living* student text provides an appealing format for introducing students to comprehensive family and consumer sciences concepts. The written presentation is supplemented by lively photographs, which help maintain interest. The organization of the text, the special features, and the visual presentation combine to make the book a positive learning experience for all students.

Understanding the Organization of the Text

UNITS The text is divided into five units. Each unit brings together chapters that have a common theme. They can be used in sequence or presented in the format that best fits your needs. The units are:

Unit 1: *Personal Development* —building self-concept, making decisions, developing citizenship and leadership skills, setting personal and career goals.

Unit 2: *Relationships* —understanding family and friends; communication and conflict-resolution skills; and understanding and caring for children.

Unit 3: *Consumer Skills and Home Management* —managing resources, time, and money; making wise consumer choices; keeping a home clean and safe; and protecting the environment.

Unit 4: *Foods and Nutrition* —following healthy guidelines, making informed food choices, and preparing nutritious snacks and meals.

Unit 5: *Clothing and Textiles* —planning a wardrobe, making clothing choices, and using clothing construction skills.

CHAPTERS This edition of *Young Living* includes 18 chapters. Each chapter contains three to six self-contained lessons and teaches about a major topic. Built-in learning aids in each chapter include:

- **Chapter Opener.** Each chapter begins with a two-page spread that includes a full-page photograph and an article titled "Teens Making a Difference." This article relates stories of teens who are active in their families, schools, or communities, promoting leadership skills and demonstrating responsibility.

- **Chapter Review.** At the end of each chapter is a two-page review of the chapter materials. It is divided into the parts noted to the right.

LESSONS Each chapter is divided into self-contained lessons designed for classroom management and flexibility. Each lesson includes the following built-in learning aids:

- **Lesson Objectives.** Objectives appear at the beginning of each lesson. These are written in an informal style and help focus students' reading.

- **Words to Know.** The Words to Know section at the beginning of each lesson introduces important content-related vocabulary. When first used in the text, each term appears in boldface type with a definition. All vocabulary terms are included in the Glossary at the end of the book. A Spanish Glossary is also included.

- **Lesson Review.** Each lesson concludes with a three-part review that includes several vocabulary and recall questions, several critical thinking questions, and activities in which students apply the lesson's concepts.

Inside the Student Text

Chapter Summary provides the main points of each lesson's content in bulleted list form.

Thinking Critically challenges students with questions that require them to use higher level thinking skills, such as analysis, synthesis, and evaluation.

Family and Community provides students with a variety of activities they can pursue at home, in school, or in the community at large to promote the understanding of family and consumer sciences issues.

CHAPTER 4 REVIEW

Chapter Summary

- Your choice of a career will be one of the most important decisions you will ever make. Since you will be spending a large part of your life working, you should choose work you will enjoy.
- You can prepare for your future career by setting goals, researching careers, continuing your education, and working part-time.
- In school you learn the basic skills of reading, writing, math, science, speaking, and listening. Knowing how to use a computer is also an important basic skill.
- Job hunting requires organization. Before starting your search, decide what kind of job you want and when you can work.
- You can find job openings by asking family and friends, looking at the help-wanted ads, calling possible employers, and visiting employment agencies.
- Dressing appropriately is important for a job interview. Your appearance is usually the first thing an employer notices.
- Good communication skills, flexibility, and team spirit will help you succeed on the job.
- Your work record includes a description of your work habits and how well you handled problems.
- Getting promotions or finding new employment will depend on a good work record.

Words to Know

Using complete sentences, answer the following questions on a separate sheet of paper.

1. What is the purpose of an *aptitude test*?
2. How might *proofreading* help you in a job?
3. Whom should a person list as *references* on a job application?
4. At work, what words might mean the same as *supervisor*?
5. Give an example of *flexibility* on the job.
6. Describe what an *entrepreneur* does.

Review Questions

Using complete sentences, answer the following questions on a separate sheet of paper.

1. Why is it important to decide on career goals while you are in school?
2. How can you find a job or career that is right for you?
3. Why are reading, writing, math, science, speaking, and listening skills called basic skills?
4. Describe the process of getting a job.
5. What can you do to promote good teamwork on the job?
6. Give three examples of good work habits.

Thinking Critically

Using complete sentences, answer the following questions on a separate sheet of paper.

1. **Explain** Why might aptitude tests give people an incomplete picture of career possibilities?
2. **Analyze** Do you think that computers make learning to read, write, and do math less important? Why or why not?
3. **Apply** What questions would you ask an employer at a job interview?
4. **Describe** Why is team spirit such an important quality for employees to have? When might it not be very important?
5. **Apply** What would you do if a coworker was not doing his or her job?

Cooperative Learning

1. With a group of your classmates, make an employment guide for young teens. Include descriptions of jobs suitable for teens, information on how to find jobs in your community, and tips on how to succeed on the job. Each member of the group can be responsible for writing a different section of the guide. Make your guide available to other students in your school.
2. Gather information about a career that interests you. Find out the education required for jobs in that field, responsibilities or duties to be expected, working conditions, and employment outlook. Exchange information with a small group of your classmates.

Family & Community

1. One reason why teens may not know much about their parents' jobs is that they rarely see their parents at work. Arrange to spend some time with a parent or any adult family member at his or her workplace during a vacation from school. Find out about the adult's duties and responsibilities and how he or she uses basic skills at work. Report your findings to the class.
2. Look for resources in your community that help teens start their own businesses. You might find books on teen entrepreneurship at the public library or in bookstores. Programs such as Junior Achievement or Future Business Leaders of America provide teens with business training.

Building A Portfolio

1. Parent-teacher-student conferences and report cards provide a "performance review" of the job you are doing in school. Use information from these sources to list some goals for improving your performance. Place a copy of your list of goals in your portfolio, and use it to measure your progress.
2. Write a business letter to a nearby college, vocational school, community college, or technical school. Request information about available training for careers that interest you. Place a copy of your letter and the information you receive in your portfolio.

Review Questions assesses students' abilities to recall basic factual information.

Words to Know assesses students' knowledge of vocabulary terms presented in the chapter.

Cooperative Learning provides students with group activities that give practical application of the chapter concepts.

Building a Portfolio offers a variety of activities that involve students in projects that can become part of their permanent family and consumer sciences portfolio. Many of these activities draw on infor-mation gathered throughout their study of the chapter.

Inside the Student Text

Chapter Features

CHAPTER ACTIVITIES Each chapter ends with one page of activities, which are designed to encourage discussion, promote critical thinking, and provide hands-on learning opportunities.

- **Chapter Articles** The top half of the Chapter Activities pages includes articles drawn from the following menu:

A Global View gives students an understanding and appreciation of the wide variety of cultural groups in the world today.

Technology explores how technology affects students' lives today and in their future.

Consumer Focus asks students to explore the truth and relevance of information found in the media—reports of new studies or treatments, advertisements, product endorsements, and so on.

Friends & Family focuses on ways that family members and friends can help students with a variety of tasks, such as setting goals. These articles also provide students with ways that they can involve family members and friends in activities such as cooking and sewing.

- **Curriculum Connections** The bottom half of the Chapter Activities pages provides cross curricular relevance of the Family and Consumer Sciences program to math, science, social studies, literature, and technology.

Chapter 7 Activities

A Global View "I'LL TRADE YOU..."
You are used to paying money for goods and services. Another way to get the items you need is by bartering, or trading goods and services without the use of money. You have probably bartered without even knowing it. When you and a friend swap comic books or baseball cards, you are bartering.
Try This!
Arrange to barter services with a friend or parent. Report on your bartering to the class.

TECHNOLOGY
How Did They Do That?
Artists use computers to create amazing special effects for television advertising. Two techniques they use are "warping"—changing one part of a picture at a time—and "morphing"—changing one image into another image. Advertisers spend millions of dollars on these ads. They hope that the special effects will help you remember the ad—and the brand name.
Try This!
Write your own script for a special effects ad.

FRIENDS & FAMILY
THE ALLOWANCE DEBATE
Not all families agree on whether an allowance should be tied to doing chores around the house. Some parents believe that paying their children to do household tasks helps them see the

MATH CONNECTION
THE $1,300 SNACK
Imagine that you spend $5 a week on soft drinks, candy bars, and pretzels. Did you know that in five years your snack habit could cost you more than $1,300?
When you put money in a savings account, the money earns **interest**, or *a fee the bank pays to use your money*. The interest is added to the **principal**, or *the money in your account*.

Chapter 5 Activities

TECHNOLOGY
The New Post Office
Writing letters has once again become fashionable. Many people stay in touch with friends through electronic mail, or E-mail. A computer and a phone line are all they need. They can send messages through the Internet, and their friends can receive them in seconds.
Try This!
Find out more about E-mail and the Internet. If possible, interview someone who uses them. Write a short report on your findings.

FRIENDS & FAMILY
SHARING A ROOM
Matt shares a bedroom with his brother, Josh. Over the last week they have been constantly arguing. Josh never finishes his homework early enough for Matt to have time to listen to music before going to bed. Matt's light bothers Josh when he is trying to sleep.
TRY THIS!
List three possible solutions for the problem that are fair for both Matt and Josh.

Consumer Focus
"I Just Have to Have..."
Did you ever buy shoes or another clothing item just to be like other teens your age? Wanting to follow fads is a normal part of adolescence.
The next time you want to buy something, however, think about whether it's right for you.
Try This!
Make a list of any items you bought simply to fit in with your peers. Analyze if they were right for *you*.

LITERATURE CONNECTION
MAMA IS A SUNRISE
When she comes slip-footing through the door,
she kindles us
like lump coal lighted,
and we wake up glowing.
She puts a spark even in Papa's eyes
and turns out all our darkness.

Evelyn Tooley Hunt

Follow Up
Reading literature can give you words to describe your feelings about the people closest to you.
Find another poem or a song about families or friends. It might describe how you feel about a relationship. It might describe relationships in an entertaining or a thought-provoking way. You could even try writing your own poem or song lyrics. Read your poem or lyrics to a small group of your classmates and explain what it means to you.

CHAPTER 5 ACTIVITIES 147

T8

Inside the Student Text

Special Features

The special features in each chapter are designed to increase students' interest. The features focus on activity-oriented themes. The special features include:

- **Tips for Living** presents tips students can use to help them develop life skills. Students read about topics that pertain to them, such as how to make decisions, how to reach short-term and long-term goals, or how to save time on sewing projects.

- **Skills in Action** focuses on specific skills presented in the lesson. This feature provides activities that help students actively practice the skill. For example, students practice trying out creative and nutritious breakfast combinations or practice sewing handmade gift items.

You—just like anyone else—want to feel safe in your own neighborhood. There are steps you can take to protect yourself. You and your family can join or help set up a Neighborhood Watch group in which neighbors look after one another and one another's homes. Members of such groups are trained by the police to identify and report suspicious activities. When you walk down the street, keep alert—especially at night. Pay attention to the people around you and to what they are doing.

TIPS for living

STRANGER DANGER

Although most people you meet in stores and on the streets are kind and helpful, you still need to be careful around people you don't know. Follow these tips to stay safe.
- Don't get too close to a car if a stranger calls out for directions. It's easy for a stranger to pull you into a car.
- Beware of strangers who offer you gifts or money or ask you to help find a lost dog or cat.
- If a stranger follows or grabs you, run away, scream, and make lots of noise.
- Always let your family know where you will be.
- Tell your parents or other trusted adults if someone makes you feel uncomfortable.

262 CHAPTER 9: YOUR ENVIRONMENT

Skills IN ACTION

Pressing Fabrics

Whenever you sew, you will need to use the iron to press seams and other work. Follow these safety tips:
- Always rest the iron on its heel.
- To see if the iron is hot, try it on a scrap of fabric, not on your finger.
- Unplug the iron when you finish.
- Coil the cord so that no one trips over it or pulls the iron off the ironing board.

Try This!

As a class, assemble fruit baskets or boxes for shut-ins or elderly residents in your neighborhood. Everyone should bring in a few pieces of fresh fruit. Decorate your fruit baskets or boxes with ribbons, bows, and handmade greeting cards.

Cooking Fruit

Ben's grandmother likes ... vorites are baked apples an... them in a conventional ove... microwave oven. There is n... the fresh fruit, and she know... ing microwave cooking as we...

Sabrina likes to cook frui... of water to her favorite fres... lid. To reduce the amount of... a heavy-bottomed pan and ... perature. She refrigerates th... plain yogurt for an afternoo...

Fruits taste and look be... During cooking, small amou... and vitamin C—are lost. Som... destroyed by heat and air. T... heat and as little water as po...

Serving Fruit

The ways in which you ... your taste and imagination.

392 CHAPTER 14: LET'S COOK

- **Try This!** presents hands-on activities that help students to become responsible to themselves and to others. The activities suggest ways for students to become involved with their family, school, or community.

Teacher's Wraparound Edition

The Teacher's Wraparound Edition provides teaching suggestions printed in the margin beside the actual student text page, which has been slightly reduced in size. The Teacher's Manual you are reading explains the program components and how to use the components.

Unit Opening Pages

To introduce the unit, these two pages provide an overview of chapters within each unit, along with suggestions for introducing the unit by discussing the up-close, unit-opening photographs and overhead color transparencies.

Projects and games specific to the unit are provided in the Teacher's Classroom Resources and are identified in a special Unit Projects box. Helpful hints on promoting your Family and Consumer Sciences program are highlighted in a box on the right-hand side margin. Across the bottom of the Unit opening pages you will find ideas for preparing bulletin board displays to use throughout the unit.

Chapter Planning Guide

To assist the teacher in course planning, a two-page Chapter Planning guide has been inserted in the Teacher's Wraparound Edition immediately preceding the beginning of every chapter. The following types of information can be found on these pages.

- A list of lesson titles and page numbers.
- A list of features and teaching resources, which are available for the specific chapter.

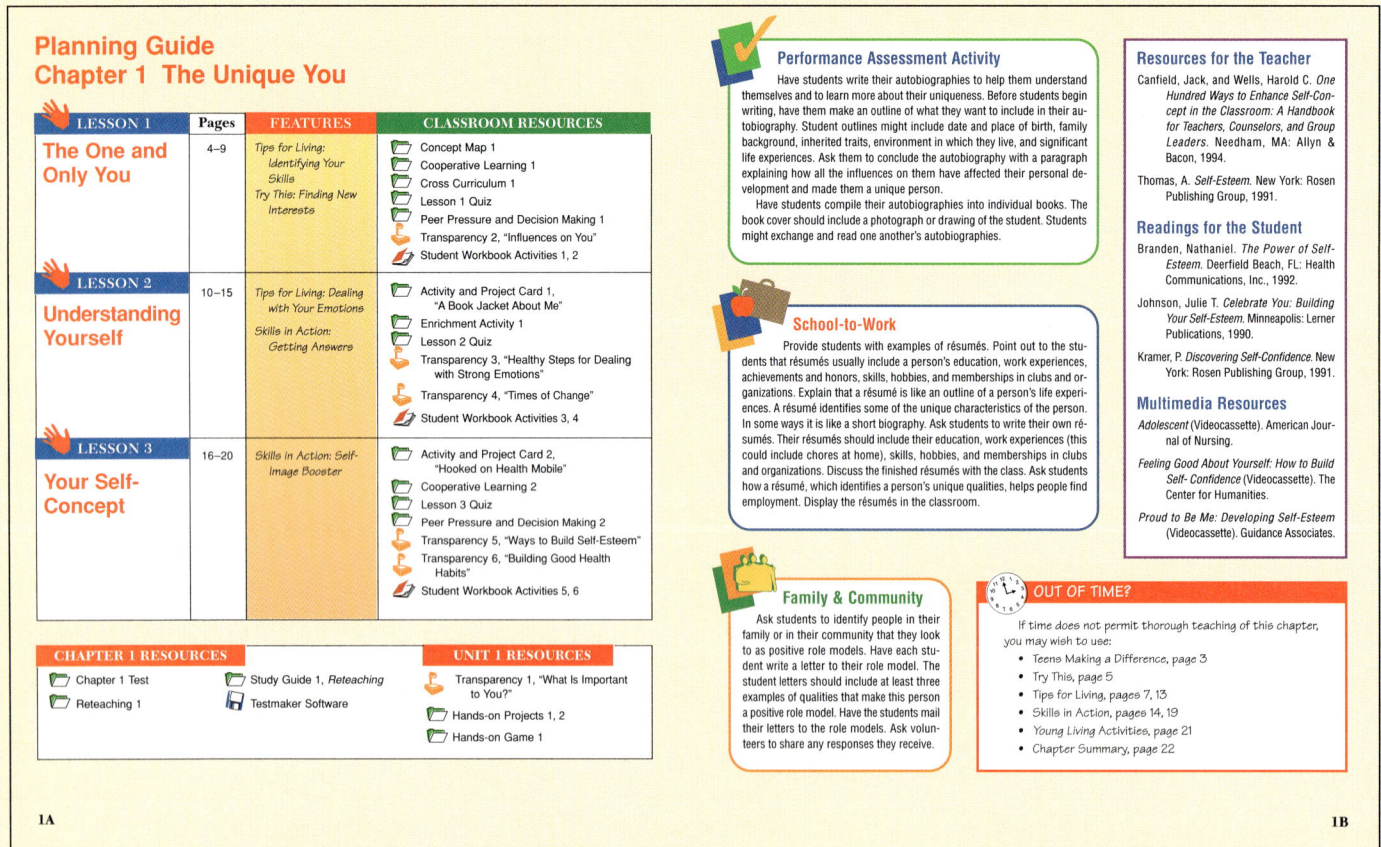

Teacher's Wraparound Edition

- A list of additional resources including books and multimedia products for the student and the teacher.
- A **Performance Assessment** activity. These activities provide a way of teaching and learning that involves both process and product. It is not just a testing strategy. Performance assessment activities provide hands-on approaches to learning concepts. Through these activities students are able to actually experience these concepts rather than just reading, writing, and listening.
- A **Family and Community** activity provides ways for students to get a broader view of the chapter concepts. These activities provide students with ways of interacting with family members, friends, and people in their community, using the main concepts in the chapter.
- A **School-to-Work** activity relates the chapter concepts to future career possibilities. These activities might involve correspondence with local businesses or interviews of professionals in the community.

Chapter Opening Pages

The two-page spread that begins each chapter has the following elements:

- **Chapter Overview.** This is a brief description of the chapter and of the specific lessons. Knowing the general content of specific lessons can be helpful in deciding which lessons to use.
- **Introducing the Chapter.** This feature includes discussion and activities that provide students with an overview of the chapter content.
- **Chapter Motivator.** This element contains many hands-on activities, designed to involve students in the chapter content.
- **Teens Making a Difference.** Teaching strategies that help to focus on and expand this feature are presented here.
- **Key to Ability Levels.** This key, appearing at the bottom margin of the left-hand page, provides a description of each of the three codes used throughout the lesson plan to identify activities designed for students of various abilities, as well as learning styles.
- **Technology in the Classroom.** A description of specific uses of technology in the family and consumer sciences classroom is provided at the bottom margin of the right-hand page.

Lesson Pages

The activities provided on the lesson pages make it easy for you to choose the teaching strategies that are appropriate for your students' abilities and learning styles. The lesson pages are organized as follows.

FOCUS Activities and suggestions presented under this heading are designed to help you focus students' attention on the lesson material.

- **Lesson Objectives.** Student objectives for the lesson are listed.
- **Motivating Activity.** This activity sparks students' interest in the lesson content.
- **Introducing the Lesson.** This activity gives closure to the Motivating Activity and focuses students on the topic of the lesson.
- **Introducing Words to Know.** This element provides an introductory vocabulary activity to help students learn the lesson vocabulary and build vocabulary skills.

TEACH The activities listed under this heading make up the suggested lesson plan.

- **Activities.** These are the activities and discussion topics recommended to develop the skills in a family and consumer sciences program. Strategies are leveled to identify those that are most appropriate for students of varying ability levels and learning styles.

Teacher's Wraparound Edition

- **Using Visuals.** This activity is designed to focus and expand on the information presented in the illustrated graphics and photographs in the lesson.
- **Did You Know?** This element provides interesting facts that supplement the lesson and increase students' interest level.
- **Teacher Talk.** This element provides some suggestions in dealing with subjects of a sensitive nature. The tips are designed to help you foster an atmosphere of mutual respect in the classroom. One way to do this is by not prying when students are reluctant to participate in discussions. To facilitate discussion you can call on volunteers, present imaginary situations, or add points to the discussion yourself. Issues of a sensitive nature deal with things such as the variety of family structures, family problems, or weight control and eating habits. Teacher Talk also provides suggestions about topics that students might need to be made aware of (for example, pointing out illegal advertising techniques that students should be aware of).
- **Teaching Features.** This element suggests strategies that help expand the information provided in the features Skills in Action, Tips for Living, and Try This activities.
- **Teacher's Classroom Resources Correlation.** References are provided throughout the lesson pages to suggest where each of the blackline master activities and color transparencies fit into the lesson content. Look for icons following each activity reference for blackline masters 📁 ; student workbook 📖 ; and color transparencies 🔦 .

ASSESS Under this heading are suggestions for reviewing the lesson and evaluating student understanding.
- **Reteaching.** Reteaching activities are provided for those students who have difficulty mastering the important lesson concepts.
- **Answers to Lesson Review.** Answers to the review questions are provided.
- **Enrichment.** These activities are designed for students who are able and willing to explore the content in greater depth.

CLOSE The strategies here are designed to bring closure to the class and to recap the important concepts of the lesson.

In addition to side column activities, each lesson includes, across the bottom of the page, several other teaching suggestions and activities. These bottom margin features include:
- **Lesson Resources.** This element provides you with a list of resources from the Teacher's Classroom Resources, blackline masters, transparencies, and activities from the Student Workbook that can be used with the lesson.
- **More About . . .** Additional information about topics presented in the lesson is included here.
- **Cooperative Learning.** These activities require students to work together to pursue a common goal and deal with topics related to the lesson content.
- **Meeting Student Diversity.** These activities incorporate cultural perspectives, strategies for the physically challenged, and strategies addressing different learning styles.
- **Home and Community Connection.** This element provides activities and strategies that allow students to use family and community members to further their understanding of lesson concepts.
- **Technology Update.** This element includes topics that illustrate latest technological changes affecting the field of family and consumer sciences. The element also includes information about ways that technology affects students' lives.

Understanding the Teacher's Classroom Resources and Testmaker

A separate *Young Living* Teacher's Classroom Resources box is designed to provide you with well-planned materials that supplement the *Young Living* student text. Creating and implementing class activities is a time-consuming process. Devising worksheets and tests that are clear, accurate, and interesting is even more so. The purpose of the Teacher's Classroom Resources box is to provide a wealth of additional material for effective teaching. You can choose the materials that fit the skill level and time framework of your class. Most pages are designed to be reproduced for classroom use. The Teacher's Classroom Resources box includes the following components:

Reteaching Activities. The activities in this booklet are designed for students who need additional help in learning the concepts presented in the chapter. There is one activity for each chapter. The Chapter Study Guide, found in the Reteaching booklet, can be given to students to help them identify the main concepts of the chapter. Students can also use the guide to review the material and to help them prepare for the test.

Enrichment Activities. This booklet contains activities that allow students the opportunity to explore concepts further. There is at least one activity for each chapter.

Cooperative Learning Activities. These activities call for students to work in small groups or teams. Each group member is responsible not only for his or her own learning but also for the learning of other team members. Two activities are provided for each chapter.

Concept Mapping Activities. The activities in this booklet help students graphically organize the material in each chapter. The activities can be used to preview a lesson's content by visually relating the concepts to be learned and allowing students to read with purpose. When used as a review strategy, the activities reinforce main ideas and clarify relationships.

Cross-Curriculum Activities. This booklet provides students with activities that relate information in the family and consumer sciences classroom with other subject areas, such as math, literature, social studies, and science. Each activity relates to one subject area, and the activities clearly identify the subject area related to. There is at least one cross-curriculum activity for each chapter.

Hands-on Projects and Games. These highly structured learning activities provide a variety of hands-on learning experiences. The projects teach students to follow directions, work independently, and solve problems. At least two of these activities are provided for each unit. Games are provided for each unit of *Young Living*. The games encourage student involvement, build and test skills, and reinforce important concepts. Games can be used to introduce or wrap up a unit.

Peer Pressure and Decision-Making Activities. The activities in this booklet are designed to help students understand and cope with both the positive and negative peer pressure that they will encounter as adolescents and throughout their lives. The activities encourage students to think about how they would react in various situations involving peer pressure. The activities also provide students with situations in which to practice and apply the six-step decision-making process.

Food and Sewing Lab Activities. The activities in this booklet give students experience with cooking and

Understanding the Teacher's Classroom Resources and Testmaker

sewing. The booklet includes recipes and instructions for preparing nutritious snacks and meals and for making sewing projects.

Transparencies. Seventy-two overhead color transparencies provide motivating visuals that can be used to introduce or reinforce a lesson. Discussion questions and suggestions for using the transparencies are provided in the Instructor's Guide.

Testing Program. Two types of reproducible tests are provided for the program. A one-page Lesson Quiz is available for each lesson. A two-page Chapter Test for each chapter covers the main concepts of the chapter.

Student Activities Workbook. The workbook provides creative and varied activity sheets to enhance student learning. One or two activity sheets, which reinforce lesson content while strengthening basic skills, are presented for each lesson. The workbook pages are perforated for easy removal of the worksheets if desired. The Student Workbook is designed as a consumable item. Therefore, it may not be reproduced in part or whole. Such reproduction is a violation of copyright laws. The Teacher's Annotated Edition of the student workbook provides answers to all questions.

Reproducible Lesson Plans. This booklet contains a lesson plan for each lesson of *Young Living*. The lesson plans are designed to help you spend less time planning, thereby giving you more time for teaching.

Testmaker. Also available for *Young Living* is a Testmaker software program. The Testmaker allows you to draw upon a test bank of hundreds of objective questions. The program allows you to prepare and print out tests quickly and easily.

Professional Family and Consumer Sciences Series

Linking Home, School, and Community. Promoting programs to students, administrators, parents, and community members, helps people develop an understanding of the value of life-management programs. They discover that the family and consumer sciences teaches skills in the areas of personal development, parenting and child development, consumer affairs and management skills, foods and nutrition, and clothing and textiles. An ongoing marketing program can help you publicize the value of family and consumer sciences programs. This booklet provides you with ideas and steps to develop partnerships and communicate effectively.

Meeting the Special Needs of Students. This booklet provides suggestions and strategies for integrating and teaching students with disabilities and learning problems, as well as for working with gifted students.

Dealing with Sensitive Issues. This booklet prepares the educator to discuss with students issues that are generally considered sensitive by providing background information and teaching strategies.

Professional Notes

Cooperative Learning

Although cooperative learning is a useful teaching strategy in many subjects, it occupies an important place in the family and consumer sciences classroom. Cooperative learning can aid in instilling communication skills and in helping students get along with others. It can also give students opportunities to practice skills such as effective listening and conflict resolution.

- **What is Cooperative Learning?**

  Cooperative learning requires students to work together to pursue a common goal. In cooperative learning, each member of the group has a specific task to perform to achieve the group's goal. Because part of each student's evaluation is based on the overall quality of the group's work, there is an incentive for all students in the group to help one another accomplish the task assigned to the group as a whole. In such an approach, cooperation replaces competition, and students learn effective interpersonal communication skills.

  Cooperative learning requires careful structuring and monitoring by the teacher in order to assure that it becomes more than just a group activity. Cooperative learning should include the following characteristics: students work face-to-face in a heterogeneous group, the activity promotes positive interdependence, each member of the group has individual accountability, and the group has a common goal or product.

- **The Teacher's Role**

  The teacher's coaching is important to successful cooperative learning. The teacher's role is important in helping groups at key moments during a project. Students might need assistance in agreeing on goals or evaluating their success. Specifically, the teacher needs to make sure that no one student in the group does most of the work.

- **Cooperative Learning in the *Young Living* Program**

  The *Young Living* program provides many opportunities for cooperative learning. Some cooperative learning activities challenge students to solve problems and to make decisions. Other cooperative learning activities involve students in hands-on research and in presenting findings to others.

  Depending on the nature of the activity, the strategies suggest that students work on tasks in pairs, small groups, or larger groups. For the most part, the ideal group size will be four to six students. The teacher should structure each group to obtain a mix of high, average, and low achievers. In addition, the teacher should strive for ethnic and gender balance.

  The Student Edition includes cooperative learning activities in each Chapter Review. They provide a variety of opportunities for students to work together on activities relating to the chapter content.

  The Teacher's Wraparound Edition includes cooperative learning suggestions in the bottom margins of each chapter. These activities offer a variety of interesting, activity-based teaching ideas.

  The Teacher's Classroom Resources includes a Cooperative Learning Activities booklet containing at least one cooperative learning activity for each chapter.

Meeting Student Diversity

There are many effective teaching strategies that teachers can use to create a positive learning environment—one that enhances instruction for every student.

Professional Notes

- **Students with Varying Ability Levels and Learning Styles**

  The Teacher's Wraparound Edition of *Young Living* provides many types of activities to support the concepts in the text. It is not intended that you use all of them. Instead, it is suggested that you select those activities that are most appropriate to the needs and abilities of your students and to your teaching methods. To assist you in this selection, each activity in the lesson plan is coded. The codes are listed in the opening pages of each chapter.

- **Students with Special Needs**

  Students with special needs are often mainstreamed in the family and consumer sciences classroom. It is important to ensure that special needs students are provided with equal opportunities when responding in the classroom.

  In some cases you will be required to alter your teaching methods when working with special needs students. For example, when an activity requires students to write on the chalkboard, students in wheelchairs may require a lowered chalkboard or the use of an overhead projector. Visually impaired students may need to give a oral responses. For hearing impaired students, you might highlight key terms and phrases on the chalkboard. Learning disabled students might need to get short, easy-to-read handouts.

- **Students with Language Diversity**

  Students with language diversity may not have trouble mastering the content. Their difficulty may be only with language. You can help these students in several ways. Allow time for students to become familiar with the structure of English. Some students may know English words but have trouble with word order. By accepting students' mistakes and praising efforts, you can build an atmosphere in which students can feel free to experiment with English.

  Students with limited English proficiency can often understand more than they can express. They can use simple sentences but may need help understanding figures of speech and words with multiple meanings. Provide peer learning by grouping English-proficient students with students with limited English proficiency. Encourage students to work in pairs or small heterogeneous groups to teach skills to one another.

- **Meeting Student Diversity in the *Young Living* Program**

  Specific suggestions for involving students with varying abilities are provided in the activities of the lesson plans in the Teacher's Wraparound Edition. Each activity is labeled with the codes described at the beginning of each chapter. In addition the bottom margin of the Teacher's Wraparound Edition provides specific activities to help you involve students with specific needs, such as the physically challenged and visually impaired, in the family and consumer sciences classroom.

Multicultural Perspectives

As the United States continues to become a more multicultural society, it is increasingly important for students to see peoples different from themselves as interesting people who have different ideas, customs, and languages, but who also share many of the same values.

Young Living addresses the issue of diversity in a variety of ways. The Student Edition reflects a multicultural population as well as diverse lifestyles. This is done

Professional Notes

by integrating examples of diversity in the text itself. The illustrations in the program reflect a varied student population and a variety of living arrangements. In addition, the *Young Living* Student Edition includes a Spanish Glossary.

The Teacher's Wraparound edition includes activities in the bottom margin element, titled Meeting Student Diversity. This element includes suggestions for ways that students can explore the ways of other cultures in regard to various concepts presented in the family and consumer sciences classroom.

Technology in the Classroom

Advances in technology are continuously being made and these changes affect all aspects of students' lives, including school. Technology provides a variety of instructional tools that you can use in the family and consumer sciences classroom, such as the computer, CD-ROMs, laserdiscs, and on-line resources. These tools can be used to provide information, to guide learning, and for evaluation. An important aspect of the instructional tools is to help students become users of technology, not just users of lessons involving technology.

Technological equipment can be used in the family and consumer sciences classroom in a variety of ways. Suggestions for using various technological tools are presented in the Teacher's Wraparound Edition in the bottom margin of the chapter opening pages. In addition, activities in the Teacher's Wraparound Edition that are appropriate for computer use include a note suggesting such use. The note is followed by the following icon:

As with all instructional materials, the teacher needs to be familiar with technological equipment and materials before using them in the classroom. Students need to be provided with guidance for the use of the equipment, clear directions, and expected outcomes.

Block Scheduling

Block scheduling differs from traditional class scheduling in the amount of time allotted to each period. In block scheduling fewer class sessions are scheduled for larger blocks of time over fewer days. For example, in block scheduling, a course might meet for 90 minutes a day for 90 days, or half a school year.

- **Advantages for School Systems**
  For schools themselves, the greatest advantage of block scheduling is that there is a better use of resources. No additional teachers or classrooms may be needed, and more efficient use is made of those resources presently in schools. These advantages are accompanied by an increase in the quality of teacher instruction and students' time on task.

- **Advantages for Teachers**
  There are several advantages for teachers who are in schools that use block scheduling. With block scheduling, teachers have responsibility for a smaller number of students at a time, so students and teachers get to know each other better. With more time, teachers are able to provide additional time and resources for meeting the individual needs of students. The extended time frame provided by block scheduling affords the teacher the opportunity to implement a greater number of cooperative learning, research-oriented, and activity-intense projects to motivate and involve their students.

Professional Notes

Teachers can also be more focused on what they are teaching. In fact, block scheduling seems to result in changes in teaching approaches, classrooms that are more student-centered, improved teacher morale, and increased teacher effectiveness.

If school days are of the same length as those that are more traditionally scheduled, teachers find the block approach more time-efficient. Block scheduling cuts in half the time needed for introducing and closing classes. Block scheduling also eliminates half of the time needed for class changes, resulting in more teaching time and fewer discipline problems.

- **Advantages for Students**
Students involved in the block-scheduling approach are found to have a greater success rate than those students with traditional scheduling because students seem to learn more and retain it better. Students benefit from better student-teacher relationships and a more manageable work load. Generally, students feel better organized and are more aware of their progress in the class.

- **Block Scheduling in the *Young Living* Program**
Activities in the Teacher's Wraparound Edition that are particularly suited to use within the block scheduling framework are identified throughout the text by the following designation: . In addition, a list of activities from the Teacher's Classroom Resources that are suitable for classrooms using block scheduling are included in the chapter opening pages of the Teacher's Wraparound Edition.

Course Presentation

The chart on this page suggests some ways classes might be structured using *Young Living*. Included are plans for a 9-week, 18-week, and 36-week course. Plans for the 18-week course can also be used in a 9-week course in classrooms that use block scheduling. These outlines can easily be adapted to meet your own particular needs.

Chapter Number	Chapter Title	DAYS SPENT ON CHAPTER		
		9-week	18-week; or 9-week, with 90-minute periods	36-week
1	The Unique You	2	4	8
2	Everyday Living Skills	3	5	10
3	Steps to Success	3	5	10
4	Careers	3	6	12
5	Your Family and Friends	3	8	15
6	Understanding and Caring for Children	2	5	12
7	Being a Wise Consumer	3	6	12
8	Your Home	2	4	8
9	Your Environment	2	4	8
10	Nutrition and You	2	4	8
11	Developing Healthy Habits	2	4	8
12	Working in the Kitchen	3	6	12
13	Preparing to Cook	2	4	8
14	Let's Cook	3	5	10
15	Looking Good	2	4	6
16	Planning Your Wardrobe	2	5	10
17	Preparing to Sew	2	4	8
18	Sewing Skills	4	7	15
		45 days	90 days	180 days

Scope and Sequence	Chapter 1 The Unique You	Chapter 2 Everyday Living Skills
Personal Development	Influence of heredity and environment (1-1) Role development (1-1) Personality development (1-2) Physical and emotional changes (1-2) Positive self-concept (1-3) Self-esteem (1-3)	Benefits of positive attitude (2-1) Breaking bad habits (2-1) Combating shyness (2-2) Skills and talents (2-4) Personal resources (2-4)
Self-Responsibility	Self-respect (1-2) Controlling emotions (1-2) Developing positive self-concept (1-3)	Maturity (2-1) Manners (2-1) Avoiding time wasters (2-4)
Decision Making/Management	Taking care of self (1-3) Health habits (1-3)	Types of resources (2-4) Resource management (2-4) Management steps (2-4) Trading and substituting resources (2-4) Time management (2-4) Setting priorities (2-4)
Consumer Skills	Choosing grooming products (1-3)	
Citizenship/Leadership	Being a role model (1-1)	Citizenship skills (2-3) Leadership skills (2-3) Teamwork (2-3) Volunteerism (2-3) People as resources (2-4)
Relating to Others	Role modeling (1-1) Understanding emotions (1-2) Controlling anger (1-2) Accepting criticism (1-3)	First impressions (2-1) Stereotypes (2-1) Getting along with others (2-1) Communication skills (2-2) Nonverbal communication (2-2) Teamwork (2-3)
Health, Safety, Nutrition	Laughter (1-2) Practicing good health habits (1-2) Taking care of self (1-3)	Breaking bad habits (2-1)
Skill Development	Identifying skills (1-1)	Management skills (2-4) Time management (2-4)
Career Exploration	Personal skills (1-1) Role models (1-1)	Citizenship (2-3) Volunteering (2-3)
Technology		Forms of communication (2-2)

Chapter 3 Steps to Success	Chapter 4 Careers	Chapter 5 Your Family and Friends
Needs and wants (3-1) Personal value system (3-1) Short- and long-term goals (3-4) Goal setting (3-4)	Identifying skills and interests (4-1) First impressions on the job (4-4) On the job (4-4) Being flexible on the job (4-4)	Building relationship skills (5-1) Influence of family (5-2) Family traditions (5-2) Causes of conflicts (5-6)
Identifying personal values (3-1) Showing responsibility (3-2) Making responsible decisions (3-3)	Filling out a job application (4-3) Starting a business (4-3) Being a responsible employee (4-4)	Avoiding harmful substances (5-5) Making responsible decisions (5-5)
Refusal skills (3-1) Types of decisions (3-3) Steps in decision making (3-3) Risk taking (3-3) Managing resources (3-4)	Organizing a job hunt (4-3) Finding job openings (4-3) Applying for a job (4-3) Handling problems on the job (4-4) Managing income (4-4)	Adapting to change (5-3) Life changes (5-3) Managing stress (5-3) Changes in friendships (5-4) Peers and decision making (5-5) Handling peer pressure (5-5)
Advertising appeal (3-4)		Shopping under peer pressure (5-5)
Showing responsibility (3-2)	Team spirit (4-4) Getting along with others (4-4)	Preserving family memories (5-2) Making new friends (5-4) Keeping in touch with friends (5-4)
Differences in values (3-1) Responsibility to others (3-2) Showing respect (3-2) Seeking advice (3-3)	References (4-3) Dressing for interviews (4-3) Meeting supervisors and coworkers (4-4) Communicating with supervisors and coworkers (4-4) Getting along with coworkers (4-4) Showing respect for others (4-4)	Importance of relationships (5-1) Importance of family life (5-2) Getting along with parents (5-2) Getting along with siblings (5-2) Importance of friendships (5-4) Making and keeping friends (5-4) Being part of a group (5-4) Peer pressure (5-5) Ways to prevent conflict (5-6) Learning to compromise (5-6) Peer mediation (5-6)
Wellness as a value (3-1)		Coping with stress (5-3) Laughter (5-3) Avoiding harmful substances (5-5)
Refusal Skills (3-1) Learning responsibility (3-2) Setting goals (3-3)	Developing basic skills (4-2) Computer skills (4-2) Improving study skills (4-2) Writing business letters (4-2) Practicing good work habits (4-4) Communication skills (4-5)	Relationship skills (5-1) Making friends (5-4) Being assertive (5-5) Conflict resolution (5-6)
Technology and future (3-4)	Setting career goals (4-1) Part-time employment (4-1) Starting a career search (4-1) Job preparation (4-1) Choosing a career (4-1) Applying for a job (4-3) Job interview (4-3) Using references (4-3) Entrepreneurship (4-4)	Peer mediator training (5-6)
Technology skills (3-4)	Researching careers (4-1)	E-mail (5-6)

T21

Scope and Sequence	Chapter 6 Understanding and Caring for Children	Chapter 7 Being a Wise Consumer
Personal Development	Developmental tasks (6-2)	Being a wise consumer (7-1)
Self-Responsibility	Responsibilities of parenting (6-1) Babysitting (6-5)	Responsibilities as a consumer (7-4)
Decision Making/Management	Planning appropriate activities for children (6-5)	Influences on buying decisions (7-1)
Consumer Skills	Selecting toys (6-2)	Identifying advertising techniques (7-2) Evaluating advertisements (7-2) Evaluating media messages (7-2) Being a skillful shopper (7-3) Comparison shopping (7-3) Selecting a store (7-3) Reading warranties (7-3) Mail-order shopping (7-3) Making refunds and exchanges (7-4) Writing letters of complaint (7-4)
Citizenship/Leadership	Providing guidance (6-1)	Rights as a consumer (7-4)
Relating to Others	Interacting positively with children (6-1) Guiding children (6-1) Encouraging independence (6-1) Expectations of children (6-2) Children with special needs (6-2) How children learn (6-2) Child's play (6-3)	Influence of peers on buying decisions (7-1)
Health, Safety, Nutrition	Toy safety (6-3) Keeping children safe (6-4) Preventing common accidents (6-4) Playground safety (6-4) Nutritious snacks (6-5) Handling emergencies (6-5)	Reading labels (7-3) Identifying quackery (7-4)
Skill Development	Parenting skills (6-1) Child-care skills (6-5)	Shopping skills (7-3) Reading labels (7-3)
Career Exploration	Babysitting (6-5)	Money management (7-5)
Technology	Software for children (6-5)	Electronic shopping centers (7-3)

Chapter 8 Your Home	Chapter 9 Your Environment	Chapter 10 Nutrition and You
		Food and appearance (10-1)
Redecorating your room (8-2) Taking care of your room (8-3)	Avoiding unnecessary risk (9-3)	Making wise food choices (10-1)
Organizing living space (8-1) Storage space (8-1) Dividing chores (8-1) Designing living space (8-2) Managing cleaning tasks (8-3)	Conserving natural resources (9-1) Energy conservation (9-1) Reducing, reusing, recycling waste (9-2)	Making food choices (10-1)
Choosing accessories (8-2)	Conserving resources (9-1) Reducing and reusing (9-2)	Understanding food terms (10-2) Evaluating nutrition claims (10-3)
	Encouraging people to recycle (9-2)	
Sharing space (8-1) Respecting privacy (8-1) Working together in a home (8-3)	Protecting the environment (9-1)	Reasons for eating (10-1) Food and tradition (10-1)
Home safety (8-3) Home security (8-3)	Acting safely (9-3) Bicycle and skating safety (9-3) Preventing violence (9-3)	Food and health (10-1) Proteins, carbohydrates, fats (10-2) Vitamins, minerals, and water (10-3) Hunger vs. appetite (10-1) Nutrients for health (10-1)
Using design elements (8-2) Using accessories (8-2) Principles of design (8-2)	Using water wisely (9-1) Acting safely (9-3) Preventing violence (9-3)	
Decorating and designing (8-2)		
Home safety equipment (8-3) Automation in the home (8-3)	Recycling methods (9-2) Alternative energy sources (9-3)	

Scope and Sequence	Chapter 11 Developing Healthy Habits	Chapter 12 Working in the Kitchen
Personal Development	Following healthy guidelines (11-2)	
Self-Responsibility	Eating healthful foods (11-1) Choosing a balanced diet (11-2) Reducing fat in the diet (11-2) Reducing salt and sugars in the diet (11-2)	Kitchen cleanup (12-1)
Decision Making/ Management	Using the Food Guide Pyramid (11-1) Choosing healthful snacks (11-3) Choosing a restaurant (11-3) Starting a fitness program (11-4) Weight control (11-4) Cutting calories (11-4) Avoiding fad diets (11-4)	Storing leftovers (12-1) Making a work plan (12-5) Saving time in the kitchen (12-5)
Consumer Skills	Checking food labels (11-1) Eating out (11-3)	Buying wisely (12-5)
Citizenship/Leadership	Fitness program (11-4)	Teamwork in the kitchen (12-5)
Relating to Others		Meals on wheels (12-1)
Health, Safety, Nutrition	The Food Guide Pyramid (11-1) The food groups (11-1) Maintaining healthy weight (11-2)	Food safety (12-1) Kitchen cleanup (12-1) Kitchen safety (12-1) Using a fire extinguisher (12-2)
Skill Development	Following healthy guidelines (11-2)	Using kitchen tools and equipment (12-3) Microwave cooking (12-4)
Career Exploration		
Technology	Fat substitutes (11-4)	Microwave cooking (12-4)

Chapter 13 Preparing to Cook	Chapter 14 Let's Cook	Chapter 15 Looking Good
		Healthy appearance (15-1)
Shopping etiquette (13-2)		Practicing good health habits (15-1)
Planning a meal with the Food Guide Pyramid (13-1) Meal-planning resources (13-1) Analyzing meal patterns (13-1) Storing foods (13-2)	Choosing nutritious foods (14-3) Cooking methods (14-5)	Making clothing decisions (15-2)
Food shopping (13-2) Coupons (13-2) Food labels (13-2) Dated products (13-2)	Using meat substitutes (14-5) Extending meats (14-5)	Clothing choices (15-1) Checking clothing labels (15-3)
Managing meals (13-2)		
Meal patterns (13-1)		Reasons for wearing clothes (15-2) Dressing appropriately (15-2)
	Packing a sack lunch (14-3)	Skin care (15-1) Hands, feet, nail care (15-1) Hair care (15-1) Tooth care (15-1) Eye care (15-1)
Table setting (13-1) Table manners (13-1) Reading and following recipes (13-3) Preparing convenience foods (13-3) Measuring ingredients (13-4)	Choosing fruit (14-1) Cooking fruit (14-1) Serving fruit (14-1) Storing fruit (14-1) Preparing, cooking, and serving vegetables (14-2) Cooking soups and salads (14-2) Preparing breads and cereals (14-3) Preparing sandwiches (14-3) Cooking pasta and rice (14-3) Cooking with milk, cream, yogurt, and cheese (14-4) Preparing meat, poultry, fish, dry beans, eggs, and nuts (14-5)	Selecting color, line, and texture (15-3) Using design elements (15-3)
High-tech packaging (13-4)	Genetically-engineered food (14-5)	Plastic products (15-3)

Scope and Sequence	Chapter 16 Planning Your Wardrobe	Chapter 17 Preparing to Sew
Personal Development		Caring for equipment (17-1)
Self-Responsibility		Managing time in the sewing lab (17-1) Selecting a pattern (17-2)
Decision Making/ Management	Planning a wardrobe (16-1) Developing a shopping plan (16-3) Caring for clothes (16-4) Storing clothes (16-4)	Sew or buy (17-3)
Consumer Skills	Evaluating quality fabrics (16-2) Evaluating quality construction (16-2) Selecting comfortable clothes (16-2) Reading clothing labels (16-3) Stretching the clothing budget (16-3)	Choosing fabrics (17-3) Choosing notions (17-3)
Citizenship/Leadership		Recycling clothes (17-2)
Relating to Others	Wardrobe and appearance (16-1)	Working in the sewing lab (17-1)
Health, Safety, Nutrition		Safety in the sewing lab (17-1)
Skill Development	Taking a wardrobe inventory (16-1) Extending your wardrobe (16-1) Identifying fabrics (16-2) Choosing shoes (16-2) Clothing care (16-4)	Operating a sewing machine (17-1) Measuring for pattern size (17-2) Using sewing kits (17-2)
Career Exploration		
Technology	Electronic clothes shopping (16-4)	

| Chapter 18
Sewing Skills		
Making clothing repairs (18-5)		
Time-saving tips for sewing (18-1)
Storing patterns (18-4)		
Recycling clothing (18-5)		
Working in the sewing lab (18-1)		
Sewing safety (18-2)		
Following a guide sheet (18-1)
Preparing fabric (18-1)
Preparing patterns (18-2)
Learning to stitch (18-2)
Using a serger (18-3)
Sewing construction techniques (18-4)
Finishing seams (18-4)
Reducing seam bulk (18-4)
Hand sewing (18-5) | | |
| | | |
| Uses for a serger (18-3)
Smart sewing machines (18-5) | | |

Using Community Resources

Al-Anon, Alateen Group Headquarters
P.O. Box 862 Midtown Station
New York, NY 10018-0862
(212) 302-7240

American Cancer Society
1599 Clifton Road
Atlanta, GA 30329
(404) 841-0700

American Dietetic Association
216 W. Jackson Blvd.
Chicago, IL 60606
(312) 899-0040

American Heart Association
7272 Greenville Avenue
Dallas, TX 75231
(214) 373-6300
http:\\www.amhrt.org

American Institute of Nutrition
9650 Rockville Pike
Bethesda, MD 20814
(301) 530-7050
http:\\www.nutrition.org\nutrition\

American Lung Association
1740 Broadway
New York, NY 10019
(212) 315-8700

American Medical Association
515 North State Street
Chicago, IL 60610
(312) 464-5000
http:\\www.ama-assn.org

American Optometric Association
243 North Lindbergh
St. Louis, MO 63141
(314) 991-4100

Association for Children and Adults with Learning Disabilities
4156 Library Road
Pittsburgh, PA 15234
(412) 341-1515

Asthma and Allergy Foundation of America
1125 15th St., Suite 502
Washington, DC 20005
(202) 466-7643

Centers for Disease Control and Prevention (CDC)
4770 Buford Highway, NE
Atlanta, GA 30341

Child Care Information Service/ National Association for the Education of Young Children
1509 16th St., N.W.
Washington, DC 20036
(800) 424-2460

Children's Defense Fund
25 E St., N.W.
Washington, DC 20001
(202) 628-8787
cdf@tmn.com

Educational Resource Information Center (ERIC) Early Childhood Education
University of Illinois
805 W. Pennsylvania Avenue
Urbana, IL 61801
(217) 333-1386

Family Services
11700 Westlake Park Drive
Milwaukee, WI 53224
(414) 359-1040

Food and Drug Administration
5600 Fishers Lane
Rockville, MD 20857
(301) 594-6740

International Food Information Council (IFIC)
1100 Connecticut Ave., N.W., Suite 430
Washington, DC 20036
(202) 296-6540

March of Dimes Birth Defects Foundation
1275 Mamaroneck Avenue
White Plains, NY 10605
(914) 428-7100

National Committee for the Prevention of Child Abuse
332 So. Michigan Avenue, Suite 1600
Chicago, IL 60604
(312) 663-3520

National Congress of Parents and Teachers, Alcohol Education Program
330 N. Wabash Ave., Suite 2100
Chicago, IL 60611-3690
(312) 670-6782

National Dairy Council
6300 North River Road
Rosemont, IL 60018

National Institute of Allergy and Infectious Diseases, Information Office
9000 Rockville Pike
Bethesda, MD 29892
(301) 496-5717

National Institute of Child Health and Human Development
Research on Mothers and Children
6100 Executive Blvd., Rm. 4B05K
Rockville, MD 20852
(301) 496-4000

National Mental Health Association
1025 Prince Street
Arlington, VA 22314
(703) 684-7722

National Safety Council
1121 Spring Lake Drive
Itasca, IL 60143-3201
(708) 285-1121

National Wildlife Federation
1400 16th Street NW
Washington, DC 20036

Sierra Club
730 Polk Street
San Francisco, CA 94109

The Skin Cancer Foundation
245 5th Ave,. Suite 2402
New York, NY 10016
(212) 725-5176
(800) 754-6490

USDA Food and Nutrition Service
National Agricultural Library
Information Center 304
10301 Baltimore Boulevard
Beltsville, MD 20705
(301) 504-5719

Young Living

SEVENTH EDITION

GLENCOE
McGraw-Hill

New York, New York   Columbus, Ohio   Mission Hills, California   Peoria, Illinois

Teacher Reviewers

Sue Eng Chang
Mandarin High School
Jacksonville, Florida

Bonnie Jenuine
Carpinteria Middle School
Carpinteria, California

Marva F. Randolph
Baltimore City Public Schools
Baltimore, Maryland

Teri Gemar
Sutton Public Schools
Sutton, Nebraska

Sandra Fleming Kingdon
Wright Middle School
Nashville, Tennessee

Lori Scanlon
Oakland Middle School
Columbia, Missouri

Brenda T. Graham
A.C. Reynolds Middle School
Asheville, North Carolina

Suzanne C. Kroepsch
Campus Middle School
Englewood, Colorado

Marcia Elaine Sharrard
South Miami Middle School
Miami, Florida

Debbie Harvey
Pleasanton Middle School
Pleasanton, California

Brenda W. Owen
Morton Middle School
Lexington, Kentucky

Beth H. Trojahn
Grant Middle School
Springfield, Illinois

Glencoe/McGraw-Hill
A Division of The McGraw-Hill Companies

Editorial services provided by Visual Education Corporation, Princeton, NJ.

"Mama Is a Sunrise" by Evelyn Tooley Hunt is reprinted by permission from the author.

Copyright © 1997 by Glencoe/McGraw-Hill.
All rights reserved. Except as permitted under the United States Copyright Act, no part of this publication may be reproduced or distributed in any form or by any means, or stored in a database or retrieval system, without prior written permission from the publisher.

Send all inquiries to:
Glencoe/McGraw-Hill
15319 Chatsworth Street
P.O. Box 9609
Mission Hills, California 91346-9609

ISBN 0-02-642816-4 (Student Text)
ISBN 0-02-642817-2 (Teacher's Wraparound Edition)

Printed in the United States of America.

1 2 3 4 5 6 7 8 9   VHJ   03 02 01 00 99 98 97 96

Table of Contents

UNIT 1 Personal Development 1

CHAPTER 1   The Unique You 2
Lessons
1. The One and Only You 4
2. Understanding Yourself 10
3. Your Self-Concept 16

Activities 21

CHAPTER 2   Everyday Living Skills ... 24
Lessons
1. Making a Good Impression 26
2. Communicating with Others 31
3. Being a Citizen and a Leader 36
4. Managing Your Life ... 42

Activities 49

CHAPTER 3   Steps to Success 52
Lessons
1. What's Important to You? 54
2. Acting Responsibly 59
3. Using the Decision-Making Process 64
4. Setting Goals 70

Activities 75

CHAPTER 4   Careers 78
Lessons
1. Looking Ahead to Careers 80
2. School to Work 86
3. Getting a Job 92
4. Being Successful on the Job 98

Activities 105

TABLE OF CONTENTS   iii

UNIT 2 Relationships 108

CHAPTER 5 Your Family and Friends 110

Lessons
1. Getting Along with Others 112
2. Family Relationships 117
3. Changes Within Families 123
4. Developing Friendships 130
5. Peers and Decision Making 136
6. Resolving Conflicts 141

Activities 147

CHAPTER 6 Understanding and Caring for Children .. 150

Lessons
1. Parenting Skills..................... 152
2. Ages and Stages.................... 158
3. Child's Play 165
4. Child Safety..................... 171
5. Caring for Children............... 176

Activities 183

UNIT 3 Consumer Skills and Home Management ... 186

CHAPTER 7 Being a Wise Consumer 188

Lessons
1. Influences on Buying Decisions ... 190
2. Evaluating Media Messages 194
3. Comparison Shopping 200
4. Consumer Rights and Responsibilities 206
5. Managing Your Money 212

Activities 217

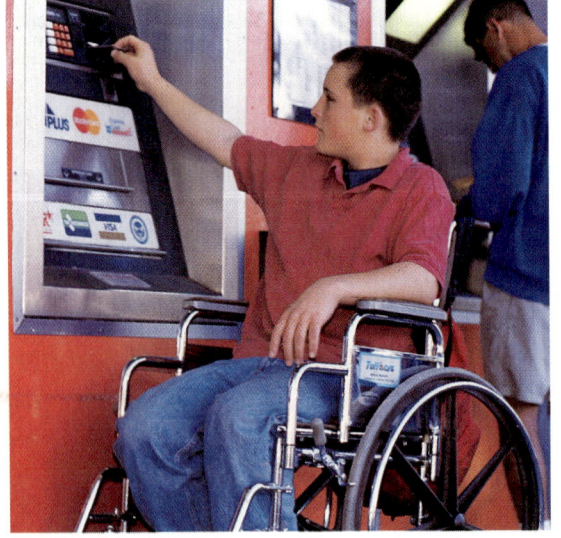

CHAPTER 8 Your Home 220
Lessons
1. Making the Most of Your Home ... 222
2. Designing Your Space 229
3. Keeping a Home Clean and Safe ... 235

Activities 241

CHAPTER 9 Your Environment 244
Lessons
1. Protecting Your Environment 246
2. Keeping Your Environment Clean 252
3. Your Personal Safety and Violence Prevention 258

Activities 265

UNIT 4 Foods and Nutrition 268

CHAPTER 10 Nutrition and You 270
Lessons
1. What Food Does for You 272
2. Nutrients: Proteins, Carbohydrates, and Fats 278
3. Nutrients: Vitamins, Minerals, and Water 284

Activities 291

CHAPTER 11 Developing Healthy Habits ... 294
Lessons
1. The Food Guide Pyramid 296
2. Following Healthy Guidelines 303
3. Snacking and Eating Out 310
4. Exercise and Weight Control 316

Activities 323

CHAPTER 12 **Working in the Kitchen** **326**

Lessons
1. Food Safety and Sanitation 328
2. Kitchen Safety 332
3. Kitchen Tools and Equipment 337
4. Microwave Cooking 343
5. The School Foods Lab 350

Activities **355**

CHAPTER 13 **Preparing to Cook** **358**

Lessons
1. Planning a Menu 360
2. Food Shopping and Storage 366
3. Following Recipes and Directions 373
4. Measuring Ingredients 380

Activities **385**

CHAPTER 14

Let's Cook ... **388**

Lessons
1. Fruits 390
2. Vegetables 394
3. Breads, Cereals, Rice, and Pasta 399
4. Milk, Yogurt, and Cheese 406
5. Meat, Poultry, Fish, Dry Beans, Eggs, and Nuts 413

Activities **421**

vi TABLE OF CONTENTS

UNIT 5 Clothing and Textiles 424

CHAPTER 15 Looking Good 426
Lessons
1. Personal Health and Grooming 428
2. Making Clothing Decisions ... 434
3. Clothing Design 440

Activities 447

CHAPTER 16 Planning Your Wardrobe ... 450
Lessons
1. Deciding What You Need 452
2. Evaluating Quality and Fit 458
3. Shopping for Clothes 466
4. Clothing Care 472

Activities 477

CHAPTER 17 Preparing to Sew 480
Lessons
1. The Sewing Lab and Equipment 482
2. Choosing a Sewing Project 489
3. Choosing Fabrics and Notions 494

Activities 499

CHAPTER 18 Sewing Skills 502
Lessons
1. Preparing Your Pattern and Fabric 504
2. Starting to Sew 510
3. Using a Serger 516
4. Making Your Project 523
5. Repairing and Altering Your Clothes 529

Activities 535

Glossary 538
Glossary/Glosario 547
Index 558

TABLE OF CONTENTS **vii**

Features

TEENS MAKING A DIFFERENCE

1. Say Cheese, Please.................3
2. Improving a Neighborhood.........25
3. Helping Others....................53
4. Junior Entrepreneur...............79
5. Story Time.......................111
6. Friendship Matters...............151
7. Clothes from Recycled Plastic....189
8. Treasure Bags....................221
9. Buddy Service....................245
10. Community Service Club..........271
11. The School Store................295
12. Meals on Wheels.................327
13. Community Food Drive............359
14. School Bake Sale................389
15. Recycling Clothes for Charity...427
16. The Boutique Look...............451
17. Clothes for Children............481
18. Sewing for Dolls................503

Skills IN ACTION

Getting Answers...........................14
Self-Image Booster........................19
Volunteering..............................39
Acting on Your Values.....................55
Evaluating Past Decisions.................69
Starting Your Own Business................96
On the Job...............................100
Using "I" Messages.......................113
Making New Friends.......................133
Learning to Compromise...................144
Making Friends...........................155
Guiding Preschoolers.....................162
Selecting Toys...........................166
Treasure Chest...........................181
Money Savers.............................192
Shopping by Television...................195
Evaluating Clubs.........................203
Identifying Quackery.....................208
Using Water Wisely.......................248
Bicycle and Skating Safety...............261
Creative Breakfasts......................275
Finding the Sugar in Foods...............281
Starting a Fitness Program...............320
How to Use a Fire Extinguisher...........334
Which Tool?..............................338
Converting Conventional Oven Recipes.....348
Rating the Team's Success................353
Practicing Good Table Manners............362
Shopping Etiquette.......................368
Organizing Recipes.......................374
Creative Vegetables......................398
Brown-bagging It.........................401
Using Yogurt Instead.....................409
Meat Extenders...........................418
Dressing Appropriately...................437
The Right Lines for You..................444
Identifying Fabrics......................459
Earning Money for Clothes................469
Hand Washing Clothes.....................475
Pressing Fabrics.........................487
Expressing Yourself Through Fabric.......496
Home Decorating..........................508
Sewing for Fun and Profit................521
Recycling Your Clothes...................532

TIPS for living

Identifying Your Skills 7
Dealing with Your Emotions . . 13
Breaking Bad Habits 28
Making Up Your Mind 65
Reaching Your Goals 72
Reading the Want Ads 84
Improving Your Study Skills . . 88
Filling Out a Job Application . 95
Getting Along with
    Coworkers 102
Laughter is the Best
    Medicine 124
Handling Peer Pressure 139
Helping Children Become
    Independent 156
Sparking a Child's
    Imagination 163
Teaching Children to Share . 169
Playground Safety 173
Handling Emergencies 180
Writing a Complaint Letter . 210
Clearing the Clutter 226
The Principles of Design 231
Drawing a Floor Plan 234
How to Recycle 255
Stranger Danger 262
Understanding Food Terms . 280
Reducing the Fat 307
Where's the Fat? 313
Calories for Fitness 318
Microwave Tricks 347
Saving Time in the Kitchen . . 352
Setting the Table 361
Rare, Medium,
    or Well-Done? 417
Taking Care of Your Eyes . . . 432
Shaping Up 445
Choosing Shoes 464
The Hidden Costs 469
Using Sewing Kits 491
Timesaving Notions 497
Serger Terms 517

Try This!

Finding New Interests 5
Stereotyping 27
Needs and Wants 58
Helping Charitable
    Organizations 63
Matching Your Skills
    with a Job 82
Writing a Business Letter 88
Good Work Habits 102
Gifts from the Heart 114
Special Memories 118
A Feeling of Well-being 129
Keeping in Touch 135
Recognizing Peer Pressure . . 137
Peer Mediation 145
Safety Tips 174
Comparing Labels 196
Secondhand Treasures 205
Stretching Your Money 215
Sharing Space 223
Home Safety Checklist 238
Conserving Natural
    Resources 247
Is Your Diet Healthful? 276
Vitamin Supplements 285
Can Food Labels
    Mislead You? 288
Eyeballing Serving Sizes 297
Reducing Salt in Your Diet . . 309
Snack Attacks 311
Dish-washing Safety 329
Stretching Food Dollars 371
Using Seasonings 382
Making Fruit Baskets 392
Health-booster Veggies 396
Milk's Many Forms 408
Protective Wear 436
Donating Clothes 453
Keeping the Lab Neat 483
Sewing Safety 514
Storing Patterns 525
Hand-sewing Skills 530

CONNECTIONS

SCIENCE	Pass It On 21
SOCIAL STUDIES	Everyday Citizens 49
TECHNOLOGY	Technology and Your Future . . . 75
MATH	Gross Pay Versus Net Pay 105
LITERATURE	Mama Is a Sunrise 147
ART	Children in Art 183
MATH	The $1,300 Snack 217
TECHNOLOGY	Automation in the Home 241
SCIENCE	Alternative Sources
of Energy 265
SOCIAL STUDIES	Foods Around the World 291
MATH	Getting Active 323
SCIENCE	Friction Produces Heat 355
MATH	Recipe Conversions 385
TECHNOLOGY	Genetically Engineered
Food 421
TECHNOLOGY	Recycled Plastic 447
SOCIAL STUDIES	Clothing and Climate 477
MATH	Product Pricing 499
SOCIAL STUDIES	Clothing Customs 535

TABLE OF CONTENTS ix

UNIT 1 Personal Development

Unit Overview

In Unit 1 students explore personal development. The unit focuses on ways that students' individuality, self-concept, and interpersonal and communication skills can contribute to personal and career success.

Chapter 1 helps students explore personal development and develop an understanding of how to build a positive self-concept. In Chapter 2 students learn to develop interpersonal, communication, citizenship, leadership, and management skills. Chapter 3 discusses the process of evaluating wants, needs, and values and its relationship to making decisions and setting goals. Chapter 4 details ways that students can develop career goals and be successful in their jobs.

Introducing the Unit

- **Parent Letters** As you begin the study of this unit, you may wish to send home copies of the Parent Letter and Activities found in the *Linking Home, School, and Community* booklet in the TCR.
- **Using Visuals** Discuss the Unit Opener photograph with students. Ask how the teen shown in the picture is developing her own personal self-concept.
- **Using the Color Transparency** Present Color Transparency 1, "What Is Important to You?" Have students use the example in the transparency to begin thinking about what they feel is most important in their own lives.

Chapter 1: The Unique You

Chapter 2: Everyday Living Skills

Chapter 3: Steps to Success

Chapter 4: Careers

BULLETIN BOARD IDEAS

What Makes You a Star? Divide the bulletin board into two categories: *Heredity* and *Environmental Influences*. Cut out nine star shapes. Print the words *eye color, sex, hair color,* and *height* on four stars and place them under the category *Heredity*. Print the words *interests, friends, school, family,* and *hobbies* on the five stars that are left. Place these stars under the category *Environmental Influences*.

UNIT PROJECTS 1

Encourage students to complete one or two Hands-on Projects for this unit found in the Teacher's Classroom Resources.
- Hands-on Project 1, "Personal Banner," helps students understand their own unique qualities as they design a banner for themselves.
- Hands-on Project 2, "Start Your Own Business," reinforces skills learned in Chapters 3 and 4 as students work together to start and run their own small business.

Unit Closure

- Allow class time at the end of this unit to reinforce students' understanding of the material by playing Hands-on Game 1, "Personal Password," found in the TCR.
- Create your own Unit Test using the Testmaker Software to evaluate students' comprehension.

Promoting Family & Consumer Sciences

Administrators Information is provided at the opening of each Unit to help you recognize opportunities for forming partnerships with parents, coworkers, and community members. You will find suggestions for effectively communicating your program's accomplishments and documenting students' achievements. You may also wish to refer to the *Linking Home, School, and Community* booklet in the TCR.

BULLETIN BOARD IDEAS

Where the Jobs Are: Get a Piece of the Pie! Draw a large pie on poster board. Divide the pie into eight pieces and label each piece with one of the following terms: *vocational, service, industry, social services, education, professional, engineering, business,* and *conservation.* You may wish to use different colors of poster board for each of the eight pie pieces. Use the classified section of the newspaper as the background for the bulletin board.

Planning Guide
Chapter 1 The Unique You

LESSON 1	Pages	FEATURES	CLASSROOM RESOURCES
The One and Only You	4–9	*Tips for Living: Identifying Your Skills* *Try This: Finding New Interests*	Concept Map 1 Cooperative Learning 1 Cross Curriculum 1 Lesson 1 Quiz Peer Pressure and Decision Making 1 Transparency 2, "Influences on You" Student Workbook Activities 1, 2
LESSON 2 **Understanding Yourself**	10–15	*Tips for Living: Dealing with Your Emotions* *Skills in Action: Getting Answers*	Activity and Project Card 1, "A Book Jacket About Me" Enrichment Activity 1 Lesson 2 Quiz Transparency 3, "Healthy Steps for Dealing with Strong Emotions" Transparency 4, "Times of Change" Student Workbook Activities 3, 4
LESSON 3 **Your Self-Concept**	16–20	*Skills in Action: Self-Image Booster*	Activity and Project Card 2, "Hooked on Health Mobile" Cooperative Learning 2 Lesson 3 Quiz Peer Pressure and Decision Making 2 Transparency 5, "Ways to Build Self-Esteem" Transparency 6, "Building Good Health Habits" Student Workbook Activities 5, 6

CHAPTER 1 RESOURCES
- Chapter 1 Test
- Reteaching 1
- Study Guide 1, *Reteaching*
- Testmaker Software

UNIT 1 RESOURCES
- Transparency 1, "What Is Important to You?"
- Hands-on Projects 1, 2
- Hands-on Game 1

Performance Assessment Activity

Have students write their autobiographies to help them understand themselves and to learn more about their uniqueness. Before students begin writing, have them make an outline of what they want to include in their autobiography. Student outlines might include date and place of birth, family background, inherited traits, environment in which they live, and significant life experiences. Ask them to conclude the autobiography with a paragraph explaining how all the influences on them have affected their personal development and made them a unique person.

Have students compile their autobiographies into individual books. The book cover should include a photograph or drawing of the student. Students might exchange and read one another's autobiographies.

School-to-Work

Provide students with examples of résumés. Point out to the students that résumés usually include a person's education, work experiences, achievements and honors, skills, hobbies, and memberships in clubs and organizations. Explain that a résumé is like an outline of a person's life experiences. A résumé identifies some of the unique characteristics of the person. In some ways it is like a short biography. Ask students to write their own résumés. Their résumés should include their education, work experiences (this could include chores at home), skills, hobbies, and memberships in clubs and organizations. Discuss the finished résumés with the class. Ask students how a résumé, which identifies a person's unique qualities, helps people find employment. Display the résumés in the classroom.

Family & Community

Ask students to identify people in their family or in their community that they look to as positive role models. Have each student write a letter to their role model. The student letters should include at least three examples of qualities that make this person a positive role model. Have the students mail their letters to the role models. Ask volunteers to share any responses they receive.

Resources for the Teacher

Canfield, Jack, and Wells, Harold C. *One Hundred Ways to Enhance Self-Concept in the Classroom: A Handbook for Teachers, Counselors, and Group Leaders.* Needham, MA: Allyn & Bacon, 1994.

Thomas, A. *Self-Esteem*. New York: Rosen Publishing Group, 1991.

Readings for the Student

Branden, Nathaniel. *The Power of Self-Esteem*. Deerfield Beach, FL: Health Communications, Inc., 1992.

Johnson, Julie T. *Celebrate You: Building Your Self-Esteem*. Minneapolis: Lerner Publications, 1990.

Kramer, P. *Discovering Self-Confidence*. New York: Rosen Publishing Group, 1991.

Multimedia Resources

Adolescent (Videocassette). American Journal of Nursing.

Feeling Good About Yourself: How to Build Self-Confidence (Videocassette). The Center for Humanities.

Proud to Be Me: Developing Self-Esteem (Videocassette). Guidance Associates.

OUT OF TIME?

If time does not permit thorough teaching of this chapter, you may wish to use:

- Teens Making a Difference, page 3
- Try This, page 5
- Tips for Living, pages 7, 13
- Skills in Action, pages 14, 19
- Young Living Activities, page 21
- Chapter Summary, page 22

CHAPTER 1
The Unique You

Chapter Overview
Chapter 1 discusses the physical and emotional changes associated with adolescence. The chapter gives examples of ways adolescents can develop a positive self-concept.
LESSON 1 identifies the factors that influence individual differences.
LESSON 2 describes the impact of physical and emotional changes during adolescence.
LESSON 3 explains the importance of a positive self-concept and how to build a positive self-concept.

Introducing the Chapter
Have students skim the lesson titles and photographs in the chapter. Based on the titles, ask them to write two questions for each lesson that they would expect the lesson to answer. Ask students to write the questions on index cards and have them answer the questions after they have studied the chapter.

Chapter Motivator
Refer students to the chapter title, "The Unique You." Then on a slip of paper have students write a description of themselves that they think makes them unique. Collect the slips and choose one randomly. Read the description to the class and have students identify the person who wrote each description.

CHAPTER 1
The Unique You

LESSON ONE
The One and Only You

LESSON TWO
Understanding Yourself

LESSON THREE
Your Self-Concept

KEY TO ABILITY LEVELS
Teaching strategies that appear throughout the chapter have been identified by one of three codes to give you an idea of their suitability for students of varying learning styles and abilities.

L1 Level 1 strategies should be within the ability range of all students. Often full class participation is required. Teacher direction is usually needed.

L2 Level 2 strategies are for average to above-average students or for small groups. Some teacher direction is necessary.

L3 Level 3 strategies are designed for students able and willing to work independently. Minimal teacher direction is necessary.

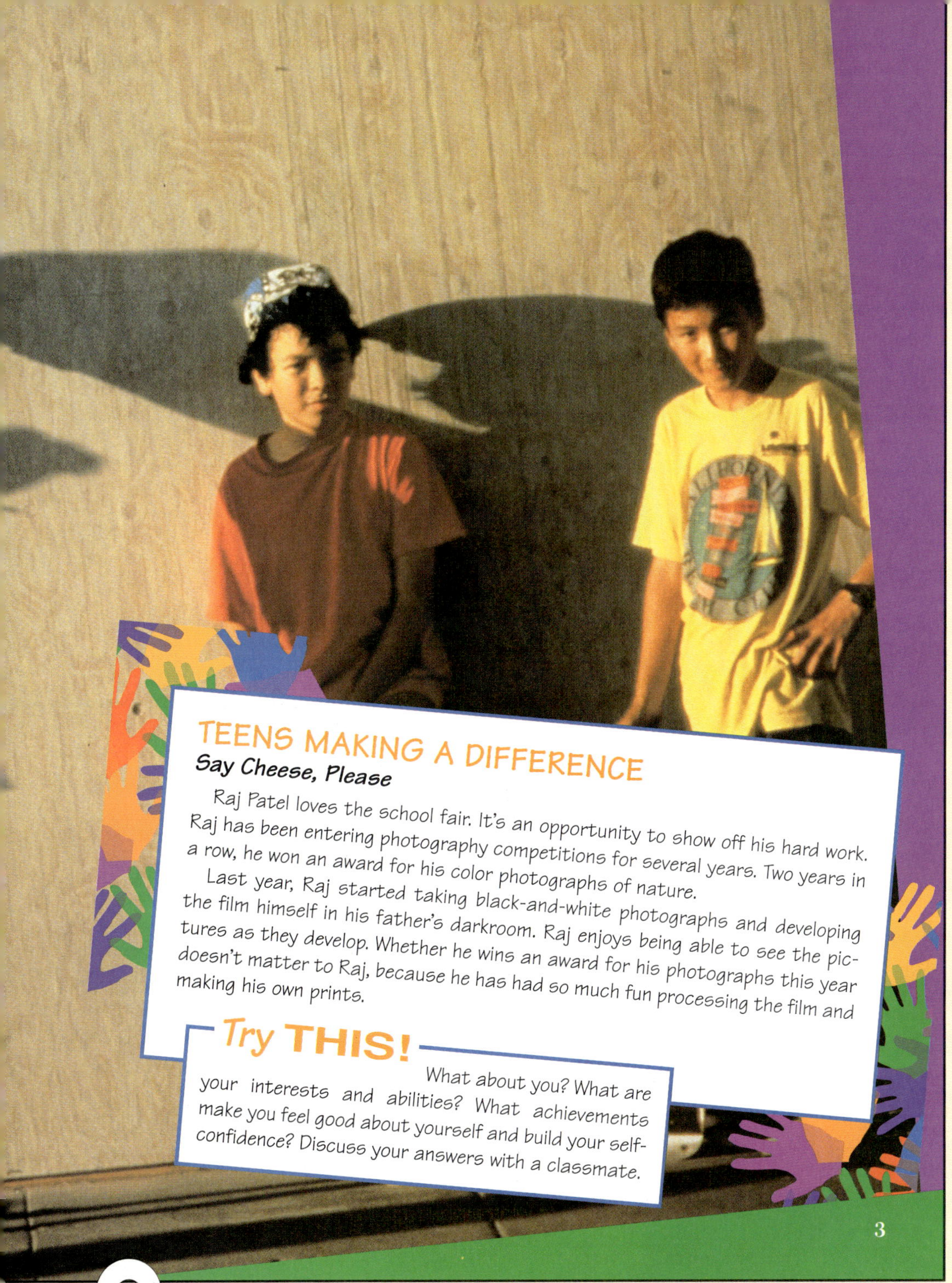

TEENS MAKING A DIFFERENCE
Say Cheese, Please

Raj Patel loves the school fair. It's an opportunity to show off his hard work. Raj has been entering photography competitions for several years. Two years in a row, he won an award for his color photographs of nature.

Last year, Raj started taking black-and-white photographs and developing the film himself in his father's darkroom. Raj enjoys being able to see the pictures as they develop. Whether he wins an award for his photographs this year doesn't matter to Raj, because he has had so much fun processing the film and making his own prints.

Try THIS!

What about you? What are your interests and abilities? What achievements make you feel good about yourself and build your self-confidence? Discuss your answers with a classmate.

CHAPTER 1

TEENS MAKING A DIFFERENCE

Have students read "Teens Making a Difference." Ask students to identify the qualities of Raj that make him unique. (Students might indicate his interest in photography.) Tell students that people's interests and abilities are important factors in developing a positive self-concept.

Ask students to answer the questions from the TRY THIS activity on their own. Then have them work with a classmate to discuss the answers. Encourage students to be open and honest in discussing their responses.

BLOCK SCHEDULING

The following Teacher Classroom Resources are recommended for use in classrooms using Block Scheduling:
- Activity and Project Card 1, "A Book Jacket About Me"
- Activity and Project Card 2, "Hooked on Health Mobile"
- Cooperative Learning 1, "Find Out About a Classmate"
- Cooperative Learning 2, "Who We Are"

TECHNOLOGY IN THE CLASSROOM

Multimedia Equipment The use of multimedia equipment in the classroom is rapidly playing a more important role. Overhead projectors, VCRs, videodisc players, computers, and CD-ROMs are some of the examples of technology-related equipment that is becoming more commonplace in the Family and Consumer Sciences classroom. Using technology has several advantages for effective teaching and learning. It motivates students, enables them to analyze data, and provides real-life situations that can be viewed and used as discussion tools. You will find "Technology in the Classroom" in all chapter opening pages of the Teacher's Wraparound Edition to help you successfully integrate technology in your classroom.

LESSON ONE
The One and Only You

FOCUS

Lesson Objectives
After studying this lesson, students should be able to
- discuss why people are alike and different from everyone else.
- differentiate between inherited and acquired characteristics.
- describe the influence of role models.

Motivating Activity
Introduce the topic of individuality by assigning the following activity. Have students list five physical characteristics that can differ to make each individual unique.

Introducing the Lesson
Have volunteers read their responses to the Motivating Activity. (possible physical differences: height; weight; eye, skin, hair color) Then mention to the students that physical differences are just some of the factors that make a person unique. Tell them that Lesson 1 will describe other factors that contribute to the uniqueness of every individual.

Introducing *Words to Know*
Call on volunteers to read the definitions of *heredity* and *acquired* found on pages 5 and 6. Ask students to explain the differences between the two terms. Have students give examples of characteristics that are determined by heredity and characteristics that are acquired. Explain that the root word for "heredity" is *heres*, which also gives us "heir" and "heritage."

4

LESSON ONE
The One and Only You

 **WORDS TO KNOW**

unique
heredity
environment
acquired
culture
role
role models

DISCOVER...
- why people are alike and different from everyone else.
- the difference between inherited and acquired characteristics.
- the influence of role models.

Nicole and Amanda are identical twins. Most people think that the teens are exactly alike, but, in fact, they are quite different. Nicole likes to listen to rock music, while Amanda prefers jazz. Nicole loves outdoor activities. Amanda, on the other hand, would rather read a mystery book. The teens even look slightly different from each other. In fact, no two people—not even identical twins—are exactly alike. There is something special about each person. You also are **unique**— *one of a kind.* You are special and different from all others.

4 CHAPTER 1: THE UNIQUE YOU

CLASSROOM RESOURCES FOR LESSON 1

 Blackline Masters
Concept Map 1
Cooperative Learning 1
Cross Curriculum 1
Lesson 1 Quiz
Peer Pressure and Decision Making 1

 Transparencies
Transparency 2, "Influences on You"

 Student Workbook
Activities 1, 2

You probably share some interests, such as camping or watching movies, with family members or friends. During your teen years you will also begin to develop other interests on your own. You are entering the stage in your life when you will establish your individuality and become your own person.

Traits in Common

Although people are different from each other, they are also alike in many ways. Everyone must have food, water, and a place to live. Everyone needs to feel loved and accepted by others. All people need to feel safe. You, like others, have the desire to express your creativity and independence. However, the way you satisfy your needs may be different from that of other people. Like Nicole, you may enjoy outdoor activities. Your best friend may be more like Amanda and prefer playing board games and watching old-time movies.

Being an Individual

No two people act, think, or feel the same way. This is because everyone comes from a different background and has different experiences. Everything you do, everywhere you go, and everyone you know—especially your family members and friends—have influenced who you are. **Figure 1.1** on the next page shows the many influences on you that make you unique.

Heredity and Environment

Some of the characteristics that make you an individual are a result of your heredity. **Heredity** (huh-RED-i-tee) is *the passing on of traits or characteristics from parents to their children.* These traits include your eye and skin color, your facial features, and your body build.

You have other qualities that make you a unique individual. These are traits that are a result of your **environment,** or *all the living and nonliving things that surround you.* Do you live in a small town, in a big city, or in the country? Imagine how different you would be if you had been raised in a different climate or a different country.

Try This!
Think of a new activity you would like to try, such as playing tennis, starting a baseball card collection, or playing chess. Then make a list of ways you could find out more about the interest.

LESSON ONE: THE ONE AND ONLY YOU 5

HOME AND COMMUNITY CONNECTION

Explain to students that just as no two snowflakes are alike, no two sets of fingerprints are alike. Fingerprints provide the most reliable method of identifying an individual. Even identical twins have different sets of fingerprints. Invite a member of the local police department to explain to the class how fingerprinting is used as a method of identification in solving missing persons cases and criminal cases. With parental permission, fingerprint the students. Allow students time to study the differences in one another's fingerprints. Give the fingerprints to students to take home.

CHAPTER 1, LESSON 1

TEACH

Try This!
After students have read the feature ask them to choose a hobby that they might be interested in exploring. Ask them to identify ways that they would go about exploring it. Then encourage them to explore the particular hobby and to decide whether it is one that they would like to continue pursuing.

L1 Comparing and Contrasting
On the board draw a Venn diagram with two intersecting circles. Label the intersecting part of the circles "Both." Have students work with partners. Ask each pair to draw the Venn diagram shown on the board. Each person should write his or her name above one of circles. Have the partners list the characteristics they have in common with each other under the heading "Both." Have the pairs complete the rest of the diagram by listing their differing characteristics under their name. Discuss the diagrams.

L2 Analyzing
Have students print their names vertically on a piece of paper. Ask them to write nouns and adjectives starting with the letters of their name that describe their personal characteristics. These might include special interests, hobbies, and abilities. (For example, a person named "Ben" might indicate the following: "B"—baseball, "E"—energetic, "N"—nice.) Post the papers on a bulletin board titled "I am Unique."

5

CHAPTER 1, LESSON 1

USING VISUALS
Have students study the illustration showing the factors that influence who they are in Figure 1.1. Ask volunteers to discuss the influence that makes them unique. Then have students create a drawing similar to the one shown. Their illustrations should picture themselves and the specific influences that help determine who they are. Display the illustrations on a bulletin board.

L1 Using Transparencies
Present Color Transparency 2, "Influences on You," in the TCR. Use this overhead visual to reinforce concepts from this lesson.

L2 Science
Explain to students that whether they have straight, wavy, or curly hair depends on the shape of their hair shafts. This trait is a result of heredity. An oval shaft causes wavy hair. A round shaft causes straight hair. A flat shaft causes curly hair. Have students use a magnifying glass or microscope to view a strand of their hair. Ask them to determine the shape of their hair shafts based on the shape of this hair strand. Ask students how their environment can change the inherited characteristics of their hair. (Humidity can cause hair to become curlier or straighten. Sunlight can lighten hair color. People can have their hair straightened, permed, or colored.)

L2 Social Studies Connection
Assign Cross-Curriculum Activity 1 in the TCR. Students research holidays from various cultures in this activity.

 **Figure 1.1 Influences on You**
Many factors influence who you are. Which of these factors have influenced you the most?

Think about your interests, hobbies, and abilities. Some of them are **acquired,** or *learned from the people and things around you.* Perhaps your sister taught you how to skate. Maybe a friend sparked your interest in computers. These are examples of acquired skills or interests. Name three abilities that you have acquired or learned.

You have some characteristics that are influenced by both heredity and your environment. For example, body build may be inherited, but the athletic skill to play a particular sport is acquired.

Culture

Your culture also influences the person you become. **Culture** refers to *the ways of thinking, acting, dressing, and speaking shared by a group of people.* Cultures may be based

6   CHAPTER 1: THE UNIQUE YOU

TECHNOLOGY UPDATE

Crime investigators have recently starting using an individual's uniqueness to help identify criminals. DNA testing, sometimes referred to as genetic fingerprinting, relies on the uniqueness of an individual's inherited traits. Each individual's inherited traits are determined by the makeup of their DNA molecule. Experts estimate that there are trillions of different ways that the DNA molecule could be put together. Therefore, many people believe that it is highly unlikely that two people would be found with identical DNA molecules. Some critics, however, believe that the techniques used to identify the patterns in a DNA molecule are not absolutely reliable.

TIPS for living

IDENTIFYING YOUR SKILLS

Another name for an acquired ability is a skill. Everyone has skills. You might be good at playing soccer, or you might be a good listener. Identifying your skills gives you confidence to try new activities. Ask yourself the following questions.

- What activities do I most enjoy?
- What things seem easiest for me to learn?
- In what subjects do I get my best grades?
- What do my family and friends compliment me on?
- What tasks do my family and friends ask me to help them do?

on race, ethnic group, geographic location, or social class. You may not even think about your culture until you meet someone who speaks a different language at home or celebrates other holidays from yours.

Your culture may influence the food you eat or the holidays you celebrate. What might be some benefits of learning about other cultures?

Family Background

Your family has one of the strongest influences on the person you become. Are you an only child, or do you have brothers or sisters? Are you the oldest, the youngest, or in the middle? What activities do you do with family members? How important is spending time together with family members? These questions suggest some of the ways you are influenced by your family.

MEETING STUDENT DIVERSITY

Cultural Perspectives Ask students to give examples of cultural groups, such as African Americans, Native Americans, Christians, Muslims, and so on. Point out that besides race, ethnicity, geographic location, or social class, cultures may also be based on occupations, religions, interests, or age. Have students determine all the cultural groups to which they belong. Emphasize that cultural differences add to the interesting diversity we experience every day.

CHAPTER 1, LESSON 1

TIPS for living
Allow students time to answer the questions that will help them identify their skills. Ask volunteers to name the skills they identified.

DID YOU KNOW
A simple strand of your hair can tell many things about who you are. Scientists can run tests on a strand of your hair to determine your age, gender, and race. Laboratory tests using strands of hair can also determine whether or not the person has been using certain types of drugs.

L2 Social Studies
Have students learn about the culture of another young person. Provide them with the addresses of organizations that connect young people from different countries who want to be pen pals. (World Pen Pals, 1690 Como Ave., St. Paul, MN 55108, or International Pen Friends, Box 65, Homecrest Station, Brooklyn, NY 11229; this organization has special services for the blind and permanently handicapped.)

Encourage students to write letters to their pen pal describing their own culture and asking questions about their pen pal's culture.

L1 Discussing
Point out to students that their friends and peers also influence what kind of person they become. Ask students to give examples of ways their friends and peers influence them.

LESSON ONE: THE ONE AND ONLY YOU

CHAPTER 1, LESSON 1

L2 Problem Solving
Assign Peer Pressure and Decision Making 1 in the TCR. This activity gives students the opportunity to recognise peer pressure and practice decision-making skills.

L2 Cooperative Learning
Assign Cooperative Learning Activity 1, "Find Out About a Classmate," in the TCR.

L1 Student Workbook
Assign Activities 1 and 2 in the Student Workbook.

ASSESS

Evaluating the Lesson
Assign Reviewing Terms and Facts and Thinking Critically on page 9 to review the lesson; then assign the Lesson 1 Quiz in the TCR.

Reteaching
- Organize students into small groups to discuss experiences that have affected their attitudes, achievements, and outlook on life. Ask each group to select two or three examples of experiences to share with the class.
- Have students complete Reteaching Activity 1 in the TCR.
- Assign Concept Map 1 in the TCR.

Enrichment
Have students list a role model for one of the following categories: politician, athlete, or performer. Have them read a newspaper or magazine article about the person and write a paragraph explaining why the person is a positive role model.

Experiences

Each person has a unique set of experiences. For example, you may have moved several times, and perhaps you have learned to play the flute. Your best friend has lived in the same house since she was born and excels in sports. These experiences affect a person's attitudes, achievements, and outlook on life. Experiences not only include the activities you do, but also the places you go and the friends you have. During your teen years, new experiences help you grow into a unique individual.

Roles

What roles do you have? A **role** is *the way you behave when you interact with another person.* The roles you have determine how you relate to other people and how you act in various situations. For example, you may act silly when you are with your best friend but very mature when you are babysitting. You have many roles. At home you may be a daughter or a son and a brother or a sister. At school you may be a student, a best friend, and a team member. In the community you may be a volunteer for a recycling center or a member of a Scout troop. Your role varies, depending on whom you are interacting with.

You learn your roles by talking to and watching people who are important to you. **Role models** are *people who help you see what is expected of you and show you how to act in certain situations.* Role models can be parents, older siblings, relatives, teachers, coaches, or religious leaders. Who are some of your role models? How do you act as a role model to a younger sibling or neighbor?

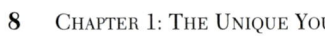

You may be a role model for someone else. How can you make sure that your role is a positive one?

8 CHAPTER 1: THE UNIQUE YOU

MORE ABOUT • • •

Your Many Roles The roles people play in their lives often have to do with their traditions or culture. In many cultures, such as in the developing countries of Africa and Asia, women continue to play a traditional role of homemaker, with home and family the center of their lives. In other cultures, such as in the United States and the former Soviet bloc countries, career opportunities for women are increasing, while the number of men who stay home to raise children is also increasing.

Although you share some things in common with other teens, you are a unique individual. What qualities do you have that make you different from your friends?

One of a Kind

You share some traits—including the need for food, shelter, and love—with other people. You also have dreams, ideas, habits, and traits that are yours alone. All of the people, places, and events in your life have influenced the person you are now and the person you will become. Whether you are shy or outgoing, funny or serious, quiet or loud—you are a special, interesting, and unique person.

LESSON ONE Review

Using complete sentences, answer the following questions on a separate sheet of paper.

Reviewing Terms and Facts

1. **Identify** What are four influences that give you a unique identity?
2. **List** What are three ways your family influences the person you become?
3. **Explain** What effect do experiences have on people?

Thinking Critically

4. **Distinguish** What is the difference between inherited traits and acquired abilities? Give two examples of each.

5. **Analyze** Choose a person you think of as a positive role model. Explain what you admire about this person.

Applying Concepts

6. List ten of your most important characteristics. Decide what percentage of these traits are inherited, what percentage have been acquired with help from other people, and what percentage are a little bit of both. Draw a pie chart showing your results.

LESSON ONE: THE ONE AND ONLY YOU   9

TECHNOLOGY UPDATE

Personalizing a Career Using special computer software, students can learn more about possible career opportunities. These programs assess students' interests and skills, and identify careers that match with their skills and interests. One program, for example, allows students to rate their abilities, list grades they receive in certain subjects, and select work-related tasks they might enjoy. The program then shows them how to apply their abilities and interests to a specific career field, such as health care or food services. Some sample jobs and job descriptions are also included.

CHAPTER 1, LESSON 1

Answers to Lesson 1 Review

1. Any four: different inherited and acquired characteristics, different environment, different family backgrounds, different experiences, different culture, different roles.
2. Whether you are an only child or have brothers or sisters; whether you are the youngest, the oldest, or in the middle; what activities you do with your family.
3. Experiences affect your attitudes, achievements, and outlook on life. New experiences help you grow into a unique individual.
4. Inherited traits are traits passed from parents to children. Acquired abilities are learned from the people and things around you. Any two inherited traits: color of eyes, facial features, height, special talents. Any two acquired abilities: interests and hobbies.
5. Students choose a positive role model and explain what they admire about the person.
6. Answers will vary. Students should list characteristics and draw a pie graph to show percentage of inherited traits, percentage acquired with help from other people, and percentage of traits that are a bit of each.

CLOSE

Stress to students that they have many roles. Ask them to enumerate their roles at home, in school, and in their community.

LESSON TWO
Understanding Yourself

FOCUS

Lesson Objectives

After studying this lesson, students should be able to
- identify ways to better understand themselves.
- explain how adolescence is a time of change.
- discuss constructive ways of dealing with emotions.

Motivating Activity

On the back of several slips of paper write an emotional state such as nervous, proud, fearful, lonely, and so on. Hand out one slip to each student. Have them decide on ways that they could act out, in pantomime, the emotion they chose.

Introducing the Lesson

Have students share their responses to the Motivating Activity by calling on them to act out the emotion they chose. Have class members guess what the emotion is. Discuss other ways the emotion might be expressed. Tell students that this lesson will help them better understand themselves and learn positive ways of dealing with their emotions.

Introducing *Words to Know*

Ask a volunteer to read the vocabulary words. Tell students that the word "adolescence" comes from the Latin verb *adolescence*, "to grow up." Ask students to think of a synonym. (youth, teen years)

LESSON TWO
Understanding Yourself

WORDS TO KNOW

adolescence
personality
emotions

DISCOVER...
- how to understand yourself better.
- how adolescence is a time of change.
- constructive ways of dealing with emotions.

Ben is worried about himself. Some days he feels happy and cheerful one moment, and sad and restless the next. He is also concerned because he is shorter than most of his classmates. Do you ever have feelings like Ben's? These are normal feelings that occur during **adolescence** (a-duhl-E-suhns), *the period of great growth and change between childhood and adulthood.*

As you grow up, you will get to know yourself better and be comfortable with yourself. You will also become aware of how you see yourself and how others see you. This helps you understand your strengths and weaknesses. It gives you confidence to show off your positive qualities and encourages you to improve the things about yourself that you want to change.

10   CHAPTER 1: THE UNIQUE YOU

CLASSROOM RESOURCES FOR LESSON 2

 Blackline Masters
Activity and Project Card 1,
  "A Book Jacket About Me"
Enrichment Activity 1
Lesson 2 Quiz

 Transparencies
Transparency 3, "Healthy Steps for Dealing with Strong Emotions"
Transparency 4, "Times of Change"

 Student Workbook
Activities 3, 4

Your Personality

Personality is *the sum total of a person's traits, feelings, attitudes, and habits.* Your personality shows in the way you look, the way you communicate, and the way you act. It is the part of you that you reveal to other people.

Your personality continues to grow and change throughout your life. It changes as you have new experiences and meet new people. You become a more interesting person when you develop your skills and talents, learn to do new things, and participate in school and community activities.

Everyone's personality is different. Perhaps you are very outgoing and friendly, while some of your friends are quiet and reserved. Do you enjoy spending time indoors reading a book, or do you prefer to be outdoors playing basketball? There is no right or wrong way to be. Learning more about yourself will help you appreciate and respect the differences in yourself and in other people.

Your Emotions

Do you remember how proud you felt when you scored the winning goal in a soccer game or got a good grade on your science project? Perhaps you remember how happy you were

No two people have the same personality. Why is it important to understand your own personality?

LESSON TWO: UNDERSTANDING YOURSELF   11

CHAPTER 1, LESSON 2

TEACH

L1 Making Comparisons
Have students bring in two pictures of themselves: one taken in first grade and one taken recently. Have them attach the pictures to a piece of paper. Ask them to study the pictures, focusing on the ways that their personalities have changed since first grade. Have them list the changes. Call on students to share their lists with the class. Help students understand that personality development continues throughout life.

L3 Journal Writing
Point out to students that one positive way of dealing with their emotions it to write about them. Have students keep a private journal for several days. They should write about their emotions, describing the emotions they feel, what caused each emotion, and how they expressed the emotion. Discuss with students how keeping a journal can help them deal with their emotions.

L2 Activity and Project Card
Allow time for students to complete Activity and Project Card 1, "A Book Jacket About Me," in the TCR.

COOPERATIVE LEARNING

Studying Emotions Organize students into small groups. Ask each group to devise a situation about a young person who is dealing with angry or sad emotions. For example, a possible scenario might be: You want to go to the mall with a group of friends, but your parents say you cannot go. Have the groups exchange the situations and create a skit depicting a healthy emotional reaction to the scenario. Direct the students to use the "Tips for Dealing with Your Emotions" on page 13 to help them write their skit. Have students present their skits to the class.

CHAPTER 1, LESSON 2

L1 Analyzing
Call on students to describe possible emotional reactions to the following scenarios. Then ask them to suggest constructive ways to deal with the emotions.
- You must give an oral report to your class.
- You cannot understand the math assignment.
- Your older brother will not let you go with him to the movies.
- Your best friend ignores you.
- You have difficulty performing a new skill in gym class.
- You are the goalie and the other team scores against you.

L1 Using Transparencies
Present Color Transparency 3, "Healthy Steps for Dealing with Strong Emotions," and 4, "Times of Change," in the TCR. Use these overhead visuals to reinforce concepts from this lesson.

---

when your father praised you for keeping your room neat. An important part of your personality is related to your emotions. **Emotions** are *feelings, such as happiness, fear,* or *love.* By understanding your emotions and why they change, you will better understand yourself.

You have many emotions. You may feel pleased and excited when you do something well. Learning how to use a computer program or completing an English report, for example, would give you a feeling of pride and satisfaction. At other times you may feel sad or frustrated, such as when you have a disagreement with a friend or you cannot figure out a math problem. Depending on the situation, you may feel joyful, angry, proud, jealous, hurt, or loved. When was the last time you experienced each of these feelings?

One of the difficult things about emotions is that you may experience different ones at the same time. You may feel both excited and scared about being in the school play. You may feel proud that your sister was accepted by a college, yet sad that she will be going away. Having two different emotions at the same time makes it hard to sort out your feelings. It is a natural part of life that you sometimes feel confused or mixed up.

During adolescence you may develop close relationships with friends. What other emotional changes take place during adolescence?

12 CHAPTER 1: THE UNIQUE YOU

MORE ABOUT •••
Adolescence Not only are there great physical changes taking place during adolescence, but there are also highly important developments occurring with regard to values, aspirations, roles, and identity. Adolescents have their own subculture, featuring special language, clothes, idols, magazines, and music. Adolescents have a strong need for self-understanding and a desire to show their independence. They tend to be idealistic—often searching for the ultimate truth, beauty, and love. They question the relevancy of social and ethical standards.

Ask students if they agree with this analysis of adolescence and to give reasons for their opinions. Then ask them to give personal examples of the characteristics of adolescence.

Changes in Your Emotions

During adolescence you will be adjusting to many changes—both physical and emotional. Don't be surprised if your emotions seem stronger and harder to control. This is common, because your body systems are developing and changing. Your feelings may be hurt more easily. You may feel ignored or become irritated easily. Positive feelings can be stronger, too. For example, you may develop a closer relationship with a friend of the opposite gender.

Adjusting to new emotions can be challenging. Today you may laugh when someone teases you, but tomorrow teasing may upset you. Sometimes you will feel happy and want to share your joy with your friends. At other times you may want to be alone and not talk to anyone. When your moods are constantly changing like this, it may seem as if you lack control over your life. In fact, you can learn to handle your feelings. See Tips for Living, "Dealing With Your Emotions."

Controlling Your Emotions

Even though these new and changing emotions are difficult to understand, you should not let them rule your life.

DEALING WITH YOUR EMOTIONS

It is normal to feel angry or sad sometimes. It's the way you handle your emotions that is important. Try these healthy ways to deal with your emotions.

- Admit how you feel. Try to figure out why you feel that way.
- Talk about your feelings with a family member, friend, teacher, or counselor.
- Write down your feelings in your journal.
- Work off your feelings by doing something physical, such as pounding a pillow or riding a bike.
- If you are angry with another person, wait until you have cooled off before speaking to him or her. Tell the person how you feel and what you need or want.

CHAPTER 1, LESSON 2

TEACHER TALK!

Dealing with Sensitive Issues

Discussing some of the emotional and physiological changes that take place during adolescence may be difficult for some students. Reassure students that although everyone experiences emotional changes and physical growth at different rates, everyone does go through these changes eventually, and the changes that occur are perfectly normal. Students who are worried about emotional or physiological changes or have specific questions about their development should be encouraged to see a school counselor or a professional health-care provider.

TIPS for living

Point out to the students that in dealing with anger they might try listening to the other person's reply without interrupting. Doing so might keep the misunderstanding from growing into a larger argument. Also, tell students that they should avoid attacking the other person verbally by making negative comments. Instead, they should calmly express how they feel.

MORE ABOUT •••

Controlling Your Emotions Explain to students that every now and then they may want to evaluate their emotional health. One way they can do this is by taking a personal inventory. Have the students number their papers from 1 to 5 and record a "yes" or "no" response to the following statements: 1) I think before I react; 2) I do what I think is right, even if it is difficult; 3) I am happy with who I am; 4) I think about how my actions will affect others; 5) I take time to listen to others. Have students write how they think they can improve in the areas that produced a "no" response.

CHAPTER 1, LESSON 2

Skills IN ACTION

After students have read "Getting Answers," have them work in small groups to make lists of phone numbers of organizations in their community that offer help to teens. Have them post the lists in places where students will have an opportunity to see them.

L1 Student Workbook
Assign Activities 3 and 4 in the Student Workbook.

ASSESS

Evaluating the Lesson
Assign Reviewing Terms and Facts and Thinking Critically on page 14 to review the lesson; then assign the Lesson 2 Quiz in the TCR.

Reteaching
- Have each student divide a sheet of paper in half lengthwise, and label the columns "Physical" and "Emotional." Then have them list examples of growth during adolescence under each heading.
- Have students complete Reteaching Activity 1 in the TCR.

It is all right to feel angry, for example. However, if you yell at someone when you are angry, you may hurt that person's feelings and say something you will regret later. At times like these it helps to remember that you can have control over the way you react to situations.

Understanding Physical Changes

You must learn to adjust to not only the emotional changes that are taking place, but also the new physical changes. Physical changes in height, weight, and body shape occur rapidly during adolescence. You may have noticed that you or your friends seem to grow inches overnight. Sometimes the different parts of your body don't all grow at the same rate. Your feet may grow longer first. Other changes are taking place within your body, and the shape of your body changes.

Skills IN ACTION

Getting Answers

You may wonder why you suddenly have acne, or why your moods are constantly changing. Where can you go for answers to your questions? Make a list of the names and phone numbers of adults you could ask for advice. Keep your personal "yellow pages" handy, and know there is always someone you can talk to.

Changes in Your Growth and Development

It can be frustrating when your body is constantly changing and growing. Just when you get used to it one way, it changes again. Adjusting to the rapid changes can be difficult. It can make you feel awkward and clumsy.

Everyone does not change and grow at the same rate. Some of your friends will grow taller before their bodies fill out. Others first put on weight and then grow taller. You might be concerned about being too tall or too short because your friends are medium height. Perhaps you wish your voice was deeper or your feet were smaller. Some people grow and change very quickly; others do so more slowly.

These changes can make you feel different from others around you. Since teens usually want to be like their peers, this can be a frustrating time. If you are the one who starts to grow first, you may feel embarrassed or out of place. Try not to worry—your classmates will soon catch up. On the other hand, if you are the one who starts to grow later, remember that you will soon catch up to the others.

14   CHAPTER 1: THE UNIQUE YOU

MEETING STUDENT DIVERSITY

Varied Learning Styles Use the following suggestions to help students who have difficulty with English:
- Pair students with native speakers of English who can restate the main ideas of the lesson in language that helps them comprehend important concepts. Then have the students with difficulty summarize the concepts.
- Encourage nonnative English speakers to translate the *Words to Know* into their native language and use each word in a sentence (in that language). Have volunteers write their sentences on the board, with the English translation written underneath the sentences.

Being Yourself

Although there are physical features that you can't change, such as your height, you can still look your best. By being well-groomed, showing good posture, and having a friendly attitude, you will emphasize your strengths.

While the teen years can often be confusing, they can also be exciting. During this time you are learning to control your varied emotions and to cope with rapid physical changes. You are learning more about yourself, which will prepare you for becoming an adult.

Everyone grows and changes at a different rate. What can you do to adjust to these changes?

LESSON TWO *Review*

Using complete sentences, answer the following questions on a separate sheet of paper.

Reviewing Terms and Facts
1. **Vocabulary** Define the term *adolescence*. Use it in an original sentence.
2. **Vocabulary** Define the term *personality*. What are three ways to develop your personality?
3. **Describe** List three physical changes that occur during adolescence.

Thinking Critically
4. **List** Identify three ways to control strong emotions, such as anger or jealousy.
5. **Suggest** What advice would you give to a friend who feels embarrassed because he is taller than his friends and classmates?

Applying Concepts
6. Think about a television show or movie you have seen in which a main character is an adolescent. What type of personality does the character display? Which emotions does he or she deal with? What, if anything, did you learn from this character? Write a paragraph or two in which you summarize your answers.

LESSON TWO: UNDERSTANDING YOURSELF   15

CHAPTER 1, LESSON 2

Answers to Lesson 2 Review

1. The period of great growth and change between childhood and adulthood. Possible sentence: My classmates and I are going through adolescence.
2. The sum total of a person's traits, feelings, attitudes, and habits. Any three: have new experiences, meet new people, develop skills and talents, learn to do new things, participate in school and community activities.
3. Changes in height, weight, and body shape.
4. Admit how you feel, talk about your feelings, take a bike ride to cool off.
5. Answers will vary but might include telling a friend that everyone does not grow at the same rate.
6. Answers will vary. Students should explain the emotions this person deals with and what has been learned.

Enrichment

- Have students imagine that they write an advice column in their school paper. Have them respond to the following question: I often feel sad and lonely. What can I do to deal with these emotions?
- Assign Enrichment 1, "Crossing the Bridge," in the TCR.

CLOSE

Have students make a time line of physical changes from birth to adolescence.

MEETING STUDENT DIVERSITY

Getting to Know Yourself Some students may have difficulty identifying their own personality traits. Try this abstract activity. Provide students with peanuts still in the shells to create their own "Personality Peanut." Have students draw expressions on their peanut shell. Have them each write a paragraph describing the peanut's personality, including information about the peanut's feelings, attitudes, habits, and physical characteristics. Students may then form small groups and introduce their peanuts. Have groups discuss how heredity, environment, culture, family background, and experiences influence the peanut's personality.

LESSON THREE
Your Self-Concept

FOCUS

Lesson Objectives

After studying this lesson, students should be able to
- examine qualities that help build a positive self-concept.
- give examples of ways to accept constructive criticism.
- explain how good health habits can contribute to a positive self-concept.

Motivating Activity

Write the following on the board for students to complete:

Choose a person whom you admire and write three reasons why you think it would be fun to be that person.

Introducing the Lesson

Have students share their responses to the Motivating Activity. Then have them think of three reasons that the person they admire might give for wanting to be them. Point out to students that knowing one's own strengths helps to build a positive self-concept. Tell them that Lesson 3 provides them with other ways to help build a positive self-concept.

Introducing *Words to Know*

Ask students to read the vocabulary list to themselves. Ask them to note the words that begin with the modifier "self." (self-concept, self-esteem, self-confidence) Explain to students that "self" as a modifier means independent, as in self-government or self-starting. Have students suggest other words that begin with the modifier "self." (self-assertive, self-respect, self-discipline)

LESSON THREE
Your Self-Concept

 **WORDS TO KNOW**

self-concept
self-esteem
self-confidence
constructive criticism

DISCOVER...
- how to build a positive self-concept.
- how to accept constructive criticism.
- how good health habits can contribute to a positive self-concept.

During the past month nothing seemed to go as Ramon planned. He did poorly on an important test and his baseball team lost the championship. Ramon is frustrated and discouraged. Have you ever had feelings similar to Ramon's?

How You See Yourself

During the teen years—and throughout your life—it is important to have a positive **self-concept**, or *mental picture of yourself.* Self-concept includes your views about your personality traits and about what activities you do well. Your

16 CHAPTER 1: THE UNIQUE YOU

CLASSROOM RESOURCES FOR LESSON 3

 Blackline Masters
Activity and Project Card 2, "Hooked on Health Mobile"
Cooperative Learning 2
Lesson 3 Quiz
Peer Pressure and Decision Making 2
Reteaching 1

 Transparencies
Transparency 5, "Ways to Build Self-Esteem"
Transparency 6, "Building Good Health Habits"

 **Student Workbook**
Activities 5, 6

self-concept is influenced by the people around you. It started forming when you were a child, and it continues developing throughout your life. Perhaps your sister teases you about the way you wear your hair, or your grandfather tells you that you are a good chess player. These comments affect your self-concept, or the image that you have of yourself.

Another term for self-concept is self-image. Your self-image does not always stay the same. It may change as the situation you are in changes. When you win a game or help a neighbor, for example, you feel really proud of yourself. On the other hand, if you get a poor grade or have an argument with a friend, you may not feel as good about yourself. Even people with a strong self-concept get discouraged with themselves when something does not work out as they planned.

Being recognized for an achievement makes you feel proud of yourself and gives your self-image a boost. In what other situations might your self-image improve?

A Positive You

Your success in life depends on developing a positive self-concept. It gives you the confidence to try new things. If you have a positive self-concept, you are willing to make new friends, go to new places, and try new activities. Why do you think that this is true?

Improving Your Self-Concept

It is possible to improve your self-concept, or the way you see yourself. Begin by concentrating on only a few traits at one time. Try to do something each day to help build the qualities you want to improve.

LESSON THREE: YOUR SELF-CONCEPT   **17**

CHAPTER 1, LESSON 3

TEACH

L1 Art
Have students use their art supplies to create symbols of characteristics they like about themselves. Have each student use the symbols to assemble a mobile. Display the mobiles in the classroom.

L3 Self-Evaluation
Have students draw a picture of themselves holding a scale with two sides, similar to the scale of justice. Have them label one side of the scale "Positive" and list their positive qualities on the scale. Have them label the other side of the scale "Negative" and list qualities they would like to improve on this scale. Discuss students' scales. Point out that they can improve their self-concept by working to increase or strengthen their positive qualities.

L2 Applying Knowledge
After students finish reading "Improving Your Self-Concept," ask them to name additional qualities that help build a positive self-concept (for example, pride and initiative) Write students' responses on the board. Then ask them to write examples of ways to develop each quality.

L1 Using Transparencies
Present Transparencies 5, "Ways to Build Self-Esteem" and 6, "Building Good Health Habits," in the TCR. Use these overhead visuals to reinforce concepts in this lesson.

HOME AND COMMUNITY CONNECTION

Have students go into their community to get tips for ways of improving themselves. Ask them to obtain pamphlets from places such as an employment agency, health-care facility, dentist's office, counseling agency, nutrition store, or health club, that give suggestions about ways that people can improve themselves. Students might look for pamphlets that give tips about developing positive qualities, building self-confidence, and developing good health habits. They might display the pamphlets on a bulletin board.

CHAPTER 1, LESSON 3

TEACH

L3 Decision Making

Reinforce how self-respect can help a person in making important decisions. Have students write a paragraph describing a situation in which their self-respect enabled them to use their own judgment instead of going along with the crowd. Students should include a description of the mental image they have of themselves as a result of their decision.

Allow class time for students to try the exercise described in "Self-Image Booster," page 19. Ask students what the exercise told them about themselves. Then ask them how they react to compliments. Point out that a person who gracefully accepts compliments has a positive self-image.

L2 Activity and Project Card

Allow time for students to complete Activity and Project Card 2, "Hooked on Health Mobile," in the TCR.

L2 Cooperative Learning

Assign Cooperative Learning Activity 2, "Who We Are," in the TCR.

L2 Problem Solving

Assign Peer Pressure and Decision Making 2 in the TCR. This activity gives students the opportunity to recognize peer pressure and practice decision-making skills.

18

When you have finished wearing your clothes or using your possessions, put them back where they belong. How do you think this will help your self-concept?

Here are some qualities that will help you build a positive self-concept.

- **Cheerfulness.** Being cheerful means being happy, friendly, and seeing the bright side of life.
- **Cleanliness and neatness.** Start each day by wearing fresh, clean clothes, and practicing good grooming habits. In addition to being neat with your personal appearance, take care of your possessions.
- **Honesty.** Telling the truth, being sincere, and being loyal are ways to show your honesty.
- **Thoughtfulness.** Think about how your actions affect other people. Help others without being asked. Use good manners, and remember to say "please" and "thank you."
- **Responsibility.** Being responsible means doing your chores and your homework and coming home on time. It also involves accepting the consequences of your actions and decisions.
- **Resourcefulness.** Resourcefulness means knowing when to ask for help and where to find information when you need it.
- **Self-control.** Thinking before you act and setting limits are ways to practice self-control. It includes using your knowledge of right and wrong as a guide for your actions. Self-control could mean learning to control your anger or refusing to try tobacco, alcohol, or other drugs.

Building Self-Esteem

When you have a positive self-concept, you like yourself. In turn, you will develop **self-esteem,** or *the ability to respect yourself.* Respecting yourself helps you to use your own judgment, resist peer pressure, and set and achieve your goals. When you care about yourself, you do nothing to hurt yourself.

18 CHAPTER 1: THE UNIQUE YOU

MEETING STUDENT DIVERSITY

Physically Challenged Invite someone who is physically challenged to give her or his views on the importance of building a positive self-concept. Have the speaker focus on the qualities that helped her or him build a positive self-concept, how positive support from others helps build a positive self-concept, and how students who are not physically challenged can build a positive self-concept by being supportive of people who are physically challenged.

Gaining Self-Confidence

You need to have self-confidence to have a positive self-concept. When you have **self-confidence,** you have *faith in your abilities*. You gain self-confidence every time you do something well—even small daily achievements, such as improving your keyboarding skills or doing your homework.

You have probably noticed that success helps you gain confidence in your abilities. Learn to recognize the things you do well. Give yourself credit for your successes instead of dwelling on your mistakes. Be realistic about your expectations, and realize that no one does everything well.

Accepting Constructive Criticism

How do you feel when someone criticizes you? Do you become defensive or just ignore it? Learning to accept constructive criticism is a good way to improve your self-concept. **Constructive criticism** is *someone's evaluation of you that encourages you and helps you become a better person.* It helps you grow and improve yourself. For example, if your music teacher suggests a better song for your voice, you can follow the advice and improve your performance. Accepting and using constructive criticism will help you to improve your skills.

Taking Care of Your Health

Good health also promotes a positive self-concept. With good health habits you have energy and a healthful appearance, and you feel good. **Figure 1.2** on the next page shows ways to build good health habits.

Self-Image Booster

Take two minutes to list your strengths (honest), then your weaknesses (lazy). Begin by choosing which weakness you want to convert to a strength. Ask a friend for feedback as you practice your new skill.

Learning a new swimming stroke might give you the confidence to try out for the swim team. What activities do you do well?

Making Improvements

You can make a difference in your life by developing personal qualities. Getting to know yourself and accepting constructive criticism are two ways to begin. Once you identify the areas in your life that need improvement, you will be on your way toward a positive self-concept.

LESSON THREE: YOUR SELF-CONCEPT

MORE ABOUT...

Caring About Yourself The holistic approach to health and wellness explores the possibilities of the human mind. This approach affirms that diseases can be cured through the powers of a positive attitude. The belief in the powers of positive thinking can also be applied to an individual's self-concept. Concentrating on the positive aspects of personality helps affirm them in the mind. For example, a person who wishes to become more outgoing and gain new friends should think, "I enjoy meeting new people. I feel good when I talk to people even if I don't know them well." This kind of affirmation works to build qualities that lead to increased self-confidence. Ask students to write an affirmation about a quality they want to improve.

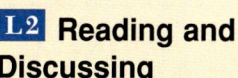

CHAPTER 1, LESSON 3

L2 Reading and Discussing

Ask students to work in small groups to write about situations that illustrate ways to use constructive criticism. Students' situations might include helping a younger sibling learn a new skill or helping a friend with an assignment. Call on a member from each group to read the group's situation. Have the class determine if the constructive criticism encouraged the people and helped them to improve themselves.

L1 Student Workbook

Assign Activities 5 and 6 in the Student Workbook.

ASSESS

Evaluating the Lesson

Assign Reviewing Terms and Facts and Thinking Critically on page 20 to review the lesson; then assign the Lesson 3 Quiz in the TCR.

Reteaching

- Provide students with the following scenario: Vivian is very unsure of herself around people she does not know well. She thinks to herself, "Why would they want to be with me or hear what I have to say?" Ask students to recommend two ways Vivian could build her self-confidence.
- Have students complete Reteaching Activity 1 in the TCR.

Enrichment

Ask students to plan a positive self-concept campaign. The campaign should be designed to remind them to feel good about themselves. Have them create posters or banners encouraging positive self-concepts to display in school halls.

CHAPTER 1, LESSON 3

USING VISUALS
Have students study the examples of ways to develop good health habits in Figure 1.2. Have students create and execute a plan for developing a good health habit in a situation that has been a problem for them in the past, such as lack of exercise or not brushing their teeth as often as they should.

Answers to Lesson 3 Review

1. Gives you confidence to try new things.
2. Any five: cheerfulness, cleanliness, neatness, honesty, thoughtfulness, responsibility, resourcefulness, self-control.
3. Use your own judgment; pay attention to what's important to you; protect your reputation; and do nothing that would hurt yourself, your parents, or your friends.
4. By your views about what you are like and what you are good at doing. It is influenced by the people around you.
5. Answers will vary. Students should list several qualities that help them feel good about themselves.
6. Criticism is not helpful when it is negative and it attacks you and tears you down.
7. Answers will vary. Students should identify a health habit to change and make a list of ways to work on improving the habit.

CLOSE
Ask students to create a jingle or slogan that will help them to improve a quality that leads to increased self-confidence.

 Figure 1.2 Building Good Health Habits
Taking care of your health will contribute to your happiness and well-being throughout your life.

LESSON THREE Review

Using complete sentences, answer the following questions on a separate sheet of paper.

Reviewing Terms and Facts
1. Recall How does a positive self-concept help you succeed?
2. List Name five qualities that help you build a positive self-concept.
3. Identify What can you do to increase your self-esteem?

Thinking Critically
4. Explain How is self-concept formed?

5. Apply Name qualities you have that help promote a positive self-concept.
6. Analyze When might criticism not be helpful?

Applying Concepts
7. Choose one health habit that you would like to change. Make a list of ways that you can work on changing the habit. For example, you might want to improve your health by increasing your exercise or eating foods low in fat. Then put your plan into action.

20   CHAPTER 1: THE UNIQUE YOU

MORE ABOUT

Taking Care of Your Health An American psychologist named Abraham Maslow developed the following hierarchy of human needs:
1) physiological needs—those that relate to the functioning of the body such as food and sleep
2) safety and physical security—needs such as shelter and protection from harm
3) love—the need for a feeling of belonging and affiliation with others
4) esteem—the need for a high self-evaluation supported and reinforced by others
5) self-actualization—the need to grow to one's fullest potential

Ask students to identify which of Maslow's hierarchy of needs involve relationships with others.

Chapter 1 Activities

FRIENDS & FAMILY

YOUR OUTLOOK ON LIFE

You inherit physical characteristics from your parents. You may not realize it, but some of your attitudes as well as your outlook on life may also come from family members. Your own outlook on life, however, is something you can work on and change.

TRY THIS!

Do you think that you have a positive outlook on life? Why or why not? Make a list of ways you could become more of an optimist.

Consumer Focus

Drugstore Dilemma

Melinda, age 13, decided to start using a moisturizer when her skin became dry and flaky. She went to the drugstore, only to find half an aisle lined with moisturizers. Melinda was overwhelmed by all the possibilities. Which brand was the best?

Try This!

Discuss this problem with a small group of your classmates. Write a list of guidelines that teens could use when shopping for personal grooming products.

 **CULTURAL CELEBRATIONS**

Your culture influences you in many ways. It may influence your personality; the way you speak, dress, and act; and the way you express your emotions. Your culture may also influence the way you celebrate birthdays, holidays, and special occasions.

TRY THIS!

What is your cultural heritage? In what ways has it influenced the way you celebrate special occasions? Write your answers in your journal.

SCIENCE CONNECTION

PASS IT ON

You have probably heard people say things like "Mike has his grandfather's nose" or "Rosie looks just like her mother." These people were talking about heredity—the passing on of physical and mental traits from parents to their children.

1. Make a list of your physical characteristics. Which traits can you identify as coming from a parent? If you have brothers and sisters, which traits do you have in common with them?

2. Which of your abilities or skills did you inherit? Which have been influenced by your environment? Explain your answers.

CHAPTER 1 Activities

FRIENDS & FAMILY

Explain that the power of positive thinking has been the basis for many books and articles. Emphasize that a positive outlook can help students get along with others, stay healthy, and succeed in life. Ask for examples of how a person who sees life in a positive way can influence those around him or her.

Describe to students an example of a cultural celebration such as the Jewish ceremony called Bar Mitzvah (for boys) or Bat Mitzvah (for girls). Ask students to describe details and influences from their own cultural heritage in their private journals for the "Try This" activity.

Consumer Focus

Tell students that personal grooming products can help people look and feel good and make them more confident about their appearance. Explain that as young teens, they may be making more of their own decisions about which grooming products to buy. They may find that the many varieties available may make it difficult to know which products to choose.

Teaching the SCIENCE CONNECTION

Show students that physical traits are inherited from parents. Exhibit photographs of various members of the same family. If possible include grandparents, parents, and children. Ask students to identify physical traits that children inherited from each parent.

 **Answers to Follow-Up**

1. Answers will vary. Students should list their physical traits that resemble their father, those that resemble their mother, and those they have in common with brothers and sisters.
2. Answers will vary. Students should explain which abilities or skills they inherited and which were influenced by their environment.

CHAPTER 1 REVIEW

Checking Comprehension

Use the Chapter Summary and the Chapter 1 Review to help students go over the most important ideas in Chapter 1.

Answers to Words to Know

1. An acquired characteristic is learned from the people and things around you.
2. Culture refers to the ways of thinking, acting, dressing, and speaking shared by a group of people. Cultures may be based on race, ethnic group, geographic location, or social class.
3. Adolescence is the period of great growth and change between childhood and adulthood.
4. Answers will vary. Student may list any ten emotions.
5. Self-concept is your mental picture of yourself. Self-esteem is the ability to respect yourself.
6. Answers will vary. Student should give an example of a constructive criticism in which an evaluation encourages and helps someone to become a better person.

Answers to Review Questions

1. People are unique because of the characteristics they inherit and because they have different backgrounds and experiences. They acquire different interests and abilities as a result of their environment. People are alike because they all have the same basic needs for food, for water, for a place to live, to feel safe, and to be loved and accepted by others.

Chapter Summary

- You are a unique individual.
- Your individual characteristics are a result of your heredity and environment, culture, family background, experiences, and roles.
- You have many roles in life—daughter or son, brother or sister, student or friend.
- Adolescence is a time of many changes, both physical and emotional.
- Your personality is a blend of all your traits, feelings, attitudes, and habits.
- Understanding and learning to handle your emotions can help to give you control over your life.
- A positive self-concept, or mental picture of yourself, is important for success in life.
- Having self-confidence and self-esteem will help you reach your goals.
- Learning to accept and use constructive criticism will help you improve your skills.

▶ Words to Know

Using complete sentences, answer the following questions on a separate sheet of paper.

1. What is an *acquired* characteristic?
2. What is a *culture*? On what are cultures based?
3. Why is *adolescence* sometimes considered a mixture of childhood and adulthood?
4. List ten *emotions*.
5. What is the difference between *self-concept* and *self-esteem*?
6. Give an example of *constructive criticism*.

▶ Review Questions

Using complete sentences, answer the following questions on a separate sheet of paper.

1. In what ways are people unique as well as similar?

22 CHAPTER 1: THE UNIQUE YOU

2. Give an example of a characteristic that is influenced by both heredity and environment.
3. Why are role models important?
4. Why is it sometimes difficult to understand yourself during adolescence?
5. How does your personality grow and change throughout your life?
6. How can you gain control over your emotions?
7. Why is it important to build a positive self-concept?
8. How can you develop a positive self-concept?
9. How does a person with a positive self-concept react to compliments? Constructive criticism? Making mistakes?
10. In what way are good health habits related to a positive self-concept?

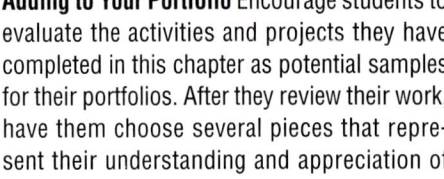

EXTRA CREDIT PROJECT

Adding to Your Portfolio Encourage students to evaluate the activities and projects they have completed in this chapter as potential samples for their portfolios. After they review their work, have them choose several pieces that represent their understanding and appreciation of key concepts, such as: recognizing their own individuality; what makes up their personality; the importance of a positive self-concept; and how having self-confidence can help them reach their goals. These examples of student work can become a part of their permanent files, and students may wish to look back on these examples to evaluate their progress later.

CHAPTER 1 REVIEW

Thinking Critically

Using complete sentences, answer the following questions on a separate sheet of paper.

1. **Analyze** Why might teens be considered a cultural group?
2. **Apply** Give an example of a role you hope to have in the future. How might you prepare yourself for that role?
3. **Interpret** Why might teens' emotions be compared to a roller coaster?
4. **Explain** What might happen to your self-concept if you didn't deal with your emotions in a healthy way?
5. **Analyze** Why might teens with a poor self-concept use tobacco, alcohol, or other drugs?

Cooperative Learning

1. As a class, choose one aspect of a culture—such as food, clothing, jewelry, celebrations, or customs regarding learning from elders. In groups of three or four, select one culture and research this aspect of it. Share your findings with the class.
2. In small groups, discuss your favorite television characters. Make a list of their desirable and undesirable personality traits. Then discuss what each character could do to improve his or her personality.

Family & Community

1. Teens can be role models for younger brothers or sisters or children in the neighborhood. Think of ways you could set a good example for someone younger than yourself. Write a pledge to be a good role model, and then be sure to live up to your promise.
2. Families share inherited traits. They also share a cultural heritage. Learn more about traditions, customs, or events that are important to your family. With your family's permission, show the class an object that represents your cultural heritage.

Building A Portfolio

1. Divide a large sheet of paper into ten sections. In each section, write, draw, or paste something that illustrates a different aspect of your life. You might have a section for your hobbies, another for your achievements, another for your family, and so on. Add the illustration to your portfolio.
2. Write a letter to a real or imaginary teen who lives in a different part of the city, state, country, or world. Describe what life is like where you live and how you think your environment influences your personality. Your letter might be in the form of an audiotape or a videotape. Put a copy of your letter in your portfolio.

CHAPTER 1 REVIEW 23

CHAPTER 1 REVIEW

2. Answers will vary. Example answer: Musical talent is inherited, but you learn to play the piano as a result of your environment.
3. They help you see what is expected of you and show you how to act in certain situations.
4. It is sometimes difficult to understand yourself during adolescence because your body grows so rapidly and you have new and intense emotions that are always changing.
5. It changes as you have new experiences and meet new people.
6. Talk to someone, pound a pillow, or take a bike ride to cool off.
7. Your success in life depends on developing a positive self-concept. It gives you confidence to try new things, make new friends, and go to new places.
8. By practicing and improving the following qualities: cheerfulness, cleanliness and neatness, honesty, thoughtfulness, responsibility, resourcefulness, and self-control.
9. Accepts compliments gracefully, uses positive criticism constructively, ignores negative criticism, and accepts responsibility for mistakes and learns from them.
10. Following good health habits helps you feel good about yourself.

Evaluate

Use the Chapter 1 Test in the TCR, or construct your own test using the Testmaker Software.

CLOSE

Have students apply their knowledge of the chapter's content by completing one of the alternative assessment activities listed under Family and Community or Building a Portfolio.

Answers to Thinking Critically

1. Teens often share ways of thinking, acting, dressing, and speaking that are different from those of other age groups.
2. Answers will vary. Student gives an example of a role and tells how he or she might prepare for it.
3. Teens' emotions are like a roller coaster because they are constantly changing like the up-and-down feelings of riding a roller coaster.
4. A person's self-concept is lowered if emotions are not dealt with in a healthy way.
5. Teens with a poor self-concept have little self-respect and may not care about their health. As a result, these teens may not follow good health habits. They may also have little self-control.

Planning Guide
Chapter 2 Everyday Living Skills

LESSON 1	Pages	FEATURES	CLASSROOM RESOURCES
Making a Good Impression	26–30	*Try This: Stereotyping* *Tips for Living: Breaking Bad Habits*	Concept Map 2 Cooperative Learning 3 Lesson 1 Quiz Transparency 7, "Getting Along with Others" Student Workbook Activity 7
LESSON 2 **Communicating with Others**	31–35		Cross Curriculum 2 Lesson 2 Quiz Peer Pressure and Decision Making 3 Transparency 8, "What's Your Communication Style?" Student Workbook Activities 8, 9
LESSON 3 **Being a Citizen and a Leader**	36–41	*Skills in Action: Volunteering*	Activity and Project Card 3, "Teen Hero Poster" Concept Map 3 Lesson 3 Quiz Transparency 9, "Teamwork" Student Workbook Activities 10, 11
LESSON 4 **Managing Your Life**	42–48		Activity and Project Card 4, "Resources Arcade" Cooperative Learning 4 Enrichment 2 Lesson 4 Quiz Peer Pressure and Decision Making 4 Transparency 10, "Timesaving Techniques" Student Workbook Activities 12, 13

CHAPTER 2 RESOURCES

- Chapter 2 Test
- Reteaching 2
- Study Guide 2, *Reteaching*
- Testmaker Software

Performance Assessment Activity

Have students evaluate for one day how well they perform the following everyday living skills: getting along with others, verbal communication, and listening skills. Students should develop an inventory sheet that they can use to help with their evaluations. For each skill, have them write statements that reflect guidelines that they can observe. For example, an inventory statement for getting along with others might say "Tries to understand how other people feel," and an inventory statement for listening skills might say "Gives full attention to the speaker and makes eye contact." Students should refer to the guidelines for these skills in Chapter 2 to develop their inventory forms. At the end of the day, ask students to fill out the inventory forms. Have them use the evaluations to develop a list of skills that they need to improve.

School-to-Work

Ask students to find classified advertisements in the newspaper or in a book about careers. Have them find several job descriptions for typical managers in the ads, and have them choose one of the advertisements. Then refer students to the guidelines for effective verbal communication skills, for listening skills, and the basic steps of management, as presented in Chapter 2. Ask students to explain how a manager in a workplace can use these guidelines and steps to do his or her job. Students should present their explanations in the form of a chart that lists the skills and steps in one column and the ways a manager can use them in a second column.

Family & Community

As a class or in small groups, have students identify a problem in their community, such as increasing litter in the streets, insufficient park space, or the need for a stop sign at a particular intersection. Ask them to list possible solutions to the problem. Have them demonstrate their citizenship skills by planning strategies that can help solve the problem. Plans can involve both teamwork and individual efforts. Students should make posters advertising their plans. For example, a poster may read "Join Your Neighbors Saturday for 'Clean Up the Streets Day.'" Display posters in the classroom.

Resources for the Teacher

Forsyth, Patrick. *First Things First: Managing Your Time for Maximum Performance.* London: Institute of Management Foundation, 1994.

Wilson, Marlene. *You Can Make a Difference: Helping Others and Yourself Through Volunteering.* Boulder, CO: Volunteer Management Associates, 1990.

Readings for the Student

Dykstra, Gretchen. *Real Life Citizenship.* New York: Scholastic Book Service, 1990.

Salzman, Marian, and Reisgies, Teresa. *One Hundred Fifty Ways Teens Can Make a Difference.* Princeton, NJ: Peterson's Guides, Inc., 1991.

Wing, Ralph. *Just Do It! Time Management.* St. Louis: Pangaea Press Staff, Division of Pangaea Group, Inc., 1990.

Multimedia Resources

Body Language Analysis. (Two disks). Orange Juice Software Systems.

Communicating with Parents: Volume 11. (Videocassette, teacher's guide). The Power of Choice Series. LiveWire Video.

Communicate! (Disk). Orange Juice Software Systems.

OUT OF TIME?

If time does not permit thorough teaching of this chapter, you may wish to use:

- Teens Making a Difference, page 25
- Tips for Living, page 28
- Try This, page 27
- Skills in Action, page 39
- Young Living Activities, page 49
- Chapter Summary, page 50

CHAPTER 2

Everyday Living Skills

Chapter Overview

In Chapter 2 students learn to develop interpersonal, communication, citizenship, leadership, and management skills.

LESSON 1 describes ways of making a good impression.
LESSON 2 explores effective communication skills for getting along with others.
LESSON 3 focuses on ways of being a good citizen and leader.
LESSON 4 describes the basic steps of the management process; identifies personal, material, and community resources; and describes time-management tools.

Introducing the Chapter

Write the chapter title on the board. Discuss with students what the term *living skills* refers to. *(Students might indicate skills that people need on a daily basis.)* Ask students to list the skills that they consider "living skills." Record students' responses on the board and compare the responses with the skills discussed in the chapter.

Chapter Motivator

Refer students to the lesson titles. Then organize the class into four groups. Assign one of the lesson titles to each group. Ask students in each group to draw a picture or cartoon that illustrates the title and reflects what they think the content of the lesson will be. Display students' work. After students complete the chapter, discuss how closely the pictures or cartoons reflect the lessons' contents.

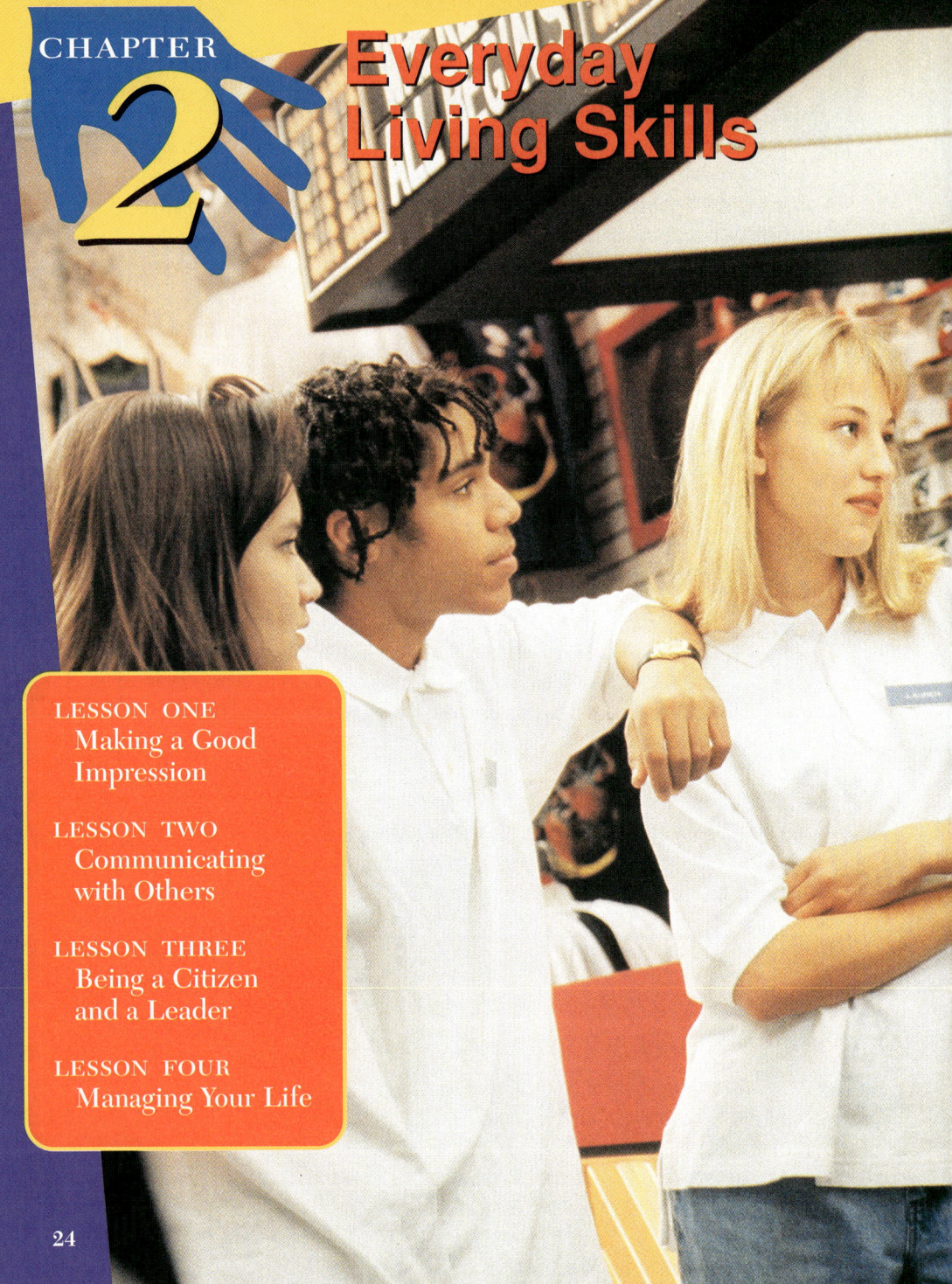

CHAPTER 2
Everyday Living Skills

LESSON ONE
Making a Good Impression

LESSON TWO
Communicating with Others

LESSON THREE
Being a Citizen and a Leader

LESSON FOUR
Managing Your Life

KEY TO ABILITY LEVELS

Teaching strategies that appear throughout the chapters have been identified by one of three codes to give you an idea of their suitability for students of varying learning styles and abilities.

L1 **Level 1** strategies should be within the ability range of all students. Often full class participation is required. Teacher direction is usually needed.

L2 **Level 2** strategies are for average to above-average students or for small groups. Some teacher direction is necessary.

L3 **Level 3** strategies are designed for students able and willing to work independently. Minimal teacher direction is necessary.

CHAPTER 2

TEENS MAKING A DIFFERENCE

Call on a volunteer to read "Teens Making a Difference." Then discuss with students what personal qualities they think Tanya has. *(Students might suggest that she is generous, creative, and a good leader.)*

Then have students complete TRY THIS! Call on students to read the newspaper articles or their own accounts about volunteers in their community. You might also ask students to describe volunteer work that they have done in their community.

BLOCK SCHEDULING

The following Teacher Classroom Resources are suggested for use in classrooms with Block Scheduling.
- Activity and Project Card 3, "Teen Hero Poster"
- Activity and Project Card 4, "Resources Arcade"
- Cooperative Learning 3, "Actions Speak Louder Than Words"
- Cooperative Learning 4, "Settlers In Space"

TEENS MAKING A DIFFERENCE
Improving a Neighborhood

Twelve-year-old Tanya Jenkins lives in a large city. When Tanya was younger, she played in a playground near her home. In the past few years, though, the playground fell into disrepair. The lot became overgrown with weeds and littered with trash. The swing set and jungle gym were no longer safe for children to use.

Tanya decided to do something about cleaning up the playground. With the permission of her teacher, Tanya got the help of her entire English class. The class spent one Saturday cleaning up the trash and pulling the weeds. To raise money for new playground equipment, the class held a bake sale and a flea market.

Today Tanya feels proud that she played an important part in helping to improve her neighborhood.

Try THIS!

Do you know of any volunteers who are working to make life better for the people in your community? Bring in newspaper articles describing their activities, or write your own account of their work.

TECHNOLOGY IN THE CLASSROOM

Slides You can use slides in a way that best suits the needs of your students. Even with little skill in photography, a teacher can take slide pictures or make them. Slides are an excellent way of showing detail, such as when portraying natural scenes or close-ups of furniture. The major advantage of using slides is that you can make ones that show items of interest in the local community, such as people in a local work environment and local architectural styles. Students working in groups can make their own slides to accompany their group projects.

LESSON ONE
Making a Good Impression

FOCUS

Lesson Objectives

After studying this lesson, students should be able to
- explain how to make a good impression.
- state the disadvantages of stereotypes.
- describe the effects of a positive attitude.

Motivating Activity

Play a game with students so that they can understand the importance of first impressions. Send two students out of the classroom. Direct remaining students to select slips of paper that identify an emotion to act out. Have students act out the emotions they chose. Have the two outside students come back to the class. Tell them to give their first impression of the acting students.

Introducing the Lesson

Have the two students tell what thoughts ran through their minds when they saw the students in the Motivating Activity. Tell students that this lesson defines *impression* and discusses the importance of making a good first impression.

Introducing *Words to Know*

Write the Words to Know on the chalkboard. Call on volunteers to give definitions for each word. Write acceptable definitions on the board. If students cannot define a term, have them look it up in the Glossary.

LESSON ONE
Making a Good Impression

impression
first impression
stereotype
maturity
empathy

DISCOVER...
- how to make a good impression.
- the disadvantages of stereotypes.
- the effects of a positive attitude.

Kelly and her brother Dan just moved to a new town. On their first day at school Kelly was polite and friendly. She wanted to make a good impression. Dan, on the other hand, started showing off and claiming to be the world's greatest soccer player. He was trying to impress people. Can you see the difference between trying to impress people and making a good impression? An **impression** is *an image you present or others present to you*. When you try to impress people, you pretend to be someone other than who you really are. When you make a good impression, you have presented yourself in the best way possible.

26 CHAPTER 2: EVERYDAY LIVING SKILLS

CLASSROOM RESOURCES FOR LESSON 1

 Blackline Masters
Concept Map 2
Cooperative Learning 3
Lesson 1 Quiz

 Transparencies
Transparency 7, "Getting Along with Others"

 **Student Workbook**
Activity 7

First Impressions

People form an opinion about you the first time they meet you. This *instant opinion, or image,* is called a **first impression.** It is based on certain clues, such as the way you look and talk and act. First impressions are important because they help people decide whether they want to know you better. What type of first impression do you make when you are considerate of others? In contrast, what do people think if you have poor manners?

When people judge you by only a few clues, the clues may be misleading. For example, you may wear a baseball cap but not like to play baseball. What other kinds of clues may mislead people about you?

First impressions are not always accurate. When people have a chance to get to know you better, they may change their opinion. Sometimes, however, the first impression is the only chance you have to make a good impression.

Try This!

General statements such as "All people who wear glasses are smart" or such descriptions as "Dumb jocks" are stereotypes. List stereotypes that you have heard people use. Then write a paragraph explaining why stereotypes should be avoided.

Avoiding Stereotypes

Sometimes people form opinions about you without even knowing you. They may expect you to act a certain way. *An idea or image formed in advance about all members of a group* is called a **stereotype.** The belief that all teens like rock music or that all elderly people are hard of hearing is an example of stereotyping. Some stereotypes are based on gender. For example, some people may think that all boys like sports or that all girls like to cook.

When people form their opinions of you based on a stereotype, their idea or image is usually unfair, untrue, or exaggerated. The only way for people to learn what you and others are really like is to get to know each person as an individual.

By talking and listening to someone, you can get to know that person as an individual. Why is this important?

LESSON ONE: MAKING A GOOD IMPRESSION 27

CHAPTER 2, LESSON 1

TEACH

Try This!

Ask students to read their paragraphs to the class. Then urge them to work together to develop a summary statement that explains why stereotypes should be avoided.

L2 Role-Playing

Ask students to work in pairs to develop an interview that addresses the topic "Making a Good Impression." One student should take on the role of the interviewer and the other the role of the expert. Students should use the information in this lesson to develop the questions and answers for the interview. Have each pair present their interview to the class.

L1 Analyzing

Show students pictures of ten people who represent an assortment of age groups and ethnic backgrounds. Have them write their first impressions of the people pictured. Then have students read the section on "Avoiding Stereotypes" to see if their impressions display stereotypical responses.

L2 Applying

Organize the class into small groups. Ask the groups to prepare guidelines for making a good first impression in the following situations: the first day at school, meeting a new friend's parents, interviewing for a babysitting job. Discuss each group's guidelines.

COOPERATIVE LEARNING

Organize the class into small groups. Have each group discuss the meaning of stereotypes and stereotypical thinking. Then have each group develop a list of ways that people can eliminate stereotypical thinking. (For example, avoiding sexist language, being open-minded, avoiding prejudging people.) Each group should present their ideas in an illustrated chart that can be displayed and referred to in the classroom.

CHAPTER 2, LESSON 1

L3 Critical Thinking

Write the following expression on the chalkboard: "When life gives you lemons, make lemonade." Have students discuss the meaning of this expression (choosing to make the best of a bad situation). After students have read the information under "Having a Positive Attitude," ask them to think of other expressions that illustrate a positive attitude or the benefits of a positive attitude. Write students' expressions on the chalkboard and discuss.

L2 Cooperative Learning

Assign Cooperative Learning 3, "Actions Speak Louder Than Words," in the TCR.

TIPS for living

After students have read "Breaking Bad Habits," ask them to identify a habit they would like to break. Have them use some of the suggestions listed and write a report describing their efforts. Students should indicate whether or not they were successful and should speculate as to why they were or were not.

Showing Good Behavior

You can make a good impression on others by being pleasant and sincere. Showing that you have confidence in yourself will make you more interesting to others.

Using good manners and being thoughtful of others help you create a good impression. Having good manners means more than just saying "please" and "thank you" or using the right fork when you eat. It means respecting other people's rights and helping them feel comfortable. Thinking about how your behavior affects others will help you practice good manners.

Being Mature

When you act maturely, you make a good impression on other people. **Maturity** means *making wise decisions, practicing self-control, and acting responsibly*. It means learning to express your feelings in a positive way and accepting responsibility for your actions. If you make a mistake, you don't get angry or defensive. Instead you know that making mistakes is part of the learning process.

Having a Positive Attitude

Have you ever wondered, "Why does this have to happen to me?" Most people feel that way sometimes. You can't

TIPS for living

BREAKING BAD HABITS

Bad habits, such as tapping your fingers or interrupting other people when they're talking, make a poor impression. Try the following tips to help you break a bad habit.

- Ask family members and trusted friends to help you identify a bad habit that you may not be aware of. Then have them give you a secret signal every time they see you practicing your habit.
- Figure out why you have the habit. Maybe you twist your hair around your finger when you're nervous. Try to remove the reason for the habit. For example, studying more for a test will help you feel less nervous.
- Find an acceptable substitute behavior. For example, try breath mints in place of biting your nails.

28 CHAPTER 2: EVERYDAY LIVING SKILLS

MORE ABOUT...

Maturity Tell students that part of being mature is being able to handle stress or the pressures of life. Point out to students that being able to do so is essential for avoiding both mental and physical illness. Tell them that the next time stress occurs, they should look for its source and try to eliminate it or reduce it. Tell them that discussing a problem with a friend, relative, or some other person may help relieve their stress.

When something goes wrong, try to keep a positive attitude. How is this teen showing a positive attitude?

always control the things that happen to you. However, you can control how you react to the things that happen. When something unpleasant happens, you can choose to be positive and look on the bright side. You can choose to make the best of a bad situation. For example, if you don't make the school band, you might decide to spend more time practicing and try again next year. You might decide to try out for the school play instead. A positive attitude will help you make a good impression on teachers, friends, and parents.

Getting Along with Others

Getting along well with other people is an important part of the impression you make on others. If you can get along with your family, friends, classmates, teachers, and community members, you will make a good impression on them. Here are some qualities that will help you get along with other people.

- **Consideration.** Think about other people and their feelings. Treat people the same way you would like to be treated.
- **Friendliness.** Be pleasant and friendly. Greet people. Invite new students to join you and your friends for lunch. Let others know that you want to be a friend.
- **Cooperation.** Pitch in and do your share of work. At home you can keep your room clean. At school you can do your part on group assignments.

LESSON ONE: MAKING A GOOD IMPRESSION   29

COOPERATIVE LEARNING

Introductions Being at ease when faced with introducing people for the first time is a communication skill that can give students self-confidence in many situations as they mature. Assign partners to practice making introductions. Begin by suggesting techniques to use when introducing friends to parents, friends to peers, or younger people to older people. Have partners work together to write down sentences to use in several different situations, such as in school, at a family gathering, at a church or club event. Then have pairs work together to practice making introductions using sentences they have prepared.

CHAPTER 2, LESSON 1

L2 Creating a Poster
Have students review the qualities for getting along with others in this lesson. Organize the class into groups, and assign one of the qualities to each group. Have the groups make a poster illustrating various ways that teens can exhibit the assigned quality. Display completed posters in the classroom.

L1 Using Transparencies
Present Color Transparency 7, "Getting Along with Others," in the TCR. Use this overhead visual to reinforce concepts from this lesson.

L1 Student Workbook
Assign Activity 7 in the Student Workbook.

ASSESS

Evaluating the Lesson
Assign Reviewing Terms and Facts and Thinking Critically on page 30 to review the lesson; then assign the Lesson 1 Quiz in the TCR.

Reteaching
- Have students write a paragraph describing a scenario in which a teen tries to make a good impression. Have them use each of the "Words to Know" in the paragraph.
- Have students complete Reteaching Activity 2 in the TCR.
- Assign Concept Map 2 in the TCR.

Enrichment
Ask students to visit a library or select a book from home to find a story about characters who display empathy. Have them share the story with the class.

CHAPTER 2, LESSON 1

Answers to Lesson 1 Review

1. Making a good impression is being yourself; trying to impress people is pretending to be someone else.
2. An idea or image formed in advance about all members of a group. Possible examples: all teens like rock music, all girls like to cook, all elderly people are hard of hearing.
3. Being polite, respecting other people's rights, making others feel comfortable, thinking about how your behavior affects others.
4. Makes wise decisions, practices self-control, and acts responsibly.
5. Consideration, friendliness, cooperation, reliability, and understanding.
6. Because it helps you decide if you want to know a person better. Sometimes a first impression is the only chance a person gets to make a good impression.
7. Answers will vary. Students could choose to be positive and look on the bright side of things. They can also choose to make the best of a bad situation.
8. Cartoon characters will vary, but students should identify the features that stereotype the characters.

CLOSE

Ask students to write a paragraph about a person who has left a lasting impression on them. Ask them to describe the qualities of the person that contributed to the lasting impression.

Cooperating is an important part of getting along with others. How do you cooperate with others at home and at school?

- **Reliability.** Do you do what you say you will do? People like to know they can depend on you. Prove to them that you will keep your word.
- **Understanding.** Try to understand how other people feel. Show **empathy,** or *the ability to put yourself in another person's place.* Respect that person's viewpoint and feelings.

A Lasting Impression

As you have learned, people form an impression of you as soon as they meet you. Often that first impression lasts for a long time. You can see why it is important to make sure that the first impression is positive. You can continue to make a good impression by having a positive attitude and practicing the skills for getting along well with other people.

LESSON ONE Review

Using complete sentences, answer the following questions on a separate sheet of paper.

Reviewing Terms and Facts

1. **Compare** What is the difference between making a good impression and trying to impress someone?
2. **Vocabulary** Define the term *stereotype.* Give an example.
3. **Describe** What does it mean to have good manners?
4. **Identify** What are three characteristics of a mature person?
5. **List** Name five qualities that can help you get along with other people.

Thinking Critically

6. **Explain** Why is a first impression so important?
7. **Evaluate** In general, do you think that you have a positive attitude? Why or why not? How could you develop one?

Applying Concepts

8. Look through magazines and newspapers to find examples of cartoon characters who are stereotyped. Identify the feature the cartoonist has exaggerated to produce the stereotype, and share your findings with the class.

30   CHAPTER 2: EVERYDAY LIVING SKILLS

 HOME AND COMMUNITY CONNECTION

Guest Speaker Invite a personnel director or an employer in your community to speak to the class. Have the individual discuss the importance of first impressions in job interviews. Ask the speaker to describe the qualities that a person who makes a good first impression exhibits, and to give students a list of Do's and Don'ts in presenting oneself in an interview. Ask the speaker to answer questions that students may have.

LESSON TWO
Communicating with Others

DISCOVER...
- skills that will help you communicate better with others.
- verbal and nonverbal communication techniques.
- the importance of being an effective listener.

Dylan likes to talk on the telephone. Jason smiles and waves to his next-door neighbor. Amber confides all her hopes and dreams to her best friend, Rachel. How do you communicate with other people? Learning how to communicate effectively takes effort, but it has many rewards.

WORDS TO KNOW
communication
nonverbal communication
body language
conversation
gossip

LESSON TWO: COMMUNICATING WITH OTHERS   31

LESSON TWO
Communicating with Others

FOCUS

Lesson Objectives
After studying this lesson, students should be able to
- identify skills that help communicate better.
- describe verbal and nonverbal communication techniques.
- explain the importance of being an effective listener.

Motivating Activity
Write the word *communication* on the board. Ask students to work in small groups to brainstorm their own definitions for the term.

Introducing the Lesson
Have students from each group share their responses to the Motivating Activity. Write the students' definitions of *communication* on the chalkboard. Stress to students that there are many ways to communicate. Tell them that in Lesson 2 they will learn how to communicate effectively.

Introducing *Words to Know*
Have students use the terms in Words to Know to write a paragraph about different kinds of communication. Call on volunteers to read their paragraphs. Have students determine their understanding of the terms by checking the definitions of the terms in the Glossary.

CLASSROOM RESOURCES FOR LESSON 2

 Blackline Masters
Cross Curriculum 2
Lesson 2 Quiz
Peer Pressure and Decision Making 3

 Transparencies
Transparency 8, "What's Your Communication Style?"

Student Workbook
Activities 8, 9

31

CHAPTER 2, LESSON 2

TEACH

L1 Creating a Collage
Organize the class into small groups. Have them look through magazines to find pictures illustrating communication. Tell them to find examples of various kinds of verbal and nonverbal communication. Ask them to combine the pictures in a collage titled "What Is Communication?" Display collages in the classroom.

L3 Analyzing
Discuss with students who they have the most difficult time communicating with—parents, teachers, friends, or other adults. Then ask students to work in pairs, with one student assuming the role of a writer of an advice column and the other the role of a teen writing for advice about a communication problem with one of the people mentioned above. Have the student representing the teen write a letter describing the problem. Have the student representing the advice columnist write a response, offering a solution to the problem by using the guidelines for verbal communication on this page. Have each pair read the solution and the response to the rest of the class. Call on volunteers to evaluate the solutions.

L1 Demonstrating
Write examples of various emotions on slips of paper (anger, surprise, frustration, etc.). Ask volunteers to choose one slip of paper and demonstrate an example of nonverbal communication that illustrates the emotion they chose. Discuss with the class whether or not they agree on the meaning of the nonverbal message portrayed.

Types of Communication

There are many forms of communication. **Communication** is *the process of sending and receiving messages*. Communication can be verbal or nonverbal.

Verbal Communication

Verbal communication begins with selecting the right words to express yourself. Next, it is important to be honest. Say what you really think and feel, but be polite. Other guidelines for effective verbal communication include the following:

- **Speak for yourself.** Make "I" statements. Talk about your own experiences and feelings. Don't assume that other people know what you think, how you feel, or what you want. You have to tell them.

- **Avoid speaking for others.** Don't assume that you know what other people think, how they feel, or what they want. Ask them.

- **Be clear and direct.** Tone of voice reveals your feelings. You send mixed messages if your tone does not match the words you are using. Mixed messages are confusing.

- **Be aware of your listener.** Check to see that your listener understands what you are saying.

- **Ask questions.** Ask "who," "what," "where," "when," and "how" questions. These help others share their thoughts and feelings.

Talking on the telephone is one way to communicate verbally. Why do you think that it is especially important to speak clearly when using the telephone?

Nonverbal Communication

Much of our communication is **nonverbal communication,** or *messages sent without using words*. When you use nonverbal communication, you show how you feel about yourself and others. **Figure 2.1** shows some forms of nonverbal communication.

MORE ABOUT • • •

Communication Communication skills are vital to success in many areas of life. The importance of these skills stems from the fact that everyone continuously communicates with those within range of sight and sound. It is impossible not to communicate. Lack of communication skills has been reported by employers to be the primary deficiency of today's workers. Communication breakdown is said to be a major factor in marriage and family problems. On the other hand, skillful communication enhances human interactions. Have students consider how good communication skills could enhance the student/teacher relationship.

CHAPTER 2, LESSON 2

USING VISUALS
Refer students to Figure 2.1. Ask students to work in small groups and suggest examples of nonverbal communication for each boxed item. Have them indicate what their examples communicate.

Figure 2.1 Forms of Non-verbal Communication
Nonverbal communication is an important way to convey messages. What forms of nonverbal communication do you use?

DID YOU KNOW
In recent years various technological advances have greatly advanced communication. Teleconferencing allows a number of people to communicate simultaneously using telephone lines or radio signals linked to audio, video, or computer connections. The Internet is a web of computer networks that links millions of people, allowing them to communicate with one another whenever they are in the system. One of the services available through the Internet is electronic mail (E-mail), which allows users to transmit memos and messages through a computer network. Facsimile transmission (fax) allows graphic information to be transmitted via normal telephone lines. The speed of this type of communication has made it popular in time-sensitive business transactions.

The Importance of Listening

The ability to listen is just as important as the ability to express yourself. Studies indicate that 60 percent of the time that you are communicating is spent listening. If you are a poor listener, you are probably a poor communicator. Listening is not the same as hearing. When you hear, you are aware of the words being said. When you listen, you try to understand the message.

Listening is one of the hardest communication skills to learn. You can improve your listening skills by using the following guidelines.

- Give your full attention to the speaker, and make eye contact.
- Concentrate on what the speaker is saying, not on what you will say next.

LESSON TWO: COMMUNICATING WITH OTHERS   33

L1 Using Transparencies
Present Color Transparency 8, "What's Your Communication Style?" in the TCR. Use this overhead visual to reinforce concepts from this lesson.

MEETING STUDENT DIVERSITY

Cultural Diversity Tell students that the way people use verbal and nonverbal communication to show their feelings can vary from culture to culture. In some African cultures members of tribes point with the lower lip instead of with the forefinger. In Italy, sports fans express their disapproval by whistling instead of by booing. However, for the most part people all over the world express their emotions with the same facial expressions. That is what researchers determined when they conducted a comparison of human responses to emotion-provoking stimuli. They discovered that people in industrialized nations as well as in developing nations smile when they are happy, raise their eyebrows when they are surprised, and frown when they are sad.

CHAPTER 2, LESSON 2

L2 Evaluating

Organize the class into groups of three or four. Arrange for each group to have access to a video camera. Have the members of each group take turns videotaping the other two members in the group in normal conversation. When all three tapes have been completed, ask the group to play them back and evaluate one another's listening skills using the guidelines for effective listening in this lesson.

L2 Problem Solving

Assign Peer Pressure and Decision-Making Activity 3 in the TCR. This activity gives students the opportunity to recognize peer pressure and practice decision-making skills.

L2 Technology Connection

Assign Cross-Curriculum Activity 2, "Exploring the Internet," in the TCR. Students learn about on-line communication in this activity.

L1 Student Workbook

Assign Activities 8 and 9 in the Student Workbook.

ASSESS

Evaluating the Lesson

Assign Reviewing Terms and Facts and Thinking Critically on page 35 to review the lesson; then assign the Lesson 2 Quiz in the TCR.

Reteaching

- Have students write on one side of an index card a statement that illustrates a guideline for effective verbal communication, and on the other side one for effective listening.
- Have students complete Reteaching Activity 2 in the TCR.

34

- Show your interest by leaning toward the speaker and nodding.
- Listen for the overall meaning, not just the details.
- Remember to notice nonverbal cues.
- Avoid making quick judgments.
- Resist distractions.
- Do not interrupt. Ask questions only when necessary.
- Give active feedback to indicate you have understood.

Having a Conversation

Conversation is *the sharing of ideas, thoughts, and feelings*. It is a two-way street. You must be willing to express yourself as well as to listen to others.

For a conversation to be interesting, it is important for each person to have a chance to talk. You have probably been bored by a situation in which one person took over the conversation. Keep it lively by including others.

Asking Questions

You can draw others into conversation by finding out what their interests are. Most people like to talk about television, movies, and current events. They usually like to talk about their own experiences, too.

When someone is speaking, give that person your full attention. Why is listening such an important skill to learn?

COOPERATIVE LEARNING

Questions for Conversations Discuss with the class what conversation is and what makes it interesting. Stress to students the importance of asking good questions to make a conversation interesting. (For example, instead of saying "Do you play soccer?" say "What sports do you like playing?") Then organize the class into small groups. Ask the groups to brainstorm ten questions that could be asked to encourage an open-ended conversation rather than to bring a conversation to a standstill. Have groups share their questions with the rest of the class, and have the rest of the class evaluate their effectiveness.

Asking good questions helps you find out about other people's interests. Ask questions that give people something definite to talk about. Consider the following example: Rena asks, "Do you like baseball?" Eric answers, "Yes." End of conversation. It has nowhere to go.

Suppose Rena asks, "What did you think of the game today?" If Eric is interested in baseball, he will have something definite to say. The conversation is off to a good start.

Avoid asking "why" questions. A question such as "Why did you change your mind?" forces the other person to explain or defend his or her actions. You also should avoid questions that lead the other person. For instance, the question "Don't you think that…?" is really a statement of what you think. It is designed to get the other person to agree with you.

Avoiding Problem Areas

Do you know people who gossip? **Gossip** is *talking about other people and their personal lives*. Gossip can destroy friendships and ruin a person's reputation. Gossip can also turn into rumors that spread and can lead to violent confrontations. By avoiding gossip and rumors in your conversations, you can show that you are a mature and responsible person.

Gossip can cause many problems in relationships. What would you do if someone wanted you to spread gossip?

LESSON TWO Review

Using complete sentences, answer the following questions on a separate sheet of paper.

Reviewing Terms and Facts

1. **List** Name four forms of nonverbal communication.
2. **Vocabulary** Define the term *body language*. Give an example.
3. **Explain** Why are gossip and rumors dangerous?

Thinking Critically

4. **Evaluate** Which of the listening skills do you think you do well? Which do you need to work on? Explain your answers.

5. **Analyze** Why is it important to avoid asking "why" questions?

Applying Concepts

6. Divide into groups of three or four students. One student should locate and read aloud the first paragraph or two from a newspaper article. After listening, the other students in the group should write down answers to the following questions: "Who, what, where, when, how?" Compare your answers to those of the other people in your group to see who was listening effectively.

LESSON TWO: COMMUNICATING WITH OTHERS

HOME AND COMMUNITY CONNECTION

Guest Speaker Find a family counselor in your community. Ask the counselor to visit your class to talk to the students about ways that a family can improve communication among its members. Ask the counselor to give examples of speaking and listening skills that can help to enhance this communication. Have students ask the counselor questions that they may have about the topic. Remind them to take notes during the presentation. After the counselor completes the presentation, students should compile the counselor's suggestions in a chart titled "Communication Guidelines for Families" to be used as a reference.

CHAPTER 2, LESSON 2

Answers to Lesson 2 Review

1. Touching, personal space, body language, physical appearance.
2. The look on your face, gestures, and body stance. Examples include frowning, smiling, and drooping shoulders.
3. They can lead to violent confrontations.
4. Answers will vary but should include reasons.
5. It forces a person to explain or defend his or her actions and puts that person on the spot.
6. Answers will vary but should demonstrate use of listening skills.

Enrichment

Point out to students that people from different cultures have different ways of communicating social courtesies. For example, in some cultures people shake hands upon meeting, while people in other cultures hug each other when they meet. Ask students to ask members of their family or community to give examples of cultural courtesies and have students share them with their classmates. Ask the class to analyze the ways verbal and nonverbal communication are used in these courtesies.

CLOSE

Have students write an answer to the following question: Why are both good speaking skills and good listening skills necessary for effective communication? Discuss students' answers.

LESSON THREE
Being a Citizen and a Leader

FOCUS

Lesson Objectives
After studying this lesson, students should be able to
- identify ways to build and demonstrate citizenship and leadership skills.
- describe how group members can work together to achieve goals.

Motivating Activity
Write the following open-ended statement on the chalkboard for students to complete:

I am a citizen of . . .

Introducing the Lesson
Have students share their responses to the Motivating Activity. List the responses on the chalkboard. Ask students if it is possible to be a citizen of more than one group. Tell them that in Lesson 3 they will learn what a citizen is and how they can develop their citizenship skills.

Introducing *Words to Know*
Refer students to the terms in Words to Know. Ask them to identify three words that describe roles of individuals *(volunteers, citizen, leader)*. Ask them to identify a compound word *(teamwork)*. Then tell students that the word *volunteer* can be used as a noun, adjective, or verb. Ask students to give an example of each. *(Answers will vary. Sample sentences follow: Volunteers are unpaid. That is a volunteer position. They volunteered their services.)*

36

LESSON THREE
Being a Citizen and a Leader

WORDS TO KNOW

volunteer

citizen

teamwork

leader

DISCOVER...
- ways to build and demonstrate your citizenship and leadership skills.
- how group members can work together to achieve goals.

On Saturdays Selena helps out at a community recycling center. Kyle picks up groceries for his elderly neighbor. Have you ever volunteered? A **volunteer** is *a person who donates time and energy without pay to do a service for others*. Being a volunteer has many benefits. The most important one is that it makes you feel good about yourself. Volunteers also gain valuable experience and the sense of accomplishment that comes from a job well done.

36   CHAPTER 2: EVERYDAY LIVING SKILLS

CLASSROOM RESOURCES FOR LESSON 3

 Blackline Masters
Activity and Project Card 3, "Teen Hero Poster"
Concept Map 3
Lesson 3 Quiz

 Transparencies
Transparency 9, "Teamwork"

 **Student Workbook**
Activities 10, 11

Being a Citizen

Why does being a volunteer make you feel good? When you have helped out, you discover that what you have given of yourself is helpful to another person. This gives you a sense of self-worth. Many organizations, including museums, hospitals, and nursing homes, rely on help from volunteers.

There are many ways you can help others and volunteer your talents and skills. For example, you can collect used clothing for the needy or hand out magazines and newspapers to people in a hospital or nursing home. Teaching computer skills or giving piano lessons to a neighbor is another way you can volunteer.

When you volunteer, you show that you are a good citizen. A **citizen** is a *member of a community, such as a city, state, or country*. There are many other ways to be a good citizen, such as offering to work as part of a team. When people use **teamwork,** *everyone in the group cooperates and works together to reach a goal*. For example, you use teamwork and demonstrate your citizenship skills when you

- participate in a school fund-raiser.
- join the student council.
- pitch in to help your family do yard work.
- take part in a walkathon.

This teen is volunteering his skills by reading to young children. What are some other ways to volunteer?

CHAPTER 2, LESSON 3

TEACH

L2 Illustrating
Review the meaning of *teamwork* with students. Ask them to give examples of ways that teamwork can help make their community a better place to live. Have students illustrate their examples in a bulletin-board display titled "Teamwork Works."

L2 Discussing
Ask students to list different ways they can help the needy in their community (shopping for the elderly, reading to children with disabilities). Ask students how doing the volunteer work they listed could help them later in life.

L1 Making a Mural
Organize the class into small groups. Ask each group to draw a mural that illustrates ways that students can demonstrate citizenship skills at home and in school. Display finished murals in the classroom.

L1 Using Transparencies
Present Color Transparency 9, "Teamwork," in the TCR. Use this overhead visual to reinforce concepts from this lesson.

MORE ABOUT • • •

Teamwork A major goal of many employers in both large and small companies is having a workforce in which teamwork, not competition, is the motivating force. Good team members express approval of their coworkers, giving a kind word or smile. They are thoughtful, writing thank-you notes for personal and business favors. Good team members are considerate, listening to others' opinions. A successful team effort requires loyalty, dependability, and commitment to the team's goals. Ask students if they consider themselves to be good team members—in sports, clubs, and other organizations.

CHAPTER 2, LESSON 3

L1 Demonstrating
Put the following items on a display table: a library book, a rented videocassette tape, and a school basketball. Ask students to give ideas on what can be done to make people more responsible in taking care of shared property.

L2 Analyzing
Ask students to work in pairs. Have them write the term *leader* vertically on a blank sheet of paper. Then ask pairs of students to brainstorm characteristics of a good leader starting with each of the letters of the word. Have them write each characteristic next to its letter. Ask students to share their characteristics with the class.

TEACHER TALK!

Getting Involved

Stress to students how becoming more involved with people and activities in their community now will carry over into their adult lives. It will give them experience and self-confidence and help develop their leadership skills.

You can show your citizenship skills by pitching in and doing your share of the work. In what community-sponsored events have you participated?

The examples just mentioned are ways of showing your citizenship skills by working as part of a team. However, some things that you do by yourself also show your citizenship skills. For example, you can

- take a moment to pick up litter and discard it in the proper place.
- return lost items to the lost-and-found department or to the rightful owner.
- care for pets when neighbors go out of town.

What other ways can you think of to show your citizenship skills?

Whether you demonstrate your citizenship skills in a group or alone, being a good citizen helps you in many ways. It gives you a sense of belonging and a feeling of pride. You are able to share community facilities, such as libraries, parks, and museums. In addition, you are able to develop skills that will help throughout your lifetime and possibly even lead you into a career.

Citizenship Skills

It is easy to be a good citizen if you remember these three guidelines:

- **Do your share.** Offer to pitch in and help. Look for ways that you can lend a hand to family members, neighbors, teachers, and friends. Volunteer to help at school or in your community. Get involved in a community-sponsored event, such as a park cleanup, Neighborhood Watch, or recycling campaign. Ask teachers and neighbors what you can do to lend a hand.

- **Show respect for others.** Treat them as you—and they—would like to be treated. For example, wait your turn instead of trying to get to the front of a line. Give

---

MEETING STUDENT DIVERSITY

Hearing Impaired If any student in the class has a hearing impairment, arrange the necessary measures for the student to ensure his or her grasp of the lesson materials. These measures may involve having an individual in the class who can sign to the student. They may also involve the teacher's learning some basics of American Sign Language to foster better communications between the teacher and student. Because the students are at an age when they may not completely understand physical challenges in people, ensure that other students show respect to the hearing-impaired student but do not mistake pity for respect.

others in your family a chance to use the telephone. Speak respectfully to adults, such as grandparents, teachers, and police officers. Greeting adults and calling them "Mr.," "Ms.," or "Mrs." is another way to show your respect. What other ways to be courteous can you think of?

Remember to show respect to everyone, not just people you know well or especially like. Help all students. Make new students feel comfortable, and introduce them to other people. If someone holds different values from yours, be open and accepting. If you disagree with someone, give that person a fair chance to explain his or her opinion.

- **Take good care of shared property.** Be as careful with a library book or park equipment as you would be with your own possessions. Then the next person will be able to use and enjoy them too. The same is true for other property that you share, such as recreation areas, the school building, and streets and sidewalks.

Being a Leader

Every group needs a **leader,** *a person with the ability to guide and motivate others.* Leadership is the direction, or guidance, from the leader that helps a group accomplish its goals.

Sometimes leaders are chosen or elected. For example, the captain of your hockey team, your student body officers, and the mayor of your community were probably elected.

At other times the job of a leader is not a formal one. For example, when you organize a birthday party for a friend or get your siblings to help rake the leaves without being asked, you are being a leader.

Leadership Skills

Sometimes leaders are out in front of the team, showing the way. At other times they may be in the background, encouraging others. At all times leaders must use good communication skills and know how to work with people. **Figure 2.2** on the next page shows some ways to build leadership skills.

LESSON THREE: BEING A CITIZEN AND A LEADER

Volunteering

Volunteering gives you a chance to meet new people and learn new things. Make a list of your skills and interests. Then match your skills and interests with a volunteer job.
- Do you enjoy exercise? Mow lawns or shovel walks for an elderly neighbor.
- Can you play a musical instrument? Play your instrument for residents of a nursing home.
- Do you like to be outdoors? Deliver flyers for community organizations.

CHAPTER 2, LESSON 3

After students have read the feature, have them identify a career they are interested in. Encourage them to talk to persons in the field to learn about opportunities for volunteer work. If possible, suggest that students do volunteer work in their chosen career field for three to four weeks. Have them report their experience to the class.

L2 Analyzing
Ask students to think of an individual whom they consider to be a good leader. Then ask them to complete the following statement: _____ is a good leader because _____. In the first blank, have students identify the person. In the second blank, have them describe the leadership skills the person has. Call on volunteers to read their statements and compare the skills.

L2 Activity and Project Card
Assign Activity and Project Card 3, "Teen Hero Poster," in the TCR.

HOME AND COMMUNITY CONNECTION

Community Involvement Many people believe that citizens also have a duty to help out in their communities. Across America thousands of citizens are getting involved in their communities and trying to make a difference. Businesses are encouraging their employees to do volunteer work in the community. Schools, churches and synagogues, and other organizations are creating programs to help those in need. Explain to students that when people work together, they can accomplish great things. Being able to make an improvement, even a small one, makes people feel good about themselves and gives them a sense of power.

CHAPTER 2, LESSON 3

USING VISUALS
Refer students to Figure 2.2. Ask them to give examples of ways that the leader in this illustration could use good communication skills (both verbal and nonverbal).

L2 Applying
After students have read the lesson, ask them to list organizations in their community that help people and need volunteers. Then ask them to combine their information in a telephone directory, listing the organization, the address and telephone number, and the kinds of tasks volunteers for the organization perform. Students should refer to the directory when they want to volunteer in their community.

L1 Student Workbook
Assign Activities 10 and 11 in the Student Workbook.

ASSESS

Evaluating the Lesson
Assign Reviewing Terms and Facts and Thinking Critically on page 41 to review the lesson; then assign the Lesson 3 Quiz in the TCR.

Serve as part of the team, not the boss. Get everyone involved. Ask for and listen to everyone's opinion. Let group members help set goals and make decisions.

Figure 2.2
Building Leadership Skills
Being a good leader involves working with others to accomplish a goal.

Working as a Team

A group, such as a family, a school, or a community, needs all of its members to work together successfully to achieve its goals. Without the cooperation and support of all members, a group cannot operate effectively.

It is up to you to decide how you can best contribute. For example, if your club is organizing a fund-raiser, think of a few of the tasks involved: deciding on the date, deciding on the type of fund-raising event, getting people to help.

Ask yourself: "How can I best contribute to this effort?" Then volunteer your services!

Developing Your Skills

Developing your team-member and leadership skills is an important part of becoming an adult. When you use your skills to help others, you feel good about yourself and also gain valuable experience.

40   CHAPTER 2: EVERYDAY LIVING SKILLS

COOPERATIVE LEARNING

Teamwork Experience Have the class select a charitable organization and plan how the class could raise funds for this charity. Fund-raising ideas could include a car wash, bake sale, craft fair, or bike-a-thon. Ask the students to identify the tasks involved in the fund-raising and decide what committees are needed to accomplish them. Have students select a leader and members for each committee and work together to plan and carry out the activity.

Encourage team spirit. Be enthusiastic and positive. Use effective communication skills.

Show appreciation. Thank people who help the group reach its goal. Tell people that you appreciate their efforts.

LESSON THREE *Review*

Using complete sentences, answer the following questions on a separate sheet of paper.

Reviewing Terms and Facts
1. Identify What are some benefits of being a volunteer?

2. Vocabulary Define the term *teamwork*. Use it in an original sentence.

3. Explain Why is it important to take good care of shared property?

4. Identify List three ways to build leadership skills.

Thinking Critically
5. Give Examples Name two ways that you show your citizenship skills.

6. Analyze Why is being a good team member just as important as being a good leader?

Applying Concepts
7. Select a person whom you consider to be a leader. Write a list of the leadership qualities that you think the person has. Is this person a formal or informal leader? Write a list of guidelines that other people could use to develop leadership skills.

LESSON THREE: BEING A CITIZEN AND A LEADER   41

HOME AND COMMUNITY CONNECTION

Help make students aware of the people in their community who demonstrate citizenship skills and teamwork. Have them look through newspapers for articles that describe how people help others. Ask each student to cut out the article and paste it onto a sheet of paper. Next to the article students should identify the citizenship skills that the person or persons have demonstrated. If appropriate, students might also indicate how the individual demonstrated leadership skills. Combine students' articles into a booklet titled "Citizens and Leaders in Our Community."

CHAPTER 2, LESSON 3

Reteaching
- Ask students to work in pairs to list the responsibilities of leaders and group members. Have them share their list with the class.
- Have students complete Reteaching Activity 2 in the TCR.
- Assign Concept Map 3 in the TCR.

Enrichment
Ask each student to identify an individual as a recipient of a "Leadership Medal." The person could be a famous one or one whom the student knows personally. Have students write the speech they will deliver when presenting this award. The speech should include information about the person's leadership qualities and accomplishments.

Answers to Lesson 3 Review
1. Volunteers gain experience and personal satisfaction, and they feel good about themselves.
2. A group cooperating and working together to reach a goal. Sentences will vary.
3. So that others can use it.
4. Get everyone involved, encourage team spirit, and show appreciation.
5. Examples will vary but could include skills used in a group and skills that are developed individually.
6. For a group to be able to achieve its goals, everyone should work together and support the group.
7. Leadership qualities and guidelines will vary.

CLOSE
Ask students to identify two ways that they can demonstrate citizenship and leadership skills every day.

41

LESSON FOUR
Managing Your Life

FOCUS

Lesson Objectives
After studying this lesson, students should be able to
- explain the basic steps of the management process.
- identify resources that can be used to reach goals.
- describe time-management tools and techniques that can help them make better use of time.

Motivating Activity
That time is an important factor can be seen by considering the many expressions in the English language that refer to time. "Time heals all," "time marches on," and "when time stood still" are some examples of such expressions. In addition, we speak of an idea "whose time has come" and of "being in the right place at the right time." Ask students to give examples of other "time" expressions.

Introducing the Lesson
Have students share their responses to the Motivating Activity by reading examples aloud. Explain to them that Lesson 4 will identify skills that can be used to manage time and resources.

Introducing *Words to Know*
Ask students to locate the definitions for the terms in Words to Know as they appear in the Lesson. Using short paraphrases of the definitions as clues, have students create crossword puzzles containing the terms. Students can exchange their puzzles with a partner and solve them.

42

LESSON FOUR
Managing Your Life

 **WORDS TO KNOW**

management
evaluate
resource
talent
prioritize
procrastinate

DISCOVER...
- the basic steps of the management process.
- resources that can be used to help you reach your goals.
- time-management tools and techniques.

Megan and her friend Theresa are opposites. While Theresa always has her homework done on time, Megan is often working on hers until the last minute. Theresa is never late to student council meetings, but Megan usually rushes in and is often unprepared. Theresa gets more accomplished than Megan because Theresa practices good management skills. **Management** is *using what you have to get what you want, being organized, and planning ahead.*

42   CHAPTER 2: EVERYDAY LIVING SKILLS

CLASSROOM RESOURCES FOR LESSON 4

 Blackline Masters
Activity and Project Card 4, "Resources Arcade"
Cooperative Learning 4
Enrichment 2
Lesson 4 Quiz
Peer Pressure and Decision Making 4
Reteaching 2

 Transparencies
Transparency 10, "Timesaving Techniques"

 Student Workbook
Activities 12, 13

Learning Management Skills

People who manage well accomplish more with greater ease. They use their time, money, and energy wisely. Theresa is a good manager. So are Katie and Hassan. Katie has learned to save money by putting part of her earnings into a savings account. Hassan gets to school a half hour early so that he can work in the computer lab.

Management Steps

You can be a good manager if you learn to follow certain basic steps. These steps can be followed if you are writing a report or organizing a bake sale for the school band.

- **Step 1: Decide on your goal.** Determine what your goal is, and write it down on a piece of paper. Maybe you want to earn $50 or complete your science project. Writing down your goal helps you commit to it.

- **Step 2: Make a plan.** Decide how you want to achieve the goal. Maybe the goal can be broken into smaller parts, or short-term goals, that are easier to reach. For example, if you want to earn $40, perhaps you will plan to earn $20 this week and $20 next week.

- **Step 3: Put the plan into action.** Begin working on your plan. If you are going to try out for the cheerleading squad, don't just talk about it—practice.

- **Step 4: Evaluate the results.** The last step is to evaluate the outcome of your plan. When you **evaluate,** you *determine the value of what you accomplished*. Are you satisfied with the way your plan worked? If not, what would you do differently the next time?

By learning the basic steps of management, you can accomplish tasks more easily. What is the first step of management?

Managing Your Resources

To be a good manager you must make full use of the resources that you have. A **resource** is *a source of information or expertise that you can use to help you meet your goals*. The three types are personal resources, material resources, and community resources.

LESSON FOUR: MANAGING YOUR LIFE   43

CHAPTER 2, LESSON 4

TEACH

L1 Applying
Provide students with the following situation:

Tara must learn three pages of a new song on the cornet by the end of next week. She also wants to keep up with her homework and finish chores by the weekend. She has the following tasks to do after school: go to cornet lesson, mow the lawn, finish a reading assignment, and return a library book.

Have students create a flow chart in which they illustrate how Tara will complete her tasks and accomplish her goal using the basic steps of management. Discuss students' completed flow charts.

L2 Writing
Ask students to write a short story about a person who is a good manager. The story could have a contemporary or a fairy-tale focus. The story should illustrate ways that the person practices good management skills. If computers are available, encourage students to write their stories using a word processing program and print them out.

L2 Evaluating
Have students list some areas of their life that could be improved through better management. Have them choose one area and use the steps of management to plan, do, and evaluate the activity. Discuss with students how using the steps of management helped them do a better job.

HOME AND COMMUNITY CONNECTION

Ask students to interview an adult family member to find out how the person manages a home or a business. Students might ask the following questions: What kinds of tasks do you accomplish daily? How do you make sure that the tasks get done? Students should take notes during the interview and then use the notes to evaluate to what extent the basic steps of management are used by the person being interviewed. Ask students to share the results of their interviews with one another.

CHAPTER 2, LESSON 4

L2 Analyzing
On a sheet of paper, have students create a chart titled "Managing Personal Resources." Tell students that the chart will be an inventory of their personal resources. Have them use the categories listed in the lesson as column heads: Time, Energy, Knowledge, Skills and Talents, and People. Ask them to complete the chart by writing an example of personal resources in each category. (For example, under "Knowledge" students might write "good in history" or "know a lot about electronics." Under "Skills and Talents" students might write "play piano well" or "in-line skating.")

L1 Finding Examples
Stress to students that knowledge is an important personal resource. Ask them to list examples of ways that they can gain knowledge (reading, listening to other people, visiting museums, watching informational television programs). Have them create a poster that illustrates these ways.

L3 Writing
Ask students to choose one of their material resources. Have them write a paragraph describing this resource and explaining how this possession, object, or money helps them do what they want to do. Call on volunteers to share their paragraphs with the class.

L2 Activity and Project Card
Assign Activity and Project Card 4, "Resources Arcade," in the TCR.

Your skills and talents are part of your personal resources. How can you improve your skills?

Personal Resources

Personal resources are time, energy, knowledge, skills and talents, and people. How well you use your personal resources makes a difference in how successful you are and how much you accomplish.

- **Time.** Everyone has 24 hours a day. Much of this time is spent eating, sleeping, grooming, studying, working, and playing. The time that is left over can be used for special activities. Learn to use time wisely.

- **Energy.** Energy is the power or ability to be active. It has to do with the strength of the body and mind to do things—to work and play. Much of your energy depends on getting enough sleep, eating nutritious foods, and following a regular exercise program. Your attitude toward what has to be done also affects how energetic you may feel.

- **Knowledge.** Knowledge is information and understanding. Throughout your life you will continue to learn.

- **Skills and talents.** A skill is an ability that comes from training or practice. You have reading, writing, math, and computer skills. You may also have other skills, such as the ability to play the piano, which you learned from taking lessons. Talents are different from skills. A **talent** is *natural ability*. You may have a talent for drawing, singing, or playing tennis. In order to develop your talent, however, you need to practice and train.

- **People.** People are valuable resources. Strong relationships with family and friends will provide help and

44   CHAPTER 2: EVERYDAY LIVING SKILLS

COOPERATIVE LEARNING

Using Personal Resources Have students work in groups of four or five. Assign one of the following personal resources to each group: time, energy, knowledge, skills and talents, and people. Have each group develop tips that students can use to help conserve or better use the assigned resource. Have a member of each group prepare the tips on a sheet of paper that can be reproduced and handed out to class members. Students should combine the handouts into a reference booklet for ways to use their personal resources.

support all your life. The encouragement of family and friends can help you gain confidence and strengthen your self-concept.

Material Resources

Material resources are possessions, objects, and money. They make it easier to do what you want to do. Your personal possessions might include a bike, a stereo, or books. Objects might include a refrigerator, a table, or a microwave oven.

How do these possessions and objects help you do what you want to do? Personal possessions give you enjoyment and satisfaction. Riding your bike and listening to your stereo are a few ways that you gain enjoyment from your possessions. Objects make life easier. For example, using a washing machine to wash clothes is easier than washing them by hand.

Community Resources

Every community provides a variety of resources for its citizens to use. These include schools, hospitals, and police and fire departments. Among other community resources are youth programs, parks, and recreational facilities. Some communities have interesting places to visit, such as museums or important historic buildings.

Communities also provide resources for people who have special kinds of problems. Most communities offer programs for the homeless, the elderly, people with low income, and people who have problems with alcohol and other drugs. There are also programs to protect battered spouses and abused children.

Using Resources

There are several ways to obtain resources that you may not have. Resources can be traded or substituted. For example, you can use your time and energy to mow lawns for pay. Then you can use the money to buy a CD player. You might trade your knowledge and skill by tutoring a friend in math in exchange for guitar lessons.

Sometimes you can substitute one resource for another. If you want some posters for your room, for example, you could

Communities provide resources, such as parks, where people can enjoy many types of activities. What resources does your community provide?

LESSON FOUR: MANAGING YOUR LIFE **45**

CHAPTER 2, LESSON 4

L2 Writing
Ask students to choose an athlete, artist, or skilled craftsperson to find out how that person perfected her or his skills. Have students report their findings by writing a biographical profile of the person for a magazine article titled "Developing Personal Resources." Have students share their profiles with their classmates.

L2 Applying
Ask students to name a resource that could be traded or substituted in each of the following examples:
- Dan does not have the money he needs to buy a model he saw at the hobby store.
- Santina needs to have a yellow shirt when she sings in the school choir.
- Bridget knows how to sew clothes. She would like to learn to play the guitar.

L2 Problem Solving
Assign Peer Pressure and Decision-Making Activity 4 in the TCR. This activity gives students the opportunity to recognize peer pressure and practice decision-making skills.

L1 Using Transparencies
Present Color Transparency 10, "Timesaving Techniques," in the TCR. Use this overhead visual to reinforce concepts from this lesson.

MEETING STUDENT DIVERSITY

Language Diversity You might try the following strategies for students who experience language difficulties:
- Have these students make use of a buddy system. This system will allow their individual strengths to complement each other by having students work in pairs.
- Have such students focus on the lesson subheads. The subheads are designed to focus students on the basic information in the lesson.

CHAPTER 2, LESSON 4

L3 Math

Ask students to make a time schedule for the jobs regularly done at home. Ask them to determine how much time is devoted to each of these jobs. Then have them make a circle graph that illustrates what percentage of the total amount of time available in one week is devoted to the various jobs. Display students' graphs. Discuss with them how better time management could reduce the percentage of time needed to perform the jobs. Have students use a computer software program with calendar or scheduling capabilities if available.

L2 Critical Thinking

Organize the class into small groups. Challenge the groups to develop a list of criteria that could be used when they must choose between two activities that occur at the same time. Have a member from each group present the criteria to their classmates.

L1 Demonstrating

Use a timer to give students a sense of time passing. Set the timer for three minutes. Ask students to perform one activity, such as writing their name or reading only one paragraph from the textbook over and over. Call out one-minute intervals. At the end of the three minutes, discuss with students what more could have been accomplished in that three-minute time period.

L2 Cooperative Learning

Assign Cooperative Learning Activity 4, "Settlers in Space," in the TCR.

use your money resources to buy them. You could also substitute your personal resources of time, energy, and skills for money and make the posters yourself.

Managing Your Time

Using good time management skills will help you in all areas of your life. You will have more time for special activities that you want to do, such as playing basketball or starting a stamp collection. You won't constantly be late or forget to do important tasks. You will have more time for yourself and others.

Time Management Tools

Calendars, lists, and schedules help people keep track of activities and get more done. It doesn't matter what method you use as long as it works well for you.

- **Calendars.** On the calendar make a note of upcoming activities or appointments; important dates, such as birthdays and holidays; and other events that you want to remember. At a glance you can check to see what upcoming events are planned.

- **Lists.** Some people use a list each day as a reminder of tasks to complete. Once a day or once a week, you can make a "To-Do List" for the next day or week. As you complete each task, you can cross it off the list and see how much you have accomplished.

- **Time Schedules.** A time schedule is a list of hours in the day with tasks to be done filled in at the right time. It could also be a chart that combines the days of the week and the hours of the day.

Making a "To-Do List" is one way to keep track of the tasks you need to accomplish. How do you keep track of your activities?

Time Management Problems

Time management includes dealing with problems that may arise. You may find that two activities occur at the same time. If you cannot make room for both or change the time for one, you may have to make a choice. This will be difficult if

46   CHAPTER 2: EVERYDAY LIVING SKILLS

COOPERATIVE LEARNING

Time-Management Tools Organize the class into small groups. Assign each group one of the following time-management tools: using a calendar, using a list, making a time schedule. Ask each group to use the assigned tool to keep track of activities in the classroom (homework assignments, tests, field trips). Students should make a calendar, develop a "To Do" list, or a time schedule of the tasks to be done. When groups have completed their assigned time-management tool, have them share the tools with the rest of the class. Ask the class to decide which time-management tool is most effective to use in the classroom.

you must choose between two things you really want to do. Your choice may be between play rehearsals and gymnastics practice. Think about what is most important to you, and make a choice. Then act on your decision.

Sometimes you have several things you want to accomplish during a day. It may be difficult to know where to begin. In this case, you can *rank the tasks in order of importance,* or **prioritize** them. If you are using a "To-Do List," put an **A, B,** or **C** next to each task. Activities marked with an **A** are top-priority items. They need to be done first. **B** activities are completed next. **C** activities are the least important activities. If they are not done, they can wait until the next day.

Another challenge is dealing with unexpected changes. Sometimes schedules and lists do not work out exactly as planned. A friend may have to cancel the shopping trip to the mall you had scheduled. The rain may prevent you from raking leaves. Whatever the case, stay flexible. Make the most of your time by having ideas for alternate activities.

Figure 2.3 Timesaving Techniques
There are many ways to save time. What other ways can you think of?

Establish daily routines for eating and sleeping. Set a specific time each day for study and exercise.

Avoid interruptions. If a friend calls while you are doing your homework, tell your friend that you will call back when you have finished.

Learn to say no. If your friends want you to go to the movies but you haven't finished writing your report, you need to say no.

Divide big jobs into small tasks. For example, you can study for a test for 30 minutes before dinner and 30 minutes after dinner.

Simplify work. If something takes too much time, try to figure out ways to reduce the time.

Stick with a task until it is done. When you're cleaning your room, don't stop to read a magazine you picked up off the floor.

Do two tasks at the same time. For example, you can memorize a poem for English class while washing the car.

LESSON FOUR: MANAGING YOUR LIFE 47

MORE ABOUT • • •

Time To help students rate their time-management skills, have them answer the following questions with *yes* or *no.* Are you almost always in a hurry? Do you leave tasks or chores incomplete? Do you feel as if you are working hard but not accomplishing much? Do you have enough time for rest or for personal relationships? Are you regularly late with assignments and for appointments? Do you often try to do several things at once? Do you have trouble deciding what to do next? Tell students that if most of their answers are yes, their time-management skills need improvement. Suggest that they use the time-management techniques discussed in the lesson to improve their time-management skills.

CHAPTER 2, LESSON 4

L2 Writing Poetry
Assemble a group of products on a table, such as a calendar, a watch, stackable bins, drawer organizers, and so forth. Have each student select one item and write a rhyme about how the item is a beneficial organizational tool. Post the rhymes.

L2 Evaluating
Ask students to complete the following sentence: The biggest waste of time I've ever experienced was when I . . .

USING VISUALS
Refer students to Figure 2.3. Ask them to identify the time-saving techniques that they have used. Then have them brainstorm other time-saving techniques that they have used and found to be effective.

L1 Student Workbook
Assign Activities 12 and 13 in the Student Workbook.

ASSESS

Evaluating the Lesson
Assign Reviewing Terms and Facts and Thinking Critically on page 48 to review the lesson; then assign the Lesson 4 Quiz in the TCR.

Reteaching
- Have each student give one example of a way that good management could help him or her get more out of life.
- Have students complete Reteaching Activity 2 in the TCR.

47

CHAPTER 2, LESSON 4

Answers to Lesson 4 Review

1. Decide on your goal, make a plan, put the plan into action, evaluate.
2. Personal, material, and community resources.
3. Skills are abilities that come from training or practice. Talents are natural abilities that a person possesses.
4. Using a calendar, using a list, and making a time schedule.
5. Any four: establish daily routines, simplify work, divide big jobs into small tasks, do two tasks at the same time, stick with a task until it is done.
6. You can trade or substitute one resource for another.
7. Answers will vary but may include that people procrastinate when they are not sure how to do something.
8. Projects and plans will vary.

Enrichment

- Tell students that not only is it important not to waste their own time, but it is also important to be considerate of other people's time. Ask students to create paper cut-outs of clock faces with friendly reminders to illustrate ways that students can be considerate of other people's time. Hang the clock faces around the classroom.
- Assign Enrichment Activity 2 in the TCR.

CLOSE

Have students complete the following statement: "If I manage my resources and time wisely, . . ." Ask them to share their statements with classmates.

You can avoid wasting time by organizing everything you need before you start a task. What are some other ways to avoid wasting time?

Saving Time

As you begin to pay more attention to time, you will find many ways to save it. **Figure 2.3** on page 47 gives some suggestions that can save you time each day.

Making Time Count

Have you ever turned on the television to watch one show and later realized that you were watching television for hours? Perhaps you have spent a lot of time looking for your math book, only to find it under a stack of papers. Precious time can be lost. Here are some ways to avoid wasting time.

- **Avoid putting things off.** If you **procrastinate,** or *put things off,* you can waste a lot of time thinking and worrying about the task you need to do. Usually the job itself doesn't take very long when you finally do it.

- **Get organized.** Almost any task goes faster when you are organized. Before you begin the task, gather the tools or equipment you need and find out how to do the task.

- **Take care of yourself.** If you have ever thought that you could make more time by sleeping less, you have probably found out that it doesn't work. It is hard to concentrate when you are tired. Often you end up getting less done, instead of more, because you are tired.

LESSON FOUR Review

Using complete sentences, answer the following questions on a separate sheet of paper.

Reviewing Terms and Facts

1. **List** Name the four steps of the management process.
2. **Identify** What are three types of resources?
3. **Vocabulary** What is the difference between *skills* and *talents*?
4. **Name** List three time management tools.
5. **Recall** Name four timesaving techniques.

Thinking Critically

6. **Explain** What can you do if you don't have the resources that you need?
7. **Analyze** What are some reasons why people might procrastinate?

Applying Concepts

8. Think of a project you want to complete in the next few weeks. Write a plan for how you will manage the project. Include the resources you will use and a time schedule.

48 CHAPTER 2: EVERYDAY LIVING SKILLS

TECHNOLOGY UPDATE

Time-Management Tools Bring to class catalogs with examples of high-tech, time-management tools such as the following: car phones, answering machines, electronic watches with alarms, calculator-message computers, computer notepads and calendars. Organize the class into small groups, and assign one of the tools to each group to find out what it does, where it is used, how much it costs, and so on. Have each group report their findings, focusing on how the tool helps in time management.

Chapter 2 Activities

Consumer Focus

TECHNOLOGY

Saving Time

Not long ago a television ad showed nervous, upset people rushing into a bank and asking to withdraw time. "I need another 24 hours," a worried customer says to the bank teller.

Try This!

Do you use time wisely? Keep a list for one day of exactly how you spend your time. Then think of ways that you might manage your time more effectively.

"Netiquette"

People who communicate via on-line computer services and the Internet are expected to follow certain guidelines, called "netiquette." For example, before asking a basic question, polite on-line users should "FAQ-check," or look up "Frequently Asked Questions."

Try This!

Find out more about modern technology and good manners. Write your own rules of etiquette for renting videos, talking on cellular phones, or listening to portable stereos. Share the guidelines with your classmates.

FRIENDS & FAMILY

THE EXPERIENCE GAP

Teens don't always understand their parents' world, and parents sometimes forget what it's like to be a teen. You can help to close "the experience gap."

TRY THIS!

Try taking a few minutes each day to exchange experiences with your parents. It may help you and your parents to communicate and understand each other better.

SOCIAL STUDIES CONNECTION

EVERYDAY CITIZENS

Citizens of the United States have many rights, including freedom of speech and freedom of religion. In exchange for these rights, they have certain responsibilities. The government, for example, requires citizens to obey laws and pay taxes. Citizens have other responsibilities that are not required by law. These include the duty to vote and the duty to keep informed.

 **Follow Up**

1. What things can you learn in school that will help prepare you for participating in your community?

2. As a class or in small groups, identify a problem, such as graffiti. Find out if anything is being done about it. If so, join the effort. If not, plan a way to meet the need or help solve the problem and carry out your plan. Write an account of the group's efforts for a local newspaper.

CHAPTER 2 ACTIVITIES 49

CHAPTER 2 Activities

Consumer Focus

Have students think of all the "instant" or "ready-in-minutes" products found on supermarket shelves. Discuss how merchants use the idea of time to get people into their stores: *Hurry! Time is running out on our gigantic sale! Only 3 days left!* Assign the "Try This" activity.

TECHNOLOGY

Draw the following symbols on the chalkboard: :-) Ask students if they recognize this as an on-line symbol called a "smiley." When viewed sideways it looks like a happy face. Many similar symbols are in use to express emotions over the Internet. Have students invent some original smileys.

FRIENDS & FAMILY

To introduce this activity, read the following comparisons to students. Then ask them to recall similar experiences they can relate to. *Kevin is worried about finishing his social studies report on time.* (Kevin's father is worried about whether the important package he shipped will arrive on time.) *Everything went wrong for Marissa at school today.* (Marissa's mother had a bad day at work.)

Teaching the SOCIAL STUDIES CONNECTION

Ask students to describe community activities that they have been involved in. Tell students that some people believe that all Americans should be required to perform some type of compulsory community service to the country in peacetime as well as in war. Ask students if they agree that American citizens should be required to perform some kind of community service and to give reasons for their opinion.

 **Answers to Follow-Up**

1. Answers will vary. Students might say that school projects can prepare them for community projects.
2. Students' newspaper accounts will vary.

49

CHAPTER 2 REVIEW

Checking Comprehension

Use the Chapter Summary and the Chapter 2 Review to help students go over the most important ideas presented in Chapter 2.

Answers to Words to Know

1. A first impression is an instant image that people make when they first meet someone; a stereotype is an image formed in advance about all members of a group.
2. You could show empathy by consoling your friend and pointing out his or her positive traits.
3. The look on your face, gestures, and body stance.
4. Every person has a chance to talk, no one takes over the conversation, you ask questions that get others involved in the conversation.
5. Examples will vary but should include people who donate their time and energy without pay to do a service for others.
6. Possessions, objects, and money.
7. To rank them in order of importance.

Answers to Review Questions

1. Answers will vary but might include that the teen might not have good manners, act mature, have a positive attitude, or get along well with others.
2. Basing opinions on stereotypes gives you a limited viewpoint, and you miss out on getting to know the real person.
3. Listening means that you understand the message. It helps you understand the speaker's viewpoint and shows that you are interested.

CHAPTER 2 REVIEW

Chapter Summary

- Making a good first impression is important. Being mature, having a positive attitude, and getting along with others are all ways of making a good impression.
- To get along with other people, show consideration, friendliness, cooperation, reliability, and understanding.
- By practicing good communication skills—choosing the right words and using appropriate nonverbal communication—you send a clear, direct message.
- Nonverbal communication is any message sent without words. It may be body language, the use of personal space, touching, or physical appearance.
- Conversation is a two-way street that involves listening as well as talking.
- Doing volunteer work is a good way to show your citizenship and to develop team-member and leadership skills.
- Being a good citizen and leader means using teamwork.
- Being a good citizen includes doing your share, showing respect for others, and taking good care of shared property.
- Good management requires deciding on a goal, making a plan, putting the plan into action, and evaluating the results.
- Using your personal, material, and community resources will help you achieve your goals.
- Time management tools, such as calendars, lists, and time schedules, can help you make the best use of your time.

Words to Know

Using complete sentences, answer the following questions on a separate sheet of paper.

1. What is the relation between a *stereotype* and a *first impression*?
2. How might you show *empathy* for a friend who didn't make the team?
3. What are three types of *body language*?
4. Describe the characteristics of a good *conversation*.
5. Give an example of *volunteers* in your community.
6. Name the three types of material *resources*.
7. What does it mean to *prioritize* tasks?

Review Questions

Using complete sentences, answer the following questions on a separate sheet of paper.

1. How could a teen with the latest clothes and hairstyle still make a poor impression?
2. Why is it important to treat people as individuals rather than stereotyping?
3. Why is listening such an important communication skill?

50 CHAPTER 2: EVERYDAY LIVING SKILLS

EXTRA CREDIT PROJECT

Extending Chapter Content Students may wish to make a Living Skills Bookmark as a reminder to make use of the living skills covered in Chapter 2. Provide students with strips of poster board, 2 x 8 inches (5 x 20 cm). Have them go back through the chapter and note key points from each lesson by noting the headings, illustrations, and bulleted lists. Each student should make notes from these key points and create a design for the bookmark that highlights skills that he or she can refer to during day-to-day experiences. Encourage students to make their bookmarks bright and decorate them with attractive borders or illustrations.

CHAPTER 2 REVIEW

4. How does asking questions promote good conversation?
5. Why is being able to work in a group an important part of being a good citizen?
6. How does being a good citizen benefit you?
7. In what ways can other people be a resource in meeting your goals?
8. What are the benefits of good time management?

Thinking Critically

Using complete sentences, answer the following questions on a separate sheet of paper.

1. **Describe** In what types of situations would it be especially important for teens to make a good first impression?
2. **Analyze** What stereotypes might adults have of teens? What can be done to break these stereotypes?
3. **Contrast** In what ways does a conversation on the telephone differ from a conversation that takes place in person?
4. **Explain** What responsibilities do citizens have to their leaders?
5. **Suggest** How could you show your consideration for other people's time?

Cooperative Learning

1. In small groups, role-play ways in which teens might make a good impression in various situations. The situations might include showing understanding and empathy for a new student or meeting a friend's parents for the first time. Try to show good communication skills.
2. As a class or in small groups, plan and carry out a project to meet a need in your school. Use the management process to guide your planning.

Family & Community

Try having a family "roundtable" discussion once a week. Gather everyone in one room. Go around the group and give each person a chance to report on his or her activities during the past week. Encourage family members to talk by using good listening skills and body language.

Building A Portfolio

1. Have a conversation with a parent or other adult. Ask the person about his or her experiences as a teen. Tell the person about your life as a teen. You might share photos and other souvenirs, such as school yearbooks. With the other person's permission, tape-record the conversation. Put the tape in your portfolio and listen to it again in the next few weeks. Reviewing the tape will remind you of how to use your communication skills.
2. Take an inventory of your resources. Divide a sheet of paper into three columns: Personal Resources, Material Resources, and Community Resources. List the resources you have in each column. Place the inventory sheet in your portfolio. The next time you have a goal to accomplish, use your inventory sheet to remind you of your resources.

CHAPTER 2 REVIEW **51**

CHAPTER 2 REVIEW

4. Asking people about their own interests and experiences promotes good conversation.
5. Because a citizen is a part of a group, such as a family, school, community, or nation. These groups of people get tasks done by working as part of a team.
6. It gives you a sense of belonging and a feeling of pride, and it helps others.
7. Strong relationships provide help and support. The encouragement of family and friends can help you gain confidence and strengthen your self-concept.
8. You can get more done and have time to do special things. You will be able to do important tasks and be on time. You will have more time for yourself and others.

Evaluate

Assign Chapter 2 Test in the TCR, or create your own Chapter Test using the Testmaker Software.

CLOSE

Have students apply their knowledge of the chapter's content by completing one of the alternative assessment activities listed under Family and Community or Building a Portfolio.

Answers to Thinking Critically

1. Situations will vary but might include interviewing for a job or meeting the parents of a new friend.
2. Stereotypes will vary but might include that all teens like rock music. Adults need to get to know the teens as individuals.
3. A telephone conversation involves only verbal communication, but a conversation in person involves both verbal and nonverbal communication.
4. To be cooperative and supportive.
5. Answers will vary but might include that teens and seniors can contribute different viewpoints to a project.

Planning Guide
Chapter 3 Steps to Success

LESSON 1	Pages	FEATURES	CLASSROOM RESOURCES
What's Important to You?	54–58	*Skills in Action:* Acting on Your Values *Try This:* Needs and Wants	Activity and Project Card 5, "Creating Values Symbols" Cooperative Learning 5 Cross Curriculum 3 Lesson 1 Quiz Peer Pressure and Decision Making 5 Transparencies 11 & 12, "Which Value Do You Consider 'Tops'?" Transparency 13, "Refusal Skills" Student Workbook Activities 14, 15
LESSON 2 **Acting Responsibly**	59–63	*Try This:* Helping Charitable Organizations	Concept Map 4 Lesson 2 Quiz Student Workbook Activities 16, 17
LESSON 3 **Using the Decision-Making Process**	64–69	*Tips for Living:* Making Up Your Mind *Skills in Action:* Evaluating Past Decisions	Concept Map 5 Lesson 3 Quiz Transparency 14, "Factors that Affect Decisions" Student Workbook Activity 18
LESSON 4 **Setting Goals**	70–74	*Tips for Living:* Reaching Your Goals	Activity and Project Card 6, "Go for the Goal" Cooperative Learning 6 Enrichment 3 Lesson 4 Quiz Peer Pressure and Decision Making 6 Transparency 15, "Goal Management" Student Workbook Activities 19, 20

CHAPTER 3 RESOURCES

Chapter 3 Test   Study Guide 3, *Reteaching*   Testmaker Software
Reteaching 3

Performance Assessment Activity

Ask students to conduct interviews with classmates or other acquaintances about setting and achieving goals. Each student should prepare a list of questions in advance. Questions might include: What goals have you set for yourself? Have your goals been realistic goals? What priorities have you had to set to balance different goals? If you don't set goals, why not? What are some goals you have reached? What did you do to reach your goals? How did reaching the goals make you feel?

Students might want to tape their interviews and play them to the rest of the class. Have students form small groups and use the information from the interviews to create posters that convey the importance of goal setting. Display completed posters in the classroom.

School-to-Work

Ask students to look through the classified want ads in their local newspaper. Have them choose a job that they find interesting and that they might like to have as an adult. Tell students that they should list the job as their long-term goal. Ask them to focus on the personal qualifications and skills the job requires. Then have students think of short-term goals that they could set to help them achieve the long-term goal of obtaining a similar job. Hold a class discussion to evaluate students' short-term goals.

Family & Community

Bring in articles clipped from your local newspaper concerning community issues on which people tend to take opposing positions. For example, articles might address issues such as whether or not to build a discount store in the community or whether or not schools should have a dress code. Organize the class into groups and have each group apply the six-step decision-making process to the issue in an effort to reach a decision. Assist students in getting additional information they might need in order to reach a decision.

Resources for the Teacher

March, James G. *A Primer on Decision Making: How Decisions Happen.* New York: Maxwell Macmillan International, 1994.

Rudman, Gerald J. *Decision-Making Skills for Middle School Students.* Washington, DC: NEA Professional Library, National Education Association, 1985.

Readings for the Student

Johnson, Linda Carlson. *Responsibility.* New York: Rosen Publishing Group, 1990.

Milios, Rita. *Discovering How to Make Good Choices.* New York: Rosen Publishing Group, 1992.

Smith, Sandra Lee. *Coping with Decision Making.* New York: Rosen Publishing Group, 1993.

Multimedia Resources

Acting on Your Values. Volume 2 (Videocassette, teacher's guide). Live Wire Video.

Decision Making: A Methodical Approach (Disk). Orange Juice Software Systems.

Making Decisions: You Can Learn How (Two filmstrips, teacher's guide). Sunburst Communications.

OUT OF TIME?

If time does not permit thorough teaching of this chapter, you may wish to use:

- Teens Making a Difference, page 53
- Tips for Living, pages 65, 72
- Try This, pages 58, 63
- Skills in Action, pages 55, 69
- Young Living Activities, page 75
- Chapter Summary, page 76

CHAPTER 3

Steps to Success

Chapter Overview

Chapter 3 examines various actions students can take to be successful. The chapter emphasizes students' involvement in achieving success.

LESSON 1 identifies needs, wants, and values and explains how values influence an individual's actions.

LESSON 2 focuses on the importance of acting responsibly.

LESSON 3 explores the six-step decision-making process and how to use the process to make responsible decisions.

LESSON 4 differentiates between short-term and long-term goals and describes ways to reach goals.

Introducing the Chapter

As students look at the photograph of happy teens on the opening pages, ask them to describe what success feels like to them. Have students write a journal entry to finish the sentence "I always feel great when I can . . ."

Chapter Motivator

Ask each student to write down one thing they wish they could accomplish. Explain that answering the question in the first lesson title "What's Important to You?" can be the first step toward accomplishing a goal. Have students read the rest of the lesson titles for this chapter. Then ask for volunteers to explain how they imagine each of these ideas can help them achieve success. Explain that in this chapter they will learn how acting responsibly, making wise decisions, and setting goals are all important steps to success.

CHAPTER 3 Steps to Success

LESSON ONE
What's Important to You?

LESSON TWO
Acting Responsibly

LESSON THREE
Using the Decision-Making Process

LESSON FOUR
Setting Goals

KEY TO ABILITY LEVELS

Teaching strategies that appear throughout the chapter have been identified by one of three codes to give you an idea of their suitability for students of varying learning styles and abilities.

L1 Level 1 strategies should be within the ability range of all students. Often full class participation is required. Teacher direction is usually needed.

L2 Level 2 strategies are for average to above-average students or for small groups. Some teacher direction is necessary.

L3 Level 3 strategies are designed for students able and willing to work independently. Minimal teacher direction is necessary.

TEENS MAKING A DIFFERENCE
Helping Others

Thirteen-year-old Keesha James and her friends are popular visitors at the Twin Oaks Nursing Home. When Keesha's grandmother moved to the nursing home, Keesha started visiting her. She spent time playing cards with her.

One Saturday, Keesha brought a few friends with her. When some of the other people in the nursing home saw Keesha's grandmother and the girls playing cards, they joined in the game too. Everyone had such a good time that the teens decided to visit the nursing home every other Saturday.

The teens have made many new friends at the nursing home. They enjoy making the residents happy and seeing their smiling faces.

Try THIS!

Start a collection of newspaper articles that show teens helping others. Put the articles in your portfolio. Circle the activities that you would like to do.

53

CHAPTER 3

TEENS MAKING A DIFFERENCE

Have students read the article about helping others. Ask students to suggest places in their community where they might find opportunities to help in the way Keesha has helped people at the nursing home. Ask what benefits might be gained from working in their own community to offer time or energy to help others. Assign the TRY THIS! activity. Encourage students to keep an article file in their portfolios, or collect the most interesting articles and keep them in a classroom article file. These may be kept for students who are absent or for future use throughout the program.

BLOCK SCHEDULING

The following Teacher Classroom Resources are suggested for use in classrooms with Block Scheduling.
- Activity and Project Card 5, "Creating Values Symbols"
- Activity and Project Card 6, "Go for the Goal"
- Cooperative Learning 5, "Wheel of Needs"
- Cooperative Learning 6, "Looking Ahead"

TECHNOLOGY IN THE CLASSROOM

Transparencies You will find a range of options to introduce technology into this program. Overhead transparencies are available for use with each of the chapters. They continue to be an excellent media source because they allow the teacher to work facing the class. Bright colors and bold, easy-to-read captions and callouts keep students' attention as the teacher points out or highlights concepts displayed on a large screen that can be visible from anywhere in the classroom. Transparencies are easy to use and store, and can be used in a well-lighted room at any time during the lesson. The *Young Living* Transparency Package found in the Teacher's Classroom Resources includes 72 full-color transparencies for use with this program.

LESSON ONE
What's Important to You?

FOCUS

Lesson Objectives
After studying this lesson, students should be able to
- differentiate between wants and needs.
- explain the importance of identifying personal values.
- describe the influence of values on actions.

Motivating Activity
Wrap three boxes in brightly colored paper. Ask students to pretend that these are wishing boxes and that anything they want can be inside the boxes. Ask students to list the things that they would want each box to contain.

Introducing the Lesson
Have students share their responses to the Motivating Activity. Have students identify what their lists suggest is important to them. Tell students that this lesson discusses the importance of students knowing what their values are.

Introducing *Words to Know*
Ask each student to write a sentence for each word in the Words to Know list. Ask them to form small groups and have each group use their sentences to develop a definition for each word. Discuss the similarities and differences among the students' definitions and the ones provided in the lesson.

LESSON ONE
What's Important to You?

WORDS TO KNOW
- needs
- potential
- wants
- values
- refusal skills

DISCOVER...
- the difference between wants and needs.
- the importance of identifying your personal values.
- the influence of your values on your actions.

Can you list the things that are important to you? You might think of a good family life, close friends, and enough food each day. Other teens might add having enough spending money or the chance to play on the hockey team to their list of things that are important to them. If you know what is important to you, it is easier to set goals and to achieve happiness in life.

54 CHAPTER 3: STEPS TO SUCCESS

CLASSROOM RESOURCES FOR LESSON 1

 Blackline Masters
Activity and Project Card 5, "Creating Values Symbols"
Cooperative Learning 5
Cross Curriculum 3
Lesson 1 Quiz
Peer Pressure and Decision Making 5

 Transparencies
Transparencies 11 & 12, "Which Value Do You Consider 'Tops'?"
Transparency 13, "Refusal Skills"

 Student Workbook
Activities 14, 15

Basic Needs

You share the same basic needs that all people have. **Needs** are *things that you have to have in order to live*. There are different types of needs. Physical needs are basic to your survival and well-being. They include air, food, water, sleep, a place to live, and clothing.

Remember how pleased you were to see all your friends on the first day of school? You have emotional needs, too. Emotional needs include your need to belong and to be accepted by other people. Getting along with other people is an important need that everyone has. Another emotional need is the need to be safe and secure. That means feeling comfortable and protected from harm. The need to be loved and the need to be respected and recognized for your work and your actions are also emotional needs. When your emotional needs are met, you feel good about yourself.

Another need that you share with other people is the need to reach your full potential. **Potential** is *the capacity to grow and develop*. When you strive to reach your full potential, you use your skills, talents, and abilities to try to be everything you are capable of becoming.

Wants

Wants are different from needs. **Wants** are *things that you would like to have but that are not necessary for survival*. You may want the latest CD, but you can live without it.

Sometimes people confuse wants and needs. Have you ever wanted something so much that you convinced yourself that you really needed it? Perhaps you felt that you could not live without a new camera. Did you really need it, though, or was it something you simply wanted to have? Wants are not basic to your survival as food and water are.

Values

The way you satisfy your needs and wants is based on your **values**, *ideas about right and wrong and about what is important in your life*. Most people share common values, such

Acting on Your Values

It's not always easy to act on your values—to do the right thing. One helpful idea is to practice what you will say or do in difficult situations. Think of a situation in which your values might be challenged. Then write a short skit to show how you stand up for what you believe is important.

LESSON ONE: WHAT'S IMPORTANT TO YOU?

MEETING STUDENT DIVERSITY

Physically Challenged Discuss with students—or ask physically challenged students in the class to lead a discussion on—the special needs of people with physical challenges in terms of needing to belong and to be accepted by others and in terms of reaching their full potential. (They may feel rejected by other students or may have limitations that prevent participation in some activities.) Have physically challenged students describe the steps they take to meet their physical and emotional needs.

CHAPTER 3, LESSON 1

TEACH

Stress to students that developing a value system is important in helping them make decisions and dealing with conflicting situations. Then refer students to the Skills In Action feature. Allow time for students to create their skits. After students have presented their skits, ask the class to identify the values the students stood up for in each skit.

L1 Finding Examples

On the chalkboard, make a table with two columns titled "Needs" and "Wants." Have students give examples of each. Write students' responses under the appropriate heading. Ask students to evaluate the lists, reminding them that needs are necessary for survival and that wants are not. Have them check whether or not wants appeared on the needs list.

TEACHER TALK!

Talking About Values

When students are asked to discuss values, you might find that talking in the third person (about fictitious people or situations) will avoid any invasion of students' privacy.

L2 Cooperative Learning

Assign Cooperative Learning Activity 5, "Wheel of Needs," in the TCR.

CHAPTER 3, LESSON 1

L1 Analyzing
On slips of paper write values that are commonly held, such as honesty, loyalty, friendship, and freedom. Use play money, and auction the values to students, having them bid on those of personal importance. After all values have been sold, ask students to comment on why they bought the value, why it is important, and if there was another value they would have liked to have bought.

L1 Using Transparencies
Present Color Transparencies 11 and 12, "Which Value Do You Consider 'Tops'?" Use these overhead visuals to reinforce concepts from this lesson.

L2 Role-Playing
Provide students with the following scenarios:
- Jamie's family is having a party for Jamie's grandmother's 75th birthday. Jamie's best friend, however, wants him to go to a party at a mutual friend's house.
- Miranda is on the school basketball team. Her team is playing on Friday evening. Miranda's friends are planning to go to the movies that evening and want her to come with them.

Ask students to work in pairs to role-play each scenario. Have them deal with the conflict by using refusal skills. Ask the rest of the class to evaluate each scenario in terms of how effectively the person used refusal skills to deal with the conflict.

L2 Language Arts Connection
Assign Cross-Curriculum Activity 3 in the TCR. Students learn how proverbs can express values in this activity.

A good family life is a common value shared by most people. What are some other common values?

as a good family life, freedom, honesty, trust, and health. Other values are individual, such as being a good student and playing a sport well.

Sharing Values

Many of your values come from your family and from other people who are important to you, such as teachers and religious leaders. Like most young people, you probably grew up sharing your family's values. You learned values from your family related to such things as food, money, religion, education, and marriage. Perhaps your family placed a value on traditions, such as how birthdays and holidays are celebrated.

As you get older, you may begin to add other values. Some of these values will come from your environment, the people and the things around you. For instance, if your community starts a recycling campaign, you may learn to value reusing and recycling in your home.

Differences in Values

People have different values because their interests and experiences vary and because they come from diverse backgrounds. What values do you have that differ from the values of your friends?

The way you prioritize, or rank, your values may also be different from the way others rank their values. For example, some people put a high priority on exercising regularly; some don't. Some of your friends may work extra hard at getting good grades; some may care little about grades. You can learn to respect other people's values and priorities even though these values and priorities are different from yours. In return, other people should respect your values and priorities.

56 CHAPTER 3: STEPS TO SUCCESS

MORE ABOUT • • •

Emotional Needs and Self-Esteem Remind students that when their emotional needs are met, they feel good about themselves. Point out to students that high self-esteem is important for a healthy, happy life. Self-esteem affects every aspect of a person's life. It affects success in school, relationships, decisions, and self-respect. Explain that people with high self-esteem trust their own reactions, accept themselves as they are, take responsibility for their actions, and are willing to try things even if they sometimes fail. Ask the class to brainstorm examples of ways that self-esteem influences important areas of life. (For example, people with low self-esteem may not believe that they can do well in school, so they do not bother to try.)

Your Own Value System

It is important to develop your own set of values based on what you believe to be right or wrong. Knowing what is important to you will help you make decisions about your personal life and your career.

As you develop your value system, you may notice that some of your values are in conflict with each other. For example, if getting good grades is important to you, you may want to spend the afternoon finishing your math assignment. What if your friends are going to the movies and they encourage you to join them? You will have to decide which value is more important—completing your math homework and turning it in on time or being with your friends.

At times, your values may also be in conflict with other people's values. To remain true to what you believe is right and wrong, you may need to use **refusal skills,** or *ways to say no effectively*. **Figure 3.1** gives examples of refusal skills.

Figure 3.1 Refusal Skills
Sometimes you will need to use refusal skills to stay true to your beliefs and values.

- State exactly how you feel, directly and honestly.
- Do not apologize for your decisions—or for your values.
- Use direct eye contact to show that you mean what you say.
- Use a firm yet friendly tone of voice.
- Use the other person's name.
- Suggest an option that is more acceptable to you.
- Avoid compromise, which can be a slow way of saying yes.

LESSON ONE: WHAT'S IMPORTANT TO YOU? 57

CHAPTER 3, LESSON 1

USING VISUALS
Have students study the examples of refusal skills in Figure 3.1. Have students recall which, if any, of the examples they have used. How well did it work? Ask them which skill they consider most effective.

L1 Using Transparencies
Present Color Transparency 13, "Refusal Skills," in the TCR. Use this overhead visual to reinforce concepts from this lesson.

L2 Activity and Project Card
Provide time for students to complete Activity and Project Card 5, "Creating Values Symbols," in the TCR.

L2 Problem Solving
Assign Peer Pressure and Decision Making 5 in the TCR. This activity gives students the opportunity to recognize peer pressure and practice decision-making skills.

L1 Student Workbook
Assign Activities 14 and 15 in the Student Workbook.

ASSESS

Evaluating the Lesson
Assign Reviewing Terms and Facts and Thinking Critically on page 58 to review the lesson; then assign the Lesson 1 Quiz in the TCR.

COOPERATIVE LEARNING

Family Values Have students work together to create a bulletin-board display illustrating family values based on tradition. Have a group of students draw a world map and label the continents. Then have each student identify the area from which their family originated and connect one end of a string or colored ribbon to the area and the other end to a place on the bulletin board outside the map. (For some students, more than one area may be identified as place of origin.) At this end of the string, ask students to provide an illustration of how their family values have been influenced by the culture of their area of origin.

CHAPTER 3, LESSON 1

Reteaching

- Bring a newspaper editorial to class and read it aloud. Then ask: If you could write an editorial on the same topic, what position would you take?
- Have students complete Reteaching Activity 3 in the TCR.

Enrichment

Provide students with a list of about 10 commonly-held values. (courage, honesty, loyalty, etc.) Ask students to choose the value that they consider to be most important. Then have them write a short position paper defending their choice. Call on volunteers to read their paper to the class.

Answers to Lesson 1 Review

1. Physical, emotional, reach full potential. Examples will vary.
2. Using your skills, talents, and abilities to try to be everything you are capable of becoming.
3. Needs are things you have to have in order to live. Wants are things that you would like to have but are not necessary for survival.
4. Any three: a good family life, freedom, honesty, trust, and health.
5. Answers will vary.
6. Answers will vary, but might include values are based on family values, the environment, interests and experiences.
7. Examples will vary
8. Descriptions will vary, but need to include the way the perfect day reflects students' values.

CLOSE

Refer students to the lesson title "What's Important to You?" Have them create a collage in which they answer that question.

58

Try This!

Most people have only a few real needs but lots of wants. Practice telling the difference by making a back-to-school shopping list. Divide the list into two columns—"Needs" and "Wants." Estimate how much money you would save if you bought only the items in your "Needs" column.

Some of your values—such as freedom and health—will be important to you all your life. Other values may become more or less important as you have new experiences and meet new people. For example, you may learn to value the outdoors as a result of taking a science class in school. You will want your life to include the values that are the most important to you.

Your values serve as guides to your actions. For example, if you value honesty, you will not lie to a friend. If you value your family, you will help out at home. If you value excellence as a singer, you will practice. Your values help you decide what to do and how to act.

Your Values and Your Life

Your values are influenced by your family, friends, and environment. When you decide on your personal values, you will be able to satisfy your needs and wants in ways that contribute to a happy, successful life.

LESSON ONE Review

Using complete sentences, answer the following questions on a separate sheet of paper.

Reviewing Terms and Facts

1. **Identify** List three kinds of basic needs, and give an example of each.
2. **Explain** What does reaching your full potential mean?
3. **Vocabulary** What is the difference between *needs* and *wants*?
4. **List** Name three common values that most people share.

Thinking Critically

5. **Evaluate** Which has influenced your values more—your family or the environment? Explain your answer.
6. **Explain** Why does each individual have a unique set of values?
7. **Relate** Give an example of how your values determine your actions.

Applying Concepts

8. Write a description of what a perfect day would be like for you. How would you spend your time, what would you eat, and with whom would you spend the day? Compare your description with those of your classmates. How does the description reflect your values?

58 CHAPTER 3: STEPS TO SUCCESS

COOPERATIVE LEARNING

Refusal Skills Organize the class into small groups. Ask each group to compile a list of strategies, phrases, or behaviors that work when they want to say no. Then have students create mobiles that illustrate the refusal techniques that they have listed. Provide paper and cardboard backing for illustrations, and have students use coat hangers to construct their mobiles. Hang the mobiles in the classroom for students to use as a quick reference in dealing with a situation that calls for refusal skills.

LESSON TWO
Acting Responsibly

DISCOVER...
- the meaning of responsibility.
- ways you can act responsibly.
- the importance of acting responsibly.

During the teen years you will have more opportunities to act responsibly. Acting responsibly earns you the trust of other people and builds good relationships. It makes you feel good about yourself and helps you keep safe.

WORDS TO KNOW

responsibility
respect
commitments
initiative

What Is Responsibility?

Responsibility means *making choices and being able to answer for those choices.* As you get older, you will have more

---

CLASSROOM RESOURCES FOR LESSON 2

 **Blackline Masters**
Concept Map 4
Lesson 2 Quiz

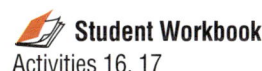 **Student Workbook**
Activities 16, 17

LESSON TWO
Acting Responsibly

FOCUS

Lesson Objectives
After studying this lesson, students should be able to
- define responsibility.
- give examples of ways that a person can act responsibly.
- explain why it is important to act responsibly.

Motivating Activity
Write the following on the chalkboard for students to complete:
I think that _____ is a responsible person because _____.
Tell them to fill in the first blank with the name of a person whom they consider responsible and in the second blank to tell why they think the person is responsible.

Introducing the Lesson
Have students share their responses to the Motivating Activity. Based on the completed sentences, discuss with students what qualities responsible people seem to have. Ask students to compare their descriptions of responsible people with the description in Lesson 2.

Introducing *Words to Know*
Provide each student with four blank cards. Have students write one of the Words to Know on one side of a card. On the other side, have them use another word or phrase to describe the word. Then have each student work with a partner to play a game in which they take turns reading each other's descriptions and trying to identify the word that the descriptions refer to.

CHAPTER 3, LESSON 2

TEACH

L1 Creating Posters

Have students identify the ways that they can show responsibility to their family. Then ask them to create posters that illustrate the ways. Suggest to students that they display their posters in their home as a reminder to them of ways that they can act responsibly there.

L1 Comparing

Ask students to think of situations in a television program or movie in which individuals did not show responsibility for themselves, to their family members, or to friends or other members of their community. Ask students to describe how these individuals would have responded to the situation if they had showed responsibility.

TEACHER TALK!

Learning Responsibility

A teacher is often the adult who students look to when assuming new responsibilities in the classroom. Encourage students to ask questions to ensure understanding of what is expected of them. (For example, if you expect students to do research papers, explain what you expect them to do: decide on a topic, take notes, record sources, write first draft.) Increase students' responsibilities gradually. Finally, encourage students to keep trying when their first attempts at learning a new responsibility fail.

---

opportunities to make your own choices. It is important to know how to handle the responsibility that comes with those choices. This is an important part of becoming an adult.

Responsibility for Yourself

You are responsible for your own behavior and actions. Each day you make many choices. You can show responsibility for yourself by making wise choices. For example, you can take care of your health by choosing to eat healthful foods, to exercise, and to get enough rest. At school you can choose to complete your schoolwork on time and to try to do your best.

Responsibility to Others

In addition to being responsible for yourself, you have a responsibility to other people. These people include your family members, your friends, and the members of your community. By being honest and dependable, you show that you care about other people.

Your Family

Showing responsibility to your family means being polite, arriving home on time, and being reliable. You can show your family that you are reliable by doing the chores and other tasks that are expected of you.

Acting responsibly at home also includes following the rules and showing **respect,** or *consideration,* for other people's feelings and concerns. Showing respect for family members means asking permission before using their things, calling home to let someone know if you are going to be late, and cleaning up after yourself.

One way to show your family that you are dependable is to do your chores without being asked. What other ways can you think of?

Your Friends

An important part of friendship is showing responsibility to

60 CHAPTER 3: STEPS TO SUCCESS

MEETING STUDENT DIVERSITY

Learning Styles Students with special learning needs might benefit from concrete examples to help them understand abstract concepts such as *responsibility* and *commitment.* Have students find the definitions of these terms in the lesson. Also, have them look at the photos in the lesson. Ask them how the photos illustrate the concepts of responsibility and commitment. Then have students find other examples of these terms in their homes, school, and community.

your friends. This includes honoring your **commitments,** or *promises*. If you said that you would help paint scenery for the school play, your friends can count on you to be there.

You can also act responsibly by helping a friend in need. Sometimes this means simply comforting a friend who is sad. Other times, however, a friend may have a serious problem or may be involved in something dangerous. In these situations you should try to get your friend to talk to an adult, such as a parent or teacher. If this doesn't work, you should tell an adult about the problem so that your friend can get professional help.

Your Community

In your community, your responsibilities include respecting public and private property and showing concern for the environment. Acting responsibly can be as simple as making sure that your garbage goes into a trash can instead of onto the street, and not destroying community property.

You can also show responsibility by helping out in your community. You might volunteer to collect food for the needy, or take part in a walkathon. When people act responsibly, they help to make their community a better place to live.

Being a volunteer in your community is a good way to show responsibility. Have you ever been a volunteer?

Showing Responsibility

The more you show that you are accountable now, the more freedom and trust you will be given in the future. Here are a few of the many ways to show responsibility.

- **Obey rules.** Families, schools, and communities have rules that help maintain order and keep people safe. Your parents probably have rules about what time you

LESSON TWO: ACTING RESPONSIBLY **61**

CHAPTER 3, LESSON 2

L2 Writing Poetry

Organize the class into groups of three to four. Assign one of the ways to show responsibility that is listed under "Showing Responsibility" to each group. Ask students in each group to work together to write a poem in which they illustrate the way that was assigned to them. Call on a member of each group to read the group's poem to the class.

L2 Applying

Ask students the following question: What are some ways to show responsibility in the workplace? Have students answer the question by using the bulleted list on pages 61–62 and providing specific examples for each item. Call on volunteers to share their examples with the class.

L3 Creating

If your school does not have a handbook, have students work in groups to create a handbook that addresses students' responsibilities in following school rules and procedures. Encourage groups to illustrate their handbook. Display finished handbooks in the classroom. Handbooks might also be photocopied and shared with other classes. If computers are available, encourage students to make use of desktop publishing software to create their handbooks.

HOME AND COMMUNITY CONNECTION

Have students look through their local newspapers to find articles that illustrate responsibility in the community. Ask them to work in pairs to develop a television news broadcast that highlights the person or event described in the article. Students might use a regular news broadcast or a talk-show format. Have each pair present their broadcasts to the class. As part of a class discussion, have students determine which of the ways discussed under "Showing Responsibility" are evident in the example presented by each pair of students.

CHAPTER 3, LESSON 2

Try This!

Have students read the "Try This" activity on page 63. Have them post these organizations and their phone numbers in a bulletin-board display. Encourage students to refer to the display when choosing a way to give a helping hand in their community.

L1 Student Workbook
Assign Activities 16 and 17 in the Student Workbook.

ASSESS

Evaluating the Lesson
Assign Reviewing Terms and Facts and Thinking Critically on page 63 to review the lesson; then assign the Lesson 2 Quiz in the TCR.

Reteaching
- Ask students to imagine that they have been asked to write an article for the "Kids Want to Know" section of a local newspaper. The article is to address these questions: What is responsibility? How can I show responsibility? Tell students that the audience for the article is people of their age group. Call on volunteers to read their articles to the class.
- Have students complete Reteaching Activity 3 in the TCR.
- Assign Concept Map 4 in the TCR.

---

must be home after school. Your school most likely has rules against running in the halls. You act responsibly when you follow the rules.

- **Help others.** Responsible people look out for their families, friends, and neighbors—not just for themselves. If you see someone in trouble, try to help.

- **Carry out tasks or duties.** If it is your job to clear the table, do it without being told. If you see other tasks that need to be done, take the initiative. **Initiative** is *taking action without being asked*.

- **Keep your promises.** If you told a friend that you would help him study for a test, you have an obligation to keep that promise. In this way you will show friends and others that they can count on you.

- **Have a positive attitude.** If there are chores to be done, do them without complaining.

- **Show maturity.** There are many ways to show maturity. One way is to be honest and admit your mistakes. If you forgot that it was your turn to walk the dog, apologize and offer to do it the next time.

Helping others will make you feel good about yourself. Why do you think this is true?

Characteristics of Responsible People

Certain characteristics go along with being responsible. Responsible people

- are reliable.
- admit their mistakes and don't blame others.
- are trustworthy.
- show respect for other people and their property.
- keep their word.

62 CHAPTER 3: STEPS TO SUCCESS

MORE ABOUT •••

Showing Responsibility Remind students that people show responsibility for themselves by making wise choices. Point out that making wise choices is a part of being a wise consumer. Tell students that being a wise consumer includes shopping in a way that gives the most value for what you spend. It also includes checking labels to be aware of what you are buying, and knowing what to do if there is a problem with a purchase. Discuss with students other ways of being a wise consumer.

Learning Responsibility

Not everyone has the same responsibilities, and people's responsibilities change over time. As a young child, your main task may have been to take care of your toys. As a young teen, however, you will be expected to assume more complex jobs, such as preparing dinner.

Learning responsibility can be hard, but it has many rewards. You will feel good about yourself, and other people will respect you and start treating you like an adult. Try following these guidelines.

- **Find out what is expected of you.** Listen carefully. Ask questions if you don't understand.
- **Look to adults as role models.** Ask them to help you learn the right thing to do.
- **Take on new tasks gradually.** You will avoid stress if you don't take on too much at once.
- **Be patient with yourself.** If you forget to do something or do it wrong, learn from your mistake and try harder the next time.

Try This!

Check the Yellow Pages for charitable organizations in your community. Choose one and find out how you can lend a helping hand. Report your findings to the class.

LESSON TWO Review

Using complete sentences, answer the following questions on a separate sheet of paper.

Reviewing Terms and Facts

1. Recall In what ways can you act responsibly at home?

2. Vocabulary Define the term *respect*. Use it in an original sentence.

3. Vocabulary What is another word for *commitment*?

4. Identify Name three characteristics of responsible people.

Thinking Critically

5. Describe Give two examples of ways that you could take the initiative at home.

6. Predict What do you think would happen if people did not act responsibly in their community?

Applying Concepts

7. An important way to show responsibility is to help others. Think of an opportunity you have to lend a helping hand to someone, and then act on it. Describe your experience to a small group of your classmates.

LESSON TWO: ACTING RESPONSIBLY   63

CHAPTER 3, LESSON 2

Answers to Lesson 2 Review

1. Answers will vary but might include being polite, arriving home on time, being reliable, following the rules, and showing respect for other people's feelings and concerns.

2. *Respect* means consideration. Sentences will vary.

3. Promise.

4. Any three of the following: They are reliable, admit their mistakes and don't blame others, are trustworthy, show respect for other people and their property, and keep their word.

5. Examples will vary but should show ways that students do things at home without being asked.

6. Answers will vary but might include that the community could become an unsafe and unhealthy place to live.

7. Answers will vary. Students might describe what they did and how it made them feel about themselves.

Enrichment

Have students choose a historical figure whom they believe possessed the characteristics of a responsible person. Ask students to present an oral report in which they describe the characteristics of the person and the ways that the person showed responsibility.

CLOSE

Ask students to write a short paragraph that completes the following phrase: "If everyone in the world acted responsibly, . . ." Call on volunteers to read their paragraphs to the class.

COOPERATIVE LEARNING

Showing Responsibility Organize the class into small groups to create pamphlets that show preschool and kindergarten children how they can act responsibly. Students in each group should discuss the ways that a young child can act responsibly. After students have agreed on the examples, have them develop the pamphlet. Have each group divide tasks among its members. Encourage them to illustrate the pamphlet, using drawings that would appeal to young children. Point out that any text should use vocabulary that is appropriate for the particular age group. You might have students give completed pamphlets to local kindergarten and preschool classes.

LESSON THREE
Using the Decision-Making Process

FOCUS

Lesson Objectives
After studying this lesson, students should be able to
- differentiate between routine and major decisions.
- describe how to use the six-step decision-making process.
- explain how to make responsible decisions.

Motivating Activity
Ask students to read the lesson opening paragraph. Then have them write the most difficult decision they recently have made.

Introducing the Lesson
Call on volunteers to describe the decision identified in the Motivating Activity. Discuss with students how they made their decision. For example, did they consider all options? Also, ask them if they feel they made the right decision. Tell students that Lesson 3 will explore the decision-making process.

Introducing *Words to Know*
To introduce the Words to Know list, write the following on the chalkboard: "Winners make things happen; losers let things happen." Ask students which vocabulary terms illustrate the statement. *(decisions and default)*

Ask students which term is a synonym for "practice" *(habit)*, "choices" *(options)*, and "effects" *(consequences)*.

64

LESSON THREE
Using the Decision-Making Process

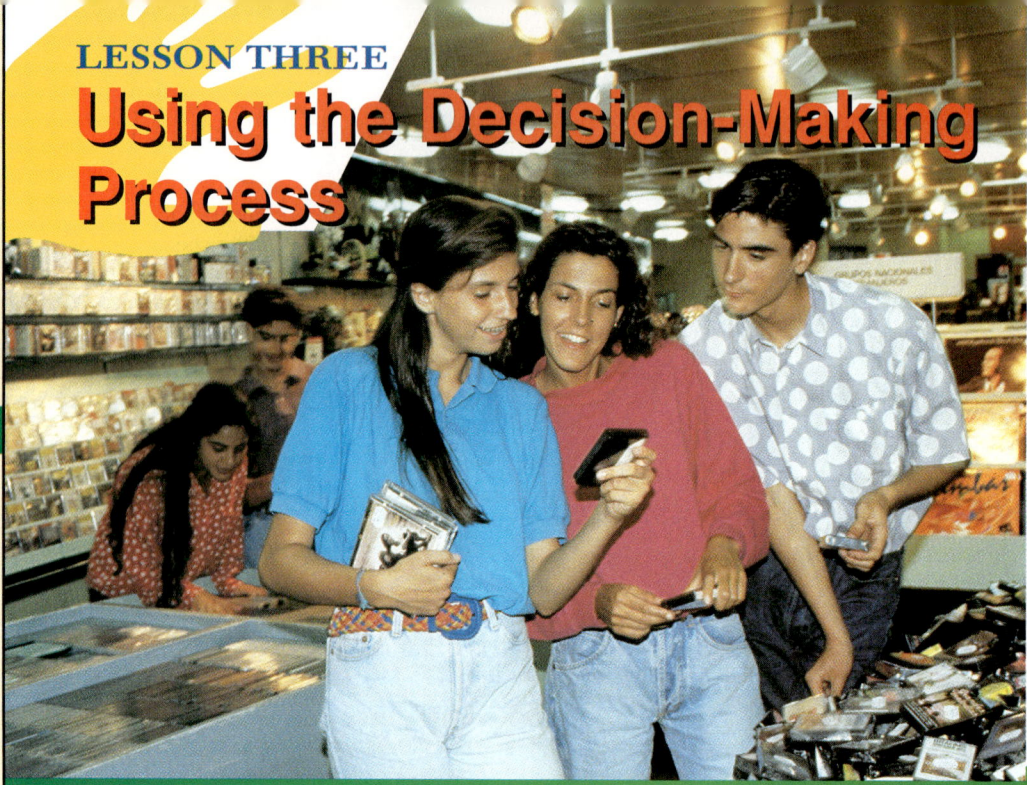

WORDS TO KNOW
- decision
- default
- habit
- options
- consequences

DISCOVER...
- the difference between routine and major decisions.
- how to use the six-step decision-making process.
- how to make responsible decisions.

You have many choices in your life. Each day you have the choice of what to eat for lunch, what to do with your free time, and how hard to study. In fact, life is made up of all kinds of decisions. A **decision** is *a choice a person makes about what action to take*.

Types of Decisions

Decisions are made in several different ways. Sometimes you make decisions by responding to something that has happened, such as deciding to start an exercise routine after doing

64 CHAPTER 3: STEPS TO SUCCESS

CLASSROOM RESOURCES FOR LESSON 3

 Blackline Masters
Concept Map 5
Lesson 3 Quiz

 Transparencies
Transparency 14, "Factors that Affect Decisions"

 Student Workbook
Activity 18

poorly in gym class. You also make decisions that cause something to happen, such as deciding to be honest so that your family can trust you. Even if you decide not to decide, such as not responding to an invitation to a party, you have made a decision—by default. Making a decision by **default** means *failing to make a decision and leaving the outcome to chance*.

Making Routine Decisions

Some decisions are minor or routine. These are choices that you make every day. They usually do not require a lot of time or thought. Deciding what clothes to wear is a routine decision. It is important to you at the time, but it really does not affect your life very much.

Some routine decisions become habits. A **habit** is *a behavior pattern that is repeated without thinking about it*. You probably have habits like taking a shower every morning and doing your homework each evening.

Making Major Decisions

Major decisions are the choices that have long-term effects on your life. They require much time and thought and may be difficult to make. You do not make major decisions as often as you make routine decisions.

Some of the major decisions you will make as a teenager are what classes to take in school, whether to get a part-time job, or who your friends will be. Some major decisions, such as whether or not to go to college, can be life changing.

TIPS for living

MAKING UP YOUR MIND

Do you find it difficult to make decisions? Here are some tips.
- Realize that not all decisions are worth agonizing over.
- When faced with a decision, put your choices in writing. Make a list of all your options, along with the pros and cons of each.
- Limit your choices. Identify all of your options, and then narrow down your choices to three. This may make it easier to decide on one.

LESSON THREE: USING THE DECISION-MAKING PROCESS

CHAPTER 3, LESSON 3

L2 Analyzing
Ask students to write a story recalling a situation in which they procrastinated too long in making a decision. Their stories should also include the results of their procrastination. Call on volunteers to share their stories with the class.

TEACHER TALK!

Using Decision-Making Steps

You might give students opportunities to make decisions in the classroom. For example, when assigning projects provide a few topics for them to choose from. Use positive reinforcement for good decisions and for poor decisions use constructive suggestions for improving decision making skills.

L1 Using Transparencies
Present Color Transparency 14, "Factors that Affect Decisions," in the TCR. Use this overhead visual to reinforce concepts from this lesson.

When making decisions, try writing down all of your options and comparing them. How might this help you?

Why Decision Making Is Important

You will find that being successful in life depends a lot on your ability to make wise decisions. Learning to make routine decisions will help you develop the self-confidence to make more difficult decisions as you get older. The ability to make decisions gives you a sense of freedom and independence.

The decisions you make now will affect the choices you have in the future. For example, deciding now to explore different careers will make you aware of your options and will expand your choices later. What other ways can you think of in which the decisions you make now will affect your future choices?

Steps in Decision Making

Making a decision is easier if you break the problem into smaller parts. If you approach decision making as the six-step process shown in **Figure 3.2,** you will learn to make wise decisions. This process is particularly helpful when you need to make major decisions. The decision-making process includes the following six steps.

66   CHAPTER 3: STEPS TO SUCCESS

COOPERATIVE LEARNING

Making a Decision Give students a set of six index cards each. Ask each student to write one step of the decision-making process on one side of each of the six cards. Have the set of cards laminated for students to use in this and other activities that demonstrate the decision-making process. Next, on slips of paper write brief descriptions of situations that require decisions. Provide cooperative groups with a set of laminated cards, and have each group apply the decision-making process to a situation from the slips of paper. Have students record each step on the back of each laminated card with washable markers. Have groups read the solutions aloud, and ask the class to evaluate the application of the steps.

Figure 3.2 The Six Steps of Decision Making

It is helpful to use the six-step decision-making process if you have to make an important decision.

1. State the situation — Identify the decision you must make. You need to be clear about the real question facing you before you can find the best answer. Stating the situation also allows you to concentrate on one decision at a time.

2. List the options — Options are possible choices. Usually more than one choice is available to you. You may have several options.

3. Weigh the possible outcomes — Think about the advantages and disadvantages of each possible choice. Ask yourself, "What would happen if I…?" Consider your needs, wants, and goals. Thinking through all the possibilities will help you make better decisions.

4. Consider your values — Use your beliefs, or what is important to you, as guidelines in your decision making. You will not be happy with a decision that goes against your values or your family's values.

5. Make a decision and act — This is the point where you actually decide. A decision is not a real decision until you take action on your choice. After you have made your decision, you must take the responsibility to see it through.

6. Evaluate the decision — Making a decision and then acting on it is not the end of the decision-making process. You must judge whether the decision you made was the best one. Analyzing the outcome of your decision will help you in future decision making.

LESSON THREE: USING THE DECISION-MAKING PROCESS **67**

CHAPTER 3, LESSON 3

USING VISUALS
Have students study the six steps in decision making shown in Figure 3.2. Ask students in what kinds of situations they would use all six steps and in what kinds of situations they would not.

L2 Critical Thinking
Point out to students that making decisions at the right time is an important part of making responsible decisions. Have students list five major decisions they expect to make in the next five years. Call on volunteers to read their entries to the class and have them compare their potential decisions with those of other classmates. Discuss with students how being aware of decisions they may need to make in the future can help them control how things happen.

L3 Evaluating
Organize the class into small groups. Have each group identify situations in which it would be important to consider the consequences of a decision. Ask each group to illustrate the situation in a cartoon titled "Think Before You Act." Display and discuss completed cartoons.

MORE ABOUT • • •

Making Decisions at the Right Time Remind students that putting off a decision too long is called *procrastination*. Ask them to speculate as to why some people procrastinate more than others. Tell them that research indicates that perpetual procrastinators put off making decisions because they are not confident of the outcome of their decisions. They may then think of themselves as lazy or unworthy because of their procrastination. This helps create a negative self-image, which reinforces the problem. Ask students to describe a situation in which they procrastinated. Ask them to relate the situation to their self-confidence.

CHAPTER 3, LESSON 3

Skills IN ACTION

After students read the feature on page 69, ask why evaluating a decision is an important step in the decision-making process. Encourage students to use the evaluations in their private journals to help them make decisions in the future.

L1 Student Workbook
Assign Activity 18 in the Student Workbook.

ASSESS

Evaluating the Lesson
Assign Reviewing Terms and Facts and Thinking Critically on page 69 to review the lesson; then assign the Lesson 3 Quiz in the TCR.

Reteaching
- Have students use the decision-making steps to work through a problem and come up with the best solution. Students should make a flow chart that shows the six steps.
- Have students complete Reteaching Activity 3 in the TCR.
- Assign Concept Map 5 in the TCR.

Enrichment
Have students find articles in newspapers or magazines that illustrate situations in which a good decision by a young person helped someone else.

When faced with a difficult decision, ask for advice from your parents or other trusted adults. Why is their advice valuable?

Making Responsible Decisions

Learning to make responsible decisions will give you a sense of control over your life. Instead of accepting whatever happens to you, you can help control how things happen. Here are some suggestions to help you make responsible decisions.

- **Make your decisions at the right time.** Avoid making quick decisions. Give yourself time to consider all the facts. On the other hand, don't put off a decision too long. If you do, you may find that some of your options are no longer available.

- **Consider the consequences. Consequences** (CON-suh-kwen-sez) are *the results of your choice.* Think about how your choice will affect your life now and in the future. How will it affect your family members or friends?

- **Be willing to take risks.** Any time you make a decision, there is a risk involved. There is always a chance that you will make a mistake. You must have the courage to act on your decisions despite the risk.

68 CHAPTER 3: STEPS TO SUCCESS

MORE ABOUT • • •

Procrastination Write on the board the following statement: "Never put off till tomorrow what you can do today." Then review with students the meaning of procrastination—putting off tasks rather than being disciplined and accomplishing chores or responsibilities. People often avoid tasks that appear to them to be difficult, boring, or unpleasant. Suggest the following tips students should use to avoid procrastination: Ask questions if you are not sure what to do; Break a large project into smaller, more manageable steps; Set a certain time to begin a certain project; Remember to reward yourself for starting and for finishing a project.

- **Seek advice when you need it.** Advice from family members and friends can help you make the right decisions. Sometimes they have had to make similar decisions. Listen to others and use their advice if it is helpful.
- **Accept responsibility for your decisions.** Making your own decisions means accepting responsibility for the choices you make. You cannot make excuses or blame others when you make a poor decision. Accepting responsibility for your decisions and the consequences of those decisions is a sign of maturity.

Your Decisions

Decisions will become more complex as you grow older. Knowing how to handle routine decisions can give you practice and help you feel confident when you have to make major decisions. The six-step decision-making process will help you explore your options and make responsible decisions that you can feel pleased with.

Evaluating Past Decisions

Think about an important decision you made recently. Ask yourself questions such as:
- Am I satisfied with the results?
- Was there a better option than the one I chose?

If you discovered you made a mistake, write down how you could make a better decision in the future.

LESSON THREE Review

Using complete sentences, answer the following questions on a separate sheet of paper.

Reviewing Terms and Facts

1. **Vocabulary** Define *habit* and give an example.
2. **Recall** How are routine decisions different from major decisions?
3. **Recall** Why is it important to learn how to make decisions?
4. **List** Name the six steps of the decision-making process.
5. **Identify** What are four tips for making responsible decisions?

Thinking Critically

6. **Analyze** Why do people sometimes make decisions by default?
7. **Predict** What might be the consequences of deciding to smoke cigarettes?

Applying Concepts

8. Write a list of ten decisions you make in an average day. Next to each item on your list, note whether it is a minor decision or a major decision. Then number each decision in order of importance, with 1 being the most important and 10 being the least important.

LESSON THREE: USING THE DECISION-MAKING PROCESS **69**

HOME AND COMMUNITY CONNECTION

Remind students that seeking advice from family and friends can help them make better decisions. Then ask students to identify other sources of advice available to young people when they need help in making decisions. Students might write the name of each of these sources on a card and combine the cards into a "Sources of Advice" directory.

CHAPTER 3, LESSON 3

Answers to Lesson 3 Review

1. *Habit* is a behavior pattern that is repeated without thinking about it. Examples will vary, but might include such things as brushing your teeth.
2. Routine decisions are minor choices you make every day. They usually do not require much time or thought. Major decisions are choices that have long-term effects. They are more difficult to make, require much time and thought, and are not made very often.
3. Success in life depends on your ability to make wise decisions. It gives you a sense of freedom and independence. The decisions you make now will affect the choices you have in the future.
4. State the situation, list the options, weigh the possible outcomes, consider your values, make a decision and act, evaluate the decision.
5. Any four: make your decisions at the right time, consider the consequences, be willing to take risks, seek advice when you need it, accept responsibility for your decisions.
6. Answers will vary but might include that they might not be willing to risk making a mistake.
7. Answers will vary but might include that deciding to smoke might result in respiratory problems.
8. Decisions and rankings will vary.

CLOSE

Ask students to explain how practicing making decisions ahead of time can benefit them when making future decisions.

LESSON FOUR
Setting Goals

FOCUS

Lesson Objectives
After studying this lesson, students should be able to
- differentiate between short-term and long-term goals.
- explain how to set realistic goals.
- identify resources that will help them reach their goals.

Motivating Activity
Ask students to list skills they have tried to master in the last few years. For example, students might list trying to learn how to use in-line skates.

Introducing the Lesson
Call on volunteers to share their lists. Tell them that skills they want to master and things they want to accomplish are goals. Tell students that Lesson 4 describes different kinds of goals and discusses ways of achieving them.

Introducing *Words to Know*
Ask students to write a definition for each term in Words to Know. Then ask them to use each word in a sentence. Call on volunteers to read their sentences and correct any misconceptions.

LESSON FOUR
Setting Goals

WORDS TO KNOW
goal
realistic goal
resource
trade-off

DISCOVER...
- short-term and long-term goals.
- how to set realistic goals.
- resources that will help you reach your goals.

What do you want to achieve in life? Do you want to be a guitar player? An Olympic gymnast? An architect? Knowing what you want to do makes life more interesting and rewarding. It gives purpose to your life and helps you do your best.

70   CHAPTER 3: STEPS TO SUCCESS

CLASSROOM RESOURCES FOR LESSON 4

 Blackline Masters
Activity and Project Card 6, "Go for the Goal"
Cooperative Learning 6
Enrichment 3
Lesson 4 Quiz
Peer Pressure and Decision Making 6
Reteaching 3

 Transparencies
Transparency 15, "Goal Management"

 Student Workbook
Activities 19, 20

Setting Personal Goals

Goals are essential for success in life. A **goal** is *something you want to achieve*. Your goal may be becoming the class treasurer, learning how to fly a plane, or earning a college degree. A goal serves as a guide for what you do and gives you something to work toward. Personal goals help you do your best and achieve the things you want in life.

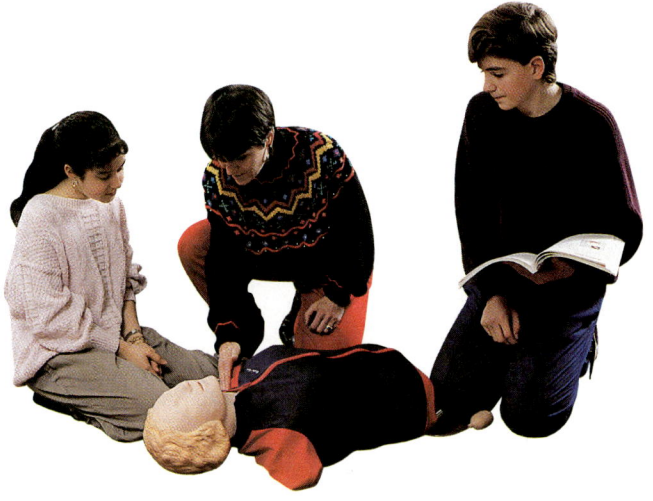

Setting short-term goals, such as completing a CPR course, can prepare you for your long-term goal of becoming an emergency medical technician. What are your short-term goals?

Long-term and Short-term Goals

Even though you may not often think about setting goals, you do it all the time. Some of your goals may take a long time to reach—months or even years. These are called long-term goals. Your long-term goals may include learning to drive a car, going to college, or saving enough money to buy a computer.

Short-term goals can be reached more quickly, perhaps in a few days or weeks. Your short-term goals might include completing a science project or getting an A on a math test. Short-term goals are usually specific and can be met in a definite time period.

Sometimes short-term goals can help you achieve a long-term goal. For example, a long-term goal of making the school choir could be broken down into the following short-term goals.

LESSON FOUR: SETTING GOALS **71**

CHAPTER 3, LESSON 4

TEACH

L1 Making a Time Line
Ask students to do the following: Make a time line by drawing a horizontal line across a blank piece of paper. On the far left write today's date. On the far right of the time line write the date ten years in the future. Draw perpendicular lines, and write anticipated goals with projected dates for accomplishment. (Make sure that the distance between the lines corresponds to the length of time between the projected dates.) Have students place a circle around their three most important goals.

L2 Drawing a Mural
Organize the class into small groups. Have students in each group discuss some of the goals that their school has. Then have the students create murals illustrating these goals.

L2 Activity and Project Card
Allow time for students to complete Activity and Project Card 6, "Go for the Goal," in the TCR.

L2 Cooperative Learning
Assign Cooperative Learning 6, "Looking Ahead," in the TCR.

COOPERATIVE LEARNING

Organize the class into groups of four to five. On slips of paper write long-term goals that students in the class might want to reach. For example, goals might include going to college, earning money to buy a bicycle, or learning to play an instrument. Ask each group of students to choose a slip of paper. Have them brainstorm ways to break the long-term goal into several short-term goals that would help to achieve the long-term goal. When students finish, discuss each group's results. Have other students suggest additional short-term goals that could help achieve the long-term goal.

CHAPTER 3, LESSON 4

L2 Analyzing
Ask students to list their goals. Have them rank the goals in order of importance to them. Tell them that ranking the goals will help to set priorities for their goals. Then ask students to identify the possible trade-offs that setting priorities for their goals may involve.

L3 Reading
Ask students to use newspapers, magazines, and books to find examples of people, other than sports figures, who achieved goals that made a difference to themselves and to others. Have students identify the person's goals and discuss ways that the person's attitude made it easier to reach her or his goals. Have students share their examples with the class.

L2 Creating Slogans
Ask students to write slogans that illustrate the importance of a positive attitude in achieving goals. Have students create signs that include these slogans. Display the signs around the classroom and, if possible, in the school hallways.

TIPS for living
After students have read "Tips for Living," discuss why it is important to set personal goals. Tell students that planning is an important step in reaching goals. Emphasize that unrealistic goals can lead to frustration.

L2 Problem Solving
Assign Peer Pressure and Decision Making 6 in the TCR. This activity gives students the opportunity to recognize peer pressure and practice decision-making skills.

- Take voice lessons to improve your singing.
- Plan time each day to practice your singing.
- Sign up for an audition.
- Choose a song to use at the audition.
- Practice the song.
- Audition for the choir.

In this example, reaching each short-term goal is one step toward achieving the long-term goal.

Setting Realistic Goals

When you set goals, you need to make sure that they are realistic. A **realistic goal** is *one that you can reach*. If your goals are too hard to reach, you may become discouraged and give up. If they are too easy, you may lose interest in them. Realistic goals are both reachable and challenging.

Achieving Your Goals

Achieving your goals is not something that just happens. You have to plan how you will reach each goal. Writing the goal down is a good first step. This will help you get a clear picture of what you want to accomplish.

REACHING YOUR GOALS
The way you set your goals has a lot to do with your success. Your goals should be:

Specific—so that you will have something toward which to work.

Challenging—so that you will stay interested.

Organized—so that you know which goal to work on first, second, and so on.

Realistic—so that you can reach your goals.

Evolving—so that you can change your plans if you need to.

72 CHAPTER 3: STEPS TO SUCCESS

HOME AND COMMUNITY CONNECTION

Guest Speaker You might wish to invite a successful member of your community to speak to the class about goal setting. Ask the person to address the benefits and rewards of setting goals and to describe resources that were available to him or her. Also, ask the individual to address the importance of having a positive attitude and setting priorities for their goals. Before the speaker comes to their class, have students prepare questions to ask the speaker about how he or she set goals and attained them.

You need to determine what resources will be required to reach your goal. A **resource** is *something you need to accomplish a goal*. Your resources include your time, money, energy, knowledge, and skills. Your family and friends are also resources that are available to you. Using your resources wisely helps you achieve the goals you set for yourself.

You also need to plan more than one way to reach your goal in case your first plan doesn't work. For example, suppose that you want to take up a new sport. If you find that you don't like team sports, you could try an individual sport such as swimming, jogging, or biking.

Your Attitude

A positive attitude goes a long way toward helping you achieve your goals. Your attitude is the way you feel about something. A positive attitude helps you do your best even if the task is something you do not enjoy. It helps you tackle a difficult job rather than putting it off. It also helps you be flexible when things don't go exactly as you had planned. A positive attitude will help you to be successful in whatever you try to accomplish.

Your family and friends are valuable resources that can help you achieve your goals.

Setting Priorities

Some of your goals will be more important to you than others. You may even find that two or more goals are in conflict with each other. When this happens, you need to set priorities for your goals. This will let you concentrate on the goals that are most important to you.

Setting priorities for your goals may involve making trade-offs. A **trade-off** is *something that you give up in order to get something more important*. For example, if being on the debate team is very important to you, you may need to give up other after-school activities and put off trying out for the band.

LESSON FOUR: SETTING GOALS   73

CHAPTER 3, LESSON 4

L1 Using Transparencies
Present Color Transparency 15, "Goal Management" in the TCR. Use this overhead visual to reinforce concepts from this lesson.

L1 Student Workbook
Assign Activities 19 and 20 in the Student Workbook.

ASSESS

Evaluating the Lesson
Assign Reviewing Terms and Facts and Thinking Critically on page 74 to review the lesson; then assign the Lesson 4 Quiz in the TCR.

Reteaching
- Ask students to create how-to pamphlets titled "Setting Goals." Students should use the subhead titles in Lesson 4—"Setting Personal Goals," "Achieving Your Goals," and "Having Successful Experiences"—as the main section titles in their pamphlets.
- Have students complete Reteaching Activity 3 in the TCR.

Enrichment
- Encourage students to carry out a project that would meet a school need or goal, such as school beautification, nutrition awareness, or school pride. Have students determine the short-term goals they will achieve and the resources they have available to accomplish the project. After students have completed the project, discuss the benefits to the school.
- Assign Enrichment Activity 3 in the TCR.

 **HOME AND COMMUNITY CONNECTION**

Remind students that when they achieve a goal, they should be proud of their accomplishments, but also recognize that they may have had help along the way. Parents, teachers, and friends may have provided assistance and support. Have students look back at a recent goal they have achieved and identify family members, friends, and acquaintances who helped them reach their goal. Once students have identified the people who have helped them achieve a recent goal, encourage them to show their appreciation by writing a letter or making a thank-you card for one of the people. Tell them to describe the way the person has helped them in their letter or card.

CHAPTER 3, LESSON 4

Answers to Lesson 4 Review

1. A long-term goal takes a long time to reach; a short-term goal can be reached more quickly.
2. One that is within reach; sentences will vary.
3. Any five: time, energy, money, knowledge, skills, family, friends.
4. To help you concentrate on the goals that are most important to you.
5. Answers will vary but might include that goals serve as a guide for what to do and give a person something to work toward. Goals also help people do their best and achieve the things they want in life.
6. Answers will vary.
7. Goals will vary but should include the long-term goal and the short-term goals to achieve it.

CLOSE

Ask students to write a paragraph that answers the following question: How will setting and working toward personal goals help me have successful experiences in life?

Having Successful Experiences

Have you ever heard the expression "Nothing succeeds like success"? True success is made up of many little successes along the way. Having successful experiences will help you grow and develop during your teen years. As you experience success in reaching your goals, you will begin to feel good about yourself. You will want to set new goals and to try new things. This will add to your sense of personal worth.

There may be times when you do not achieve all the goals you set for yourself. If you fail to reach a goal, try to figure out what went wrong. Was your goal realistic? Did you have a clear picture of what you wanted to accomplish? Did you use your resources wisely and plan alternative ways to reach your goal? Did you have a positive attitude? Did you set priorities? Knowing what went wrong will help you improve your chances for success the next time.

Having successful experiences as a teen will help you achieve success throughout your life. Why do you think this is so?

LESSON FOUR Review

Using complete sentences, answer the following questions on a separate sheet of paper.

Reviewing Terms and Facts

1. **Compare** What is the difference between a long-term goal and a short-term goal?
2. **Vocabulary** Define the term *realistic goal*. Use it in an original sentence.
3. **Identify** List five resources that can help you achieve your goals.
4. **Explain** Why is it necessary to set priorities for your goals?

Thinking Critically

5. **Explain** Why is it important to set goals?
6. **Illustrate** Give an example of a trade-off you have had to make.

Applying Concepts

7. Write down one long-term goal you are interested in working toward. Then list all the short-term goals that could help you achieve your long-term goal.

74   CHAPTER 3: STEPS TO SUCCESS

MORE ABOUT • • •

Success Success can be defined in various ways. In the late 1800s Horatio Alger wrote of a poor boy who became successful through hard work. His success was defined in terms of power, money, and prestige. A contemporary educator defines success as "doing what you do best and liking it." Interestingly, current research shows that men consider money to be an indicator of success, while women relate success to being good at their jobs. Ask students to consider their personal definition of success.

Chapter 3 Activities

A Global View — FAMILY VALUES

Many people in the United States belong to families that came here from other countries. Sam's great-grandparents, for example, came from China. Katerina's parents were born in Germany. Although these teens may seem very different, they share many of the same values.

TRY THIS!
Find out about ethnic or cultural celebrations with your friends. Then analyze what common values these celebrations represent.

Consumer Focus

The Appeal of Advertising

Advertising—especially for clothes and personal care products—often appeals to people's emotions. Advertising may appeal to people's desire to be attractive to others, to be loved, or to fit into a group.

Try This!
Find a magazine advertisement for a product you want, or think about a TV ad for the product. Write a paragraph analyzing how the advertiser appealed to your emotions.

FRIENDS & FAMILY

SCORING GOALS

Having goals, or something to shoot for, gives purpose and direction to life. Just as in sports, scoring life goals takes strategy and skill. Others can help you achieve your goals. Just as in sports, you will feel a sense of accomplishment when you reach your goal.

TRY THIS!
Talk to your family and friends about the goals they have for their lives, and share your goals with them.

TECHNOLOGY CONNECTION

TECHNOLOGY AND YOUR FUTURE

Nearly any job you choose will require technology skills. To be prepared for the future and to reach your full potential, you should learn as much about technology as you can. Take advantage of the opportunities you have in school to learn about it and to work on the computer.

 **Follow Up**

1. Make a list of your computer skills that you could show an employer. Include the training you have had and the systems and software you have used. Find out ways you could improve your skills.

2. Think of a job you might like to have. Use a reference book on occupations to find out how technology is used in that job. Report your findings to the class.

CHAPTER 3 ACTIVITIES 75

CHAPTER 3 Activities

A Global View

As students read the activity on Family Values, explain that each of the people discussed have learned the value of honesty, trust, and hard work from their families. Tell students that if they were invited to visit each of their homes for dinner, they would see that having strong family ties is a value that these teens share.

Consumer Focus

Discuss how the images often used by advertisers suggest that buying a soft drink, for example, will make the buyer as attractive and popular as the teens in the advertisement. Explain that there is nothing illegal about this approach, but students should be sure that what the advertiser is selling really fits their wants and needs.

FRIENDS & FAMILY

Point out to students that when they think of the word *goal*, they probably think of goals in sports. Scoring a goal in a favorite sport makes players feel proud that their hard work has paid off. Tell students they can have a similar feeling of accomplishment if they set life goals and work toward accomplishing their goals.

Teaching the TECHNOLOGY CONNECTION

Point out that in 1994 about 37 percent of households in the United States owned computers. Ask students to interview an older sibling or other adult family members about the changes in technology that they have witnessed in their lifetime. Ask students to give examples of ways that they use technology in school or at home.

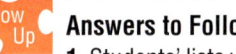 **Answers to Follow-Up**

1. Students' lists will vary but should be detailed, listing the systems and software they have used. Students might ask their school counselor to find courses that might improve or extend their computer skills.

2. Students might report their findings in the form of a job want ad.

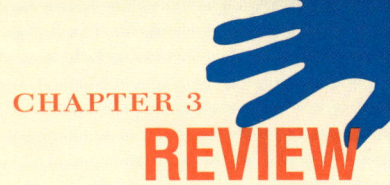

CHAPTER 3 REVIEW

Checking Comprehension

Use the Chapter Summary and the Chapter 3 Review to help students go over the most important ideas presented in Chapter 3.

Answers to Words to Know

1. Potential.
2. Answers will vary but should include commitments to a job, marriage, and children.
3. The other team failed to make the right decision or follow a certain rule, thereby leaving the outcome, in this case a victory for the opposing team, to chance.
4. The results of a choice. Examples will vary.
5. Examples might include two of the following: time, money, energy, knowledge, skills, family, friends.

Answers to Review Questions

1. Because you may adopt new values as you have new experiences and meet new people.
2. Knowing what is most important to you in life helps you make decisions. Your values serve as guides to your actions.

Chapter Summary

- Needs are those things that are necessary for survival, such as air, food, clothing, and shelter.
- Wants are things that you would like to have but that are not necessary for survival.
- Values are ideas about right and wrong and about what is important in your life. Some common values are honesty, trust, a good family life, and good health.
- Acting responsibly means making choices and being answerable for those choices.
- You can show responsibility in many ways, including obeying rules, helping others, and keeping promises.
- A good way to learn responsibility is by following the example of an adult role model.
- You make many decisions each day. Decisions are made in response to an event, by default, and by habit.
- Use the six-step decision-making process for major decisions, and make your decisions responsibly.
- To be successful, you must set realistic goals throughout your life. You will have both long-term and short-term goals.
- Planning how to reach your goals requires using your resources.

Words to Know

Using complete sentences, answer the following questions on a separate sheet of paper.

1. The U.S. Army uses the slogan "Be all that you can be" to encourage young people to join the military. What term from this chapter fits this slogan?
2. What are some major *commitments* that most people make during their lives?
3. Sports teams sometimes win games by *default*. What does this mean?
4. What are *consequences*? Give an example.
5. List two personal *resources* that most teens have.

Review Questions

Using complete sentences, answer the following questions on a separate sheet of paper.

1. Why do some of your values change over time?
2. Why is it important for you to define your own values?
3. What are some rewards for acting responsibly?
4. Give an example of a decision you might make now that could affect your life in the future.
5. How can short-term goals contribute to long-term goals?
6. Why is it important to set realistic goals?

EXTRA CREDIT PROJECT

Group Project Working in small groups, have students create their own group crest. Provide each group with a poster board and have them draw the crest and divide it into four sections. Label each section with: values, needs, wants, and goals. After students come to a consensus about ideas for each section they share with other group members, have them illustrate the crest with appropriate icons. When crests are completed, ask a representative from each group to explain what the crest illustrates. Display the crests in the classroom.

CHAPTER 3 REVIEW

Thinking Critically

Using complete sentences, answer the following questions on a separate sheet of paper.

1. **Suggest** Why might a "value" in one culture be considered an undesirable quality in another culture? Give an example to support your answer.
2. **Explain** Why is it important to learn responsibility at an early age? What would you teach a five- or six-year-old child about acting responsibly?
3. **Analyze** Sometimes friends make decisions by saying "I'll go if you go" or "I'll do it if you do it." What is wrong with this approach to decision making?
4. **Apply** How might achieving an important goal affect your self-concept? How might it affect your attitude toward other goals?

Cooperative Learning

1. In groups of four or five, share the plot of a movie, television show, or book you have read in which one of the main characters holds two conflicting values. Discuss the character's solution to the problem. Justify the decision with explanations of goals, wants, needs, and values.
2. Goal setting can provide direction to groups as well as to individuals. Along with your classmates, decide on a project you would like to accomplish. Some ideas for a long-term goal include improving the school grounds by planting flowers or a tree, or purchasing new equipment for the school. Plan together the short-term goals, or steps, you will need to reach your long-term goal. Decide on the resources you have for accomplishing your long-term goal. If possible, put your plan into action.

Family & Community

1. Talk to your family members about the goals you have as a family. Choose one of your family's goals, and draw a newspaper ad for it. Use the title "Go for the Goal!" for your ad. Ask for permission to display the ad in your home.
2. Write an article about yourself or a friend showing responsibility. Post a copy of your article on the classroom bulletin board.

Building A Portfolio

1. Put a small object or a picture in your portfolio that represents a value you have. Include a paragraph describing your value.
2. Think of a major decision you made recently. Apply the six steps of the decision-making process you followed to make the specific decision. On a piece of paper, write the process you used, and keep the paper in your portfolio as a model for future decision making.
3. Look over your written work on personal goal setting. Select one of your goals (a long-term goal plus short-term goals) to include in your portfolio. Once a week, look at your goal and check your progress. Assigning a completion date for each short-term goal will help keep you on track.

CHAPTER 3 REVIEW 77

Planning Guide
Chapter 4 Careers

LESSON 1	Pages	FEATURES	CLASSROOM RESOURCES
Looking Ahead to Careers	80–85	Try This: Matching Your Skills with a Job Tips for Living: Reading the Want Ads	Activity and Project Card 7, "Qualified Teen Seeking Employment" Cooperative Learning 7 Lesson 1 Quiz Transparency 16, "Career Decisions" Student Workbook Activities 21, 22
LESSON 2 **School to Work**	86–91	Try This: Writing a Business Letter Tips for Living: Improving Your Study Skills	Concept Map 6 Lesson 2 Quiz Transparency 17, "School to Work" Student Workbook Activities 23, 24
LESSON 3 **Getting a Job**	92–97	Tips for Living: Filling out a Job Application Skills in Action: Starting Your Own Business	Activity and Project Card 8, "Want Ads" Cooperative Learning 8 Cross Curriculum 4 Lesson 3 Quiz Peer Pressure and Decision Making 7 Transparency 18, "Preparing for a Job Interview" Student Workbook Activities 25, 26
LESSON 4 **Being Successful on the Job**	98–104	Skills in Action: On the Job Tips for Living: Getting Along with Coworkers Try This: Good Work Habits	Enrichment 4 Lesson 4 Quiz Peer Pressure and Decision Making 8 Transparency 19, "Relationships on the Job" Transparency 20, "Evaluating Earnings and Deductions" Student Workbook Activities 27, 28

CHAPTER 4 RESOURCES

Chapter 4 Test   Study Guide 4, *Reteaching*   Testmaker Software
Reteaching 4

Performance Assessment Activity

Ask students to create a "Guide to Finding a Job and Keeping It." Have them use the information in the chapter to help them write this guide. The guide should have a magazine-style format—short, catchy articles with many visuals. Students might create advertisements that feature careers as a theme in their magazine. Have students write a rough draft of the guide, including suggestions for illustrations. Then organize the class into small groups to critique one another's guides. Tell students to contribute constructive criticism so that the authors can improve their guides. Allow students time to complete their final drafts.

When students have finished their guides, display them in the school library.

School-to-Work

Have students work in groups to find local businesses to research. Have them write letters inquiring what employee skills are required for success within these companies. Perhaps your school has a partnership or mentoring program with a local company that students could contact. Suggest students call the Chamber of Commerce for names and addresses of locally-owned businesses. Ask students to prepare a list of questions that focus on the role that the following skills play in helping employees to be successful at their jobs: a positive attitude, communication skills, flexibility, and a team spirit. Students should inquire about the role that these skills play in making employees successful at their jobs within these companies. Have them ask about other skills that employees need to be successful. Allow time for groups to share responses to their inquiries with the class.

Family & Community

Bring to class various samples of business cards from members of the students' families and from other community members and businesses. Discuss the use of business cards and the kinds of information they include: the name of the employee; the job title or a description of the job the person does; the name, address, and phone number of the business; the business fax number; the E-mail number; and a logo. Then ask students to choose a job that they have done or can do (babysitting, raking the lawn) and design their own business cards.

Resources for the Teacher

Herman, Marcia. "Careers Video Tours for Junior/Middle School Students." *School Library Journal,* Sept. 1995.

Hirsch, Arlene S. *Career Checklists.* Lincolnwood, IL: NTC Publishing Group, 1991.

Readings for the Student

Fry, Ron. *How to Study.* Hawthorne, NJ: Career Press, 1994.

Hopke, William. *Activities for Career Discovery Encyclopedia.* Bloomington, IL: Meridian Education Corporation, 1991.

Multimedia Resources

Encyclopedia of Careers and Vocational Guidance (CD-ROM). Ninth Edition. Zenger Media.

Effective Listening Skills: Listening to What You Hear (Videocassette). Media Concepts. Social Studies School Service.

Jobs for the 21st Century (Videocassettes, set of 3). Guidance Associates. Zenger Media.

Taking Science from School to Work (CD-ROM). School Company. Zenger Media.

OUT OF TIME?

If time does not permit thorough teaching of this chapter, you may wish to use:

- Teens Making a Difference, page 79
- Tips for Living, pages 84, 88, 95, 102
- Try This, pages 82, 88, 102
- Skills in Action, pages 96, 100
- Young Living Activities, page 105
- Chapter Summary, page 106

CHAPTER 4
Careers

Chapter Overview
Chapter 4 explains preparations for careers, how to get a job, and how to be successful on the job.
LESSON 1 identifies career preparation techniques.
LESSON 2 explains that the basic skills learned in school are essential for success in the workplace.
LESSON 3 describes the skills needed to find a job.
LESSON 4 identifies the skills necessary for job success.

Introducing the Chapter
Have students refer to the chapter title, "Careers." Ask them to explain what they think is meant by *careers.* (the work that people do through life) Have students skim the pictures in the chapter and identify the careers shown in them. Then have students read the lesson titles and write a few sentences explaining what they think each lesson will cover. After students have completed the chapter, ask them if the lessons included the topics they expected to be covered.

Chapter Motivator
Ask students to think about a career they would like to pursue. Have them visualize themselves in a career. Ask students to draw a picture of themselves working at a job in their chosen career. Collect the pictures. Show each picture one at a time to the class and have students identify the career and the person who drew it.

CHAPTER 4 Careers

LESSON ONE
Looking Ahead to Careers

LESSON TWO
School to Work

LESSON THREE
Getting a Job

LESSON FOUR
Being Successful on the Job

KEY TO ABILITY LEVELS

Teaching strategies that appear throughout the chapter have been identified by one of three codes to give you an idea of their suitability for students of varying learning styles and abilities.

L1 **Level 1** strategies should be within the ability range of all students. Often full class participation is required. Teacher direction is usually needed.

L2 **Level 2** strategies are for average to above-average students or for small groups. Some teacher direction is necessary.

L3 **Level 3** strategies are designed for students able and willing to work independently. Minimal teacher direction is necessary.

TEENS MAKING A DIFFERENCE
Junior Entrepreneur

Bobby Vasek started a car-cleaning service when he was 13 years old. His business was inspired by his love of cars and his need to earn some spending money. Now, at age 17, Bobby and three of his friends still wash, wax, and polish cars after school and on weekends.

Bobby is an entrepreneur—a person who runs his own business. Bobby's hard work is paying off: he will soon have enough money saved to buy his own car.

Try THIS!

Is starting a business something you would like to do? List five personal characteristics that you think a successful entrepreneur needs.

CHAPTER 4

TEENS MAKING A DIFFERENCE

Have students read "Teens Making a Difference." Ask students to identify Bobby's personal characteristics that helped him become an entrepreneur. (*Students might indicate Bobby's interest in cars, his need to earn money, his understanding of the value of good service in getting and keeping customers, and his determination.*) Tell students that an entrepreneur's dedication to his or her business is an important factor in its success.

Ask students to answer the questions at the end of the feature on their own. Call on volunteers to identify the characteristics a successful entrepreneur would need. Compile the responses in a class list on the board.

BLOCK SCHEDULING

The following Teacher Classroom Resources are suggested for use in classrooms with Block Scheduling.
- Activity and Project Card 7, "Qualified Teen Seeking Employment"
- Activity and Project Card 8, "Want Ads"
- Cooperative Learning 7, "What Will I Be?"
- Cooperative Learning 8, "Practicing Job Interviews"

TECHNOLOGY IN THE CLASSROOM

Faxing Faxing is a quick and convenient way for you and your students to request or receive information. You can fax requests for such things as catalog information or availability of audio-visual materials. You might suggest that students fax letters of inquiry to local businesses when requesting information about such things as job availability or job requirements. They might also use the fax machine to voice their opinion or concern about a particular issue.

LESSON ONE
Looking Ahead to Careers

FOCUS

Lesson Objectives
After studying this lesson, students should be able to
- explain reasons why people work.
- identify considerations for choosing a career.
- describe various ways to prepare for work.

Motivating Activity
Have students identify three academic subjects and three recreational activities that they enjoy.

Introducing the Lesson
Have students share their responses to the Motivating Activity. List some responses on the board. Then ask students to identify jobs that would match some of the academic subjects and recreational activities listed. Explain to students that this lesson will focus on ways that personal interests can be matched to career skills.

Introducing *Words to Know*
Explain that "apprentice" comes from the Old French *aprendre,* meaning "to learn and teach." Also, tell students that "career" comes from the Old French *cariere,* meaning "road," relating to "life work."

LESSON ONE
Looking Ahead to Careers

WORDS TO KNOW
aptitude test
career research
job preparation
apprenticeship programs

DISCOVER...
- reasons why people work.
- considerations for choosing a career.
- various ways to prepare for work.

"What do you want to be when you grow up?" You have probably heard that question many times. Have you really thought about your answer? Perhaps you are interested in becoming a gourmet chef or a fashion designer. Maybe you have always dreamed of a career in computers or medicine. You have many choices, and it is not too soon to start thinking about some careers you might want to pursue.

80   CHAPTER 4: CAREERS

CLASSROOM RESOURCES FOR LESSON 1

 Blackline Masters
Activity and Project Card 7, "Qualified Teen Seeking Employment"
Cooperative Learning 7
Lesson 1 Quiz

 Transparencies
Transparency 16, "Career Decisions"

 Student Workbook
Activities 21, 22

The World of Work

People work for many reasons. The main reason, of course, is to earn a living, but there are other benefits. People take pride in their work and get a feeling of accomplishment from a job well done. Work is a way to meet people and make friends.

Most people choose jobs based on their interests and skills. Some people enjoy physical tasks, such as repairing machinery or installing new roofs. Others prefer creative work, such as taking photographs or designing homes. Still others want jobs in which they can help people: responding to medical emergencies, for example, or caring for young children.

Most people spend a large part of their lives working. They may spend 40 or more years in the workforce. Wouldn't you rather spend that time doing something you enjoy?

If you enjoy science and have an aptitude for it, there are many careers to explore in scientific fields. What is one career you might like to know more about?

Thinking About Careers

It is a good idea to begin planning a career path while you are still in school. Thinking ahead will give you time to learn some of the specific skills that will help you get a job. It will also help you determine what kind of training and education you will need for the career you choose.

Matching Yourself to a Job

It can be a challenge to match yourself to a job. A few people decide early in life what they want to do and begin to prepare for a career right away. For example, if they enjoy math or science in school, they may choose careers in accounting or medicine.

LESSON ONE: LOOKING AHEAD TO CAREERS 81

MORE ABOUT • • •

The Perfect Career Why are some people invigorated by their job, while others are tired or burned out? Does it have to do with the amount of physical energy expended? Is it a result of the number of hours spent on the job? Does it have to do with the amount of money a person is paid for the job? Researchers have found that the key ingredient that makes a job invigorating is the matchup of a person's talents and skills with a sense of commitment to and interest in the job. Poll students to find out if they have had an invigorating job experience.

CHAPTER 4, LESSON 1

TEACH

L2 Finding Examples
Have students identify the careers that interest them. Have them find a magazine or newspaper article about one of the careers. Ask students to read the article and summarize the content of the article to the class. Have them place the articles on a bulletin board so that other interested students can read them.

L2 Critical Thinking
Arrange to have students bring an object that illustrates a hobby or special leisure-time interest to share with the class. Ask them to describe their hobby or special interest and identify the skills they developed because of it. Have class members brainstorm careers or jobs related to the hobby or special interest.

L1 Writing
Ask students to write a journal entry in which they describe their "dream career." Tell them to indicate in their entries what they think is attractive about the career, how the career reflects their interests, and how they think the career would benefit their lives.

L2 Cooperative Learning
Assign Cooperative Learning Activity 7, "What Will I Be?" in the TCR.

CHAPTER 4, LESSON 1

After students have identified their skills and job ideas, ask them to find pictures in magazines that show people at jobs using the skills they listed. Have students arrange the pictures in a collage titled "Matching Jobs and Skills." Display the collages around the school.

L1 Discussing

Ask students to discuss the benefits of career exploration before entering high school. *(They can take specialized classes to learn more about their field.)* Ask students to identify what jobs are related to the school subjects they are taking. Ask them how they can learn which subjects will be helpful in specific careers? *(by talking to teachers, counselors, and parents)*

L2 Writing

Emphasize to students that it helps to identify their values and goals before they explore career possibilities. Have them write a paragraph describing the values and goals that will affect their career decisions. Ask volunteers to share their paragraph with the class.

L2 Research

Have students identify a career of interest to them. Have them use the bulleted list under "Looking for Answers" to find the answers to the list of things they will want to know about the related jobs in the career of their choice. Ask students to present their findings in an oral report to the class. Encourage use of computer resources.

You will be happiest if you choose work that matches the interests and skills you already have. Make a list of your skills and interests.

Now match each skill on your list with a job that uses that skill. Look in career books for ideas. If possible, use a computer software program to match your skills and interests with various jobs.

You will probably have several jobs during your lifetime. One of the first steps in finding work that will satisfy you is to consider what you are interested in. Do you have special skills that could be useful in a particular type of work? Could you volunteer or work part-time to strengthen those skills?

When considering a career, you should also think about your values and goals. What do you want to do with your life? What is important to you? Do you want to help other people? Consider a career in health services. Do you like to build things? Look into construction or architecture. Knowing your values and goals will help you focus on an area that suits the sort of person you are.

If you still can't decide, there are special tests that can help you discover your aptitudes. Aptitudes are natural abilities or talents. An **aptitude test** is *a test that predicts a person's ability to learn certain skills.* A test of this kind can help by revealing your strengths.

Researching Careers

When you have chosen a few possibilities, you can look for answers to questions you may have about various kinds of jobs. **Career research** is *the process of finding out all you can about a field of work that interests you.*

Looking for Answers

If you know what to expect from a job, it will be easier to decide which kind is best for you. Here are some of the points you will want to research about various jobs:

- Education required for the job
- Responsibilities or duties expected
- Salary or wages for entry-level and experienced workers
- Chances for promotion
- Working conditions, including protection against safety hazards
- Possible need for more workers in this field in the future

82   CHAPTER 4: CAREERS

TECHNOLOGY UPDATE

Speeding Along the Information Highway Not only can people use computers to access the most recent career information, but employers can use computers to access information about potential employees. Many people send computer disks that contain a copy of their résumé to employment agencies or to job fairs. The résumés are copied to computer files categorized by career choice. Employers can quickly see whom they want to interview for new openings. Some help-wanted ads request that résumés be sent by fax to the personnel department. People do not need to own a fax machine to accomplish this task. Many businesses, such as office-supply stores, will let people use their fax for a fee.

You can learn about careers through computer programs or on-line services. Ask your librarian to recommend some.

You can find out some of these facts about various careers by talking with people who work in the fields in which you are interested. You can also look in the library for books on careers; *The Occupational Outlook Handbook* or the *Dictionary of Occupational Titles (DOT)* are useful references. The *DOT* lists 20,000 different kinds of jobs.

Choosing a Career

You might find that there are two or three career areas that really interest you. If so, over the next few years try to find out more about each of them. Talk over the possibilities with family members, school counselors, and teachers. They can advise you or answer questions.

Preparing for Work

The learning required to get and keep the kind of job you want is called **job preparation.** You will need to be willing to study and work for specific jobs as well as for promotions. Here are some of the benefits of preparing for work.

- Job preparation means a better life for you and those you might have to support.

- You will have a better chance for success and financial security.

LESSON ONE: LOOKING AHEAD TO CAREERS 83

CHAPTER 4, LESSON 1

L1 Applying Life Skills
Have students brainstorm job possibilities for young teens. Examples could include entertaining at children's parties, petsitting, cake decorating, and running errands. Ask students to explain how a job today can lead to a career tomorrow. How can a part-time job help prepare a teenager for the world of work?

L1 Using Transparencies
Present Color Transparency 16, "Career Decisions," in the TCR. Use this overhead visual to reinforce concepts from this lesson.

L1 Discussing
Invite a school counselor to speak to the class about the opportunities for students to continue their education after high school. Have students identify the kinds of careers they are interested in. Ask the counselor to describe the continuing education opportunities available in the community that would help the students get a job in their chosen career.

L2 Activity and Project Card
Allow time for students to complete Activity and Project Card 7, "Qualified Teen Seeking Employment," in the TCR.

COOPERATIVE LEARNING

Guest Speaker Invite a person who is in an apprenticeship program to speak to the class. Organize the class into small groups. Before the speaker arrives, have each group prepare questions to ask the apprentice. (Possible questions might include: How are you preparing for a career? What on-the-job training are you receiving? What education do you need to meet the requirements of your job? How did high school prepare you for your apprenticeship?) Have a representative from each group ask the questions, and have all the students record the answers. When students have completed their questions, hold a class discussion evaluating an apprenticeship position.

CHAPTER 4, LESSON 1

L2 Math
Have students survey five adults about how they found their present job and record their answers. In class, tally the responses and make a graph showing the best sources of job leads.

TIPS for living
Have students look in the want ads of a newspaper. Have them select a job they are interested in and write a letter of interest explaining why they would be qualified for the job.

L1 Student Workbook
Assign Activities 21 and 22 in the Student Workbook.

ASSESS
Evaluating the Lesson
Assign Reviewing Terms and Facts and Thinking Critically on page 85 to review the lesson; then assign the Lesson 1 Quiz in the TCR.

Reteaching
- Have students draw a sketch or cartoon of themselves working in a career that interests them. Tell them to write a caption for the sketch that explains why they chose this career.
- Have students complete Reteaching Activity 4 in the TCR.

Many skilled workers learn their jobs by participating in a formal apprenticeship program.

- If a job is one you really like, it will give you enjoyment and satisfaction.

Without a high school education, your job opportunities are limited. Many fields of work require education beyond high school.

Continuing to Learn

There are many ways to continue your education after high school. You may want to:

- attend college. Community colleges, four-year colleges, and universities offer courses and degrees in a wide variety of fields.

- enroll in a course at a vocational trade center. A vocational program can teach you skills for specific occupations, such as computer programming, plumbing, or the food industry.

- get a job with a company that teaches its employees the special skills they need. Some companies have **apprenticeship programs,** which are *formal programs that use on-the-job training to teach job skills.*

TIPS for living
READING THE WANT ADS

You can find a job by looking at help-wanted ads. Here are some tips to remember.

- The Sunday paper has the largest number of job ads.
- Most newspapers divide job listings into sections, such as "Part-Time."
- Newspaper ads use abbreviations. For example, "PT" means part-time.
- Note the qualifications for a job, the hours required, and other information. Make sure that the job is right for you before answering an ad.

84   CHAPTER 4: CAREERS

HOME AND COMMUNITY CONNECTION

Job Fair Invite local businesses and parents of students to participate in a job fair. Encourage participants to bring in information or products to share with students. Divide the meeting room so that people representing similar careers are grouped together. Allow students ample time to visit with people in the careers that interest them. Ask them to write a one-page report describing their findings.

Working Part-Time

Before you look for a full-time job, you will probably have worked at part-time jobs. You can get valuable experience by working in restaurants, businesses, and stores, or by baby-sitting or delivering newspapers.

Part-time employment can be part of your preparation for full-time employment. Part-time work helps you:

- learn to get along with your supervisor and coworkers.
- find out how you like a certain type of work.
- gain work experience that will be helpful when you apply for a full-time job.
- become aware of job requirements and other qualities that you need to acquire for full-time work.

By asking other people how they got started in a career, you might get ideas for your own life. With whom could you talk about a career that interests you?

Exploring Your Options

It is a good idea to start exploring career opportunities now. That way you will be better prepared to make a career choice. When you think about your options, consider your interests, abilities, values, and goals. Decisions based on these factors will lead you to work you enjoy.

LESSON ONE Review

Using complete sentences, answer the following questions on a separate sheet of paper.

Reviewing Terms and Facts
1. **List** Name three reasons why people work.
2. **Recall** What should you consider when matching yourself to a career?
3. **Vocabulary** Define the term *apprenticeship program*. Use it in an original sentence.

Thinking Critically
4. **Analyze** When you begin to research careers, which three factors do you feel will be most important to you?
5. **Explain** How can you narrow down possible career choices?
6. **Interpret** Why is part-time employment valuable?

Applying Concepts
7. Using some item such as a toy, a book, or a box of cake mix, work with a group of students to make a list of as many jobs as you can think of that would be involved in the creation of the product. Find out what training is needed for the job that interests you.

LESSON ONE: LOOKING AHEAD TO CAREERS

CHAPTER 4, LESSON 1

Answers to Lesson 1 Review

1. To earn a living, to meet people and make friends, and to gain a sense of accomplishment.
2. Favorite school subjects, interests and skills, values and goals, and aptitudes.
3. A formal program that uses on-the-job training to teach people skills. Example sentence: "I am in an apprenticeship program to learn the skills needed for carpentry."
4. Any three: education requirements, responsibilities or duties expected, salary or wages for entry-level and experienced workers, chances for promotion, working conditions, and the future need for more workers in the field.
5. Talk over the possibilities with family members, school counselors, and teachers.
6. You have a chance to learn how to get along with your supervisor and coworkers, find out how you like a certain type of job, gain work experience, and become aware of job requirements.
7. Answers will vary. Students might create a two-column chart listing the careers in one column and the training needed for each one in the second column.

Enrichment

Have students interview three adults to find out why they work. Make a chart showing the responses.

COOPERATIVE LEARNING

Choosing a Career Organize the class into small groups. Ask students in each group to imagine they are career placement specialists. Have each group design a survey of ten questions that try to narrow down a person's skills. Each group should make several copies of its survey. Students who have access to a computer may wish to use a word-processing program to prepare their survey forms. Have groups exchange and complete the surveys. Students should return their completed survey to the group that designed it. Have members of the group advise the respondents about the types of jobs that might be suitable for them.

CLOSE

Have students finish the following statement: "When I am 18 years old, I want to be . . ." Then have them complete the statement again, replacing "18 years old" with "21," "30," and "40." Ask students to share their answers and explain their choices.

LESSON TWO
School to Work

FOCUS

Lesson Objectives

After studying this lesson, students should be able to
- explain how basic skills—reading, writing, math, science, speaking, and listening—contribute to success at work.
- discuss why computer skills are essential in the workplace.

Motivating Activity

On a table display the following items: a newspaper ad, a checkbook, an application form, a computer diskette, a measuring cup, a city map, a telephone. Ask students to write down the kinds of skills—reading, writing, math, science, speaking, listening, computer—that are used with each item.

Introducing the Lesson

Have students share their responses to the Motivating Activity. Then ask them to read the lesson opening paragraph. Tell students that this lesson will help them better understand the importance of developing skills in reading, writing, math, science, speaking, listening, and computers.

Introducing *Words to Know*

Ask students to pronounce and read the definition of the vocabulary words. Explain that "software" was coined from the word *hardware*, which is used when referring to a computer machine. Software is the symbolic language essential for the operation of computers.

86

LESSON TWO
School to Work

WORDS TO KNOW

comprehension
proofread
software

DISCOVER...
- how basic skills—reading, writing, math, science, speaking, and listening—contribute to success in life.
- why computer skills are essential in the workplace.

Imagine what your life would be like if you did not have reading, writing, math, science, speaking, and listening skills. You would not be able to read a magazine article, a CD cover, or a store advertisement. You could not complete your class assignments. How would you count your spending money? You would have trouble communicating with your friends, family, and classmates.

86   CHAPTER 4: CAREERS

CLASSROOM RESOURCES FOR LESSON 2

 **Blackline Masters**
Concept Map 6
Lesson 2 Quiz

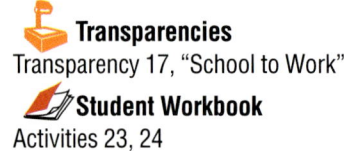 **Transparencies**
Transparency 17, "School to Work"

Student Workbook
Activities 23, 24

Developing Basic Skills

The most important key to your success is developing skills in the basics: reading, writing, math, science, speaking, and listening. These skills are called *basic* because they serve as tools to help you function in life. More and more, computer skills are considered basic, too.

Basic skills are important to you not only now but also in the future, especially at work. For example, you will need reading and writing skills to fill out a job application or write a résumé. To understand the information on your paycheck and to budget your money, you will need math skills. Skills in science will help you understand how technology affects people and their environment. Listening and speaking skills will be essential when you meet with prospective employers.

Using your reading, writing, math, science, speaking, and listening skills every day is the best way to develop them. When you leave your language arts, math, and science classes, continue to use your basic skills. Find ways to apply them in practical situations. What ways can you think of to do this?

Reading

Reading is one of the most important basic skills. It provides a foundation for other skills. Without reading skills, you could not write, read directions, understand and solve math problems, or use a computer.

By using your basic skills every day, you will continue to improve them. How is this teen using basic reading skills?

LESSON TWO: SCHOOL TO WORK

CHAPTER 4, LESSON 2

TEACH

L1 Applying
Have students make a chart titled "Skills for Careers" using the following column heads: "Reading," "Writing," "Math," "Science," "Speaking," "Listening." Under each heading have students identify a career in which the particular skill is needed. When students complete their individual charts, call on volunteers to read their responses and compile the responses in a class chart on the board.

L2 Reading
To provide students with practice in improving comprehension skills, bring articles about careers from a business section of a newspaper. Have students working in pairs each read an article and write a one-paragraph summary of it. Have them exchange articles with their partners and evaluate their comprehension of the article.

L2 Reading and Writing
Have students practice reading and writing skills. Ask them to read business magazines or newspaper sections to find short biographies about people in a particular occupation or job. Ask them to use the writing skills discussed on this page and write a paragraph on the person they read about. Call on volunteers to share their paragraphs with the class. Hold a class discussion evaluating how well students used writing skills.

L1 Using Transparencies
Present Color Transparency 17, "School to Work," in the TCR. Use this overhead visual to reinforce concepts from this lesson.

MORE ABOUT • • •

Study Skills Some students fail to do their best on tests because they are nervous. Help students conquer test-taking anxiety by offering them the following tips: Break down the material that needs to be studied. Study a manageable amount at a time. Use a calendar to help plan when you will study. The night before the test, get eight to nine hours of sleep. The morning of the test, eat a nutritious breakfast and allow time for a quick review of the materials. Before taking the test, take a few deep, relaxing breaths. Use all the time allotted for taking the test. Review your answers for errors. Tell students that planning ahead and being prepared for a test will give them the confidence they need to succeed.

CHAPTER 4, LESSON 2

Try This!

Help students find samples of business letters to follow as they write their own. Also, bring to class copies of the Yellow Pages or a business telephone directory for the local community. Encourage students to share their responses from the businesses with the class.

L3 Science

Ask students: What happens when food boils and freezes? Ask what they need to know in order to answer the question. (*Students will need to know that substances are made up of molecules and they will need to know that molecules slow down and are more tightly packed when they are cooled.*)

Then ask students to compile a list of science or math skills they could make use of in the kitchen. Have students share their lists with the class.

TIPS for living

To further encourage students to improve their study skills, have them design an ideal study center. Ask them to look through catalogs of office furniture to get ideas for styles and arrangements. Tell them to sketch the arrangement of the study center, explaining where it would be located and listing the supplies that would be stored there. Ask them to share their sketches with classmates.

Try This!

Knowing how to write a business letter is important for getting and keeping a job. It follows a special format and must be neatly prepared. Ask your English teacher for samples.

Type or print your letter on plain white paper, or use a word processor. Ask a friend or family member to proofread your letter.

Building your vocabulary is one way to develop your reading skills. Use a dictionary to learn to pronounce words correctly and find out what they mean. You must also learn how to follow written directions. For example, if you are reading an instruction manual in a computer class, you must be able to follow the directions in order to do the work correctly.

The main goal of reading is comprehension. **Comprehension** means *understanding what you read*. With practice, you can improve your comprehension. You can even think beyond the facts that are given. For example, you can read advertisements for competing products and decide which one is probably the best.

Writing

Writing is a way to express your ideas. Your writing is a reflection of you. Developing writing skills will help you feel good about yourself and make a positive impression on others. The ability to express yourself clearly in writing will improve your chances for getting and keeping a job.

You can improve your writing skills by taking time to organize your thoughts. Think about the purpose of what you are going to write. Perhaps you are writing a letter to a prospective employer. How can you convince the employer to call you in for an interview? If the letter is long, first outline the major points. Use a dictionary to be sure that you are using the right words and spelling them correctly.

TIPS for living — IMPROVING YOUR STUDY SKILLS

Good study skills can improve your learning and your grades. A good school record is important for getting a job. Here are some ways to improve your study skills.

- Arrange a study area. Keep supplies within easy reach, including a dictionary.
- Set aside a specific time each day for studying.
- Be sure that you understand all assignments.
- Avoid distractions such as TV and stereo. If you get a phone call, arrange to call back later.

88 CHAPTER 4: CAREERS

MORE ABOUT •••

Best Buy Ask students to bring the following items to class: boxes of cereal, bags of chips, tubes of toothpaste, juice packs, and boxes of raisins. Ask them to put the purchase price on each item. Arrange the items in groups, by category. Then organize the class into small groups. Provide each group with one of the groups of items. Have the students practice their math skills by computing the unit price of each of the items, and have them determine the best buy. Ask each group to share its findings with the class in the form of a bar graph. Students may prepare graphs on computers if they are available.

Write a rough draft, and reread it to see if it can be improved. Does it say what you want it to say? **Proofread,** or *check for errors in your grammar, punctuation, and spelling.* Retype or input a final copy, and check to be sure that your work is neat and accurate. You want to make a good first impression with your letter.

Math and Science

You use math and science skills every day in ways you may not even think about. For example, you use math and science when you compare prices, prepare a meal, or remove stains from your clothes.

Some of the math skills you must develop are the basic processes: addition, subtraction, multiplication, and division. You also need to master fractions, decimals, and percentages. These basics will help you figure out your weekly earnings if you are paid by the hour, or the cost of getting to work. Correct use of a calculator is another essential math skill. Developing good math skills now will open the door to many opportunities later.

Whether or not you plan to become a scientist, you can use science skills every day. Knowing how chemical and physical reactions occur is useful in many practical situations. For example, what happens when food is cooked or frozen? Science skills will also help you develop an appreciation for nature and your environment. You will understand how to select clothing that will protect you in extreme weather.

Speaking

Communication takes place between a sender and a receiver. The speaker is sending a message to the receiver, or listener. However, just speaking to another person does not guarantee good communication. If someone talks too fast, for instance, the message may not get through. Speaking and listening are basic skills that need to be learned and practiced.

You may not be aware of how many times a day you use math skills. How do you use math at a grocery store? At a restaurant? When you are preparing a meal?

LESSON TWO: SCHOOL TO WORK

CHAPTER 4, LESSON 2

L1 Communication Skills

Point out to students that an effective communicator encourages responses from his or her listeners. Draw a chart with two columns on the board. In the first column write the title "Openers," and record the following phrases: What do you think? How would you feel? Has this ever happened to you? You are a good problem solver. In the second column write the title "Enders," and record the following phrases: How would you know? You have no idea how I feel. How could you be so dumb? Do you think you know everything? Discuss with students the kinds of phrases that encourage communication and those that stop communication. Ask students to add phrases to the chart.

L2 Role-Playing

Have students work with partners using speaking and listening skills to role-play the parts of the teacher and the student in the following scenario:

Your math teacher has asked to speak with you about your grades. You're having difficulty in math class. You have forgotten your homework a few times and received a failing mark on a unit test.

Have the partners switch roles, allowing each person a chance to play each role. Then ask the rest of the class to evaluate the conversations, based on how effectively each pair of students used speaking and listening skills.

MEETING STUDENT DIVERSITY

Cultural Perspectives Tell students that when people communicate with another person, they use their experiences to construct their message. The listener uses his or her experiences to understand the message. It may be difficult for people from one culture to understand figures of speech from another culture. For example, the expression "I'm so hungry, I could eat a horse!" might make someone from another culture wonder if the person has a craving for horse meat. Stress to students that the only way to know if a message is understood is to get feedback from the listener. Listeners need to give the speaker feedback so that he or she knows that they understood the message.

CHAPTER 4, LESSON 2

TEACHER TALK!

Improving Listening Skills

Point out to students that an important listening skill is empathy. This is the ability to put oneself in someone else's shoes. Tell students that being able to understand how another person feels helps one become a better listener and helps one hear the whole message.

L1 Student Workbook

Assign Activities 23 and 24 in the Student Workbook.

ASSESS

Evaluating the Lesson

Assign Reviewing Terms and Facts and Thinking Critically on page 91 to review the lesson; then assign the Lesson 2 Quiz in the TCR.

Reteaching

- Ask students to give one example of how learning academic, communication, and computer skills will help them obtain, keep, and succeed in a job.
- Have students complete Reteaching Activity 4 in the TCR.
- Assign Concept Map 6 in the TCR.

90

Could this trainee learn to do the job if it were not explained clearly? What could be done to improve understanding?

Speaking is just as important in the workplace as reading and writing. Developing the ability to express your thoughts clearly will help you perform well on the job, no matter what career you choose. You can improve your speaking skills by:

- thinking before you speak in order to organize your ideas.
- speaking in a direct and straight-forward manner.
- making sure that the other person understands what you are saying.
- finding a different way to express your idea if your listener does not understand you.

Listening

The second part of good communication is listening. To be an effective listener, you need to hear, think about, and respond to what the speaker is saying. On the job, you will need to make a real effort to understand what others say to you. If you do not understand what your employer wants you to do, you may not do the job correctly. You can improve your listening skills by:

- concentrating on what the other person is saying.
- allowing the other person to finish talking without interrupting.
- listening even if you do not agree with everything the other person is saying.
- letting the other person know that you are listening.

Computer Skills

Computers are changing the way we live and work. Today computers are used for many purposes, including education,

90 CHAPTER 4: CAREERS

COOPERATIVE LEARNING

Remind students that knowing the proper manners for introductions is an important communication skill while on the job. Point out that when they introduce two people, introductions should be clear and concise. For example, when introducing a new worker to his or her supervisor, they might say, "Mary Greene, I would like you to meet your supervisor, Beth Banner." It is helpful to add information about the people to help begin a conversation. Explain that it is customary for the people being introduced to shake hands. Organize students into groups to role-play the introduction of a new worker to his or her supervisor and coworkers. Encourage students to practice using a firm handshake, smiling, and acting in a friendly manner.

communication, and entertainment. Knowing how to use a computer is essential for certain jobs in almost every field.

Computers have a great impact on your life. They are used almost everywhere, including factories, offices, restaurants, stores, and repair shops. At home, people use computers to manage finances, write reports, locate information, and communicate with others.

If you have not spent much time using a computer, now is a good time to practice your skills. You can learn to use **software,** which is *a computer program or set of instructions.* Most computer software is "user-friendly." That means that it is designed to help you make computers work for you even if you know little about them.

Such skills as speaking a foreign language may not be basic, but they can contribute to your qualifications for a job. What jobs can you think of in which you could use foreign language skills?

Your Future Success

All workers need basic skills to be successful. You need reading and writing skills to read a job posting and apply for a promotion. Your math and science skills will help you keep up with technological advances. When you work with other people, you use speaking and listening skills. Computer skills are required in just about every occupation.

LESSON TWO

Using complete sentences, answer the following questions on a separate sheet of paper.

Reviewing Terms and Facts

1. **Recall** What is the best way to develop your reading, writing, math, science, speaking, and listening skills?
2. **Vocabulary** What do you do when you *proofread?*
3. **Explain** Why might computer skills be considered basic?

Thinking Critically

4. **Analyze** Why is it important to develop basic knowledge and skills?

5. **Apply** Give three examples of ways in which you use math and science skills in your daily life.
6. **Integrate** Name a specific work skill you would need for a particular job.

Applying Concepts

7. Keep a record of how often you use math, reading, writing, and communication skills during a single day. Did you use science or computer skills? Make a graph to show which skills you used most often.

LESSON TWO: SCHOOL TO WORK   91

TECHNOLOGY UPDATE

Computer Jargon Knowing computer terms makes it easier to read and talk about computers. A *microprocessor chip* is a computer chip the size of a fingernail. It can store and process hundreds of thousands of pieces of information. *Hardware* is the physical equipment that makes up the computer system. It includes the "brain," a disk driver, a typewriterlike keyboard, and a video screen that looks like a television screen. Ask students to identify other computer terms such as *input, output, database, mouse, modem,* and *Internet.* Students might make a dictionary of common computer terms and their definitions.

CHAPTER 4, LESSON 2

Answers to Lesson 2 Review

1. By using them every day in practical situations.
2. Check for errors in your grammar, punctuation, and spelling.
3. Knowing how to use computers is essential for working in almost every field.
4. These skills serve as tools to help you function in life; they help you handle the demands of adult life.
5. Compare prices, prepare meals, remove stains from your clothes.
6. Answers will vary. Students should name a work skill needed for a particular job.
7. Answers will vary. Students should keep a record and make a graph showing what basic skills are used most often.

Enrichment

Ask students to interview an adult they know to learn ways the person uses basic skills on the job.

CLOSE

Give students two minutes to list ways computers affect their personal lives. Ask them to share their responses.

LESSON THREE
Getting a Job

FOCUS

Lesson Objectives
After studying this lesson, students should be able to
- explain how to find and apply for a job.
- discuss how to prepare for a job interview and make a good impression.

Motivating Activity
Ask students to brainstorm a list of jobs that are appropriate for middle-school students.

Introducing the Lesson
Have students share their responses to the Motivating Activity. Ask them to describe the ideal job for them ten years from now. Tell students that this lesson will describe the skills needed to help them get their ideal job.

Introducing *Words to Know*
Call on a volunteer to read the Words to Know. Then ask students to write a paragraph using all the terms. Have them check the definitions of the terms in the Glossary to see if they used the terms correctly in their paragraph.

LESSON THREE
Getting a Job

WORDS TO KNOW

job opening
job application
references
job interview
job applicant

DISCOVER...
- how to find and apply for a job.
- how to prepare for a job interview and make a good impression.

Getting a job requires good management skills. Marla learned about these skills when she looked for an after-school job. Her mother told her that the first thing she needed to do was to gather the required forms. Next Marla had to learn how to find the kind of job she wanted. Then she had to apply for the job and get an interview. Marla decided that getting a job was not going to be easy. By following the guidelines in this lesson, however, she got a part-time job at a garden center.

92 CHAPTER 4: CAREERS

CLASSROOM RESOURCES FOR LESSON 3

 Blackline Masters
Activity and Project Card 8, "Want Ads"
Cooperative Learning 8
Cross Curriculum 4
Lesson 3 Quiz
Peer Pressure and Decision Making 7

 Transparencies
Transparency 18, "Preparing for a Job Interview"

 **Student Workbook**
Activities 25, 26

Looking for a Job

No matter what type of work you have done before, perhaps yard work or babysitting, you will eventually need to seek out possible employers—businesses that can offer you a job. By learning job-hunting skills now, you will be prepared to find a part-time job while you are still in school or a full-time job when you have finished school.

Getting Organized

Before you look for a job, you need to get organized. You must get a social security card if you do not already have one. You will need a copy of your birth certificate or other proof that you are a United States citizen. Depending on where you live, you may also need a work permit, or employment certificate, if you are under the age of 16 or 18. Your school counselor can help you get one.

Once you have the necessary papers, you are ready to plan your job hunt. First, decide what kind of job you want. A look at your career goals, favorite subjects and activities, and past experiences should help you focus your attention on jobs that would be most suitable for you. Next, decide when and for how many hours you can work. For example, can you work after school or on weekends only? Now decide when you should look for a job. If you want a summer job, you should start looking in the spring. If you want a job during winter or spring vacation, start looking before the vacation begins. If you want an after-school job, look for it after school. Do not miss school to apply for a job. An employer may think you will also miss work if you want to do something else.

▲ Finding employers who have jobs available is only one part of looking for a job. Why is it important to learn job-hunting skills now?

LESSON THREE: GETTING A JOB 93

MORE ABOUT • • •

Looking for a Job There are more than 20,000 different occupations available in the United States. The United States Department of Education has classified the occupations into 15 career clusters. Career clusters include occupations related to one another in the interests and abilities they require but that need different kinds of preparation. The 15 career clusters are agribusiness and natural resources, business and office, communications and media, construction, fine arts and humanities, home economics, health, hospitality and recreation, manufacturing, marine science, marketing and distribution, environment, personal services, public service, and transportation.

CHAPTER 4, LESSON 3

TEACH

L1 Discussing
Discuss with students how people use management skills to find a job. (Students might need to refer to chapter 2 to review management skills.)

L2 Activity and Project Card
Allow time for students to complete Activity and Project Card 8, "Want Ads," in the TCR.

L2 Identifying Sources
Point out to students that many job openings never appear in newspapers, but instead are filled as a result of recommendations or by word-of-mouth. Have students make a list of all the people they know who are good sources of job leads. (family, friends, neighbors, teachers, acquaintances)

DID YOU KNOW

Every two years the United States Bureau of Labor Statistics publishes *The Occupational Outlook Handbook,* which describes job requirements, probable earnings, and predicts employment opportunities. The U.S. Department of Labor publishes the *Dictionary of Occupational Titles,* which describes about 20,000 jobs. This department also publishes the *Guide for Occupational Exploration,* which classifies occupations by interests and abilities.

L2 Cooperative Learning
Assign Cooperative Learning 8, "Practicing Job Interviews," in the TCR.

93

CHAPTER 4, LESSON 3

L2 Making a Chart
Help students identify their skills and talents. Provide them with a copy of a chart titled "Skills and Talents Identification." The chart should include five columns with the headings: "Job," "Skills Developed," "What I Liked," "What I Disliked," "Accomplishments Achieved." To complete the chart, tell students to think of the jobs they have had (both paid and unpaid), the skills that they developed as a result of the job, what they liked and disliked about the job, and what they accomplished as a result of performing the job. Ask students to use their completed charts to help them focus on skills that they have that could be transferred to a future career.

USING VISUALS
Have students study the examples of ways to find job openings in Figure 4.1. Have students identify which, if any, of the examples they have used. Ask: How well did it work? Which example do you think is most effective? Why?

L2 Language Arts Connection
Assign Cross-Curriculum Activity 4 in the TCR. Students practice writing their own résumés in this activity.

L1 Using Transparencies
Present Color Transparency 18, "Preparing for a Job Interview," in the TCR. Use this overhead visual to reinforce concepts from this lesson.

▲ **Figure 4.1
Ways to Find
Job Openings**
What other ways can you think of to find a job opening?

Finding a Job Opening

Now you are ready to look for job openings. A **job opening** is *a job that is not filled.* **Figure 4.1** shows some common ways to find job openings.

Applying for a Job

When you find a job opening that interests you, contact the employer to apply for the job. You may be asked to fill out a job application and come in for an interview when you apply for a job.

A **job application** is *a form on which you supply information about yourself that will help an employer make a hiring decision.* You will need to write down information about your education, skills, activities and interests, and work experience. If you fill out the application at the job site, you will need to have that information with you. Be sure to complete the application form neatly without skipping any questions.

HOME AND COMMUNITY CONNECTION

Guest Speaker If possible, invite an employee of a local employment agency to speak to the class about how her or his employment agency helps people find suitable jobs. Have students prepare questions for the speaker ahead of time. Students might create a poster that illustrates the ways the employment agency helps people find suitable jobs.

On an application form, you may be asked to give the names of several references. **References** are *people who can tell an employer about an applicant's character and quality of work.* Your references should be adults (not parents or other relatives) who know and like you. You might choose teachers, counselors, family friends, coaches, previous employers, club leaders, or religious leaders. Be sure to ask their permission before you use their names as references. Sometimes you can get adults to write letters of reference for you. The employer may call or write to your references to ask questions about your character or your abilities.

If the employer thinks that you might be suitable, you will be invited to interview for the job. A **job interview** is *a face-to-face meeting between an employer and a job applicant.* A **job applicant** is *a person who wants a job.* The interview gives the employer a chance to meet you and learn more about your qualifications for the job. The interviewer may ask, "Why do you think you can do this job well?" or "What are your strengths and weaknesses?" The interview also gives you a chance to learn more about the job and the business. It is an opportunity to ask questions about the job or about the place of employment. You might ask where and when you would work and what your duties would be.

TIPS for living

FILLING OUT A JOB APPLICATION

The way you fill out a job application can make a lasting impression. Here are some rules to follow.

- To avoid putting information in the wrong place, read the application form carefully before you start filling it in.
- Read the instructions, and follow them exactly.
- Print as neatly as possible, using blue or black ink.
- Answer all questions that apply to you. If a question does not apply, write "NA" (not applicable) in the space.
- Be prepared to describe your education, skills, past work experience, and references.
- Check to make sure that you have answered every question.

LESSON THREE: GETTING A JOB

CHAPTER 4, LESSON 3

L2 Writing
Have students write ten questions to ask an employer during an interview. Ask students to share their questions with the class. Tell them that there are some questions an employer cannot ask them during an interview. Point out to students that interviewers should not ask questions about such things as the job applicant's marital status or religious and ethnic background. Explain why an employer cannot ask such a question.

L3 Decision Making
Ask students to list in their private journals four people whom they would use as references. Have them explain their choices in their journals. Emphasize that students should always ask a person's permission before using that person as a reference. Have students compose a letter to one of the people on their list asking permission to use them as a reference.

TIPS for living
Give students practice in filling out a job application. Emphasize the importance of filling it out completely, neatly, and correctly.

L2 Problem Solving
Assign Peer Pressure and Decision Making 7 in the TCR. This activity gives students the opportunity to recognize peer pressure and practice decision-making skills.

MEETING STUDENT DIVERSITY

Varied Learning Styles Students who have difficulty reading and/or writing may need additional help when completing a job application. Suggest they pick up an application ahead of time, photocopy it, and use the copy as a rough draft. Help students read through the entire application, especially the instructions, to avoid duplication of information and to note any additional information. If something is unclear, tell students to ask for help, even if that means calling the company. Have students fill out the rough draft. Have them proofread the rough draft for accuracy. Tell them to make sure that the final copy is neat and legible. If possible, have the student type the final copy.

CHAPTER 4, LESSON 3

Skills IN ACTION

Allow students time to share their advertisement or commercial with the class. Have the rest of the class critique the advertisements and commercials.

L1 Student Workbook
Assign Activities 25 and 26 in the Student Workbook.

ASSESS

Evaluating the Lesson
Assign Reviewing Terms and Facts and Thinking Critically on page 97 to review the lesson; then assign the Lesson 3 Quiz in the TCR.

Reteaching
- Have students write a newspaper column titled "Tips for Getting a Job." Photocopy the columns and distribute them to the class.
- Have students complete Reteaching Activity 4 in the TCR.

Enrichment
Provide students with sample letters of inquiry for job openings. Instruct them to write a letter of inquiry for a job opening they read about in the newspaper.

An interview gives you a chance to see if you are really interested in the job. What questions would you ask during an interview?

Skills IN ACTION

Starting Your Own Business

Lawn mowing, babysitting, and dog walking are common teen businesses, but there are many other possibilities. Be inventive! Then create a flyer or business card. You might even tape-record a radio commercial or videotape a television commercial. Share your business idea with your classmates.

96   CHAPTER 4: CAREERS

The Job Interview

You can improve your chances of getting a job by making a good impression during the job interview. The moment you walk through the door for an interview, you start making an impression on the employer. The first thing the employer usually notices is the applicant's appearance—dress, hair, and grooming.

Your posture and manners are also important parts of the first impression. Employers look for an applicant who has good posture, walks confidently, and looks people in the eye. They are impressed by an applicant who smiles, speaks clearly, and seems friendly and enthusiastic.

You can prepare for a job interview by learning all you can about the employer and practicing for the interview. Practice by having a friend ask you questions; respond as if you were really being interviewed.

Dressing for the Interview

Plan carefully what you will wear to a job interview to make a good first impression. Your clothes should be

---

MEETING STUDENT DIVERSITY

Practicing Interviews Preparing for a job interview can be a difficult challenge for students whose native language is other than English. Encourage non-native students by offering them the opportunity to role-play with a partner whose native language is English. Have partners practice by first preparing a script for an in-person interview, and then role-playing the situation. Students can also gain experience with telephone inquiries and setting up interviews by phone. Have them practice with partners what they will say ahead of time and then role-play telephone conversations.

appropriate for the interview, clean, and neatly pressed. Be sure that your shoes are also clean and polished.

Pay attention to details as you dress for a job interview. Be sure that you have a clean body, shiny hair, white teeth, and clean fingernails. Many interviewers notice these details. An effort to appear neat and clean tells an employer that the job is important to you.

Using Your Skills to Get a Job

It is easier to find a job if you organize your search. When you find a job opening that interests you, be prepared to fill out an application and go to an interview. Your chances for a successful interview improve if you are well-groomed and neatly dressed. If you make a good impression on the employer, you will be more likely to get the job.

Which job applicant do you think will make a better first impression? Which one would you hire?

LESSON THREE *Review*

Using complete sentences, answer the following questions on a separate sheet of paper.

Reviewing Terms and Facts

1. Recall What papers must you have before you look for a job?

2. Vocabulary Define the term *job application*.

3. List Name the three things that contribute to an employer's first impression of you.

4. Describe How can you prepare for a job interview?

Thinking Critically

5. Summarize What do you need to do when planning your job hunt?

6. Explain What are the purposes of a job interview?

7. Suggest What would you wear to an interview for a job in an office? For an interview for babysitting? For a fast-food job?

Applying Concepts

8. With a classmate, take turns role-playing the parts of an applicant and an employer in a job interview. Be sure to agree on the type of job the applicant is looking for. Analyze your performance in each role.

LESSON THREE: GETTING A JOB   97

MEETING STUDENT DIVERSITY

Cultural Perspectives Eye contact is important in the United States. During a job interview, it is important to look the interviewer directly in the eyes for at least some of the interview. Many people believe that making eye contact means that a person is self-assured, friendly, and honest. By contrast, people in some cultures believe it is rude to look directly into a person's eyes while talking. Explain to students that the increase in international business has placed a greater importance on understanding the customs of other nations. Ask students to name areas in which cultural differences may affect business situations.

CHAPTER 4, LESSON 3

Answers to Lesson 3 Review

1. A Social Security card, a copy of your birth certificate or other proof that you are a United States citizen; and if you are under the age of 16 or 18, you may need a work permit or employment certificate.

2. A form on which you supply information about yourself that will help an employer make a hiring decision.

3. The applicant's appearance, posture, and manners.

4. By learning all you can about the employer, practicing for the interview, and planning what you will wear to the interview.

5. Decide what job you want, decide when you can and will work, and decide when you should look for a job.

6. Gives the employer a chance to learn more about the job applicant's qualifications for the job and gives the job applicant a chance to learn more about the job and business and to ask questions.

7. Answers will vary. Students should point out that the clothes should be appropriate for the interview, clean, and neatly pressed; clean and polished shoes.

8. Role-playing situations will vary but students should analyze their performances.

CLOSE

Have students discuss how they could get information about an employer before going on an interview.

LESSON FOUR
Being Successful on the Job

FOCUS

Lesson Objectives
After studying this lesson, students should be able to
- identify steps to becoming a responsible employee.
- explain why building a good work record is important.
- discuss how they can advance at work.

Motivating Activity
Ask students to write ten qualities of a successful student.

Introducing the Lesson
Have students reread their responses to the Motivating Activity and underline the three most important qualities needed to be a successful student. Ask students to explain their choices to the class. Then tell them that this lesson describes qualities that are essential for success in a job.

Introducing *Words to Know*
Ask volunteers to read the definitions of *supervisor* and *coworkers*. Explain that "supervisor" comes from the Latin *super*, meaning "over," and the Latin *videre*, meaning "to see." The prefix "co-" in "coworker" comes from the Latin *cum*, meaning "with" or "joining." Point out that the word "entrepreneur" came into English from the French in 1828. It was derived from *entreprende*, "to undertake." Today it means one who undertakes a business venture, generally someone self-employed.

LESSON FOUR
Being Successful on the Job

WORDS TO KNOW
coworkers
supervisor
employee manual
flexibility
teamwork
work record
promotion
entrepreneur

DISCOVER...
- steps to becoming a responsible employee.
- why building a good work record is important.
- how you can advance at work.

Caitlyn is a junior in high school. She has always dreamed of becoming a professional photographer. When she heard about a part-time job as an assistant in a photography studio, she jumped at the opportunity. She filled out a job application and went for an interview. The employer was impressed by Caitlyn's good grades and her positive attitude. Caitlyn got the job and now works one day a week after school and every Saturday. She enjoys her work, and her **coworkers,** *the people she works with,* and customers like her enthusiasm. Each week Caitlyn puts part of her paycheck into a savings account. She hopes to open her own photography studio someday.

98　Chapter 4: Careers

CLASSROOM RESOURCES FOR LESSON 4

 Blackline Masters
Enrichment 4
Lesson 4 Quiz
Peer Pressure and Decision Making 8
Reteaching 4

 Transparencies
Transparency 19, "Relationships on the Job"
Transparency 20, "Evaluating Earnings and Deductions"

 Student Workbook
Activities 27, 28

Becoming a Responsible Employee

The key to success in any job is to be a responsible employee. You are a responsible employee when you know what your job responsibilities, or duties, are and you fulfill them.

There are some responsibilities that every employee has in every job situation. These responsibilities include having a positive attitude and using good communication skills. It is also important to be a good team member.

If you think about it, these job responsibilities are similar to your responsibilities at school. At work, as in school, you need to arrive on time, follow rules, and do your share of the work. Of course, you also know that you should always be honest and do your best. What other general responsibilities can you think of?

To become a responsible employee, follow these three steps.

- **Step 1: Know your job responsibilities.** Besides general job responsibilities, every job also has specific

Skills that you develop in school, such as working as a member of a team, will help you in your future career. What other skills do you need to be a responsible employee?

LESSON FOUR: BEING SUCCESSFUL ON THE JOB

MORE ABOUT •••

Knowing Your Job Responsibilities Many businesses have job descriptions that are included in the employee manual. This helps the employees know exactly what is expected of them. An employee who is unsure of his or her responsibilities should write down what he or she believes are the responsibilities if there is no manual. The employee should share the job description with his or her supervisor for approval. In this way the employee knows what to do to fulfill his or her job responsibilities. Have students write their job responsibilities as a student, a part-time employee, or a member of a family. Ask them to share their job descriptions with the class. Have other students add to the descriptions.

CHAPTER 4, LESSON 4

TEACH

L1 Applying Life Skills
Provide students with copies of your school's student handbook or manual. Explain that it is a book of rules that students must follow. Point out that the student handbook or manual is similar to an employee manual. Review some of the contents of the manual, such as attendance policy, dress code, insurance, sexual harassment policy, and survey of private information. Explain that these are some of the issues that employee manuals address. Ask students to discuss the advantages of having a book of rules for an employee to follow.

L1 Discussing
Inquire about good work habits practiced in class. Check to see if all students have and use an assignment notebook. Explain that students who write down their assignments every day at school are learning a valuable work habit that they will most likely carry over into their job. Point out that keeping a daily list of job responsibilities helps employees organize their day, manage their time, and become successful.

L2 Problem Solving
Assign Peer Pressure and Decision Making 8 in the TCR. This activity gives students the opportunity to recognize peer pressure and practice decision-making skills.

L1 Using Transparencies
Present Color Transparency 19, "Relationships on the Job," in the TCR. Use this overhead visual to reinforce concepts from the lesson.

CHAPTER 4, LESSON 4

Skills IN ACTION

Allow students time to share their skits with the class. Ask students to give examples of phrases used in the skits that showed respect for others. *(Excuse me. May I help you? Pardon me. Thank you for your help.)* Point out to students that the tone in which these phrases are said must also be respectful. Discuss how body language can indicate respect.

L3 Research
Have students research the career they are interested in and make a flow chart showing advancement opportunities. Encourage students to use on-line sources for their research.

L2 Reading
Ask students to read a magazine or newspaper article or article from an encyclopedia about a famous entrepreneur such as Henry Ford, William Gates, or Oprah Winfrey. Ask them to imagine they are successful entrepreneurs and give motivational speeches to the class.

DID YOU KNOW
Many states have a law that gives all employees the right to see their personnel records. Employees may make a formal, or written, request to see what's in their personnel files at least once a year. Documents from the file may be copied, but nothing may be removed. If employees find information in the file that is not true or that they disagree with, they can include a note of explanation in the file.

Skills IN ACTION

On the Job
You will have many opportunities to use communication skills at work. Here are a few examples:
- Finding out customers' needs and wants
- Getting acquainted with coworkers
- Handling problems

Think of an on-the-job situation requiring good communication skills. Ask a classmate to role-play the situation with you.

COOPERATIVE LEARNING

Working Together Have students work in small groups to plan and make a poster that teaches one idea from this lesson. (making a good first impression on the job, meeting the supervisor and coworkers, being flexible on the job, team spirit, or working together) Each poster should include a heading, information from the text, and appropriate drawings or pictures from magazines. Have students share their posters with the class. Then discuss how the members of each group worked together. Ask: Was everyone part of the team? Did teammates cooperate with one another? If not, how could teammates have gotten along better?

---

duties. If you work in a flower shop, for example, your duties might include making flower arrangements, dealing with customers, and operating the cash register.

How do you know what your responsibilities are? You will probably learn about some of them during your job interview. In your first week of work, your specific responsibilities will be explained to you by your **supervisor,** *the person who checks your work and evaluates your performance.* You may be given an **employee manual,** *a book of rules that employees must follow.* You will have to understand and obey these rules.

- **Step 2: Fulfill your job responsibilities.** A key to success at work is just to *do* your job. This sounds simple, and it is. You would be surprised, though, at how many people fail to follow this simple rule.

  Sean had a part-time job as a salesperson at a music store in the mall. Sean's friends would often visit him at work. When Sean was talking to his friends, he would ignore customers. Because Sean didn't do his job, he was fired. The lesson to learn from Sean's experience is that you are at work to do your work. Arrive on time, ask questions if you do not understand something, and make your job responsibilities your top priority.

- **Step 3: Evaluate yourself.** At the end of each workday you should evaluate your performance on the job. Did you fulfill your responsibilities? How could you have done your job better? Did you use good communication skills?

Success on the job requires hard work. Following these steps, however, will help you become a good employee and reach your career goals.

Flexibility

Even when you plan carefully, you cannot always control the ways things turn out. People who are flexible accept that plans may be affected by forces they cannot control. **Flexibility** is *the ability to adjust easily to new conditions.* Because conditions on the job can change often, most work situations require flexibility. For example, computer technology is constantly changing, and as a result, workers must learn new skills and new ways to accomplish tasks.

Flexibility is also important when dealing with coworkers. You cannot always control the ways tasks are done. Sometimes coworkers must each give in a little to reach an agreement.

Team Spirit

When you go to work, you become part of a team. As a member of a team, you should work with and listen to others and have a helpful attitude. That builds **teamwork,** or *cooperation while working together to reach a goal*. When coworkers cooperate with one another and share feelings of pride in their work, they get along better and can reach their goals more effectively. **Figure 4.2** shows some ways to be a good team member.

- Show loyalty.
- Be flexible.
- Have a positive attitude.
- Focus your attention on each task.
- Speak in a pleasant way to others.
- Listen attentively to others.
- Do your full share of the work.
- Be truthful.

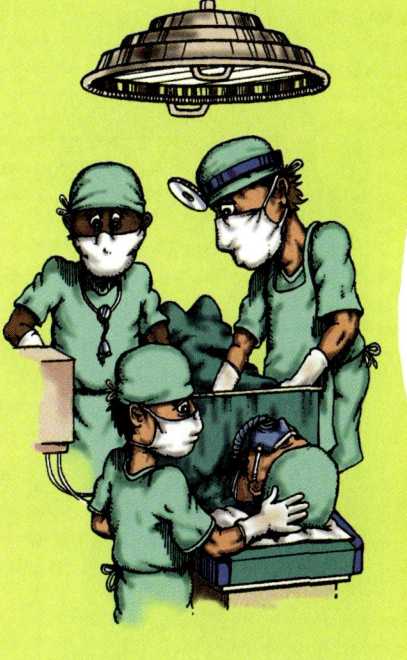

Figure 4.2 Working as a Team Member
Sharing goals and responsibilities as part of a team is an experience that is valuable to everyone.

LESSON FOUR: BEING SUCCESSFUL ON THE JOB   101

CHAPTER 4, LESSON 4

USING VISUALS
Have students work in small groups to illustrate the message in Figure 4.2. Provide each group with a piece of cardboard. Have them draw and cut apart a puzzle with eight pieces. Ask them to write one responsibility of a team member on each of the puzzle pieces. Then have each group exchange puzzle pieces with another group and reconstruct the puzzles. Point out that, just like the finished product of a team, the puzzle doesn't fit together properly if any of the responsibilities of a team member are forgotten.

L2 Writing
Ask students to write a magazine article for an issue dealing with jobs. Students should use the skills suggested in the lesson, but they should provide specific examples of how these skills can be used. Students may wish to use computers to write their articles. Call on volunteers to share their articles with the class.

L1 Applying
Have students consider how the following statement relates to being a good team member: "A winning team can lose the game if a team member drops the ball." Then have them work in groups to create more slogans that exemplify successful teamwork. Display slogans on the bulletin board.

MORE ABOUT ● ● ●

Being a Team Member If possible, invite someone who coaches an athletic team or a scholastic team to speak to the class. Ask the coach to give an inspirational speech to the class about the importance of working together as a team. Allow students time to ask the coach questions about ways of being a good team member. Encourage them to prepare questions ahead of time to ask the coach, and tell them that they may note additional questions they may think of during the speech.

CHAPTER 4, LESSON 4

Try This!

As students work on this activity, remind them to consider personal, material, and community resources they identified in Chapter 2. Have them think of ways to manage these resources to develop their lists of good work habits.

L2 Problem Solving

Present the following scenario to students:

You are babysitting. One of the children falls and hits his head quite hard.

Write a note to a friend explaining what happened and how you handled the problem. When students have finished writing their notes, ask them to reread the notes and evaluate their performance on the job. Have students share their notes and evaluations with the class.

TIPS for living

Have students make a list of tips for getting along with teammates. Ask students to compare their lists with the list of tips for getting along with coworkers. Point out to students that coworkers are part of a team. In order to get the job done, coworkers must cooperate and get along with one another. Point out that more people are fired from their jobs for not being able to get along with people than for lack of skills.

Try This!

Employers want workers who manage their time, energy, and material resources wisely. With a group of your classmates, make a list of good work habits such as "Get to work on time" or "Be honest."

Getting Along with Others

Relationships are an important part of every job. You have to learn to get along with your employer, supervisor, and coworkers, and perhaps customers or clients. The better your relationships are with these people, the more you will enjoy work and experience success.

Your Work Record

Do you know someone who has a reputation as a nice person? Maybe you know someone with a reputation for good grades. What kind of reputation do you have? You probably know that once you get a reputation, it's hard to change it.

As you work, you will develop a reputation based on your work record. A **work record** is *a written record of how well an employee performs on the job.* Your work record shows how well you have fulfilled your job responsibilities. It mentions how often you were late and how often you missed work. You can also expect to find comments about your attitude and how well you followed instructions.

TIPS for living

GETTING ALONG WITH COWORKERS

You will do a better job and enjoy your work more if you get along with your coworkers. To build good working relationships:

- **Do your share.** If you don't, others may resent getting stuck with extra work.
- **Be prompt.** Arrive at work early, and return from breaks on time.
- **Help others.** If you finish your work early, offer to help someone else.
- **Accept differences.** Keep an open mind, and see what you can learn from others.
- **Stay positive.** People like to work with others who smile and think positively.
- **Avoid gossip.** Stay neutral and don't get involved when people gossip or spread rumors at work.

102   CHAPTER 4: CAREERS

MORE ABOUT • • •

The Schoolwork Record Emphasize to students that the record of their schoolwork in junior high school and in high school will become important when applying for and entering college. Tell students that colleges look for good grades as well as extracurricular and leadership activities that applicants were involved in during high school. Ask students to speculate on why involvement in such activities would be a factor that colleges would take into consideration when deciding whether or not to admit an individual.

If you apply for a job with a new company, that employer will probably check your work record along with other references. A good work record will improve your chances of being hired. You can see that your work record will follow you like your reputation, so it pays to build a good one.

Advancement Opportunities

As you know, to be promoted means to move forward. In the world of work, a **promotion** is *a move up to a better job with more responsibility.* For example, you might be promoted from stock clerk to assistant manager. A promotion usually includes a raise in salary. Another way to advance is to accept a better job—one with more responsibilities and higher pay—with another company.

Becoming an Entrepreneur

For some people, the way to begin a career or to advance is to strike out on their own. An **entrepreneur** is *a person who starts and runs his or her own business.* Running your own business has many advantages. You are your own boss. You get credit for all of your successes. Of course, when you are an entrepreneur you are also responsible for every part of the business. If the business does not do well, you lose money. Do you know anyone who is an entrepreneur? If you were an entrepreneur, what type of business would you have?

Taking Initiative

Everyone who is successful on the job has one thing in common: initiative. Initiative means starting something on your own and working to complete it. You will use your initiative to get a job and to advance in your career. By taking initiative, you will gain the self-esteem that comes from success in your work.

You can gain experience as an entrepreneur by starting a business at home. For example, a neighbor might agree to pay you for doing chores.

LESSON FOUR: BEING SUCCESSFUL ON THE JOB

HOME AND COMMUNITY CONNECTION

Conduct a workshop on teenage entrepreneurship. Invite teenage entrepreneurs to class to explain how they planned, financed, and managed their own business ventures. Ask students to suggest local teens they are familiar with who have experience in starting or running their own businesses. Have them invite these teens to participate. Allow students time to interact with the entrepreneurs. If no local teen entrepreneurs are available, have students bring in articles from newspapers and magazines, or have them prepare summaries of television reports about teens who run their own businesses. Display these articles in the classroom and allow students to discuss each teen business.

CHAPTER 4, LESSON 4

L1 Student Workbook
Assign Activities 27 and 28 in the Student Workbook.

ASSESS

Evaluating the Lesson
Assign Reviewing Terms and Facts and Thinking Critically on page 104 to review the lesson; then assign the Lesson 4 Quiz in the TCR.

Reteaching
- Have students create illustrations that demonstrate the three steps to being a responsible employee.
- Have students complete Reteaching Activity 4 in the TCR.

Enrichment
- Have students compute how much money they will save if they put away five dollars a week for a year. Then have them compute the amount of interest they will have accrued based on the current interest rate for a savings account at a local bank.
- Assign Enrichment Activity 4 in the TCR.

L1 Using Transparencies
Present Color Transparency 20, "Evaluating Earnings and Deductions," in the TCR. Use this overhead visual to reinforce concepts from this lesson.

CHAPTER 4, LESSON 4

Answers to Lesson 4 Review

1. Know your job responsibilities, fulfill your job responsibilities, evaluate yourself.
2. The ability to adjust easily to new conditions. Sentences will vary.
3. A written record of how well an employee performs on the job; an evaluation of an employee's work. A work record includes the results of performance reviews.
4. You will be able to reach your goals.
5. Answers will vary. Students should point out that a person who has a good work record may advance faster and higher than a person with a poor work record.
6. Answers will vary. Students should identify their dream job and describe how two skills discussed in this lesson will help them achieve their dream job.
7. Interviews will vary but should include the steps the person took to become successful.

CLOSE

Ask students to debate the following statement: "The way to advance in a job is to toot your own horn."

Managing Your Income

Have you ever heard of a millionaire who went bankrupt? It does happen. Earning an income is not enough; you have to manage your money carefully. Managing your income is a way to get what you want out of life. If you make a habit of saving part of every paycheck, you will be able to set and reach financial goals. Perhaps you want to save enough money to buy a computer or a stereo. It is not too early to start saving now for a future goal, such as buying a car or going to college. Remember that how you manage your income is as important as how much money you earn.

By managing your income carefully, you can save money to reach a goal. What would you buy with your savings?

LESSON FOUR Review

Using complete sentences, answer the following questions on a separate sheet of paper.

Reviewing Terms and Facts

1. List Identify three steps you can take to become a responsible employee.
2. Explain Define the term *flexibility*. Use it in an original sentence.
3. Vocabulary Define the term *work record*. Then write a sentence explaining what it includes.
4. Explain Why is it important to manage your income?

Thinking Critically

5. Contrast Write a paragraph contrasting the advancement of an employee who has a good work record with that of an employee who has a poor work record.
6. Apply Describe your dream job, and explain how two skills you learned in this lesson might help you achieve it.

Applying Concepts

7. Interview the owner of a small business. Write a paragraph explaining the steps that person took to achieve success. Share your findings with the class.

104   CHAPTER 4: CAREERS

HOME AND COMMUNITY CONNECTION

Guest Speaker Ask an employee of a local bank to explain to the student how to manage their money through checking and savings accounts. The bank employee should explain the bank's policy for opening checking and savings accounts for students. Ask the bank employee to show the students how to deposit and withdraw money in checking and savings accounts. The bank employee might also show students how to balance a checking account.

Chapter 4 Activities

Consumer Focus

Career Information
Helping people find satisfying work has become a big business. Stores sell a wide range of books, videos, and software on career planning. Now a growing number of educators are developing career awareness materials for middle school students.

Try This!
Begin looking for information on careers that interest you. Start a job file where you can keep the materials you find.

TECHNOLOGY

Job Search
Did you know that you can use a computer to help you choose a career? Special software packages let the computer match your answers to questions about your personal job preferences with the characteristics of hundreds of jobs.

Try This!
Ask for a more detailed description of any of the jobs. In this way, you can learn about jobs that might be right for you.

A Global View

GLOBAL MARKETPLACE
You live in a global marketplace. In the past, marketplaces tended to be close to customers' homes. Today, however, modern transportation and communication systems make it easier to buy and sell goods and services around the world. What do you think that you can do now to get ready for a job in the global marketplace?

TRY THIS!
Find out the name of a company that does business worldwide. Read about the types of jobs available in that business's global marketplace.

MATH CONNECTION

GROSS PAY VERSUS NET PAY
Clearing tables at The Heritage Diner was Zach Ryan's first "real" job. After two weeks, he looked forward to receiving his first paycheck. Zach soon learned that his earnings, or *gross pay*, would not be the same as his take-home pay, or *net pay*. Zach's gross pay was $166.25, while his net pay was $136.58. What is the reason for the difference? Deductions!

Follow Up
1. Alicia earns $6.25 an hour as a cashier at Martin's Variety Store. Last week she worked 38 hours. She had the following deductions: F.I.C.A.—$18.17, federal income tax—$6.49, state income tax—$4.00, and medicare—$3.44. What was Alicia's gross pay? What was her net pay?

2. Interview a self-employed person to find out how he or she pays taxes and insurance. Write a paragraph or two on your findings.

CHAPTER 4 Activities

Consumer Focus
Ask students to find out what career planning information is available in your school. Have students volunteer to check with the counseling office or the school librarian for pamphlets or booklets. Have them find out where these materials are available for students and report to the class.

TECHNOLOGY
Assign volunteers to look in computer software catalogs to locate sources of software packages that will give information on job characteristics. Ask students what other technologies are available to assist individuals seeking employment.

A Global View
Ask volunteers to note clothing products that were manufactured outside the United States. Tell them that teens in Taiwan, Italy, Mexico, and other countries buy many products with the "Made in the U.S.A." label. The global marketplace promises to become even more important in the years ahead. Ask how this trend will provide career opportunities both in the United States and in other countries.

Teaching the MATH CONNECTION
Have students make a pie graph showing how Zach's income for one paycheck was distributed. Students must calculate each deduction's percentage of the gross pay and the net pay's percentage of the gross pay. The pie graph will show: FICA *(about 7%)*; Federal Income Tax *(about 6%)*; State Income Tax *(about 4%)*; Medicare *(about 1%)*; net pay *(about 82%)*.

Answers to Follow-Up
1. $237.50; $208.84.
2. Answers will vary. Students should explain that self-employed people must pay income tax in estimated quarterly installments. Self-employed people must buy their own insurance if they are not covered by their spouse's insurance.

CHAPTER 4 REVIEW

Checking Comprehension

Use the Chapter Summary and the Chapter 4 Review to help students go over the most important ideas in Chapter 4.

Answers to Words to Know

1. To discover a person's natural abilities or talents.
2. It helps you to catch mistakes.
3. People who can tell an employer about an applicant's character and quality of work.
4. *Boss* or *manager*.
5. Answers will vary. Students should give an example of flexibility on the job, such as being willing to learn new skills to accomplish tasks.
6. Starts her or his own business.

Answers to Review Questions

1. So that you can learn the skills needed for your career and take related courses while you are in school.
2. Find out about career areas that interest you. Talk over the possibilities with parents, school counselors, and teachers.
3. They serve as tools to help you function in life and help you handle the demands of adult life.

Chapter Summary

- Your choice of a career will be one of the most important decisions you will ever make. Since you will be spending a large part of your life working, you should choose work you will enjoy.
- You can prepare for your future career by setting goals, researching careers, continuing your education, and working part-time.
- In school you learn the basic skills of reading, writing, math, science, speaking, and listening. Knowing how to use a computer is also an important basic skill.
- Job hunting requires organization. Before starting your search, decide what kind of job you want and when you can work.
- You can find job openings by asking family and friends, looking at the help-wanted ads, calling possible employers, and visiting employment agencies.
- Dressing appropriately is important for a job interview. Your appearance is usually the first thing an employer notices.
- Good communication skills, flexibility, and team spirit will help you succeed on the job.
- Your work record includes a description of your work habits and how well you handled problems.
- Getting promotions or finding new employment will depend on a good work record.

Words to Know

Using complete sentences, answer the following questions on a separate sheet of paper.

1. What is the purpose of an *aptitude test*?
2. How might *proofreading* help you in a job?
3. Whom should a person list as *references* on a job application?
4. At work, what words might mean the same as *supervisor*?
5. Give an example of *flexibility* on the job.
6. Describe what an *entrepreneur* does.

Review Questions

Using complete sentences, answer the following questions on a separate sheet of paper.

1. Why is it important to decide on career goals while you are in school?
2. How can you find a job or career that is right for you?
3. Why are reading, writing, math, science, speaking, and listening skills called basic skills?
4. Describe the process of getting a job.
5. What can you do to promote good teamwork on the job?

106 CHAPTER 4: CAREERS

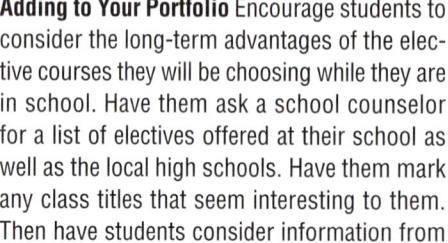

EXTRA CREDIT PROJECT

Adding to Your Portfolio Encourage students to consider the long-term advantages of the elective courses they will be choosing while they are in school. Have them ask a school counselor for a list of electives offered at their school as well as the local high schools. Have them mark any class titles that seem interesting to them. Then have students consider information from Chapter 4 about preparing for and making career choices. Have them note any electives that they feel might help them gain experience or skills for careers they would like to consider. Have students keep a copy of these classes and special notes in their portfolios to refer to when making class selections.

CHAPTER 4 REVIEW

6. Give three examples of good work habits.

Thinking Critically

Using complete sentences, answer the following questions on a separate sheet of paper.

1. **Explain** Why might aptitude tests give people an incomplete picture of career possibilities?
2. **Analyze** Do you think that computers make learning to read, write, and do math less important? Why or why not?
3. **Apply** What questions would you ask an employer at a job interview?
4. **Describe** Why is team spirit such an important quality for employees to have? When might it not be very important?
5. **Apply** What would you do if a coworker was not doing his or her job?

Cooperative Learning

1. With a group of your classmates, make an employment guide for young teens. Include descriptions of jobs suitable for teens, information on how to find jobs in your community, and tips on how to succeed on the job. Each member of the group can be responsible for writing a different section of the guide. Make your guide available to other students in your school.
2. Gather information about a career that interests you. Find out the education required for jobs in that field, responsibilities or duties to be expected, working conditions, and employment outlook. Exchange information with a small group of your classmates.

Family & Community

1. One reason why teens may not know much about their parents' jobs is that they rarely see their parents at work. Arrange to spend some time with a parent or any adult family member at his or her workplace during a vacation from school. Find out about the adult's duties and responsibilities and how he or she uses basic skills at work. Report your findings to the class.
2. Look for resources in your community that help teens start their own businesses. You might find books on teen entrepreneurship at the public library or in bookstores. Programs such as Junior Achievement or Future Business Leaders of America provide teens with business training.

Building A Portfolio

1. Parent-teacher-student conferences and report cards provide a "performance review" of the job you are doing in school. Use information from these sources to list some goals for improving your performance. Place a copy of your list of goals in your portfolio, and use it to measure your progress.
2. Write a business letter to a nearby college, vocational school, community college, or technical school. Request information about available training for careers that interest you. Place a copy of your letter and the information you receive in your portfolio.

CHAPTER 4 REVIEW

4. Gather the necessary papers—Social Security card, birth certificate or other proof that you are a United States citizen, and a work permit or employment certificate; decide what kind of job you want; decide when you will work; look for job openings; complete job applications; interview for the job.
5. Work with and listen to others and have a helpful attitude; learn to get along with your employer, supervisor, coworkers, customers, and clients.
6. Answers will vary. Students might include the following: dress neatly; be on time; know your job responsibilities; fulfill your job responsibilities; evaluate yourself.

Evaluate

Assign the Chapter 4 Test in the TCR, or create your own Chapter test using the Testmaker Software.

CLOSE

Have students apply their knowledge of the chapter's content by completing one of the alternative assessment activities listed under Family and Community or Building a Portfolio.

Answers to Thinking Critically

1. When deciding on a career, you need to think about your interests, skills, values, and goals. Aptitude tests only predict a person's ability to learn certain skills.
2. Answers will vary. Students should compare and contrast the importance of computer skills to reading, writing, and math skills.
3. Answers will vary. Students should write several questions they would ask an employer at a job interview.
4. People in most jobs work with other people to get the job done. Team spirit may not be important if a person is self-employed.
5. Answers will vary. Students may suggest talking to the coworker about doing his or her share of the work or talking to the supervisor.

UNIT 2
Relationships

Unit Overview

Unit 2 identifies the relationship skills that are needed to successfully get along with family members, friends, and acquaintances. Unit 2 also describes successful parenting skills and helps students to understand child development and child care.

In Chapter 5 students learn the qualities of a strong relationship and develop skills in compromise, communication, and conflict resolution. In Chapter 6 they learn what to expect of children at different stages and ages. Students are also presented with child care and safety procedures to be used when caring for younger children.

Introducing the Unit

- **Parent Letters** As you begin the study of Unit 2, you may wish to send home copies of the Parent Letter and Activities found in the *Linking Home, School, and Community* booklet in the TCR.
- **Using Visuals** Have students look closely at the mother and daughter in the picture. Ask them to relate possible scenarios to describe what they think might be going on between the two people.
- **Using the Color Transparency** Present Transparency 21, "Relationships," in the TCR. Discuss with students the importance of relationships in people's lives.

UNIT 2
Relationships

Chapter 5:
Your Family and Friends

Chapter 6:
Parenting and Children

BULLETIN BOARD IDEAS

Travel the Family Express Mount green construction paper on the bulletin board and draw a set of railroad tracks meandering across it. Make one engine shape and print *Family Express* on the engine. From different colored construction paper cut out pieces in the shape of train boxcars. On five of the cars print techniques for strengthening family bonds, such as sharing interests and activities; planning family vacations; attending religious services; discussing books, movies, and current events; and participating in sporting activities. Mount the train cars on the bulletin board. Then give a paper car to each student and have him or her list a favorite family activity. Arrange students' boxcars behind the train cars already on the tracks.

UNIT PROJECTS 2

Encourage students to work on two Hands-on Projects for this unit found in the Teacher's Classroom Resources.
- Hands-on Project 3, "Create a Toy," gives students the opportunity to design and make a developmentally-appropriate toy for a child.
- Hands-on Project 4, "Friendship Frames," directs students to create a message about friendship and a personalized frame.

Unit Closure

- Allow class time at the end of this unit to reinforce students' understanding of the material by playing Hands-on Game 2, "Relationship Squares," found in the TCR.
- Create your own Unit Test using the Testmaker Software to evaluate students' comprehension.

Promoting Family & Consumer Sciences

Administrators Individuals from the school administration can provide support and resources essential to your program. Communicate regularly with them by providing copies of correspondence and updates of your class activities and events. Administrators can be an essential link to community events, new partnerships, and public relations.

BULLETIN BOARD IDEAS

A Child Blossoms Through Play Draw a large sunflower on poster board. Print one of the following on each flower petal: *colors; imagination; coordination; creativity; sizes and shapes; muscle control; body control; how to walk, run, kick, and climb; how to push, pull, throw, pound, and stack*. Cut out four leaves from green construction paper and place them at the base of the flower stem. Label each leaf with one of the following: *emotional growth, mental growth, physical growth,* and *social growth.* Place an illustration of a watering can in the top right-hand corner. Print *Play teaches* on the spout. Use blue construction paper to make raindrops. Show the raindrops being poured from the watering can.

Planning Guide
Chapter 5 Your Family and Friends

LESSON 1	Pages	FEATURES	CLASSROOM RESOURCES
Getting Along With Others	112–116	Skills in Action: Using "I" Messages Try This: Gifts from the Heart	Lesson 1 Quiz Transparency 22, "Skills for Success in Relationships" Student Workbook Activities 29, 30
LESSON 2 **Family Relationships**	117–122	Try This: Special Memories	Enrichment 5 Lesson 2 Quiz Peer Pressure and Decision Making 9 Transparency 23, "Improving Communication with Your Parents" Student Workbook Activities 31, 32
LESSON 3 **Changes Within Families**	123–129	Tips for Living: Laughter Is the Best Medicine Try This: A Feeling of Well-Being	Concept Map 7 Lesson 3 Quiz Transparency 24, "Managing Stress" Student Workbook Activities 33, 34
LESSON 4 **Developing Friendships**	130–135	Skills in Action: Making New Friends Try This: Keeping in Touch	Activity and Project Card 9, "Friendship Chain" Lesson 4 Quiz Peer Pressure and Decision Making 10 Transparency 25, "To Have a Friend, Be a Friend" Student Workbook Activities 35, 36
LESSON 5 **Peers and Decision Making**	136–140	Try This: Recognizing Peer Pressure Tips for Living: Handling Peer Pressure	Cooperative Learning 9 Cross Curriculum 5 Lesson 5 Quiz Peer Pressure and Decision Making 11 Transparency 26, "Peer Pressure" Student Workbook Activities 37, 38

LESSON 6	Pages	FEATURES	CLASSROOM RESOURCES
Resolving Conflicts	141–146	*Skills in Action:* Learning to Compromise *Try This:* Peer Mediation	Activity and Project Card 10, "What Causes Conflict?" Concept Map 8 Cooperative Learning 10 Lesson 6 Quiz Peer Pressure and Decision Making 12 Transparency 27, "Peer Mediation" Student Workbook Activities 39, 40

CHAPTER 5 RESOURCES

- Chapter 5 Test
- Reteaching 5
- Study Guide 5, *Reteaching*
- Testmaker Software

UNIT 2 RESOURCES

- Transparency 21, "Relationships"
- Hands-on Projects 3, 4
- Hands-on Game 2

Performance Assessment Activity

Explain to students that Native Americans of the Pacific Northwest erected totem poles, tall wooden poles with carved images of people and animals or other natural objects symbolizing the tribe or family. Have students make drawings, carvings, or sculptures of personal totem poles showing the story or history of the relationships between their family and friends. Have them include totems for: themselves, friends, family members; the type of family they belong to; how they fit into the family; interests, goals, customs, values of family and friends; or life changes. Organize the class into small groups to explain each totem pole. Display the totem poles in the classroom.

OUT OF TIME?

If time does not permit thorough teaching of this chapter, you may wish to use:

- *Teens Making a Difference,* page 111
- *Tips for Living,* pages 124, 139
- *Try This,* pages 114, 118, 129, 135, 137, 145
- *Skills in Action,* pages 113, 133, 144
- *Young Living Activities,* page 147
- *Chapter Summary,* page 148

Resources for the Teacher

Creighton, Allan, and Kivel, Paul. *Helping Teens Stop Violence: A Practical Guide for Counselors, Teachers, and Parents.* Alameda, CA: Hunter House, 1992.

Readings for the Student

Cannon, Carol. *Never Good Enough: Growing Up Imperfect in a "Perfect" Family. How to Break the Cycle of Codependency and Addiction for the Next Generation.* Boise, ID: Pacific Press Publishing, 1993.

Multimedia Resources

Communicating with Parents (Videocassette with Teacher's Guide). Live Wire Video. Social Studies School Service.

Coping with Pressures (Videocassette with Teacher's Guide). Live Wire Video. Social Studies School Service.

CHAPTER 5
Your Family and Friends

Chapter Overview

Chapter 5 explains the value and importance of relationships. Students learn that family life and friendships are important now and in the future. Students are given strategies to help them cope with peer pressure, making decisions, changes in relationships, and conflicts.

LESSON 1 identifies the skills needed to build strong relationships.
LESSON 2 describes the importance of family life.
LESSON 3 identifies strategies for dealing with the changes in life.
LESSON 4 explains how friendships require giving and receiving.
LESSON 5 describes the positive and negative influences of peers.
LESSON 6 describes ways to resolve conflicts peacefully.

Introducing the Chapter

Refer students to the chapter title, "Your Family and Friends." Have students skim the lesson titles and the pictures throughout the chapter. Ask students to write in their private journals their own thoughts on the subjects of each lesson title. Ask volunteers to read their sentences aloud.

Chapter Motivator

Point out to students that this chapter is about relationships with family members and friends. Provide each student with ten strips of construction paper, five blue and five yellow. Have them write the ways they give in a relationship on the blue strips. On the yellow strips, have them write the ways they receive in a relationship. Discuss the responses with the class. Then have students loop the strips of paper together to form a relationship chain.

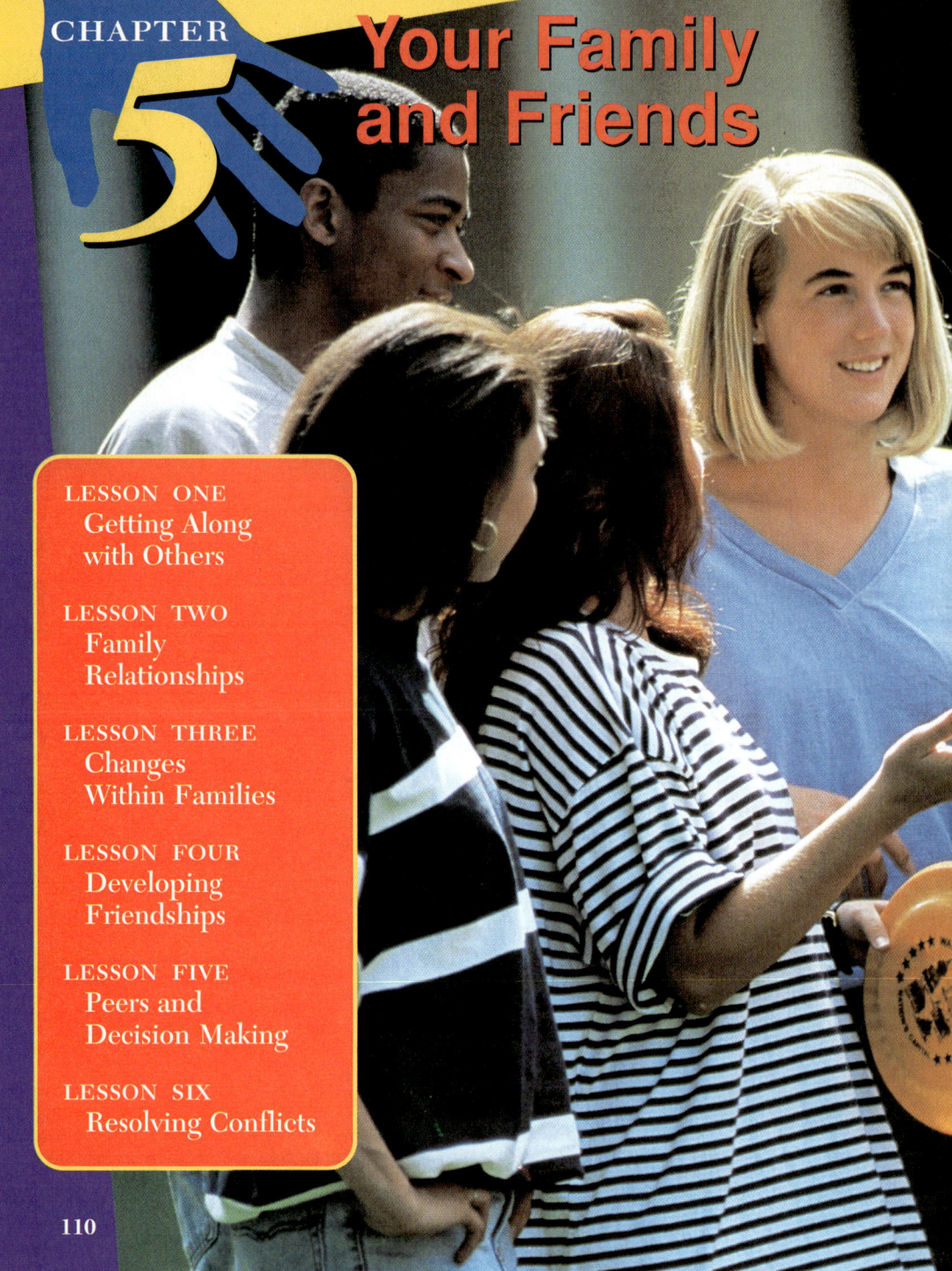

CHAPTER 5
Your Family and Friends

LESSON ONE
Getting Along with Others

LESSON TWO
Family Relationships

LESSON THREE
Changes Within Families

LESSON FOUR
Developing Friendships

LESSON FIVE
Peers and Decision Making

LESSON SIX
Resolving Conflicts

KEY TO ABILITY LEVELS

Teaching strategies that appear throughout the chapter have been identified by one of three codes to give you an idea of their suitability for students of varying learning styles and abilities.

L1 Level 1 strategies should be within the ability range of all students. Often full class participation is required. Teacher direction is usually needed.

L2 Level 2 strategies are for average to above-average students or for small groups. Some teacher direction is necessary.

L3 Level 3 strategies are designed for students able and willing to work independently. Minimal teacher direction is necessary.

CHAPTER 5

TEENS MAKING A DIFFERENCE

Have students read "Teens Making a Difference." Ask students to identify the relationships that Tara had developed as a result of her volunteer work. *(Tara had developed a close relationship with the children in the hospital where she volunteered, especially with a girl named Cindy.)* Point out to students that volunteers often develop relationships with the people through their volunteer work. Ask students to name other benefits of volunteering.

BLOCK SCHEDULING

The following Teacher Classroom Resources are suggested for use in classrooms with Block Scheduling.
- Activity and Project Card 9, "Friendship Chain"
- Activity and Project Card 10, "What Causes Conflict?"
- Cooperative Learning 9, "New Student Information Sheet"
- Cooperative Learning 10, "Play a Role"

TEENS MAKING A DIFFERENCE
Story Time

One Monday, in creative writing class, Tara could not think of any ideas for her next story. Tara's teacher suggested that Tara think about the children she has met through her volunteer work at the hospital.

Tara thought about a little girl named Cindy who was very scared about being in the hospital. When Cindy's mother was not there, Tara would read stories to the girl.

Just then, Tara got an idea. She asked, "Could our class write a collection of stories for the children?" Everyone thought that it was a great idea. When the collection was finished, the class dedicated it to the children at the hospital.

Try THIS!

What could you do to help a young friend or family member who was scared about something? Write down five ideas, and share them with a classmate.

111

TECHNOLOGY IN THE CLASSROOM

Filmstrips This audiovisual format can be adapted to the needs of your class and can be shown in part or whole. You can ask and answer questions and lead a discussion with students as the frames are being shown. Manuals or teacher's guides that provide additional information are often included. Filmstrips are useful in providing closeup views of work that might be difficult to see clearly in a demonstration, at the same time cutting down on the time and possible cost of having an actual demonstration. Filmstrips are available with or without sound. Sound filmstrips require the use of a sound projector or a tape recorder.

LESSON ONE
Getting Along with Others

FOCUS

Lesson Objectives

After studying this lesson, students should be able to
- explain the importance of relationships.
- identify the skills needed to develop strong relationships.
- describe ways to practice relationship skills.

Motivating Activity

Have students fold a paper in half. Have them write the name of a person they like and respect on the top line of each half of the paper. Under each name, ask students to list five reasons why they like and respect the person.

Introducing the Lesson

Have students share their responses to the Motivating Activity. Use the responses as a basis for discussing qualities needed to build strong relationships. Explain to students that this lesson will help them understand the benefits of developing strong relationships.

Introducing *Words to Know*

Ask a volunteer to read the definitions of the vocabulary words. Then on the board write the word "relationship" in a large circle. Create a word web using the Words for Living and their definitions in this lesson.

LESSON ONE
Getting Along with Others

WORDS TO KNOW
belonging
security
cooperation
considerate

DISCOVER...
- the importance of relationships.
- the skills needed to develop strong relationships.
- ways to practice relationship skills.

People often take relationships for granted. They may not realize how important another person is to them until something changes in their relationship. For example, if your brother went away to college or your best friend went to summer camp, you would miss that person a great deal.

Why Are Relationships Important?

Relationships are important because they help you meet your social and emotional needs. Everyone needs to feel

112   CHAPTER 5: YOUR FAMILY AND FRIENDS

CLASSROOM RESOURCES FOR LESSON 1

Blackline Masters
Lesson 1 Quiz

Transparencies
Transparency 22, "Skills for Success in Relationships"

Student Workbook
Activities 29, 30

accepted and liked by others. How well your relationships meet these needs influences your feelings about yourself and others.

Belonging

Relationships with friends and family members give you a sense of **belonging,** or *feeling included.* Belonging helps you feel good about yourself and builds your self-esteem. It allows you to feel at ease and comfortable.

To feel that you belong, you need to feel loved and accepted by others. This gives you a sense of **security**—*feeling safe and protected.* When you know that you can count on family and friends to love and accept you the way you are, you feel that you are secure and that you belong.

You can add to your own feelings of security by making others feel loved and secure in turn. When you care for others, their needs become as important as your own. If you comfort your younger sister after a classmate has said something mean to her, you make her feel that she is secure and that she belongs. If you bring your dad a glass of lemonade when he is washing the car, you make him feel loved. Showing others that you care about them makes you feel giving and unselfish.

Approval

The approval and recognition of family and friends also build your self-esteem. Think about how good you feel when someone compliments or thanks you. "Great haircut!" or

Using "I" Messages

The next time you're upset with a family member or a friend, try sending an "I" message instead of saying, "You always…" You might say, for example, "I feel angry because…" "I" messages allow you to express how you feel without putting others down or making them feel defensive. With a partner, role-play sending "I" messages.

When family members help each other, they build strong relationships. In what ways do you help members of your family?

LESSON ONE: GETTING ALONG WITH OTHERS   113

CHAPTER 5, LESSON 1

TEACH

Skills IN ACTION

After students have role-played sending "I" messages with partners, ask each set of partners to role-play an "I" message response to a situation for the class. Discuss with students the importance of body language in each message.

L2 Diagramming

Have students draw illustrations showing themselves and all the social groups to which they belong, such as family, school, clubs, organizations, work, and religion. Ask students to write a caption for each illustration explaining their involvement in each group. Hold a discussion with students about the sense of security they feel as a result of belonging to each group.

DID YOU KNOW

A person's well-being is based on a health triangle—mental, physical, and social health. People should strive for a balanced health triangle. This means that you should work to keep each side of the triangle healthy. Ask students to define *social health*. (the ability to have positive relationships with the people around you) Ask them to name some qualities that people with good social health possess. (*good team members accept differences in others, meet people easily, make and keep friends*)

MEETING STUDENT DIVERSITY

Tactile Learning Have students work in pairs. Assign each pair one of the skills that can help make relationships more satisfying. Ask each pair of students to create mobiles that depict the assigned skill. Encourage partners to brainstorm creative ways of illustrating the skill. Then have them work together to construct the mobiles from construction paper, poster board, or cardboard. Students may wish to cut pictures from magazines to illustrate the mobiles. Provide markers, paints, or other art supplies, and string and wire hangers to make the mobiles. Display completed mobiles in the classroom.

113

CHAPTER 5, LESSON 1

Try This!

Have students give their gift certificates to a friend or family member. Have them describe the results to the class.

L2 Critical Thinking

Write the following relationship traits on the board: *acceptance, security, belonging, humor, responsibility, approval, communication, cooperation, trust.* Have students write the traits on a piece of paper in rank order from most important (1) to least important (9). Have students discuss and defend their rankings with classmates.

DID YOU KNOW ?

At least 3,000 languages are currently spoken in the world. The word *language* comes from the Latin word *lingua,* meaning "tongue." Ask students to describe other methods of communication besides spoken language.

L2 Role-Playing

Organize the class into five groups. Assign each group one of the suggestions for showing that you care described in the bulleted list. Ask students to write a scenario for their assigned suggestion. Then have each group role-play the scenario for the class.

L1 Using Transparencies

Present Color Transparency 22, "Skills for Success in Relationships," in the TCR. Use this overhead visual to reinforce concepts from this lesson.

114

Try This!

Are you looking for that perfect gift for a family member or a special friend? Sometimes the best choice isn't something that costs a lot of money. For example, make a gift certificate that says "This certificate entitles (name) to 'one car wash' or 'three games of checkers.'"

When you cooperate with others, you do your share of the work. What are some other ways to show that you are cooperative?

114

"Thanks for your help" are comments that everyone likes to hear. Such comments make you feel good about yourself.

You have probably heard little children shout, "Look at me!" when they build a tower with blocks or run a race. Their need for recognition is so great that they persist until you look at them and say, "Very good!" When you show others a special art project or a poem you wrote, you are also seeking approval. It is natural to feel happy when you receive a compliment for something you are proud to have done. Likewise, you can make your family members or friends happy by complimenting them on their accomplishments.

Developing Relationship Skills

There are several skills that can make your relationships more satisfying. These skills will help you get along better with both your family and your friends. They will also help prepare you for future relationships.

Communication

A key to good relationships is practicing communication skills. That means learning to express your thoughts clearly and listening to what others say. Good communication brings people closer together. Share your problems or concerns with your family and friends. Express your joys and dreams. When family members and friends are talking, listen closely to what they are saying. Try to understand the message from their point of view. Use positive body language, such as a smile or a nod of approval, to show that you are listening.

Cooperation

For relationships to work, the people involved need to cooperate with one another. **Cooperation** is *working together for the*

COOPERATIVE LEARNING

Developing Relationship Skills Organize the class into groups of four or five students and have them work together on an art project. Have them choose the focus of the project, and choose any medium that is practical in the classroom as long as the finished art project relates to developing relationships. For example, students might make collages that illustrate the basic relationship skills. Display finished projects. Then ask the groups to explain how they used communication, cooperation, trust, and thoughtfulness to complete the assignment.

good of all. At school, cooperation may involve sharing equipment in gym class or doing your share of the work on a social studies project. At home, cooperation may mean taking turns using the telephone or helping out by preparing dinner.

Building Trust

The ability to build trust is also necessary in relationships. To earn the trust of parents, adults, and friends, you need to show them that you can handle new experiences and responsibilities. For instance, taking out the trash without being reminded or getting up on time are ways of showing that you are trustworthy.

Another way to earn trust is to be reliable and honest with people. This means that you do what you say you are going to do. For example, if you say that you will take care of a new kitten, it is important to keep your word.

Being Considerate

It takes practice to consider others' needs and feelings. Being **considerate,** or *thoughtful,* is an important part of getting along with others.

How do you act around your family and around your friends? Is there a difference? Using a pleasant, friendly tone of voice and thinking before you speak will make others feel accepted and respected. Your actions show how considerate you are. Here are some ways to show your family and friends that you care. Can you think of other ways?

- **Respect others' privacy.** Don't listen to their conversations or borrow things without asking.
- **Be thoughtful about noise.** Make sure that your music or television isn't disturbing others.
- **Notice others' feelings.** If your father is tired or your friend is upset, find ways to help out.

Showing consideration for others is an important relationship skill. How is this teen being considerate of someone else?

CHAPTER 5, LESSON 1

L1 Discussing
Make a two-column chart on the board. Title one column "Negative Actions" and the other column "Positive Actions." Ask students to name ways that young people seek approval and recognition. Have them identify the actions as negative or positive. Complete the chart with students' responses. Discuss the effects of negative actions on relationships.

L1 Student Workbook
Assign Activities 29 and 30 in the Student Workbook.

ASSESS

Evaluating the Lesson
Assign Reviewing Terms and Facts and Thinking Critically on page 116 to review the lesson; then assign the Lesson 1 Quiz in the TCR.

Reteaching
- Have students make an outline titled, "Building Relationships." Their outline should include the two main headings "Why Are Relationships Important?" and "Developing Relationship Skills." Have students refer to the material in Lesson 1 to supply supporting details for the main headings.
- Have students complete Reteaching Activity 5 in the TCR.

LESSON ONE: GETTING ALONG WITH OTHERS

MORE ABOUT

Relationships As a social being, your lasting satisfactions and meanings come from relationships with others. You need to love and be loved, to appreciate others and be appreciated. How well you can enter into a meaningful relationship with others begins with the relationship you have with yourself. If you are overly critical of yourself, you will be so with others. If you expect too much from yourself, you will do so with others. If you have a sense of self-worth and self-love, you will be better able to establish positive relationships with others. Ask students to identify where they can go for help if they suffer from low self-esteem.

CHAPTER 5, LESSON 1

Answers to Lesson 1 Review

1. Social and emotional needs.
2. Feeling safe and protected. I have a sense of security when I am with my family and friends.
3. Communication, cooperation, building trust, and being considerate.
4. Show that you can handle new experiences and responsibilities, by being honest and truthful.
5. Use a pleasant, friendly tone of voice; think before speaking; respect the privacy of others; be thoughtful about noise; read others' feelings; show your appreciation; help people with disabilities.
6. The project the team is working on may not get finished or done properly.
7. Answers will vary. Students should give two examples of ways to show appreciation at home. Students might suggest doing chores without complaining or being reminded or hugging a family member.
8. Answers will vary. Students should list ten ways they could be more considerate of family members and friends. They should star five ideas to start doing immediately.

Enrichment

Have students write poems regarding friendships. Have them read and discuss the ideas of the poems with the class.

CLOSE

Have students give three examples of how they build trust in their relationships.

- **Show your appreciation.** Say thank you or return the favor when someone has done something nice for you.
- **Help people with disabilities.** Open a door for someone in a wheelchair, or offer to carry a package for someone with crutches.

The Value of Relationships

You can see why good relationships are important to people. Strong relationships give you a sense of security, acceptance, and approval. Practicing relationship skills at home, at school, and with friends is worth the effort. You will be happier, make those around you happier, and feel better about yourself.

▶ Learning how to develop strong relationships is a skill that will help you throughout your life. Why do you think that this is so?

LESSON ONE Review

Using complete sentences, answer the following questions on a separate sheet of paper.

Reviewing Terms and Facts

1. **Name** What two types of needs do relationships fulfill?
2. **Vocabulary** Define the term *security*. Use it in an original sentence.
3. **List** Name four skills that help people develop strong relationships.
4. **Recall** How can you earn trust?
5. **Explain** What are some ways to show family and friends that you care about them?

Thinking Critically

6. **Analyze** What might happen if team members did not cooperate?
7. **Apply** Give two examples of ways you could show appreciation at home.

Applying Concepts

8. List ten ways in which you could be more considerate of family members or friends. Put a star next to five ideas that you could start doing immediately. Make plans to carry out the other ideas on your list.

116   CHAPTER 5: YOUR FAMILY AND FRIENDS

COOPERATIVE LEARNING

Voicing Your Emotions Organize the class into groups of five students. Provide each group with a slip of paper with the following statement: *Did you say John called?* Have each student in each group read the sentence. To help students get an idea of how much their tone of voice can change a message, each student is to put the stress on a different word in the sentence. Have students start by stressing the first word, and so on. Then have each group discuss the following questions: Which of the readings simply sounded like a question? Which sounded angry, emotional, or like an accusation? Each group might try the same exercise with other sentences.

LESSON TWO
Family Relationships

DISCOVER...
- several types of family structure.
- the importance of family ties and traditions.
- ways to get along with family members.

What comes to mind when you think of *family*? Can you create a description of what a family is? Is it being together for a holiday? Is it the group of people next door? Perhaps you think of a family you see on a favorite television program. There are many groups of people that function as families.

WORDS TO KNOW

family
siblings
traditions

LESSON TWO: FAMILY RELATIONSHIPS   117

LESSON TWO
Family Relationships

FOCUS

Lesson Objectives
After studying this lesson, students should be able to
- differentiate among the types of family structure.
- discuss the importance of family ties and traditions.
- identify ways to get along with family members.

Motivating Activity
Have students finish the following sentence, "A family is . . ."

Introducing the Lesson
Have students share their responses to the Motivating Activity. Write their responses on the board. Point out that there are many definitions of a family because there are so many types of families. Tell students that this lesson will help them better understand their family.

Introducing *Words to Know*
Have students read the vocabulary words and their definitions. Ask volunteers to identify their siblings and the birth order of the children in their family. Ask students to describe some examples of family traditions.

CLASSROOM RESOURCES FOR LESSON 2

 Blackline Masters
Enrichment 5
Lesson 2 Quiz
Peer Pressure and Decision Making 9

 Transparencies
Transparency 23, "Improving Communication with Your Parents"

 Student Workbook
Activities 31, 32

117

CHAPTER 5, LESSON 2

TEACH

Try This!

Ask students to share ways they record family events and traditions. Suggest that they try one of the projects suggested in the feature for creating family memories. Have them report to the class how their family reacted to the project.

L2 Categorizing

Have students use magazine pictures to make collages of each of the different types of families described in this lesson. Students should label the type of family depicted in the collage. Display the collages in the classroom.

L2 Applying Life Skills

For one week, have students keep a daily log of ways they kept in touch with family members who share their household. At the end of the week, ask students to share their log entries with the class. Discuss how making time for family members makes them feel.

USING VISUALS

After students have studied the types of families in Figure 5.1, ask them if they can think of examples of each type of family.

Try This!

Every family has special stories and memories. Try one or more of the following to preserve your family memories.
• Volunteer to organize family photos into a photo album.
• Videotape special family events.
• Tape-record a collection of family stories.
• Put together a scrapbook that highlights vacations.

Figure 5.1
Family Types
These are some common types of families.

What Is a Family?

A **family** is *a group of two or more people who care about each other and are committed to each other*. Usually, the members of a family live together, and in most cases they are related by marriage, birth, or adoption. **Figure 5.1** describes some of the common family structures.

The Importance of Families

Regardless of the structure, a healthy family life is a source of pleasure and growth for its members. Healthy families consist of people who care about each other and work together as a team. Family members work together to

- provide food, clothing, and a place to live.
- create a loving environment.
- encourage independence.
- teach values and life skills.
- give friendship, guidance, and emotional support.

In what ways do you and the members of your family meet these needs?

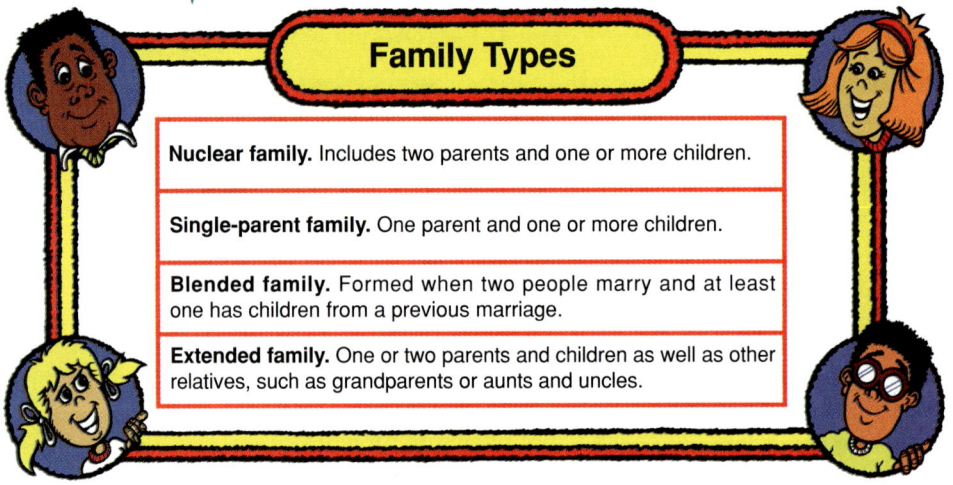

Family Types

Nuclear family. Includes two parents and one or more children.

Single-parent family. One parent and one or more children.

Blended family. Formed when two people marry and at least one has children from a previous marriage.

Extended family. One or two parents and children as well as other relatives, such as grandparents or aunts and uncles.

118 CHAPTER 5: YOUR FAMILY AND FRIENDS

TECHNOLOGY UPDATE

New developments in home building promise to make life easier for all members of a family. In a test house, called Smart House, researchers are experimenting with voice-activated controls. Also, special control panels would enable a person to perform tasks from a central location. For example, you could lock doors, turn off any light in the house, check burners on the stove, and adjust the thermostat from your bed. Ask students how such technology could benefit all families.

Strengthening Family Relationships

Families can become closer when they spend time together. By becoming involved in each other's daily lives and participating in similar activities, hobbies, and interests, family members strengthen their ties with each other.

Think about the activities you like to share with your mother, father, and **siblings,** or *brothers and sisters.* Perhaps you like to go biking or hiking with your parents or shopping with your sister. Even sharing daily events, such as talking about what happened at school or fixing dinner, can help build long-lasting and satisfying family relationships. Other ways to enrich family life include the following:

- sharing games or hobbies
- attending religious services
- planning holiday celebrations
- discussing books, movies, and current events

What do you enjoy doing with your family? What other activities might you suggest to them?

In healthy families, members do things with and for each other. When her mother had a baby, Maya helped out by making dinner each night until her mother felt stronger. Maya's older brother pitched in and did the laundry. These actions increase the bonds of affection and provide emotional support for the family unit. They are especially helpful if members are faced with difficulties, such as someone losing a job or becoming ill. At times like these, it helps if everyone can join together to be supportive and make ends meet.

The traditions you practice with family members help make your family unique. What traditions does your family have?

Your Unique Family

The people who make up a family have different skills, talents, and possessions. For example, your father may be an artist. Your sister may play on the soccer team. Your brother

LESSON TWO: FAMILY RELATIONSHIPS **119**

CHAPTER 5, LESSON 2

L1 Display

Make a bulletin board titled, "Strengthen Family Ties." From different colors of construction paper, cut pieces in the shape of neckties. On each tie print a technique for strengthening family bonds, such as sharing interests and activities; discussing books, movies, and current events; attending sporting events; celebrating holidays; vacationing together. Then provide each student with a paper necktie. Have them list a favorite family activity that reflects the technique stated on the tie they were given. Arrange the ties on the board.

L3 Problem Solving

Ask students to pretend that they write an advice column for a newspaper. Have them give advice to the reader who wrote the following letter:
Dear Advisor,
  I am in junior high. I love my parents and siblings, but I don't feel like they love me. Sometimes I feel alone in my house even when everyone is home. What can I do to feel better about my family?
  Sincerely,
  Home Alone in a Full House

COOPERATIVE LEARNING

Comparing and Contrasting Families Ask student volunteers to participate in a panel discussion of family differences and likenesses. (If possible, try to arrange to have a panel of students from diverse cultures.) Have a moderator work with the rest of the class to come up with meaningful questions to ask the panel of volunteers. Possible questions include: How does your family spend time together? What holidays does your family celebrate? What traditions does your family follow when celebrating these holidays?

CHAPTER 5, LESSON 2

L2 Applying Life Skills

Have students write the name of a family member at the top of a piece of paper. Then have them fold the paper in half lengthwise. In the left column have them list six characteristics they admire about the person. In the right column have them write a compliment to give the person based on one of the characteristics. Urge students to follow through and give the compliments.

USING VISUALS

After students have studied the tips to improve communication with their parents in Figure 5.2 on page 121, point out the importance of keeping the lines of communication open with their parents and other family members. Explain that the family is the single most influential component of a society. It is from the family that children learn personal habits as well as problem-solving techniques that will be used in interpersonal relations. The family is seen as the main determining factor in an individual's educational and occupational achievements.

L1 Using Transparencies

Present Color Transparency 23, "Improving Communication with Your Parents," in the TCR. Use this overhead visual to reinforce concepts from this lesson.

L2 Problem Solving

Assign Peer Pressure and Decision Making 9 in the TCR. This activity gives students the opportunity to recognize peer pressure and practice decision-making skills.

---

may own a drum set and play in a band. The skills, talents, and possessions of its members make each family unique.

Families also have different ways of expressing themselves and their emotions. You have probably noticed that some show their love for each other more openly than others. They may show affection by hugging and kissing one another and saying, "I love you." This does not mean that families who hug and kiss less feel less love. They just express it in different ways.

It is not surprising that families have different ways of expressing themselves. Families have various **traditions,** *customs and beliefs handed down from one generation to another.* These traditions might influence, for example, how they celebrate holidays, the foods they like, and their religious beliefs. Even people in different parts of this country have their own customs. It is important to realize that customs can be different without being wrong. By sharing ideas with a variety of people, you can learn more about them. At the same time, they will learn more about you as well.

Talking openly with your parents will bring you closer together.

Getting Along with Family Members

Within your family, you practice the skills of communication, cooperation, trust, consideration, respect, and appreciation. These skills help you get along with other family members and prepare you for relationships with others.

You and Your Parents

As you move toward independence, it helps to understand that parents are people, too. They have strengths and weaknesses, interests, and skills. They, too, are working toward goals. Perhaps they are going back to school or saving for a family vacation. Sometimes they face trouble at work, financial difficulties, or health problems. In these cases, it helps to recognize your parents' point of view. Just like you, they have good days and bad days and worries and hopes. If you give

COOPERATIVE LEARNING

Varying Family Profiles Make up packs of three, four, or five index cards. Each pack should represent a different family profile. (For example, a pack of three cards might have *father, young child,* and *teen* listed, one on each card. A pack of five cards might have *father, mother, grandfather, teen,* and *infant* listed on the cards.) Distribute the packs to groups of corresponding size, and have members of each group choose cards at random. Have students in each group work together to figure out how daily chores and responsibilities might be divided within its assigned "family." When groups have worked out an arrangement that best meets the needs of all the family members, have each group share its arrangement with the class.

Figure 5.2 Improving Communication with Your Parents
Following these guidelines will help you communicate with your parents. Why is communication so important?

them love, understanding, patience, and cooperation, your family life will go more smoothly.

Communicating with parents is especially important during your teen years. Talk openly to your parents about your problems and concerns. Many times this helps both you and your parents understand one another's feelings. Try the tips in **Figure 5.2** to improve communication with your parents.

Getting Along with Siblings

You may enjoy many activities with your brothers and sisters. However, sometimes you may have difficulty getting along with them.

Learning to get along with siblings helps you learn to get along with others away from home. Here are some suggestions to improve your relationships with siblings.

- Avoid teasing them. Accept the way they act and what they say.
- Share your belongings with them, and ask permission before you use or borrow theirs.

LESSON TWO: FAMILY RELATIONSHIPS   **121**

CHAPTER 5, LESSON 2

L1 Student Workbook
Assign Activities 31 and 32 in the Student Workbook.

ASSESS

Evaluating the Lesson
Assign Reviewing Terms and Facts and Thinking Critically on page 122 to review the lesson; then assign the Lesson 2 Quiz in the TCR.

Reteaching
- Have students draw a diagram showing four different types of families. Diagrams should illustrate that families come in various shapes and sizes.
- Have students complete Reteaching Activity 5 in the TCR.

Enrichment
- Have students read literature that addresses family-life situations, such as *Little Women, Little Men, Cheaper by the Dozen, Ramona, Matilda, The Great Brain,* and *Little House on the Prairie.* Ask them to describe the strengths and weaknesses of the families discussed in the books.
- Assign Enrichment Activity 5 in the TCR.

 HOME AND COMMUNITY CONNECTION

Interview Have students interview their parents, grandparents, or elderly neighbors to determine how family life was different when that person was the students' age. Students should prepare questions for their interview such as the following: What type of family did you have when you were growing up? Which type of family was most common in the past? Has family life changed over the years? If so, what has caused the change in family life? What disagreements were common between teens and parents when you were a teen? If possible, with permission of the interviewee, have students videotape their interviews and share them with the class.

CHAPTER 5, LESSON 2

Answers to Lesson 2 Review

1. A blended family is formed when two people marry and one or both people have children from a previous marriage. An extended family includes one or two children as well as other relatives, such as grandparents or aunts and uncles.
2. Any three: create a loving environment; provide physical care; encourage independence; teach values and life skills; provide food, clothing, and a place to live; give friendship, guidance, and emotional support.
3. By doing things for and with each other.
4. Any three: choose a time when your parent is not busy or upset; begin the conversation with positive comments; keep emotions in control; try to understand the position of your parents; make it a habit to talk with your parents every day.
5. Learning to get along with family members teaches you how to get along with people in future relationships.
6. Their ages, interests, and ideas may cause disagreements.
7. Answers will vary. Students should list suggestions for improving communication in the family.

CLOSE

Have students debate the following statement: "No other influence in society has as far-reaching an impact on a person as family."

Take time to have fun with your family. Sharing activities can bring you closer together.

- Do your share of the work. Don't leave it for them to do.
- Compliment them when you can, and speak kindly about them.

Enjoying Family Life

Your family provides you with physical care and gives you love, guidance, and friendship. The ties and traditions that you share with them will influence your personal development and relationships for the rest of your life.

LESSON TWO Review

Using complete sentences, answer the following questions on a separate sheet of paper.

Reviewing Terms and Facts
1. **Vocabulary** What is the difference between a *blended family* and an *extended family*?
2. **Identify** Name three ways family members support one another.
3. **Explain** How are family ties strengthened?
4. **Identify** What are three guidelines that you could follow if you have a difficult time talking with your parents?

Thinking Critically
5. **Analyze** How can learning to get along with family members now help to improve your relationships in the future?
6. **Discuss** Why do siblings sometimes not get along with each other?

Applying Concepts
7. Discuss the guidelines for improving communication with one or both of your parents. Ask them which suggestion they believe would be most effective in your family.

122   CHAPTER 5: YOUR FAMILY AND FRIENDS

HOME AND COMMUNITY CONNECTION

Family Enjoyment Point out to students places in the community where families can go to enjoy activities together. Suggestions include the YMCA, parks, park district programs, scouts, museums, libraries, and movie theaters. Ask students for other suggestions. Make a list on the chalkboard of student suggestions. Have them use telephone books to find additional possibilities. Ask for volunteers to compile all the places identified and make a list for a file to be kept in the classroom for student reference.

LESSON THREE
Changes Within Families

DISCOVER...
- the changes that occur naturally throughout the life cycle of a family.
- how to adapt to change.
- how to cope with stress.

Change is a normal part of life. Over the years, almost everything changes, from clothing to technology. Just as fashions and technology change, families also change. Sometimes it's easier to deal with a new computer in the classroom than it is to adjust to a divorce or the birth of a sibling. It helps to understand the change and know how to adapt to it.

WORDS TO KNOW
life changes
stress
cope

Life Changes

Think of how you have changed over the years. Think of how your life has changed. Some changes are unimportant,

LESSON THREE: CHANGES WITHIN FAMILIES 123

LESSON THREE
Changes Within Families

FOCUS

Lesson Objectives
After studying this lesson, students should be able to
- explain how to understand family change.
- discuss how to adapt to changes.
- describe how to cope with stress.

Motivating Activity
Have students write down a change in their community or in the world during their lifetime.

Introducing the Lesson
Ask students to share their responses to the Motivating Activity. Ask them how these changes affected their lives. Explain that in this lesson they will explore ways to prepare for and adjust to change.

Introducing *Words to Know*
Have volunteers read the vocabulary words and terms and their definitions. Then write the term *life changes* on the board. From this term draw an arrow and write the word *stress*. Explain to the students that life changes can cause stress. Next, draw an arrow from *stress* and write the word *cope*. Point out to the students that learning to cope with stress in a positive way is healthy.

CLASSROOM RESOURCES FOR LESSON 3

 Blackline Masters
Concept Map 7
Lesson 3 Quiz

 Transparencies
Transparency 24, "Managing Stress"

 **Student Workbook**
Activities 33, 34

123

CHAPTER 5, LESSON 3

TEACH

L1 Finding Examples

Draw two columns on the chalkboard. At the top of one column write *Life Changes a Person Cannot Control*. At the top of the second column write *Life Changes a Person Can Control*. Ask students to identify examples of the two kinds of changes and write them under the appropriate heading. Discuss students' examples.

L3 Critical Thinking

Ask students to reflect privately upon changes that have occurred in their families. Ask: Were the changes expected or unexpected? How have these changes affected your role in the family? What emotions have you felt as a result of these changes? What have you done to adjust to the changes? Students should record their answers in a private journal entry. Emphasize to students that the reflections are for their personal use and need not be shared with anyone else.

TIPS for living

Encourage students to bring their favorite comic strips to class. Set aside bulletin-board space for displaying the comic strips. Think of a title for the display, such as "De-Stressed."

---

but others are **life changes,** or *major ways your life is altered by events that you may or may not be able to control.* Sometimes these events present you with a new way of life.

Some life changes are the result of things you do, or don't do. For example, if you need to make up a class but do not go to summer school, you will not be promoted to the next grade.

Other life changes you cannot control. If your family moves to a new house, you may have to go to a different school. If your parents have a new baby, you are no longer an only child. An accident or serious illness can put you in the hospital. Whether you want to or not, you may experience changes.

Understanding Family Changes

Families undergo changes just as their members do. As each individual grows and changes, the rest of the family adapts and changes. This is called the life cycle of the family. Your roles change as members grow and change. If your older sister gets married, you may find that you have more chores to do at home. You may also find that you have more time to spend with your parents. Sometimes the changes are planned or expected, such as children gaining more responsibility as they get older. Other times they come as a surprise.

TIPS for living

LAUGHTER IS THE BEST MEDICINE

Have you ever heard, "Laughter is the best medicine"? Humor is often a healthy way of dealing with emotions. Laughter even keeps your body fit. When you laugh, your chest, heart, lungs, and other body parts are exercised. Laughing can also increase your heartbeat. After a good laugh, all systems return to normal, resulting in less stress and an all-around good feeling. Here are some ways to add humor to your life.

- Read the cartoons and comic strips in the newspaper daily.
- Watch your favorite situation comedy on television.
- Find friends who have a good sense of humor. Some people have a talent for seeing the funny side of life.

124 CHAPTER 5: YOUR FAMILY AND FRIENDS

HOME AND COMMUNITY CONNECTION

Dealing with Family Problems Point out to students that some family changes are too serious to be worked out within the family. When this happens, a family needs outside help. If help is not sought and the problem is not solved, the family and the personal well-being of each family member are at risk. Invite a social worker from the school or the community to speak to the class about the kinds of family matters that may require outside intervention. Ask the social worker to explain to students where they can get help if they and their family are experiencing a crisis.

CHAPTER 5, LESSON 3

L3 History
Have students research to find out about technological advances in the last 10 years. Ask them to make a time line showing when these advances took place. Display the time lines in the classroom. Discuss with students how these technological advances have caused changes in families.

L2 Writing
Have students identify situations involving family change. Ask them to write letters to an advice column expressing concern over one example they choose and asking how they should handle the change. Collect the letters and redistribute them so that each student gets someone else's letter. Have students write responses to the letters. Again collect the letters and discuss the questions and responses with the class.

TEACHER TALK!

Handling Sensitive Issues
Point out to students that a common problem that arises out of divorce or family separation is guilt. Children often feel guilty because they hold the erroneous belief that they are responsible for the divorce or separation. Students who have such feelings should be encouraged to discuss those feelings with their parents or a counselor.

▲ Changes may result in your having to take on new roles and responsibilities at home. What roles do you have within your family?

Changing Family Roles

When Justin's father remarried, Justin was surprised at how many changes took place in his family. His stepmother brought her two young children to live with Justin and his father. Now Justin has found himself in a new role—as an older brother and sometimes as a babysitter.

Maria's family also has had changes in roles. Maria's mother has a new job in the city, and she often works in the evening. Now Maria must take care of her younger sister after school and make dinner for the family.

Both Justin and Maria have learned to accept their changing roles. They discovered that when someone in their family was adjusting to a new situation, they could help out.

Changes Within the Family

Sometimes changes occur in the structure of your family. Family members may be born or adopted. Older brothers or sisters may move out of the home.

LESSON THREE: CHANGES WITHIN FAMILIES   125

COOPERATIVE LEARNING

Extending the Welcome Mat Organize the students into small groups. Have a moderator in each group lead a discussion about the changes a person experiences when moving to another community. Then ask the groups to develop guidelines to help students in their school make new students feel welcome. When each group has finished its guidelines, have the groups come together to read and discuss the ideas. Have students choose three of the best ideas, and have a representative from the class present the ideas to members of the Student Council.

CHAPTER 5, LESSON 3

L2 Speculating
Ask students to predict the kinds of changes they can expect when they go to high school. Have them give suggestions of steps they can take to adjust to these changes. You might invite a high-school student to explain the changes she or he experienced and to give any suggestions she or he has for coping with the changes.

L1 Applying Concepts
Have students identify a stressful situation that happened to them personally or to a friend. Ask them to explain why it was stressful. Have them consider whether it was positive or negative stress. Then ask them to identify tips from the lesson that could have helped them deal with this stressful situation.

DID YOU KNOW ?
According to a recent survey, most teenagers in today's schools think housework should be shared by both sexes. A majority of the males and females surveyed felt that food shopping, meal preparation, dish washing, housecleaning, and laundry should be shared. Females were in favor of shared household tasks in larger percentages than males.

Other changes are the result of separation and divorce. Families must learn to accept changes, even painful ones. After a divorce, one or both parents may remarry. This causes more changes. New stepbrothers or stepsisters may join the family.

One of the most difficult changes for a family to deal with is the death of one of its members. People find it hard to accept that a part of the family is gone. They sometimes feel guilty about what they did not say or do when the person was alive. These reactions are normal. Everyone in the family can support and comfort one another. Some families seek professional counseling to help them deal with the loss of a family member.

Changes Outside the Family

Some changes are the result of the economy. A job may be lost and the family has less money to spend. The increase in the number of women working outside the home has changed people's ideas about the roles of men and women. Men are helping more often with child rearing. Social issues, such as poverty, child or spouse abuse, and substance abuse, affect everyone.

Today both parents in many households work outside the home.

126   CHAPTER 5: YOUR FAMILY AND FRIENDS

MORE ABOUT • • •

Family Changes Point out to students that with the increase in the number of two-income families, there is an increase in the need for time off from work to tend to the needs of dependents. In response to this need, Congress passed the Family and Medical Leave Act, which went into effect in August 1993. Under this law, any employer with more than 50 employees is required to give his or her employees (both male and female), who need to care for a new baby, an adopted child, or a sick child up to 12 weeks of unpaid leave. An employee can also get a leave to care for an ill adult family member or for the employee's own illness. Afterward, the employee is entitled to return to the same or an equivalent job.

Adjusting to Change

Not all changes are sad, of course. Getting your own bedroom and making a new friend are examples of happy changes. No matter what changes occur in your life, though, you will have to adjust to them. Here are some positive ways to accept change.

- **Plan ahead.** If you know about the change in advance, prepare for it even if you do not want it to happen. For example, if you are transferring to a new school, you can find out about the school before your first day.
- **Talk about your feelings.** Your family and friends can be a great source of strength and encouragement. Teachers, school counselors, coaches, religious leaders, and family service agency workers can also help you understand and handle the new situation.
- **Discover something positive about the change.** Remember that changes are part of life and they will help you grow. It does not help to keep thinking about what is wrong or different. What can you learn from the experience?
- **Be supportive.** When your family faces changes, you can help just by being there. If your brother is nervous about going to a new high school, point out his strengths and help him to manage his weaknesses. If something goes wrong for the family, do not waste time and energy blaming or finding fault. Be patient and understanding. Listen and help one another.

Understanding Stress

When change occurs in your life, you may experience stress. **Stress** is *the body's reaction to changes around it.* Both pleasant and unpleasant events cause stress. For example, performing a solo in a school concert may be stressful even though you enjoy singing. Whatever the situation, remember that stress is a natural part of life.

Many teens would find this situation stressful. How would you cope with this kind of stress?

LESSON THREE: CHANGES WITHIN FAMILIES **127**

CHAPTER 5, LESSON 3

L2 Applying Knowledge
Have students write questions anonymously regarding family changes and stress. (Emphasize to students that they may use fictional changes and stresses and that they should feel free to keep personal information to themselves.) Place the questions in a box. Allow classmates to offer solutions to the problems and situations. Reinforce how to adapt to family changes and cope with stress.

L2 Categorizing
Have students work in groups to list examples of stress. Write responses on the board. Then have each group categorize its examples as positive stress and negative stress. Share each group's responses with the class. Discuss students' categories.

L1 Using Transparencies
Present Color Transparency 24, "Managing Stress," in the TCR. Use this overhead visual to reinforce concepts from this lesson.

MEETING STUDENT DIVERSITY

Cultural Perspectives In the United States, people tend to be constantly in a rush to get from one place to another. People are expected to be punctual. Being late is considered rude and inconsiderate. This emphasis on punctuality can cause negative stress. Other cultures have a more relaxed attitude toward time. In some cultures punctuality is not as important as stopping to talk to a friend. Ask students to discuss the advantages and disadvantages of expecting people to be punctual.

CHAPTER 5, LESSON 3

Try This!

After students have read the feature on page 129, have them share their exercise plans with the class. Ask students to keep a record of their exercise each day for a week, recording the type and length of exercise and how they felt after exercising. Discuss the results with the class.

USING VISUALS

Have students study the tips for handling stress shown in Figure 5.3. Encourage them to develop a program on managing stress and present the program to the class.

L1 Student Workbook
Assign Activities 33 and 34 in the Student Workbook.

ASSESS

Evaluating the Lesson
Assign Reviewing Terms and Facts and Thinking Critically on page 129 to review the lesson; then assign the Lesson 3 Quiz in the TCR.

Reteaching
- Have students list five suggestions that will help in managing stress.
- Have students complete Reteaching Activity 5 in the TCR.
- Assign Concept Map 7 in the TCR.

Effects of Stress

How much stress you feel depends on how much change there is in your life and how you see the event. For instance, adjusting to a new school and making new friends would be somewhat stressful to most people. To a person who has never changed schools before and feels scared, it would be more stressful. If the person is handling another major life change at the same time, such as the parents' separation, the stress would be even greater.

Stress can also motivate and challenge you. It can help you accomplish your goals in life. The stress of wanting to make

Figure 5.3 Managing Stress
Some techniques for managing stress are shown here. What other techniques can you think of?

128   CHAPTER 5: YOUR FAMILY AND FRIENDS

COOPERATIVE LEARNING

No More Excuses Discuss with students whether they ever feel they cannot exercise because they lack the right athletic shoes, clothing, or exercise equipment. Remind them that they don't need these expensive items to get exercise and relieve the effects of stress. Simple walking or running shoes and some old shorts or sweats are all they need to be comfortable while working out. Have students work in groups to brainstorm excuses for not exercising regularly. Have them work together to write song lyrics or jingles that offer positive alternatives to the excuses.

the soccer team, for example, would motivate you to exercise and practice.

Constant stress, however, can have a negative effect on a person. It can cause depression and a lack of physical or mental energy. People who are unable to **cope,** or *adjust to a difficult situation,* may become unhappy, depressed, or seriously ill. Sometimes they try to run away from their problems by turning to alcohol or other drugs.

Coping with Stress

Learning to cope with stress in a positive way is important to your health and well-being. **Figure 5.3** shows some ways to manage stressful situations.

Try This!
Researchers believe that exercise changes body chemicals that affect the brain, resulting in a feeling of well-being. Keeping the benefits of exercise in mind, choose a sport or physical activity that you enjoy. Then develop an exercise plan.

Living with Change

During your teen years, you will probably experience many changes in your life. Although you will not be able to control all of these changes, viewing them as challenges and opportunities to learn and to develop new skills may help you to avoid negative stress and keep a positive outlook.

LESSON THREE Review

Using complete sentences, answer the following questions on a separate sheet of paper.

Reviewing Terms and Facts
1. **Vocabulary** Define the term *life changes.* Use it in an original sentence.
2. **Give Examples** What are three examples of changes that can occur within the family?
3. **Identify** List four ways in which you can adjust to changes.
4. **Recall** What are three ways to manage stress?

Thinking Critically
5. **Analyze** In what ways can you benefit from changes?
6. **Explain** Why might two people experience different amounts of stress from the same event?

Applying Concepts
7. Imagine that a friend's parents are getting a divorce. Write a letter to the friend, offering support and making suggestions on how he or she might cope with the change.

LESSON THREE: CHANGES WITHIN FAMILIES   129

COOPERATIVE LEARNING

Healthful Ways to Relax Organize students into small groups. Have each group brainstorm healthful ways to relax to relieve stress. Groups should make lists of all suggestions and then review their lists for the best four ideas. Ask each group to make a poster of their ideas. Have them title their posters "Healthful Ways to Relax." Students should then illustrate each of the four suggestions, and explain the benefits of each suggestion in a caption. Display posters in the classroom or around the school so that other students may benefit from these illustrated relaxation tips.

CHAPTER 5, LESSON 3

Answers to Lesson 3 Review

1. Major ways your life is changed by events that you may or may not be able to control. Possible sentence: Life changes can bring about a new way of life.
2. Any three: Family members may be born or adopted. A grandparent or relative may come to live with you. Older brothers and sisters may move out of the home. Parents may separate or divorce. Parents may remarry. New stepbrothers or stepsisters may join the family. A family member may die.
3. Plan ahead, talk about your feelings, discover something positive about change, be supportive.
4. Any three: Gather a support system, set priorities, realize that you are not alone, practice good health habits, keep a positive attitude.
5. Changes give you opportunities to learn new skills, avoid negative stress, and keep a positive outlook.
6. The amount of stress people experience depends on how people see the event and on whether or not a person is handling another major life change at the same time.
7. Answers will vary. Student letters should offer support and suggestions for helping a friend cope with his or her parents' divorce.

Enrichment

Have students develop a scenario of a major change in a family and the steps the family took to cope.

CLOSE

Ask students to write a sentence explaining the following statement: "The only thing that stays the same is change."

129

LESSON FOUR
Developing Friendships

FOCUS

Lesson Objectives
After studying this lesson, students should be able to
- explain what it means to be a friend.
- discuss the qualities of a friend.
- explain why friendships may change.

Motivating Activity
Ask students to list 15 people they know other than family members.

Introducing the Lesson
Have students reread their responses to the Motivating Activity. Then ask them to consider how many of these people they think of as friends. Ask them to review their lists and explain that they will be learning about their relationships with others. Tell them that this lesson will describe the skills needed to make and keep friends.

Introducing *Words to Know*
Ask students to read the vocabulary list to themselves. Explain that all these words refer to people they come in contact with. Explain that "acquaintance" refers to a relationship less intimate than friendship. The root word *acquaint* means "to become informed or aware about something, but not with a detailed knowledge of particulars."

LESSON FOUR
Developing Friendships

WORDS TO KNOW

acquaintance

peers

peer groups

expectations

DISCOVER...
- what it means to be a friend.
- the qualities of a friend.
- why friendships may change.

Who are your friends? Are they people you can talk to about your secrets and ambitions? Are they other teens who also like to go to the movies? Are they your teammates or the people in your science club? Can you really define your friends in such simple terms? You probably can't. Friends may be all those things, but they are also much more.

What Is a Friend?

A friend is someone you like and who likes you. It is someone you can talk to. A friend is a person who shares similar

130   CHAPTER 5: YOUR FAMILY AND FRIENDS

CLASSROOM RESOURCES FOR LESSON 4

Blackline Masters
Activity and Project Card 9, "Friendship Chain"
Lesson 4 Quiz
Peer Pressure and Decision Making 10

Transparencies
Transparency 25, "To Have a Friend, Be a Friend"

Student Workbook
Activities 35, 36

interests, goals, or values with you. For instance, you may enjoy collecting stamps or working on the computer with your friend. Perhaps you study with your friend. You and your friend may have the same career goal of becoming a lawyer or a fire fighter. The important quality you have in common is that you care about one another's lives.

How Do Friendships Begin?

Friendships begin and develop when people meet and like each other. You do not automatically have a friend just because you meet someone. Some people are only acquaintances. An **acquaintance** is *a person you greet or meet fairly often but do not have a close relationship with.* It may be a neighbor, the librarian at school, or the bus driver.

Friendships usually develop from the acquaintances that you have. They are formed with people you are interested in knowing better. They grow into true and lasting friendships as people learn more about one another.

Give and Take

Good friendships are based on a give-and-take relationship. No two people are alike in what they give to you as a friend or in the benefits they receive from you. Some people may just be casual friends. You may enjoy their company at school or play street hockey with them in your neighborhood. Others may become close friends whom you know very well and in whom you confide. Almost all friends learn from each other. They have something to offer one another. Some of the ways that friends share and contribute to each other's lives are by

- giving companionship and happiness.
- sharing good times.
- demonstrating a feeling of acceptance.

As people get to know each other better, they often develop lasting friendships. How did you meet your friends?

COOPERATIVE LEARNING

Healthful Group Activities Organize the class into three groups. Have each group brainstorm healthful activities to do with several friends in the home, school, or community. For example, a group might suggest playing a board game or organizing a game of basketball at home. Have the groups choose one of their ideas and design an advertisement of their idea in the form of a billboard. The advertisements should stress the idea of healthful activities. Display the billboards in the hallways at school.

CHAPTER 5, LESSON 4

TEACH

L2 Writing
Write on the board one example of an "icebreaker," such as: "Hi! How did you like the game last night?" Have students write at least five statements or questions that make good icebreakers for meeting people. Ask students to share their statements or questions.

L2 Activity and Project Card
Allow time for students to complete Activity and Project Card 9, "Friendship Chain," in the TCR.

L2 Problem Solving
Assign Peer Pressure and Decision Making 10 in the TCR. This activity gives students the opportunity to recognize peer pressure and practice decision-making skills.

DID YOU KNOW

The American Quakers of 1679 refused to use titles when addressing one another, so they simply called each other Friend. About 100 years later they became known as the Religious Society of Friends. They have no formal creed, rites, liturgy, or priesthood, and reject violence in human relations, including war.

L1 Using Transparencies
Present Color Transparency 25, "To Have a Friend, Be a Friend," in the TCR. Use this overhead visual to reinforce concepts from this lesson.

CHAPTER 5, LESSON 4

L2 Illustrating
Have students work with partners to make illustrations depicting items in the bulleted list in the text of ways friends share and contribute to each other. Display the pictures in the classroom.

L3 History
Have students read biographies of famous people in history, such as Thomas Jefferson or Jane Addams, to find out who their friends were and what qualities their friends had. Ask students to report their findings to the class. If computers are available, encourage students to research CD-ROM encyclopedias for their reports.

L2 Hands-on Project
Assign Hands-on Project 3 in the TCR. Students create a decorative framed message about friendship in this activity.

TEACHER TALK!

Handling Sensitive Issues

Sometimes young people have difficulty expressing sympathy to a friend who has lost a parent or sibling. You might suggest appropriate statements that students can offer their friends at such a difficult time. Also point out to students that people who experience grief need to talk to their friends about their feelings.

- depending on each other to listen when they need to talk about their problems.
- offering help when it is needed.
- being loyal to one another.

What are some other ways that friends show that they care about each other?

Making New Friends

Beginning a new friendship is not always easy, but you can be successful if you make the effort. Everyone has to make new friends at times. Old friends may move away, or friendships may change as you grow and develop new interests. For example, you may want a new buddy to go swimming with or a person who shares your love of crafts. Making new friends is a skill that you can learn.

As you go through life, you will have many opportunities to develop new friendships. Some may begin easily. Others take more effort, and you may need to keep trying. However, not all the friendships will work out. The person with whom you hoped to be friends may be too busy or have different interests. With experience you will recognize what friendships are worth pursuing.

What Makes a Friend?

When friendships are formed, they are based on caring, sharing, and good communication. These qualities, along with trust and reliability, help to strengthen friendships. They show others that you want to be a good friend. However, in order to have friends, you cannot be on the receiving end all the time. You have to be willing to contribute something. Listening to your friend and offering your help when it is needed are signs of a good friend. For instance, have you ever helped

As you develop new interests, you will want to make new friends who share those interests. What interests do you have in common with your friends?

132 CHAPTER 5: YOUR FAMILY AND FRIENDS

MEETING STUDENT DIVERSITY

Physically Challenged Discuss with students—or ask physically challenged students in the class to moderate a discussion on—the special needs of people with physical challenges in the area of making and keeping friends. Students with physical challenges may have limitations that prevent participation in some of the activities common among members of their age group. Have students investigate efforts at school and in the community to include students with physical challenges in organized activities.

Your peer group can be a major influence on the way you feel about yourself. Why are peer groups important?

a friend practice for baseball tryouts or finish chores so that you both could go to the movies? Doing your part when working with others and praising your friends when they do well are also ways to show that you are a good friend.

Being Part of a Group

During adolescence, most teens seek approval from their peers. **Peers** are *people of the same age as you.* Your peers' acceptance and recognition help you develop a sense of belonging. Acceptance by your peers strengthens your self-esteem.

Most teens strive to become part of a peer group. **Peer groups** are *groups of people of the same age.* Your peer group helps to fill your need for companionship and support. Within the group, you practice skills that can be used in other groups throughout your life.

Changes in Friendships

Your friendships will probably change over the years. Some of your friends may move away or transfer to different schools. Some of your friends may have new responsibilities

Skills IN ACTION

Making New Friends

Here are some suggestions for making new friends.
- **Be friendly.** Don't be afraid to smile and greet other people.
- **Take an interest in others.** Ask questions. Listen to what the other person has to say.
- **Enjoy yourself.** Your happiness will be contagious.

With your classmates, brainstorm a list of ways to meet people and make new friends.

LESSON FOUR: DEVELOPING FRIENDSHIPS

CHAPTER 5, LESSON 4

L1 Music
Have students listen to songs about friendships, such as "You've Got a Friend" or "That's What Friends Are For." Ask them to determine the message of the music. Ask them to work in groups to compile lists of more songs about friendship.

L2 Writing
Ask students to write a short story about a friendship that has changed. The story should include an explanation of the reasons for changes in the friendship. The story could be fiction or nonfiction. Have students share stories.

L2 Charting
Have students make a chart showing changes in their friendships over time. Have them name their best friend in kindergarten, second grade, fourth grade, and sixth grade. Next to each name, students should explain how their friendship with this person has changed, noting reasons for the changes. Charts may be created using appropriate computer software if available.

Skills IN ACTION

On the board, write the following reasons why young people make and keep friends: similar interests, similar values, personal qualities, same school or neighborhood. Have students discuss which category seems to be the most important reason for choosing friends.

MORE ABOUT • • •

Friendships A key to having lasting friendships is allowing the friend to maintain his or her own identity. Tell students that they should not expect to make their friend be just like them or have the exact same interests. They should not expect perfection in their friend. Instead, they should learn to enjoy their friend's uniqueness and ignore minor faults. Have students consider how they are different from their best friend.

CHAPTER 5, LESSON 4

Try This!

Encourage students to follow through with one or more of the suggestions in the feature on page 135. Point out that they can use the suggestions to strengthen their friendships with people they see on a regular basis as well as those who live far away.

L1 Student Workbook

Assign Activities 35 and 36 in the Student Workbook.

ASSESS

Evaluating the Lesson

Assign Reviewing Terms and Facts and Thinking Critically on page 135 to review the lesson; then assign the Lesson 4 Quiz in the TCR.

Reteaching

- Ask students to write a paragraph explaining the difference between an acquaintance and a friend. Have students complete
- Reteaching Activity 5 in the TCR.

Enrichment

Have students make caricature sketches showing how they met a friend and what they enjoy doing together.

134

---

after school. Friendships may also change, as you and your friends discover new interests and activities.

The important point to remember about changes in friendships is that you can grow and learn from them. You may not have chosen the changes, but you can use them to understand more about yourself and others.

Differences in Expectations

Has there ever been a time when a friend let you down? Some changes in friendships are due to changing expectations. **Expectations** are *a person's ideas of what should be or should happen.*

A common expectation in friendships is to have and to be a best friend. Best friends expect to be able to confide in and trust each other and share common interests. Changes in friendships may occur when someone who was your best friend develops different interests and no longer shares as much with you. Perhaps a new friend, someone you enjoyed being with

Friendships can change if one friend develops new interests. What are some other reasons why friendships change?

134   CHAPTER 5: YOUR FAMILY AND FRIENDS

MORE ABOUT • • •

Interpersonal Skills Keep in mind that the diversity of the classroom is representative of the diversity in the world. Skills that students learn in school will help them in their future, in higher education, and in job situations. Getting along with others includes a sensitivity to people with disabilities and diverse cultural backgrounds. Include a discussion of how behavior toward others will have an influence on relationships that can affect a person's success. Remind students that developing interpersonal skills can be an important part of their education.

at summer camp, expects to become your best friend. During the early teen years, changes in best friends are common, as young people learn what to expect from certain friends and what their friends expect from them.

Expectations in friendships between boys and girls also change often during the teen years. Sometimes a boy and girl who have just been friends develop a boyfriend-girlfriend relationship. This usually means that they have special caring feelings for one another. Problems may arise when one friend expects more from the relationship than the other friend wants to give.

The Importance of Friendships

Friendships help you grow and learn more about yourself and other people. Sometimes, people form a childhood friendship that lasts a lifetime. More often they make new friends as they move to high school and beyond. As you expand your circle of friends, you will discover new ways to interact with others.

Try This!

If you or a friend must move away, it doesn't mean you have to stop being friends.
- Write a friendly letter. Ask questions that will encourage your friend to write back.
- Send greeting cards on special occasions. Make your own cards for a more personal touch.
- Make an audiotape or a videotape. Your friend will enjoy hearing your voice and seeing how you look.

LESSON FOUR Review

Using complete sentences, answer the following questions on a separate sheet of paper.

Reviewing Terms and Facts
1. **Recall** How do friendships begin and develop?
2. **List** Name four ways in which friends share and contribute to one another's lives.
3. **Vocabulary** Define the term *peer group*. Use it in an original sentence.
4. **Identify** What are some benefits of being part of a peer group?

Thinking Critically
5. **Contrast** What is the difference between an acquaintance and a friend?
6. **Evaluate** Which qualities are the most important ones in your friendships?
7. **Analyze** In what ways can you benefit from changes in friendships?

Applying Concepts
8. Make a collection of cartoons, quotations, captions, and articles about friendship. Put them in a scrapbook or file. Create your own poem, saying, or cartoon about friendship, and add it to the file.

LESSON FOUR: DEVELOPING FRIENDSHIPS

CHAPTER 5, LESSON 4

Answers to Lesson 4 Review

1. When people meet and like each other.
2. Any four: giving companionship and happiness, sharing good times, giving a feeling of acceptance, depending on one another, offering help, being loyal to one another.
3. Groups of people of the same age. Possible sentence: I have many good friends in my peer group.
4. Fills your need for companionship and support, allows you to practice skills that can be used throughout your life.
5. An acquaintance is someone you greet or meet fairly often, but do not have a close relationship with. A friend is someone you do have a close relationship with.
6. Answers will vary. Students will list the qualities that are most important in their friendships, such as caring, sharing, good communication, trust, and reliability.
7. Answers will vary. Possible answer: You can grow and learn from changes.
8. Students should compile cartoons, quotations, captions, and articles about friendship in a scrapbook. They should also write their own poem, quotation, or cartoon about friendship to add to the scrapbook.

CLOSE

Ask students to write a sentence that interprets the following verse: "Make new friends, but keep the old. One is silver, the other is gold."

HOME AND COMMUNITY CONNECTION

Using Positive Peer Pressure Encourage students to develop a project that enlists the support of peers through positive pressure to perform an act that will benefit the community at large. Possible projects include assisting senior citizens on routine shopping trips, teaching younger students soccer skills, or holding a fund-raiser for a community cause. Have students work individually or with partners to brainstorm other ideas for the project. Ideas may then be presented for the class to decide upon one project to follow through on.

LESSON FIVE
Peers and Decision Making

FOCUS

Lesson Objectives
After studying this lesson, students should be able to
- differentiate between the positive and negative influences of peer pressure.
- identify ways to handle peer pressure.
- describe how to be assertive.

Motivating Activity
Have students brainstorm various kinds of pressure. *(cabin pressure, barometric pressure, blood pressure, parental pressure, peer pressure)* Ask them to write their responses.

Introducing the Lesson
Have students share their responses to the Motivating Activity. Then discuss how a person feels when these kinds of pressures are exerted on her or him. Tell students that this lesson discusses some of the positive and negative pressures exerted on them by their friends and other people they know.

Introducing *Words to Know*
Ask volunteers to read the definition of *addiction*. Explain that "addiction" is often followed by "to" plus a noun. The Latin root is *addictus*, meaning "give over (as a slave)." Ask students to identify addictions other than drugs. *(Answers may include the following: alcohol, tobacco, gambling, overeating, overworking, overexercising, overspending.)*

LESSON FIVE
Peers and Decision Making

WORDS TO KNOW

peer pressure
popularity
addiction
assertive

DISCOVER...
- the positive and negative influences of peer pressure.
- ways to handle peer pressure.
- how to be assertive.

Everyone wants to be accepted and liked by peers. In many situations, the desire to belong to a peer group is a positive influence. There are times, however, when peers can be a negative influence in your life. Learning to recognize the differences between these types of influences will help you decide whether to go along with the group or act as an individual.

136   CHAPTER 5: YOUR FAMILY AND FRIENDS

CLASSROOM RESOURCES FOR LESSON 5

 Blackline Masters
Cooperative Learning 9
Cross Curriculum 5
Lesson 5 Quiz
Peer Pressure and Decision Making 11

 Transparencies
Transparency 26, "Peer Pressure"

 Student Workbook
Activities 37, 38

The Influence of Peers

Having good friends and being part of a peer group can be a positive influence in your life. Their attitudes toward school, sports, or after-school activities can encourage you to do your best. The support and confidence peers give you can help you gain confidence. At times, your peers may expect you to join in their actions and activities or adopt their beliefs. **Peer pressure** is *the influence you feel to go along with the behavior and beliefs of your peers.*

Positive Peer Pressure

The acceptance and recognition of your peers help you feel good about yourself. A peer group can give you a sense of belonging and strengthen your self-esteem. A peer group can give you support and encourage positive behavior. Suppose that you were competing in a tennis match. Wouldn't you feel good knowing that your friends were there cheering you on? You would feel confident and want to do your best. This type of peer pressure is a positive force.

Negative Peer Pressure

Sometimes peer pressure is a negative force. Some groups make outsiders feel uncomfortable, unpopular, or unwanted. It may be difficult for you to go against the wishes of your

Try This!

Recognizing peer pressure is the first step in deciding how to deal with it. With a partner, decide whether the following situations represent positive or negative peer pressure.
• Your friends urge you to run for student council president.
• A popular classmate wants to copy your math homework.
• Your friends tease you about getting good grades.

How have you used positive peer pressure to encourage your friends?

MORE ABOUT • • •

Factors That Influence Decisions Peer pressure is not the only factor that helps people make decisions. Other factors include self-esteem; resources—money, time, and materials; and values. Ask students to give examples of situations in which they made decisions based on factors other than peer pressure. Have them identify the factor that influenced their decision. Point out that some decisions may be influenced by several factors.

CHAPTER 5, LESSON 5

TEACH

Try This!

Have students determine whether the situations described in the feature represent positive or negative peer pressure by answering the following questions:
Did the peer pressure inspire you to improve your health or appearance?
Did the peer pressure challenge you to work hard?
Did the peer pressure encourage you to do your best?
Did the peer pressure get you to do something worthwhile?
Would you be proud to tell your parents about the situation?
Point out to students that if they answered yes to any of the questions, then the situation probably represents positive peer pressure.

L2 Cooperative Learning
Assign Cooperative Learning Activity 9, "New Student Information Sheet," in the TCR.

L2 Comparing
Have students find magazine and newspaper articles about young people who acted in response to peer pressure. Ask them to categorize the peer pressure in each article as positive or negative pressure. Have them explain their reasoning.

L2 Problem Solving
Assign Peer Pressure and Decision Making 11 in the TCR. This activity gives students the opportunity to recognize peer pressure and practice decision-making skills.

137

CHAPTER 5, LESSON 5

L2 Role-Playing

Write the following assertiveness tips on the board:
Be firm; mean what you say.
Speak calmly.
Look your peers in the eye when you speak.
Don't give in.
Offer alternatives to the negative idea.

Then have students draw pictures of the following scenarios, adding thought bubbles that contain appropriate assertiveness tips for each illustration:
Your friends want to skip school to go to the mall.
You are at a party and your friends decide to make prank phone calls to strangers.
Your friend forgot to do her homework and asks to copy yours.

L2 Science Connection

Assign Cross-Curriculum Activity 5 in the TCR. Students learn the importance of deciding against the use of harmful substances in this activity.

L3 Math

Have students research the latest statistics on mortality rates of adolescents over the past 45 years. Statistics can be found in *The American Almanac: Statistical Abstract of the United States.* Students should use their findings to make a line graph. Ask students to explain the trend shown on the graph. *(Since 1960 the mortality rate among adolescents has risen.)* Then ask students what role negative peer pressure may play in this trend toward using harmful substances. Computer resources may be used for this activity.

---

peers—for instance, to be friendly to someone the group has excluded. If one member of a group is critical or has a bad attitude, it may influence the entire group.

Another negative kind of peer pressure is when you feel pushed to participate in activities that go against your values. Maybe you have been faced with making a choice about skipping school, smoking, drinking alcohol, or doing something else that you think is wrong or know is dangerous or illegal.

Making Responsible Decisions

Eventually, most teens are faced with decisions about following the group or following their own conscience. When this happens, they need to ask: Are the wishes of a few people more important than what they believe is right? If they did something only because of peer pressure, would they regret it later?

Avoiding Harmful Substances

Everyone wants to be liked and accepted, but some people feel that gaining **popularity,** or *the state of being well liked,* is essential. Some people think that they can become popular by smoking cigarettes or using alcohol or other drugs. They may do these things to impress friends or because their friends have coaxed or dared them to take part. It is important to learn to use refusal skills (see page 57) when you feel pressured to engage in activities that you believe are wrong.

If you are faced with negative peer pressure, sometimes it is best just to say no and walk away.

138 CHAPTER 5: YOUR FAMILY AND FRIENDS

HOME AND COMMUNITY CONNECTION

Dealing with Negative Peer Pressure Invite a spokesperson from a local hot line to speak to the class about phone calls he or she has received from students who feel negative pressure from peers to engage in high-risk activities. Ask the spokesperson to give the students advice on how to handle situations that involve negative peer pressure. Have students prepare, in advance, written explanations of situations they face that involve negative peer pressure. Have the spokesperson address these situations. Ask students to develop a schoolwide campaign to combat negative peer pressure.

TIPS for living

HANDLING PEER PRESSURE

Here are some ways to deal with negative peer pressure.

- **Think ahead.** Decide in advance what you will do if certain situations arise. You might even practice what you will say and do.
- **Practice refusal skills.** If your friends suggest that you do something that is wrong or against your values, use your refusal skills.
- **Suggest other activities.** Think of things to do that are fun, healthy, safe, and legal. Let your friends know that you would like to be with them, but not if it means doing something that goes against your values.
- **Choose your friends carefully.** Develop friendships with peers who share your values and interests.
- **Talk to parents and counselors.** Let them know if you're having problems. They can give you the support and encouragement you need to resist giving in.

If you have ever thought about trying alcohol or other drugs, think again about the reasons why. Consider carefully the long-term effects of such a decision. Using alcohol and other drugs does not make a person popular, build up self-confidence, or solve problems. What alcohol and other drugs can do is trap a person. These harmful substances slow down the ability to act and think normally, and they weaken the ability to make sound decisions.

Many people who try tobacco, alcohol, or other drugs soon find themselves addicted. **Addiction** is *a person's physical or mental need for a drug or other substance.* Many people die each year from alcohol and drug abuse.

Avoiding High-Risk Behavior

Certain kinds of negative peer pressure cause more than just regrets. Accepting a ride from someone who has been drinking alcohol can result in injury or death from a serious accident. Sexual involvement can result in pregnancy or can have harmful, even life-threatening, results in the form of AIDS (acquired immunodeficiency syndrome) and other sexually transmitted diseases. Responsible people avoid such risks, knowing that a healthy future is at stake.

LESSON FIVE: PEERS AND DECISION MAKING   139

MORE ABOUT...

Harmful Effects of Smoking How popular is it to be sick? Studies show that cigarette smoking is a health hazard that can lead to cancer, stroke, and heart and lung disease. Smoking also stains teeth and fingers, causes gum disease and bad breath, dulls the senses of taste and smell, decreases athletic ability, and costs money. Have students role-play a situation in which they use positive peer pressure to help a friend stop smoking.

CHAPTER 5, LESSON 5

TIPS for living

Have students work in small groups and role-play how they would handle peer pressure in the following situations. Tell students to use one of the tips suggested in "Tips for Living."

"You have to try smoking cigarettes. It looks so cool, and everyone is doing it."

"When I run out of money, I just shoplift what I want. Come on, I'll show you how it's done."

"Let's invite the new kid to have lunch with us. He's such a dork. We can make fun of him."

L1 Student Workbook

Assign Activities 37 and 38 in the Student Workbook.

ASSESS

Evaluating the Lesson

Assign Reviewing Terms and Facts and Thinking Critically on page 140 to review the lesson; then assign the Lesson 5 Quiz in the TCR.

Reteaching

- Organize the class into small groups. Have students in each group create a poster titled "Positive Influences of Peers." The posters should illustrate ways that peers can be a positive influence.
- Have students complete Reteaching Activity 5 in the TCR.

CHAPTER 5, LESSON 5

Answers to Lesson 5 Review

1. Gives you a sense of belonging and helps strengthen your self-esteem.
2. You will be liked and accepted more for your individual qualities than for what you do or wear to impress others, and it will improve your self-esteem.
3. The body's physical or mental need for a drug or other substance.
4. Any three: explains their needs and opinions clearly; speaks in a confident manner; does not give in to others; stands up for what he or she believes in; makes suggestions for activities.
5. Answers will vary. Possible response: Teens are still learning about who they are. They are more unsure of their values and beliefs than adults.
6. Answers will vary.
7. Answers will vary. Students should explain which way of saying no worked best in their role-play situation.

Enrichment

Have students read articles about the effects of smoking, drinking, or using drugs. Ask them to use information from the article to create an advertisement that uses positive peer pressure to urge against using these harmful substances.

L1 Using Transparencies

Present Color Transparency 26, "Peer Pressure," in the TCR. Use this overhead visual to reinforce concepts from this lesson.

CLOSE

Discuss with students how a strong self-concept and an understanding of their values can help them handle peer pressure responsibly.

140

The next time you and your friends are looking for something to do, practice being assertive by suggesting a fun, healthy activity. What other ways can you think of to be assertive?

Being Assertive

You will be better prepared to handle negative peer pressure if you learn how to use refusal skills and to act assertively. Being **assertive** means *standing up for yourself in firm but positive ways*. Assertiveness means speaking in a confident manner, not giving in to others when you feel something is wrong, and standing up for what you believe in. Assertive teens don't wait for someone else to decide what the group is going to do. They are the ones who suggest going in-line skating, renting a video, or playing a computer game. Learning how to act assertively will make you feel more in control of your life.

LESSON FIVE Review

Using complete sentences, answer the following questions on a separate sheet of paper.

Reviewing Terms and Facts

1. **Recall** Name an advantage of being part of a peer group.
2. **Explain** Why is it important to be yourself, no matter who your friends are?
3. **Vocabulary** Define the term *addiction*.
4. **Identify** List three qualities of an assertive person.

Thinking Critically

5. **Analyze** Why do you think that peer pressure is more common among teens than among adults?

6. **Evaluate** Do you consider yourself to be assertive? Why or why not?

Applying Concepts

7. With a classmate, role-play a situation involving negative peer pressure. One of you should act as the person who uses negative peer pressure, and the other should act as the person who resists the pressure. Use the refusal skills you learned in Chapter 3, Lesson 1. Then switch roles and try a different way of saying no. Which way worked best? Why?

140   CHAPTER 5: YOUR FAMILY AND FRIENDS

MORE ABOUT • • •

Friendships and Responsible Decisions Tell students that in order to develop a strong self-concept and an understanding of values, a person needs to spend time alone to get to know what his or her likes and dislikes are. Point out to students that one way to do this is to make room in their busy schedule for something they enjoy doing by themselves. Having a strong sense of who they are will give them the strength to stand up to negative peer pressure even if they are the only ones to do so.

LESSON SIX
Resolving Conflicts

DISCOVER...
- reasons why conflicts occur.
- ways to prevent conflicts.
- how conflicts can be resolved.

Do you get along with everyone all of the time? If you are like most people, your answer is probably no. In fact, you might even find that lately you are getting into more arguments than you did when you were younger. That's because you are developing more opinions and beliefs that are your own. Learning how to handle these differences in a positive way is an important part of becoming an adult.

WORDS TO KNOW
conflict
prejudice
compromise
negotiation
peer mediation

LESSON SIX: RESOLVING CONFLICTS 141

CLASSROOM RESOURCES FOR LESSON 6

Blackline Masters
Activity and Project Card 10, "What Causes Conflict?"
Concept Map 8
Cooperative Learning 10
Lesson 6 Quiz
Peer Pressure and Decision Making 12
Reteaching 5

Transparencies
Transparency 27, "Peer Mediation"

 Student Workbook
Activities 39, 40

LESSON SIX
Resolving Conflicts

FOCUS

Lesson Objectives
After studying this lesson, students should be able to
- identify reasons why conflicts occur.
- give examples of ways to prevent conflicts.
- explain how conflicts can be resolved.

Motivating Activity
Write the following on the board: *Civil War, World War I, a fist fight, a verbal argument.* Ask them to identify what these four things have in common.

Introducing the Lesson
Ask volunteers to give their response to the Motivating Activity. *(examples of conflicts)* Point out that although the Civil War and World War I were more encompassing than the other two examples of conflict, all conflicts are detrimental to people. Tell students that this lesson explains ways to avoid and resolve conflicts.

Introducing *Words to Know*
Have volunteers read the vocabulary words and terms and their definitions. Ask students to identify the word that is a cause of conflicts. *(prejudice)* Explain that the word *prejudice* comes from the Latin word *praejudicium,* meaning "previous judgment." Then have students identify the words or terms that describe ways of resolving conflicts. Explain that the prefix "com" in *compromise* means "together."

141

CHAPTER 5, LESSON 6

TEACH

L1 Ranking
Refer students to the causes of conflicts listed in the lesson. Have students write the causes on a sheet of paper. Ask them to determine which cause is the one most likely to create conflict for people their age. Have them rank that cause as "1" and then rank the remaining causes in decreasing order of occurrence. Compare students' rankings. Discuss reasons for the rankings.

L2 Activity and Project Card
Allow time for students to complete Activity and Project Card 10, "What Causes Conflict?" in the TCR.

L2 Problem Solving
Assign Peer Pressure and Decision Making 12 in the TCR. This activity gives students the opportunity to recognize peer pressure and practice decision-making skills.

L2 Discussing
Ask students to describe a conflict they recently had. Have them identify the cause of the conflict, how the conflict could have been prevented, and how the conflict was resolved. Have students discuss alternative resolutions to the conflict.

What Are Conflicts?

A **conflict** is *any struggle, disagreement, or fight.* Conflicts can occur just about anywhere, and everyone experiences them at one time or another. You have probably had disagreements with both friends and family members. Conflicts don't just occur between individuals, though. They also happen on a large scale, such as when two countries disagree and go to war.

Causes of Conflicts

Think about the last time that you had a disagreement. Can you remember the cause? Maybe you felt that someone wasn't respecting your feelings. Perhaps you and the other person wanted two different things. Then again, maybe you wanted the same thing. Here are some reasons why conflicts occur.

- **Misunderstandings.** Arguments often occur when people don't communicate effectively. Sometimes one person doesn't take the time to listen closely to what the other person is saying.

- **Differing Beliefs or Opinions.** You have your own beliefs and opinions about a wide range of topics. If someone put down your favorite football team, for example, you might take that remark as an attack on you personally. You might feel a need to defend yourself.

- **Gossip and Teasing.** When people gossip about or tease someone, they usually hurt that person's feelings and may start a conflict. For instance, if a group of peers started teasing your best friend about his braces, your friend would probably feel hurt and angry. You might feel angry, too.

- **Jealousy.** When one person wants something that someone else has, a disagreement may occur. If you and a friend both tried out for the lead in the school play and your friend got the part, you might have a conflict.

- **Prejudice.** Some conflicts are caused by **prejudice** (PRE-juh-dis), *an opinion about people that is formed*

When two people want the same thing, they may have a disagreement. How would you handle this situation?

142   CHAPTER 5: YOUR FAMILY AND FRIENDS

HOME AND COMMUNITY CONNECTION

Resolving Conflicts Through Mediation Have students research situations in which real-life conflicts have been resolved through mediation. Ask them to work in small groups to find examples of such situations in their local school, community, or in the news. Examples might include: local land-use issues such as a new shopping center being built in a vacant lot. Ask students to investigate how mediation was used to resolve each conflict. Also, have each group speculate what might have happened in each situation if the conflict had not been resolved by mediation. Students might summarize their findings in writing and share them with the rest of the class.

without facts or knowledge about those people. Prejudice causes people to judge others without taking the time to get to know them. Prejudice often leads to heated arguments and angry clashes.

Preventing Conflicts

You can prevent some conflicts by heading off problems before they even start. The best way to do this is to pay attention to your own behavior. How do you treat others? Why do you say or do certain things? By exploring your actions, you may find that there are some qualities you can improve in yourself. For example, you might work on accepting other people as they are, even if they are different from you, and try looking at situations from their point of view.

Learning to control your anger is another important way to prevent conflicts. Controlling anger is not always easy and takes a great deal of practice. When you feel yourself getting angry, you can try one or more of the following.

- Take a deep breath and count to ten.
- Go for a walk or a bike ride.
- Take a few minutes to have a "talk" with yourself. Remind yourself of the reasons why you don't want to act angry.
- Think about why you are feeling angry.

Ways to Resolve Conflicts

If you do find yourself in a conflict, how do you handle it? Your heart may start to pound. You may have the urge to turn and run—or to leap in and fight. These are all very emotional reactions, and they are quite natural. They will not solve your problems, however.

Resolving a conflict means that you and the other person work out your differences in a way that satisfies both of you. To resolve a disagreement, you and the other person must

If you are angry, try doing something physical, such as exercising. What are some other ways to cool off?

CHAPTER 5, LESSON 6

TEACHER TALK!

Arguing Fairly
Tell students that sometimes arguments can't be prevented. Encourage them to keep their arguments fair by following these rules:
- Focus on the behavior, not the personality.
- Don't bring up past hurt or anger.
- Listen to the other person's side without interrupting.
- Don't use name-calling or insults.

L2 Creating a Brochure
Have students work in pairs to create a brochure that explains and illustrates ways of resolving conflicts. Students should incorporate the information from Lesson 6 in their brochures. Have them share their brochures with their classmates. If computers are available, encourage students to design brochures using word-processing or other appropriate software.

L2 Cooperative Learning
Assign Cooperative Learning Activity 10, "Play a Role," in the TCR.

MEETING STUDENT DIVERSITY

Cultural Perspectives Tolerance is the ability to accept other people as they are. Learning about the cultures and traditions of people from different races, religions, and ethnic groups promotes acceptance. Tolerance helps prevent conflict caused by prejudice. Have students identify events in school or the community that promote learning about other cultures. Ask them to share their findings with the class.

CHAPTER 5, LESSON 6

DID YOU KNOW

Resolving conflict through peer mediation provides several positive benefits. It increases students' self-esteem. Students respond to peer mediators because they feel they understand the situation. Students feel they have an active role in decision-making in the community.

L2 Applying Knowledge

Tell students that compromise is known as a win-win situation—in other words, when a compromise is achieved, both parties have agreed to a solution that satisfies them. Have students write a conversation between a young person and his or her parent in which a compromise is achieved. Provide students with the following situation: You want to go to the movies, but you have homework to do.

Have students make a set of compromise cards. They can use the situations described in "Skills in Action" as ideas for their cards. Have students describe the conflict situation on one side of a card. For the other side of the card, have them come up with a compromise idea for the situation.

144

---

work as a team. Instead of thinking of the situation as the two of you against each other, think of it as the two of you against the problem.

Communication

The first step in conflict resolution is to open the lines of communication. Choose a neutral location that is quiet and free of groups of people. You and the other person must both be willing to listen to each other and to explain your own point of view.

You should explain how you feel and how you see the problem. When you are talking, try not to start sentences with the word *you*. The other person might feel attacked and stop listening. Start sentences with the word *I* instead. See the "Skills in Action" feature in Lesson 1 of this chapter for more about "I" messages. Express your point of view as clearly as possible. Try to stay calm, and avoid using an angry tone of voice.

When you are talking, you want the other person to listen. You should do the same. When you listen, look directly at the speaker. Don't interrupt. If you have questions, save them for when the other person has finished. It is helpful if you sum up the other person's point of view to make sure that you understand it.

As you know, body language is another important part of communication. The way you look at a person, the way you stand, and the way you move your hands and arms all communicate your feelings to others. You want your body language to show the same feelings as your words.

Even if you are not involved in a disagreement yourself, you can help other people solve a problem through communication. Instead of taking sides in an argument or a fight, try to get the people involved to talk out their problems. Giving friends this kind of support will help them see that they don't have to fight to impress anyone.

Compromise

Resolving a conflict often means that the people involved must reach a compromise. A **compromise** (KAHM-pruh-myz)

Learning to Compromise

The ability to compromise is a skill that will help you in every relationship. Think of a situation in your life that calls for a compromise. Write a paragraph describing how you could work out an agreement with the other person.

144   CHAPTER 5: YOUR FAMILY AND FRIENDS

COOPERATIVE LEARNING

Advertising the Message Organize students into groups to make infomercials about conflict resolution. Have students in each group create a conflict situation. Have them use the information about resolving conflicts in the lesson as the basis for their infomercial. Arrange time for students to put together and practice the infomercial. Have the groups present their infomercial to the class. Hold a class discussion to evaluate each group's work. If possible, videotape the presentation to share with other classes.

is *an agreement in which each person gives up something in order to reach a solution that satisfies everyone.*

Negotiation is one of the best ways to compromise. **Negotiation** (ni-GOH-shee-AY-shuhn) is *the process of talking about a conflict and deciding how to reach a compromise.* This requires a lot of give and take, in which both people give up some demands and make promises.

For negotiation to work, both sides must be willing to stop asking for certain things or at least change their demands. For instance, Rachel gets angry when her younger brother, Mark, borrows her CDs without asking. Mark, however, cannot always ask because she is at basketball practice when he has time to listen to them. Perhaps Rachel could agree to let him borrow certain CDs when she is not home. In return, Mark could let her borrow his handheld electronic game without asking, when she wants to play it after he has gone to bed.

When you are negotiating you must also make sure that you can follow through with your promises. If you agree to behave differently, you must actually do so. Otherwise, your agreement might crumble. For example, if you have agreed to stop teasing a friend about her haircut and she has agreed to stop teasing you about your clothes, you must both keep your promises.

Sometimes compromises can best be reached with the help of a third person who is not involved in the conflict. This person may be a parent, teacher, school counselor, or other

Try This!

The idea behind peer mediation programs is that students often feel more comfortable discussing their differences in front of someone their own age rather than an adult. Find out more about peer mediation by asking the following questions:
- What training do mediators get?
- What kinds of situations are best handled by peer mediation?
- What are some typical rules for mediation sessions?

A specially trained peer mediator can work with teens to resolve a conflict. What personal qualities do you think that a peer mediator should have?

CHAPTER 5, LESSON 6

Try This!

Have students ask a school administrator or counselor the questions listed. If your school does not have a peer mediation program, have interested students ask a school administrator about starting a program.

L1 Student Workbook
Assign Activities 39 and 40 in the Student Workbook.

ASSESS

Evaluating the Lesson
Assign Reviewing Terms and Facts and Thinking Critically on page 146 to review the lesson; then assign the Lesson 6 Quiz in the TCR.

Reteaching
- Have students make a poster illustrating rules for conflict resolution.
- Have students complete Reteaching Activity 5 in the TCR.
- Assign Concept Map 8 in the TCR.

Enrichment
Have students learn more about peer mediation. If their school has a peer mediation program, direct students to talk to the peer mediators about the types of conflicts they help resolve, the methods they use, and the training they receive.

MORE ABOUT • • •

Peer Mediation Programs NAME, the National Association for Mediation in Education, is a support network and materials clearinghouse for educators wanting to help others develop conflict resolution skills. The organization works with individuals and groups around the country, helping them learn about conflict resolution. It publishes books, makes training videos, puts out a newsletter, and helps people network and set up peer mediation programs. For more information about the organization or for help in setting up a peer mediation program in your school, contact NAME, 1726 M Street NW, Suite 500, Washington, D.C. 20036. (202) 466-4764.

CHAPTER 5, LESSON 6

Answers to Lesson 6 Review

1. Misunderstandings, differing beliefs or opinions, gossip and teasing, jealousy, prejudice.
2. An opinion about people that is formed without having facts or knowledge of those people. Possible sentence: Prejudice is a result of people forming opinions about people before getting to know them.
3. You and the other person work out your differences in a way that satisfies both of you.
4. A compromise is an agreement in which each person gives up something in order to reach a solution that satisfies everyone. Negotiation is the process of talking about a conflict and deciding how to reach a compromise.
5. Specially trained students help other students find a solution to a problem.
6. Answers will vary. Students may respond that close friends can have misunderstandings, differences in beliefs or opinions, and jealous feelings toward each other.
7. Answers will vary. Students give an example of a situation in which they had to negotiate.
8. Answers will vary.

L1 Using Transparencies

Present Color Transparency 27, "Peer Mediation," in the TCR. Use this overhead visual to reinforce concepts from this lesson.

CLOSE

Ask students to discuss the importance of patience. Ask students to cite examples of when their patience helped them avoid a conflict.

146

When you need help solving a problem, it is best to seek advice from an adult. Whom would you ask for help with a problem?

adult. Sometimes this third person is a peer. **Peer mediation** is *a process by which specially trained students help other students find a solution to a problem.* A peer mediator does not take sides in the conflict.

Avoiding Conflicts

Let's say that you have tried everything. You have made every effort to head off problems before they spark conflicts. You have tried to resolve problems through communication, negotiation, and compromise. Still, a conflict is growing to a dangerous point. You are at school and a classmate is bullying you. What do you do? Sometimes, as hard as it may be, the best response is to walk away. In such situations it is helpful to seek out an adult at school or at home to talk to. You can't solve every problem alone. No one can. What is important is that you do your best to behave in a way that reflects your values.

LESSON SIX Review

Using complete sentences, answer the following questions on a separate sheet of paper.

Reviewing Terms and Facts

1. **Identify** List five causes of conflicts.
2. **Vocabulary** Define the term *prejudice*. Use it in an original sentence.
3. **Explain** What does it mean to resolve a conflict?
4. **Vocabulary** What is the difference between *compromise* and *negotiation*?
5. **Describe** How can peer mediation be used to solve a problem?

Thinking Critically

6. **Analyze** Why might close friends have conflicts?
7. **Interpret** Give an example of one situation in which you had to negotiate.

Applying Concepts

8. In small groups, discuss a book or a story you have read in which two characters had a conflict. How did they solve the problem? Could they have benefited from the help of a peer mediator?

146 CHAPTER 5: YOUR FAMILY AND FRIENDS

MEETING STUDENT DIVERSITY

Varied Learning Styles If you have students who experience language difficulties or take an inordinately long time to complete a lesson, you might use one or more of the following strategies:
- Permit such students to make use of a buddy system. Allow students' individual strengths to complement each other by having students work in pairs and trios.
- Have such students focus on the section headings. The headings in this program are designed to "telegraph" information to the student about the topic. Such information may prove invaluable to students with a limited grasp of the language.

Chapter 5 Activities

TECHNOLOGY
The New Post Office

Writing letters has once again become fashionable. Many people stay in touch with friends through electronic mail, or E-mail. A computer and a phone line are all they need. They can send messages through the Internet, and their friends can receive them in seconds.

Try This!
Find out more about E-mail and the Internet. If possible, interview someone who uses them. Write a short report on your findings.

Consumer Focus

"I Just Have to Have..."

Did you ever buy shoes or another clothing item just to be like other teens your age? Wanting to follow fads is a normal part of adolescence.

The next time you want to buy something, however, think about whether it's right for you.

Try This!
Make a list of any items you bought simply to fit in with your peers. Analyze if they were right for *you*.

FRIENDS & FAMILY

SHARING A ROOM

Matt shares a bedroom with his brother, Josh. Over the last week they have been constantly arguing. Josh never finishes his homework early enough for Matt to have time to listen to music before going to bed. Matt's light bothers Josh when he is trying to sleep.

TRY THIS!
List three possible solutions for the problem that are fair for both Matt and Josh.

LITERATURE CONNECTION

MAMA IS A SUNRISE

When she comes slip-footing through the door,
she kindles us
like lump coal lighted,
and we wake up glowing.
She puts a spark even in Papa's eyes
and turns out all our darkness.

Evelyn Tooley Hunt

Follow Up

Reading literature can give you words to describe your feelings about the people closest to you.

Find another poem or a song about families or friends. It might describe how you feel about a relationship. It might describe relationships in an entertaining or a thought-provoking way. You could even try writing your own poem or song lyrics. Read your poem or lyrics to a small group of your classmates and explain what it means to you.

CHAPTER 5 ACTIVITIES 147

Teaching the LITERATURE CONNECTION

Discuss the poem line by line with students. Ask them to identify the adjectives, adverbs, metaphors, and similes used in the poem to describe Mama. Discuss how these words and phrases describe the relationship Mama has with her family. Have students illustrate the poem. Display the illustrations in the classroom.

Follow Up — Answers to Follow-Up

The poet compares Mama to a sunrise. Mama is an upbeat person, full of love and warmth for her family. Mama gives the rest of the family hope and reassurance that all is well. The poet loves her mother. Students' poems or song lyrics will vary.

CHAPTER 5 Activities

TECHNOLOGY

Explain to students that various forums and discussion groups also meet on the Internet to share thoughts on subjects such as sports, movies, books, and computers. Point out that there are pen pal services for those who want to communicate with people from other parts of the world.

Consumer Focus

As students read the article, point out that there can be problems with buying items just to be like everyone else. Remind them that some styles may not suit everyone. Have students consider that the item may be something they really cannot afford. Have students take these problems into consideration as they compile their lists.

FRIENDS & FAMILY

Discuss with students some possible solutions to the problems Matt is having because he shares a room. Have students suggest what Matt could do to cooperate. *(He might agree to do part of his homework at the kitchen table. He might get a small reading light so that he won't bother his brother.)*

CHAPTER 5 REVIEW

Checking Comprehension

Use the Chapter Summary and the Chapter 5 Review to help students go over the most important ideas in Chapter 5.

Answers to Words to Know

1. Safe and protected.
2. Thoughtful.
3. One or two parents and children as well as other relatives, such as grandparents or aunts and uncles.
4. Answers will vary. Students should give an example of a tradition, such as celebrations, foods, or religious beliefs.
5. Answers will vary. Students give two examples of life changes.
6. Adjust, handle, deal with.
7. The body has a physical or mental need for a drug or other substance.
8. Explain your needs and opinions clearly while respecting the needs and opinions of others.
9. Struggle, disagreement, or fight.

Answers to Review Questions

1. Relationships help you meet your social and emotional needs and feel accepted and liked by others.
2. Any example: being courteous, using good manners, waiting your turn, being fair, lending a hand, giving in a little sometimes.

CHAPTER 5 REVIEW

Chapter Summary

- Relationships, the bonds you form with others, give you a sense of belonging, security, and self-esteem.
- A successful relationship depends on communication, cooperation, trust, and consideration.
- There are many types of families. Examples include nuclear, single-parent, blended, and extended families.
- An important part of family life is learning to get along with family members.
- Change is a part of life. Changes occur in family roles and structure.
- Stress is the emotional and physical tension caused by change. Learning to manage stress is an important life skill.
- A friend is someone who shares your interests, goals, and values. An acquaintance is someone you see fairly often but do not know very well.
- Building and maintaining friendships means forming a give-and-take relationship. Friendships can change over time.
- Peer pressure can be either positive or negative. Being assertive and standing up for what you believe in will help you resist negative peer pressure.
- Conflicts in relationships occur for many reasons, including misunderstandings, differing beliefs or opinions, gossip and teasing, jealousy, and prejudice.
- Learning how to prevent or resolve conflicts peacefully is an important part of becoming an adult.

Words to Know

Using complete sentences, answer the following questions on a separate sheet of paper.

1. How do you feel when you have a sense of *security*?
2. What does it mean to be *considerate*?
3. Describe an *extended family*.
4. Give an example of a *tradition*.
5. Give two examples of *life changes*.
6. What are some words that mean the same as *cope*?
7. What does it mean to have an *addiction*?
8. If you practice *assertiveness* when confronted with negative peer pressure, what do you do?
9. What is meant by *conflicts* in a relationship?

Review Questions

Using complete sentences, answer the following questions on a separate sheet of paper.

1. Why are relationships important?
2. Give an example of a way to show cooperation.
3. In what ways are families different? In what ways are they alike?

148   CHAPTER 5: YOUR FAMILY AND FRIENDS

EXTRA CREDIT PROJECT

Class Project Have volunteers work together to create and promote a class celebration called "Appreciation Day." The purpose of the celebration is to let students express their appreciation of their family and friends. Have students design cards with illustrations and messages to give to friends and family members. If cameras are available to students have them take pictures of people in relationships (friends, siblings, parents/children). These pictures can be used to help illustrate the cards or to help illustrate advertisements for "Appreciation Day."

CHAPTER 5 REVIEW

4. Why is it important to learn to adjust to life changes?
5. How can stress be both positive and negative?
6. How can you be a good friend?
7. Explain how peer pressure can be either positive or negative.
8. How can you prevent some conflicts from occurring?
9. What is the first step to take in resolving a conflict?

Thinking Critically

Using complete sentences, answer the following questions on a separate sheet of paper.

1. **Analyze** Which do you think is the most important relationship skill: communication, cooperation, trust, or consideration? Explain your choice.
2. **Analyze** Why do you think that some teens use negative peer pressure on others?
3. **Suggest** What are some ways a teen could cope with a move to a new school or to a new community?
4. **Recommend** What do you think is the best way to deal with a conflict?

Cooperative Learning

1. As a class, make a friendship quilt. Each person should decorate a sheet of paper. Include your name and a drawing that reflects something about you, such as a hobby, pet, or favorite activity. Tape all of the sheets together, and hang the quilt on a bulletin board.
2. Read a short story. Think about the relationship between the main character and one of the other characters. Are these two people relatives, friends, or acquaintances? Did any changes occur in the relationship? Discuss your ideas about the story in small groups.

Family & Community

1. Gather information about clubs or organizations for teens in your community. Find out about activities and meeting times. Choose and join a group that interests you. Encourage your friends to go with you, or use the group to make new friends.
2. Make a poster that shows one way to prevent or resolve conflicts. If possible, display the poster in your school or community.

 Building A Portfolio

1. Paste a photograph of your family at the top of a piece of paper, or draw a picture of your family. Underneath the picture, write a description of your family. Include names and ages of family members and information about each person's skills and talents. Describe an activity you like to do together. Keep your family portrait in your portfolio.
2. Make a time line to show the major changes that have happened to you over the years. Choose one of your life changes. Write one or more paragraphs describing how the change affected your life, how you coped with the change, and what you might have done differently. Place your time line and your description in your portfolio.

CHAPTER 5 REVIEW 149

CHAPTER 5 REVIEW

3. Each family is different because families are made up of people who have different skills, talents, and possessions. Families also have different ways of expressing themselves and their affection. Families have different traditions. Families are alike because the members care about each other and are committed to each other. Usually the members live together and are related.
4. It is important to learn to adjust to life changes in order to manage stressful situations and make your life happier.
5. Some stress can affect health in harmful ways. Positive stress can motivate and challenge you.
6. You can be a good friend to someone else by sharing and contributing to your friend.
7. Positive—gives you a sense of acceptance and belonging, strengthens your self-esteem, gives you support, and encourages positive behavior. Negative—you may feel pressured to do something that goes against your values.
8. You can prevent some conflicts from occurring by heading off problems before they even start and learning to control your anger.
9. The first step in resolving a conflict is to open the lines of communication.

Evaluate

Use the Chapter 5 Test in the TCR, or construct your own test using the Testmaker Software.

CLOSE

Have students apply their knowledge of the chapter's content by completing one of the alternative assessment activities listed under Family and Community or Building a Portfolio.

Answers to Thinking Critically

1. Answers will vary. Students should explain which of the following relationship skills is most important: communication, cooperation, trust, or consideration.
2. Answers will vary. Students may note that some teens use negative peer pressure to manipulate others to get what they want.
3. Find out about the school ahead of time. Talk about their feelings. Discover something positive about the change. Be supportive of their family.
4. You and the other person must work together as a team to solve the problem.

149

Planning Guide
Chapter 6 Understanding and Caring for Children

LESSON 1	Pages	FEATURES	CLASSROOM RESOURCES
Parenting Skills	152–157	Skills in Action: Making Friends Tips for Living: Helping Children Become Independent	Lesson 1 Quiz Peer Pressure and Decision Making 13 Transparency 28, "Parenting: Meeting Children's Needs" Student Workbook Activity 41
LESSON 2 **Ages and Stages**	158–164	Skills in Action: Guiding Preschoolers Tips for Living: Sparking a Child's Imagination	Activity and Project Card 11, "Be an Author" Concept Map 9 Cooperative Learning 11 Lesson 2 Quiz Transparency 29, "Patterns of Children's Development" Student Workbook Activities 42, 43
LESSON 3 **Child's Play**	165–170	Skills in Action: Selecting Toys Tips for Living: Teaching Children to Share	Cooperative Learning 12 Cross Curriculum 6 Enrichment 6 Lesson 3 Quiz Transparency 30, "Choosing Toys for Children" Student Workbook Activities 44, 45
LESSON 4 **Child Safety**	171–175	Tips for Living: Playground Safety Try This: Safety Tips	Concept Map 10 Cross Curriculum 7 Lesson 4 Quiz Student Workbook Activity 46

LESSON 5	Pages	FEATURES	CLASSROOM RESOURCES
Caring for Children	176–182	*Tips for Living: Handling Emergencies* *Skills in Action: Treasure Chest*	Activity and Project Card 12, "Calling All Babysitters" Enrichment 7 Lesson 5 Quiz Peer Pressure and Decision Making 14 Student Workbook Activities 47, 48

CHAPTER 6 RESOURCES

- Chapter 6 Test
- Reteaching 6
- Study Guide 6, *Reteaching*
- Testmaker Software

Performance Assessment Activity

Tell students they will stage a TV talk show on the subject of Parenting and Children. The show will have five 20-minute segments—one corresponding to each of the lesson headings. Organize students into five groups and assign each group one of the lesson headings. Tell them they should work as a group to outline their segment. They should decide among themselves who should perform specific tasks such as writing; contacting guest hosts and speakers; preparing graphics such as charts, graphs, and other visuals; presenting; and selecting music. Students might even plan several commercials aimed at parents and other caregivers. If possible, have students present their programs at a PTA meeting.

OUT OF TIME?

If time does not permit thorough teaching of this chapter, you may wish to use:

- *Teens Making a Difference*, page 151
- *Tips for Living*, pages 156, 163, 169, 173, 180
- *Try This*, page 174
- *Skills in Action*, pages 155, 162, 166, 181
- *Young Living Activities*, page 183
- *Chapter Summary*, page 184

Resources for the Teacher

Gonzalez-Mena, Janet. *Infants, Toddlers, and Caregivers.* Mountain View, CA: Mayfield Publishers, 1993.

Stoppard, Miriam. *Complete Baby and Child Care.* New York: Dorling Kindersley, Inc., 1995.

Readings for the Student

Burgeson, Nancy. *The Baby-Sitter's Guide.* Mahwah, NJ: Troll Associates, 1991.

Stuhring, Celeste. *Kid Sitter Basics: A Handbook for Babysitters.* Kansas City, MO: Westport Publishers, Inc., 1994.

Multimedia Resources

The Baby-Safe Home: Don't Let Your Child Become a Victim. (VHS Video). Nelson Entertainment, Inc.

Baby-Sitting Basics. (VHS Video). Marshfilm Enterprises, Inc.

Babysitting the Responsible Way. (VHS Video, Manual). Cambridge Career Products.

CHAPTER 6
Understanding and Caring for Children

Chapter Overview

Chapter 6 examines how good parenting skills can help students respond and interact positively with children. This chapter emphasizes the skills and understandings students need to become good caregivers.

LESSON 1 describes the differences between parenting and parenthood and the role of a caregiver.

LESSON 2 explains the developmental tasks of infants, toddlers, and preschoolers.

LESSON 3 explores the importance of child's play.

LESSON 4 identifies guidelines for keeping children safe.

LESSON 5 focuses on child-care skills.

Introducing the Chapter

Write one of the following titles on each of five pieces of poster board:
- Parenting is . . .
- Children are . . .
- Playtime for children . . .
- Children's safety . . .
- Babysitting is like . . .

As students come into the room, have them write their comments on the posters. Tell them that Chapter 6 addresses these topics.

Chapter Motivator

Write the following on the chalkboard: "What It Means to Be a Parent." Ask students to write a paragraph on this theme. You might suggest that students skim the lesson titles and the photographs in the chapter to get some ideas. Call on volunteers to read them to the class.

CHAPTER 6
Understanding and Caring for Children

LESSON ONE
Parenting Skills

LESSON TWO
Ages and Stages

LESSON THREE
Child's Play

LESSON FOUR
Child Safety

LESSON FIVE
Caring for Children

KEY TO ABILITY LEVELS

Teaching strategies that appear throughout the chapter have been identified by one of three codes to give you an idea of their suitability for students of varying learning styles and abilities.

L1 Level 1 strategies should be within the ability range of all students. Often full class participation is required. Teacher direction is usually needed.

L2 Level 2 strategies are for average to above-average students or for small groups. Some teacher direction is necessary.

L3 Level 3 strategies are designed for students able and willing to work independently. Minimal teacher direction is necessary.

TEENS MAKING A DIFFERENCE
Friendship Matters

Two years ago, as a sixth grader, Ricky Rodriguez decided to participate in a cross-age peer mentoring program. Once a week the mentors spent an hour with elementary school children who needed one-on-one attention.

Ricky was paired with Josh, a shy and withdrawn first grader. Soon Ricky's visits became the highlight of Josh's week. In fact, Josh asked if Ricky could be his mentor again the next year.

The second year there was a noticeable difference in Josh. His schoolwork improved and he was more outgoing. Because of his experience with Josh, Ricky is thinking about becoming a teacher or a social worker.

Try THIS!

Do you know any younger children who look up to you? Write a paragraph or two describing how you can be a good role model to them.

CHAPTER 6

TEENS MAKING A DIFFERENCE

Have students read "Friendship Matters." Discuss with students how friendship mattered to Josh. *(Students might indicate that the fact that Ricky became Josh's friend helped to make Josh feel better about himself, thereby helping to make him more confident and outgoing.)*

Ask students to answer the questions at the end of the feature. Call on volunteers to relate how being looked up to by a younger child made them feel.

BLOCK SCHEDULING

The following Teacher Classroom Resources are suggested for use in classrooms with Block Scheduling.
- Activity and Project Card 11, "Be an Author"
- Activity and Project Card 12, "Calling All Babysitters"
- Cooperative Learning 11, "Create a Storybook"
- Cooperative Learning 12, "Linda's Birthday Party"

TECHNOLOGY IN THE CLASSROOM

Films You will find a variety of subjects on film for use in the Family and Consumer Sciences classroom. Films are especially useful for showing events in sequence that in reality have considerable time lapses, such as the developmental levels of children. Films also provide students with a common experience on which to base discussion about interpersonal relationships. Educational films are available from a variety of sources. Professional organizations, universities, nonprofit associations, and your local school district often lend, rent, or sell films. As with other audiovisual materials, unfamiliar films should always be previewed before they are shown to the class.

LESSON ONE
Parenting Skills

FOCUS

Lesson Objectives
After studying this lesson, students should be able to
- differentiate between parenthood and parenting.
- describe the commitment involved in becoming a parent.
- explain how parenting skills can help them respond and interact positively with children.

Motivating Activity
Bring to class an assortment of magazines. Ask students to find a picture that depicts the word *parenting*. Have students write answers to the following questions: How is parenting depicted in the picture you selected? What do you think of when you hear the word *parenting*? Do you think the person in the picture is the child's parent? What qualities or skills does a good parent have?

Introducing the Lesson
Call on volunteers to share their responses to the Motivating Activity as you write their responses on the chalkboard. Leave the responses on the chalkboard for use with the "Close" Activity. Then ask students if they think there is a difference between parenthood and parenting. Tell them that this lesson explains that difference and describes the qualities or skills necessary for parenting.

Introducing *Words to Know*
Ask students to look at the Words to Know. Ask them if all parents are caregivers. Then ask if the reverse is true.

LESSON ONE
Parenting Skills

 **WORDS TO KNOW**

caregiver
parenthood
parenting
guidance
discipline
punishment
child abuse
consistent

DISCOVER...
- the difference between parenthood and parenting.
- the commitment involved in becoming a parent.
- how parenting skills can help you interact positively with children.

Do you remember who taught you to ride a bike, tie your shoes, or tell time? Was it your mother, father, grandmother, grandfather, brother, or sister? You can probably think of many people who have taught you what you know today. These people have been your caregivers. A **caregiver** is *a person who takes care of a child or a sick or elderly person.* A caregiver can be a relative, babysitter, teacher, child care worker, nurse, or neighbor. Who are the caregivers who have had a major influence in your life?

152   CHAPTER 6: UNDERSTANDING AND CARING FOR CHILDREN

CLASSROOM RESOURCES FOR LESSON 1

 Blackline Masters
Lesson 1 Quiz
Peer Pressure and Decision Making 13

 Transparencies
Transparency 28, "Parenting: Meeting Children's Needs"

 Student Workbook
Activity 41

Parenthood—A Lifelong Commitment

If you were asked to apply for a job that required a lifelong commitment, 24-hour duty, and some extra benefits, how would you respond? That job description fits **parenthood,** or *the function of being a parent.* Parenthood is a major decision and a lifelong commitment. It takes love, patience, guidance, and financial resources to be an effective parent.

Parents are the primary caregivers. They are responsible for providing a safe, loving, and stimulating environment for their children. They must fulfill a child's physical needs as well as provide emotional support. Can you see why this is a 24-hour job?

Many new parents are surprised to find how demanding parenthood can be in terms of time, energy, and money. Parents often have to make adjustments or give up their personal desires in order to provide for their children. For example, parents may have to give up traveling if their children are in school.

Parenthood can bring many joys, however. The special relationship that develops between a parent and child is a fulfilling and enriching experience. All over the world parents claim that parenthood brings them special extra benefits such as happiness, love, and pride.

Responsible Parenting

Parents and other caregivers need to use good parenting skills. **Parenting** is *the process of caring for children and helping them to grow and learn.* This process can be very rewarding, but it also takes a lot of hard work.

Do you use parenting skills? Perhaps you help care for a younger brother or sister, or

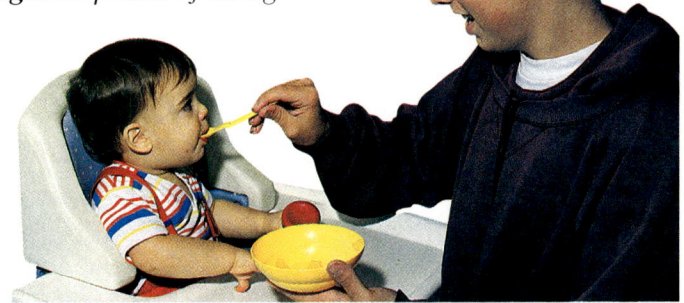

Babysitting or caring for a younger sibling requires parenting skills. How can you improve your parenting skills?

LESSON ONE: PARENTING SKILLS   153

MORE ABOUT • • •

Nurturing The most important attribute of good caregivers is a nurturing disposition—a feeling of warmth and caring toward other people. Caregivers can show their concern for the welfare of children through affection, kindness, and care. In addition to nurturing attitudes and behavior, caregivers need patience, consistency, trust, respect, interest, courage, confidentiality, motivation, enthusiasm, empathy, and strength of character. Ask students to describe how caregivers in their lives have displayed these characteristics.

CHAPTER 6, LESSON 1

TEACH

L1 Creating a Chart
Create a chart on the chalkboard with "Children's Needs" as the major heading and four columns labeled "Physical," "Social," "Emotional," and "Intellectual." Have students work in small groups to give examples of each. Then ask each group to give their responses as you add them to the chart on the chalkboard. If computers are available in the classroom, allow students to make their charts using the computer, and print them out for class discussion.

L1 Role-Playing
To emphasize the point that parenting is a 24-hour-a-day job, have students role-play being a parent for one 24-hour period. Using an item such as a five-pound sack of flour, ask them to "care for it" as they would an infant. Remind students that within this 24-hour period they must "feed, change diapers, and care for" the "infant" as they would a real infant. Tell them to set a timer to go off every 20 minutes for a whole day. Each time the timer goes off, the students should stop what they're doing and care for the "baby" for five minutes. Also, remind students that they cannot leave the infant alone if it is in their care. Have volunteers report their experiences in class.

L2 Comparing
Have students take part in a simulation called "You Be the Child." Have them use the "wrong" hand to use a thick crayon to draw a picture of the place where they live. Have students sit on the floor, using their chairs as work tables. Also, have students work in pairs to feed each other applesauce. When students have completed their simulations, have them write a paragraph describing their experiences.

153

CHAPTER 6, LESSON 1

TEACHER TALK!

Shaken Baby Syndrome

Five studies conducted between 1982 and 1990 noted that 25 to 50 percent of teenagers and adults did not know that shaking a baby is dangerous. Point out to students that persistent crying by an infant can sometimes be irritating and frightening. Emphasize, however, that at no time should they shake the infant in an attempt to stop its crying. Infants can be easily injured when shaken. Because infants' neck muscles are not strong enough to control head movements, rapid movement of the infant's head can result in the brain being bruised from banging against the wall of the skull. The injuries may include seizures, partial or total blindness, paralysis, mental retardation, or death.

L2 Problem Solving

Assign Peer Pressure and Decision Making 13 in the TCR. This activity gives students the opportunity to recognize peer pressure and practice decision-making skills.

---

maybe you babysit for children in your neighborhood. You can improve your parenting skills by watching your parents, by taking a child development class, and by reading this chapter and other books on the topic. The more you know about children, the more comfortable you will be with them. You will find that the way you handle children affects the way they behave and their friendliness toward you.

Responding to Children's Needs

Young children, just like everyone, have physical, emotional, social, and intellectual needs that must be met. While you are caring for, playing with, and teaching children, it is up to you to fulfill these needs.

- **Physical Needs.** All children have basic physical needs. They need healthful food, appropriate clothing, good hygiene, rest and sleep, and a safe and stimulating environment. Babies and young children indicate their needs by crying. Crying is their way of telling you they are hungry, wet, tired, frightened, ill, or unhappy. As children become older and their language skills increase, they are better able to use words or sentences to communicate their needs.

Playing with children helps to improve their intellectual skills. What are some other ways to meet children's intellectual needs?

- **Intellectual Needs.** Children have intellectual needs, too. They need a stimulating environment, language activities, and opportunities to explore. Reading books, playing with puzzles and blocks, and selecting toys of different shapes and sizes helps to develop children's intellectual abilities.

- **Emotional and Social Needs.** Children also need to have their emotional and

154   CHAPTER 6: UNDERSTANDING AND CARING FOR CHILDREN

COOPERATIVE LEARNING

Positive Parenting Have students work in pairs to create skits about positive parenting. Have one student role-play a preschooler and the other student role-play a caregiver. Skits should include the caregiver making negative statements to the preschooler. Have the class watch each pair's skit and take notes about all the negative statements the caregiver made. Then discuss the negative statements and as a class change the negative statements to positive statements. Present skits to the PTA or another interested community group if possible.

social needs met. They need to be held, cuddled, and comforted. Sometimes a kiss, hug, or gentle pat is all children need to be reassured that someone cares. Children are very sensitive to your feelings about them. Be warm and friendly with them. Speak kindly to them. They can tell by the way you touch, hold, or talk to them that they are loved.

Providing Guidance

Caregivers need to give children **guidance,** or *direction.* That is how children learn basic rules for behavior. These rules help children stay safe, learn self-control, and learn to get along with others.

Discipline is *the task of teaching a child which behavior is acceptable and which is not.* Children need guidance in learning appropriate behavior, and as they are learning they may use inappropriate behavior. **Punishment** is *a way of discouraging inappropriate behavior.* Some forms of punishment may be effective in helping a child learn self-control; others may not. *Physical or emotional mistreatment of a child* is called **child abuse.**

When guiding children, it is important to be **consistent,** which means *reacting the same way to the same situation each time it occurs.* It also means that you follow through and do what you say you will do. For example, if you say that you will take away a toy the next time a child throws it, you should do so. When you are consistent, children know what to expect.

In addition to being consistent, avoid making false threats. For example, telling a child that you will leave her at home alone if she misbehaves is a false threat, because you know that it would be unsafe to leave the child at home without supervision.

Communicating Positively

Children, like adults, respond better to positive statements than to negative ones. Keep your sentences simple. For instance, say "Let's play outside for awhile" instead of "Don't play in the living room." Emphasize what the children are allowed to do rather than what they should not do. You may also need to explain why. "Try to climb on the jungle gym this way, so you won't fall and get hurt."

Making Friends

Here are some tips to help children feel comfortable with you.
- When talking to children, sit or kneel so that you are at their eye level.
- Be patient—don't jump in to finish their sentences.
- Ask children how you can join in their play. "How about if I be the mailman who delivers mail to your store?"

LESSON ONE: PARENTING SKILLS **155**

CHAPTER 6, LESSON 1

After students have read the feature, have them share instances when they might have the opportunity to try these tips to make children feel comfortable. Encourage students to practice these skills the next time they have an opportunity to be with young children.

L3 Writing
Have students work in pairs to write a want ad for a parent. Want ads should describe a parent's qualifications, duties, work hours, and pay.

L3 Applying Life Skills
Have students brainstorm other ways that independent skills can be encouraged. Have interested students make a display of children's clothing and accessories that promote independence. Collect appropriate items and create a display for a showcase in the classroom, the library, or a community location.

L1 Using Transparencies
Present Color Transparency 28, "Parenting: Meeting Children's Needs," in the TCR. Use this overhead visual to reinforce concepts from this lesson.

MORE ABOUT • • •

Parenthood Parents and caregivers need to provide children with several things: (1) a sense of personal worth, (2) consistency in discipline, (3) firm guidelines, (4) religious training, (5) privacy, (6) respect, and (7) a set of decent standards and solid values. Ask students if they can add to this list and/or generate a list of what children can give to their parents.

CHAPTER 6, LESSON 1

TIPS for living

Have students read the feature. Ask them to give further tips for independence that they remember from their own childhood or learned from watching caregivers dealing with children. Have students interview their parents about further tips for increasing a child's independence and share them with the class.

L1 Student Workbook

Assign Activity 41 in the Student Workbook.

ASSESS

Evaluating the Lesson

Assign Reviewing Terms and Facts and Thinking Critically on page 157 to review the lesson; then assign the Lesson 1 Quiz in the TCR.

Reteaching

- Have each student review the needs and wants of children and the responsibilities of parenthood. Ask them to make a Venn diagram showing where needs, wants, and responsibilities overlap.
- Have students complete Reteaching Activity 6 in the TCR.

Children will learn to look at life in a positive way if you set a good example. How can you use body language to communicate positively?

Praise is another way of focusing on the positive. You might say to a young child, "I think you did a terrific job finding all those marbles that spilled—you have really sharp eyes."

Encouraging Independence

Children want to become independent and be able to perform tasks by themselves. As they try to do new tasks on their

TIPS for living

HELPING CHILDREN BECOME INDEPENDENT

As children perform more tasks for themselves, they learn to be more independent—an important part of growing up. Here are some ways to encourage independence.

- A step stool by the sink lets children reach the faucet and wash their hands by themselves.
- Child-size utensils encourage children to feed themselves.
- Child-size toothbrushes, combs, and hairbrushes help children learn to groom themselves.
- Allowing children to make choices about what story to read or what game to play makes them feel important. Even a choice between two options is better than no choice at all.

156 CHAPTER 6: UNDERSTANDING AND CARING FOR CHILDREN

MORE ABOUT • • •

Individual Differences Many children have sensitive personalities from birth. If the parents are also quiet and sensitive, children often demonstrate the same personalities. Caregivers may find it difficult to communicate with sensitive children until they get to know the child better. Caregivers can help put the child at ease by providing a warm and accepting atmosphere when caring for these children. When babysitting for a sensitive child, students should use patience and encourage children to be themselves, so that they will develop self-confidence and become more at ease.

own, they will probably make mistakes at first. It takes practice to learn skills such as using a fork, brushing teeth, or tying a shoe. Just like you, they learn from their mistakes.

You can encourage children to become more independent. If you always help children with something they could do themselves, they will not think they can do it alone, or they may not want to try. If they make mistakes, encourage them to keep trying. Praise their efforts, even when the results are not perfect.

Positive Parenting

Because everything that happens to a child helps to shape the child's personality, it is important that you interact with children in a positive way. When you practice parenting skills, you will be able to respond to children's needs and help them feel secure. Your encouragement and consistent guidance will also help them grow to be healthy, caring, and secure individuals.

Encouraging children to become independent will help them grow and develop. What can you do to help encourage a child's sense of independence?

LESSON ONE Review

Using complete sentences, answer the following questions on a separate sheet of paper.

Reviewing Terms and Facts

1. **Vocabulary** Define the term *caregiver*. Give three examples of people who could be caregivers.
2. **Recall** What are some ways for teens to acquire parenting skills?
3. **Identify** What are ways that you can help fulfill a child's emotional and social needs?
4. **Name** Identify three ways that you could communicate positively with a young child.

Thinking Critically

5. **Contrast** What is the difference between parenting and parenthood?
6. **Analyze** Why is it important to be consistent when guiding young children?

Applying Concepts

7. Imagine that you are a parent and that you are looking for a caregiver for your child. Write a help-wanted advertisement listing the personal qualities that you are looking for in a caregiver.

LESSON ONE: PARENTING SKILLS   157

COOPERATIVE LEARNING

Parenting Advice Pair students and tell each pair their task is to create a letter that parents seeking advice on parenting might write to an advice columnist of a parenting magazine. Letters should focus on one of the topics discussed in this lesson, such as how to respond to children's needs, how to provide guidance, how to communicate positively, or how to encourage independence. Have pairs exchange letters and write the columnist's response using information from the lesson.

CHAPTER 6, LESSON 1

Answers to Lesson 1 Review

1. A person who cares for children on a short-term or long-term basis. Any three: parent, relative, brother or sister, babysitter, teacher, day-care worker, neighbor.
2. By watching parents; taking a child development class, reading this chapter and books on the topic.
3. By holding, cuddling, comforting, kissing, hugging, and patting.
4. Any three: keep sentences simple, use positive statements, be sincere and encouraging, speak at eye level, ask about their likes, play guessing games, use praise.
5. Parenting can be done by any caregiver, including parents. The main caregivers have the job of parenthood. They are the persons responsible for meeting the child's physical, mental, emotional, and social needs.
6. So that you do not confuse children. Instead, you help children know what to expect.
7. Advertisements will vary but should include the personal qualities reflected in the lesson.

Enrichment

Have students find out the approximate cost of raising children for a one-week period. They should include the costs for food, clothing needs, entertainment, school activities, and rent and utilities. Have them multiply the amount by 52 to get the cost for one year.

CLOSE

Call students' attention to the statements on the board about "parenting" from the Motivating Activity. Ask them what they might add to these statements now that they have studied this lesson.

157

LESSON TWO
Ages and Stages

FOCUS

Lesson Objectives
After studying this lesson, students should be able to
- explain how babies and children develop.
- analyze what to expect when interacting with babies and children.
- describe how to help children learn.

Motivating Activity
Arrange to have each student bring a photograph of himself or herself as a baby, toddler, or preschooler. Have them write their name and age on the back of the photo. Collect the photographs as students enter the room. Display the pictures on a bulletin board titled "The Fantastic Photo Gallery." Group the pictures under the headings "Babies," "Toddlers," and "Preschoolers." Allow students time to study each picture and guess who the student is in each photograph. Ask students to write down the individual differences and point out growth and characteristics for each developmental stage that they note.

Introducing the Lesson
Have students share their responses to the Motivating Activity as you list them under each heading on the chalkboard. Tell them that this lesson explains the developmental differences between infants, toddlers, and preschoolers.

LESSON TWO
Ages and Stages

WORDS TO KNOW

developmental tasks
conscience
toddlers
preschoolers

DISCOVER...
- how infants and children develop.
- what to expect when interacting with infants and children.
- how to help children learn.

What comes to mind when you think about young children? Do you remember your two-year-old niece who is just learning to talk? Do you think of the children you babysit for who like the bedtime stories you read to them? Perhaps you think about your best friend's younger brother and how he enjoys playing games with you. Knowing what to expect of children at different ages and stages makes your time with them more enjoyable.

158 CHAPTER 6: UNDERSTANDING AND CARING FOR CHILDREN

CLASSROOM RESOURCES FOR LESSON 2

 Blackline Masters
Activity and Project Card 11, "Be an Author"
Concept Map 9
Cooperative Learning 11
Lesson 2 Quiz

 Transparencies
Transparency 29, "Patterns of Children's Development"

 Student Workbook
Activities 42, 43

Developmental Tasks

The concept of developmental tasks is important to understand when caring for children. **Developmental tasks** are *achievements or milestones, such as walking and talking, that can be expected of children at various ages and stages of growth.*

The sequence, or order, of developmental tasks follows a set pattern. Infants crawl before they walk, for example. Some children achieve these milestones faster than others, however. Janie learned to walk by the age of 12 months, but Marta did not take her first step until 15 months. Both are normal. Toddlers babble sounds before they learn to say words. They say individual words before they speak in complete sentences.

Most toddlers enjoy activities that allow them to use their physical skills. What are some other physical tasks that children learn?

Developmental tasks are useful for explaining what the typical child can do by certain ages. However, each child is a unique individual. Just as children do not grow at the same rate physically, they do not all perform developmental tasks at the same time.

Types of Development

Children develop physically, intellectually, emotionally, socially, and morally. For example, walking and climbing are

LESSON TWO: AGES AND STAGES 159

MORE ABOUT •••

Infancy Sucking is the sole method by which an infant gets its nourishment during the first three to four months of life. Thus, it is easy to understand why thumb, finger, toe, and blanket sucking are common habits in infants. The habit established during infancy may continue into preschool years. At this stage of development, the sucking habit is usually associated with fatigue, unhappiness, or boredom. The child may suck his or her thumb or blanket while drifting off to sleep, when not feeling well, or when watching television. Thumb, finger, toe, or blanket sucking is usually harmless, but it may cause improper positioning of the teeth. Ask students to explain what they would do if a child they were caring for was sucking his or her thumb.

CHAPTER 6, LESSON 2

L3 Design
Have students sketch three toys. Ask them to describe how children of different ages would use the toy and describe how each toy would help a child develop physically, mentally, or socially. Discuss developmental tasks that are accomplished at different ages.

L2 Cooperative Learning
Assign Cooperative Learning Activity 11, "Create a Storybook," in the TCR.

L3 Writing
Ask students to use their imagination and creativity to write a poem or short story about a preschooler playing make-believe or about a special-needs child. Have them share their story with classmates.

L3 Analyzing
Have students look at toy catalogs and study a selection of toys for preschoolers. Ask: How are these toys appropriate for the developmental tasks of toddlers? Which toys can be used by both toddlers and preschoolers? How does their use aid the steps in any or all of the developmental tasks of children?

---

physical tasks. Talking and singing are intellectual tasks. Kissing and hugging are emotional tasks. Playing with others and sharing are social tasks. Understanding right from wrong and learning how to be fair are moral tasks.

- **Physical Development.** During the first 12 months of Anna's life, she put on weight, grew longer, and gained the muscle coordination to hold her head up, sit up, and crawl. Her first food was mother's milk, but by the age of 6 months she began eating solid foods.

- **Intellectual Development.** During the first few years of her life, Anna also developed the ability to think, reason, and solve simple problems. She learned to recognize familiar faces and places. As Anna learned to talk, that became another sign of her intellectual development.

- **Social Development.** During the first weeks of life, Anna began to learn how to relate to others. She began by smiling when she saw her mother's or father's face. During her toddler years, she learned to play with other children, make friends, and share toys.

- **Emotional Development.** When Anna was an infant, her needs were met as soon as she cried. Anna learned to trust her caregivers—the first stage of emotional

Although children master developmental tasks in the same order, each child develops at his or her own rate. What skills do toddlers learn?

160   CHAPTER 6: UNDERSTANDING AND CARING FOR CHILDREN

MORE ABOUT • • •

Child Development Why can a seven-year-old answer the question "Who was born first, you or your mother?" but a four-year-old can't? The answer has to do with intellectual development in children. According to one expert in the field of children's intellectual development, Jean Piaget, intelligence develops gradually as a child grows. Piaget spent years questioning, observing, and playing games with babies and young children. He found that younger children think in a different way than older children and adults. Therefore, he concluded that intellectual development involves changes in the amount of information a child has as well as changes in the manner of thinking.

Infant (Birth to 1 year)
- Coos, Laughs (Birth–6 months)
- Grasps at Rattle (2 months)
- Smiles (2 months)
- Rolls Over (3–6 months)
- Puts Objects in Mouth (2 months)
- Sits Up Alone (4–6 months)
- Says Single Words (6–12 months)
- Crawls (7–9 months)
- Pulls Self Up (9–12 months)
- Plays Pat-A-Cake, Peek-A-Boo (10–12 months)

Toddler (1–3 years)
- Walks
- Learns Meaning of "No"
- Follows Simple Instructions
- Feeds Self with Spoon
- Identifies Pictures
- Climbs Stairs
- Undresses Self
- Plays Beside Others
- Puts Words into Sentences
- Begins Toilet Training

Preschooler (3–5 years)
- Opens Doors
- Dresses Self
- Recognizes Colors
- Rides a Tricycle
- Repeats Rhymes, Songs
- Brushes Teeth
- Speaks in Sentences
- Begins Cooperative Play

**Figure 6.1
Patterns of Children's Development**
At what stage do most children learn how to use a spoon? Throw a ball? Brush their teeth?

development. As she gets older, Anna will also learn to express her feelings in acceptable ways to parents, siblings, and others.

- **Moral Development.** Anna's parents are teaching her a system of rules to guide her behavior. They want her to develop a sense of right and wrong, fairness, justice, and consideration for others. Around the age of four or five, Anna will begin to develop a **conscience,** *the internal moral code that directs people's behavior.*

What to Expect of Children

It is important to treat each child as an individual. Even children who have the same parents experience different growth rates and patterns. After you spend some time with children and get to know them, you will have an idea of what you can expect from each child. **Figure 6.1** shows some of the tasks learned by children at various stages of development.

LESSON TWO: AGES AND STAGES   **161**

CHAPTER 6, LESSON 2

L1 Using Transparencies

Present Color Transparency 29, "Patterns of Children's Development," in the TCR. Use this overhead visual to reinforce concepts from this lesson.

USING VISUALS

Stress to students that an understanding of the patterns of children's development is necessary in order to appropriately meet the needs of children at various ages and stages. Then refer students to Figure 6.1 on this page. Write each developmental task for each stage on an index card. Then put all the cards in a box and mix them. Post the headings "Infant," "Toddler," and "Preschooler" on the bulletin board. Then ask students to take turns selecting a card from the box and placing it in the correct column on the bulletin board.

L2 Hands-on Project

Assign Hands-on Project 4, "Child's Play," in the TCR. Students create toys for children in this activity.

COOPERATIVE LEARNING

Ages and Stages Organize students into groups of three. Tell them their task is to design a child's bed quilt. The unique thing about this quilt is that it will illustrate the characteristics of infants, toddlers, and preschoolers. Assign each student in the group one of the stages and ask them to create or cut from magazines illustrations that might appear on the quilt. You may wish to assign a project for sewing baby quilts for donation to a community service organization.

CHAPTER 6, LESSON 2

Have students read the feature. After each group prepares its list, you might have a volunteer in each group present it to the class. Eliminate duplicate ideas and prepare a class list of ideas for guiding and motivating preschoolers.

L3 Researching

Have students research and read several magazine articles by or about parents of children with special needs. Students should look for ways the parents encourage and motivate their children to become independent. Then have students present their findings to the class. Students might also invite willing parents to talk to the class about the special ways they motivate their children.

👉 TIPS for living

After students have read the feature on page 163, discuss other ideas they may have to inspire children's imaginations. Have them use one of the activities, or choose one of the ideas from the discussion, to spark the imagination of a child they know. Have them describe the results to classmates.

Guiding Preschoolers

Preschoolers are ready to learn appropriate behavior and to follow rules. With a small group of classmates, compile a list of ways to guide preschoolers. Here are some ideas to get you started.

- Set a good example.
- Stick by any limits you set.
- Give brief, simple reasons for the rules you set.

Infants

Katrina, a newborn baby, eats every few hours. She sleeps 16 to 20 hours each day. As she gets older, she will stay awake longer and eat less often. In the first few months, her parents will gradually develop a schedule so that Katrina can learn to have a regular time for eating, bathing, sleeping, and playing.

Katrina will have many developmental tasks to learn, such as how to eat, sit alone, pick up objects, and crawl. She will learn how to play with toys and be comfortable with different people and places. Katrina will also need a great deal of love and attention.

Toddlers

Toddlers are *children who are one to three years old.* The name comes from the unsteady way they walk, or toddle. Toddlers are usually full of energy and ideas. They are learning to be more independent by doing tasks for themselves and by being less dependent on the people who care for them. As a part of this new independence, they often use the word *no*. These are some tasks that toddlers can learn to do:

- Come to the table for meals when called.
- Eat food without dawdling or being bribed.
- Follow safety rules such as not touching something hot.

Preschoolers

Preschoolers are *children who are three to five years old.* Preschoolers interact more with their playmates and like to play with children of all ages. They like to talk. Preschool children may carry on a conversation with make-believe playmates or dolls. They might imitate their heroes or pretend to be superhuman.

Children with Special Needs

Some children have special needs. Jake walks with a leg brace. Peter wears a hearing aid. Joanna has emotional problems. Each of these children has a particular disability, yet what they need most is to learn how to develop their abilities

CHAPTER 6: UNDERSTANDING AND CARING FOR CHILDREN

MEETING STUDENT DIVERSITY

Physically Challenged Explain to students that some children with special needs develop at a slower rate. For example, some children may be late in physical growth, as well as in social, emotional, and mental development. In other cases, development may be slow in only one area. For example, a child confined to a wheelchair because of physical problems may be advanced in social and intellectual growth. Consider borrowing a wheelchair for classroom experience in which students use the wheelchair to see what it's like. Remind students that events such as the Special Olympics are an example of how children with disabilities can participate in rewarding competitive events.

and enjoy a good life. For example, they need to learn to be as independent as possible, and they need encouragement to develop a positive self-concept. The attitudes of people around them are important in making this possible.

How Young Children Learn

Young children learn from exploring their environment with their five senses—sight, hearing, taste, touch, and smell. Children learn something from everyone and everything around them, including toys. Their first toys might help them develop their body and coordination or help them learn to focus, perhaps on a brightly colored object. As children grow, activities and toys can help them improve their intellectual abilities. Some toys teach shapes, colors, letters, numbers, and others teach reasoning skills.

Children with special needs benefit from caregivers who encourage their independence.

TIPS for living

SPARKING A CHILD'S IMAGINATION

Try these ideas to jump start a youngster's journey into imagined worlds.

- Ask open-ended questions—questions that don't have a yes or no answer. "What do we need to build a dream castle?"
- Write a group story. Start off the story in some such way as, "Once upon a time there was a frog who didn't have any friends." Ask each child to contribute a sentence.
- Here's a rainy day idea: Ask children to help plan a make-believe outing in their home. Maybe they will go camping and make a tent out of a blanket spread over a table. Encourage as many ideas from the children as possible.

LESSON TWO: AGES AND STAGES 163

CHAPTER 6, LESSON 2

L1 Student Workbook
Assign Activities 42 and 43 in the Student Workbook.

ASSESS

Evaluating the Lesson
Assign Reviewing Terms and Facts and Thinking Critically on page 164 to review the lesson; then assign the Lesson 2 Quiz in the TCR.

Reteaching
- Present students with the following situation: Joe said, "I'm going to care for my two-year-old brother on Saturday. He'll give me a real workout!" Have students work in pairs to develop a list of learning activities that Joe might use when caring for the toddler.
- Have students complete Reteaching Activity 6 in the TCR.
- Assign Concept Map 9 in the TCR.

Enrichment
Have each student organize a bag of three carefully selected items for an infant, toddler, or preschooler that would assist that child in his or her physical, mental, and social development. Have students share the items with classmates and explain why the items were selected.

COOPERATIVE LEARNING

Video Project Students may work in small groups to prepare a video production showing effective child care practices to be used while babysitting. Have students review the chapter for key points to include in their video production. They may use dolls to represent infants and children, or perhaps get permission from families to include younger siblings in segments showing games and toys appropriate for toddlers and children. Groups should determine who will film the video, who will be narrator and who will demonstrate various skills and tips to be used while babysitting. Go over plans with the group before they begin filming, and review the video for appropriateness before sharing with the class.

CHAPTER 6, LESSON 2

Answers to Lesson 2 Review

1. Developmental tasks are achievements that can be expected of children at various ages or stages of growth. Examples are walking and talking.
2. Each child is unique and progresses at his or her own rate.
3. Physical, mental, social, emotional, and moral development.
4. Any five: exploring, doing the same task over and over, listening to sounds and conversation, handling objects, having new experiences, gaining praise and approval.
5. Knowing what to expect of children at different ages and stages makes the time spent with them more enjoyable. This knowledge also helps one plan appropriate activities that will be meaningful and educational to the child.
6. Any one: physical—walking, climbing; mental—talking, singing; social—smiling, playing with others; emotional—hugging, kissing; moral—fairness, consideration for others.
7. Toddlers are unsteady walkers but are full of energy and ideas. They are just learning to do tasks for themselves. On the other hand preschoolers can do many tasks for themselves. They like to talk and interact more with playmates.
8. Guides will vary but should incorporate appropriate activities for the age group intended.

CLOSE

Refer students to the lesson title "Ages and Stages." Ask them to explain in a brief statement how an understanding of ages and stages can help them in caring for young children.

164

▲ Young children learn through hands-on discovery, using the five senses: touch, taste, smell, sight, and hearing.

Young children also learn by practicing tasks over and over again, observing and imitating others, and exploring objects in their environment. They also learn from being exposed to such interesting places outside the home as an aquarium, a science museum, a historic house, a children's theater, or a pick-your-own strawberry patch.

◆ Understanding Children

Although every child is unique, most children go through a similar pattern of growth and development. As an older brother or sister or as a babysitter, you can help children learn and discover new things by interacting with them. Show children that you are interested in them and that what they say matters to you.

LESSON TWO *Review*

Using complete sentences, answer the following questions on a separate sheet of paper.

Reviewing Terms and Facts

1. **Vocabulary** Define the term *developmental tasks*. Give two examples.
2. **Explain** Why don't all children of the same age perform developmental tasks at the same time?
3. **List** Name the five main areas of development.
4. **Identify** What are five ways in which children learn?

Thinking Critically

5. **Analyze** Why is it helpful to understand when young children should accomplish certain developmental tasks?
6. **Describe** Give an example of each of the five main areas of development.
7. **Compare** How are toddlers and preschoolers similar? How are they different?

Applying Concepts

8. Divide into groups of four or five. Review the section in this lesson called "How Young Children Learn." Think of one simple game or activity for young children for each of the five senses. Try to make one or two of your activities appropriate for outdoors. Have someone in the group take notes. Compile the activities from all the groups into a babysitter's activity guide.

164   CHAPTER 6: UNDERSTANDING AND CARING FOR CHILDREN

HOME AND COMMUNITY CONNECTION

Field Trip Take a field trip to a day-care center or preschool. Before students make the trip suggest that they collect old clothes appropriate for children to use when playing dress-up to give to the center as a thank-you for the trip. Have students record activities of the children, focusing on the physical, mental, emotional, social, and moral development of the various ages represented. Discuss the observations.

LESSON THREE
Child's Play

DISCOVER...
- how infants, toddlers, and preschoolers learn through play.
- how to select safe toys.
- the different types of play activities.
- the advantages of quiet play.

Beep, beep! Gabrielle's school bus honks at the cars and trucks in the traffic jam on the floor. Gabrielle is working hard at an important job for a child—learning through play. Through play with other children and with toys, children develop physically, intellectually, emotionally, socially, and morally. Play teaches children about sizes and shapes, colors, and numbers. It teaches them about their world and helps them grow.

WORDS TO KNOW
attention span
solitary or independent play
parallel play
cooperative play
group play

LESSON THREE: CHILD'S PLAY   **165**

LESSON THREE
Child's Play

FOCUS

Lesson Objectives
After studying this lesson, students should be able to
- explain how infants, toddlers, and preschoolers learn through play.
- determine how to select safe toys.
- differentiate between the types of play activities.
- explain the advantages of quiet play.

Motivating Activity
Have students write the name of a favorite toy, game, or activity that they enjoyed as a child. Then have them read the opening paragraph.

Introducing the Lesson
Have students share their responses to the Motivating Activity. Then discuss the following questions: How old were you when you played with this toy? Why did you find it enjoyable? What did you learn from playing with the toy? Tell students this lesson explains how a child develops through play and why safety precautions are necessary when children are at play.

Introducing *Words to Know*
Write each of the three Words to Know on the board. Have students look up each of the terms in the Glossary or find them in the chapter. When finished, have students write a sentence for each word in the list. Call on volunteers to share their sentences.

CLASSROOM RESOURCES FOR LESSON 3

 Blackline Masters
Cooperative Learning 12
Cross Curriculum 6
Enrichment 6
Lesson 3 Quiz

 Transparencies
Transparency 30, "Choosing Toys for Children"

 Student Workbook
Activities 44, 45

165

CHAPTER 6, LESSON 3

TEACH

 IN ACTION

Emphasize that selecting appropriate toys for infants is important not only to their development but also to their safety. Then ask students to read the feature. After the students complete their reading, have them write an article for their local newspaper describing the characteristics of toys that would be appropriate gifts for different-aged children.

L1 Evaluating

On a display table feature a selection of toys for babies. Have students evaluate each toy using the criteria listed in the text. Emphasize that parents who have older children must be especially careful to keep toys with small parts away from the babies.

L2 Making Comparisons

Have students devise a chart to compare how child's play is similar to adult work and activities. Students should create two-column charts, with the first column labeled "Adult Work" and the second column labeled "Child's Play." Have students list an activity performed by an adult in the first column and list a child's play activity that is a preparation for adult "work" in the second column.

L2 Cooperative Learning

Assign Cooperative Learning Activity 12, "Linda's Birthday Party," in the TCR.

Skills IN ACTION

Selecting Toys

As a class, prepare a display of toys that are safe for babies—no parts small enough to be swallowed. Here's how you can do it without actually buying anything.
- Borrow a toy.
- Draw a toy.
- Bring in a picture from a toy catalog.

Allow class members to evaluate each selection.

How Infants Learn Through Play

Baby Nicholas is happy waving his arms and kicking his legs. He likes to have someone play with him and enjoys being moved from place to place so he can look at new sights. A walk outside or to the grocery store is very interesting to him.

Nicholas does not stay with one toy for very long. He, like other infants, has a short **attention span,** *the length of time a person can concentrate on any one thing.* This means that toys and other objects hold his interest for only a short amount of time.

When infants discover their hands and can hold a toy, play becomes more important to them. They gradually learn to pick up a toy and hold it. It is natural for them to play happily, picking up first one toy, then another. Playing with toys is one way babies learn about the world around them. For example, when they shake a rattle, it causes a sound.

Playing helps infants get the exercise they need. When they first throw a toy, it may go in any direction. They keep trying until they finally learn to control their muscles enough to toss the toy toward another person.

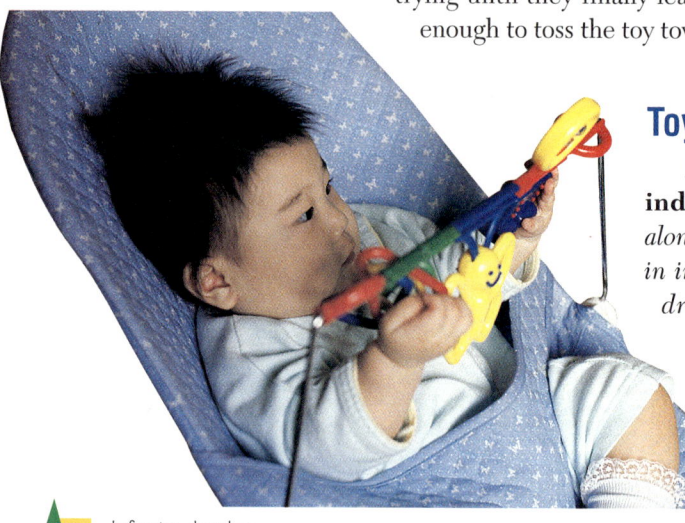

Infants develop their senses by playing with toys. Which senses is this baby developing?

Toys for Infants

Infants engage in **solitary** or **independent play**—*playing alone and showing little interest in interacting with other children.* Infants play with their hands, toes, toys, or other objects. Toys that are easy to pick up and hold with tiny fingers are best for first toys. Infants like toys that are pleasant to touch, see, and chew on. Musical toys, squeeze toys, and stacking and nesting blocks are good toys for a baby. Even small kitchen items, such as plastic measuring cups and spoons and pots and pans, can be

166   CHAPTER 6: UNDERSTANDING AND CARING FOR CHILDREN

MORE ABOUT • • •

Child's Play Not only is child's play fun, but research shows those children who develop complex play through pretend games also develop language skills. To encourage such language development, experts suggest that caregivers (1) allow free, unstructured time for play; (2) furnish some props (e.g., a doctor's kit) to suggest various themes; (3) encourage activities that involve language use, such as "playing house"; and finally (4) limit the child's television time.

entertaining toys. **Figure 6.2** provides suggestions for choosing toys for infants as well as for toddlers and preschoolers.

Playtime for Toddlers

Play is toddler's work, and toys are their tools. Playing helps children develop their minds, bodies, and social skills.

Toddlers are curious about everything and spend much of their time exploring. They pull out various toys, look them over, and go on to something else. Most toddlers play alone or

Figure 6.2 Choosing Toys for Children
What kinds of toys are good choices for a child who is six months old? Two years old? Five years old?

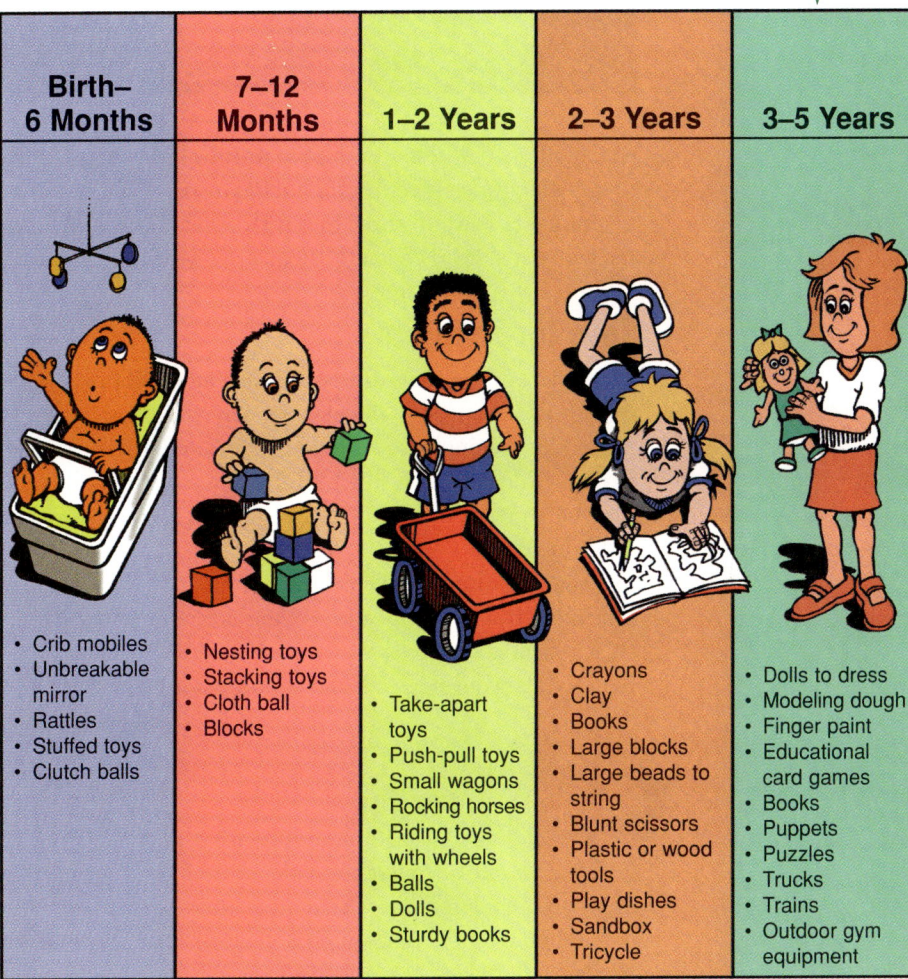

Birth–6 Months
- Crib mobiles
- Unbreakable mirror
- Rattles
- Stuffed toys
- Clutch balls

7–12 Months
- Nesting toys
- Stacking toys
- Cloth ball
- Blocks

1–2 Years
- Take-apart toys
- Push-pull toys
- Small wagons
- Rocking horses
- Riding toys with wheels
- Balls
- Dolls
- Sturdy books

2–3 Years
- Crayons
- Clay
- Books
- Large blocks
- Large beads to string
- Blunt scissors
- Plastic or wood tools
- Play dishes
- Sandbox
- Tricycle

3–5 Years
- Dolls to dress
- Modeling dough
- Finger paint
- Educational card games
- Books
- Puppets
- Puzzles
- Trucks
- Trains
- Outdoor gym equipment

LESSON THREE: CHILD'S PLAY   167

HOME AND COMMUNITY CONNECTION

Selecting Toys for Children Have students work in small groups to develop a presentation for a PTA meeting on selecting the correct toys for young children. Assign one of the following tasks to each group: handling publicity, researching and selecting toys, checking for safety standards, preparing a bibliography for parents, and making the presentation.

CHAPTER 6, LESSON 3

USING VISUALS
After students have studied Figure 6.2, organize the class into five groups. Assign each group one of the ages in the illustration and ask them to find pictures in parenting magazines or toy catalogs that illustrate the appropriate toys listed for their assigned age. Have them use the pictures to create a graphic display for the bulletin board.

L1 Using Transparencies
Present Color Transparency 30, "Choosing Toys for Children," in the TCR. Use this overhead visual to reinforce concepts from this lesson.

TEACHER TALK!

Toy Safety
Caution students about allowing young children to play with toys that are inappropriate for their age. Young children often choke on small parts of toys. To prevent choking, objects and parts of toys can be checked by a choke hazard tester to see if they are small enough to lodge in a child's windpipe. If the object slips into the tester—which looks like a small, clear plastic prescription bottle—it is possible that the object could be dangerous to the child.

CHAPTER 6, LESSON 3

TIPS for living

After students read the feature on page 169, point out to them that one of the most encouraging things a caregiver can do with a child is to share him- or herself with the child. By setting aside a consistent, special time to be with the child, the caregiver lets the child know that she or he can count on this special time. Point out that many teachers have also reported that taking a few minutes after school for mutual sharing with a child has provided encouragement to children, even enough to stop them from misbehaving. Ask students to write a paragraph about how someone shared time with them and how they felt because of it. Students might also write a poem for young children about the importance of sharing.

L2 Language Arts Connection

Assign Cross-Curriculum Activity 6 in the TCR. Students learn about how to evaluate and choose books for children in this activity.

L2 Reading

Have each student select a story or book appropriate for a young child and practice reading the story aloud, using sound effects and expression in their voice. Then have students read their story to the class or to a group of young children. Have them report the children's reactions to the class.

Toddlers do not yet have the social skills to play with other children. Instead, they play alongside other children. What is this type of play called?

watch others play. They engage in **parallel play,** or *play that occurs alongside of, rather than with, a friend.* They are just beginning to learn to share toys with others. The idea of taking turns or sharing means little to a two-year-old.

Toys for Toddlers

Toddlers need toys for both active and quiet play. Their toys should help them develop socially and physically. Toys for toddlers should also help them think and use their imagination. Older toddlers like toys that do something, but they may be startled by toys like a jack-in-the-box or toys that move too fast.

Toddlers also enjoy vehicle toys. Toy cars, bulldozers, tractors, and airplanes will capture their attention and stimulate their imagination. Action toys, such as riding toys and balls, help toddlers develop skill and coordination.

Playtime for Preschoolers

Preschoolers engage in **cooperative play**—*playing together with one or two other children and sharing toys.* Play helps preschoolers learn to take turns, share, and make friends with other children. As they get older, they enjoy **group play,** or *play with several other children,* especially those their own

168 CHAPTER 6: UNDERSTANDING AND CARING FOR CHILDREN

MORE ABOUT • • •

Toys For centuries children have been learning through playing with toys. Research indicates that marbles were a favorite toy of Egyptian children around 3000 B.C. At about the same time, Babylonian children were playing with clay tops with sides etched with animal and human forms. The first rattles designed for children's amusement appeared in Egypt around 1360 B.C. Have students research the history of other early toys.

168

TIPS for living

TEACHING CHILDREN TO SHARE

Young children often fight over toys. Although two-year-olds may be too young to understand the concept of sharing, preschoolers can learn to share. Use the following tips to teach children about sharing.

- Use "sharing" words—such as share, take turns, wait your turn.
- Ask one child to show another child how a toy works.
- Help children find ways to share materials and play together. For instance, make an airplane out of chairs and create roles for everyone: pilots, flight attendants, and passengers.
- Praise the children when you see them sharing.

age. The benefits of playtime for preschoolers include taking turns and sharing with others, learning how to get along with and play with a group, and becoming more creative.

Toys for Preschoolers

As children develop, their interest in playthings gradually changes. New toys help keep pace with their natural development. Preschoolers enjoy action toys that encourage physical exercise—tricycles, climbing equipment, and balls. Toys for pretend play can include household props and occupational props—lab coats and briefcases, dress-up clothes, and non-toxic art materials.

When preschoolers play together, they learn about cooperation and sharing. What other skills do you think that these children are learning?

169

MEETING STUDENT DIVERSITY

Students with Special Needs Students with special needs might share with the class the types of toys their parents bought or developed to adapt to their special needs when they were infants, toddlers, and preschoolers. The class as a whole might work in small groups to design toys for students with special needs. They might also write to the Crestwood Company, 6625 Sidney Place, Milwaukee, WI 53209 (414-352-5678) to obtain a catalog that includes toys adapted for children with special needs.

CHAPTER 6, LESSON 3

L1 Critical Thinking

Organize the class into groups of four to investigate ways to introduce young children to music, such as singing songs with motions, playing records and tapes, using homemade musical instruments, and dancing. Have the groups demonstrate how to use one of these activities with young children.

L1 Student Workbook

Assign Activities 44 and 45 in the Student Workbook.

ASSESS

Evaluating the Lesson

Assign Reviewing Terms and Facts and Thinking Critically on page 170 to review the lesson; then assign the Lesson 3 Quiz in the TCR.

Reteaching

- Show students pictures of children engaged in play. Have the students determine whether the children are involved in parallel or group play and discuss the type of learning that is taking place. (Students could also watch children in the kindergarten playroom.)
- Have students complete Reteaching Activity 6 in the TCR.

Enrichment

- Ask students to watch a children's program on television, note the positive and negative influences of the show, and evaluate the influence of the commercials shown during the show. Have them report their observations to the class.
- Assign Enrichment Activity 6 in the TCR.

CHAPTER 6, LESSON 3

Answers to Lesson 3 Review

1. Attention span is the length of time a person can concentrate on any one thing. Sentences will vary.
2. Any three: pick up a toy and hold it, learn about the world around them, control muscles, how to use hands, how to use their legs, how to handle toys.
3. Action toys, vehicle toys, imaginative toys.
4. Any four: seeing the value in taking turns and sharing with others; learning to get along with and play with a group; having opportunities to help others; continuing to develop their bodies by running, climbing, and jumping; becoming more creative; getting practice in solving problems.
5. Any three: Puzzles, puppets, creative materials, stories and books, computer software programs, listening to music, singing, dancing, television, videotapes.
6. Parallel play occurs alongside, rather than with, a friend. Group play is play with other children of all ages.
7. Quiet play helps children relax and helps develop their imagination. Without quiet play, children wear themselves out quickly, and may become irritable.
8. Students' lists will vary but should be compared with the list in the lesson.

CLOSE

Have students use the major headings and subheadings in this lesson to prepare a mural for the bulletin board that shows pictorially the major concepts of the lesson.

170

Computer software programs can open up a whole new world of learning for children. What might be some of the advantages of helping a child develop an interest in computers at an early age?

Quiet Play

Quiet play is helpful before meals, naptime, or bedtime to help children relax. Quiet play can also help to calm an upset child. Here are some suggestions for quiet play activities:

- Drawing with crayons or markers, painting, making collages from old magazines
- Playing with clay
- Making up stories, listening to books read aloud
- Listening to music

Learning Through Play

Stop to think about the favorite toys you have had over the years. Did you realize you had learned so much through playing? Through playtime and toys, infants, toddlers, and preschool children develop physically, intellectually, emotionally, socially, and morally.

LESSON THREE Review

Using complete sentences, answer the following questions on a separate sheet of paper.

Reviewing Terms and Facts

1. **Vocabulary** Define the term *attention span*. Use it in an original sentence.
2. **Identify** What are three developmental tasks that infants learn through play?
3. **List** Name three types of toys for toddlers.
4. **Recall** What are four ways in which play benefits preschoolers?
5. **Give Examples** Name three types of quiet play activities for children.

Thinking Critically

6. **Contrast** What is the difference between parallel play and group play?
7. **Analyze** Why is quiet play important for children? What might happen if a child did not have any quiet play?

Applying Concepts

8. Ask a preschooler you know what his or her favorite toys are. Share your results with your classmates and put together a "top ten" list of favorite toys for preschoolers. How does the list compare with the suggestions in this lesson?

170   CHAPTER 6: UNDERSTANDING AND CARING FOR CHILDREN

MORE ABOUT • • •

Toys Fad toys are attractive to children, but their thrill fades quickly. There is good reason that the same toys are played with generation after generation. The same wooden blocks, crayons, puzzles, trucks, dolls, games, and cuddly bears are all as appropriate today as they were in years past. These toys meet the needs that young children have always had, and will always have: to express themselves, to be creative, and to show love and affection. Ask students to debate the following statement: Many of today's mechanized toys do not allow children to build their creative powers.

LESSON FOUR
Child Safety

LESSON FOUR
Child Safety

FOCUS

Lesson Objectives
After studying this lesson, students should be able to
- explain how to keep children safe.
- describe how to prevent common accidents.

Motivating Activity
Ask students to write on a slip of paper what they think is the most common cause of accidents for young children.

Introducing the Lesson
Have students share their responses to the Motivating Activity as you write responses on the chalkboard. Tell students that this lesson explains the common accidents that children have, what they can do to prevent these accidents, and other ways they can keep children safe.

Introducing *Words to Know*
Refer students to the Words to Know list. Have them survey the lesson and find the definitions of the terms. Ask them to write the definition of each term.

DISCOVER...
- how to keep children safe.
- how to prevent common accidents.

Children do not understand the dangers that surround them. In their eagerness to explore, they can easily hurt themselves or try to play with a dangerous object or substance. There are precautions you can take, however, to help keep children safe and prevent them from getting hurt.

WORDS TO KNOW
childproof
intruder
smoke alarm
poison control center

Keeping Children Safe

Many families make their homes **childproof,** or *safe for children to play and explore in.* Childproofing includes putting

LESSON FOUR: CHILD SAFETY   **171**

CLASSROOM RESOURCES FOR LESSON 4

 Blackline Masters
Concept Map 10
Cross Curriculum 7
Lesson 4 Quiz

 **Student Workbook**
Activity 46

171

CHAPTER 6, LESSON 4

TEACH

L1 Critical Thinking
Organize the class into small groups and have them list ways to prevent intruders from entering when they babysit. Have each group share its list with the class. After the lists have been combined, ask each group to create a public service announcement that could be used to teach others how to prevent home intrusions.

L1 Reading
Have students study a first-aid book and demonstrate the correct procedure for treating an injury that might happen to a child while they are babysitting.

L2 Critical Thinking
Brainstorm with students potential fire hazards in a person's home. Ask students if there are additional considerations to be made in someone else's home. Also discuss what a caregiver can do when babysitting to prevent a fire from ever starting.

L3 Math
Show students how to draw a floor plan. Have them draw one of their own home and draw the escape routes they would use from different areas. Then discuss why escape routes should be checked before a fire starts.

All babies put objects into their mouths. That is why toys that are safe must be too large to swallow.

safety latches on cabinet doors and drawers. It also includes using safety gates at the top and bottom of stairs, putting safety caps on electrical outlets, and moving cleaning supplies and other dangerous items so that they are out of children's reach. Even if a home has been childproofed, you still need to watch children to make sure that they are safe.

There are different safety concerns for children of different ages. Because babies put objects in their mouths, you need to make sure that anything that could result in harm or anything small enough to be swallowed is kept out of reach. Toddlers must be watched every minute because they move quickly, climb, and get into everything. Although preschoolers have a better idea of what they should not do, they may still get into dangerous situations unless their behavior is monitored.

Intruders

Keeping children safe involves taking care to protect the children and yourself from intruders. An **intruder** is *someone who uses force to get into a home.* Caregivers need to take the following precautions—day or night.

- Make sure that all doors and windows are locked.
- Do not open the door for any stranger.
- Call a neighbor or another trusted adult, or dial 911 (emergency center) if a stranger approaches and does not go away.

Preventing Accidents

Some common accidents are falls and injuries, fires, and poisoning. When caring for young children, you need to take special precautions to prevent accidents. To learn how to take care of basic injuries, such as a small cut or a nosebleed, you might consider taking a first-aid course or studying a book on first aid. If a child gets hurt and you do not feel capable of handling the situation, stay calm and call for help. A broken bone, lots of bleeding, a burn, or an animal bite can be

---

MORE ABOUT • • •

First Aid Tell students that infants explore their environment by putting objects in their mouths. If a child they are watching swallows something and is coughing hard, let the coughing continue. This is the body's way of getting rid of a foreign object in the throat or windpipe. If the child can't talk, breathe, or cough at all, do the following things for a baby or very small child: Hold the child upside down in a jackknife position over your arm; give several quick blows to the child's back, between the shoulder blades; repeat as necessary until the swallowed object "pops out."

dangerous. Call the child's parents, a neighbor, or dial 911 for help.

Falls and Injuries

Falls are the leading cause of accidental death at home in the United States. When caring for children, follow these guidelines to prevent falls and injuries.

- Never leave an infant alone on a changing table, sofa, or bed. The infant may roll over and fall off.
- Restrict crawling babies and toddlers to places that they can explore safely.
- Keep all young children away from electrical wires and outlets and breakable or dangerous objects.
- Make sure that toys are age appropriate and that they are smooth and free of loose parts.
- Keep plastic bags away from children to prevent suffocation.

If you care for children, you should know how to handle routine accidents. What should you do to avoid unsafe situations?

TIPS for living

PLAYGROUND SAFETY

To keep children safe on outdoor play equipment, explain that the following behavior can cause accidents.

- Standing on a swing, walking in front or in back of a moving swing, swinging empty seats, pushing other children off the swing, twisting the chains
- Climbing up the front of the slide
- Jumping off the seesaw unexpectedly
- Overloading climbing equipment
- Roughhousing on the jungle gym

LESSON FOUR: CHILD SAFETY 173

MORE ABOUT • • •

Cuts and Scrapes A cut or scrape can be very upsetting to a child, especially if it bleeds a lot. To stop bleeding, apply pressure directly on the wound with a clean cloth. Press firmly and continuously for about five minutes or until bleeding stops. If you can, raise the injured part higher than the child's head; this makes bleeding stop more quickly. Once bleeding stops, clean the wound gently with soap and water. Apply an antiseptic on the bandage, not the wound, so it won't sting or hurt the child.

CHAPTER 6, LESSON 4

L2 Science

In small groups have students make a list of poisons that might be found in the home. Have them find out the symptoms of each type of poisoning and how a person should be treated if the poisoning occurs. Have students look up the telephone number of the nearest poison control center. Caution them that the wrong type of treatment for poisoning could be life-threatening.

DID YOU KNOW

House and garden plants can appear very tasty to a young child—but can be dangerous. While usually not fatal, eating certain plants can cause unpleasant symptoms ranging from skin irritation to nausea and vomiting, depending on the type of plant. Local poison control centers may have a list of poisonous and nonpoisonous plants found in the area. A free pamphlet, "Poison Plant Guide," is available from the McKennan Poison Control Center in Sioux Falls, SD (1-605-336-3894).

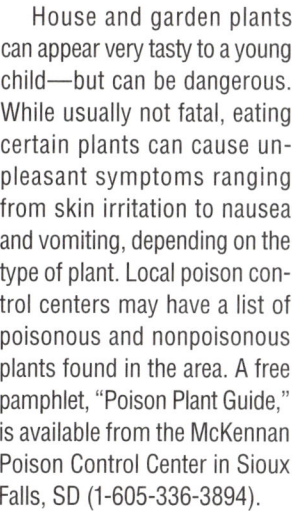

TIPS for living

Have students read the feature. Then have them work in small groups to develop cartoon-like posters to illustrate the Do's and Don'ts of playground safety. Have students display their posters in a kindergarten room.

CHAPTER 6, LESSON 4

L2 Science Connection
Assign Cross-Curriculum Activity 7 in the TCR. Students learn about treating burn victims in this activity.

Have students read the feature. After they have read it, organize students into five groups and assign each group one of the ideas suggested in the feature for teaching children basic safety rules. Have students in each group develop their assigned plan and present it to the kindergarten class in your school.

L1 Student Workbook
Assign Activity 46 in the Student Workbook.

ASSESS

Evaluating the Lesson
Assign Reviewing Terms and Facts and Thinking Critically on page 175 to review the lesson; then assign the Lesson 4 Quiz in the TCR.

Reteaching
- Have students list questions a babysitter should ask parents about their home to ensure the safety of the children. Have groups present their lists to the rest of the class.
- Have students complete Reteaching Activity 6 in the TCR.
- Assign Concept Map 10 in the TCR.

174

Car seats are designed to prevent children from getting hurt in a car accident.

- Keep knives and breakable dishes away from children.
- Outside, always watch toddlers to prevent them from running into the street.
- In a car, children should always ride in a child car seat, no matter how short the trip is.

Fires

Fires are the second leading cause of accidental death in the United States. To prevent fires, follow these guidelines.

- Use the stove and oven properly. Turn pot and pan handles away from the edge of the stove. When cooking, avoid wearing clothes with long, full sleeves.
- Keep all matches and lighters away from children.
- Be sure that there are smoke alarms on every floor of your home. A **smoke alarm** is *a device that sets off an alarm when smoke is present.*

If you smell smoke or see a fire when you are caring for children, first get the children out safely. Then call the fire department from a neighbor's home. Do not try to put out the fire yourself or to save items from the home.

If you are trapped by smoke or fire, try not to panic. Stay close to the floor. If you can, put a wet cloth over your nose and mouth and over the children's, and crawl to safety. If you cannot get out, stay in a room—the bathroom is good if it has a window—close the door to the room, and stuff wet towels around the cracks in the door. Turn on the light, and call out the window for help.

Caregivers need to teach children how to be safe. You might try one of the following ideas:
- Write a safety story and read it to the children.
- Make a safety poster for the children to color.
- Put on a puppet show.

174   CHAPTER 6: UNDERSTANDING AND CARING FOR CHILDREN

HOME AND COMMUNITY CONNECTION

Guest Speaker Invite a firefighter or emergency or rescue-squad worker to class to explain the most common causes of home fires and the actions that should be taken if a fire occurs while students are babysitting. Have students prepare questions in advance to ask the speaker. Have the speaker emphasize that if a fire occurs when they are babysitting, they should not leave the children alone in the house or leave them after they get out.

Poisonings

Common-sense prevention is the best way to keep children away from dangerous household substances. All poisonous items should be kept in locked cabinets or stored in drawers that have safety latches on them. If that is not possible, keep the items on a high shelf, out of the children's reach.

If you suspect that a child has been poisoned, the first step to take is to call the **poison control center,** *a medical facility with staff trained to help in poisoning emergencies.* You can find the number of the nearest poison control center by looking in the telephone book or by calling directory assistance.

Be Prepared

Have you ever heard the expression, "An ounce of prevention is worth a pound of cure"? When it comes to child safety, it means that you can prevent many common accidents by being prepared. Learn basic first-aid procedures. Make sure the homes where you care for children are childproofed. Ask parents to leave you emergency numbers for their community. These simple steps may save a life.

Many common household items are poisonous and should be kept in a locked cabinet or on a high shelf away from children. What should you do while babysitting to prevent an accidental poisoning?

LESSON FOUR Review

Using complete sentences, answer the following questions on a separate sheet of paper.

Reviewing Terms and Facts

1. **Explain** What does it mean when you make a home *childproof?*
2. **Describe** If you smell smoke or see fire, what should you do first? Next?
3. **Identify** Where can you call for help if a child swallows poison?

Thinking Critically

4. **Evaluate** What is the single best way to keep young children safe?
5. **Analyze** What can happen if you rely solely on childproofing to keep children safe?

Applying Concepts

6. Check for smoke alarms in your home. They should be located on every level, especially outside bedroom areas. Test the batteries in your smoke alarms to see if they work. If your home needs more smoke alarms or the batteries are dead, ask a parent to help you install more alarms or to replace the batteries.

LESSON FOUR: CHILD SAFETY

CHAPTER 6, LESSON 4

Answers to Lesson 4 Review

1. Childproofing means making a place safe for children to play and explore in.
2. Check to make sure there is fire or smoke. Then get the children out and call the fire department from a neighbor's house.
3. Poison control center. Look up the number in the telephone book or call information.
4. By never leaving them alone so that you can prevent accidents and handle emergencies right away.
5. Childproofing may give a false sense of security; even if a home is childproof, children can move quickly and get into dangerous situations if not watched closely.
6. Ask students to report on their search for smoke alarms.

Enrichment

Encourage interested students to research the most recent statistics available regarding injuries to babies, toddlers, and infants. Instruct them to represent the statistics in a pie chart or circle graph. Use computer programs, if available, to complete charts.

CLOSE

Go around the room and ask each student to name one way he or she could ensure a child's safety. List responses on the chalkboard.

COOPERATIVE LEARNING

Childproofing a House Organize students into groups and tell them that their task is to develop a mural that depicts ways to childproof a house. Students might divide the task by rooms, such as kitchen, bedroom, bathroom, living/dining area. Students might use an illustration of a cross-section of a house or a child's dollhouse and index cards on which they can list ways to childproof each room. They can extend strings from each room to its index-card listing.

LESSON FIVE
Caring for Children

FOCUS

Lesson Objectives
After studying this lesson, students should be able to
- explain how to prepare for babysitting.
- describe how to care for infants, toddlers, and preschoolers.

Motivating Activity
Have students write a brief paragraph about the most difficult, the funniest, or the most memorable experience they have had while taking care of a child.

Introducing the Lesson
Have several students share their responses to the Motivating Activity. Point out that babysitting provides a good employment opportunity, and it is perhaps one of the most responsible jobs they will ever have. Tell students that this lesson explains how to prepare for babysitting as well as how to care for infants, toddlers, and preschoolers.

Introducing *Words to Know*
Call on a student to pronounce the vocabulary term. Explain that "distract" means to draw (the mind, attention, etc.) away in another direction. Ask students if they can think of a synonym *(divert)*. Have students write sentences using the word.

LESSON FIVE
Caring for Children

WORDS TO KNOW

redirect

DISCOVER...
- how to prepare for babysitting.
- how to care for infants, toddlers, and preschoolers.

Babysitting is usually the easiest kind of job for young people to find, and it provides good employment experience. However, caring for children is a big responsibility. You will be better able to handle it if you prepare in advance. Then, the more frequently you care for children, the more you will know about keeping them safe and happy.

Babysitting

When you babysit, you take the place of the children's parents. You are totally responsible for the safety and well-being

176 CHAPTER 6: UNDERSTANDING AND CARING FOR CHILDREN

CLASSROOM RESOURCES FOR LESSON 5

 Blackline Masters
Activity and Project Card 12, "Calling All Babysitters"
Enrichment 7
Lesson 5 Quiz
Peer Pressure and Decision Making 14
Reteaching 6

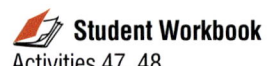 **Student Workbook**
Activities 47, 48

of the children in your care. If you do your job well, you will gain valuable experience and earn money. You will also have an opportunity to play with children and teach them new things.

Preparation

Before you begin looking for a babysitting job, you can prepare by taking a course in babysitting and first aid through a 4-H group, a local hospital, or a community center. You could also volunteer as a parent's helper—someone who cares for an infant or a young child under a parent's supervision.

Be sure to ask around to determine what the usual rate of pay is in your community. When you are starting out, you might be willing to charge a little less in order to get your first jobs.

When parents ask you to babysit, find out the following information before you accept the job:

- The number and ages of the children
- The time you will be needed
- How long the parents plan to be gone
- The rate of pay you will receive

If everything about the job is agreeable to you, check with your parents to make sure that the job meets with their approval. After you accept the job, write down the date, time, and place. Give your parents the phone number where you can be reached.

On the Job

The first time you babysit for a family, ask the parents if you can arrive a little early. That way, you will have a chance to get to know the

When you babysit for a new family, ask for a tour of the house. Why is this important?

LESSON FIVE: CARING FOR CHILDREN **177**

COOPERATIVE LEARNING

Preparing for Babysitting Tell students they will work as a class to develop a course outline for a class on babysitting. Organize the class into five groups and assign each group one of these topics: How to Get Started Babysitting, Tips for Caring for Infants, Tips for Caring for Toddlers, Tips for Caring for Preschoolers, Suggestions for Safety. Have each group develop an outline for their topic, suggest visuals they might use in the course presentation, make a list of suggested handouts for class attenders, and prepare a bibliography of helpful materials.

CHAPTER 6, LESSON 5

TEACH

L1 Critical Thinking
Working in small groups, have students develop a pamphlet titled "Before You Babysit." They can use the major headings from this lesson as topics to be included in the pamphlet.

L2 Keeping Records
Students may wish to start a card file as they gather information on families they contact for babysitting jobs. Suggest that they organize the file by family name. On each card they might include information about the children's ages, work phone numbers of parents, and emergency contacts. Once the student has watched the children, he or she can make notes about the children's likes and dislikes and special things to remember. Students with card-file capabilities on their home computers might keep the records on electronic files.

L2 Activity and Project Card
Allow time for students to complete Activity and Project Card 12, "Calling All Babysitters," in the TCR.

CHAPTER 6, LESSON 5

L2 Creating a Form

Have students work in small groups to write a "Code of Behavior for Babysitters." The first line should state: "A good babysitter . . ." Then have them list 12 items descriptive of an effective caregiver. This form may be created on a computer if one is available.

USING VISUALS

Have students study Figure 6.3. Based on their own experiences, ask them to add other items to the list that they consider helpful when babysitting.

DID YOU KNOW

Campfire Boys and Girls, the Red Cross, and local hospitals not only have beginning babysitters' classes, but in some areas offer a "special sitters" class so that teens can learn to care for developmentally delayed and disabled children.

**Figure 6.3
Babysitter's Checklist**
When you babysit, be sure to get this information from the parents before they leave. Is there anything else you need to know?

- Where the parents will be and a phone number where they can be reached.
- The name and phone number of an adult you can call if the parents can't be reached.
- The phone numbers of the police and fire departments and the rescue squad.
- The address where you are babysitting.
- The location of first-aid supplies.
- The location of toys, diapers, and other items you may need.
- The children's usual routine for eating and sleeping.
- The time the parents will be home.

children while the parents are still at home. During this time, you can also ask the parents for the information shown in **Figure 6.3.**

It is a good idea to ask the parents to go over a few of the family rules—television viewing, homework time, friends' visits, snacks, and bedtime—in front of the children. Discuss rules or limits that might cause problems later, such as television viewing, homework time, friend's visits, snacks, and bedtime.

If you are friendly and caring with the children, they will feel comfortable with you in charge. Show the children that you enjoy being with them and that you are interested in what they would like to do. Try to get them involved in something enjoyable for them so that they stay happy and busy—and won't have the opportunity to behave inappropriately.

178   CHAPTER 6: UNDERSTANDING AND CARING FOR CHILDREN

TECHNOLOGY UPDATE

On-Line Advice Rather than flipping through magazines or books, parents who have computers can, in the comfort of their homes, now use on-line services to get quick advice about caregiving. What users like about the service is the quick replies and the opportunity to immediately share and discuss problems with others. Have students investigate the type of information about child growth and development available from various on-line services and report their findings to the class. If there are students in class who are experienced at using on-line services, they might provide a demonstration for the rest of the class.

Reliable babysitters get asked back again and again and can establish a good relationship with the parents and children. Show that you are reliable by

- keeping a constant, careful watch on the children.
- keeping an accurate list of phone messages.
- leaving the house as neat as you found it.
- not allowing your friends to visit.
- not opening the door to strangers.

Television Tips

When you babysit, you should not rely on the television to keep the children busy. Ask the parents the following questions about television viewing ahead of time.

- Is it all right for the children to watch television? If so, how long may they watch?
- What programs or videotapes are OK to watch?

Caring for Children

Caring for children is a serious and important task, but it can also be enjoyable and creative. Children of different ages have different needs and require different types of care. Learning how to take care of infants, toddlers, and preschoolers will help you meet their needs and enjoy your time with them.

Caring for Infants

Infants are cute, fun to cuddle, and easy to entertain. Because they cannot do things for themselves, they rely on their caregiver for all their needs. Babies communicate their needs for sleep, food, comfortable clothing, and attention by crying.

When infants cry, first check to see if they are hungry or have dirty

One of the best ways to acquire skills for babysitting is to help your parents care for your younger brothers and sisters. What are some other ways to acquire these skills?

LESSON FIVE: CARING FOR CHILDREN 179

CHAPTER 6, LESSON 5

L2 Applying Skills
Have students work in pairs to brainstorm a list of good work habits that they should develop when tackling the job of caregiver. Ask them to use the list to write a cover letter explaining how these skills have helped them to prepare for other jobs they might wish to pursue.

L3 Critical Thinking
Emphasize that it is normal for toddlers to feel anxious when separated from their parents. Working in small groups, have students make a list of things a babysitter can do to comfort toddlers when their parents leave.

L2 Problem Solving
Assign Peer Pressure and Decision Making 14 in the TCR. This activity gives students the opportunity to recognize peer pressure and practice decision-making skills.

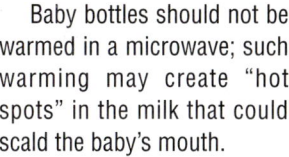

DID YOU KNOW
Baby bottles should not be warmed in a microwave; such warming may create "hot spots" in the milk that could scald the baby's mouth.

MORE ABOUT • • •

Infant Development A newborn needs to be fed often, usually every three to four hours, and kept clean, dry, and warm. During the infant's second and third months, personality and physical control begin to emerge. The baby may turn his or her head, learn to smile, and begin to reach for items. As children approach six months of age, they can hold their heads up, turn over, and begin to learn to sit with support. Between six and nine months, children learn to sit alone and begin to crawl.

CHAPTER 6, LESSON 5

TIPS for living

Have students read the feature. You might have them check the newspaper for several days to look for articles about emergency situations that confronted caregivers of young children. The articles should explain how the caregivers dealt with the emergencies. Make room on the bulletin board to post these articles.

L1 Demonstrating

Have students bring a doll and demonstrate the following: how to hold an infant, how to change the infant's diaper, how to feed the infant, how to put the infant to bed. Ask the class to evaluate the methods demonstrated.

DID YOU KNOW

Food allergies can cause behavior disorders and learning disabilities in children. It may not be just the particular food that children are allergic to; the vast array of additives present in food may contribute to the problem. In 1950 approximately 14 percent of the U.S. population had known food or substance allergies, according to the National Institutes of Health. By 1985, the figure rose to 33 percent, and projections for 1995 are close to 50 percent.

TIPS for living

HANDLING EMERGENCIES

In a serious emergency, you will need to call for help. If you live in an area with 911 emergency service, dial 911. If not, carry an emergency card with phone numbers of the police and fire departments, rescue squad, and poison control center listed on it. Know the house number and street where you are babysitting. Here are some tips for making an emergency phone call.

- Remain calm.
- Explain that you are the babysitter and give the street address where you are.
- State the type of emergency.
- Listen to and follow any directions you are given.
- Do not hang up until you are told to do so.

When you pick up an infant, grasp the baby's entire body rather than just the arms. Hold the baby firmly and rest it against your shoulder or cradle it in your arms.

diapers. Sometimes they may be too hot or too cold, or may need to be burped. If none of these problems exist, try holding, rocking, or walking them.

The first time you take care of an infant, have the parent show you the following.

- **How to hold the baby.** Infants can't hold their heads up without help. To support an infant's head, place one hand under the head and the other hand and arm under the lower part of the baby's back. Then you can lift the baby safely to your shoulder or cradle the baby in the bend of your arm and elbow area.

- **How to change diapers.** Ask the parent to show you the diaper-changing procedure and where to put dirty diapers. When you change a diaper, assemble everything you need before you begin. Babies can roll off changing tables and beds, so never leave them unattended.

- **What to feed the baby and when.** A young baby drinks milk or formula. Cradle the baby in your arm when you give a bottle. After the baby stops drinking, hold the baby over your shoulder, and lightly pat the back until you hear a burp. It may take a minute or two

180   CHAPTER 6: UNDERSTANDING AND CARING FOR CHILDREN

HOME AND COMMUNITY CONNECTION

Emergency Medical Dispatcher Point out to students that calls to 911 are answered by a professional called an emergency medical dispatcher. It is the dispatchers' responsibility to make sure they obtain the correct information about the emergency and to dispatch emergency workers to the correct location. You might ask an emergency medical dispatcher to talk to the class in order to emphasize the importance of providing the correct information when calling 911.

for the burp to come. Be patient. Also know that babies do not always burp.

- **Where and when to put the baby to sleep.** Place the baby on the side or back, never on the stomach. Be sure to pull up the side of the crib and fasten it securely. When the baby is sleeping, check frequently to make sure that everything is all right.

Caring for Toddlers and Preschoolers

Toddlers require a lot of attention. They need help and understanding as they grow and make new discoveries. They also demand much attention because they are busy moving from one thing to another. Unless a toddler is sleeping, a caregiver must constantly keep him or her in sight.

While toddlers are beginning to enjoy showing off their budding independence, most will need special comforting when their parents leave. You may need to redirect them with a favorite toy, puzzle, or game. When you **redirect** children, you *turn their attention to something else.* They will usually get over missing their parents in a few minutes.

If the toddler has learned to use the toilet, you may have to help him or her in the bathroom. Unfasten the toddler's clothes, and help him or her get onto the toilet or potty seat.

Preschoolers are curious and often look forward to being with caregivers they like. You can share such activities as reading, coloring, and pretend play with preschoolers.

Treasure Chest

Children will look forward to seeing a babysitter who brings surprise activities and goodies. Here are some ideas for the treasure chest.
- A few inexpensive toys
- Colorful bandage strips
- Materials for making puppets—old clean socks, yarn, glue, tape, and scraps of fabric
- Storybooks, crayons and colored paper
- Cassette tapes or compact discs of children's songs

▸ Toddlers enjoy playing with caregivers they like. What kinds of play activities would you enjoy with toddlers?

LESSON FIVE: CARING FOR CHILDREN **181**

TECHNOLOGY UPDATE

Baby Monitors Point out to students that some parents use baby monitors that allow them to keep in touch with their baby even when the baby is in another room. The monitors come in two parts—the baby's transmitter, which is placed in the infant's room, and the parents' receiver, which travels with the parents. Most models have a belt clip for the parents' receiver and run on AC current or batteries. Lights indicate whether the batteries are low or the baby unit is out of range.

CHAPTER 6, LESSON 5

Have students read the feature. Then have them develop their own babysitter's treasure chest. Tell them that even if they don't babysit, they can use it when children visit their home. You may want to suggest that they develop a "Babysitter's Bag of Tricks" to sell as a fundraiser for the PTA.

L3 **Critical Thinking**

Have students write articles for a classroom publication, *Babysitter's Gazette,* on why it is important for caregivers to follow parents' instructions for naptime and bedtime routines.

L1 **Student Workbook**

Assign Activities 47 and 48 in the Student Workbook.

ASSESS

Evaluating the Lesson

Assign Reviewing Terms and Facts and Thinking Critically on page 182 to review the lesson; then assign the Lesson 5 Quiz in the TCR.

Reteaching

- Have students bring pictures of infants, toddlers, and preschoolers to class. Have them use these pictures as the center of concept maps which illustrate the various characteristics of each group.
- Have students complete Reteaching Activity 6 in the TCR.

CHAPTER 6, LESSON 5

Answers to Lesson 5 Review

1. How many children are there and what are their ages? What are your responsibilities while babysitting? What time should you arrive? How long will the parents be gone? What is the rate of pay?
2. They are busy darting from one thing to another.
3. When you redirect a child, you turn his or her attention to something else.
4. Discuss with the parents and in front of the children rules or limits that might cause problems.
5. By taking a course in babysitting, by talking with other babysitters.
6. Students' lists should be similar to the list in the chapter.

Enrichment

- Suggest that students investigate safety precautions for preparing and serving foods to toddlers. Have them find out what foods are likely to cause choking and what should be done if a child chokes on food. Ask them to report their findings to the class.
- Assign Enrichment Activity 7 in the TCR.

CLOSE

Ask students to complete the following sentence. "When caring for children, a good caregiver . . ." Write student responses on the chalkboard.

Babysitting can be a rewarding and valuable experience. What are some benefits of babysitting?

Toddlers need their food cut into small bites, and they may need help using a spoon or a fork. During meals and snacks, serve only foods that parents have specified and provided. Children may have allergies of which you are unaware.

When caring for toddlers and preschoolers, keep the children's normal bedtime routine. Ask parents what time each child goes to bed. Also, find out if the child always has a bedtime story.

The Rewards of Babysitting

Babysitting is not only an excellent way to develop good work habits but also an enjoyable and challenging job. As you gain more experience, you will become more confident about meeting children's needs.

LESSON FIVE *Review*

Using complete sentences, answer the following questions on a separate sheet of paper.

Reviewing Terms and Facts
1. **Recall** What questions should you ask before you accept a babysitting job?
2. **Explain** Why do toddlers require a lot of attention?
3. **Vocabulary** How do you *redirect* a child?

Thinking Critically
4. **Recommend** As a babysitter, what could you do to prevent children from objecting to family rules?

5. **Describe** How might you get recommended for babysitting jobs?

Applying Concepts
6. Make a list of questions to ask parents before you accept a babysitting job and when you arrive at their home. Leave space for answers as well as for names and addresses. Then look up local phone numbers for the police, fire department, ambulance, poison control center, and directory assistance. Add these phone numbers to your list.

MEETING STUDENT DIVERSITY

Cultural Diversity Invite students in the class who grew up in other cultures to discuss the differences in child caregiving in their countries. Students might explain the different types of games, books, and toys used in their native lands to teach young children. If possible, have the students bring in samples of such toys, books, and games to show to the class. Students might also explain different customs or techniques used for caregiving.

Chapter 6 Activities

TECHNOLOGY
Software for Kids

Matthew and Nathan, four-year-old twins, crowd into a chair in front of the computer. Nathan pushes the *P* key. "P is for piano," says the computer.

Educational computer games are being created specifically for young children. These programs teach preschoolers the names and sounds of letters and numbers, and such concepts as color, shape, and size.

Try This!
If possible, try out one of the programs for preschoolers, and report to the class.

FRIENDS & FAMILY
BABYSITTING DILEMMA

Cherise and Katie wanted to start babysitting to earn extra money, but they needed a great idea to help them stand out from the competition. One day they saw a Red Cross ad saying: "Child safety and CPR class—open to parents and babysitters." *That* was what would give them an edge over other babysitters!

TRY THIS!
Why do you think that the Red Cross course will help?

A Global View
BRINGING UP CHILDREN

Adolescents in many cultures play an important role in caring for younger children and teaching them new skills. For example, instead of being taught directly by adults, many Native American children observe the way their older siblings perform a task. Then they practice the skill on their own and test themselves.

TRY THIS!
Why do you think that adolescents have more child-rearing responsibilities in some cultures than in others? Share your ideas with your classmates.

ART CONNECTION
Follow Up: CHILDREN IN ART

1. Although Eakins's *Baby at Play* was painted over 100 years ago, it tells us that children loved to play with toys that are still popular today. Besides providing a visual record of people, times, and places, what other values does art have?

2. Bring examples of children's art to class, and discuss why young children love to paint, draw, and make things.

Thomas Eakins. *Baby at Play.* 1876. National Gallery of Art, Washington, D.C. John Hay Whitney Collection.

CHAPTER 6 ACTIVITIES 183

CHAPTER 6 Activities

TECHNOLOGY
Gather several computer software catalogs for students to browse through after they read this article. Have them choose several of the computer programs they think would interest a preschool child and tell why they think children would enjoy them.

FRIENDS & FAMILY
After students read the article, ask where they think they might find classes on child safety, first aid, or CPR in their communities. If possible, bring to class brochures or booklets on child care and safety from local agencies to share with students.

A Global View
Ask volunteers to do research on the subject of "Bringing Up Children" in other cultures. Suggest they use magazine and newspaper articles, CD-ROM encyclopedias, or on-line resources to gather information to share with the class.

Teaching the ART CONNECTION
Have students work in small groups to create ideas for a painting called *Babies at Play in the 1990s*. Then have each group work together to create a painting using their ideas. Arrange to have the paintings displayed somewhere in the school for students to enjoy.

Follow Up: Answers to Follow-Up
1. Enjoyment, stimulation of creativity and imagination.
2. Have students display the sample children's artwork and discuss why children love to paint, draw, and make things. You might also have your school's kindergartners show samples of their artwork to the class.

183

CHAPTER 6 REVIEW

Checking Comprehension

Use the Chapter Summary and the Chapter 6 Review to help students go over the most important ideas presented in Chapter 6.

Answers to Words to Know

1. Provide direction so that children learn the basic rules of behavior.
2. Being consistent means doing what you say you will do and avoiding saying things you do not mean.
3. Preschoolers are children who are three, four, or five years old. Preschoolers like to talk and to play with children of all ages.
4. Attention span is the length of time a person can concentrate on any one thing.
5. Group play is playing with other children of all ages. Preschoolers—children aged three, four, and five—are ready for group play.
6. An intruder is someone who uses force to get into a home.
7. Smoke alarms are important because they set off an alarm when smoke is present and alert people to the possibility of fire.
8. Answers will vary but might include talking soothingly to the child, reading a story, or giving the child a favorite toy.

Answers to Review Questions

1. To be prepared for babysitting jobs, to help with younger siblings at home, and to prepare for the future task of parenting.
2. Making positive statements, praising children, encouraging independence.

CHAPTER 6 REVIEW

Chapter Summary

- Parenting is the process of caring for children and helping them grow and learn.
- Children need guidance, discipline with a positive focus, and encouragement to do tasks for themselves.
- Children progress through predictable physical, intellectual, emotional, social, and moral developmental stages. Learning about these stages helps you know what to expect from children at different ages.
- Some children have special physical, intellectual, or emotional needs. Love, understanding, and extra attention can help these children develop their abilities.
- Types of play include solitary or independent play, parallel play, cooperative play, group play, and quiet play.
- Child safety is one of a caregiver's main concerns. You should know how to prevent common accidents and what to do if an accident occurs.
- Babysitting is an important job that requires responsibility and planning. Babysitters should make sure that they have all of the information and instructions they need before the parents leave.
- Caring for infants and young children may involve changing diapers, feeding, and putting children to bed. You should know the correct procedures for these tasks.

 ## Words to Know

Using complete sentences, answer the following questions on a separate sheet of paper.

1. What do you do when you give children *guidance*?
2. Explain what it means to be *consistent* when taking care of children.
3. Define the term *preschoolers*. What are two characteristics of preschoolers?
4. Explain what is meant by a child's *attention span*.
5. What is *group play*? At what age are most children ready for group play?
6. What is an *intruder*?
7. Why are *smoke alarms* important?
8. How could you *redirect* a child?

Review Questions

Using complete sentences, answer the following questions on a separate sheet of paper.

1. Why should a young teen learn parenting skills?
2. Give three examples of positive parenting.
3. What are the developmental tasks of infants?
4. Name four ways in which young children learn.
5. What are typical play activities for infants?

184 CHAPTER 6: UNDERSTANDING AND CARING FOR CHILDREN

EXTRA CREDIT PROJECT

Adding to Your Portfolio Have students prepare a section in their portfolios to reinforce what they have learned about understanding and caring for children. Encourage students to locate photographs, illustrations, or artworks of children from magazines and books. Illustrations may demonstrate the following: positive parenting skills; children playing safely; various ages and stages of development; or ways of caring for children. Encourage students to consider works of fine art found in catalogs or encyclopedias. Have students collect or duplicate these illustrations and write captions that explain how each one demonstrates a concept from the chapter.

CHAPTER 6 REVIEW

6. How does play benefit toddlers?
7. What should you do if a child becomes seriously injured while in your care?
8. How can you prevent children from getting into poisonous substances?
9. Describe a reliable babysitter.

Thinking Critically

Using complete sentences, answer the following questions on a separate sheet of paper.

1. **Compare** How are the needs of young children similar to your own needs?
2. **Analyze** Why do you think that it is important to stimulate a child's imagination?
3. **Suggest** What would you do if two toddlers wanted to play with the same toy?
4. **Explain** Why must caregivers watch children closely even if the home has been childproofed?

Cooperative Learning

1. As a class, organize a used-toy drive. Use your management skills to advertise the event and collect the toys. Be sure that all of the toys you collect are clean and safe for children. Donate the toys to the children's ward of a local hospital or to an organization that helps children with special needs.
2. Working in small groups, discuss child-care skills that a babysitter should have. Have each group member explain a skill to the group. If possible, use a doll to demonstrate the skill. Choose from this list: how to feed and burp a baby, how to hold a baby, how to change a diaper, how to bathe a baby, how to soothe a crying baby, how to play with a baby.

 Family & Community

1. Check the safety of the play equipment at a nearby playground. Look for such items as missing bolts, sharp edges, and worn or shaky anchoring structures. Report anything that you think is unsafe to the playground supervisor, or write a letter to the city department in charge of the playground.
2. Find out about a babysitting or first-aid class. The local chapter of the Red Cross, the YWCA, a 4-H club, a local hospital, or community education programs may offer classes for babysitters. If possible, sign up for a class. Share what you learn with your classmates.

 Building A Portfolio

1. Write down as many facts as you can remember about yourself as a young child. Who were your playmates? What were your favorite toys? Which stories did you enjoy? Put a list of facts about yourself, along with childhood photos or artwork, into your portfolio.
2. Collect cartoons and comic strips that feature young children. Share your findings with your classmates. Discuss how the cartoons and comic strips are related to information you found in this chapter. Keep your collection in your portfolio.

CHAPTER 6 REVIEW 185

CHAPTER 6 REVIEW

3. Answers should include those tasks listed in Figure 6.1, page 161.
4. Any four: exploring to find out things around their home, doing the same thing over and over again, observing and imitating others, listening to sounds and conversations that go on around them, handling objects they use and see others use, having new experiences, gaining praise and approval.
5. Waving arms, kicking legs, swinging, pulling, throwing, pushing, pounding, banging, and stacking.
6. Develops their minds, bodies, and social skills, especially the social skill of learning to share.
7. Contact the child's parents, a neighbor, or a relative so that they can provide the appropriate care. In poisoning cases, call the poison control center or 911.
8. Watch children closely; keep all poisons locked in cabinets and drawers that have safety latches.
9. One who looks after the safety and welfare of the child in her or his care and meets the child's physical, emotional, social, intellectual, and moral needs.

Evaluate

Use the Chapter 6 Test in the TCR, or construct your own test using the Testmaker Software.

CLOSE

Have students apply their knowledge of the chapter's content by completing one of the alternative assessment activities listed under Family and Community or Building a Portfolio.

Answers to Thinking Critically

1. People of all ages have physical, emotional, social, intellectual, and moral needs that must be met.
2. So that the child can develop creativity and curiosity.
3. Explain that they must share in playing with the toy. Let one child play with the toy for a while, then switch it to the other child. Meanwhile, you might entertain the child not playing with the toy by reading, giving the child another toy, and so on.
4. Because infants can put anything in their mouths, toddlers move quickly and get into everything, and preschoolers can get into dangerous situations unless their behavior is monitored.

185

UNIT 3
Consumer Skills and Home Management

Unit Overview

Unit 3 explains consumer rights and responsibilities. The unit also describes the benefits of keeping a home clean and safe and encourages recycling.

Chapter 7 identifies influences on consumer behavior and ways of managing money. In Chapter 8 students discover how they can maximize and personalize their living area. The chapter also presents students with effective ways of keeping their homes safe and clean. Chapter 9 explores ways that students can protect their environment. The chapter also explains what students can do to help avoid accidents and prevent violence in their lives.

Introducing the Unit

- **Parent Letters** As you begin study of this unit, you may wish to send home copies of the Parent Letter and Activities found in the *Linking Home, School, and Community* booklet in the TCR.
- **Using Visuals** Have students examine the photo and explain how the teen in the photo is demonstrating consumer skills.
- **Using the Color Transparency** Present Color Transparency 31, "Managing Your Life," in the TCR. Ask students to identify which of the areas called out in the transparency they feel they can manage well.

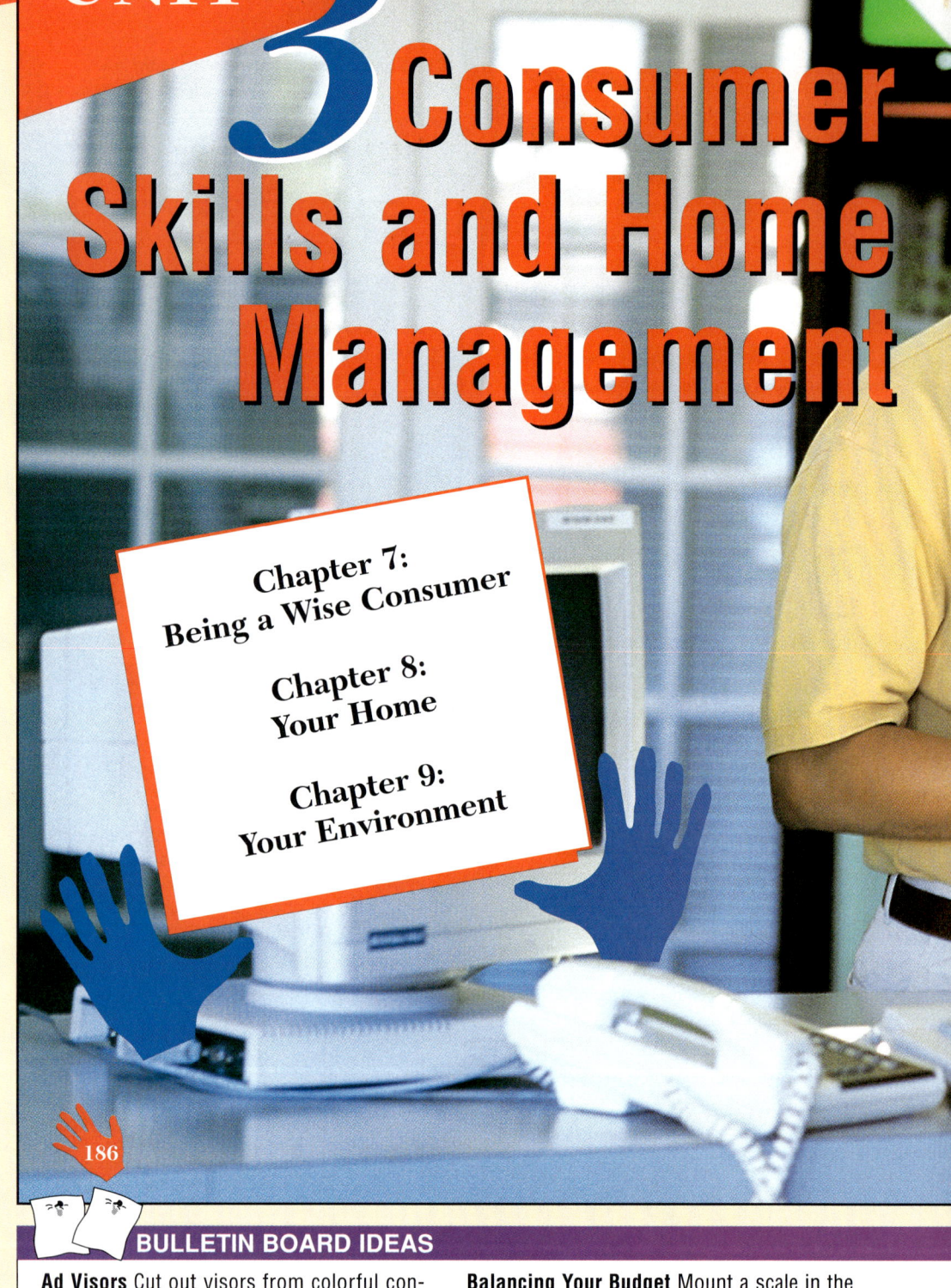

UNIT 3
Consumer Skills and Home Management

Chapter 7:
Being a Wise Consumer

Chapter 8:
Your Home

Chapter 9:
Your Environment

BULLETIN BOARD IDEAS

Ad Visors Cut out visors from colorful construction paper. On each visor list a technique associated with advertising, such as *informative, persuasive, public-service message, misleading, catchy slogans, endorsements,* and *bright colors*. Mount visors on the bulletin board. Next to each visor attach an actual advertisement that demonstrates the technique.

Balancing Your Budget Mount a scale in the center of the bulletin board. On one side of the scale, put words to indicate income, such as *gifts, salary, allowance*. On the other side of the scale list expenses, such as *school supplies, clothes, snacks, entertainment*.

UNIT PROJECTS 3

Encourage students to work on three Hands-on Projects for this unit found in the Teacher's Classroom Resources.
- Hands-on Project 5, "T-Shirt Art for the Earth," guides students to design and decorate a T-shirt expressing a message about conservation.
- Hands-on Project 6, "Plastic Bag Dispenser," directs students to make a useful dispenser for storing plastic grocery bags.
- Hands-on Project 7, "Design a Room," has students work together to draw up plans for decorating a room of their choice.

Unit Closure

- Allow class time at the end of this unit to reinforce students' understanding of the material by playing Hands-on Game 3, "Personal and Home Management Jeopardy," found in the TCR.
- Create your own Unit Test using the Testmaker Software to evaluate students' comprehension.

Promoting Family & Consumer Sciences

Parents Take opportunities to reach out to parents whenever possible. Conduct workshops on topics of interest to parents. Plan a breakfast for working parents and ask for their input on tips for your classroom. Have students fix and serve the breakfast.

BULLETIN BOARD IDEAS

Storage Space On the bulletin board show a "before" and "after" scene of a clothes closet. In the first scene draw a closet with one clothes bar going across the top of the closet. In the second scene show the closet divided with clothes bars at different levels for shirts, pants, and dresses. Divide part of the closet space with drawers and shelves for sweaters and shoes.

Don't Trash It—Reuse It! Divide the bulletin board into two parts. On the left side of the board mount items that many times are discarded, such as berry baskets, thread spools, and tissue boxes. On the right side of the board show ways to recycle the items, such as for storage of toys, kitchen items, or collections.

187

Planning Guide
Chapter 7 Being a Wise Consumer

LESSON 1	Pages	FEATURES	CLASSROOM RESOURCES
Influences on Buying Decisions	190–193	*Skills In Action:* Money Savers	Lesson 1 Quiz Peer Pressure and Decision Making 15 Transparency 32, "Influences on Consumer Choices" Student Workbook Activities 49, 50
LESSON 2 **Evaluating Media Messages**	194–199	*Skills In Action:* Shopping by Television *Try This:* Comparing Labels	Concept Map 11 Cooperative Learning 13 Lesson 2 Quiz Student Workbook Activities 51, 52
LESSON 3 **Comparison Shopping**	200–205	*Skills in Action:* Evaluating Clubs *Try This:* Secondhand Treasures	Enrichment 8 Lesson 3 Quiz Transparency 33, "Smart Shopping" Student Workbook Activity 53
LESSON 4 **Consumer Rights and Responsibilities**	206–211	*Skills in Action:* Identifying Quackery *Tips for Living:* Writing a Complaint Letter	Activity and Project Card 13, "Consumer Letter" Concept Map 12 Cooperative Learning 14 Lesson 4 Quiz Peer Pressure and Decision Making 16 Transparency 34, "Refunds and Exchanges" Student Workbook Activities 54, 55

LESSON 5	Pages	FEATURES	CLASSROOM RESOURCES
Managing Your Money	212–216	*Try This: Stretching Your Money*	Activity and Project Card 14, "A Budgeting Game" Cross Curriculum 8 Lesson 5 Quiz Transparency 35, "Writing a Check" Transparency 36, "Recording Checks" Student Workbook Activities 56, 57

CHAPTER 7 RESOURCES
- Chapter 7 Test
- Reteaching 7
- Study Guide 7, *Reteaching*
- Testmaker Software

UNIT 3 RESOURCES
- Transparency 31, "Managing Your Life"
- Hands-on Projects 5, 6, 7
- Hands-on Game 3

Performance Assessment Activity

Ask students to choose a magazine advertisement and ask a family member or friend to evaluate the message. Each student should prepare a list of questions in advance.

When students have completed the evaluation, organize the class into small groups. Have the students in each group share their advertisements and evaluations with the other members. Then ask them to develop an evaluation form that they could use to judge how useful and how truthful the messages in ads really are.

OUT OF TIME?

If time does not permit thorough teaching of this chapter, you may wish to use:
- Teens Making a Difference, page 189
- Tips for Living, page 210
- Try This, pages 196, 205, 215
- Skills in Action, pages 192, 195, 203, 208
- Young Living Activities, page 217
- Chapter Summary, page 218

Resources for the Teacher

Celsi, Teresa Noel. *Ralph Nader: The Consumer Revolution.* Brookfield, CT: Millbrook Press, 1991.

Dappen, Andy. *100s of Ways You Can Save 1000s of Dollars.* Brier, WA: Brier Books, 1992.

Readings for the Student

Gay, Kathlyn. *Caution: This May Be an Advertisement: A Teen Guide to Advertising.* New York: Watts, 1992.

New Board Games. Zillions (February/March 1995), pp. 4–8.

Multimedia Resources

Survival Finances: A Personal Money Management Simulation. (Apple disk) J. Weston Walch.

Why You Buy: How Ads Persuade (Videocassette with teacher's guide). Learning Seed. Zenger Media.

Writing Checks Right (Videocassette with student workbook, manual). Cambridge Career Production. Zenger Media.

CHAPTER 7

Being a Wise Consumer

Chapter Overview

Chapter 7 introduces students to the skills needed to be a wise consumer. Students also learn about their consumer rights and responsibilities.
LESSON 1 identifies factors that influence buying decisions.
LESSON 2 describes the techniques used by advertisers to sell products.
LESSON 3 explains how to compare price, quality, and warranty among products.
LESSON 4 discusses consumer rights and responsibilities.
LESSON 5 describes money-management skills.

Introducing the Chapter

Have students skim the lesson titles and subheads in the chapter. Have them make an outline of the chapter using the chapter title, lesson titles, and subheads. As students read each lesson, have them add details to the outline. Encourage them to use their outlines as study aids for the chapter test.

Chapter Motivator

Refer students to the chapter title, "Being a Wise Consumer." Have students complete the following sentence: "Being a wise consumer means . . ." Ask volunteers to read their responses to the class. Discuss responses. Record accurate responses on the board. Have students use the responses to make a concept web of ways to be a wise consumer.

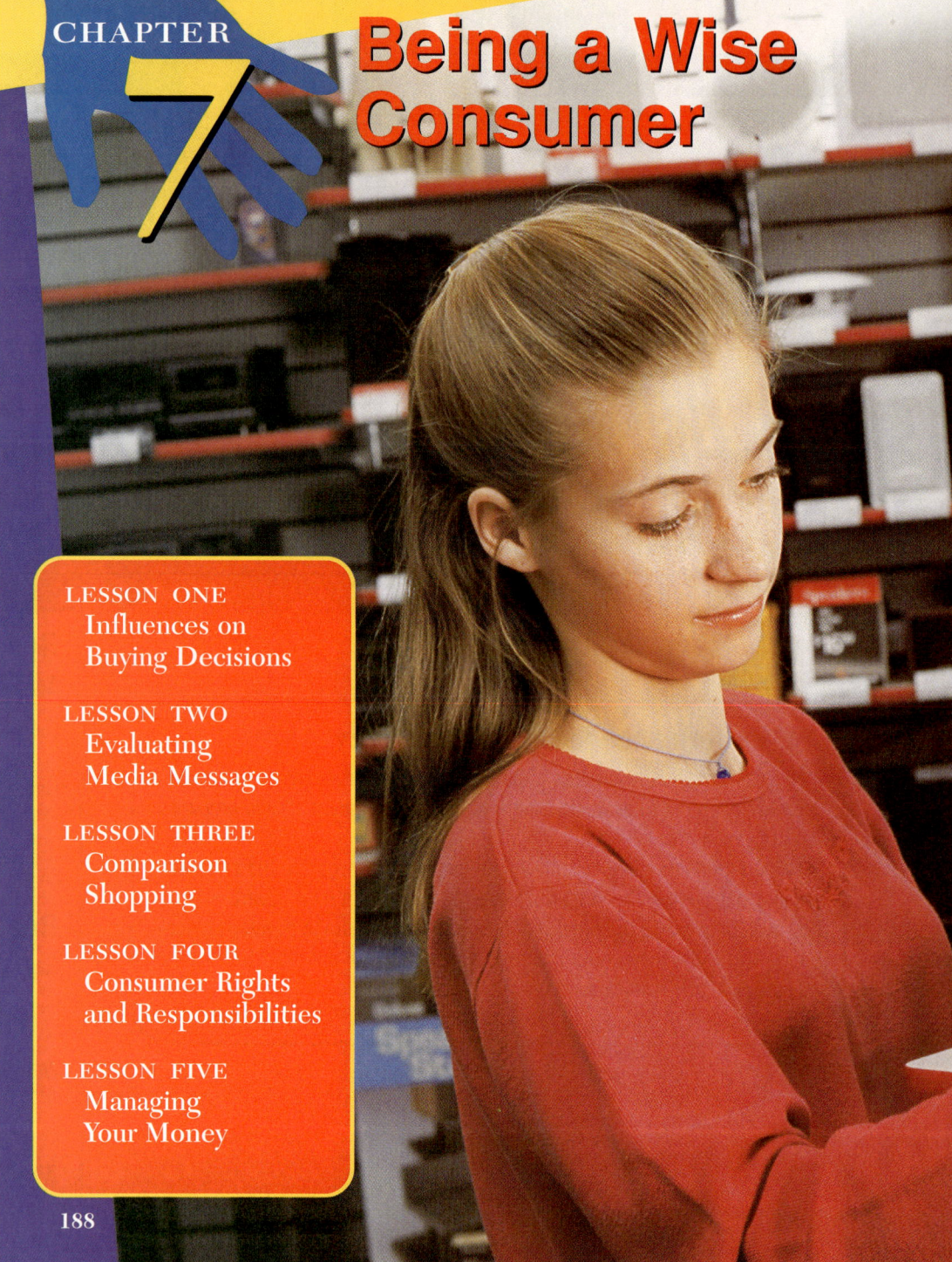

CHAPTER 7 Being a Wise Consumer

LESSON ONE
Influences on Buying Decisions

LESSON TWO
Evaluating Media Messages

LESSON THREE
Comparison Shopping

LESSON FOUR
Consumer Rights and Responsibilities

LESSON FIVE
Managing Your Money

KEY TO ABILITY LEVELS

Teaching strategies that appear throughout the chapter have been identified by one of three codes to give you an idea of their suitability for students of varying learning styles and abilities.

L1 Level 1 strategies should be within the ability range of all students. Often full class participation is required. Teacher direction is usually needed.

L2 Level 2 strategies are for average to above-average students or for small groups. Some teacher direction is necessary.

L3 Level 3 strategies are designed for students able and willing to work independently. Minimal teacher direction is necessary.

CHAPTER 7

TEENS MAKING A DIFFERENCE

Have students read "Teens Making a Difference." Ask them to identify the ways the students in the article make a difference by recycling. Have students participate in a discussion of ways that they make a difference in the environment by recycling. Encourage them to brainstorm ways that recycling can become part of their everyday life. Have students make posters using these ideas. Display the posters throughout the school.

Ask students to work with a partner to answer the questions at the end of the feature. Ask volunteers to share their responses with the class.

BLOCK SCHEDULING

The following Teacher Classroom Resources are suggested for use in classrooms with Block Scheduling.

- Activity and Project Card 13, "Consumer Letter"
- Activity and Project Card 14, "A Budgeting Game"
- Cooperative Learning 13, "Ads—Fact or Fantasy?"
- Cooperative Learning 14, "Rally Around Your Rights"

TEENS MAKING A DIFFERENCE
Clothes from Recycled Plastic

In social studies class, Rachel Davis and her friend Maria learned that most of the millions of plastic beverage bottles that are thrown out daily are never recycled. Just recently, however, the teens found clothes made from recycled plastic in a mail order catalog. The jackets were made of polyester fleece, but most of the fabric was made from recycled bottles. Rachel and Maria have decided to buy at least some clothes that are good for the environment as well as useful to them.

Try THIS!

How can you help the environment through your shopping decisions? Make a chart of items you buy regularly for which environmentally safe choices are available. Share your chart with your classmates.

189

TECHNOLOGY IN THE CLASSROOM

Software Programs Choosing quality software is essential to the quality of instruction in the Family and Consumer Sciences classroom. The software you select should be the kind that will attain the objectives of the course. You can obtain information about software from a variety of sources. These include journals and publications, catalogs, software stores, exhibits at professional meetings and conferences, and educational resource centers.

LESSON ONE
Influences on Buying Decisions

FOCUS

Lesson Objectives
After studying this lesson, students should be able to
- explain what it means to be a consumer.
- identify how peers, habits, and advertising influence buying decisions.

Motivating Activity
Have students write the name of a major item they would like to purchase. Ask them to name three people they would ask for advice before they make their purchase.

Introducing the Lesson
Have students share their responses to the Motivating Activity. Make a chart on the board with the following headings: Peers, Parents, Teachers, Siblings, Salespeople. Tally student responses in the chart. Discuss the major influences on students' buying decisions. Point out that seeking advice before making a large purchase is often helpful.

Introducing *Words to Know*
Ask a volunteer to read the vocabulary words and their definitions. Ask students to write a paragraph using all the vocabulary words. Have them share their paragraphs with the class.

190

LESSON ONE
Influences on Buying Decisions

WORDS TO KNOW
goods
services
consumer
advertisement

DISCOVER...
- what it means to be a consumer.
- how peers, habits, and advertising influence your buying decisions.

Do you remember every T-shirt, magazine, notebook, or CD you bought last year? Are you, or is one of your friends, saving money to buy something special, such as concert tickets or a new jacket? As a teen, you are a member of a group with a great deal of spending power. Many companies that make clothing, magazines, and soft drinks take teen interests very seriously. Some of these companies even specialize in products designed specifically for teens.

190   CHAPTER 7: BEING A WISE CONSUMER

CLASSROOM RESOURCES FOR LESSON 1

 Blackline Masters
Lesson 1 Quiz
Peer Pressure and Decision Making 15

 Transparencies
Transparency 32, "Influences on Consumer Choices"

 Student Workbook
Activities 49, 50

Teens as Consumers

On what do teens spend their money? Like all people, they buy goods and services. **Goods** are *products made for sale*, such as in-line skates, computer games, or jeans. **Services,** or *work performed by one person for others*, include the work done to repair your bike, tutor you, dry-clean your clothes, or teach you karate. Even if you don't spend a great deal of money, you can be a smarter shopper if you know what factors influence your consumer decisions. A **consumer** is *a person who buys goods and services*.

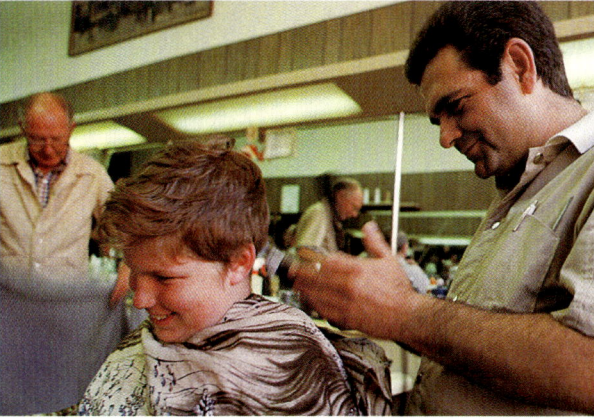

A haircut is a service. What other services do you buy?

As a consumer you have many choices to make. You must decide what to buy, where to buy, and when to buy. You have to decide how to get the best value for your money. By making wise purchases, you will be a satisfied consumer.

Factors That Influence Buying Decisions

When you bought your last CD or pair of athletic shoes, what influenced your decision? Did your friends convince you that you needed the CD? Did you buy the same brand of shoes that you always buy? Maybe your decision was based on price. Perhaps you saw an advertisement that encouraged you to purchase the product. An **advertisement** is a *message to persuade consumers to buy*

Peers

Because friends are an important part of the lives of most teens, their ideas and tastes can be influential. Have you ever tried out a new shampoo because some of your friends were using it? Have you ever decided to buy a new backpack because a friend bought one?

LESSON ONE: INFLUENCES ON BUYING DECISIONS 191

MORE ABOUT • • •

Buying Goods and Services Consumer educators offer the following tips for purchasing goods and services:
- When calculating what you can afford to pay for a good, consider the extra costs of upkeep or maintenance.
- Ask others for references when buying services, because services cannot be inspected in advance.
- Check recommendations on products and brands in such magazines as *Zillions, Consumer Reports for Kids,* or *Consumer Reports.*

CHAPTER 7, LESSON 1

TEACH

L2 Math
Have students divide a paper in half and mark one side of the paper "Goods" and the other "Services." Give students five minutes to list each product or service they purchased within the last week and estimate the total cost of these goods and services. Have them determine if they spent more money on goods or on services. Then compute the total money spent by the class on goods and services.

L2 Economics
Have students keep a log for the last two weeks of the goods they purchased. Their log should include the following information: kind of good, where it was bought, who or what influenced their decision to buy. Have them make a chart showing the results of their logs. Computers may be used to keep logs and create charts.

L3 Math
Have students estimate the money that they have spent in the last week. Have them total the sum for the entire class and find the average per student. Then have them multiply by the number of students in their school. Discuss the conclusions that can be reached about young people's spending power.

L2 Problem Solving
Assign Peer Pressure and Decision Making 15 in the TCR. This activity gives students the opportunity to recognize peer pressure and practice decision-making skills.

L1 Using Transparencies
Present Color Transparency 32, "Influences on Consumer Choices," in the TCR. Use this overhead visual to reinforce concepts from this lesson.

CHAPTER 7, LESSON 1

Have students list four brand-name products they use. Ask them to take their list to a store where these products are sold. Ask students to write the cost and the ingredients or materials next to the name of each product. Then have them find a generic brand of the item and record the cost and the ingredients. Have them compare and contrast the ingredients or materials and the prices. As a class, discuss the advantages and disadvantages of buying brand-name goods versus generic goods.

L1 Student Workbook

Assign Activities 49 and 50 in the Student Workbook.

ASSESS

Evaluating the Lesson

Assign Reviewing Terms and Facts and Thinking Critically on page 193 to review the lesson; then assign the Lesson 1 Quiz in the TCR.

Reteaching

- Have students write a paragraph describing something they bought that they did not need. Ask them to explain what influenced their decision to buy the item and what they learned from the experience.
- Have students complete Reteaching Activity 7 in the TCR.

192

Money Savers

Often, store brands and generic brands are made from the same ingredients or materials. The only difference may be the amount of money spent on packaging and advertising. The extra cost is passed on to consumers. Why not save some money and try the less expensive item?

Before buying goods or services, think about why you want to make the purchase. Are you being influenced by your peers?

192   CHAPTER 7: BEING A WISE CONSUMER

Sometimes one or two popular students can spread a fad that was started by a movie, concert, or sports event. Other students may see them carrying a certain kind of bag or wearing a certain brand of shoes that a celebrity wears and decide to do the same. These items may even become status symbols, or signs of popularity and importance.

Teens who belong to a certain group often dress similarly. They may think that wearing a particular kind of clothes is a way of expressing who they are. For example, athletes may wear sweats and baseball caps, whereas surfers may like T-shirts and baggy shorts. Other groups may prefer preppy clothes or leather jackets.

What really matters is that you buy for yourself what is best for *you*. As you make a buying decision, ask yourself the following questions.

- Am I buying an item that is popular today but will soon be out of fashion?
- Am I getting the best value for my money?
- Am I spending a lot more money for a name-brand item?

Before you make a purchase, evaluate the product and analyze your decision. If it is not best for you, you may choose to wait or to buy something else. Do what is best for you, and be proud of your individuality.

Habit

As you have probably discovered, many of your buying decisions are influenced by your habits. If you always shop at the same store, you may be passing up good prices offered at another store. Sometimes you need to evaluate your habits to make sure that you are being a careful shopper.

Advertising

Advertising is another important influence on people's buying decisions. Advertising is everywhere you look—in newspapers and magazines, on television and radio, and on taxis and buses. It even appears on clothing and on some on-line computer services.

COOPERATIVE LEARNING

Ad Them Up Organize the students into small groups. Provide each group with a popular teen magazine. Have the members of the group calculate the percentage of the magazine that is made up of advertisements. Have them discuss whether they read the advertisements in magazines and if the advertisements affect their buying decisions. Then have the group members choose three advertisements in the magazine that they think might strongly influence young people to buy the product. Have each group share its findings with the class.

The major advantage of advertising is that it lets consumers know what goods and services are available. Ads introduce new products and point out their benefits. In addition, they let people know about sales. Looking at the weekly advertising circulars in the newspaper is a great way to compare prices.

Some ads deliver a public service message. They may warn people about the dangers of tobacco, alcohol, and other drugs. Other advertisements ask people to conserve natural resources or donate money to charitable organizations.

There are also disadvantages to advertising. Sometimes ads persuade people to buy items they don't need, especially if the product is endorsed by a celebrity the consumers like or admire. Advertising can be misleading. Some ads make exaggerated claims. One ad, for example, states that four out of five dentists surveyed recommend a particular brand of toothpaste. How many dentists were questioned? How were they chosen? Think carefully about such claims.

You can improve your consumer skills by learning what factors influence your buying decisions.

LESSON ONE Review

Using complete sentences, answer the following questions on a separate sheet of paper.

Reviewing Terms and Facts

1. **Vocabulary** What is the difference between *goods* and *services*?
2. **List** What choices do you have to make as a consumer?
3. **Identify** Name three factors that influence your buying decisions.
4. **Recall** Where might you find advertisements?

Thinking Critically

5. **Interpret** Why is it important to analyze your buying decisions before going along with your peer group?
6. **Explain** Why might it be hard to change buying decisions based on habit?
7. **Analyze** Do you think that the advantages of advertising outweigh its disadvantages? Explain your answer.

Applying Concepts

8. Make a list of eight or ten items that you purchased recently. Next to each item identify what most influenced your buying decision—peers, habit, or advertising. Compare your list with those of your classmates. Do you see any similarities between your buying behavior and that of your peers?

LESSON ONE: INFLUENCES ON BUYING DECISIONS   193

COOPERATIVE LEARNING

Experimenting Have students work in small groups to identify an advertisement that makes a claim, such as that a certain paper towel holds more liquid than any other brand on the market. Then have the students set up an experiment to prove or disprove the claim. Have each group perform their experiment for the class. Discuss the results of the experiments. Remind students to beware of advertisements that make claims.

CHAPTER 7, LESSON 1

Answers to Lesson 1 Review

1. Goods are products made for sale. Services are work performed by one person and sold to others.
2. Decide what to buy, where to buy it, and when to buy it.
3. Peers, habit, advertising.
4. In newspapers and magazines, on television, radio, subways, taxis, buses, on-line computer services, and billboards.
5. Analyzing buying decisions before going along with the peer group can save money and make you proud of your individuality.
6. Habits are hard to break. Choices based on habit may cause you to pass up good prices.
7. Answers will vary. Students should mention that advertising allows consumers to know what goods or services are available, it introduces new products and tells people about the benefits of the products, and it lets people know about sales. Some advertising has a public-service message. Advertisements encourage people to buy items they don't need and are sometimes misleading.
8. Students should list items they purchased recently, identify what influenced their buying decision, and compare their buying behavior to that of peers.

Enrichment

Have students write a consumer advice column for a school newspaper that gives examples of influences on purchasing behavior.

CLOSE

Ask students to name one thing they will change about their buying behavior because of the information they have received in this lesson.

LESSON TWO
Evaluating Media Messages

FOCUS

Lesson Objectives
After studying this lesson, students should be able to
- describe the messages advertisers use to convince people to buy their products.
- discuss the types of media that carry messages.
- explain how to evaluate advertising messages.

Motivating Activity
Ask students to write down a description of their favorite advertisement—what product is advertised, who the audience is, what it is about the advertisement that captures their attention.

Introducing the Lesson
Have students share their responses to the Motivating Activity. Use the responses as a basis for discussing the factors that make an advertisement appealing and memorable. Explain to students that this lesson will help them understand the powerful effects of advertising.

Introducing *Words to Know*
Have students read the vocabulary words and their definitions. Point out that *media* is the plural for *medium*, which means "method of communication." Tell them that the word *infomercial* is a combination of the words *informational commercial*. Explain that until recently there was no such word.

LESSON TWO
Evaluating Media Messages

WORDS TO KNOW

information ad
image ad
media
infomercial

DISCOVER...
- the messages advertisers use to convince people to buy their products.
- the types of media that carry the messages.
- how to evaluate advertising messages.

How many advertisements do you see and hear in a single day? Do the ads tempt you to try a soft drink or see a new movie? To be a wise consumer, you need to learn to evaluate, or judge, just how useful and truthful the messages in ads really are.

194   CHAPTER 7: BEING A WISE CONSUMER

CLASSROOM RESOURCES FOR LESSON 2

 Blackline Masters
Concept Map 11
Cooperative Learning 13
Lesson 2 Quiz

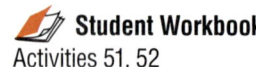 **Student Workbook**
Activities 51, 52

Why Do Companies Advertise?

Advertisements, or ads, are designed to catch the attention of consumers and convince them to buy a product or service. Ads influence consumers by presenting goods or services in an attractive way. Ads also inform consumers about new products, remind them of old products that are still available, and attract them to special sales.

Types of Advertisements

Advertisements generally fall into one of two categories: information ads and image ads. Each type of ad sends a different kind of message.

- **Information ads** are *ads that describe the features of a product or service and give facts about its price and quality.* Information ads appeal to the practical side of people. They send the message that an item gives good value for the money or that an item is a good buy because of its high quality.

- **Image ads** are *ads that connect a product or service to a lifestyle that consumers would like to have.* Image

Shopping by Television

If shopping by television, keep these points in mind.
- You can't judge the quality of an item by the way it looks on the screen.
- Shipping and handling adds to the price of the item.
- If you don't like the item after you receive it, you will probably have to pay for return postage.

Identify the image that this ad projects. Would the ad convince you to buy the product?

LESSON TWO: EVALUATING MEDIA MESSAGES

TECHNOLOGY UPDATE

Many stores now use in-store videos to sell products and services. For example, in an accessories department, you may be able to watch a video that explains several ways to use jewelry. In a hardware store, you may be able to watch a video that promotes a certain brand of floor tiles or tools. Such videos catch the attention of shoppers, provide information, and save salespeople's time. Discuss with students the advantages and disadvantages of such videos.

CHAPTER 7, LESSON 2

TEACH

Skills IN ACTION

Have students make a public-service announcement for television warning of the disadvantages of shopping by television. Have students present their messages for the class.

L2 Economics

Have students jot down the types of advertisements that they see or hear in one day. Then ask them to write a one-page report evaluating and analyzing the advertisements by answering the following questions: What products and services were advertised? How many advertisements were information ads? How many were image ads? What was the message of each ad? How did the ads catch your attention? What types of media presented the ads? Did any of the ads convince you to buy a product or service? If so, explain why. Have students share their findings.

DID YOU KNOW

People who are tired of getting a mailbox full of "junk mail" can write to the following address requesting that their name be removed from all direct-mail lists:
Mail Preference Service
Direct Marketing Association
Box 9008, Farmingdale, NY 11735

CHAPTER 7, LESSON 2

Try This!

Provide samples in the classroom of various products mentioned in the activity for students to examine the labels. Encourage students to also look for labels at home to add to their comparisons.

L2 Math

Point out to students that economists estimate that 20 to 40 percent of the purchase price of products goes into advertising. Have students bring in a list of prices or sales receipts of five brand-name items they or their family buys. Ask them to calculate the approximate cost of advertising for each item by figuring the percentage. Ask students to share their findings. Have them use the information to draw conclusions about the cause of differences in prices of generic and brand-name items. Have them test their conclusions by comparing the difference in price.

L2 Analyzing

Explain to students that another technique used in advertising that can mislead a consumer is the use of deceptive wording. For example, a shampoo ad might state that its product "fights dandruff." The ad is not promising that the product will *stop* dandruff; it only promises to fight it—a battle the consumer may very well lose. Tell students that they should look for facts in advertising rather than vague statements or opinions. Have students choose a product and make two ads—one using deceptive wording and one using facts. Ask students to share their ads.

Try This!

Labels help you compare features of different products. Try to find labels for each of the following:
• Two brands of toothpaste that claim to fight cavities
• Two brands of quick-cooking hot cereal
• Two brands of laundry detergent

Compare the labels of the products in each group. Is one a better value? Report your findings to the class.

ads often use actors, sports stars, or other celebrities to endorse, or recommend, a product. They send the message that consumers will be more attractive or popular, or perhaps smarter or healthier, if they use the product or service. Image ads are often used to promote fashions, cosmetics, and other items that a person may want but does not actually need.

Media Messages

Now you know about the kinds of messages advertisers use, but how do these messages reach you? *The means of communication by which advertisers send their messages* are called **media.** What types of media can you think of?

Types of Media

The three most commonly used types of media are print, electronic, and direct mail.

- **Print media** are newspapers and magazines. Food and clothing stores often place ads in newspapers to reach their local customers. Companies that sell products nationwide, such as breakfast cereal or shampoo, may take out ads in national magazines. Items that appeal to a specific audience might be advertised in specialty magazines. For example, hiking boots are likely to be advertised in magazines about hiking and climbing.

- **Electronic media** are radio, television, and the Internet. The ads that appear on radio and television are also called *commercials.* Radio commercials are generally aimed at a local audience. The ads are often designed to attract a particular group of consumers such as teens.

  Many of the ads that appear on television are aimed at people nationwide. By advertising during national shows, companies can reach millions of consumers. Sometimes advertisers use a special kind of television commercial called an infomercial. **Infomercials** are *extended-length informational commercials that appear*

196 CHAPTER 7: BEING A WISE CONSUMER

TECHNOLOGY UPDATE

The use of photography can make products look different than they actually are. Using certain angles, lighting, or camera lenses can make items appear to be smaller, larger, brighter, darker, fatter, or thinner than they are in reality. Computer-generated graphics can also change the look of products. When evaluating advertisements, it is wise to remember the old sayings, "Looks can be deceiving," and "You can't judge a book by its cover."

on television. These ads usually promote mail-order products and provide a toll-free number for consumers to call.

Advertising is also found on some on-line services and the Internet. When computer users are on-line, ads sometimes appear on the computer screen. In addition, consumers who are looking for a specific product or service can go to on-line "shopping malls" and look for the ads that sellers place.

- **Direct mail** includes mail-order catalogs, store circulars, and packets of ads and coupons that come in the mail. Some companies that do business nationwide use only direct mail to advertise. Catalog houses and local businesses also send ads through the mail.

Signs and displays are two other types of media that you have seen many times. Advertising signs can appear on billboards, buses, taxis, and storefronts. Advertising displays are seen in store windows and inside stores to attract buyers.

Much of what you find in your mailbox, along with letters and bills, is direct-mail advertising.

Advertising Techniques

After hearing a commercial on the radio, did you ever discover that you couldn't get the jingle out of your head? Advertisers use special techniques to get you to notice and remember their products. **Figure 7.1** on the next page shows some of the techniques they use to get their messages across.

LESSON TWO: EVALUATING MEDIA MESSAGES

CHAPTER 7, LESSON 2

L1 Analyzing
Have students choose and view a television commercial and write an analysis of it using the methods for evaluating advertising claims in "How to Evaluate Messages." Ask students to share their evaluations with the class.

L2 Cooperative Learning
Assign Cooperative Learning Activity 13 in the TCR. Students work in groups to evaluate advertisements in this activity.

TEACHER TALK!

Resisting the Pitch
Remind students that salespeople are trained to sell products. Whether or not the customer needs the product is generally not a concern to salespeople. Tell students that the way to resist a sales pitch is to remember that they are buying something for *them,* not for the salesperson. It is their money and their decision to make. The salesperson will not pay the bill or use the product.

HOME AND COMMUNITY CONNECTION

Guest Speaker Invite a local merchant or marketing representative to speak to the students about the decisions involved in advertising his or her company's goods or services. If possible, ask the merchant or representative to bring in all advertisements used by his or her company. Have students prepare questions for the speaker, such as: What type of media does the company or business use to advertise? About what percentage of the company's or business's revenue is spent on advertising?

CHAPTER 7, LESSON 2

USING VISUALS
After students have studied the techniques for sending messages in Figure 7.1, have them find examples of each technique and make a collage using their examples. Display the collages in the classroom.

L1 **Student Workbook**
Assign Activities 51 and 52 in the Student Workbook.

ASSESS

Evaluating the Lesson
Assign Reviewing Terms and Facts and Thinking Critically on page 199 to review the lesson; then assign the Lesson 2 Quiz in the TCR.

Reteaching
- Provide each student with examples of three advertisements. Have them evaluate the message of each, using skills they learned in this lesson.
- Have students complete Reteaching Activity 7 in the TCR.
- Assign Concept Map 11 in the TCR.

Slogans. Advertisers use slogans and jingles to remind people of their products.

Endorsements. Advertisers use famous people, including actors, athletes, and musicians, to promote their products.

Product Characters. A popular technique is to use cartoon characters to advertise products.

Emotional Appeals. With this technique, advertisers tell you that you will be happier, healthier, and more popular if you use their products.

Figure 7.1 Techniques for Sending Messages
Which of these advertising techniques have you seen or heard?

How to Evaluate Messages

Before you decide to buy a service or product, be sure to analyze the advertising claims. Here are some ways.

- **Advertisements mention only the best features of a product.** Before buying, think about what you need to know about the product to decide which brand is best for you. Then look for that information in the ads.
- **Separate emotional appeals from facts.** Does the ad suggest that the product will make the buyer healthier, more attractive, or even happier than is realistic?
- **Don't trust endorsements.** Famous people appear in ads to get your attention, but they are seldom experts in nutrition, medicine, or fashion. Remember, those who look like average people are actors who are well paid to say positive things about the products.
- **Beware of slogans.** They may make certain items memorable, but they are not a guarantee of quality.

198   CHAPTER 7: BEING A WISE CONSUMER

MORE ABOUT • • •

Endorsements Beware of celebrity endorsements. What you hear may not be the truth! Businesses pay famous people thousands of dollars to advertise products. A law governing advertisements states that a famous person who advertises a product must actually *use* the product. However, the law does not say that the famous person has to *like* the product. Ask students to describe some image ads that have influenced them to buy products. Discuss: Does knowing that the celebrities may not believe what they say in image ads change your mind about the products?

Getting More Information

Although the federal government requires advertisers to make truthful claims, companies often exaggerate how good their products are. You don't have to depend on ads for all your information about a product or service, however. Other sources of useful information are available to you.

One of the most reliable sources of information is very close to you—the people you know. Ask your family and friends what brand of a product they use, whether it works well, and if the item was worth the money they paid. Another good source is consumer magazines. Consumer organizations test products, survey the people who use them, and then report their findings. Magazines such as *Consumer Reports* publish these findings. A third source of information is the labels on the products themselves. Learning what a product is made of and how much care it needs can help you determine if it is the right one for you.

If you are trying to decide which brand of a product to purchase, ask family members and friends for recommendations. What are some other sources of information about products?

LESSON TWO Review

Using complete sentences, answer the following questions on a separate sheet of paper.

Reviewing Terms and Facts
1. **Recall** Explain why companies advertise.
2. **Vocabulary** Define the term *information ad*. Use it in an original sentence.
3. **List** What are the three most commonly used types of media?
4. **Recall** Name four advertising techniques.
5. **Identify** List four points to keep in mind when evaluating media messages.

Thinking Critically
6. **Explain** Why are image ads rather than information ads often used to sell products that consumers may want but don't really need?
7. **Analyze** What kinds of emotional appeals would work in an ad for breakfast cereals? For in-line skates?

Applying Concepts
8. Make up a product and create a television commercial for it. Find or make props and visual aids, and use music if possible. Be sure to include at least one of the advertising techniques you learned about in your ad.

LESSON TWO: EVALUATING MEDIA MESSAGES 199

MEETING STUDENT DIVERSITY

Cultural Perspectives An advertisement that is successful in the United States may be offensive in another country because of differences in cultural perspective. For example, since it is not appropriate to kiss in public in some countries, an ad that shows two people kissing might be banned or disapproved of in those countries. The advertiser may only need to make a slight adjustment in order for the ad to be successful. However, the advertiser is at a disadvantage if he or she does not understand the culture of the country where the advertisements are being run. Ask students how an advertiser can avoid offending people in another country.

CHAPTER 7, LESSON 2

Answers to Lesson 2 Review

1. To catch the attention of consumers and convince them to buy a company's product or service.
2. Ads that describe the features of a product or service and give facts about its price and quality. Original sentences will vary.
3. The three most commonly used types of media are print media, electronic media, and direct mail.
4. Four advertising techniques are slogans, endorsements, product characters, and emotional appeals.
5. Look for the best brand for you, separate emotions from facts, don't trust endorsements, and beware of slogans.
6. They appeal to the emotions. They send the message that consumers will be more attractive, popular, happier, or healthier if they use the product or service.
7. Answers will vary. Students may answer that an emotional appeal ad for breakfast cereal would probably suggest that the cereal will make the buyer healthier. An ad for in-line skates would suggest that they can be part of a group if they buy a certain brand of skates.
8. Students should create a television commercial using advertising techniques they learned in the lesson.

Enrichment

Suggest that students visit a local mall and analyze the attention-grabbing techniques used in stores or in window displays. Have students give oral reports of their findings.

CLOSE

Ask students to analyze the following statement when applied to media messages: "Buyer beware."

LESSON THREE
Comparison Shopping

FOCUS

Lesson Objectives
After studying this lesson, students should be able to
- explain how to become a skillful shopper.
- discuss how to compare price and quality.
- describe how to pay for purchases.

Motivating Activity
Ask students to complete the following: "The worst purchase I ever made was . . ."

Introducing the Lesson
Have students share their responses to the Motivating Activity. Ask them to explain why the purchase was bad and what they learned from making the poor purchase. Point out to students that in this lesson they will learn important shopping skills that will help them get the best value for their money.

Introducing *Words to Know*
Have each student write the Words to Know and the definition of each on a sheet of paper. Then have students exchange papers and use each word correctly in a sentence. Ask each student to return the paper to its owner for that person to evaluate how accurately the sentences reflect the definitions of the words.

LESSON THREE
Comparison Shopping

 **WORDS TO KNOW**

impulse buying
department store
specialty store
chain store
factory outlet
discount store
warranty

DISCOVER...
- what it means to be a skillful shopper.
- how to compare items for price and quality.
- how to read product labels.

Did you ever save your money to buy something you wanted, such as a camera or video game? Then, only days after making your purchase, did you see a similar item for less money, or one that had more features or was of higher quality? By learning a few rules that skillful shoppers follow, you can often prevent this situation from happening.

200   CHAPTER 7: BEING A WISE CONSUMER

CLASSROOM RESOURCES FOR LESSON 3

 Blackline Masters
Enrichment 8
Lesson 3 Quiz

 Transparencies
Transparency 33, "Smart Shopping"

 Student Workbook
Activity 53

The Skillful Shopper

Skillful shoppers get the best value for their money. As you develop your shopping skills, you will get greater satisfaction from the purchases you make and save a great deal of money over the years.

Now is the time to learn how to be an informed shopper. Begin by reading labels on food, clothing, and appliances. Compare prices at different stores and among different brands. Look closely at merchandise to judge its quality. Check to see whether the manufacturer will replace or repair the item if it breaks. It is possible to find out some of this information before you even walk into a store.

Gathering Information

Before you make a major purchase, it is wise to learn as much about the item as possible. Collect information about products from friends and family members, magazines, and advertisements. Gathering information before you shop will help you avoid impulse buying. **Impulse buying** means *making a sudden decision to buy.* Did you ever decide to buy candy or a magazine while you were standing in the checkout line? When people buy on impulse, they often purchase things they don't need or that are not worth the money.

Word of mouth is one of the best and easiest ways to gather information. Begin your investigation of a product by asking friends or family members who have used or owned a similar type of item. Ask them such questions as:

- Are you satisfied with the product?
- What do you like or dislike about it?
- Would you purchase the product again?

Magazines such as *Consumer Reports* compare the prices, quality, and features of several brands of the same product. They evaluate the different brands for ease of use, cost,

▲ You can make wise purchasing decisions by gathering information about a product before you buy it. What information can you find in a newspaper advertisement?

LESSON THREE: COMPARISON SHOPPING **201**

MORE ABOUT • • •

Impulse Buying Some people buy on impulse because they are influenced by the thought that they are getting a bargain. Never mind that they may never use the item—they saved money! Impulse buying, or binge buying, can be very costly and it can fill a closet, garage, or house with items rarely or never used. Before buying, a person should ask, "Do I really need this?" "Can I live without this?" Sometimes people shop and buy clothing or other items to make themselves feel good. In this case their emotions have influenced their buying behavior. Instead, they might take a walk, work on a hobby, or read. Impulse buying or binge buying can become addictions. People who have these problems may need to seek help from a counselor.

CHAPTER 7, LESSON 3

TEACH

L1 Home Economics
Have students read the labels of food products to determine the main ingredients. Explain that, by law, labels on food products must list the ingredients in descending order of weight. Ask them how knowing this can help them become a more skillful shopper.

L2 Critical Thinking
Ask students to make a bulletin-board display titled, "Be an Informed Consumer." Have students draw a cartoon illustrating a suggestion given in the lesson. Display the cartoons on the bulletin board.

L1 Transparencies
Present Color Transparency 33, "Smart Shopping," in the TCR. Use this overhead visual to reinforce concepts from this lesson.

TEACHER TALK!

Bait and Switch
Bait and switch advertising claims that an item is on sale. When you go to the store to buy the item, the store employee claims that the item is either of inferior quality or out of stock. Then the person tries to sell another, more expensive item. Tell students that if this situation happens to them, they should ask for a "rain check" for the original item they wanted to buy. By law, stores must give rain checks to consumers who wish to purchase the advertised item.

CHAPTER 7, LESSON 3

L2 Categorizing

Have students work in small groups to generate a list of 20 stores in their community. Then have students categorize the stores listed as department stores, specialty stores, factory outlets, grocery stores, and so on. Then have each group discuss the following questions: What types of merchandise would you expect at each store? How convenient is each store? How pleasant is each store to shop in? When the groups are finished, have them compare their results.

DID YOU KNOW?

Some people get as much pleasure from shopping as they do from other leisure-time activities. A recent survey asked people if they enjoyed shopping as much as or more than certain other activities. The following are some of the activities with the percentage of those questioned who said they enjoy shopping as much as or more than the particular activity: watching television—49 percent; going to the movies—46 percent; playing sports—40 percent; eating and drinking—37 percent; traveling—24 percent. Ask students to rate the enjoyment they get from shopping. Students may wish to conduct a survey at school and compare results to this information.

---

frequency of repairs, and other such concerns. The reports also comment on how well each brand performs its function. This information helps consumers determine which brand they prefer.

Newspaper advertisements can also be helpful. Use them to find out which stores in your area carry the product you want and what price they charge for it. You can use this information to comparison shop in advance.

Selecting a Store

What types of stores are familiar to you? Different kinds of stores carry different selections of merchandise. The best store for you depends on the particular item you want to buy, the price you are willing to pay, and the service you need.

Prices for the same item often vary among stores. Suppose that you are looking for a CD player. You may go to a **department store,** *a store that carries a wide range of merchandise.* Most department stores sell clothes, shoes, household items, and electronic equipment. Department stores usually offer many services, such as customer services, delivery, and credit. You will find a moderate selection of CD players at a range of prices.

You may choose a **specialty store,** *a store that carries only a specific type of merchandise.* In a store that specializes in electronic equipment, you will probably find a very large selection of CD players. The prices in a specialty store may be higher than in a department store, unless the store is very large or part of a chain.

Chain stores are *groups of stores that bear the same name and carry the same merchandise.* There are chains of department stores as well as of specialty stores. Some specialty chains—such as clothing, shoe, and record stores—cater specifically to teens and young adults.

Another type of store is the **factory outlet,** *a store that carries only one manufacturer's products.* Outlets have a limited selection of styles, and some items may be imperfect, but you will find low prices.

Price, selection, and services may vary widely among different types of stores. What factors are most important to you?

202 CHAPTER 7: BEING A WISE CONSUMER

MORE ABOUT • • •

Selecting a Store Convenience shopping is an important factor in deciding where goods are purchased. Some convenience food stores often charge high prices for their goods. Shoppers must decide what is more important—their time or their money. On the other hand, shoppers may be able to find good bargains at the "club" food stores. At such membership stores, goods are often packaged in large quantities or in bulk. It is possible to save a great deal of money at such stores, but shoppers may not need such large quantities of items, or the items might spoil before they can eat them. These stores are generally very large, and shopping takes much longer there than in smaller stores. Ask students to discuss their experiences at convenience and club stores.

Discount stores are *stores that carry a limited selection of items at low prices.* Some discount stores specialize in a particular kind of merchandise, such as household linens, men's or women's clothing, or athletic shoes. Others carry a wide variety of products. Few customer services are provided, but the prices are among the lowest available. Other stores that sell merchandise at discounted prices include membership warehouses and thrift shops.

Another shopping option is to buy products from catalogs. Some catalogs are associated with stores and carry merchandise that the stores cannot keep in stock. Other catalog companies do business only by phone and mail.

Electronic shopping centers are similar to catalogs, but they are found on on-line services and the Internet. Consumers can view pictures and descriptions of the merchandise offered by many different stores and manufacturers. While on-line, they can place an order that will be received instantly.

When choosing a store, you may want to consider how important it is to you to see the merchandise yourself. Also keep in mind how convenient it is to get to the store and whether it is a clean, pleasant place to shop.

Before You Buy

After you have chosen a store, you will need to practice your shopping skills and consider certain factors before making your purchase. Checking quality and prices and reading labels and guarantees will help you get the best value for your money.

Checking Quality and Price

Some people think that price is an indicator of how good a product is. They think that a more expensive product must be superior. That is not always the case. You need to check both the quality and the price of an item you want to buy.

Before you purchase something, examine it closely for quality. For example, when you buy clothing, check the stitching on the seams and the width of the hem. Does the item seem well made? Is the material durable and easy to clean?

LESSON THREE: COMPARISON SHOPPING

Evaluating Clubs

Compact disc, video, and book clubs are very popular. When people join a club, they get to purchase a large number of items for a small charge—sometimes as little as one cent. Are these clubs really a bargain, though? Compare the price of the club item with the price of a similar item in a store. Don't forget to add handling and postage to the price of the club item. See if there are any hidden costs to belonging to the club. Report your findings to the class.

COOPERATIVE LEARNING

Healthy Comparisons Have students work in small groups to compare the nutrition of several cereals. Students should make visual aids such as charts, graphs, and tables where appropriate to show a comparison of the information on the nutrition labels. When they have completed their comparisons, have them use their findings to decide which cereal is most nutritious. Then have them use their visual aids to make an advertisement for the most nutritious cereal. Have each group show its advertisement to the class.

CHAPTER 7, LESSON 3

Ask students to share their findings about mail-order clubs. Have the class draw a conclusion about the cost of belonging to such buying clubs versus buying the items at local stores.

L2 Health

Have students bring to school labels of foods that manufacturers claim are "low fat," "reduced fat," or "fat free." Ask students to check the labels for fat content of each food. Point out that 1 gram of fat contributes 9 calories. Fat should not contribute more than 30 percent of daily caloric intake. For each food item, have students note which products exceed 30 percent of the calories per serving as listed on the label. Have students decide which foods deserve the claims "low fat" or "reduced fat."

L3 Math

Have students compare prices of items by using the unit price of the items. Supermarkets usually have labels on the shelves showing how much each product costs by one unit of weight. With unit prices, students can compare the cost for two items that come in different-sized packages. Have students compare the prices of three different-sized packages for the same brands of a product. (Suggestions include: laundry detergent, chips, cookies, toilet tissue, toothpaste.) To calculate the unit price, divide the price of the package by the number of units in the package. Ask students to share their findings. Have students use their findings to make a generalization about what sizes—smaller or larger—are more inexpensive.

CHAPTER 7, LESSON 3

Try This!

After they read the activity on page 205, ask students to bring in items that they have purchased secondhand. Discuss the advantages and disadvantages of shopping for such items.

L1 Student Workbook

Assign Activity 53 in the Student Workbook.

ASSESS

Evaluating the Lesson

Assign Reviewing Terms and Facts and Thinking Critically on page 205 to review the lesson; then assign the Lesson 3 Quiz in the TCR.

Reteaching

- Have students compose the top ten rules for being a skillful shopper.
- Have students complete Reteaching Activity 7 in the TCR.

Enrichment

- Have students choose an item that young people often buy, such as athletic shoes, clothing, or CDs. Have them compare the cost at a department store, specialty store, and factory outlet and report their findings to the class.
- Assign Enrichment Activity 8 in the TCR.

When you purchase clothing, do you know how reading the label can save you money? If clothes must be professionally dry-cleaned, you will spend extra money every time they need cleaning.

Items that are on sale may be less expensive than regular-priced items, but may not be of the same quality. Stores sometimes have sales of merchandise that they have bought at special, lower prices. The quality of these items may also be lower than that of their regular merchandise. You need to look at products on sale to see if they are, in fact, bargains.

Higher-priced items may be of good quality, but they may also contain features that you don't need. For instance, having an additional five speeds on your bike may not be a feature you consider to be worth the extra money.

Reading Labels

Labels give useful information about the features and the use and care of the product. Labels also give information required by law on products such as clothing and food.

A clothing label must contain the name of the manufacturer, country of origin, fiber content, and instructions for care. Labels on foods list ingredients, with the greatest quantity first. If a can of chili lists beans before meat, you can expect to see more beans than meat when you open the can. Food labels must also contain the name of the product, the name and

204 CHAPTER 7: BEING A WISE CONSUMER

COOPERATIVE LEARNING

Consumer Tips Remind students of the title of the chapter, "Being a Wise Consumer." Have students work in small groups. Have them read the lesson titles for the chapter. Ask groups to summarize the information in each lesson by writing the summaries in the form of a consumer tip. For example, students might summarize the title "Comparison Shopping" in the form of the following consumer tip: "Always check labels carefully to find the best product for the lowest cost." Have groups decide on their favorite tips and compile them into a book or pamphlet to share with classmates.

address of the manufacturer, weight of the contents, and a nutrition label on all processed foods. Food labels also give information on how to prepare the food.

Checking Warranties

Many items come with a guarantee or a warranty. A **warranty** is *the manufacturer's written promise to repair or replace a product if it does not work as claimed.* Be sure to read the warranty so that you know what is promised. Some warranties apply only to certain parts of the product or only under specific conditions. For example, the frame of your bike may be covered by the warranty, but the tires may not be covered.

Proof of Purchase

There are several ways to pay for purchases. You can use cash, a check, a credit card, or a debit card. You will learn about these payment methods in Lesson 5 of this chapter. Regardless of the way you pay for an item, however, remember to keep the receipt as proof of your purchase. Keep the receipt and the warranty in a safe place. If you decide to return the item, you will need the receipt.

Secondhand stores, thrift shops, flea markets, rummage sales, and garage sales can be great places to shop. Think carefully, however, before purchasing a used item. You will probably not be able to return it.

LESSON THREE Review

Using complete sentences, answer the following questions on a separate sheet of paper.

Reviewing Terms and Facts

1. **Identify** What are the benefits of being a skillful shopper?
2. **Recall** What factors should you consider when selecting a store?
3. **Vocabulary** Define the term *warranty*. Use it in an original sentence.

Thinking Critically

4. **Analyze** What is the relationship between price and quality? What should you consider when comparing price and quality?

5. **Suggest** Why would consumers choose to shop through catalogs or an electronic shopping center rather than at a store in person?

Applying Concepts

6. Look through an issue of *Consumer Reports* or a similar buying guide, and compare several brands of a similar product, such as blow dryers, tape players, or in-line skates. Compare prices, quality, and features. Explain to the class which brand and model you would purchase and why.

LESSON THREE: COMPARISON SHOPPING

CHAPTER 7, LESSON 3

Answers to Lesson 3 Review

1. Skillful shoppers get the best value for their money, get satisfaction from the purchases, and save a great deal of money.
2. Factors to consider when selecting a store include the item you want to buy, the price you are willing to pay, and the service you need.
3. The manufacturer's written promise to repair or replace a product if it does not work as claimed. Possible sentence: I always read the warranty of a product before I purchase it.
4. Higher-priced items may be of better quality than a lower-priced item. You need to check both the quality and the price of an item before you make a purchase.
5. Catalogs may have merchandise that stores cannot keep in stock. Some manufacturers do business only by phone and mail.
6. Students should look through a buying guide to compare price, quality, and features of a similar product and explain to the class which brand and model they would purchase and why.

CLOSE

Have students create slogans that will help them remember important shopping skills. Have them share their slogans with the class.

MEETING STUDENT DIVERSITY

Physically Challenged Discuss with students—or ask physically challenged students in the class to lead a discussion on—the special needs of people with physical challenges in terms of selecting stores for shopping. (Students in wheelchairs may have difficulty maneuvering in some stores, students who are blind may find roadblocks to shopping in some stores, and so on.) Have volunteers investigate and report to the class on efforts to ensure that the needs of physically challenged individuals are met in local stores.

LESSON FOUR
Consumer Rights and Responsibilities

FOCUS

Lesson Objectives
After studying this lesson, students should be able to
- explain their consumer rights.
- discuss how to be a responsible consumer.
- demonstrate how to make refunds and exchanges.

Motivating Activity
Ask students to name rights they have as a consumer.

Introducing the Lesson
Have students read their responses to the Motivating Activity. Ask them to give examples of situations they've experienced in which they felt their rights as a consumer were not met. Tell students that in this lesson they will learn about their rights and their responsibilities as consumers.

Introducing *Words to Know*
Have students write the Words to Know on a large sheet of paper. Next to each word, have them write its definition. Then ask them to make an illustration of each word or concept.

LESSON FOUR
Consumer Rights and Responsibilities

WORDS TO KNOW
- redress
- expires
- shoplifting
- exchange
- refund

DISCOVER...
- your consumer rights.
- how to be a responsible consumer.
- how to make refunds and exchanges.

Kayla was in a hurry. She had to buy a swimsuit for a pool party that afternoon, and she didn't have much time. She grabbed two suits that she liked from the rack. She decided to try them on at home, chose one, and return the other at a more convenient time. What do you think will happen when Kayla tries to return the swimsuit? Do you know why?

206 CHAPTER 7: BEING A WISE CONSUMER

CLASSROOM RESOURCES FOR LESSON 4

 Blackline Masters
Activity and Project Card 13, "Consumer Letter"
Concept Map 12
Cooperative Learning 14
Lesson 4 Quiz
Peer Pressure and Decision Making 16

 Transparencies
Transparency 34, "Refunds and Exchanges"

 Student Workbook
Activities 54, 55

Your Rights as a Consumer

Consumers have rights that protect them from false advertising and unsafe products. The law requires manufacturers to put labels on food and clothing and to make products that are safe to use. Your rights make it possible for you to voice a complaint if you are not satisfied with a product or service.

Your consumer rights may have helped you already. For example, if you returned a telephone that didn't work or a pair of shoes that didn't fit, you exercised some of your rights. Perhaps you noticed the safety warnings on your younger sister's toys. These are just a few of the ways in which consumers are protected. The following are included among your specific rights as a consumer:

- **The right to safety.** Products must be well designed and, if used properly, must not cause harm or injury.

- **The right to be informed.** Advertisements and labels give you information about products. Laws protect you from false or misleading advertisements.

- **The right to choose.** Consumers are entitled to choose from a variety of products. They have the right to select the items that fit their needs.

- **The right to be heard.** Consumers can speak out about a product if they are not satisfied with it.

- **The right to redress. Redress** is *action taken to correct a wrong.* Consumers can seek redress if they have a problem with a product.

- **The right to consumer education.** Consumers are entitled to learn about their rights.

Consumer rights protect you and help you get the best product for your money. However, along with those rights you also have responsibilities.

As a consumer, you have the right to choose from a variety of products. What are some of your other consumer rights?

LESSON FOUR: CONSUMER RIGHTS AND RESPONSIBILITIES   207

MORE ABOUT • • •

Consumer Rights Agencies Point out to students that there are a number of agencies that help to protect consumers. Have students research the responsibilities associated with one of the following federal agencies: Consumer Product Safety Commission, Department of Agriculture, Federal Communications Commission, Federal Trade Commission, Food and Drug Administration, and Office of Consumer Affairs. There are also private organizations that work to protect consumers. These include Underwriter's Laboratories, Public Citizen, Consumer Federation of America, and Conference of Consumer Organizations. You may wish to invite a representative from a local organization to speak to the class.

CHAPTER 7, LESSON 4

TEACH

L1 Discussing
Have students describe instances in which they felt that their consumer rights were violated. Discuss what recourse the students had in each situation. Point out to students that they have the right to politely ask to speak to a manager if they are unhappy with the salesperson's solutions to their problem.

L3 Finding Examples
Have students find an article about product safety in a magazine or newspaper. Ask them to summarize the problem identified and the proposed solution. Articles may be compiled and put into a file for future reference, or for students who were absent.

L1 Creating a Poster
Organize the class into groups. Ask each group to make a poster showing the consumer rights that are discussed in the lesson. Encourage students to add illustrations to their posters to make them more attractive. Display finished posters in the classroom for students to use as a reference tool.

L2 Activity and Project Card
Allow time for students to complete Activity and Project Card 13, "Consumer Letter," in the TCR.

L2 Cooperative Learning
Assign Cooperative Learning Activity 14, "Rally Around Your Rights," in the TCR.

207

CHAPTER 7, LESSON 4

Skills IN ACTION

Tell students that there are some ways to spot a quack. Quacks tend to work alone, selling their products through the mail or door-to-door, so they are harder to catch. Quacks usually want cash for their products rather than payment with checks or credit cards.

L2 Applying Knowledge

Have students explain what they should do in the following situation: You bought a compact-disc player. After a week of using the player, one of the push buttons is stuck.

L2 Reading

Bring to class a variety of product instructions. Have students read the instructions for using the products. Ask: What instructions for using the products are given? What safety precautions are given? What care instructions are provided? Why should you read product instructions?

Teacher Talk!

Responsible Consumers
Tell students that some products have a money-back guarantee. If they are not happy with a product, the manufacturer promises to return their money. Tell students to look for such a guarantee on the packaging and read the details to learn their responsibilities for getting money back.

Skills IN ACTION

Identifying Quackery

Beware of quackery—the sale of worthless products and treatments by means of false claims. An example of quackery is an acne cream that is said to make pimples disappear in a few hours. Bring a "quack" ad to class, and tell why you think it isn't truthful.

Your Responsibilities as a Consumer

Do you consider yourself a responsible consumer? Being courteous, counting your change, handling merchandise carefully, and getting the information you need are all part of being a responsible consumer.

Being Courteous

Courtesy is everyday thoughtfulness that you show to other people. It means being polite and respectful to salespeople and other customers in a store. It means that you wait your turn in line. You also show courtesy when you hold the door open for other people.

When you have to return an item to the store, you do so in a polite way. Calmly explain to the salesperson what the problem is, and state how you would like to resolve it. For example, do you want your money back, or do you want to trade the item for another size or color? Remember to bring your receipt with you.

Part of your responsibility as a consumer is to follow the manufacturer's instructions. What are some other ways to be a responsible consumer?

208

COOPERATIVE LEARNING

Shopping By Mail Organize the class into small groups. Provide each group with a mail-order catalog. Ask them to read the catalog and make a list of consumers' responsibilities and the catalog company's responsibilities. Have the groups discuss the advantages and disadvantages of shopping by mail. Have a spokesperson from each group report their findings to the class.

Behaving Responsibly

The manufacturer also has responsibilities—to produce a product that is good and safe and reasonably priced. As a responsible consumer, you need to read and follow the instructions. Experts, who understand the product, prepare instructions that provide for your safety and satisfaction. It is important to follow them. If, for example, the instructions say to wash a shirt by hand, do not put the shirt in the washing machine.

Another way to behave responsibly is to handle merchandise with care. This applies to more than breakable items. Clothing can also be easily damaged while you are trying it on. Remove your shoes before trying on pants. Return clothes that you have tried on in the dressing room to their hangers and leave the dressing room neat.

When you buy such items as watches and stereos, you will receive a warranty. If you get a warranty card with the product, fill it out and send it to the manufacturer. The date on the card lets the manufacturer know when the warranty **expires,** or *runs out.* Keep your warranties, sales slips, and special instructions together in one place.

Being Honest

When paying cash for your purchases, pay attention to the change you receive. If you receive too much change, return it to the salesperson. Otherwise that person may be responsible for replacing the money.

Some teens do not realize the seriousness of shoplifting. **Shoplifting,** or *taking items from a store without paying for them,* is stealing. It is a crime that costs businesses billions of dollars each year. These losses are passed on to customers as increased prices. Some teens look at shoplifting as a prank. Their friends may dare them to do it. Shoplifting, however, is a serious crime for which a person may go to jail. It is a crime that remains on that person's record.

If an item that you want to buy is marked "As Is," be sure to try it on and check it carefully for defects. Why is this important?

LESSON FOUR: CONSUMER RIGHTS AND RESPONSIBILITIES **209**

CHAPTER 7, LESSON 4

L2 Role-Playing

Have students role-play the following situations regarding refunds and exchanges:
- *You are a clerk in a department store. A customer is returning a dress she bought ten days ago. It has makeup around the collar, it is very wrinkled, and the skirt is stained.*
- *Greg washed a shirt, following the instructions on the label. The shirt shrunk. He is returning it to the store where he purchased it.*
- *Marta bought a battery-operated watch two months ago. It stopped running. It has a six-month warranty. She is returning it to the store.*
- *Juan bought a compact disc three days ago. When he played the disc for the first time, he found it had a large scratch in it. He has thrown away the receipt, but he decides to take the compact disc back anyway.*

L2 Problem Solving

Assign Peer Pressure and Decision Making 16 in the TCR. This activity gives students the opportunity to recognize peer pressure and practice decision-making skills.

MORE ABOUT • • •

Shoplifting In many instances shoplifting has little to do with stealing because of lack of money to purchase an item. Instead some shoplifters steal because of the sense of excitement involved; they enjoy gambling with the risk of getting caught. Other shoplifters steal because of a feeling of entitlement; they believe that an item is due them. Many shoplifters do not acknowledge to themselves that they are lawbreakers. They often have an exaggerated view of their own cleverness and invulnerability and are surprised and shocked when they are caught. Ask students what they would do if a friend wanted to shoplift an item.

CHAPTER 7, LESSON 4

TIPS for living

After students have read the feature, help them write a business letter. On the board, draw a diagram of a business letter, showing students where the date, business address, salutation, and closing should be placed. Have students write a sample letter of complaint about a product to a business, using the correct business-letter format.

L1 Using Transparencies

Present Color Transparency 34, "Refunds and Exchanges," in the TCR. Use this overhead visual to reinforce concepts from this lesson.

L1 Student Workbook

Assign Activities 54 and 55 in the Student Workbook.

ASSESS

Evaluating the Lesson

Assign Reviewing Terms and Facts and Thinking Critically on page 211 to review the lesson; then assign the Lesson 4 Quiz in the TCR.

Reteaching

- Have students write examples of situations in which consumers' rights could be violated.
- Have students complete Reteaching Activity 7 in the TCR.
- Assign Concept Map 12 in the TCR.

210

TIPS for living

WRITING A COMPLAINT LETTER

What would you do if you were dissatisfied with a product you had purchased? You might decide to throw it away and forget about it. A better idea, however, would be to write a letter of complaint to the manufacturer. Here are some pointers for writing a complaint letter.

- Follow a regular business letter format. Include your name, address, phone number, and the date.
- Get the address of the company from the product label.
- State the product name, style, and model number. Include the name and address of the store where you bought the item and the date of purchase.
- Send photocopies of the receipt, bills, or warranties. Keep the originals.
- Explain why you are unhappy with the product and how you would like the problem solved.
- Keep the tone of the letter positive and courteous, and allow time for a response and action.

Knowing About Refunds and Exchanges

Like most people, you have probably purchased a product with which you were unhappy. It may not have worked properly. Perhaps it was the wrong color or size. What did you do? You may have asked for an **exchange,** *a trade of one item for another,* or a **refund,** *the return of your money in exchange for the item.* Whenever you make an exchange or ask for a refund, follow these guidelines:

- **Know the store's policy.** Every store sets its own return and exchange policy. The policy is usually posted where you pay for the item. Read the policy. If you don't understand it, ask the clerk before paying for the purchase. Never assume that you can return an item.
- **Keep proof of your purchase.** The store receipt is proof of the price, date of purchase, and store where you bought an item. Most stores require you to show your receipt in order to receive a refund.

210 CHAPTER 7: BEING A WISE CONSUMER

HOME AND COMMUNITY CONNECTION

Emphasizing Skills Make use of frequent opportunities to remind students that the skills they practice in the classroom have applications to their personal lives as well as future careers. Guide students to understand how and why these skills are important. For example, after doing activities in this chapter on consumer skills and money management, have students brainstorm the connection between what they did and how they can use it in real life.

- **Determine if you are entitled to a refund.** Some items that are defective or on sale are marked "As Is" or "All Sales Final." In these cases you are not entitled to a refund. Certain products, such as bathing suits, underwear, and pierced earrings, are usually not returnable because of health codes.
- **Be ready to process your claim.** If you are entitled to a refund, take your merchandise and sales receipt (and perhaps your warranty, if any) to the store. You may be asked to fill out a form with your name, address, and reason for returning the item. If the item is defective, be sure to provide this information so that the store can notify the manufacturer.

Knowing your rights and responsibilities as a consumer will help you now and in the future.

LESSON FOUR Review

Using complete sentences, answer the following questions on a separate sheet of paper.

Reviewing Terms and Facts
1. **Identify** List your consumer rights.
2. **Give Examples** What are two ways to show that you are a courteous shopper?
3. **Explain** How does shoplifting affect the price you pay for goods?
4. **Vocabulary** What is the difference between an *exchange* and a *refund*?

Thinking Critically
5. **Analyze** Do you think that consumers have enough rights? Explain your answer.

6. **Describe** What procedure would you follow when returning an item?
7. **Interpret** Why is it important to read instructions before using or operating a product?

Applying Concepts
8. Develop a file that organizes receipts, warranties, and special instructions to use in your home. Suggest ways to encourage family members to use the file. Discuss ideas with your classmates.

LESSON FOUR: CONSUMER RIGHTS AND RESPONSIBILITIES

HOME AND COMMUNITY CONNECTION

Guest Speaker Invite a security guard from a local store or a police officer from the community to explain what happens when a person is caught shoplifting. Have the guard or officer explain who pays for the losses caused by shoplifting, why people shoplift, and the punishment a shoplifter might receive. Have students prepare questions ahead of time to ask the officer or guard. Allow students to discuss the consequences of shoplifting after the speaker has given his or her presentation to the class.

CHAPTER 7, LESSON 4

Answers to Lesson 4 Review

1. The right to safety, the right to be informed, the right to choose, the right to be heard, the right to redress, the right to consumer education.
2. Any two: Being polite and respectful to the salesperson and other customers in a store. Wait your turn in line. Avoid pushing and shoving. Hold the door open for others.
3. It costs businesses millions of dollars each year. These losses are passed on to customers as increased prices.
4. An exchange is a trade of one item for another. A refund is a return of an item so you get your money back.
5. Answers will vary. Students should explain whether they think consumers have enough rights.
6. The procedure depends on the store's return policy.
7. Instructions are provided for your safety and satisfaction.
8. Students should develop files to organize receipts, warranties, and special instructions. Students should suggest ways to encourage family members to use the file.

Enrichment

Have students get information about the refund and exchange policies of a store where they shop. Ask: What proof of purchase is required? What procedures should you follow to make a refund or exchange? Have students report their findings to the class.

CLOSE

Ask students to explain the relationship between consumer rights and responsibilities.

LESSON FIVE
Managing Your Money

FOCUS

Lesson Objectives
After studying this lesson, students should be able to
- identify sources of income.
- explain how to develop a plan for spending and saving money.
- describe how to get the most for their money.

Motivating Activity
Write the following statements on the board. Ask students to write a sentence telling what the statements have in common.
- A penny saved is a penny earned.
- Stay within your budget.
- Save for a rainy day.
- Penny wise, pound foolish.

Introducing the Lesson
Have students share their responses to the Motivating Activity. *(The statements have to do with saving or managing money.)* Discuss with students the importance of managing money well. Tell them that this lesson discusses some money-management techniques to help them stretch their buying power.

Introducing *Words to Know*
Ask a volunteer to read the vocabulary words and terms and their definitions. Then have students use the vocabulary words to write a short newspaper article titled "Managing Your Money." Ask students to share their articles with a partner.

212

LESSON FIVE
Managing Your Money

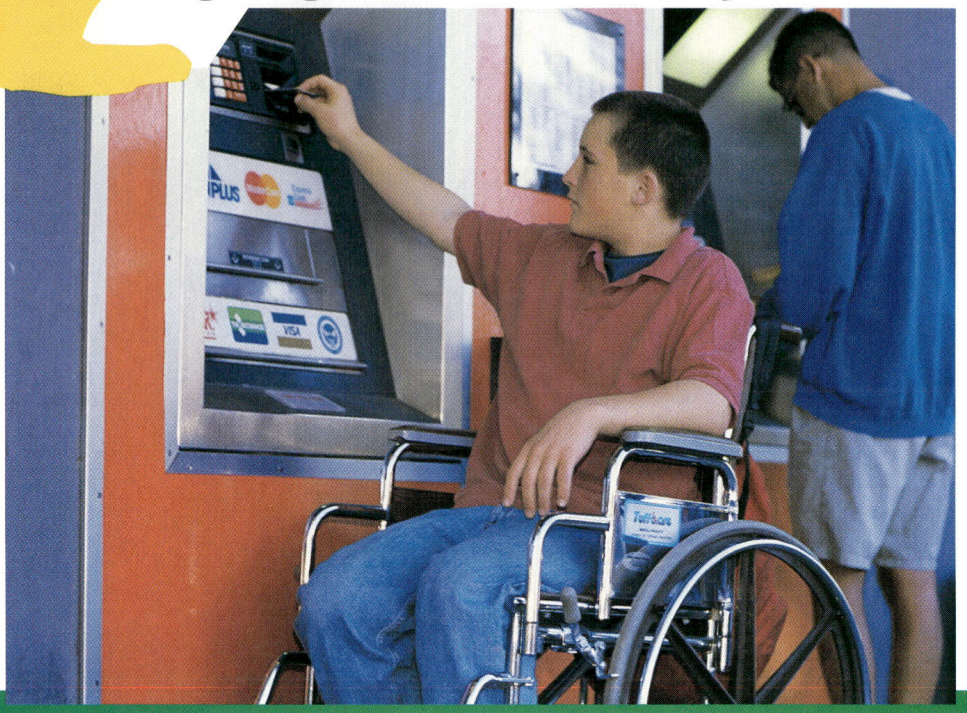

 **WORDS TO KNOW**

income
expenses
fixed expenses
flexible expenses
budget
interest
layaway plan
debit card
credit

DISCOVER...
- your sources of income and your expenses.
- how to develop a plan for spending and saving money.
- ways to get the most from your money.

Do you ever think about how you spend your money? When you have a little extra, what do you do with it? Do you buy a new CD or go to a movie? Do you save it to buy a birthday present or your own television? The way people manage their money reflects their needs and wants. Marco likes music and is saving his money for a stereo. Nicole enjoys working with children and wants to become a teacher. She is saving part of her allowance for college. How do your needs and wants influence your spending?

212 CHAPTER 7: BEING A WISE CONSUMER

CLASSROOM RESOURCES FOR LESSON 5

 Blackline Masters
Activity and Project Card 14, "A Budgeting Game"
Cross Curriculum 8
Lesson 5 Quiz

 Transparencies
Transparency 35, "Writing a Check"
Transparency 36, "Recording Checks"

 Student Workbook
Activities 56, 57

How to Manage Your Money

You will be earning, spending, and saving money all of your life. Even if you have only a small amount to spend, you can stretch your buying power by learning to buy and save wisely. The key to managing your money is to remember that how much you have to spend is less important than how you spend what you have.

To manage your money wisely you will need to

- know where your money is coming from.
- determine how much money you will have.
- look at how much money you are spending.
- evaluate what you are buying.

Your Income and Expenses

Your **income** is *the amount of money you earn or receive regularly.* Your **expenses** are *the money you spend to buy goods and services.* **Figure 7.2** shows some of the many possible

Figure 7.2
Income and Expenses
There are many ways for teens to earn and spend money. What other sources of income and expenses can you think of?

Income
- Allowance/gifts
- Babysitting
- Yard work
- Washing cars
- Paper route
- Dog walking

Expenses
- Sports equipment
- School supplies
- Entertainment
- Snacks
- Clothes
- Grooming supplies

TECHNOLOGY UPDATE

Shoppers in some areas of the country can now shop without using cash, checks, or credit cards. After purchases have been totaled at the checkout counter, the customer presents a plastic card that contains bank account information. A computer uses this information to automatically transfer funds from the customer's account to the store's account. This new technology moves us one step closer to becoming a cashless, checkless society. Ask students: What are the advantages and disadvantages of such a society?

CHAPTER 7, LESSON 5

TEACH

L2 Critical Thinking
Ask students to make an illustration with labels showing how the tips for managing money will help them stretch their buying power.

USING VISUALS
Have students make a list of sources of income and expenses similar to the lists in Figure 7.2. Ask students to brainstorm ways they could increase their income and ways they could decrease their expenses. Ask them to share their ideas with the class.

L3 Math
Have students plan a budget for an income of $12 per week. Remind them to do the following: Examine personal values and goals. Set aside enough money for weekly expenses. Decide how much should be saved. Encourage students to use computers with budget-planning software if available.

L2 Math Connection
Assign Cross-Curriculum Activity 8 in the TCR. Students learn about making wise consumer choices in this activity.

LESSON FIVE: MANAGING YOUR MONEY

CHAPTER 7, LESSON 5

L1 Using Transparencies

Present Color Transparencies 35, "Writing a Check," and 36, "Recording Checks," in the TCR. Use these overhead visuals together to reinforce concepts from this lesson.

L2 Applying Life Skills

Have students make a chart similar to the one shown in the lesson. Ask them what information is kept on this expense record, how a record like this is kept, and how this information is used to make a budget. Then have them use their expense record to record their expenses for one week. Have students write an evaluation of their spending trends based on their charts. Ask them to explain how they can improve their buying habits.

L2 Creating

Have students think of a concept for a bank commercial. The purpose of the commercial is to encourage people to save their money at the bank. Have students use techniques that catch the attention of consumers and convince them to buy the services offered at the bank. The commercial should include ways people can be wise consumers so that they have money to save at the bank. Have students write their ideas for commercials and share them with the class. Discuss which commercials students feel would be most effective.

214

---

sources of income and expenses. If you manage your money well, you will not spend more on expenses than you receive as income. What are your sources of income? What are your expenses?

Keeping Track of Your Money

You can improve your spending habits by keeping an expense record, or an organized account of what you buy and how much you spend. To keep an expense record, make a chart like the one shown on the left. Each day list the date, the items you buy, and the amount you spend that day. At the end of the week, add up each expense category. Some expenses are fixed, and some are flexible. **Fixed expenses** are *expenses that are always the same*, such as the fee for your weekly karate lesson. **Flexible expenses** are *expenses that vary*, such as the amount you spend for a concert ticket.

By looking at the totals on your expense record, you can evaluate how you spend your money. Decide if you are buying useful items or if you would like to improve your buying habits.

Setting Up a Budget

Before you set up a **budget**, or *plan for using your money*, you need to examine your personal values and goals. Do you want to save enough money for a new skateboard? Do you want to pay for singing lessons so that you can try out for the musical at school? Are you saving money to buy your parents an anniversary gift?

Once you have determined your income, have a record of your expenses, and understand your goals, you can set up a budget. Begin by setting aside enough money to cover your expenses. If your income does not cover your expenses, you will need to make some adjustments. You may choose to cut back on some of your expenses or to find new ways to add money to your weekly income.

Keeping an expense record can help you manage your money. What items would you list on your expense record?

214   CHAPTER 7: BEING A WISE CONSUMER

 HOME AND COMMUNITY CONNECTION

Guest Speaker Invite a spokesperson from a local bank or savings and loan to speak to the class and explain the various banking services available to students. Ask the speaker to discuss the benefits of planning and saving as part of good budgeting skills. During the visit, discuss with students the responsibilities involved in opening a checking or savings account and keeping good records. If possible, look into the possibility of opening a branch of a local bank or savings and loan in your school.

Starting a Savings Plan

Your budget should include a savings plan. A savings plan helps you put money aside for unexpected needs and for the future. Many people find it easier to save when they set goals, such as having money for holiday activities, trips, or hobbies. Some teens begin saving for a car or a college education. Unless you plan ahead and save regularly, it might be difficult to achieve your goals.

To start a savings plan, set aside about 10 percent of your income each week. Figure out how much money you could save in a year. What could you buy with *your* savings?

It's a good idea to put the money you save in a savings account in the bank. The bank pays **interest,** or *a fee paid to use your money.* The interest is added to the money in your savings account. In this way your money grows.

Ways to Pay for Purchases

Teens generally pay for their purchases with cash. You may not always have enough cash to buy what you want, however. In that case, you may want to use a layaway plan. A **layaway plan** is *a scheduled payment plan in which you put a small amount of money down and make regular payments until you have paid for the item.* When the item has been paid for in full, you take it home.

> **Try This!**
> Good money managers know how to get the most for their dollars. Working in groups, list ways teens can stretch their money. Here are two ideas. Can you think of others?
> • Make your own cards and gifts.
> • Instead of buying books, CDs, or tapes, borrow them from the library.

Using a layaway plan is one way to pay for purchases. How can a layaway plan help you to be responsible with your purchases?

MORE ABOUT • • •

Credit Point out to students that before they make a major purchase on an installment plan, the credit grantor will check their income and how well they have paid bills in the past. Point out to students that their record of paying bills is known as a credit rating. If they have a poor record of paying bills, credit may not be granted. Stress to students that it is important when seeking credit to make sure that they can meet the payments out of future income. A good record of paying bills will allow them to establish a good credit rating.

CHAPTER 7, LESSON 5

> **Try This!**
> Ask students to brainstorm other suggestions for saving money for future spending. Have them make a poster showing their suggestions. Display the posters in the classroom.

L3 Applying Life Skills

Have students try various computer software packages that help keep spending records. Ask them to rank the software in order of preference.

L2 Activity and Project Card

Allow time for students to complete Activity and Project Card 14, "A Budgeting Game," in the TCR.

L1 Student Workbook

Assign Activities 56 and 57 in the Student Workbook.

ASSESS

Evaluating the Lesson

Assign Reviewing Terms and Facts and Thinking Critically on page 216 to review the lesson; then assign the Lesson 5 Quiz in the TCR.

Reteaching

- Ask students to write three things they can do to get the most from their income. Ask them to explain how their suggestions work.
- Have students complete Reteaching Activity 7 in the TCR.

CHAPTER 7, LESSON 5

Answers to Lesson 5 Review

1. Determine how much money you will have. Know where your money is coming from. Look at how much money you are spending. Evaluate what you are buying.
2. Making an expense record can improve your spending habits.
3. It helps you save for unexpected events and for the future.
4. Credit is a method of payment that lets you buy now and pay later. You promise to make payments until the item is paid for.
5. Answers will vary. Students should indicate that a budget helps you learn about your spending habits and where you can cut expenses, and it helps you save money for the future.
6. Advantage: to buy expensive items. Disadvantage: interest on unpaid balance.
7. Answers will vary. Students should estimate how much money they would save in a week, a year, and two years out of their weekly earnings from two jobs. They should explain how they would use the savings.

Enrichment

Have students write an article for the school newspaper on the proper care of sports equipment, bicycles, skateboards, clothes, or stereo equipment. Explain how caring for these items is part of money-management skills.

CLOSE

Ask students to use the information in Lesson 5 to explain the meaning of the following statement: "How much you have to spend is less important than how you spend what you have."

216

Credit allows people to purchase large, expensive items that they need and might not have enough cash on hand to buy.

Another way to pay for purchases is with a check. A check is a written order directing a bank to pay the person or business named on the check. In order to pay by check, a person must open a checking account with a bank. A checking account is a convenient way of handling larger amounts of money without keeping a lot of cash on hand.

Many people use debit cards to pay for purchases. A **debit card** is a *card that is issued by a bank and is used to withdraw money directly from a person's bank account.* For example, people can use debit cards to pay for groceries.

When you rent a video or pay back money that you borrowed, you are using credit. **Credit** is *a method of payment that lets you buy now and pay later.* Either the seller or a bank must trust in the ability of the purchaser to make payments until the item is paid for. Many families use credit to buy such expensive items as furniture, large appliances, and cars. Credit fees, or interest on the unpaid balance, are charged for the use of credit.

One way to use credit is to have a charge account with a particular store. The store issues a charge card that can be used instead of money when shopping there. Within 30 days the store sends you a bill for your purchases.

LESSON FIVE *Review*

Using complete sentences, answer the following questions on a separate sheet of paper.

Reviewing Terms and Facts

1. **List** Name four things you need to know before you can begin to manage your money.
2. **Explain** What is the purpose of keeping an expense record?
3. **Recall** Why should your budget include a savings plan?
4. **Vocabulary** Define the term *credit*. What kind of promise are you making when you use credit to pay for a purchase?

Thinking Critically

5. **Explain** Why is it important to budget your money?
6. **Analyze** What might be some advantages and disadvantages of buying on credit?

Applying Concepts

7. Imagine that you earn $40 a week from yard work and a paper route. How much money should you put in a savings account? How much money would you have saved after a year? After two years? How would you use your savings?

216   CHAPTER 7: BEING A WISE CONSUMER

MEETING STUDENT DIVERSITY

Varied Learning Styles To help students with a variety of learning styles, have students work in pairs. Ask each pair of students to create a crossword puzzle using the vocabulary words in the lesson. Tell them that the clues to the crossword puzzles should be definitions of the vocabulary words. Provide each pair with graph paper to help them with the grid for the crossword puzzle.

Chapter 7 Activities

A Global View — "I'll Trade You…"

You are used to paying money for goods and services. Another way to get the items you need is by bartering, or trading goods and services without the use of money. You have probably bartered without even knowing it. When you and a friend swap comic books or baseball cards, you are bartering.

Try This!
Arrange to barter services with a friend or parent. Report on your bartering to the class.

Technology — How Did They Do That?

Artists use computers to create amazing special effects for television advertising. Two techniques they use are "warping"—changing one part of a picture at a time—and "morphing"—changing one image into another image. Advertisers spend millions of dollars on these ads. They hope that the special effects will help you remember the ad—and the brand name.

Try This!
Write your own script for a special effects ad.

Friends & Family — The Allowance Debate

Not all families agree on whether an allowance should be tied to doing chores around the house. Some parents believe that paying their children to do household tasks helps them see the connection between working and earning money. Other parents feel that children should help around the house without getting paid.

Try This!
Form small groups to discuss the allowance debate. Write an allowance policy considering both the point of view of the parents and the children. Share your policy with your classmates.

Math Connection — The $1,300 Snack

Imagine that you spend $5 a week on soft drinks, candy bars, and pretzels. Did you know that in five years your snack habit could cost you more than $1,300?

When you put money in a savings account, the money earns **interest**, or *a fee the bank pays to use your money.* The interest is added to the **principal**, or *the money in your account.*

Follow Up
1. Imagine that instead of buying junk food you put $5 a week in a savings account that pays 6 percent interest. How much would you have after one year?
2. Many savings accounts require a minimum balance. List three ways you could earn the money.
3. Contact a bank and find out about the types of savings accounts and the rates of interest. Share your findings with your classmates.

Chapter 7 Activities

A Global View

After students read the article, explain that before the invention of money, bartering was the usual way people conducted their business. Point out that bartering is still practiced in many places in the world today, including the United States. Ask students if they can think of examples such as neighbors exchanging tools and labor to fix up their homes.

Friends & Family

After students have read the feature and done the "Try This" activity, have them also discuss issues such as how much an allowance should be, what expenses an allowance should cover, and how often teens should receive a raise in their allowance. Encourage students to share their own experiences and opinions.

Technology

Describe this amusing television advertisement: A young boy with a straw in his mouth sips from a bottle of soda. Then, right before your eyes, the boy shrivels up and sucks himself inside the bottle. Ask students to share other advertisements that show impossible and amazing special effects that they have seen.

Teaching the MATH CONNECTION

Ask students who have savings accounts to find out the interest rate and how it is compounded at the bank that has their account. Write all the responses on the board. Have students find out about the kinds of services performed by commercial banks, savings and loans, and credit unions. How are they similar? How are they different?

Answers to Follow-Up
1. $275.60
2. Answers will vary. Students should explain how they could earn the money required to open a savings account.
3. Answers will vary. Students will explain the types of savings accounts available and the rate of interest they pay.

CHAPTER 7 REVIEW

Checking Comprehension

Use the Chapter Summary and the Chapter 7 Review to help students go over the most important ideas in Chapter 7.

Answers to Words to Know

1. Answers will vary. Example answers: clothing, magazines, school supplies, sports equipment, entertainment, compact discs.
2. Answers will vary but might include: bike repairs or tutoring.
3. An image ad is used to promote items that a person may want but does not actually have.
4. Print media includes newspapers and magazines.
5. This type of buying often involves something you don't need or something that may not be worth the money.
6. Read a warranty to know what promise is made.
7. *Redress* means the opportunity to seek a solution to a problem.
8. It means the warranty runs out.
9. You make a plan for using your money.
10. Buying on credit is placing trust in the purchaser to make payments until the item is paid for.

Chapter Summary

- Goods are products made for sale. A service is work performed by one person for another.
- A consumer is someone who buys goods and services.
- Your buying decisions may be influenced by your peers, your habits, or advertising.
- Advertisements are generally considered to be either information ads or image ads.
- To get their messages across, advertisers use print media, electronic media, and direct mail.
- You can shop at a wide variety of stores, including department stores, specialty stores, discount stores, factory outlets, and membership warehouses.
- A careful shopper compares price and quality, reads labels, and checks warranties.
- Knowing your consumer rights and fulfilling your consumer responsibilities are part of responsible buying.
- As a consumer, you have the right to ask for a refund or an exchange.
- The money that you earn or receive regularly is called your income. The money that you spend on goods and services is called your expenses. There are fixed and flexible expenses.
- Keeping an expense record, setting up a budget, and starting a savings plan are smart methods of money management.
- There are several ways to pay for your purchases: cash, check, debit card, credit, or layaway plan.

Words to Know

Using complete sentences, answer the following questions on a separate sheet of paper.

1. Give examples of *goods* teens might buy.
2. What *services* could teens perform?
3. Explain the purpose of an *image ad*.
4. Give two examples of print *media*.
5. Identify a drawback of *impulse buying*.
6. Why should you read a *warranty*?
7. What is meant by right to *redress*?
8. Describe what happens when a warranty on a product *expires*.
9. What do you do when you *budget* your money?
10. How is buying on *credit* like making a promise?

Review Questions

Using complete sentences, answer the following questions on a separate sheet of paper.

1. What choices must a consumer make?
2. Besides advertising, what are two sources of product information?
3. Name three ways to get information about a product *before* you go into a store.

218 CHAPTER 7: BEING A WISE CONSUMER

EXTRA CREDIT PROJECT

Group Project Challenge students to apply money management skills to plan a family vacation. Tell each group of four students they should decide on a vacation for a family of four. They will plan where to travel, how to get there, and how long the vacation will last. They must stay within a fixed budget amount determined by you. Students should work together to plan expenses, including travel, lodging, food, admission fees, and entertainment for each person. Have groups prepare an itinerary. Tell them they may need to try several times to remain within their budget. Have groups report to the class explaining their vacation plans and how they managed their expenses.

CHAPTER 7 REVIEW

4. What should you do to be a skillful shopper once you are in a store?
5. Name six rights you have as a consumer.
6. How do your personal needs and wants influence your management of money? Give an example.

Thinking Critically

Using complete sentences, answer the following questions on a separate sheet of paper.

1. **Apply** Describe a situation in which a teen should resist peer influence when making a buying decision.
2. **Evaluate** Name five emotions or feelings to which advertisers appeal. Give an example of a specific ad that supports one of your answers.
3. **Analyze** Why might it be important for people to read a product label for ingredients?
4. **Explain** Why is writing a complaint letter both a consumer right and a consumer responsibility?
5. **Suggest** What advice would you give someone who has just started to use a credit card?

Cooperative Learning

1. Working in a group, create a fictitious teen. Make up facts about the teen's finances, including income and expenses. Give the information to another group. Have the group create a budget for the teen and work out any money-management problems.
2. As a class, start a consumer column in your school newspaper, or publish your own consumer newsletter for teens. Take turns writing articles. The articles could contain tips on the best places for teens to shop for goods and services in your community. You could interview classmates about their experiences with various products.

Family & Community

Ask to be involved in the next major purchase your family makes, such as a new refrigerator, a new car, or a family vacation. Help the family research different brands or models and weigh the pros and cons of each. Does advertising ever influence their preferences? If so, how?

Building A Portfolio

1. Think of a major purchase you would like to make, such as a stereo or a computer. Gather information about the product, and look for the best place to buy it. Begin to save money for your purchase. If you don't have enough income to make your goal realistic, think of ways you could earn extra money. Put a photo or drawing of the item you would like to buy in your portfolio to remind you of your goal.
2. Take an inventory of your clothes closet. Make a list of clothes you need. Ask your family to help you set a budget for clothes shopping. Watch for sale ads before you go shopping. Put the receipts from any purchases in your portfolio, along with your evaluation of how well you managed your money.

CHAPTER 7 REVIEW 219

CHAPTER 7 REVIEW

Answers to Review Questions

1. Decide what to buy, where to buy it, and when to buy.
2. Other sources are consumer magazines, and labels on products.
3. Talk to family and friends, read consumer magazines, and check advertisements.
4. Check quality and prices and read labels and guarantees.
5. The right to safety, to be informed, to choose, to be heard, to redress, and to consumer education.
6. Your personal needs and wants help you decide how to spend your money. Possible example: If you want to learn to sing, you may spend money on singing lessons.

Evaluate

Use the Chapter 7 Test in the TCR, or construct your own test using the Testmaker Software.

CLOSE

Have students apply their knowledge of the chapter's content by completing one of the alternative assessment activities listed under Family and Community or Building a Portfolio.

Answers to Thinking Critically

1. Answers will vary. Students describe a situation in which a teen should resist peer influence when making a buying decision.
2. Answers will vary. Students name five emotions or feelings to which advertisers appeal, such as loneliness or happiness. Students give an example of a specific ad that appeals to one of the emotions listed.
3. Labels provide product information, ingredients, and instructions.
4. Answers will vary. Students should point out that a complaint letter exercises the consumer's right to be heard. It is also a consumer responsibility because it lets the manufacturer know what is unsafe or what you do not like about the product.
5. Answers will vary.

219

Planning Guide
Chapter 8 Your Home

LESSON 1	Pages	FEATURES	CLASSROOM RESOURCES
Making the Most of Your Home	222–228	Try This: *Sharing Space* Tips for Living: *Clearing the Clutter*	Cross Curriculum 9 Lesson 1 Quiz Transparency 37, "Guidelines for Room Arrangement" Student Workbook Activities 58, 59
LESSON 2 **Designing Your Space**	229–234	Tips for Living: *The Principles of Design* Tips for Living: *Drawing a Floor Plan*	Activity and Project Card 15, "Design a Movie Set" Activity and Project Card 16, "Create a Color Wheel" Cooperative Learning 15 Lesson 2 Quiz Peer Pressure and Decision Making 17 Transparency 38, "The Personal Touch" Student Workbook Activities 60, 61
LESSON 3 **Keeping a Home Clean and Safe**	235–240	Try This: *Home Safety Checklist*	Concept Map 13 Cooperative Learning 16 Enrichment 9 Lesson 3 Quiz Peer Pressure and Decision Making 18 Student Workbook Activities 62, 63

CHAPTER 8 RESOURCES

Chapter 8 Test

Reteaching 8

Study Guide 8, *Reteaching*

Testmaker Software

Performance Assessment Activity

Organize students into groups of four. Provide each group with a large sheet of paper to be divided into four parts. In each of the four parts have students sketch a floor plan for living space for a family for each of the following stages in life: a just-married couple, a couple with a toddler, a couple with two preschool children and one parent who works in a home office, a couple with two teenaged children. When students have finished, allow time for each group to share its floor plans. Have students explain how the home described in each of the four plans fills the needs of the people living there at various stages of their lives.

School-to-Work

Arrange for the class to interview a decorator or an interior designer about the work he or she does. Work with students to generate a list of questions to begin the interview. Questions might deal with what training is needed, what a typical day on the job is like, what are some of the person's favorite projects, and so on. Have students summarize what they have learned about the job in a "help wanted" ad that describes the job and the requirements needed for the job.

Family & Community

Have students list public buildings in their community (schools, library, fire station, police station, government office building). Ask them to identify ways that safety measures are used in the buildings to keep people who visit and work there safe. Students might visit the buildings or they might call and find out. Students should focus on measures taken to protect people from fire, from falling, and from being hurt by machinery or equipment. Have students share their information with their classmates.

Resources for the Teacher

Barnard, Nicholas. *Complete Home Decorating Book.* New York: Dorling Kindersley, Inc., 1994.

Hiller, Karl J. *Family Safety Handbook.* Farmington, UT: Jackson Publishers, 1991.

Manroe, Candace O. *Storage Made Easy: Great Ideas for Organizing Everything in Your Home.* New York: Doubleday & Co., Inc., 1995.

Readings for the Student

Everett, F., and P. Woods, eds. *Decorate Your Room.* Tulsa, OK: EDC Publishing, 1989.

Wirths, Claudine G., and Mary Bowman-Kruhm. *Where's My Other Sock? How to Get Organized and Drive Your Parents and Teachers Crazy.* New York: Thomas Y. Crowell Co., 1989.

Multimedia Resources

Accidentally Yours (16 mm film). International Film Bureau.

For Safety's Sake (Video). New World Video.

Interior Design (Video). Crystal Productions.

Where We Live (16 mm film). Canadian Television Network.

OUT OF TIME?

If time does not permit thorough teaching of this chapter, you may wish to use:

- Teens Making a Difference, page 221
- Tips for Living, pages 226, 231, 234
- Try This, pages 223, 238
- Young Living Activities, page 241
- Chapter Summary, page 242

219B

CHAPTER 8
Your Home

Chapter Overview
Chapter 8 introduces students to the importance of a home to a person's physical and emotional well-being and provides practical tips for creating a pleasant and safe home.

LESSON 1 explains that homes provide shelter, security, and a place to express oneself, and describes ways to organize and share living space.

LESSON 2 presents the elements of design and suggests ways to personalize living space.

LESSON 3 explains the advantages of keeping a home clean and safe.

Introducing the Chapter
Organize the class into three groups. Assign one of the lessons to each group. Then ask students in each group to skim their assigned lesson and choose a picture that they think illustrates the lesson title and the content of the lesson. Ask them to write a new caption that includes the lesson title for the picture they choose. Tell them that Chapter 8 deals with the home: how it fills people's needs, how living space in it can be organized and designed, and how it can be taken care of.

Chapter Motivator
Have each student begin a web with the word *Home* in the center. Ask them to jot down topics related to home. Suggest that students skim the headings and photographs in the chapter to help them complete the web. After students have completed their webs, discuss how each word in the web relates to home.

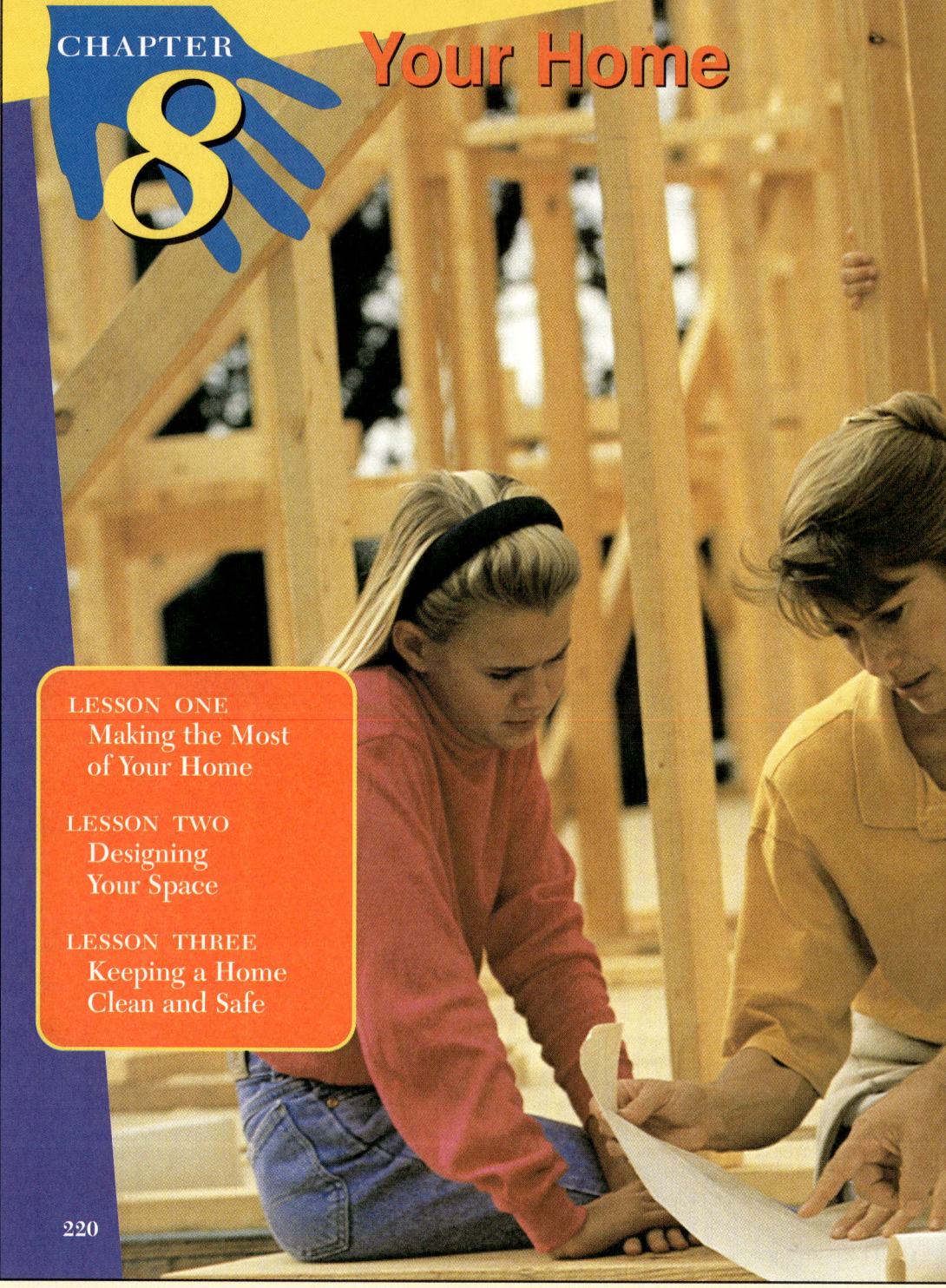

CHAPTER 8
Your Home

LESSON ONE
Making the Most of Your Home

LESSON TWO
Designing Your Space

LESSON THREE
Keeping a Home Clean and Safe

KEY TO ABILITY LEVELS

Teaching strategies that appear throughout the chapter have been identified by one of three codes to give you an idea of their suitability for students of varying learning styles and abilities.

L1 Level 1 strategies should be within the ability range of all students. Often full class participation is required. Teacher direction is usually needed.

L2 Level 2 strategies are for average to above-average students or for small groups. Some teacher direction is necessary.

L3 Level 3 strategies are designed for students able and willing to work independently. Minimal teacher direction is necessary.

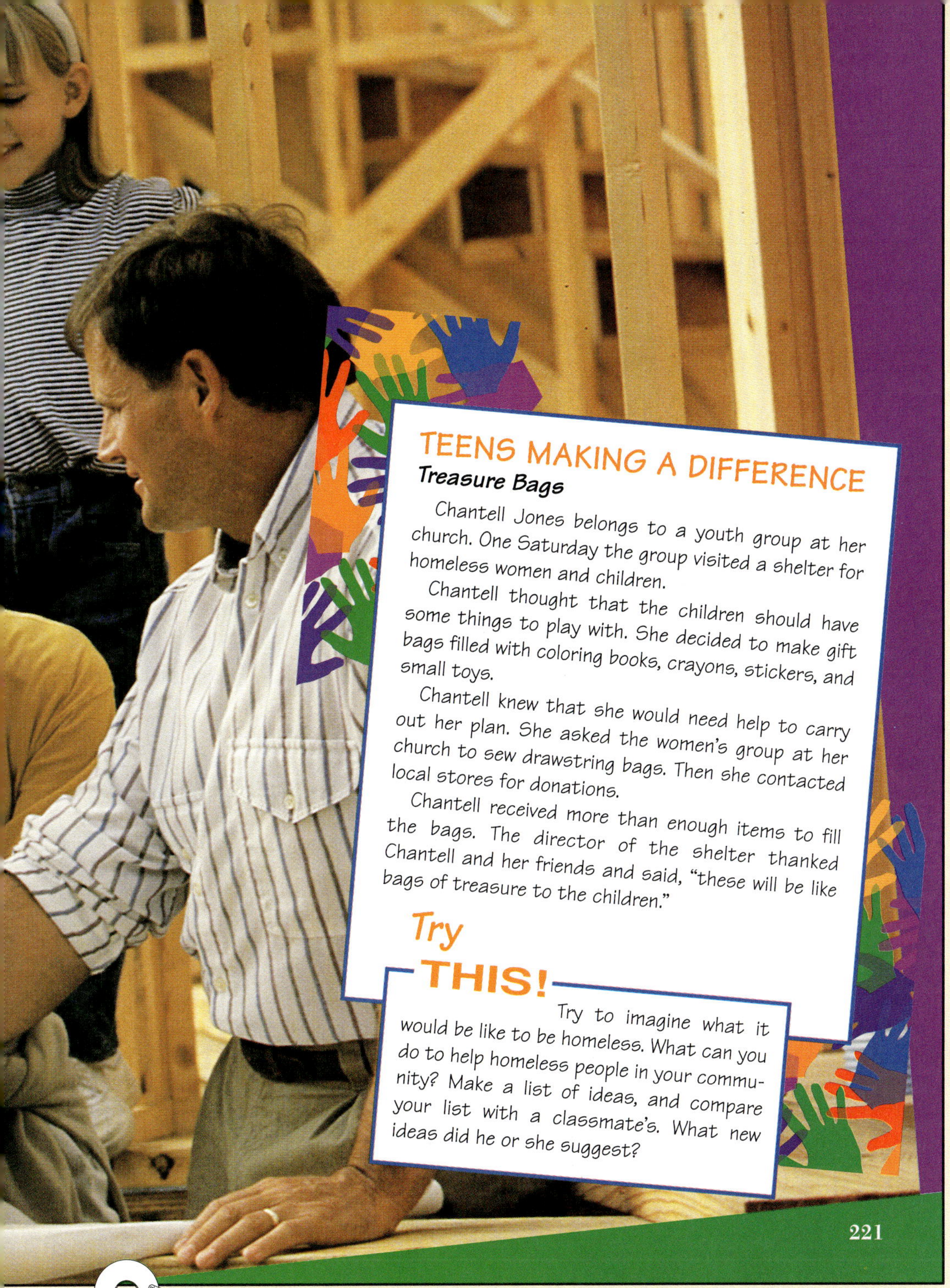

CHAPTER 8

TEENS MAKING A DIFFERENCE

When students have finished reading the feature, ask them what kinds of qualities Chantell had as a person. *(Students' responses might include that she was empathetic, caring, and organized.)* Then ask them how they think the children in the shelter felt when they received their "bags of treasure."

After students have completed their list of ideas, you might work with them to implement some of the ideas.

BLOCK SCHEDULING

The following Teacher Classroom Resources are suggested for use in classrooms with Block Scheduling.
- Activity and Project Card 15, "Design a Movie Set"
- Activity and Project Card 16, "Create a Color Wheel"
- Cooperative Learning 15, "A Designer's Touch"
- Cooperative Learning 16, "Safe and Snug at Home"

TEENS MAKING A DIFFERENCE
Treasure Bags

Chantell Jones belongs to a youth group at her church. One Saturday the group visited a shelter for homeless women and children.

Chantell thought that the children should have some things to play with. She decided to make gift bags filled with coloring books, crayons, stickers, and small toys.

Chantell knew that she would need help to carry out her plan. She asked the women's group at her church to sew drawstring bags. Then she contacted local stores for donations.

Chantell received more than enough items to fill the bags. The director of the shelter thanked Chantell and her friends and said, "these will be like bags of treasure to the children."

Try THIS!
Try to imagine what it would be like to be homeless. What can you do to help homeless people in your community? Make a list of ideas, and compare your list with a classmate's. What new ideas did he or she suggest?

TECHNOLOGY IN THE CLASSROOM

Computer-Aided Design (CAD) Several drawing software programs are available for use in the Family and Consumer Sciences classroom. Before selecting any type of software, you need to make sure that it is useful for the specific purpose intended. Also, you need to make sure that the computer hardware you have is capable of running the software. Computer-Aided Design (CAD) programs are among the most effective software programs for design. However, as with other software, these programs require time for the user to learn. CAD software is available for both house design and clothing and fabric design. The software enables students to lay out everything from textiles to houses on a computer screen.

LESSON ONE
Making the Most of Your Home

FOCUS

Lesson Objectives
After studying this lesson, students should be able to
- explain what a home provides.
- describe ways to organize living space.
- describe how to share space.

Motivating Activity
Ask students to complete the following statement: "A home is . . ."

Introducing the Lesson
Call on volunteers to share their responses to the Motivating Activity by writing them on the board. Have students note the similarities in their responses. Point out to students that a home fills some basic needs for people. Tell the class that this lesson discusses these needs.

Introducing *Words to Know*
Ask students to read the terms in Words to Know. Ask them to find two meanings for *function*. (Students might indicate that *function* can mean "use" or "the way something works" and that it can also mean "an event," such as a dance.) Ask students to think of a sentence for each definition of *function*.

Then ask students what comes to mind when they hear the term *traffic*. Ask them to speculate on the meaning of *traffic pattern*. Have them check their definitions with the one in the lesson.

222

LESSON ONE
Making the Most of Your Home

WORDS TO KNOW
function
traffic pattern

DISCOVER...
- how a home provides shelter, security, and a place to express yourself.
- how to organize your living space.
- how to share space in a home.

People live in many types of homes—apartments, mobile homes, duplexes, townhomes, single-family houses, and condominiums. Homes come in all shapes, sizes, and colors, but all of them have one common feature. To the people living there, each one is called "home."

The Importance of Homes

Homes satisfy the basic need for shelter. They are built to protect people from the weather—rain, snow, wind, or

222   CHAPTER 8: YOUR HOME

CLASSROOM RESOURCES FOR LESSON 1

 Blackline Masters
Cross Curriculum 9
Lesson 1 Quiz

 Transparencies
Transparency 37, "Guidelines for Room Arrangement"

 Student Workbook
Activities 58, 59

extreme temperatures. Homes also provide a place for you to take care of your personal needs. In your home you can bathe, prepare meals, and sleep comfortably. You also have a place to keep your clothes and personal possessions.

You get a sense of well-being and peace of mind, or a feeling of security, in your home. It is a place to relax and be yourself. It is a place where you can enjoy leisure activities, such as listening to music, playing video games, or reading. It is a great place to spend time with family members and friends.

You can also use your home to express yourself. Take a look at your room. What do the objects in your room reveal about your interests? Does your room reflect your personality?

Special Living Areas

Most homes are divided into special living areas in order to meet people's needs and interests. Some areas, such as bedrooms, are designed for privacy. Other areas, such as living rooms, are used for gathering with family members and entertaining friends. Dividing space into special areas makes the home more convenient and easier to manage.

When you share space with family members, it helps if everyone works together to get the chores done. One way to accomplish this goal is to organize a work schedule. Try these ideas.
- With your family, list chores that need to be done.
- Decide who will do what chores.
- Make a chore chart. Write down the list of chores that need to be done and who will do them.

Most homes are divided into special areas, such as a kitchen, a living room, a bathroom, and bedrooms. Some areas serve more than one function. What are some functions of a kitchen?

LESSON ONE: MAKING THE MOST OF YOUR HOME   223

CHAPTER 8, LESSON 1

TEACH

As students read the activity, discuss with them the importance of communication when there are issues involving sharing space. Have students use one of the suggestions for dividing chores in their homes and then report on how well it worked.

L1 Generalizing

Organize the class into small groups. Ask students in each group to look in magazines to find and cut out several pictures of different types of homes—apartments, mobile homes, duplexes, townhomes, single-family houses, and condominiums. Have students identify the type of home in each picture. Then ask each group to write a generalization that states what the homes have in common. Ask a representative from each group to read its statement to the class.

L1 Creating a Chart

Have each student create a chart identifying the rooms family members use to perform each of the following activities: listening to music, watching TV, reading, cooking, eating, doing homework, and relaxing. Students should use the names of the activities as the row headings and the names of the rooms as the column headings. Have students place an *X* under the type of room or rooms in which each activity is performed. Then have students identify rooms that have multiple purposes and those that have single purposes.

MEETING STUDENT DIVERSITY

Cultural Diversity Ask students to investigate the ways that people of different cultures and in different climates fill their need for shelter. Organize the class into small groups. Have students in each group research information about the homes of people in other parts of the world. For example, students might find out about homes in the South American tropical rain forest or in the Sahara, or homes of the Inuit in Alaska. Have each group present the information in a written report. Encourage students to include pictures or shoe-box displays to illustrate their reports.

223

CHAPTER 8, LESSON 1

TEACHER TALK!

Talking About Homes

Be sensitive to values people place on size and location of homes. Some students may be reluctant to share ideas about their homes if they feel they or their families will be judged by others. You might have students use the third person or a fictional situation when talking about homes.

L2 Describing

Ask students to identify a leisure activity they enjoy. Have them brainstorm how space could be provided for this activity in their home. Then have them draw a picture of the space, describing the type of facilities and equipment that would be needed. Have students include captions with their pictures and display them on a bulletin board titled "My Special Area."

L2 Critical Thinking

Write the following terms on the chalkboard: "a tall stool," "a chest of drawers," "a table," and "a bookcase." Encourage students to be creative in thinking of unique ways to use these items. Have them consider using the items in various places such as the kitchen, a bedroom, a family room, and a bathroom. Have students draw pictures of the uses and include a caption explaining the uses. Ask volunteers to share their ideas.

The way you organize your living space depends on the activities in which you and your family like to participate.

By organizing the rooms for more than one **function**, or *use*, you can make the best use of space, equipment, and furniture. For example, you probably use your bedroom not only for sleeping but also for studying, reading, relaxing, and listening to music. Besides cooking or eating meals, your family may use the kitchen for other activities, such as doing homework, paying bills, or playing games.

Organizing Your Living Space

To organize the space within your home, begin by thinking of the various activities of all your family members. What area would be best for each activity? For example, would exercise equipment be better located in a bedroom, the basement, or the family room? Should the family computer be set up in a bedroom or in the den?

How do you and your family use the living space now? Are there improvements that could be made? If a shelving unit or different lighting was added, could the space be expanded to serve an additional function? **Figure 8.1** shows some guidelines for arranging rooms.

Selecting Furniture

Furniture style is a matter of personal taste. You may like furniture with sleek, modern lines. Your sister may prefer country-style furniture. Try looking in magazines and books to find the furniture styles you like best.

Some furniture can serve more than one purpose. A desk that has a large surface area may be used as a computer station.

224 CHAPTER 8: YOUR HOME

MORE ABOUT • • •

Special Living Areas For centuries the hearth was a focal point of a home. The Romans believed that the household gods lived near the hearth. In western Europe, people believed that the hearth was the home of the brownies and other fairies who brought good luck to the household. The reverence for the hearth continues in a tradition passed on in some parts of Great Britain. When a family moves to a new house, embers are taken from the old fireplace and burned in the new one. Have students consider the connection between the British tradition mentioned and the custom of having a housewarming party in a new house.

Figure 8.1 Guidelines for Room Arrangements

Here are some tips for creating a practical arrangement. Which ones can you use in your space?

1. Consider the traffic pattern in the room. The **traffic pattern** is *the path people take to move around and in and out of the room.* Furniture should be placed so as not to get in the way. If you find that you have to constantly walk around a chair, you should try a different arrangement.

2. Leave space around furniture so it can be used comfortably. Drawers and doors require extra space for opening and closing.

3. Place furniture in groupings that are functional, or useful and convenient. For example, a small table and a lamp placed next to a bed create a functional grouping.

4. Group related items together. For example, by storing cassettes next to a tape player, listening to music becomes quicker and easier.

LESSON ONE: MAKING THE MOST OF YOUR HOME 225

CHAPTER 8, LESSON 1

USING VISUALS
Refer students to Figure 8.1. Then ask them to make a scale drawing of the floor plan of their bedroom, including the present furniture arrangement. Have them list the functions this room serves. Ask students to sketch an alternative floor plan and rearrange the furniture, taking into consideration the basic rules of good room arrangement described in the figure.

L1 Using Transparencies
Present Color Transparency 37, "Guidelines for Room Arrangement," in the TCR. Use this overhead visual to reinforce concepts from this lesson.

L2 Applying
Ask students to list activities of family members. Have them identify the rooms in which these activities take place and the kinds of furnishings and equipment that are necessary.

Then ask students to imagine that they are writing an article for a home-decorating magazine that gives tips on efficiently arranging rooms. Have them choose one of the rooms and make recommendations for ways to better organize the room, using the guidelines for room arrangement described on this page. Ask students to explain how their suggested changes can improve the enjoyment of these rooms.

L2 Social Studies Connection
Assign Cross-Curriculum Activity 9 in the TCR. Students learn about homes in various cultures in this activity.

MEETING STUDENT DIVERSITY

Physically Challenged Discuss with students—or ask physically challenged students in the class to lead a discussion—on the special needs of people with physical challenges in terms of housing. Consider these issues: getting in and out of a home, moving from room to room, using kitchen facilities, and so on. Have students find out what equipment is available to aid physically challenged people. Have them also find out how homes and rooms can be tailored to meet the needs of physically challenged people.

225

CHAPTER 8, LESSON 1

L2 Writing

Have students use magazines and decorating books to find pictures of furniture in styles they like. Have them attach the pictures to a piece of cardboard. Then have them write two or three paragraphs explaining why they like the styles and how they would use the furniture pictured. Display completed work.

L2 Demonstrating

Today many building-supply stores sell closet-organizing equipment and storage equipment. In recent years "container" stores have opened that specialize in containers and other storage equipment. Bring in brochures from these stores that illustrate a variety of storage equipment. Then organize students into small groups. Provide each group with a brochure. Have students in each group brainstorm ways that the items shown in the brochures can be used to help get organized and to create storage space. Have each group demonstrate their ideas.

👉 TIPS for living

Invite students to share their messy closet stories. Then discuss the tips for clearing clutter. Ask students to offer other suggestions for keeping a closet neat.

▲ Furniture is available in many different styles. Which furniture styles do you like?

A small table draped with fabric could conceal an item that isn't used year-round, such as a fan.

Arranging Special Areas

Changing the placement of your furniture can make an area look quite different. Rearranging the furniture can also help you save space. Maybe your bookcase could fit on one side of the desk instead of along the wall. Arranging two single beds in an L shape may take up less room than placing them parallel to each other. By following a few basic rules, you will be able to arrange your furniture in the most effective way.

Storage Space

Having enough storage space is essential for a functional room. Decide what objects should be stored in a space. For example, paper, pens and pencils, and a dictionary should be stored in a study area. Items that would not be used in this area, such as videotapes, should be stored elsewhere.

TIPS for living

CLEARING THE CLUTTER

A crowded, messy closet can be like a black hole. If you put something in there, you may never see it again. To get organized, follow these steps.

- Clean out your closet. Stack everything that you don't wear or want. Donate these items to charity, hand them down to a younger brother or sister, or sell them at a garage sale.
- Categorize your clothes. Group garments by type, season, color, or body part (top half, bottom half, or whole body). Group together similar items, such as shoes or belts. Store seasonal items in underbed boxes.
- Use double hanging rods, hooks, and clear plastic boxes to increase storage space.

226 CHAPTER 8: YOUR HOME

COOPERATIVE LEARNING

Evaluating Space Invite students to work in small groups to evaluate the classroom and make a report of how well it is organized. Ask them to consider storage, furniture grouping, traffic patterns, and so on. Students should indicate the parts of the room that are organized well and give reasons why they are. Then have students brainstorm ideas and sketch out recommendations for the areas of the room that they believe are not organized as well. Call on groups to share their findings with one another, or have them present their ideas in an oral report to the class.

The best storage places are closets, drawers, and shelves. If these spaces already seem full, look for ways to make them more useful. Start sorting your belongings. Give away or discard what you don't need.

There are many ways to make drawer space more effective. Drawer dividers, plastic trays, and shoe boxes can help.

Closets can also be made more functional. Small hooks on the closet door can hold small items. Stackable bins, see-through wire drawers, and plastic boxes help to organize storage space. What other ways can you think of?

Sharing Space

Whether you are sharing a bedroom, a bathroom, the kitchen, or a computer area, you must work with other family members to keep the space organized and clean. Sharing space will be easier if you remember the following guidelines.

- **Respect other people's privacy.** If someone's door is closed, knock and wait for a response before entering. Keep your music or television turned low, or use headphones if another person wants to sleep or study. Of course, never read another person's mail or look through others' belongings without getting their permission.
- **Be considerate of others.** Show your consideration by not leaving your belongings in someone else's way. When you have finished using the kitchen or the bathroom, be sure to leave it at least as clean as you found it.
- **Cooperate with family members.** For example, is there a "morning rush hour" in your home? This can happen when several family members are trying to get ready for work or school at the same time. The morning will go more smoothly if everyone agrees on a schedule.

With careful planning, even a small space can store a great many things. How can you modify your closet to get the most use out of it?

LESSON ONE: MAKING THE MOST OF YOUR HOME **227**

CHAPTER 8, LESSON 1

L2 **Role-Playing**
Provide students with the following scenarios and have them work in pairs or small groups to role-play each scenario. Have them resolve each of the conflicts by using one or more of the guidelines for sharing space.
- *You share a room and your little sister is always in your stuff.*
- *One of your parents has started to work at home and has taken over the family room.*
- *Mom, Dad, and Burt all have to leave the house by 7:35. Mom leaves first at 6:45, and Dad takes Burt to school. They share one bathroom.*

L1 **Student Workbook**
Assign Activities 58 and 59 in the Student Workbook.

ASSESS

Evaluating the Lesson
Assign Reviewing Terms and Facts and Thinking Critically on page 228 to review the lesson; then assign the Lesson 1 Quiz in the TCR.

Reteaching
- Ask students to imagine that they are planning to organize a particular room in their home. Have them list questions that should be asked when organizing a particular space. *(Questions should focus on types of equipment and furniture to include, ways of arranging the space, and amount of storage space needed.)* Call on volunteers to share their questions with the class.
- Have students complete Reteaching Activity 8 in the TCR.

 HOME AND COMMUNITY CONNECTION

Guest Speaker Invite a realtor or a builder to visit the class and talk about current trends in the housing market. Have students generate questions before the visit. Questions might include the following: How many bathrooms do new houses have? What kind of "special" rooms do home buyers find attractive? What are the latest ideas for storage? Groups of students might work together to summarize the information they learn during the interview into a feature article for the school newspaper. Display the articles in the classroom.

227

CHAPTER 8, LESSON 1

Answers to Lesson 1 Review

1. Any three: shelter, place to take care of physical needs, place to keep possessions, security, place to express oneself.

2. Answers may vary. A sample might be a bedroom, which can be used for sleeping, getting dressed, studying, and relaxing.

3. Traffic pattern is the path people take to move around and in and out of the room. Furniture should be placed so that it does not get in the way.

4. Furniture should be arranged in functional groupings. Related items should be grouped together. Space should be left around furniture so that it can be used comfortably.

5. Be considerate of others, respect other people's privacy, cooperate with family members, compromise.

6. Adequate storage space means you can get to and use items easily; storing things correctly makes them last longer; and good storage makes things convenient.

7. You can follow the guidelines for sharing space and be sensitive to ways people's needs change.

8. Responses will vary but should be based on ideas learned in the lesson.

Enrichment

Ask each student to organize the space for a "dream" room. Have students use the suggestions about organizing living space presented in the lesson to organize their space. Ask each student to draw a sketch or create a diorama of the room.

CLOSE

Refer students to the closing photograph. Have them give examples of ways that a home benefits them and their families.

- **Try to compromise.** Sometimes you will need to compromise to avoid conflicts. This means that each person gives up something he or she wants in order to reach a solution that satisfies both people. For example, suppose that you like rock music, but you share a bedroom with your brother who likes country. How could you compromise? You might take turns listening to music on different days or at different times during the day.

A home is an enjoyable place to spend time with family members. What activities does your family enjoy together?

LESSON ONE Review

Using complete sentences, answer the following questions on a separate sheet of paper.

Reviewing Terms and Facts

1. Identify What three basic needs does a home help satisfy?

2. Recall Give an example of a room that has more than one function. What are the functions of this room?

3. Vocabulary Define the term *traffic pattern*. How does traffic pattern affect furniture placement?

4. List Name three guidelines for room arrangements.

5. Identify What are four points to remember when sharing space with others?

Thinking Critically

6. Analyze Why is it important to have enough storage space?

7. Describe How can you show consideration for family members who share your home?

Applying Concepts

8. Read an article in a home-decorating magazine that gives hints on decorating and personalizing a bedroom. Summarize the article for the class. Tell which ideas you liked and which ones you didn't like and why.

228 CHAPTER 8: YOUR HOME

 HOME AND COMMUNITY CONNECTION

The Cost of Utilities Have students work in small groups to investigate the cost of utilities—gas, electricity, water—in their community. Ask them to contact local utility companies for information about average costs, seasonal costs, and amounts of usage in their community. Students might also use their family's utility bills to find out about the costs and amount of usage of utilities in their own homes. Students can make poster-sized charts of the information they gather for display in the classroom.

LESSON TWO
Designing Your Space

DISCOVER...
- how to use design elements.
- how to give your living space a new look.
- how to add accessories to personalize your space.

Are you happy with your bedroom at home? There are many easy, inexpensive ways to turn the space you have now into a place that you can be proud of and enjoy.

Design in Your Room

Why do some rooms look more inviting than others? How can a room seem large, even though it is actually small? The

WORDS TO KNOW
design
illusion
diagonal
texture
floor plan
accessories

LESSON TWO: DESIGNING YOUR SPACE   **229**

LESSON TWO
Designing Your Space

FOCUS

Lesson Objectives
After studying this lesson, students should be able to
- identify the design elements of space, shape, line, texture, and color and explain their use.
- describe ways to create a new look for a living space.
- explain the importance of accessories.

Motivating Activity
Display a magazine picture of an imaginatively decorated room. Ask each student to write down three features of the room that catch their eye.

Introducing the Lesson
Call on volunteers to share their responses to the Motivating Activity. In the discussion, introduce these concepts: color, shape, line, and texture. Then explain that students will learn more about how they can use these elements in their own decorating.

Introducing *Words to Know*
Have students match each of the Words to Know with a definition:
- feeling that something is different from the way it really is (illusion)
- diagram of a room arrangement (floor plan)
- the way something feels or looks as if it would feel (texture)
- the art of combining elements in a pleasing way (design)
- interesting items added to make a space more personal (accessories)
- on an angle (diagonal)

CLASSROOM RESOURCES FOR LESSON 2

 Blackline Masters
Activity and Project Card 15, "Design a Movie Set"
Activity and Project Card 16, "Create a Color Wheel"
Cooperative Learning 15
Lesson 2 Quiz
Peer Pressure and Decision Making 17

Transparencies
Transparency 38, "The Personal Touch"

Student Workbook
Activities 60, 61

CHAPTER 8, LESSON 2

TEACH

L2 Demonstrating
Organize the class into small groups. Assign one element of design to each group. Ask each group to demonstrate the use of its assigned element in designing a room. Students can present their ideas in construction paper cutouts, magazine pictures, photographs, or miniature models. Students should identify and explain how they used the assigned design element.

L1 Discussing
Have students observe and categorize the lines in the classroom. Ask questions such as the following to begin the discussion: What forms the lines? What types of lines do you see (horizontal, vertical, diagonal)? How do the lines affect the feel of the room? Point out that combining lines helps balance the shapes in a room in a pleasing way.

L2 Activity and Project Card
Allow time for students to complete Activity and Project Card 15,"Design a Movie Set," in the TCR.

L2 Cooperative Learning
Assign Cooperative Learning Activity 15 in the TCR. Students work in groups to create a room design in this activity.

---

way a room looks depends a great deal on how design was used—or not used—to create an overall effect. **Design** is *the art of combining elements in a pleasing way.* You can use design to create the type of look you want in a room.

The Elements of Design

The elements of design are space, shape, line, texture, and color. Each contributes its own special effect to the final design.

- **Space.** Space helps draw attention to objects. For example, a vase on a shelf will stand out and be seen if some space is left on either side of it. On the other hand, too much space between objects can result in a bare, empty look. You can create many illusions just by dividing space in various ways. An **illusion** is *a feeling that something is different from the way it really is.*

- **Shape.** Shape refers to the outline or form of solid objects. For example, a bed has a rectangular shape. A table may be rectangular, square, or round. Attractive designs use shape effectively. Having too many different shapes in one room makes most people feel uncomfortable.

- **Line.** Lines are very important to design. If you look around a room, you can see them in many places—the legs of a table, the frame of a door, or the stripes on a curtain. Straight lines make objects seem strong and dignified. Curved lines make objects seem softer and more graceful. Lines that are vertical go straight up and down and suggest height. They can make objects look taller. Lines that are horizontal move straight across and seem to widen objects. Lines that move at a **diagonal,** or *on an angle,* suggest action.

- **Texture. Texture** is *the way something feels or looks as if it would feel.* A rug might feel soft and fuzzy. A polished table feels hard and smooth. Texture provides visual interest in a room, and you can add more interest by using a variety of textures. Textures can also affect the mood of a room. Soft, fuzzy, and nubby surfaces

230 CHAPTER 8: YOUR HOME

MEETING STUDENT DIVERSITY

Varied Learning Styles Provide a concrete way to understand the concept of texture with the following activity. Fill a brown paper bag with a variety of objects that have different textures. Without looking at the object, have students feel each object in the bag and describe its texture (slippery, scratchy, puffy, etc.). Write the descriptions on the chalkboard as students provide them. When students are finished with their descriptions, take the objects out of the bag, and have students match each object with their texture descriptions.

make a room look cozy. Smooth, hard surfaces create a clean, modern effect.

- **Color.** Color probably has the greatest effect on the appearance of a room. A change of color can make a room look completely different. Color can also be used to create illusions. For example, white or light colors on the walls make a room look larger. Using darker colors or many different hues will make a room seem smaller.

Colors are often described as warm or cool. Red, yellow, and orange are warm colors. If a room does not get much sunlight or is cold in winter, warm colors can make the room seem more cozy. Blue, green, and violet are cool and restful. A cool color is a good choice for a room that gets hot or has too much sunlight. You can also use cool colors to set a relaxing mood.

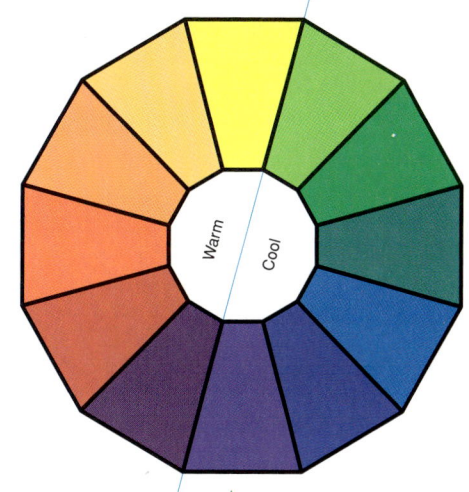

A color wheel shows the relationship of colors to one another. What are your favorite colors, and how might you use them to accent your room?

TIPS for living

THE PRINCIPLES OF DESIGN

The principles of design are rules that govern how artists organize the elements of design. Here is how to use them:

- **Balance.** Use elements, such as two similar shapes, to provide equal visual weight, or stability.
- **Emphasis.** Create contrast by using one element to dominate the others. Try a red pillow to provide punch.
- **Harmony.** Combine similar elements to accent their similarities by using repetition and gradual changes.
- **Variety.** Combine a number of different things of a particular kind—for example, a collection arranged on a shelf.
- **Movement.** Create the look and feeling of action by guiding the viewer's eye. Line helps guide the eye.
- **Rhythm.** Create a visual tempo, or beat, by placing elements carefully. Hang your posters to create a beat!
- **Proportion.** Keep an eye on the relationship of certain elements to the whole and to each other.

LESSON TWO: DESIGNING YOUR SPACE

TECHNOLOGY UPDATE

CD-ROMs for Room Design Designing tasks can now be completed on the computer, using CD-ROM software. These software programs let you design a home or plan an addition to an existing home. The programs can also help you decorate various rooms. You can choose furniture (from the libraries of furniture that come with the software) and experiment with furniture positioning without actually having to haul heavy pieces around a room. Some CD-ROMs are also capable of providing you with a 3-D walk-through of the designs you select.

CHAPTER 8, LESSON 2

L2 Language Arts

Have students write the words they associate with these colors: yellow, blue, orange, green, violet, white, black, and red. Ask: Which colors seem warm? Why? Which colors seem cool? Why? How does color affect your mood? Invite volunteers to share their responses. Discuss with students why it is important to consider color when determining the function of a room.

L3 Applying Life Skills

Have students think about how they would like to change a room in their home. Tell them to make two plans for changing the room. In the first plan, they should change only one design element, for example, color. In the second plan, they should change two or more design elements. They might add furniture with different lines, add fabric drapes and pillows for texture, and so on. Students might make "before" and "after" pictures of their rooms.

TIPS for living

After students have read "The Principles of Design," have them find examples of ways that the principles are used. Provide students with home-decorating magazines. Organize the class into small groups and have each group find examples in the magazines of the principles of design being used.

L2 Activity and Project Card

Allow time for students to complete Activity and Project Card 16, "Create a Color Wheel," in the TCR.

CHAPTER 8, LESSON 2

L3 Creative Thinking
Challenge students to think of ways that they can create a new look by identifying decorative uses for a bedsheet. (Uses might include slipcovers, curtains, fabric shades, pillows, lamp shades, rag rugs, stuffed toys, wall hangings, and quilts.)

L2 Hands-on Project
Assign Hands-on Project 5, "Design a Room," in the TCR. Students create a room design in this activity.

L1 Writing
Ask students to imagine that they are writing an article for a teen magazine. The article is for an issue that deals with making a room personal. Ask students to write an article describing ways that teens could use their hobbies, interests, or collections to add a personal touch to their living space. Encourage students to use computers to write their articles. Call on volunteers to share their articles with the class.

L2 Problem Solving
Assign Peer Pressure and Decision Making 17 in the TCR. This activity gives students the opportunity to recognize peer pressure and practice decision-making skills.

Your Own Style

Before you start planning a bedroom makeover, you need to think about the look that you want for your space. In part, that depends on what you have to start with, but it also depends on your personal taste. Of course, if you share a room you will also need to consider the taste of the other person.

The elements of design can be used in many different ways with pleasing results, but not all of them will appeal to you.

First consider what kind of mood you want to create—soft and feminine, bold and bright? What are your interests? Do you want a theme, such as sports, rock and roll, or a hobby? Do you want your space to be cool and restful or bright and lively? Are you looking for ways to make the room seem larger? Keep in mind that you will probably have to live with your changes for a long time. Be sure of your decisions before starting any work on a new look.

Creating a New Look

Once you have decided on the mood and style that you want, you can plan how to achieve that look in your room. Making a plan before you start will help everything go smoothly.

Perhaps you would like a new color scheme. What parts of the room will be easiest to change? Walls can be painted a new color, and you can hang new pictures. Carpet, on the other hand, is difficult and expensive to replace. Fortunately, you can often work around the features you can't change.

If you decide to paint the walls, check with your parents first. Then choose your new color carefully. Paint a small test section on the wall to be sure that the color will create the effect you want.

▶ If you are thinking about creating a new look for your bedroom, you can get ideas from decorating magazines and books. Where else could you look for ideas?

232 CHAPTER 8: YOUR HOME

MEETING STUDENT DIVERSITY

Cultural Diversity Have students investigate the folk art of various cultures. Many cultures produce beautiful and functional items—such as baskets, woven fabrics, pottery, and wooden items—that are often used as accessories. Bring to class or ask students to bring books about design and decorating that include pictures of these items. Students who have folk-art items at home might bring them to class to show classmates. Students may create a display for these items for the school office or library. Discuss ways that the items might be used as accessories in a room.

Paint is great for furniture as well as walls. You can paint mismatched furniture the same or similar colors to give your room a finished look.

Fabric can add interest to a wall or turn a sturdy carton into an attractive covered table. There are books that explain how to cover chests and other pieces with cloth. You can make a simple slipcover and matching curtains, and use leftover fabric to make pillows, chair pads, lamp shades, and many other items.

Using Accessories

No room is complete without accessories. **Accessories** are *interesting items added to make a space more personal.* **Figure 8.2** shows some of the many ways that you can use accessories to give a room a personal touch.

Figure 8.2
The Personal Touch
Many different kinds of items can make your space uniquely yours. What kinds of accessories express who you are?

LESSON TWO: DESIGNING YOUR SPACE 233

COOPERATIVE LEARNING

Organize the class into small groups. Ask students in each group to imagine what homes in the year 2050 would be like. Have them imagine the following: What types of houses would be available? What methods would be available for pet care in the home? What safety measures would the home of the future include? Ask students to show these features in an illustrated and captioned poster titled "The House of the Future." If possible, interested students might use CAD software to help them design living space for their houses of the future. Display finished posters in the classroom.

CHAPTER 8, LESSON 2

USING VISUALS
Refer students to Figure 8.2. Then ask them to generate a list of no-cost or inexpensive accessories (trophies, wall hangings, plants, posters).

L1 Using Transparencies
Present Color Transparency 38, "The Personal Touch," in the TCR. Use this overhead visual to reinforce concepts from this lesson.

L1 Student Workbook
Assign Activities 60 and 61 in the Student Workbook.

ASSESS

Evaluating the Lesson
Assign Reviewing Terms and Facts and Thinking Critically on page 234 to review the lesson; then assign the Lesson 2 Quiz in the TCR.

Reteaching
- Ask students to write a paragraph or two explaining how color, line, texture, shape, and space are demonstrated in the bedroom shown in Figure 8.2. Accept all reasonable responses.
- Have students complete Reteaching Activity 8 in the TCR.

Enrichment
Conduct a scavenger hunt outdoors. Instruct students to find natural examples of two of the following elements of design: shape, line, texture, and color. Have students display and group objects by design element.

CHAPTER 8, LESSON 2

TIPS for living

Provide students with graph paper, scissors, and ruler to practice drawing a floor plan for this feature. Have them work in pairs to come up with the best arrangement of furniture.

Answers to Lesson 2 Review

1. Space, shape, line, texture, and color.
2. A feeling that something is different from the way it really is.
3. Answers will vary but should include some of the following ideas: Space helps draw attention to objects. Shape adds interest to a room. Lines add interest. Texture provides variety and interest to a room. Color creates an overall mood.
4. Red, yellow, and orange are warm colors. Blue, green, and violet are cool colors.
5. An accessory is an interesting item you add to make your space more personal. Examples include posters, wall hangings, plants, and trophies.
6. Color has the greatest effect overall, but each of the other elements contributes to a pleasing room.
7. Soft, fuzzy, nubby textures make a room seem cozy. Smooth, hard surfaces give a clean, modern effect.
8. Accessories say who a person is; they help personalize a room. Accessories make your room your own.
9. Responses will vary, but should discuss shape, use of space, color, line, and texture.

CLOSE

In a brief paragraph, ask students to choose the design element they think is most important and to explain why.

234

TIPS for living

DRAWING A FLOOR PLAN

Have you ever worn yourself out moving furniture around to find the best arrangement? Make a **floor plan,** or *diagram of a room arrangement,* to save time and trouble. To make one, do the following.

● Measure the room and the furniture in it.
● Draw the dimensions of the room on a piece of graph paper. Have one or two squares equal each foot of space in the room.
● Show where the doors, windows, and other fixed features are. Draw a dotted line to show which way the doors open.
● On another sheet of graph paper draw each piece of furniture. Cut out and label the pieces.
● Move the pieces of furniture around on the floor plan until you get a satisfying arrangement. Allow space for walking and for drawers to open.

LESSON TWO *Review*

Using complete sentences, answer the following questions on a separate sheet of paper.

Reviewing Terms and Facts

1. List What are the five elements of design?
2. Vocabulary Define the term *illusion.* Use it in an original sentence.
3. Identify How does each element of design contribute to the overall effect of a room?
4. Recall Which colors are considered warm? Which ones are considered cool?
5. Vocabulary Define the term *accessories.* Give four examples of accessories.

Thinking Critically

6. Analyze Which element of design do you think is the most important? Explain your answer.
7. Describe How can texture affect the mood of a room?
8. Explain Why are accessories an important part of any room?

Applying Concepts

9. Look through magazines, and choose a picture of a room you like. Write a few paragraphs explaining how the design elements have been used to create an appealing look.

234 CHAPTER 8: YOUR HOME

MORE ABOUT •••

Technology vs. Folk Art Futurists contend that as technological advances lead to mechanization and impersonalization in other areas, decorating styles in homes will reflect just the opposite. The emphasis will be placed on comfort, personalization, and togetherness. Interior design will feature soft colors and cozy and nostalgic looks. Folk art and handmade items will increase in popularity. Ask students to think about how this idea is already becoming a reality in homes. Can students think of examples of technologically advanced cooking equipment and homemade accessories in the same kitchen? Ask them to point to similar examples in other rooms of the home.

LESSON THREE
Keeping a Home Clean and Safe

DISCOVER...
- the value of keeping a home clean and safe.
- how to manage cleaning tasks.
- how to prevent accidents.

WORDS TO KNOW

sanitary
precautions
cleaning plan

Do you feel proud of your home when it is clean and neat? Do you feel good knowing that your home is safe and secure? Keeping your home clean, neat, safe, and secure is worthwhile for many reasons.

- **It saves time and energy.** You waste time and energy when you have to search for items that you need. For example, have you ever wasted time looking for a missing notebook or shoe?

LESSON THREE
Keeping a Home Clean and Safe

FOCUS

Lesson Objectives
After studying this lesson, students should be able to
- discuss advantages of a clean and safe home.
- list suggestions for managing cleaning tasks.
- develop strategies for preventing accidents.

Motivating Activity
Have each student complete the following statement: "My least favorite chore is . . ."

Introducing the Lesson
Call on volunteers to read their responses to the Motivating Activity. Generate a list of the chores on the board and brainstorm ways to simplify these tasks. Then explain that this lesson suggests ways to manage cleaning chores.

Introducing *Words to Know*
Help students see ways the vocabulary words are related to a clean and safe home. Ask for original sentences using two of the words. For example, A *cleaning plan* can help keep a kitchen *sanitary*. Taking *precautions* to keep kitchen counters clean helps to keep a kitchen *sanitary*. Point out that *clean* is a synonym for *sanitary*.

CLASSROOM RESOURCES FOR LESSON 3

 Blackline Masters
Concept Map 13
Cooperative Learning 16
Enrichment 9
Lesson 3 Quiz
Peer Pressure and Decision Making 18
Reteaching 8

 **Student Workbook**
Activities 62, 63

CHAPTER 8, LESSON 3

TEACH

L2 Critical Thinking
Remind students that cooperation within a family helps a home run more smoothly and efficiently. Tell students that even small children can help to complete cleaning tasks in a home. Ask students to make lists of jobs that can be done by children in each of the following age groups: 4–5 years old, 6–7 years old, 8–9 years old, and 10–12 years old. Students might post their lists in their homes.

L2 Cooperative Learning
Assign Cooperative Learning Activity 16 in the TCR. Students work in groups to devise a list of safety measures for each room of a house in this activity.

TEACHER TALK!

Handling Emergencies

In addition to knowing what precautions to take to prevent accidents, students need to know what to do in case of an emergency.

Having emergency reference material on hand can prove useful until qualified help arrives. You might help students familiarize themselves with this material by providing first-aid books for students to browse through.

- **Clothes and other possessions last longer.** If you take care of your belongings, they last longer and do not need to be replaced as often.
- **Family members stay healthier in a clean home.** A clean home is **sanitary,** or *free from germs.*
- **Most home accidents can be prevented.** By practicing safety **precautions,** or *steps to avoid danger,* family members can keep many home accidents and injuries from occurring.
- **Security measures can keep a home safe.** If a home has adequate window and door locks, it will be more difficult for intruders to break into the home.

Families may find that managing cleaning tasks is easier if they use a cleaning plan to organize the work. What items are included in a cleaning plan?

Organizing the Cleaning Tasks

Routine cleaning tasks are those that must be done every day or every week. These chores include washing dishes, emptying the dishwasher, making beds, cleaning floors, keeping rooms picked up, emptying wastebaskets, and hanging up clothes. Routine tasks keep the home clean and neat so that heavy cleaning is needed less often.

A cleaning plan can help families manage their cleaning tasks. A **cleaning plan** is *a list of daily, weekly, and occasional household jobs and of the family member or members who are responsible for each job.* To make a cleaning plan, decide with other members of the family what jobs need to be done and who will perform each task.

Cleaning Shared Space

When each person takes responsibility for keeping his or her personal space in order, much of the housekeeping gets done

236   CHAPTER 8: YOUR HOME

HOME AND COMMUNITY CONNECTION

Researching Cleaning Services Ask students to look in a local telephone book to locate information about home-cleaning services. With supervision, have students call for information about the services, including what services are provided, how much they cost, who provides equipment and supplies, and so on. Have students report their findings to the class.

automatically. To get your share done with ease, you need to establish some routine habits. For example, hanging up clothes or putting them in a hamper is a habit that takes no more time than dropping clothes on the bed or in a corner. If you are cooking in the kitchen, clean up as you go along so that the cleanup at the end is easier.

Because the bathrooms and the kitchen are used by all family members, every person must help keep them in order. Rinse the bathtub and sink after each use. Hang towels and washcloths neatly in the same place after each use. Return personal grooming items to their proper place to avoid clutter.

In the kitchen leave the counter and sink clean. Wash and dry the dishes, or put them in the dishwasher. What are some other ways to keep the kitchen clean and neat?

Cleaning Up Your Room

It will be easier to keep your room clean if you take time each day to put it in order. All the tasks do not have to be done at the same time. For instance, a good plan may be to hang up your clothes and straighten the dresser and desk at night. It doesn't take long to make your bed in the morning. You can dust or empty the wastebasket in the afternoon after you finish your homework. Put away your belongings as soon as you finish using them.

Keeping your clothes closet organized helps you find what you need. It also helps to keep your room looking neat. Try these ideas.

- Hang up your clothes according to categories. For example, put all of your shirts or blouses, pants or skirts, and sweaters together.

▲ By spending a few minutes straightening your room each day, you can keep it neat and attractive. How much time do you spend cleaning your room each day?

CHAPTER 8, LESSON 3

L2 Investigating
Ask volunteers to visit a store that sells smoke detectors. Have them compare several smoke detectors, considering the prices and the manufacturers' claims. Ask students to share their findings with the class.

L2 Language Arts
Ask each student to scan a local newspaper for an article about a household accident, such as a fire or a fall. Allow time for students to present an oral report describing the accident and telling what precautions might have prevented it. Articles may be added to a classroom file for future reference.

L3 Applying Life Skills
Have students inspect their homes for hazards that could cause falls or might lead to accidental poisoning. Have them prepare a checklist in class to help in their inspection. Suggest that students discuss any hazards they find with family members and together make recommendations to correct these hazards.

L2 Problem Solving
Assign Peer Pressure and Decision Making 18 in the TCR. This activity gives students the opportunity to recognize peer pressure and practice decision-making skills.

LESSON THREE: KEEPING A HOME CLEAN AND SAFE **237**

MEETING STUDENT DIVERSITY

Learning Styles Tactile learners might benefit from demonstrating ways to handle safety devices. Whenever possible, bring in safety devices. Have students handle the devices and role-play how they can be used in the home. Have students select a room in the house and become experts on safety in that room. Have them illustrate ways of making the selected room safe and share their illustrations with the class.

237

CHAPTER 8, LESSON 3

After students have read the ways to secure a home, have them use the checklist to evaluate how secure their home is. Students might then make a checklist identifying the security measures that would make their homes safer.

L2 Applying Concepts

Remind students that many everyday household products are poisons. Have students bring in one or two labels from household cleaning products. Collect all the labels for a display. Have students work in class to annotate the display with information about how to use and store the products safely and what to do in case of poisoning.

DID YOU KNOW

Of all home accident deaths in 1993, 32 percent were a result of falls, 25 percent a result of poisoning, and 14 percent a result of fire.

Use this checklist to see if your home and family are safe from intruders.
1. Is there exterior lighting over every entrance?
2. Is shrubbery trimmed near doors and windows?
3. Are there secure locks on doors and windows?
4. Are there other safety devices, such as peepholes, door chains, and motion detector lights?
5. Are doors locked at all times?
6. Are garage doors kept locked when not in use?
7. Do you avoid opening the door to strangers?

- Clean soiled shoes and clothes before putting them in the closet, and keep your shoes in a shoe bag or on a shoe rack.
- Keep small articles that you use only occasionally in shoe boxes or plastic boxes. Label the outside of the boxes so that you can find the items easily.

What other closet-organizing tips can you think of?

Home Safety

Many of the accidents that happen in homes could be prevented or avoided with a little care. Don't let someone in your family be hurt by carelessness. Read over the following rules, and then take the time to make your home safe.

Protect your home from fire by following these safety rules.

- Make sure that smoke alarms are installed in the home. Alarms should be installed near the kitchen, outside the bedrooms, and at the top of the stairs. Check smoke alarms once a month to be sure that they are working properly, and change the batteries routinely.
- Do not let curtains, towels, or pot holders get too close to the stove. If you are cooking, avoid wearing a shirt with loose sleeves that might easily catch fire.
- Keep the area around the stove free of grease. Grease burns easily and can spread a fire.
- Make sure that all electrical cords are in good condition. A damaged cord can cause surrounding material to catch fire.
- If you have a fireplace in your home, make sure that it is used properly. Keep flammable objects away from the fireplace, and be sure to use a screen.
- Keep a fire extinguisher in the home, and learn how to use it properly.

To protect people from falls in your home, follow these safety rules.

238   CHAPTER 8: YOUR HOME

MORE ABOUT • • •

Electricity and Safety Students should be aware of other ways to prevent electrical shock. They can share the following with family members:
- Never turn on a light switch while in the bathtub or standing in water.
- Do not allow children to poke metal objects or fingers into electrical outlets.
- Do not stand outdoors in an electrical storm.
- Wear shoes with rubber soles when using power tools.
- Never use aluminum ladders near power lines.

- Make sure that the stairs are in good repair, well lit, and free from clutter. Stairs should also have handrails.
- If something is spilled on a bare floor, wipe it up immediately.
- Place nonskid pads under small rugs so that they don't slide.
- Be sure to use nonskid strips or mats in bathtubs and showers.

If you spill something on the floor, clean it up right away so that no one slips and falls. How else can you protect people from falls in the home?

Other Safety Precautions

In addition to fires and falls, there are many other types of accidents that can happen in homes. If there are small children in the family, poisoning is a particularly serious danger. Make sure that all cleaning products and chemicals are kept out of the reach of the children. Don't forget to store lawn products carefully. Read the label on any chemical or cleaning product before using it so that you will know how to handle it correctly. If anyone in your family accidentally swallows a poisonous substance, immediately call a poison control center or a hospital.

Power tools and sharp knives can also cause injuries if they are not used with care. Learn how to handle such equipment properly. Knives and other potentially dangerous objects should be kept out of the reach of children.

LESSON THREE: KEEPING A HOME CLEAN AND SAFE **239**

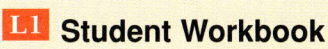

CHAPTER 8, LESSON 3

L1 Student Workbook
Assign Activities 62 and 63 in the Student Workbook.

ASSESS

Evaluating the Lesson
Assign Reviewing Terms and Facts and Thinking Critically on page 240 to review the lesson; then assign the Lesson 3 Quiz in the TCR.

Reteaching
- Ask students to work in small groups to create illustrated posters that describe ways of preventing accidents. Display completed posters in the classroom and school hallways.
- Have students complete Reteaching Activity 8 in the TCR.
- Assign Concept Map 13 in the TCR.

Enrichment
- Divide the class into groups and have each group research and demonstrate for the class how to properly clean such items and surfaces as wood furniture, stainless steel sinks, silver objects, tile floors, miniblinds, and plastic surfaces.
- Assign Enrichment Activity 9 in the TCR.

HOME AND COMMUNITY CONNECTION

School-to-Work Encourage students to research careers available in architecture and housing maintenance. Have them prepare a list of careers and then identify classes available in school that would help them in each of the careers they have listed. Students may wish to contact local businesses that employ architects, maintenance, or home repair workers for suggestions of classes that are most helpful to people working in that area. When students have gathered the information, have them design a chart or write a report of their findings.

CHAPTER 8, LESSON 3

Answers to Lesson 3 Review

1. A *precaution* is a step taken to avoid danger. A sample sentence: June took the precaution of unplugging the toaster before taking out the toast.
2. Answers might include washing dishes, making beds, emptying wastebaskets, cleaning floors, and hanging up clothes.
3. Put away things as soon as you are finished with them; organize your closet; take 10–15 minutes each day to straighten and pick up the room.
4. Answers should include four of the following: keeping curtains away from stove, avoiding wearing garments with loose sleeves while cooking, keeping the stove area clean of grease, installing smoke detectors, making sure electrical cords are in good condition, using a fireplace screen, and keeping a fire extinguisher in the house and knowing how to use it.
5. Falls can be prevented by keeping stairs in good repair, wiping up spills, keeping clutter off stairs, using non-skid rugs, and using nonskid strips in bathtubs.
6. Establishing routine cleaning habits means you do not have to do all the cleaning at once. Also, cleaning little by little means the task is easier overall.
7. All the precautions from the lesson apply, but people should be especially alert to storing and using cleaning products safely and keeping small children away from stairways, matches, and sharp objects.
8. Responses will vary depending on what the tasks are and who will do them.

CLOSE

Ask each student to respond in writing to explain the following: The safest place for us can also be the most unsafe place.

Improper use of electrical appliances is another common cause of accidents. Be sure to connect and disconnect any electrical appliance with dry hands. Do not use any appliance that has a damaged cord. Do not use a hair dryer while in the bathtub or while standing on a wet spot.

Keeping your home clean and safe will benefit all members of the family. What are some of these benefits?

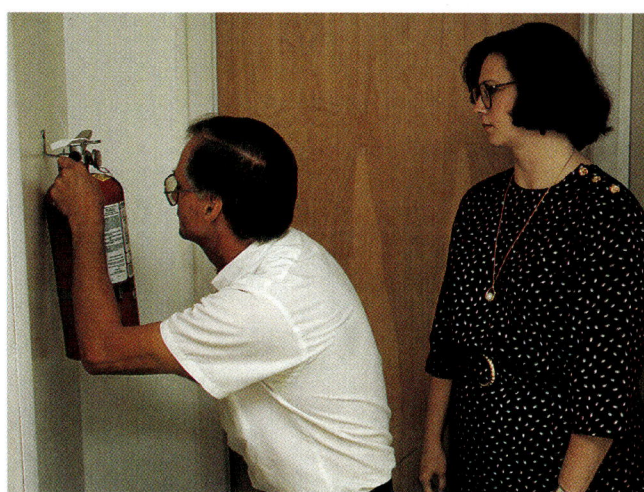

LESSON THREE *Review*

Using complete sentences, answer the following questions on a separate sheet of paper.

Reviewing Terms and Facts

1. **Vocabulary** Define the term *precautions*. Use it in an original sentence.
2. **Recall** What are routine cleaning tasks? Give four examples of these tasks.
3. **List** What are three tips for keeping your bedroom neat?
4. **Name** List four ways to protect your home from fire.
5. **Identify** Name four safety rules for preventing falls in the home.

Thinking Critically

6. **Explain** How can establishing routine cleaning habits save you time?
7. **Analyze** What special safety precautions should be taken if young children live in a home?

Applying Concepts

8. Make a cleaning plan for your home. First list the cleaning tasks that need to be done on a daily, weekly, and occasional basis. Then discuss with family members who can do which chores on which days. Make sure that the work is divided fairly. On the computer or by hand, create a chart that shows the cleaning tasks and each family member's assignments for a one-month period. Put your plan into effect.

COOPERATIVE LEARNING

Community Safety Workers Ask students to generate a list of those people in their community who work to keep people safe. These include police officers, firefighters, health workers, and many others. When the list is complete, have the class decide who they would like to interview about safety. Arrange for a person from the field the students choose to speak to the class. Organize the class into small groups. Have them generate a list of questions to ask the person. After the interview, ask students to create visuals, such as posters or murals, that summarize the information they received from the speaker. Display visuals in the classroom or school hallways.

Chapter 8 Activities

Consumer Focus

Fido and Fluffy

Pets can help make a home feel friendly, warm, and safe. They can also make it difficult to keep a home clean and sanitary. Many dogs and cats shed, and pets sometimes leave unpleasant stains and odors.

Fortunately, deodorizers and other products are available to help people clean up after pets.

Try This!
Consult a book on household cleaning tips for ways to remove pet stains and odors. Report to the class on your findings.

A Global View

HOME SWEET HOME

In Nigeria, Yakuba and his family reside in a mud hut with a straw roof. Chong and her parents live on a houseboat in the harbor of Singapore. Kadir and his family are nomads in Saudi Arabia. They travel across the desert and set up tents whenever they stop.

TRY THIS!
Cut out or draw pictures of different types of housing. Assemble your pictures for a classroom display. Write a paragraph about people's need for homes, and put it with your artwork.

FRIENDS & FAMILY

ACCIDENTS WAITING TO HAPPEN

Every year thousands of adults and children are seriously hurt or die as a result of home accidents.

Some accidents happen because of careless behavior. Other accidents occur as a result of unsafe conditions, such as frayed electrical cords. Most home accidents can be prevented.

TRY THIS!
Learn more about home safety hazards. Then make a home safety checklist. Use the checklist to discover potential hazards in your home. Work with your family on accident prevention.

TECHNOLOGY CONNECTION

AUTOMATION IN THE HOME

Many homes are equipped with features that help people stay safe, save energy and money, and make their lives easier.

Lights and appliances can be programmed to turn on and off at set times. Heating and cooling systems can be set to operate automatically. With a computer, modem, and fax machine, people can stay in touch with coworkers anywhere.

Follow Up
1. What role do you think that computers play in home automation?
2. What other types of automation would you like to see in homes of the future? Make a list of ideas, and exchange lists with a classmate.
3. How might home automation benefit people with physical disabilities? Write down two or three examples.

CHAPTER 8 Activities

Consumer Focus

As students complete the "Try This" activity, you might ask students who have pets to bring in samples of special cleaning products or deodorizers that they have used in their homes. Allow students to set up a table to display special soaps and brushes and let them demonstrate chew toys, scratching posts, or other methods used to keep their pets occupied.

A Global View

Discuss with students the different types of housing people in the United States live in—single-family houses, apartment buildings, or mobile homes. Point out that environment, culture, economic conditions, family size, and values influence the type of housing in which people live. No matter what a home looks like, it fulfills the same basic needs for those who live in it.

FRIENDS & FAMILY

Ask students to describe other common actions that can cause accidents in the home, such as putting a fork into the toaster to retrieve a piece of bread that is stuck. Discuss the students' descriptions and let them use these examples to begin their lists for accident prevention in the activity.

Teaching the TECHNOLOGY CONNECTION

Before students read the feature, bring in advertisements from hardware and house-supply stores that advertise some of the kinds of products discussed in the feature. Have students review the advertisements and explain what these products have in common.

Follow Up — Answers to Follow-Up
1. Answers will vary but students might indicate that many home-automation devices require computerized devices to work.
2. Ideas will vary. Encourage students to work with partners to evaluate their ideas.
3. Examples will vary, but students should indicate how automation would be used to help physically disabled people.

CHAPTER 8 REVIEW

Checking Comprehension
Use the Chapter Summary and the Chapter 8 Review to help students go over the most important ideas presented in Chapter 8.

Answers to Words to Know
1. Kitchen: for cooking meals; Table: studying; Shelf: for storing clothing.
2. The pathway people take into, out of, and through a room.
3. The art of making things look good by combining them in a pleasing way.
4. Diagonal lines suggest action.
5. Nubby, soft, fuzzy, and smooth
6. *Sanitary* means clean.
7. Safety precautions help keep people safe from accidents.
8. A cleaning plan contains a list of daily, weekly, and occasional cleaning chores and who will do them.

Answers to Review Questions
1. A home provides a place to keep possessions, relax, and express yourself.
2. Different living areas serve the many different needs of modern families.
3. Answers should include some of the following: pick up one's belongings, clean up after using rooms, knock before opening closed doors, and keep music low when the other is sleeping or studying.

242

CHAPTER 8 REVIEW

Chapter Summary
Your home not only provides the shelter you need but also reflects your personality.

- You can make your home both appealing and functional by choosing your furniture and arranging your living space with care.
- Sharing living space with others requires respect for others' privacy, consideration, cooperation, and compromise.
- The elements of design are space, shape, line, texture, and color.
- Before you change the look of your room, it is a good idea to plan how you will make the changes.
- The accessories you add to a room help define your style and give your living space a personal touch.
- There are many advantages to keeping a home clean and safe, including saving time and energy, keeping the home free of germs, and preventing accidents.
- It is much easier to keep the home clean if everyone shares the tasks and follows a cleaning plan.
- Take safety precautions to guard against accidents, fires, falls, and intruders in the home.

 ### Words to Know
Using complete sentences, answer the following questions on a separate sheet of paper.

1. Name one *function* of each of the following: a kitchen, a table, a shelf.
2. Explain what is meant by the *traffic pattern* in a room.
3. What is *design*?
4. Draw a *diagonal* line. What effect do diagonal lines suggest?
5. Name four kinds of *texture*.
6. What does *sanitary* mean?
7. Why is it important to practice safety *precautions* in the home?
8. What is listed in a *cleaning plan*.

242   CHAPTER 8: YOUR HOME

Review Questions
Using complete sentences, answer the following questions on a separate sheet of paper.

1. What does your home provide for you besides physical shelter?
2. Why are homes divided into special living areas?
3. How could a teen who shares a bedroom with a brother or sister show respect for the other person's privacy?
4. How can color be used to affect the appearance of a room?
5. Before you start a room makeover, what should you do?
6. Why should a teen maintain a clean, neat bedroom?

EXTRA CREDIT PROJECT

Extending Chapter Content Students may participate in a Home Scavenger Hunt to locate features and elements of housing design and living space that are covered in the chapter. Prepare a list for students to work from that includes various functional furniture placement, design elements, accessories, and safety features. Have them form teams or work individually and check their own homes, or they may wish to use school or office spaces. If possible, have them use cameras to take pictures of as many examples as they can find from the list. Have groups tally the number of examples their team located and report to the class.

CHAPTER 8 REVIEW

7. List three ways to manage your cleaning time efficiently.
8. Give two examples of ways to prevent falls in the home.

Thinking Critically

Using complete sentences, answer the following questions on a separate sheet of paper.

1. **Suggest** How might a family's values influence living space? Give examples.
2. **Analyze** What aspects of day-to-day living do you think an architect has to consider when designing a living space? Explain your answer.
3. **Recommend** How could you use the elements of design to create a room that looks large and efficient?
4. **Apply** How would you design living space to meet the needs of a family member who uses a wheelchair?

Cooperative Learning

1. Working with a partner, look in home-decorating magazines for a color picture of a room. Cut out the picture, and paste it on a piece of construction paper. Write a paragraph describing how the elements of design have been used in the room. Then exchange pictures with another pair of students. Discuss the design elements in the new picture, and see if the description the other pair wrote matches the picture.
2. Working in groups of three or four, choose a cleaning technique, such as how to wash dishes, clean glass, or clean a bathtub. Look in a book on household hints for information on your cleaning technique. Then demonstrate your technique to the class or make a poster explaining the technique.

Family & Community

1. Discuss with your family a free or inexpensive way to improve the living space in your home. For example, you might agree on a cleaning schedule, rearrange the furniture in the living room, paint the kitchen, or make the house childproof. Make a plan and then carry it out.
2. Identify a local group that helps people safeguard their homes and be good neighbors. This may be a block club, a Neighborhood Watch program, or a community organization. Find out about the work of the group, and report your findings to the class.

Building A Portfolio

1. Plan a makeover for your personal living space. Think about how you could improve your space, and then put your plan into action. Your plan could involve redecorating, rearranging the furniture, or cleaning. Use photos or drawings to show "Before" and "After." Place the photos or drawings in your portfolio.
2. List the accessories you have in your personal living space, such as posters, collections, and knickknacks. Tell what each accessory reveals about your interests. Are your accessories similar to or different from those you kept in your living space when you were younger? Put the list in your portfolio.

CHAPTER 8 REVIEW 243

CHAPTER 8 REVIEW

4. Color can make a room appear larger (light colors), smaller (dark colors), warmer (reds and oranges), cooler (blues and greens), cheerful (warm colors), or relaxing (cool colors).
5. Create a plan and check it out with other family members.
6. Clean bedrooms save time, show respect for possessions and for other family members, and make cleaning tasks easier.
7. Examples: make a cleaning plan, keep personal things in their places, keep cleaning supplies orderly and close-at-hand, clean only one thing at a time, clean up messes as soon as they happen.
8. Examples: use nonskid rugs, wipe up spills, clean clutter on stairways, use nonskid mats in bathtubs.

Evaluate

Use the Chapter 8 Test in the TCR, or construct your own test using the Testmaker Software.

CLOSE

Have students apply their knowledge of the chapter's content by completing one of the alternative assessment activities listed under Family and Community or Building a Portfolio.

Answers to Thinking Critically

1. What a family thinks is important will be reflected in how they use space. A family who values learning and education might have space for books, computers, tables for working, and so on.
2. Lifestyles that include working parents; less cleaning and cooking time; home offices; children with many activities; and people of different generations living together. Design features must reflect this lifestyle.
3. Light colors, space between objects and furniture, straight lines, and smooth surfaces will help make a room look large and efficient.
4. Answers should include ways to make moving about in a wheelchair easy and working surfaces that meet the needs of a seated person.

243

Planning Guide
Chapter 9 Your Environment

LESSON 1	Pages	FEATURES	CLASSROOM RESOURCES
Protecting Your Environment	246–251	Try This: Conserving Natural Resources Skills In Action: Using Water Wisely	Activity and Project Card 17, "Preserving the Environment" Cooperative Learning 17 Lesson 1 Quiz Peer Pressure and Decision Making 19 Transparency 39, "Protect the Environment" Student Workbook Activity 64
LESSON 2			
Keeping Your Environment Clean	252–257	Tips for Living: How to Recycle	Concept Map 14 Cooperative Learning 18 Lesson 2 Quiz Transparency 40, "Makeup of U.S. Waste" Student Workbook Activities 65, 66
LESSON 3			
Your Personal Safety and Violence Prevention	258–264	Skills in Action: Bicycle and Skating Safety Tips for Living: Stranger Danger	Activity and Project Card 18, "Speak Out Against Violence" Concept Map 15 Cross Curriculum 10 Enrichment 10 Lesson 3 Quiz Peer Pressure and Decision Making 20 Transparency 41, "The Accident Chain" Student Workbook Activities 67, 68

CHAPTER 9 RESOURCES

- Chapter 9 Test
- Reteaching 9
- Study Guide 9, *Reteaching*
- Testmaker Software

Performance Assessment Activity

Ask students to conduct interviews with classmates or other acquaintances about protecting their environment. Each student should prepare a list of questions in advance. Students might want to tape their interviews and play them to the rest of the class. Consider presenting some of the taped interviews to PTA community groups. When students have completed their interviews, have small groups use the information from the interviews to create posters that convey the importance of protecting the environment. Display the completed posters in the classroom.

School-to-Work

Ask students to research a job that they might like to have as an adult that involves working with the environment or personal safety. You might have the class brainstorm a list of job titles or descriptions, then have each student choose one job to research. Ask students to find out what education is required for the job, what personal characteristics would be beneficial, and what duties and responsibilities are involved in the job.

Family & Community

Bring in articles clipped from local newspapers concerning people or groups that work to prevent accidents or acts of violence. For example, articles might address safety programs designed to teach home security or shelters that offer safe havens for abused spouses and children. Organize the class into groups and have each group analyze the stories for how they promote personal safety and/or violence prevention. Have groups discuss how these individuals or groups aid the community. Then ask students to write a short fiction story about a teen's plan to promote personal safety.

Resources for the Teacher

Earth Works Group. *50 Simple Things You Can Do to Save the Earth.* Berkeley, CA: EarthWorks Press, 1989.

Saunders, Carol Silverman. *Safe at School: Awareness and Action for Parents of Kids Grades K-12.* Minneapolis: Free Spirit Publishers, 1994.

Rathje, William L., and Cullen Murphy. *Rubbish!: The Archaeology of Garbage.* New York: HarperCollins Publishers, 1992.

Readings for the Student

Chaiet, Donna. *Staying Safe at School.* New York: Rosen Publishing Group, 1995.

Chaiet, Donna. *Staying Safe on the Streets.* New York: Rosen Publishing Group, 1995.

Love, Ann, and Jane Drake. *Take Action: An Environmental Book for Kids.* New York: Beech Tree, 1993.

Multimedia Resources

Home Alone (Videocassette). Hi-Tops Video.

Kids in the Crossfire: Violence in America. (Videocassette). MPI Home Video, 1993.

Safety Monkey (Interactive Multimedia). IVI Publishing, 1994.

OUT OF TIME?

If time does not permit thorough teaching of this chapter, you may wish to use:
- Teens Making a Difference, page 245
- Tips for Living, pages 255, 262
- Try This, page 247
- Skills in Action, pages 248, 261
- Young Living Activities, page 265
- Chapter Summary, page 266

CHAPTER 9
Your Environment

Chapter Overview
Chapter 9 examines various actions students can take to protect themselves and their environment. The chapter emphasizes students taking action and assuming personal responsibility.

LESSON 1 identifies natural resources and explains ways to conserve resources and use energy wisely.

LESSON 2 focuses on disposal of waste and what it means to reduce, reuse, and recycle.

LESSON 3 explores how to avoid accidents and unnecessary risk, and how to prevent violence.

Introducing the Chapter
Refer students to the chapter title and the lesson titles. Have them use the lesson titles as the main heads of an outline. Then have them skim the lessons and look at the photographs to find two supporting details to write under each main heading. Have students exchange their outlines with a partner and review them as a preview of the chapter. Tell them that Chapter 9 focuses on the environment and on ways that they can help protect it and themselves.

Chapter Motivator
Write the word *pollution* on the board. Then provide students with magazines to look through to find examples of pollution. Have them categorize their examples of pollution as air, water, land, and noise pollution. Then ask students to brainstorm ways in which they can help stop the various kinds of pollution and help protect the environment. After they complete the chapter, have them compare the ways they listed with the ways suggested in the chapter.

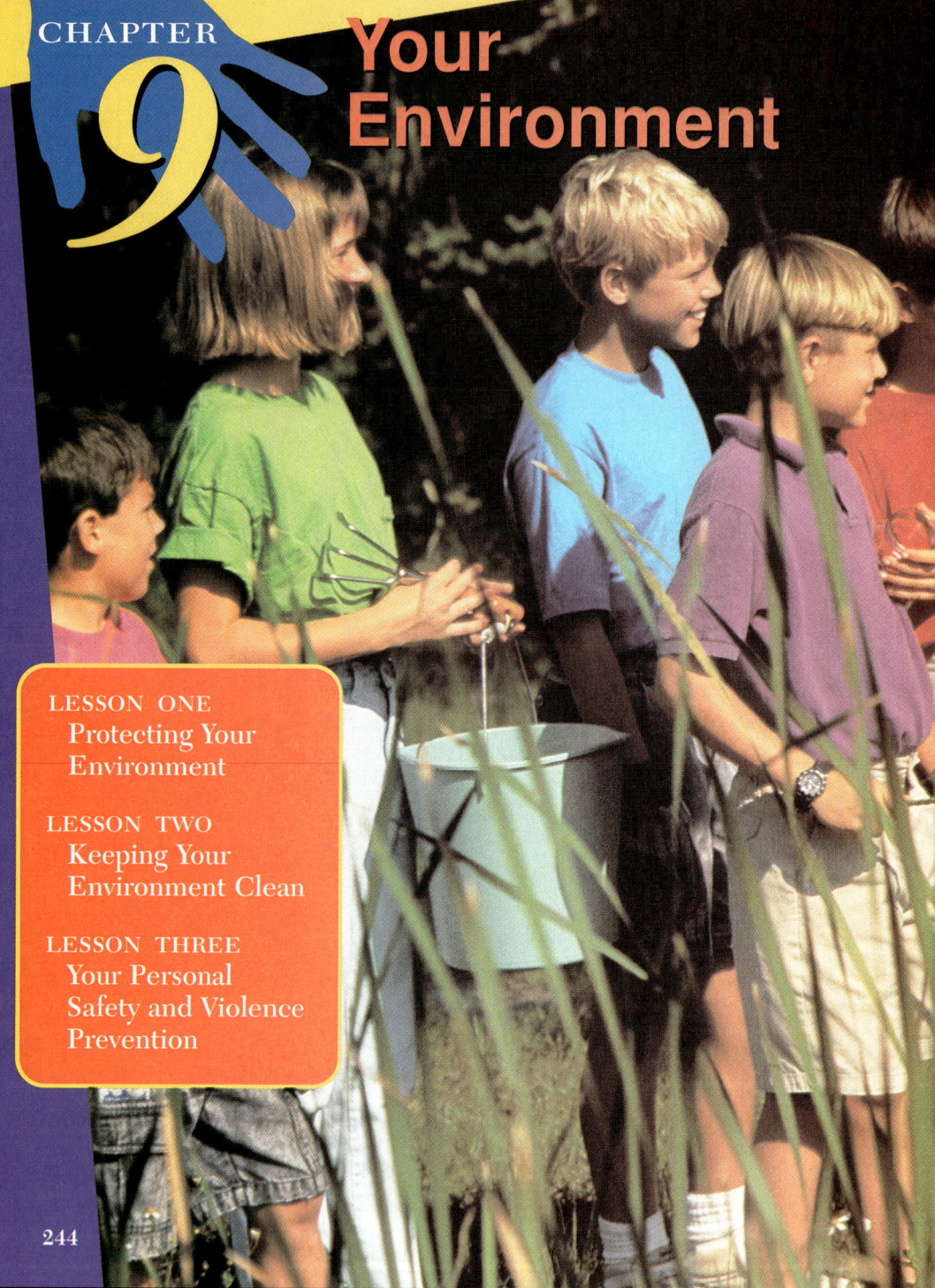

CHAPTER 9
Your Environment

LESSON ONE
Protecting Your Environment

LESSON TWO
Keeping Your Environment Clean

LESSON THREE
Your Personal Safety and Violence Prevention

KEY TO ABILITY LEVELS

Teaching strategies that appear throughout the chapter have been identified by one of three codes to give you an idea of their suitability for students of varying learning styles and abilities.

L1 Level 1 strategies should be within the ability range of all students. Often full class participation is required. Teacher direction is usually needed.

L2 Level 2 strategies are for average to above-average students or for small groups. Some teacher direction is necessary.

L3 Level 3 strategies are designed for students able and willing to work independently. Minimal teacher direction is necessary.

CHAPTER 9

TEENS MAKING A DIFFERENCE

Call on a volunteer to read the feature. Ask students what other ways teens can be "buddies" to younger children. List these ways on the board.

Then have each student complete the activity at the end of the feature. When students have completed their paragraphs, ask them to read their paragraphs to a classmate and evaluate them.

BLOCK SCHEDULING

The following Teacher Classroom Resources are suggested for use in classrooms with Block Scheduling.

- Activity and Project Card 17, "Preserving the Environment"
- Activity and Project Card 18, "Speak Out Against Violence"
- Cooperative Learning 17, "Using Resources Responsibly"
- Cooperative Learning 18, "Don't Refuse to Reuse"

TEENS MAKING A DIFFERENCE
Buddy Service

Seventeen-year-old Kevin Chang started a buddy service to help young teens in his community stay safe. Kevin's 12-year-old brother Thomas often asked Kevin to drive him home from school because Thomas felt unsafe walking home alone. Some of Thomas's friends started asking Kevin to drive them home too. That is when Kevin asked some of his friends to help him make the buddy service a business.

Kevin and his friends now take appointments and charge hourly rates for their buddy service. Parents don't mind paying for the service to ensure that their children get home safely.

Try THIS!

Do you think that a buddy service would be useful at your school? Why or why not? Write a paragraph or two explaining your answer.

245

TECHNOLOGY IN THE CLASSROOM

Computers There are three general types of software available for use in the Family and Consumer Sciences classroom. These three include word processing, database, and spreadsheet programs. Students can use word processing for any assignment that requires writing. A database is an organized collection of information. Students can use a database to categorize, organize, manipulate, and evaluate information. Spreadsheets are used to calculate numbers. Most spreadsheets also automatically calculate functions such as averages. Students can use spreadsheets for activities such as calculating and comparing the cost of burning a 60-watt bulb and the cost of burning a 100-watt bulb for a certain length of time.

245

LESSON ONE
Protecting Your Environment

FOCUS

Lesson Objectives
After studying this lesson, students should be able to
- explain what natural resources are.
- describe ways to conserve natural resources.
- list ways to use energy wisely.

Motivating Activity
Write the following statement on the board for students to complete: "I conserve natural resources when I . . ."

Introducing the Lesson
Write the following headings on the board: Land, Air, Water, Energy. Have students share their responses to the Motivating Activity by writing them under the appropriate resource that their responses illustrate. Tell students that Lesson 1 illustrates other ways to protect the environment.

Introducing *Words to Know*
Ask each student to write a sentence for each term in the Words to Know list. When students have finished, ask them to form small groups and share their sentences with group members. Ask each group to use their sentences to develop a definition for each term. Then have a student from each group share the definitions with the rest of the class. After all groups have reported, discuss the similarities and differences among the students' definitions and the ones provided in the lesson.

LESSON ONE
Protecting Your Environment

WORDS TO KNOW

natural resources
pollution
conservation
insulation
energy efficient

DISCOVER...
- the natural resources that make up the environment.
- ways to conserve natural resources.
- ways to use energy wisely.

Do you like to spend time at the beach or in the mountains? Have you ever gone swimming or fishing in a lake or an ocean? Enjoying outdoor activities is one of the greatest pleasures of life. In addition, you could not survive without the elements that nature provides.

246 CHAPTER 9: YOUR ENVIRONMENT

CLASSROOM RESOURCES FOR LESSON 1

 Blackline Masters
Activity and Project Card 17, "Preserving the Environment"
Cooperative Learning 17
Lesson 1 Quiz
Peer Pressure and Decision Making 19

 Transparencies
Transparency 39, "Protect the Environment"

 **Student Workbook**
Activity 64

What Are Natural Resources?

Natural resources are *materials that are supplied by nature.* You might not think about them very often, and you may even take them for granted. However, your health and well-being depend on several key natural resources. These include air, water, soil, and the energy derived from coal, oil, and gas.

At one time these resources seemed almost limitless. Some, however, are nonrenewable, and if they are used up or permanently damaged, they will no longer be available. This damage is often caused by pollution. **Pollution** is *the changing of air, water, and land from clean and safe to dirty and unsafe.*

Air

Your body uses the oxygen in air to produce energy. Plants use the carbon dioxide in air to produce food and oxygen. Plants, animals, and people could not live without clean air.

Unfortunately, the air you breathe is not completely clean. It may contain dust, smoke, chemical particles, and smog.

Every day the earth's natural resources are being polluted, misused, or damaged. Think of at least one way *you* could help to correct or prevent air pollution, water pollution, or depletion of nonrenewal fuels. Share your ideas with the class.

The air that you breathe is an important natural resource. Why do you think that running would be difficult if you didn't have enough fresh, clean air to breathe?

LESSON ONE: PROTECTING YOUR ENVIRONMENT

CHAPTER 9, LESSON 1

TEACH

Stress to students that each individual must take responsibility for helping to care for the resources of the planet. Then refer students to the feature. Allow time for students to make their lists of ways to correct or prevent the problems. Have them share their ideas with classmates.

L2 Science

Have small groups of students coat microscope slides with a thin layer of petroleum jelly. The slides should be placed in various indoor and outdoor locations where they will not be disturbed for two days. When retrieving the slides, students should note their locations. Then have students use a microscope or hand lens to observe the particle pollution collected on each slide. Discuss the amount and kinds of particles seen on each slide.

L3 Researching

Ask interested students to read about lead, a dangerous chemical pollutant in drinking water. Suggest they contact the local health department for information about how lead gets into drinking water and how to test for lead in drinking water. Have students write a paragraph about their findings.

L2 Cooperative Learning

Assign Cooperative Learning Activity 17, "Using Resources Responsibly," in the TCR.

MEETING STUDENT DIVERSITY

Cultural Diversity Discuss with students the traditional Native American belief that people should seek to live in balance with the natural world and not take more from it than is necessary. The earth provides for people and people must take care of it for future generations. Ask students to contrast this attitude with that of Europeans who colonized North America. (Europeans attempted to conquer the wilderness and took from the land without regard to future generations.) Ask students how Native American beliefs can be seen today in the environmental movement.

CHAPTER 9, LESSON 1

L3 Researching
Ask interested students to use references and back issues of magazines to find out about toxic waste disposal at Love Canal, New York, and how it affected the people who live in that community.

L2 Comparing
Ask small groups of students to work together to write and illustrate a children's story about how life might be different if a country ran out of oil and other sources of energy. After groups have completed their stories, have a member of each group read the story aloud to the class and show the illustrations. These stories may be donated to a children's shelter or a day-care center.

L3 Researching
Ask students to find out how nuclear waste has been handled in the past, what current practices are, and what plans are for the future. Also ask students to research on-line environmental groups that are especially concerned with the issues of nuclear waste disposal.

L2 Problem Solving
Assign Peer Pressure and Decision Making 19 in the TCR. This activity gives students the opportunity to recognize peer pressure and practice decision-making skills.

Have students discuss how each suggestion mentioned can help conserve water. Then ask them to list other steps that could be taken at home or at school to conserve water.

These substances, which are all forms of air pollution, can be harmful to your health. Some causes of air pollution are

- the release of poisonous gases such as car exhaust fumes that combine with the atmosphere to create smog when fuels are burned to provide energy.
- smoke from such sources as fireplaces, barbecues, and burning leaves.
- chemicals, including those that kill insects and those used as cooling agents in air conditioners and refrigerators.

Using Water Wisely

Here are some ways you can conserve water.
- Run the washing machine only with a full load.
- Turn off the water when brushing your teeth.
- Take short showers instead of baths.
- Repair leaky faucets.
- Ask your family to install water-saving showerheads and toilets.

Water

Water, like air, is necessary to all living things. In fact, water is your body's most essential nutrient. It is needed for every bodily function.

You may think that there is plenty of water. After all, about 70 percent of the earth's surface is covered by water. Most of it, however, is salt water. Many plants and animals cannot use that water. They need clean, fresh water to survive.

Much of the earth's water is polluted by wastes. Common sources of water pollution are human wastes, detergents, and the chemicals used to kill insects or to fertilize crops. Polluted water can cause people to become sick or even die.

Soil

The earth's land is made up of soil, the loose material in which plants can grow. Plants get the nutrients and water they need from the soil. People, in turn, need the nutrients that plants provide in order to live.

Energy

What would happen if there wasn't any gasoline left for cars, trucks, and buses? How would we heat homes, schools, and office buildings if we ran out of oil and other kinds of fuel? You may think that this could never happen. However, many sources of energy—such as oil, natural gas, and coal—are in limited supply. Once they are used up, they cannot be replaced.

248   CHAPTER 9: YOUR ENVIRONMENT

MORE ABOUT

Energy Alternative energy sources offer one solution to the problem of limited supplies of oil, natural gas, and coal. Wind energy can turn windmills that contain generators to produce electricity. The energy of moving water in rivers and ocean tides can also turn generators. Geothermal energy—heat energy from inside the earth—can be used to heat water for heating buildings or to produce steam for electricity generators. Solar energy can be used to heat buildings or to generate electricity.

Conservation Measures

You may feel that the problems of pollution and a shrinking supply of natural resources are overwhelming and beyond your control. There are many ways, however, that you can make a difference. One important way is to practice **conservation,** *the saving of resources.* The best way to conserve a resource is to use less of it. For example, turn off the faucet to save water when you are brushing your teeth. Whenever possible, walk or use a bicycle—instead of riding in a car—to reduce smog. Reuse paper bags and return plastic bags to grocery stores.

Families can also work together to conserve natural resources. Some families have added more insulation to their homes to save fuel. **Insulation** is *a material installed in the attic or walls of a building to keep it cooler in summer and warmer in winter.* How does your family conserve resources? You will learn more about conservation in Lesson 2 of this chapter.

These teens are helping to conserve natural resources and reduce air pollution. What are some other ways to do this?

Using Energy Wisely

An important way to conserve resources is to learn to use energy wisely. Look for appliances that are **energy efficient,** or *made to use less energy.* By using energy efficiently, you not only conserve resources but also reduce pollution of the environment.

You can save energy at home in many ways. Most of the energy used at home is for heating and cooling. Depending on the season, you can reduce the heating temperature or increase the cooling temperature. The rest of the energy used in homes is for heating water, lighting the home, and running appliances. When your family members buy new appliances, they can look for the most energy-efficient ones by comparing guides that list energy costs per year. **Figure 9.1** on the next page shows other ways to be energy efficient.

LESSON ONE: PROTECTING YOUR ENVIRONMENT   249

CHAPTER 9, LESSON 1

DID YOU KNOW

In the early 1970s, shortages caused motorists to wait in extremely long lines for gasoline that had increased tremendously in price. Largely as a result of this crisis, the federal government created the Department of Energy in 1977 to promote energy conservation and the development of new energy sources.

L3 Research

Ask students to check the appliances in their homes to see if any are labeled with an energy efficiency ratio (EER). If so, ask them to note the appliance, what kind of energy source it uses (such as electricity, natural gas, or propane), and what the EER number on the tag is. Suggest that students post their information on the chalkboard, grouped according to appliances, and compare the various appliances. If labels are not still attached to appliances, have volunteers contact utility companies to get information on recommended EER for conservation, and/or rate reduction on bills.

L2 Activity and Project Card

Allow time for students to complete Activity and Project Card 17, "Preserving the Environment," in the TCR.

MORE ABOUT

Energy-Efficient Appliances Most household appliances are now marked with a number called an energy efficiency ratio (EER). The number on the tag of an appliance gives the consumer an idea of how much energy the appliance uses. For example, the higher an electric hot water heater's EER, the more heating it does for the same amount of electricity. The higher the EER, the cheaper the appliance is to use. Therefore, even if a high-EER appliance costs more to buy, it will save money in the long run.

249

CHAPTER 9, LESSON 1

USING VISUALS
Have volunteers describe and elaborate on each of the tips for energy efficiency shown in Figure 9.1. As each tip is covered, ask the students how many of them currently do or have done what is suggested. Then ask if they can think of any other tips that could be added to the diagram to increase energy efficiency.

L1 Using Transparencies
Present Color Transparency 39, "Protect the Environment," in the TCR. Use this overhead visual to reinforce concepts from this lesson.

L1 Student Workbook
Assign Activity 64 in the Student Workbook.

ASSESS

Evaluating the Lesson
Assign Reviewing Terms and Facts and Thinking Critically on page 251 to review the lesson; then assign the Lesson 1 Quiz in the TCR.

Reteaching
- Have students identify three rooms in their homes and write three conservation tips for each room.
- Have students complete Reteaching Activity 9 in the TCR.

250

**Figure 9.1
Tips for Energy Efficiency**
Which of these ways of saving energy have you and your family tried?

- In cold weather, wear warm clothing and layers of closely woven fabric.
- Turn off the lights when you are not using them.
- Use hot water sparingly.
- Repair leaky faucets.
- Keep doors to closets and unused rooms closed. There is no need to heat or cool those spaces.
- Whenever possible, use the microwave oven.
- Keep the air-conditioner thermostat turned up in summer.
- Run the dishwasher only with a full load.
- Keep the thermostat turned down to 68°F in winter.
- Use lined drapes to keep the cold out in the winter.
- Seal and close up cracks around the doors and window.
- Avoid leaving the refrigerator door open for an extended period of time.
- When you use the oven, cook several items at the same time.
- Avoid opening oven doors while foods are cooking.

250   CHAPTER 9: YOUR ENVIRONMENT

COOPERATIVE LEARNING

Creating Posters Let students work together in small groups to make posters similar to Figure 9.1, representing areas in their homes and labeling specific ways their families could use energy wisely. Encourage students to bring in photographs of various areas of their homes to add to the posters. Students may choose to make separate sections of the poster for each home, or organize the posters by areas such as: kitchen, living room, garage, and so on. Ask students to present their posters to the class and to explain how they have shown energy efficiency.

There are many ways for people to get involved in cleaning up their community. How might you volunteer in your area?

Other Ways to Help

Protection of natural resources and the environment begins with people like you. There are plenty of ways for you to make a difference. You can use air, water, land, and energy wisely. You can make an effort to be energy efficient at home. You can be a concerned citizen who cares about the environment and works with others to keep it clean.

LESSON ONE *Review*

Using complete sentences, answer the following questions on a separate sheet of paper.

Reviewing Terms and Facts

1. Vocabulary Define the term *pollution*. List the natural resources that pollution affects.

2. List Name the major causes of air pollution.

3. Recall What is the best way to conserve a resource?

Thinking Critically

4. Analyze Why do you think that some people are not careful with natural resources?

5. Predict What might happen to our natural resources if we don't take care of them?

6. Explain Who benefits when people use energy efficiently? How do they benefit?

Applying Concepts

7. Read the label on a cleaning product at home or in a store. List the product's uses and whether it contains harmful or poisonous substances. If it does, look in a store for a substitute product that is not harmful. Share your results with the class.

LESSON ONE: PROTECTING YOUR ENVIRONMENT **251**

HOME AND COMMUNITY CONNECTION

Family Conservation Encourage students to share what they have learned about conserving resources with other family members. Have students identify what the family is already doing at home, on the road, at school, and in the workplace to conserve natural resources. Ask them to survey family members to determine what else they are willing to do. Suggest that students work with family members to make an action plan to show their commitment to saving resources.

CHAPTER 9, LESSON 1

Answers to Lesson 1 Review

1. Pollution is the changing of air, water, and land from clean and safe to dirty and unsafe. Pollution affects the resources of air, land, and water.
2. The major causes of air pollution are the burning of fuels, including gasoline; other sources of smoke, such as burning leaves or trash; and chemicals, including those that kill insects and those used as cooling agents.
3. The best way to conserve a resource is to use less of it.
4. Some people might not know the importance of conserving natural resources or might think it's too difficult or expensive to worry about conserving resources.
5. If natural resources are not taken care of, some of them will be used up and people won't be able to replace them.
6. When people conserve energy, they save money by using less resources. Everybody benefits when resources are conserved, especially future generations.
7. Product descriptions and substitutions will vary, but should include reasonable substitute products.

Enrichment

Ask students to list five things they would be willing to give up in order to conserve energy. Then have them create a story or a poster showing how they gave up an item to conserve energy.

CLOSE

Refer students to the lesson title "Protecting Your Environment." Have them create a collage in which they illustrate ways that they could accomplish that task.

LESSON TWO
Keeping Your Environment Clean

FOCUS

Lesson Objectives

After studying this lesson, students should be able to
- explain where waste goes when it is thrown away.
- describe ways to limit the amount of waste in their environment.
- tell what it means to reduce, reuse, and recycle.

Motivating Activity

Bring a full garbage can from your school cafeteria into the classroom. Ask students to make a list of what they think is in the garbage can and then tell where they think the garbage will go.

Introducing the Lesson

Have students share their responses to the Motivating Activity. Then ask: Does it matter to you what happens to all the trash in the school? In the town? In the state? In the world? Why or why not? Explain to students that in this lesson they will learn more about what happens to trash and why trash disposal is important.

Introducing *Words to Know*

Have students check the definitions of Words to Know in the Glossary. Ask them to prepare a set of study cards, with each word to know on one side of an index card and its definition on the other side.

252

LESSON TWO
Keeping Your Environment Clean

WORDS TO KNOW

landfills
decompose
incineration
precycle
biodegradable
recycling

DISCOVER...
- where trash goes after you throw it away.
- ways to limit the amount of waste in your environment.
- what it means to reduce, reuse, precycle, and recycle.

You may think that as long as you don't litter, you are doing your part to keep your community clean. There is much more to it than that, however. Since about the middle of the 20th century we have lived in a "throwaway" society. Many items are used only once and then thrown away. As a result, we now have a serious problem because we have too much waste and not enough safe ways to get rid of it.

252 CHAPTER 9: YOUR ENVIRONMENT

CLASSROOM RESOURCES FOR LESSON 2

 Blackline Masters
Concept Map 14
Cooperative Learning 18
Lesson 2 Quiz

 Transparencies
Transparency 40, "Makeup of U.S. Waste"

 Student Workbook
Activities 65, 66

Where Does Waste Go?

Billions of tons of trash and garbage are disposed of every year in the United States. Where does it all go? Where *should* it all go? These questions are urgent because the mountain of waste created by Americans continues to grow.

You can work to change the situation. Even though the trash problem is a national issue, the solution depends on individual actions. Your actions can help to make a difference.

Landfills

About 80 percent of the waste in the United States is disposed of in landfills. **Landfills** are *huge pits where waste is dumped and buried between layers of earth.* Most large communities have landfills, or dumps, somewhere on their outskirts. These landfills are carefully designed to control the odors, germs, and other unpleasant or unhealthy situations that are created by piles of trash and garbage. Away from towns and carefully buried, the waste doesn't pose a threat to people's health.

Landfills do cause problems, however. They take up huge amounts of space, and no one wants to live near a landfill. Garbage buried in landfills is supposed to **decompose,** or *break down,* so that it becomes part of the soil. However, recent studies have shown that certain kinds of discarded waste, such as plastic foam, do not break down for a long time.

Incineration

Another common way to dispose of trash in the United States is by incineration. **Incineration** means *disposing of waste by burning it.* About 10 percent of the waste in the United States is incinerated. Burning trash, however, causes air pollution. When trash that is poisonous is burned, its smoke is especially dangerous. The problem is so great that many communities do not allow trash to be burned.

There are thousands of landfills like this one all across the country. Why can't we continue to rely on them as a way to dispose of all of our waste?

LESSON TWO: KEEPING YOUR ENVIRONMENT CLEAN

CHAPTER 9, LESSON 2

TEACH

L1 Math
Save the trash that accumulates in your classroom wastebasket for one day. Ask students to guess the weight of the trash. Then place the trash in a plastic bag and weigh it. Ask students to calculate how much trash would come from your classroom each week, assuming this sample was an average one. How much trash would be produced in a month? In a school year? Students may wish to weigh trash from other classrooms for a day and compare.

L3 Research
Have interested students find out how many wastebaskets are in the entire school and, from that number, estimate the weight of the trash hauled away from the school in one school year. Then have them find out what happens to the school trash. Ask them to share their findings with the class.

DID YOU KNOW
The United States Environmental Protection Agency estimates that by the year 2000, more than 25 U.S. states will have no more landfill space. Waste disposal fees have been increasing rapidly because landfills are quickly reaching capacity.

COOPERATIVE LEARNING

Reducing School Trash Ask small groups of students to work together to come up with ways to reduce the amount of trash that is produced by the school. Have each group make a poster illustrating one or more of their ideas. Posters could be displayed around the school as part of a "Trash Awareness Day," when all students in the school are encouraged to produce less trash.

Limiting the Amount of Waste

Burying waste in landfills and incinerating it both have serious drawbacks. What should Americans do about the problem? The key is to reduce the amount of waste we create. All Americans can do their part by following the "three R's"—Reduce, Reuse, Recycle.

Reduce

The first step is to reduce the amount of trash created. To start reducing the amount of trash you create, you can

- reduce the amount of paper you throw away by using both sides of notebook paper and by using only washable cups and plates.
- **precycle,** or *avoid buying products that use more packaging than necessary.*
- plan meals carefully so there is little waste.
- avoid buying disposable products.
- use cloth grocery bags instead of paper or plastic ones.
- buy products that are **biodegradable**—*able to degrade, or break down, and be absorbed by the environment.* Biodegradable products don't fill up landfills.

Check to see if the products your family uses are biodegradable. How can this help the environment?

Reuse

The second of the "three R's" is *reuse.* The idea is simple: you can limit the amount of waste you create by reusing items you might otherwise throw away. If you use your imagination, you can probably think of many ways to reuse items. Here are a few ideas.

- Buy products packed in containers that can be refilled or used for something else.
- Keep boxes, bottles, and cans to use as storage containers.

254 CHAPTER 9: YOUR ENVIRONMENT

MEETING STUDENT DIVERSITY

Cultural Diversity Students might assume that every person on earth produces about the same amount of trash. Help students realize that trash is a product of wealth. People who live in wealthy, industrialized nations produce far more trash than people elsewhere. For example, it has been estimated that people in the United States throw out almost half the food they buy. Ask students to speculate on the amount of trash that might be produced in developing countries in Africa or Latin America and to explain why the amount would be substantially less than in industrialized countries.

CHAPTER 9, LESSON 2

L3 Research

Have interested students research the benefits of composting food wastes, grass clippings, and leaves. Have them find out how composting can be done at home, what items should not be included in a compost pile, and where people can go for information and help with composting. Local parks and recreation departments may have this information available.

TEACHER TALK!

Protecting the Environment

Have students discuss the pros and cons of disposing of trash in a landfill versus incineration of trash. Help them realize that since neither is an ideal solution for trash disposal, limiting the amount of garbage is an important step in protecting the environment.

L2 Research

Have small groups of students find out what actually happens to waste from their area. Students should trace the waste collection process from home to its final destination—a landfill, an incinerator, or another location. Groups could make charts to illustrate what they find out.

L2 Cooperative Learning

Assign Cooperative Learning Activity 18, "Don't Refuse to Reuse," in the TCR.

With a little imagination, many items can be reused instead of thrown away. What items have you reused recently?

- Save old towels and clothes to use as rags.
- Always think twice before throwing something away. Ask yourself: "What else can I do with this?"

Reusing means being creative; it can be fun. What other ideas can you add to the list?

Recycle

You already know that Americans throw out millions of tons of trash. Have you ever wondered just what all that trash is? Is it mostly plastic bottles, discarded papers, or

TIPS for living

HOW TO RECYCLE

To make recycling a habit at home and at school, follow these steps.

- Find out where to recycle in your area. Cans, bottles, and newspapers may be picked up at your home or school, or they can be sold to a recycling center.
- Set up a recycling system at home or at school. Have separate, labeled containers for glass, cans, plastic, paper, and other recyclable items.
- Learn how to prepare items for recycling. For example, you may have to rinse out and flatten plastic containers.
- Find out the days and times for recycling in your area.

LESSON TWO: KEEPING YOUR ENVIRONMENT CLEAN   255

COOPERATIVE LEARNING

Reuse Challenge Bring into class a box of assorted objects that might normally be thrown out, such as an empty thread spool, coffee can and plastic lid, egg carton, cardboard tube from paper towels, a plastic soda bottle or milk jug, and so on. Challenge small groups to come up with creative ways to reuse each of the items. Each group should prepare a drawing and a written description of how each item could be reused. After the ideas are shared, the class could vote on which was the most creative way to reuse each item in the box.

CHAPTER 9, LESSON 2

L2 Applying Knowledge

Set up a classroom display of common grocery items in various kinds and sizes of packaging. Then ask small groups of students to evaluate which items best fit into a program of avoiding products with more packaging than necessary. Ask groups to suggest alternative ways the "overpackaged" products might be repackaged. They may wish to reinvent a package for a product and demonstrate how their design will help the environment.

L3 Critical Thinking

Ask students to write paragraphs in response to this question: If you had to choose between saving money by buying a less expensive product and buying a more expensive product that was better for the environment, which would you choose and why?

TIPS for living

Point out to students that each individual must take responsibility for recycling. Then refer students to the Tips for Living feature. Assign different groups of students to carry out one of the tips. After students have completed the tips, have them share their information with classmates.

L1 Using Transparencies

Present Color Transparency 40, "Makeup of U.S. Waste," in the TCR. Use this overhead visual to reinforce concepts from this lesson.

255

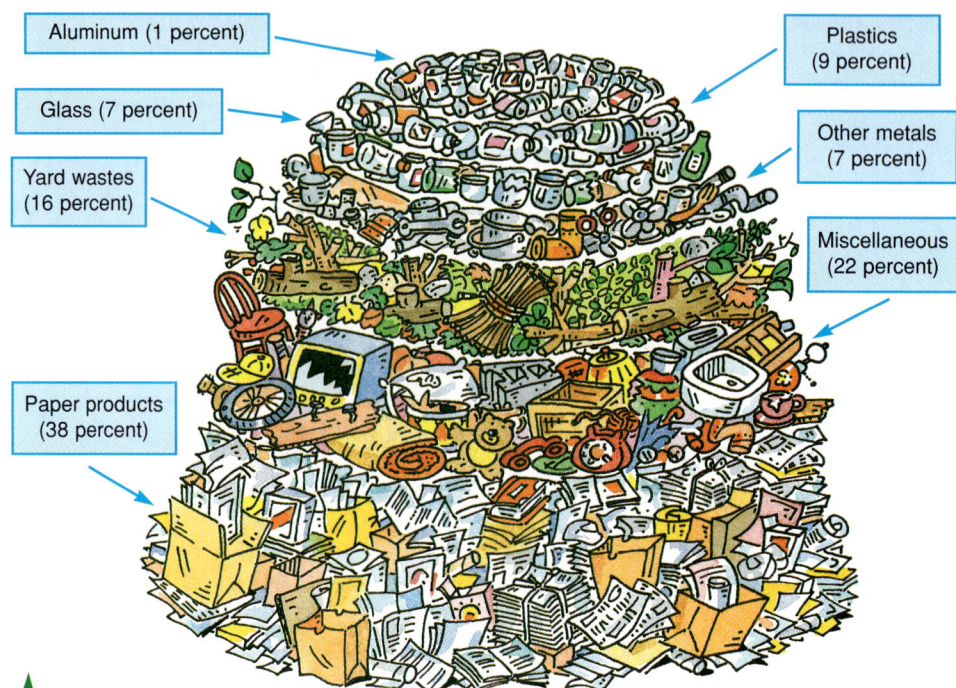

Figure 9.2
Makeup of U.S. Waste
What do you think the most commonly thrown-away products are made of? Paper? Plastics? Glass?

other material? The makeup of America's waste is shown in **Figure 9.2**.

These statistics provide a clue as to how we can cut down on waste. Many of the materials we throw away can be easily recycled. **Recycling** is *turning waste items into products that can be used.* For example, newspapers can be turned into pulp to make new paper. Aluminum cans can be melted down and turned into new cans and other products. Many plastics can also be recycled. Because over half of the trash we create is recyclable, a commitment to recycling can greatly reduce the amount of waste in the country.

Other Ways to Reduce Waste

Recycling means much more than simply taking cans and newspapers to recycling centers. When you donate clothes, books, and other items to charities, for instance, you are recycling them. You also recycle if you give or receive hand-me-down clothes or trade magazines with a friend after

256   CHAPTER 9: YOUR ENVIRONMENT

TECHNOLOGY UPDATE

New Use for Recycled Plastic Recycled plastic has traditionally gone into carpets and clothing, but recently it has also been approved for reuse in some food containers. Several companies have gotten approval from the Food and Drug Administration to market recycled polyethylene terephthalate (PET), currently used in soda bottles and plastic salad dressing bottles, for use in food containers. In recycling, a chemical process breaks down PET into individual monomers, using methanol, heat, and pressure. This process purifies it before it is repolymerized.

reading them. Can you see how holding a garage sale is also a way to recycle? All of the actions suggested in this lesson may seem small, but every one helps to limit the amount of waste. By applying the "three R's" to your own life, you will do your share to make our environment a much better place.

Instead of throwing away furniture and buying new items, try repainting, refinishing, reupholstering, or using slipcovers. Besides reducing the amount of waste, what are some other benefits of this approach?

LESSON TWO *Review*

Using complete sentences, answer the following questions on a separate sheet of paper.

Reviewing Terms and Facts

1. **Vocabulary** Define the terms *landfill* and *incineration*. What do they have in common?
2. **Explain** How can *biodegradable* products help the environment?
3. **Identify** List three ways to reduce the amount of trash discarded in the United States.
4. **List** Name four ways to reuse items.

Thinking Critically

5. **Explain** Why are current methods of waste disposal inadequate?

6. **Suggest** Think of something you threw away recently. Describe two ways that you could have reused it.
7. **Predict** Do you think that reducing the amount of waste produced will be enough to solve the waste-disposal problem? Why or why not?

Applying Concepts

8. Write a letter to the editor of your local newspaper encouraging the people in your community to reduce, reuse, and recycle. Identify ways to encourage people to follow the plan. Then post your letter on the bulletin board.

LESSON TWO: KEEPING YOUR ENVIRONMENT CLEAN   257

HOME AND COMMUNITY CONNECTION

Home Recycling Have students plan and design a simple home recycling center that would make it easier for family members to sort items for recycling. Suggest students find out what items are recycled in your community and include containers for these items in their design. Encourage students to take their plans home and, with the help of an adult family member, build their recycling center. Students may wish to report back to classmates how well their home recycling centers succeed.

CHAPTER 9, LESSON 2

Answers to Lesson 2 Review

1. A landfill is a huge pit where garbage is dumped and buried between layers of earth. Incineration is the disposing of garbage by burning it. Both are ways to dispose of garbage.
2. Biodegradable products break down and are absorbed by the environment. They don't fill up landfills.
3. Avoid buying disposable products. Use cloth grocery bags instead of paper or plastic ones. Avoid buying products that use more packaging than needed.
4. Reuse old boxes, bottles, and cans as storage containers. Reuse paper and plastic shopping bags instead of getting new ones. Save old towels and clothes to use as rags. Repaint or refinish old furniture for reuse.
5. Incineration causes air pollution, and some landfills leak poisonous substances into the soil and water. Places are also running out of room for landfills.
6. Items and ways of reusing them will vary, but reuses suggested should be reasonable for the item identified.
7. Responses will vary, but should indicate an understanding that unless all individuals actively participate in reducing the amount of waste they produce, the waste problem will not be solved.
8. Students' letters should reflect an understanding of what is meant by reduce, reuse, and recycle and should stress the benefits to the community.

CLOSE

Have each student complete the following sentence: "The best way to reduce, reuse, and recycle is . . ."

LESSON THREE
Your Personal Safety and Violence Prevention

FOCUS

Lesson Objectives
After studying this lesson, students should be able to
- describe how the accident chain works.
- list how to avoid unnecessary risks.
- identify ways to prevent violence.

Motivating Activity
Write the word *accident* on the chalkboard. Ask students to write down lists of word or phrases that come to mind when they think of the word. Then organize the class into small groups and ask them to work together to write a short scenario of an accident.

Introducing the Chapter
Ask a representative from each group to read aloud their scenario from the Motivating Activity. Discuss the different ideas that groups had of an accident scenario.

Introducing *Words to Know*
Review the Words to Know with students. Let volunteers share what they already know about each term, including experiences and ideas about safety. Then ask them to check the formal definition of each word in the Glossary.

LESSON THREE
Your Personal Safety and Violence Prevention

WORDS TO KNOW
risk
hazard
pedestrian
violence

DISCOVER...
- how the accident chain works.
- how to avoid unnecessary risks.
- how to prevent violence.

Are there any small children in your family who are not yet steady on their feet? Do you or any members of your family enjoy sports or hobbies that might be dangerous? Have you or your friends ever been bothered by a bully at school? For safety and peace of mind, it is important for everyone to take precautions that prevent accidents or injuries.

258 CHAPTER 9: YOUR ENVIRONMENT

CLASSROOM RESOURCES FOR LESSON 3

 Blackline Masters
Activity and Project Card 18, "Speak Out Against Violence"
Concept Map 15
Cross Curriculum 10
Enrichment 10
Lesson 3 Quiz
Peer Pressure and Decision Making 20
Reteaching 9

 Transparencies
Transparency 41, "The Accident Chain"

 **Student Workbook**
Activities 67, 68

Acting Safely

Have you ever been annoyed at yourself for behaving carelessly so that you were bruised or scratched, or a favorite article was broken or torn? Knowing how to work or play in the right way or the safe way is not always enough. When people act unsafely out of habit or laziness, they **risk** or *take a dangerous chance of hurting themselves or others.*

Accidents are the leading cause of death among teens. Sadly, most accidents could have been prevented. Avoidable accidents often happen when people take unnecessary risks. These accidents frequently follow a pattern called the *accident chain*. The accident chain has five steps.

- **Step 1: an unsafe situation.** For example, while wearing in-line skates, Jake wants to cross a four-lane road to skate at a park on the other side.

- **Step 2: an unsafe habit.** To get to where he wants to go, Jake often skates on busy streets instead of walking.

- **Step 3: an unsafe act.** Still on skates, Jake begins to cross the road.

- **Step 4: an accident.** Realizing that he doesn't have enough time to get to the other side of the road before the light changes, Jake doubles back to the median strip and falls.

- **Step 5: the result.** Jake twists his ankle and scrapes his arm.

Fortunately, such accidents can be avoided. That does mean, though, that a person has to take the time to think of a safer way of doing or getting what he or she wants. Any of the

By following the rules and avoiding unnecessary risks, you can prevent most accidents from happening. How are these teens acting safely?

LESSON THREE: YOUR PERSONAL SAFETY AND VIOLENCE PREVENTION   259

CHAPTER 9, LESSON 3

TEACH

L2 Comprehending

Let students work with a partner to make their own accident chains. They can use five strips of construction paper and tape to make a chain. Each link should be labeled with one part of an accident chain. Let each pair of students share their accident chains with the rest of the class and explain how the chain could be broken by changing one of the first three links.

L1 Current Events

Ask students to clip and bring in newspaper accounts of accidents. Have students read the articles aloud and discuss what might have caused the accident and what possible things might have been done to avoid the accident. Keep the articles in a file for future use. If students have access to on-line services they may wish to search for and print out articles from this computer source.

DID YOU KNOW

According to National Safety Council estimates, every 10 minutes accidental injuries cost Americans approximately $8.4 million. On the average, there are 11 accidental injury deaths and about 2,120 disabling injuries every hour.

L1 Using Transparencies

Present Color Transparency 41, "The Accident Chain," in the TCR. Use this overhead visual to reinforce concepts from this lesson.

MEETING STUDENT DIVERSITY

Physically Challenged Discuss with students—or ask physically challenged students in the class to lead a discussion on—the special needs of people with physical challenges in terms of avoiding accidents. Have physically challenged students describe some of the steps they take to avoid accidents. If possible, borrow a wheelchair from a community organization that provides equipment to handicapped individuals for students to experiment with. Have them try navigating around the classroom to feel how easy it is for accidents to occur without taking proper precautions.

CHAPTER 9, LESSON 3

L1 Discussion

Help students discuss the differences between risks that cannot be avoided and unnecessary risks. Have students make two lists on the chalkboard—natural risks and unnecessary risks. For each natural risk, ask students to describe actions they could take to lessen the risk. *(Students might list riding a bicycle as a natural risk and the actions taken to lessen the risk could include wearing a bike helmet, obeying traffic signals, and indicating turns.)*

L2 Comprehending

Have students work in small discussion groups in which they write guidelines for acting safely in specific recreational activities. Each group could be assigned a different activity, such as boating, skiing, bicycling, swimming, skateboarding, hiking, and so on. After each group has developed their safety guidelines, have them share them with the class.

TEACHER TALK!

Talking About Home Safety

Review with students the home safety precautions they learned about in Chapter 8, Lesson 3. Ask them to describe how these precautions can break an accident chain.

L2 Social Studies Connection

Assign Cross-Curriculum Activity 10 in the TCR. Students learn about safety procedures in this activity.

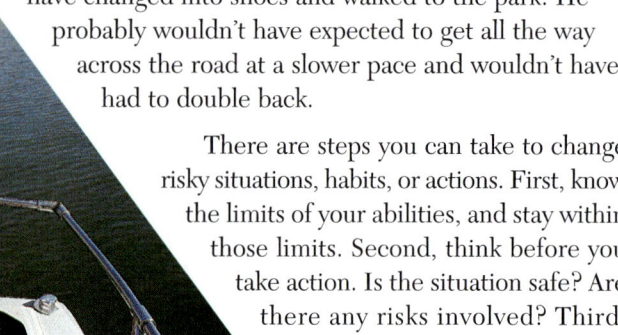

Many activities involve some risk. If you stay within the limits of your abilities and take safety precautions, however, you will greatly reduce your risk of accident or injury.

first three steps of the accident chain can be changed to achieve one's goal safely.

- **The situation can be changed.** Jake could have looked for a safer route to the park.
- **The unsafe habit can be changed.** Jake should skate only in areas without traffic.
- **The unsafe action can be changed.** Jake could have changed into shoes and walked to the park. He probably wouldn't have expected to get all the way across the road at a slower pace and wouldn't have had to double back.

There are steps you can take to change risky situations, habits, or actions. First, know the limits of your abilities, and stay within those limits. Second, think before you take action. Is the situation safe? Are there any risks involved? Third, don't let other people pressure you into doing what you know—or even sense—is not a good idea.

At Home

Every home has some **hazards,** or *dangers.* Some hazards are unavoidable in the course of everyday life. For instance, wet bathtubs and showers are slippery, but people need to bathe or shower regularly. Likewise, detergents are poisonous, but clothes need to be washed.

On the Road

Whether you travel on foot, on skates or a bike, or in a car, the most important way to keep safe is to know and follow the rules of the road. As a **pedestrian,** or *a person who travels on foot,* you must stay aware of what drivers and other pedestrians are doing. Always cross at crosswalks or intersections, and look out for vehicles turning right on a red light. In a car, make sure that you wear a seat belt—both the lap belt and the shoulder harness—and never distract the driver.

260 CHAPTER 9: YOUR ENVIRONMENT

TECHNOLOGY UPDATE

Side Airbags Many cars are now equipped with front airbags which, when used with seat belts, reduce the chances of serious injury or death in head-on collisions. Side impacts, however, account for 21 percent of all accidents and 36 percent of fatalities. Side-impact airbag systems, designed to reduce these statistics, are scheduled to appear in several 1997 model cars. In one system, a hollow, flexible tube inflates on impact and pops out of the side of the roof to protect the occupant's head while a door-mounted bag inflates to protect the occupant's body. Survey students to find out whether their family cars are equipped with air bags.

Outdoors

Have you ever been sunburned from being outdoors without sunscreen or gotten blisters from walking too long in new shoes? Outdoor safety requires common sense—just like safety at home and on the road. Whether you enjoy water sports or hiking or winter sports, you need to take precautions to make the most of your outing.

- **Water activities.** The most important precaution when participating in water sports is knowing how to swim very well. If you plan to swim, make sure that you go with a buddy and that there is a lifeguard on duty. If you go boating, wear a life jacket, and be sure that you know how to handle the boat properly.

- **Hiking and camping.** When hiking or camping, make sure that you wear the right clothing for the weather. You should also be careful to use marked trails and designated campsites. Tell someone where you are going and when you expect to return.

- **Winter sports.** When you think of winter sports, you might imagine boots, gloves, and heavy sweaters. Wearing appropriate clothing and dressing in many layers are necessary precautions for enjoying the outdoors in winter. You also have to check to see that the conditions are good for the sport you have in mind. For instance, check ahead of time to be sure that the ice is thick enough for safe skating.

No matter what activity you choose or where it takes place—beach, mountain, or field—there are certain precautions you should always take.

- Know how much you are really capable of doing. Pushing yourself beyond your training and ability is taking unnecessary risks.

- Use the correct equipment for the sport or activity.

Bicycle and Skating Safety

Bicycling and in-line skating can be great fun when you follow safety rules.

For information on safety workshops in your community, contact your local police department or parks and recreation department. Demonstrate safe bicycling and skating for younger children in your neighborhood.

When you take part in winter sports, it is important to protect your hands and feet by wearing gloves, boots, and extra socks.

LESSON THREE: YOUR PERSONAL SAFETY AND VIOLENCE PREVENTION **261**

CHAPTER 9, LESSON 3

L2 Making Posters
Have students work with partners to select one type of outdoor activity. Then let the partners plan and make an attractive poster illustrating the appropriate precautions that should be taken to safely enjoy that activity.

Stress to students that attending a safety workshop and applying what is learned there can greatly reduce the chances of accidents and injuries. Then refer students to the Skills in Action feature. Ask volunteers who have attended such workshops to share what they learned with the class. Interested students might want to contact the local police department or parks and recreation department and make a poster alerting students to the workshops available in their area.

L2 Applying Concepts
Have students work with a partner to plan a day hike or bicycle trip. Have them list clothing and equipment they would need, draw a map of their route, and make a timetable for the hike. Have each pair of students share their plan with the class and explain how their plan takes safety precautions into account.

L2 Problem Solving
Assign Peer Pressure and Decision Making 20 in the TCR. This activity gives students the opportunity to recognize peer pressure and practice decision-making skills.

HOME AND COMMUNITY CONNECTION

Safety Outdoors With the help of several parent volunteers, have students plan and hold a Safety Outdoors fair at your school. The fair should include information about and examples of safety equipment. Encourage students to collect equipment for display. Students should arrange for talks by individuals from local organizations. Have students collect or prepare posters and brochures on outdoor safety. Encourage students to present their fair on a day when other students can attend and to publicize the fair with posters in the community.

- Know the safety rules for your activity and follow them.
- Remember to warm up before and cool down after an activity to avoid injury.
- Practice the buddy system. When people pair up during activities, they can look after each other and help each other in an emergency.
- Use sunscreen to protect your skin from ultraviolet rays.
- Check the weather conditions where you plan to go. Avoid being out in extreme temperatures and electrical storms.

In Your Community

Have you ever been startled by a loud noise as you sat on your porch lost in thought? Have you ever felt uneasy when you walked home from a friend's house at dusk?

You—just like anyone else—want to feel safe in your own neighborhood. There are steps you can take to protect yourself. You and your family can join or help set up a Neighborhood Watch group in which neighbors look after one another and one another's homes. Members of such groups are trained by the police to identify and report suspicious activities. When you walk down the street, keep alert—especially at night. Pay attention to the people around you and to what they are doing.

TIPS for living

STRANGER DANGER

Although most people you meet in stores and on the streets are kind and helpful, you still need to be careful around people you don't know. Follow these tips to stay safe.

- Don't get too close to a car if a stranger calls out for directions. It's easy for a stranger to pull you into a car.
- Beware of strangers who offer you gifts or money or ask you to help find a lost dog or cat.
- If a stranger follows or grabs you, run away, scream, and make lots of noise.
- Always let your family know where you will be.
- Tell your parents or other trusted adults if someone makes you feel uncomfortable.

CHAPTER 9, LESSON 3

L1 Discussion

Write the following question on the chalkboard: "When and where do you feel unsafe or wonder whether you're really safe?" Before asking for volunteers to answer the question, explain that everyone worries about their safety at least sometimes. After volunteers have described places or situations that make them feel unsafe, explain that knowing how to behave to protect their own safety can make them feel safer and more secure.

TEACHER TALK!

Dealing with Sensitive Issues

Discussing violence may be difficult for many students. Students need to know how to *feel* safe, so it is important to deal with this topic in a sensitive manner. The topic of violence is likely to be very troublesome for students whose home lives include violence.

TIPS for living

Stress to students the importance of taking responsibility for their own safety and not placing themselves in circumstances where they are likely to become victims. Then refer students to the Tips for Living feature. After reading the feature, have students add to the list of safety tips.

MORE ABOUT • • •

Preventing Violence in Society The 1994 Omnibus Violent Crime Control and Prevention Act was passed by Congress and signed by President Clinton. Among its provisions are stiffer penalties for violent and drug crimes committed by gangs; block grants for local communities to set up anti-gang programs, establish partnerships between senior citizen groups and law enforcement agencies to combat crimes against the elderly; sponsorships of boys and girls clubs; and programs to allow victims of violent crimes to speak at the sentencing of their assailants.

Stay away from dangerous areas and poorly lighted streets. Avoid taking any unnecessary risks.

What Is Violence?

Violence is *the use of physical force to harm someone.* Violence often takes place between people who know each other, but some violent acts are directed at complete strangers.

Why Violence Occurs

Why do some conflicts turn violent? You have probably seen teens argue over a boyfriend or a girlfriend or get angry at what someone else said about them behind their backs. If arguments get heated or anger gets out of control, fights can break out. Here are some reasons why violence occurs:

- **Strong emotions.** People who lack healthy ways of handling strong emotions may break into violence when they are upset. *Jealousy* over a boyfriend or a girlfriend may cause teens to act violently toward someone whom they are dating or toward someone whom they fear is threatening their relationship. Some teens, not knowing how to handle a confrontation, may let themselves be baited or taunted into fighting. They don't realize that when they take the bait they are actually letting the other person control them. The desire for *revenge* is another strong emotion that leads to teen violence. If Kristen is the subject of unpleasant rumors or Marc is made to look foolish in an argument, the desire to get even may lead to a fight.

- **Drugs and alcohol.** Violent acts are often committed by people who are under the influence of drugs and alcohol. These substances prevent people from thinking clearly and may even make them act violently.

Strong emotions, such as anger and jealousy, can lead to heated arguments and sometimes to violence. What would you do if two of your friends got into a fight?

LESSON THREE: YOUR PERSONAL SAFETY AND VIOLENCE PREVENTION

CHAPTER 9, LESSON 3

L2 Activity and Project Card

Allow time for students to complete Activity and Project Card 18, "Speak Out Against Violence," in the TCR.

L1 Student Workbook

Assign Activities 67 and 68 in the Student Workbook.

ASSESS

Evaluating the Lesson

Assign Reviewing Terms and Facts and Thinking Critically on page 264 to review the lesson; then assign the Lesson 3 Quiz in the TCR.

Reteaching

- Ask small groups of students to create several fictitious situations that might be dangerous. Situations could involve being the possible victim of an accident or violence. Then have groups exchange situations and brainstorm ideas for dealing with the situations. Have each group present their ideas to class.
- Have students complete Reteaching Activity 9 in the TCR.
- Assign Concept Map 15 in the TCR.

MEETING STUDENT DIVERSITY

Avoiding Potential Problems It is important for teachers of gifted students to be aware of potential problems with peers. Peer relationships can be a cause of stress for some gifted students who have difficulty making and keeping friends. They may feel they have little in common with their peers or that their friends do not understand them, and may have to endure teasing and name-calling. Even remarks not intended to be cruel can make gifted students feel they are being singled out. Teachers should be aware of these stresses and try to facilitate understanding and tolerance to help these students avoid confrontation.

CHAPTER 9, LESSON 3

Answers to Lesson 3 Review

1. The five steps of the accident chain are an unsafe situation, an unsafe habit, an unsafe act, an accident, and the results.

2. A hazard is a danger. Student sentences will vary but should convey an understanding of what a hazard is. A sample sentence might be: Walking on an icy sidewalk is a hazard.

3. Know how much you are capable of doing and don't push yourself. Use the correct equipment for the sport or activity. Practice the buddy system. Check the weather conditions where you plan to go.

4. Four reasons violence occurs are strong emotions, drugs and alcohol, peer pressure, and prejudice.

5. The person doing the baiting and taunting is trying to make the person react. If the person doesn't think for himself or herself, the baiter has control.

6. Students' lists will vary but should reflect an understanding of behaviors that reduce unnecessary risks.

Enrichment

- Have students think of ways they could help reduce violence in schools. Then ask them to create a poster that presents their idea. Posters could be displayed in classrooms or school hallways.
- Assign Enrichment Activity 10 in the TCR.

CLOSE

Ask each student to identify one important habit he or she plans to develop or change as a result of studying this lesson.

Traveling with a friend is a good way to keep yourself safe from violence. What are some other ways?

- **Peer pressure.** Teens sometimes pressure their peers to look and act like the rest of the group. Sometimes teens feel that they have to prove their loyalty to a group by conforming to the group's standards, even when it means going against their personal values.

- **Prejudice.** When a person forms an opinion about another person without factual knowledge of that individual, hostile feelings can develop and may lead to acts of violence.

Preventing Violence

There are many precautions you can take to keep yourself safe and help prevent violence in your school and community.

- Carry yourself with confidence to avoid looking like a potential victim.
- Travel with friends, and stay out of unfamiliar areas.
- Don't give in to baiting and taunting. Remember that the baiter is trying to get a reaction out of you.
- Try to resolve conflicts peacefully.
- Tell a parent, a counselor, or another responsible adult if you feel threatened.

LESSON THREE Review

Using complete sentences, answer the following questions on a separate sheet of paper.

Reviewing Terms and Facts

1. Recall List the five steps of the accident chain.

2. Vocabulary Define the term *hazard*. Use it in an original sentence.

3. List When participating in outdoor activities, what are four precautions you should always take?

4. Identify Name four reasons why violence occurs.

Thinking Critically

5. Explain Why is the person who takes the bait and fights when taunted letting the baiter control him or her?

Applying Concepts

6. Take a personal safety inventory. Think about the safety precautions mentioned in this lesson. Do you follow these rules and avoid risks in all situations? Prepare two lists: one of precautions that you already take and one of ways in which you could act more safely.

264 CHAPTER 9: YOUR ENVIRONMENT

COOPERATIVE LEARNING

Getting Rid of Guns In 1993, more than 39,000 people died from gunshot wounds. Thousands more were injured. Because of gang violence, including drive-by shootings, many communities want to get rid of as many guns as possible. Some communities are using gun buy-back programs. People who turn in guns to the police are given money or credit at local stores that participate in the program.

Chapter 9 Activities

FRIENDS & FAMILY

SAVING A CREEK
Twelve-year-old Jordan Taylor noticed that a creek near her home was littered with waste. Jordan organized family members and friends to help with the cleanup.

TRY THIS!
Identify an area in your community that is in need of repair. Make a list of ways that you can help. Then put your plan into action.

 A Global View

LONG-DISTANCE POLLUTION
Damage to the environment in one part of the world affects other parts of the world as well. The sulfur in drifting smoke mixes with moisture and falls as acid rain. Scientists believe that chemicals released into the atmosphere have created holes in the ozone layer. The burning of rain forests adds to global warming.

TRY THIS!
What can you do at a local level that will help the environment worldwide? Write down some ideas and share them with your classmates.

TECHNOLOGY

Homes 2000
Early science fiction writers described homes in the year 2000 as looking like the interior of a spaceship. People would roar around wearing jet packs, and dinner would consist of a power-packed capsule. These predictions aren't likely to come true, but you can be sure that housing will become more environmentally sound.

Try This!
Look in home-decorating magazines for examples of conservation of resources in home building and remodeling. Share your examples with the class.

SCIENCE CONNECTION

ALTERNATIVE SOURCES OF ENERGY
Scientists have many ideas for new energy sources. Alternative energy sources must be renewable, nonpolluting, practical to obtain, and affordable. Natural resources can provide alternative sources of energy. For example, some possible sources come from geothermal energy, hydropower, tidal power, wind, and solar power.

 Follow Up

1. As a class, conduct an energy conference. In groups of three or four, research one alternative source of energy per group. Find out how the energy is produced and its advantages and disadvantages. Each group should report its findings to the class.
2. How might you use your human energy as an alternative energy source? What are the advantages and disadvantages of human energy?

CHAPTER 9 ACTIVITIES **265**

Teaching the SCIENCE CONNECTION
Pass around two calculators, a solar-powered one and a battery-operated one. Ask students what makes each one work. Lead students to conclude that the battery must be periodically replaced in the one calculator, but the solar-powered calculator runs on light. Ask students to identify the advantages of using a solar-powered device.

 Follow Up
Answers to Follow-Up
1. Groups' reports will vary but should be detailed.
2. Answers will vary, but may include: dress to retain body heat in cold weather; walk or ride bicycles instead of automobiles.

CHAPTER 9

Activities

FRIENDS & FAMILY

Discuss with students how Jordan could have recognized the creek was in trouble. Ask them what the consequences might be if no one takes the initiative to begin cleaning up a littered natural area. *(The natural environment can become polluted and harm wildlife and plants in the area.)* Explain that an action as simple as picking up trash and planting wildflower seeds can have a positive impact.

 A Global View

Write the following statement on the chalkboard: "Think Globally, Act Locally." Tell students this is the motto of people concerned about the environment. Ask them to explain what they think this statement means and how it applies to them. Encourage them to think of actions they can take on a local level as they do the "Try This" activity.

TECHNOLOGY

Point out that building contractors today use more recycled materials in home construction. Special wiring and sensors automatically adjust indoor heating and cooling. Built-in recycling centers encourage families to make recycling a daily habit.

265

CHAPTER 9 REVIEW

Checking Comprehension

Use the Chapter Summary and the Chapter 9 Review to help students go over the most important ideas presented in Chapter 9.

Answers to Words to Know

1. Pollution damages natural resources such as air, water, and land. This damage is difficult or even impossible to repair.
2. The purpose of conservation is to save natural resources.
3. An energy-efficient appliance uses less energy, conserving resources and reducing pollution.
4. A landfill is a huge pit where garbage is dumped and buried between layers of earth.
5. A biodegradable product is one that can be broken down and absorbed by the environment.
6. A hazard is a danger. Examples will vary.
7. Violence is the use of physical force to harm someone.

Review Questions

1. Many natural resources cannot be replaced once they are used up.
2. Students' lists will vary but might include using air, water, land, and energy wisely and not taking them for granted. They might also mention making an effort to be energy efficient at home and working with others to reduce, reuse, and recycle.

Chapter Summary

- Natural resources include air, water, land, coal, oil, and gas. Some natural resources are in limited supply, and if they are used up they will no longer be available.
- Ways to conserve natural resources include using less of them and using energy efficiently.
- Americans create an enormous amount of waste. Disposing of waste each year has become a national problem.
- You can help solve the waste crisis by reducing the amount of trash you create, reusing items instead of throwing them away, precycling, and recycling.
- Your environment includes the natural environment and the people, events, and conditions around you. Your home and your community are part of your total environment.
- You can help keep your environment safe by avoiding unnecessary risks and by taking precautions.
- Violence among teens is a growing problem. Jealousy and anger, drugs and alcohol, peer pressure, and prejudice are some of the reasons why teens fight.

Words to Know

Using complete sentences, answer the following questions on a separate sheet of paper.

1. Explain the effect of *pollution* on natural resources.
2. What is the purpose of *conservation*?
3. What does an *energy-efficient* appliance do?
4. Describe a *landfill*.
5. What is a *biodegradable* product?
6. Give an example of a *hazard* in the home.
7. Define the term *violence*.

Review Questions

Using complete sentences, answer the following questions on a separate piece of paper.

1. Why do we need to conserve our natural resources?
2. List ways in which you can contribute to solving the larger problems associated with pollution and waste disposal.
3. Why can't Americans depend on landfills for disposal of waste?
4. Why is incineration not a good answer to the waste problem?
5. What are two methods of recycling?
6. What are some precautions you can take to avoid a sports injury?

266 CHAPTER 9: YOUR ENVIRONMENT

EXTRA CREDIT PROJECT

Group Project Have students create an environmental design from collections of cleaned-out food containers, wood or plastic scraps, and other found objects that can be recycled into a model of a park playground for children. Groups should brainstorm ideas for play equipment that can be made by combining the recyclable materials they collect. Have them design forms that include places to climb, swing on, jump over, balance on, or crawl through. Provide large cardboard bases on which students may combine their objects and attach them with glue, tape, or pins. Encourage groups to decorate the models with paints, markers, or colored paper.

CHAPTER 9 REVIEW

7. What are some precautions you can take to keep yourself safe in your school and your community?

Thinking Critically

Using complete sentences, answer the following questions on a separate sheet of paper.

1. **Suggest** What effect do you think that a dirty environment has on people?
2. **Explain** Why do you think that people had less trash to throw out 50 years ago than people do today?
3. **Analyze** Why do you think that many teens take risks?

Cooperative Learning

1. Working in a group of five, form an "accident chain." Have one person think of an unsafe situation, the next person an unsafe habit, and so on. Present your chain to the class, and discuss ways the accident could be avoided.
2. As a class, decide on a project to improve your school's environment. For example, you could plant a tree, conduct an antilitter campaign, or make safety posters. You might conduct an "energy audit" of your school and recommend ways for the school to conserve energy. Use your management skills to carry out the project.

Family & Community

1. Talk to family members about ways to become more energy efficient at home. Have each family member name one change he or she will make. For example, your sister may offer to turn off her radio when she is not listening to it. After two weeks, ask family members whether or not the change was easy to make.
2. Join a clean-up campaign in your neighborhood or start one of your own. You might adopt a certain block, a bus shelter, or a walking trail and pick up litter on a regular basis.

Building A Portfolio

1. Make a list of the trash you throw away during a week. Every time you throw out an item, add it to the list. At the end of the week, look over your list. Put a circle around each item you could have used again, a square around each item you could have recycled, and a star next to each item you probably didn't need in the first place. Keep the list in your portfolio as a reminder to follow the "three R's."
2. Enroll in a class or workshop in your school or community that teaches safety to teens. You might choose a class on boating safety, a Red Cross lifesaving course, a workshop on violence prevention, or a demonstration of self-defense. When you finish the class, put your certificate of attendance in your portfolio.

CHAPTER 9 REVIEW **267**

CHAPTER 9 REVIEW

3. Many landfills are filling up and we are running out of room to build more landfills.
4. Incineration causes air pollution and because of this many places don't allow waste to be burned.
5. Old newspapers can be turned into pulp from which new paper can be made, and aluminum cans can be melted down and made into new cans.
6. Remember to warm up and cool down before and after an activity to avoid injury. Use the correct safety equipment for the sport.
7. Keep alert when you're walking down the street, pay attention to people around you and what they're doing, stay away from dangerous areas and poorly lighted streets, and avoid taking any unnecessary risks.

Evaluate

Use the Chapter 9 Test in the TCR, or construct your own test using the Testmaker Software.

CLOSE

Have students apply their knowledge of the chapter's content by completing one of the alternative assessment activities listed under Family and Community or Building a Portfolio.

Answers to Thinking Critically

1. People's health and well-being depend on clean air, water, and land. A dirty environment increases the health risks for all people.
2. Fifty years ago there weren't as many prepackaged foods as there are today. There also were no fast-food restaurants that packaged food in nonreusable containers.
3. Often peer pressure leads teens to want to be part of the group, and they allow themselves to be pressured into doing things they know aren't safe.

267

UNIT 4
Foods and Nutrition

Unit Overview

In Unit 4 students examine the relationship of proper nutrition and exercise in promoting good health. Students are also introduced to various cooking methods for preparing healthy meals.

In Chapter 10 students learn to identify nutrient-rich foods. Chapter 11 introduces students to guidelines that promote healthy eating habits. Chapter 12 explains food and kitchen safety and sanitation techniques. The chapter also tells students about microwave cooking. In Chapter 13 students find out about cooking preparation: planning a menu, shopping, food storage, and following recipes. Chapter 14 identifies cooking procedures for various kinds of foods.

Introducing the Unit

- **Parent Letters** As you begin study of this unit, you may wish to send home copies of the Parent Letter and Activities found in the *Linking Home, School, and Community* booklet in the TCR.
- **Using Visuals** Have students look closely at the photograph and explain how they can tell that the teens in the picture understand the importance of nutrition and health.
- **Using the Color Transparency** Present Transparency 42, "Food, Family, and Friends," in the TCR. Have volunteers share with the class some pleasant experiences they have had while sharing food with family or friends.

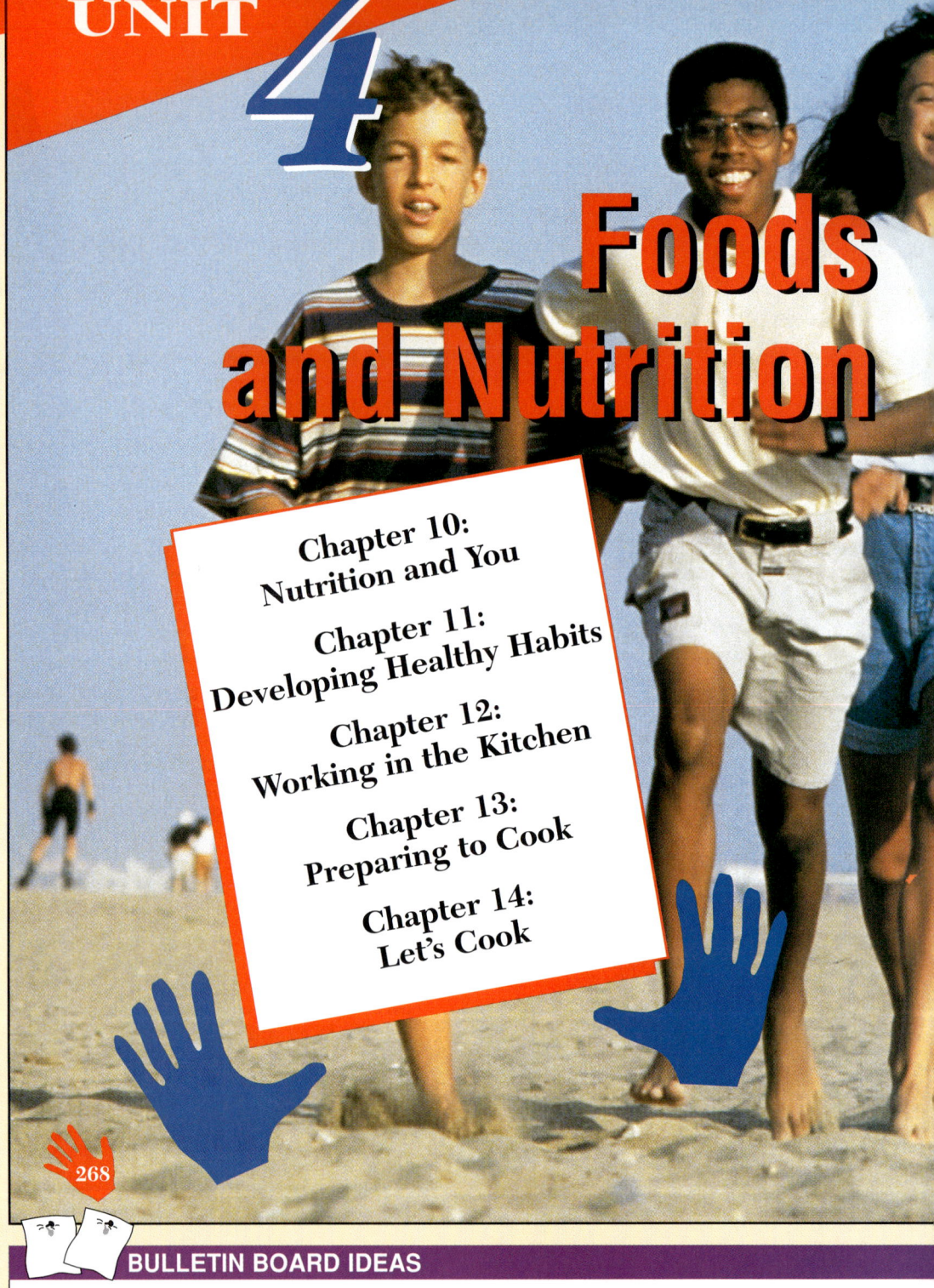

UNIT 4
Foods and Nutrition

Chapter 10:
Nutrition and You

Chapter 11:
Developing Healthy Habits

Chapter 12:
Working in the Kitchen

Chapter 13:
Preparing to Cook

Chapter 14:
Let's Cook

BULLETIN BOARD IDEAS

What Kind of Eater Are You? Place a first-place ribbon on the bulletin board and label it *Health Hero*. Mount a picture of a racing sailboat, and label it *Admirable Food Adventurer*. Draw a picture of a jester riding a tightrope, and label it *Diet Daredevil*. Mount a picture of a knight, and label it *Super Snacker*.

Signs of Good Health From bright yellow construction paper cut out road signs. On each sign list one of the following: healthy skin, hair, nails, teeth, and eyes; ideal weight; pep and vitality; and good posture. Arrange the road signs along a curved path stretching across the bulletin board.

UNIT PROJECTS 4

Encourage students to complete one or two Hands-on Projects for this unit. These can be found in the Teacher's Classroom Resources.
- Hands-on Project 8, "Veggie Creativity," shows students how to make an appetizing raw vegetable snack.
- Hands-on Project 9, "Gifts to Cherish from the Kitchen," shows students how to create either a salsa or herb vinegar recipe suitable for gift-giving.

Unit Closure

- Allow class time at the end of this unit to reinforce students' understanding of the material by playing Hands-on Game 4, "Nutrition and Food Bingo," found in the TCR.
- Create your own Unit Test using the Testmaker Software to evaluate students' comprehension.

Promoting Family & Consumer Sciences

Teachers Develop connections with teachers in various disciplines whenever possible. Ideas for team projects with students from different classes might include planning a household budget with the math teacher; analyzing cultural diversity with a social studies teacher; or organizing a fitness day with physical education teachers.

BULLETIN BOARD IDEAS

Be a Safety Sleuth On poster board draw a kitchen that has various safety hazards, such as frayed cords, water spilled on the floor, towels too close to the burner, electric cords hanging over the dish water, and pot handles turned out. Mount the board on the bulletin board.

The Snack Shack Draw a side profile of a house and mount it in the center of the bulletin board. Include five windows in the house, or divide one large window into five panes to represent the five food groups. Clip pictures from magazines of different healthy snack foods. Place them in the appropriate food group.

Planning Guide
Chapter 10 Nutrition and You

LESSON 1	Pages	FEATURES	CLASSROOM RESOURCES
What Food Does for You	272–277	*Skills in Action:* Creative Breakfasts *Try This:* Is Your Diet Healthful?	Cooperative Learning 19 Lesson 1 Quiz Peer Pressure and Decision Making 21 Transparency 43, "Looking Good, Feeling Good" Student Workbook Activities 69, 70
LESSON 2 **Nutrients: Proteins, Carbohydrates, and Fats**	278–283	*Tips for Living:* Understanding Food Terms *Skills in Action:* Finding the Sugar in Foods	Lesson 2 Quiz Peer Pressure and Decision Making 22 Transparency 44, "Nutrient Know-How: Proteins, Carbohydrates, and Fats" Student Workbook Activities 71, 72
LESSON 3 **Nutrients: Vitamins, Minerals, and Water**	284–290	*Try This:* Vitamin Supplements *Try This:* Can Food Labels Mislead You?	Activity and Project Card 19, "Nutrition Puzzles" Activity and Project Card 20, "Nutrient Campaign" Concept Map 16 Cooperative Learning 20 Cross Curriculum 11 Enrichment 11 Lesson 3 Quiz Transparency 45, "Nutrient Know-How: Vitamins, Minerals, and Water" Transparency 46, "Food Sources of Vitamins and Minerals" Student Workbook Activities 73, 74

CHAPTER 10 RESOURCES

- Chapter 10 Test
- Reteaching 10
- Study Guide 10, *Reteaching*
- Testmaker Software

UNIT 4 RESOURCES

- Transparency 42, "Food, Family, and Friends"
- Hands-on Projects 8, 9
- Hands-on Game 4

Performance Assessment Activity

Tell students they will plan a Nutrition Fair to be held in their classroom. The focus of the fair will be to raise the attendees' awareness of healthy eating habits. Organize students into three groups and assign each group one of the lessons in Chapter 10. Tell each group that their task is to develop a booth that focuses on the content of the lesson. Students should divide tasks such as: making posters to advertise the fair; distributing handouts of information; contacting guest speakers; developing a questionnaire; preparing sample recipes, and so on.

School-to-Work

Have students create a learning center called "Careers in Nutrition" in the corner of the classroom and use three sides of a cardboard box to create a bulletin board that can be set on a table. Have students research various careers using newspapers and magazines to find articles and photographs of individuals working in nutrition careers to post on the board. They might also look in the library for books on careers in nutrition. Have students prepare handouts about specific careers in nutrition for the learning center. A useful resource is *Opportunities in Nutrition Careers* by Carol Coles Caldwell (NTC Publishing Group, 1992).

Family & Community

Point out to students that many communities conduct food drives to help the hungry and homeless in the community. Suggest that students plan a school-sponsored food drive. Organize students into groups and assign the following tasks: generating publicity, designating donation locations or pickups, boxing and delivering donations.

Resources for the Teacher

Landis, Robyn. *BodyFueling.* New York: Warner Books, 1994.

USDA. *Nutrition: Eating for Good Health.* USDA, 1995.

The New Food Label: There's Something in It for Everybody. IFIC Publications. 1100 Connecticut Ave., N.W., Suite 430, Washington, D.C. 20036.

Readings for the Student

Nardo, Don. *Vitamins and Minerals.* New York: Chelsea House Publishers, 1994.

Salter, Dr. Charles A. *Looking Good, Eating Right.* Brookfield, CT: Millbrook Press, 1991.

Tips to Healthy Eating for Kids. (Pamphlet) IFIC Publications. 1100 Connecticut Ave., N.W., Suite 430, Washington, D.C. 20036.

Multimedia Resources

Food for Life (VHS Video). Perennial Education.

Food for Thought (VHS Video). Visual Education Productions.

Nutrition Kit: Eating Sensibly in the 1990's (VHS Video/Booklets). Cambridge Career Products.

OUT OF TIME?

If time does not permit thorough teaching of this chapter, you may wish to use:

- Teens Making a Difference, page 271
- Tips for Living, page 280
- Try This, pages 276, 285, 288
- Skills in Action, pages 275, 281
- Young Living Activities, page 291
- Chapter Summary, page 292

CHAPTER 10
Nutrition and You

Chapter Overview
Chapter 10 introduces students to the study of nutrition and explains how daily meals and snacks based on the six kinds of nutrients contribute to a healthful diet.

LESSON 1 explains how the six kinds of nutrients help the human body and protect against illness.

LESSON 2 explains the role of proteins, carbohydrates, and fats in the body.

LESSON 3 lists the good food sources of vitamins and minerals and emphasizes the importance of water in the diet.

Introducing the Chapter
Write "Food" and "Nutrients" on the board. Have each label be the center of a web. Have students skim the lesson titles, subtitles, and photographs in Chapter 10 to add to the web. Students should complete the "Food" web by writing the ways in which food affects an individual. (It helps a person look good and feel good; it satisfies hunger.) Students should complete the "Nutrients" web by listing the kinds of nutrients there are. Tell students that they will learn more about these topics in Chapter 10.

Chapter Motivator
Take a survey of how many students take vitamin and/or mineral supplements. Ask them to share reasons why they take the supplements. Discuss whether the supplements are prescribed by a physician, or if they are self-prescribed. Discuss the pros and cons of taking supplements and have students brainstorm situations when vitamin supplements might be necessary.

CHAPTER 10
Nutrition and You

LESSON ONE
What Food Does for You

LESSON TWO
Nutrients: Proteins, Carbohydrates, and Fats

LESSON THREE
Nutrients: Vitamins, Minerals, and Water

KEY TO ABILITY LEVELS

Teaching strategies that appear throughout the chapter have been identified by one of three codes to give you an idea of their suitability for students of varying learning styles and abilities.

L1 Level 1 strategies should be within the ability range of all students. Often full class participation is required. Teacher direction is usually needed.

L2 Level 2 strategies are for average to above-average students or for small groups. Some teacher direction is necessary.

L3 Level 3 strategies are designed for students able and willing to work independently. Minimal teacher direction is necessary.

CHAPTER 10

TEENS MAKING A DIFFERENCE

Call on a volunteer to read the feature. Ask students to describe how all the people involved in the community service club benefit from the club's work.

You might start a community service club in your own classroom. Interested students might organize a food drive involving the entire school. The food that is collected might be given to various organizations in your community.

BLOCK SCHEDULING

The following Teacher Classroom Resources are suggested for use in classrooms with Block Scheduling.
- Activity and Project Card 19, "Nutrition Puzzles"
- Activity and Project Card 20, "Nutrient Campaign"
- Cooperative Learning 19, "A Message on Food and Health"
- Cooperative Learning 20, "Nutrient Roundtable"

TEENS MAKING A DIFFERENCE
Community Service Club

One Saturday, when Jillian Thompson was helping out at her family's restaurant, she noticed how much leftover food got thrown away. Jillian wondered if there was a way for that food to be used to feed hungry people. Jillian's father suggested that she call a local soup kitchen to see if they could use the food.

Jillian then asked her social studies teacher to help her set up a community service club at school. Many students volunteered to help, and their parents agreed to take turns doing the driving. Now good, nutritious food serves to keep people healthy instead of going to waste.

Try THIS!
Talk to your teachers, guidance counselor, or librarian to learn about programs in your community that help feed people in need. Find out what you can do to help.

271

TECHNOLOGY IN THE CLASSROOM

On-Line Services The Family and Consumer Sciences classroom can be enhanced by various on-line services. By adding a modem to a computer and connecting the computer to a phone line, you can easily access information, data, and resources from outside the classroom. Electronic bulletin boards provide current information and announcements. You can access up-to-date information on home economics topics from the extensive database of home economics extension services. Investigate ways to communicate with others about topics of interest. Classrooms and schools throughout the world can now electronically connect, providing students with an increased understanding of other cultures.

LESSON ONE
What Food Does for You

FOCUS

Lesson Objectives
After studying this lesson, students should be able to
- describe how food affects the way they feel.
- state the difference between hunger and appetite.
- list factors that influence food choices.

Motivating Activity
Ask students to write a list of five foods they like and five foods they dislike.

Introducing the Lesson
Call on several students to read the lists they prepared for the Motivating Activity. As a class, discuss whether these are healthy food choices. Explain that the food a person eats is his or her diet and there are guidelines for choosing foods that help a person grow, go, and glow.

Introducing *Words to Know*
Introduce the vocabulary terms. Begin by pointing out that the word *diet* means "the food you eat." *Diet* comes from the Greek *diaita*, meaning "mode of life." Ask students to write their own definitions for the other words in the list. Have them check their definitions against the definitions in the Glossary.

LESSON ONE
What Food Does for You

WORDS TO KNOW
nutrients
diet
hunger
appetite
calorie
nutrition
digestion

DISCOVER...
- how food affects the way you look and feel.
- the difference between hunger and appetite.
- factors that influence food choices.

Carly's favorite foods are pizza, salads, and yogurt. Even though these foods are healthful, Carly knows that she needs to eat a variety of foods to supply her body with the nutrients it needs. **Nutrients** (NOO-tree-ents) are *substances in food that are important for the body's growth and maintenance.* Carly still eats her favorite foods, but she balances her diet by including many different choices. **Diet** means *everything you regularly eat and drink.*

272 CHAPTER 10: NUTRITION AND YOU

CLASSROOM RESOURCES FOR LESSON 1

 Blackline Masters
Cooperative Learning 19
Lesson 1 Quiz
Peer Pressure and Decision Making 21

 Transparencies
Transparency 43, "Looking Good, Feeling Good"

Student Workbook
Activities 69, 70

Looking Good

Your diet affects the way you look. Eating healthful foods can help you look your best. Exercise, adequate rest, and personal hygiene also contribute to your appearance. Most healthy young teens have these physical characteristics:

- Normal growth
- Average weight
- Sparkling eyes
- Good posture
- Healthy teeth
- Shiny hair

Skin problems are common among teens, but they usually go away as people get older. Contrary to popular belief, eating such foods as chocolate or potato chips does not cause skin problems. However, eating a nutritious diet, washing your face every day, and getting enough rest will help keep your skin healthy.

Eating nutritious foods helps keep up your energy level. What activities might be more fun if you had more energy?

Feeling Good

Have you ever noticed how young children get cranky when they are hungry? Along with exercise and rest, food affects how you feel, no matter what your age. Feeling good and being healthy go hand in hand. A healthy person is

LESSON ONE: WHAT FOOD DOES FOR YOU   **273**

HOME AND COMMUNITY CONNECTION

Many grocery stores are now helping shoppers become more nutrition conscious. For example, they may hand out pamphlets about nutritious meal planning; use color-coded shelf tags that identify foods for calorie-controlled, fat-modified, or sodium-restricted diets; display store posters or weekly advertisements of healthy foods and preparation tips flagged by a "heart-smart" logo; or offer recipe cards that feature nutritious entrées. Ask students the next time they go food shopping to make a list or obtain actual handouts of ways the grocery store assists shoppers in becoming more nutrition conscious. Results can be displayed as collages or a bulletin-board project.

CHAPTER 10, LESSON 1

TEACH

L1 Diagramming
Have students develop a concept map or word web of the physical qualities of healthy young people. Have them write "healthy people" on a piece of paper and circle it. On lines radiating from the circle have them write the qualities of healthy people.

L2 Research
Suggest that students do library research to find a recent article on how wise food choices reduce the chances of getting certain diseases, such as heart disease and cancer. Have several students present their articles to the class and post the remaining articles on the bulletin board under the heading "Diet and Disease." Students may wish to search on-line resources for their articles if computers are available.

L3 Journalism
Have students play the role of an extraterrestrial journalist who has come to Earth. The journalist's assignment is to write an article on the nutrition of Americans for the *Extraterrestrial Tribune*. Ask the journalists to watch TV commercials for several hours and to describe the diet of Americans based solely on what they saw in the food advertisements they observed on television. Have several students read their articles to the class. Then discuss whether the articles give an accurate picture of the nutrition habits of Americans.

L1 Using Transparencies
Present Color Transparency 43, "Looking Good, Feeling Good," in the TCR. Use this overhead visual to reinforce concepts from this lesson.

CHAPTER 10, LESSON 1

L2 Comparing
Have students make a list of the foods they eat over the next two days. After each item they eat, have them write the word "hunger" or "appetite." Have volunteers discuss their lists with the class.

L3 Analyzing
Using the same list they prepared in the previous activity, have students research the number of calories in each food on their list. Then have them analyze which food choices had more calories—those driven by hunger or those driven by appetite. If possible, have students use computers for this project. Have them compare their lists.

L2 Problem Solving
Assign Peer Pressure and Decision Making 21 in the TCR. This activity gives students the opportunity to recognize peer pressure and practice decision-making skills.

L2 Cooperative Learning
Assign Cooperative Learning Activity 19 in the TCR. Students work in groups to create a health message in this activity.

L2 Design
Have students work in small groups to design a menu for the Healthy Huddle restaurant. Point out that this menu will differ from traditional menus in that it will list the nutrients and calories in each food item. This activity can be done on computers if available. Have groups present their menus to the class.

- energetic and not easily tired.
- mentally alert.
- calm, not stressed.
- rarely sick.

Food is your source of energy for physical and mental activities. You need energy to perform well in school, in sports, and in all your other activities. Without adequate food and nutrients, you may tire easily and feel less alert.

A healthful diet protects you from illness. By getting the nutrients you need, your body is better able to fight infections, heal wounds, and recover quickly if you do get sick.

The sight and smell of some foods can cause people to develop an appetite even when they are not hungry.

Satisfying Your Hunger

When your stomach growls or feels empty, you are experiencing signs of hunger. **Hunger** is *the physical need to eat*. Once you eat, that empty feeling goes away. Hunger tells you that your body needs food, but it does not tell you what to eat. You must learn to select healthful foods. You must also learn how much to eat.

Appetite is different from hunger. **Appetite** is *the desire to eat*. When you smell fresh strawberries or see a chocolate layer cake, you might develop an appetite without really being hungry.

When hunger is satisfied, it may be time to stop eating. Some people still have an appetite, however, so they continue

274   CHAPTER 10: NUTRITION AND YOU

MORE ABOUT • • •

Diet and Cancer The American Cancer Society suggests the following guidelines to help the body protect itself from certain forms of cancer: (1) eat more high-fiber foods such as fruits and vegetables and whole-grain cereals; (2) include dark-green and deep-yellow fruits and vegetables, which are rich in vitamins A and C; (3) include cabbage, broccoli, brussels sprouts, kohlrabi, and cauliflower; (4) be moderate in the consumption of salt-cured, smoked, and nitrite-cured foods; (5) cut down on total fat intake from animal sources and vegetable fats and oils; (6) avoid obesity; (7) be moderate in the consumption of alcoholic beverages.

to eat. If they eat too much food, or food that is too high in calories, they may gain excess weight. A **calorie** is *a unit of heat that measures the energy available in food.* Food provides energy for your daily activities. If you eat food that has more calories than your body uses, however, the extra energy is stored as fat.

What Influences Your Food Choices?

Like most people, you eat for many reasons. Food helps keep you healthy. Some foods may be part of family traditions. For example, you may have a favorite menu for a particular holiday meal. Some people eat because they are bored or depressed. Food is usually part of social gatherings. You have probably eaten snacks or cake and ice cream at a birthday party.

Have you ever thought about why you choose to eat the foods you do? Of course, you have likes and dislikes, but other factors also influence your food choices:

- **Family.** Your family has taught you about food. Over the years, you have learned to eat and enjoy foods that are part of your family's habits, lifestyle, and traditions.

- **Cultural background.** You may like foods that are part of your culture. Foods from many cultures are popular in the United States.

- **Religion.** Some religious teachings forbid certain foods. For example, Hindus don't eat beef. Many Jewish people and Muslims don't eat pork.

- **Friends.** As you get older, your friends may introduce you to new food experiences.

Creative Breakfasts

Try the following nutritious breakfast ideas for a change of pace:
- Plain yogurt with fruit and granola
- A breakfast burrito—an egg scrambled with ham and rolled in a warm tortilla
- Hot or cold sandwiches, such as grilled cheese, tuna, or turkey

Your family influences your food choices. What could you do to influence their choices?

LESSON ONE: WHAT FOOD DOES FOR YOU   275

MEETING STUDENT DIVERSITY

Cultural Diversity Ethnic foods—those associated with a particular group or country—are popular in the United States. The western part of the country, which accounts for about one-third of the nation's population, has about one-half of the nation's ethnic restaurants, with Asian and Mexican food being the most popular. The people in the Middle Atlantic states favor Italian food. Other types of ethnic restaurants are Greek, Chinese, Vietnamese, German, and so on. Take a poll to find out the favorite ethnic foods of the class and what factors affect their preferences.

CHAPTER 10, LESSON 1

After students have read the Skills in Action feature, discuss their reactions to the suggested meals. Ask them to share their own recipes for nontraditional breakfasts. Discuss whether each suggested breakfast provides the nutrition they need. Suggest to students who say they don't need breakfast that they try eating a nutritious breakfast for a week. Then have them report how, or if, eating breakfast changed the way they felt.

L1 Interviewing
Have students make a list of the factors that influence food choices. Have them list what factors influence their own personal food choices. Then have them use the list to interview family members about their food likes and dislikes.

L2 Critical Thinking
Have students write a paragraph describing how changing lifestyles have affected the way we eat.

L3 Debate
Have students debate the following: Food advertisements on television have little effect on people's food choices.

L3 Analyzing
Have students collect food advertisements and analyze the type of nutritional claims made by the advertisements. They might compare selected advertisements for the same type of product, such as salad dressing, and make a display comparing the nutritional claims made by each advertiser.

CHAPTER 10, LESSON 1

After students have read the feature, point out that good eating habits are only part of a healthy lifestyle. Challenge students to make a schedule and keep a record of their health habits for one week. They should plan how much time they will spend exercising; the type of exercise they will do; how much sleep they need; and when they should bathe, wash their hair, and brush their teeth. Have them make a chart to keep track of their health habits.

L1 Student Workbook
Assign Activities 69 and 70 in the Student Workbook.

ASSESS

Evaluating the Lesson
Assign Reviewing Terms and Facts and Thinking Critically on page 277 to review the lesson; then assign the Lesson 1 Quiz in the TCR.

Reteaching
- Ask students to cut pictures of their favorite foods from magazines and categorize them according to the different classes of nutrients. Ask them to identify foods that could not be categorized and discuss whether they are nutritious.
- Have students complete Reteaching Activity 10 in the TCR.

How healthful is your diet? Rate your eating habits by answering the following questions.
- Do you eat breakfast every morning?
- Do you eat meals at regular intervals?
- Do you eat a varied diet?

If you answered no to some of these questions, make a plan to improve your diet.

- **Convenience.** People who have little time to cook may choose foods that are easy to prepare.
- **Cost.** To get more for their money, many people choose less expensive foods.
- **Area where you live.** You may eat foods that are popular and easily available in your part of the country. For example, fish is common in the coastal areas.
- **Advertising.** You may be persuaded to buy and eat certain foods because of television, radio, and magazine advertisements.
- **Health.** When you know about food and nutrition, you can choose foods that promote your health.

Nutrients for Health

When you make food choices, the factor that should influence you most is your health. Nutrients in food keep you healthy, help you grow, and give you energy. Eating a variety of foods will provide you with good nutrition. **Nutrition** (noo-TRI-shuhn) is *the study of nutrients and how they are used by the body.*

There are six kinds of nutrients: proteins, carbohydrates, fats, vitamins, minerals, and water. Each one has an important function.

- **Proteins** help build, repair, and maintain body cells and tissues.
- **Carbohydrates** provide energy and fiber.
- **Fats** provide energy and supply essential fatty acids for normal growth and healthy skin.
- **Vitamins, minerals, and water** help regulate the work of the body's systems.

Nutrients are released from food during digestion. **Digestion** is *the process of breaking down food into a form the body can use.* Nutrients are absorbed into the bloodstream and carried to cells to do their work.

▶ Eating nutritious foods is essential to keep your body running smoothly. This snack is satisfying and healthy.

276 CHAPTER 10: NUTRITION AND YOU

COOPERATIVE LEARNING

Tracking Nutrition Have students work in pairs. Each member of the pair should chart the foods they eat for three days, grouping them according to the six kinds of nutrients. Partners should then exchange charts and play the role of a nutritionist. Have them analyze their partner's diet and tell him or her what is missing from the diet, things that should be added to the diet to make it healthy, and healthful snacks that could be substituted for unhealthy snacks.

The food choices that you make will affect your health now and for years to come. How can you be sure that you are making the right choices?

Nutrients affect all your body processes, such as your heartbeat, blood flow, and breathing. These processes, in turn, affect the way you feel and how much energy you have. They also affect how you look—the quality of your skin, hair, and nails.

Your body, like everything else that belongs to you, requires good care. To keep your body functioning properly, you must choose foods that supply enough of each nutrient. Lack of nutrients can cause health problems now or in the future.

LESSON ONE *Review*

Using complete sentences, answer the following questions on a separate sheet of paper.

Reviewing Terms and Facts

1. List Name five characteristics of a healthy person.

2. Explain How does diet affect your energy level?

3. Vocabulary Define the term *nutrition*. Use it in an original sentence.

4. Recall List the six nutrients and their functions.

Thinking Critically

5. Explain Why is it so important to get the necessary nutrients from your diet?

6. Contrast What is the difference between hunger and appetite?

7. Analyze Identify five factors that affect your food choices. Which one most strongly influences your diet? Explain your answer.

Applying Concepts

8. Identify your personal eating habits. Are you a picky eater? Do you eat only a limited number of foods? Do you eat fruits and vegetables only when forced to? Write a paragraph or two describing your eating habits. Do you need to make changes in your diet? Have your eating habits changed since you were younger?

LESSON ONE: WHAT FOOD DOES FOR YOU   **277**

CHAPTER 10, LESSON 1

Answers to Lesson 1 Review

1. Any five: normal growth, good posture, average weight, teeth free of cavities, sparkling eyes, clean, shiny hair.
2. Since food is your source of energy, you tire easily and are less alert without adequate food and nutrients.
3. The study of nutrients and how they are used by the body.
4. Proteins—help build, repair, and maintain body cells and tissues. Carbohydrates—provide energy and fiber. Fats—provide energy, supply essential fatty acids. Vitamins, minerals, and water—help regulate the body's work.
5. Because nutrients affect all your body processes. To keep the body running smoothly, you need to make food choices that supply enough of each nutrient.
6. Hunger is the physical need to eat. Appetite is the psychological, or mental, desire to eat.
7. Students' answers will vary but should include the factor(s) listed on pages 275–276.
8. Students' answers will vary but should reflect an understanding of how the findings apply to their own diet.

Enrichment

Suggest that students research foods associated with a particular region of the country or a food custom of a particular religion. Have them make a brief report to the class.

CLOSE

Have students use the Words to Know in a paragraph titled "What Food Does for You."

MORE ABOUT • • •

Nutrients Explain to students that chemical compounds called antioxidants play an important role in keeping the body healthy. Tell them that these compounds, which include vitamins C and E, rid the body of free radicals. Free radicals are naturally occurring substances that damage body tissues and blood fats. Tell students that scientists believe that the damage brought on by free radicals is one cause of cancer, heart disease, and heart attacks. Point out to students that foods rich in antioxidants include fruits and vegetables.

LESSON TWO

Nutrients: Proteins, Carbohydrates, and Fats

FOCUS

Lesson Objectives

After studying this lesson, students should be able to
- explain the functions of proteins, carbohydrates, and fats in the human body.
- list the types of foods that are good sources of proteins, carbohydrates, and fats.

Motivating Activity

Write the following questions on the chalkboard and have students write their responses.
- Which nutrient builds and repairs body cells?
- Name a food high in carbohydrates.
- What are two sources of fat?

Introducing the Lesson

Call on students to share their responses to the Motivating Activity. Correct any incorrect responses. Then tell students that in this lesson they will learn about the sources and benefits of proteins, carbohydrates, and fats.

Introducing *Words to Know*

Scramble the letters for each of the Words to Know and write each scrambled word or phrase on an index card. Display one of the cards and read the definition of it. Have students try to unscramble the letters and figure out what the word or phrase is.

LESSON TWO

Nutrients: Proteins, Carbohydrates, and Fats

WORDS TO KNOW

proteins
amino acids
carbohydrates
fiber
whole grains
saturated fats
unsaturated fats
cholesterol

DISCOVER...
- the functions of proteins, carbohydrates, and fats in the human body.
- the types of foods that are good sources of proteins, carbohydrates, and fats.

Tyler has learned a lot about nutrients while training for the track team. He knows that he needs to eat plenty of foods that contain proteins, carbohydrates, and fats. These nutrients provide calories and energy. The body needs large amounts of them to stay healthy.

278 CHAPTER 10: NUTRITION AND YOU

CLASSROOM RESOURCES FOR LESSON 2

 Blackline Masters
Lesson 2 Quiz
Peer Pressure and Decision Making 22

 Transparencies
Transparency 44, "Nutrient Know-How: Proteins, Carbohydrates, and Fats"

 **Student Workbook**
Activities 71, 72

278

Proteins

Proteins are *nutrients that are needed to build, repair, and maintain body cells and tissues.* All of your body tissues—including your skin, hair, blood, muscles, and vital organs—are made of proteins. During the teen years, you need proteins to help your body grow and develop to its adult size. Even after you stop growing, you still need proteins to help your body repair itself. Billions of worn-out body cells are replaced every day, and proteins are used to make those new cells.

Each protein is a different combination of amino acids. **Amino** (uh-MEE-noh) **acids** are *chains of building blocks that make up proteins.* Your body can manufacture some amino acids. Others, called essential amino acids, can't be made by your body. They must come from the food you eat.

Some foods contain all the essential amino acids. These foods, called *complete proteins,* come from animals. Meat, fish, poultry, milk, cheese, and eggs are examples of complete proteins. Other foods are good sources of protein, but they lack one or more of the essential amino acids. These foods, called *incomplete proteins,* come from plants. Dry beans, nuts, and grains are examples of incomplete proteins.

Combining Proteins

You can combine incomplete protein sources to make complete proteins. These combinations provide all the amino acids needed for the body to grow and repair itself. Proteins from dry beans and nuts lack some amino acids. Grain proteins lack other amino acids. By combining these types of foods, however, you can get all the essential amino acids. Such combinations include

- bread and peanut butter.
- cereal with nuts.
- rice and beans.

By combining proteins from grains with proteins from dry beans and nuts, you can get all the essential amino acids that your body needs. Twelve to fifteen percent of daily calorie intake should come from protein.

LESSON TWO: NUTRIENTS: PROTEINS, CARBOHYDRATES, AND FATS

CHAPTER 10, LESSON 2

TEACH

L1 Creating Posters
Pair students and have them create a display that illustrates what proteins do for the body (help the body grow and repair itself). Students' displays should also illustrate the foods that contain complete and incomplete proteins.

L2 Writing
Ask students to write an article for a newspaper's food section. The article should discuss the importance of protein and amino acids, and include visuals of foods that contain complete and incomplete proteins. The articles should include the effects of not getting enough protein in the diet. Computers may be used for this activity.

L2 Problem Solving
Assign Peer Pressure and Decision Making 22 in the TCR. This activity gives students the opportunity to recognize peer pressure and practice decision-making skills.

L1 Using Transparencies
Present Color Transparency 44, "Nutrient Know-How: Proteins, Carbohydrates, and Fats," in the TCR. Use this overhead visual to reinforce concepts from this lesson.

MORE ABOUT • • •

Protein and Athletes A widely held misconception is that athletes and others who participate regularly in sports and exercise need to consume huge quantities of protein to maintain energy, strength, and power. The truth is that the reason athletes need more total protein in their diet is that they need more calories overall. The best nutritional preparation for physically intense activities is a high-carbohydrate, well-balanced diet consisting of adequate levels of proteins, fats, vitamins, minerals, and liquids. A diet providing 70 percent of total calories from carbohydrates and 12 percent from proteins has been shown to be the best for athletes and others involved in physically intensive activities.

CHAPTER 10, LESSON 2

TIPS for living

After students have read the feature, ask them to bring in food labels and wrappers that include the terms defined in the feature. Have them create a collage for each term using the labels and wrappers.

L3 Research

Have students do research to find out the latest recommendations for the amount of fat needed in the diet. Also ask them to find out why Americans have been using less fat in their diet in recent years.

DID YOU KNOW

Seventy percent of the sugar in our diets is hidden in processed foods such as peanut butter, catsup, cereal, and soda. The average person in the United States eats approximately 130 pounds of sugar each year.

TIPS for living

UNDERSTANDING FOOD TERMS

Have you ever compared food labels and wondered what the difference was between *lite* and *low-calorie* or *low-fat* and *fat-free* foods? Understanding the terms used on food labels has become much easier, because the government has standardized the meanings of these terms. The following definitions refer to a single serving.

- **Light or lite:** one-third fewer calories or 50 percent less fat than the traditional version of the product
- **Low-calorie:** 40 calories or fewer
- **Low-fat:** 3 grams of fat or less
- **Fat-free:** less than 0.5 gram of fat
- **Reduced sugar:** 25 percent less sugar than the typical product
- **Sugar free:** less than 0.5 gram of sugar
- **Low sodium:** 140 milligrams of sodium or less
- **High fiber:** 5 grams of fiber or more

Carbohydrates

Carbohydrates are *the starches and sugars that give the body most of its energy.* Almost all carbohydrates come from plant sources, which also provide fiber.

Starches and Sugars

Starches and sugars are excellent energy sources. Starches are found in grains, such as oats, rice, and wheat. Foods made from grain—including bread, tortillas, pasta, and cereals—also provide starch. Potatoes, corn, dry beans, and nuts are additional sources of starch.

Natural sugars are found in fruits and milk. These foods are good sugar sources because they are also high in other nutrients. Foods such as candy, cake frosting, and soft drinks also contain sugar, but they are not beneficial sources of it. These prepared foods are high in calories but low in other nutrients, so they should be eaten sparingly.

280   CHAPTER 10: NUTRITION AND YOU

MORE ABOUT • • •

Carbohydrates This nutrient is the principal source of energy for the body. In addition, carbohydrates are the most economical types of foods. Nutritionists distinguish between two types of carbohydrates: simple carbohydrates and complex carbohydrates. Simple carbohydrates are the sugars. Complex carbohydrates are primarily starches. The major sources of complex carbohydrates are grains such as bread, rice, and pasta and vegetables such as potatoes and beans. For a long time, people thought that complex carbohydrates were fatty and to be avoided. The truth is that complex carbohydrates have fewer calories and more nutrition than any other food group.

Fruit is a good source of natural sugars. Why are natural sugars an important part of your diet?

Fiber

Fiber is *the tough, stringy part of raw fruits, vegetables, and grains that your body cannot digest.* Although fiber is not a nutrient, eating the right amount of fiber-rich foods helps the body function normally. Fiber provides bulk, which helps move food through your digestive system. It also helps your body eliminate wastes.

Eating foods that contain fiber is important for digestion. Without enough fiber, digestion can slow down. This may cause constipation, or infrequent bowel movements. In addition, a diet rich in high-fiber foods can reduce the risk for certain diseases, including colon cancer.

Good sources of fiber include foods made from whole grains. **Whole grains** are *foods that contain all of the edible grain, including the outer layer, the bran, and the germ.* Whole-wheat breads, whole-wheat cereals, and popcorn are whole-grain foods. Fruits and vegetables—especially those with edible skins, stems, and seeds—also contain fiber.

Fats

Like carbohydrates, fats are an important source of energy. Fats contain twice as many calories, ounce for ounce, as carbohydrates. Your body relies on fat cells to store energy and to help regulate body temperature. Your skin needs fats to stay

Finding the Sugar in Foods

Because sugar comes in so many forms, you may not realize how much of it is added to the foods you eat. Here are some snack foods and the amount of sugar per serving:
- Cola—9 teaspoons
- Sweetened cereal— 8 teaspoons
- Yogurt with sweetened fruit— 7 teaspoons
- Popcorn— 0 teaspoons

What are your favorite snacks? Check the labels to see how much sugar has been added.

LESSON TWO: NUTRIENTS: PROTEINS, CARBOHYDRATES, AND FATS

CHAPTER 10, LESSON 2

L1 Science

Using brown paper bags, have students test for the fat content of various foods. Have them rub various foods on the paper bag. If the food contains fat, a translucent spot will appear. Based on their experiment, have students make a list of foods that have fat content and those that do not. (Note: Water will produce a translucent spot, but a water spot disappears when the water dries.)

After students identify their favorite snacks, have them share their lists with the class. After they have checked labels and identified added sugar content, ask them to cross out the snacks with the highest sugar content and make a list of snacks they might substitute for these. Encourage students to choose natural, healthful snack substitutes.

COOPERATIVE LEARNING

Examining Sugars, Fiber, and Fats Organize the class into groups of four. Tell them that nutritionists recommend that a cereal should have at least 3 grams of fiber, less than 8 grams of sugar, and no more than 2 grams of fat. Have students examine six nutrition labels from empty cereal boxes and make bar graphs to show the following: The first graph should show the fat content; the grams of fat should appear on the vertical axis and the cereal names on the horizontal axis (each cereal is a separate bar). The second graph should show the sugar content. The third graph should show the fiber content. Each group should prepare three graphs. Have students evaluate the cereals to see how closely they meet nutritionists' recommendations.

CHAPTER 10, LESSON 2

USING VISUALS

After students have studied Figure 10.1, have them list the foods they ate for breakfast, lunch, and dinner yesterday and find out the amount of calories from fat or the fat content in each food item. Point out that the best way to lose one's taste for fat is to use naturally low-fat choices that will train your taste buds to prefer low-fat foods. Have students select low-fat foods for two weeks. They should keep a log of each time they replace a fatty food with a natural low-fat substitute and record the fat content of the foods. At the end of two weeks, they should calculate the amount of fat they didn't eat.

L1 **Student Workbook**

Assign Activities 71 and 72 in the Student Workbook.

ASSESS

Evaluating the Lesson

Assign Reviewing Terms and Facts and Thinking Critically on page 283 to review the lesson; then assign the Lesson 2 Quiz in the TCR.

Reteaching

- Have students list the following words vertically on their paper: "protein," "carbohydrate," and "fat." Give them ten minutes to think of a healthy food source beginning with each letter of each nutrient. Have students share their lists with the rest of the class.
- Have students complete Reteaching Activity 10 in the TCR.

Figure 10.1
Tips for Reducing Fat
By following these guidelines, you can reduce the amount of fat in your diet but still eat delicious food.

1. Start your day with breakfast.
Choose a healthful breakfast to start your day. Did you know that a doughnut and a glass of whole milk have a total of 22.1 grams of fat? Instead, try a bagel with nonfat cream cheese and a glass of skim milk, which have a total of only 1.5 grams of fat.

2. Choose a healthful lunch.
What is your favorite lunch food? If you enjoy a tuna sandwich, keep in mind that tuna packed in oil and served on white bread contains a total of 11.4 grams of fat. A healthier choice is tuna packed in water and served on whole-wheat bread, which contains a total of only 3.8 grams of fat.

4. Make wise choices for dinner.
The way in which food is prepared makes a big difference in the food's fat content. A dinner of fried chicken and french fries, for example, contains a total of 18.7 grams of fat. By choosing grilled chicken and a baked potato instead, you can still eat the foods you like but with a total of only 3.3 grams of fat.

3. Snack smart.
Some snack foods are loaded with fats. Potato chips have 39.8 grams of fat; chocolate chip cookies, 30.1 grams; and premium ice cream, 16.1 grams. For a snack that is lower in fat, try nonfat frozen yogurt, with 0 grams of fat; an apple, with .6 grams; or pretzels, with 4.5 grams.

282   CHAPTER 10: NUTRITION AND YOU

MEETING STUDENT DIVERSITY

Active Learners Students will carry more with them from the classroom to the workplace if they are actively involved in their own learning process. You can offer choices about what activities will be part of a lesson, for example. Use the suggestions provided for the illustration on this page. You may shift the responsibility for planning activities, implementing them, and assessing progress to students themselves. They will see learning as a process that offers real-life rewards in the form of improved skills, and they will be willing to invest more of their time and energy.

smooth, and your nervous system needs them to work properly. Fats also carry several vitamins needed by the body, such as vitamin A.

Fats come from both animal and plant sources of food. **Saturated fats** are *fats found in food from animal sources.* Meats, egg yolks, cheese, and butter contain saturated fats. Eating too much saturated fat can cause health problems, including an increased risk of heart disease. **Unsaturated fats** are *fats that come from plants.* They are generally liquid at room temperature and are found mainly in vegetable oils, such as olive, corn, or canola oil. No more than 30 percent of the calories you consume should come from fat, preferably unsaturated fats. **Figure 10.1** gives some tips for reducing the amount of fat in your diet.

Saturated fats contain **cholesterol** (kuh-LES-tuh-rawl), *a waxlike substance our bodies produce and need in small amounts.* Since your body produces all the cholesterol it needs, you don't need cholesterol in your diet. In fact, diets high in cholesterol have been linked to an increased risk of heart disease.

Eating a diet with enough of the proper nutrients will give your body the energy it needs. Which foods might you eat before a race?

LESSON TWO *Review*

Using complete sentences, answer the following questions on a separate sheet of paper.

Reviewing Terms and Facts
1. **Recall** What do proteins do for the body?
2. **Describe** What are complete proteins? Name three foods that provide complete proteins.
3. **List** What foods are good sources of carbohydrates?
4. **Vocabulary** Define the term *saturated fats.* List three foods that contain saturated fats.

Thinking Critically
5. **Suggest** How can you make sure that you are eating foods that contain all the essential amino acids?

6. **Contrast** What are the advantages of eating foods that contain natural sugars over eating foods with sugar added?
7. **Explain** Why is fiber important? List three foods you eat that are good sources of fiber.

Applying Concepts
8. Create a poster about proteins, carbohydrates, and fats. Cut out or draw pictures of various foods that contain these nutrients. Group them according to the nutrients found in them. Then, below each group of foods, list the functions in the human body for that nutrient.

LESSON TWO: NUTRIENTS: PROTEINS, CARBOHYDRATES, AND FATS

MEETING STUDENT DIVERSITY

Students with Special Needs Some students in the class may have diseases, such as diabetes, or allergies to certain foods. You might ask for volunteers who are willing to explain to the class how this affects their diet and how they compensate for the foods they are unable to eat. If volunteers are not available, provide students with pamphlets on special diets for diabetes and allergies and allow time for them to read about foods that are included in special diets.

CHAPTER 10, LESSON 2

Answers to Lesson 2 Review

1. Help build, maintain, and repair the body.
2. Proteins that have all the essential amino acids. Any three: meat, fish, poultry, milk, cheese, and eggs.
3. Grains, foods made from grain, potatoes, dry beans and peas, corn, and nuts.
4. Fats found in meats and dairy products. Any three: beef, poultry, eggs, milk, cheese, and butter.
5. By combining incomplete protein sources to make complete proteins.
6. Both supply calories for energy. However, unlike natural sugar sources, sugars in prepared foods contain very few other nutrients.
7. Provides bulk, which helps move food through the digestive system and helps eliminate body wastes. Students' answers will vary but should include fiber sources listed in the lesson.
8. Posters will vary but should be checked to be sure nutrients are properly placed and the list of functions is correct.

Enrichment
Have students research the artificial fats in the marketplace, such as Simplesse or Olestra.

CLOSE
Ask students to think of a title for this lesson other than "Proteins, Carbohydrates, and Fats." Suggest that they use the sources or functions of these nutrients as a substitute.

LESSON THREE
Nutrients: Vitamins, Minerals, and Water

FOCUS

Lesson Objectives
After studying this lesson, students should be able to
- explain the functions of vitamins, minerals, and water in the human body.
- list the types of food that are good sources of vitamins, minerals, and water.

Motivating Activity
Ask students to complete the following:
Vitamins are important for . . .
Minerals are important for . . .
Water is important for . . .

Introducing the Lesson
Have students share their responses to the Motivating Activity. Then discuss the sources of information for students' responses. Tell them that this lesson will explore the importance of vitamins, minerals, and water in the diet.

Introducing *Words to Know*
Write each Word to Know on an index card; then write the definition for each on a separate card. Make several sets of the term-and-definition cards. Organize the class into small groups. Give each group a set of cards and let students in each group take turns matching each term with its definition.

LESSON THREE
Nutrients: Vitamins, Minerals, and Water

 **WORDS TO KNOW**

vitamins
enriched
minerals
calcium
osteoporosis
iron

DISCOVER...
- the functions of vitamins, minerals, and water in the human body.
- the types of food that are good sources of vitamins, minerals, and water.

Brittany loves to eat junk food—potato chips, cookies, and candy. She rarely eats fruits and vegetables, and she doesn't like the taste of milk. Brittany doesn't worry about her health, however, because she is careful to take a multiple vitamin once or twice a week. Lately, though, Brittany has been feeling tired all the time. She seems to get colds often, too. Do you think that Brittany's problems may be related to her diet? What could she do to improve her health?

284 CHAPTER 10: NUTRITION AND YOU

CLASSROOM RESOURCES FOR LESSON 3

 Blackline Masters
Activity and Project Card 19, "Nutrition Puzzles"
Activity and Project Card 20, "Nutrient Campaign"
Concept Map 16
Cooperative Learning 20
Cross Curriculum 11
Enrichment 11
Lesson 3 Quiz

Reteaching 10
 Transparencies
Transparency 45, "Nutrient Know-How: Vitamins, Minerals, and Water"
Transparency 46, "Food Sources of Vitamins and Minerals"

 Student Workbook Activities 73, 74

The Need for Vitamins

Vitamins are *substances needed in small quantities to help regulate body functions.* Vitamins are important for many reasons. They help your body use other nutrients, store and use energy, and fight infection. **Figure 10.2** on pages 286–287 shows what some vitamins and minerals do for your body.

There are many types of essential vitamins, including the following: A, B-complex, C, D, and E. Because your body can't make most vitamins, you must get them from the foods you eat. These nutrients can easily be obtained from a variety of delicious foods, such as those listed in Figure 10.2.

Vitamin A

Have you ever walked into a dark room after being in the bright sunlight? Did you notice that your eyes had to adjust to less light before you could see again? Vitamin A enables your eyes to adjust to the dark. It also helps keep your skin healthy and helps your body resist infection. Dark green, leafy vegetables, deep yellow vegetables, and dairy products are good sources of vitamin A.

B-Complex Vitamins

The B-complex vitamins—riboflavin, thiamine, and niacin—give you energy by helping your body use calories from carbohydrates, fats, and proteins. Riboflavin also helps keep your eyes and skin healthy. Thiamine and niacin promote a healthy nervous system.

B-complex vitamins come from many different foods. Dairy products are the best sources of riboflavin. Thiamine and niacin are found in meat, dry beans, and some grain products. When selecting grain products, such as flour and bread, choose whole-grain or enriched foods. When wheat and other whole grains are turned into flour, nutritious parts of the grain are often lost. If these foods have been **enriched,** *the lost nutrients have been replaced in the same quantity or in greater quantity than the unprocessed food originally contained.*

LESSON THREE: NUTRIENTS: VITAMINS, MINERALS, AND WATER

Vitamin supplements are not a substitute for a balanced diet. They do not contain protein, carbohydrates, or fiber. Design a dinner menu that will provide the nutrients, vitamins, and minerals necessary for your good health.

CHAPTER 10, LESSON 3

TEACH

L1 Analyzing
Display several empty vitamin bottles, each with a vitamin's letter posted on it. Ask students to create labels on a sheet of paper for each bottle, listing or showing pictures of the foods from which the particular vitamin is obtained and the functions of each vitamin.

L2 Activity and Project Card
Allow time for students to complete Activity and Project Card 19, "Nutrition Puzzles," in the TCR.

L1 Design
Have students design a sweatshirt that emphasizes the importance of vitamins and minerals in the diet. Suggest that students not only create a slogan for the sweatshirt but also design a visual that emphasizes the concept.

After students have read the feature, ask them to list the vitamins that a multivitamin supplement provides. Then have students work with a partner to make a list of foods they could eat that would provide them with the same vitamins. Discuss students' lists.

MEETING STUDENT DIVERSITY

Reading Disabled Students with reading disabilities will often skip over chart and table material because it looks too difficult. The charts of vitamins and minerals can be broken down into smaller segments for students with learning problems. Have them work with partners or in small groups. For example, have students cover the bottom of the vitamins chart with a sheet of paper so that only the vitamin A row is visible. Have them read aloud this portion of the chart. Then have students slide the paper down so that only the vitamin B portion is showing, and have them read this portion aloud. Continue in this way until the entire chart is studied. Proceed in a similar manner with the sections on the minerals chart.

CHAPTER 10, LESSON 3

USING VISUALS

Have students review the information in Figure 10.2. Then ask them to name the vitamin or mineral that could help the following conditions:
- Lately Jean has no appetite. *(thiamine)*
- Earl's gums bleed when he brushes his teeth. *(Vitamin C)*
- Matt seems to bleed a lot whenever he gets cut. *(Vitamin K)*
- It takes longer than normal for Scott's eyes to adjust to a dark movie theater. *(Vitamin A)*

L1 Using Transparencies

Present Color Transparencies 45, "Nutrient Know-How: Vitamins, Minerals, and Water," and 46, "Food Sources of Vitamins and Minerals," in the TCR. Use these overhead visuals to reinforce concepts from this lesson.

L2 Writing

Have students work in small groups to design a magazine cover and a table of contents for a *Nutrition News* magazine. Tell them this is a special issue focusing on the importance of vitamins and minerals in the diet. Have each group member research one of the topics and write a brief article that might appear in the magazine.

L2 Create a Quiz

Have students work in pairs to create a true/false quiz based on the information in Figure 10.3. Have pairs exchange quizzes and take the quiz. Have pairs grade each other's quizzes and then, as a class, change all false questions to true questions.

Figure 10.2 Benefits and Food Sources of Vitamins and Minerals
Vitamins and minerals are essential for good health. What are some benefits of vitamin B? Which foods are good sources of iron?

Vitamins

Benefits	Food Sources
Vitamin A • helps eyes adjust to darkness. • helps keep skin healthy. • protects linings of nose, mouth, throat, and other organs from infection.	Dark green vegetables, deep yellow vegetables and fruits, eggs, whole milk, fortified low-fat milk
B-Complex Vitamins* • help carbohydrates, fats, and proteins produce energy.	Whole-grain and enriched breads and cereals, pork, organ meats, dry beans, peas
Thiamine • promotes growth, appetite, and digestion. • helps keep nervous system healthy.	Whole-grain and enriched breads and cereals, pork, organ meats, dry beans, peas
Riboflavin • helps keep eyes and skin healthy.	Milk, cheese, yogurt, eggs, organ meats, poultry, fish, enriched breads and cereals
Niacin • keeps digestive tract working normally. • helps keep nervous system and skin healthy.	Whole-grain and enriched breads and cereals, liver, meat, fish, poultry, nuts

*Other B complex vitamins—vitamin B6, folic acid, vitamin B12, pantothenic acid, and biotin—also help the body use carbohydrates, fats, and proteins.

Vitamin C (also called ascorbic acid) • helps the body fight infection. • helps wounds heal. • helps keep gums healthy.	Oranges, grapefruit, other citrus fruits, berries, melon, broccoli, spinach, potatoes, tomatoes, green pepper, cabbage
Vitamin D • works with calcium to build strong bones and teeth.	Fortified milk, fish-liver oil
Vitamin E • keeps oxygen from destroying other nutrients and cell membranes.	Vegetable oil, salad dressing, margarine, grains, fruits, some vegetables
Vitamin K • helps blood clot	Green leafy vegetables, egg yolk

286 CHAPTER 10: NUTRITION AND YOU

COOPERATIVE LEARNING

Have students develop a puppet show for younger children that explains the benefits of vitamins and minerals. Students should divide tasks among themselves. One group can write the script, another design the puppets, another create the puppet stage, and another narrate the presentation. Provide cardboard, paper, cloth scraps, felt scraps, glue, scissors, craft sticks, markers, and other art supplies for students to create their puppets and stage. Allow time for groups to present their puppet shows to the class. Encourage students to arrange for presentation of their shows at local preschools or elementary schools.

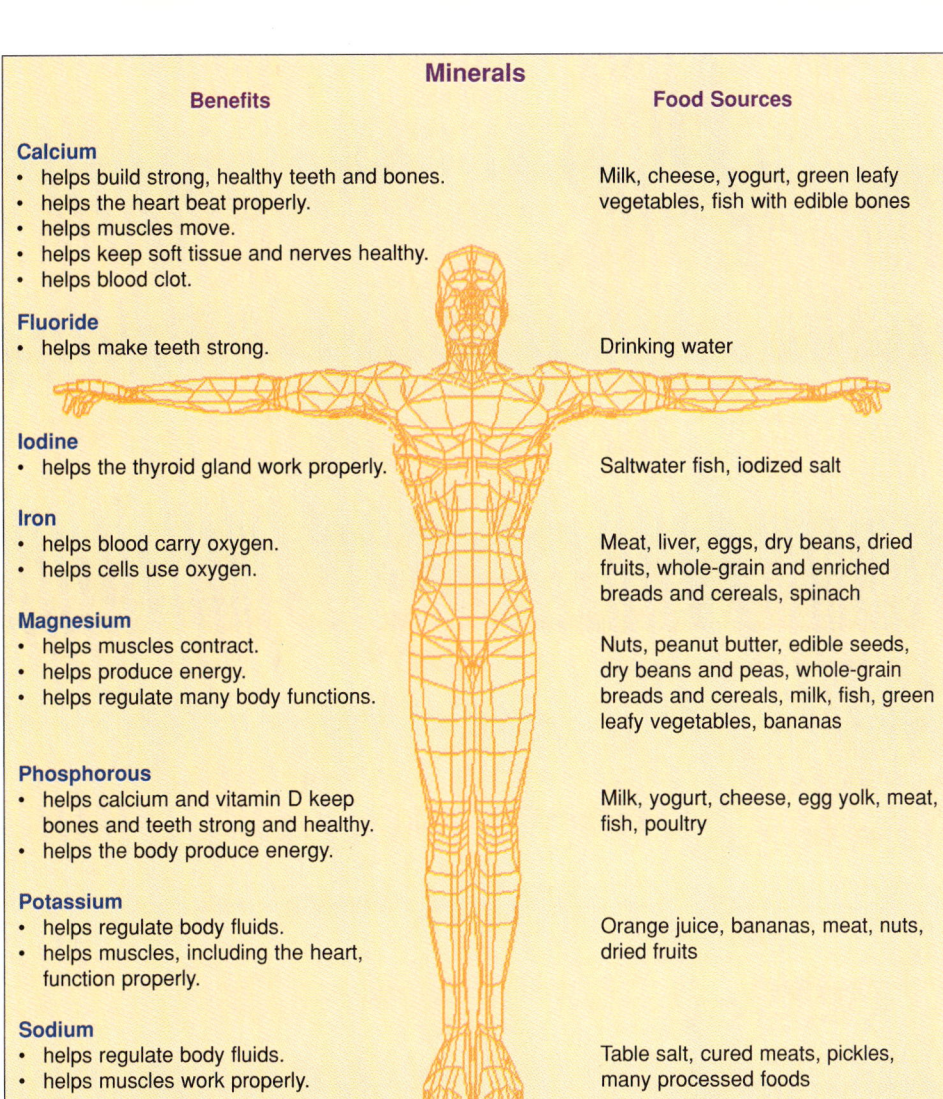

Minerals

Benefits	Food Sources
Calcium • helps build strong, healthy teeth and bones. • helps the heart beat properly. • helps muscles move. • helps keep soft tissue and nerves healthy. • helps blood clot.	Milk, cheese, yogurt, green leafy vegetables, fish with edible bones
Fluoride • helps make teeth strong.	Drinking water
Iodine • helps the thyroid gland work properly.	Saltwater fish, iodized salt
Iron • helps blood carry oxygen. • helps cells use oxygen.	Meat, liver, eggs, dry beans, dried fruits, whole-grain and enriched breads and cereals, spinach
Magnesium • helps muscles contract. • helps produce energy. • helps regulate many body functions.	Nuts, peanut butter, edible seeds, dry beans and peas, whole-grain breads and cereals, milk, fish, green leafy vegetables, bananas
Phosphorous • helps calcium and vitamin D keep bones and teeth strong and healthy. • helps the body produce energy.	Milk, yogurt, cheese, egg yolk, meat, fish, poultry
Potassium • helps regulate body fluids. • helps muscles, including the heart, function properly.	Orange juice, bananas, meat, nuts, dried fruits
Sodium • helps regulate body fluids. • helps muscles work properly.	Table salt, cured meats, pickles, many processed foods
Zinc • speeds healing of wounds. • affects growth, taste, appetite, and smell.	Meat, organ meats, eggs, poultry, seafood, cheese, milk

Vitamin C

Vitamin C helps keep you well. When you cut or bruise yourself, for example, vitamin C helps the wound heal. It keeps your gums healthy and helps your body fight infection. Good sources of vitamin C include such fruits as oranges, melons,

LESSON THREE: NUTRIENTS: VITAMINS, MINERALS, AND WATER

CHAPTER 10, LESSON 3

USING VISUALS

Have students use Figure 10.2 to identify the vitamins or minerals each of these foods contains: liver, pickles, bananas, yogurt, peanut butter, eggs, cod, salmon, spinach, salad dressing, fortified milk, broccoli, oranges, oatmeal, and carrots. Small groups might compete to find the greatest number of correct nutrients.

L2 Comparing

Display an assortment of cereal products. Have students study the food labels on the cereal products and read the labels to find out which B-complex vitamins each product contains. Ask them to compare products to find out which contains the most B-complex vitamins.

L2 Health Connection

Assign Cross-Curriculum Activity 11 in the TCR. Students learn about food sources from around the world in this activity.

L2 Home Economics

Explain that except for calcium, deficiencies of the major minerals are rare. However, some scientific studies find that many teens and adults do not have enough calcium in their diets. Tell students that if they do not consume enough calcium, their body will take the calcium it needs for body processes from their bones and teeth. Have students look through cookbooks to find five recipes that include ingredients high in calcium. Ask them to keep copies of these recipes for future use.

MORE ABOUT • • •

Minerals The benefits of reducing sodium intake have long been known. Recent studies have substantiated the idea that reduced salt intake results in a decrease in blood pressure and in cardiovascular disease. A not-so-obvious source of sodium is breakfast food. Many of the favorite breakfast cereals contain more sodium per 1-ounce serving than an equal amount of potato chips. Therefore, in trying to reduce one's sodium intake, it is important to watch for sodium even in sources that don't taste salty. Emphasize to students that they need to read the labels to know how much salt they are eating and how it fits into their total daily intake.

CHAPTER 10, LESSON 3

L1 Concept Mapping
Write the word "Water" on the chalkboard and circle it. Draw lines radiating from the circle and ask students to name all the foods they can that contain water.

L2 Cooperative Learning
Assign Cooperative Learning Activity 20 in the TCR. Students work together on a nutrient roundtable in this activity.

L2 Activity and Project Card
Allow time for students to complete Activity and Project Card 20, "Nutrient Campaign," in the TCR.

L3 Music
Have students choose a favorite song and write new lyrics that emphasize the importance of vitamins, minerals, and water in the diet.

Have students share the results of their brand comparisons with the class. Then have them work in pairs to create two food products—one that has exaggerated nutrition claims and another that is a truly healthy food. Have pairs share their product ideas with the class.

▲ Vitamin C helps your body heal wounds and keep them from becoming infected. Which foods contain vitamin C?

Not all foods labeled *low-fat,* or *sugar-free* are necessarily healthful. For instance, cereals made with whole grains may also be high in fat.
The next time you are at the market, compare several brands of an item to see which one is really healthiest.

and berries. Some dark green, leafy vegetables—such as spinach and broccoli—also contain vitamin C.

Vitamins D and E

Vitamin D helps your body use minerals, such as calcium and phosphorus. It is also essential for normal bone and tooth development. If you get enough sunlight, your body makes its own vitamin D. Foods that provide vitamin D include fortified milk, fish oils, beef, butter, and egg yolks.

To keep red blood cells healthy, your body needs vitamin E. You can find it in vegetable oils, yellow vegetables, grains, nuts, and green leafy vegetables.

The Function of Minerals

When you hear the word *minerals,* you may think of the minerals found in rocks and soil. Food also contains many **minerals,** which are *elements needed in small amounts for sturdy bones and teeth, healthy blood, and regular elimination of body wastes.* Like vitamins, minerals are essential to good health.

288   CHAPTER 10: NUTRITION AND YOU

MORE ABOUT •••

Iron Iron-deficiency anemia affects about one-fourth of the American population, especially young children, teenage girls, and women of childbearing age. These groups should be sure to eat plenty of iron-rich foods. Excellent sources of iron are liver, clams, lean beef, canned peas, and prune juice. Very good sources are sardines, corned beef, bean soup, cooked apricots, raisins, and peanuts. Good sources are egg yolks, tuna fish, cooked asparagus, broccoli, tomato juice, dates, bran flakes, cooked oatmeal, and enriched rice. Suggest that students evaluate the foods they have eaten in the past three days to determine which of the foods are good sources of iron.

Each one has a special job to perform. Look again at Figure 10.2, which shows some of the many functions of minerals.

Every day your body uses small amounts of minerals. Some, such as calcium, phosphorus, and magnesium, are needed in greater amounts than others. Trace elements, such as iron, zinc, and iodine, are needed only in tiny amounts. The minerals your body needs can be found in various types of food, many of which are listed in Figure 10.2.

Calcium

You need calcium to grow and to stay healthy. **Calcium** is *a mineral that helps build bones and teeth and ensures normal growth.* Young people need to get enough calcium to develop strong teeth and bones. Calcium is necessary throughout life, particularly for women, to reduce the risk of **osteoporosis,** *a condition in which bones gradually lose their mineral content and become weak and brittle.* Calcium also has other functions, including helping your muscles move and your heart beat. When you bleed, calcium aids vitamin K in helping the blood to clot. Calcium also helps to keep your nerves and soft tissues healthy. The best sources of calcium are dairy products.

Iron

Like calcium, iron is one of the most important nutrients. **Iron** is *an essential component of blood.* It helps carry the oxygen you breathe to your brain, your muscles, and all of your body's cells. Oxygen helps your body produce energy to keep body processes going and for physical activity. Females need about twice as much iron as males, because they lose blood during menstruation.

The best sources of iron are meat, poultry, dry beans, dried fruits, and dark green, leafy vegetables.

Water

Although you may not think of water as a nutrient, you can't live without it. Water helps regulate body functions and

▲ Your body needs calcium to build strong bones and teeth. What foods are good sources of calcium?

LESSON THREE: NUTRIENTS: VITAMINS, MINERALS, AND WATER **289**

TECHNOLOGY UPDATE

Dinner in Ten Minutes or Less Convenience foods have changed the way people cook dinner. Thanks to microwave ovens and better techniques of preserving food, dinner doesn't take nearly as long to prepare and cook as it used to. This convenience allows variety and choice for a busy lifestyle, and students can ensure that proper nutrients are included in every meal, even when time is short. Have students check labels on several different convenience foods. Have them read the ingredients and note whether the convenience foods contain the six kinds of nutrients.

CHAPTER 10, LESSON 3

L1 Student Workbook
Assign Activities 73 and 74 in the Student Workbook.

ASSESS

Evaluating the Lesson
Assign Reviewing Terms and Facts and Thinking Critically on page 290 to review the lesson; then assign the Lesson 3 Quiz in the TCR.

Reteaching
- Ask students to make a poster that illustrates to younger children the importance of vitamins, minerals, and water for a healthy body. Students' posters should explain the function of vitamins, minerals, and water and the types of food that are good sources of each. If possible, students might display their posters in the classrooms of the lower grades.
- Have students complete Reteaching Activity 10 in the TCR.
- Assign Concept Map 16 in the TCR.

Enrichment
- Suggest that students research the history of vitamin C to find out how it was discovered. Encourage the use of computer-encyclopedia programs for this research. Have them report their findings to the class.
- Assign Enrichment Activity 11 in the TCR.

CHAPTER 10, LESSON 3

Answers to Lesson 3 Review

1. Lost nutrients added back in the same or greater quantity than unprocessed food originally contained. Sentences will vary.
2. Vitamin C helps wounds heal, helps fight infection, and keeps gums healthy.
3. Iron in the blood helps carry oxygen to cells, and oxygen helps produce energy.
4. Any two: helps regulate body functions, helps digestion, carries nutrients to body cells, helps control body temperature, helps eliminate body wastes.
5. They control the way other nutrients in the body work.
6. Calcium helps teeth and bones grow stronger. Strong bones protect against bone disease during the adult years.
7. About two-thirds of the body is made up of water, and it is water that helps regulate body functions. If the body does not get enough water, it becomes dehydrated and this negatively affects body functions.
8. Students' charts will vary, but students should become aware of vitamins or minerals they are lacking in their diets.

CLOSE

Have students write a paragraph that explains the statement "Food becomes you." Have students share their paragraphs with the class.

290

When you exercise, it is important to replace the fluids you lose through sweat. How can you do that?

carries nutrients to body cells. It aids in digestion, removes wastes, and helps control your body temperature.

Because water is lost through perspiration, urine, and breath, you must replace it. You should drink between six and eight glasses of water each day in addition to other beverages. When you play basketball, tennis, or other active sports, your body perspires a great deal, and you need additional water.

LESSON THREE Review

Using complete sentences, answer the following questions on a separate sheet of paper.

Reviewing Terms and Facts

1. Vocabulary Define the term *enriched*. Use it in an original sentence.
2. Recall How does vitamin C keep you healthy?
3. Explain What is the purpose of iron in your body?
4. List Name two functions of water in your body.

Thinking Critically

5. Describe Why are vitamins and minerals called regulators?

6. Explain Why is it especially important for young people to get enough calcium in their diets?
7. Analyze The body can survive without food for longer than it can survive without water. What might be the reason for this?

Applying Concepts

8. Make a list of all the foods you ate and beverages you drank yesterday. Next to each item, write down the vitamins and minerals supplied by that food. (Refer to Figure 10.2 for help.) Are there any vitamins or minerals lacking in your diet? What foods could you eat to improve your nutrition?

290   CHAPTER 10: NUTRITION AND YOU

TECHNOLOGY UPDATE

Gene Splicing Gene splicing may lead to tastier and more nutritious foods in the future by combining a single gene from a fruit or vegetable with a beneficial gene from a mammal, a bacterium, or another plant. Scientists are presently testing more than fifty products that include virus-resistant cantaloupes, longer-lasting peppers, herbicide-resistant soybeans, higher-starch potatoes that absorb less fat, cooking oils with lower saturated fat content, and drought-resistant grain. When these foods hit the marketplace, they will not have a special label, unless in the process of production a substance is added to the food that is known to cause allergic reactions in certain people.

Chapter 10 Activities

A Global View — ETHNIC CUISINE

Have you ever eaten Italian, Mexican, or Chinese food? Has your family ever been to a Japanese, Greek, or Indian restaurant? Many popular ethnic foods have been brought to the United States from other countries.

TRY THIS!

Test your knowledge of ethnic cuisine by taking the quiz below. Match the foods on the left with the country or culture on the right.

1. burrito
2. croissant
3. grits
4. wonton soup
5. fettuccine Alfredo
6. pita
7. couscous
8. curry
9. baklava
10. sushi

a. North Africa
b. Japan
c. Greece
d. Middle East
e. India
f. France
g. China
h. United States
i. Mexico
j. Italy

Answers: 1. i; 2. f; 3. h; 4. g; 5. j; 6. d; 7. a; 8. e; 9. c; 10. b

Consumer Focus

The Vitamin Diet

You have probably seen advertisements for vitamin pills. Some ads suggest that vitamins alone can keep you healthy and energetic. Some even claim that certain diseases can be cured simply by taking vitamins. In reality, however, vitamin supplements are not a substitute for a nutritious diet.

Try This!

Draw a magazine ad for a nutrient-dense food. Think of a catchy logo to promote your product.

SOCIAL STUDIES CONNECTION

FOODS AROUND THE WORLD

Many factors influence the kinds of foods that people eat. One major factor is where people live. Climate, soil conditions, and availability of water determine which foods can be grown. Certain regions have typical dishes. Rice is eaten with different varieties of beans in parts of Latin America, and Italy is famous for its pasta dishes. Many Indian curry dishes are flavored with a mixture of herbs and spices called *masala*.

 Follow Up

1. What are the favorite ethnic or cultural foods among people in your class? As a class, make a chart or map showing how many parts of the world influence your diet.

2. In small groups, discuss cultural food traditions in your families. What foods have been passed down by grandparents that have become family favorites? Have some families continued to eat more of these traditional foods than others?

CHAPTER 10 ACTIVITIES **291**

CHAPTER 10 Activities

A Global View

Discuss with students how various factors influence food choices around the world, including people's culture and religion. Many religions have dietary laws or traditions. Explain that Buddhism, for example, encourages its followers to avoid meat and alcohol. Jewish dietary laws spell out the kinds of meat and fish that may be eaten. Islamic law does not allow the use of pork. In trying dishes from other cultures students may experience very different flavors and combinations of foods that have developed because of these traditions.

Consumer Focus

Remind students that to maintain good health, it is important to get the vitamins and minerals your body needs from the foods you eat. As students do the activity, encourage them to develop advertisements for foods that they would choose to eat themselves. Their ads should demonstrate their knowledge of the importance of choosing healthful, nutritious foods.

Teaching the SOCIAL STUDIES CONNECTION

Have students work in small groups and use the information in the feature as a starting point for a mural on Foods in Other Countries. Students each select a country and research the foods that are prevalent in the diets of the people who live there. They might then put this information on index cards and, using a world map, use strings extending from each country to connect to the index cards.

 **Answers to Follow-Up**

1. Answers will vary, but have students discuss their responses and explain their maps.
2. Allow groups to discuss traditions and ideas.

CHAPTER 10 REVIEW

Checking Comprehension

Use the Chapter Summary and the Chapter 10 Review to help students go over the most important ideas presented in Chapter 10.

Answers to Words to Know

1. The foods a person eats.
2. Unit of heat that measures the energy available in food.
3. The process of breaking down food into a form the body can use.
4. In proteins.
5. Whole grains, vegetables, fruits with edible skins or seeds, dry beans and peas, nuts, and seeds.
6. Because they contain all of the edible grain—outer layer, bran, and germ—which has the most fiber and nutrients.
7. Because it is needed to build bones and teeth and ensure normal growth.
8. Because it helps carry oxygen to the body, which helps produce energy.

CHAPTER 10 REVIEW

Chapter Summary

- Eating nutritious foods can help you look and feel your best.
- Food provides you with energy for physical and mental activity. A healthful diet also protects you from illness.
- Hunger is the physical need to eat, whereas appetite is the desire to eat. You can have an appetite without being hungry.
- Your food choices are influenced by many factors, including family, cultural background, religion, and friends.
- To stay healthy, your body needs six kinds of nutrients: proteins, carbohydrates, fats, vitamins, minerals, and water.
- Proteins are needed to build, maintain, and repair your body.
- Carbohydrates, or starches and sugars, provide energy. Fiber is not a nutrient, but it helps move food through the digestive system and eliminate wastes.
- Fats provide energy, help keep your skin smooth, help your nervous system work, and carry several vitamins. Unsaturated fats are more healthful than saturated fats.
- Vitamins are substances your body needs in small quantities to regulate its functions.
- Minerals help your body work properly. The minerals your body needs, including calcium and iron, are found in a variety of foods.
- Water is essential for life. It carries nutrients to body cells and aids in digestion, temperature control, and removal of wastes.

Words to Know

Using complete sentences, answer the following questions on a separate sheet of paper.

1. Explain what a person's *diet* consists of.
2. What is a *calorie*?
3. Define the term *digestion*.
4. Where can you find *amino acids*?
5. Which foods contain *fiber*?
6. Why are *whole grains* good fiber sources?
7. Explain why you need *calcium* to stay healthy.
8. Why does your body need *iron*?

Review Questions

Using complete sentences, answer the following questions on a separate sheet of paper.

1. Name four factors that affect the way you look and feel.
2. What happens if you eat food that has more calories than your body needs?
3. Explain how each of the following factors influences your food likes and dislikes: family, advertising, and health.

292   CHAPTER 10: NUTRITION AND YOU

EXTRA CREDIT PROJECT

School-to-Work Students may prepare for jobs in the food industry by finding out where different foods originate. Have teams of students begin by listing ingredients in a favorite meal or recipe. Tell them the first step is to determine where each of the food ingredients is grown or made. The next task is to identify what steps are needed in the collection, preparation, packaging, transport, marketing, and serving of the food items. Finally, have students list the job title or description of each person involved in the process of getting the foods to the table. Once students have compiled the list of job titles, have them identify any jobs they might be interested in pursuing.

CHAPTER 10 REVIEW

4. What foods contain carbohydrates?
5. Explain what might happen if a person's diet has too little fiber.
6. Why do you need to drink water every day?

Thinking Critically

Using complete sentences, answer the following questions on a separate sheet of paper.

1. **Explain** Do you think that a person can be healthy if he or she doesn't eat meat? Why or why not?
2. **Analyze** Why do you think that some people overeat?
3. **Contrast** What is the difference between a complete protein and an incomplete protein?
4. **Apply** Why should you avoid foods that contain added sugar?
5. **Suggest** How can you get enough calcium in your diet if you don't like milk?

Cooperative Learning

1. Bring in a food advertisement. In groups of three or four, evaluate the advertisements by answering the following questions: How does the advertisement try to influence your food choices? Is it successful? Would you buy the food? Why or why not?
2. In groups of four or five, research a nutrient. Write an analysis that includes the benefits of the nutrient, the problems that result from a lack of it, and the foods that contain it. Find two recipes that use a food or foods rich in that nutrient. Share your group's findings with the class.

Family & Community

1. Examine two or three convenience foods that you and your family eat regularly for dinner. Read the labels to determine which nutrients can be found in these foods. Do they contain saturated or unsaturated fats? Discuss with family members whether those convenience foods are healthful choices for your family.
2. Take a survey of ten friends and family members to find out what factors most influence their food choices. Ask each person to name his or her three favorite foods and explain why they are favorites. Which factor influenced the most people? What conclusions can you draw from your survey?

Building A Portfolio

1. Write down everything you eat for one day. You can use this textbook and information from labels or a computer program to categorize the foods as proteins, carbohydrates, or fats. Then break each item down further as complete protein, incomplete protein, starch, sugar, fiber, saturated fat, or unsaturated fat. Is your diet varied? Are you getting too much or too little of any food category? Write a paragraph summarizing your results, and put it in your portfolio.
2. Write a paragraph about a family food tradition. Explain how the tradition has been passed down from generation to generation. Put your paragraph in your portfolio.

Chapter 10 Review **293**

CHAPTER 10 REVIEW

Answers to Review Questions

1. Food, exercise, rest, and personal hygiene.
2. The extra energy is stored as fat.
3. Answers will vary, but students should explain how each of the factors influences them.
4. Any foods containing starches and sugars, such as grains, potatoes, dry beans, corn, nuts.
5. Lack of fiber slows digestion and may cause constipation and infrequent bowel movements.
6. Water helps regulate body functions, carries nutrients to the body cells, aids digestion, helps control body temperature, and helps remove wastes. Since the body loses water in sweat, urine, and breath, this loss must be replaced or the body becomes dehydrated and weak.

Evaluate

Use the Chapter 10 Test in the TCR, or construct your own test using the Testmaker Software.

CLOSE

Have students apply their knowledge of the chapter's content by completing one of the alternative assessment activities listed under Family and Community or Building a Portfolio.

Answers to Thinking Critically

1. Answers will vary, but should focus on the fact that a person cannot be healthy if healthful foods are not eaten, since nutrients in food keep the body functioning properly.
2. They eat too much of unhealthy foods and do not just eat to satisfy hunger or appetite.
3. Complete proteins are foods that come from animals—meat, fish, poultry, milk, cheese—and that contain all the amino acids. Incomplete proteins come from plant foods—dry beans and peas, nuts, and grains—but lack one or more of the essential amino acids.
4. Because these foods are high in calories but low in other nutrients.
5. By eating more cheese; yogurt; dark green, leafy vegetables; and fish with bones.

293

Planning Guide
Chapter 11 Developing Healthy Habits

LESSON 1	Pages	FEATURES	CLASSROOM RESOURCES
The Food Guide Pyramid	296–302	*Try This:* Eyeballing Serving Sizes	Cross Curriculum 12 Lesson 1 Quiz Transparency 47, "The Food Guide Pyramid" Student Workbook Activities 75, 76
LESSON 2 **Following Healthy Guidelines**	303–309	*Tips for Living:* Reducing the Fat *Try This:* Reducing Salt in Your Diet	Concept Map 17 Enrichment 12 Lesson 2 Quiz Transparency 48, "The Picture of Wellness" Student Workbook Activity 77
LESSON 3 **Snacking and Eating Out**	310–315	*Try This:* Snack Attacks *Tips for Living:* Where's the Fat?	Activity and Project Card 21, "Restaurant Art" Cooperative Learning 21 Food Lab Activity 1, "Snack Smorgasbord" Lesson 3 Quiz Peer Pressure and Decision Making 23 Transparency 49, "Snacks: Empty-Calories or Nutrient-Dense?" Student Workbook Activities 78, 79
LESSON 4 **Exercise and Weight Control**	316–322	*Tips for Living:* Calories for Fitness *Skills in Action:* Starting a Fitness Program	Activity and Project Card 22, "Health Tips Pamphlet" Concept Map 18 Cooperative Learning 22 Enrichment 13 Food Lab Activity 2, "High-Speed Breakfasts" Lesson 4 Quiz Peer Pressure and Decision Making 24 Transparency 50, "Fitness: The Choices Are Yours!" Student Workbook Activities 80, 81

CHAPTER 11 RESOURCES

Chapter 11 Test
Reteaching 11
Study Guide 11, *Reteaching*
Testmaker Software

Performance Assessment Activity

Ask students to prepare survey questions to give to friends and acquaintances as inventories about their diet and exercise habits. Each student should prepare questions that focus on the Dietary Guidelines and tips for including exercise. Students should request that questions be answered anonymously. When students have received the completed surveys, organize the class into small groups. Have each group use the information from the surveys to create posters that convey the importance of developing healthy habits. Display completed posters in the classroom.

School-to-Work

Ask students to research jobs that are related to food, nutrition, and exercise. These jobs might include food scientists, farmers, cafeteria or restaurant managers, dietitians, sports medicine specialists, physical therapists, coaches, or fitness trainers. Ask students to find out the personal qualifications, skills, and education a person must have for the job they chose to research. Ask them to share their information with classmates. Survey the class to find out how many students might be interested in each job presented.

Family & Community

Ask students to bring in a copy of a recipe for a healthful favorite family dish. Have students work in small groups to evaluate the dish for its nutritional value. Have them suggest other foods that might be included in a menu to make a nutritious, balanced meal. Combine the recipes and the suggestions for accompanying foods to make a cookbook. Encourage students to take the cookbook home and share the meal plans with their families.

Resources for the Teacher

DeLorme, R., and F. Stransky. *Fitness and Fallacies.* Dubuque, IA: Kendall/Hunt Publishing Company, 1990.

Snyder, S.H., M.D., ed. *Nutrition and the Brain.* New York: Chelsea House, 1992.

A Practical Guide for Parents: Advertising, Nutrition, and Kids (Pamphlet). IFIC Publications. 1100 Connecticut Ave., N.W., Suite 430, Washington, D.C. 20036.

Readings for the Student

Jacobson, M.F., et al. *Safe Food: Eating Wisely in a Risky World.* Los Angeles: Living Planet Press, 1991.

Lee, Sally. *New Theories on Diet and Nutrition.* New York: Franklin Watts, Inc., 1990.

Salter, C.A. *Looking Good, Eating Right: A Sensible Guide to Proper Nutrition and Weight Loss.* New York: Millbrook Press, 1991.

Multimedia Resources

Diet: Health and Disease (Videocassette). Human Relations Media.

Nutrition for Health: The Food Pyramid/Wellness: Moderation in Eating (Videodisc). AIMS Media.

OUT OF TIME?

If time does not permit thorough teaching of this chapter, you may wish to use:

- Teens Making a Difference, page 295
- Tips for Living, pages 307, 313, 318
- Try This, pages 297, 309, 311
- Skills in Action, page 320
- Young Living Activities, page 323
- Chapter Summary, page 324

CHAPTER 11
Developing Healthy Habits

Chapter Overview

Chapter 11 explores the relationship among diet, exercise, and rest. The chapter emphasizes students' involvement in making healthy choices.

LESSON 1 identifies the foods that make up the five food groups in the Food Guide Pyramid.

LESSON 2 focuses on how the Food Guide Pyramid can be used to promote health, emphasizing ways to reduce sugar, salt, and fat in the diet.

LESSON 3 explores how to choose healthful snacks and how to make healthy choices when eating out.

LESSON 4 explains why fitness is important and what students can do to maintain a healthy weight.

Introducing the Chapter

Have students skim the chapter and lesson titles and the photographs in the chapter. Based on the scan of the chapter, ask each student to write three questions that they think will be answered in the chapter. Tell them that Chapter 11 provides practical information that they can use to develop healthy habits.

Chapter Motivator

Ask students to complete the following statement: "To get the proper foods and the right amount of exercise, I. . . ." Call on volunteers to read their statements, and record the responses in the form of a concept web, with "Developing Healthy Habits" labeled in the hub. Have students compare their responses with the information in Chapter 11.

CHAPTER 11
Developing Healthy Habits

LESSON ONE
The Food Guide Pyramid

LESSON TWO
Following Healthy Guidelines

LESSON THREE
Snacking and Eating Out

LESSON FOUR
Exercise and Weight Control

KEY TO ABILITY LEVELS

Teaching strategies that appear throughout the chapter have been identified by one of three codes to give you an idea of their suitability for students of varying learning styles and abilities.

L1 Level 1 strategies should be within the ability range of all students. Often full class participation is required. Teacher direction is usually needed.

L2 Level 2 strategies are for average to above-average students or for small groups. Some teacher direction is necessary.

L3 Level 3 strategies are designed for students able and willing to work independently. Minimal teacher direction is necessary.

TEENS MAKING A DIFFERENCE
The School Store

The student council at Kennedy Middle School operates a student store. The store sells pencils, notebook paper, school caps and T-shirts—and candy bars.

After learning about good nutrition in class, a majority of the council members voted to stop selling candy bars. The council decided to sell apples, oranges, and small cans of fruit juice instead.

At first, some students grumbled about not being able to buy candy at school. However, many more students said that they liked the tasty red apples and the sweet, juicy oranges. The fruit juice, they said, really hit the spot.

Try THIS!
Consider how good nutrition is promoted in your school. Think of changes you could suggest that would improve students' nutrition.

CHAPTER 11

TEENS MAKING A DIFFERENCE

Have students read "The School Store." Ask them to identify other foods rich in nutrients that could be substituted for snacks such as chocolate bars.

Then ask students to work in small groups to complete TRY THIS! Have a representative from each group present the group's suggestions to the rest of the class.

BLOCK SCHEDULING

The following Teacher Classroom Resources are suggested for use in classrooms with Block Scheduling.
- Activity and Project Card 21, "Restaurant Art"
- Activity and Project Card 22, "Health Tips Pamphlet"
- Cooperative Learning 21, "And Now, a Word About Snacks"
- Cooperative Learning 22, "Working on Working Out"

TECHNOLOGY IN THE CLASSROOM

CD-ROMs CD-ROM discs contain data that is read on a CD-ROM drive. The advantage of CD-ROM discs is that they can contain huge amounts of information that would be impossible to handle on other types of storage media. This high capacity for storage allows software companies to create complex games and huge databases. Hundreds of CD-ROMs are available for use in the Family and Consumer Sciences classes. Teachers can choose among information discs such as encyclopedias and dictionaries, as well as discs that deal with topics such as interior decorating and cooking.

LESSON ONE
The Food Guide Pyramid

FOCUS

Lesson Objectives

After studying this lesson, students should be able to
- recognize the Food Guide Pyramid.
- list the five basic food groups and describe where they appear in the Food Guide Pyramid.
- explain how the Food Guide Pyramid can be used to plan healthy meals.

Motivating Activity

Ask students to imagine they have just won a contest at a large grocery store. As a winner, they can select enough food to feed a family of four for a week. Ask students to write a grocery shopping list of the items they would choose.

Introducing the Lesson

Have students share their responses to the Motivating Activity. Have them group the items in categories and discuss the categories they made. Tell them that this lesson discusses the five food groups and the nutrients they provide.

Introducing *Words to Know*

Ask each student to write a sentence for each word in the Words to Know list. When they have finished, ask them to form small groups and share their sentences with group members. Ask each group to develop a definition for each word. Then have each group share their definitions.

LESSON ONE
The Food Guide Pyramid

Food Guide Pyramid
food group
serving
vegetarian

DISCOVER...
- the Food Guide Pyramid.
- the foods that make up the five food groups.
- how to use the Food Guide Pyramid to plan healthful meals.

Knowing which nutrients your body needs is a first step toward a healthful diet, but how do you know which foods you should eat to get those nutrients? How much of each kind of food should you eat? That is where the Food Guide Pyramid comes in handy.

296   CHAPTER 11: DEVELOPING HEALTHY HABITS

CLASSROOM RESOURCES FOR LESSON 1

 Blackline Masters
Cross Curriculum 12
Lesson 1 Quiz

 Transparencies
Transparency 47, "The Food Guide Pyramid"

 Student Workbook
Activities 75, 76

What Is the Food Guide Pyramid?

The **Food Guide Pyramid** is *a set of guidelines to help you choose what and how much to eat to get the nutrients you need.* It is easy to plan healthful meals if you follow the Food Guide Pyramid. You can use it to choose foods that suit your tastes and lifestyle as well as to meet your nutritional needs.

The Food Groups

Look carefully at the Food Guide Pyramid in **Figure 11.1**. Notice that it is divided into six sections. Each section lists foods from a general category. *Each category of foods on the Food Guide Pyramid* is called a **food group.** Notice also that the sections are not all the same size. As you move up from the base of the Pyramid, the sections get smaller. This

Try This!

You can learn to "eyeball" correct serving sizes.
• An ounce of cheese is about the size of a walnut.
• One-half cup of rice or pasta is about the size of a tennis ball.
• A three-ounce serving of meat or fish is about the size of a deck of cards.

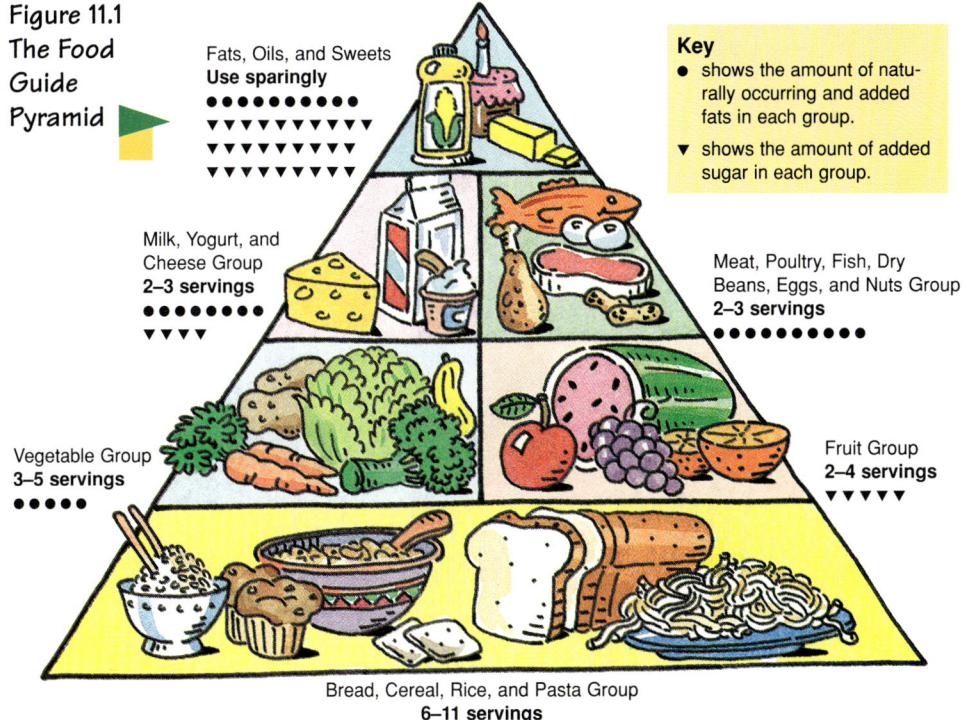

Figure 11.1 The Food Guide Pyramid

Fats, Oils, and Sweets — Use sparingly

Milk, Yogurt, and Cheese Group — 2–3 servings

Meat, Poultry, Fish, Dry Beans, Eggs, and Nuts Group — 2–3 servings

Vegetable Group — 3–5 servings

Fruit Group — 2–4 servings

Bread, Cereal, Rice, and Pasta Group — 6–11 servings

Key
● shows the amount of naturally occurring and added fats in each group.
▼ shows the amount of added sugar in each group.

LESSON ONE: THE FOOD GUIDE PYRAMID 297

HOME AND COMMUNITY CONNECTION

Guest Speaker If possible, invite a dietitian or nutritionist from a local hospital to speak to the class. Encourage students to prepare questions in advance to ask the individual. Questions should focus on how the dietitian uses the Food Guide Pyramid and the five food groups to plan healthful meals for patients in the hospital. Students should use the dietitian's responses to their questions to prepare a one-page written summary of the presentation.

CHAPTER 11, LESSON 1

TEACH

Try This!

To help students better visualize serving sizes, pass around a walnut, a tennis ball, and a deck of playing cards. Discuss whether the servings they eat are larger, smaller, or about the same size as the items being passed around.

L1 Discussion

Discuss with students the importance of each food group. Reinforce the idea that each group provides nutrients that are necessary for good health. Stress that foods from one group cannot be substituted for those in another group. Ask students to explain why fats, oils, and sweets are at the top of the pyramid.

DID YOU KNOW ?

Vegetarians prefer not to eat meat, poultry, or fish. Strict vegetarians eat only foods from plants—not even eggs or milk products. To prevent deficits of nutrients that are found in animal products, such as iron, vegetarians need to eat other foods that are rich in these nutrients. These foods include dried fruits, legumes, leafy greens, and enriched grains.

L1 Using Transparencies

Present Color Transparency 47, "The Food Guide Pyramid," in the TCR. Use this overhead visual to reinforce concepts from this lesson.

CHAPTER 11, LESSON 1

L1 Applying
Ask students to think of additional specific examples of foods they eat from each food group. Then have them create word webs for each group.

L1 Discussion
Ask students to discuss some of the foods they think Americans eat that are considered fatty. Help students share what they know about high-fat foods and encourage them to suggest alternative foods that are fat-free or low in fat.

L3 Research
Have students research special diets for people with food allergies or enzyme deficiencies and report their findings to the class. Students may wish to use computer on-line resources to do their research.

DID YOU KNOW?

The labeling on 2 percent milk was changed from "low fat" to "reduced fat" because 2 percent milk contains 5 grams of fat per serving.

---

tells you at a glance which groups of food should be more plentiful in your diet and which should make up a smaller part of it. The larger the section of the Pyramid a food group occupies, the more servings of that group you need to eat. A **serving** is *a portion of food that a person would be likely to eat at one time* (such as one apple or one slice of bread).

The five lower sections of the Pyramid show the five food groups. Each group provides you with some of the nutrients necessary for good health. The five food groups include the

- Bread, Cereal, Rice, and Pasta Group.
- Vegetable Group.
- Fruit Group.
- Milk, Yogurt, and Cheese Group.
- Meat, Poultry, Fish, Dry Beans, Eggs, and Nuts Group.

The tip, or smallest section, of the Pyramid includes fats, oils, and sweets—items that you should eat only in small amounts. **Figure 11.2** on pages 300 and 301 provides more information about the five food groups.

Making wise food choices is easy if you use the Food Guide Pyramid to plan meals.

Using the Food Guide Pyramid

Kimberly has invited two of her friends to sleep over on Friday night. This afternoon Kimberly and her mother are planning the meals. Kimberly's mom suggests that Kimberly plan to serve a snack on Friday night as well as dinner because the girls will probably stay up later than usual. That means that Kimberly has to decide what foods to eat for three meals, and she wants to make each one different and interesting. Saturday's breakfast will be easy. Everyone likes fresh fruit and cereal or bagels. What about dinner, though? Where can Kimberly get some ideas?

298 CHAPTER 11: DEVELOPING HEALTHY HABITS

MEETING STUDENT DIVERSITY

Physically Challenged Good nutrition is especially important for individuals with disabilities. For example, it is crucial that individuals with diabetes mellitus maintain a well-balanced diet in order to prevent both acute and long-term medical problems. People with food allergies must know what foods to avoid, regardless of peer pressure. Many less-active physically challenged individuals who lead more sedentary lives must select their foods carefully to ensure proper nutrition while limiting their calorie intake to avoid obesity. Ask physically challenged students to volunteer to share their special dietary concerns with classmates.

Planning Meals

The Food Guide Pyramid is a great source of ideas. It tells you which foods fit into which group and how many servings of each group you should eat in a day.

Kimberly and her mom decide to plan a dinner that will require very little last-minute preparation. After looking over the Food Guide Pyramid, they build the meals from the base up and make sure that they include all five food groups. They choose chicken sandwiches on whole-wheat bread and a platter of raw vegetables for dinner. Because Kimberly wants to serve brownies for dessert, she decides to have fruit and yogurt shakes as a nutritious late-night snack.

As you look over the Food Guide Pyramid, you will notice that there is a range of recommended servings for each of the five food groups. A range is given because different people have different nutritional needs. People who are physically active, for example, need to eat more than less active people. The important point to remember is that you need to eat enough servings of all five food groups to get the nutrients you need.

Another fact to keep in mind is that many dishes are made up of foods from more than one food group. For example, spaghetti with meatballs and tomato sauce includes foods from the bread group (pasta), the meat group (meatballs), and the vegetable group (tomatoes).

People who follow special diets may wonder if the Food Guide Pyramid can help them plan meals. For example, a **vegetarian** is *a person who eats mainly fruits, vegetables, and grains.* Some vegetarians eat fish and dairy products. Others do not eat any animal products, not even dairy foods. A person who follows such a diet must be especially careful to get all of the vitamins, minerals, and protein needed for good health.

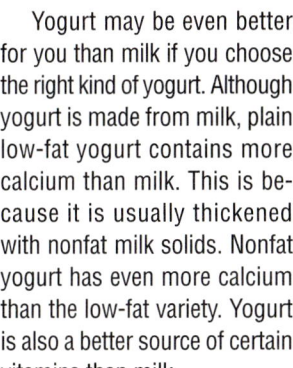

By trading off, you can eat foods with small amounts of fat and sugar while still getting the nutrients you need. What trade-offs might you make in your food choices?

Making Trade-offs

Remember how Kimberly served fruit and yogurt shakes as a snack so that she could have brownies for dessert? She made a trade-off, or chose a food that is lower in sugar at snack time so that she could serve one that is high in sugar at dinner.

LESSON ONE: THE FOOD GUIDE PYRAMID 299

COOPERATIVE LEARNING

Planning a Menu Have students imagine they have been placed in charge of planning the menu for their family for one week. Allow them to work in small groups to plan menus for breakfasts, lunches, and dinners for seven days. Tell students that each day's meals have to include a balanced number of servings from all five food groups. Tell them that as they plan their menus they should keep track of the number of recommended servings. Students should also make sure to limit the fat and sugar content of the foods and to strive for a variety of foods. When menus are completed, encourage groups to share menus and to comment on each other's ideas.

CHAPTER 11, LESSON 1

L1 Discussion
Ask students to tell which food groups each of the foods chosen by Kimberly and her mother belong to. Then ask them to name at least two nutrients found in each of those foods.

L2 Science Connection
Assign Cross-Curriculum Activity 12 in the TCR. Students learn about vegetarian diet requirements in this activity.

DID YOU KNOW
Yogurt may be even better for you than milk if you choose the right kind of yogurt. Although yogurt is made from milk, plain low-fat yogurt contains more calcium than milk. This is because it is usually thickened with nonfat milk solids. Nonfat yogurt has even more calcium than the low-fat variety. Yogurt is also a better source of certain vitamins than milk.

L2 Planning Menus
Have small groups of students research foods associated with a particular region or a food custom of a particular region. Have each group plan a menu for a balanced meal based on what they learned. Have groups share their menu with the class. If possible, plan a day for students to bring examples of foods or food customs to share and demonstrate.

CHAPTER 11, LESSON 1

USING VISUALS
Have students study the five food groups in Figure 11.2. Ask them where each of the groups fits into the Food Guide Pyramid shown in Figure 11.1 on page 297. Ask them to tell how many servings a day they should have from each group, and give examples of a serving. Then ask from which group they need the most servings every day.

L3 Research
Planning vegetarian meals that are balanced can be more challenging, since foods must be combined to provide the proper combinations of essential amino acids. Have students look in a library for books about vegetarian cooking that contain recipes for vegetarian meals. Have students search computer on-line sources as part of their research. Have them plan a menu of vegetarian meals for one day and share the information with the class.

L2 Applying
Ask students to make a list of their five favorite foods. Then have them work in small groups to determine how many of their lists include foods from more than one food group, and list the food groups represented by that food. Have groups share their information with the class.

Figure 11.2
The Five Food Groups
For a healthful diet, choose foods from each of the five food groups. What is an example of a single serving from the Bread, Cereal, Rice, and Pasta Group?

The Bread, Cereal, Rice, and Pasta Group
Nutrients
Carbohydrates, iron, B-complex vitamins
Servings Per Day
6–11
Sample Serving Sizes
1 slice bread
½ bagel or ½ English muffin
½ cup (125 mL) cooked cereal, rice, or pasta
1 ounce (28 g) ready-to-eat cereal

The Vegetable Group
Nutrients
Vitamins A and C, iron, and fiber
Servings Per Day
3–5
Sample Serving Sizes
½ cup (125 mL) chopped raw or cooked vegetables
1 cup (250 mL) raw, leafy vegetables

300   CHAPTER 11: DEVELOPING HEALTHY HABITS

MORE ABOUT • • •

Different Kinds of Fat Although fats should be used in moderation, some fat is essential in the diet. Fats serve as a carrier for the fat-soluble vitamins—vitamins A, D, E, and K. They provide an essential fatty acid—linoleic acid. Fats are the most concentrated source of energy for the body. Saturated fats are those that come from animal sources; they are generally solid at room temperature. Unsaturated fats come from plant sources and are usually liquid at room temperature. Unsaturated fats are recommended to be included in moderate amounts in a well-balanced diet. Ask students to generate a list of various types of saturated and unsaturated fats.

The Fruit Group

Nutrients
Vitamins A and C, carbohydrates, and fiber

Servings Per Day
2–4

Sample Serving Sizes
1 medium apple, banana, or orange
¾ cup (175 mL) fruit juice
½ cup (125 mL) canned fruit
¼ cup (50 mL) dried fruit

The Milk, Yogurt, and Cheese Group

Nutrients
Calcium, phosphorus, riboflavin, vitamins A and D

Servings Per Day
2–3

Sample Serving Sizes
1 cup (250 mL) milk or yogurt
1½–2 ounces (42–56 g) cheese

The Meat, Poultry, Fish, Dry Beans, Eggs, and Nuts Group

Nutrients
Protein, iron, B vitamins

Servings Per Day
2–3

Sample Serving Sizes
2–3 ounces (56–84 g) cooked lean meat, poultry, or fish

Foods that count as 1 ounce (28 g) of meat
½ cup (125 mL) cooked dry beans
1 egg
2 tablespoons (30 mL) peanut butter
⅓ cup (75 mL) nuts

LESSON ONE: THE FOOD GUIDE PYRAMID **301**

COOPERATIVE LEARNING

Food Group Teams Divide the class into four teams and have two teams compete with one another. Have one team name a food group. Have each person on the opposing team name a food in that group. Set a time limit for each team to answer. If each person successfully names a food, the teams trade roles.

CHAPTER 11, LESSON 1

L1 Discussion
Ask each student to name a food they like that is high in sugar, fat, and/or salt. List the foods on the chalkboard as they are named. Then ask students to suggest a more nutritious trade-off for each food.

L1 Student Workbook
Assign Activities 75 and 76 in the Student Workbook.

ASSESS

Evaluating the Lesson
Assign Reviewing Terms and Facts and Thinking Critically on page 302 to review the lesson; then assign the Lesson 1 Quiz in the TCR.

Reteaching
- Have students prepare meal plans for themselves for one day. Their meal plans should include the recommended number of servings from each food group.
- Have students complete Reteaching Activity 11 in the TCR.

Enrichment
Provide each student with a copy of a restaurant menu. You might wish to ask students to bring in menus from local restaurants for this activity. Ask them to plan meals for one day from the choices on the menu. Remind them that their meal plans should include the recommended number of servings from each food group.

CHAPTER 11, LESSON 1

Answers to Lesson 1 Review

1. The Food Guide Pyramid is a guideline to help people choose what and how much to eat to get the nutrients they need.

2. A food group is a category of foods on the Food Guide Pyramid. The five food groups are (1) grains, (2) vegetables, (3) fruits, (4) milk products, and (5) meats, poultry, fish, eggs, and dry beans.

3. All the foods are high in protein, and most include important vitamins and minerals.

4. Because people have different nutritional needs.

5. It is a useful strategy to make sure you get enough servings of foods from the food group at the bottom because you need the greatest number of servings from this group. You can then add the fewer servings needed from the food groups farther up the pyramid.

6. Meal examples will vary, but should include foods from all five groups.

7. A person following a special diet might not get the proper number of servings from each of the food groups.

8. Charts and comparisons with the Food Guide Pyramid will vary, but need to include an analysis of the students' eating habits and needed changes in those habits.

CLOSE

Ask students to name the five food groups, tell their position on the Food Guide Pyramid, and summarize the major nutrients found in each group.

Trading off allows you to have small amounts of the foods at the tip of the Food Guide Pyramid while still eating a nutritious diet.

Checking Food Labels

An easy way to figure out what foods can be traded off is to check the nutrition labels on food packages. These labels tell you the amount of each essential nutrient as well as the amount of fat, sugar, and sodium (salt) in each serving of a particular food. In addition, the labels list the number of calories per serving. You will learn more about nutrition labels in Chapter 13, Lesson 2.

Developing healthy eating habits now will contribute to good health throughout your life.

LESSON ONE *Review*

Using complete sentences, answer the following questions on a separate sheet of paper.

Reviewing Terms and Facts

1. Recall What is the Food Guide Pyramid?

2. Vocabulary Define the term *food group*. List the five food groups.

3. Identify What nutrients are provided by the milk, yogurt, and cheese group?

4. Explain Why is a range of servings given in the Food Guide Pyramid?

Thinking Critically

5. Analyze Explain why it is useful to plan a meal by starting at the bottom of the Food Guide Pyramid and going up.

6. Apply Give an example of a meal that includes foods from all five food groups. Explain your choices.

7. Interpret Why could a person who follows a special diet be at risk of not getting the proper nutrients?

Applying Concepts

8. Write down all the foods you ate yesterday. Next to each item, note the amount you ate. Compare your diet with the Food Guide Pyramid. Add up the number of servings you had from each food group and check against the suggested number. How well did your diet follow the guidelines? Write down some possible ways of improving your diet.

302 CHAPTER 11: DEVELOPING HEALTHY HABITS

COOPERATIVE LEARNING

Reading Food Labels Divide the class into small groups and give each group a different kind of cereal package. Ask them to use the food label to determine serving size, number of servings per container, the calories per serving, percentages of nutrients, and ingredients. Then have groups exchange cereal packages and repeat the procedure. After each group has examined the label on each package, discuss which cereal they think would be the best choice as part of a healthy breakfast.

LESSON TWO
Following Healthy Guidelines

DISCOVER...
- how the Dietary Guidelines can be used to promote health.
- ways to cut down on fat, sugar, and salt in the diet.

Andrew's health is especially important to him. He wants to be a major league pitcher some day. Andrew knows that to be at his best he needs to feel good physically and mentally. You could say that Andrew works for wellness. **Wellness** is *a high level of overall health.* The foods you eat play an essential role in determining your level of wellness.

WORDS TO KNOW

wellness
Dietary Guidelines
balanced diet
moderation
sodium

LESSON TWO: FOLLOWING HEALTHY GUIDELINES   303

CLASSROOM RESOURCES FOR LESSON 2

 Blackline Masters
Concept Map 17
Enrichment 12
Lesson 2 Quiz

 Transparencies
Transparency 48, "The Picture of Wellness"

 **Student Workbook**
Activity 77

LESSON TWO
Following Healthy Guidelines

FOCUS

Lesson Objectives
After studying this lesson, students should be able to
- identify how the Dietary Guidelines can be used to promote health.
- describe how to avoid too much fat, sugar, and salt in their diets.

Motivating Activity
Write the following sentence starters on the chalkboard and ask students to complete them. "I should include more . . . in my diet because. . . ." and "I should eat less . . . because. . . ."

Introducing the Lesson
Have students share their responses to the Motivating Activity. Explain to students that in this lesson they will learn more about making healthy food choices and what they should avoid or limit in their diets.

L1 Using Transparencies
Present Color Transparency 48, "The Picture of Wellness," in the TCR. Use this overhead visual to reinforce concepts from this lesson.

Introducing *Words to Know*
Write each of the Words to Know on the board. Have students look up each term in the Glossary at the back of the student text. Ask them to write sentences for each term, defining the term in their own words.

303

CHAPTER 11, LESSON 2

TEACH

USING VISUALS
Have students read each of the Dietary Guidelines in Figure 11.3. Ask them why the lead lines from some of the guidelines go to the green light, while others go to the amber light, and one goes to the red light. *(The guidelines connected to the green light are things you should do; those with lines going to the amber light indicate things you should use caution with; and the one with the line going to the red light is something you should avoid or stop.)*

DID YOU KNOW ?
Following a diet that is high in fiber and low in salt, fat, and cholesterol has significant health benefits. A diet that is high in salt can lead to high blood pressure. One that is high in fat and cholesterol can lead to a buildup of fatty deposits in the arteries. Both of these conditions can lead to heart disease.

L1 Discussion
Ask students to recall the sources of nutrients they studied in Lesson 1. Discuss how what they learned about nutrients explains why they need to eat a variety of foods. *(Because different foods are good sources of different nutrients, it is important to eat a variety of food so that you get all the essential nutrients.)*

The Dietary Guidelines

How can you make sure that your diet contributes to your wellness? First, you can use the Food Guide Pyramid. It shows you visually how to follow the Dietary Guidelines for Americans.

The **Dietary Guidelines** are *advice on what Americans should eat to stay healthy.* These guidelines were developed by the U.S. Department of Agriculture (USDA) and the U.S. Department of Health and Human Services using recommendations by nutrition authorities. The guidelines take into account the important effect diet has on health. By following them, you can ensure that you are eating the right types of foods. You can also reduce your chances of developing certain health problems, such as heart disease and high blood pressure.

Of course, food alone can't make you healthy. Good health also depends on your heredity and environment. Your lifestyle—for example, your exercise habits—is also important to your health. However, a diet based on these guidelines can help keep you healthy, perhaps even help improve your health. **Figure 11.3** shows the Dietary Guidelines for Americans.

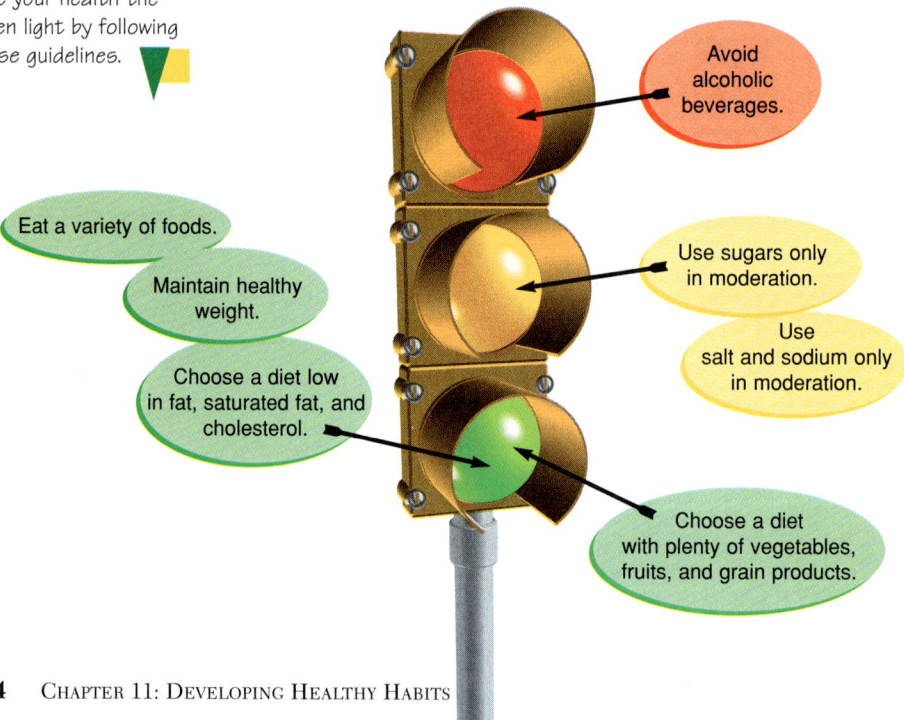

Figure 11.3 Dietary Guidelines for Americans
Give your health the green light by following these guidelines.

304   CHAPTER 11: DEVELOPING HEALTHY HABITS

MEETING STUDENT DIVERSITY

Cultural Diversity Explain to students that while most milk that people drink in the United States comes from cows, people in other countries get their milk from different animals. People in Lapland (part of Finland) drink reindeer milk; in other parts of Europe people drink goat milk; in Tibet and Mongolia people drink yak milk; and in parts of India people drink water-buffalo milk. Cheeses and yogurt in these areas are also usually made from the milk of those animals. If possible, bring in some goat cheese for students to sample.

Eat a Variety of Foods

How many different foods do you eat during a typical day? The first guideline says that variety is the key to good nutrition and good health. You need more than 40 different nutrients for good health. No single food or food group can supply all of these nutrients in the amounts you need. To get the nutrients you need, you must balance your food choices. A **balanced diet** is *a diet that is made up of a variety of foods with nutrients in the recommended amounts.*

One way to be assured of a balanced diet is to choose foods each day from all five food groups. Remember that these include grain products, vegetables, fruits, milk and milk products, and meats and meat alternatives. Refer back to pages 300 and 301 for information on recommended servings per day and serving sizes.

Maintain Healthy Weight

A person who is at a healthy weight is not too fat or too thin. Being too fat is linked with many illnesses, including high blood pressure, heart disease, stroke, diabetes, certain cancers, and others. Although being too thin is less common, it is also linked with disease and a greater risk of early death.

How can you know if your weight is "healthy"? You can't compare your weight with that of your friends. There are differences among people of the same age. For example, people with a large body frame usually weigh more than people of the same height with a smaller body frame. At this time in your life, growing and gaining weight are normal.

To determine if your weight is right for you, consult your doctor. He or she can consider all the factors that contribute to a healthy weight for you.

You can't compare your own best weight with that of your friends. There are differences among people of the same age. Do you know what those differences are?

LESSON TWO: FOLLOWING HEALTHY GUIDELINES

CHAPTER 11, LESSON 2

L2 Writing Skits
Have students work in small groups to write short skits about teens and their concern about their weight. Encourage students to write skits that focus on a teen's problem and the teen's constructive solution to the problem. Students may wish to videotape their skits.

L3 Research
The eating disorders bulimia and anorexia nervosa can cause serious health problems and can even result in death. Have students research these eating disorders and report their information to the class. Research may be done using CD-ROM encyclopedias or on-line services if computers are available.

L3 Applying
If appropriate software is available, students can use the computer to create menus that contain ingredients that are rich in carbohydrates and low in fat. Depending on the type of software they have available, students may be able to tell the computer what ingredients they would like to use and then include recommended requirements for a healthy diet, and the computer will provide a menu that is complete with recipes.

HOME AND COMMUNITY CONNECTION

Fast-Food Restaurants Following healthy guidelines is often difficult for students and often beyond their control. Families who eat many of their meals at fast-food restaurants can find it almost impossible to eat meals that are low in salt and fat. If possible, you might ask a manager of a local fast-food restaurant to speak to the class about ways that the restaurant is trying to provide healthy food choices for its customers. Students might suggest additional ways that restaurants can help their customers make healthy food choices.

CHAPTER 11, LESSON 2

L3 Research
Ask students to find a newspaper or magazine article that describes health problems caused by eating foods that are high in fat and cholesterol. Ask them to make a brief report on the article to the class.

L2 Analyzing
Have students work in small groups to analyze a typical fast-food menu. You might have them collect flyers and brochures from local fast-food restaurants that explain the nutritional content of their menus. Ask them to determine which foods are high in fat, whether the fat occurs naturally or is added by frying, and how they could avoid getting too much fat when eating at a fast-food restaurant.

L3 Investigate
Have students investigate the two kinds of cholesterol (HDL and LDL). Have them find out what "good" cholesterol is and what "bad" cholesterol is. Ask them to write short reports based on their research. Students may wish to use computers for research and for writing their reports.

Choose a Diet Low in Fats and Cholesterol

Fat is an important nutrient that provides energy. If you are like many Americans, however, your diet is too high in fat. Health experts recommend a diet that is low in fat and cholesterol.

Why is eating too much fat harmful? A diet high in fat leads to such health problems as obesity and certain types of cancer. A diet high in saturated fat and cholesterol is linked to an increased risk of heart disease.

You can reduce the fats in your diet by using nonstick pans and baking or broiling foods. Why isn't frying a recommended way of cooking food?

The amount of fat in your diet depends on what you eat over several days, not on one meal or type of food. For example, if you like a small amount of butter on your baked potato, you will not be getting too much fat as long as you limit the amount of other fats you eat.

Some foods that contain fats and cholesterol—meats, milk, cheese, and eggs—also contain high-quality protein and important vitamins and minerals. To reduce fats and cholesterol, choose low-fat versions of these foods such as nonfat milk and cheese.

Eat Plenty of Vegetables, Fruits, and Grains

Vegetables, fruits, and grain products are an essential part of a varied and healthful diet. They contain complex carbohydrates, fiber, and other nutrients that contribute to good health. In addition, these foods are usually low in fats. If you eat the suggested amounts of them, you are also likely to decrease the fat in your diet and get more fiber.

Complex carbohydrates, such as starches, are essential to good nutrition. Starches give you long-lasting energy as well as

306 CHAPTER 11: DEVELOPING HEALTHY HABITS

COOPERATIVE LEARNING

Making Posters Organize the students into small groups. Ask each group to work together to design and make a poster showing foods that are good choices for a low-fat diet. Students might include photos or drawings of the foods. Encourage them to make their posters attractive. Display the posters in the classroom.

Beware of foods whose labels list sugar by its other names: glucose, fructose, maltose, lactose, corn sweetener, high-fructose corn syrup, molasses. Where can you look to find out if products contain sugars?

vitamins and minerals. Starch is found in breads, cereals, pasta, rice, dry beans, peas, potatoes, and corn.

Fiber helps to keep your digestive system healthy. Fiber is found naturally in whole-grain breads and cereals, dry beans and peas, vegetables, and fruits.

Use Sugars Only in Moderation

Sugar is a type of carbohydrate that is found in many foods. Sugar provides calories, and most people like the way it tastes. Fruit contains natural sugar. Many processed foods, such as cookies and soft drinks, contain refined sugar.

This guideline calls for **moderation**—*avoiding extremes* in diet. That means that although eating too much sugar may not be healthful, it isn't necessary to eliminate sugar from your diet entirely. To cut down on the sugar in your diet, you can

TIPS for living

REDUCING THE FAT

Reducing the amount of fat in your diet can help you maintain a healthy weight. Here are some suggestions.

- Avoid foods made with saturated fats, such as ice cream, cookies, and frosted cakes.
- Choose lean meats, and trim extra fat from your meat.
- Choose nonfat or reduced-fat milk.
- Avoid snacking on chips.

LESSON TWO: FOLLOWING HEALTHY GUIDELINES

MORE ABOUT • • •

Sugars Despite people's concerns about calories and cavities, Americans have eaten more candy than ever in the last five years—an average of 21 pounds per person annually. According to Hershey, the nation's leading candy maker, candy is eaten by more than 90 percent of Americans, and more is eaten on Friday than on any other day.

CHAPTER 11, LESSON 2

L1 Discussion

Discuss with students the importance of eating vegetables, fruits, and grains. Ask them to bring in examples of foods that are high in starches and foods that are high in fiber. Display foods in the classroom.

DID YOU KNOW

People today don't think of salt as important or precious, but the ancient Chinese used salt as the basis of their taxation system. The Romans also used salt for payment. The word *salary* comes from "salarium," the salt given to Roman soldiers as payment for their military service.

L2 Applying

Have students collect and study food labels to identify hidden sources of sugar in the diet. Ask them to find words that identify sugar in a list of ingredients. Have them circle the hidden sources of sugar and make a collage of the labels.

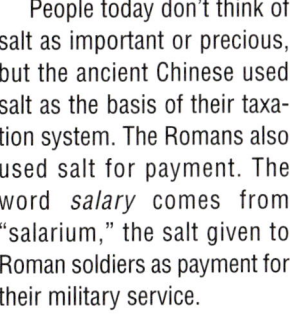

TIPS for living

Suggest that students try to follow the suggestions for limiting fat for three days and keep a log of what they did to reduce fat in their diets. Have them share what they did with classmates.

CHAPTER 11, LESSON 2

Student Workbook
Assign Activity 77 in the Student Workbook.

ASSESS

Evaluating the Lesson
Assign Reviewing Terms and Facts and Thinking Critically on page 309 to review the lesson; then assign the Lesson 2 Quiz in the TCR.

Reteaching
- Have students refer to the Dietary Guidelines. Have them analyze their school lunch menu against these guidelines. Students might suggest ways that the lunches might be adjusted to meet all the guidelines.
- Have students complete Reteaching Activity 11 in the TCR.
- Assign Concept Map 17 in the TCR.

Enrichment
- Tell students that the average American consumes one-third of a pound of sugar each day. Have students find out how refined sugar contributes to tooth decay. Ask them to draw an illustration showing how tooth decay occurs.
- Assign Enrichment Activity 12 in the TCR.

One way to reduce the amount of sodium in your diet is to cook with and eat fresh ingredients.

- eat fresh fruit instead of desserts with added sugars.
- eat less of all foods with added sugars.
- keep nutritious snacks on hand.

Use Salt and Sodium Only in Moderation

Salt contains **sodium,** *a mineral that helps regulate the amount of fluid in our bodies.* You need some sodium to stay healthy. However, most Americans eat more sodium than they need.

For some people, too much sodium can lead to high blood pressure. High blood pressure makes the heart work too hard. Cutting back on sodium can benefit everyone. To cut down on sodium, you can

- use very little salt, if any, in cooking and at the table.
- limit the amount of salted foods you eat, such as chips, pretzels, and nuts.
- eat less processed food, such as packaged sandwich meat, canned soup, and cheeses.

308   CHAPTER 11: DEVELOPING HEALTHY HABITS

MEETING STUDENT DIVERSITY

Cultural Diversity Point out to students that while government nutritionists have established the Dietary Guidelines, many religious or cultural groups have their own special dietary guidelines. Have students work in small groups to research dietary guidelines of various religious or cultural groups. Have the groups share their information with the class.

Avoid Alcoholic Beverages

The last guideline concerns the use of alcohol. Drinking alcoholic beverages is illegal for young people. Even for adults, it is not recommended. Although alcohol supplies calories, it has no other nutritional value.

Drinking alcohol does not benefit your health—in fact, it is linked with many health problems. People who drink before driving increase their risk of having accidents. A pregnant woman who drinks alcohol may damage her unborn baby's health.

Balancing Your Diet

Following the Dietary Guidelines can help you choose a diet that contributes to wellness. The first two guidelines form the foundation of a balanced diet: *Eat a variety of foods* for the nutrients you need and in the right amounts to *maintain a healthy weight*. The other guidelines offer advice on which types of foods to eat and which types of foods to limit to ensure that your diet is healthful.

About 75 percent of the sodium in your diet comes from canned and packaged foods. One way to reduce the sodium in your diet is to read food labels and buy brands with less added sodium chloride (salt), monosodium glutamate, disodium phosphate; sodium alginate, benzoate, sulfite, hydroxide, propionate; or brine.

What are some other ways of reducing the salt in your diet?

LESSON TWO Review

Using complete sentences, answer the following questions on a separate sheet of paper.

Reviewing Terms and Facts

1. **Vocabulary** What are the *Dietary Guidelines*?

2. **Recall** How can you be sure that your diet is well balanced?

3. **Explain** Why are complex carbohydrates essential to good nutrition?

4. **List** Name three ways to cut down on added sugars in your diet.

Thinking Critically

5. **Analyze** Why should you follow the Dietary Guidelines?

6. **Explain** Why can too much fat and cholesterol be harmful?

7. **Apply** How can you determine which processed foods are high in sodium?

Applying Concepts

8. Read the section of a nutrition, biology, or life sciences textbook that describes how the body uses fat and cholesterol and what happens to the body when you eat too much. In your own words, write a few paragraphs to explain the process.

LESSON TWO: FOLLOWING HEALTHY GUIDELINES

HOME AND COMMUNITY CONNECTION

Family Meals Have students record their family meals for three days and analyze them to determine if they meet the Dietary Guidelines. If they do not, have students write up a list of suggestions for changes in the family diet. They might also offer to help plan or prepare meals. Caution them to be sensitive in their suggestions as certain foods may be part of a family tradition.

CHAPTER 11, LESSON 2

Suggest that students might look for brands of their favorite soups and vegetables that are labeled as containing low or reduced salt or sodium. You might organize a tasting party where students compare their favorite canned soup and a low-sodium version of the same soup.

Answers to Lesson 2 Review

1. Advice on what Americans should eat to stay healthy.

2. Choose foods each day from the five food groups.

3. Give you long-lasting energy and provide many vitamins and minerals.

4. Eat fresh fruit instead of desserts with added sugars. Eat less of all foods with added sugars. Avoid eating sweets between meals.

5. To maintain, or improve, your health and to reduce your chances of getting certain diseases.

6. A diet high in fat and cholesterol leads to health problems, including obesity and certain types of cancer.

7. You can read the food labels on processed foods to determine which are high in sodium.

8. Paragraphs will vary but should include the fact that the body uses dietary fats for their essential fatty acids, components our bodies can't make. Fats also carry the four fat-soluble vitamins—A, D, E, and K.

CLOSE

Have students summarize the Dietary Guidelines and identify one specific thing they could do to meet each guideline.

LESSON THREE
Snacking and Eating Out

FOCUS

Lesson Objectives
After studying this lesson, students should be able to
- identify nutritious snacks.
- explain how to choose a restaurant.
- discuss how to order healthful foods from a restaurant menu.

Motivating Activity
Have students complete the following statements:
- Between meals I eat . . .
- The snacks I eat most often are . . .
- My favorite foods to eat at a restaurant are . . .

Introducing the Lesson
Have students share their responses to the Motivating Activity. Have students tell which snacks and foods named they think are healthful. Tell them that this lesson discusses how they can use the Food Guide Pyramid and Dietary Guidelines to help them eat nutritious foods when snacking or eating out.

Introducing *Words to Know*
Write each Word to Know on an index card; then write the definition for each word on a separate card. Make several sets of the term-and-definition cards. Divide the class into small groups. Give each group a set of cards and let students in each group take turns matching each term with its definition.

 **WORDS TO KNOW**

snacks

nutrient-dense foods

empty-calorie foods

menu

DISCOVER...
- what makes a healthful snack.
- how to choose a restaurant.
- how to order from a restaurant menu.

How often do you grab a bite to eat on the go? Do you think about the nutritional value of the food, or do you just look for something to keep you going until the next meal? When you are at a restaurant, do you pay attention to the nutrient content of the foods you order, or are you likely just to choose something that seems tasty? Both snacking and eating out can be healthful. Just remember to follow the Food Guide Pyramid and the Dietary Guidelines when you eat between meals and away from home.

CLASSROOM RESOURCES FOR LESSON 3

 Blackline Masters
Activity and Project Card 21, "Restaurant Art"
Cooperative Learning 21
Food Lab Activity 1, "Snack Smorgasbord"
Lesson 3 Quiz
Peer Pressure and Decision Making 23

 Transparencies
Transparency 49, "Snacks: Empty-Calories or Nutrient-Dense?"

 **Student Workbook**
Activities 78, 79

Eating Snacks

Tanya plays softball and runs in the off-season to stay in shape. Even though she is active and gets very hungry by mealtime, she finds that the recommended servings from the bread group are more than she can eat in just three meals. Tanya now carries a bagel and fresh fruit as morning and afternoon snacks. **Snacks** are *foods eaten between meals.*

The key to healthy snacking is to treat snacks as part of your regular diet. To do so, follow these guidelines.

- Count the calories in snacks as part of your total calories for the day.
- Choose foods that help you get the number of servings your body needs from each of the food groups.
- Time your snacks so that you don't eat too close to lunch or dinner.

"Snack attacks" occur quite often during the school day. Working in small groups, create a list of healthy snacks. All items should be high in nutrients and low in calories. Share your list with other groups.

Choosing Nutrient-Dense Snacks

What are your favorite snacks? Do you choose **nutrient-dense foods**—*foods that are rich in the nutrients your body needs to stay healthy?* These foods supply proteins, carbohydrates, vitamins, minerals, and water. For nutrient-dense snacks, choose from the five food groups, as Tanya did. Select whole-grain items from the bread group. A wide variety of nutrient-dense snacks can be found in the fruit and vegetable groups.

By choosing nutrient-dense snacks, you will help your body stay healthy. What are some examples of nutrient-dense snacks?

311

HOME AND COMMUNITY CONNECTION

Healthful Snacks To help all members of their families develop healthy snacking habits, suggest that students talk to their families about setting up snack centers in the kitchen. This could be done by designating part of one refrigerator shelf as a snack center and keeping it stocked with containers filled with cheese chunks, cut-up fruits and vegetables, and juices. Another snack center could hold snacks that don't have to be refrigerated, such as raisins, crackers, bagels, muffins, or individually-sealed containers of unsweetened applesauce.

CHAPTER 11, LESSON 3

TEACH

With permission from your school administrator, have students set up and operate a school snack bar for a fundraiser for an after-school event. Money from the sale of snacks might be earmarked for a particular purpose, such as for new books for the school library or new equipment for gym classes. Survey students to find out their favorite healthy snacks.

L1 Using Transparencies

Present Color Transparency 49, "Snacks: Empty-Calories or Nutrient-Dense?" in the TCR. Use this overhead visual to reinforce concepts from this lesson.

L1 Making a Snack Cookbook

Have each student write a recipe for a healthy snack they would enjoy eating. Encourage them to be creative in their recipes, such as stuffing celery sticks with peanut butter and raisins or blending skim milk, low-fat yogurt, and fresh fruit to make a shake. Compile the recipes into a Healthy Snack Cookbook and make a copy for each student. Encourage students to use the recipes to make snacks for their family. Cookbooks may be shared with younger students, perhaps as an activity with an elementary-school class.

311

CHAPTER 11, LESSON 3

L3 Math
Have students keep a record of the snacks they eat for one week. Ask them to also record the amount of money spent on each snack. At the end of the week ask them to calculate the total amount of money spent on snacks.

DID YOU KNOW

The following snacks are all under 100 calories: 3-inch diameter apple; 1 large navel orange; 1 cup unsweetened applesauce; 6-ounce container of low-fat, plain yogurt; 1 small bran muffin; 10 1-inch plums; 11 thin wheat crackers; 3 fresh apricots; 3 graham crackers; 2 cups popcorn popped with oil; 2½-ounce strawberry frozen-yogurt bar; or 1 extra-large hard-boiled egg.

L2 Critical Thinking
Ask students why it might be easier to eat a nutritious, balanced meal at a cafeteria than at a fast-food restaurant or other restaurant. Have them list foods from each menu, compare the lists, and then write a summary of their findings.

L2 Food Lab
Allow time for students to complete Food Lab Activity 1, "Snack Smorgasbord," in the TCR.

L1 Discussion
Ask students to summarize what tips they should follow when eating out to be sure they are eating balanced meals.

Avoiding Empty-Calorie Snacks

Empty-calorie foods are *foods that are high in calories but low in nutrients.* The foods we usually think of as "junk food"—such as potato chips, candy, and soft drinks—are empty-calorie foods. Many of these foods are found at the tip of the Food Guide Pyramid. They often contain large amounts of sugar, salt, and fat, all of which should be eaten sparingly. A candy bar, for example, provides lots of calories in the form of sugar and fat, but little nutrition.

Eating Out

Do you enjoy eating out? Maybe you like getting together with friends over a meal. Perhaps your family enjoys eating at a restaurant to try new foods. When you eat out, remember to choose your meals with the same eye to nutrition as when you eat at home.

Selecting a Restaurant

What types of restaurants do you like? You are probably familiar with fast-food restaurants. They give quick service, are

The food choices, types of service, and price ranges vary greatly from one restaurant to another. At what types of restaurants have you eaten?

312 CHAPTER 11: DEVELOPING HEALTHY HABITS

COOPERATIVE LEARNING

Planning a Party Ask small groups of students to imagine that they are planning a party menu. They should select a theme for the party, decide what foods to serve, and determine how they could prepare the foods so that they would be attractive and fun to eat. They can use newspaper supermarket flyers to calculate costs of foods they will include. Have each group prepare an illustrated brochure to show the foods and to describe the preparation.

TIPS for living

WHERE'S THE FAT?

You can follow the example of people around the world for a low-fat diet. Try the ideas listed below.

- Many Mexican, Indian, and Asian dishes use spices—rather than butter or margarine—to perk up flavor of vegetables and rice.
- Most French people eat their bread without butter.
- Italians apply pizza toppings sparingly and barely cover their pasta with sauce.
- In France and Italy, meat is served in much smaller portions than in the United States.

fairly inexpensive, and serve popular foods, such as hot sandwiches, french fries, salads, and shakes.

A second type of restaurant is a cafeteria, similar to your school cafeteria. Customers take a tray and choose foods while going through a serving line. Cafeterias are also fairly inexpensive, charging separately for each item. Many selections are offered in each food category.

Some restaurants offer meals at a fixed price. Customers pay a set price and are entitled to eat whatever foods are offered. In many cases, these restaurants feature all-you-can-eat buffets and salad bars.

Another common type of restaurant is one that provides table service. After you are seated at a table, a waiter or waitress takes your order and brings your food.

Restaurants also vary widely in the kinds of foods they offer. Some specialize in certain types of dishes, such as seafood, steaks, or pancakes. Ethnic restaurants specialize in the food of a particular country or region.

Choosing Wisely from the Menu

What exactly is a menu? A **menu** is *a list of all the dishes a restaurant serves, organized by category.* The categories might include appetizers, salads, main dishes, side dishes, desserts, and beverages. Menus also generally list the price for each dish. Some menus feature low-fat choices.

LESSON THREE: SNACKING AND EATING OUT 313

CHAPTER 11, LESSON 3

TIPS for living

Survey students to find out which of the tips their family already follows. Discuss which of the tips they would find easiest to follow.

L2 Problem Solving

Assign Peer Pressure and Decision Making 23 in the TCR. This activity gives students the opportunity to recognize peer pressure and practice decision-making skills.

L1 Discussion

Discuss with students what they can do when they feel the urge for a sugary, salty, or fatty snack. Remind them that they don't have to completely eliminate these things from their diet. Reinforce the idea of trade-offs covered in Lesson 1.

L2 Activity and Project Card

Allow time for students to complete Activity and Project Card 21, "Restaurant Art," in the TCR.

MEETING STUDENT DIVERSITY

Cultural Diversity Plan a day for students to share their cultural differences with classmates by sharing foods. Have students make and bring in a dish that represents their ethnic or religious heritage. Discuss ahead of time the various dishes that students will bring and which cultures will be represented. Have each student describe the ingredients and preparation of his or her dish. Allow students to sample various dishes.

CHAPTER 11, LESSON 3

L2 Cooperative Learning

Assign Cooperative Learning Activity 21 in the TCR. Students work in groups to plan a variety of healthful snacks in this activity.

L1 Student Workbook

Assign Activities 78 and 79 in the Student Workbook.

ASSESS

Evaluating the Lesson

Assign Reviewing Terms and Facts and Thinking Critically on page 315 to review the lesson; then assign the Lesson 3 Quiz in the TCR.

Reteaching

- Have students use magazine pictures or grocery store ads to make collages that show healthy snacks and restaurant meals. Ask each student to explain why each part of the collage is a healthy food choice.
- Have students complete Reteaching Activity 11 in the TCR.

Enrichment

Give students an opportunity to hold a taste-testing party featuring nutritious snacks. Have students make a chart showing the nutritional value of these foods.

Many restaurants post their menus outside the door. How might that be helpful to customers?

As you look at a menu, the most important point to remember is to choose foods from all five food groups—just as you would do if you were planning a meal at home. Here are some tips for ordering when you eat out.

- Select dishes that are low in fat, sugar, salt, and calories. Baked potatoes have much less fat than french fries.

- Choose nutrient-dense dishes. At Italian restaurants, have whole-wheat or vegetable pasta. Instead of soft drinks or milk shakes, have juice or milk.

- Limit the number of treats you allow yourself. If you really want dessert, make a trade-off. If you can't resist the fried ice cream at a Mexican restaurant, have simmered beans instead of refried beans, and avoid the tortilla chips.

- Remember that sauces and salad dressings add calories. When eating Italian foods, choose red sauces, made with tomatoes, rather than white sauces made with butter and cream.

- Most portion sizes are larger than a serving. Bring leftovers home in a box.

- Eat only until you feel satisfied.

314 CHAPTER 11: DEVELOPING HEALTHY HABITS

MORE ABOUT • • •

Eating Out or Eating In Most people eat more carefully at home than in restaurants. According to a 1995 survey, more than half of Americans (53 percent of men and 61 percent of women) monitor very closely what they eat and drink at home. Far fewer (22 percent of men and 25 percent of women) do the same thing when they eat out. Tell students that when Americans eat out at restaurants (other than fast-food restaurants), their favorite choices are: fried chicken, roast beef, spaghetti, turkey, baked ham, fried shrimp, beef stew, meatloaf, fish, macaroni and cheese, pot roast, and Swiss steak. Poll the class to find out students' favorites.

Take-out Food

A popular alternative to eating at a restaurant is getting food "to go." Take-out food includes food that you pick up, have delivered, or get at a drive-through window. Pizza, tacos, and Chinese food are popular take-out items. When ordering take-out food, try to include foods from all five food groups.

Making Healthy Food Choices

Snacking and eating out can be both enjoyable and nutritious. Remember, however, that the food choices you make when snacking or eating out are part of your overall diet. By following the Food Guide Pyramid, choosing nutrient-dense foods, and avoiding empty-calorie foods, you will help keep your body healthy.

If you choose wisely, take-out food can be nutritious.

LESSON THREE *Review*

Using complete sentences, answer the following questions on a separate sheet of paper.

Reviewing Terms and Facts
1. **Identify** What are *nutrient-dense* foods?
2. **Contrast** What is the difference between a cafeteria and a restaurant with table service?
3. **Vocabulary** Define the term *menu*. What categories are usually found on a menu?
4. **List** Name four guidelines for selecting foods at a restaurant.

Thinking Critically
5. **Analyze** Why do you think that some people gain weight from eating snacks? How could this problem be avoided?
6. **Interpret** Why is it a good idea to look over an entire restaurant menu before ordering?

Applying Concepts
7. Create a simple menu for a new fast-food restaurant. Offer healthy choices from the five food groups, and be sure to include beverages and desserts. Exchange menus with a classmate.

LESSON THREE: SNACKING AND EATING OUT   315

COOPERATIVE LEARNING

Making a Newspaper Have small groups of students make a *Good Nutrition* newspaper. They can collect and use articles from newspapers and magazines and write some articles of their own based on what they learned. Encourage them to look for interesting facts they can tell people about different kinds of foods. Have groups share the newspapers with the class.

CHAPTER 11, LESSON 3

Answers to Lesson 3 Review

1. Nutrient-dense foods are foods that are rich in the nutrients the body needs to stay healthy.
2. In cafeterias, customers place their selections on a tray as they go through the serving line, but at restaurants with table service, a server takes the customers' order and brings their food.
3. A menu is a list of the dishes a restaurant serves, organized by category. Categories may include appetizers, salads, main dishes, side dishes, desserts, and beverages.
4. Answers will vary but should include four of the following: choosing foods from all five food groups; selecting dishes that are low in fat, sugar, salt, and calories; choosing nutrient-dense dishes; limiting the number of treats you give yourself; choosing sauces, stuffings, and toppings that are low in calories.
5. Answers will vary but students should indicate that people gain weight from eating snacks because they choose snacks that are high in calories. This problem could be avoided by choosing snacks that are nutrient-dense.
6. By looking over the entire menu, you can see if there are healthier alternatives to more calorie-laden items; see if you can trade off fats or sugars to have a special treat; and keep track of the cost of your dinner.
7. Answers will vary but should include selections from all five food groups.

CLOSE

Have students write a brief summary of strategies that they can use to make healthy food choices when snacking or eating out.

LESSON FOUR
Exercise and Weight Control

FOCUS

Lesson Objectives
After studying this lesson, students should be able to
- explain why fitness is important.
- describe how exercise helps maintain fitness.
- describe ways to maintain a healthy weight.

Motivating Activity
Ask students to name physical activities they enjoy. List these activities on the chalkboard. For each activity named, ask how many students in the class participate in that activity and write the number of students beside the activity.

Introducing the Lesson
Ask students how each of the activities listed on the board from the Motivating Activity might help them be physically fit. Ask them which of the activities they think would help most. Tell students that this lesson discusses how they can stay fit and what they can do to maintain a healthy weight.

Introducing *Words to Know*
Have students write the definition of each Word to Know next to the word on a chart. Then have them draw or paste pictures on the chart that relate to the meaning of each word.

316

LESSON FOUR
Exercise and Weight Control

WORDS TO KNOW
fitness
stamina
obesity
aerobic exercise
fad diet

DISCOVER...
- why fitness is important.
- how exercise can help you stay fit.
- what you can do to maintain a healthy weight.

Aaron has a lot of responsibilities. Schoolwork takes up much of his time. He has chores to do at home, and he delivers flyers for some local restaurants. Aaron spends time with friends too. Even though Aaron is busy, he still finds time to exercise and to eat well. He stays fit by riding his bike, skating, and swimming at the community pool.

316   CHAPTER 11: DEVELOPING HEALTHY HABITS

CLASSROOM RESOURCES FOR LESSON 4

 Blackline Masters
Activity and Project Card 22, "Health Tips Pamphlet"
Concept Map 18
Cooperative Learning 22
Enrichment 13
Food Lab Activity 2, "High-Speed Breakfasts"
Lesson 4 Quiz

Peer Pressure and Decision Making 24
Reteaching 11

 Transparencies
Transparency 50, "Fitness: The Choices Are Yours!"

 Student Workbook
Activities 80, 81

The Importance of Fitness and Physical Activity

When you are physically fit, you look and feel your best. **Fitness** is *the ability to handle day-to-day events in a healthy way.* Fitness means that you

- have enough energy to do your schoolwork, have fun, and handle problems.
- can keep your weight at the right level for you.
- can deal with stress and the ups and downs of life.
- are confident about your abilities.
- make exercise and activity a part of your life every day.

Exercise and Fitness

You cannot be fit unless you exercise. By exercising regularly, as long as you also eat well, you will enjoy all the benefits of fitness.

- You will feel positively about yourself. Knowing you're taking care of your body is good for your self-esteem.
- You will look your best. Exercise helps control weight and gives you a healthy glow.
- Day-to-day tasks will seem easy because you will have the energy you need.
- You will be able to relax and sleep easily.
- You will have physical and mental stamina. **Stamina** is *the ability to focus on a single activity for a long time.* For example, you will be able to

Exercise can be a way for teens to have fun together. What activities do you enjoy with your friends?

CHAPTER 11, LESSON 4

TEACH

L1 Discussion
Ask students to privately consider their own fitness and rate it on a scale of 1 (completely unfit) to 10 (ready for anything). Encourage students to analyze why they rate themselves as they do. Then ask them to identify in their private journals their goals for where they would like to be in terms of total fitness. Stress to them that their rating and goals will remain private.

L3 Research
Many sports and other leisure activities that are commonly enjoyed in the United States originated in other cultures or countries. Ask each student to research one sport and prepare a short report describing its history and how it is played. Some suggestions for sports to research are: cycling, snowboarding, ice hockey, jumping rope, soccer, squash, swimming, field hockey, handball, bowling, tennis, football, and volleyball.

L2 Problem Solving
Assign Peer Pressure and Decision Making 24 in the TCR. This activity gives students the opportunity to recognize peer pressure and practice decision-making skills.

L1 Using Transparencies
Present Color Transparency 50, "Fitness: The Choices Are Yours!" in the TCR. Use this overhead visual to reinforce concepts from this lesson.

HOME AND COMMUNITY CONNECTION

Corporate Fitness Programs Tell students that fitness and exercise are becoming a part of many corporate settings. Many companies in the United States now have exercise facilities and supervised exercise programs for their employees. Research has shown that exercise relieves stress. As a result, many employers believe that employees who are less stressed are more productive and healthy. Have students interview adults they know to find out if any local companies have fitness programs and report their findings to the class.

317

CHAPTER 11, LESSON 4

L2 Critical Thinking
Provide students with the following situation: Beverly wants to lose 5 pounds. Every day when she comes home after school, she watches television, and snacks on cookies or chips and soda until it is time for dinner. Have students write a letter to Beverly in which they explain how she can change her habits to lose 5 pounds. Call on volunteers to share their letters with the class. Evaluate the suggestions given in the letters.

L1 Applying
Have students work in small groups to brainstorm ways they could get more exercise. Point out to students that they may want to consider alternatives to the labor-saving devices they usually depend on, like using a push mower instead of a power mower, or washing the car themselves instead of taking it to a car wash. Then ask each group to create a poster illustrating ways that students could get more exercise. Display the posters around the school.

TIPS for living
Remind students that the loss of one pound per week is generally considered safe; losing more can be hazardous to their health. Emphasize that to lose one pound in a week, you would need to reduce your calorie intake or increase the number of calories you burn in exercise by a total of 500 calories a day, or 3,500 calories a week. Most people successfully lose weight by a combination of reducing calorie intake and increasing calories burned.

---

dance without getting very tired, and you can pay attention in class and learn easily.

- You will be able to deal with stress.

There are plenty of enjoyable, inexpensive ways to exercise. What's important is that you make exercise a regular part of your life. For example, Jennifer walks to school instead of taking the bus. Although walking takes longer, she enjoys that time alone. Her friend Nick prefers organized exercise. He plays on a softball team and enjoys getting together with friends to play volleyball on weekends.

Your Healthy Body Weight

Are you happy with your weight? Do you think that you're too heavy or too thin? People who maintain a healthy body weight are neither overweight nor underweight.

Being overweight can lead to obesity, one of our country's leading problems. **Obesity** is *a condition in which a person's weight is 20 percent or more above his or her healthy weight.* Obese people are at greater risk for such illnesses as heart disease and diabetes.

TIPS for living

CALORIES FOR FITNESS

Fitness involves more than just exercising regularly. It also includes avoiding empty-calorie foods and eating foods that are rich in nutrients. Follow these eating tips for physical fitness.

- Avoid high-calorie foods, such as french fries, pastries, and candy, and cake with frosting.
- Turn down second helpings, except for low-calorie vegetables and fruits.
- Eat regular meals with average-size portions.
- Have a nutrient-dense snack between meals to keep your energy level up.
- Enjoy fresh fruit instead of sweet desserts.
- Eat slowly. You will be less likely to overeat because it takes 20 minutes for your brain to signal that you have eaten enough.

MEETING STUDENT DIVERSITY

Physically Challenged Some of the exercises and activities suggested in Lesson 4 may not be appropriate for students with physical limitations or disabilities. You might ask physically challenged students to describe alternative activities they like to do that have the same exercise benefits as those presented in the lesson. Then ask students to work in small groups to plan a fitness fair for physically challenged younger children. Students might plan activities and exercises that help develop strong muscles, build endurance, and improve flexibility.

Being underweight is unhealthy too. People who are underweight often aren't eating enough, or aren't eating properly. This means that they aren't getting the nutrients they need. For instance, Tina thinks that being thin is all that matters. She eats very little so that she won't gain weight. What she doesn't realize is that the foods she eats are usually "fast" foods, such as french fries, that are high in fat and calories and low in nutrients. If she ate a well-balanced diet with lots of fruits and vegetables, she would be healthier and still able to control her weight.

What is your healthy body weight? That depends on you—your height, your frame size, your gender. Each person has a weight that is best for him or her. By looking in the mirror, you can probably see how well your weight suits you. If you're unsure, consult a doctor or a school nurse who can help you evaluate your weight.

Controlling Your Weight

Many teens are concerned about their weight. They want to look their best, and they often think that this means losing or gaining weight. They may believe that they have to give up certain foods or skip specific meals to control their weight. For example, Kenny has tried several times to lose 10 pounds. The problem is that he can never seem to go for more than one week eating prepackaged diet foods. He thinks that skipping breakfast will help him cut down on calories, but that doesn't work either. Kenny needs to learn the basics about eating and exercising to control weight.

A Balancing Act

Think of controlling your weight as a balancing act: you have to balance the calories you get from the foods you eat with the

You can control your weight and still eat your favorite foods as long as you balance the calories you eat with the amount of exercise you get.

LESSON FOUR: EXERCISE AND WEIGHT CONTROL **319**

TECHNOLOGY UPDATE

Body Fat Measurement There is no established standard for ideal body fat percentage. Most fitness programs aim for 18 to 22 percent of total weight for women and up to about 25 percent for men. One way to determine the percentage of body fat is by measuring the skin fold thickness of three different parts of the body, using calipers. Other methods include weighing an individual under water, measuring total body water, or determining the distribution of fat-soluble gases in the body. Yet another method, called bioelectrical impedance, involves passing a mild electric current through the body to measure resistance.

CHAPTER 11, LESSON 4

DID YOU KNOW

A very muscular person may show up as overweight, and a person with excessive fat may show up as normal on height and weight charts because muscle weighs more than an equal volume of fat.

L2 Activity and Project Card

Allow time for students to complete Activity and Project Card 22, "Health Tips Pamphlet," in the TCR.

L2 Food Lab

Allow time for students to complete Food Lab Activity 2, "High-Speed Breakfasts," in the TCR.

TEACHER TALK!

Dealing with Sensitive Issues

Weight and weight control may be uncomfortable or embarrassing topics for some students. De-personalizing discussions by focusing on fictional characters may ease the situation. You might have students write an advice column to fictitious teens needing suggestions on weight control and nutrition.

L2 Applying

Ask small groups of students to list three nutritious snacks that would be appropriate for people who are trying to gain weight, for people who are trying to lose weight, and for people who are trying to maintain their weight.

CHAPTER 11, LESSON 4

L1 Discussion
Emphasize to students that regular exercise will help people lose weight, but not overnight. Point out that by jogging for 20 minutes a day, 7 days a week, for one year, you can lose more than 20 pounds (without reducing your intake of food). Discuss the misconception that an increase in physical activity automatically causes an increase in appetite. Point out that research has shown that mild to moderate exercise will actually decrease appetite in most people.

L3 Research
Have students find an article about a fad diet in a newspaper or magazine. Ask them to evaluate the diet by comparing it with the five food groups and the recommended number of daily servings to determine whether the diet is balanced.

L2 Cooperative Learning
Assign Cooperative Learning Activity 22, "Working on Working Out," in the TCR.

Skills IN ACTION
Help students understand the benefits of developing healthy habits during their teen years. Ask them to review the benefits of an exercise program and encourage them to begin a fitness program. Have them evaluate the results after they have engaged in the program for two or three weeks.

---

calories you use for energy. To maintain your weight, you must make sure that the calories you eat equal those you burn as energy. If you take in more calories than your body uses, you gain weight. If your body uses more calories than it takes in, you lose weight.

To control your weight, you need to eat a balanced diet from the five food groups. Include foods you enjoy, but limit the number of servings you eat of fats, oils, and sweets. To lose weight, eat fewer calories than your body uses. The healthiest way to lose fat is to take in fewer calories and exercise more. That helps you burn the calories you take in while also burning body fat.

The Benefits of Exercise

Exercise is necessary if you want to reach and maintain a healthy body weight. Whether you want to lose weight, gain weight, or maintain your weight, exercise has many benefits.

- **Exercise burns calories.** The harder and longer you exercise, the more calories you burn. **Figure 11.4** shows how many calories you can burn doing different types of exercise.

- **Exercise helps your heart and lungs work better.** Aerobic exercise is the best kind for this purpose. **Aerobic exercise** is *nonstop, repetitive, vigorous exercise that increases breathing and heartbeat rates.* Bicycling, swimming, dancing, and jogging are all examples of aerobic exercise.

- **Exercise tones your muscles.** This improves the shape of your body.

- **Exercise helps you control your appetite.** It also relieves tension that could lead to overeating or loss of appetite.

Avoiding Fad Diets

Achieving fitness and a healthy body weight through a well-balanced diet and exercise takes time. If you are overweight or obese, you might be tempted to lose weight quickly

Skills IN ACTION

Starting a Fitness Program

Use your knowledge of exercise and a balanced diet to get started on a personal fitness program. Follow these steps.
1. Choose an activity you enjoy.
2. Set your own personal goals, but be realistic.
3. Be sure to warm up and cool down every time you exercise.

COOPERATIVE LEARNING

Developing an Aerobic Exercise Routine Have students work in small groups to plan an aerobic dance or exercise routine set to music they enjoy. Have groups determine which piece of music they will choose. Then direct groups to decide what type of exercises or movements should be included in the routine. Allow time for students to try out their planned routines and practice the steps, or encourage students to get together after school to practice. After each group has developed their routine, have them perform it for the class. If possible, arrange for students to perform their routines for a school assembly or parent-teacher meeting.

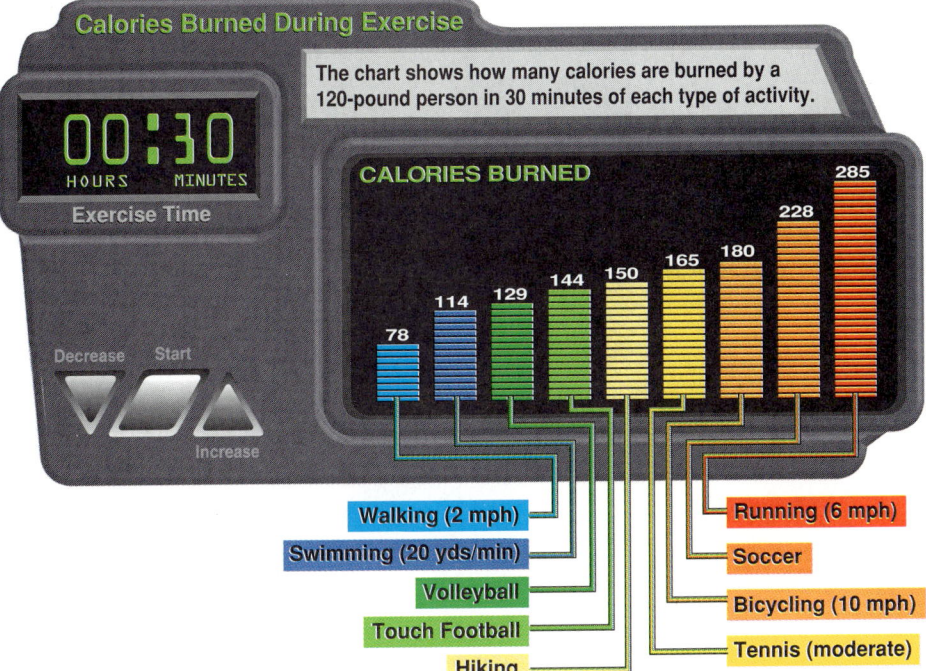

▲ Figure 11.4
Calories Burned During Exercise
The chart shows how many calories are burned by a 120-pound person in 30 minutes of each type of activity.

by going on a fad diet. A **fad diet** is *a diet that promises quick weight loss through unusual means.*

Fad diets are rarely successful in controlling weight. It is hard to stay on fad diets because they cut out certain foods, lack variety, and don't usually satisfy people's appetites. Most people who lose weight on a fad diet gain the weight back—and sometimes more. For example, Gretchen tried a fad diet in which she drank a milk shake for breakfast and lunch but ate a sensible meal for dinner. She stuck with it for two days. Then she started snacking in the afternoon and evening because she craved food. By the fifth day, Gretchen gave up and found herself eating more than before. When she weighed herself on the seventh day, she discovered that she had gained a pound!

A more serious problem is that fad diets are unbalanced—so they don't provide the nutrients you need to be healthy and fit. Some may even cause physical harm, especially to people who don't follow them under the guidance of a physician.

LESSON FOUR: EXERCISE AND WEIGHT CONTROL 321

CHAPTER 11, LESSON 4

USING VISUALS
Have students study the visual in Figure 11.4. Ask students whether they would burn more calories if they played tennis or soccer for an hour. *(soccer)* Then ask them to compare calories burned by bicycling for two hours and by swimming for one hour. Ask each student to identify one or two activities that he or she would enjoy doing and that would burn 300 calories in a day (equal to the calories in a cheeseburger).

L1 Student Workbook
Assign Activities 80 and 81 in the Student Workbook.

ASSESS

Evaluating the Lesson
Assign Reviewing Terms and Facts and Thinking Critically on page 322 to review the lesson; then assign the Lesson 4 Quiz in the TCR.

Reteaching
- Organize the class into four groups. Have each group make a list of activities to do instead of eating when they feel bored. Then have them work together to list the benefits of these activities. Have groups share their lists with classmates.
- Have students complete Reteaching Activity 11 in the TCR.
- Assign Concept Map 18 in the TCR.

COOPERATIVE LEARNING

Creating Menus Have students work in small groups to create menus for a day that includes three meals and two snacks. The goal of the menu is that it provide foods that are high in carbohydrates and low in fats. Provide each group with a poster board on which they can list their daily menu in an attractive manner, and have them include a slogan that would encourage people to follow that menu for a day. When posters are completed, ask a representative from each group to explain the choices of food on the menu. Display the menus in the classroom.

CHAPTER 11, LESSON 4

Answers to Lesson 4 Review

1. Answers will vary but should include three of the following: you will feel better about yourself; you will look better; day-to-day tasks will be easier; your heart, muscles, and bones will be healthier; you will be able to relax and sleep better; you will have greater physical and mental stamina.
2. People who are underweight aren't eating enough or aren't eating properly, so they aren't getting the nutrients they need.
3. The calories you get from the foods you eat with the calories you burn.
4. A fad diet is a diet that promises quick weight loss through unusual means. Such diets are rarely successful because they are hard to stay on long enough to lose weight.
5. By adjusting the calories you take in and the calories you burn, you can gain, lose, or maintain weight.
6. Weight control is balancing the calories from foods you eat with calories used for energy. Weight loss is using more calories than you take in.
7. Charts and letters will vary but should indicate an understanding of the benefits of fitness and exercise.

Enrichment

- Ask students to identify weight-loss products that claim weight loss can be quick and easy. Then have them write an editorial for a nutrition magazine explaining why these claims must be false and supporting the idea that weight loss takes time and effort.
- Assign Enrichment Activity 13 in the TCR.

CLOSE

Ask students to list five reasons why regular exercise is important to their personal health.

322

You need to make exercise a part of your lifestyle to be physically fit and healthy. Which types of exercise do you enjoy the most?

A more sensible approach to controlling your weight is to combine a good diet with exercise. If you plan a diet with foods you like from the five food groups, you will probably stick with it. In the long run, you will maintain your health while losing weight. You'll be more likely to keep the weight off too.

LESSON FOUR *Review*

Using complete sentences, answer the following questions on a separate sheet of paper.

Reviewing Terms and Facts
1. **List** What are three benefits of fitness?
2. **Explain** Why is being underweight unhealthy?
3. **Identify** What do you have to balance to control your weight?
4. **Vocabulary** What is a *fad diet*? Why are fad diets rarely successful?

Thinking Critically
5. **Relate** How are calories related to your diet and the amount of exercise you get?
6. **Contrast** What is the difference between weight control and weight loss?

Applying Concepts
7. Make a two-column chart entitled "The Benefits of Fitness and Exercise." In one column list the physical benefits. In the second column list the mental benefits. Then write a letter to yourself to convince yourself to exercise regularly.

322   CHAPTER 11: DEVELOPING HEALTHY HABITS

 HOME AND COMMUNITY CONNECTION

A Family Exercise Program Have students create a program of activities that members of their family could do together to increase family fitness. Remind them to take into account the ages, current fitness levels, and interests of family members when developing their programs. Encourage them to share their programs with family members and have them report back on the success of their family fitness programs.

Chapter 11 Activities

Consumer Focus

Choosing Snacks

How many times have you seen carrot or celery sticks advertised as snack foods on television? Probably never. On the other hand, you have seen countless ads for cookies, chips, and soft drinks. Advertisers know how to create a desire for sweet, salty, and greasy snacks.

Try This!

Look for a TV ad for an empty-calorie snack. Take notes on the methods the advertiser uses to sell the product. Discuss the ad with your classmates.

 TECHNOLOGY

Having Your Cake and Eating It Too

Imagine being able to eat a scoop of rich ice cream without worrying about the fat and calories! Simplesse, developed in 1982, was one of the earliest fat substitutes. Made from milk and egg protein, it greatly reduces the fat content of frozen desserts when substituted for cream or other fats. For example, 4 ounces of ice cream normally contains 15 grams of fat. When made with Simplesse, it has less than 1 gram of fat.

Try This!

Find out more about fat substitutes. Summarize your findings in a brief report.

FRIENDS & FAMILY

EXERCISING THE FAMILY

Teens have found that it's easier to begin an exercise program if other family members are involved. You can start by discussing your plan with parents. Tell them what your goals are and how you would like to reach them. For example, you may want to start exercising four times a week.

TRY THIS!

Talk to family members about types of exercises you could do together. Then plan a weekly schedule of specific exercise sessions.

 MATH CONNECTION

GETTING ACTIVE

Several factors influence the number of calories you burn during physical activity. One factor is the type of activity. Aerobic exercise—such as jogging, bicycling, and swimming—gives your heart and lungs a workout and burns the most calories per minute. Another factor is your weight. The heavier you are, the more calories you will burn.

 Follow Up

1. Choose a sports activity from the chart on page 321. Plan to spend 30 minutes at that activity three times a week. Approximately how many calories will you burn in a week?

2. Sports and regular exercise routines are two ways to get active. What are some other ways you can add physical activity to your daily life at home and at school?

CHAPTER 11 ACTIVITIES 323

Teaching the MATH CONNECTION

Discuss with students how much of their time they are inactive. Point out that they sit all day in school. Ask how many sit in a bus, subway, or car when traveling to and from school. They probably sit at home while doing homework and relaxing. Tell them that all that sitting puts them at risk for weight gain, especially if they consume too many calories at the same time. Encourage students to find ways to incorporate physical activities into their lives to keep the calories in food from turning into excess fat.

 Follow Up

Answers to Follow-Up
1. Answers will vary.
2. Answers will vary but might include walking to school, the library, or the store.

CHAPTER 11

Activities

Consumer Focus

Ask students to name and describe examples of advertisements they have seen that use any of the following methods to make snack products more appealing: animation, bright colors, celebrity endorsements, special computer effects. Discuss whether these advertisements appear more for healthful foods or for snack items.

 TECHNOLOGY

Discuss possible reasons why food companies have developed replacements for fat. Ask students whether they have ever tried any of the foods containing these substitutes. Have them share their opinions about the quality and tastes of the foods they have tried.

 FRIENDS & FAMILY

Encourage students to ask parents or siblings to help them in preparing a weekly fitness schedule so that they can set aside time to take part in exercise sessions together. Point out that working toward physical fitness with family members is a great way to spend time together and become healthier in the process.

323

CHAPTER 11 REVIEW

Checking Comprehension

Use the Chapter Summary and the Chapter 11 Review to help students go over the most important ideas presented in Chapter 11.

Answers to Words to Know

1. Answers will vary according to which food group student chooses.
2. A vegetarian is a person who eats no meat. Some vegetarians eat no meat or meat products.
3. Wellness is the achievement of a high level of overall health.
4. Moderation means avoiding extremes in doing something.
5. Nutrient-dense foods are rich in the nutrients the body needs to stay healthy. Examples will vary but should include foods that are rich in proteins, carbohydrates, vitamins, minerals, and water.
6. Candy, chips, cola, and sweet desserts are called empty-calorie foods because they are high in calories but low in nutrients.
7. Stamina is the ability to perform a single activity for a long time without stopping.
8. Aerobic exercise is nonstop, repetitive, vigorous exercise that increases breathing and heartbeat rates. Swimming and jogging are aerobic exercises.

Answers to Review Questions

1. The larger area at the base of the pyramid shows that you need more servings of foods in that group. As you go up the pyramid and the areas get smaller, you need fewer servings of those foods.

324

Chapter Summary

- The Food Guide Pyramid shows you how to plan a healthful diet for each day. It suggests a number of daily servings for each category of food.
- The five food groups are grains; vegetables; fruits; milk products; and meat, poultry, fish, eggs, dry beans, and nuts. Each category of food contains different nutrients.
- Following the Dietary Guidelines will help you stay healthy: Eat a variety of foods; maintain healthy weight; choose a diet low in fat—especially saturated fat—and cholesterol; eat plenty of vegetables, fruits, and grains; use sugar, salt, and sodium only in moderation; avoid alcoholic beverages.
- A balanced diet is necessary to provide your body with the nutrients it needs.
- Eating healthful snacks can be part of your daily meal plan. You should eat snacks that are nutrient-dense and avoid empty-calorie snacks.
- By choosing wisely, you can eat nutritious meals in restaurants.
- Physical fitness brings many benefits, such as feeling healthy and having stamina.
- The key to controlling your weight is to balance the number of calories you get from the foods you eat with the amount of energy you use.
- Exercise is necessary to reach and maintain a healthy body weight.

Words to Know

Using complete sentences, answer the following questions on a separate sheet of paper.

1. Select a *food group* and name five foods that are in that group.
2. What is a *vegetarian*?
3. Describe *wellness*.
4. If you do something in *moderation*, what do you do?
5. What are *nutrient-dense foods*? Give two examples of nutrient-dense snacks.
6. Why are candy, chips, cola, and sweet desserts called *empty-calorie foods*?
7. What does it mean when you have *stamina*?
8. What is *aerobic exercise*? Give an example.

Review Questions

Using complete sentences, answer the following questions on a separate sheet of paper.

1. How does the shape of the Food Guide Pyramid help you remember what to eat each day?
2. How do you know how many servings to eat from each food group?
3. Why is it important to eat a variety of foods?

324   CHAPTER 11: DEVELOPING HEALTHY HABITS

EXTRA CREDIT PROJECT

Extending Chapter Content Have students prepare a debate or speech arguing the validity of the following statements about healthy habits: "Early to bed and early to rise makes a man healthy and wealthy and wise;" or "Healthy Mind in a Healthy Body." Ask students first to try to locate where the statement originated. Have them work in teams, each team taking sides on whether or not they feel the statement is true. Have teams develop arguments using information from Chapter 11 to defend or explain their position. After teams rehearse their sides, allow them to hold debates in front of the class.

CHAPTER 11 REVIEW

4. List the Dietary Guidelines for Americans.
5. What guidelines should everyone follow when choosing snacks?
6. How can you select healthy foods when eating out?
7. How does exercise help you control your weight?
8. Why are fad diets generally unsuccessful in helping people control their weight?

Thinking Critically

Using complete sentences, answer the following questions on a separate sheet of paper.

1. **Analyze** Why do you think that many teens have poor eating habits?
2. **Explain** Why do manufacturers of food products aim a large portion of their advertising at children and teens?
3. **Evaluate** Do you think that the American lifestyle contributes to physical fitness? Why or why not?

Cooperative Learning

1. Working in groups of four or five, plan menus for your school's lunch program. Have each group member write a menu for one day of the week. Base your menus on the Food Guide Pyramid and the Dietary Guidelines for Americans. Exchange weekly menu plans with another group and evaluate each other's ideas.
2. Working with a partner, invent a sweet, salty, or greasy food product. Design the packaging for your product. Include a warning label that lists the health hazards of eating the food. Display your design on the class bulletin board.

Family & Community

1. Plan some family fitness fun. Organize backyard games, such as volleyball or badminton, or get your family to go bowling together on a Saturday afternoon. Think of other ways to encourage your family to be physically active.
2. Find out about organized exercise programs and sports activities for young teens in your community. These programs may be sponsored by schools, community centers, parks, or youth groups. If you are not already participating in a program, make plans to join one.

Building A Portfolio

1. Make two changes in your behavior each day that reflect healthful choices. They can be small changes, such as eating an apple instead of a candy bar or walking up a flight of stairs instead of taking an elevator. Record these healthful choices in a daily diary. Keep your diary in your portfolio.
2. Plan a meal based on the Food Guide Pyramid and Dietary Guidelines. Prepare the meal for your family. Then write a report on how the meal turned out. Place your report and your menu in your portfolio.

Chapter 11 Review   325

CHAPTER 11 REVIEW

2. The Food Guide Pyramid indicates how many servings of food you need from each food group.
3. You need more than 40 different nutrients for good health, and no single food or food group can supply all the nutrients in the amounts you need.
4. Eat a variety of foods; maintain healthy weight; choose a diet low in fat, saturated fat, and cholesterol; eat plenty of vegetables, fruits, and grains; use sugars only in moderation; use salt and sodium only in moderation; avoid alcoholic beverages.
5. Count snacks in your total calories for the day; choose food from each of the food groups; space out your snacks.
6. Select foods that are low in fat, sugar, salt, and calories; choose nutrient-dense dishes; limit treats; remember that sauces, stuffings, and toppings can add calories.
7. By balancing the calories you get from food with the calories you burn during exercise, you can lose, gain, or maintain your weight.
8. Fad diets cut out certain foods, lack variety, and don't usually satisfy people's appetites. They are hard to stay on long enough to lose weight.

Evaluate

Use the Chapter 11 Test in the TCR, or construct your own test using the Testmaker Software.

CLOSE

Have students apply their knowledge of the chapter's content by completing one of the alternative assessment activities listed under Family and Community or Building a Portfolio.

Answers to Thinking Critically

1. Teens generally need more nutrients and calories than adults, since their bodies are growing. They may not eat enough of a variety of foods. Teens also snack a lot and often eat on the go, and they may not pay attention to the nutritional value of what they eat. Many teens are concerned about weight and may not know the proper way to lose weight.
2. Children and teens watch a lot of television, where most of the ads appear. They often ask their parents to buy foods they see advertised.
3. Answers will vary, but students should give reasons for their opinion.

Planning Guide
Chapter 12 Working in the Kitchen

LESSON 1	Pages	FEATURES	CLASSROOM RESOURCES
Food Safety and Sanitation	328–331	Try This: Dish-washing Safety	📁 Concept Map 19 📁 Cross Curriculum 13 📁 Lesson 1 Quiz 📓 Student Workbook Activities 82, 83
LESSON 2 **Kitchen Safety**	332–336	Skills in Action: How to Use a Fire Extinguisher	📁 Cooperative Learning 23 📁 Lesson 2 Quiz 📁 Peer Pressure and Decision Making 25 🖥 Transparency 51, "A Safe and Sanitary Kitchen" 📓 Student Workbook Activities 84, 85
LESSON 3 **Kitchen Tools and Equipment**	337–342	Skills in Action: Which Tool?	📁 Activity and Project Card 23, "Measuring Equipment" 📁 Enrichment 14 📁 Lesson 3 Quiz 🖥 Transparency 52, "Kitchen Tools for Kitchen Tasks" 📓 Student Workbook Activity 86
LESSON 4 **Microwave Cooking**	343–349	Tips for Living: Microwave Tricks Skills in Action: Converting Conventional Oven Recipes	📁 Food Lab Activity 3, "Mexico from the Microwave!" 📁 Lesson 4 Quiz 🖥 Transparency 53, "Microwave Musts" 📓 Student Workbook Activities 87, 88
LESSON 5 **The School Foods Lab**	350–354	Tips for Living: Saving Time in the Kitchen Skills in Action: Rating the Team's Success	📁 Activity and Project Card 24, "It's All in the Game" 📁 Cooperative Learning 24 📁 Lesson 5 Quiz 📁 Peer Pressure and Decision Making 26 📓 Student Workbook Activity 89

CHAPTER 12 RESOURCES

📁 Chapter 12 Test 📁 Study Guide 12, *Reteaching* 💾 Testmaker Software
📁 Reteaching 12

Performance Assessment Activity

Have students work in pairs to create public service announcements or advertisements about working in the kitchen. Have students choose from the following topics: Sources of food contamination; Handling food safely; Kitchen cleanup; Preventing falls in the kitchen; Preventing fires and burns in the kitchen; Preventing cuts in the kitchen; Preventing electrical shocks in the kitchen; Proper use of kitchen tools; Proper use of kitchen appliances; Teamwork in the kitchen. Have pairs present their public service announcements or advertisements to the class.

School-to-Work

Invite people from the food service industry in the local community to give a panel presentation for the students, discussing careers in this field. The panel might consist of a food server, cafeteria worker, restaurant manager, grocery store manager, sanitation inspector, caterer, and dining room attendant. Have students ask prepared questions regarding entry-level skills, special training, or education needed for particular jobs; starting wages; responsibilities; promotions; and job benefits.

Family & Community

Suggest that students work with family members to analyze the food safety and sanitation practices in their home kitchen. Have students and family members brainstorm problems they have associated with food handling, food preparation, kitchen cleanup, and dishwashing. Ask them to discuss with family members solutions to each problem they identified. Have the family use these ideas to formulate a checklist of Do's and Don'ts to post in the kitchen. The issue of safety and sanitation may be a sensitive one within some families. Stress to students that family discussions and checklists can be kept private and need not be shared with the class.

Resources for the Teacher

Bridge, Fred, and Jean F. Tibbetts. *The Well-Tooled Kitchen.* New York: Morrow, 1992.

Goodman, Robert. *A Quick Guide to Food Safety.* San Diego: Silvercat Publications, 1992.

"Toaster Ovens & Broilers." *Consumer Reports* (October 1994), p. 634.

Readings for the Student

Cappellini, Nancy. *Ethnic Cooking the Microwave Way.* Minneapolis: Lerner Publications, 1994.

Lansky, Vicky. *Microwave Cooking for Kids.* New York: Scholastic, Inc., 1992.

Weaver, Rebecca, and Rodney Dale. *Machines in the Home.* New York: Oxford University Press, 1993.

Multimedia Resources

Kitchen Safety: What Would You Do If . . . (Apple, 2 disks). Orange Juice Software Systems, Inc.

Safety Sense (Videocassette). Great Plains National.

OUT OF TIME?

If time does not permit thorough teaching of this chapter, you may wish to use:

- Teens Making a Difference, page 327
- Tips for Living, pages 347, 352
- Try This, page 329
- Skills in Action, pages 334, 338, 348, 353
- Young Living Activities, page 355
- Chapter Summary, page 356

CHAPTER 12

Working in the Kitchen

Chapter Overview

Chapter 12 introduces students to kitchen safety and sanitation skills. They learn what measures to take to prevent accidents in the kitchen. Students also learn how to use small and large kitchen tools and equipment. Students compare the similarities of working in the kitchen at school and at home.

LESSON 1 describes food safety and sanitation principles.
LESSON 2 explains how to prevent spills and falls, burns and fires, and cuts and electrical shocks.
LESSON 3 describes how to use kitchen tools and small and large appliances.
LESSON 4 discusses how to use microwave ovens.
LESSON 5 describes how to follow a work plan and work as a team member in the school foods lab.

Introducing the Chapter

Have students skim the titles of the lessons in this chapter. Ask them to identify the lesson in which they are likely to find the answer to each question. How can I prevent falls in the kitchen? *(Lesson 2)* What causes food poisoning? *(Lesson 1)* How can work duties in the kitchen be organized? *(Lesson 5)* What basic tools and cookware are needed in a kitchen? *(Lesson 3)* How do I prepare food for cooking in a microwave oven? *(Lesson 4)*

Chapter Motivator

Have students write short answers to the following questions: About how many times a week do you prepare a meal in your kitchen? What kinds of meals do you prepare? What is your favorite food item to prepare?

CHAPTER 12 Working in the Kitchen

LESSON ONE
Food Safety and Sanitation

LESSON TWO
Kitchen Safety

LESSON THREE
Kitchen Tools and Equipment

LESSON FOUR
Microwave Cooking

LESSON FIVE
The School Foods Lab

326

KEY TO ABILITY LEVELS

Teaching strategies that appear throughout the chapter have been identified by one of three codes to give you an idea of their suitability for students of varying learning styles and abilities.

L1 Level 1 strategies should be within the ability range of all students. Often full class participation is required. Teacher direction is usually needed.

L2 Level 2 strategies are for average to above-average students or for small groups. Some teacher direction is necessary.

L3 Level 3 strategies are designed for students able and willing to work independently. Minimal teacher direction is necessary.

TEENS MAKING A DIFFERENCE
Meals on Wheels

Every Saturday, Eric goes to work in a church kitchen where he helps prepare 200 meals. He is a volunteer for Meals on Wheels, a national program that prepares and delivers meals to elderly shut-ins. Whether he's peeling potatoes or mixing muffins, Eric's help is always needed.

Once prepared, the meals are delivered by Eric and other volunteers. It's clear to Eric that for most of the people he serves, his smiling face and cheery hello are the high point of their day. The feeling that he's making a difference is all that Eric needs to keep up the hard work—and to give up his Saturdays.

Try THIS!
Learn more about the Meals on Wheels program in your community. How can you volunteer? Do you think that it's something you would like to do?

TECHNOLOGY IN THE CLASSROOM

Technology in the Kitchen Computers are used everywhere today, even in the kitchen. With the right software, a computer can help do many things. You can use the software to plan a menu. If you input how many people you want to feed and some of the ingredients you would like to use, the computer will print out a menu, complete with recipes. If you know that one of your guests loves blueberries, the software will give you a list of recipes using blueberries. It can also adjust the amount of ingredients in a recipe, based on the number of people you want the recipe to serve. You can also print a shopping list, making it easy to know what you need to buy.

CHAPTER 12

TEENS MAKING A DIFFERENCE

Have students read "Teens Making a Difference." Ask students to identify the kinds of volunteer work Eric does to pitch in for Meals on Wheels. (*peels potatoes, mixes muffins, delivers the meals*) Discuss with students the benefits Eric receives as a result of his work. Then ask them to describe the kinds of volunteer work they do or would like to do.

Have students research to find the answers to the questions at the end of the feature. Ask them to share their findings with the class.

BLOCK SCHEDULING

The following Teacher Classroom Resources are suggested for use in classrooms with Block Scheduling.
- Activity and Project Card 23, "Measuring Equipment"
- Activity and Project Card 24, "It's All in the Game"
- Cooperative Learning 23, "The Do's and Don'ts of Kitchen Safety"
- Cooperative Learning 24, "Working Together in Food Preparation"

LESSON ONE
Food Safety and Sanitation

FOCUS

Lesson Objectives
After studying this lesson, students should be able to
- identify the sources of food contamination.
- explain how to handle food safely.
- describe ways to keep the kitchen clean.

Motivating Activity
Have students list three examples and descriptions of sanitation practices they follow in their kitchens at home.

Introducing the Lesson
Write students' responses to the Motivating Activity on the board. Ask students to explain how the sanitation practices that they follow in the kitchen help keep them healthy. Tell them that in this lesson they will learn how to prevent the growth of harmful bacteria in food.

Introducing *Words to Know*
Ask a volunteer to read the vocabulary words and their definitions. Ask students to use the vocabulary words to write a paragraph about food safety.

LESSON ONE
Food Safety and Sanitation

WORDS TO KNOW

contamination
salmonella
perishable

DISCOVER...
- the sources of food contamination.
- how to handle food safely.
- ways to keep the kitchen clean.

When Samantha gets home from school, she washes her hands in warm, soapy water and looks for a snack. She finds some leftover chicken in the refrigerator, but because it smells funny, she throws it out. She uses a clean spoon to dish out a bowl of applesauce. Before she takes the bowl to the kitchen table, she puts the jar of applesauce back in the refrigerator. Why do you think Samantha is so careful with food?

328 CHAPTER 12: WORKING IN THE KITCHEN

CLASSROOM RESOURCES FOR LESSON 1

 Blackline Masters
Concept Map 19
Cross Curriculum 13
Lesson 1 Quiz

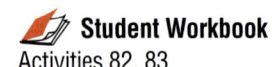 **Student Workbook**
Activities 82, 83

Keeping Food Safe

Samantha knows that eating unsafe food can make people very sick. Her eating habits and cleanliness help to prevent **contamination,** or *becoming infected with bacteria.*

You may think that food contamination is not a serious problem. In mild cases of food poisoning, people may experience headaches, stomach cramps, and fever. In more severe cases, however, medical attention may be necessary. The good news is that you have the power to reduce the risk of food contamination by understanding what causes it. Then you can follow some simple procedures when handling and preparing food to protect yourself from food poisoning.

A few types of bacteria cause most food poisoning. One of the most serious forms of food poisoning is caused by **salmonella** (SAL-muh-NELL-uh), or *bacteria that are often found in raw or undercooked foods, such as meat, eggs, fish, and poultry.* Salmonella grow quickly at room temperature and can be spread by hands and cooking utensils. For this reason, you must thoroughly cook all meat, poultry, fish, and eggs. You should also wash your hands, knife, and cutting board with soap and hot water whenever you cut raw meat, fish, or poultry.

Another way to reduce the risk of food poisoning is to handle perishable foods carefully. Foods that are **perishable** are *likely to spoil quickly.* Common perishable foods include meat, poultry, fish, eggs, and dairy products. Bacteria grow quickly at temperatures between 60°F and 125°F (16°C and 52°C). Therefore hot foods, such as hamburgers, should be kept hot, and cold foods, such as yogurt, should be kept cold until they are eaten. Keep hot foods at 140°F (60°C) or above and cold foods at 40°F (4°C) or below.

Foods that have been cooked should not stand at room temperature for more than two hours. If you are packing food for a school lunch or a picnic, use cold packs and a cooler to keep the cold foods cold.

> **Try This!**
> To make sure that you are washing dishes as safely and efficiently as possible, soak cooked-on food in pots and pans while you are eating so that they are easier to wash later. To avoid injury, wash knives and other sharp objects separately. Wash dishes in hot, soapy water, and rinse them with plenty of hot water.

Why is it important to wash a cutting board with soap and hot water?

LESSON ONE: FOOD SAFETY AND SANITATION

HOME AND COMMUNITY CONNECTION

Field Trip Have a group of volunteers organize an after-school visit to a local grocery store to observe how foods are cared for and stored to ensure food safety. Have students contact the manager of the store ahead of time to arrange the visit. Ask the manager to explain food-handling procedures in departments that contain perishables, such as the dairy, meat, deli, and produce departments. Have students check items in the store for dating codes on various products, such as milk, bread, canned foods, meats, and cereal boxes.

CHAPTER 12, LESSON 1

TEACH

> **Try This!**
> Ask students to make a poster for a dishwashing detergent. Tell them to write directions on the poster for washing dishes using their dish detergent. Have them share their poster with the class.

L2 Discussing
On a table in the classroom, display several items that can cause food contamination in the kitchen and several foods that spoil easily. The items and foods might include: roach or insect killer, wood cutting board, cutting knife, kitchen towels, baster, eggs, milk, chicken, and fish. Ask students to determine the relationship between the items and the foods and food safety. Discuss the proper handling of each item and of the food in order to avoid food contamination.

L1 Finding Examples
Have students use magazines to find examples of foods that are perishable. Have them place their examples on a large sheet of paper. Next to each example, have them write a caption explaining the proper handling of the perishable item to prevent food poisoning.

L2 Science Connection
Assign Cross-Curriculum Activity 13 in the TCR. Students learn about dangers in the kitchen in this activity.

CHAPTER 12, LESSON 1

TEACHER TALK!
More Sanitation Tips
Point out other kitchen sanitation tips to students, such as keeping appliances clean. Note that bacteria can grow in refrigerators, freezers, ovens, and toasters. Remind students that these appliances should be unplugged before cleaning them with warm soapy water.

USING VISUALS
Have students describe and demonstrate each safety guideline shown in Figure 12.1. Ask students to identify other safety guidelines to follow in preventing food contamination.

L1 Student Workbook
Assign Activities 82 and 83 in the Student Workbook.

ASSESS
Evaluating the Lesson
Assign Reviewing Terms and Facts and Thinking Critically on page 331 to review the lesson; then assign the Lesson 1 Quiz in the TCR.

Reteaching
- Have students make a concept map on food contamination.
- Have students complete Reteaching Activity 12 in the TCR.
- Assign Concept Map 19 in the TCR.

330

How to Store Leftovers

To keep leftovers from spoiling, refrigerate or freeze them immediately after the meal. Put leftovers in a tightly covered shallow container, and store them in the refrigerator. Many leftovers can also be frozen for use at a later date. When freezing leftovers, pack them in an airtight container, and label them with the name of the food and the date. Freezing foods keeps bacteria from growing until the food is thawed out. Most foods can be stored in the freezer for several months. **Figure 12.1** shows other ways to prevent food contamination.

Figure 12.1
Preventing Food Contamination
For your health and the health of others, it is important to handle foods safely and to keep the kitchen clean.

330 CHAPTER 12: WORKING IN THE KITCHEN

COOPERATIVE LEARNING
Food Inspector Have students work in small groups to prepare food in the foods lab. Have students in each group take turns serving as a food inspector for the group. Have the inspectors watch how food is handled and whether sanitary cleanup procedures are followed. If a video camera is available, group activity may be videotaped for one day, and inspectors can critique the tape for the class. Ask the inspectors to write up an evaluation of the group's sanitary practices. Have the inspectors discuss their evaluations with the group.

Keeping the Kitchen Clean

Jeff and his dad always clean up the kitchen as they cook. They wipe up spills immediately and clean off the countertops. As they finish using pots, pans, and cooking utensils, they wash them in hot, soapy water. By keeping the kitchen clean, Jeff and his dad make it a more healthful and pleasant place to work.

A Safe, Clean Kitchen

Properly stored leftovers will be safe for later use. Why should you write the date on these leftovers?

The best defense against food poisoning in the kitchen is to work actively to prevent it. That means following the procedures suggested in this lesson. Put these ideas into practice to keep food safe and to keep the kitchen clean.

LESSON ONE Review

Using complete sentences, answer the following questions on a separate sheet of paper.

Reviewing Terms and Facts
1. **Describe** What are the symptoms of mild food poisoning?
2. **Recall** What causes food poisoning?
3. **Vocabulary** Define the term *perishable*. Give two examples of perishable foods.
4. **Identify** What should you do to keep leftovers from spoiling?

Thinking Critically
5. **Apply** What could you do in your kitchen to prevent food from becoming contaminated?
6. **Explain** Why is a dirty kitchen unhealthy and unpleasant?

Applying Concepts
7. Write two food safety slogans you might find helpful. If possible, display them in the kitchen at home or at school.
8. Imagine that your class is having a dinner party for parents. Your job is to make sure that the food served is safe to eat. Write down ten procedures you would follow to make the food safe as well as delicious.

LESSON ONE: FOOD SAFETY AND SANITATION

MEETING STUDENT DIVERSITY

Varied Learning Styles As students consider food safety techniques, some class members may benefit from physical examples and from brief, focused role-playing activities. Whenever possible, have students perform or role-play the suggestions in the lesson's "Tips for Living" feature. Pair students with partners and have partners work together to perform or demonstrate the appropriate tips. Evaluate students' demonstrations and encourage cooperative learning techniques.

CHAPTER 12, LESSON 1

Answers to Lesson 1 Review

1. Headaches, stomach cramps, and fever; in some cases symptoms are severe enough to require medical attention.
2. A few types of bacteria cause most food poisoning.
3. Spoil quickly. Any two: eggs, meat, milk.
4. Any five from the illustration "Preventing Food Contamination," Figure 12.1 on page 330.
5. Clean as you cook. Wipe up spills immediately, and wipe counters clean. Fill the sink with warm soapy water and wash the cooking utensils as you finish using them.
6. A dirty kitchen can cause food contamination and it looks and feels unpleasant.
7. Answers will vary. Students write two food safety slogans.
8. Answers will vary. Students write down ten steps to make food safe as well as delicious.

Enrichment

Have students research first-aid measures for someone with food poisoning. Ask them to write a health pamphlet describing the symptoms and treatment of food poisoning.

CLOSE

Ask students to make a menu for a picnic lunch to take to the beach on a warm day.

LESSON TWO
Kitchen Safety

FOCUS

Lesson Objectives
After studying this lesson, students should be able to
- identify causes of common kitchen accidents.
- describe ways to prevent spills and falls, burns and fires, cuts and electrical shocks in the kitchen.

Motivating Activity
Have students write a kitchen safety rule.

Introducing the Lesson
Have students share their responses to the Motivating Activity. Point out that the variety of responses indicates that there are many hazards in the kitchen. Tell students that in this lesson they will learn many tips for preventing accidents in the kitchen.

Introducing *Words to Know*
Have students read the vocabulary words and their definitions. Ask them to write a sentence defining each word and give an example of each.

LESSON TWO
Kitchen Safety

flammable

conduct

DISCOVER...
- the causes of common kitchen accidents.
- ways to prevent common accidents from occurring in the kitchen.

When Michael realizes that he has only 20 minutes before he has to leave for practice, he grabs a dining room chair, stands on it, and starts looking through a high cabinet for a snack. As he reaches for the crackers on the top shelf, the chair wobbles, and Michael falls to the kitchen floor. He picks up most of the crackers that spilled out and throws them away. Then he pours himself a glass of milk and takes his food into the dining room.

332 CHAPTER 12: WORKING IN THE KITCHEN

CLASSROOM RESOURCES FOR LESSON 2

 Blackline Masters
Cooperative Learning 23
Lesson 2 Quiz
Peer Pressure and Decision Making 25

 Transparencies
Transparency 51, "A Safe and Sanitary Kitchen"

 Student Workbook
Activities 84, 85

Preventing Accidents

Michael's fall is a typical kitchen accident. The most common accidents that occur in the kitchen include

- falls.
- burns.
- cuts.
- electric shocks.

These types of accidents and injuries are usually preventable if people develop good, safe work habits.

Falls

The same day that Michael fell, Michael's sister Marcie ran into the kitchen, slipped on cracker crumbs, and also fell. Because Michael was rushing to practice, he hadn't done a good job of cleaning up the mess he had made. Although neither Michael nor Marcie was badly hurt, one or both of them might have been. To prevent falls, Michael and Marcie now follow these guidelines.

- Keep cupboard doors and drawers closed when not in use.
- Stand on a short stepladder or a sturdy step stool with a waist-high hand bar to get at high or hard-to-reach items.
- Turn pot and pan handles toward the center of the stove or counter so that the pots or pans won't get knocked over.
- Clean up spilled foods or liquids immediately.

Burns

Jenny was cooking french fries on the stove when the phone rang. She left the kitchen to answer it. After a few minutes, Jenny heard the smoke alarm go off. She ran into the kitchen and found that the pan was smoking and popping. Jenny hadn't realized how quickly a grease fire can start.

▲ If you need to reach for something on a high shelf, use a small stepladder or step stool. What else can you do to prevent falls from occurring in the kitchen?

LESSON TWO: KITCHEN SAFETY **333**

CHAPTER 12, LESSON 2

TEACH

L2 Observe
Pantomime several incorrect safety practices for the students, such as standing on a folding chair to reach an item in a high cabinet, cutting a carrot toward your body, and placing a pot handle toward the walkway. Have students jot down the kinds of safety violations they observe. Discuss the observations and what the consequences can be when people follow unsafe kitchen practices.

L2 Applying Life Skills
Explain to students that accidents often happen as a result of a pattern of five elements known as an accident chain. Review with students the concept introduced in Chapter 9, Lesson 3. Draw on the board a chain with five links. Inside each link write, in order, the following elements: situation, unsafe habit, unsafe act, accident, and results of accident. Have students choose an unsafe kitchen practice to illustrate the elements of an accident chain. Then explain that most kitchen accidents can be prevented if any one of the first three elements of the chain is changed.

L1 Using Transparencies
Present Color Transparency 51, "A Safe and Sanitary Kitchen," in the TCR. Use this overhead visual to reinforce concepts from this lesson.

MORE ABOUT • • •

Safety in the Kitchen Point out to students that a common accident in the kitchen is choking. To help a choking victim, you must dislodge the object blocking the airway. Review with students the first aid for choking. Have them practice the following steps for first aid for choking on a large doll: 1) Stand behind the victim, wrapping your arms around his or her waist. Put the thumb side of your wrist against the person's abdomen, just above the navel. 2) Grasp your fist with the other hand and apply pressure inward and up toward the diaphragm with quick, upward thrusts until the person is no longer choking. Do not thrust the ribs.

333

CHAPTER 12, LESSON 2

Ask students to locate the fire extinguisher in the foods lab. Have a volunteer read the instructions for using the fire extinguisher. Also remind students that another safety feature that should be located near all kitchens is a smoke detector. Tell students that it is important to read the directions on a smoke-detector label.

L1 Role-Playing

Have students review ways to prevent kitchen accidents by practicing safe work habits. Ask volunteers to role-play the kitchen safety rules in the following situations:
Washing sharp objects.
Using a knife and cutting board to cut apples.
Disconnecting electrical appliances before cleaning.
Using a pot holder to remove food from an oven.

L3 Critical Thinking

Have students draw cartoons of a kitchen with safety hazards present. Allow them to exchange drawings and list the hazards found in the cartoons.

L2 Problem Solving

Assign Peer Pressure and Decision Making 25 in the TCR. This activity gives students the opportunity to recognize peer pressure and practice decision-making skills.

L2 Cooperative Learning

Assign Cooperative Learning Activity 23, "The Do's and Don'ts of Kitchen Safety," in the TCR.

How to Use a Fire Extinguisher

Every kitchen should be equipped with a fire extinguisher. To learn how to use one, study the following steps.
1. Pull the ring.
2. Stand back several feet from the fire, point the nozzle at the base of the flames, and squeeze the handle.
3. Spray the foam back and forth across the base of the fire.

You can prevent most fires and burns in the kitchen if you follow these safety precautions.

- Avoid leaving the kitchen if you have food cooking. Fires can spread in seconds.

- Use medium or low temperatures for cooking greasy foods, such as french fries or fried chicken. If a grease fire starts, turn off the heat and smother the fire with a tight-fitting lid. Never use water—it will make a grease fire spread.

- Keep all flammable objects away from the stove. **Flammable** means *capable of burning easily.* Be especially careful with paper bags, pot holders, kitchen towels, curtains, and plastic containers.

- Use dry pot holders when cooking hot foods and liquids or removing them from the stove, oven, or microwave.

- When cooking, remove pan lids by tilting them away from you. This allows steam to escape safely at the back of the pot, away from your hands and face.

- Don't wear clothing with long, loose-fitting sleeves when cooking. The sleeves can easily catch fire.

- If your hair is long, tie it back.

- Keep a fire extinguisher in or near the kitchen where you can reach it quickly and safely. Be sure that you know how to use it properly.

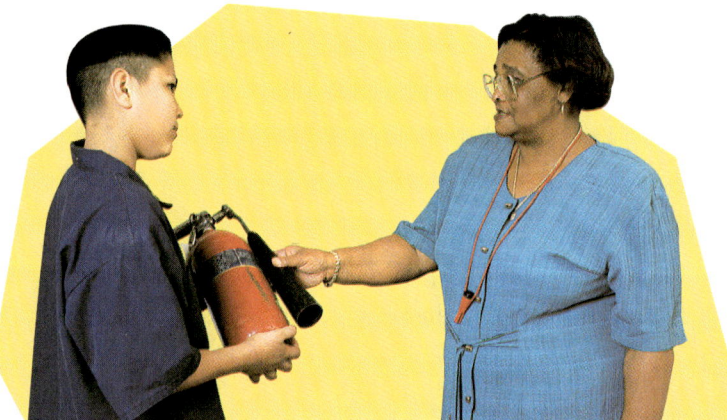

If you cook, you should know how to use a fire extinguisher. Where should it be kept?

334 CHAPTER 12: WORKING IN THE KITCHEN

COOPERATIVE LEARNING

Applying Kitchen Safety Rules Organize the class into four groups. Assign each group one of the following topics: spills and falls, burns and fires, cuts, and electrical shock. Have each group refer to the text to help members write a script to perform the kitchen safety rules for their topic. Each member of the group should have a part in the presentation. If possible, have the students use the lab kitchen as the stage to present their script.

334

Cuts

Belinda wanted to make a salad for lunch. Since she couldn't find the cutting board, she decided to peel and chop the vegetables over the sink. The good knives were all dirty, so she found an old knife in the back of the drawer. As she was slicing a tomato, she cut her finger. Belinda probably could have avoided cutting herself if she had followed a few safety precautions. To prevent kitchen cuts, observe the following safety rules.

To prevent cuts, use a cutting board when you chop food. In which direction should you cut food?

- Keep knives sharp. Sharp knives are safer than dull ones.

- Cut food away from your body. Use a cutting board for all cutting jobs—even if it's only a single apple.

- Wash knives and sharp objects separately from other utensils.

- Store knives in a special compartment in the drawer or in a knife holder. Put them away immediately after cleaning them.

- Never pick up broken glass with bare hands. Sweep it into a dustpan immediately. Then wipe the floor with several thicknesses of damp paper towel, put broken pieces into a bag, and place the bag in a trash can.

Electric Shocks

Emilio was making breakfast when his bagel got stuck in the toaster. Emilio's mother told him to unplug the toaster and then use a fork or tongs to get the bagel out.

Electrical appliances make kitchen tasks easier, but they can also cause electric shocks. To prevent shocks, take the following precautions.

LESSON TWO: KITCHEN SAFETY

CHAPTER 12, LESSON 2

L2 Reading

Have students collect newspaper and magazine articles about home accidents and determine where most accidents in the home occur. Ask them to analyze each article and state safety practices that could have been followed to prevent the accident. Save these articles in a file for future reference.

L1 Student Workbook

Assign Activities 84 and 85 in the Student Workbook.

ASSESS

Evaluating the Lesson

Assign Reviewing Terms and Facts and Thinking Critically on page 336 to review the lesson; then assign the Lesson 2 Quiz in the TCR.

Reteaching

- Have each student write on a slip of paper a question about kitchen safety. Example questions: Why should cabinet doors and drawers be kept closed? Why should appliances be unplugged before cleaning? Place the slips in a box. Divide the class into two teams. Ask each team to take turns answering questions on the slips drawn from the box.

- Have students complete Reteaching Activity 12 in the TCR.

MEETING STUDENT DIVERSITY

Cultural Perspectives Students who are still acquiring English skills may need assistance in understanding kitchen safety practices. Provide photographs and/or descriptions to help them identify each. Encourage the students to work in groups to design universal symbols to warn of the dangers of kitchen accidents. Have groups share their symbols with the class.

CHAPTER 12, LESSON 2

Answers to Lesson 2 Review

1. Falls, burns, cuts, and electrical shocks.
2. Clean up spills immediately. Keep cupboard doors and drawers closed. Turn pot and pan handles in over the top of the range or counter. Use a short stepladder or a sturdy step stool with a waist-high hand bar to reach high or hard-to-get items. Put items on high shelves in boxes or baskets.
3. Capable of burning easily. Any one example: paper bags, pot holders, kitchen towels, curtains, and plastic containers.
4. Never pick up glass with bare hands. Sweep broken glass into a dustpan immediately. Wipe the floor with several thicknesses of damp paper towels, put broken pieces into a bag, and place the bag in a trash can.
5. To make the kitchen a safe environment.
6. Answers will vary. Students give an example of ways to improve their work habits.
7. You might get an electrical shock.
8. Answers will vary. Students write a paragraph on treatment of a minor bump, burn, or cut.

Enrichment

Have students draw a floor plan of their home. Have them draw routes to escape from all rooms of the house in the event of a kitchen fire.

CLOSE

Ask students to identify three safety issues in their kitchen at home that they will address with family members. Have them explain how they will make their kitchen safer.

336

- Always unplug a toaster before trying to pry food from it. Forks, knives, or other metal utensils can **conduct**, or *carry electricity*, and cause an electrical shock.
- Avoid using any appliance that has a frayed or worn cord.
- Dry your hands thoroughly before touching electrical equipment.
- Disconnect appliances by pulling out the plug, not by tugging on the cord.
- Keep portable appliances unplugged when not in use.

To avoid electric shocks, you need to be careful when using kitchen appliances. What is this teen doing to prevent a shock?

Safety in the Kitchen

Family members tend to spend a lot of time in the kitchen. Many of the accidents that occur in the kitchen can be prevented. By following the rules outlined in this lesson, you can make the kitchen a safe place to work and eat.

LESSON TWO Review

Using complete sentences, answer the following questions on a separate sheet of paper.

Reviewing Terms and Facts

1. **Recall** What are the four most common types of kitchen accidents?
2. **List** Name five ways to prevent kitchen falls.
3. **Vocabulary** Define the term *flammable*. Give two examples of objects that are flammable.
4. **Describe** Explain the safest way to pick up broken glass.

Thinking Critically

5. **Explain** Why is it necessary to develop good, safe work habits in the kitchen?
6. **Apply** How can you improve your work habits in the kitchen to make them safer?
7. **Predict** What might happen if you plugged in a blender with wet hands? Explain your answer.

Applying Concepts

8. Read about first-aid procedures in a health textbook. Find out how to treat a minor burn, or cut. Write a paragraph explaining the proper procedure and listing the supplies you would need.

336   CHAPTER 12: WORKING IN THE KITCHEN

 **HOME AND COMMUNITY CONNECTION**

Guest Speaker Invite to school a firefighter, paramedic, nurse, or doctor to explain and demonstrate first-aid procedures for falls, burns, cuts, and electrical shocks. Ask the guest to review emergency procedures in your community for serious injuries. Have students prepare questions in advance. Allow time for discussion after the presentation. Encourage students to practice the procedures and techniques that are demonstrated.

LESSON THREE
Kitchen Tools and Equipment

DISCOVER...
- how to use basic kitchen tools.
- the purposes of small kitchen equipment.
- the types of major appliances used in a kitchen.

Molly decided to bake a cake for her mother's birthday, so she bought a cake mix and vanilla icing. Because Molly had never baked a cake before, she asked her friend Chelsea to help. Chelsea said that she would bring some cookware and kitchen tools that would make their job easy. What do you think that Chelsea brought? Do you know the basic kitchen tools, cookware, and appliances to use to make your cooking tasks easier?

WORDS TO KNOW

utensils

small appliances

major appliances

microwave oven

LESSON THREE: KITCHEN TOOLS AND EQUIPMENT   337

CLASSROOM RESOURCES FOR LESSON 3

 Blackline Masters
Activity and Project Card 23, "Measuring Equipment"
Enrichment 14
Lesson 3 Quiz

 Transparencies
Transparency 52, "Kitchen Tools for Kitchen Tasks"

 **Student Workbook**
Activity 86

LESSON THREE
Kitchen Tools and Equipment

FOCUS

Lesson Objectives
After studying this lesson, students should be able to
- explain the proper use of kitchen tools.
- discuss the advantages of small equipment.
- describe the special features of major appliances.

Motivating Activity
Display several kitchen utensils on a table, labeling each with a number. Have students number their papers with the corresponding numbers of the utensils displayed. Next to each number, ask students to write the name of the utensil and explain its purpose.

Introducing the Lesson
Have students share their responses to the Motivating Activity. Then ask them to decide which of the tools displayed are essential for everyday cooking tasks. Tell students that in this lesson they will learn about the advantages of kitchen tools and appliances and how to use them.

Introducing *Words to Know*
Have each student write the Words to Know and the definition of each on a sheet of paper. Then have students exchange papers and use each word correctly in a sentence. Ask them to return the paper to its owner for that person to read and evaluate.

337

CHAPTER 12, LESSON 3

TEACH

Discuss with students the tools needed for the jobs listed in the article. Encourage them to take the tool list home to see how many of the kitchen tools they have and note where they are located. Ask students to decide whether tools are kept in safe, convenient locations.

L2 Applying Knowledge

Ask students to design an ad for a small cooking utensil. The ad should tell what the tool does and how it makes cooking easier. The ad should make the utensil seem indispensable. Have students share their ads with the class.

L1 Finding Examples

Have students compare the list of utensils in the textbook with those they find in their kitchen. Have them name and describe other utensils that they have in their kitchens. Ask them to draw a picture of each utensil and explain how their family uses it. Ask students to share their pictures and explanations with the class. Discuss whether families sometimes have different names for these utensils.

L2 Analyzing

Have students work with family members to analyze the use of storage space in their kitchen. Have them design a storage system that makes use of the suggestions described above and that the family members agree to.

Which Tool?

Test your kitchen know-how by naming the right tool for each of the following jobs:
- Turning hamburgers on the grill
- Mixing dry ingredients for a cake
- Shredding cheese to put on a pizza
- Draining the water from cooked pasta

▲ Many people use food processors to save time when chopping such foods as vegetables. Which small appliances have you used?

Small Equipment

Not all kitchen tools and cookware are essential. For example, you don't have to have a vegetable peeler to peel a carrot. You can do the job with a small knife. However, a kitchen equipped with the basic tools and cookware makes food preparation much easier.

A variety of **utensils,** or *kitchen tools,* and cookware is available. The most commonly used utensils include those for cooking, mixing, and slicing or cutting. The best cookware to use depends on the type of food you are cooking and where you are cooking it. For instance, you could use a metal cake pan to bake cookie bars in a conventional oven but not in a microwave oven. **Figure 12.2** on pages 339–341 describes some of the most basic kitchen tools and cookware.

Small Appliances

When Molly made the cake, she used a hand mixer to beat the batter. A hand mixer is a **small appliance,** or *small, electrically powered kitchen equipment.* Commonly used small appliances include toasters, food processors, and blenders.

Large Appliances

Molly needed to use one major appliance to bake her cake. **Major appliances,** or *large kitchen equipment,* include the stove, oven, refrigerator, dishwasher, and microwave oven. A **microwave oven** is *an appliance that cooks by vibrating the molecules in food.* Some major appliances, such as a stove and a refrigerator, are needed in every kitchen. Others, such as a microwave oven and a dishwasher, make food preparation easier but are not essential.

The cost of major appliances varies, depending on the extra features that are included. Each family must decide which features would be most useful to them. For example:

- Stoves usually come with conventional ovens. Some stoves also include microwave ovens, while others include convection ovens. (Continued on page 342.)

MORE ABOUT •••

Buying Small Kitchen Equipment People should buy small kitchen equipment according to the kinds and frequency of kitchen tasks performed. For example, an apple slicer might be a handy utensil if the people using it like to eat sliced apples or if they make apple pies. However, if they prefer eating their apples whole and rarely make apple pies, an apple slicer would not be a wise purchase. People should buy kitchen equipment that is well-designed, easy to operate, and durable. They should also try out the handles for comfort.

COOKING TOOLS

Figure 12.2 Kitchen Tools and Cookware
Which kitchen tools and cookware do you think are essential?

TONGS Used for lifting and turning hot foods.

COLANDER Used for draining liquids from cooked food or for rinsing fruits and vegetables.

ROTARY BEATER Used for beating light mixtures or adding air to eggs.

RUBBER SCRAPER Used for cleaning foods completely from sides of bowl.

SPATULA Used for lifting and turning foods such as pancakes and hamburgers.

LARGE SPOON Used for stirring and spooning ingredients.

KITCHEN FORK Used for lifting and turning food.

MIXING BOWLS Used for mixing ingredients. Usually come in different sizes.

LESSON THREE: KITCHEN TOOLS AND EQUIPMENT

CHAPTER 12, LESSON 3

USING VISUALS
Have students refer to Figure 12.2, showing kitchen tools and cookware, to identify the tools and cookware needed to prepare the following foods: peanut butter cookies, beef roast, tuna casserole, soup, banana bread, cupcakes, vegetable salad.

L1 Using Transparencies
Present Color Transparency 52, "Kitchen Tools for Kitchen Tasks," in the TCR. Use this overhead visual to reinforce concepts from this lesson.

DID YOU KNOW
You can save time and energy in the kitchen by properly storing your kitchen tools and equipment. These items should be stored where they are most likely to be used, with like tools and equipment, and according to the frequency of use. For example, cooking utensils should be located near the stove. Slicing and cutting tools should be stored together. Items such as a kitchen fork and a turner should be in a handy place, since these are used frequently. Organizers such as cutlery trays and turntables help make storage easier.

L2 Activity and Project Card
Allow time for students to complete Activity and Project Card 23, "Measuring Equipment," in the TCR.

MORE ABOUT •••

Using Small Kitchen Equipment Demonstrate safety techniques when using the following utensils: meat thermometer, electric mixer, and grater. Remind students to unplug an electric mixer before putting on or taking off beaters or before cleaning the mixer. Emphasize that students should keep other utensils, fingers, and hair away from rotating beaters. Demonstrate how when using a grater, they should hold the food in their writing hand and grasp the handle of the grater with the other hand. Tell them to move the food from top to bottom over the teeth of the grater and back up again in a continuous motion. Stress that they should keep fingertips and knuckles away from the grater.

CHAPTER 12, LESSON 3

L2 Applying Knowledge
Select a recipe and divide it into the same number of steps as there are class members. Write each step on an index card. Number the cards sequentially. As students arrive in class, hand out the cards. Call the steps in numerical order. Have individuals demonstrate the steps using the proper utensils and equipment.

L3 Math
Have students work with partners to learn about the features available on major kitchen appliances such as dishwashers, refrigerators, ranges, and microwaves. Have them analyze newspaper ads or catalogs from stores that sell such appliances. Ask them to estimate the cost of added features on appliances. Have them share their findings with the class.

L3 Critical Thinking
Ask students to name the different slicing and cutting tools. Ask them which they would choose if they could choose only three slicing and cutting tools. Have them explain why.

DID YOU KNOW
In 1990 about 79 percent of households in the United States had microwave ovens. Ownership increased from about 14 percent of households in 1980.

MIXING TOOLS

WIRE WHISK Used for beating and blending. Especially good for beating egg-white mixtures and stirring sauces.

SIFTER Used for removing lumps and adding air to flour before measuring. Can also combine dry ingredients.

PEELER Used for peeling fruits and vegetables.

CHEF'S KNIFE Used for cutting, mincing, slicing, and dicing food.

SLICING AND CUTTING TOOLS

CUTTING BOARD Used to protect the counter when cutting.

PARING KNIFE Small knife used for peeling and cutting fruits and vegetables.

GRATER Used for grating, shredding, or slicing vegetables and cheese.

SLICING KNIFE Used for slicing meat and poultry.

340 CHAPTER 12: WORKING IN THE KITCHEN

HOME AND COMMUNITY CONNECTION

Field Trip Ask for volunteers to visit a housewares department in a local store. Have these students preplan the trip by requesting that the store have a salesperson demonstrate how to use some of the small kitchen equipment they sell. Then have students make a comparison chart of small kitchen equipment sold at the store. Their charts should compare prices, materials, and quality of the items. Have students share their charts with classmates.

COOKWARE

COOKIE SHEET
Used for baking cookies or pizza.

MUFFIN TIN
Used for baking muffins, cupcakes, and rolls.

ROASTING PAN WITH RACK
Used for roasting meat and poultry.

PIE PAN
Used for baking pies and quiches.

LOAF PAN
Used for baking bread and meat loaf.

DOUBLE BOILER
Used for foods that burn easily, such as milk and sauces.

CAKE PANS
Used for baking cakes and bar cookies. Available in square, round, rectangular, and tube.

CASSEROLES
Ovenproof dishes, which come in a variety of sizes.

SAUCEPANS
Used for top-of-the-stove cooking. Have one long handle and a lid. Available in different sizes.

LESSON THREE: KITCHEN TOOLS AND EQUIPMENT   341

COOPERATIVE LEARNING

Cooking with Utensils Organize students into small groups. Provide each group with recipe books. Have each group chose a recipe and write its ingredients and instructions on an index card. Then have groups exchange index cards. Tell them to decide what small kitchen equipment is needed to complete the recipe. Have students add this list to the recipe instructions. Then have each group work in the kitchen lab to gather all the small kitchen equipment needed to prepare the recipe.

CHAPTER 12, LESSON 3

L1 Student Workbook
Assign Activity 86 in the Student Workbook.

ASSESS

Evaluating the Lesson
Assign Reviewing Terms and Facts and Thinking Critically on page 342 to review the lesson; then assign the Lesson 3 Quiz in the TCR.

Reteaching
- Have students make a matching game. Ask them to fold a piece of paper in half lengthwise. On the first half of the paper, ask them to write a description of ten cooking steps, such as "Peel raw potatoes for stew." On the other half of the paper, ask them to write (in random order) the name of the utensil they would use to complete the cooking step. Have students exchange papers and complete the matchup.
- Have students complete Reteaching Activity 12 in the TCR.

Enrichment
- Have students write sentences explaining the uses of the following cooking tools: garlic press, mallet, pastry brush, scoops, kitchen shears, and baster.
- Assign Enrichment Activity 14 in the TCR.

CHAPTER 12, LESSON 3

Answers to Lesson 3 Review

1. For draining liquids from cooked food or for rinsing fruits and vegetables.
2. Any five: mixing bowls, rotary beater, rubber scraper, sifter, wire whisk.
3. Any one: double boiler, saucepans. Any one: cake pan, casserole, cookie sheet, loaf pan, muffin tin, pie pan, roasting pan with rack.
4. An appliance that cooks by vibrating the molecules in food. It makes food preparation faster and easier.
5. Answers will vary.
6. Answers will vary. Possible answer: A small appliance can make cooking easier because it usually simplifies the cooking steps and decreases the amount of time needed to cook. For example, a mixer saves time and energy, since the cook does not need to mix the ingredients by hand.
7. Answers will vary.
8. Answers will vary. Students explain how they would prepare a food without a particular utensil and how the utensil would have made their work easier.

CLOSE

Ask students to make a list of ten kitchen tools and equipment that would be essential in a first apartment or home. Have them explain their choices.

342

Major appliances come in a variety of sizes, colors, and brands and may have many different features. What features would you like in a new refrigerator?

A convection oven uses a high-speed fan to circulate hot air throughout the oven, which speeds up the cooking. Conventional ovens may be self-cleaning or continuous cleaning. An automatic timer that can turn the oven on or off is another possible feature.

- Microwave ovens are fast, convenient, and easy to use. They come in a variety of sizes and have a range of power settings. You will learn more about microwave ovens in Lesson 4 of this chapter.
- Refrigerators may have the freezer on the top, on the bottom, or on the side. Some are self-defrosting and have extra freezer space, ice makers, or ice cube and water dispensers.

Cooking with Ease

You can cook just about anything if you have the most basic kitchen utensils, cookware, and appliances and know how to use them. Preparing food will be easier, more enjoyable, and safer when you select the right tools for the job.

LESSON THREE Review

Using complete sentences, answer the following questions on a separate sheet of paper.

Reviewing Terms and Facts

1. **Recall** What is a colander used for?
2. **List** Identify five kitchen tools you would use to mix ingredients.
3. **Identify** Name one type of cookware you would use on the stove top and one type you would use in the oven.
4. **Vocabulary** Define the term *microwave oven*. What are the advantages of using a microwave oven?

Thinking Critically

5. **Analyze** If you could have only four pieces of cookware, which ones would you choose? Explain your answer.
6. **Describe** How do the small appliances in your kitchen make cooking easier?
7. **Apply** If you were buying a refrigerator, what features would be most important to you? What features would be least important?

Applying Concepts

8. Suppose that you do not have one of the utensils you need. Describe how you could prepare the food without that utensil. Explain how the utensil would have made your work easier.

342 CHAPTER 12: WORKING IN THE KITCHEN

MEETING STUDENT DIVERSITY

Cultural Perspectives People who cook ethnic foods may have kitchen tools and equipment that differs from those discussed in this lesson. Have students ask friends and neighbors what kinds of ethnic dishes they make and if they need to use special tools and equipment to make them. Ask students to report their findings to the class. Also, ask students to research what special tools are needed to make the following ethnic dishes: ravioli (pasta maker), en papillate (oiled paper), kabobs (skewers), soufflé (soufflé pan), plum pudding (ring mold), krumkake (krumkake iron).

LESSON FOUR
Microwave Cooking

DISCOVER...
- how a microwave oven works.
- how to use a microwave oven.
- ways to prepare foods for microwave cooking.

Gino's family rarely eats dinner together on weekdays. His mom and older brother fix dinner and eat before they go to work at the hospital. When Gino's dad gets home from work, he and Gino reheat the food in the microwave oven. The microwave doesn't dry out the food, and it is fast and easy to use.

Many people use microwave ovens for jobs that, in the past, could be done only by stoves and conventional ovens. In fact, microwave ovens have features that make them more versatile than many other kitchen appliances. It is no wonder that they are changing the way people cook.

WORDS TO KNOW
defrosting
arcing
rotating
variables

LESSON FOUR: MICROWAVE COOKING   343

CLASSROOM RESOURCES FOR LESSON 4

 Blackline Masters
Food Lab 3, "Mexico from the Microwave!"
Lesson 4 Quiz

 Transparencies
Transparency 53, "Microwave Musts"

 Student Workbook
Activities 87, 88

LESSON FOUR
Microwave Cooking

FOCUS

Lesson Objectives
After studying this lesson, students should be able to
- explain how a microwave oven works.
- demonstrate how to use a microwave oven.
- discuss variables to consider when using the microwave oven.

Motivating Activity
Allow students two minutes to write down ways they could use a microwave oven.

Introducing the Lesson
Make four columns on the board with the following headings: "Cooking," "Reheating," "Defrosting," "Other." Have students read their responses to the Motivating Activity. Write student responses in the appropriate column on the board. Discuss the variety of uses of microwaves. Tell students that in this lesson they will learn more about microwave cooking.

Introducing *Words to Know*
Have students write the Words to Know on a large sheet of paper. Ask them to find the definitions in the lesson. Then ask students to make an illustration of each word or concept.

343

CHAPTER 12, LESSON 4

TEACH

L1 Science
Have students rub their hands together quickly. Discuss the heat that this action makes. Explain that this rubbing creates friction. Ask them to read "How a Microwave Oven Works" and to describe the part friction plays in microwave cooking.

L3 History
Point out to students that microwaves have important uses other than in cooking. Have students research microwaves. Ask them to report to the class about the discovery of microwaves, how they were originally used, and their other functions today.

DID YOU KNOW
Pot holders should be used when taking containers out of microwave ovens. It is true that microwaves pass right through containers and into the food, thereby leaving the containers cool. Once the food is hot, however, it can transfer heat to the container and continue to transfer heat as it cooks outside the oven, thus causing the container to heat up.

L1 Using Transparencies
Present Color Transparency 53, "Microwave Musts," in the TCR. Use this overhead visual to reinforce concepts from this lesson.

How a Microwave Oven Works

Although microwave ovens vary in size, power, and features, they all operate the same way. They produce microwaves, or energy waves that penetrate food and agitate its molecules. This process results in heat that cooks the food. Unlike conventional ovens, microwave ovens heat only the food—the container usually does not get hot.

Microwave ovens are a fast and convenient way to cook. Foods cook up to 75 percent faster than in a conventional oven. You can reheat leftover food, cook food, or defrost frozen food. **Defrosting** means *thawing or unfreezing frozen food.*

Because microwave ovens cook food so quickly, they use less electricity than other methods of cooking. The nutrients in food are better preserved because of this quick cooking time and because such foods as vegetables require little or no added water.

Because vegetables take less time to cook in a microwave, they taste better than those cooked on a stove. What guidelines do you use when cooking vegetables in a microwave?

344

COOPERATIVE LEARNING

Infomercial Organize students into small groups. Have each group gather information from sales catalogs or newspaper advertisements describing the latest features offered on new models of microwave ovens. Have them use this information and other facts they learned in this lesson to write a script for an infomercial about a new microwave. Have each group design a microwave for their infomercial and present information about their microwave to the other groups.

344

Using a Microwave Oven

The amount of power that an appliance uses is measured in watts. Most household microwave ovens use a maximum of 500 to 700 watts. The higher the wattage, the faster most foods will cook. If you are unsure of the wattage, you can look it up in the instruction manual or on the label attached to the oven.

Although you cannot control the wattage, you can control the amount of power with which you cook. The power control on the microwave oven may be a control panel or a single dial. Some control panels are numbered from 1 to 10, so that "1" means 10 percent of the available power and "10" means 100 percent. Other control panels simply have settings for low, medium, and high.

To determine which power setting to use and how long to cook a particular food, consult a recipe or the instruction manual. Some control panels list common foods with specific power settings and cooking times.

The control panels vary among different microwave ovens. What are some of the more common power settings you have seen?

Choosing Cookware

Kendra thought that it was all right to use any plastic, glass, or ceramic container in the microwave oven. Then one day, while she was reheating leftovers in a plastic container, the plastic started to melt. Since then, she has learned to make sure that containers are labeled "microwave safe" before using them in the microwave oven. These containers will not get too hot, melt, crack, or shatter from the heat produced in the oven. Round containers allow more even heating and cooking than square or rectangular ones.

Because the microwaves that heat the food cannot pass through metal, metal containers should never be used in a microwave oven, and aluminum foil should not be used as a cover.

LESSON FOUR: MICROWAVE COOKING

CHAPTER 12, LESSON 4

L1 Finding Examples
Point out to students that some common cookware items may be suitable for the microwave, so it is not always necessary to buy specialized equipment. Explain that glass measuring cups, oven-proof casserole dishes, and glass mixing bowls can be used in the microwave. Have students refer to Lesson 3 in Chapter 12. Ask students to identify the items shown in Lesson 3 that could be safely used in the microwave.

L2 Analyzing
Bring in several examples of cookware made specifically for microwaves. Have students analyze the claims by the manufacturer as to why these items should be purchased. Ask students to decide which items could be replaced by a similar item that would already be in most kitchens. Have students prepare similar foods in different containers, then compare and contrast the results of using different cookware.

L2 Applying Knowledge
Display several examples of small kitchen equipment on a table. Ask students to fold a piece of paper in half lengthwise. Title half the paper "Microwave Safe," and the other half "Unsafe for Microwave." Have students write the name of each example in the appropriate column, with an explanation of why the example is safe or unsafe for use in a microwave oven.

HOME AND COMMUNITY CONNECTION

Guest Speaker Invite to class a parent or community member who frequently uses a microwave for cooking. Ask the speaker to demonstrate how to cook a meal using a microwave, explaining the process step-by-step. Encourage students to ask questions during the demonstration.

CHAPTER 12, LESSON 4

L2 Diagramming
Have students make a flowchart showing how to use a microwave oven. If computers are available, encourage students to make their flowcharts on the computer and print them out.

L2 Giving Examples
Ask students to draw examples of the four variables in microwave cooking discussed on page 348. Display the illustrations in the classroom.

DID YOU KNOW ❓

Some microwave ovens come with built-in turntables that rotate the food for you. Removable turntables can also be purchased and placed inside a microwave. These turntables must be wound up before you begin cooking in the microwave.

L2 Food Lab
Allow time for students to complete Food Lab Activity 3, "Mexico from the Microwave!" in the TCR.

Metal can also cause **arcing**, or *electrical sparks that can damage a microwave oven and start a fire.* Brown paper bags and other products made from recycled paper should also be avoided because they can catch fire.

Cooking Preparation

Because microwave ovens cook food differently from conventional ovens, you need to follow specific guidelines when preparing food for cooking.

- Choose a container that will fit into the microwave oven without touching the sides or the top. To keep liquids from boiling over, use a container that has extra space in it.

- Arrange the food so that it can heat up or cook evenly. Cut foods into pieces of the same size so that they will cook at the same rate. Place the thickest pieces toward the outside of the container, where they will receive the most energy.

- Use a fork or knife to pierce foods that are encased in a skin, such as whole potatoes and hot dogs. This will ensure that the steam does not build up and cause them to burst.

- Cover foods so that they hold in their moisture and do not spatter. You can use paper towels, waxed paper, plastic wrap, or covers that come with microwavable containers. Cover the food *loosely*, or make a vent by turning back a corner of the plastic wrap to let the steam escape.

Before you cook food in a microwave oven, you may need to use special techniques to prepare it. What technique is this teen using?

The Cooking Process

You will often need to use special techniques when cooking foods in a microwave oven.

346 CHAPTER 12: WORKING IN THE KITCHEN

MORE ABOUT • • •

The Cooking Process There are many tips for making microwave cooking successful. For example, food in a wide, shallow dish will heat faster than food in a narrow, deep dish. Bread, rolls, and sandwiches can get soggy while they are reheated. This can be avoided if they are wrapped in paper towels or paper napkins. Foods with skins or membranes—such as egg yolks, potatoes, squash, and tomatoes—must be pierced with a fork to allow steam to escape to avoid explosions.

- **Stirring.** To help some foods, such as soups and stews, to cook evenly, stir them after they are partly cooked. Since the outside cooks first, stir from the outer edge of the container toward the center.
- **Rearranging.** Some foods, such as baking potatoes, might have to be rearranged or turned over after a few minutes. Move pieces that have been on the outer edges of the container into the center so that they can heat up, defrost, or cook evenly.
- **Rotating.** Some foods need to be rotated. **Rotating** means *turning the dish a quarter-turn or a half-turn in the oven.* This allows the microwaves to enter the food on all sides. The package directions or the recipe you are following will usually specify how often to rotate the food. Most newer microwave ovens have a turntable that automatically rotates whenever the oven is in use.
- **Standing time.** Microwave recipes tell you to let the food stand after the power shuts off. It can stand on the counter if you need to put another dish into the oven. This standing time is required to let the temperatures equalize. In fact, standing time is almost as important as cooking time for the food to turn out just right.

MICROWAVE TRICKS

Here are some quick microwave tricks to try.
- Soften hard ice cream by microwaving a half gallon for 45 to 60 seconds at the defrost setting.
- Freshen soggy pretzels, crackers, or popcorn by microwaving 2 cups for 45 seconds at high power and then letting it stand for 1 minute.
- Make your own microwave dinners by freezing leftovers in divided plates. Then reheat them at a later date.
- Microwave juice oranges or lemons for 30 seconds each at high power before squeezing. They will be easier to squeeze, and you will get more juice.

LESSON FOUR: MICROWAVE COOKING   347

MEETING STUDENT DIVERSITY

Physically Challenged For students with physical limitations or disabilities, some of the steps discussed in microwave cooking may be difficult. Ask physically challenged students to describe difficulties they may have in using a microwave, such as reaching microwave ovens, preparing foods for cooking in microwaves, rotating or stirring foods as they cook, and safely using microwave ovens. Have students determine whether the microwave in the school foods lab is conveniently placed and easy to reach. Help all students come up with a variety of solutions to the problems the physically challenged identify.

CHAPTER 12, LESSON 4

L2 Role-Playing

Have students demonstrate the precautions to take when using a microwave in the following scenarios:
- *Preparing to reheat lasagna in a microwave oven.*
- *Plugging a microwave oven into an electrical circuit.*
- *Removing covers from containers of microwaved foods.*
- *Unusual sounds coming from a microwave oven.*

DID YOU KNOW

Before cleaning a microwave oven, bring a cup of water to a boil in the microwave oven. This helps loosen dried food particles that may have accumulated in the oven. Be sure to follow cleaning instructions given by the manufacturer of the microwave oven.

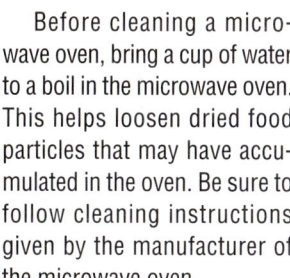

Have students work with partners in the foods lab. Have them try the microwave tricks discussed in "Tips for Living." Ask one partner to use the conventional method to accomplish the task. Have the other partner use the microwave tip. Partners should explore the effectiveness and advantages of using a microwave for these tasks. Ask students for other "tried and true" microwave tricks they may know about.

CHAPTER 12, LESSON 4

Skills IN ACTION

Have students convert recipes for a conventional oven to microwave recipes using the guidelines in "Skills in Action." Point out to students that conversion directions are often provided on packages for foods such as noodles, frozen vegetables, and fish. Students might refer to one of these when choosing recipes to convert.

L1 Student Workbook
Assign Activities 87 and 88 in the Student Workbook.

ASSESS

Evaluating the Lesson
Assign Reviewing Terms and Facts and Thinking Critically on page 349 to review the lesson; then assign the Lesson 4 Quiz in the TCR.

Reteaching
- Have students work in small groups to write five questions they would ask before purchasing a microwave oven.
- Have students complete Reteaching Activity 12 in the TCR.

Enrichment
Have students work in small groups to prepare a microwave cookbook. Encourage students to divide tasks among the members of the group. Students might add illustrations to their cookbooks. Display cookbooks for students to use as references.

348

Skills IN ACTION

Converting Conventional-Oven Recipes

If your time is limited and you need to bake a dish in a hurry, you can often convert a recipe meant for a conventional oven to a microwave recipe. Here are some general guidelines to follow.
- Reduce liquid ingredients by 1 or 2 tablespoons per cup.
- Reduce cooking time by about 50 to 75 percent.
- Add very little salt to meats and vegetables—it dries out foods during microwave cooking.

Variables in Microwave Cooking

When you use a microwave oven, you need to follow different procedures to cook different types or sizes of food. That is because of variables in microwave cooking. **Variables** are *conditions that determine how long a food needs to be cooked and at what power level.* Variables include the following:

- **Density.** The denser the food, the longer it takes to cook. The heavier a food feels for its size, the denser it is. For example, a slice of meat is denser than a slice of bread of the same size.
- **Volume of food.** The amount, or number of servings, determines how much power and time are needed. Generally, the smaller the amount of food, the faster it cooks.
- **Shape of food.** Round foods, such as pancakes, cook more evenly than foods that have corners, such as lasagna. This is because the corners can overcook. Thin pieces cook more quickly than thick pieces.
- **Temperature of food.** If food is at room temperature, it will heat faster than food taken directly from the refrigerator or freezer.

Safe Use of Microwave Ovens

Cooking in a microwave oven can be easy and safe as long as you take a few basic precautions.

- To avoid fires and other accidents, use dishes labeled "microwave safe."
- Remove covers slowly after food is cooked, tilting the cover or removing the plastic wrap so that steam escapes away from you.
- Do not microwave foods in containers that are completely sealed. When pressure from steam builds up, the container can burst.

348 CHAPTER 12: WORKING IN THE KITCHEN

COOPERATIVE LEARNING

Model Kitchen Have small groups work together to construct a three-dimensional model of a kitchen, diorama style, from a shoebox and smaller containers or stiff paper. The model should include representations of a kitchen counter, stove, sink, refrigerator, and cupboards. Smaller containers or boxes may be covered with plain paper, decorated, and placed inside the shoebox to represent the equipment to be included. Have group members each take one section of the kitchen diorama and label it with paper signs or drawings indicating safety and sanitation procedures to be followed for each section. Have them refer to the chapter to be sure they include all important points.

- Do not use an extension cord with a microwave oven or plug it into the same electrical outlet as other large electrical appliances.
- If the oven door does not close tightly or if you hear unusual sounds coming from the oven, tell an adult.
- If there are sparks inside the oven or if there is a fire, turn off the oven or unplug it immediately and get help.

Although some people are concerned that it is unsafe to stand in front of a microwave oven while the oven is on, it is generally safe to do so.

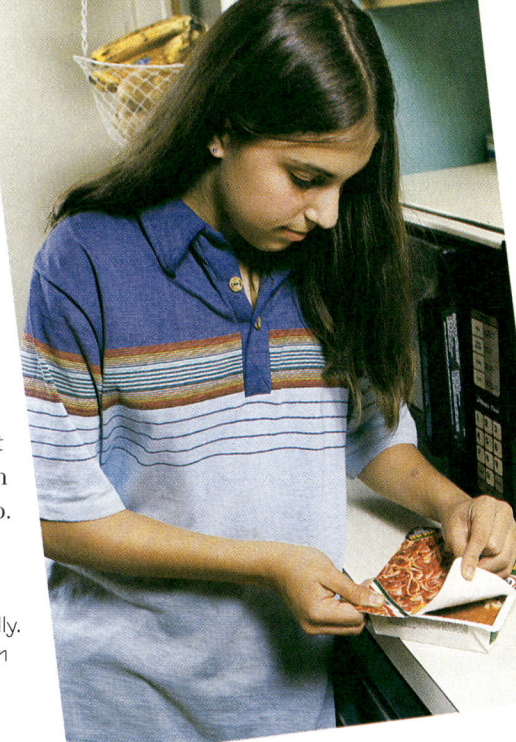

Because steam builds up in a covered container, you need to remove the cover carefully. What are some other safety rules to keep in mind when using a microwave oven?

LESSON FOUR Review

Using complete sentences, answer the following questions on a separate sheet of paper.

Reviewing Terms and Facts
1. **Vocabulary** Define the term *arcing*. How can arcing be avoided?
2. **Recall** Why is it important to rotate foods while they are cooking?
3. **Identify** What are the four variables to consider when you cook foods in a microwave oven?
4. **List** Name six safety precautions to take when using a microwave oven.

Thinking Critically
5. **Evaluate** Do you think that there are any disadvantages to cooking food in a microwave oven? If so, what are they?
6. **Analyze** Why would an egg crack if it were cooked with the shell on in a microwave oven?
7. **Predict** Which food would cook faster in a microwave oven—a slice of steak or a slice of meat loaf the same size? Explain your answer.

Applying Concepts
8. Find a recipe with directions for cooking a dish you like in the microwave oven. Make a list of all the techniques used, such as piercing and rotating, that make the recipe suitable for use in a microwave oven.

LESSON FOUR: MICROWAVE COOKING

TECHNOLOGY UPDATE

The Latest Model New features are constantly being added to new models of microwave ovens. Some of the latest features include one-touch cooking—oven automatically calculates cooking times and power level for different types of food such as popcorn, pizza, and baked potato; multistage cooking—oven can cook foods using different power levels during one setting; menu-action screen—step-by-step instructions scroll across the display; auto-weight defrost—weight of frozen food is entered into microwave program and the correct defrost time is automatically programmed. Have students discuss advantages and disadvantages of adding such features to new models of microwaves.

CHAPTER 12, LESSON 4

Answers to Lesson 4 Review

1. Sparks that will damage or start a fire in the microwave. Avoid this by using cookware that does not contain metal.
2. This allows the microwaves to enter the food on all sides.
3. The type of food, volume of food, shape of food, and temperature of food before being put in the microwave.
4. Use dishes labeled "microwave safe"; remove covers slowly after food is cooked, tilting the cover so that steam escapes away from you; do not microwave foods in containers that are completely sealed; do not use an extension cord or plug the microwave into an electrical outlet that other appliances already run on; tell an adult if the door does not close tightly or if you hear unusual sounds; turn off or unplug the microwave immediately and get help if there are sparks inside the oven or if there is a fire.
5. Answers will vary but might include that cooking in microwave ovens is fast and convenient.
6. Pressure from the steam inside the egg would cause the eggshell to crack.
7. Meat loaf, because it is less dense than steak.
8. Recipes will vary, but students should list the techniques that make the recipe suitable for microwave cooking.

CLOSE

Have each student describe something new they learned about microwave cooking from studying this lesson.

LESSON FIVE
The School Foods Lab

FOCUS

Lesson Objectives
After studying this lesson, students should be able to
- discuss how to work as a team member in the school foods lab.
- explain how to make and follow a work plan.

Motivating Activity
Have students write down any cooking duties they have at home.

Introducing the Lesson
Have students share their responses to the Motivating Activity. Use the responses to discuss how cooking duties are divided among family members in the students' homes. Then ask students to consider ways in which cooking in the home may differ from cooking in school labs. *(Time is more structured in school. Teamwork may not be stressed at home. Choice of recipes is more flexible in the lab.)* Then tell students that in this lesson they will learn how to make and follow a work plan as a team member.

Introducing *Words to Know*
Ask a volunteer to read the vocabulary words and terms and their definitions. Then have them use the Words to Know to write a short newspaper article titled "Working in the School Foods Lab."

350

LESSON FIVE
The School Foods Lab

WORDS TO KNOW

work plan
dovetailing

DISCOVER...
- how to work as a team member in the school foods lab.
- how to make and follow a work plan.

Once a week, Adam plans, shops for, and prepares one meal for his family. When he plans the meal, he takes into account the nutrition principles he learned in the school foods lab. When he prepares the meal, he uses cooking techniques that he learned in class.

Cooking in your kitchen at home is not the same as cooking in a foods class. At school, you have to work closely with your classmates. At home, you may be alone or you may be working with only one other person. With these differences in mind, how can you make the best use of the school foods lab?

350 CHAPTER 12: WORKING IN THE KITCHEN

CLASSROOM RESOURCES FOR LESSON 5

 Blackline Masters
Activity and Project Card 24, "It's All in the Game"
Cooperative Learning 24
Lesson 5 Quiz
Peer Pressure and Decision Making 26
Reteaching 12

 **Student Workbook**
Activity 89

Cooking Teams

A school foods lab session needs to be carefully planned, organized, and managed. Typically, the class is divided into cooking teams of three to six members each. Just as in any successful team, every member has specific responsibilities, or duties to perform. In addition, all team members must be able to

- get along with other team members.
- read and follow directions.
- handle food safely and follow safety precautions.
- help other team members. For example, if you have finished stir-frying the vegetables for your team, you can help the student who is slicing bread.

Creating a Work Plan

Before each team can begin to work, team members must create a work plan for the group. A **work plan** is *a list of the jobs that need to be done and the name of the person who will do each job.* For instance, a work plan might list a task such as "Chop two small onions," with Dave's name printed beside it. Plans also list the equipment and the ingredients the team needs and give step-by-step directions on how to combine the ingredients.

The following tasks are a part of each team's work plan:

- **Pre-preparation.** Team members need to put out all the supplies, equipment, and ingredients; wash food if necessary; and measure ingredients, using the correct measuring utensils. For example, to measure two teaspoons of vanilla, you need a measuring teaspoon, not a regular spoon.

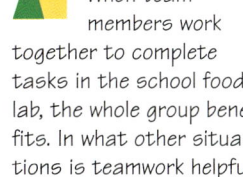

When team members work together to complete tasks in the school foods lab, the whole group benefits. In what other situations is teamwork helpful?

LESSON FIVE: THE SCHOOL FOODS LAB **351**

CHAPTER 12, LESSON 5

TEACH

L1 Discussing
Invite a school sports coach to speak to the class about the importance of teamwork. Then ask students to interpret the following statement: A team is only as strong as its weakest member.

L2 Critical Thinking
Review with the students some oaths or pledges that people make to show their loyalty and support for their country, organization, or team. Ask students to write an oath or pledge for members of cooking teams. Have them vote for their favorite oath or pledge. Have a student copy the winning oath or pledge in large letters and display it in the classroom.

L2 Problem Solving
Assign Peer Pressure and Decision Making 26 in the TCR. This activity gives students the opportunity to recognize peer pressure and practice decision-making skills.

L2 Activity and Project Card
Allow time for students to complete Activity and Project Card 24, "It's All in the Game," in the TCR.

MEETING STUDENT DIVERSITY

Learning Styles Students with special learning needs can be grouped with mainstream students to carry out tasks in the foods lab. Often you will find these students are successful in the foods lab because it provides hands-on experience. They may have difficulty reading recipes. Always encourage teamwork. In assessing the performance of such groups, use criteria—such as positive interdependence—that reflect the capacity of the group members to work together effectively.

351

CHAPTER 12, LESSON 5

L3 Critical Thinking
Remind students of the importance of dovetailing tasks to save time in the school foods lab. Have students work in pairs. Provide each pair with a recipe. Have them make a list of food preparation and cleanup tasks that can be dovetailed while preparing their recipe. Have students share their lists with the class.

L2 Experimenting
Point out to students that pans containing certain foods clean better using cold water, and others clean better using very warm water. Ask students to experiment with cold soapy water and with warm soapy water when cleaning pans containing the following foods: sugar, grease, egg, milk, syrup, cereal, starch, and flour. You might set this up as a lab experiment, having students observe the experiments and summarize the results. Based on the results of the experiments, ask students to make recommendations for cleaning pans containing various kinds of foods.

L2 Cooperative Learning
Assign Cooperative Learning Activity 24, "Working Together in Food Preparation," in the TCR.

TIPS for living
Have students make posters explaining the time-saving tip for working with foods described in "Tips for Living."

- **Mixing and preparation.** Team members must combine ingredients and prepare food. For instance, in making baked apples, you need to combine sugar and cinnamon, fill the apple centers with the mixture, and then bake the apples.
- **Table setting and serving the food.** Team members must set the table and serve the food correctly.
- **Cleaning up.** Team members should clean up as they go along so that they don't have to rush to clean up at the last minute.

In a well-run foods lab, the tasks are divided so that they can be dovetailed. **Dovetailing** means *fitting different tasks together smoothly and efficiently*. For example, Jesse may wash the lettuce while Allison makes the salad dressing. Each time a new work plan is made, these tasks are moved from one person to another. That way, Jesse can learn to measure and combine ingredients the next time while Allison learns how to prepare vegetables.

How to Follow the Work Plan
A work plan is easy to follow when all team members understand the tasks to be done, who is to do each task, and how to do their own tasks correctly. Any questions should be resolved before each team begins cooking.

TIPS for living
SAVING TIME IN THE KITCHEN

Make the most of your time by following these timesaving tips.
- **Plan ahead.** Read the entire recipe, make sure that you understand each instruction, and plan each step before you begin.
- **Get organized.** Assemble all the necessary ingredients and equipment.
- **Share the work.** Divide tasks among lab partners or family members, and help others when your job is done.
- **Dovetail tasks.** When possible, overlap the jobs you are doing. For example, prepare salad while the pasta cooks.
- **Clean as you go.** Keep the counters wiped clean, and soak dirty dishes in a sink filled with hot, soapy water.

HOME AND COMMUNITY CONNECTION

Field Trip If possible, arrange a field trip to a local restaurant to observe teamwork in a kitchen. Ask the manager of the restaurant to explain the responsibilities of every member of the cooking team and describe their work plan. You might arrange for a team of two or three students to videotape a few minutes in a kitchen. Upon returning to the classroom, have the students show the video and evaluate the restaurant's work plan.

Following a work plan, team members should check off steps as they are completed. Why is this important?

Following a work plan will help you stay on schedule. After each member completes a step, he or she should check it off. That way, the steps will be completed in the correct order.

Does the Plan Work?

When the work is completed, team members need to evaluate, or judge, their work plan, so that they understand what they did correctly, what could be improved, and whether they reached their goal. For example, when team members evaluate their oven-baked french fries, they may decide that the potatoes would not have burned if two team members had checked the baking time.

As you continue to complete projects in the school foods lab, you will gain experience and learn from your team's evaluations. In time, you can take on more difficult tasks. For example, your first project may be to make grilled cheese sandwiches, but in a short time you may find yourself helping to prepare full meals.

A Successful Lab Team

Being a good team member in the foods lab is the same as being a good member of any team. If team members have a

LESSON FIVE: THE SCHOOL FOODS LAB   353

Skills IN ACTION

Rating the Team's Success

Take this quiz to rate the success of your foods lab team.
- Was the work schedule followed?
- Did team members work together willingly and help each other?
- Was each step of the recipe followed properly?
- Did the food look and taste good?
- Was kitchen cleanup completed on time?

If you answered no to any of the questions, think about how you can do better next time.

CHAPTER 12, LESSON 5

Skills IN ACTION

Have students read the quiz to rate the success of their foods lab team. Ask them to make a grading system for the school's foods lab based on these criteria.

L1 Student Workbook
Assign Activity 89 in the Student Workbook.

ASSESS

Evaluating the Lesson
Assign Reviewing Terms and Facts and Thinking Critically on page 354 to review the lesson; then assign the Lesson 5 Quiz in the TCR.

Reteaching
- Have students pretend they are a "cooking coach." Have them write ten suggestions for assisting members of a cooking team to work together and get the job done.
- Have students complete Reteaching Activity 12 in the TCR.

Enrichment
Have students copy their favorite family recipe. Have classmates determine if the recipe could be made in the foods lab, considering skills, budget, and time to prepare the recipe.

COOPERATIVE LEARNING

Video Series Tell students that they have been hired by a cable company to produce a TV series about working in the school foods lab. The show will have four episodes—one corresponding to each step in creating a work plan. You might assign students to the following groups in creating the television series: writing staff, acting staff, art staff, and production staff. Members of the writing staff might use ideas from the lessons and articles to create a short script for each episode. Members of the acting staff should learn and perform their parts for each episode. Members of the art staff should create or gather props needed for each episode. Members of the production staff should block out the scenes for each episode.

CHAPTER 12, LESSON 5

Answers to Lesson 5 Review

1. Perform specific responsibilities; get along with other team members; read and follow directions; handle food safely and follow safety precautions; help other team members.
2. A list of the jobs that need to be done and the name of the person who will do the job; preparation, mixing and preparation, table setting and serving the food, cleaning up.
3. So that you can learn to do a variety of tasks.
4. By checking off each step as it is completed.
5. Answers will vary.
6. Answers will vary, but might include painting a room or working on a school project with someone.
7. Evaluating helps the team understand what was done correctly and what could be improved. Answers will vary. Possible answer: Your team might finish step three before step two. You might forget to add an ingredient to the recipe.
8. Answers will vary. Students should choose a recipe and write a work plan.

CLOSE

Have students write an analogy for being members of teams in sports and in the school foods lab.

When team members carefully detail, organize, and carry out their work plan, they can enjoy a successful meal. plan, follow it, perform their assigned tasks, and work together cooperatively, cooking projects will be easier and more enjoyable for everyone involved.

LESSON FIVE Review

Using complete sentences, answer the following questions on a separate sheet of paper.

Reviewing Terms and Facts
1. Recall List the duties that all team members should be able to perform.
2. Vocabulary What is a *work plan*? Identify the four tasks that are part of the work plan.
3. Explain Why are foods-lab tasks moved from one person to another?
4. Identify How do team members ensure that steps are performed in the correct order?

Thinking Critically
5. Analyze Which tasks do you think would be the most difficult when working with a team? Which do you think would be the easiest? Explain your answers.
6. Apply Make a list of other activities, besides cooking, in which dovetailing would be helpful.
7. Explain Why is it important to evaluate the work plan? What might happen if team members fail to evaluate it?

Applying Concepts
8. Choose a recipe you would like your team to use in the foods lab. Be sure to determine that your team has the skills, budget, and time to prepare the dish you choose. Then create a work plan with job assignments.

354   CHAPTER 12: WORKING IN THE KITCHEN

COOPERATIVE LEARNING

Making and Following a Work Plan Organize students into cooking teams. Assign each group a different recipe to make in the school foods lab. Have the groups create a work plan, follow the work plan, and evaluate the work plan. Allow groups to share their completed dishes before cleaning up. After the cooking projects are completed, have each group report to the class on how successful their work plan was.

Chapter 12 Activities

Consumer Focus

Buying Wisely
Check these before you buy:
- **The expiration date.** This is the date by which the product should be eaten.
- **Signs of spoilage.** Cans should not have dents or bulges.
- **Signs of tampering.** Make sure that the safety seal is unbroken.

Try This!
Find out the meanings of the following types of dates found on product labels: pull date, sell by, and pack date. Share your findings with your class.

Technology

Computers in the Kitchen
Some kitchen appliances use computer technology. For example, there are computer cookbooks. Can't think of anything to fix for dinner? Type in a list of foods you have on hand, and with special software, your computer will print out recipes you can make with those ingredients.

Try This!
Visit a store that sells software. Find out what programs are available to help you shop for, prepare, or cook food. Make a list of the titles and their prices.

A Global View

FROM EARTH OVENS TO MICROWAVES
People all over the world have been using ovens for thousands of years, yet the way ovens work has changed very little. Microwave ovens, which were invented in the 1940s, introduced the first real change in oven technology in thousands of years.

TRY THIS!
Bake one potato in a microwave oven and another potato in a conventional oven. Compare cooking times and the texture of the potatoes. Which potato do you prefer? Write a paragraph on the results.

SCIENCE CONNECTION

FRICTION PRODUCES HEAT
In a conventional oven, food is heated mainly by the radiation of heat waves from the hot oven walls. The food heats by conduction—the transfer of heat through the exchange of energy.

The waves produced by a microwave oven penetrate the food, where they quickly pull the food particles back and forth. The movement creates friction, and the friction, in turn, produces heat.

Follow Up
1. Explain why quickly rubbing your hands together is similar to the operation of a microwave oven. Try it, and see if your hands feel warmer.
2. Electromagnetic waves are attracted to water, fat, and sugar. How might that affect the rates at which different foods cook in a microwave oven?

Teaching the SCIENCE CONNECTION
Ask students to refer to the feature to draw diagrams showing how a conventional oven works and how a microwave oven works. Display the diagrams in the classroom.

Have students interview members of their family or neighbors to find out how they use conventional and microwave ovens. Have students share their findings with the class.

Answers to Follow-Up
1. Rubbing hands together causes friction similar to the friction in microwave ovens.
2. Foods that contain water, fat, and/or sugar cook faster than foods without these ingredients.

CHAPTER 12 Activities

Consumer Focus
Remind students that food safety begins with proper packaging and handling. Explain that if the label on a package reads "sell by," the product must be used within a few days of that date. Tell them that frozen foods should be free of ice spots and frost.

TECHNOLOGY
Point out that while computer skills are important at school and at work, students may need to use computer skills to cook, too. Tell them that appliances such as coffeemakers and ovens can be programmed to start and stop whenever you want them to—whether or not you are in the kitchen.

A Global View
Tell students that the earliest ovens were rock-lined pits in which a wood fire was built. Around the year 1800, an English scientist named Rumford developed an enclosed metal box that was heated by an outside fire through one of the walls. All the other walls were insulated to reduce heat loss. Today's home oven is essentially a Rumford box.

CHAPTER 12 REVIEW

Checking Comprehension

Use the Chapter Summary and the Chapter 12 Review to help students go over the most important ideas in Chapter 12.

Answers to Words to Know

1. Being infected with bacteria. In mild cases, people may experience headaches, stomach cramps, and fever.
2. Foods that are likely to spoil quickly. Any two examples: meat, poultry, fish, eggs, and dairy products.
3. Capable of burning easily.
4. Any two utensils: colander, kitchen fork, large spoon, tongs, turner, meat thermometer, rubber scraper, wire whisk, bread knife, chef's knife, grater, paring knife, peeler, slicing knife.
5. Sparks that can damage a microwave oven and start a fire. Metal, metal containers, and aluminum foil put in the microwave oven can cause arcing.
6. A list of the jobs that need to be done and the name of the person who will do each job. You need to make a work plan before a cooking team can begin to work.
7. Doing more than one task at the same time.

Answers to Review Questions

1. Kitchen cleanliness helps prevent food contamination, which causes food poisoning.
2. Because bacteria grow quickly at temperatures between 60°F and 125°F (16°C and 52°C).

Chapter Summary

- Food contamination is a serious health hazard. Handling, preparing, and storing food safely can prevent food contamination.
- Perishable foods—such as eggs, meat, and milk—must be kept at the proper temperature to avoid spoiling. Keep hot foods hot and cold foods cold.
- When handling food, wash your hands frequently to prevent the spread of germs. Wash cutting boards and countertops after using them.
- Common types of accidents in the kitchen are falls, burns, cuts, and electric shocks.
- Most kitchen accidents can be prevented by developing safe work habits.
- There are many types of kitchen tools and equipment. Knowing how to use them properly will make cooking tasks much easier.
- Microwave ovens cook food quickly and preserve the nutrients in food.
- When using a microwave oven, you need to use microwave-safe cookware, follow specific guidelines for preparing food, and use special cooking techniques.
- Variables to consider when using a microwave oven include the density, volume, shape, and temperature of food.
- Teamwork is essential in the foods lab. Each member of the group has specific responsibilities.
- When members of the foods lab team follow a work plan, complete their tasks, and cooperate, success is almost guaranteed.

 ## Words to Know

Using complete sentences, answer the following questions on a separate sheet of paper.

1. Define the term *contamination*. What can happen to a person as a result of food contamination?
2. Give two examples of *perishable* foods.
3. Define the word *flammable*.
4. Give two examples of *utensils*.
5. What is *arcing*, and how is it caused?
6. What is a *work plan*, and when do you need to make one?
7. Define the term *dovetailing*.

 ## Review Questions

Using complete sentences, answer the following questions on a separate sheet of paper.

1. Why is kitchen cleanliness necessary for food safety?
2. Explain why it is important to keep hot foods hot and cold foods cold.
3. Give two examples of each of the following: cooking tools, mixing tools, slicing and cutting tools.

356 CHAPTER 12: WORKING IN THE KITCHEN

EXTRA CREDIT PROJECT

Adding to Your Portfolio Students may wish to designate a special section of their portfolios to organize, remember, and review the cooking practices and procedures they have learned in the chapter. Have them design a packet or envelope for this purpose. Suggest that they include an outline of procedures from each lesson, as well as charts and tables that illustrate kitchen equipment, microwave use, and work plans. Students may personalize their packets with illustrations or notes about their own kitchen or special information to help them when working in the school foods lab.

CHAPTER 12 REVIEW

4. Why is it important to use microwave-safe containers when cooking food in a microwave oven?
5. Why is standing time necessary after food is cooked in a microwave oven?
6. List the four types of tasks each team must complete in the school foods lab.
7. What is the final step of the foods lab?

Thinking Critically

Using complete sentences, answer the following questions on a separate sheet of paper.

1. **Explain** If you were taking food to a picnic on a hot summer day, how could you make sure that it stayed safe to eat?
2. **Suggest** List some small appliances that might have more than one purpose and describe each purpose.
3. **Interpret** Why do many people own both a microwave oven and a conventional oven?
4. **Analyze** What kinds of cooperative behavior, besides those mentioned in the text, do you think would help the school foods lab run more smoothly?

Cooperative Learning

1. In small groups, choose one illness caused by improperly cooked or handled food. Research the illness to find out how it is caused, its symptoms, and ways to prevent it. Present your findings in class.
2. In teams of three or four, choose a dish to prepare. Then create a work plan for your team, including all the steps outlined in Lesson 5 of this chapter. If possible, prepare your dish in the foods lab.

Family & Community

1. Choose a restaurant to visit, and evaluate it for cleanliness and safety. Rate the restaurant on a scale of 1 to 10, with 1 meaning *unacceptable* and 10 meaning *excellent*. Make a list of reasons why you chose the rating you did, and discuss them in class.
2. Go through your kitchen with a parent or another older relative. Have that person explain or demonstrate how to use any tools or equipment with which you are not familiar. Based on what you learned in this chapter, discuss items you would recommend purchasing for the kitchen.

Building A Portfolio

1. Evaluate your safety consciousness and cleanliness when working in the kitchen at home. Do you handle, prepare, and cook food as discussed in the text? How do you store leftovers? Do you have safe work habits? Write down your answers to these questions and suggest improvements. Put your assessment in your portfolio.
2. Think of a situation in your life in which you work as part of a team. Evaluate your behavior as a team member. Are you cooperative? Do you contribute as much to the group effort as others do? Are you responsible, prompt, and good at following directions? Write a summary of your strengths and weaknesses, and keep it in your portfolio.

CHAPTER 12 REVIEW **357**

CHAPTER 12 REVIEW

3. Any two cooking tools: colander, kitchen fork, large spoon, tongs, turner. Any two mixing tools: mixing bowls, rotary beater, rubber scraper, sifter, wire whisk. Any two slicing and cutting tools: bread knife, chef's knife, cutting board, grater, paring knife, peeler, slicing knife.
4. These containers will not get very hot, melt, crack, or shatter from the heat produced in the oven.
5. This standing time lets the food finish cooking even though the oven is not on.
6. Pre-preparation, mixing and preparing, table setting and serving the food, cleaning up.
7. Evaluating the work plan. It helps the members understand what they did correctly, what could be improved, and whether they reached their goal.

Evaluate

Use the Chapter 12 Test in the TCR, or construct your own test using the Testmaker Software.

CLOSE

Have students apply their knowledge of the chapter's content by completing one of the alternative assessment activities listed under Family and Community or Building a Portfolio.

Answers to Thinking Critically

1. Use cold packs or a cooler to keep cold foods cold.
2. Answers will vary. Possible small appliances: toasters, food processors, blenders, and crock pots. Students should provide an explanation of uses of the appliances.
3. Answers will vary. Students may indicate that people have a preference for cooking certain foods in each appliance.
4. Answers will vary. Students describe cooperative behavior that would help the school foods lab run more smoothly.

357

Planning Guide
Chapter 13 Preparing to Cook

LESSON 1	Pages	FEATURES	CLASSROOM RESOURCES
Planning a Menu	360–365	*Tips for Living:* Setting the Table *Skills in Action:* Practicing Good Table Manners	Activity and Project Card 25, "What's to Eat?" Concept Map 20 Cooperative Learning 25 Food Lab Activity 4, "Cooking with Herbs" Lesson 1 Quiz Peer Pressure and Decision Making 27 Transparency 54, "Meal Appeal" Student Workbook Activities 90, 91
LESSON 2 **Food Shopping and Storage**	366–372	*Skills in Action:* Shopping Etiquette *Try This:* Stretching Food Dollars	Activity and Project Card 26, "Shopping for the Best Buys" Cooperative Learning 26 Lesson 2 Quiz Transparency 55, "Reading a Food Label" Transparency 56, "Using Unit Pricing" Student Workbook Activities 92, 93
LESSON 3 **Following Recipes and Directions**	373–379	*Skills in Action:* Organizing Recipes	Concept Map 21 Cross Curriculum 14 Enrichment 15 Food Lab Activity 5, "Delicious Dinners in Minutes" Lesson 3 Quiz Transparency 57, "Reading a Recipe" Student Workbook Activities 94, 95
LESSON 4 **Measuring Ingredients**	380–384	*Try This:* Using Seasonings	Cross Curriculum 15 Food Lab Activity 6, "Mmmm . . . Desserts!" Lesson 4 Quiz Student Workbook Activities 96, 97

CHAPTER 13 RESOURCES

Chapter 13 Test   Study Guide 13, *Reteaching*   Testmaker Software
Reteaching 13

Performance Assessment Activity

Ask students to conduct interviews with adults about their cooking experiences and favorite recipes. Each student should prepare a list of questions in advance. When students have completed their interviews, organize the class into small groups. Have each group use the information from the interviews to write a short story titled "Adventures in Cooking." Have a representative read each group's story to the class.

School-to-Work

Ask students to research jobs that are related to food shopping, menu planning, and cooking. These jobs might include grocery-store workers, dietitians, chefs, cookbook editors, farmers, or food-processing plant workers. Ask them to find out the personal qualifications, skills, and education a person must have for the job they chose to research. Ask students to share their information with classmates. Survey the class to find out how many students might be interested in the jobs presented.

Family & Community

Ask students to collect recipes from family members and bring them to class. Have students rewrite all the recipes in the standard format and organize them by categories into a cookbook. Students can draw illustrations for the cookbook and design a cover. Encourage students to share the cookbook with their families.

Resources for the Teacher

Better Homes and Gardens Healthy Family Cookbook. Des Moines: Better Homes and Gardens Books, 1995.

Crocker, Betty. *Betty Crocker's Do-Ahead Cookbook.* New York: Macmillan, 1995.

Lair, Cynthia. *Feeding the Whole Family: Down-to-Earth Cookbook and Whole Foods Guide.* San Diego: LuraMedia, 1994.

Readings for the Student

George, Jean Craighead. *Acorn Pancakes, Dandelion Salad & Other Wild Dishes.* New York: HarperCollins Publishers, 1995.

Robbins, Meyera. *Great Food for Great Kids: Quick and Easy Recipes for a Healthy Family.* Studio City, CA: Michael Wiese Productions, 1994.

Robson, Denny. *Cooking.* New York: Gloucester Press, 1991.

Multimedia Resources

Braising and Stewing (Videocassette). International Video Network.

My First Cooking Video: A Kids' Guide to Making Fun Things to Eat (Videocassette). Sony Kids' Video.

OUT OF TIME?

If time does not permit thorough teaching of this chapter, you may wish to use:

- Teens Making a Difference, page 359
- Tips for Living, page 361
- Try This, pages 371, 382
- Skills in Action, pages 362, 368, 374
- Young Living Activities, page 385
- Chapter Summary, page 386

CHAPTER 13
Preparing to Cook

Chapter Overview

Chapter 13 introduces students to the processes of planning menus and preparing foods. Emphasis is placed on how to plan nutritious meals, how to make wise food choices when shopping, and how to store foods properly. Students also learn how to follow recipes and food preparation directions and how to measure ingredients.

LESSON 1 describes how to plan balanced meals based on resources, budget, time, and skills.

LESSON 2 discusses how to find the best food buys and how to store foods properly.

LESSON 3 explains how to prepare foods by following recipes and how to prepare convenience foods.

LESSON 4 compares customary and metric measurements and discusses tools and techniques for measuring ingredients.

Introducing the Chapter

Have students read the lesson titles in the chapter. Based on the titles, ask them to share their personal experiences with menu planning, food shopping and storage, following recipes, and measuring ingredients.

Chapter Motivator

Refer students to the chapter title, "Preparing to Cook." Pass out slips of paper and ask each student to write a tip that would be useful when preparing to cook. Ask students to read aloud and discuss their helpful hints. Tell students that Chapter 13 will provide them with other hints in preparing to cook.

CHAPTER 13 Preparing to Cook

LESSON ONE
Planning a Menu

LESSON TWO
Food Shopping and Storage

LESSON THREE
Following Recipes and Directions

LESSON FOUR
Measuring Ingredients

KEY TO ABILITY LEVELS

Teaching strategies that appear throughout the chapter have been identified by one of three codes to give you an idea of their suitability for students of varying learning styles and abilities.

L1 Level 1 strategies should be within the ability range of all students. Often full class participation is required. Teacher direction is usually needed.

L2 Level 2 strategies are for average to above-average students or for small groups. Some teacher direction is necessary.

L3 Level 3 strategies are designed for students able and willing to work independently. Minimal teacher direction is necessary.

TEENS MAKING A DIFFERENCE
Community Food Drive

Boy Scout Troop 196 decided to sponsor a food drive to benefit a food pantry for needy families. First the Scouts persuaded a supermarket to donate grocery bags. Then they wrote a letter about the food drive, saying that donations should be nutritious, nonperishable, and easy to store.

The Scouts stapled a copy of the letter to every grocery bag and delivered a bag to each house in the community. Residents were asked to fill the bag and leave it on their doorsteps the next week. When the Scouts returned, they collected 1,200 pounds of groceries for the pantry!

Try THIS!

Make a list of food products that would be good donations for this type of drive. Then work with your classmates to compile a master list to use for your school's next food drive.

TECHNOLOGY IN THE CLASSROOM

Computerized Cookbooks You will find a range of software programs appropriate for use in the Family and Consumer Sciences classroom. One type of database available to students to help them with their study of cooking is the computerized cookbook. Recipes in computerized cookbooks are usually categorized by type as in printed cookbooks. However, you can also locate recipes in computerized cookbooks by a search for specific ingredients such as blueberries or garlic. Computerized cookbooks also have the capability of changing the quantities of the ingredients before printing the recipe for use.

TEENS MAKING A DIFFERENCE

Have students read "Teens Making a Difference." Ask them why the Scouts requested donations of foods that were nonperishable and easy to store. (*Students should mention that food had to be collected, taken to the food pantry, and stored until it could be distributed.*)

Ask students to make their own list of food items before compiling a master list. Have students read their lists aloud. (*Students might mention such things as canned tuna or canned meats, canned fruits, vegetables, soups, and juices, jars of baby food, or boxes of cereal or pasta.*)

BLOCK SCHEDULING

The following Teacher Classroom Resources are suggested for use in classrooms with Block Scheduling.

- Activity and Project Card 25, "What's to Eat?"
- Activity and Project Card 26, "Shopping for the Best Buys"
- Cooperative Learning 25, "Teaching Children Table Manners"
- Cooperative Learning 26, "Safety Guidelines for Food Storage"

LESSON ONE
Planning a Menu

FOCUS

Lesson Objectives
After studying this lesson, students should be able to
- describe how to plan balanced meals that fit their lifestyle.
- explain the importance of variety in meal planning.
- explain how to evaluate the available resources in menu planning.

Motivating Activity
Ask students to recall what they had for breakfast that morning. Have them list the foods they ate.

Introducing the Lesson
Have students share their lists from the Motivating Activity. Ask them to explain why they chose to eat what they did. Ask students for suggestions for other food options for breakfast. Tell them that in this lesson they will find out how to plan a balanced menu and how to include variety in their meals.

Introducing *Words to Know*
Have students work with partners to look up and discuss the definition of each of the Words to Know. Then let partners work together to write original sentences using each of the words in context.

LESSON ONE
Planning a Menu

 **WORDS TO KNOW**

appetizer
meal pattern
texture
garnish
time schedule

DISCOVER...
- how to plan balanced meals that fit your lifestyle.
- the importance of variety in meal planning.
- how to evaluate your available resources.

Whether you are throwing a birthday party for a friend or cooking a meal for your family, it is best to start by making a plan. Serving tasty, attractive, and nutritious meals requires more than just being a good cook. It takes management skills.

The first step in creating a meal is planning ahead. It is best to plan all your meals for an entire day. This way, you can be sure that you are getting the right number of calories and enough servings from each food group.

360   CHAPTER 13: PREPARING TO COOK

CLASSROOM RESOURCES FOR LESSON 1

 Blackline Masters
Activity and Project Card 25, "What's to Eat?"
Concept Map 20
Cooperative Learning 25
Food Lab Activity 4, "Cooking with Herbs"
Lesson 1 Quiz
Peer Pressure and Decision Making 27

 Transparencies
Transparency 54, "Meal Appeal"

 Student Workbook
Activities 90, 91

The Planning Stage

As you plan your menu, think of meals that are simple and nutritious. Include a variety of foods, and consider your skills, time, and money. Plan your meals around the Food Guide Pyramid and your own eating patterns.

Using the Food Guide Pyramid

You learned in Chapter 11, Lesson 1, that the Food Guide Pyramid divides foods into five basic groups. For good nutrition, you should plan meals that include foods from each group.

- **The Bread, Cereal, Rice, and Pasta Group.** You need 6 to 11 servings every day. Some foods in this group, such as pasta, can be used as the basis of a main dish. Others, such as rice and bread, are usually served as side dishes.

Meals are more enjoyable if the table is attractive and properly set. What guidelines do you follow when setting your table?

TIPS for living

SETTING THE TABLE

Setting the table is an important part of meal preparation. Follow these guidelines to set a formal table.

- If you use a tablecloth, spread it over the table evenly and smoothly.
- If you use place mats, position them near the edge of the table.
- Center the plates on the place mats or at each place on the tablecloth.
- Place a knife to the right of each plate and a fork to the left of each plate. The cutting edge of the knife should be turned toward the plate.
- Place a spoon to the right of each knife.
- Set a water or beverage glass near the tip of each knife.
- Place a napkin beside each fork.
- If using a salad or bread-and-butter plate place it near the tip of each fork.

LESSON ONE: PLANNING A MENU   **361**

MORE ABOUT •••

Appetizers Appetizers should stimulate, not dull, the appetite for the meal to come. It is best when there are not too many and not too much. They can be served as the first course at the table, but more often they are served from trays before people sit down to a meal. Hors d'oeuvres, served in France, often consist of small pieces of cheese, meat, fish, and olives. In Italy, a common appetizer is thinly sliced prosciutto (Italian-style ham) served with thin wedges of cantaloupe or honeydew melon. Common American appetizers include fruit cups, seafood cocktails, fruit or vegetable pieces with dip, stuffed mushrooms, cheese and crackers, or even miniature pizzas.

CHAPTER 13, LESSON 1

TEACH

L1 Discussion
Discuss with students the advantages to planning meals for an entire day, rather than planning just one meal at a time. Then review the five food groups in the Food Guide Pyramid and ask students to name examples of foods from each group and to state how many servings from each group are needed daily.

L2 Planning an Appetizer
Have students work in small groups to plan an appetizer tray they could serve to their family before a meal. Remind students that appetizers do not have to be just vegetables. Encourage them to be creative in planning their appetizers. Have a representative from each group share their ideas with the class. Allow the class to vote on their favorite idea. If possible, prepare the favorite appetizer and allow students to sample it.

L2 Activity and Project Card
Allow time for students to complete Activity and Project Card 25, "What's to Eat?" in the TCR.

TIPS for living
Tell students that items included in a place setting depend on the foods in the menu. After students have read "Tips for Living," have them work in small groups to create unique place settings for different menus.

361

CHAPTER 13, LESSON 1

Skills IN ACTION

Have each pair of students role-play for the rest of the class the table manners suggested in the feature and discuss the table manners illustrated. Have the class work in small groups to write and illustrate a children's book designed to teach table manners. Have them use the guidelines in the feature to help them plan the book. Students might present their books to the younger classes.

L2 Cooperative Learning
Assign Cooperative Learning Activity 25, "Teaching Children Table Manners," in the TCR.

L1 Analyzing Meal Patterns
Ask students to illustrate their meal patterns. Provide each student with a paper plate. Have them do the following: Divide the plate into three sections. In the first section have students draw foods they typically eat for breakfast; in the second section, foods they typically eat for lunch; and in the third section, foods they typically eat for dinner. Tell students to list snacks in the center of the plate. Ask them to exchange their plates with a partner and check each other's menus for adequate servings from each of the food groups. Display the plates around the classroom.

Skills IN ACTION
Practicing Good Table Manners

The next time you sit down to a meal with your family or friends, you can show good manners by following these rules.
- Avoid putting your elbows on the table.
- Lift the food to your mouth instead of lowering your head.
- Don't talk with your mouth full.
- Ask someone to pass food that is out of your reach.
- Lay your knife and fork across the center of your plate when you finish eating.
- Lay your napkin neatly beside your plate when the meal is over.

- **The Vegetable Group.** Three to five servings are needed every day. Raw vegetables can be eaten as a salad, a snack, or an **appetizer**—*a dish served before the meal.* Raw or cooked vegetables can be served as a side dish.
- **The Fruit Group.** From this group, you need two to four servings every day. These may include fresh, frozen, dried, and canned fruit as well as fruit juice. Fruit can be part of any meal.
- **The Milk, Yogurt, and Cheese Group.** As a growing teen, you need three servings every day. Foods from this group can accompany any meal.
- **The Meat, Poultry, Fish, Dry Beans, Eggs, and Nuts Group.** Two to three servings are needed every day. Foods from this group are usually served as the main dish in a meal.

Analyzing Your Meal Pattern

Most people follow a **meal pattern,** or *habit that determines when and what they eat each day.* They may eat a main meal at noon or in the evening. They usually select similar types of foods each day for breakfast, lunch, dinner, and snacks. For example, your meal pattern for the day might be as follows:

- **Breakfast:** cereal with fruit and nuts, juice, milk
- **Lunch:** sandwich, fruit or vegetable, dessert, milk
- **Dinner:** meat or poultry, vegetable, rice or pasta, milk
- **Snack:** fruit

If you are aware of your meal pattern and use the Food Guide Pyramid, menu planning is easy. Simply choose a combination of foods from the five food groups that fit the meal pattern. To plan a lunch for the meal pattern above, you might choose a tuna salad sandwich, carrot sticks, oatmeal cookies, and milk. Meal patterns should be flexible. Your schedule may change, you may be trying to gain or lose weight, or you may be invited to eat at a friend's home.

362   CHAPTER 13: PREPARING TO COOK

MEETING STUDENT DIVERSITY

Cultural Diversity Have students work in small groups to research meal patterns in other cultures. Invite students from other cultures—from your class or from other classes in the school—to contribute their own personal experiences as part of the research. Ask each group to make a poster that shows a daily menu following the meal pattern and specific foods from one culture. Display the posters in the classroom.

Meal Appeal

Including a variety of foods in your meals makes eating more interesting. Meals planned with variety in mind can look and taste better. Eating many different foods also makes it easier to get all the nutrients you need. One way to add variety is to vary the way foods are prepared. Another way is to choose foods that provide different textures, colors, sizes and shapes, flavors, and temperatures.

- **Texture.** Foods with different textures add more variety. **Texture** means *the way food feels when it is eaten.* Rolls may be crusty, raw vegetables are crisp, and pudding is smooth. One way to vary the textures of foods is by preparing them in different ways. For example, think of the difference in texture between raw carrots and cooked carrots.

- **Color.** Choosing foods of different colors will make the meal look more interesting. For instance, salad with green lettuce, red tomatoes, and orange carrots will add color to your meal. Adding a **garnish**, *a small amount of a food or seasoning to decorate the food,* is another way to provide more color. Parsley, lemon wedges, and orange slices are garnishes.

- **Size and Shape.** Varying the sizes and shapes of foods will give you a much more appealing meal. For example, a dinner of fish sticks, zucchini sticks, and french fries would seem dull. How would you change this menu?

- **Flavor.** Combine flavors that vary and complement each other. Turkey and mashed potatoes, steak and onions, and broccoli and cheese are some flavors that go well together.

- **Temperature.** Vary the temperatures of food in a meal. Plan some hot and some cold food.

If you plan wisely, you can prepare some foods ahead of time. How would this help you?

LESSON ONE: PLANNING A MENU 363

CHAPTER 13, LESSON 1

L1 Discussion
Ask students for examples of various main dishes. (*meat loaf, roasted chicken, grilled lamb chops, swiss steak, and fish sticks*) Discuss with students what variety in meal planning involves. (*foods of different colors, textures, shapes and sizes, flavors, and temperatures*) Then have students find pictures in magazines and make a collage showing the variety of foods available. From these foods, have students plan menus for one day.

L1 Using Transparencies
Present Color Transparency 54, "Meal Appeal," in the TCR. Use this overhead visual to reinforce concepts from this lesson.

L2 Math
Have students work in small groups to prepare a time schedule for the following menu: green pepper and mushroom omelette, bacon, grapefruit sections, toasted English muffins, and milk. Remind students to include time for setting the table, serving the food, and cleaning up.

L2 Problem Solving
Assign Peer Pressure and Decision Making 27 in the TCR. This activity gives students the opportunity to recognize peer pressure and practice decision-making skills.

L2 Food Lab
Allow time for students to complete Food Lab Activity 4, "Cooking with Herbs," in the TCR.

COOPERATIVE LEARNING

Analyzing Resources Have students work in small groups to plan a meal. Have them use cookbooks to select recipes based on the resources they might have at home. Prepare several different sample pantry inventories from which groups can choose available food resources. Have them indicate the resources they have available for the meal they chose.

CHAPTER 13, LESSON 1

L1 Student Workbook
Assign Activities 90 and 91 in the Student Workbook.

ASSESS

Evaluating the Lesson
Assign Reviewing Terms and Facts and Thinking Critically on page 365 to review the lesson; then assign the Lesson 1 Quiz in the TCR.

Reteaching
- Organize students to work in small groups. Assign each group one of the following meals: breakfast, lunch, dinner. Ask students in each group to make posters that illustrate basic food patterns for their meal for display in the classroom. Have students suggest specific foods to use in the menus and evaluate the meals for variety and inclusion of foods from the five food groups.
- Have students complete Reteaching Activity 13 in the TCR.
- Assign Concept Map 20 in the TCR.

Enrichment
Provide students with a list of foods such as baked potato, cauliflower, baked fish, and jello. Ask them to describe how they could use garnishes to make the foods look more attractive.

Planning Ahead

As you plan your menus, take time to read through the recipes carefully and make sure that you have all of the resources you will need.

- **Skills.** If you are a beginning cook, you may want to avoid complicated recipes. Could you choose convenience foods for part of the meal? For instance, you might make a dessert from a mix rather than cook it from scratch.
- **Equipment.** Some recipes call for a specific utensil. Make sure that you have all of the necessary tools and equipment.
- **Ingredients.** Do you have all the ingredients the recipe calls for? If you don't, think of substitutions that could be made.
- **Money.** Do the ingredients fit your food budget? Can you save money with coupons or use foods that are less expensive because they are in season?
- **Time.** If you know that you will be working within a time frame, such as having only one hour in which to cook dinner, you must choose foods that can be prepared within the time allowed.

Using a Time Schedule

An important part of planning a meal is making a time schedule. A **time schedule** is *a plan to make sure that all foods are ready to serve at the right time.* Some dishes take longer than others to prepare, and some foods take longer than others to cook. For this reason, you must know what to do first and when to do it. A sample time schedule is shown in **Figure 13.1**.

Managing Meals

Taking time to plan ahead helps you create nutritious, attractive meals that fit your lifestyle, skills, and budget. With a little practice, the planning will become so natural that you will hardly even have to think about it.

364   CHAPTER 13: PREPARING TO COOK

COOPERATIVE LEARNING

Videotaping Explain that students are going to stage a program called "Preparing to Cook," which will be videotaped for later broadcast to the school and to families of students. Organize the class into four groups. Assign one of the chapter lessons to each group. Tell students in each group that they will be responsible for creating a segment of the program based on the concepts in their assigned lesson. Students in each group might divide up the following tasks: on-camera hosts, segment coordinators and script writers, sound/video technicians, and design crew.

Figure 13.1 Sample Time Schedule
Using a time schedule helps you make sure that all foods are ready at the right time.

First list the job that will take longest to do. Then list in order the other jobs to be done until you have listed them all.

Some foods take longer to cook than others, so you must plan what to do first and when to do it.

Besides cooking time, consider that some dishes take longer to prepare than others.

Don't forget to allow time for setting the table, serving the food, and cleaning up.

Plan a time schedule backward, from the end to the beginning. First decide at what time you will serve the meal. Then figure out how much time you will need to prepare each of the different foods.

It is easier to follow a time schedule if the preparation jobs are listed in the order in which they are to be done.

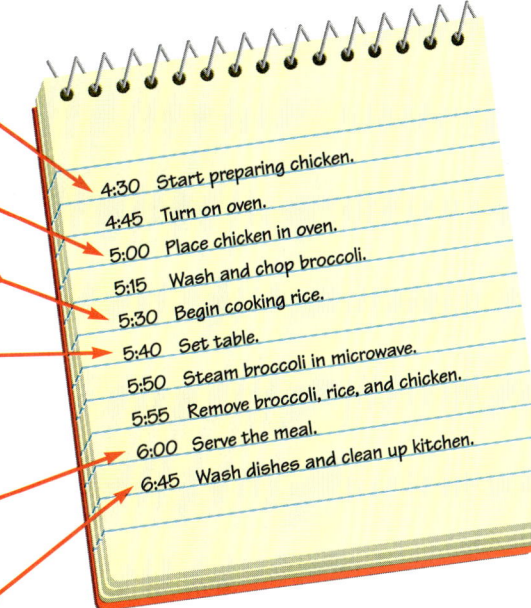

- 4:30 Start preparing chicken.
- 4:45 Turn on oven.
- 5:00 Place chicken in oven.
- 5:15 Wash and chop broccoli.
- 5:30 Begin cooking rice.
- 5:40 Set table.
- 5:50 Steam broccoli in microwave.
- 5:55 Remove broccoli, rice, and chicken.
- 6:00 Serve the meal.
- 6:45 Wash dishes and clean up kitchen.

LESSON ONE Review

Using complete sentences, answer the following questions on a separate sheet of paper.

Reviewing Terms and Facts
1. **Recall** Why should meal patterns be flexible?
2. **List** Name five ways to add variety to meals.
3. **Vocabulary** Define the term *texture*. Describe the textures of three different foods.
4. **Name** List five resources that you should consider before preparing a meal.

Thinking Critically
5. **Explain** What is the advantage of planning meals for a whole day?
6. **Analyze** Why is it important to include variety when planning meals?

Applying Concepts
7. Write down your typical meal pattern. Then plan a daily menu that follows the recommendations of the Food Guide Pyramid and fits your meal pattern.

LESSON ONE: PLANNING A MENU   365

COOPERATIVE LEARNING

Planning a Menu Ask students to work in small groups to plan a menu for a day that meets the recommendations of the five food groups and provides variety. Groups should divide several tasks among their members. For example, one student should be responsible for checking the nutritional values of the foods. One student should research recipes and list the preparation tasks and the time required for the recipes. Another student should analyze cooking times and plan the use of oven, stovetop, microwave, or chilling times. Still another student should estimate cleanup time. Then group members should work together to compile their meal plan.

CHAPTER 13, LESSON 1

USING VISUALS
Ask students to look at the sample time schedule in Figure 13.1. Have them identify what should be done first and why. (*The thing that takes the longest time to prepare should be started first.*) Have students choose a dish they would like to cook and prepare a time schedule for it.

Answers to Lesson 1 Review
1. Your schedule might change, you might be trying to gain or lose weight, or you might be invited to eat at a friend's house.
2. Vary the way foods are prepared and choose foods that vary in texture, color, size and shape, flavor, and temperature.
3. Texture is the way food feels when it is eaten. Descriptions of textures will vary.
4. Before preparing a meal, you should consider your skills, equipment, ingredients, money, and time.
5. The advantage is that you can be sure of getting the right number of servings from each food group and the right amount of calories.
6. Variety makes eating more interesting, meals look and taste better, and it is easier to get all the nutrients you need.
7. Meal patterns and daily menus will vary, but should meet recommendations of the Food Guide Pyramid.

CLOSE

Have students write a paragraph explaining important points involved in planning and preparing healthful meals.

LESSON TWO
Food Shopping and Storage

FOCUS

Lesson Objectives
After studying this lesson, students should be able to
- explain why planning before food shopping is helpful.
- describe how to make wise food purchases.
- identify ways of storing food safely.

Motivating Activity
Display packages of food products that come in a variety of brands and package sizes. Be sure to include a store brand and a generic product. Write the prices of the products on the chalkboard, without the brand names. Ask students to make a list of the brands, along with the price from the chalkboard that they think matches each one.

Introducing the Chapter
Have students share their responses to the Motivating Activity. Ask them to explain their reasoning for matching products and prices as they did. Tell them that this lesson provides them with guidelines for making wise food purchases.

Introducing *Words to Know*
Ask students which of the food products from the Motivating Activity are store-brand products and which are generic products. Explain that generic products were introduced in 1977 and are available in 80 percent of supermarkets.

LESSON TWO
Food Shopping and Storage

WORDS TO KNOW
- staples
- national-brand products
- store-brand products
- generic products
- grade labeling
- unit pricing
- open dating

DISCOVER...
- why it is helpful to plan before you shop for food.
- how to make wise food purchases.
- how to store foods safely.

Have you ever helped with the family grocery shopping? You probably know how many different brands and food items there are to choose from. Learning good shopping skills can help you make wise food choices. You can learn how to buy foods that provide nutrition and flavor and still get the most for your money.

366   CHAPTER 13: PREPARING TO COOK

CLASSROOM RESOURCES FOR LESSON 2

 Blackline Masters
Activity and Project Card 26, "Shopping for the Best Buys"
Cooperative Learning 26
Lesson 2 Quiz

 Transparencies
Transparency 55, "Reading a Food Label"
Transparency 56, "Using Unit Pricing"

 Student Workbook
Activities 92, 93

Before You Shop

Before you head for the store, make a list of everything you need for the meals you have planned. Review the recipes, and don't forget to check your staple foods. **Staples** are *foods that you are likely to use often.* Examples of staples include milk, eggs, salt, and pepper.

You can save money by adjusting your menus to take advantage of weekly specials. Check supermarket advertisements in your local newspaper to find out what items are on sale.

Smart Shopping

Learning how to find the best buys is an important part of being a smart shopper. Some brands are better buys than others. Store brands and generic products, for example, are usually less expensive than national brands.

- **National-brand products** are *those products that you see advertised on television or in newspapers or magazines.* These products often cost more than others because the manufacturer spends a great deal of money on advertising. This advertising cost is added to the price of the product.

- **Store-brand products** are *foods and household items that have the store's name or another name used only by that store on the label.* They usually cost less because there is little or no advertising cost. They often have the same ingredients and nutrients as national brands.

- **Generic products** are *products with labels listing only the product name and nutritional information.* These cost even less than store-brand products.

Clipping coupons is one way to make the most of your family's food dollars. What are some other ways?

LESSON TWO: FOOD SHOPPING AND STORAGE **367**

HOME AND COMMUNITY CONNECTION

Comparing Brands Have students compare nutrition information and price of a national brand, store brand, and generic brand of a similar food product the next time their family goes to the grocery store. Suggest that students share the information with their family members and discuss which product might be a better choice for their family.

CHAPTER 13, LESSON 2

TEACH

L1 Discussion
Ask students to name other items that they would consider to be staples. (*Answers might include shortening, specific spices, pastas, or rice.*) Discuss whether some items might be considered staples in one household but not another. For example, corn meal might be a staple in a household that frequently makes corn tortillas or cornbread, but might rarely or never be used in other households.

L2 Organizing Coupons
Provide small groups of students with a variety of different manufacturers' or store coupons. Ask students to develop a filing system to divide the coupons by category so that they would be easier to use when shopping. Have groups share their coupon categories. Ask if there are additional categories they would add for foods for which they had no coupons. Ask each group to determine how much money they could save if they used all the coupons they had while shopping.

L2 Activity and Project Card
Allow time for students to complete Activity and Project Card 26, "Shopping for the Best Buys," in the TCR.

CHAPTER 13, LESSON 2

Discuss with students why each of the shopping etiquette rules is important. Then ask them to suggest additional rules that could be added to the list.

L1 Discussion

Ask students to describe the uses for which they would want to choose the top grade of food product available. Then ask them for what uses lower grades would be appropriate.

L1 Math

Ask students to calculate the unit price for each of the following pairs of products to determine which is a better value: a 1-pound box of crackers for $2.09 or an 8-ounce box for $1.29; a 227-gram can of green beans for $0.69 or a 425-gram can for $1.39; a 12-ounce box of cereal for $2.59 or an 18-ounce box for $3.29; a bottle of salad dressing that contains 0.35 liters for $2.65 or a 0.47-liter bottle for $3.29.

L1 Using Transparencies

Present Color Transparency 55, "Reading a Food Label," in the TCR. Use this overhead visual to reinforce concepts from this lesson.

L1 Discussion

Ask students to name products that are labeled with open dating. Discuss whether they should buy a product just before the date on the package.

368

Shopping Etiquette

The next time you go to the supermarket, remember these rules of shopping etiquette.

- Handle food items with care, especially fruits and vegetables.
- Don't open a container until you have paid for the item.
- If you decide that you don't want an item, put it back where you got it.
- Return shopping carts to their appropriate place.

What can you add to this list?

Higher grades of meat may have a better flavor than lower grades, but they are more expensive.

368   CHAPTER 13: PREPARING TO COOK

It takes practice to find which brands give you the most for your money. You will want to compare national-brand, store-brand, and generic products to see which ones you prefer.

Understanding Grade Labeling

Understanding and using grade labeling can also help you when you shop. **Grade labeling** is *a measurement of food quality using standards set by the government.* Many food items—including eggs, poultry, and meat—are graded. The highest grade is the highest in quality. For example, Grade AA eggs are of higher quality than Grade A eggs.

Reading Food Labels

Food labels also give you valuable shopping information. By law, food labels must provide the following:

- The name of the food
- The name and address of the product's manufacturer
- The nutritional content, including serving size, calories, and nutrient amounts per serving
- A list of ingredients in order of amount (so that a dry cereal might list oat flour first, then sugar, followed by

MORE ABOUT •••

Grade Labeling Grade A milk meets government health standards. Eggs and butter are graded AA, A, and B. Grades A and B are fine for cooking and baking. For meat, prime is the top grade. Choice grade is sold in most stores. Good grade is less flavorful, but less expensive. Both Grades A and B of poultry are good quality, but Grade A is meatier. Canned and frozen fruits are available in Grades A (Fancy), B (Choice), and C (Standard). Grade A is the largest and most perfect fruit, Grade B is somewhat smaller, and Grade C has pieces that are not all the same size and shape. Canned and frozen vegetables are graded the same as fruits. For example, Grade C vegetables would be fine for use in soups or stews.

other ingredients, to show that oat flour is the main ingredient, then sugar, and so on)

- The total weight

Labels give other helpful information as well. **Figure 13.2** shows a sample label and the kinds of information provided.

You can use the weight and volume information on the label to compare quantities and find the best buy. For

**Figure 13.2
Nutrition Facts**
A great deal of important information is provided on the Nutrition Facts label. How much fat does one serving of this product contain?

1. Serving size is an important reference because calorie and nutrient content are based on this amount. Foods that are similar, such as breakfast cereals, will have similar serving sizes.
2. Knowing the number of calories from fat can help you meet Dietary Guidelines. These guidelines state that 30 percent or less of your daily calories should come from fat.
3. Percent Daily Values are based on a diet of 2,000 calories a day. You can adjust the Percent Daily Values to your own diet and calorie intake.
4. Nutrient content is provided in metric amounts (grams or milligrams) and by Percent Daily Values. This information is useful for comparing foods.
5. Information about certain nutrients is required on the label. These nutrients are total fat, saturated fat, cholesterol, sodium, total carbohydrate, dietary fiber, sugars, protein, vitamins A and C, calcium, and iron.
6. A reference chart provides information for both 2,000- and 2,500-calorie diets. The chart shows the highest amount of total fat, saturated fat, cholesterol, and sodium that a person should consume. It also shows the ideal intake for total carbohydrate and dietary fiber.
7. Some labels show the number of calories supplied by one gram of fat, carbohydrate, and protein.

LESSON TWO: FOOD SHOPPING AND STORAGE 369

COOPERATIVE LEARNING

Comparing Foods for Nutrition Ask students to list various food products advertised on television during children's programs. Have students work in small groups to examine and compare nutrition labels from these foods. Ask students to determine which of the foods are most nutritious and to rank the foods according to the amount of each of the nutrients listed on the labels. Have groups prepare a table or a bar chart to demonstrate the results of their findings. Allow time for groups to present tables and charts to the class and to explain how they reached their conclusions.

CHAPTER 13, LESSON 2

DID YOU KNOW

All meat shipped in interstate commerce is federally inspected. The round, purple U.S. Inspected and Passed stamp on a cut of meat guarantees that the meat came from a source judged wholesome by a federal inspector and that the plant where it was processed complied with sanitary regulations.

L3 Research

Have students research what can happen to cause canned foods to spoil and why dented or bulging cans should not be purchased. Suggest that they also find out about the safety precautions needed for home canning of foods.

L1 Analyzing

If possible, arrange a field trip or ask a group of volunteers to plan a visit to a local supermarket. Have students look for examples of the following: unit pricing information on the shelves; displays designed to attract sales; what services the store offers to customers; and the location of generic items, brand-name items, and store brands. Then have students prepare a summary of the services, variety, and convenience offered to customers shopping at that store.

USING VISUALS

As you go over each of the numbered nutrition facts in Figure 13.2, ask volunteers to locate the information on the label and read it aloud.

Before purchasing dairy products, check the open dating to be sure that the food is fresh. What happens to the food after that date?

example, which is a better value—a 1-pound (500-gram) bag of tortilla chips for $1.99 or an 11-ounce (300-gram) bag for $1.49?

Unit pricing makes these kinds of price comparisons simpler. **Unit pricing** means *showing the cost of the product per unit.* Examples of units include ounce, pound, gram, liter, and gallon. Look for the unit pricing label on the front of the store shelf. It will give you the product name, the size, and the price per unit. You can easily decide which size is the best buy.

Checking for Freshness

Products that are packaged fresh—such as bread, milk, yogurt, and meat—also have a date on their labels. **Open dating** is *the display of a freshness date on packaged food.* The date shown is generally the last day a food may be sold as fresh.

Shopping for Quality

There is more to smart shopping then just reading the labels. You need to know how to judge food quality and safety, too. Here are some tips to remember.

- Buy meat, poultry, and fish that is wrapped in fresh, undamaged packaging material.
- Buy fresh fruits and vegetables in season that are firm and do not have spots.
- Never buy dented or bulging cans. The food may be spoiled.
- Pick up frozen and refrigerated foods last.

Food Storage

When you get home from the supermarket, you will need to store the food you bought. Heat, light, time, and moisture destroy vitamins. They can also affect the flavor and spoil

370 CHAPTER 13: PREPARING TO COOK

foods. Storing foods properly helps them keep their freshness, flavor, and nutrients.

Refrigerated and Frozen Foods

The first foods you should put away are frozen foods. Put them in the freezer so that they won't thaw out. Place perishable foods in the refrigerator immediately too. Perishable foods are those that spoil quickly without refrigeration. Milk, meat, poultry, and fish should be stored in the back of the refrigerator—the coldest part.

If fresh meat is to be frozen, remove the store wrapping and wrap the meat in special freezer paper. You can also put meat in a plastic bag made for freezing or wrap it in heavy aluminum foil. Eggs should be kept in the egg carton.

Fresh Fruits and Vegetables

Most fruits need to be stored in the refrigerator. Salad vegetables, such as lettuce and celery, should be stored in plastic wrap, bags, or containers in the refrigerator. Before storing root vegetables—carrots and radishes, for instance—remove any tops. Certain vegetables, such as potatoes and whole onions, can be stored in a vegetable bin in a cool, dry place. Wash all fruits and vegetables well before cooking or eating them.

Nonperishable Foods

Nonperishable foods are usually packaged in cans, bottles, or boxes. They may include soup, tuna, bottled beverages, pasta, and cake mix. These foods should be stored in a cabinet where they will stay cool and dry. As you unpack groceries, move the older nonperishable items to the front of the shelf and place the newest items at the back. This helps keep your food supply fresh by making sure that the older items get used first.

Once they are opened, many nonperishable items become perishable. Mayonnaise, salad dressing, and spaghetti sauce can be stored in a cool cabinet only until they are opened. After that, they should be kept tightly covered in the refrigerator. Refrigerate bottles of juice, jams and jellies, ketchup, and mustard after they are opened as well.

Try This!
Use these tips to get the most from your family's food budget. Don't shop when you are hungry. If you do, you may buy items that you don't need. Use coupons. Some stores double the face value of manufacturers' coupons. Take advantage of sales.

LESSON TWO: FOOD SHOPPING AND STORAGE 371

MORE ABOUT • • •

Storing Foods in a Freezer The low temperatures of a freezer tend to draw moisture from foods, causing them to lose flavor, volume, and texture. Foods placed in a freezer should be placed in vapor-proof packaging. Foods should also be labeled and dated. Generally, beef, lamb, veal, fruits, and vegetables can be kept frozen for up to a year. Pork, poultry, and fish can be kept for four to six months. Ground beef can be kept for about two months, cooked and baked foods up to three months, and ham and ice cream up to one month. After these time periods, the foods lose quality.

CHAPTER 13, LESSON 2

L1 Student Workbook
Assign Activities 92 and 93 in the Student Workbook.

ASSESS

Evaluating the Lesson
Assign Reviewing Terms and Facts and Thinking Critically on page 372 to review the lesson; then assign the Lesson 2 Quiz in the TCR.

Reteaching
- Organize the class into small groups. Have each group make a poster titled "Making Good Decisions at the Supermarket." The poster should illustrate the following: grade labeling, open dating, name and address of the manufacturer, ingredient lists, and nutrition labeling.
- Have students complete Reteaching Activity 13 in the TCR.

Enrichment
Hold a taste-testing comparison of a national brand, a house brand, and a generic brand of the same food item. Items that might be used include corn chips, dry cereal, or canned fruit. Items for tasting should be placed in dishes marked A, B, and C so that students cannot identify brands. Ask students to taste samples and rate each food for appearance, color, texture, and flavor. Ask them which samples they prefer and why. Reveal brands after the taste test.

CHAPTER 13, LESSON 2

Answers to Lesson 2 Review

1. Staples are foods that are likely to be used often. Examples: sugar, flour, and salt.
2. Store brands are foods that have the store's name or another name just for that store on the label. Generic products list only the name and nutritional information of the product and are less expensive than store brands.
3. Any four: name of the food, name and address of the product's manufacturer or distributor, nutrient content, a list of ingredients in order of amount, total weight.
4. Meat, poultry, and fish should be wrapped in fresh, undamaged packaging material and should be odorless. Choose vegetables that are firm and do not have spots. Never buy dented or bulging cans. Pick up frozen and refrigerated foods last.
5. Frozen foods should be put in the freezer first so that they won't thaw out. Perishable foods should be refrigerated so they won't spoil.
6. Unit pricing lets you compare the price per unit between similar products to help you find the best buy.
7. Answers will vary. Students may think that most foods that do not have open dating will probably be used up long before they would spoil.
8. Tips will vary. After compiling a master list of tips, suggest that students take a copy home to share with their families.

CLOSE

Have students create a brochure that provides guidelines for shopping and storing food. Students might illustrate the brochures and display them in the classroom for reference.

372

When storing nonperishable foods, rotate the oldest items to the front of the shelf. Why is this important?

A Well-Stocked Kitchen

Knowing how to shop wisely and store food correctly will make meal preparation easier. You will have the ingredients you need, ready to use, when you begin cooking. You can serve tasty and nutritious meals while also making the most of your food dollars.

LESSON TWO Review

Using complete sentences, answer the following questions on a separate sheet of paper.

Reviewing Terms and Facts

1. **Vocabulary** Define the term *staples*. Give three examples of staples.
2. **Contrast** What is the difference between a store brand and a generic product?
3. **List** Name four types of information that are provided on a food label.
4. **Identify** List four tips for judging food quality and safety.
5. **Recall** When unpacking groceries, what foods should you store first? Explain your answer.

Thinking Critically

6. **Explain** How can you use unit pricing to save money?
7. **Analyze** Do you think that all food labels should contain open dating? Why or why not?

Applying Concepts

8. Ask two or three adults for tips on judging freshness, quality, and value when food shopping. Compare your findings with those of your classmates. Then compile a master list of the most popular tips.

372   CHAPTER 13: PREPARING TO COOK

COOPERATIVE LEARNING

Designing a Floor Plan Ask students to work in small groups to draw a floor plan of a grocery store, labeling each area or aisle with the foods that are located there. Then have them write a grocery shopping list that would include a variety of items from each area of the store. Have each group exchange their floor plan and list with another group. Then have each group draw a route through the store that would be efficient and allow for the selection of all the items on their list and for selection of refrigerated and frozen foods last.

LESSON THREE
Following Recipes and Directions

DISCOVER...
- how to follow different recipe formats.
- the meanings of abbreviations and preparation terms.
- how to prepare convenience foods.

Just about everyone knows how to cook something. Maybe you're a whiz at scrambled eggs or pancakes. Perhaps you are already in charge of preparing entire meals once in a while. Whatever level of experience you have in the kitchen, this lesson will help you improve your cooking skills.

WORDS TO KNOW
recipe
yield
standard format
narrative format
convenience foods

The Importance of Recipes

Almost all good cooks use recipes. A **recipe** is *a list of ingredients and directions for preparing a specific food.* If you

LESSON THREE: FOLLOWING RECIPES AND DIRECTIONS 373

LESSON THREE
Following Recipes and Directions

FOCUS

Lesson Objectives
After studying this lesson, students should be able to
- identify different recipe formats.
- define abbreviations and preparation terms used in recipes.
- explain how to prepare convenience foods.

Motivating Activity
Have students write a recipe for a turkey, lettuce, and tomato sandwich, including all the necessary steps.

Introducing the Chapter
Have students share their recipes from the Motivating Activity. Ask them to evaluate each recipe for accuracy of the instructions. Discuss why a well-written recipe is important to ensure a successful result.

Introducing *Words to Know*
Have students look up each term listed in Words to Know in the Glossary at the back of the textbook. Then ask them to write sentences for each word, defining the terms in their own words.

CLASSROOM RESOURCES FOR LESSON 3

 Blackline Masters
Concept Map 21
Cross Curriculum 14
Enrichment 15
Food Lab Activity 5, "Delicious Dinners in Minutes"
Lesson 3 Quiz

 Transparencies
Transparency 57, "Reading a Recipe"

 **Student Workbook**
Activities 94, 95

373

CHAPTER 13, LESSON 3

TEACH

L2 Looking at Cookbooks

Bring in an assortment of cookbooks. Ask small groups of students to look at several cookbooks to identify each of the parts of a recipe mentioned in the text. Then have them determine if the recipes follow the standard format or the narrative format.

L1 Discussion

Discuss guidelines to follow when writing a recipe for others to follow. Be specific about the kind and amount of ingredients. For example, note whether the 2 cups of flour should be wheat, cake, or all-purpose. Be sure to organize the steps in sequence. For example, include a step to sauté onions before a step to add sautéed onions to bread crumbs. Include descriptive terms, such as "sauté onions until translucent," and/or timing hints, such as "heat the sauce for about 10 minutes." Then have students read a recipe to evaluate it for these hints.

Discuss why it is important to organize recipes by category. Ask students to suggest additional categories they might want to add to their recipe file. Suggest that students follow the suggestions for organizing their recipe collections and share their results with the class.

You can find recipes in cookbooks or magazines, or by asking friends and relatives. Start a recipe file or notebook in which to keep your favorites.

know how to read and follow recipes, you will greatly increase your chances of success in the kitchen.

Not all recipes are written in the same way. Some are easier to follow than others. While you are learning to cook, look for simple, easy-to-read recipes that

- list the necessary ingredients.
- state the amount of each ingredient.
- provide step-by-step instructions on how to combine the ingredients.
- mention the sizes of pans that will be needed.
- specify the cooking time and temperature.
- estimate the **yield,** or *the number of servings*.

Look at the recipes on page 375. Which would be easier for you to follow? Can you find each of the parts of a recipe mentioned above in the one you chose?

Recipe Formats

The type of recipe you will see most often is the standard format. A recipe in a **standard format** is *a list of all the ingredients in order of use and step-by-step directions for preparing the food.* **Figure 13.3** shows a recipe in this format.

Figure 13.3 shows the same recipe in a **narrative format,** or *a paragraph description of the steps and ingredients in order of use*. This format is sometimes used in newspapers and magazines because it takes up less space.

Skills IN ACTION

Organizing Recipes

To get the best use out of your recipe collection, do the following:

- Tape loose recipes to index cards so that they will be easier to use.
- Sort recipes into categories such as meat dishes, vegetable dishes, appetizers, and desserts.
- Find a small box to hold your recipes, or buy a recipe box.

374 CHAPTER 13: PREPARING TO COOK

 **HOME AND COMMUNITY CONNECTION**

Making a Classroom Cookbook Ask each student to bring in a favorite family recipe or a recipe from a cookbook. Have students work together to divide the recipes into categories, such as main dishes, appetizers, vegetable dishes, salads, and desserts. Assign each category to a small group and have them organize and copy those recipes on one or more sheets of plain paper. Ask each group to design a cover for the cookbook. Combine each group's recipes into a cookbook. If possible, make enough copies for students to take home to share with their families.

Whatever the recipe format, the procedure for following the recipe remains the same. Here are some general guidelines for using recipes. Read through the entire recipe. Make sure that you understand all the terms and abbreviations. Then, assemble all the ingredients and equipment before you start. Next, do any necessary preparation, such as turning on the oven or greasing the pan.

The Language of Recipes

Recipes have their own special language. To be able to follow them, you need to know some common cooking terms and abbreviations.

Preparation and Cooking Terms

You probably already know the meaning of some of the words used in recipes. *Boil* and *bake* are cooking terms that are easy to understand. However, can you explain the

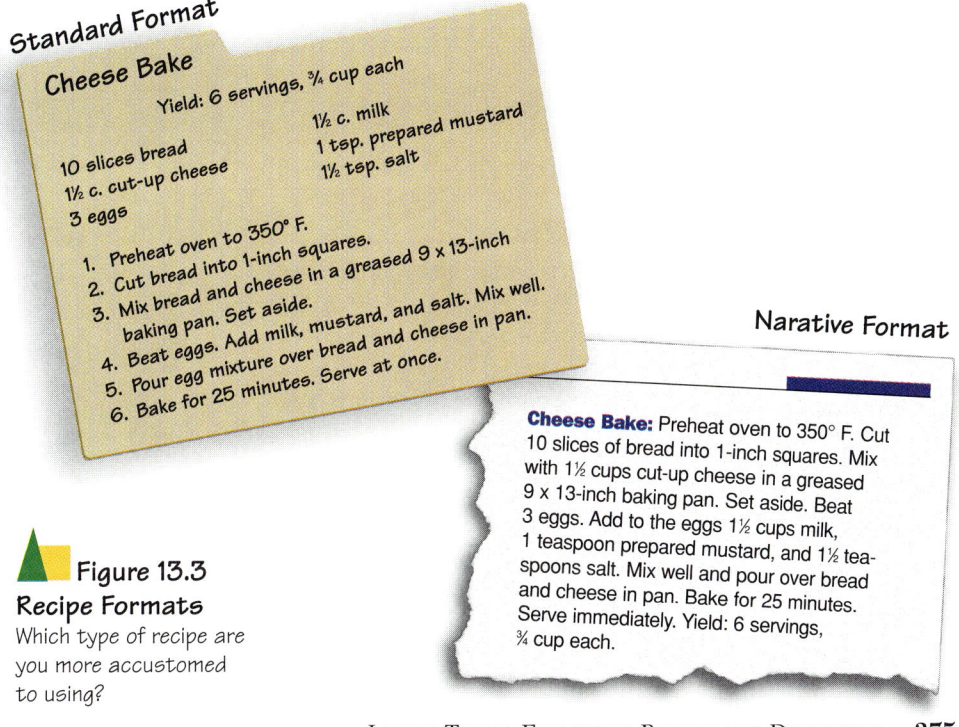

Figure 13.3
Recipe Formats
Which type of recipe are you more accustomed to using?

TECHNOLOGY UPDATE

Cooking Videos Cookbook videos allow you to learn the techniques of some great chefs at home. The videos allow you to profit from an expert's advice and detailed instructions. Ingredients and measurements are often captioned on the screen to help you. Rather than purchasing cooking videos, you might check your local library's video selections or your local video rental store. Present these videos to the class during discussions to demonstrate measuring techniques, preparation of ingredients, and kitchen safety and sanitation.

CHAPTER 13, LESSON 3

L1 Discussion

Ask students to look at the standard-format recipe for cheese bake in Figure 13.3 on the previous page. Have them follow the guidelines for using recipes by first reading through the entire recipe. Discuss whether they understand all the terms and abbreviations used in the recipe. Then ask them to name the ingredients and equipment they would need to make the recipe. Finally, ask them what preparations they need to make before following the recipe.

L2 Looking at Convenience Foods

Have small groups of students look at a variety of packaged convenience foods. Ask them to group them into ready-to-eat foods and ones that require some preparation. Have them look at the directions on several boxes of cake, bread, or muffin mixes. Ask them to list ingredients they need to make the food that are not included in the mix. Discuss the advantages of using these convenience foods.

USING VISUALS

Refer students to the common cooking terms in Figure 13.4. Then ask them to find recipes that they have used that include one of these terms. Have them determine which of the terms are used most often in the recipes.

Figure 13.4 Common Cooking Terms
There are many ways to cook foods. Which is your favorite method for cooking chicken? Meat? Vegetables?

difference between *simmering* and *steaming*? **Figure 13.4** illustrates many commonly used cooking terms.

It is equally important to understand preparation terms. For example, do you know how to *shred* cabbage? Can you describe how *chopping* differs from *mincing*? **Figure 13.5** explains the meaning of common preparation terms.

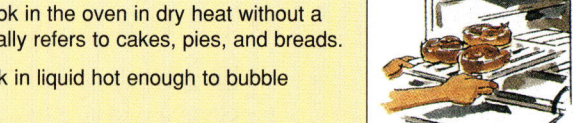

Bake—Cook in the oven in dry heat without a cover. Usually refers to cakes, pies, and breads.

Boil—Cook in liquid hot enough to bubble rapidly.

Braise—Simmer gently in a small amount of liquid in a covered pan. Meat may be browned first.

Broil—Cook under direct heat.

Brown—Cook in a small amount of fat over high heat to brown the surface.

Chill—Put in the refrigerator until cold.

Cook—Prepare food by dry heat, moist heat, or direct heat.

Cook by dry heat—Cook food uncovered without adding any liquid.

Cook by moist heat—Cook in a covered pan with added liquid.

Deep-fat-fry or French-fry—Cook in fat deep enough to cover or float the food.

Fry—Cook in hot fat.

Preheat—Heat the oven to the right temperature before putting in the food.

Roast—Cook in the oven in dry heat. Usually refers to meat.

Sauté—Fry in a small amount of fat until done.

Scald—Heat milk until it steams and just begins to bubble around the edge of the pan.

Simmer—Cook to just below the boiling point. The liquid will just barely bubble.

Steam—Cook by steam over boiling water.

Stew—Cook slowly in liquid.

Stir fry—Cook quickly in a small amount of fat at high heat.

376 CHAPTER 13: PREPARING TO COOK

COOPERATIVE LEARNING

Identifying Preparation Terms Have students work in small groups to locate recipes in magazines or newspapers that use the preparation terms listed in Figure 13.4. Ask them to circle each term they find with colored markers. Then have them make a collage of the recipes and display the collages in the classroom.

Figure 13.5
Common Preparation Terms
Which of these preparation methods have you used?

MIXING TERMS

Blend. Stir until the ingredients are completely mixed.

Cream. Blend until smooth and fluffy.

Toss. Tumble ingredients lightly with a spoon and fork.

Whip. Beat fast with an electric mixer, rotary beater, or wire whip to add enough air to make the mixture fluffy.

Beat. Mix or stir quickly, bringing the contents of the bowl to the top and down again.

Stir. Move the ingredients in a circular motion to mix or to prevent burning.

Combine. Mix two or more ingredients together.

CUTTING TERMS

Chop. Cut into small pieces.

Grate. Rub back and forth on a grater to make small pieces.

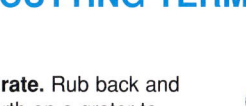

Mince. Cut or chop into very fine pieces.

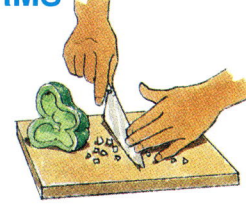

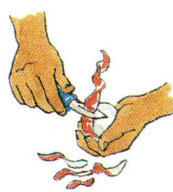

Peel. Remove the skin from a fruit or vegetable with a peeler, knife, or rind remover. Some peelings can be removed by hand.

Shred. Shave or cut off in long, narrow pieces with a knife or grater; also, tear food apart into long pieces.

LESSON THREE: FOLLOWING RECIPES AND DIRECTIONS

CHAPTER 13, LESSON 3

USING VISUALS
Have students study the terms in Figure 13.5. Then refer students back to Lesson 3 of Chapter 12 to identify the kitchen tools that could be used to perform each of the preparation tasks shown in the figure.

LI Creating Cartoons
Have students create cartoons to demonstrate their knowledge of preparation terms, cooking terms, and correct abbreviations. Ask students to create cartoons that answer the following questions: What would happen if you used a tablespoon of salt instead of a teaspoon of salt in a cookie recipe? What would happen if you stirred whipping cream instead of whipping it? What would happen if you broiled a cake instead of baking it? Display the cartoons in the classroom.

DID YOU KNOW ?
Stir-frying is traditionally used in Chinese cooking. It involves cooking thin strips or slices of meats and vegetables in a small amount of fat at high heat in a cooking utensil called a wok. Because stir-frying causes food to cook quickly, all the ingredients should be cut, measured, and assembled before starting. Once the food is added to the wok, it is stirred and tossed with a large spoon or spatula.

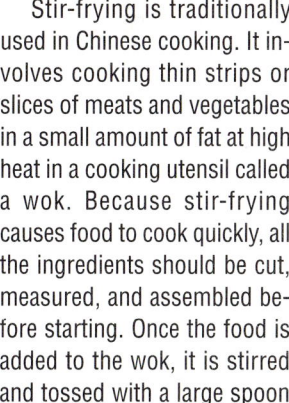

MORE ABOUT • • •

Basic Ingredients Each of the following basic ingredients in a recipe is used for a specific purpose. Flour provides the structure for baked products and is used to thicken liquids. Sugar adds flavor, improves texture, and aids in browning. Shortening helps food brown evenly and helps keep foods fresh. Milk adds flavor and helps preserve foods. It moistens ingredients so that they can be blended and will hold together. Eggs add flavor, color, tenderness, and lightness to breads and cakes. Eggs bind ingredients together in dishes such as meat loaf. They are used to thicken foods, such as custards and sauces. Spices add flavor and help keep foods fresh.

CHAPTER 13, LESSON 3

USING VISUALS
Refer students to Figure 13.6. Then write a recipe on the chalkboard with all words spelled out. Have students copy the recipe using the abbreviation for each of the appropriate words.

L1 Student Workbook
Assign Activities 94 and 95 in the Student Workbook.

ASSESS

Evaluating the Lesson
Assign Reviewing Terms and Facts and Thinking Critically on page 379 to review the lesson; then assign the Lesson 3 Quiz in the TCR.

Reteaching
- Write cooking terms and preparation terms on one side of index cards and the meanings of the terms on the other side. Have one student in each group hold up a term and have other group members explain its meaning.
- Have students complete Reteaching Activity 13 in the TCR.
- Assign Concept Map 21 in the TCR.

Enrichment
- Hold a create-a-sandwich competition. Encourage students to be creative in combining ingredients to make a unique hot or cold sandwich. Students should name their sandwiches and write complete recipes for them.
- Assign Enrichment Activity 15 in the TCR.

CUSTOMARY

teaspoon	tsp. (or t.)
tablespoon	Tbsp. (or T.)
cup	c. (or C.)
pint	pt.
quart	qt.
gallon	gal.
ounce	oz.
pound	lb.
degrees Fahrenheit	°F

METRIC

milliliter	mL
liter	L
gram	g
degrees Celsius	°C

Figure 13.6 Common Abbreviations Why is it important to understand these common abbreviations?

Abbreviations

Recipes often show measurements in shortened form to save space. To follow the recipe, it is essential to understand what the abbreviations mean. **Figure 13.6** explains the customary and metric abbreviations most often used. Abbreviations for "teaspoon" and "tablespoon" can be confusing, so be sure that you know the difference. Can you imagine how your vegetable soup would taste if you added one tablespoon of salt instead of one teaspoon?

The Basic Ingredients

Now that you know how to read a recipe, you are ready to begin combining the ingredients. Remember that the success of your dish depends in part on following step-by-step instructions. As you learn to cook, you will notice that a few common ingredients are found in most recipes. These basic ingredients are flour, sugar, shortening (fats such as butter, oil, or margarine), milk, eggs, and spices. Each ingredient in a recipe is used for a specific purpose. Leaving one out could ruin the dish.

378 CHAPTER 13: PREPARING TO COOK

MORE ABOUT • • •

Mixes Point out to students that many mixes have suggestions for changes or additions to the ingredients that are added to the mix. For example, a nut bread mix may offer suggestions for adding dried fruits—such as apricots or cranberries—or chocolate chips, or substituting orange juice for water. The package may also include a recipe for making a glaze for the nut bread. These suggestions allow the consumer to make a variety of foods from the same basic mix.

Using Packaged Foods

Sometimes you may want to use convenience foods when you cook. **Convenience foods** are *foods that are already partly prepared to save you time.* For instance, you might buy a bag of tossed salad instead of purchasing all the ingredients and cutting them up yourself. One common type of convenience food is a mix. Many people use cake and muffin mixes instead of baking from scratch. Using instant pudding mix is quicker than cooking pudding.

Following Package Directions

When you use convenience foods, you should follow the directions given on the package, just the way you would any other recipe. Make sure that you have all the ingredients and utensils you will need and that you understand all the instructions.

If you are using a general-purpose baking mix, use only the recipes provided on the box. Don't try to substitute the mix for ingredients in another recipe.

Convenience foods can cut preparation time. Why is it important to read and follow the package directions?

LESSON THREE *Review*

Using complete sentences, answer the following questions on a separate sheet of paper.

Reviewing Terms and Facts

1. **List** Name five pieces of information that a good recipe should give you.
2. **Vocabulary** What are the two types of *recipe formats*?
3. **Identify** Give the meaning of the following abbreviations: *tsp., Tbsp., mL, L.*
4. **Recall** Define the word *yield*, and use it in an original sentence.

Thinking Critically

5. **Analyze** What problems might result if you didn't read through an entire recipe before starting to cook?

6. **Compare** Explain the differences among chopping, grating, and shredding.
7. **Evaluate** What are some advantages of using convenience foods? What might be some disadvantages?

Applying Concepts

8. Create a cookbook of your family's recipes. Can you find out exactly what makes Grandpa's spaghetti sauce so good, or why the French toast always tastes better when your sister makes it? Write down your family's special recipes in a notebook. Decorate the cover with a drawing or a family snapshot.

LESSON THREE: FOLLOWING RECIPES AND DIRECTIONS 379

MEETING STUDENT DIVERSITY

Cultural Diversity Many foods that are now included in the American diet actually originated in other countries and cultures. Have pairs of students research the culture or country of origin for several of the following foods and find recipes for them: pizza, gazpacho, sushi, goulash, paella, tortilla, jambalaya, scones, borscht, hummus, baklava, quiche, sauerkraut, curry, pâté, matzo, cocoa, waffle, and egg roll. Ask them to provide pictures of these foods whenever possible, and include the pictures in a report of their findings.

CHAPTER 13, LESSON 3

Answers to Lesson 3 Review

1. A good recipe should include necessary ingredients, the amount of each ingredient, instructions on how to combine the ingredients, the size of pans needed, the cooking time and temperature, and the yield.
2. The two types of recipe formats are standard format and narrative format.
3. The abbreviations stand for teaspoon; tablespoon; milliliter, and liter.
4. The number of servings. Sentences will vary.
5. You might discover you did not have all the necessary ingredients or kitchen tools. You might not realize that you have to preheat the oven while you are preparing the recipe.
6. Chopping is cutting into small pieces with a knife; grating in rubbing back and forth on a grater to make small pieces; shredding is shaving or cutting off in long, narrow pieces with a knife or grater.
7. Convenience foods save time because they are already partly prepared. Disadvantages of convenience foods are that they are usually more expensive than making a food from scratch and that the package may contain or make more of a food than you need.
8. Family cookbooks will vary. Suggest that students make copies of the cookbooks to give to family members.

CLOSE

Have students write a paragraph explaining how learning to follow recipes can make them successful cooks.

LESSON FOUR
Measuring Ingredients

FOCUS

Lesson Objectives
After studying this lesson, students should be able to
- list customary and metric measurements.
- identify the best measuring tools for the job.
- explain how to measure dry and liquid ingredients.

Motivating Activity
Ask students to write what they think might happen if they were given the following recipe for preparing sugar cookies: 1 large bowl sifted cake flour, 1 medium bowl granulated sugar, 2 eggs, 2 splashes vanilla extract, pinch of salt, 1 small bowl soft shortening, some milk, handful of baking powder

Then ask students to guess the amount of each ingredient.

Introducing the Lesson
Have students share their responses to the Motivating Activity. Then have them compare their guessed measurements with the following sugar cookie recipe: 4 cups sifted cake flour, 1½ cups granulated sugar, 2 eggs, 1 teaspoon vanilla extract, ½ teaspoon salt, ⅔ cup soft shortening, 4 teaspoons milk, 2½ teaspoons baking powder

Tell students that Lesson 4 discusses the proper ways of measuring ingredients.

Introducing *Words to Know*
Write each of the Words to Know on the chalkboard. Have students look up each term in the Glossary at the back of the textbook.

LESSON FOUR
Measuring Ingredients

WORDS TO KNOW
metric measurement
customary measurement
graduated measuring cups
leavening agent

DISCOVER...
- customary and metric units of measure.
- the best measuring tool for each job.
- techniques for measuring dry and liquid ingredients.

Recipes your great-grandparents might have used were not always precise in their measurements. Long ago, recipes often called for "butter the size of a walnut," a "scant cup of sugar," or "two handfuls of flour." These measurements worked all right for experienced cooks, but they must have been pretty difficult for beginners! Fortunately, modern recipes are much more precise. They tell us the exact amount of each ingredient to use.

380   CHAPTER 13: PREPARING TO COOK

CLASSROOM RESOURCES FOR LESSON 4

 Blackline Masters
Cross Curriculum 15
Food Lab Activity 6, "Mmmm . . . Desserts!"
Lesson 4 Quiz
Reteaching 13

 **Student Workbook**
Activities 96, 97

Measure Up

By measuring accurately, using the proper measuring tools, and following directions, you will ensure that your recipes turn out the same every time you use them. You will also gain the confidence to try new dishes.

Types of Measurement

You have probably studied metric measurement in math and used it in your science classes. **Metric measurement** is *a system of measurements based on multiples of ten.* Some metric units used in cooking are liters and milliliters for volume and grams and kilograms for weight. When you cook, you will probably use *traditional units of measure,* or **customary measurement.** Examples of customary units used in cooking are fluid ounces and cups for volume, and ounces and pounds for weight. **Figure 13.7** shows equivalent measurements in the two systems.

Figure 13.7 Equivalent Measurements
You may use any of these three different types of measurements when you cook. What types of recipes may use metric measurements?

Customary	Customary Equiv.	Approximate Metric Equiv.
1 teaspoon	⅓ tablespoon	5 milliliters
1 tablespoon	3 teaspoons	15 milliliters
½ cup	8 tablespoons	125 milliliters
1 cup	16 tablespoons 8 fluid ounces	250 milliliters
2 cups	1 pint	500 milliliters
4 cups	1 quart	1000 milliliters or 1 liter
1 pound	16 ounces	500 grams

LESSON FOUR: MEASURING INGREDIENTS

MORE ABOUT • • •

The Metric System The version of the metric system now used is the International System of Units. It is usually referred to by its French initials, SI (from Système International d'Unités). In 1996, the only two countries not using the metric system in daily life were the United States and Myanmar. The metric system is a decimal system, based on multiples of ten. Units of length, area, volume, and mass can be converted from one unit to another by multiplying or dividing by a multiple of ten.

CHAPTER 13, LESSON 4

TEACH

L2 Demonstrating Measuring

Have students work in small groups taking turns to demonstrate how to measure the following: ¾ cup water, ½ cup flour, ½ teaspoon baking soda, ¼ cup brown sugar, ⅛ cup shortening, and 1 tablespoon vegetable oil. Have group members evaluate one another's measuring techniques.

L2 Food Lab

Allow time for students to complete Food Lab Activity 6, "Mmmm . . . Desserts!" in the TCR.

USING VISUALS

Refer students to Figure 13.7. Then write the following recipe for cheese sauce on the chalkboard and ask students to convert the recipe from metric to customary measurements:
125 grams butter (*4 ounces*)
375 milliliters all-purpose flour (*1½ cups*)
250 milliliters milk (*1 cup*)
250 milliliters chicken stock (*1 cup*)
5 milliliters nutmeg (*1 teaspoon*)
2.5 milliliters white pepper (*½ teaspoon*)
2.5 milliliters salt (*½ teaspoon*)
100 grams grated cheddar cheese (*about 3 ounces*)
45 milliliters chopped parsley (*3 tablespoons*)

CHAPTER 13, LESSON 4

Many spice containers list foods in which the spice can be used. Bring in a variety of spices and let students look at the containers for suggestions. Ask them if they have ever experimented with spices in a recipe. If so, ask them to tell what the results were.

L2 Math Connection

Assign Cross-Curriculum Activity 15 in the TCR. Students learn about using math in the kitchen in this activity.

DID YOU KNOW

Baking powders are classified according to the acid ingredients they contain. There are three types of baking powder, and when following a recipe it is important to use the kind the recipe calls for. Double-acting baking power reacts very slowly, releasing up to one-third of its leavening in the cold mixture and the rest in the heat of the oven. Phosphate baking powder reacts slowly and requires heat to liberate some of its leavening. Tartrate baking powder reacts rapidly and begins its action at room temperature as soon as liquid is added.

Adding seasonings will make almost any food taste better. Try one of the following in your own cooking: Fresh mint, ginger, basil, sage, or thyme.
You might even try growing your own herbs.

Some recipes show ingredients in both metric and customary amounts. You can use either system, as long as you have the right measuring utensils.

Measuring Equipment

The right kinds of measuring equipment make cooking easier. Here are several items you will want to have handy.

- **Graduated measuring cups** are *sets of measuring cups in commonly used sizes.* They are also called dry measuring cups because they are usually used to measure dry ingredients, such as flour, sugar, and oats. Customary measuring cups usually come in sets of four: ¼ cup, ⅓ cup, ½ cup, and 1 cup. A set of metric dry measures usually includes 50 mL, 125 mL, and 250 mL sizes.

- **Liquid measuring cups** are used to measure such ingredients as milk, water, and oil. These cups are usually made of glass or clear plastic so that you can accurately see the amount of liquid. They have a handle, a pouring spout, and space beyond the top measuring line to allow for a full measure without danger of spilling. Liquid measuring cups are marked on the side with specific graduated amounts.

- **Measuring spoons** are used to measure smaller amounts of all types of ingredients. A typical set of customary measuring spoons includes ¼ teaspoon, ½ teaspoon, 1 teaspoon, and 1 tablespoon. Metric measuring spoons include 1 mL, 5 mL, 15 mL, and 25 mL.

Using the right measuring utensil will make cooking easier. Which of these tools are used to measure dry ingredients? Liquid ingredients?

Measuring Techniques

The reason you need many tools is that different ingredients require different measuring techniques. Knowing the proper technique to use is just as important as having the right equipment. **Figure 13.8** shows how to measure some common ingredients.

382   CHAPTER 13: PREPARING TO COOK

TECHNOLOGY UPDATE

Food Measurements Accurate measurement of foods is especially important for people who plan menus for special diets. Computer programs can be used to get a comprehensive and accurate analysis of a person's food intake. Programs can be used to analyze a recipe, a single food, or a meal. Computer programs are also used to increase amounts in a recipe to determine a shopping list for serving large numbers of people. Printouts and graphs make the results easy to understand.

Figure 13.8 Measuring Basics
Learning how to measure different types of ingredients will help you prepare successful meals. Which of these measuring techniques have you used?

Flour. Presifted and whole-wheat flour must be stirred with a fork before measuring. Regular flour may have tiny lumps and must be sifted first. In all cases carefully spoon the flour into the dry measuring cup. Level off with a metal spatula or the back of a knife. Avoid tapping a cup to level flour because that packs it again.

Butter and margarine. The wrappers on a stick of butter or margarine are marked in tablespoons. Just cut off the amount you need.

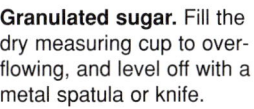

Granulated sugar. Fill the dry measuring cup to overflowing, and level off with a metal spatula or knife.

Shortening. To measure shortening, press it into a dry measuring cup, making sure there are no air pockets. Level with a metal spatula. Remove shortening with a rubber spatula.

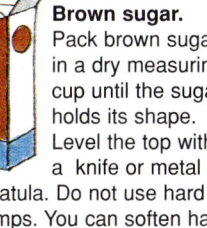

Brown sugar. Pack brown sugar in a dry measuring cup until the sugar holds its shape. Level the top with a knife or metal spatula. Do not use hard lumps. You can soften hard lumps by heating them for a short time in the oven or a microwave.

Liquids. Place the liquid measuring cup on a flat surface, pour to the marker line, and check it at eye level. For smaller amounts, dip the measuring spoon into the liquid.

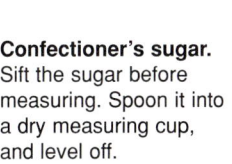

Confectioner's sugar. Sift the sugar before measuring. Spoon it into a dry measuring cup, and level off.

Leavening agents and spices. Baking powder and baking soda are two types of **leavening agents,** which are *ingredients that make baked foods rise.* Baking powder, baking soda, and spices must be stirred first to remove any lumps. Dip in the measuring spoon, and then level.

LESSON FOUR: MEASURING INGREDIENTS   **383**

CHAPTER 13, LESSON 4

USING VISUALS
Refer students to Figure 13.8. Ask them to describe the differences between the way granulated sugar, brown sugar, and confectioner's sugar should be measured. Explain to students that lumps can also be removed from brown sugar by rolling them with a rolling pin on waxed paper. Show students the markings on the wrapper of a stick of butter or margarine. Write several amounts of butter on the chalkboard and ask students to tell how many sticks or parts of sticks they would need for each amount.

L1 Student Workbook
Assign Activities 96 and 97 in the Student Workbook.

ASSESS

Evaluating the Lesson
Assign Reviewing Terms and Facts and Thinking Critically on page 384 to review the lesson; then assign the Lesson 4 Quiz in the TCR.

Reteaching
- Display a variety of measuring equipment. Give each student an amount of an ingredient and have them choose the correct equipment needed to measure it. For example, you might ask a student to show what he or she would use to measure 1 cup of sugar, 1 tablespoon of salt, ⅔ cup of flour, ½ cup of milk, and so on.
- Have students complete Reteaching Activity 13 in the TCR.

HOME AND COMMUNITY CONNECTION

Practicing Measuring Suggest that students demonstrate their measuring abilities to their families by following a recipe of their choice. Students might look through cookbooks to find something their families would enjoy or they could use a family recipe. They might choose to make a main dish, casserole, bread, cake, or cookies. Ask students to share their experience with classmates. In order to receive credit for a homework assignment, have students write a description of the measuring techniques they used while preparing the recipe and have their paper signed by a family member.

CHAPTER 13, LESSON 4

Answers to Lesson 4 Review

1. Metric measurements are based on multiples of ten and include units such as grams and liters. Customary measurements are those traditionally used in the United States and include units such as cups and ounces.
2. Weight is measured in grams and kilograms; volume is measured in liters and milliliters; temperature is measured in degrees Celsius.
3. Graduated measuring cups, liquid measuring cups, and measuring spoons.
4. Water, milk, and oil.
5. Dry measuring cups come in a set of separate cups in graduated sizes and are filled to the top to measure dry ingredients. Liquid measuring cups are usually clear glass or plastic, have a pour spout and an overflow rim, and are used to measure liquid ingredients.
6. The ingredients for cakes, cookies, and other baked goods must be measured accurately to ensure good results. If they are not accurately measured, cakes may not rise or cookies may spread and burn.
7. Measuring techniques should follow those described on pages 382–383.

Enrichment

Ask students to prepare a simple recipe using metric measures. Have them present the food to the class and tell the class what equipment they used and whether the food was satisfactory.

CLOSE

Ask students to write instructions for the steps needed in measuring brown sugar, water, granulated sugar, margarine, and baking soda.

Accuracy in Measuring

While you are still a beginner, it is best to measure all ingredients exactly. As you become more experienced, you will discover where and when it is safe to be less precise.

Some foods—such as cakes, cookies, and other baked goods—require accurate measurements for good results. If ingredients are not measured accurately, the cake may not rise or the cookies may spread and burn. With other foods—such as soups, stews, and casseroles—it is not necessary to be quite so careful. In these cases you can more easily experiment and add leftovers. For example, if you are making beef vegetable soup, you can add small amounts of leftover vegetables in addition to the ingredients the recipe calls for.

When you want to be sure that your recipe will come out just right, it is always best to be accurate. That means using the right tools and the right techniques. Then you can be sure of getting the right result—a successful product.

Measuring accurately is essential to success in the kitchen. What might happen if this teen did not measure accurately?

LESSON FOUR *Review*

Using complete sentences, answer the following questions on a separate sheet of paper.

Reviewing Terms and Facts

1. **Vocabulary** What is the difference between *metric measurement* and *customary measurement*?
2. **Recall** What units are used to measure weight, volume, and temperature in the metric measuring system?
3. **List** Name three common types of measuring equipment.
4. **Give Examples** Name three ingredients that could be measured in a liquid measuring cup.

Thinking Critically

5. **Compare** Explain the differences between dry and liquid measuring cups.
6. **Explain** What types of food require the most accurate measurements? Why?

Applying Concepts

7. With a partner, take turns demonstrating the proper measuring technique for two of the ingredients mentioned in this lesson. Ask your partner to assess your technique based on the instructions in the text.

384 CHAPTER 13: PREPARING TO COOK

COOPERATIVE LEARNING

Measuring Equipment Pass around a variety of customary and metric measuring equipment. Have small groups of students make a sketch of each piece of equipment and beside their sketch write what type of measurements it shows and how it is used. Have students combine their sketches in a pamphlet titled "Tools for Measuring Ingredients." You might use the pamphlet as a classroom reference.

Chapter 13 Activities

TECHNOLOGY
High-tech Packages
New high-tech food packaging will not only protect and identify products but also may have an effect on the food it contains. For example, when a package of potato nuggets is placed in a microwave oven, special sensors inside the package will heat up to make the nuggets brown and crispy.

Try This!
Imagine that you could improve a food package in any way that you choose. Explain what you would change.

A Global View — CHOOSING FOOD

Do you know anyone who goes to a market or grocery store every day? It's most likely that you don't. In some cultures, however, it is common for people to shop for food every day. Often they may not even have access to refrigerators or freezers to store their food.

TRY THIS!
Research a culture and plan a menu for a nutritious main meal in that culture's ethnic tradition.

Consumer Focus
Food Shopping Lures
Some food-store managers give out free samples of snack foods as well as coupons for those products. Impulse items, such as candy and magazines, are displayed in checkout lanes. These techniques can lure shoppers into buying items they may not want or need.

Try This!
What can you do to resist impulse buying? First, make a shopping list before you go to the store. Once you're in the store, stick to your list.

MATH CONNECTION
RECIPE CONVERSIONS
Recipes are written to yield a certain number of servings. You can make more or less of a dish by converting, or changing, the amount of each ingredient. This is called recipe conversion. To increase the number of servings, multiply all the ingredients by the same number. To decrease, divide all the ingredients by the same number.

Follow Up
1. Look at the Cheese Bake recipe on page 375. Convert the recipe so that it yields twice as many servings.
2. Find a recipe that yields an average number of servings (for example, six or eight). Convert the recipe so that it yields twice as many servings. Then convert the recipe so that it yields half as many servings. Exchange recipes with your classmates for more practice in recipe conversion.

CHAPTER 13
Activities

A Global View
Ask students: How many times a week does someone from your family shop for food? Point out that such foods as bread may not include preservatives and therefore may not remain fresh. Tell them that in some countries—France, for example—meal planning includes buying fresh foods each day.

TECHNOLOGY
Discuss with students that in the grocery store, they may see food products in plastic, glass, and aluminum packages. Explain that packages of the future may include labels that would indicate whether the contents got too hot or too cold during shipping, or a special film on microwave dinners that heats only certain parts of the dinner.

Consumer Focus
Ask students whether they have noticed that commonly purchased foods, such as bread and milk, are often placed at the far end of the store so that customers must pass by other tempting items along the way. Discuss other food shopping lures. Remind them that it is also a good idea to eat before they shop. If they feel hungry, they may buy something they don't need.

Teaching the Math CONNECTION
Discuss with students the importance of considering the measuring equipment they will use when converting a recipe. Point out that they may need to use larger or smaller measuring cups and spoons. Also point out that they may need to adjust the size of the pan they will use to cook or bake the ingredients in.

Answers to Follow-Up
1. 20 slices bread, 3 c. cheese, 6 eggs, 3 c. milk, 2 tsp. prepared mustard, 3 tsp. (or 1 T.) salt.
2. Recipes will vary. Remind students to check their partner's conversions for accuracy.

CHAPTER 13 REVIEW

Checking Comprehension

Use the Chapter Summary and the Chapter 13 Review to help students go over the most important ideas presented in Chapter 13.

Answers to Words to Know

1. Texture is the way food feels when it is eaten. Raw vegetables are crisp and pudding is smooth.
2. Adding a garnish is a way to provide more color to food.
3. A time schedule should include all the jobs that have to be done to prepare a meal, in the correct order, including setting the table, serving the food, and cleaning up.
4. Staples are foods that are likely to be used often, such as sugar, flour, or salt.
5. Grade labeling uses standards set up by the government to measure food quality.
6. Open dating is the display of a freshness date on packaged food. It shows the last date a food may be sold as fresh.
7. The yield is the number of servings a recipe makes.
8. A standard-format recipe lists all the ingredients in order of use and gives step-by-step directions for preparing the food. A narrative-format recipe gives a paragraph description of the steps and ingredients in order of use.

Chapter Summary

- It is best to plan meals ahead of time. Remember to follow the Food Guide Pyramid and try to keep your meal patterns flexible.
- For variety in your meals, choose foods that have different textures, colors, sizes and shapes, flavors, and temperatures.
- Good shopping skills include planning before you shop and choosing the best buys. Smart shopping makes meal preparation easier and saves money.
- Storing foods properly helps prevent spoiling.
- A recipe is a list of ingredients and directions for preparing a specific food.
- Recipes are written in either standard or narrative format.
- To follow a recipe, you must understand common abbreviations and cooking terms.
- If you use convenience foods, the work of preparation has been partially done to save you time. You need to follow the package directions, just as you would follow a recipe.
- There are several basic types of measuring tools: graduated, or dry, measuring cups; liquid measuring cups; and measuring spoons.
- There are different ways to measure different types of ingredients. It is important to learn how to measure accurately.

Words to Know

Using complete sentences, answer the following questions on a separate sheet of paper.

1. Explain what is meant by the *texture* of food. Give two examples.
2. Why might you add a *garnish* to food?
3. Describe what a *time schedule* for meal preparation should include.
4. What are *staples*? Give an example.
5. Explain the purpose of *grade labeling*.
6. What is meant by *open dating* on food products?
7. What does *yield* mean on a recipe?
8. How is a recipe in *standard format* different from a recipe in *narrative format*?

Review Questions

Using complete sentences, answer the following questions on a separate sheet of paper.

1. What are three ways to use management skills in meal preparation?
2. Why is it important to include variety in meals?
3. What are three ways to save money when shopping for groceries?
4. Explain how you would store each of the following foods: an unopened jar of spaghetti

386   CHAPTER 13: PREPARING TO COOK

EXTRA CREDIT PROJECT

Using Convenience Foods Suggest that students work with a family member to prepare a food from a general-purpose baking mix at home and report to the class on the success of their experience. If students have access to a video camera at home, suggest that they videotape the procedure. Then students might share their video on baking with a mix with the rest of the class. Students may wish to bring in samples of what they prepared to share with classmates.

CHAPTER 13 REVIEW

sauce, a head of lettuce, a carton of ice cream, an opened jar of mayonnaise, and eggs.

5. List five preparation terms and five cooking terms you might see in a recipe.

6. What technique is recommended for measuring dry ingredients?

Thinking Critically

Using complete sentences, answer the following questions on a separate sheet of paper.

1. **Analyze** Think about the ways to ensure variety in meals—texture, color, size and shape, flavor, and temperature. Which of these do you think is most important to vary for an appealing meal? Which do you think is least important to vary? Explain your answers.

2. **Suggest** When might lower-grade food products be preferable to higher-grade food products?

3. **Explain** Why are sets of dry measuring cups called *graduated* cups? Why don't dry measuring cups have extra space for overflow?

Cooperative Learning

1. Working in a small group, conduct a nutrient review. Have each group member bring a Nutrition Facts label to class. Then have each person select a nutrient from the label and tell the group about food sources of the nutrient, its benefits to health, and the effects of eating too much or too little of it.

2. Make a class cookbook. Have everyone contribute a favorite recipe. Write all the recipes in standard format, and use correct abbreviations. Make sure that directions are clear and complete. Divide the responsibilities for compiling and distributing the cookbook.

Family & Community

1. With a parent or another adult in your family, make a weekly meal plan for your household. Work together to make a shopping list, and shop for the food items you need. Use the information on product labels and unit pricing to help you select items. Be sure to store the groceries properly when you return from the supermarket. Write a summary of your planning session and shopping trip.

2. Make a directory of neighborhood food stores that could be helpful to someone new to your community. Include wholesale grocery stores, large supermarkets, convenience stores, specialty stores, and farmers' markets. Explain the advantages and disadvantages of each type of store.

Building A Portfolio

1. Write a story about your favorite childhood memory of food. You might describe the first time you tried to cook something by yourself, or you could tell about learning to cook with a family member. What did you cook? Exchange and discuss stories with a classmate. Then put your story in your portfolio.

2. Start a file of menu ideas. Be sure that each menu includes a variety of foods, textures, colors, sizes and shapes, flavors, and temperatures. Keep your file in your portfolio.

CHAPTER 13 REVIEW **387**

CHAPTER 13 REVIEW

Answers to Review Questions

1. Plan ahead, use the five food groups and meal patterns, check resources, and make a time schedule.

2. Varying colors, textures, sizes and shapes, flavors, and temperatures of foods makes meals look and taste better.

3. Any three: make a shopping list, check the weekly specials, compare brands, read labels, check grades and quality, buy seasonal fruits and vegetables.

4. Spaghetti sauce should be stored in a cabinet where it will stay cool and dry. Lettuce should be washed and stored in plastic wrap, a plastic bag, or a container in the refrigerator. A carton of ice cream should be stored in the freezer. An opened jar of mayonnaise should be tightly closed and stored in the refrigerator. Eggs should be stored in the egg carton in the refrigerator.

5. Cooking terms include any five shown in Figure 13.4. Preparation terms include any five shown in Figure 13.5.

6. Spoon the ingredient into a dry measuring cup and level off with a metal spatula or the back of a knife.

Evaluate

Use the Chapter 13 Test in the TCR, or construct your own test using the Testmaker Software.

CLOSE

Have students apply their knowledge of the chapter's content by completing one of the alternative assessment activities listed under Family and Community or Building a Portfolio.

Answers to Thinking Critically

1. Answers will vary. Students should be able to explain their answers with logical reasons.

2. Answers will vary. Students might mention that lower-grade eggs can be used for cooking and baking and lower-grade vegetables can be used in soups or stews.

3. Dry measuring cups come in sets that are graduated in size. They don't have a space for overflow because you use a metal spatula or the back of a knife to level off the dry ingredients when you measure.

387

Planning Guide
Chapter 14 Let's Cook

LESSON 1	Pages	FEATURES	CLASSROOM RESOURCES
Fruits	390–393	*Try This:* Making Fruit Baskets	Food Lab Activity 7 Lesson 1 Quiz Student Workbook Activities 98, 99
LESSON 2 **Vegetables**	394–398	*Try This:* Health-booster Veggies *Skills in Action:* Creative Vegetables	Food Lab Activity 8 Lesson 2 Quiz Transparency 58, "Produce: Select the Freshest, Cook Wisely" Student Workbook Activities 100, 101
LESSON 3 **Breads, Cereals, Rice, and Pasta**	399–405	*Skills in Action:* Brown-bagging It	Cooperative Learning 27 Food Lab Activities 9, 10 Lesson 3 Quiz Transparency 59, "Cooking Rice and Pasta" Student Workbook Activities 102, 103
LESSON 4 **Milk, Yogurt, and Cheese**	406–412	*Try This:* Milk's Many Forms *Skills In Action:* Using Yogurt Instead	Cooperative Learning 28 Enrichment 16 Lesson 4 Quiz Transparency 60, "Milk, Yogurt, and Cheese Group" Student Workbook Activities 104, 105
LESSON 5 **Meat, Poultry, Fish, Dry Beans, Eggs, and Nuts**	413–420	*Tips for Living:* Rare, Medium, or Well-done? *Skills in Action:* Meat Extenders	Activity and Project Card 27, "Create a Cookbook" Activity and Project Card 28, "Critic's Corner" Concept Map 22 Cross Curriculum 16 Lesson 5 Quiz Peer Pressure and Decision Making 28 Transparency 61, "Methods for Cooking Meat and Fish" Student Workbook Activity 106

CHAPTER 14 RESOURCES

- Chapter 14 Test
- Reteaching 14
- Study Guide 14, *Reteaching*
- Testmaker Software

Performance Assessment Activity

Ask students to make a day's menu for breakfast, lunch, dinner, and snacks. Tell them that the menu must meet the daily food requirements listed on the Food Guide Pyramid and include the foods discussed in each lesson of Chapter 14. Have students include all recipe instructions for each dish on the menu. Have them prepare the suggestions in the menu for their family. Ask them to survey family members about their likes and dislikes on the day's menu. When students have completed their menu and survey with family members, organize the class into small groups. Have group members share their menus and surveys with the group.

School-to-Work

Provide students with examples of careers in the food-service industry, such as cook, baker, food server, chef, restaurant manager; the food-processing industry, such as canning and food freezing worker, meat cutter, butcher, food tester, food technologist; and the home economics industry, such as nutritionist or dietitian. Have students work in pairs to skim the want ads for jobs in these industries. Ask pairs to note whether most jobs are in food service, food processing, or home economics. Ask them to identify the technical, educational, and personal skills required for each job. Discuss how the classes that students are taking in school could help prepare them for a career in a food-related industry.

Family & Community

Bring in recipes clipped from your local newspaper. Have students analyze the recipes and identify the food groups represented in each recipe. Ask them to determine whether the recipes are healthful. Have them rewrite recipes that can be changed to be more healthful. For example, a recipe that requires whole milk might be revised to include skim milk instead, and so on.

Resources for the Teacher

Ceserani, V., and Ronald Kinton. *Practical Cookery.* New York: Halsted Press, 1993.

Macmillan, Norma. *Cook's Kitchen Bible.* New York: Smithmark, 1995.

Nobles, Anita K. *Hey Mom . . . I'll Cook Dinner: Recipes That Turn a Kid into the Family Chef.* Memphis: Impress Ink, 1994.

Readings for the Student

Clark, Raymond C. *Potluck: Exploring American Foods and Meals.* Brattleboro, VT: Pro Lingua, 1994.

Jones, Norma, et al., eds. *Food: What We Eat and Where Does It Come From?* Wylie, TX: Info Plus TX, 1992.

Salter, Charles A. *The Vegetarian Teen.* Brookfield, CT: Millbrook Press, 1991.

Multimedia Resources

Food Preparation Words and Terms (Videocassette). Home Economics School Service.

The Way to Cook Soups, Salads, and Bread (Videocassette). Home Economics School Service.

OUT OF TIME?

If time does not permit thorough teaching of this chapter, you may wish to use:
- Teens Making a Difference, page 389
- Tips for Living, page 417
- Try This, pages 392, 396, 408
- Skills in Action, pages 398, 401, 409, 418
- Young Living Activities, page 421
- Chapter Summary, page 422

CHAPTER 14
Let's Cook

Chapter Overview

Chapter 14 introduces students to the techniques of preparing foods from the five food groups. They discover methods of cooking foods that retain nutrients and quality.

LESSON 1 identifies methods for choosing, cooking, and serving fruits.

LESSON 2 describes methods of preparing, serving, and cooking vegetables.

LESSON 3 explains how to make and prepare breads, cereals, pasta, and rice.

LESSON 4 discusses preparation techniques for milk and milk products.

LESSON 5 describes methods for preparing meats, poultry, fish, dry beans, eggs, and nuts.

Introducing the Chapter

Have students skim the lesson titles. Then have them make a concept map of the five food groups. Have them add details to the concept map as they read each lesson. Encourage students to use their concept map as a study aid for the chapter test.

Chapter Motivator

Refer students to the chapter title, "Let's Cook." Ask them to name three foods they like to prepare and record responses on the board. Then have students use the foods listed to make a graph showing the top ten favorite foods. Tell students that Chapter 14 discusses ways to prepare foods from the five food groups.

CHAPTER 14 Let's Cook

LESSON ONE
Fruits

LESSON TWO
Vegetables

LESSON THREE
Breads, Cereals, Rice, and Pasta

LESSON FOUR
Milk, Yogurt, and Cheese

LESSON FIVE
Meat, Poultry, Fish, Dry Beans, Eggs, and Nuts

388

KEY TO ABILITY LEVELS

Teaching strategies that appear throughout the chapter have been identified by one of three codes to give you an idea of their suitability for students of varying learning styles and abilities.

L1 Level 1 strategies should be within the ability range of all students. Often full class participation is required. Teacher direction is usually needed.

L2 Level 2 strategies are for average to above-average students or for small groups. Some teacher direction is necessary.

L3 Level 3 strategies are designed for students able and willing to work independently. Minimal teacher direction is necessary.

CHAPTER 14

TEENS MAKING A DIFFERENCE

Have students read "Teens Making a Difference." Ask them to identify the ways the students in the article make a difference by holding a bake sale. (*Students raise money for the school's computer lab.*) Ask them to sequence the steps taken by the Lincoln Junior High students to hold a bake sale. Have them describe fundraising activities in which they have participated.

Ask students to work with a classmate to complete TRY THIS! at the end of the feature. Ask pairs to share their list with the class.

BLOCK SCHEDULING

The following Teacher Classroom Resources are suggested for use in classrooms with Block Scheduling.
- Activity and Project Card 27, "Create a Cookbook"
- Activity and Project Card 28, "Critic's Corner"
- Cooperative Learning 27, "Packing Some Punch Into Lunch"
- Cooperative Learning 28, "Encouraging Children to Drink Milk"

TEENS MAKING A DIFFERENCE
School Bake Sale

Last fall the students at Lincoln Middle School planned several events to raise money for the school's computer lab. Angela Martinez and her friends volunteered to put on a bake sale. They arranged to hold the sale at a shopping mall near their school. Then they sent flyers home with the students, asking families to donate baked goods.

On the morning of the sale, the teens set up card tables for the baked goods and made price tags. By early afternoon, the bake sale had sold out with profits of more than $500. Just a few more bake sales, thought Angela, and the school could buy a new computer!

Try THIS!

Locate four recipes for baked goods that you feel would be popular and appropriate to make for a bake sale. Compare recipes with your classmates.

TECHNOLOGY IN THE CLASSROOM

Modems Modems are devices that permit computers to communicate with each other through telephone lines. A modem converts the signals sent by a computer to the kinds of signals used by telephone lines. The receiving computer reconverts the signals. Adding a modem to a computer and connecting it to a phone line can provide a wealth of information for students in the Family and Consumer Sciences classroom. Having a modem allows computers to have access to databases with up-to-date information on home economics topics. Modems also provide access to electronic bulletin boards, which contain current information on a variety of topics.

LESSON ONE
Fruits

FOCUS

Lesson Objectives
After studying this lesson, students should be able to
- explain how to choose fruits.
- identify ways to cook fruits.
- describe how to serve fruits.

Motivating Activity
Have students write down the name of their favorite fruit and whether they like to eat it fresh, dried, cooked, canned, frozen, or as juice.

Introducing the Lesson
Have students share their responses to the Motivating Activity. Discuss with students when they like to eat their favorite fruit—at breakfast, lunch, dinner, or snack time. Point out that in this lesson they will learn the best ways to choose, cook, and serve fruit.

Introducing *Words to Know*
Ask a volunteer to read the vocabulary words and their definitions. Ask students to write a paragraph about apples, using all the vocabulary words. Have them share their paragraphs with the class.

LESSON ONE
Fruits

WORDS TO KNOW
produce
seasonal
processed

DISCOVER...
- how to choose fruit.
- ways to cook fruit.
- how to serve fruit.

Every June, Lauren and her father go to the local strawberry fields and fill buckets with freshly picked strawberries. In addition to eating some of the strawberries plain, they make their own strawberry jam and pies, use some berries in fruit salad, and freeze some for later use. Of all the fresh fruit Lauren eats in the summer, strawberries are her favorite.

390 CHAPTER 14: LET'S COOK

CLASSROOM RESOURCES FOR LESSON 1

 Blackline Masters
Food Lab Activity 7, "Recipes with Fruit"
Lesson 1 Quiz

 **Student Workbook**
Activities 98, 99

Fruit—From Appetizers to Desserts

Besides tasting great, fruit provides important vitamins and minerals, carbohydrates, and fiber. It's easy to get the recommended number of daily servings because fruit goes well with any meal or snack. Vanessa likes to eat dried fruit on her breakfast cereal. Luke enjoys an apple or orange with his lunch.

Choosing Fruit

You can buy fruit in many different forms. Most supermarkets carry frozen, canned, and dried fruit in addition to the fresh fruit found in the produce section. **Produce** means *fresh fruits and vegetables.* When selecting produce, be sure that it is truly fresh and in good condition. Damaged fruit loses nutrients and will not keep well. **Figure 14.1** explains how to choose fruit.

Figure 14.1 Buying Fresh Fruit
The next time you select fresh fruit, follow these guidelines.

- Test a fruit by pressing it gently. Choose fruit that feels firm but not hard.
- Avoid fruits that look dry or withered, or that feel especially soft or hard.
- Look for fruit that has a good color. Avoid fruits that have spots or bruises.
- Look at the shape of the fruit. If it appears misshapen, it may not taste good.
- Smell fruits that have a hard rind, such as cantaloupe. Ripe fruits usually have a pleasant smell.
- Check the heaviness of fruit. If it feels heavy, it is usually juicy.

LESSON ONE: FRUITS

CHAPTER 14, LESSON 1

TEACH

L2 Applying
Have students keep a log for several days of the fruits they eat. Their log should include the following information: kind of fruit, the amount of fruit eaten, when it was eaten, and how it was prepared. Have students evaluate their log to see if they are eating at least three fruit servings a day. If students find they are falling short of three fruit servings a day, ask them to analyze how they can increase their intake of fruit. Discuss the findings with students.

L3 Health
Review with students the information contained in nutrition labels. Have students choose a type of fresh fruit and write a nutrition label for it. They can research nutritional information about fruits in nutrition books such as the *Nutrition Almanac* by J. D. Kirschmann and Levon J. Dunne.

L2 Food Lab Activity
Allow time for students to complete Food Lab 7, "Recipes with Fruit," in the TCR.

USING VISUALS
Have students study the illustration showing how to buy fresh fruit in Figure 14.1. Ask students to use this information to choose fruit at the grocery store for their family. Have them report their experience to the class.

HOME AND COMMUNITY CONNECTION

Field Trip Arrange a field trip to a local grocery store or produce market with a produce manager. Ask if the produce manager can be available to give students a tour of the produce department and answer students' questions about fruits and vegetables. Have students prepare questions prior to the field trip. Questions might include the following: Where are the fruits and vegetables grown? How are they transported to the store? How does the store purchase the fruits and vegetables? How are the fruits and vegetables prepared for sale? What are some tips for buying fresh fruits and vegetables?

CHAPTER 14, LESSON 1

L1 Finding Examples
Help students create a bulletin-board display showing the months of the year and when seasonal fruits are available locally. Ask students to bring in pictures of seasonal fruits from old magazines to add to the bulletin-board display.

L2 Economics
Have students use the sales circulars in the local newspaper to select fruits for a family of four for about one week. Have students estimate the cost of the fruits and share the cost with the class. Ask them to describe ways to serve the fruits fresh and cooked.

Try This!

Ask students to write directions for the proper storage of the following fresh fruits: pears, blueberries, grapefruits, and peaches. Have students work in small groups to assemble the fruit baskets. If possible, have the class deliver the baskets to shut-ins or elderly residents.

L1 Student Workbook
Assign Activities 98 and 99 in the Student Workbook.

ASSESS

Evaluating the Lesson
Assign Reviewing Terms and Facts and Thinking Critically on page 393 to review the lesson; then assign the Lesson 1 Quiz in the TCR.

 Improvements in storage, transportation, and packaging make it possible to enjoy a variety of fresh fruits from around the world.

Try This!

As a class, assemble fruit baskets or boxes for shut-ins or elderly residents in your neighborhood. Everyone should bring in a few pieces of fresh fruit. Decorate your fruit baskets or boxes with ribbons, bows, and hand-made greeting cards.

Some produce, like Lauren's strawberries, is **seasonal**, or *more plentiful, more readily available, and less expensive at certain times of the year.* When you buy produce in season, you get the best possible quality while also saving money. Produce that is available out of season may be more expensive and less nutritious because it is often artificially ripened or shipped a long distance.

If fresh fruits are not available or if you want the fruit in another form, you might choose processed fruits. **Processed** means that a food is *changed from its raw form before being sold.* Fruits that are frozen, canned, or dried are considered processed, as are fruit juices.

Cooking Fruit

Ben's grandmother likes to bake fruit for dessert. Her favorites are baked apples and baked pears. She used to bake them in a conventional oven, but now she prefers to use the microwave oven. There is no change in the color or flavor from the fresh fruit, and she knows that fewer nutrients are lost during microwave cooking as well.

Sabrina likes to cook fruit on the stove. She adds a little bit of water to her favorite fresh fruit and covers the pan with a lid. To reduce the amount of nutrients lost in cooking, she uses a heavy-bottomed pan and cooks the fruit at a low, even temperature. She refrigerates the fruit after it cools and adds it to plain yogurt for an afternoon snack.

Fruits taste and look best when they're cooked properly. During cooking, small amounts of some vitamins—B vitamins and vitamin C—are lost. Some dissolve in water, and some are destroyed by heat and air. To minimize nutrient loss, use low heat and as little water as possible.

Serving Fruit

The ways in which you can serve fruit are limited only by your taste and imagination. You can leave the edible skins or

COOPERATIVE LEARNING

Comparison Shopping Organize students into small groups. Assign each group a fruit. Provide each group with the following forms of the fruit: fresh, frozen, canned, dried, and juice. Have the students taste each form of the fruit. (Be sure the frozen fruit has time to defrost.) Then have each group write an informational article for the school newspaper in which they compare the following aspects of each form of its assigned fruit: nutritional value, price, taste, and texture. Ask students in each group to rank the forms of fruit on the basis of best value for the money. Ask groups to share their articles with the class.

peels on many fresh fruits. They provide fiber as well as nutrients. Just be sure to wash fruit thoroughly under cold running water to remove dirt, bacteria, and pesticides.

You may prefer to peel your fruit before eating it. Some fruits—such as apples, bananas, pears, and peaches—darken in color if they are peeled and not eaten right away. You can prevent this discoloration by sprinkling the cut surfaces with lemon juice and wrapping the fruit in plastic or another airtight covering. You can also dip them in a bowl of water with lemon juice added.

A Healthful Treat

Fruits are an important part of a well-balanced diet. They are available in a variety of forms and are a healthful addition to any meal or snack. To get the most nutrients from the fruits you eat, be sure that they are in good condition, and prepare them properly.

When cooking fruit, use as little water as possible, and cover the pan with a lid. Why is this important?

LESSON ONE Review

Using complete sentences, answer the following questions on a separate sheet of paper.

Reviewing Terms and Facts

1. Recall What should you look for when selecting fresh fruits?

2. Vocabulary What is meant by the term *seasonal*? Give an example of a seasonal fruit.

3. List Name the types of processed fruits.

4. Identify When cooking fruit on the stove, how can you limit the amount of nutrient loss?

5. Explain How can you prevent fruits from darkening in color after you peel them?

Thinking Critically

6. Compare and Contrast How are fresh, frozen, canned, and dried fruits similar? How are they different?

7. Explain Why is it important to cook fruits properly?

Applying Concepts

8. Survey your friends and relatives to find out which fruits they like best. Do they have any favorite recipes? As a class, compile a list of the top five favorites. If possible, prepare one dish in class.

LESSON ONE: FRUITS   393

COOPERATIVE LEARNING

Experimenting Have students work in small groups to create a new way to prepare and serve a fruit. Have each group prepare and serve their fruit to the class. Encourage students to serve their fruit in an attractive manner. Each group should keep notes during preparation, recording the steps and techniques required. Have each group make a recipe card, or write the recipes on sheets of paper, and display the recipes for the rest of the class as the fruit is served. Discuss the taste and nutritional value of the fruit.

CHAPTER 14, LESSON 1

Reteaching

- Have students create a week's menu of healthful snacks that include fruit.
- Have students complete Reteaching Activity 14 in the TCR.

Answers to Lesson 1 Review

1. Be sure they are truly fresh and in good condition.
2. More plentiful, more available, and less expensive at certain times of the year. An example of seasonal fruits is strawberries.
3. Fruit juices and frozen, canned, and dried fruits are processed fruits.
4. Use a heavy-bottomed pan and cook at a low, even temperature.
5. Sprinkle the cut surfaces with lemon juice and wrap the fruit in plastic or another airtight covering.
6. Frozen fruits have a softer texture than fresh fruits, they retain almost as many nutrients, and keep their flavor and color better than canned fruits. Canned fruits are available in many forms. Dried fruits are high in nutrients and fiber, but their color, flavor, and texture are very different from fresh fruits.
7. Fruits taste and look best when cooked properly.
8. Students' surveys will vary.

Enrichment

Have students write a consumer advice column that gives examples of ways to choose fresh fruits and suggestions for preparing them.

CLOSE

Ask students to name three tips about choosing fruits that they learned about in this lesson.

LESSON TWO
Vegetables

FOCUS

Lesson Objectives
After studying this lesson, students should be able to
- describe how to prepare, serve, and cook vegetables.
- discuss how to make different types of salad.
- explain ways to use vegetables in soups.

Motivating Activity
Ask students to write down the name of their favorite vegetable and a description of the way they like the vegetable prepared.

Introducing the Lesson
Have students share their responses to the Motivating Activity. Use the responses as a basis for discussing different kinds of vegetables and the various ways vegetables can be prepared. Explain to students that this lesson will help them learn new and interesting ways to prepare vegetables.

Introducing *Words to Know*
Have students read the vocabulary words and their definitions. Ask them to prepare a dinner menu that includes all the vocabulary words.

LESSON TWO
Vegetables

 **WORDS TO KNOW**

casserole
salad
dressing
broth
dehydrated

DISCOVER...
- how to prepare, serve, and cook vegetables.
- how to make salads.
- ways to use vegetables in soups.

Dylan didn't like to eat vegetables until other family members started trying new and interesting ways to prepare them. Now they add vegetables to spaghetti sauce, stir-fry them with chicken and sweet-and-sour sauce, and add them to soups and muffins. Dylan likes several vegetable dishes so much that he even prepares them himself.

394 CHAPTER 14: LET'S COOK

CLASSROOM RESOURCES FOR LESSON 2

 Blackline Masters
Food Lab Activity 8, "Salad Bar Supreme"
Lesson 2 Quiz

 Transparencies
Transparency 58, "Produce: Select the Freshest, Cook Wisely"

 **Student Workbook**
Activities 100, 101

Vegetables—Good Anytime

Vegetables are a delicious part of a well-balanced diet. They are also valuable sources of carbohydrates, fiber, and many important vitamins and minerals. New varieties are developed every year, including miniature versions of such old favorites as squash and eggplant.

Selecting and Preparing Vegetables

Like fruits, vegetables are most nutritious when they are fresh. Although vegetables are seasonal, most are available year-round. If you prefer processed vegetables, you can usually buy them frozen, canned, or dried.

Fresh vegetables need to be refrigerated until you are ready to use them. For best results, they should be used within a few days after you buy them. Before serving fresh vegetables, wash them carefully under cold running water. If you plan to eat them raw, you may want to peel them and blot them dry. To keep raw vegetables crisp, do not wash them too far in advance of serving them.

Cooking Vegetables

Vegetables can retain their nutrients and keep their shape, texture, flavor, and color if they are cooked properly. To prevent vitamin and mineral loss during cooking, add as little water as possible, use a lid to speed cooking time, and avoid overcooking. Cook vegetables until they are tender and crisp, not soft, so that they keep their flavor and color.

To determine whether vegetables are overcooked, look for color changes. Vegetables that are cooked properly have a somewhat brighter color than raw ones. Green beans are bright green when they are done and olive green when they have cooked too long.

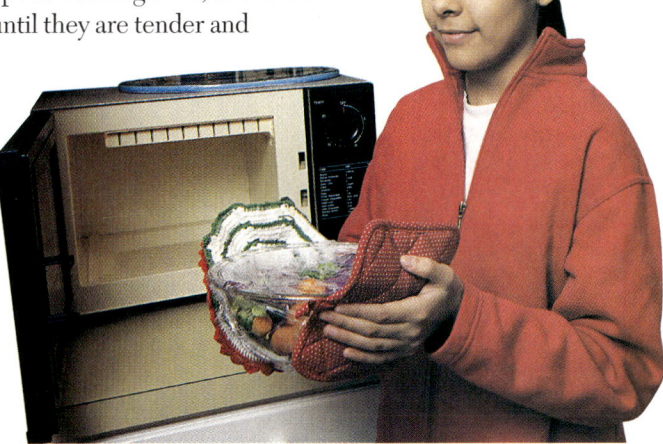

To retain nutrients in vegetables, cook them in a microwave oven so that they need little or no water. What are some other healthful ways to cook vegetables?

LESSON TWO: VEGETABLES

TECHNOLOGY UPDATE

Picking and Transporting Vegetables Vegetables must be picked and transported rapidly from farms to the marketplace in order to ensure freshness and quality. In the past, vegetables were picked, then taken to a building where they were washed, sorted, packaged, and labeled. Some farm machines today, however, can pick, sort, wash, package, and label the vegetables as they move through the farm fields. This means that consumers can purchase fresher vegetables than they were able to in the past.

CHAPTER 14, LESSON 2

L3 Math

Have students choose a vegetable. Have them locate recipes or cooking charts to determine times for cooking the vegetable using the six most common methods: steaming, simmering, baking, frying, stir-frying, and microwave cooking. Have them draw a graph ranking or comparing the cooking times for the vegetable. Students may make graphs on computers if available.

L2 Advertising

Have students prepare a public-service announcement for television explaining the health benefits of eating vegetables. Have students present their messages to the class.

DID YOU KNOW?

The darker the vegetable leaf, the more nutrients the vegetable contains. Green leaf lettuce contains more nutrients than head lettuce.

Try This!

Have students share their magazine and newspaper articles with the class. Display the articles and the students' reports on a bulletin board.

To avoid overcooking vegetables, pay attention to their color. Vegetables should be bright when they are cooked properly. Cook them just until they are tender-crisp.

Try This!

New studies show that eating carrots may help to prevent certain kinds of cancer. Find out more about this link between carrots and cancer prevention, or find a magazine or newspaper article about a study related to other vegetables and the prevention of diseases. Prepare a brief written report.

Vegetables can be cooked and served as a side dish or added to other ingredients to make a main dish, such as a casserole. A **casserole** is *a combination of ingredients cooked and served in a baking dish*. There are many different ways to cook vegetables. The most common are listed below:

- **Steaming.** To steam vegetables, place them in a steamer over simmering water in a covered pan. They should not touch the water.

- **Simmering.** To simmer, cook vegetables in a small amount of liquid, just below the boiling point. Cover the pan with a tight-fitting lid. If large puffs of steam come from the pan, the water is boiling and the heat needs to be turned down.

- **Baking.** Some vegetables, such as potatoes, are baked with their skins on. Before placing them in the oven, be sure to pierce the skins several times to prevent them from bursting.

- **Frying.** Some vegetables, such as potatoes and zucchini squash, can be cooked in fat. This cooking method is not as healthful as others, however.

- **Stir-frying.** To stir-fry, cook vegetables quickly over high heat while stirring them in only a small amount of oil.

MEETING STUDENT DIVERSITY

Varied Learning Styles Use the following suggestions to help students who have difficulty with English:

- Pair those learners with native speakers of English. Have pairs cut out pictures of vegetables from magazines. Then have them make a glossary of vegetables using the pictures and the English name of each.

- Have students cook vegetables using the six most common methods—steaming, simmering, baking, frying, stir-frying, and microwave cooking. Then have them draw a picture and label each method of cooking vegetables. Add the drawings and labels to the glossary of vegetables. Encourage students who have difficulty with English to use the glossary as a study aid.

- **Microwave cooking.** You may need to cut vegetables in pieces, place them in an appropriate container, and cover them while cooking. Refer back to Chapter 12, Lesson 4, for microwave cooking techniques.

Making Delicious Salads

One popular way to eat vegetables is in salads. A **salad** is *a food or a combination of foods, usually served cold with a dressing.* A **dressing** is *a sauce that adds flavor to a dish.* Dressings may be made with oil and vinegar, yogurt, tomato sauce, or mayonnaise. Many types of ready-made salad dressings—such as ranch-style, French, and Italian—are sold in supermarkets.

Tips for Good Salads

To make fresh and delicious salads, handle the ingredients with care. Follow these guidelines:

- Keep ingredients cold until you are ready to prepare them.
- Remove discolored or bruised sections of vegetables or fruits.
- Tear tender salad greens, such as lettuce, instead of cutting them.
- Cut vegetable pieces large enough to identify but small enough so that they are bite-sized.
- Wait until just before serving the salad to add dressing, which can wilt leafy greens if added too soon.

Salads are a delicious way to eat vegetables. What ingredients do you like in your salad?

LESSON TWO: VEGETABLES 397

Making Soups

How can you fit foods from all five food groups into one bowl? The answer is by

---

CHAPTER 14, LESSON 2

L1 Art
Ask students to pretend they are in charge of setting up a salad bar in a local restaurant. Have them make a drawing of the layout and the kinds of salads, dressings, and other foods they would have in the salad bar.

L2 Food Lab
Allow time for students to complete Food Lab 8, "Salad Bar Supreme," in the TCR.

L1 Student Workbook
Assign Activities 100 and 101 in the Student Workbook.

ASSESS

Evaluating the Lesson
Assign Reviewing Terms and Facts and Thinking Critically on page 398 to review the lesson; then assign the Lesson 2 Quiz in the TCR.

Reteaching
- Have students make a brochure of helpful hints for preparing vegetables so that they look and taste fresh and delicious.
- Have students complete Reteaching Activity 14 in the TCR.

Have students read the feature on page 398 and write a review of the vegetable recipe they try. Combine the recipes and reviews into a cookbook titled "Creative Vegetables." Students may take pictures or make drawings of the vegetable dishes to add to the cookbook.

HOME AND COMMUNITY CONNECTION

Guest Speaker Invite a local cook or chef to speak to the students about making creative salads, soups, and vegetable dishes. If possible, have the cook or chef demonstrate how to prepare a salad, soup, or vegetable dish for the students. Have students prepare questions for the speaker, such as: What types of vegetable dishes are most popular at your restaurant? What are your favorite herbs and spices to add to vegetable dishes? If a speaker is not available, have students bring in menus from local restaurants. Have them compare the cost of various meals on the menu with the estimated cost of preparing the dish at home.

CHAPTER 14, LESSON 2

Answers to Lesson 2 Review

1. Add as little water as possible, use a lid to speed cooking, and avoid overcooking.
2. Steaming, simmering, baking, frying, stir-frying, microwave cooking.
3. Any three tips: keep ingredients cold, remove discolored or bruised sections, tear salad greens, cut into bite-size pieces, wait until serving to add dressing.
4. Answers will vary. Students compare the advantages and disadvantages of two methods of cooking vegetables.
5. Hot or cold, hearty or light, creamy or clear, homemade or convenience soups. A friend might make a canned or dehydrated soup, since these soups are already made and only require adding milk or water and heating. Someone looking for the best flavor would probably enjoy a homemade soup, since the ingredients are probably fresher.
6. Students create a salad recipe using unusual combinations of foods. Each ingredient should be labeled by its food group. Students explain with what part of the meal the salad should be served and with what it should be served.

Enrichment

Have students prepare a new vegetable dish for their family. Ask them to share their family's response to the new dish.

CLOSE

Discuss the following saying with the class: "An apple a day keeps the doctor away." Ask students to make up a health slogan for their favorite vegetable.

398

Creative Vegetables

With a little effort, you can serve vegetables that are colorful, flavorful, and appealing.

Find a recipe for an interesting new way to prepare vegetables. The recipe might call for an unusual seasoning or sauce. Try out the recipe on your family, and report the results to the class.

---

making soup. Soup is a nutritious way to combine ingredients from any or all of the food groups. Soup can be hot or cold, hearty or light, and creamy or clear.

- For a main dish, try hot vegetable soup, corn chowder, or bean-and-ham soup.
- Creamy soups are hearty. Usually they contain milk and are thickened with flour. Soups of this kind should be cooked over low heat and stirred often to avoid lumping and burning.
- For a side dish, you might use beef or chicken broth. **Broth** is *the liquid left when meat, poultry, fish, or vegetables have been cooked in water.* You can add vegetables, meat, or noodles to broth to make a main dish.

Many people do not have the time to make soups from scratch. Instead, they may enjoy using convenience soups because they can simply follow the directions on the label. Soups that are **dehydrated,** or *dried so that all or most of the liquid has been taken out*, come in packets. They must have water added to them before they are heated.

LESSON TWO Review

Using complete sentences, answer the following questions on a separate sheet of paper.

Reviewing Terms and Facts

1. **Explain** How can you prevent vegetables from losing vitamins and minerals during cooking?
2. **List** Name six common ways to cook vegetables.
3. **Identify** Give three tips for making good salads.

Thinking Critically

4. **Compare and Contrast** Think of two methods of cooking vegetables. What are the advantages and disadvantages of each method?

5. **Recommend** List the different ways of preparing soup. Which would you recommend to a friend who is looking for convenience? Which would you recommend to a friend who is looking for the best flavor? Explain your choices.

Applying Concepts

6. Create your own salad recipe. Be creative and try to think of unusual combinations. Write down your recipe, labeling each ingredient by its food group. Explain what part of a meal your salad would be and what you might serve with it.

398   CHAPTER 14: LET'S COOK

MORE ABOUT • • •

Microwave Cooking Vegetables People often overcook vegetables. This causes the vegetables to lose flavor and nutrients. To avoid this problem when microwave cooking vegetables, it is best to shut off the oven before the food is done because the food continues to cook after the food has been removed from the oven. For example, the center of a potato that has been microwaved for five minutes will be too hard at first but will be cooked thoroughly after five minutes of standing at room temperature. Have students cook various types of vegetables in the microwave and compare the cooking and standing times.

LESSON THREE
Breads, Cereals, Rice, and Pasta

DISCOVER...
- how to make and use breads.
- how to prepare sandwiches.
- what you need to know to cook pasta and rice.

Lori is planning a menu for the class picnic. She wants to serve something besides the usual hamburgers, chips, and brownies. She thinks that she may include crusty rolls and breads and several kinds of cheeses and meats. She also has a favorite pasta salad recipe that she thinks everyone would like. For dessert, she might serve apple-granola crisps. What other foods would you suggest?

WORDS TO KNOW

dough
sandwich
pasta

LESSON THREE: BREADS, CEREALS, RICE, AND PASTA   399

CLASSROOM RESOURCES FOR LESSON 3

 Blackline Masters
Cooperative Learning 27
Food Lab Activity 9, "Cooking with Grains and Cereals"
Food Lab Activity 10, "Pasta Possibilities"
Lesson 3 Quiz

 Transparencies
Transparency 59, "Cooking Rice and Pasta"

 Student Workbook
Activities 102, 103

LESSON THREE
Breads, Cereals, Rice, and Pasta

FOCUS

Lesson Objectives
After studying this lesson, students should be able to
- explain how to make and prepare breads.
- discuss how to prepare different types of sandwiches.
- describe what they need to know to cook grains such as pasta and rice.

Motivating Activity
Ask students to describe the ingredients of their favorite sandwich.

Introducing the Lesson
Have students share their responses to the Motivating Activity. Ask: Why is this your favorite sandwich? Is the sandwich nutritional? Why or why not? What food groups are represented in your sandwich? Point out to students that in this lesson they will learn, among other things, how to prepare different types of sandwiches.

Introducing *Words to Know*
Have each student write the Words to Know and the definition of each on a sheet of paper. Then have them exchange papers and use each word correctly in a newspaper advertisement for a restaurant. Ask students to return the paper to its owner for that person to read and evaluate.

399

CHAPTER 14, LESSON 3

TEACH

L1 Home Economics
Bring in several labels of bread products. Have students compare the labels of the bread products to determine the main ingredients. Remind students that labels on food products must list the ingredients in descending order of weight. Ask them how knowing this can help them choose the most nutritious bread products.

L2 Analyzing
Have students list the grains used in breads. (*wheat, rye, corn, barley, oats, rice, and so on*) If possible, have students bring in samples and taste each type of bread. Then have them compare the nutrient content of various whole-grain breads. Ask students to describe the flavors and textures of the breads.

L2 Science
Have students perform the following experiment to see how yeast works: Place yeast, sugar, and warm water in a test tube. Cover the end of the test tube with a balloon. Have students observe the reaction. Students may then experiment with yeast by adding vinegar to the water, using cold rather than warm water, and using only water and yeast without the sugar. Ask them to write a conclusion to the question: What does yeast do in bread?

Bread is a popular part of most meals. What are your favorite breads to eat for breakfast, lunch, and dinner?

Preparing Breads

How many foods did Lori think of that were breads? People serve breads at many meals—from toast at breakfast to buns and rolls at picnics. Breads are made from the flour of many grains. Some of the most common flours are wheat, rye, white, and corn. Other ingredients are added to give each type of bread its particular flavor, texture, and appearance.

Making Quick Breads

Kenny likes to bake quick breads—such as muffins, biscuits, and coffee cakes—because they are fast and easy to make. He simply mixes the ingredients together to make a **dough,** *a thick mixture of flour, liquid, and other ingredients.* Then he places the dough in a pan and bakes it.

Air bubbles, which form during baking, make quick breads light and fluffy. Two ingredients used in quick bread—baking powder and baking soda—cause the air bubbles to form, making the dough rise quickly as it bakes.

When preparing quick breads, it is important to mix the dough just long enough to blend the ingredients. Too much mixing makes quick breads flat and heavy.

Making Yeast Breads

Yeast breads are another type of bread. They take longer to prepare than quick breads. Yeast breads are also made with

400   CHAPTER 14: LET'S COOK

MEETING STUDENT DIVERSITY

Cultural Perspectives Point out to students that bread is often called the "staff of life" because it is part of the food group that forms the base of the Food Guide Pyramid. Bread is a universal food, and different kinds of breads have developed throughout the world. Have students research the following breads to find out what country the bread originated in, how it is made, and what its ingredients include: kouloura, grissini, kugelhupf, chapati, tortilla, matzo. Ask students to share their findings with the class.

dough, but with this type of bread, it is yeast that makes the bread rise. Most store-bought sandwich bread, French and Italian bread, and hamburger buns are yeast breads.

A dough made with yeast must rise twice. First, you must let it rise in a warm place outside the oven for an hour or more. Then you punch it down, shape it, and let it rise in the pan before baking. If you want to take a short cut, you can buy frozen dough. Then all you have to do is let the dough warm to room temperature and rise until it is ready to be baked.

When you bake quick breads such as muffins, baking soda or baking powder causes the bread to rise quickly. What are some other examples of quick breads?

Serving Bread

There are many ways to serve bread for meals. To make garlic bread, you can slice French bread, spread it with butter to which you have added minced garlic, wrap the bread in foil, and heat it in the oven.

Another way to use bread, even if it is several days old, is to make French toast. Soak one slice at a time in a mixture of milk and beaten eggs. Then brown the slices in a skillet with a little butter or margarine. You can top them with fresh fruit.

Making Basic Sandwiches

One of the most popular ways to eat bread is as part of a sandwich. A **sandwich** is usually *two pieces of bread*

Skills IN ACTION

Brown-bagging It

A packed lunch can be nutritious and delicious. Here are some ideas:
- Include a hearty food, such as a sandwich or hard-cooked eggs.
- Pack fresh fruit or raw vegetables.
- Put milk or juice in a reusable container.
- Nutritious cookies, such as oatmeal or peanut butter, are a good dessert choice.

LESSON THREE: BREADS, CEREALS, RICE, AND PASTA **401**

CHAPTER 14, LESSON 3

L2 Critical Thinking

Give students the following lunch menus. Have them suggest foods that could be added to each of these lunches to make them more nutritious.
- Oranges and milk
- Cheese and crackers
- Juice and meat sandwich
- Banana and hard-cooked eggs

Skills IN ACTION

Have students work with a partner to share their record of what they put in their lunch each day. Ask the partners to analyze the records to determine if the lunches were nutritionally balanced. Have partners give each other ideas on how they might fill nutritional gaps in their lunch menus.

L2 Cooperative Learning

Assign Cooperative Learning Activity 27, "Packing Some Punch Into Lunch," in the TCR.

TEACHER TALK!

Unenriched White Bread

Tell students that unenriched white bread has been stripped of most of the vitamins, minerals, and fiber found in other breads. Students may not realize that unenriched white bread does not add to the goal of achieving a well-balanced diet.

MORE ABOUT •••

The History of Pancakes Historians believe that pancakes were first made in ancient Egypt. They were made out of a wheat-flour gruel and baked on a flat, hot stone. Later, the Egyptians added leavening to the gruel and cooked the "pancakes" in an oven. Pancakes became part of Lenten observances. In these observances the flour symbolized the staff of life, the milk symbolized innocence, and the egg symbolized rebirth. The Pilgrims who came to our country made pancakes from cornmeal. The French introduced thin fruit- or cheese-filled pancakes called "crepes." Jewish people introduced another type of filled pancake called "blintzes."

CHAPTER 14, LESSON 3

L3 Health

Have students pretend they are opening a specialty sandwich shop. Each sandwich in their shop includes ingredients from the five basic food groups. For example, a sandwich named Thanksgiving Turkey includes the following ingredients: whole wheat bread, mayonnaise, turkey, Swiss cheese, lettuce, orange slices, and cranberry sauce. Ask students to prepare a menu with five specialty sandwiches. Have them give their sandwiches catchy names.

L2 Food Lab

Allow time for students to complete Food Lab 9, "Cooking with Grains and Cereals," in the TCR.

DID YOU KNOW

Pizza can be delicious and good for you if you use low-fat toppings like vegetables. Skip the sausage and pepperoni and go easy on the cheese or use a low-fat or fat-free cheese. Have students try this recipe for muffin pizza: Toast whole-wheat English muffins. Spread a tablespoon of tomato sauce over the muffins. Add a dash of pepper and oregano. Top with chopped onion, mushroom, and green pepper. Cover with thin slices of part-skim mozzarella cheese. Broil until the cheese melts—about 3 or 4 minutes.

---

surrounding a filling, such as meat or cheese. Although there are many kinds of sandwiches, all good sandwiches include

- bread that is fresh.
- butter, margarine, mayonnaise, or another spread to keep the bread moist.
- a filling, such as chicken salad, spread to the corners of the bread, or slices of meat or cheese.
- ingredients for extra flavor and texture, such as lettuce or tomato.

You can make sandwiches with any type of bread, including whole wheat, enriched white, rye, pumpernickel, seven-grain, and oatmeal. Pita bread, croissants (krah-SAHNZ), and French bread are also good choices. A variety of sandwich fillings will help you fulfill your daily nutritional requirements.

 When choosing breads and other grains, remember that whole-grain products are higher in nutrients and fiber than breads made from refined flour, such as white bread.

Making Special Sandwiches

Do you ever feel as if your sandwiches are getting a little dull? If so, you may want to try something different. Sandwiches don't have to be cold. For variety, you can make a tuna melt by putting tuna and cheese on a bagel or bread and melting the cheese in the oven or broiler. Peanut butter with banana slices on oatmeal bread provides foods from three food groups.

Grains

Some foods made from grains must be cooked before you eat them. These include some breakfast cereals, rice, and pasta. Since they all contain starch, some of the cooking techniques are similar for each one.

402   CHAPTER 14: LET'S COOK

COOPERATIVE LEARNING

Healthy Comparisons Have students work in small groups to prepare a rice or pasta dish. Have each group prepare a work plan for cooking the dish. Refer students to Lesson 5 of Chapter 12 to review the idea of a work plan. Students in each group should divide the following tasks from the work plan: pre-preparation, mixing and preparation, table setting and serving the food, and cleaning up. Ask each group to follow its work plan and evaluate it. After the class has sampled each group's dish, hold a class discussion about the type of rice or pasta and the methods of cooking used in making the dishes.

How to Make Cooked Cereals

When you think of cereal, do you think about the kind you pour out of the box and eat cold with milk? Many people also enjoy eating cooked cereals, such as oatmeal, grits, and cream of wheat.

Like other grains that are cooked, cereals expand to two or three times their original volume. They can be cooked with water or milk on the stove or in the microwave oven.

How to Cook Rice

One type of grain that must be cooked is rice. Rice should be simmered in water, not boiled. When cooked properly, rice is light and fluffy, never heavy or gummy. When you cook rice, follow these tips:

- Don't rinse rice, because rinsing removes some nutrients.
- Use a little oil in the cooking water to help keep the grains separate and to prevent foaming.
- Don't remove the lid while the rice is cooking.
- Because all of the water is absorbed during cooking, rice does not need to be drained.
- Fluff the rice with a fork before serving.

Before you cook rice, read the directions on the package. Different kinds of rice require different amounts of water and lengths of cooking time.

There are many ways to serve rice. For example, rice can be rolled in a flour tortilla with cooked chicken and beans. It is also an important ingredient in chicken-rice soup and rice pudding. What other ways do you like to eat rice?

When you cook rice, be sure to follow the package directions. Why is this important?

LESSON THREE: BREADS, CEREALS, RICE, AND PASTA   **403**

CHAPTER 14, LESSON 3

L1 Estimating

Display several sizes of pots and pans on a table. Have students estimate the size of pot or pan needed to cook different amounts of breakfast cereal, rice, and pasta. If possible, cook some of the grains to see if the students' estimates are correct.

L1 Using Transparencies

Present Color Transparency 59, "Cooking Rice and Pasta," in the TCR. Use this overhead visual to reinforce concepts from this lesson.

DID YOU KNOW

Brown rice contains important vitamins and minerals, especially vitamins B and E, iron, calcium, and phosphorus. White rice has been processed, which strips it of these vitamins and minerals. Have students compare and contrast the nutrition-facts labels on packages of white and brown rice.

L3 Comparing

Have students study the package directions for cooking breakfast cereals, rice (regular, quick-cooking, and instant), and pasta. Ask them to compare the cooking techniques for these foods.

MORE ABOUT

Eating Grains Corn is a grain, so popcorn is a food made from grain. Popping corn was begun by Native Americans about 5,000 years ago. At first the whole ear of corn was popped on a stick. Later, corn was popped in a heated clay vessel full of sand. Pilgrims ate popcorn with milk as a breakfast cereal. A recent study estimates that 192 million pounds of popcorn are consumed annually in the United States. Nutritionists have identified unsalted, unbuttered popcorn as an acceptable snack for people eating a well-balanced diet. Have students try a snack of popcorn and sliced apples. Ask them to suggest other combinations of popcorn and healthy foods such as raisins and other dried fruits.

403

CHAPTER 14, LESSON 3

L1 Finding Examples
Have students bring in a variety of pastas. Discuss the shapes, sizes, and colors of the pastas. Ask students to name the kinds of dishes in which each pasta might be used.

USING VISUALS

Demonstrate how to cook pasta using the steps shown in Figure 14.2. Demonstrate safety tips as you cook.

L2 Food Lab
Allow time for students to complete Food Lab 10, "Pasta Possibilities," in the TCR.

L1 Student Workbook
Assign Activities 102 and 103 in the Student Workbook.

ASSESS

Evaluating the Lesson
Assign Reviewing Terms and Facts and Thinking Critically on page 405 to review the lesson; then assign the Lesson 3 Quiz in the TCR.

Reteaching
- Have students make a poster using pictures of breads, cereals, rice, and pasta and showing some different ways these foods can be served in meals.
- Have students complete Reteaching Activity 14 in the TCR.

Figure 14.2 Cooking Pasta
Follow these guidelines when cooking pasta. What texture should pasta have when it is cooked properly?

How to Cook Pasta

If you have eaten spaghetti, macaroni, or noodles, then you have eaten pasta. **Pasta** is *a food made from flour and water and formed into shapes,* including noodles, spirals, shells, and many others.

❶ Choose a large enough pot. Pasta doubles in size when it is cooked.

❷ Measure water and salt into a large pot. You'll need 2 quarts (2 L) water and an optional 1 teaspoon (5 mL) salt for every 8 ounces (224 g) pasta. Add one teaspoon (5 mL) cooking oil to the water. This helps to keep the water from boiling over. It also helps keep the pasta from sticking together.

❸ Bring the water to a boil.

❹ Add the pasta slowly to the water. The water should continue to boil. If it stops, the pasta might stick together.

❺ Stir the pasta from time to time. This also helps keep it from sticking. Cook the pasta only until it's tender. The package directions tell you how long.

❻ Pour the pasta into a colander to drain. Don't rinse the pasta with water.

404   CHAPTER 14: LET'S COOK

MORE ABOUT •••

Wild Rice Bring a package of wild rice to class. Explain to students that although it is called a rice, it is actually a grain that is not related to rice. Wild rice grows in shallow lakes in Minnesota, Wisconsin, and central Canada. It is high in protein and vitamins. One way of harvesting it is by bending the heads of the 4- to 8-foot-high stalks over a canoe. The heads of the stalks are beaten with sticks to loosen the grain, and the grain falls into the canoe. Have students find recipes that include wild rice.

Pasta is usually dried. It becomes soft enough to eat when it is cooked. Properly cooked pasta is slightly firm, not soft, limp, or mushy. **Figure 14.2** describes how to cook pasta.

Healthy Grain Choices

Breads, cooked cereals, rice, and pasta provide you with important nutrients: iron, B vitamins, carbohydrates, and fiber. Once you know how to cook and prepare grains, you will see that there are many ways to include them in your diet every day.

Pasta should keep its shape and stay firm even after it has been cooked.

LESSON THREE Review

Using complete sentences, answer the following questions on a separate sheet of paper.

Reviewing Terms and Facts

1. **Recall** What is the purpose of using baking soda and baking powder in quick breads?
2. **Recall** Describe the appearance of rice that has been cooked properly.
3. **Vocabulary** What is *pasta*? Give three examples of types of pasta.

Thinking Critically

4. **Apply** Imagine that you are going on a picnic. Give examples of three types of sandwiches that would need to be kept in a cooler and two types of sandwiches that could be packed in a brown bag.
5. **Explain** How do you know how much liquid to use when cooking a grain? Why is it important to cook it properly?
6. **Compare and Contrast** What are the similarities and differences between cooking rice and cooking pasta?

Applying Concepts

7. Write seven menus for one week of dinners, using breads, rice, and pasta. For example, one dish might be lamb curry over rice; another might be pita pockets with chicken salad, tomato, cucumber, and onion. Remember to vary your menus as much as possible.

LESSON THREE: BREADS, CEREALS, RICE, AND PASTA   **405**

MEETING STUDENT DIVERSITY

Physically Challenged Discuss with students—or ask physically challenged students in the class to lead a discussion on—the special needs of people with physical challenges in terms of food preparation. (Students in wheelchairs may have difficulty maneuvering in the kitchen, students who are blind may find roadblocks to preparing foods in some kitchens, and so on.) Have volunteers investigate and report to the class about appliances, special kitchen equipment, and cookbooks that help to ensure that the needs of physically challenged individuals are met in kitchens.

CHAPTER 14, LESSON 3

Answers to Lesson 3 Review

1. Baking soda and baking powder cause air bubbles to form, making quick breads light and fluffy. Baking powder makes the dough rise quickly as it bakes.
2. Light and fluffy.
3. A food made from flour and water and formed into shapes. Any three examples: noodles, ravioli, spirals, shells, green spinach noodles, orange pumpkin noodles, brown whole-wheat noodles.
4. Answers will vary. Students may answer turkey, chicken, ham, egg salad, or tuna salad need to be kept in a cooler. Peanut butter or vegetable sandwiches could be placed in a brown bag.
5. Package directions tell how much liquid to use. This minimizes the amount of nutrients lost during cooking.
6. Both rice and pasta are cooked using water and oil. Both rice and pasta expand in size during cooking. Rice is simmered; pasta is boiled. Rice absorbs all the water it is cooked in. Pasta needs to be drained. Neither rice nor pasta should be rinsed.
7. Students write menus for dinners, using breads, rice, and pasta.

Enrichment

Have students research the food processing of rice or pasta. Have them draw flow charts on poster boards showing the steps taken to process rice or pasta from harvesting to preparation for eating. Encourage students to prepare their charts using computers.

CLOSE

Ask students to give reasons why breads, cereals, rice, and pasta could be given a "Best Buy" award.

LESSON FOUR
Milk, Yogurt, and Cheese

FOCUS

Lesson Objectives
After studying this lesson, students should be able to
- explain how to add milk to their diet.
- discuss the many ways they can use dairy products.
- demonstrate how to prepare dairy foods.

Motivating Activity
Ask students to write a short explanation of the meaning of the slogan, "Milk—it does a body good."

Introducing the Lesson
Have students read their responses to the Motivating Activity. Ask them to give examples of ways they include milk in their diet. Tell them that in this lesson they will learn ways to add milk and milk products to their diet.

Introducing *Words to Know*
Ask a volunteer to read the vocabulary words and terms and their definitions. Then have students use the vocabulary words to write an introductory paragraph for a cookbook titled "Cooking with Dairy Products."

LESSON FOUR
Milk, Yogurt, and Cheese

WORDS TO KNOW
dairy foods
scald
curdles

DISCOVER...
- how to add milk to your diet.
- the many ways you can use dairy products.
- how to prepare dairy foods.

When Emily gets home from softball practice, she grabs a tall glass and pours herself some milk. She finds milk refreshing and thirst-quenching. Her brother Rob opens the freezer and takes out a strawberry frozen yogurt bar. He enjoys having something sweet and creamy for an afternoon snack.

Milk and other dairy foods provide you with calcium and other nutrients, including vitamins A, B, and D. **Dairy foods** are *foods made from milk*. For good health, you need to include dairy foods in your diet every day. Which dairy foods do you like best?

406   CHAPTER 14: LET'S COOK

CLASSROOM RESOURCES FOR LESSON 4

 Blackline Masters
Cooperative Learning 28
Enrichment 16
Lesson 4 Quiz

 Transparencies
Transparency 60, "Milk, Yogurt, and Cheese Group"

Student Workbook
Activities 104, 105

The Many Uses of Milk

People of all ages drink milk at mealtimes and with snacks. In addition, milk is used in many recipes. What foods can you think of that are made with milk?

Cooking with Milk and Cream

Have you ever cooked foods whose ingredients included milk, buttermilk, or cream? For example, you might use milk or cream to make creamy soups, sauces, puddings, and custards. Milk and buttermilk are often used in cakes, breads, and muffins.

When cooking with dairy foods, it is important to be especially careful. Milk products burn, or scorch, easily if the temperature is too high or if they are cooked too long. To cook milk you need to **scald** it, or *bring the food slowly to a temperature just below the boiling point.* Never let milk boil. Heat only until little bubbles begin to appear around the edge.

If you do not handle milk properly, it may curdle. When milk **curdles,** it *separates into little particles (curds).* Adding anything acidic—such as fruit, tomato, or fruit juices—to milk may cause curdling. To avoid this, add these foods very slowly and stir the milk constantly.

Thick, creamy sauces add flavor to many dishes. For example, a basic white sauce made with milk can be served over vegetables or noodles. For extra flavor, add cheese or herbs to the sauce.

To keep milk from burning when you cook it, use a double boiler or a heavy pan. What else should you do to prevent milk from burning?

Preparing Milk Drinks

For a delicious cold drink, blend milk with fruit, juice, ice cream, or yogurt in a blender or food processor. You can also mash the fruit, combine all the

LESSON FOUR: MILK, YOGURT, AND CHEESE **407**

COOPERATIVE LEARNING

Adding Calcium to Your Diet Organize students into small groups. Have each group brainstorm ways to add calcium to their diet. Have them think of slogans or jingles to express their ideas. Ask them to select several of their favorite ideas and use them to make illustrations on poster board about adding calcium to a diet, and add the slogans or jingles they created. Have students share their posters with the class and let the class vote on the best posters. Display the posters in the school cafeteria.

CHAPTER 14, LESSON 4

TEACH

L1 Discussing
Have students describe instances in which they use milk as an ingredient in foods they prepare.

L3 Finding Examples
Have students find recipes for dishes that include milk as an ingredient. Ask them to bring recipes to share with the class.

L1 Using Transparencies
Present Color Transparency 60, "Milk, Yogurt, and Cheese Group," in the TCR. Use this overhead visual to reinforce concepts from this lesson.

L2 Cooperative Learning
Assign Cooperative Learning Activity 28 in the TCR. Students work in groups to come up with creative ideas on how to serve milk to children in this activity.

CHAPTER 14, LESSON 4

Try This!

Encourage students to check the nutrition-facts labels for each form of milk listed. Compare the fats and calories versus the nutritional value of each form. Stress the fact that skim milk has the same amount of calcium as whole milk, but less fat and fewer calories.

L2 Applying Knowledge

Have students cut out advertisements for dairy foods in teen magazines. Ask them to analyze the message in each advertisement. Then have them create their own advertisement about their favorite dairy food. Display the advertisements on a bulletin board.

L2 Writing

Have students choose a dairy food for the "Best-Tasting Dairy Food Award." Have them write a persuasive speech about their award-winning dairy food. Ask volunteers to give their speech to the class.

L2 Role-Playing

Have students role-play a cook on television. Have them explain the cooking instructions for a dish that includes cheese.

Try This!

Milk comes in many forms—nonfat, low-fat, whole milk, half-and-half, cream, whipping cream, evaporated milk, sweetened condensed milk, nonfat dry milk, and buttermilk! Bring samples of these products to class. Taste and compare. Discuss the characteristics of each.

ingredients in a covered container, and shake it well. Try some of these combinations:

- **Orange shake:** 1 cup (250 mL) buttermilk, 3 tablespoons (45 mL) orange juice concentrate, and 1 teaspoon (5 mL) honey
- **Banana milk:** ¾ cup (175 mL) milk, 1 mashed banana, 5 crushed ice cubes, and 1 teaspoon (5 mL) sugar
- **Lemon-strawberry yogurt smoothie:** ½ cup (125 mL) lemon yogurt, ½ cup (125 mL) milk, ¼ cup (50 mL) sliced strawberries, and 1 teaspoon (5 mL) sugar
- **Coffee shake:** ½ cup (125 mL) coffee ice cream and ½ cup (125 mL) milk

Yogurt—Plain or Fancy

Yogurt is a dairy product that contains most of the same nutrients as milk. Because yogurt is easier to digest than milk, many people who cannot drink milk can still eat yogurt. From

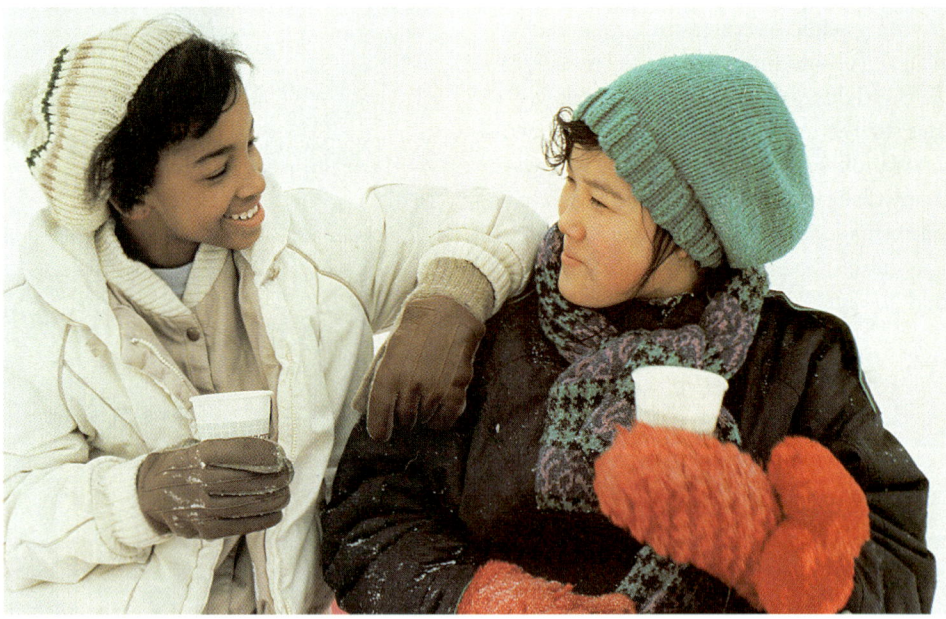

Hot chocolate is an alternative to plain milk. What other beverages supply you with calcium?

408 CHAPTER 14: LET'S COOK

COOPERATIVE LEARNING

Using Small Appliances Have students work in small groups to prepare the milk drinks listed on this page. First, have the groups prepare the milk drinks without using a blender or food processor. Then have them prepare the recipe using a blender or food processor. Ask them to record the differences in preparation time and in the texture of the finished drinks. Ask each group to answer the following questions: How do small appliances simplify food preparation? Which drinks did you prefer—those mixed by hand or those mixed with a blender or food processor? Is the extra cleanup when using a blender or food processor worth the difference in preparation time and taste? Have groups share their responses.

Yogurt is a versatile food. You can eat it plain, add toppings, and even cook with it. Have you ever tried yogurt instead of sour cream on a baked potato?

plain or vanilla to kiwi or papaya, yogurt comes in a wide variety of flavors. It is also available in several forms, including regular, low-fat, and nonfat. In addition, yogurt can be used instead of sour cream or mayonnaise in some recipes.

Cheese—Many Variations

Can you imagine what some of your favorite foods would taste like without cheese? Pizza and lasagna just wouldn't be the same. What other foods do you eat that would lack flavor and appeal if the cheese were left out?

Cooking with Cheese

Cheese is an important ingredient in many recipes. For the best results, though, it must be cooked carefully. If you cook cheese too long or at high temperatures, it may burn or

Using Yogurt Instead

If you don't like to drink milk, eat yogurt instead. Yogurt has the same nutrients as milk, and it is easier to digest. Eat yogurt instead of high-fat, high-calorie snacks. Low-fat or nonfat yogurt has only a fraction of the calories, and it tastes smooth and refreshing! Yogurt can also be used in salad dressings, dips, and dessert toppings.

LESSON FOUR: MILK, YOGURT, AND CHEESE 409

CHAPTER 14, LESSON 4

DID YOU KNOW

Making yogurt cheese is an easy process and can be a welcome addition to sandwiches, salads, or desserts. Line a colander with two layers of clean cheesecloth. Place the colander over a cake pan. Place 1 pint (500 mL) plain nonfat or low-fat yogurt in the colander. Cover with waxed paper. Refrigerate and allow yogurt to drain for 8 to 10 hours. Remove yogurt cheese from cheesecloth. Pack it into a storage container. Discard liquid that dripped into the pan. Cover yogurt cheese tightly and refrigerate.

L2 Science

Have students cook cheese at different temperatures and record the results. Have them draw a conclusion about the best temperature to cook cheese.

Encourage students to experiment with yogurt as a substitute in recipes calling for sour cream or mayonnaise. Ask students to describe the results of the experiments.

MORE ABOUT •••

Consuming Cheeses Cheese is a food that is naturally high in protein and fat. It is also relatively expensive. Have students compare the calorie and fat contents of various cheeses and their unit prices. Have them make a bar graph to show their findings. Ask students to choose the five best cheese buys. Then have volunteers identify ways to use these cheeses in recipes.

CHAPTER 14, LESSON 4

L2 Language
Ask students to recite the nursery rhyme "Little Miss Muffet." Point out to them that in the nursery rhyme, Dr. Muffet's daughter, Patience, sat on a tuffet (a low stool) eating her curds and whey. Have them research the meaning of the words *curds* and *whey*.

L1 Taste Test
Conduct a cheese-tasting lab to introduce students to kinds of cheeses they may not have tasted before. Have them describe flavors. Discuss uses for each type of cheese.

L2 Listening Skills
Read the following recipe to the students. Have them identify the ingredients and the food groups represented. Then ask students to help you compile a list of equipment that would be needed to make this dessert. Crush 20 graham crackers with a rolling pin. Set aside. In a small saucepan, melt 1/3 cup margarine. Using a fork, stir together crackers and melted margarine. Place mixture in the bottom of an 8 x 8 x 8-inch baking dish. Set aside. Place 8 ounces of plain yogurt in a mixer bowl. Add 1 small package instant vanilla pudding and 1 cup milk. Mix for 1 minute. Scrape sides of bowl with a spatula. Mix again. Pour over graham cracker mixture in baking dish. Top with fresh sliced strawberries. Chill and serve.

---

become rubbery or stringy. When cooking with cheese, follow these tips:

- Use low to medium heat, and avoid overcooking.
- Grate or shred hard cheeses, such as cheddar, before adding them to other ingredients. The cheese will blend faster and more evenly.
- Add cheese to sauces or casseroles at the end of the cooking time, if possible, so that the cheese won't become overcooked.

Cheese comes in many varieties: soft, semisoft, hard, or processed. Cheeses range in flavor from mild to tangy, sharp, and strong. Which types of cheese do you like?

Enjoying Cold Cheeses

Besides cooking with cheese, you can also enjoy cheese cold, either by itself or added to a variety of foods. For example, try sprinkling grated cheese on soups, chili, baked potatoes, spaghetti, and burritos. For an easy snack, eat cheese with crackers, crusty bread, or fresh fruit. Firm cheeses that can be sliced, such as cheddar and Swiss cheese, taste best at room temperature. Take them out of the refrigerator about an hour before they will be eaten.

MEETING STUDENT DIVERSITY

Varied Learning Styles If there are students in the class who have special interests in cooking or baking, have them use their interests to create healthy, nutritious, and fun recipes for desserts made with dairy foods. Let interested students work individually, with partners, or in small groups to create recipes and compile them into a specialty cookbook for desserts. Then, if possible, allow them to prepare some of their recipes for the rest of the class.

Desserts Made with Dairy Foods

Besides tasting good, many desserts made with dairy foods are also nutritious. Have you ever made custard or pudding for dessert? Maybe you enjoy eating ice cream or frozen yogurt as an after-dinner treat.

Custards and Puddings

Custards are made with milk, eggs, and flavorings. The eggs are used to thicken the custard. Some custards are baked in the oven, while others are cooked in a saucepan on the stove. Either way, custards should be cooked at low temperatures, and not for too long. After custard cools, it should be chilled in the refrigerator.

Another dairy dessert that may be cooked is pudding. The thickening agent in pudding is flour or another starch, rather than eggs. Pudding is made by blending flour with milk and then adding other ingredients. Cook pudding over low heat, and stir it often. Puddings are also usually chilled before serving. An easier way to make custards and puddings is to use packaged mixes.

Dairy Treats

When people think about getting enough calcium each day, they usually think about drinking milk. However, there are many other ways to add dairy foods to your diet. You can cook with milk or cheese, add cold cheese to other foods, and enjoy dairy desserts. When choosing a frozen

Pudding is a nutritious dairy dessert that can be cooked or made from an instant mix. How would you prefer to make pudding?

CHAPTER 14, LESSON 4

TEACHER TALK!

Cholesterol Control
As students read about desserts made from dairy foods, remind them that custard includes eggs. If they are watching their cholesterol intake, they need to count the eggs in custard toward their weekly egg consumption.

L1 Student Workbook
Assign Activities 104 and 105 in the Student Workbook.

ASSESS

Evaluating the Lesson
Assign Reviewing Terms and Facts and Thinking Critically on page 412 to review the lesson; then assign the Lesson 4 Quiz in the TCR.

Reteaching
- Have students write three examples of recipes that include a dairy product.
- Have students complete Reteaching Activity 14 in the TCR.

Enrichment
- Have students find recipes for nutritious desserts that contain each of the following: yogurt, pudding, skim milk, and ricotta cheese.
- Assign Enrichment Activity 16 in the TCR.

TECHNOLOGY UPDATE

Increasing Milk Production In 1994 some dairy farmers in the United States began injecting a bovine growth hormone (BGH) into their dairy cows. This hormone increases the milk production in dairy cows. Some people fear that this synthetic drug might affect the milk from treated cows. After studying the effects of the hormone on cow's milk, the Food and Drug Administration (FDA) said that special labeling of milk from BGH-treated cows was unnecessary. The FDA states that milk from hormone-treated cows is the same as milk from nontreated cows.

CHAPTER 14, LESSON 4

Answers to Lesson 4 Review

1. Foods made from milk. Any two examples: milk, cream, pudding, custard, cheese, ice cream, yogurt.
2. Slowly add foods that cause curdling in milk and stir the milk constantly.
3. It would get rubbery, stringy, or burnt.
4. Custard and pudding. Flour or another starch is used to thicken them.
5. Milk and cheese burn easily when cooked. To avoid this, scald them slowly at low temperatures. Milk and cheese may curdle when cooked. To avoid this, add foods slowly to milk and stir constantly. Grate or shred hard cheeses before adding them to other ingredients. When milk is heated it may form a skin on the surface. Prevent this by covering the pot with a lid or by stirring the milk while it is cooking.
6. Answers may vary. Students may respond that yogurt is popular because it is easier to digest than milk, it comes in a variety of flavors and forms, it can be used instead of sour cream or mayonnaise in some recipes, and it has fewer calories and fat than some other dairy foods.
7. Answers will vary. Students list cheeses they like to eat and suggest some foods to add these cheeses to.
8. Students keep a record of dairy products eaten for three days. They compare their intake with the amount recommended in the Food Guide Pyramid. Students make suggestions to increase the amount of dairy foods in their diet, if needed.

CLOSE

Ask students to explain the importance of dairy products in a person's diet.

412

▲ Pizza is a popular food that provides calcium because it is topped with cheese. What other popular foods are made with dairy products?

dessert, check the nutrition labels carefully. Many low-fat and nonfat products taste delicious and contain far less fat and fewer calories than regular ice cream or frozen yogurt.

LESSON FOUR *Review*

Using complete sentences, answer the following questions on a separate sheet of paper.

Reviewing Terms and Facts

1. **Vocabulary** Define *dairy foods.* Give two examples of dairy foods.
2. **Recall** How can you prevent milk from curdling?
3. **Describe** What would happen to cheese if you cooked it too long?
4. **Identify** Name two cooked dairy desserts. What ingredients are used to thicken them?

Thinking Critically

5. **Summarize** What are three problems you might have when cooking with milk and cheese? How can you avoid these problems?
6. **Analyze** Why do you think that yogurt has become so popular?
7. **Recommend** Make a list of cheeses that you like to eat. Then suggest some foods to which you could add these cheeses to increase the amount of dairy foods in your diet.

Applying Concepts

8. For three days, keep a record of all the dairy foods you eat and drink. Then compare your intake with the number of servings recommended in the Food Guide Pyramid. Do you eat and drink enough dairy foods? If not, how could you increase the amount in your diet?

412   CHAPTER 14: LET'S COOK

HOME AND COMMUNITY CONNECTION

Visiting a Restaurant If possible, arrange a field trip to a restaurant that serves a variety of dairy foods. Ask the restaurant manager if a cook could show the students how dairy foods are stored and prepared for restaurant dishes. Ask the cook to demonstrate the preparation of a dish served at the restaurant that includes dairy foods.

LESSON FIVE
Meat, Poultry, Fish, Dry Beans, Eggs, and Nuts

DISCOVER...
- how to prepare meat, poultry, fish, dry beans, and eggs.
- ways to include lower-cost protein in your diet.
- how to make a small amount of meat go farther.

Carrie and Chris volunteered to plan and prepare dinner for their parents' anniversary on Saturday. They decided that they needed to choose a main dish first. They narrowed down their choices to meat loaf, grilled chicken, or salmon steaks.

WORDS TO KNOW
moist-heat cooking

dry-heat cooking

hard-cooked eggs

meat extenders

LESSON FIVE: MEAT, POULTRY, FISH, DRY BEANS, EGGS, AND NUTS   413

LESSON FIVE
Meat, Poultry, Fish, Dry Beans, Eggs, and Nuts

FOCUS

Lesson Objectives
After studying this lesson, students should be able to
- identify how to prepare meat, poultry, fish, beans, and eggs.
- explain ways to include lower-cost protein in their diet.
- describe how to make a small amount of meat go further.

Motivating Activity
Have students make a list of the types of meat, fish, poultry, beans, or eggs that they eat. Collect the lists.

Introducing the Lesson
Read to students the lists from the Motivating Activity. Have students indicate preferences for the foods: thumbs up for those they like, thumbs down for those they dislike, and crossed arms for those they have never tried. Point out to the students that in this lesson they will learn how to prepare meat, poultry, fish, beans, eggs, and other sources of protein.

Introducing *Words to Know*
Have students write the Words to Know on a large sheet of paper. Next to each word, have them write its definition. Then ask students to make an illustration of each word or concept.

CLASSROOM RESOURCES FOR LESSON 5

 Blackline Masters
Activity and Project Card 27, "Create a Cookbook"
Activity and Project Card 28, "Critic's Corner"
Concept Map 22
Cross Curriculum 16
Lesson 5 Quiz

Peer Pressure and Decision Making 28
Reteaching 14

 Transparencies
Transparency 61, "Methods for Cooking Meat and Fish"

 Student Workbook
Activity 106

CHAPTER 14, LESSON 5

TEACH

L1 Discussing
Point out to students that cooking tenderizes meat and brings out its natural flavor. It also improves the texture of meat. Have students identify the most popular way of cooking meat in their home.

DID YOU KNOW?
When Air Force captain Scott O'Grady was shot down in Bosnia in 1995, he survived for six days by eating insects. Insects contain a sizeable amount of protein. For example, the *escamole* ant found in Mexico gets 60 percent of its calories from protein. Have students investigate the nutritional value of other insects. Have them research to find out the kinds of insects that are part of people's diets in different parts of the world.

L2 Problem Solving
Assign Peer Pressure and Decision Making 28 in the TCR. This activity gives students the opportunity to recognize peer pressure and practice decision-making skills.

Preparing Meat, Poultry, and Fish

When Carrie and Chris chose a few main dishes they could cook, they selected foods made with meat, poultry, and fish. These protein-rich foods are popular main dishes, partly because of their versatility. They are not only cut and sold in a variety of ways but can also be prepared in countless ways.

The dish Carrie and Chris chose to make was meat loaf. Because ground meat has no bones, it yields more servings per pound. You can find many types of ground meat at the supermarket—beef, chicken, turkey, veal, and pork. You can use your favorite or vary the meats you use in such dishes as hamburgers, chili, lasagna, taco filling, and spaghetti sauce.

When you prepare meat, poultry, or fish, the two basic cooking methods you will use are moist heat and dry heat. The method you choose depends on the recipe you are following and the tenderness of the meat or poultry. **Figure 14.3** shows some common methods used for cooking with moist heat and dry heat.

When you prepare stew, you can add a variety of ingredients to make your own special recipe. What foods or seasonings would you add?

414   CHAPTER 14: LET'S COOK

MORE ABOUT • • •

Where Did the Hamburger Originate? The first hamburger did not originate in fast-food restaurants. Ground beef originated during the Middle Ages. Warring Mongolians and Turkish tribes discovered that shredding their beef made the meat taste and digest better. Germans in the seaport town of Hamburg named ground beef "hamburg steak." Ground beef was introduced to England in the nineteenth century by Dr. J. H. Salisbury, hence the English name "Salisbury steak." German immigrants to America brought their hamburg steak. It was later renamed hamburger steak, and finally hamburger. Students may wish to research when the hamburger was first served on a bun.

414

**Figure 14.3
Methods for Cooking Meats**

Meat, poultry, and fish can be cooked in a variety of ways. Which of these cooking methods do you prefer?

Roasting and Baking. Place the meat, poultry, or fish on a rack in a shallow pan, uncovered, in the oven.

Braising. To braise food, such as a pot roast, brown the meat. Then put the food in a covered pan with a small amount of liquid. Cook it slowly until tender.

Stewing. Cut meat into small pieces. Cover with liquid and cook slowly according to recipe directions.

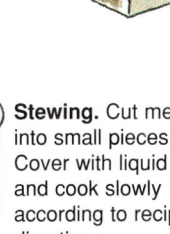

Frying. Meat, poultry, or fish can be fried in oil, butter, or margarine. Thin slices of meat, poultry, or fish can be stir-fried, which means that they are cooked quickly in a small amount of fat at a high temperature.

Microwave Cooking. Meat, poultry, and fish can be cooked in a microwave oven. They won't brown much, however.

Broiling. Place the meat, fish, or poultry on a broiler pan under the oven broiler. High heat from the broiler cooks food from the top. Turn the food over so that it cooks on both sides.

Deep-fat Frying. Chicken and fish are sometimes fried in a lot of oil. The oil must be hot, but not too hot. Chicken and fish are usually coated with a batter before deep-fat frying.

LESSON FIVE: MEAT, POULTRY, FISH, DRY BEANS, EGGS, AND NUTS   415

CHAPTER 14, LESSON 5

USING VISUALS
Have students read the information in Figure 14.3. Then ask them to identify whether each method illustrated uses dry-heat or moist-heat cooking.

L1 Using Transparencies
Present Color Transparency 61, "Methods for Cooking Meat and Fish," in the TCR. Use this overhead visual to reinforce concepts from this lesson.

L2 Research
As students read the information about preparing dishes that combine meat with other ingredients such as stews, tell them that many ethnic dishes often combine meats with such foods as vegetables, beans, or pastas. Ask students to research cookbooks from various cultures and identify two or three recipes that combine meat with other foods in one dish. Students may wish to use CD-ROM or on-line resources for their research.

MEETING STUDENT DIVERSITY

Cultural Perspectives The traditional methods for preparing and cooking various ethnic dishes may result in a large quantity of fat in the meal. For example, perhaps the meats are fried in oils or perhaps large quantities of cheeses are used in most dishes. Help students brainstorm alternative methods and ingredients for preparing traditional foods at home. For example, they might suggest using a vegetable oil for frying meats, or a low-fat cheese for the cheese dishes. If students feel they cannot change the traditional foods, help them brainstorm ways to avoid eating too much fat. For example, the students might eat a smaller portion of the traditional foods and add fresh vegetables and fruits to their meal.

CHAPTER 14, LESSON 5

USING VISUALS
Refer students to Figure 14.4. Ask students to read the chart on this page and describe the cooking methods to use for each: pot roast, turkey, spareribs, sirloin steak.

L2 Critical Thinking
Ask students to make an illustration showing how the tips for cooking with meat substitutes will help them stretch their buying power.

L1 Demonstrating
Have students cook two eggs. Boil one for 15 minutes. Simmer the other one for 15 minutes. Have students peel the eggs and compare their appearance. Ask them to determine which egg is more appetizing. Ask them why this is so.

L2 Social Studies Connection
Assign Cross-Curriculum Activity 16 in the TCR. Students learn about cooking terms from different languages in this activity.

Cooking With or Without Liquid

Have you ever eaten pot roast or beef stew? If so, then you have tasted meat cooked with moist heat. **Moist-heat cooking** is *cooking in liquid.* It involves cooking food slowly in a covered container, usually with water, broth, or a sauce.

Moist-heat cooking methods are good to use with less expensive, tougher cuts of meat and poultry. When you cook them slowly in liquid, they become more tender and flavorful.

Do you enjoy eating roast turkey, broiled steak, or baked fish? Each of these foods is cooked with dry heat. **Dry-heat cooking** is *cooking without liquid.* It is best to use dry heat when cooking tender cuts of meat and poultry. Fish is often cooked with dry heat too. **Figure 14.4** shows which cuts of meat and poultry to cook with moist heat and which to cook with dry heat.

Some meats can be cooked to different levels of doneness. The three levels are *rare, medium,* and *well-done.* Rare meat is pink on the inside. Well-done meat is thoroughly cooked inside and out. Medium is in between rare and well-done. Beef can be cooked to any of these levels. Pork, poultry, and fish, on

**Figure 14.4
Cuts of Meat and Poultry**
How does cooking with moist heat improve less tender cuts of meat and poultry?

Tender Meat and Poultry
(Use dry heat.)

Beef rib roast
Sirloin steak
Ground beef, pork, turkey
Pork chops
Ham
Pork sausage
Leg of lamb
Frying chicken

Less Tender Meat and Poultry
(Use moist heat.)

Stew meat
Pot roast
Round steak
Chuck roast
Corned beef
Spareribs
Pork blade steak
Stewing chicken

416 CHAPTER 14: LET'S COOK

MORE ABOUT • • •

Grades of Meat The United States Department of Agriculture grades most meat as to quality. The three top USDA grades for beef, veal, and lamb are prime, choice, and select. Prime is the top grade and contains the most marbling (fat flecks that run throughout the meat). Choice is high quality and has enough marbling, but not as much as prime. Select grade has less fat and flavor. It is still nutritious, however, and less expensive.

416

TIPS for living

RARE, MEDIUM, OR WELL-DONE?

When you cook meat, you may not be able to tell how well-done it is simply by looking at it. Here's what to do:

- Use an instant-read meat thermometer to measure the internal temperature of meat that you're broiling or roasting. Beef that is rare will register 140°F; medium will register 160°F; well-done will register 170°F. Pork, poultry, and fish should all be cooked until they are well-done!

- If you don't have a thermometer, prick the meat with a cooking fork. If the juice runs red, the meat is rare; pink, medium rare; colorless, well-done.

the other hand, must be cooked until they are well-done. Otherwise, they are not safe to eat.

Meat Substitutes

Other high-protein foods can be used as a main dish instead of meat, poultry, or fish. Beans and eggs are good substitutes. Not only are they high in protein, vitamins, and minerals, but they are also low in cost. In fact, they are two of the most versatile and nutritious foods you can cook.

Cooking with Dry Legumes

Dry beans and peas come in a variety of tastes and textures. Have you ever seen or tried cooking with red kidney beans, black beans, white beans, lentils, lima beans, split peas, or black-eyed peas? These and other legumes offer healthful alternatives to more familiar main dishes.

When you buy dry beans, they will be hard. To soften them, soak them in water for several hours. Then they can be prepared in many ways. For example, you can make baked beans or use beans in burritos, rolled in tortillas with rice and cheese. To save time, you can buy most types of beans in cans.

Although dry beans are a good source of protein, they are not quite as good a source as eggs, meat, or cheese.

LESSON FIVE: MEAT, POULTRY, FISH, DRY BEANS, EGGS, AND NUTS

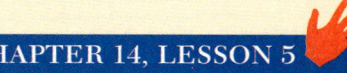

CHAPTER 14, LESSON 5

TIPS for living

Remind students that poultry and fish should always be completely cooked through. The terms *rare*, *medium*, and *well done* do not apply to these foods. Poultry and fish must be cooked thoroughly to kill the bacteria that may be present in the foods. To test the doneness of fish, pierce with a cooking fork. The fish should flake easily with a fork. To check the doneness of chicken, check for tenderness with a fork. Also, when the chicken is pierced, the juice should be clear.

L2 Finding Examples

Bring several kinds of dry beans to school. Have students look for recipes that use these ingredients. For example, they might find a recipe for a three-bean salad. Ask them to bring the recipes to class. Discuss the cooking methods described in the recipes.

L2 Discussing

Explain to students the following tips and uses for beans. They can be added to soups and casseroles. Cooking in a covered pan or dish will result in softer beans. For firmer texture, they should not be covered while cooking. Point out that canned beans have already been cooked. They only need to be heated or added to recipes. For fast cooking, canned beans may be poured into a microwave-safe dish and heated in the microwave.

COOPERATIVE LEARNING

Making Posters Have students work in small groups to brainstorm suggestions for meat extenders. Assign each group one of the following meats: ground beef, chicken, sirloin steak. Have groups use cookbooks to research recipes containing various meat extenders for their assigned meat. Then have groups make a poster demonstrating their recipes and including their own suggestions. Display the posters in the classroom.

CHAPTER 14, LESSON 5

L2 Reading

Ask students to read cookbooks to find out how to cook quiches and omelets. Have interested students report their findings to the class. Ask them to explain how the cooking methods for these kinds of egg dishes differ from making fried and scrambled eggs.

TEACHER TALK!
Cutting the Fat

Encourage students who are watching calories, yet enjoy eating eggs, to try poaching eggs in water. This method uses no butter or fat to cook the eggs. In a saucepan, heat water (2–3 inches deep) to boiling. Reduce to simmer. One at a time, break the eggs into a measuring cup and slip them into the water. Cook eggs at a simmer for 3 to 5 minutes. Lift eggs from water with a slotted spatula. Serve on toast.

Have students try some of the meat extender tips suggested in the feature. Ask them to estimate the amount of money they saved by using these tips.

Beans are a good meat substitute. They are inexpensive, are easy to cook with, and come in many varieties. With what foods can beans be combined to make complete proteins?

Meat Extenders

Find a recipe for one or more of the following ways to extend meat. Share your recipe with the class. If possible, try out the recipe on your family.
- Rice combined with meat in a casserole
- Bread crumbs or oatmeal mixed with ground meat to make meat loaf or meatballs
- Pasta combined with fish or chicken to make a cold salad

418   CHAPTER 14: LET'S COOK

You can, however, make beans a complete protein by combining them with other ingredients, such as grain products or nuts. Examples of nutritious, high-protein combinations include

- rice and beans in Mexican meals.
- peanut butter on bread (peanuts are actually a kind of legume, not a nut).
- kidney beans on a corn tortilla.

Cooking Eggs

What is your favorite way to cook eggs? No matter how you like them, there are two basic rules to follow.

- Keep the temperature low so that the eggs don't get tough.
- Cook eggs thoroughly so that the whites and yolks are firm. Harmful bacteria in raw or undercooked eggs can make you sick.

 **HOME AND COMMUNITY CONNECTION**

Egg Varieties Have students look at menus of local restaurants that serve breakfast. Ask them to read the menus for their egg dishes. Have them report to the class about some of the unusual combinations of food served with eggs. For example, students might describe the ingredients in eggs Benedict, eggs Florentine, or a Denver omelet.

When you cook eggs in the shell, cover the eggs with cold water and gradually bring the water to a boil. Let the eggs stand in the hot water, covered, after they have reached the boiling point. **Hard-cooked eggs** are *eggs that are left in hot water, covered, for 15 to 18 minutes.* That allows both the whites and the yolks to become hard. After cooking, immediately run cold water over the eggs to stop the cooking process.

Fried eggs are usually cooked in fat—butter, margarine, or oil. To fry an egg, crack the shell gently, and slip the white and the unbroken yolk into a greased frying pan. Eggs can also be cooked without fat in a nonstick pan.

To make scrambled eggs, beat the whites and yolks together. Then pour the eggs into a little hot fat in a frying pan, or use a nonstick pan or spray. Cook eggs slowly over low heat, stirring them gently and frequently so that they cook evenly. You can also make scrambled eggs in a microwave oven.

Eggs can also be used in more elaborate dishes, such as quiches and omelets. A quiche is a main-dish pie filled with eggs, cream, cheese, and such other ingredients as ham, spinach, and mushrooms. An omelet is a well-beaten egg that is first cooked in a frying pan without stirring. Then it is topped with other ingredients—such as mushrooms, peppers, and cheese—and folded over. Quiches and omelets are convenient because they can be filled with almost anything you might have on hand.

Although you may think of eggs as a breakfast dish, there are many ways to prepare them for dinner. What fillings do you like in an omelet?

Stretching Meat

How can you make your grocery dollars stretch farther when planning main dishes made with meat? The answer is to use meat extenders. **Meat extenders** are *foods added to meat to make a small amount of meat go farther.* Dry beans, nuts, and grain products are meat extenders. For example, by adding rice and beans to a chicken dish, you can double the number of servings. A small amount of ground beef will feed more people if you combine it with pasta, tomato sauce, and cheese.

LESSON FIVE: MEAT, POULTRY, FISH, DRY BEANS, EGGS, AND NUTS

CHAPTER 14, LESSON 5

L2 Activity and Project Card
Allow time for students to complete Activity and Project Card 27, "Create a Cookbook," in the TCR.

L2 Activity and Project Card
Allow time for students to complete Activity and Project Card 28, "Critic's Corner," in the TCR.

L1 Student Workbook
Assign Activity 106 in the Student Workbook.

ASSESS

Evaluating the Lesson
Assign Reviewing Terms and Facts and Thinking Critically on page 420 to review the lesson; then assign the Lesson 5 Quiz in the TCR.

Reteaching
- Ask students to write six main dishes they could prepare for dinner for their family. Students should use the foods listed in the Lesson 5 title.
- Have students complete Reteaching Activity 14 in the TCR.
- Assign Concept Map 22 in the TCR.

COOPERATIVE LEARNING

Bean Sprouts Have students grow their own sprouts from dry beans or from seeds. Supply students with soy beans, mung beans, pumpkin, alfalfa, sunflower, or sesame seeds; a glass jar (7 to 8 times the volume of the seeds); a piece of cheesecloth to cover the jar; and a piece of string. Have students wash the seeds and place them in the bottom of the jar. Cover the seeds with warm water. Tie the cheesecloth over the mouth of the jar. Put jar in warm place overnight. The next day, strain off water. Then dampen seeds with more warm water. Put jar in a warm spot on windowsill. Repeat this every day until the seeds have sprouted at least 2 inches. Store sprouts in a plastic bag in the refrigerator. Use in sandwiches or salads.

CHAPTER 14, LESSON 5

Answers to Lesson 5 Review

1. Any five: Dry-heat: roasting and baking, microwave cooking, broiling; moist-heat: stewing, braising, frying, deep-fat frying. Descriptions will vary but should basically include information in Figure 14.3 on page 415.
2. They are high in protein, vitamins, and minerals, but low in cost.
3. Soft-cooked eggs are simmered for 4 to 6 minutes. Hard-cooked eggs are simmered for 15 to 20 minutes.
4. Foods added to meat to make a small amount of meat go further. Possible example: rice and beans with chicken.
5. Moist-heat cooking involves cooking with liquids, whereas dry-heat cooking is cooking without liquids. Tougher cuts of meat and poultry are best for moist-heat cooking. Tender cuts of meat and poultry are best for dry-heat cooking.
6. Pork chops—dry heat; meatballs—dry heat; stew meat—moist heat; flounder—dry heat.
7. Meat substitutes are used instead of meat, poultry, or fish. Meat extenders are foods added to meat to make a small amount of meat go further.
8. Students list the main dishes they ate for a week. They note the cooking method, cut of meat or meat substitute, and whether meat extenders were used.

Enrichment

Have students write an article for the food section of the local newspaper on ways to include low-cost protein in their diet.

CLOSE

Write the word *protein* on the board. Have students name as many protein foods as they can think of beginning with each letter of *protein*.

420

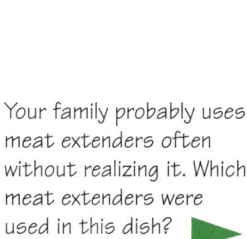

Your family probably uses meat extenders often without realizing it. Which meat extenders were used in this dish?

LESSON FIVE Review

Using complete sentences, answer the following questions on a separate sheet of paper.

Reviewing Terms and Facts

1. Identify Name five moist-heat or dry-heat methods of cooking. Describe two of them.
2. Explain Why are beans and eggs good alternatives to meats as main dishes?
3. Recall What are the two basic rules to follow when you prepare eggs?
4. Vocabulary Define the term *meat extender*. Give an example of a main dish that includes meat extenders.

Thinking Critically

5. Contrast What are the differences between cooking with moist heat and cooking with dry heat? Which types of meats are best for each? Why?
6. Recommend Describe the method you would use to cook each of the following foods: pork chops, meatballs, stew meat, flounder.
7. Explain What is the difference between a meat substitute and a meat extender?

Applying Concepts

8. List the main dishes you ate this week. Next to each item, note which cooking method was used, which cut of meat was used, or if meat substitutes or meat extenders were used.

420 CHAPTER 14: LET'S COOK

MORE ABOUT • • •

Eggs The Department of Agriculture classifies eggs as Grade AA, A, and B. They determine the grades of eggs based on the condition of the shell, yolk, and white. The yolk of the egg is a good source of vitamins A and D. The white of the egg is a good source of most of the B vitamins.

Chapter 14 Activities

FRIENDS & FAMILY

PERSONALIZED RECIPES
Some people name recipes after family members or friends. For example, a recipe might be called "Aunt Helen's Chicken Soup," or "Grandma's Spice Bars." Personalized recipes not only tell you how to cook something good to eat but also remind you of special people in your life.

TRY THIS!
Think of an entrée, salad, soup, sandwich, or dessert that could be named for you. Write the recipe on a card, including your name, and give it to a friend.

A Global View

TROPICAL FRUIT BASKET
People who live in the United States are familiar with bananas, pineapples, and coconuts. Until recently, other tropical fruits—including carambolas, pomelos, kiwi fruit, mangoes, papayas, and passion fruit—were less familiar to many Americans.

TRY THIS!
Find out more about one tropical fruit that is new to you. In what countries is the fruit grown? What does it look like? Share your findings with the class.

TECHNOLOGY

Grocery Shopping by Computer
Years ago, many people shopped for groceries from home by making a shopping list and telephoning the store. Store employees filled the order and delivered it.

Home shopping for groceries is making a comeback—this time via computers and modems. The only charge customers pay is for home delivery.

Try This!
What are the advantages and disadvantages of shopping for groceries by computer? Compare your answers with those of your classmates.

TECHNOLOGY CONNECTION

GENETICALLY ENGINEERED FOOD
Imagine eating bananas that stay yellow for weeks or grain with more protein. Genetic engineering is making these foods a reality. In 1994 scientists identified the gene in tomatoes that promotes rotting, copied it, and put it back in—but backward. As a result, "Flavr Savr" tomatoes became the first genetically altered food.

 **Follow Up**

1. How might genetically engineered fruits and vegetables that stay fresh longer affect the job of a produce manager in a supermarket?

2. Learn more about genetically engineered food. Then have a class debate on its pros and cons.

3. Find out how genetic engineering is different from traditional animal or plant crossbreeding. Write a brief explanation.

Teaching the TECHNOLOGY CONNECTION
Ask students to make a flow chart showing the major steps involved in genetically engineering food. Ask students to share their flow charts with the class.

 **Answers to Follow-Up**
1. Answers will vary. Students may indicate that a produce manager's job will be more complicated, since genetically engineered foods will add to the number of items in the produce department.
2. Answers will vary. Students debate the pros and cons of genetically engineering foods.
3. Answers will vary. Students compare genetic engineering and traditional crossbreeding.

CHAPTER 14
Activities

FRIENDS & FAMILY
Encourage students to review their recipe files at home to find foods that may have been named for their own family members. Students may choose a food because they have a special way of preparing it, or they may choose a food they love to eat. Students may wish to invent special recipes for this exercise.

A Global View
Explain to students that the fruits they read about come from tropical regions of the world, such as Central America and islands in the South Pacific. They are delicious and rich in vitamins. Encourage students to try them plain or in salads, desserts, and main dishes.

TECHNOLOGY
Tell students that a store can create a catalog of its inventory on computers which customers can then access through their home computers. Experts estimate that by the year 2005, at least 10 percent of all groceries will be ordered by computer and delivered to homes. Ask students: Do you think your family would like to shop this way? Why or why not?

CHAPTER 14 REVIEW

Checking Comprehension

Use the Chapter Summary and the Chapter 14 Review to help students go over the most important ideas in Chapter 14.

Answers to Words to Know

1. Fresh fruits and vegetables.
2. A combination of ingredients cooked and served in a baking dish.
3. The main ingredient is flour.
4. A food made from flour and water and formed into shapes.
5. Any three: milk, cream, yogurt, cheese, custards, puddings, ice cream, ice milk, sherbet.
6. A meat extender is put in a meat dish *in addition to* meat. A meat substitute is a protein that is used in a main dish *instead of* meat.

Answers to Review Questions

1. There is no change in color, flavor, or texture, and fewer nutrients are lost.
2. Any four: steaming—place in steamer over simmering water in a covered pan; simmering—cook in small amount of liquid, just below the boiling point; baking—cook in the oven; frying—cook in fat; stir-frying—cook quickly in a small amount of oil; microwave cooking—place in appropriate container and cover while cooking in oven.
3. Creamy soups are made with flour. Broth is the liquid left when meat, poultry, fish, or vegetables are cooked in water.
4. A variety of sandwich fillings can help fulfill nutritional requirements.

Chapter Summary

- Fruits are a nutritious addition to any meal. They are available fresh, frozen, canned, dried, or as juices.
- Fruits should be served fresh or cooked carefully to retain vitamins A, B, C, D, and E and potassium.
- Vegetables can be served as appetizers, salads, or part of soups and main dishes.
- A salad is a food or a combination of foods served cold, usually with a dressing.
- Soups are nutritious because they can be made with ingredients from any or all of the five food groups.
- Quick breads and yeast breads complement any meal and contain fiber and nutrients. Baking powder and baking soda cause quick-bread dough to rise quickly while baking. Yeast breads take longer to prepare than quick breads.
- Rice and pasta are high-energy grain products that must be cooked.
- Drinking milk or beverages made with milk, cooking with milk, eating yogurt, and adding cheeses to foods are some ways to include dairy foods in your diet.
- Meat, poultry, and fish are usually cooked with moist heat or dry heat and are often served as main dishes.
- Meat substitutes, such as beans and eggs, can serve as main dishes.
- Meat extenders make a small amount of meat go farther and help stretch your grocery dollars.

 Words to Know

Using complete sentences, answer the following questions on a separate sheet of paper.

1. What would you find in the *produce* section of the supermarket?
2. What is a *casserole*?
3. What is the main ingredient in bread *dough*?
4. What is *pasta*?
5. Name three *dairy foods*.
6. Explain the difference between a *meat extender* and a meat substitute.

 Review Questions

Using complete sentences, answer the following questions on a separate sheet of paper.

1. Why is it important to cook fruits properly?
2. List four ways to cook vegetables, and briefly describe each one.
3. What is the difference between a creamy soup and broth?
4. Explain how sandwiches can be nutritious.
5. Give three tips for cooking with cheese.
6. Give four examples of desserts made with dairy foods.

EXTRA CREDIT PROJECT

School-to-Work Many career opportunities in the food industry exist in public schools. Have students contact the school cafeteria supervisor or the district office and inquire about job titles that come under the heading of foods, food preparation, diet, nutrition, health, or other related fields. Students may then make a listing of these job titles and research job descriptions for each of these positions. Have them write a short description for each of the jobs they identify, and place these in a book or file for class reference.

CHAPTER 14 REVIEW

7. How would you determine the appropriate cooking method for a particular cut of meat?
8. What is the difference between stir-frying and deep-fat frying?

Thinking Critically

Using complete sentences, answer the following questions on a separate sheet of paper.

1. **Interpret** Why is fresh fruit more nutritious than processed fruit?
2. **Analyze** Why do you think that the cooking directions for frozen vegetables call for only ¼ to ½ cup of water?
3. **Apply** The package directions for quick bread said to mix the dough for two minutes. Jenna thought that she would do an extra-good job and mix the dough for five minutes. When she took the bread out of the oven, it was flat and heavy. Why didn't the bread rise?
4. **Explain** Why would plain yogurt with fresh raspberries be more nutritious than raspberry yogurt?

Cooperative Learning

1. Divide into five groups, each group choosing one of the five food groups. Brainstorm ways to encourage teens to eat nutritious foods from your group. Share your ideas with the class.
2. In groups of four or five, choose a single food, such as eggs, potatoes, or hamburger. Each student in the group should find one low-fat recipe containing that food. Compare the preparation steps and cooking methods used in the recipes.

 Family & Community

1. Encourage your family to try a new fruit or vegetable. Make a list of suggestions, and be sure that you know where to buy the fruit or vegetable. Volunteer to try out a recipe using the family's selection.
2. Ask friends and neighbors about cooking methods, special foods, and recipes from their cultural heritage. Share what you learn with the class, and discuss similarities in cooking traditions. Your class might sponsor an ethnic cooking fair.

Building A Portfolio

1. Compile all the techniques you have learned for cooking various foods into a *How to Cook...*cookbook. For example, include directions for cooking pasta, rice, and vegetables. Keep the cookbook in your portfolio for reference.
2. Visit food stores in your neighborhood, and look for "point-of-purchase" information. This is information provided at the particular place in the store where you would purchase a specific food. You might find directions for cooking various cuts of meat in the meat department or recipes for using cheese in the dairy department. Compare your findings with the information in this chapter. Add your point-of-purchase information to your portfolio.

CHAPTER 14 REVIEW 423

CHAPTER 14 REVIEW

5. Use low to medium heat, and avoid overcooking; grate or shred hard cheeses before adding them to other ingredients, which helps prevent overcooking; add cheese to sauces or casseroles at the end of the cooking time so that the cheese won't become overcooked.
6. Custard, pudding, ice cream, frozen yogurt.
7. Less expensive, tougher cuts of meat are best cooked with moist heat. Tender cuts of meat should be cooked with dry heat.
8. Food that is stir-fried is cooked quickly in a small amount of fat at a high temperature. Food that is deep-fat fried is cooked in a large amount of hot, but not too-hot, oil. Deep-fat fried food is usually coated with a batter before deep-fat frying.

Evaluate

Use the Chapter 14 Test in the TCR, or construct your own test using the Testmaker Software.

CLOSE

Have students apply their knowledge of the chapter's content by completing one of the alternative assessment activities listed under Family and Community or Building a Portfolio.

Answers to Thinking Critically

1. Most processed foods lose nutrients.
2. A smaller amount of water used in cooking vegetables means that fewer nutrients are lost.
3. Answers will vary. Students should state that too much mixing prevents air bubbles from forming. Air bubbles cause quick breads to be light and fluffy.
4. Answers will vary. Students may note that the raspberries in raspberry yogurt have been processed and therefore have lost some of their nutrients.

UNIT 5
Clothing and Textiles

Unit Overview

In Unit 5 students learn how personal grooming and proper clothes selection can help them feel good about themselves. Students also learn about developing a wardrobe and about basic sewing skills.

Chapter 15 describes how grooming, clothing choices, and clothing care can be used to create a positive first impression. Chapter 16 tells students how to select clothing based on quality construction and fit. Chapter 17 demonstrates the proper use of small and large sewing equipment. The chapter also explains how to use sewing skills to construct a sewing project. Chapter 18 introduces students to the skills needed to lay out, mark, cut, and sew a sewing project. The chapter also presents sewing skills students can use to make minor repairs and alterations on their clothes.

Introducing the Unit

- **Parent Letters** As you begin the study of this unit, you may wish to send home copies of the Parent Letter and Activities found in the *Linking Home, School, and Community* booklet in the TCR.
- **Using Visuals** As students examine the photograph on these pages, ask them how the picture shows that these teens are feeling good about themselves.
- **Using the Color Transparency** Present Transparency 62, "What Does It Take to Look Good?" in the TCR. As they view the transparency, have students consider what it means to look and to feel good.

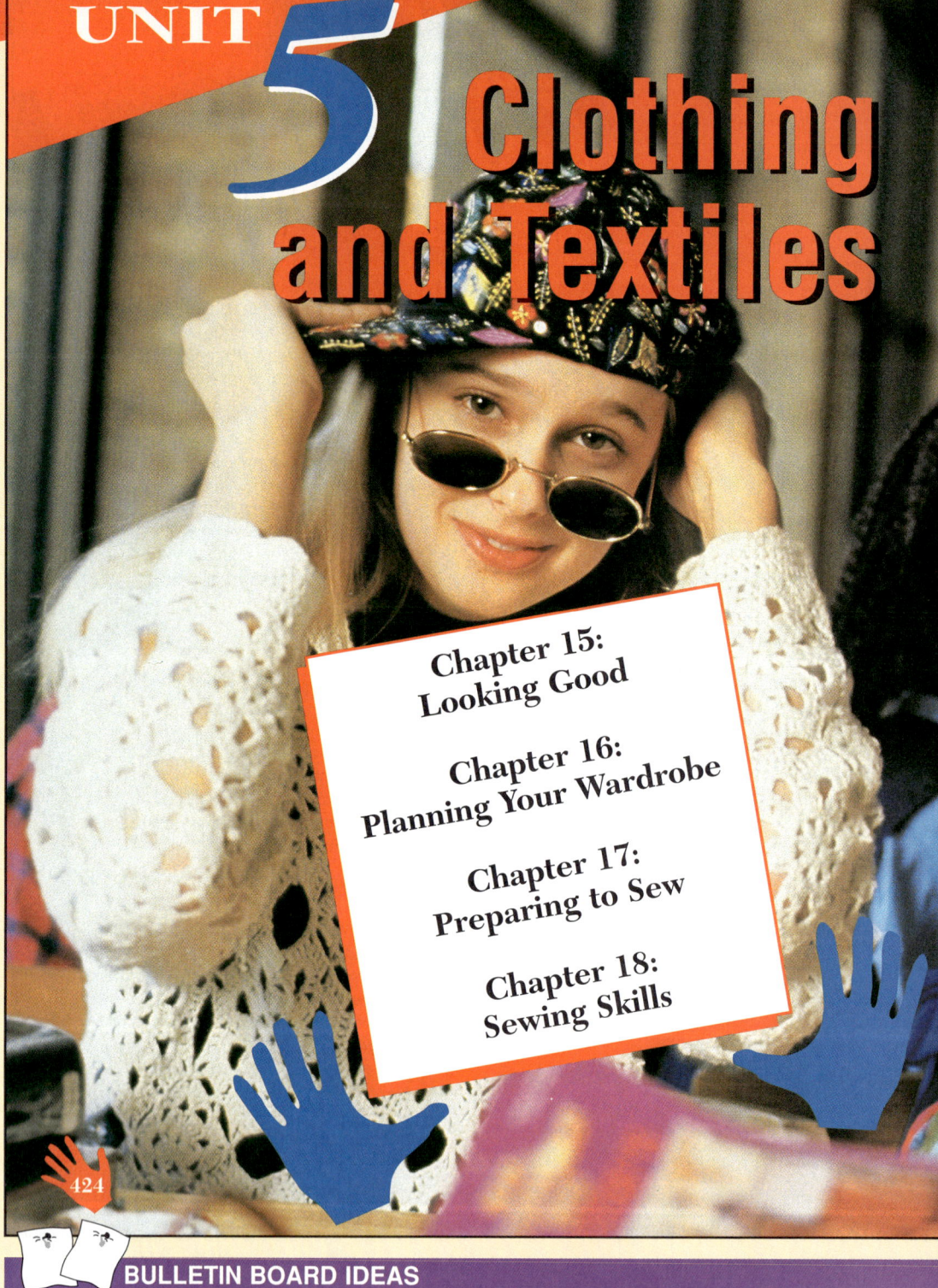

UNIT 5
Clothing and Textiles

Chapter 15:
Looking Good

Chapter 16:
Planning Your Wardrobe

Chapter 17:
Preparing to Sew

Chapter 18:
Sewing Skills

BULLETIN BOARD IDEAS

A Case of Wardrobe Needs Cut out shapes to represent suitcases and label each with one of the following: *seasons, personal activities, lifestyles,* and *where you live.* Mount suitcase shapes on the bulletin board. Clip pictures from magazines to illustrate each concept. Place the pictures in the appropriate suitcase as indicated: *seasons*—snowman, sun, leaves, flowers; *personal activities*—football, bike, trumpet, television; *lifestyles*—radio, dollar sign, graduation hat, house; *where you live*—igloo, mountains, beach, desert.

BULLETIN BOARD IDEAS

The Keys to Successful Sewing Cut out eight key shapes from an assortment of colorful construction paper. On each key print one of the following sewing guidelines: preshrink fabric; check grain; use layout for your pattern view, size, and fabric width; staystitch; press as you go along; follow pattern guide sheet. Arrange keys on the bulletin board.

Dress for the Job Select pictures of appropriate clothing for different types of jobs, such as a fast-food server, clothing store sales clerk, construction worker, auto mechanic, and office worker. Arrange pictures on the bulletin board under the heading "Dress for the Job."

UNIT PROJECTS 5

Encourage students to complete one or two Hands-on Projects for this unit. These can be found in the Teacher's Classroom Resources.
- Hands-on Projects 11, 12, 13, and 14 give directions for students to create simple yet practical sewing items for their own use or to share with a friend or family member.

Unit Closure

- Allow class time at the end of this unit to reinforce students' understanding of the material by playing Hands-on Game 5, "Clothing and Textile Pursuit," found in the TCR.
- Create your own Unit Test using the Testmaker Software to evaluate students' comprehension.

Promoting Family & Consumer Sciences

Community Form partnerships by involving the local community. Explore problems and ask for tips about various subjects covered in the lessons from experts in the field. Arrange with businesses for students to tour local companies and meet with members of community organizations in order to extend the content you are teaching in the classroom.

Planning Guide
Chapter 15 Looking Good

LESSON 1	Pages	FEATURES	CLASSROOM RESOURCES
Personal Health and Grooming	428–433	*Tips for Living:* Taking Care of Your Eyes *Try This:* Protective Wear	Activity and Project Card 29, "A Look at Grooming Products" Concept Map 23 Cooperative Learning 29 Peer Pressure and Decision Making 29 Lesson 1 Quiz Transparency 63, "The Sun's Harmful Rays" Student Workbook Activity 107
LESSON 2 **Making Clothing Decisions**	434–439	*Skills in Action:* Dressing Appropriately	Cooperative Learning 30 Enrichment 17 Lesson 2 Quiz Peer Pressure and Decision Making 30 Student Workbook Activities 108, 109
LESSON 3 **Clothing Design**	440–446	*Skills in Action:* The Right Lines for You *Tips for Living:* Shaping Up	Activity and Project Card 30, "Clothing Collage" Concept Map 24 Cross Curriculum 17 Lesson 3 Quiz Transparency 64, "Using the Color Wheel" Transparency 65, "Color Schemes" Student Workbook Activities 110, 111

CHAPTER 15 RESOURCES
- Chapter 15 Test
- Reteaching 15
- Study Guide 15, *Reteaching*
- Testmaker Software

UNIT 5 RESOURCES
- Transparency 62, "What Does It Take to Look Good?"
- Hands-on Projects 11, 12, 13, 14
- Hands-on Game 5

Performance Assessment Activity

Have students work in small groups to create a pamphlet titled "Looking Good." Pamphlets should contain answers to the following questions: What is the best way to keep your skin, hair, hands, feet, nails, and teeth healthy? Why should you use sunscreen? What factors influence the type of clothes people wear? How can clothing affect the impression you make? How can color, line, and texture be combined when selecting clothes? Suggest to students that each question constitute one section of their pamphlets. Encourage them to use pictures from magazines to illustrate their pamphlets.

School-to-Work

Ask students to research jobs that involve helping people look good. Jobs might include manicurist, hair stylist, dermatologist, dentist, dental hygienist, orthodontist, color consultant, clothing designer, or clothing sales clerk. Have students find out what personal and educational qualifications are needed for each job. Ask students to share with classmates what they find out about each job.

Family & Community

Have students work in small groups to plan a puppet show on good grooming habits that they can present to a group of young children. Some groups may want to present their puppet shows to elementary-school children, while others might choose a day-care center or a Cub Scout or Brownie troop. Remind students to gear their presentation to the age group they have chosen.

Resources for the Teacher

Daria, Irene. *The Fashion Cycle: A Behind the Scenes Look at a Year with Bill Blass, Liz Claiborne, Donna Karan, Arnold Scaasi, and Adrienne Vittadini.* New York: Simon and Schuster, 1990.

Goldsmith, Olivia. *Simple Isn't Easy: How to Find Your Personal Style and Look Fantastic Every Day!* New York: HarperPaperbacks, 1995.

Readings for the Student

Baker, Wendy. *Fashion.* New York: Thomson Learning, 1994.

Silverstein, A., et al. *Overcoming Acne: The How and Why of Healthy Skin Care.* New York: Morrow Junior Books, 1990.

Smith, Sandra Lee. *Great Grooming for Girls.* New York: Rosen Publishing Group, 1993.

Multimedia Resources

Color Confidence! with Jinny Beyer (Videocassette). Concepts Videos.

Color Me Beautiful (Videocassette). Kartes Video Communications.

Health, Fashion, and Beauty (Videocassette). Sandra Carter Enterprises, distributed by PBS Video.

OUT OF TIME?

If time does not permit thorough teaching of this chapter, you may wish to use:

- Teens Making a Difference, page 427
- Tips for Living, pages 432, 445
- Try This, page 436
- Skills in Action, page 437, 444
- Young Living Activities, page 447
- Chapter Summary, page 448

CHAPTER 15
Looking Good

Chapter Overview

Chapter 15 introduces students to personal health and grooming habits and the principles of clothing design. Emphasis is placed on learning how they can look their best by practicing good health and grooming habits and by combining color, line, and texture in clothing. Students learn how to care for their skin, hands, feet, nails, hair, and teeth. They also discover the factors that influence clothing choices and learn the difference between fad, fashion, and style.

LESSON 1 describes good health and grooming habits.

LESSON 2 explains the difference between fads, fashions, and styles, and describes how clothing affects the impression made on people.

LESSON 3 explains how color, line, and texture affect appearance and describes how to combine design elements in clothing.

Introducing the Chapter

Have students read the lesson titles and look at the photos in the chapter. Then ask students to come up with two questions that they would like to see answered in each lesson. After students have finished the chapter, have them answer the questions.

Chapter Motivator

Show students photographs of people that illustrate a variety of grooming and clothing styles. Ask students what they find attractive and unattractive about each person pictured. Tell students that Chapter 15 discusses factors that can contribute to helping people look good.

CHAPTER 15
Looking Good

LESSON ONE
Personal Health and Grooming

LESSON TWO
Making Clothing Decisions

LESSON THREE
Clothing Design

KEY TO ABILITY LEVELS

Teaching strategies that appear throughout the chapter have been identified by one of three codes to give you an idea of their suitability for students of varying learning styles and abilities.

L1 Level 1 strategies should be within the ability range of all students. Often full class participation is required. Teacher direction is usually needed.

L2 Level 2 strategies are for average to above-average students or for small groups. Some teacher direction is necessary.

L3 Level 3 strategies are designed for students able and willing to work independently. Minimal teacher direction is necessary.

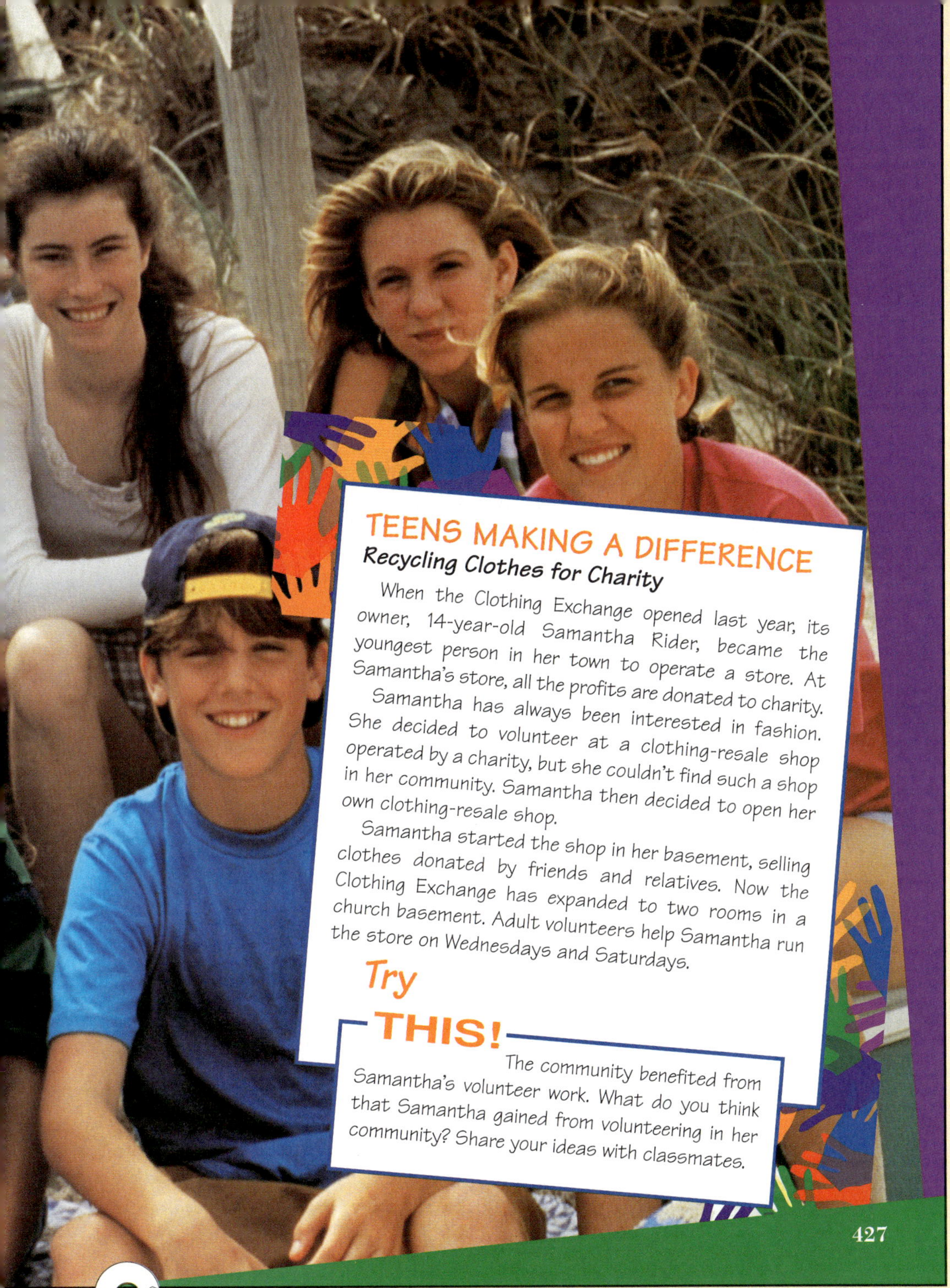

TEENS MAKING A DIFFERENCE
Recycling Clothes for Charity

When the Clothing Exchange opened last year, its owner, 14-year-old Samantha Rider, became the youngest person in her town to operate a store. At Samantha's store, all the profits are donated to charity.

Samantha has always been interested in fashion. She decided to volunteer at a clothing-resale shop operated by a charity, but she couldn't find such a shop in her community. Samantha then decided to open her own clothing-resale shop.

Samantha started the shop in her basement, selling clothes donated by friends and relatives. Now the Clothing Exchange has expanded to two rooms in a church basement. Adult volunteers help Samantha run the store on Wednesdays and Saturdays.

Try THIS!

The community benefited from Samantha's volunteer work. What do you think that Samantha gained from volunteering in her community? Share your ideas with classmates.

TECHNOLOGY IN THE CLASSROOM

Videotapes A variety of subjects are available in videotape format, which can be used to enhance the Family and Consumer Sciences classroom. Topics range from communication and family relationships to hands-on food, clothing, and recipe preparation. Classroom discussion may be held after viewing the video, or teachers may pause at any time to explain or ask questions. Students may view details of skills being taught without the necessity of repeated teacher demonstration. Teachers and districts may compile libraries of videotapes that can be shared, thus offsetting the expense of purchasing several titles for each classroom. Remember that tapes should always be previewed before being shown in the classroom.

CHAPTER 15

TEENS MAKING A DIFFERENCE

Have students read "Teens Making a Difference." Ask students why they think operating a clothing resale store for charity is a good idea. (*Students might mention it is a good way to recycle clothing that might otherwise be thrown out, it provides less-expensive clothing for families who could not afford new clothing, and the profits are donated to charity to help people.*)

Have students respond to the question about what Samantha gained from volunteering in her community. Then ask students to share any experiences they have had doing volunteer work in their community and how the work made them feel.

BLOCK SCHEDULING

The following Teacher Classroom Resources are suggested for use in classrooms with Block Scheduling.
- Activity and Project Card 29, "A Look at Grooming Products"
- Activity and Project Card 30, "Clothing Collage"
- Cooperative Learning 29, "Gear Up for Good Grooming"
- Cooperative Learning 30, "An Outfit for Every Occasion"

LESSON ONE
Personal Health and Grooming

FOCUS

Lesson Objectives
After studying this lesson, students should be able to
- explain how good health and good grooming can help them look and feel their best.
- describe how to care for skin, hands, feet, nails, hair, and teeth.

Motivating Activity
Write the following statement on the chalkboard for students to complete:
When I am at my best, I look _____ and feel _____.

Introducing the Lesson
Call on volunteers to share their responses to the Motivating Activity. Compile a list on the chalkboard of the characteristics of looking and feeling good. Tell students that Lesson 1 discusses ways of helping them look and feel their best.

Introducing *Words to Know*
Ask each student to write a sentence for each word in the Words to Know list. When they have finished, ask them to form small groups and share their sentences with group members. Ask each group to use their sentences to develop a definition for each word. Then have a student from each group share the definitions with the rest of the class. Have students compare their definitions with the ones in the text.

LESSON ONE
Personal Health and Grooming

WORDS TO KNOW
- hygiene
- acne
- dermatologist
- sunscreen
- plaque
- flossing

DISCOVER...
- how good health and good grooming help you look and feel your best.
- how to care for your skin, hands, feet, nails, hair, and teeth.

Bonnie takes care of herself because she knows that when she looks her best, she feels good. Friends often ask her what her secret is—she has such attractive skin, hair, and teeth. She tells them that there's no secret, but that she makes good grooming and healthful habits a part of her everyday routine.

428 CHAPTER 15: LOOKING GOOD

CLASSROOM RESOURCES FOR LESSON 1

Blackline Masters
Activity and Project Card 29, "A Look at Grooming Products"
Concept Map 23
Cooperative Learning 29
Peer Pressure and Decision Making 29
Lesson 1 Quiz

Transparencies
Transparency 63, "The Sun's Harmful Rays"

Student Workbook
Activity 107

The Importance of Good Health

Health affects your appearance in many ways. People who are in good health

- are full of energy.
- maintain a healthy weight.
- have good posture.
- have healthy skin, nails, hair, and teeth.

Eating healthful foods is the first step to good health. You learned in Chapter 10 that your body needs the nutrients in food to stay in good condition. Nutrients protect your body and help it look and feel better too.

Regular exercise not only helps you maintain a healthful weight but also improves your posture, the health of your skin, and your circulation. Rest is also essential to good health. On the average, you need about eight hours of sleep a night. Sleep gives your body a chance to grow and repair skin tissues.

Practicing good posture is another healthful habit to develop. Your posture is the way you hold your body. When you have good posture, you stand or sit erect with your head held high. You can improve your posture by sitting straight in your chair, standing with equal weight on both feet, and walking with your head upright.

Your posture is a reflection of your health and your attitude. Which teen has better posture?

Building Good Grooming Habits

How many magazine and television advertisements have you seen about grooming aids for teens? These ads may lead you to believe that it takes time, money, and certain products to look good. The fact is that you can look your best by following a basic hygiene routine every day. **Hygiene** involves *practices that promote health.*

LESSON ONE: PERSONAL HEALTH AND GROOMING **429**

CHAPTER 15, LESSON 1

TEACH

L1 Making a Collage
Have students use pictures from magazines to make collages that illustrate what it means to be in good health. Display the collages in the classroom or make arrangements to share them with elementary-school classes.

L2 Looking at Magazine Ads
Have students work in small groups to look through magazines for ads that feature grooming and hygiene products. Have them display the ads on a poster board divided into the following columns: Skin Care; Hair Care; Hands, Feet, and Nail Care; and Teeth Care. Have students place the magazine ads in the appropriate columns. Then have students in each group discuss which products they feel are the most important to use. Have a representative share each group's ideas with the class. Then discuss with the class whether it takes a lot of money and time for people to look their best.

DID YOU KNOW

In many magazine and television ads, grooming products are recommended by famous people such as models, actors, or sports figures. According to law, a famous person must actually use a product before he or she can recommend it. Ask students whether they have ever purchased a grooming product because it was endorsed by a famous person. Point out that the law does not require famous people to like the products they endorse.

MORE ABOUT • • •

Acne Contrary to popular belief, acne is not caused by eating chocolate or greasy foods, or by poor hygiene. Sebum, a waxy substance secreted from sebaceous glands within hair follicles, normally lubricates the skin. If the channel leading from the gland to the skin becomes clogged, pimples can begin to develop. Factors believed to contribute to acne are increased levels of male hormones, which stimulate the glands; bacteria on the skin; excessive humidity; some cosmetics; and some drugs such as steroids and antiepilepsy medications. Severe acne can be treated with antibiotics and/or retinoic acid, a derivative of vitamin A. It should not be taken during pregnancy because it can cause birth defects.

CHAPTER 15, LESSON 1

DID YOU KNOW

Contact dermatitis is a skin inflammation caused by physical contact with a substance to which a person is allergic. Symptoms of contact dermatitis include itchy skin, red rashes, flaking or blistering skin, or oozing skin blisters. Some of the most common causes of contact dermatitis include grooming products such as soaps, detergents, perfumes, cosmetics, shaving lotions, and chemicals used in hair dyes.

USING VISUALS

Refer students to Figure 15.1. Have them use the items as a checklist to evaluate how well they take care of their skin. Have students determine for themselves how they might improve the way they care for their skin.

L2 Cooperative Learning

Assign Cooperative Learning Activity 29 in the TCR. Students work in groups to examine good grooming habits in this activity.

L1 Using Transparencies

Present Color Transparency 63, "The Sun's Harmful Rays," in the TCR. Use this overhead visual to reinforce concepts from this lesson.

Your Skin

Many teens are concerned about their skin. During the teen years, the oil glands in your skin begin to work harder. The extra oil can clog pores and cause skin problems. Many teens get **acne,** *a skin condition caused by overly active oil glands.* Acne is usually mild enough to take care of at home. Teens who have more severe acne may need to consult a **dermatologist,** *a doctor who treats skin disorders.*

It is important to keep your skin healthy and protect it from the wind and sun. Use a moisturizer and a **sunscreen,** *a lotion that guards the skin against harmful rays of the sun.* **Figure 15.1** explains how to care for your skin.

To take care of your skin properly, you should know what type of skin you have. The most common types are dry skin, oily skin, and sensitive skin. Which type of skin do you have?

- Amy has dry skin that looks rough and flaky. She may have underactive oil glands, or her diet may lack essential nutrients, including water. Amy needs to be sure to drink

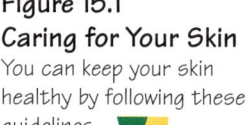

Figure 15.1 Caring for Your Skin
You can keep your skin healthy by following these guidelines.

- Eat a balanced diet.
- Get enough rest and exercise.
- Drink six to eight glasses of water each day.
- Wash your face and neck with mild soap and water at least twice a day.
- Use over-the-counter medications if blemishes are a problem. Do not pick at or squeeze pimples.
- Choose grooming products that will not irritate your skin. Look for products that are labeled "mild" or "hypoallergenic."
- Protect your skin from the sun. Use a sunscreen with a sun protection factor (SPF) of at least 15, and reapply the sunscreen if you go swimming.

430 CHAPTER 15: LOOKING GOOD

MORE ABOUT

Skin The skin is the body's largest organ. Skin has two layers. The outer layer, the epidermis, continuously makes new skin cells to replace old ones. Dead skin cells on the surface are worn off or washed away daily. The inner layer of skin, the dermis, is where blood vessels, nerve endings, hair roots, and oil and sweat glands are found. Ask students to use reference books to locate a diagram of the skin and have them draw and label the parts of the skin.

at least eight glasses of water daily. She should wash with a mild soap and apply a moisturizer afterward.

- Julio has oily skin that is usually shiny and feels greasy. He has overactive oil glands, a common condition during the teen years. Julio should wash frequently and gently to remove excess oil and dirt. After washing, he can apply an astringent to help control the oil.

- Rachel has sensitive skin that develops rough patches and rashes and is easily irritated by weather or by certain ingredients found in grooming products. To find products that won't irritate her skin, she should look for labels that read "mild" or "hypoallergenic," found on cosmetics that have little likelihood of causing an allergic response.

Your Hands, Feet, and Nails

Good hygiene includes care of your hands, feet, and nails. To look their best, your hands, feet, and nails should always be kept clean and neat. Wash hands often using plenty of mild soapsuds to wash away dirt, dead skin, and germs. Feet should be washed every day to prevent foot odor. After washing, be sure to dry your feet thoroughly.

Caring for nails means washing them regularly and giving them special care once a week. To trim and shape them, first clip them with a nail clipper. Then shape and smooth them with a file or emery board. Toenails, which need to be trimmed occasionally, should be cut straight across and kept short.

Why is it important to wash your hands often?

Your Hair

For many teens, hair is a means of self-expression. Regardless of the hairstyle you prefer, your hair is most attractive when it is clean and healthy. To keep it that way, wash and brush it regularly. Brushing your hair helps to distribute the natural oils, keeps hair from becoming dry.

LESSON ONE: PERSONAL HEALTH AND GROOMING   431

MORE ABOUT

Dry Skin The most common cause of itching without any sign of a skin rash is dry skin. Many people suffer from dry skin during winter when indoor air is very dry, but the problem can also occur in excessively humid weather. To combat dry skin, a person should soak in a tub of lukewarm water for fifteen minutes to restore skin moisture, then gently towel dry, and immediately apply all over the body a moisturizing cream or lotion that contains oils.

CHAPTER 15, LESSON 1

L2 Problem Solving

Assign Peer Pressure and Decision Making 29 in the TCR. This activity gives students the opportunity to recognize peer pressure and practice decision-making skills.

L3 Science

Have students research how vaporizers and humidifiers work and what scientific principles are involved. Have them report on how using these appliances can aid skin care.

DID YOU KNOW

Two types of ultraviolet light from the sun have damaging effects on skin. UVB rays are the main cause of sunburn, and UVA rays contribute to wrinkles and premature aging of the skin.

L2 Making Comparisons

Organize the class into small groups to research hair-care products. Have one group analyze the claims made for these products and directions for their use. Have another group check prices for each of the products. Have this group determine the unit price for each and compare the prices in the form of a bar graph. Ask yet another group to check product comparisons made by a consumer product research group and report the information to the class.

L2 Activity and Project Card

Allow time for students to complete Activity and Project Card 29, "A Look at Grooming Products," in the TCR.

CHAPTER 15, LESSON 1

TIPS for living

Ask how many students wear sunglasses. Have them indicate whether their sunglasses are rated for protection against ultraviolet rays. Ask them to research reasons why this is becoming more and more important to their health.

L1 Art

Have students work in small groups to make a mobile illustrating grooming tips. Each mobile should contain tips on hair care, care of teeth and gums, posture, skin care, and hand and foot care. Display completed mobiles in the classroom.

L1 Student Workbook

Assign Activity 107 in the Student Workbook.

ASSESS

Evaluating the Lesson

Assign Reviewing Terms and Facts and Thinking Critically on page 433 to review the lesson; then assign the Lesson 1 Quiz in the TCR.

Reteaching

- Ask students to fold a sheet of paper to form four sections. Label the sections: Skin Care; Hands, Feet, and Nail Care; Hair Care; and Teeth Care. Have students list three grooming tips for each topic in the correct section.
- Have students complete Reteaching Activity 15 in the TCR.
- Assign Concept Map 23 in the TCR.

432

TIPS for living

TAKING CARE OF YOUR EYES

Many people have a hard time imagining a life without eyesight, yet they don't often think about taking care of their eyes. Here are some suggestions.

- Protect your eyes from the sun with a good pair of sunglasses.
- Avoid eyestrain by using plenty of light for close work.
- Prevent eye injuries by wearing eye-safety gear for sports and other dangerous activities.
- Detect and treat vision problems and eye disease by getting regular eye exams—every year if you wear glasses or contact lenses, every other year if you don't wear them.

When you buy shampoo, check the labels to find one that matches your type of hair. Why do you think that this is important?

Choose a shampoo made for your type of hair—normal, dry, or oily. Shampoo your hair gently, using your fingertips (not your fingernails) to work the lather through your hair. Be sure to rinse hair thoroughly. If you use a conditioner after shampooing, follow the directions on the bottle.

The high heat of blow dryers, curling irons, or hot rollers can damage hair. If possible, let your hair dry by itself, or lower the temperature setting on your blow dryer.

Your Teeth

Your teeth affect not only your appearance but also your health. Your teeth help you chew food and shape your mouth and your smile. Taking care of your teeth will help prevent cavities and gum diseases. The best way to avoid these problems is to keep your teeth clean. Teeth start to decay when plaque is left on them too long. **Plaque** (PLAK) is *a soft, sticky film created by the bacteria that live in your mouth.*

Keeping your teeth clean and your gums healthy begins with brushing and flossing regularly. Choose a brush with soft bristles, and use a toothpaste that contains fluoride. To brush, use gentle up-and-down strokes to clean between the teeth and massage the

432 CHAPTER 15: LOOKING GOOD

HOME AND COMMUNITY CONNECTION

Guest Speaker Invite the following people from your community to speak to the class: a dermatologist, a manicurist, a dental hygienist, and an orthodontist. Ask the dermatologist to speak about teenage skin problems and the causes of the problems. Have the manicurist demonstrate nail care and explain the tools needed for it. Ask the dental hygienist to demonstrate proper brushing and flossing of teeth. Ask the orthodontist to discuss proper care of teeth for persons who wear braces. Before the visits, students might compile a list of questions to ask the speakers.

gums. Brush all tooth surfaces and your tongue at least twice a day.

Flossing should be a part of your hygiene routine once a day. **Flossing** means *pulling dental floss back and forth between your teeth at the gum line to remove food particles.* Ask your dentist or dental hygienist to show you the proper technique.

Good dental care also includes eating nutritious foods and avoiding sweet and sticky foods. Regular dental checkups are also important.

Your Appearance and Grooming

Good grooming contributes to your overall appearance and helps you feel positively about yourself. You don't have to spend a lot of time or money on personal hygiene products. All you need to do is follow a few daily routines to get the benefits of good grooming and hygiene.

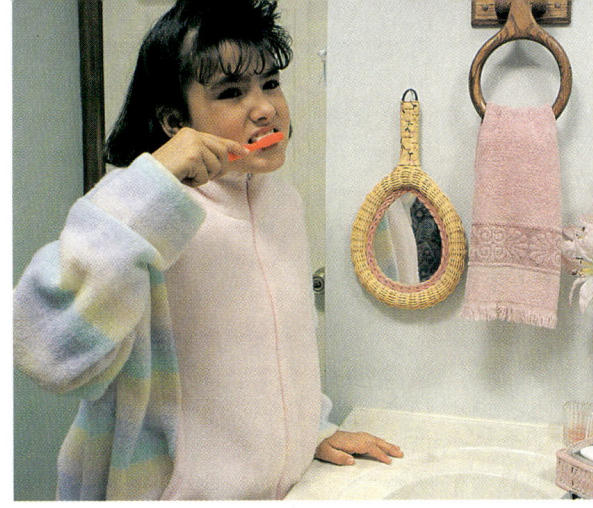

Brushing regularly will help you keep your teeth and gums healthy. What else should you do to take care of your teeth?

LESSON ONE Review

Using complete sentences, answer the following questions on a separate sheet of paper.

Reviewing Terms and Facts

1. **List** What are the four signs of good health?
2. **Vocabulary** What causes *acne*?
3. **Identify** Name three common skin types.
4. **Recall** How can you keep your teeth clean and healthy?

Thinking Critically

5. **Analyze** Why do you think that advertisers try to make people believe they need certain grooming products to look and feel good?
6. **Suggest** Why do you think that hairstyles are important to teens?
7. **Apply** Make a list of the basic grooming products you should have on hand to complete your hygiene routine every day.

Applying Concepts

8. Working in groups, evaluate three different brands of the same product. Compare labels and prices. Determine which is the best buy, and report your findings to the class.

LESSON ONE: PERSONAL HEALTH AND GROOMING   433

COOPERATIVE LEARNING

Making a Video Have students work in small groups to make a videotape that demonstrates the proper way to brush and floss teeth. The videotapes should be appropriate for younger students. Students should be sure to explain why proper care of teeth is important. View the videotapes and have students present their tapes to the class. Arrange to show the videotapes to younger grades in the local elementary school.

CHAPTER 15, LESSON 1

Answers to Lesson 1 Review

1. The four signs of good health are that a person is full of energy, maintains a healthy weight, has good posture, and has healthy skin, nails, hair, and teeth.
2. Acne is a skin condition caused by overly active oil glands.
3. Three common skin types are dry skin, oily skin, and sensitive skin.
4. To keep teeth clean and healthy, you should brush twice a day with a fluoride toothpaste and floss once a day. Regular dental checkups are also necessary.
5. Advertisers are trying to sell products. The more people they convince to buy their products, the more money they make.
6. Choosing how to wear their hair gives teens a chance to express themselves. Teens might also want to fit in with the styles worn by their peers.
7. Specific lists will vary, but should include sunscreen, toothpaste, dental floss, soap, hairbrush, and shampoo, and may include hair conditioner, body lotions, deodorant, blow dryer, nail clipper, emery board, and others.
8. Reports will vary but students should determine the best buy.

Enrichment

Have each student keep a record of money spent on the family's personal-care products for one week. Students might analyze the spending for various categories such as hair-care products; hand, foot, and nail products; and teeth products.

CLOSE

Have students make a weekly personal-grooming chart. Have them include all grooming habits they feel are necessary.

433

LESSON TWO
Making Clothing Decisions

FOCUS

Lesson Objectives
After studying this lesson, students should be able to
- identify the factors that influence the types of clothing people wear.
- explain the differences between styles, fashions, and fads.
- describe how people's clothing affects the impression they make on others.

Motivating Activity
Show students a variety of pictures of people dressed in various outfits, such as a bathing suit, shorts and T-shirt, jeans, dress, suit, cocktail dress, and tuxedo. Ask students to write situations in which each type of clothing would be considered appropriate attire.

Introducing the Lesson
Have students share their responses to the Motivating Activity. Ask them to give reasons for their answers. Then ask them how they would decide what to wear if they were invited to a party. Discuss how their choice of clothing might differ depending on the season, the location of the party, and the other people attending the party.

Introducing *Words to Know*
Have students write the definition of each Word to Know on charts. Then, next to each word and its definition, ask students to draw or paste pictures that relate to the meaning of the word.

LESSON TWO
Making Clothing Decisions

 **WORDS TO KNOW**
status
logos
modesty
style
fashions
fads
classic styles

DISCOVER...
- the factors that influence your clothing choices.
- the different meanings of styles, fashions, and fads.
- how clothing affects the impression you make on other people.

Danielle and Brianna are sisters, but you would never know it by the clothes they wear. Danielle likes clothing in bold, flashy colors. She wears the same styles that her friends wear. Brianna likes clothes that are comfortable. She wears jeans and T-shirts most of the time. She is not influenced by what other people wear. Why does each sister choose the type of clothing she does? What made you choose the clothes you

434 CHAPTER 15: LOOKING GOOD

CLASSROOM RESOURCES FOR LESSON 2

 Blackline Masters
Cooperative Learning 30
Enrichment 17
Lesson 2 Quiz
Peer Pressure and Decision Making 30

 **Student Workbook**
Activities 108, 109

are wearing now? Do you like your clothing choices? What would you change if you could?

The Purpose of Clothing

People first wore clothing to protect themselves against the wind, snow, rain, cold, and heat. That first clothing was made from animal skins. As time went on, people decorated their clothes with stains and powders made from natural materials, such as earth and clay. Seeds, stones, and shell beads were sometimes added to clothing to show a person's **status,** or *level of importance*.

Today, clothing choices are much more varied than they used to be, but the purpose of clothing has not changed. Learning why you wear the clothes you do and what influences your clothing decisions will help you choose the clothes that are best for you. **Figure 15.2** describes the reasons why people select specific types of outfits.

Figure 15.2 Reasons for Clothing Choices
People wear clothes for many reasons. What other reasons can you think of?

Protection. Clothing keeps you comfortable and protects you from the weather and climate.

Status. Some garments are worn to reflect a person's status. Jeans with designer labels and sneakers with company **logos,** or *identification symbols,* can give a person a feeling of importance.

Decoration. Clothes, such as caps and vests, are used as decoration.

Modesty. The way you wear your clothes and the type of clothing you wear suggests your personal sense of **modesty,** or *what people feel is the proper way for clothing to cover the body.*

Identification. Clothes tell as much about you as what you say. For example, uniforms may signify that you work at a particular restaurant, play in a school band, or are part of an athletic team.

LESSON TWO: MAKING CLOTHING DECISIONS 435

CHAPTER 15, LESSON 2

TEACH

DID YOU KNOW

Ancient Minoans on the island of Crete wore clothing that many students would not feel comfortable with. Women wore long, colorful, bell-shaped skirts with tiers and flounces and short-sleeved, narrow-waisted bodices. Men's clothing was colorful, but brief: loincloths, sandals, and small, feathered hats.

L2 Clothing Collages

Ask students to work in small groups to make a poster using magazine pictures that illustrate all the reasons for wearing clothes.

USING VISUALS

As you discuss the reasons for wearing clothes presented in Figure 15.2, ask students to describe examples from their own clothing that correspond to each reason. Ask each student to write down his or her favorite outfit, then analyze which reasons for wearing clothes fit that particular outfit.

MEETING STUDENT DIVERSITY

Cultural Diversity Point out to students that styles and modesty standards of clothing vary among different people, cultures, and societies. For example, kilts are often worn by men in the British Isles, and the plaid in Scottish kilts varies from clan to clan. The plain, handmade clothing worn by many Amish people reflects their belief in a simple lifestyle. In Afghanistan, many women wear traditional garments called chadri which cover them from head to ankle. Suggest that students look in travel or geographic magazines to find photographs that show other examples of traditional styles and modesty standards from other cultures.

435

CHAPTER 15, LESSON 2

If possible, show students a lab apron or lab coat and safety goggles used in science classes and discuss how these articles are designed for protection during experiments. Allow students to share their examples of protective clothing or gear with classmates.

L2 Evaluating
Ask students to work in small groups to find examples of magazine pictures that illustrate styles, fashions, and fads in clothing. Have groups share their pictures with the class and explain why they placed the pictures in the different categories.

L1 History
Have students research the fashions of different historical eras and make labeled drawings of the fashionable clothing of the day. Display the drawings in the classroom.

L2 Cooperative Learning
Assign Cooperative Learning Activity 30 in the TCR. Students work in groups to design outfits for various occasions in this activity.

Clothing and other gear can protect you not only from the weather but also from injury. For example, cyclists wear helmets to protect their heads, and firefighters wear insulated suits that are flameproof to protect themselves from burns.

With a group of classmates, brainstorm other examples of clothing or gear that helps protect people from injury.

Making Clothing Decisions

When Danielle and Brianna buy clothes, they choose different styles. A **style** is *the design of a garment.* For example, a *bomber* jacket, a *straight* skirt, and *baggy* pants are all styles.

Not all styles of clothing are considered fashions. **Fashions** are *styles of clothing that are accepted as popular at a particular time.* Fashions change frequently. Some practical clothing, such as jeans, are popular season after season. Only a few changes in the style are made to give them a fresh, new look. Fashions may include changes in skirt length, jacket length, collar shape, or width of pant legs. At any one time, however, you can find some new fashions coming in, some going out, and other styles that continue to remain popular.

Some fashions become popular very quickly but then lose their appeal. *Fashions that are very popular for a short time* are called **fads.** Fad clothing may be fun to wear, especially if your friends are wearing it. Because a fad does not last very long, however, it is not a good idea to spend a lot of money on fad items. Instead, you can choose **classic styles,** which are *styles that remain in fashion for a long time.* Classics include a blazer, crew neck shirt, and cardigan sweater. To update your look, you can buy trendy accessories, such as belts, hats, and jewelry.

The Right Clothes for the Occasion

The occasion or activity for which you are dressing helps to determine your clothing choices. For instance, you would wear different clothes to a basketball game than to a formal dance. For some events, such as having lunch with friends at the mall or going to a movie, casual clothing is acceptable. Other occasions, such as going to a fancy restaurant or a wedding, require dressier clothes.

Clothing—The Message It Sends

Even clothing that is comfortable or casual tells others something about you. People often use clothing as a way to

436 CHAPTER 15: LOOKING GOOD

MEETING STUDENT DIVERSITY

Physically Challenged Some physically challenged people need specially designed, or adaptive, clothing to make dressing easier and to make clothing more comfortable for them. Discuss how difficult it is to find such clothing. Ask a volunteer to contact a nearby children's hospital to see if the hospital would share the names of catalog companies that manufacture adaptive clothing. Students might write to the companies to have catalogs sent to the class. The catalogs could be saved as a classroom resource. Ask physically challenged students to discuss the restrictions of their clothing. Students could brainstorm ideas for reinventing clothes.

 Fad clothing does not remain popular for very long. Do you know when this type of clothing was popular?

express themselves. How do you express yourself through your clothing choices?

Self-Expression

Your clothing can tell others a lot about your personality. If you are an outgoing person, you may prefer bold colors and patterns. Your best friend, who is quiet, may prefer to wear clothes that are simple and subdued.

Your moods can also affect your clothing choices. When you are feeling happy, you may choose to wear bright colors. On days when you're feeling thoughtful and quiet, you may

Dressing Appropriately

If you want to dress for success, remember these tips:
- For job interviews, select clothes that are neat, businesslike, and conservative.
- At school, wear clothes that are appropriate for learning.
- For outdoor activities, consider the weather when you dress so that you will not be too cold or too hot.

LESSON TWO: MAKING CLOTHING DECISIONS **437**

CHAPTER 15, LESSON 2

Skills IN ACTION

After discussing each tip in "Dressing Appropriately," ask students to brainstorm tips for occasions not mentioned in the feature, such as parties, graduations, or church ceremonies. Have students write out their ideas and have volunteers read their additonal tips to the class.

L1 Selecting Clothes

Write a list on the chalkboard of activities such as a school dance, a baseball game, a picnic, dinner at a nice restaurant, shopping at the mall, aerobics class, a wedding, and work. Have students describe an appropriate outfit for each occasion. Provide clothing catalogs for students to browse through while they compile their lists.

L1 Evaluating First Impressions

Show students pictures of people in a variety of clothing. For example, you might show someone in jeans, western shirt, and boots; someone in a football or baseball jacket and a cap; someone in a business suit; and someone in a sweatsuit. Ask students to write their first impressions of the people in the pictures. Then ask them to describe how the people pictured could change their appearance to create a different first impression.

L2 Problem Solving

Assign Peer Pressure and Decision Making 30 in the TCR. This activity gives students the opportunity to recognize peer pressure and practice decision-making skills.

MORE ABOUT • • •

The Right Clothes for the Right Occasion Some fashion rules from the past now seem silly, but they were once taken very seriously. For example, a properly dressed woman would never go anywhere without her white gloves; when dining at a nice restaurant, men always wore jackets and ties and women wore dresses, never pants; jeans were only appropriate for people whose jobs required rugged clothes; and only people who worked on ranches or farms wore boots.

CHAPTER 15, LESSON 2

L1 Student Workbook
Assign Activities 108 and 109 in the Student Workbook.

ASSESS

Evaluating the Lesson
Assign Reviewing Terms and Facts and Thinking Critically on page 439 to review the lesson; then assign the Lesson 2 Quiz in the TCR.

Reteaching
- Have students work in small groups to identify clothing used as identification and as status symbols by groups in their school. Have them compare their ideas with those of other groups.
- Have students complete Reteaching Activity 15 in the TCR.

Enrichment
- Ask students to imagine that they are living fifty years in the future. Have them describe or make drawings of the clothing they would have in their wardrobes. Remind them to consider the factors that might influence the style of clothing worn.
- Assign Enrichment Activity 17 in the TCR.

People's clothing needs differ depending on their interests. What purpose do uniforms serve?

select pale or dark colors. Some people use clothes to help change their moods. For example, Stephanie always wears a bright red shirt when she's feeling a little down, because it lifts her spirits.

First Impressions

The clothes you wear contribute to the impression you make on other people. People will form an impression of you the first time they meet you. That impression is partly influenced by what you are wearing.

Have you ever decided you wanted to meet someone because of his or her appearance? Perhaps what you liked most was the way that person was dressed. People make the same judgments about you. Their ideas about you are based on your personality and your appearance. If a person met you now, would he or she want to get to know you better?

438   CHAPTER 15: LOOKING GOOD

COOPERATIVE LEARNING

Surveying Have students work in groups to prepare surveys to find out how classmates and friends choose grooming and clothing items. Suggest that surveys should cover the following areas: How do you choose hair-styling products? What hair-care products do you use regularly? How do you react when you see advertisements for cosmetics? What factors would you consider if you are going to try a new cosmetic? What do you try to communicate through your choice in clothing?

Choosing Clothing Wisely

You make clothing decisions for a variety of reasons. Even though there are many different styles of clothing available, you can learn to choose clothes that flatter you. Keep in mind that no matter what you wear, it reflects your personality and sends out messages to other people.

If you understand basic styles and fashions, you can make wise clothing decisions. How can you improve the choices you make?

LESSON TWO Review

Using complete sentences, answer the following questions on a separate sheet of paper.

Reviewing Terms and Facts

1. **List** Name five reasons why people wear clothes.
2. **Explain** Why is it best not to spend a lot of money on fad clothing?
3. **Give Examples** Name two situations in which you might wear dressy clothing.
4. **Identify** Give an example to show how clothing could be used to express someone's personality.

Thinking Critically

5. **Relate** What are some examples of clothes that people wear purely for status? Do you think that these clothes are worth the price? Why or why not?
6. **Compare and Contrast** What are the similarities and differences among styles, fashions, and fads?
7. **Analyze** Do you think that it is fair to judge a person by his or her clothing? Why or why not?

Applying Concepts

8. Make a list of fad clothing that is currently popular. Survey ten friends or classmates to determine how many wear these fad items. Which items are the most popular? Why? Discuss results with your classmates.

LESSON TWO: MAKING CLOTHING DECISIONS

CHAPTER 15, LESSON 2

Answers to Lesson 2 Review

1. People wear clothes for protection, for modesty, for identification, for status, and for decoration.
2. Fad clothing is popular for only a short time.
3. Dressy clothing would be appropriate for having dinner at a nice restaurant or attending a wedding.
4. Answers will vary. An athletic person might wear sweatsuits and tennis shoes; an outgoing person may wear bold, bright colors; and a conservative person may avoid loud, faddish clothes.
5. Answers will vary. Students might mention certain brands of sports shoes or designer jeans. Students should be able to support their answers with logical reasoning.
6. Styles, fashions, and fads all relate to types of clothing. A style is a distinctive type of clothing with a particular design. A fashion is a style that is currently popular. A fad is a fashion that catches on quickly but usually does not last very long.
7. Answers will vary. Students should be able to support their answers with logical reasoning. For example, some students may point out that it is not fair because a person may not be able to afford the latest fashions.
8. Fad items will vary, as will the number of people wearing them.

CLOSE

Ask students to explain how clothing choices are influenced by fads, fashions, and self-expression.

COOPERATIVE LEARNING

Clothing Styles Have students work in small groups to make drawings of clothing styles of popular music or entertainment personalities. Have them compile a list of personalities they might draw, and then let them determine how to choose which one the group will work on. Groups may wish to browse popular magazine articles for ideas. Students in each group should display their drawings in the classroom. Ask a representative from each group to explain how the clothing represents the personality chosen by the group.

LESSON THREE
Clothing Design

FOCUS

Lesson Objectives
After studying this lesson, students should be able to
- describe how color, line, and texture of clothing affect a person's appearance.
- explain how to combine design elements successfully when selecting clothes.

Motivating Activity
Write the following question on the chalkboard: What is your favorite outfit and why do you like it? Ask students to write their answers on a sheet of paper.

Introducing the Lesson
Have volunteers share their responses to the Motivating Activity. Survey the class to determine how many students like an outfit because of its color; because of its fabric or texture; because they feel good in it; because people compliment them when they wear it; or because it makes them look taller, shorter, thinner, or heavier. Explain to students that this lesson will help them discover how to combine design elements when selecting clothes so that they will look their best.

Introducing *Words to Know*
Write each of the Words to Know on the chalkboard. Have students look up each term in the Glossary at the back of the student text. Ask students to write a sentence for each term, defining the term in their own words.

LESSON THREE
Clothing Design

 **WORDS TO KNOW**

hues
value
intensity
color wheel
neutral color
shape
texture

DISCOVER...
- how color, line, and texture of clothing affect your appearance.
- how to combine design elements when selecting clothes.

Tim's favorite outfit is a baseball jersey and navy blue sweatpants. He feels comfortable in it. Tim doesn't pay much attention to how clothing affects his appearance. He just wears clothes he likes. Tamara is quite different. Her favorite is a jeans outfit with boots. She likes the way the color and styles flatter her appearance, and people always compliment her when she wears this outfit.

440   CHAPTER 15: LOOKING GOOD

CLASSROOM RESOURCES FOR LESSON 3

 Blackline Masters
Activity and Project Card 30, "Clothing Collage"
Concept Map 24
Cross Curriculum 17
Lesson 3 Quiz
Reteaching 15

 Transparencies
Transparency 64, "Using the Color Wheel"
Transparency 65, "Color Schemes"

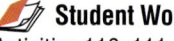 **Student Workbook**
Activities 110, 111

▸ These teens are wearing their favorite outfits. They may like these clothes best because of the colors, types of fabric, or the way they look in them. What do you like best about your favorite outfit?

How Color Affects Appearance

Why do some colors look better on you than others? If you become familiar with the relationships among colors, you will understand how colors affect your appearance and the way clothes look on you.

To understand the basic principles of color, you need to know *the names of the colors,* or the **hues.** The three basic hues are red, yellow, and blue. They are called the *primary* colors because all other colors can be made from them. The *secondary* hues are orange, green, and violet. Orange is made by combining equal amounts of red and yellow. Equal amounts of blue and yellow make green, and violet is made by combining red and blue.

Another basic element to consider is the **value,** or *the lightness and darkness of color.* For instance, blue can vary in value from very light blue to navy blue. A light value of a hue is called a *tint.* A dark value of a hue is called a *shade.* The

LESSON THREE: CLOTHING DESIGN   **441**

MEETING STUDENT DIVERSITY

Varied Learning Styles Ask students to draw three rows of five small boxes on a piece of poster board. Have them label the first row "Red," the second row "Orange," and the third row "Green." Give students small amounts of red, yellow, blue, black, and white paint and a paintbrush. Ask them to paint the middle box in each row the color labeled at the beginning of the row. Then ask them to create two different shades and two different tints of red, orange, and green by mixing paints together. Have them paint the shades and tints, from light to dark, in the boxes, starting at the box farthest left in each row. Have students compare their finished work with classmates. Discuss why all the shades and tints are not exactly the same.

CHAPTER 15, LESSON 3

TEACH

L1 Applying
Have small groups of students look through magazines to find pictures of clothing that illustrate various color schemes. Ask groups to share the pictures they find with the class.

L3 Science
Have students find out how the primary colors of light differ from the primary colors of pigment and what colors result from mixing the primary colors of light. (*The primary colors of light are red, blue, and green. Mixing red and blue light produces magenta; mixing blue and green light produces cyan; and mixing red and green light produces yellow.*) If possible, allow students to demonstrate mixing colors of light, using two slide projectors and red, blue, and green colored cellophane to cover the lenses.

L2 Fine Arts Connection
Assign Cross-Curriculum Activity 17 in the TCR. Students learn about the effects of color in this activity.

L1 Demonstrate
Ask students to define and give examples of hue, value, tint, shade, and intensity. Show students some primary blue poster paint. Demonstrate what happens to the color if a small amount of black paint is mixed with a sample of blue paint. Ask students what changed. (*the value, because the blue became darker*) Then mix some white paint with a sample of primary blue. Ask students what changed. (*the value, because the blue became lighter*) Then ask which of the blues is a tint and which is a shade. (*The blue mixed with black is a shade and the blue mixed with white is a tint.*)

441

CHAPTER 15, LESSON 3

USING VISUALS

Have students look at the color wheel in Figure 15.3 and name the warm colors and cool colors on it. Ask what they notice about the location of warm and cool colors. (*Warm colors are on one side of the color wheel and cool colors are on the other side.*) Ask if there are colors that are mixtures of warm and cool colors. (*yes, yellow-green and red-violet*) Ask where these colors are located on the color wheel. (*opposite each other*)

L1 Making a Color Wheel

Give students red, yellow, and blue paints or colored pencils. Have them make a color wheel by mixing the three primary colors of paint or colored pencils. If possible, students may wish to use a paint program on a computer color monitor. Have them combine pixels of primary colors to create color wheels. Review how green paint is made. (*Mix equal parts of blue and yellow.*) Then ask how they would make yellow-green and blue-green. (*Add more yellow to make yellow-green and add more blue to make blue-green.*)

L1 Using Transparencies

Present Color Transparency 64, "Using the Color Wheel," in the TCR. Use this overhead visual to reinforce concepts from this lesson.

---

brightness or dullness of a color is called its **intensity.** Bright red is a high-intensity color. Pale pink is a low-intensity color.

Colors are considered either warm or cool. Red, yellow, and orange are warm colors. They give a sense of brightness and cheerfulness. Blue, green, and violet (purple) are cool colors. They give a sense of calm.

When you put clothes together, you can create either single-color outfits or outfits that combine colors. By following specific guidelines, you can learn to combine colors successfully. These guidelines are based on the color wheel. A **color wheel** is *an arrangement of colors that shows the relationships of colors to each other*. **Figure 15.3** shows a color wheel. **Figure 15.4** shows different ways to create color schemes for a flattering look.

Figure 15.3 Color Wheel
The color wheel shows how colors are related to one another. Why is it important to learn about the color wheel?

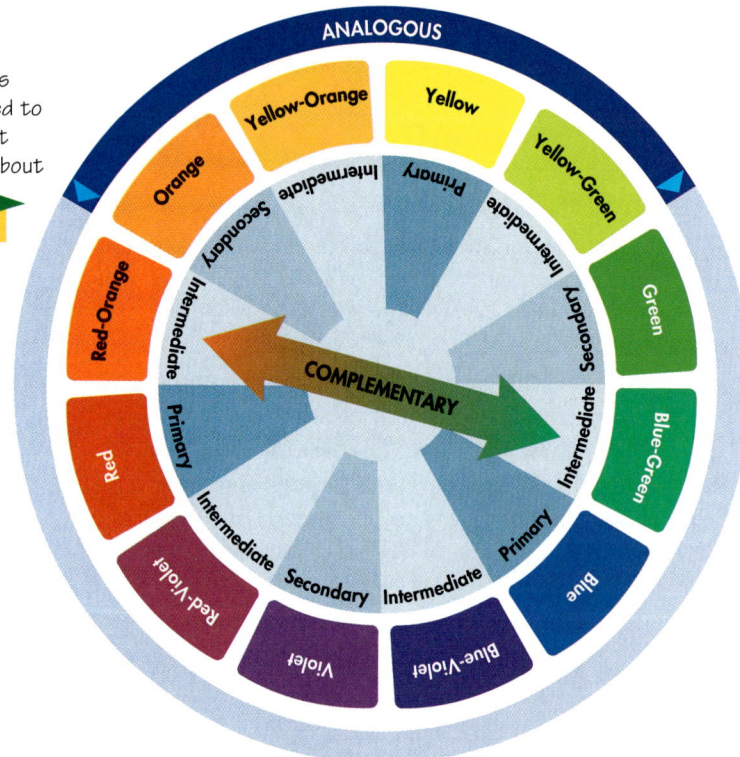

442   CHAPTER 15: LOOKING GOOD

COOPERATIVE LEARNING

Clothing Color Wheels Have small groups of students look through magazines for pictures of clothing that represent the different colors on the color wheel. Have them arrange and label the pictures to form a clothing color wheel. Provide poster board or large sheets of paper and glue for students to create their clothing color wheels. Display the color wheels in the classroom.

**Figure 15.4
Color Schemes**
Which of these types of color schemes have you tried?

Monochromatic color scheme. A monochromatic color scheme is a one-color plan. This plan involves one hue and the values, tints, and shades of that hue. A combination of light blue and medium blue is another example of a monochromatic color scheme.

Analogous color scheme. An analogous color scheme is made up of hues found next to each other on the color wheel. The colors have one common hue. A combination of red-violet, violet, and blue-violet is another analogous color scheme.

Complementary color scheme. Complementary colors are those opposite each other on the color wheel. This type of color scheme gives great contrast.

Accented neutral color scheme. A **neutral color** is *black, white, beige,* or *gray.* An accented neutral color scheme uses one of the neutral colors plus another color as the accent. A combination of black and red is an example of an accented neutral color scheme.

LESSON THREE: CLOTHING DESIGN   443

CHAPTER 15, LESSON 3

USING VISUALS
Refer students to Figure 15.4. Have them read the descriptions of the color schemes and look at the pictures illustrating each one. Emphasize that "mono" means "one," so a monochromatic color scheme involves only one hue. Ask students to name the colors shown in each color scheme and then locate those colors on the color wheel in Figure 15.3.

L1 Using Transparencies
Present Color Transparency 65, "Color Schemes," in the TCR. Use this overhead visual to reinforce concepts from this lesson.

DID YOU KNOW
Color consultants are trained to help people discover what colors are most flattering for them to wear. They usually drape people with large pieces of colored cloth and examine how each color looks with a person's skin tones, eye color, and hair color. They will then recommend certain colors or color schemes that will be most flattering. Some color consultants categorize people as seasons—winter, spring, summer, or fall. For example, "winter" people are those who look best in bright, primary colors and accented, neutral color schemes.

COOPERATIVE LEARNING

Determining Flattering Colors Provide small groups of students with 18-inch squares of different colors of material representing colors on the color wheel. Also include samples of black, white, and gray material. Ask students to take turns holding each piece of material just below their chin. Have other group members evaluate how each color affects the person's skin tones and eye and hair color. Based on observations, have each group recommend which colors look most flattering on each member of the group. Have groups share their recommendations with the class.

CHAPTER 15, LESSON 3

Show students several pictures of people wearing clothing with obvious vertical, horizontal, and diagonal lines. Ask them to describe the lines of the clothing and tell how the clothing makes the person look.

L1 Making Color Selections

Write the following color selection tips on the chalkboard: (1) you can emphasize the color of your skin, hair, or eyes by wearing the same hue; (2) bright and light colors make you look larger, while dull and dark colors make you look smaller; (3) one-color outfits make you look taller, while contrasting colors of tops and bottoms make you look shorter; (4) a contrasting color can emphasize parts of your body; (5) soft colors look better if you have a light complexion, and strong colors look better if you have a dark complexion. Have students draw and color an outfit they think would make them look their best. Display student drawings in the classroom.

L2 Activity and Project Card

Allow time for students to complete Activity and Project Card 30, "Clothing Collage," in the TCR.

L1 Art

Have students use colored pencils and typing paper to make rubbings of objects that have different textures. Suggest that they make a rubbing of a rough plaster wall, an embossed plastic tablecloth, or a corduroy jacket. Have them cut out sections of their rubbings to create a texture collage.

444

The Right Lines for You

You can change your appearance by changing the lines of your clothes. Follow these guidelines:
- Clothes with vertical lines make you look taller and thinner.
- Clothes with horizontal lines make you look shorter and wider.
- Clothes with diagonal lines can make you look taller and thinner or shorter and wider, depending on the length and angle of the lines.

The lines of a garment can affect your appearance. How do lines affect the way these teens look?

Selecting Colors

When you try different colors and color combinations, you will discover that some look better on you than others. Becoming colors make your complexion look healthy and show off your hair and eyes.

Colors affect your appearance in other ways too. They can accent or play down certain areas of your body. Light, warm, and bright colors can make you look larger. Dark, cool, and dull colors can make you look smaller. Carl wears one-color outfits so that he will look taller, whereas Judy selects contrasting colors so that she appears shorter.

Lines in Clothing

The way a garment looks on you is also affected by its lines. Lines form the outer **shape**, or *outline*, of a garment, as you can see by comparing tapered, straight-leg, and flared pants. Sometimes lines are formed by features of the garment's construction, such as seam lines and waistlines. Other lines can be part of the fabric's design, such as stripes or plaids.

444 CHAPTER 15: LOOKING GOOD

COOPERATIVE LEARNING

Determining Clothing Lines Have small groups of students look through magazines to find examples of clothing that shows vertical, horizontal, and diagonal lines. Ask them to place tracing paper over the pictures and trace the lines in the clothing pictured. Then have them label the lines in each garment. Have groups explain their line tracings to the class, using information from the lesson.

TIPS for living

SHAPING UP

Few people are completely satisfied with their bodies. However, you can change the appearance of your proportions by choosing the right clothing styles.

For example, if you want to make your waist look narrower, you can

- choose single-breasted or V-neck jackets.
- wear darker colors on top.
- avoid contrasting belts at the waist.
- wear long vests and tunics.

If you want to make your hips look smaller, you can

- wear tops with shoulder pads.
- wear shirts, sweaters, and jackets that fall below the widest part of the hips.
- avoid clothing that is too tight.

Lines can be either straight or curved. Curved lines soften a garment's appearance. Straight lines can look severe and strong. Straight lines can be

- vertical—lines that go up and down.
- horizontal—lines that go across.
- diagonal—lines that go at an angle.

When you shop for clothes, learn to look for lines. Try to see vertical lines instead of just a row of buttons or a zipper down the front. Look for horizontal lines instead of seeing only belts, waistlines, or hemlines. See diagonal or curved lines instead of necklines and collars.

Lines can be used to make you look taller or shorter, larger or smaller. See the "Skills in Action" feature on the opposite page for some tips.

Clothing comes in a variety of interesting textures. How can you use texture to change the way you look?

LESSON THREE: CLOTHING DESIGN   445

MORE ABOUT • • •

Principles of Design The principles of design are used to combine all the elements of design: line, shape, texture, and color. The principles of design include balance, proportion, emphasis, rhythm, and harmony. Balance is the way the spaces and the shapes work together. Proportion is the size relationship of each of the elements within a garment to one another and to the total look. Emphasis is the center of interest of a garment. Rhythm is the flow of the lines, shapes, space, and texture of a garment. Harmony is the pleasing arrangement of all the parts of the garment.

CHAPTER 15, LESSON 3

TIPS for living

After reading the feature, ask students to describe outfits they could wear that would combine texture, color, and line to make them look their best. Have students write their descriptions and reasons for their clothing choices in their private journals.

L1 Analyze

Place a variety of clothing articles with different textures in numbered shoe boxes. The lids should have holes so that students can reach in to feel the textures. Ask students to feel the clothing in each box and write down a description of the texture. Then remove the clothing from the boxes and ask students to compare their descriptions.

L1 Student Workbook

Assign Activities 110 and 111 in the Student Workbook.

ASSESS

Evaluating the Lesson

Assign Reviewing Terms and Facts and Thinking Critically on page 446 to review the lesson; then assign the Lesson 3 Quiz in the TCR.

Reteaching

- Have students make drawings of mix-and-match separates that create four different looks. Have them develop color schemes, lines, and textures that would be best for them. Ask students to explain their choices.
- Have students complete Reteaching Activity 15 in the TCR.
- Assign Concept Map 24 in the TCR.

445

CHAPTER 15, LESSON 3

Answers to Lesson 3 Review

1. The three primary colors are red, blue, and yellow. These colors are important because all other colors are made by combining the primary colors.
2. A color wheel is an arrangement of colors that shows their relationship to each other. It is useful in showing ways to successfully combine colors.
3. Lines in fashions are either vertical, horizontal, or diagonal.
4. Texture is created by using different yarns and weaves in making fabrics. Textures include fine or coarse, dull or shiny, heavy or light, and nubby or smooth.
5. Value is the lightness or darkness of a color. Intensity is the brightness or dullness of a color.
6. You would want to choose monochromatic color schemes and vertical lines.
7. Answers will vary depending on the physical characteristics of the individual student.

Enrichment

Ask students to write articles on clothing selection. They may choose to write about style, color, line, texture, or a combination of these. Encourage students to illustrate their articles with drawings or magazine pictures. Combine the articles to make a student newsletter on fashion and clothing selection. Computers may be used for this activity.

CLOSE

Ask students to write a paragraph explaining how knowing the effects of color, line, and texture can help them make the best clothing selections.

By understanding the effects of color, lines, and texture, you can choose clothes that will help you look your best. What do you usually consider when you make clothing choices?

The Texture of Clothing

When you choose clothing, you need to consider its **texture,** *the way something feels or looks as if it would feel.* Texture is created by using different yarns and weaves in making fabric. For instance, a wool sweater has a coarse texture that is created in the knitting process. A fabric may be dull or shiny, nubby or smooth. What textures do you prefer?

You can use textures to change the way you look. Dull textures make you look smaller. Nubby or shiny textures make you seem larger. A tall person can wear a coarse texture, but the same fabric may overpower a small person. To see which textures look best on you, try on clothing with different types of textures.

Making Fashionable Combinations

When you buy clothing, consider the effect of color, line, and texture to make selections that will help you look your best. You can use your knowledge of these design elements to emphasize your best features.

LESSON THREE Review

Using complete sentences, answer the following questions on a separate sheet of paper.

Reviewing Terms and Facts
1. **List** Name the three primary colors. Why are these colors important?
2. **Vocabulary** What is a *color wheel*? What can you learn from it?
3. **Name** What are the three main directions of lines in fashions?
4. **Describe** How is texture created? Name three types of textures.

Thinking Critically
5. **Contrast** What is the difference between value and intensity?
6. **Apply** If you wanted to look taller and thinner, what types of prints, textures, or patterned fabrics would you choose?

Applying Concepts
7. In a catalog or magazine, find a picture of an outfit that you think would look good on you. Using what you have learned about color, line, and texture, describe the outfit, and explain why you chose it.

446 CHAPTER 15: LOOKING GOOD

TECHNOLOGY UPDATE

Clothing Software Computerized clothing design offers new options for consumers. In Japan, one clothing manufacturer has installed personal computers that show 100,000 clothing designs. Using the computers, shoppers are able to design their own custom-order clothing. In the future, more-powerful clothing design systems will allow consumers to custom-make their own outfits in just minutes. Discuss with students the possibilities offered by computerized clothing design.

Chapter 15 Activities

TECHNOLOGY
Plastic Hair
Hairstyling products—such as sprays, gels, and mousses—work well because they contain polymers and resins—compounds found in plastics—that attach firmly to hair to hold it in place. However, regular shampoos can't wash them out completely.

Try This!
Read labels on some hair-care products at home or at the store. Find a "clarifying" shampoo that would help prevent or remove residue buildup. Share your findings with the class.

Consumer Focus

Label Lowdown
The manufacturers of personal care products sometimes make claims that are vague or misleading. Acne medications don't always "get rid of zits," for example, and "dermatologist-tested" beauty products aren't necessarily safer than other kinds.

Try This!
Do ads for makeup and grooming products in magazines make claims that sound too good to be true? What sources could you consult to find out whether they are true or not?

FRIENDS & FAMILY
CLOTHES COMMUNICATION
Regina and her parents sometimes disagree on the clothes she chooses for school. Her parents think that she should dress in a way that will make a good impression on her teachers. Regina wants to dress only to please herself.

TRY THIS!
Ask three or four of your teachers what kind of clothes they think students should wear to school. Report the findings of your survey to the class.

TECHNOLOGY CONNECTION

RECYCLED PLASTIC
Can you imagine wearing a fleece pullover made from empty milk jugs?

Recycled-plastic fibers have been used in carpets for years. However, it has been difficult to produce fibers soft enough for clothing—until now. You can't tell the difference between the recycled-plastic clothing and any other clothing made from synthetic materials.

Follow Up
1. Why are plastic-recycling efforts, such as making clothing from plastic soft drink bottles, as important as sorting waste materials in the first place?
2. The fibers, which are spun from used plastic bottles and other plastic products, look and feel like polyester. The finished products also cost about the same as regular clothing. Would you wear clothing made from recycled plastic? Why or why not?

CHAPTER 15 ACTIVITIES **447**

Teaching the TECHNOLOGY CONNECTION
Discuss with students what happens when plastics are sorted and collected for recycling. Ask what would happen if there weren't a market for clothing made from recycled plastics. (*Manufacturers would quit making it if it didn't sell.*) Provide a variety of mail-order clothing catalogs and ask students to look for examples of clothing described as being made from recycled plastics.

Answers to Follow-Up
1. To complete the cycle in recycling, products that consumers will buy must be made from recycled materials.
2. Answers will vary.

CHAPTER 15
Activities

TECHNOLOGY
Ask students whether they notice their hair becomes limp or dull looking after using a lot of styling products. Explain that these products can leave a residue in the hair when used for a long time. Discuss with students what they know about clarifying shampoos and how to use them. Be sure to point out that using these more than once a week can leave the hair dry.

FRIENDS & FAMILY

Students might be surprised to learn that, just like other people, teachers are greatly influenced by appearance. In a study of teachers, results showed that they are less likely to confront students who dress nicely. Teachers are also likely to give higher marks to students who dress conservatively.

Consumer Focus

Point out to students that it is possible to find makeup and personal care products made from natural ingredients. Suggest that students check store shelves for natural toothpaste containing baking soda, or lotions with ingredients such as jasmine or aloe.

CHAPTER 15 REVIEW

Checking Comprehension

Use the Chapter Summary and the Chapter 15 Review to help students go over the most important ideas presented in Chapter 15.

Answers to Words to Know

1. A dermatologist is a doctor who treats skin disorders, and a person with a serious case of acne might need to consult one.
2. A sunscreen is a lotion that guards the skin against the harmful rays of the sun.
3. Plaque is a soft, sticky film created by the bacteria that live in the mouth. Teeth start to decay when plaque is left on them too long.
4. Modesty is what is considered the proper use of clothing to cover the body. People choose clothing they feel is appropriately modest.
5. Fads usually last for only a short time.
6. Hues are the names of colors, such as red and blue.
7. Neutral colors are black, white, and gray.

Answers to Review Questions

1. Eat a balanced diet, keep your skin clean, and protect your skin from wind and sun.
2. Brushing hair helps to distribute the natural oils and keep hair from becoming dry.
3. You should brush your teeth twice a day, using gentle up-and-down strokes to clean between the teeth and massage the gums.
4. Because classic styles stay in fashion for a long time.

448

CHAPTER 15 REVIEW

Chapter Summary

- Health affects your appearance in many ways. Good health can result from eating healthful foods, exercising regularly, getting enough rest, and practicing good posture.
- You can look your best by following a basic hygiene routine every day.
- Good grooming habits include the way you care for your skin, nails, hair, and teeth.
- People wear clothing for a variety of reasons, including protection, decoration, modesty, status, and identification.
- A style is the design of a garment. A fashion is a style of clothing that is popular at a particular time. A fad is a fashion that is very popular for a short time. A classic is popular for a long time.
- Your clothing choices are influenced by the occasion and by the type of activity in which you will be participating.
- Your clothes express your unique personality and influence the impression you make on people.
- You can combine colors to create various kinds of color schemes. Monochromatic, analogous, complementary, and accented neutral are examples of color schemes.
- Colors, lines, and textures affect your appearance and how clothes look on you.

 ### Words to Know

Using complete sentences, answer the following questions on a separate sheet of paper.

1. Why might someone need to see a *dermatologist*?
2. How does *sunscreen* protect your skin?
3. What is *plaque*? When does it become a problem?
4. How does *modesty* influence clothing choices?
5. How long do *fads* usually last?
6. What are *hues*?
7. Give an example of a *neutral color*.

448 CHAPTER 15: LOOKING GOOD

 ### Review Questions

Using complete sentences, answer the following questions on a separate sheet of paper.

1. List three guidelines for caring for your skin.
2. Why is it important to brush your hair?
3. Describe the best way to brush your teeth. How often should you brush?
4. Why are classic styles good clothing choices?
5. How can clothing be used to help you make a positive first impression?
6. Name and describe the four basic color schemes.

EXTRA CREDIT PROJECT

Adding to Your Portfolio Ask students to put together a photo or video project incorporating the material from Chapter 15. Encourage students to develop a creative approach that demonstrates what they have learned about personal health, good grooming, and clothing choices. Photographs should be organized, labeled, and mounted neatly or collected in a book for display. Video projects should show careful planning and organization and should include information relevant to the chapter. Review projects and then allow students to present them to the class. These projects may then be added to students' portfolios to represent the students' understanding of the concepts.

CHAPTER 15 REVIEW

7. How can you use line and texture in clothing to improve your appearance?

Thinking Critically

Using complete sentences, answer the following questions on a separate sheet of paper.

1. **Analyze** Many teens have problems with acne. How might this problem affect a person's self-concept and self-esteem? Do you think that it should?
2. **Relate** Give two examples, other than those discussed in the text, of situations in which appropriate dress is important. Explain your choices.
3. **Apply** In terms of color, line, and texture, how would you describe your clothing choices? How do these factors affect your appearance?

Cooperative Learning

1. Working in groups of three or four, compare prices of designer items of clothing with non-designer items. Have each person in the group choose one type of garment. Group members should find out the price of the garment with a designer label and the price of a similar garment without a designer label. Then have group members compare findings and discuss whether designer items are worth the difference in price.
2. With a partner, research the clothing most often worn by people in another country. Find out how the clothing reflects the climate and culture of the country. Discuss the similarities and differences between clothing in that country and clothing worn in the United States. Present your findings to the class.

Family & Community

1. Ask your parents or grandparents to tell you about clothing styles that were popular when they were in their teens. Have them compare what they wore to certain places or events, such as school and parties, to what today's teens wear. What fads were there? Were there particular colors, lines, or textures that most teens wore? Share your findings with the class.
2. Write a one-page article about someone you know who dresses well. Describe the types of clothing the person wears and what the clothing says about the person. What could you learn from this person?

Building A Portfolio

1. For two days, keep track of your grooming habits. Write down each time you care for your skin, nails, hair, or teeth. At the end of the two days, compare your habits with those described in the chapter. Are there habits you need to change? If so, what should you do differently? Write a plan for improving your habits, and place it in your portfolio. Review it periodically.
2. Make a list of your five favorite garments or outfits. Analyze each one to determine what looks best on you in terms of style, color, line, and texture. Based on your analysis, write a conclusion about which types of clothing help you look your best. Keep the analysis in your portfolio, and refer to it the next time you shop for clothes.

CHAPTER 15 REVIEW **449**

CHAPTER 15 REVIEW

5. By dressing neatly you can make a positive first impression.
6. Monochromatic is a combination of different intensities and values of one color. Analogous is a combination of colors that are next to each other on the color wheel. Complementary is a combination of colors that are opposite each other on the color wheel. Accented neutral is a combination of a neutral color and another color as the accent.
7. Vertical lines make you look taller and thinner. Horizontal lines make you look shorter and wider. Diagonal lines can make you look either larger or smaller, depending on whether the lines are more horizontal or vertical. Shiny textures can make you look larger. Bulky textures can overwhelm a small person and make him or her appear even smaller.

Evaluate

Use the Chapter 15 Test in the TCR, or construct your own test using the Testmaker Software.

CLOSE

Have students apply their knowledge of the chapter's content by completing one of the alternative assessment activities listed under Family and Community or Building a Portfolio.

Answers to Thinking Critically

1. Answers will vary. Teens with acne may feel less attractive and may have low self-esteem and a low self-concept. A person should not be (but sometimes is) judged by outward physical appearance.
2. Answers will vary. Accept all reasonable responses.
3. Answers will vary according to the individual student and clothing choices.

449

Planning Guide
Chapter 16 Planning Your Wardrobe

LESSON 1	Pages	FEATURES	CLASSROOM RESOURCES
Deciding What You Need	452–457	*Try This:* Donating Clothes	Activity and Project Card 31, "Mix-and-Match Outfits" Concept Map 25 Cooperative Learning 31 Lesson 1 Quiz Peer Pressure and Decision Making 31 Student Workbook Activities 112, 113
LESSON 2 **Evaluating Quality and Fit**	458–465	*Skills in Action:* Identifying Fabrics *Tips for Living:* Choosing Shoes	Cooperative Learning 32 Cross Curriculum 18 Lesson 2 Quiz Student Workbook Activities 114, 115
LESSON 3 **Shopping for Clothes**	466–471	*Skills in Action:* Earning Money for Clothes *Tips for Living:* The Hidden Costs	Enrichment 18 Lesson 3 Quiz Peer Pressure and Decision Making 32 Transparency 66, "What's It Really Worth?" Student Workbook Activity 116
LESSON 4 **Clothing Care**	472–476	*Skills in Action:* Hand Washing Clothes	Activity and Project Card 32, "Zap Those Stains!" Concept Map 26 Lesson 4 Quiz Transparency 67, "Removing Stains" Student Workbook Activities 117, 118

CHAPTER 16 RESOURCES

- Chapter 16 Test
- Reteaching 16
- Study Guide 16, *Reteaching*
- Testmaker Software

Performance Assessment Activity

Ask students to generate a list of questions that pertain to buying and caring for clothes in preparation for interviewing classmates or other acquaintances. The questions might include: How do you decide what clothes you need? Who helps you decide what clothes you need? Do you shop at certain stores? If so, which ones? Do you have favorite brands? What are your techniques for saving money when you shop? How do you help take care of your clothes? Students might tape their interviews or simply keep track of the responses. When they have completed their interviews, organize the class into small groups. Have each group use the information from the interviews to create portraits of teen shoppers.

School-to-Work

Ask students to look through the classified want ads in their local newspapers for jobs that have something to do with clothing: buying, selling, manufacturing, designing, writing about fashion, laundry and dry cleaning jobs, and so on. Students might also look in books in the library about careers in fashion, design, and clothing care. Invite groups to create a visual for the classroom that shows these career possibilities. The visual might include a chart, a web that shows how the various jobs are connected, or a mural that illustrates what people in the particular jobs do. Call on volunteers to present their visuals to the class.

Family & Community

Challenge students to investigate all the possible outlets for used clothing. Students can check a telephone directory for listings of resale shops, charitable organizations, and churches that distribute used clothing. Groups of students can pool their information and create a poster that identifies all the possibilities.

Resources for the Teacher

Fit and Fabric: from Threads Magazine. Newtown, CT: Taunton Press, 1991.

Wolfe, Mary G. *Fashion: A Study of Clothing Design and Selection.* South Holland, IL: Goodheart-Willcox Co., 1993.

Readings for the Student

Hodgman, Ann. *A Day in the Life of a Fashion Designer.* Mahwah, NJ: Troll Associates, 1988.

Keeler, Patricia A. and Francis X. McCall, Jr. *Unraveling Fibers.* New York: Atheneum Books for Young Readers, 1995.

McCoy, Sharon. *Fifty Ways to Jazz up Your Jeans.* Los Angeles: Lowell House Juvenile, 1994.

Multimedia Resources

Clothing: A Consumer's Guide (color, 30 minutes). Educational Audio Visual, Inc. (EAV)

Clothing Speaks (Video). Designer Jeans (87 minutes). VHS. Videotakes.

OUT OF TIME?

If time does not permit thorough teaching of this chapter, you may wish to use:
- Teens Making a Difference, page 451
- Tips for Living, pages 464, 469
- Try This, page 453
- Skills in Action, pages 459, 469, 475
- Young Living Activities, page 477
- Chapter Summary, page 478

CHAPTER 16
Planning Your Wardrobe

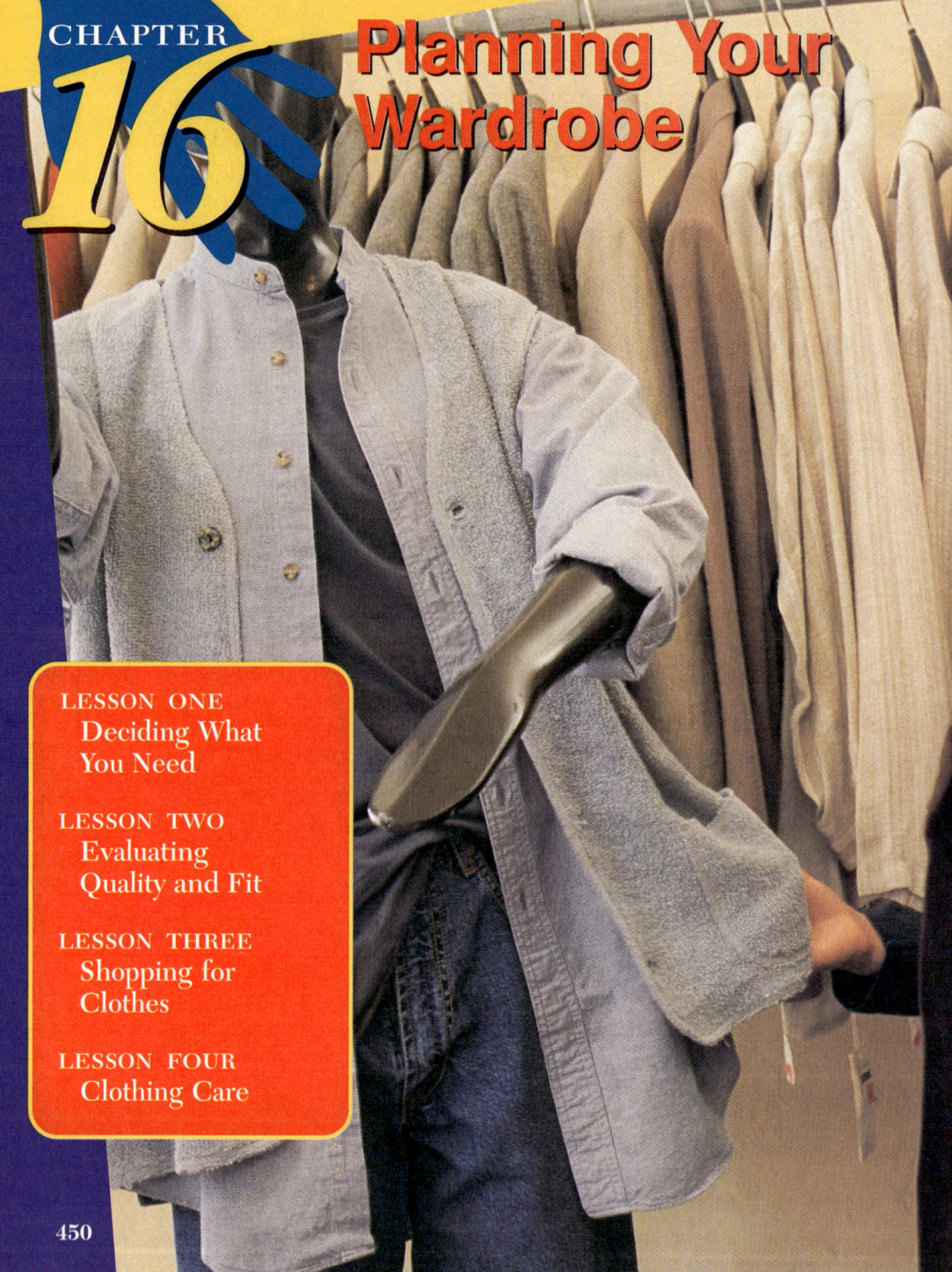

Chapter Overview
Chapter 16 examines various actions students can take to plan what clothes they need, shop for them, and care for them.

LESSON 1 describes techniques for assessing and expanding a wardrobe.

LESSON 2 describes ways to judge clothing for quality and fit.

LESSON 3 explores ways to use labels and other information to be a wise clothing shopper.

LESSON 4 provides instructions for clothing care.

Introducing the Chapter
To introduce the chapter, have students think about the clothes they wear in a week. Then ask them to create a web, with the word *wardrobe* as the hub, that illustrates the kinds of clothes that make up their wardrobe. Students might include school clothes, leisure-time clothes, clothes for sporting events, and clothes for special occasions. Tell students that Chapter 16 will provide helpful information about planning and acquiring a wardrobe.

Chapter Motivator
Provide students with newspaper and magazine advertisements showing the latest styles of clothing. Ask them to identify clothing to update their current wardrobe. Ask them to suggest inexpensive purchases that they could make to do so. Tell students that Chapter 16 will help them learn how to assess and extend their wardrobe. It will also give them tips about being smart clothes shoppers.

CHAPTER 16 Planning Your Wardrobe

LESSON ONE Deciding What You Need

LESSON TWO Evaluating Quality and Fit

LESSON THREE Shopping for Clothes

LESSON FOUR Clothing Care

KEY TO ABILITY LEVELS

Teaching strategies that appear throughout the chapter have been identified by one of three codes to give you an idea of their suitability for students of varying learning styles and abilities.

L1 Level 1 strategies should be within the ability range of all students. Often full class participation is required. Teacher direction is usually needed.

L2 Level 2 strategies are for average to above-average students or for small groups. Some teacher direction is necessary.

L3 Level 3 strategies are designed for students able and willing to work independently. Minimal teacher direction is necessary.

CHAPTER 16

TEENS MAKING A DIFFERENCE
The Boutique Look

Janine Bryant noticed that a few of her sweatshirts looked a bit drab from too many washings. Janine decided to try reviving the shirts by adding fabric paint, beads, and glitter. When she wore one of her "new" shirts to school, several people asked Janine where they could buy a shirt like the one she had made.

Janine started taking orders for her decorated shirts, but she soon had more work than she could handle. Now Janine pays a few of her artistic friends to help her.

Try THIS!

Make a list of the clothes in your closet that need repair or a new look. Next to each item, write down one or two ways in which you could improve the garment's appearance. Then follow through on one of your ideas.

TEENS MAKING A DIFFERENCE

Discuss with students the ways that they can add a new look to old clothing items in their wardrobe. Call on volunteers to share their ways. Then have students read "The Boutique Look." Have them identify the ways that Janine makes a difference.

Have students form small groups to work on the activity in TRY THIS! Have a member of each group share the group's plan with the rest of the class.

BLOCK SCHEDULING

The following Teacher Classroom Resources are suggested for use in classrooms with Block Scheduling.
- Activity and Project Card 31, "Mix-and-Match Outfits"
- Activity and Project Card 32, "Zap Those Stains!"
- Cooperative Learning 31, "Stretch the Wardrobe"
- Cooperative Learning 32, "Fibers, Fabrics, and Finishes"

451

TECHNOLOGY IN THE CLASSROOM

Interactive Videos A variety of topics can be presented in the Family and Consumer Sciences classroom by using interactive videotapes or videodiscs. This technology allows you to develop a computer lesson that will allow students to interact with the videotape or videodisc. You can input the information you want your students to learn or questions you want them to answer. At appropriate points on the tape, information can be accessed for students to analyze or respond to. You can use commercially prepared videotapes or self-made videos to develop the lesson. Topics that lend themselves to this type of technology include family interactions or decisions to make when caring for children.

LESSON ONE
Deciding What You Need

FOCUS

Lesson Objectives
After studying this lesson, students should be able to
- assess their wardrobe needs.
- explain how to take a wardrobe inventory.
- describe techniques for extending a wardrobe.

Motivating Activity
Ask students to think about three clothing items that they feel are important for a wardrobe. Tell them to consider reasons such as usefulness, stylishness, special significance, and so on.

Introducing the Lesson
Ask students to work in small groups and discuss their responses to the Motivating Activity. Ask students in each group to decide how and why people make clothing decisions. Point out that people choose clothing based on their needs, wants, and budgets. Tell the class that Lesson 1 discusses ways to determine clothing needs.

Introducing *Words to Know*
Call on a volunteer to read the vocabulary words. Ask students to determine a meaning of *accessories* for clothes, based on the meaning of the word in relation to home decorating. Explain that *versatile* means "having many uses." Have students use all the Words to Know in a short paragraph about clothes.

LESSON ONE
Deciding What You Need

 WORDS TO KNOW
accessories
personal style
versatile
wardrobe inventory
focal point

DISCOVER...
- how to assess your wardrobe needs.
- how to take a wardrobe inventory.
- ways to extend your wardrobe with accessories and smart clothing choices.

When you look in your closet, what do you see? Do you like most of your clothes and get a lot of use from them? Do you have enough casual clothes and enough dressy clothes? By thinking about what you need and what you like, and by making smart clothing choices, you can have a wardrobe that works for you without spending a lot of money.

452   CHAPTER 16: PLANNING YOUR WARDROBE

CLASSROOM RESOURCES FOR LESSON 1

 **Blackline Masters**
Activity and Project Card 31, "Mix-and-Match Outfits"
Concept Map 25
Cooperative Learning 31
Lesson 1 Quiz
Peer Pressure and Decision Making 31

 **Student Workbook**
Activities 112, 113

Looking at Your Wardrobe

A good way to begin is by taking a look at the clothes you have now. The best planning involves thinking about your entire wardrobe, not just about individual outfits. Keep in mind, too, that **accessories,** *such items as shoes, belts, scarves, hats, socks, ties, and jewelry,* are part of your wardrobe. Think about your total wardrobe needs—the different types of clothes you need for all the places you go and the activities in which you participate.

Your Wardrobe Needs

The first step in deciding what kind of clothes you need is to think about what kind of clothes you wear. Think about your various activities: you need clothes for school, casual clothes for spending time with friends, dressier clothes for special occasions, and clothes for special activities, such as sports or Scouts.

You also need to evaluate your **personal style,** *the kind of clothes you like best.* For example, do you wear a lot of tailored, buttoned shirts, or do you feel more comfortable in T-shirts?

The most practical clothes are **versatile,** or *able to be worn for many occasions.* The same sweater might be fine to wear with jeans and running shoes when you go to the mall, or with pants or a skirt and dressier shoes when you go to a restaurant with your family. A few items in neutral colors—such as white, beige, black, or gray—can be coordinated with many other items in your wardrobe.

Outer garments are part of your wardrobe, too. Because these items are often more expensive than others, it is especially important that coats and jackets be versatile. If it gets cold where you live, you will need at least one heavy jacket or coat.

Taking a Wardrobe Inventory

Now that you have a good sense of your wardrobe needs, take a look at what you already have. This would be a good

LESSON ONE: DECIDING WHAT YOU NEED   453

Rather than let old clothes take up space in your closet, you can donate them to a charitable organization. Get your clothing ready by making sure that everything is clean and in good repair.

CHAPTER 16, LESSON 1

TEACH

After students have read the feature, invite them to share their family's methods for dealing with outgrown or worn clothing. Discuss these ideas as well as those in the text. (Students might indicate exchanging clothes with friends or relatives ["hand-me-downs"], yard sales, and so on.) Ask students what is the most important thing to remember when passing on clothes to others. *(Clothing should be clean and in good repair.)*

L1 Language Arts

Organize the class into small groups to prepare a short article for a fashion magazine. The article should address teens and give them tips for what to do with clothing they do not wear. The article might be written as a result of interviews with teens and might present answers to questions asked in the interviews, such as: How did you come to have the item? Why do you keep the item? Do you think you will wear it in the future? What creative ways can you suggest for using the item? Have students share their articles with the class. Computers may be used to write reports.

MEETING STUDENT DIVERSITY

Cultural Diversity Have students investigate the ways people of different cultures and climates fill their need for clothing. You might assign small groups to locate information about different places and groups. For example, students might research the people of the South American tropical rain forest, Native Americans of Alaska, or people of the Sahara. Students might look for answers to the following questions: How does climate influence the kinds of clothing people wear? What materials do the people use for their clothing? How do people personalize their clothing? Instruct each group to share their information with the class in the form of an illustrated report.

453

CHAPTER 16, LESSON 1

USING VISUALS
Refer students to Figure 16.1. Have students complete the wardrobe inventory as a homework assignment. Remind them to consider their own personal styles and individual needs. Then ask students to sort their clothing into the categories listed. Have students determine if they have enough clothing to meet their needs.

L2 Critical Thinking
Brainstorm ways to reuse or recycle clothes no longer worn. Have students identify some creative ways to use unworn parts of fabric in those garments. Students might sketch their ideas for a display. Ideas could include making shorts from pants, tote bags or pencil cases from unworn parts of jeans, patchwork pillows, and so on. Challenge students to carry out their ideas.

Teacher TALK!

Talking About Clothing
Be sensitive to values people place on kinds and amounts of clothing. Some students may be reluctant to share ideas about their clothes if they feel they or their families will be judged by others. You might depersonalize the discussion when appropriate by using an imaginary person for discussion purposes.

**Figure 16.1
Wardrobe Inventory**
What do you think are the benefits of taking a wardrobe inventory?

Wardrobe Inventory	School	Casual	Sports	Dressy	Special Activities
Slacks					
Shirts/Blouses					
Skirts					
Dresses					
Jackets					
Accessories					

As you make your wardrobe inventory, set aside clothes that you no longer wear, and donate them to charity. Where can you donate used clothing in your community?

time to clean out your closet and drawers. Draw a chart like the one shown in **Figure 16.1**. This is called a **wardrobe inventory,** *a list of all the clothes, shoes, and accessories that you have.*

As you take your inventory, sort your clothing into the following four categories:

- **Clothes that you like and wear regularly.** Include these in your wardrobe inventory. Also, use them to help you evaluate your personal clothing style. What do you like about these clothes—style, color, fabric, texture?

- **Clothes that you no longer wear.** These might be clothes that no longer fit or that you just don't like anymore. There is no point in keeping these clothes in your inventory or in your closet. Before you set them aside, however, think about how they might still be used. If the sleeves on a shirt are too short, could they be cut off and re-hemmed to make a short-sleeved shirt instead? Clothes that you're sure you don't want can be given to friends or family members or donated to charity.

- **Clothes that you like but never seem to wear.** Make a note of these clothes. You may be able to add items to your wardrobe that will make them more useful.

- **Clothes in need of repair.** Set these to one side and see if they can be fixed. Schedule time to mend them and replace missing buttons. You will learn about repairing clothing in Chapter 18, Lesson 5.

454 CHAPTER 16: PLANNING YOUR WARDROBE

COOPERATIVE LEARNING

Versatile Clothing Organize the class into small groups. Ask each group to look through magazines and cut out pictures of versatile clothing that can be worn almost anywhere, any time of year. Have each group assemble its pictures in a collage titled "Versatile Clothing." Ask a representative from each group to explain why the group believes that the items shown in the collage would be more versatile than others. Display completed collages in the classroom.

When you have finished your wardrobe inventory, review it to see if you have enough clothing to meet all your needs. Notice which clothes can be used for more than one purpose. Be creative. Could you belt a short dress to wear as a tunic over leggings? Check to be sure that you have enough items in each category. Perhaps you have plenty of casual clothes but need to add to your dressy wardrobe.

After you have identified gaps in your wardrobe, consider what clothing items you need to fill them. Perhaps adding a basic garment, such as black pants or a white shirt, would allow for more clothing combinations. Think about what items would coordinate with clothes you already own.

Window shopping is one way to view the current styles. What are some other ways?

Extending Your Wardrobe

You now have a good idea of what clothes you need. Before you buy anything new, think about what is in style. Look at magazines, advertisements, and clothing-store displays. Observe what your friends and classmates are wearing. Study clothing combinations and ways to change the look of an outfit by adding accessories. Decide which of these current styles fit your personal style and your clothing needs.

While you are thinking about which styles you like, you should also start to note the price of the clothes and accessories that you want to buy. Another important consideration is the care these items would require. Do some of them need to be washed by hand, ironed, or dry-cleaned?

Building from the Basics

A basic wardrobe will ensure that your clothing is well planned and versatile. A good way to expand your wardrobe is by combining separates, or single pieces of clothing that mix and match. **Figure 16.2** on the next page provides some tips on planning a mix-and-match wardrobe.

LESSON ONE: DECIDING WHAT YOU NEED   455

CHAPTER 16, LESSON 1

L2 Applying Concepts
Have individual students list the clothes they would like to add to their wardrobes. When the list is completed, have them label those items they need with an *N* and those items they want with a *W*. Ask them to rank in order of importance the clothes that they identified as needed. Discuss with students what factors they use to distinguish between clothes they need and clothes they want.

L2 Critical Thinking
Have pairs of students use magazines and catalogs to create a school wardrobe for a person their age. First, have each group choose one complete outfit. Then have them add five garments to mix and match the basic outfit. Finally, have them choose two accessories. (Remind students that accessories can be essentials such as shoes or nonessentials such as jewelry.) After attaching the pictures to poster board, ask each group to display and talk about their selections.

L2 Problem Solving
Assign Peer Pressure and Decision Making 31 in the TCR. This activity gives students the opportunity to recognize peer pressure and practice decision-making skills.

L2 Cooperative Learning
Assign Cooperative Learning Activity 31 in the TCR. Students work in groups to learn about extending a wardrobe in this activity.

MORE ABOUT • • •

Weather and Wardrobe Choices Choosing the proper wardrobe items in extreme weather conditions can be important to a person's health. One cold-related condition, frostbite, can occur if the body is exposed to freezing weather without warm enough protection. Frostbite needs to be treated right away to avoid permanent damage of the affected body part. Hats, mittens or gloves, scarves, and warm, waterproof shoes or boots should be part of a wardrobe in areas where cold weather conditions frequently occur.

CHAPTER 16, LESSON 1

USING VISUALS
Refer students to Figure 16.2. Review the concept of mixing and matching items to create a wider choice of outfits. Then have students apply the suggestions given in Figure 16.2 to extend their own wardrobe. Call on volunteers to describe their experience in mixing and matching.

L3 Activity and Project Card
Allow time for students to complete Activity and Project Card 31, "Mix-and-Match Outfits," in the TCR.

L1 Student Workbook
Assign Activities 112 and 113 in the Student Workbook.

ASSESS

Evaluating the Lesson
Assign Reviewing Terms and Facts and Thinking Critically on page 457 to review the lesson; then assign the Lesson 1 Quiz in the TCR.

Reteaching
- Ask students to write a paragraph describing an item of clothing in their closet. Tell them to include the terms *wardrobe, accessories, personal style, versatile,* and *focal point* in describing the item. Call on students to share their paragraphs with the class.
- Have students complete Reteaching Activity 16 in the TCR.
- Assign Concept Map 25 in the TCR.

456

Figure 16.2
Mix and Match
Follow these suggestions when planning a basic mix-and-match wardrobe. Can you think of any other tips?

Inexpensive accessories can easily change the mood of an outfit from casual to dressy. Look through your favorite fashion magazines for new ideas.

When you go shopping, wear the clothes that you want to match.

Think again about the items that you already own. For example, a favorite shirt could be worn as a lightweight jacket. A scarf might look great as a belt.

Purchase clothes in the colors and fabrics that look good on you and fit your particular lifestyle.

Plan your wardrobe around a few favorite and flattering colors.

Combine a casual article of clothing with something more dressy. For instance, wear a silk shirt with a pair of jeans.

456   CHAPTER 16: PLANNING YOUR WARDROBE

HOME AND COMMUNITY CONNECTION

Clothing and Careers Have students talk to parents or other adults about clothing that they need for their jobs and for leisure time. Have them develop a survey to determine what types of clothing adults wear. Then invite students to create a basic wardrobe for a young person just starting a new job. Have students choose a career (engineer, construction worker, teacher, fashion consultant, and so on) and then determine the clothing they would need for work and for leisure time. Have them indicate how they could mix and match clothing items and how they could also use accessories to stretch their wardrobe. Call on students to share their wardrobe ideas.

Adding Accessories

A wardrobe is not complete without accessories. Accessories can be essentials—such as shoes and belts—or such nonessentials as ties, scarves, hats, and jewelry.

Well-chosen accessories can stretch your wardrobe by giving the same outfit an entirely different look. You can also use accessories to draw attention to your best features and away from less attractive ones. For instance, a wide belt can emphasize a slim waistline. A distinctive watchband or bracelet can draw attention to strong or graceful hands.

When using accessories, it is best to choose one *center of interest,* or **focal point.** Choose a wide belt with a big buckle, for example. Any other accessories should be less noticeable and blend in with the outfit. Too many eye-catching accessories will create a cluttered look.

A Successful Wardrobe

By building from what you have and planning what you need, you can create a versatile, coordinated wardrobe. Adding the right accessories will help you achieve different looks and give every outfit a finishing touch.

LESSON ONE Review

Using complete sentences, answer the following questions on a separate sheet of paper.

Reviewing Terms and Facts

1. **Vocabulary** Define the term *accessories*. Give two examples each of essential and nonessential accessories.
2. **Give Examples** Name some clothing items that could be used for more than one purpose.
3. **Recall** How can you turn a few clothing items into a large wardrobe?

Thinking Critically

4. **Explain** What is the purpose of a wardrobe inventory?

5. **Describe** Give an example of how accessories could be used to change the look of an outfit.

Applying Concepts

6. Look through a clothing catalog and select six basic separates from which to make a mix-and-match wardrobe. Using these separates, how many outfits can you suggest? What would the total cost be? Make a poster showing your basic wardrobe. Display your poster in class.

LESSON ONE: DECIDING WHAT YOU NEED

HOME AND COMMUNITY CONNECTION

Talking to a Store Representative Invite a clothing-store representative to speak to your class about current fashions and fashion trends. You might also invite a student in fashion design to speak to the class about internships, experience, and requirements related to his or her studies. You might have students prepare a list of questions in advance to ask the speaker. Ask the store representative or design student to show clothing combinations and various ways to accessorize the different outfits.

CHAPTER 16, LESSON 1

Answers to Lesson 1 Review

1. Accessories are items that are added to clothing. Essential accessories include shoes and belts. Nonessential accessories include ties, scarves, hats, and jewelry.
2. Examples will vary but might include a shirt that can be worn as a light jacket or a short dress that can be worn as a tunic.
3. By mixing and matching single pieces of clothing and adding accessories to a wardrobe.
4. A wardrobe inventory shows what you have so that you can figure out what you need.
5. Answers will vary but should include the way an accessory changes the outfit.
6. Posters will vary but should include the ideas presented in the lesson.

Enrichment

Ask each student to select a vacation spot, such as a ski resort, a beach resort, or a camping spot, and plan a wardrobe for a week-long vacation there. Challenge students to choose items that will fit in one standard duffel bag or small suitcase. Students can sketch or list their ideas.

CLOSE

Repeat the introductory activity, asking each student to list the three most important items in a wardrobe. Have their choices changed? Why or why not?

LESSON TWO
Evaluating Quality and Fit

FOCUS

Lesson Objectives

After studying this lesson, students should be able to
- explain how to judge quality in clothing.
- identify ways to find appropriate clothing styles and fit.

Motivating Activity

Organize the class into small groups. Give each group several swatches of fabric, each swatch made from a different type of fabric (cotton, wool, nylon, polyester, silk). Have students in each group identify the type of fabric each swatch is made of and evaluate whether each swatch is a durable fabric.

Introducing the Lesson

Call on a representative from each group to share the group's response to the Motivating Activity. Ask students to explain how they determined what type of fabric each swatch was made of. Discuss with students how they determined which fabric was durable. Then tell them that Lesson 2 will explain how to judge quality in clothing.

Introducing *Words to Know*

Create a word web on the board, using the term *fabric* as the hub. Have students place the Words to Know and their definitions in strands extending from the hub. Students might refer to the web as they study Lesson 2.

LESSON TWO
Evaluating Quality and Fit

WORDS TO KNOW
fibers
synthetic fibers
woven fabrics
knit fabrics
grain
ease

DISCOVER...
- how to judge quality in clothing.
- how to find the best style and the right fit for you.

Have you ever bought a shirt that got a hole in it after only one or two washings? Perhaps you have a sweater that you never wear because it makes you feel itchy. You can avoid these problems in the future if you learn how to judge clothing quality. Quality in an item of clothing means that it is well made, durable, and comfortable to wear. To judge clothing quality, you need to look at the fabric, the construction, and the fit.

458   CHAPTER 16: PLANNING YOUR WARDROBE

CLASSROOM RESOURCES FOR LESSON 2

 Blackline Masters
Cooperative Learning 32
Cross Curriculum 18
Lesson 2 Quiz

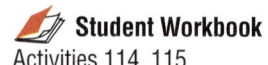 **Student Workbook**
Activities 114, 115

Recognizing Quality Fabrics

The best way to learn about fabrics is to handle and compare them for yourself. Make a trip to a fabric store. Check the labels to see the fiber content, or what the fabrics are made of. Look at the prices and compare fabrics in different price ranges. Feel various fabrics to see how they handle. When stretched or crushed, quality fabric will spring back. A basic understanding of fabrics can help you make better clothing choices.

Fibers and Fabrics

Most fabrics are made from fibers. **Fibers** are *the tiny strands that make up yarns.* Originally, all fibers came from natural sources. Some natural fibers commonly used in clothing are cotton, linen, silk, and wool. Do you know from which natural sources these fibers come?

- **Cotton**—the seed pod of the cotton plant
- **Linen**—the flax plant
- **Silk**—spun by a silkworm
- **Wool**—the hair of sheep

More recently, scientists have developed a wide variety of **synthetic fibers,** *fibers made partially or entirely from chemicals.* Polyester and nylon are two types of synthetic fibers.

All clothing must have a label that gives the fiber content of the fabric and instructions for its care and a hangtag that gives additional information.

Skills IN ACTION

Identifying Fabrics

Being able to identify different types of fabrics will help you select clothes that are well made and comfortable. Gather as many different fabric swatches (small pieces of material) as you can. Identify and label the various types of fiber (natural, synthetic, blend) and weave (woven, knit). Mount your fabrics and display your poster in class.

LESSON TWO: EVALUATING QUALITY AND FIT 459

MORE ABOUT • • •

Synthetic Fabrics Synthetic fabrics often outperform natural fabrics. Polartec and Microfleece are registered names for fabrics made from recycled plastic. At first they were used for outdoor sports clothing, but now the fabrics have gained popularity for sporty clothes of all kinds. Polartec is lightweight, warm, and dries quickly. These fabrics have a high warmth-to-weight ratio, thus keeping the wearer warm without adding weight. Coolmax and Drylete keep people warm by pulling perspiration away from the skin. Ask students to look through catalogs of clothing items made from synthetic fabrics or to bring items made of this fabric to class.

CHAPTER 16, LESSON 2

TEACH

Skills IN ACTION

After students have read the feature, have small groups work cooperatively to collect and display their fabric samples. Students might also display fabrics by color, weight, or some other property. Ask them to consider the following questions when analyzing their fabrics: Do some fabrics look best in light or dark colors? Do some fabrics seem more appropriate for some kinds of clothing than others? Call on volunteers to present their observations to the class.

L1 Understanding Concepts

Ask students to create mobiles that illustrate the terms that are used in evaluating clothing. The mobiles might illustrate the answers to the following questions: What is the difference between fabrics and fibers? *(Fabrics are made from fibers of various sorts.)* What are some natural fibers? *(cotton, wool, silk)* What are some synthetic fibers? *(polyester, nylon)*

L2 Cooperative Learning

Assign Cooperative Learning Activity 32 in the TCR. Students work in groups to evaluate fabric quality and construction in this activity.

CHAPTER 16, LESSON 2

L2 Applying
Have students investigate fabric finishes by checking labels on clothes and labels on clothing-care products in the clothing-care section of the grocery store. Have students work with partners to develop a brochure that illustrates the various types of fabric finishes, the purposes of the finishes, and the kind of care needed for fabrics with the particular finishes. Display brochures in the classroom.

L2 Social Studies Connection
Assign Cross-Curriculum Activity 18 in the TCR. Students learn about fabrics from around the world in this activity.

L3 Language Arts
Ask interested students to use library references or computer sources to research a synthetic fiber of their choice. Ask them to find answers to the following questions as well as to other questions they want answered: How is the fiber manufactured? Was it originally meant to be used for something other than clothing? What is the most popular use for the fiber? Students should report their findings in one or two brief paragraphs.

L2 Demonstrating
Provide swatches of fabrics for students to observe, including plain weave and twill weave. Have students separate the yarns so that they can see the way lengthwise and crosswise threads are interlaced. Have them unravel a thread from the swatch and examine the fibers. Students might sketch and label what they observe.

Fabrics can be made all of one fiber or by combining two or more fibers. The clothing label must tell you what percentage of each type of fiber makes up the fabric. For example, a shirt might be 100 percent cotton, or it might be a blend, such as 65 percent cotton and 35 percent polyester. A sweater might be labeled 70 percent lambs wool, 20 percent angora, and 10 percent nylon.

Fibers are made into fabrics by two main methods: weaving and knitting. The way a fabric is made affects its appearance and performance.

- **Woven fabrics** are *fabrics made on a loom by interlacing lengthwise and crosswise threads at right angles.* Several methods of interlacing are used to achieve special effects. The most durable weaves are plain and twill. The fabrics used in bedsheets and men's dress shirts are examples of plain weave. Denim used for jeans is one example of a twill weave.
- **Knit fabrics** are *fabrics made by looping threads together.* Depending on the knitting method, different fabrics can be made. Not all knits are heavy like sweaters. Cotton T-shirts are also made of knit fabric. Most knit fabrics can be stretched easily. This stretching makes them comfortable and wrinkle resistant.

Fabric Grain

Grain in fabric is *the direction in which the threads run.* Both knit and woven fabrics have a grain. The grain runs up and down and across the fabric, forming a true right angle. Well-constructed clothes should be cut on grain, with the threads running straight up and down and straight across.

Threads may sometimes be pulled off grain when the fabric goes through the finishing process. This makes the grain slant. If the fabric is off grain, the garment will appear to sag to one side, especially after a few washings.

You can test the fabric grain of a shirt by making sure that the grain is straight across the back from one underarm seam to the other. Test pants and skirts at the back of the hipline. The grain should be the same on both sides. If not, the garment probably won't look right when you wear it.

460   CHAPTER 16: PLANNING YOUR WARDROBE

HOME AND COMMUNITY CONNECTION

Flammable Fabrics Act Students should be aware that governmental agencies work to keep unsafe fabrics from being used for clothing, especially children's clothing. The Flammable Fabrics Act sets standards for the flammability of fabrics. The standards cover children's sleepwear and other apparel, as well as fabrics sold by the yard and intended for children's clothing. Carpets, rugs, mattresses, and mattress pads are also covered under the legislation. Ask students to look for information about flammability on fabric and clothing tags and to bring examples of this information to class.

460

Fabric Finishes

Manufacturers sometimes add various finishes to improve the quality or durability of fabrics. Some finishes add body or bulk. Some set or hold the threads in place so that the fabric will wear well and will not pull out at the seams. Other finishes add softness, luster, strength, crispness, or shrinkage control. Finishes can also make caring for fabrics easier.

Clothing labels often tell you what finishes have been added. For instance, a fabric may be treated to be stain- or water-repellent. Washable clothes may have a drip-dry or permanent-press finish, which means that the garment requires little or no ironing.

▲ Grain in a garment should run straight up and down and across the fabric. How might a garment look if it were off grain?

Recognizing Quality Construction

No matter from what type of fabric clothing is made, a quality garment also requires quality construction. Poor construction can ruin the appearance or durability of an otherwise attractive style. When evaluating clothing construction, use the information provided in **Figure 16.3** on the next page.

LESSON TWO: EVALUATING QUALITY AND FIT **461**

CHAPTER 16, LESSON 2

L3 Role-Playing
Ask students to work in small groups to create a skit that will "sell" a piece of clothing to the class. Provide time for students to plan their skits. They should incorporate in their skits the lesson information about recognizing quality construction. When students have finished planning, have each group present its skit to the class. Call on volunteers to evaluate the "sales presentation" and to give reasons for whether they would or would not buy the garment.

L2 Writing
Have students create a story about a favorite garment. Let the author assume the role of the garment and write in the first person. The story might include who wore me, to what occasion I was worn, how I was cared for or how I was neglected, and what became of me (recycled, sold, or traded).

DID YOU KNOW
Even when clothing is marked with a particular size, it is best not to rely on that alone to tell whether a garment will fit properly. The fit of a particular size can vary with different manufacturers and with different styles.

COOPERATIVE LEARNING

Shopping by Mail Mail-order shopping is an increasingly popular way to buy clothing. Many people find that they can save time by ordering clothes from catalogs. Collect a variety of catalogs, and have students look through them and decide on some items they would like to purchase. Ask them to choose the items they want and then report information about fabrics, style, quality of construction, and cleaning information. Have students evaluate the kind of information that catalogs provide about clothing items. Also, have students determine the kind of information about clothing that is difficult or impossible for a catalog to provide.

CHAPTER 16, LESSON 2

USING VISUALS
Invite students to share stories of the clothes they may have had that were poorly constructed. Have students note similarities in the anecdotes. Have them determine whether most of the garments fell apart on their own or because of misuse. Then refer students to Figure 16.3. Have them use the information in the chart to determine what factors contributed to the poor construction of the particular piece of clothing.

L1 Understanding Concepts
Ask students to evaluate magazine pictures of clothing for comfort. Ask students to construct a chart with the following column headings: "Clothes for School," "Clothes for Dressy Occasions," "Clothes for Athletic Activities." Have students find pictures of five clothing items that they would consider comfortable for each situation. Display students' charts and discuss what criteria students used to determine comfort. Have students compare their criteria with what was presented in the lesson.

L3 Comparing and Contrasting
Students probably know that sizes, especially for girls' and junior clothing, vary according to manufacturer. Invite students to pool their resources to find several garments of the same size but from different manufacturers. Students can measure the length, width, and size of various openings of each item and make a chart that compares measurements. What do they discover? Do sizes vary? If so, how, and why?

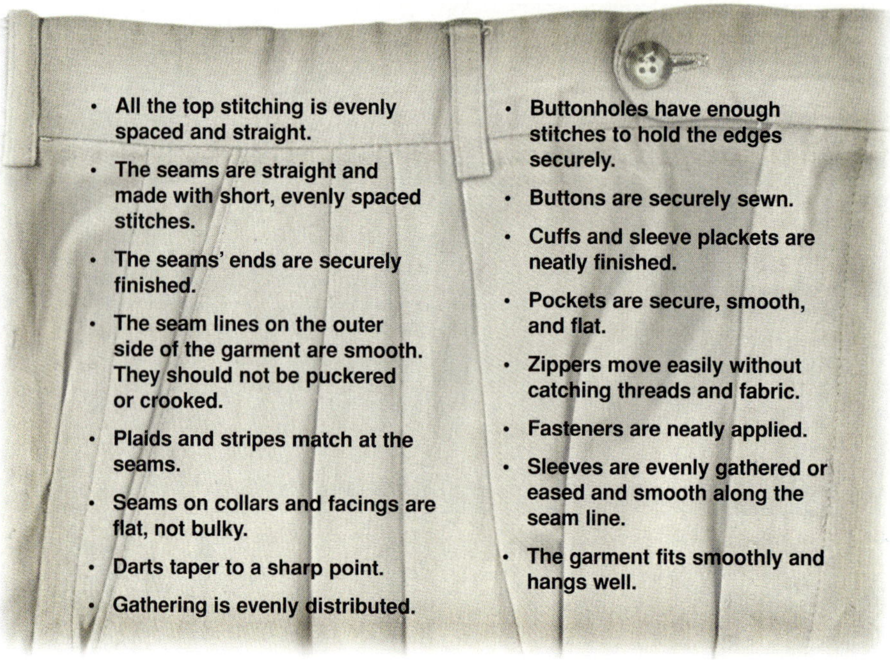

- All the top stitching is evenly spaced and straight.
- The seams are straight and made with short, evenly spaced stitches.
- The seams' ends are securely finished.
- The seam lines on the outer side of the garment are smooth. They should not be puckered or crooked.
- Plaids and stripes match at the seams.
- Seams on collars and facings are flat, not bulky.
- Darts taper to a sharp point.
- Gathering is evenly distributed.

- Buttonholes have enough stitches to hold the edges securely.
- Buttons are securely sewn.
- Cuffs and sleeve plackets are neatly finished.
- Pockets are secure, smooth, and flat.
- Zippers move easily without catching threads and fabric.
- Fasteners are neatly applied.
- Sleeves are evenly gathered or eased and smooth along the seam line.
- The garment fits smoothly and hangs well.

Figure 16.3
Signs of Quality Construction
Why is it important to check for quality construction when buying clothes?

Comfortable Clothes

To enjoy wearing your clothes, you must be comfortable in them. First, the clothes need to fit correctly. The fabric from which a garment is made and the style of the garment also affect comfort. Knowing how to evaluate these three factors will help you select clothes that you will feel comfortable wearing.

Finding the Best Fit

Clothing is sold in a variety of size categories. Each is designed for a particular body size and shape. Clothing for females comes in different sizes from clothing for males.

Female clothing is sold in girls', juniors', misses', women's, and plus sizes. Girls' sizes go up to 14 or 16 and are roughly equivalent to the age of the wearer. Juniors' sizes (such as 3, 5, 7, 9, 11, and 13) are designed for a developing figure but are usually smaller and shorter-waisted than misses sizes (such as 6, 8, 10, 12, 14, and 16). Juniors' clothes are generally styled for teens, while misses' and women's clothes cater more to

COOPERATIVE LEARNING

Clothing for Children Invite students who babysit or care for children at church or at home to create a booklet of clothing that would be appropriate for children at various ages, for example, infant, toddler, and preschool child. Students can check stores for children's clothing, clothing of small children they know, and catalogs for clothing that is easy to get on and off, safe for small children, and easy to care for. Ask students to sketch or paste pictures of their choices in their booklets and annotate the pictures, indicating which features are good and which should be avoided and why.

adult tastes. Within each size category, petite sizes are shorter in length, while tall sizes are longer.

For males there are three basic size groups: boys', teen boys', and men's. Boys' sizes are designed for small, undeveloped bodies. Teens' sizes are for slim teens and young men. Men's sizes are designed for adult figures. Men's pants are sized by the waist measurement and the inside leg measurement, or inseam. For example, jeans with a 28-inch waist and a 30-inch inseam would be labeled "Size 28/30." Dress shirts also list two measurements—the collar size and the sleeve length—such as 15/34. Sports jackets are sold by chest measurement and length, such as 38 Short or 38 Long.

For both females and males, some clothing may be sized simply as Small, Medium, Large, or Extra-large. Examples of this type of clothing include T-shirts, sweatshirts, and sweaters.

Try on and compare the fit of various brands and styles until you find one that feels comfortable to you. Check the fit by looking at yourself in a full-length mirror. Be sure also to test the fit by sitting, bending, walking, and reaching. **Figure 16.4** provides guidelines for judging the fit of garments.

CHAPTER 16, LESSON 2

L1 Applying Concepts

Display a man's shirt labeled with collar and sleeve length, a pair of jeans with length and waist given, and two articles of female clothing sized differently. Ask students to explain the meaning of the sizes. Then point out that sizes are not always true, due to manufacturers' differences.

L3 Measuring

Ask students to take their measurements and compare them to those in pattern books to get an idea of what size they are. Then have them compare their measurements to clothing charts in catalogs.

L2 Evaluating

Ask students to categorize ten garments they have at home by fiber content (natural or synthetic or blends) and ease of cleaning. They can look at the labels for this information. Collect all the information and help students make some generalizations about the kind of clothing they most frequently wear.

**Figure 16.4
Judging Fit in Garments**

For a comfortable fit in clothing, be sure to check these features. What might happen if you didn't check them before buying a garment?

SLEEVES Do long sleeves cover your wristbone? Can you lift your arms over your head with ease?

NECK OPENING Is the neck opening comfortable? If it is too large, the front of the garment falls forward and sags. If it is too small, the neck binds and the front rides up.

SHOULDER SEAMS Do the shoulder seams hit you at the shoulder? They should not go over your shoulder unless the garment is designed that way.

FASTENERS Do buttonholes, zippers, and other closures lie smoothly?

WAISTBAND AND HIPS Does the waistband feel comfortable and fasten easily? Can you sit comfortably in pants or jeans?

HEMLINE Is the hemline even around the bottom? Is the length right for you?

LESSON TWO: EVALUATING QUALITY AND FIT   **463**

USING VISUALS

Refer students to Figure 16.4. Point out that not every tip in the illustration applies to every garment. As students read and discuss the tips, ask them to list types of garments that each tip would apply to. For example, a turtleneck shirt or dress must have a comfortable neck opening.

MEETING STUDENT DIVERSITY

Clothing Diversity In various cultures, people design clothing for comfort in their particular climate. Invite students or families of students from various cultures to share their unique clothing styles. Have them explain how the styles reflect climate and comfort concerns of their cultures or countries of origin. Students can look at pictures of people in various climates and match styles with these words: *tailored, draped,* and *mixed.* Help students generalize about how the style helps keep people comfortable.

CHAPTER 16, LESSON 2

TIPS for living

After students have read the feature, ask them to evaluate how their method of buying shoes compares to the tips given. Have them determine what tips listed in the feature, if any, might help them to buy better-fitting shoes.

L1 Student Workbook

Assign Activities 114 and 115 in the Student Workbook.

ASSESS

Evaluating the Lesson

Assign Reviewing Terms and Facts and Thinking Critically on page 465 to review the lesson; then assign the Lesson 2 Quiz in the TCR.

Reteaching

- Have each student sketch an item of clothing—such as a shirt, dress, or pair of pants—and label the signs that point to a well-constructed garment. Invite volunteers to share their sketches.
- Have students complete Reteaching Activity 16 in the TCR.

TIPS for living

CHOOSING SHOES

Shoes are an important part of your wardrobe. You want to buy shoes that are both comfortable and durable. Here are some tips.

- Shop early in the day to get a more accurate fit.
- Get your feet measured so that you are sure of your size.
- Try on shoes with the type of socks or stockings that you would normally wear.
- Look for shoes that are not too tight or too loose. Be sure that you have room to wiggle your toes.
- Try on both left and right shoes, and walk around the store in them.
- If you are trying to find shoes to go with a certain outfit, wear the outfit or bring a sample of the fabric.

The Way Fabrics Feel

The fabric from which a garment is made can affect its comfort in many ways. Fabrics made of natural fibers absorb perspiration and generally feel cooler than fabrics made of synthetic fibers. Synthetic fibers usually dry faster, however, and may be more comfortable in bathing suits, for example. The fiber content of each garment must be listed on its label. Knowing the characteristics of different fibers will help you choose the most comfortable fabric.

Which fabrics do you think feel pleasant to the touch? Some people dislike the feel of slippery or clingy fabrics. Others find woolen knits rough and scratchy. You will want to buy clothes that suit your own preferences. When you buy clothes, be sure to check the feel of the fabric carefully.

If you don't like the way a fabric feels, you probably won't enjoy wearing it. From what fabrics are your favorite clothes made?

464 CHAPTER 16: PLANNING YOUR WARDROBE

MORE ABOUT • • •

Keeping Warm Fabrics and clothing styles can make a difference in keeping the body warm. Wearing several layers of lighter-weight clothing provides added insulation. Wearing natural fibers next to the skin will absorb moisture and keep you warmer. Body heat may be trapped with close-fitting collars, cuffs, and waistbands. Wearing a hat, hood, or scarf will prevent heat loss through the head. Hands and feet may be kept warm by wearing gloves, mittens, and an extra pair of socks.

Comfort and Style

Clothing style also affects its comfort. For example, a full skirt or pants with pleats may provide for more **ease**, or *ability to move freely*, in a garment. A scoop neckline or an open collar may feel less restrictive than a turtleneck sweater.

Some styles may suit your body shape better than others. Trying on a garment is the best way to decide whether a particular style is comfortable for you. A style that feels comfortable will often look flattering as well.

Understanding how to evaluate the quality and fit of garments will help you to make wise clothing choices. How might this save you money?

LESSON TWO *Review*

Using complete sentences, answer the following questions on a separate sheet of paper.

Reviewing Terms and Facts

1. **Identify** Name four natural fibers and identify the source of each.
2. **Vocabulary** How does a *woven fabric* differ from a *knit fabric*?
3. **List** Give four reasons why a finish might be added to a fabric.
4. **Recall** Name three factors that affect the comfort of clothes.

Thinking Critically

5. **Explain** How would you check the fabric grain on a shirt?
6. **Apply** What measurements would you need to know if you were buying a dress shirt for your father?
7. **Compare and Contrast** What is the difference between style and fit? How are they related?

Applying Concepts

8. Imagine that you are a clothing designer. Describe one garment that you would design and the fabric you would use to make it. Explain how the characteristics of this fabric would enhance the garment's design. Draw a sketch of your creation.
9. Working with a small group, look through a clothing catalog. Find as many terms as you can that describe the style of one type of garment, such as shirts. Make a list of these style terms, and try to define or describe the characteristics of each one.

LESSON TWO: EVALUATING QUALITY AND FIT 465

HOME AND COMMUNITY CONNECTION

Careers in Fashion and Clothing Invite a fashion designer, copywriter, or sales clerk or buyer to class to talk about a career in fashion. Have students prepare several questions in advance and then ask the person to talk about a typical day, some highs and lows of the job, and what he or she thinks the future holds for potential careers in fashion. Have students write a summary of the visit, pointing out the most interesting facts about the career presented.

CHAPTER 16, LESSON 2

Answers to Lesson 2 Review

1. Cotton, from the seed pod of the cotton plant; linen, from the flax plant; silk, a thread spun by silkworms; wool, from the hair of sheep.
2. Threads of woven fabrics are woven together on a loom, while threads of knit fabrics are looped together.
3. Any four: to add bulk or body, to extend wear, to add softness, to add luster, to add strength, to add crispness, to make a fabric water-repellent, to repel stains.
4. The fit, the kind of fabric, and the style of the garment.
5. Hold the shirt up and check the back; the grain should go straight across the back from one underarm seam to another.
6. Collar size and sleeve length.
7. The style of a garment might be loose or close-fitting, but it should still fit properly.
8. Responses will vary but should be based on some of the ideas learned in the lesson.
9. Responses will vary. Students should share ideas when defining garment characteristics and then choose the best definitions for their answers.

Enrichment

Students can investigate swatches of cotton and cotton-blend fabrics, such as broadcloth, denim, sailcloth, gingham, and muslin. Ask students to compare the fabrics. Ask each student to choose one fabric and write a sample label for it.

CLOSE

Have each student write catalog copy for their favorite garment. Post the results in a class display, possibly next to the garments.

LESSON THREE
Shopping for Clothes

FOCUS

Lesson Objectives
After studying this lesson, students should be able to
- describe how to develop a shopping plan.
- explain what clothing labels tell.
- list ways to get the most for their clothing dollar.

Motivating Activity
Write the following phrase on the chalkboard for students to complete: I think that _____ are the best brand of jeans because _____.

Introducing the Lesson
Have students share their responses to the Motivating Activity. Discuss with students what factors help determine the best kind of jeans, or other types of clothing, for them. Tell students that Lesson 3 provides helpful tips for the most effective shopping.

Introducing *Words to Know*
Explain that all the vocabulary phrases have something to do with shopping. Have students work in groups to quickly write short definitions of the phrases. Then call on representatives from the groups to share the definitions. Generate a class definition for each of the terms. Compare student-generated definitions with those in the Glossary.

LESSON THREE
Shopping for Clothes

 **WORDS TO KNOW**

shopping plan
status symbols
cost per wearing

DISCOVER...
- how to develop a shopping plan.
- what clothing labels tell you.
- how to get the most for your clothing dollars.

How do you feel about shopping for clothes? Maybe you love to shop, whereas your best friend would rather do almost anything than look for new clothes. No matter how you feel about shopping, you can be a smarter shopper by following a few simple guidelines. By planning your clothing needs and looking for the best value, you can save both time and money.

466   CHAPTER 16: PLANNING YOUR WARDROBE

CLASSROOM RESOURCES FOR LESSON 3

 Blackline Masters
Enrichment 18
Lesson 3 Quiz
Peer Pressure and Decision Making 32

 Transparencies
Transparency 66, "What's It Really Worth?"

 Student Workbook
Activity 116

Your Shopping Plan

In Lesson 1 of this chapter, you learned how to plan a wardrobe. The final step was to make a list of the clothes you needed. That list is the first step in developing a shopping plan. A **shopping plan** is *a strategy for spending the money you have available to purchase the clothing you need or want.* Before you develop a shopping plan, you should talk over your wardrobe ideas with your parents. They can help you determine how much money is available to buy the clothes you need, as well as how much of that amount you can use for other items you want.

In addition to your list of clothing needs, your shopping plan should consider these three factors:

- **Your clothing budget.** It is a good idea to set up a monthly or seasonal spending plan for your clothes. Go over your spending plan with your parents and decide how you can make your money go farther. For example, can you wait until the jacket goes on sale? Can you replace the missing buttons on your shirt instead of buying a new one?

- **How you will pay for the purchase.** You learned about several payment methods, including cash, check, credit card, and debit card, in Chapter 7, Lesson 5. Can you recall some of the advantages and disadvantages of each? For major purchases, such as a formal dress or suit, running shoes, or a winter coat, you may need to save your money. Another alternative for more expensive items is to use a layaway plan. Unlike buying on credit, layaway means that you can't take the item home until it is paid for in full.

- **Where you will shop.** In most areas, there are several stores from which to choose. Specialty stores, discount stores, and department stores are some options.

Another choice is to shop for clothes by mail order. Although you can't try on the clothes before you order them, you may prefer the convenience of shopping in your own home. Clothes that do not suit you can usually be returned.

Before you shop, you need to plan your clothing budget. Why is this important?

LESSON THREE: SHOPPING FOR CLOTHES **467**

COOPERATIVE LEARNING

Class Clothing Store Students can practice the skills of budgeting and making purchases at a "class-run" clothing store. Ask students to bring in a variety of pictures of clothing or clothing items. Call on volunteers to take on the role of sales clerks. Then have each student, using play money, try to purchase some basic items. When students have made their purchases, have them write a paragraph that evaluates their way of shopping. Students might answer the following questions in their paragraphs: How far were you able to stretch your clothing dollars? What choices did you have to make? On what basis did you make your clothing decisions?

CHAPTER 16, LESSON 3

TEACH

L1 Understanding Concepts
Talk about the concept of a shopping plan. Ask: What factors must be considered when you develop a shopping plan? *(your budget, how to pay for the clothes, and where to shop)* Why should you set up a monthly or seasonal plan for buying clothes? *(Such plans can help you budget your money and can help avoid being short of money for a needed item.)* What is a layaway plan? *(A way to buy something that allows you to put a small amount of money down and make payments on a regular basis until the item has been fully paid for.)*

L2 Applying Concepts
Invite small groups of students to choose an item such as athletic shoes or a winter jacket for a comparison study. Provide a sampling of catalogs, magazines, and newspapers for students to use to identify prices, advantages, and disadvantages of their chosen item. Ask students to find the answers to questions such as the following: How do the items vary? Do the prices of the item vary? What factors account for the differences in price? Have students in each group report their findings in a consumer magazine article about clothing. Call on volunteers in each group to share their articles with the class.

L3 Writing
Ask students to write a "Shopping Hints" article for the school newspaper or class newsletter. Articles should explain why such things as quality, style, budget, where to shop, and method of payment must be considered when making a spending plan.

467

CHAPTER 16, LESSON 3

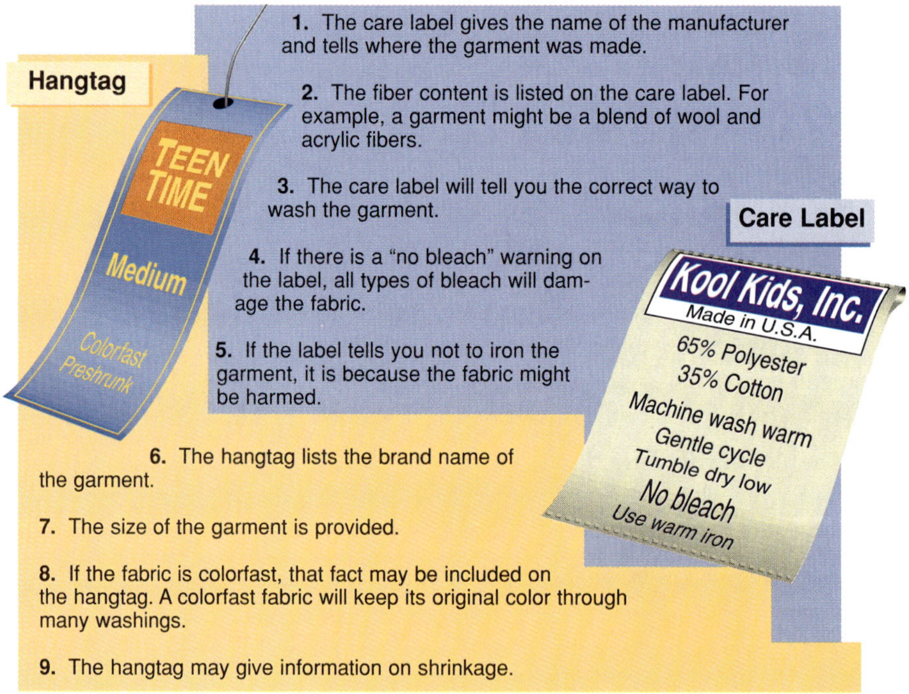

L2 Math

Ask students to list the clothes they need for the coming season. Have them allow a set amount of money for purchases. Then have them prioritize what they will buy and set up a spending plan. Have students decide how they will pay for their clothes and where they might buy the clothes. Have them present their plan in chart form. Charts may be made on computers.

USING VISUALS

Refer students to Figure 16.5. Then ask them to examine the care labels of five garments in their closet. Ask students to compare the information on these labels with the information illustrated in Figure 16.5. Then have students list the fiber content and care instructions for each of the five garments they chose.

L3 Art

Interested students can work with a partner to create a poster that demonstrates the tips about hidden costs. They might illustrate the tips with magazine pictures, or they might create a display using items of clothing with signs that provide helpful information about figuring hidden costs.

What the Label Tells You

You can find a great deal of helpful information by reading clothing labels. Taking time to check the label and the hangtag before you buy can help you determine the quality, durability, and care of garments.

Care Labels

Every item of clothing must carry a label describing its fiber content and how to care for it. This information may be on the same label or on two different labels. Look for these labels inside the collar or waist. Sometimes you will find the care label sewn into a side seam instead.

The care required depends on the fibers and finishes used in making the fabric. Check garment tags for special information about finishes, such as "little or no ironing," "wrinkle-resistant," or "water-repellent." The care label will give you specific cleaning and care instructions. **Figure 16.5** provides information about care labels.

Figure 16.5 Understanding Labels

Checking care labels before you buy clothing can save you time and money. For example, you may decide not to purchase clothing that needs to be washed by hand or dry-cleaned because the item is more difficult or expensive to care for.

1. The care label gives the name of the manufacturer and tells where the garment was made.
2. The fiber content is listed on the care label. For example, a garment might be a blend of wool and acrylic fibers.
3. The care label will tell you the correct way to wash the garment.
4. If there is a "no bleach" warning on the label, all types of bleach will damage the fabric.
5. If the label tells you not to iron the garment, it is because the fabric might be harmed.
6. The hangtag lists the brand name of the garment.
7. The size of the garment is provided.
8. If the fabric is colorfast, that fact may be included on the hangtag. A colorfast fabric will keep its original color through many washings.
9. The hangtag may give information on shrinkage.

Hangtag: TEEN TIME, Medium, Colorfast Preshrunk

Care Label: Kool Kids, Inc. Made in U.S.A. 65% Polyester 35% Cotton Machine wash warm Gentle cycle Tumble dry low No bleach Use warm iron

468 CHAPTER 16: PLANNING YOUR WARDROBE

MORE ABOUT • • •

Fashion Designers Before the late eighteenth century the clothing designer was never highlighted when a new fashion appeared. Attention was given to the garment itself—the style, detailing, color, and fabric—and to the wearer of the garment. The first fashion designer to receive fame and recognition was Rose Bertin, a Parisian milliner. Her stylish hats caught the attention of the Duchess of Chartres, who presented Rose to the Empress Maria Theresa. The Empress commissioned Rose to design clothing for her daughter, Marie Antoinette. Marie Antoinette devoted much time and money to fashion, and Rose Bertin's salon flourished as the fashion center of Paris.

Brand Name Clothing

A brand name is a trademark used by a manufacturer to identify its products. Sometimes stores have their own brand names. In addition, clothing labels may identify the designer, which is another kind of brand name. Some people use brand names as a guide in selecting clothing. Some brands may have better styles than others, and some may have better quality. Brand names and designer labels are not always signs of quality, however. They can be just **status symbols,** or *clothes or other items that give the owner a special feeling of importance.*

Through experience in wearing and comparing various articles of clothing, you will discover which brands are well made and fit well. Brand name items are usually more expensive than those with less well known names. You will have to decide if brand name clothing is worth the extra cost.

Shopping for Value

When you made your shopping plan, you had to calculate your clothing budget—how much money you had to spend. You can make that money go farther by understanding and following some simple guidelines.

Earning Money for Clothes

Have you ever needed extra money to buy the brand or style of clothes you want? For instance, Jeremy's father gave him $30 to buy a new pair of running shoes, but the pair Jeremy wants costs $50. Working with a partner, brainstorm a list of ways Jeremy, and other teens your age, can earn extra money. Then share your ideas in small groups.

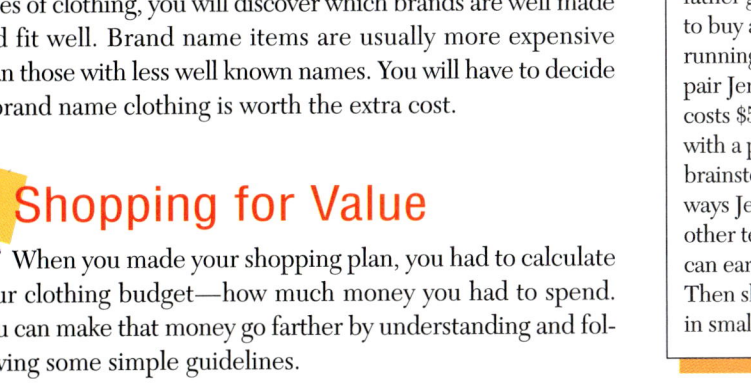

THE HIDDEN COSTS

When you shop for clothes, keep in mind that a garment may end up costing more than the price tag indicates. Beware of these hidden wastes of time and money:

- Fabrics that can't be washed in the washing machine. Dry cleaning can be expensive. Hand washing takes extra time.
- Fabrics that ball up (pill) on the surface or that snag easily. If the fabric needs to be repaired each time you wear it, you won't want to wear it much.
- Fabrics that must be ironed.
- Special features that may increase the cost of dry cleaning. For example, dry cleaners often charge extra to clean leather or to press pleats.

LESSON THREE: SHOPPING FOR CLOTHES

MORE ABOUT • • •

Shopping Options Choosing how and where to shop for clothing depends on personal preferences and budgetary requirements. Often price is a consideration and you must decide what choices are available. You will want to find out which stores carry the best selections that are suited to your preferences and have the best prices. Remember that buying on layaway means that the item cannot be taken home until it is paid for. Sometimes people enjoy finding bargains in secondhand stores. At these stores the items may not be returnable even if they don't fit or have flaws.

CHAPTER 16, LESSON 3

Be sensitive to the ways clothes are purchased in different households. Some parents have complete control over purchasing and would not allow Jeremy to purchase the more expensive sneakers even after he has earned the money. After students have finished reading the feature, call on volunteers to share ways that they earn money for things they want.

L1 Using Transparencies

Present Color Transparency 66, "What's It Really Worth?" in the TCR. Use this overhead visual to reinforce concepts from this lesson.

TIPS for living

After students have read the feature, review what a hidden cost is *(additional time and money needed to care for a clothing item)*. Then ask students to think of one garment they own. Ask them to recall the cost of purchasing this garment. Then ask them to use the information in the feature to determine any hidden costs for the clothing item.

L2 Problem Solving

Assign Peer Pressure and Decision Making 32 in the TCR. This activity gives students the opportunity to recognize peer pressure and practice decision-making skills.

CHAPTER 16, LESSON 3

L1 Student Workbook
Assign Activity 116 in the Student Workbook.

ASSESS

Evaluating the Lesson
Assign Reviewing Terms and Facts and Thinking Critically on page 471 to review the lesson; then assign the Lesson 3 Quiz in the TCR.

Reteaching
- Tell students to imagine that they have received $50 as a birthday present. They have decided to use the money to buy clothes. Ask them to make a shopping plan, using the guidelines on page 467.
- Have students complete Reteaching Activity 16 in the TCR.

Enrichment
- Ask students to find out the layaway policies in a local clothing or department store. Students should find out how much money needs to be put down and how long people have to finish paying for the purchase. Have students present the information on a poster.
- Assign Enrichment Activity 18 in the TCR.

Stretching Your Clothing Budget

You don't have to spend a great deal of money to have a wardrobe that fulfills your needs. To reduce your clothing costs, follow these tips:

- **Start with two or three basic outfits.** Add coordinated pieces to build your wardrobe around a few basic colors. You can create many different clothing combinations that way.
- **Make the best use of what you have.** Try different uses, combinations, and accessories with clothes you already own.
- **Compare cost and quality.** Keep in mind that it may not always be smart to buy the best quality. Why pay more for durability in a fad item that won't be in fashion next year?
- **Take advantage of sales.** Planning ahead and shopping during seasonal sales can be a good way to get more for your money.
- **Take good care of your clothes.** By following the directions on the care label, you can make clothes last longer.
- **Learn to sew.** Making simple repairs and simple clothing items yourself can be a way to save money and express your personality.

Shopping during sales is a good way to get more for your clothing dollars. What are some other ways?

Understanding Cost per Wearing

An easy way to find out how much value you are getting for the money you spend is to calculate the cost per wearing. **Cost per wearing** is the *amount of money spent for each time you wear an article of clothing.* To determine cost per wearing, first estimate how many times

470 CHAPTER 16: PLANNING YOUR WARDROBE

HOME AND COMMUNITY CONNECTION

Field Trip to Resale Shop Arrange for a parent or other responsible adult to accompany a small group of students to a resale or secondhand clothing shop. Direct students to take notes about what is available and at what prices. Invite discussion after the trip so that students who participated can talk about the advantages or disadvantages of shopping for some items at these stores.

you will wear a particular garment. Then add up the cost of the garment and the cost of cleaning it. Divide the total cost by the number of times you will wear the garment. This will give you an estimated cost per wearing.

Cost per wearing can help you decide where your clothing dollars will best be spent. For example, do you really want to buy an expensive ski jacket that will be worn for only one ski trip? Can you afford the better-quality leather if the same pair of shoes can be worn for school, casual wear, and dress-up occasions? A little simple math will help you develop a sound shopping plan.

A more expensive item can be a better value if it will outlast the cheaper alternative. How can cost per wearing help you decide which item to purchase?

LESSON THREE *Review*

Using complete sentences, answer the following questions on a separate sheet of paper.

Reviewing Terms and Facts

1. **List** What three factors should you consider when developing a shopping plan?
2. **Identify** Name two types of information you can find on a care label.
3. **Vocabulary** Define the term *status symbol*. Give an example of a status symbol.
4. **Recall** What are four ways to stretch your clothing budget?

Thinking Critically

5. **Compare and Contrast** How is using a layaway plan to make a purchase similar to using a credit card? How are the two payment methods different?
6. **Evaluate** Do brand names always determine quality? Why or why not?
7. **Apply** Determine the cost per wearing for a pair of jeans that cost $50, do not require dry cleaning, and will be worn 80 times.

Applying Concepts

8. Check the fabric content and care labels of clothing you own. What generalizations can you make about how fiber content is related to care? Make a chart of typical care instructions and the types of garments to which they usually apply.

LESSON THREE: SHOPPING FOR CLOTHES **471**

CHAPTER 16, LESSON 3

Answers to Lesson 3 Review

1. Total budget, method of payment, and place where you will shop.
2. Fiber content, care instructions.
3. Something that gives the wearer a special feeling of importance, such as designer jeans.
4. Any four: start with two or three basic outfits, make good use of the clothes you have, compare cost and quality, shop sales, care for clothing properly, learn to sew.
5. Both allow you to purchase without the full amount of money at the time of purchase. A credit-card payment allows you to take the garment home at the time of selection, whereas with layaway you take the garment home when it is paid for in full.
6. Construction methods, not brand names, determine quality. However, many brand names are attached to quality clothing.
7. $50.00/80 = $0.63
8. Descriptions will vary.

CLOSE

Ask students to write a paragraph describing two things they will do before they go shopping for clothes again.

MORE ABOUT ● ● ●

Clothing Care In 1984 a revision to the Care Labeling Rule went into effect. The new care labels provide more detailed information. For example, a label that recommends washing as a care procedure must also tell you the washing method, safe water temperature, and method and safe temperature for drying. However, the manufacturer is now required to list only one method of safe care, even though other methods may be used safely.

LESSON FOUR
Clothing Care

FOCUS

Lesson Objectives
After studying this lesson, students should be able to
- describe how to remove spots and stains from clothing.
- identify techniques for washing, drying, and ironing clothes.
- explain how to store clothes properly.

Motivating Activity
Write the following heading on the board: "Worst Clothing Damages." Ask volunteers to recount some of their worst cases of clothing damage, such as jeans that shrunk in the dryer or a white shirt that was washed with a pen still in the pocket. Write the responses as they are volunteered.

Introducing the Lesson
Discuss students' responses in the Motivating Activity. Ask students to describe the actions they took to fix the damage. Tell students that Lesson 4 will give them some tips about proper clothing care.

Introducing *Words to Know*
Refer students to the Words to Know. Ask them to work in pairs to write a paragraph with the following topic sentence: "There are several ways to take care of clothes." Tell students to use all the vocabulary words in their paragraphs. Call on volunteers to read their paragraphs and compare the usage of the terms in the paragraphs with the Glossary definitions.

LESSON FOUR
Clothing Care

WORDS TO KNOW
- mend
- stain
- pretreat

DISCOVER...
- how to remove spots and stains from clothing.
- techniques for washing, drying, and ironing clothes.
- how to store clothes properly.

Griffin had to get dressed quickly or he would miss the bus for school. He pulled his favorite shirt out of the closet, only to find a stain on the front. He reached for another shirt, but that one was missing a button. Finally, Griffin opened his dresser drawer to look for a T-shirt. The drawer was so overstuffed that all of the shirts were badly wrinkled. Griffin threw one on anyway and ran for the bus.

Have you ever been frustrated by not having your clothes ready to wear when you were ready to go?

472   CHAPTER 16: PLANNING YOUR WARDROBE

CLASSROOM RESOURCES FOR LESSON 4

 Blackline Masters
Activity and Project Card 32, "Zap Those Stains!"
Concept Map 26
Lesson 4 Quiz
Reteaching 16

 Transparencies
Transparency 67, "Removing Stains"

 Student Workbook
Activities 117, 118

Taking Care of Your Clothes

Keeping your clothes in ready-to-wear condition is partly just a matter of common sense. Follow these simple guidelines to take proper care of your clothes:

- Wear appropriate clothing for the activity. When doing yard work or cleaning out the garage, for example, wear old clothes so that it doesn't matter if they get very dirty.
- Dress and undress carefully to avoid snagging, ripping, or stretching garments.
- Inspect your clothes carefully after each wearing. **Mend,** or *repair,* any tears or holes before they get bigger. If you find spots or stains, remove them immediately and wash the garment as soon as possible. A **stain** is a *soiled or discolored area.*

Keeping Your Clothes Clean

Cleaning clothes properly requires a basic knowledge of fabrics and simple cleaning techniques. Handling the laundry isn't hard if you follow the instructions on clothing care labels and on laundry products and appliances.

Removing Spots and Stains

If you get a spot on your favorite shirt, it doesn't have to mean the end of the shirt. You will have the best chance of getting the spot out if you treat it as soon as possible, however. There are two basic types of stains: water based and oil based. Water-based stains include those from some foods, perspiration, grass, and washable inks. Oil-based stains come from oils, makeup, ballpoint ink, and oil-based paints. **Figure 16.6** on the next page shows how to remove common stains.

Washing Clothes

Learning the right way to launder clothes will help you keep your clothes looking newer longer. Follow these guidelines when washing your clothes:

If you protect your clothes, they will look better and last longer. Besides wearing an apron, what are some other ways to protect your clothes?

LESSON FOUR: CLOTHING CARE 473

MORE ABOUT • • •

Home Remedies for Stains Try the following remedies for stains on washable garments: *Grease:* Pour salt on a grease stain immediately. The salt will absorb the grease and prevent staining. Sprinkle talcum or cornstarch on a fresh grease stain. After it is absorbed, brush it off and blot the fabric with a damp cloth. *Ballpoint-pen ink:* To remove a ballpoint ink stain, first saturate the area with hair spray. Then rub powdered detergent into the area and wash the garment, following the instructions on the care label.

CHAPTER 16, LESSON 4

TEACH

L2 Applying Concepts
Ask students to work in small groups to create an infomercial that illustrates the guidelines for proper care of clothes. Students should include the information presented in the lesson. Encourage students to use visuals in their infomercial. Call on groups to present their infomercial to the class. If the infomercials are videotaped, you might present them to parents at a school open house.

L3 Art
Invite students to create a stain-removal guide they can place with their laundry equipment at home. First, have students collect various home remedies or do some research on how to remove common stains. Students might then make a small brochure illustrating various stain-removal tips, or they might make a small chart that can be laminated and hung in the washing area in their home.

L2 Activity and Project Card
Allow time for students to complete Activity and Project Card 32, "Zap Those Stains!" in the TCR.

L2 Science
Ask students to study the labels on several pretreatment products. Have them prepare "commercials" that answer the following questions: How does the product help remove stains? How should the product be applied? How much should be applied? Does the product guarantee stain removal? Ask students to present the commercials to the class.

473

CHAPTER 16, LESSON 4

USING VISUALS
Refer students to Figure 16.6. Ask students to identify the suggestions that they or members of their families have used successfully. If possible, ask students to demonstrate some of the stain-removal suggestions for the class. Remind students that quick attention to removing stains is the best way to get good results.

L1 Using Transparencies
Present Color Transparency 67, "Removing Stains," in the TCR. Use this overhead visual to reinforce concepts from this lesson.

L1 Writing
Students can examine the care labels in a clothing item and write step-by-step directions for how to launder the item.

L2 Demonstrating
Demonstrate the correct way to iron a shirt and then invite volunteers to iron it. Have the class evaluate the procedure by focusing on what parts of the shirt were ironed first and how well the procedure followed the care-label directions for ironing the shirt.

L3 Language Arts
Ask interested students to write a report about textile-eating insects such as moths or silverfish. Have them find out at what stage in their lives the insects eat textiles. Also, have students report on what things can be done to prevent this.

- **Pretreat stains and dirty areas.** Besides spots and stains, sleeve cuffs and the fold line on collars often need to be pretreated. **Pretreat** means *to apply a liquid detergent or stain remover on the spots before laundering.*

**Figure 16.6
How to Remove Stains**
Why is it important to remove spots and stains right away?

Blood. Soak in cold water and detergent. Use bleach if safe for fabric.

Chewing gum. Rub with an ice cube to harden the gum. With a dull knife scrape it off.

Chocolate. Soak in cool water. Rub with detergent and wash.

Grease. Use a prewash stain remover, then wash. If the stain is still visible, sponge with cleaning fluid and rinse.

Ink. Spray with hair spray or sponge with rubbing alcohol. Rinse. Then rub any remaining spots with detergent and wash.

Soft drinks. Sponge with cold water. Wash using bleach if safe for fabric.

Paint. Rub detergent into stain and wash. If some of the stain remains, sponge with mineral spirits and turpentine and rinse.

Grass. Rub detergent into stain and wash.

MORE ABOUT • • •

Detergent In 1946 the first successful clothes-washing detergent for the home became available. Using the trade name *Tide,* it appeared at the time when homemakers in America were deciding that an automatic washing machine was a necessity. *Tide's* success was rapid, and it became the forerunner of the many detergents that now crowd supermarket shelves.

- **Sort clothes.** Check care labels on clothes carefully. Then separate each pile by color: whites and light-colored fabrics, medium-colored fabrics, and dark fabrics.
- **Select the correct water temperature.** Wash your clothes in the water temperature recommended on the care label. Unless otherwise specified, most clothing can be washed in warm water and rinsed in cold.
- **Choose the correct load size.** If you are washing only a few clothes, choose a small-load setting to save water and energy. Never overload the washing machine. Clothes won't get clean if they are packed in too tightly.
- **Add detergent.** Check the detergent bottle or box for the correct amount to use. Remember to adjust for the load setting you selected.
- **If static is a problem, use a fabric softener.** Fabric softeners can be added in the washer or in the dryer. Read product labels carefully to determine which type you are using and how and when it should be added.

Drying Clothes

Clothes can generally be either line-dried or machine-dried. Line drying saves energy and money but takes longer. Line-dried clothes may feel stiff and often need to be pressed. Machine drying is quick and convenient, but it uses energy and therefore costs more.

As soon as the clothes are dry, remove them from the dryer. This will help prevent wrinkling. Hang up items such as shirts, pants, and dresses as soon as you take them out of the dryer. Then fold and sort the other items.

Ironing Clothes

Some fabrics require ironing after each wash. Even permanent-press items sometimes require touch-up pressing with a steam iron. The care label gives the proper temperature setting for the fabric. Always match the temperature setting on the iron with the fiber listed on the label. Synthetic fabrics may melt if the iron is too hot.

Hand Washing Clothes

Washing machines can damage certain fabrics. Hosiery, silk or nylon dresses and blouses, and woolen sweaters, mittens, and scarves usually need to be washed by hand. Always check labels for washing instructions. If hand washing is required, use a gentle soap. Wash the garment in cool or warm water. Rinse twice to make sure that all the soap is out. Lay the garment flat on a towel to dry.

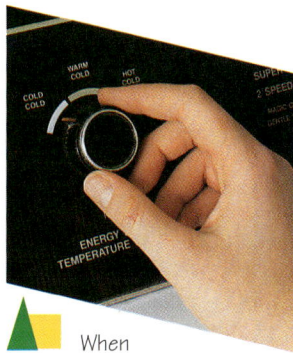

▲ When washing clothes, adjust the settings on the washing machine to match the care labels on the garments. Why should you not overload the washing machine?

LESSON FOUR: CLOTHING CARE

It is important to learn the proper techniques for ironing clothes. How do you know what temperature setting to use when ironing?

Start by ironing small areas of a garment, such as the collar, yoke, and sleeves. Then press the larger areas. This way, you avoid wrinkling areas you have already ironed.

Storing Clothes

An important, but sometimes overlooked, part of caring for clothes is storing them properly. When you hang up your clothes, take the time to close zippers and fasten buttons so that the garment will hang straight. Do not overcrowd closets and drawers, or your clothes may wrinkle.

Seasonal clothes—those that are worn only for a few months each year—or clothes that are worn only for special occasions should be given extra storage attention. Check to be sure that pockets are empty and that garments are clean and mended before putting them away. When soiled clothes are stored for a long time, stains become permanent.

Looking Your Best

You will always be well dressed if you keep your clothes fresh and neat. By learning to launder and store clothes properly, you can keep your wardrobe in good condition.

LESSON FOUR Review

Using complete sentences, answer the following questions on a separate sheet of paper.

Reviewing Terms and Facts

1. **Identify** What are three guidelines for keeping your clothes in ready-to-wear condition?
2. **Vocabulary** Define the term *stain*. Name two oil-based stains and two water-based stains.
3. **List** Identify the steps to take when machine-washing clothes.
4. **Explain** Why is proper storage especially important for seasonal clothes?

Thinking Critically

5. **Explain** How can carelessness damage your clothes?
6. **Compare and Contrast** What are the advantages and disadvantages of line-drying clothes? Of machine-drying?

Applying Concepts

7. Ask family members about home-remedy stain removers. Write a paragraph or two describing the advantages and disadvantages of using home remedies.

476 CHAPTER 16: PLANNING YOUR WARDROBE

HOME AND COMMUNITY CONNECTION

Cost of Laundry Services Ask students to investigate the costs of having a professional laundry service do the laundry for a family. Students can check the telephone directory for laundry services and make calls for information. What is the cost of doing a family's laundry? How is the cost figured? What items are sent out to a laundry more frequently than others? (For example, families may send shirts to be professionally washed and ironed.) Have students create a chart that lists the costs for various laundry services.

Chapter 16 Activities

Consumer Focus

Fun-House Mirrors

Have you ever felt surprised at your reflection in the mirror of a dressing room? It's a fact that store mirrors can reflect an inaccurate, even unflattering, image. If a mirror does not hang flat against the wall, it can change the way your body looks.

Try This!

Ask your parents or other family members for tips about trying on and purchasing clothes. Discuss their advice with your classmates.

A Global View — NATURAL FIBERS

Different plant fibers thrive in different climates. Flax, for example, grows best in cool and rainy climates. Cotton needs warm and sunny weather. Wool is processed all over the world. In ancient times, the Chinese learned how to raise silkworms, and China is still the world's leading producer of silk.

TRY THIS!

Find out the characteristics of one of these fibers. Share your findings with the class.

TECHNOLOGY

Electronic Clothes Shopping

Home-shopping channels are becoming increasingly popular. Television's selling power can be tremendous. For example, a designer recently appeared on a shopping channel and sold more than 12,000 silk blouses in less than 20 minutes.

Try This!

What do you think are the advantages and disadvantages of clothes shopping via television? Discuss your answers with a classmate.

SOCIAL STUDIES CONNECTION

CLOTHING AND CLIMATE

The main principle of clothing design in cold climates is *tailoring*—clothing follows body lines and fits snugly at the wrists and ankles to hold in body warmth.

In hot, dry areas, the first rule of clothing design is *draping*—clothes hang loosely, allowing air to flow around the body and cool it.

Follow Up

1. Find pictures that illustrate the tailored principle and the draped principle of clothing design. Discuss your pictures with the class.

2. Choose five garments from your wardrobe. Write a brief description of how each garment keeps you warm or cool.

CHAPTER 16 Activities

Consumer Focus

Ask students whether they have noticed how dressing rooms in retail stores are often cramped cubicles with long, narrow mirrors. Point out that these mirrors are often not installed properly. Suggest that students try on clothes in front of a three-way mirror.

TECHNOLOGY

Point out to students that industry experts predict that the spread of digital technology will change television shopping. Digital television will provide space for each national department store chain to have its own shopping channel. With a click of a button you will be able to view a product in an interactive shopping environment in your own home.

A Global View

Remind students that natural fibers from which cloth is made come from many different countries. Ask students to use an atlas to find out what countries might produce cotton. *(warm climates such as India, southern Russia, and the southern United States)* Point out that Australia, New Zealand, and Russia raise the largest number of sheep for wool.

Teaching the SOCIAL STUDIES CONNECTION

Talk about how a culture's clothing takes cues from the climate in which the culture is located. Students should be able to use terms such as *draped, tailored, loose, flowing,* and they might be able to describe certain fabrics such as wool, fur, linen, cotton, and so on. Explain that from a health point of view, the goal of clothing is to maintain a healthy body temperature.

Answers to Follow-Up

1. Pictures will vary, but students should find many pictures that illustrate tailored and draped clothing.

2. Selections will vary, but students should indicate how the garments keep an individual warm or cool.

CHAPTER 16 REVIEW

Checking Comprehension

Use the Chapter Summary and the Chapter 16 Review to help students go over the most important ideas presented in Chapter 16.

Answers to Words to Know

1. A scarf can be the focal point of a basic dress.
2. Versatile clothing allows a person to create many different outfits from a small number of garments.
3. A wardrobe inventory is a list of the clothes one has.
4. Fibers in woven fabric are interlaced together.
5. The grain is the direction the threads run in a fabric.
6. Ease, or the ability to move freely, is important for fit, no matter what the style is.
7. A shopping plan is a strategy for spending the money you have available to purchase the clothing you need or want.
8. Repair.
9. Apply a liquid detergent or stain remover on a stain before laundering.

Answers to Review Questions

1. Mixing and matching clothing items can help you make several different kinds of outfits with a few basic items.
2. Talk to friends, read fashion magazines, go window shopping.

Chapter Summary

- A wardrobe plan consisting of mix-and-match outfits and versatile clothing will make your wardrobe seem larger than it is.
- Accessories—such as shoes, hats, and jewelry—can update and enhance your wardrobe.
- Fabrics and fibers have different characteristics that can affect durability, style, and comfort.
- Clothing fit depends on more than choosing the correct size. When trying on garments, check the neck opening, sleeves, fasteners, waistband, shoulder seams, and hemline.
- A shopping plan will help you shop wisely and stretch your clothing budget.
- Clothing care labels help you choose clothes and care for them properly.
- Stains can be either water based or oil based. Most stains can be removed if they are taken care of immediately.
- Caring for clothes requires you to read and follow directions on clothing care labels and on laundry products and appliances.
- Proper storage helps keep clothes looking their best.

Words to Know

Using complete sentences, answer the following questions on a separate sheet of paper.

1. Give an example of an *accessory* used as an outfit's *focal point*.
2. Explain why *versatile* clothing is a good wardrobe choice.
3. What does it mean to take a *wardrobe inventory*?
4. Describe how a *woven fabric* is made.
5. Define the term *grain* as it applies to clothing.
6. Why is *ease* important in evaluating fit and style?
7. What is a *shopping plan*?
8. What is another word for *mend*?
9. Explain how to *pretreat* a stain.

Review Questions

Using complete sentences, answer the following questions on a separate sheet of paper.

1. Explain how mix-and-match dressing can stretch your wardrobe.
2. What are three ways to learn about current styles and fashions?
3. Why should you check the fabric grain when purchasing clothing?
4. Name four areas you should examine to judge the fit of a garment.

478   CHAPTER 16: PLANNING YOUR WARDROBE

EXTRA CREDIT PROJECT

Extending Chapter Content Have students apply what they have learned about wardrobe planning to create paper outfits for a "Pencil Fashion Show." Have each student fold a sheet of notebook paper into thirds and cut or tear the paper into three strips. Then have them draw outfits on the strips of paper—one each for casual, dressy, and recreational activities. Students may wish to color their outfits using markers, crayons, or colored pencils. When the outfits are completed, instruct students to punch holes 2 inches (5 cm) from the top and bottom of the strip of paper and slip their pencils into the holes to "dress" them. Have students hold a fashion show and introduce the outfits they have created.

CHAPTER 16 REVIEW

5. What three factors affect how comfortable your clothes are?
6. Describe two ways clothing labels can be useful.
7. What could be some consequences of improper laundering?

 Thinking Critically

Using complete sentences, answer the following questions on a separate sheet of paper.

1. **Apply** What can you learn from each category of clothing in your wardrobe inventory?
2. **Contrast** What are the differences between woven and knit fabrics?
3. **Evaluate** What are some advantages and disadvantages of shopping by mail?
4. **Recommend** Suppose that a friend wants to buy an expensive new dress for a special party. What advice would you give her about deciding on her purchase? About paying for it?

 Cooperative Learning

1. As a class, organize a used-clothing drive. Encourage students in your school to clean out their closets and to contribute clean items in good condition. Make minor repairs if needed. Donate the clothing to charity, or plan a one-day thrift sale.
2. Working in small groups, select five styles that are currently in fashion at your school. Evaluate each for comfort, versatility, and whether or not you would classify it as a fad. Display your evaluations in the form of a chart, and have each group present a brief report to the class.

Family & Community

1. Take a survey of the clothing stores in your community. How many fall into each category: specialty store, department store, discount store, thrift shop? How far do you have to travel to get to each? Write a one-page evaluation of your community's shopping resources.
2. Interview one or two family members or friends whose wardrobes you admire. Which types of fabrics do they prefer? What do they look for when judging clothing construction? Do they have any special tips or techniques for washing, ironing, or storing clothes? Share your findings with the class.

Building A Portfolio

1. Make an inventory of your wardrobe. List five items you need to buy. Using catalogs and sales circulars, estimate how much money it would cost to purchase these items. Then determine which garments in your wardrobe can be repaired, updated, or accessorized instead of being replaced. How much money would you save? Keep your list in your portfolio.
2. Find magazine and newspaper articles with home advice tips. Collect clippings of tips and techniques for removing specific kinds of stains. Make a folder to organize the tips for easy reference, and add the folder to your portfolio.

CHAPTER 16 REVIEW

3. A garment that is unintentionally off-grain will not hang correctly and may not fit comfortably either.
4. Any four: neck opening, sleeves, fasteners, waistband, shoulder seams, and hemline.
5. Comfort is affected by fit, style, and kind of fabric.
6. Clothing labels provide information about fabric content, which helps you judge comfort, and they provide information about how to care for the garment.
7. Some garments can be ruined by washing in water that is too hot, by using bleach, or by drying the garment at too high a temperature.

Evaluate

Use the Chapter 16 Test in the TCR, or construct your own test using the Testmaker Software.

CLOSE

Have students apply their knowledge of the chapter's content by completing one of the alternative assessment activities listed under Family and Community or Building a Portfolio.

Answers to Thinking Critically

1. Evaluating the inventory may lead to ideas about lifestyle and favorite activities. It may also lead to ideas about how important clothes are even if they are no longer useful.
2. Woven fabrics are tighter and may be stiffer than knit fabrics, which tend to be softer.
3. The advantages include saving time, possibly saving money, and allowing you to shop whenever you want to. The disadvantages include not being able to see or feel the garment or try it on.
4. Responses will vary but might include choosing an outfit that could be worn more than once, not buying an expensive dress, possibly paying for the dress on layaway, checking resale shops for dressy clothing.

Planning Guide
Chapter 17 Preparing to Sew

LESSON 1	Pages	FEATURES	CLASSROOM RESOURCES
The Sewing Lab and Equipment	482–488	Try This: Keeping the Lab Neat Skills in Action: Pressing Fabrics	Cooperative Learning 33 Enrichment 19 Lesson 1 Quiz Transparency 68, "The Parts of a Sewing Machine" Student Workbook Activities 119, 120, 121
LESSON 2 **Choosing a Sewing Project**	489–493	Tips for Living: Using Sewing Kits	Lesson 2 Quiz Peer Pressure and Decision Making 33 Transparency 69, "Reading a Pattern Envelope" Student Workbook Activity 122
LESSON 3 **Choosing Fabrics and Notions**	494–498	Skills in Action: Expressing Yourself Through Fabric Tips for Living: Timesaving Notions	Activity and Project Card 33, "Explore Fabrics and Their Uses" Activity and Project Card 34, "Prepare for Sewing Repairs" Concept Map 27 Cooperative Learning 34 Cross Curriculum 19 Lesson 3 Quiz Student Workbook Activity 123

CHAPTER 17 RESOURCES

Chapter 17 Test

Reteaching 17

Study Guide 17, *Reteaching*

Testmaker Software

Performance Assessment Activity

Have students make a work plan for preparing to sew. Students' plans should include all the necessary steps for preparing to sew that are covered in Chapter 17. Have students estimate the time each step will take. Then have them set up a time schedule of dates to accomplish each step. When students have finished their work plan, organize the class into small groups. Have the students in each group analyze the work plans. Have them identify steps that have been left out or steps that are out of sequence. Ask them to check to see if the time estimated to accomplish the steps seems appropriate. Display work plans in the classroom.

School-to-Work

Provide students with examples of careers in the fashion design, garment, and textile industries. Have students work in small groups to skim the want ads for jobs in these industries. Ask groups to identify the technical, educational, and personal skills required for each job. Discuss how the classes that students are taking in school could help prepare them for a career in a sewing-related industry.

Family & Community

Ask students to conduct interviews with family members and/or neighbors who enjoy sewing. Students should prepare a list of questions in advance. Questions might include: How did you learn to sew? What kind of sewing equipment and machine do you have? Where and how is your sewing area set up? How do you select your sewing projects? What do you look for in a pattern? Have you ever designed your own pattern? What kinds of fabrics do you like to work with? May I see some of your finished work? Students might videotape their interviews and share them with the class.

Resources for the Teacher

Argent, Jeanne. *The Complete Step-by-Step Guide to Home Sewing*. Radnor, PA: Chilton, 1993.

Evans, Mary, and William-Alan Landes. *How to Make Historic American Costumes*. Rosedale, NY: Players Press, 1993.

Keeler, Patricia A., and Francis X. McCall, Jr. *Unraveling Fibers*. New York, NY: Macmillan, 1995.

Readings for the Student

Lancaster, John. *Fabric Art*. New York, NY: Watts, 1991.

Smith, Nancy, and Linda Milligan. *Sewing Machine Fun*. Denver, CO: Possibilities Denver, 1993.

Multimedia Resources

Fabric Identification Kit (Computer software with fabric samples). Home Economics School Service.

In the Making: A How-to-Sew Video (Videocassette). Zenger Media.

Picking Your Pattern, Fabric, and Notions (Videocassette). Home Economics School Service.

OUT OF TIME?

If time does not permit thorough teaching of this chapter, you may wish to use:

- *Teens Making a Difference*, page 481
- *Tips for Living*, pages 491, 497
- *Try This*, page 483
- *Skills in Action*, pages 487, 496
- *Young Living Activities*, page 499
- *Chapter Summary*, page 500

CHAPTER 17
Preparing to Sew

Chapter Overview

Chapter 17 introduces students to the principles of choosing and making a sewing project. They learn how to manage their time in the sewing lab and how to follow safety guidelines. Students learn how to use and care for small and large equipment. They discover how to select an appropriate sewing project based on their time, money, and skill level. They examine fabrics and notions and learn to select appropriate types for their sewing project.

LESSON 1 identifies safety procedures to use in the sewing laboratory and the proper care and use of large and small equipment.

LESSON 2 describes how to select a project based on time, money, and skill level.

LESSON 3 explains how to select appropriate fabric and notions for a sewing project.

Introducing the Chapter

Refer students to the chapter title, "Preparing to Sew." Then have students skim the lesson titles and describe a sewing project they would like to try.

Chapter Motivator

Bring to school samples of five sewing projects. The projects should vary in styles, colors, and fabrics. Arrange the projects on a table in the front of the classroom. Ask students to make a chart comparing the style, color, and fabric of each sewing project. Have them share their completed charts. Point out that in this chapter they will learn the best ways to choose styles, colors, and fabrics for their sewing projects.

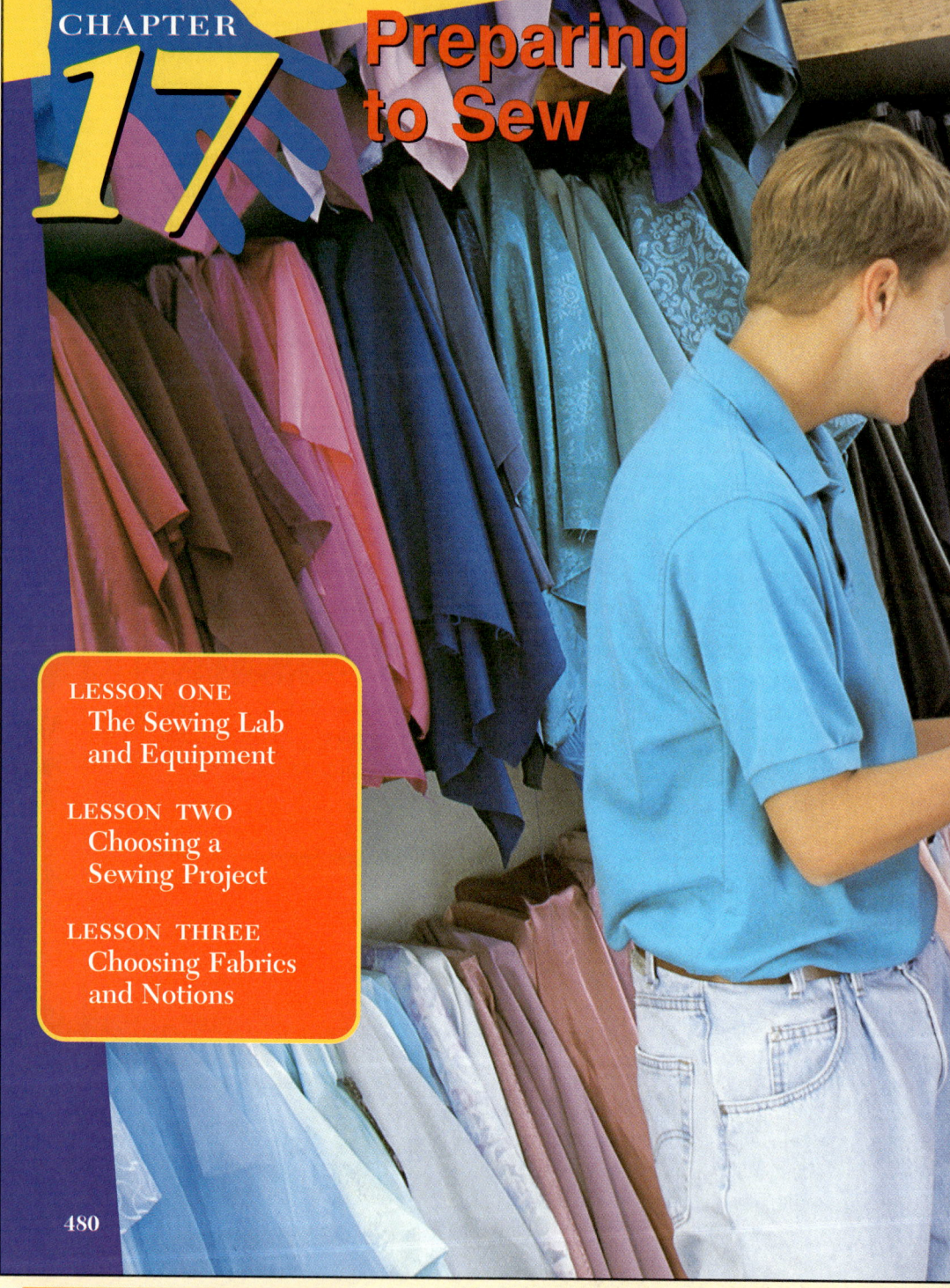

CHAPTER 17 Preparing to Sew

LESSON ONE
The Sewing Lab and Equipment

LESSON TWO
Choosing a Sewing Project

LESSON THREE
Choosing Fabrics and Notions

KEY TO ABILITY LEVELS

Teaching strategies that appear throughout the chapter have been identified by one of three codes to give you an idea of their suitability for students of varying learning styles and abilities.

L1 Level 1 strategies should be within the ability range of all students. Often full class participation is required. Teacher direction is usually needed.

L2 Level 2 strategies are for average to above-average students or for small groups. Some teacher direction is necessary.

L3 Level 3 strategies are designed for students able and willing to work independently. Minimal teacher direction is necessary.

TEENS MAKING A DIFFERENCE
Clothes for Children

Andrea's friend Kristen came to her for help in organizing a clothing drive for children in a local shelter. Kristen said that the children needed general clothing as well as specific items, such as pants, sweatshirts, and pajamas.

Andrea offered to sew some items for the children. First, she contacted the shelter to get a list of the sizes and items the children required.

The clothing drive was a huge success. Kristen collected more clothes than were needed. Andrea had fun and felt proud that she could use her sewing skills to make a difference.

Try THIS!

With a group of classmates, think of ways to use your sewing skills to help others. For example, you could make simple cloth toys for children in a homeless shelter.

TECHNOLOGY IN THE CLASSROOM

Clothing Design Technology There is a variety of computer software available for clothing and textiles. The software includes tutorials as well as simulations. The most common software includes pattern layout and sewing techniques. Computer-aided design (CAD) programs are available in which patterns are made on specialized computers that are able to convert and draw patterns in all sizes. Computers can be used to determine the best layout of pattern pieces on fabric, resulting in the use of the least amount of fabric possible. CAD programs for fabric print design are also available.

CHAPTER 17

TEENS MAKING A DIFFERENCE

Have students read "Teens Making a Difference." Ask them to identify the ways the students in the article made a difference by sewing. (*Students sewed clothes for children in a shelter.*) Ask students to describe the initiative that Andrea and Kristen took in order to make a difference in the lives of some children. Have students describe ways they have made a difference in the lives of young children.

Ask students to work with a small group to complete TRY THIS! at the end of the feature. Ask groups to share their ideas with the class.

BLOCK SCHEDULING

The following Teacher Classroom Resources are suggested for use in classrooms with Block Scheduling.

- Activity and Project Card 33, "Explore Fabrics and Their Uses"
- Activity and Project Card 34, "Prepare for Sewing Repairs"
- Cooperative Learning 33, "Sewing Machine Basics"
- Cooperative Learning 34, "The Fabric Makes the Difference"

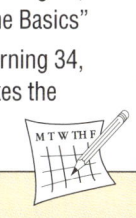

LESSON ONE
The Sewing Lab and Equipment

FOCUS

Lesson Objectives
After studying this lesson, students should be able to
- describe the keys to success in the sewing lab.
- explain how to use and care for small sewing equipment.
- describe how to operate a sewing machine.

Motivating Activity
Display several items of sewing equipment from the sewing lab in the front of the classroom. You might display pins, needles, scissors, iron, and sewing machine. Ask students to write down possible safety hazards for each item.

Introducing the Lesson
Ask students to share their responses to the Motivating Activity. Then ask them to explain how each item should be handled to avoid the safety hazard they identified. Point out to students that in this lesson they will learn how to use and care for sewing equipment.

Introducing *Words to Know*
Have each student write the Words to Know and their definitions on a sheet of paper. Then have them use each word correctly in a sales advertisement for a department store that sells sewing machines and sewing supplies. Ask volunteers to share their sales advertisements with the class.

LESSON ONE
The Sewing Lab and Equipment

WORDS TO KNOW
pinking shears
sewing gauge
bobbin
stitch regulator
presser foot

DISCOVER...
- the keys to success in the sewing lab.
- how to use and care for small sewing equipment.
- how to operate a sewing machine.

Amelia likes sewing because it gives her a chance to be creative. In her free time, she enjoys making her own clothes and pillows and other items for her room. Before Amelia started sewing at home, she learned how to sew and how to operate sewing equipment in the school sewing laboratory.

482　CHAPTER 17: PREPARING TO SEW

CLASSROOM RESOURCES FOR LESSON 1

 Blackline Masters
Cooperative Learning 33
Enrichment 19
Lesson 1 Quiz

 Transparencies
Transparency 68, "The Parts of a Sewing Machine"

 Student Workbook
Activities 119, 120, 121

The Sewing Lab

Your school's sewing lab is a great place to learn and practice basic sewing skills, including how to cut out a pattern and how to use a sewing machine. You will also learn how to work cooperatively with others and how to manage your time wisely.

Safety in the Sewing Lab

Learning how to use the supplies and equipment in the sewing lab involves learning how to operate them safely. Follow these simple safety rules:

- Keep scissors and sharp objects closed when not in use.
- Pass sharp objects with the handle toward the other person.
- Put pins and needles in a pincushion, never in your mouth.
- Keep your fingers away from the path of the sewing machine needle.
- Do not attempt to operate the machine if it is jammed or is making an unusual noise.

Managing Your Time

When you sew in the school lab, you have only a limited amount of time. The keys to making the most of your time are organization, preparation, and consideration.

- **Organization.** Put your supplies in a small container, with your name on it. If you keep your supplies neat and organized, they will be ready to use when you need them.
- **Preparation.** Bring in required fabric or supplies on the first day of the lab. That

You can do your part to keep the lab neat.

When sewing, keep your tabletop neat. Put away materials when you have finished with them. Return all sewing supplies to the proper place.

If you are having any problems with your sewing machine, tell your teacher immediately. What might happen if you try to use a machine that is not working properly?

LESSON ONE: THE SEWING LAB AND EQUIPMENT

CHAPTER 17, LESSON 1

TEACH

Have students read the activity. Then have them work in small groups to organize classroom cleanup tasks. Ask each group to explain their ideas to the class. Then have the class choose a method for cleanup that they think is most efficient.

L2 Applying Knowledge

Have students work in small groups to make public service announcements for broadcast on the radio to alert the public to safety rules that should be followed when using sewing supplies and equipment. Tell students that their announcement must not take longer than one minute. Have groups present their public service announcements to the class.

L1 Organizing

Have sewing supply items in disarray on a table in front of the classroom. Ask for volunteers to arrange the equipment neatly in a tote tray. Point out that when sewing equipment is arranged in an orderly manner and within easy reach, an individual can save time and effort.

TECHNOLOGY UPDATE

Innovations in Sewing Machines Someday sewing needles and thread may no longer be common items in a person's sewing kit. The most recent innovation in sewing machines— the ultrasonic sewing machine—welds two pieces of fabric together with very high-speed vibrations. This machine can hem, seam, tack, baste, and pleat synthetic materials of most weights and gauges. It can also be used with synthetic blends of up to 35-percent natural fibers. However, it cannot be used on fabrics that are 100-percent natural fibers, since natural fibers, such as cotton and wool, cannot be welded. Ask students to research other sewing innovations that are changing the way that clothes are made.

CHAPTER 17, LESSON 1

L1 Finding Examples

Have students help create a bulletin-board display showing the basic sewing tools available. Ask them to bring in pictures of sewing tools from catalogs and magazines to include in the bulletin-board display.

DID YOU KNOW

Needles of ivory, bone, and walrus tusk have been found in prehistoric caves. Some of the needles are estimated to be as much as 40,000 years old.

USING VISUALS

Have students study the information in Figure 17.1. Ask students to identify the sewing tool they would use to do each of the following tasks:
- Cut out fabric. (*shears*)
- Take body measurements. (*tape measure*)
- Push the needle through fabric while hand sewing. (*thimble*)
- Trim raw edges of fabric to avoid raveling. (*pinking shears*)
- Cut threads. (*scissors*)

---

way, you won't lose valuable lab time. Before you start to sew, read through the instructions for each step. If you are not sure of how to do a step, ask your teacher.

- **Consideration.** When you finish with an item, return it to where it belongs.

Sewing Equipment

To complete most projects, you will need a variety of small sewing tools in addition to the lab sewing machine and steam iron. If you buy quality tools and take care of them, they will last a long time.

Small Sewing Tools

To complete any sewing project successfully, you have to know which tools to use and how to use them. **Figure 17.1** describes some of the most basic sewing tools used for pinning, measuring, cutting, and hand sewing.

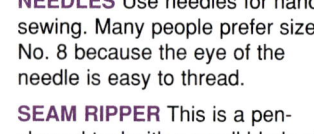

**Figure 17.1
Basic Sewing Tools**
These tools will make sewing easier. Which ones have you used?

SHEARS, SCISSORS, PINKING SHEARS Shears are a large pair of scissors that frequently have a raised handle for easier cutting. Scissors are used for trimming, clipping, and cutting threads. Pinking shears are scissors that have a zig-zag edge.

SEWING GAUGE A sewing gauge is a 6-inch (16-cm) ruler made of metal, with an adjustable pointer. Use it to measure short spaces, such as hems and seam widths.

NEEDLES Use needles for hand sewing. Many people prefer size No. 8 because the eye of the needle is easy to thread.

SEAM RIPPER This is a pen-shaped tool with a small blade at one end for removing stitches.

THIMBLE A thimble protects your finger while you're hand sewing and makes it easier to push the needle through the fabric.

THREAD Select a color that matches your fabric.

PINCUSHION The wrist pincushion is a convenient way to hold pins and needles when you're sewing.

PINS Dressmaker pins are slender, sharp-pointed, smooth, and rust-proof.

TAPE MEASURE A flexible tape is used to take body measurements.

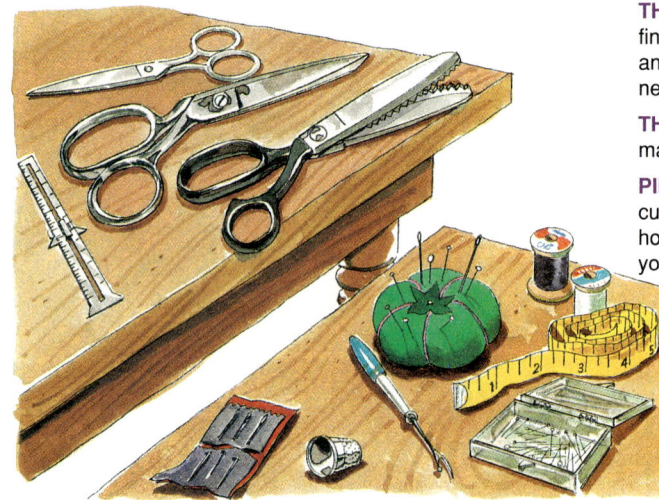

484 CHAPTER 17: PREPARING TO SEW

MEETING STUDENT DIVERSITY

Varied Learning Styles Use the following suggestions to help students who have difficulty with English: Pair those learners with native speakers of English. Have the pairs cut out magazine pictures of sewing tools and sewing equipment. Then have them make a glossary of sewing words and terms using the pictures and the English name of each tool. As students study the rest of the chapter, have them include sewing stitches in the glossary. Have the pairs draw a picture and label each sewing stitch described in their chapter. Add the drawings to the glossary of sewing words and terms. Encourage students who have difficulty with English to use the glossary as a study aid.

The Sewing Machine

Most sewing machines have the same basic parts, as identified in **Figure 17.2.** Sewing machines all operate in the same way: a needle moves up and down through the fabric, and two sets of threads interlock to form stitches.

Sewing machines vary greatly in what they can do and how much they cost. All machines sew straight stitches forward, and most sew backward too. Many sew a zigzag stitch, which can be used to finish seam edges and apply designs to a garment. Some machines can sew buttonholes, zigzag stitches, and decorative stitches.

Before using any sewing machine, be sure to read the instruction book. You can use it to find the parts on your sewing machine, and how to use its special features.

Using Your Machine

Familiarize yourself with the machine in the school lab. It is a good idea to practice winding the bobbin, threading the

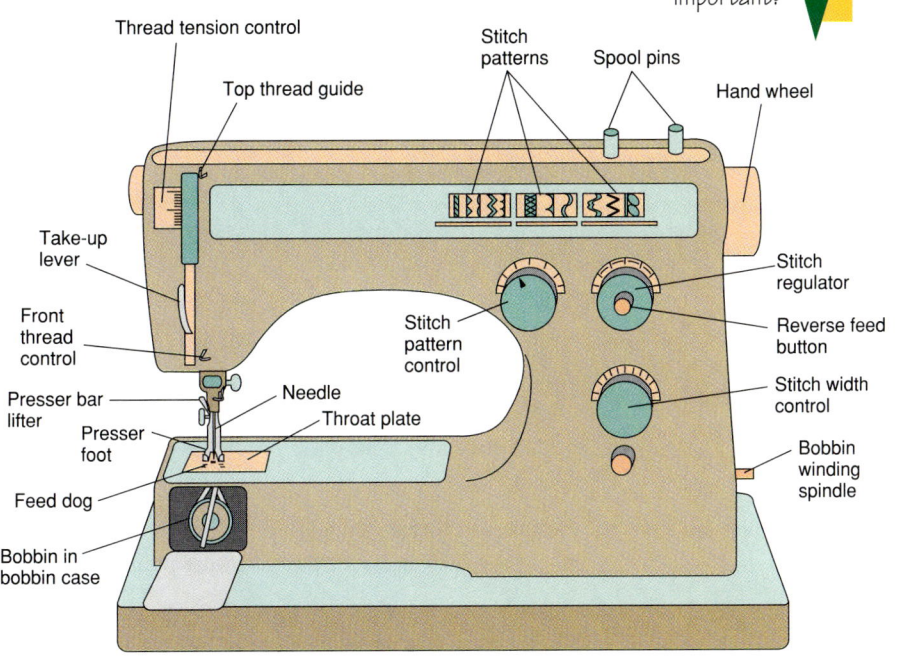

**Figure 17.2
The Parts of a Sewing Machine**
You can learn the basic parts of a sewing machine by studying this diagram and reading the instruction book for your machine. Why is this important?

L3 Reading, Writing, and Math

Provide students with consumer magazines such as *Consumer Reports* and have them research the various brands of sewing machines. Ask them to develop a graphic organizer to compare the costs, features, and durability among the various brands. Have students choose the sewing machine they believe is the best buy. Ask them to write a sentence or two explaining their choice.

USING VISUALS

Have students study the information in Figure 17.2. Point out to students that they may need to refer back to this diagram when they read the instructions for using the sewing machine. The diagram will help them locate the parts of the sewing machine they will be using.

L1 Using Transparencies

Present Color Transparency 68, "The Parts of a Sewing Machine," in the TCR. Use this overhead visual to reinforce concepts from this lesson.

LESSON ONE: THE SEWING LAB AND EQUIPMENT

 HOME AND COMMUNITY CONNECTION

Guest Speaker Invite a sewing-machine salesperson to class to demonstrate the newest models of sewing machines and sergers. Ask the demonstrator to point out the special features of each machine. Ask students to identify what features they would find most helpful.

CHAPTER 17, LESSON 1

L1 Reading

Ask students to read the direction books for the sewing machines they will use in the sewing lab to find out how to wind the bobbin and thread the machine. Have students practice these two steps.

L2 Cooperative Learning

Assign Cooperative Learning Activity 33 in the TCR. Students work in groups to practice basic sewing machine techniques in this activity.

Teacher TALK!

Handling Sensitive Issues

You may find that the sewing skills of students in your class vary greatly. Some sewing tasks require great dexterity and fine motor coordination. Students who are "all thumbs" may become frustrated with some sewing steps. Students who are proficient in winding the bobbin and threading the machine might be called upon to help students who are having difficulty with these maneuvers.

---

machine, and setting the stitch regulator. Try stitching on scraps of fabric before sewing on a project.

Winding the Bobbin

Before you can begin sewing on a machine, you must complete a few steps. The first is winding the thread you will be using from your spool onto the bobbin. A **bobbin** is *a small metal or plastic spool that holds the thread inside the machine.* Because each machine may have a slightly different procedure for winding the bobbin, you should check your instruction book to see how to do it. After you have threaded the bobbin, insert it in the bobbin case. Then insert the bobbin case into the sewing machine.

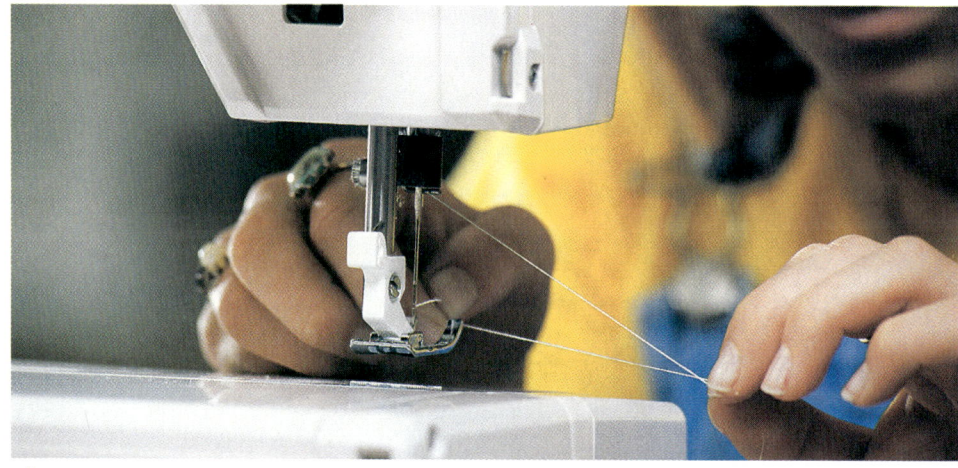

Don't try to guess how to thread an unfamiliar sewing machine. Where can you get information on the correct procedure?

Threading the Machine

The second step is threading the machine. Each type of sewing machine is threaded slightly differently. There should be a diagram in the instruction book that shows you how to thread the machine. The basic procedure for all sewing machines is as follows:

- Before you thread a machine, use the hand wheel to move the take-up lever to its highest point.

- Begin threading with the spool of thread on the spool pin located at the top of the machine.

CHAPTER 17: PREPARING TO SEW

COOPERATIVE LEARNING

Time Lines of Sewing History Have students work in small groups to research the history of sewing machines. Suggest they make use of computer encyclopedias if available. Have each group make an illustrated time line showing dates and advances in sewing machines. Provide butcher paper and art supplies for students to create their time lines. Ask each group to display their time line in the classroom.

- Then put the thread through the tension control, the take-up lever, and the needle. Use the thread guides along the way to hold the thread in place. When you thread the needle, be sure that the thread goes through the needle in the direction indicated for your machine.

Types of Stitches

The final step to complete before you can begin to sew is determining what kind of stitch to use. There are four main types of stitches:

- **Regular stitch**—a medium-length stitch (about 10 to 15 stitches per inch) used for most purposes
- **Basting stitch**—a very long stitch used for holding layers of fabric together temporarily; can be removed easily
- **Reinforcement stitch**—a short stitch used to strengthen the stitching area at a corner or a point
- **Zigzag stitch**—a sideways stitch used to make buttonholes, finish seam edges, and sew special seams

To set the stitch length on your machine, you will need to use the stitch regulator. A **stitch regulator** is *a dial or lever that controls the length of the stitches.* Machines label stitch lengths differently, but the smaller numbers are always longer stitches. For example, a stitch length of 7 would be longer than one of 14. Check the length of the stitch on a scrap of the fabric you will be using to determine if it is correct.

You can also change the tightness of the stitches with the tension control. If one thread lies flat against one side of the fabric while the other thread forms loops on the other side, you need to adjust the tension.

Operating the Sewing Machine

As with any piece of equipment, operating a sewing machine properly takes practice. Before you can begin sewing, you need to lower the needle into the fabric and drop the presser foot. The **presser foot** is *the metal piece at the end of the needle that holds the fabric in place.*

LESSON ONE: THE SEWING LAB AND EQUIPMENT **487**

Pressing Fabrics

Whenever you sew, you will need to use the iron to press seams and other work. Follow these safety tips:
- Always rest the iron on its heel.
- To see if the iron is hot, try it on a scrap of fabric, not on your finger.
- Unplug the iron when you finish.
- Coil the cord so that no one trips over it or pulls the iron off the ironing board.

CHAPTER 17, LESSON 1

L1 Illustrating
Have students draw and label a picture of each of the following types of stitches: regular stitch, basting stitch, reinforcement stitch, zigzag.

Have students read the feature. Then ask them to role-play the safety tips for pressing fabrics that are described in the feature. Ask students to provide other safety tips.

L1 Student Workbook
Assign Activities 119, 120, and 121 in the Student Workbook.

ASSESS

Evaluating the Lesson
Assign Reviewing Terms and Facts and Thinking Critically on page 488 to review the lesson; then assign the Lesson 1 Quiz in the TCR.

Reteaching
- Have students write in their own words the steps for completing the following procedures: winding the bobbin, inserting the bobbin, and threading the sewing machine.
- Have students complete Reteaching Activity 17 in the TCR.

Enrichment
- Have students write an instruction booklet for using small sewing equipment.
- Assign Enrichment Activity 19 in the TCR.

MORE ABOUT • • •

Basic Sewing Point out to students that no matter how fancy their sewing machine is, there will always be a time when they need to sew something by hand. Have students practice threading a needle. Provide each student with scissors, a needle, thread, and the following step-by-step instructions: 1) Cut, at an angle, a piece of thread about 2 feet long. 2) Put the cut end through the eye of the needle. (The thread is less likely to tangle or bunch up if it is kept running in the direction it came off the spool.) 3) Make a knot in the end of the thread that went through the eye of the needle. Have students practice the following hand stitches: running stitch, basting stitch, backstitch, hemming, and overcasting.

487

CHAPTER 17, LESSON 1

Answers to Lesson 1 Review

1. Any three: Keep scissors and sharp objects closed when not in use. Pass sharp objects with the handle toward the other person. Put pins and needles in a pincushion. Keep fingers away from the path of the sewing machine needle. Do not lean your face too close to the sewing machine. When you finish using the sewing machine, unplug the cord from the outlet and then disconnect the cord from the machine. If the machine is not working properly, tell the teacher or another adult. Do not attempt to operate.
2. The bobbin holds the thread. It is located inside the machine.
3. Any two: regular stitch—used for most purposes; basting stitch—used for holding layers of fabric together temporarily; reinforcement stitch—used to strengthen the stitching at a corner or point; zigzag stitch—used to make buttonholes, finish seam edges, and sew special seams.
4. There is only a limited amount of time to work in the sewing lab.
5. Shears are a large pair of scissors that have a raised handle for easier cutting. Scissors are used for trimming, clipping, and cutting threads. Pinking shears have a zig-zag edge.
6. Answers will vary but might include: saving money, using creativity, expressing individuality, fixing items that tear or rip.
7. Students should check each other's basic sewing skills.

CLOSE

Ask students to name three sewing safety tips they learned in this lesson.

Now you are ready to sew! Learning how to coordinate several actions at the same time can be difficult at first. You want to operate the machine at an even speed. That will produce the best stitches. To control the speed, you use either a foot pedal or a knee pedal. The harder you press, the faster the machine runs.

As you stitch, the fabric is automatically pulled through the machine. You need to use your hands to keep it straight. With practice, you will learn how to use your hands to guide the fabric and to follow the pattern markings accurately.

▶ Keeping your tools and equipment in good order will make sewing easier and more enjoyable. How has this teen organized her work?

LESSON ONE Review

Using complete sentences, answer the following questions on a separate sheet of paper.

Reviewing Terms and Facts

1. **List** Give three safety rules for the sewing lab.
2. **Vocabulary** What is the function of a *bobbin*? Where is the bobbin located?
3. **Describe** Name two types of stitches and describe the purpose of each.

Thinking Critically

4. **Analyze** Why is it important to work efficiently in the sewing lab?
5. **Compare and Contrast** What are the differences among shears, scissors, and pinking shears? For what purpose would each tool be used?
6. **Evaluate** What are two benefits of learning to sew?

Applying Concepts

7. With a partner, practice basic sewing skills on the sewing machine at school. You should become familiar with how to wind the bobbin, thread the machine, and set the stitch regulator. Then use scraps of fabric to practice operating the machine. Have your partner check your work. Then check your partner's work.

488 CHAPTER 17: PREPARING TO SEW

COOPERATIVE LEARNING

Comparing Have students work with a partner to compare and contrast the sewing machines in the lab with the diagram of the parts of a sewing machine in the text. Ask students to identify the basic parts of the machine—presser foot, tension control, take-up lever, needle, thread guide, and so on. Have pairs draw a diagram of the sewing machine in the school lab. Have them highlight the parts that are different. Ask pairs to share their diagrams with the class.

LESSON TWO
Choosing a Sewing Project

DISCOVER...
- what to look for when choosing a sewing project.
- what you can learn from the pattern envelope.
- how to determine your correct pattern size.

What do you like best about sewing? For many people, sewing is a way to express themselves. You show your individuality in the styles, fabrics, and finishing touches you choose. You can personalize your garments or even create your own designs. The key to enjoying your sewing projects is to choose ones that are suitable for your sewing ability.

WORDS TO KNOW
pattern
view
darts
alteration

LESSON TWO
Choosing a Sewing Project

FOCUS

Lesson Objectives
After studying this lesson, students should be able to
- describe what to look for when choosing a sewing project.
- discuss what can be learned from the pattern envelope.
- explain how to determine correct pattern size.

Motivating Activity
Ask students to jot down ways they personalize their clothing. (*possible examples: patches, buttons, iron-on transfers, beads, lace*)

Introducing the Lesson
Have students share their responses to the Motivating Activity. Use the responses as a basis for discussing how these items can be applied to express creativity, personality, and lifestyle. Ask students to share personal sewing experiences and how they have used their sewing skills and expressed their creativity through sewing.

Introducing *Words to Know*
Have a volunteer write each of the Words to Know in large letters on a separate index card. Write the four definitions on the board. Ask students to take one of the cards and attach it with transparent tape to the definition it matches.

CLASSROOM RESOURCES FOR LESSON 2

 Blackline Masters
Lesson 2 Quiz
Peer Pressure and Decision Making 33

 Transparencies
Transparency 69, "Reading a Pattern Envelope"

 Student Workbook
Activity 122

CHAPTER 17, LESSON 2

TEACH

L2 Analyzing
Have students study the front and back of a pattern envelope. Have them answer the following questions about the pattern envelope:
- How many views of the garment are shown?
- How is the garment described?
- How much fabric is needed for one style and size?
- What fabrics are recommended?
- What notions are required?

TEACHER TALK!

Handling Sensitive Issues

You may want to review the school dress code or school rules about gang symbols being displayed in the school. Make students aware that any items they make that break school rules will be confiscated and offending students will suffer the consequences.

L2 Problem Solving
Assign Peer Pressure and Decision Making 33 in the TCR. This activity gives students the opportunity to recognize peer pressure and practice decision-making skills.

L1 Using Transparencies
Present Color Transparency 69, "Reading a Pattern Envelope," in the TCR. Use this overhead visual to reinforce concepts from this lesson.

How to Select a Pattern

Most sewing projects call for a pattern. A **pattern** is *a plan for making a garment or project.* It contains the paper shapes of the various pieces and gives the directions for sewing. Your success in completing your project depends in part on the pattern you choose.

When you choose a sewing project, you will want one that matches your abilities and the time you have to complete it. Before you choose a pattern, consider the following:

- **Purpose.** Do you want to make clothing for yourself, a household item, or a specialty item, such as a backpack?
- **Sewing skills and experience.** If you have never worked on a project before, choose a simple pattern with few pieces.
- **Time.** Do you have enough time to complete the project? This is especially important if you are sewing at school and are sharing a sewing machine.
- **Cost.** How much money are you willing to spend?

By considering these factors, you can decide on the best pattern for your needs.

What to Look for in Patterns

When you are shopping for a pattern, start by browsing through a variety of pattern books. When you find a pattern that you like, make a note of the brand name and pattern number. Then you can find the pattern and look at the envelope for more information.

The pattern envelope provides you with all of the information you need to plan a sewing project. The front of the envelope shows a picture of the completed project. Sometimes more than one **view,** or *version of the garment,* is shown. For example, a shirt pattern may show one view with short sleeves and another with long sleeves.

The best way to find a sewing project is to look through pattern books. What information will you find in these books?

490   CHAPTER 17: PREPARING TO SEW

TECHNOLOGY UPDATE

Time-Saving Machine Time-saving machines called serger machines have been used in manufacturing for a long time. These machines stitch, trim, and finish a seam all in one step. These machines are especially good for sewing straight seams on garments such as sweatshirts.

When using a serger machine, be sure you don't sew over pins. This can damage the machine. If you need to secure the fabric when stitching, hand sew a temporary seam, using basting tape or a fabric glue stick.

On the back of the envelope, you will find the following:

- A detailed sketch showing the pattern pieces and construction features. For example, the sketch will indicate where darts are located. **Darts** are *tapered V-shaped seams used to give shape.*

- A chart that tells you how much fabric to buy for the style and size you are making

- Recommendations on the types of fabrics that can be used and additional materials you will need, such as thread and buttons

Salespeople in the fabric store are often experienced sewers. Who else could you ask for help when choosing a project?

Multisized Patterns

Some patterns may be styled to fit a range of sizes. For example, a single pattern for a belted tunic may fit sizes small to large. Loose-fitting styles such as this may be a good choice for beginning sewers, since small mistakes will matter less.

Finding Styles That Are Easy to Make

How can you find an appropriate pattern for your first project? Pattern books indicate which patterns are simple to sew and even have special sections for quick and easy projects.

TIPS for living

USING SEWING KITS

Just as you can use a mix to make a cake, you can sometimes use a kit to make a sewing project.

- Kits are faster to sew because the pieces are precut.
- With a kit, it is often easier to learn a new sewing technique, such as appliqué, because instructions are included.
- Kits contain all of the notions you need for the project—no extra shopping is required.

LESSON TWO: CHOOSING A SEWING PROJECT   **491**

MEETING STUDENT DIVERSITY

Cultural Perspective Point out to students that in many cultures knowing how to sew is a necessity. There may not be any stores nearby that sell ready-made garments. Ask students to imagine that they cannot buy any clothes in a store or from a mail-order catalog. They must make all their own clothes. Have them describe their attitude toward clothing. How large would their wardrobes be? Would they be concerned with wearing the latest styles?

CHAPTER 17, LESSON 2

L3 Writing

Have students write an article for an advice column for the school newspaper. The article should explain how to choose a sewing project that will guarantee success for a beginning sewer. Submit the best articles to the school newspaper.

DID YOU KNOW

Sometimes one pattern includes instructions for more than one size. It may also include different instructions and pattern pieces for each view. This type of pattern can be difficult for beginning sewers, since the cutting lines and instructions are usually harder to follow.

L1 Making Choices

Display several patterns for various sewing projects on a table. Have students select one of the patterns using the four items to consider when choosing a pattern. Have students explain their choices to the class.

TIPS for living

Have students find out what sewing kits are available and which ones they would be interested in using. Point out to students that they should comparison shop for kits to get the best price.

491

CHAPTER 17, LESSON 2

L2 Applying Knowledge

Ask students to determine which body measurement is most important when selecting patterns for the following: coats, jumpsuits, overalls, shorts, T-shirts.

USING VISUALS

Have students study Figure 17.3. Then have them work with same-gender partners to demonstrate how each of the following measurements should be taken: neck, chest, arm, waist, hips, bust, back waist length. Ask students to explain how the methods of taking measurements differ for females and males.

L1 Student Workbook

Assign Activity 122 in the Student Workbook.

ASSESS

Evaluating the Lesson

Assign Reviewing Terms and Facts and Thinking Critically on page 493 to review the lesson; then assign the Lesson 2 Quiz in the TCR.

Reteaching

- Have students make a brochure of helpful hints for "Sewing Success."
- Have students complete Reteaching Activity 17 in the TCR.

In addition, look for these features to help you choose an easy-to-make pattern:

- **Number of pattern pieces.** Fewer pattern pieces mean fewer pieces of fabric to cut out and stitch.
- **Number of seams.** Seams join two pieces of fabric together. The fewer seams involved, the easier it will be to complete the pattern.
- **Fit of the garment.** Loose styles are easier to sew than snug or close-fitting styles.
- **Closures.** Elastic waists, snaps, or hooks require less advanced sewing skills than do zippers and buttonholes.

Determining Your Pattern Size

Patterns, like ready-to-wear clothing, come in different sizes. They are grouped by figure types.

Figure 17.3 How to Take Measurements
Follow these guidelines to take your measurements. Why are accurate measurements important?

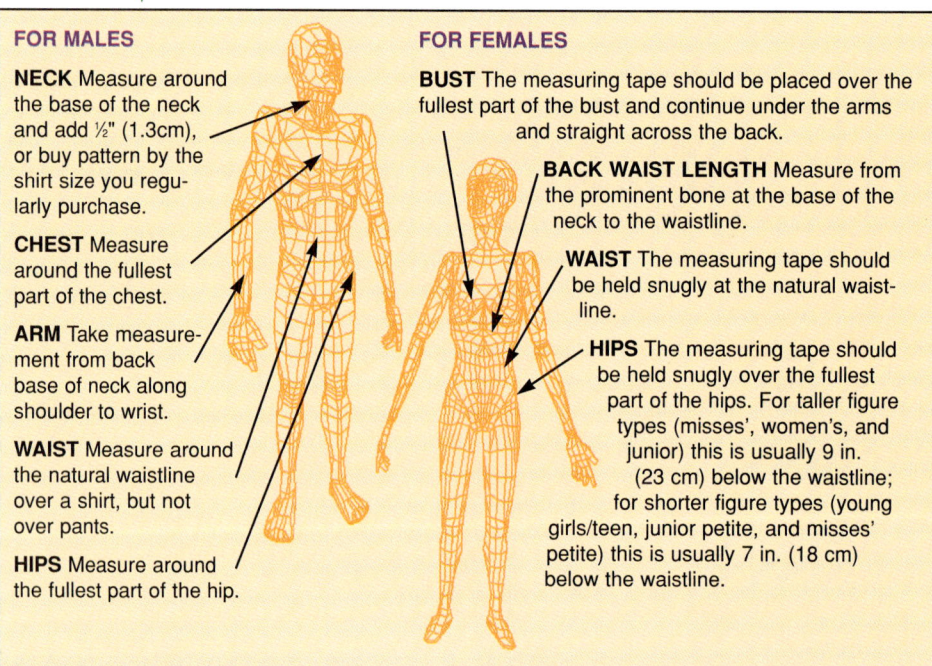

FOR MALES

NECK Measure around the base of the neck and add ½" (1.3cm), or buy pattern by the shirt size you regularly purchase.

CHEST Measure around the fullest part of the chest.

ARM Take measurement from back base of neck along shoulder to wrist.

WAIST Measure around the natural waistline over a shirt, but not over pants.

HIPS Measure around the fullest part of the hip.

FOR FEMALES

BUST The measuring tape should be placed over the fullest part of the bust and continue under the arms and straight across the back.

BACK WAIST LENGTH Measure from the prominent bone at the base of the neck to the waistline.

WAIST The measuring tape should be held snugly at the natural waistline.

HIPS The measuring tape should be held snugly over the fullest part of the hips. For taller figure types (misses', women's, and junior) this is usually 9 in. (23 cm) below the waistline; for shorter figure types (young girls/teen, junior petite, and misses' petite) this is usually 7 in. (18 cm) below the waistline.

492 CHAPTER 17: PREPARING TO SEW

 HOME AND COMMUNITY CONNECTION

Taking Measurements Have students use a measuring tape and the instructions in Figure 17.3 to take the measurements of family members. Have them arrange their findings in the form of a chart. Ask them to determine the pattern size for each family member they measured.

Pattern sizes for female clothing are based on four measurements: bust, waist, hip, and back waist length. Females need to use their measurements to determine which pattern type—girls', teens', junior, petite, or misses'—will fit best. Patterns for male clothing are based on five measurements: chest, waist, hip or seat, neck, and sleeve length. **Figure 17.3** shows you how to take your measurements. When doing so, be sure that the measuring tape is snug and held parallel to the floor.

Finding the Correct Pattern Size

After you have taken your measurements, compare them to the measurements on pattern envelopes. You want to select a size that requires very little **alteration,** or *change to make a certain size fit.* Choose the size that has the closest measurements. Use the following guidelines to decide which measurement is most important for a particular type of garment:

- For blouses and tops, fit the bust measurement.
- For shirts, fit the chest and neck measurements.
- For full skirts, fit the waist measurement.
- For pants and semifitted skirts, fit the hip measurement.

Your finished product doesn't have to look exactly like the picture on the pattern. How might you personalize a sewing project?

LESSON TWO *Review*

Using complete sentences, answer the following questions on a separate sheet of paper.

Reviewing Terms and Facts

1. **Recall** Name the factors you need to consider before choosing a pattern.
2. **List** Identify three pieces of information that you can find on the back of the pattern envelope.
3. **Name** What features should you consider when looking for easy-to-make patterns?

Thinking Critically

4. **Explain** Why is it important to evaluate your time and skill level before deciding on a sewing project?

5. **Evaluate** What are some advantages of making your own clothes? What might be some disadvantages?

Applying Concepts

6. Look through fashion magazines or advertisements for clothing styles you like. Identify several garments that you think would be the easiest to make. Then look through pattern books to find similar styles. Present your findings in the form of a chart, showing the style and listing the pattern brands and numbers that come closest.

LESSON TWO: CHOOSING A SEWING PROJECT   493

MORE ABOUT • • •

The History of Patterns The use of standard patterns did not begin until the 1860s. Before that time, clothes were cut to size by copying existing garments or cutting a garment out of muslin (an inexpensive material). The muslin was then fitted and basted on the wearer until satisfactory. Then the muslin was ripped apart and used as a pattern to cut out the more expensive fabric. Paper patterns in standardized sizes were first marketed in the 1860s. Patterns were featured in magazines and store catalogs and sold by mail order. By 1875, 10 million patterns were sold per year.

CHAPTER 17, LESSON 2

Answers to Lesson 2 Review

1. Purpose; sewing skills and experience; time; cost.
2. Detailed sketch showing the construction features. A chart that tells how much fabric to buy; recommendations on the types of fabrics that can be used and additional materials needed; a description of the garment or project that provides information about fit, design features, and special details.
3. Patterns styled to fit a range of sizes; few pattern pieces; few seams; loose styles; few gathers, folds, and pleats; elastic waists, snaps, or hooks rather than zippers and buttonholes.
4. Your success in completing the project you choose depends in part on your time and skill level.
5. Answers will vary. Possible advantages: you can save money, express individuality, and personalize your garments. Possible disadvantages: it takes time; you may not like the outcome.
6. Students make a chart of patterns they like and think they could make. The chart includes style and pattern brand and numbers.

Enrichment

Have students design an original pattern envelope. Ask them to share their designs with the class.

CLOSE

Discuss the following saying with the class: "A stitch in time saves nine." Ask students to discuss the meaning of this slogan and then make up another sewing slogan.

LESSON THREE
Choosing Fabrics and Notions

FOCUS

Lesson Objectives
After studying this lesson, students should be able to
- explain how to select the best fabric for their sewing project.
- describe which types of fabrics to avoid.
- discuss how to choose notions that match their needs.

Motivating Activity
Provide each student with a swatch of fabric. Ask them to study their swatch and write down adjectives to describe the following qualities and characteristics of the fabric: fiber blend, color, texture, design, and finish.

Introducing the Lesson
Have students share their responses to the Motivating Activity. Point out that there are many different kinds of fabrics. Explain that in this lesson they will learn how to choose the best fabric for their sewing project.

Introducing *Words to Know*
Ask a volunteer to read the vocabulary words and their definitions. Ask students to write the words and definitions on a large piece of paper and draw a picture that illustrates the word and the definition. Have them share their pictures with the class.

494

LESSON THREE
Choosing Fabrics and Notions

WORDS TO KNOW
- notions
- nap
- ravel
- interfacing

DISCOVER...
- how to select the best fabric for your sewing project.
- which types of fabrics to avoid.
- how to choose notions that match your needs.

Once you have decided on a project and a pattern, you need to choose the materials with which to make the project. When you select fabric, you should consider more than just the color and texture. You also want to be sure that the materials are of good quality and are appropriate for your project. Then you are ready to choose **notions,** *the small items that are part of the construction of the garment.*

494   CHAPTER 17: PREPARING TO SEW

CLASSROOM RESOURCES FOR LESSON 3

 Blackline Masters
Activity and Project Card 33, "Explore Fabrics and Their Uses"
Activity and Project Card 34, "Prepare for Sewing Repairs"
Concept Map 27
Cooperative Learning 34

Cross Curriculum 19
Lesson 3 Quiz
Reteaching 17

 **Student Workbook**
Activity 123

How to Choose Fabrics

Fabrics come in many different colors, textures, designs, and finishes. How do you know which fabric to buy? You will want to evaluate the fiber or fiber blend, how the fabric is made, and any finishes that have been added. In addition, you should check the grain for quality.

When selecting fabric, you can use the information on your pattern envelope. The back of the envelope provides a list of suggested fabrics and how much fabric you will need. The pattern envelope provides special instructions for fabrics with **nap,** or *one-way texture,* such as corduroy.

How to Recognize Quality Fabrics

When you shop for fabrics, you will notice that they come in many price categories. How can you tell which ones are high quality? Keep in mind that you don't have to buy the most expensive one to get a good fabric. When judging quality in fabrics, examine the following:

- **Crosswise threads.** They should be straight and at right angles to the lengthwise threads.
- **Pattern.** If you are considering a printed fabric, make sure that the pattern runs straight with the grain. If the

Check fabric carefully for flaws before you have a salesperson cut the amount you need. Why is this important?

LESSON THREE: CHOOSING FABRICS AND NOTIONS 495

HOME AND COMMUNITY CONNECTION

Visiting a Fabric Store Arrange for students to visit a local fabric store. Have a store employee point out suitable fabrics for a beginning project. Ask students to read the labels on the end of the bolts for information about the different fabrics. Have them compare the labels to determine the fiber content, shrinkage, finishes, and care. Ask them how knowing this information can help them choose the best fabric.

CHAPTER 17, LESSON 3

TEACH

L1 Writing and Analyzing
Ask students to write a definition of *quality fabric* and a sentence or two explaining how to choose a quality fabric. Then provide students with swatches of fabrics of varying quality. Ask them to use their definitions and their sentences to choose which swatches are quality fabrics.

L2 Fine Arts Connection
Assign Cross-Curriculum Activity 19 in the TCR. Students learn about the art of quiltmaking in this activity.

DID YOU KNOW
Fabrics come in a variety of widths—36 inches, 44–45 inches, and 60 inches. The amount of fabric required for a pattern varies with fabric width.

L2 Activity and Project Card
Allow time for students to complete Activity and Project Card 33, "Explore Fabrics and Their Uses," in the TCR.

L2 Cooperative Learning
Assign Cooperative Learning Activity 34 in the TCR. Students work in groups to evaluate types of fabric in this activity.

CHAPTER 17, LESSON 3

Skills IN ACTION

Have students read "Skills in Action." Then ask them to brainstorm other ways to express themselves through fabric. Encourage students to try some of the ideas described in the feature and ideas they or other students have described. Ask students who try these ideas to bring their garments to school to share with the class.

L2 Math

Have students determine the cost of the following amounts of fabric:
- 2½ yards of fabric at $2.44 per yard. (*$6.10*)
- 3 yards of fabric at $4.95 per yard. (*$14.85*)
- 1¾ yards of fabric at $4.00 per yard (*$7.00*)

L2 Matching

Display and label the following fabrics: denim, corduroy, gingham plaid, knit, gauze. Have students match each fabric with its correct description: is stretchy, has nap, will ravel easily, needs to be matched, is firm and durable. Discuss what kinds of garments each fabric would be best used for.

L2 Activity and Project Card

Allow time for students to complete Activity and Project Card 34, "Prepare for Sewing Repairs," in the TCR.

Expressing Yourself Through Fabric

Sewing can be a way to express your individuality. One way to make a garment uniquely "you" is to use fabric creatively. Try some of these ideas the next time you sew:

- Add a dash of color by using contrasting fabric for facings and undercollars or for collars and cuffs.
- Use interesting prints for the lining material of vests and jackets.

---

fabric is not printed properly, the garment will look off grain.

- **Weave.** Is it firm and durable?
- **Color.** Is it uniform throughout?
- **Finish.** Does it feel comfortable and pleasing to the touch?
- **Label.** Read the label on the end of the bolt of fabric. It gives facts about fabric width, fiber content, shrinkage, finishes, and care.

How to Select Fabric

When choosing a fabric, think about the requirements of your project. Although woven fabrics are generally the easiest to handle and sew, you should consider the following factors:

- **Whom the project is for.** If you are making something for yourself, look for colors that can be mixed and matched with other clothes you own.
- **When the garment will be worn.** The time of day and the season of the year in which the garment will be worn may affect the type of fabric and the color you choose.
- **How the item will be used.** If you are making a non-clothing item, such as a tote bag, a dark-colored fabric that doesn't show dirt may be a good choice.
- **Type of care needed.** Look for fabrics that are machine washable and that require little or no ironing.

Fabrics to Avoid

Some fabrics are difficult to work with. For example, lightweight, flimsy, and extremely soft fabrics are slippery and hard to sew. Loosely woven fabrics may not be a good choice because they tend to **ravel,** or *have threads pull out of the cut edge.* Patterns in fabrics can make a project more complicated too. For example, plaids, stripes, and large prints need to be matched at the seams.

496 CHAPTER 17: PREPARING TO SEW

MORE ABOUT • • •

The History of Fasteners The first hook-and-loop tape was invented by a Swiss mountaineer after he observed the tenacity of burs that clung to his socks and pants. After ten years he invented two strips of cotton fabric, one with tiny hooks and the other with smaller loops. Pressed together, the strips stuck until they were pulled apart. The strips were called "locking tape." Later cotton was replaced with nylon, which when woven under infrared light hardened to almost indestructible hooks and loops. The "locking tape" has been used for many applications. For example, it is used as a shoe fastener and for sealing the chambers of artificial hearts. Have students brainstorm other possible uses of "locking tape."

Selecting Notions

After you have chosen a fabric, refer to the back of the pattern envelope for a list of the type of notions you will need. Commonly used notions include the following:

- Thread
- Fasteners, such as zippers, snaps, hooks and eyes, buttons, and hook-and-loop tape
- Elastic
- Hem tape
- Interfacing. **Interfacing** is *a layer of special fabric placed between two pieces of fabric to give more shape to the garment.* It is often used in waistbands, cuffs, and collars.

When you buy notions, use your fabric to match colors. Thread should be the same color as the fabric or slightly darker because it will appear lighter when stitched.

The notions you will need for your project are listed on the pattern envelope. How can you make sure that they match your fabric?

TIPS for living

TIMESAVING NOTIONS

Even if you have plenty of time to sew, some sewing jobs, such as hemming and basting, can be downright dull. The following notions can help you complete those types of jobs faster:

- Marking pens and tracing paper with disappearing ink make it quick and easy to transfer pattern markings to fabric.
- Fabric glue sticks eliminate the need to baste hems, zippers, and trims by hand.
- Dissolving basting tape eliminates hand basting.
- Liquid seam sealant prevents fabric from raveling in a fraction of the time it takes to hem.
- Iron-on adhesive tape makes quick work of hemming, stabilizing seams, and attaching lace and other trims.

LESSON THREE: CHOOSING FABRICS AND NOTIONS   **497**

CHAPTER 17, LESSON 3

TIPS for living

Have students try one or more of the timesaving notions described in the feature. Ask them to describe their experience working with such notions. Have them discuss the success or failure of timesaving notions they have tried.

L1 Student Workbook
Assign Activity 123 in the Student Workbook.

ASSESS

Evaluating the Lesson
Assign Reviewing Terms and Facts and Thinking Critically on page 498 to review the lesson; then assign the Lesson 3 Quiz in the TCR.

Reteaching
- Have students make a diagram of a pattern envelope. The diagram should label the location of the following elements on the pattern envelope: notions, suggested fabrics, description of garment, interfacing chart, name of pattern company, pattern number, front and back views, and amount of fabric required.
- Have students complete Reteaching Activity 17 in the TCR.
- Assign Concept Map 27 in the TCR.

COOPERATIVE LEARNING

Tell students that they will produce an infomercial to demonstrate the proper use of sewing machines, sewing tools, and sewing equipment. Assign students to groups in producing the infomercial: The art staff should illustrate a background for the staging of the infomercial and any miscellaneous supplies, props, or artwork needed to produce the infomercial. Members of the writing staff might get ideas for the infomercial from the lessons in the chapter, sewing books, family members, friends, and employees of local fabric stores. The acting staff should practice their lines and actions for the infomercial. The production staff will stage the infomercial, help the actors and actresses with rehearsals, and videotape the infomercial.

497

CHAPTER 17, LESSON 3

Answers to Lesson 3 Review

1. The back of the pattern envelope tells how much fabric is needed.
2. Crosswise threads, pattern, weave, color, finish, and label.
3. Threads pull out of the cut edge. Loosely woven fabrics ravel easily.
4. Thread, fasteners, elastic, seam binding or hem tape, interfacing.
5. You don't have to buy the most expensive fabrics to get quality.
6. Answers will vary. Students should give at least two examples of items from their wardrobe that they could update using notions.
7. Students estimate the cost of a sewing project. Other factors students should consider besides cost are time and skills required.

Enrichment

Have students research to find out how textiles are dyed. Ask them to use this information to explain why colors of fabrics from different bolts may not exactly match. Ask students to share their findings with the class.

CLOSE

Ask students to write a sentence explaining how the type and quality of a fabric affects a sewing project.

498

If you calculate the total cost of fabric and notions before you buy them, you can determine whether your choices are within your budget. What can you do if they are too expensive?

Making Choices

The materials you choose will affect the cost and the success of your sewing project. Begin by reading the information on the back of the pattern envelope. Then follow the guidelines for selecting fabric and notions that you learned in this lesson. Now you're ready to start sewing!

LESSON THREE Review

Using complete sentences, answer the following questions on a separate sheet of paper.

Reviewing Terms and Facts

1. **Recall** How would you know the amount of fabric to buy for a particular sewing project?
2. **Identify** When judging fabric quality, what elements should you examine?
3. **Vocabulary** Explain what happens when a fabric *ravels*. Which type of fabric ravels easily?
4. **Give Examples** Name five commonly used notions.

Thinking Critically

5. **Analyze** Should you buy the most expensive fabric that you can afford? Why or why not?
6. **Recommend** How could you use notions to update your clothing? Give two examples of items from your wardrobe.

Applying Concepts

7. Estimate the cost of a sewing project you are interested in making. Be sure to include the cost of the pattern, fabric, and notions. How does your total cost compare with that of a similar item you could buy ready-made? What factors, besides cost, should you consider when deciding whether to make or buy this item?

498 CHAPTER 17: PREPARING TO SEW

MEETING STUDENT DIVERSITY

Physically Challenged Discuss with students —or ask physically challenged students in the class to lead a discussion on—the special needs of people with physical challenges in terms of making their own garments. (For example, students in wheelchairs may have difficulty finding patterns of clothing that make dressing convenient. Students who are blind or have other physical challenges may find roadblocks to using sewing machines and other sewing equipment, and so on.) Have volunteers investigate and report to the class about patterns and special sewing equipment that help to ensure that the needs of physically challenged individuals are met in sewing labs.

Chapter 17 Activities

FRIENDS & FAMILY

SEWING AT HOME

When selecting an area for sewing at home, consider that the ideal sewing area should be well lit and able to accommodate a sewing machine, an ironing board, and a cutting table. Where you sew also depends on when you sew and the schedules of other family members.

TRY THIS!

Think about where you could set up a sewing area in your home. Keeping in mind family schedules, when would be the best time for you to sew there?

A Global View

SEWING AROUND THE WORLD

In some cultures, appliqué sewing has developed into an art form. India is famous for its *shisha* appliqué in which tiny mirrors are sewn onto a fabric backing. In Benin, appliqué has been used for centuries on banners and ritual clothing to record the deeds of battles and the powers of kings. Cuna Native Americans are well known for their molas.

TRY THIS!

Find a picture of or additional information about one of the types of appliqué work described here. Share your findings with the class.

Consumer Focus

Sew or Buy?

The next time you're trying to decide whether to make or buy an item, consider the following factors. Would it take more time to shop for the item or to sew it? Is it less expensive to sew? Do you have the sewing skills?

Try This!

Considering time, money, and sewing skills, would it be better for you to sew or buy? Write a paragraph explaining your answer.

MATH CONNECTION

PRODUCT PRICING

Shannon Reed was sewing ten dolls for an upcoming craft fair. Her costs for materials were $68, and the entry fee to the craft fair was $10.

Each doll had taken three hours to make, and Shannon hoped to earn at least $5 per hour making and selling the dolls. Competitors charged between $20 and $30 per doll.

1. How much would Shannon have to charge per doll to make $5 per hour?

2. How much should Shannon charge per doll if materials cost $85 and she showed the dolls at two craft fairs, each with a $10 entry fee?

3. Why do you think that it was important for Shannon to check the prices of similar dolls before deciding what price to charge for her dolls?

CHAPTER 17 ACTIVITIES 499

Teaching the MATH CONNECTION

Help students work through the math procedures necessary to compute the answers to questions 1 and 2 in "Follow Up." Work out the problems as follows: Add materials costs to entry fee ($68 + $10). Divide by 10 dolls to get cost per doll ($78 ÷ 10 = $7.80). Add this total to $15 (3 hrs at $5 per hour) to get $22.80. ($85 + 20 = $105 ÷ 10 = $10.50 + $15 = $25.50)

Answers to Follow-Up

1. $22.80 per doll.
2. $25.50 per doll.
3. Answers will vary. Students should note that in order for the dolls to sell, the price Shannon charges must be competitive with similar dolls. If she charges a lot more for the dolls than people who sell similar dolls charge, Shannon will probably not sell her dolls.

CHAPTER 17

Activities

FRIENDS & FAMILY

Encourage students who enjoy sewing at school in the sewing lab to take up sewing as a hobby at home. Discuss with them places at home where they might set up a sewing center. For instance, suggest that they may find a place in the dining room after dinner, when everyone else is busy with other activities.

A Global View

Let students try a simple appliqué technique. Have them: Trace a shape onto the paper side of fusible webbing. Cut the webbing larger than the traced lines. Then iron webbing onto the wrong side of a piece of fabric and cut out the appliqué. Remove paper and iron appliqué onto garment. Machine or hand stitch decorative sewing around the edges to finish their appliqué.

Consumer Focus

Discuss with students additional questions to ask themselves when considering whether to sew or buy an item. Have them think of an item they want. Could the item easily be found on sale? Is the item difficult to fit the wearer or user? Could sewing the item make it more personalized?

499

CHAPTER 17 REVIEW

Checking Comprehension

Use the Chapter Summary and the Chapter 17 Review to help students go over the most important ideas in Chapter 17.

Answers to Words to Know

1. It controls the length of the stitches.
2. It holds the fabric in place.
3. A plan for making a garment or project.
4. A version of the garment.
5. To give the garment shape.
6. One-way texture; corduroy and velvet.
7. A layer of special fabric placed between two pieces of fabric to give more shape to the garment; waistbands, cuffs, and collars.

Answers to Review Questions

1. Any three: Shears—cut out fabric; scissors—trim, clip, and cut threads; pinking shears—trim raw edges of fabric; sewing gauge—measure short spaces; needles—hand sewing; seam ripper—remove stitches; thimble—protects finger; thread—hand and machine sewing; pincushion—hold pins; pins—hold fabrics together; tape measure—take body measurements.

CHAPTER 17 REVIEW

Chapter Summary

- When working in the sewing lab, it is important to follow safety procedures and to organize your time and supplies.
- Basic tools for sewing include needles, pins, a pincushion, a sewing gauge, a seam ripper, shears, scissors, pinking shears, a tape measure, a thimble, and thread.
- Before using any sewing machine, read the instruction book.
- A pattern is a plan for making a garment or project. The pattern envelope provides information about fabric, notions, sizes, and difficulty level.
- If you learn how to take accurate measurements, you can determine your pattern size and ensure that your completed garment will fit well.
- When judging quality in fabric, examine the crosswise threads, pattern, weave, color, finish, and label.
- Some fabrics are easier to work with than others. Woven fabrics are a good choice because they are the easiest to handle and sew.
- Notions are the small items that are part of the construction of a garment. Thread, fasteners, elastic, hem tape, and interfacing are examples of notions.

Words to Know

Using complete sentences, answer the following questions on a separate sheet of paper.

1. What does a *stitch regulator* control?
2. Describe the function of the *presser foot* on a sewing machine.
3. What is a sewing *pattern*?
4. Define the term *view* as it applies to patterns.
5. Why would a garment be designed with *darts*?
6. What is nap? Give two examples of fabrics with *nap*.
7. Define the term *interfacing*. What are three common uses for interfacing?

500   CHAPTER 17: PREPARING TO SEW

Review Questions

Using complete sentences, answer the following questions on a separate sheet of paper.

1. List three basic sewing tools, and explain the purpose of each.
2. Describe the basic procedure for threading a sewing machine.
3. What do you use to control the speed on a sewing machine?
4. Using "1" for easiest to sew and "5" for the most complex, rank in order the following five styles: a close-fitting shirt with buttons and gathered sleeves; a collarless shirt with buttons and gathered sleeves; a collarless, sleeveless shirt with snaps; a close-fitting shirt with snaps and gathered sleeves; a

EXTRA CREDIT PROJECT

Group Project Encourage students to work together on a community project by sewing infants' outfits to donate to a hospital or center for unwed mothers. Provide students with pattern books and help them choose a simple pattern appropriate for infants, taking into consideration comfort, convenience, and safety features (no buttons, loose strings, etc.). Students should decide on an appropriate, fire-retardant fabric. Parents, PTA, or other school groups may be asked to donate funds or supplies for making the outfits. Allow students time to work in the sewing lab to complete the outfits. Have them contact the facility they will donate to and arrange a time for representatives to present the finished pieces.

CHAPTER 17 REVIEW

loose shirt with a band collar, snaps, and short sleeves.

5. How do you measure the back waist length? The arm length?
6. Identify which measurement is most important for each of the following types of garments: blouses and tops, shirts, full skirts, pants, and semifitted skirts.
7. Why is it a good idea to buy fabric and notions at the same time?

Thinking Critically

Using complete sentences, answer the following questions on a separate sheet of paper.

1. **Evaluate** When choosing a sewing project, which of the following factors do you think is most important: purpose, sewing skills and experience, time, or cost? Explain your answer.
2. **Analyze** Why do you need to consider so many factors when choosing a fabric for a sewing project? What might happen if you make a selection without giving it enough thought?

Cooperative Learning

1. In small groups, brainstorm some classroom rules for the sewing lab. Take into account safety, efficiency, and consideration for others. Compare lists from each group, and combine them to make a master list. Post the rules on a bulletin board in the classroom.
2. In small groups, research one type of sewing notion (for example, snaps, hem tape, or thread). Each group should explain to the rest of the class the different types of products available within that category and the advantages and disadvantages of each type.

Family & Community

1. Think of a sewing project that you could make as a gift for a friend or a family member. Write a paragraph or two describing the person and the factors you would consider in choosing the best pattern and fabric for the project. If possible, make the item and give it to the person you chose!
2. Find out where in your community you could buy a sewing machine. Visit one store, or obtain brochures about the machines sold there. Find out whether the store offers classes in how to use the machines. Which sewing machine features do you think would be most useful? Share your findings with the class.

Building A Portfolio

1. Use a sewing machine to practice sewing various stitches on small pieces of different types of fabric. Attach notes to each piece, evaluating which stitch you would use for what purpose and how well each is suited to the type of fabric. Place the samples and notes in your portfolio.
2. Choose one item of clothing from your wardrobe. Analyze how many pieces of fabric went into its construction. Make a sketch of the pattern pieces required, labeling where each fits into the completed garment. Add the sketch to your portfolio.

CHAPTER 17 REVIEW 501

CHAPTER 17 REVIEW

2. Use the hand wheel to move the take-up lever to its highest peak. Begin threading with the spool on the spool pin. Put the thread through the tension control, the take-up lever, and the needle. Use thread guides along the way to hold thread in place.
3. Use either a foot pedal or a knee pedal.
4. 1—a collarless, sleeveless shirt with snaps; 2—a loose shirt with a band collar, snaps, and short sleeves; 3—a collarless shirt with buttons and gathered sleeves; 4—a close-fitting shirt with snaps and gathered sleeves; 5—a close-fitting shirt with buttons and gathered sleeves.
5. Measure from the prominent bone at the base of the neck to the waistline; measure from back base of neck along shoulder to wrist.
6. Blouses and tops—bust; shirts—chest and neck; full skirts—waist; pants and semifitted skirts—hips.
7. To match colors.

Evaluate

Use the Chapter 17 Test in the TCR, or construct your own test using the Testmaker Software.

CLOSE

Have students apply their knowledge of the chapter's content by completing one of the alternative assessment activities listed under Family and Community or Building a Portfolio.

Answers to Thinking Critically

1. Answers will vary. Students explain why purpose, sewing skills and experience, time, or cost is most important in choosing a sewing project.
2. Answers will vary. Students should point out that choosing the correct fabric for the kind of sewing project will help determine the success of the project.

Planning Guide
Chapter 18 Sewing Skills

LESSON 1	Pages	FEATURES	CLASSROOM RESOURCES
Preparing Your Pattern and Fabric	504–509	Skills in Action: Home Decorating	Activity and Project Card 35, "Reading a Pattern" Cooperative Learning 35 Lesson 1 Quiz Transparency 70, "Pattern Markings" Student Workbook Activity 124
LESSON 2 **Starting to Sew**	510–515	Try This: Sewing Safety	Enrichment 20 Lesson 2 Quiz Transparency 71, "Pinning, Cutting, and Marking Your Fabric" Student Workbook Activities 125, 126
LESSON 3 **Using a Serger**	516–522	Tips for Living: Serger Terms Skills in Action: Sewing for Fun and Profit	Lesson 3 Quiz Peer Pressure and Decision Making 34 Transparency 72, "The Parts of a Serger" Student Workbook Activities 127, 128
LESSON 4 **Making Your Project**	523–528	Try This: Storing Patterns	Cross Curriculum 20 Lesson 4 Quiz Sewing Labs 1, 2, 3, 4 Student Workbook Activities 129, 130
LESSON 5 **Repairing and Altering Your Clothes**	529–534	Try This: Hand-Sewing Skills Skills in Action: Recycling Your Clothes	Activity and Project Card 36, "Demonstrate Stitching Techniques" Concept Map 28 Cooperative Learning 36 Lesson 5 Quiz Sewing Labs 5, 6, 7, 8 Student Workbook Activity 131

CHAPTER 18 RESOURCES

Chapter 18 Test Study Guide 18, *Reteaching* Testmaker Software
Reteaching 18

Performance Assessment Activity

Ask students to outline the chapter. Have each student prepare a scrapbook titled "My Sewing-Skills Sampler." Ask students to make samples of each sewing skill they have learned in this chapter. Ask students to make a table of contents and glossary for their scrapbook. Interested students may wish to add a special section on serger stitches. Put the sample stitches in a scrapbook. Display student scrapbooks.

School-to-Work

Have students identify businesses in their community that provide sewing services. Have students write letters of inquiry to these businesses to find out the kinds of employment opportunities the businesses have to offer. Students' letters should inquire about the technical, educational, and personal skills required for each job. Have students share their responses with the class. Then discuss how the classes that students are taking in school could help prepare them for a job in one of these businesses.

Family & Community

Have students call or visit local tailor shops or dry cleaners to find out how much they charge to make simple repairs, to lengthen or shorten hems, or to sew on buttons. Then have students meet with their families and estimate how many items need repairing in the family per month. Ask students to compute how much family members can save by learning to repair their own clothing.

Resources for the Teacher

Black, Lynette Ranney, and Linda Wisner. *Creative Serging for the Home.* Portland, OR: Palmer/Pletsch Associates, 1991.

Mashuta, Mary. *Wearable Art for Real People.* Martinez, CA: C&T Publishing, 1989.

Readings for the Student

Hoffman, Christine. *Sewing by Hand.* New York: HarperCollins Children's Books, 1994.

Morley, Jacqueline. *Clothes for Work, Play, & Display.* New York: Watts, 1992.

Smith, Nancy, and Linda Milligan. *More Sewing Machine Fun.* Denver, CO: Possibilities Denver, 1993.

Multimedia Resources

Beginning Sewing Techniques (Videocassette). Home Economics School Service.

How Clothing Is Made (Videocassette). Home Economics School Service.

Pattern Preparation, Layout, and Cuttings (Videocassette). Home Economics School Service.

Sewing With Sergers. (Videocassette). Home Economics School Service.

OUT OF TIME?

If time does not permit thorough teaching of this chapter, you may wish to use:

- Teens Making a Difference, page 503
- Tips for Living, page 517
- Try This, pages 514, 525, 530
- Skills in Action, pages 508, 521, 532
- Young Living Activities, page 535
- Chapter Summary, page 536

CHAPTER 18
Sewing Skills

Chapter Overview

Chapter 18 introduces students to the skills needed to complete a sewing project. They learn that the secret to successful sewing is to carefully master each step from laying out a pattern to hemming a finished garment. The students are given instruction on the use of sergers. They learn construction and hand-sewing techniques.

LESSON 1 describes how to prepare a pattern and fabric.
LESSON 2 explains how to lay out, cut, mark, and sew a project.
LESSON 3 explains what a serger is and how to use one.
LESSON 4 discusses the basic steps of sewing and construction.
LESSON 5 identifies hand-sewing stitches and explains how to make clothing repairs.

Introducing the Chapter

Refer students to the chapter title "Sewing Skills." Then have them skim the lesson titles. Using the lesson titles and objectives, have them create an outline. Have them add details to their outlines as they study each lesson.

Chapter Motivator

Using a guide sheet from an easy-to-sew pattern, remove all indications of the steps involved in the sewing project. Duplicate each guide sheet. Cut apart each step. Place the steps in envelopes, so that each envelope contains all the steps. Organize students into small groups and have them arrange the guide sheets in the proper sequence. Review correct sequencing with students. Point out that in this chapter they will learn the step-by-step sewing techniques needed to complete sewing projects.

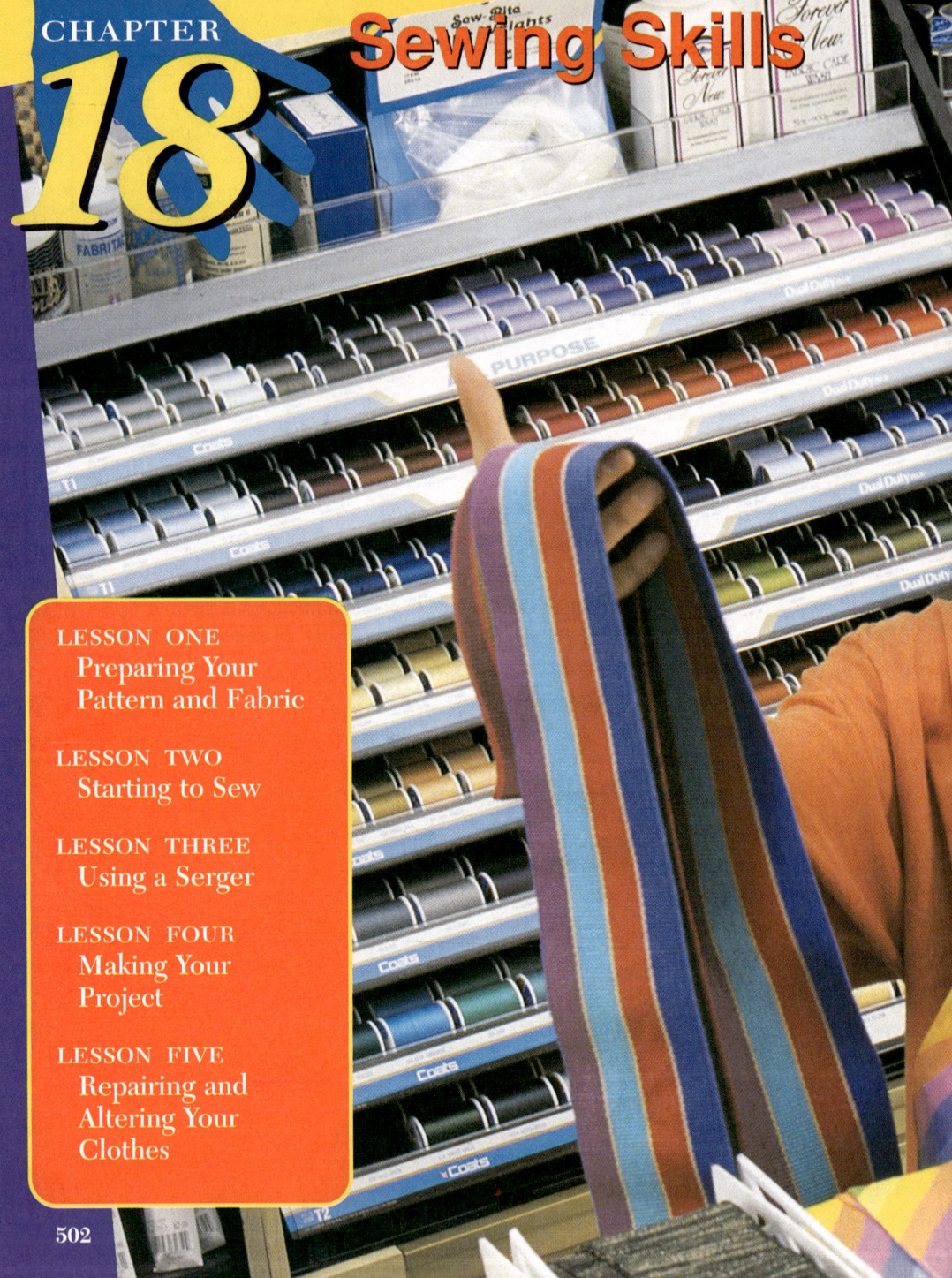

CHAPTER 18 Sewing Skills

LESSON ONE
Preparing Your Pattern and Fabric

LESSON TWO
Starting to Sew

LESSON THREE
Using a Serger

LESSON FOUR
Making Your Project

LESSON FIVE
Repairing and Altering Your Clothes

KEY TO ABILITY LEVELS

Teaching strategies that appear throughout the chapter have been identified by one of three codes to give you an idea of their suitability for students of varying learning styles and abilities.

L1 Level 1 strategies should be within the ability range of all students. Often full class participation is required. Teacher direction is usually needed.

L2 Level 2 strategies are for average to above-average students or for small groups. Some teacher direction is necessary.

L3 Level 3 strategies are designed for students able and willing to work independently. Minimal teacher direction is necessary.

CHAPTER 18

TEENS MAKING A DIFFERENCE

Have students read "Teens Making a Difference." Ask them to identify the ways the student in the article made a difference by sewing doll clothes. (*Kristi Makita started a customized sewing business as a result of her hobby of sewing doll clothes.*) Ask students to describe the initiative that Kristi Makita took in order to start a money-making sewing business. Have students describe ways they have used their skills to earn money.

Ask students to work with a partner to complete TRY THIS! at the end of the feature. Ask pairs to share their ideas with the class.

TEENS MAKING A DIFFERENCE
Sewing for Dolls

Twelve-year-old Kristi Makita loves to sew. When she was younger, she made clothes for her dolls. Now Kristi makes outfits for her younger sister's dolls. Sometimes she follows a special pattern. Other times she creates her own designs.

A few months ago Kristi displayed some of her doll clothes at a neighborhood craft fair. Several parents were impressed with Kristi's work and offered to pay her to make clothes for their children's dolls. Since then she has received more orders. Kristi has turned her hobby into a moneymaking, customized sewing business!

Try THIS!

Think of a way that you could use your sewing skills to earn, or save, money. Discuss your ideas with a classmate.

BLOCK SCHEDULING

The following Teacher Classroom Resources are suggested for use in classrooms with Block Scheduling.

- Activity and Project Card 35, "Reading a Pattern"
- Activity and Project Card 36, "Demonstrate Stitching Techniques"
- Cooperative Learning 35, "Getting Ready to Sew"
- Cooperative Learning 36, "Reject—or Recycle?"

TECHNOLOGY IN THE CLASSROOM

Camcorders The camcorder has many uses in the Family and Consumer Sciences classroom. It can be used to record presentations of guest speakers to show other classes or for later review. The camcorder can be used to videotape students in the foods and sewing labs. Students can use the videotape to evaluate their cooking and sewing techniques. Students' skits, role-playing situations, and demonstrations can be videotaped. Finally, you can use the camcorder to videotape students' activities in the Family and Consumer Sciences classroom to market the program to future students, parents, administrators, or school board members.

LESSON ONE
Preparing Your Pattern and Fabric

FOCUS

Lesson Objectives
After studying this lesson, students should be able to:
- explain how to use a guide sheet.
- describe how to check pattern pieces and measurements.
- list three steps to prepare fabric for sewing.

Motivating Activity
Cut apart a pattern and display it in front of the classroom. Cover the name of the part on each piece. Number each piece. Then ask students to try to identify the part of the garment each pattern piece represents.

Introducing the Lesson
Have students share their responses to the Motivating Activity. Identify the correct pieces as shirt front, sleeve, facing, collar, and so on. Have students read the opening paragraph. Ask them to suggest what Evan must do to prepare to sew. Tell students that in this lesson they will learn how to prepare pattern pieces and fabric for sewing.

Introducing *Words to Know*
Give students a pattern and ask them to point out the guide sheet, the layouts, and several markings. Write those words on the chalkboard, and ask students to prepare definitions for the terms based on what they have seen on the pattern. Then ask students to find the definitions of *selvage* and *raw edges*. Have them identify these two edges on a piece of fabric.

LESSON ONE
Preparing Your Pattern and Fabric

WORDS TO KNOW
- guide sheet
- layouts
- markings
- ease
- grain
- selvage
- raw edges
- bias

DISCOVER...
- how to use a guide sheet.
- how to check pattern pieces and measurements.
- how to prepare your fabric.

Evan thinks he is ready to begin his sewing project. He bought the pattern, fabric, and notions yesterday. He plans to start laying out the pattern pieces and pinning them to the fabric today. Do you know what steps Evan has left out? Do you know what he needs to do to prepare his pattern and fabric before he begins to sew?

504 CHAPTER 18: SEWING SKILLS

CLASSROOM RESOURCES FOR LESSON 1

 Blackline Masters
Activity and Project Card 35, "Reading a Pattern"
Cooperative Learning 35
Lesson 1 Quiz

 Transparencies
Transparency 70, "Pattern Markings"

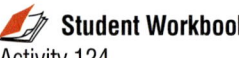 **Student Workbook**
Activity 124

Using the Guide Sheet

Before you begin sewing, you need to study the guide sheet inside your pattern envelope. A **guide sheet** is *a set of step-by-step instructions for sewing a pattern*. The guide sheet contains general information on how to use the pattern, a diagram of the pattern pieces, an explanation of the pattern markings, and layouts. **Layouts** are *diagrams of how the pattern pieces should be placed on the fabric.*

If you use the guide sheet, you will be able to sew more quickly and efficiently. For best results, follow these steps:

- Study the diagram of the pattern pieces.
- Circle the letters of the pieces needed for the view that you plan to make.
- Circle the layout diagram that you will use for your size and style.
- Read through *all* of the pattern directions before you start to work.
- As you make your project, put a check mark next to each step after you complete it.

Preparing the Pattern Pieces

After you have read through the guide sheet, you are ready to start preparing the pattern pieces. Follow these steps:

- Cut apart the pieces you will use, but do not trim them. You will cut off the margins later, when you cut the fabric.
- Put the pattern pieces that you will not use back in the envelope.
- Study each pattern piece, and refer to the guide sheet to find out what the markings mean.

To start preparing the pattern pieces, unfold them and cut them apart. Why shouldn't you trim the pieces?

LESSON ONE: PREPARING YOUR PATTERN AND FABRIC   505

MEETING STUDENT DIVERSITY

Varied Learning Styles Many students at this experience level will have difficulty understanding pattern layouts because it involves abstract representation. For these students, offer concrete experience with pattern layouts. Give them a layout sheet from a pattern; a large piece of fabric in a dark, solid color; and as many pattern pieces as should fit on the fabric. Let them pin the pattern pieces to the fabric as shown in the first layout. Repeat with subsequent layouts. When they notice that some layouts do not fit as well as others, give them another large piece of fabric with a different width. Have them repeat the layouts until they find one that fits the new fabric width without a lot of fabric left over.

CHAPTER 18, LESSON 1

TEACH

L2 Comparing and Contrasting

Organize students into small groups and give each group a guide sheet from a different pattern manufacturer. Encourage students to find out as much as they can about what kind of information is included on the guide sheet. Then have the groups exchange guide sheets and study the new ones. Repeat until each group has examined guide sheets from several different manufacturers. Have each group compare the guide sheets by answering the following questions: How are they the same, and how are they different? Which guide sheet gives you the most information? Which one would you prefer to use and why?

L2 Activity and Project Card

Allow time for students to complete Activity and Project Card 35, "Reading a Pattern," in the TCR.

L1 Analyzing

Discuss with students how using a guide sheet makes sewing easier and reduces errors. Ask them to compile information from the Comparing and Contrasting activity above into a graph or chart. Point out that pattern manufacturers have already solved many of the problems that students might encounter as they work on their projects.

L2 Cooperative Learning

Assign Cooperative Learning Activity 35 in the TCR. Students work in groups to prepare patterns for sewing in this activity.

505

CHAPTER 18, LESSON 1

L3 Math

Have students work with a partner to take their body measurements. Then provide each student with a pattern envelope. Have them compare their body measurements with those listed on the pattern envelope. Ask students to circle their size on the pattern envelope. Tell them to analyze the pattern to determine if they would need to make alterations to the pattern. If so, have students describe the kind of alterations they would need to make.

Teacher Talk!

Special Layouts

Some students may want to work with fabrics that have a difficult pattern. Point out that plaids, stripes, and checks require a special layout to ensure that they will exactly match at the side seams, center seams, shoulders, waistlines, armholes, and sleeves. Before laying out the pattern, have students match the major lines of the pattern. Pin the two sides of the fabric together with major lines matched. Then place the pattern pieces on the fabric. Check each piece to be sure that the major lines will meet when the piece is cut and sewn. Notches that are to be joined together should be on the same stripe or located in the same position on a check or plaid.

Small prints or designs can be laid out like solids. Large prints or designs, however, should be in about the same position on each side and on the front and back of the garment.

Markings are *guides on the pattern pieces for making a project*. **Figure 18.1** explains common pattern markings.

- If the pattern pieces are wrinkled, iron them with a warm, dry iron.

Checking the Pattern Measurements

Before you place a pattern on fabric, you need to make sure that the pattern you selected fits your body. To do that, compare your measurements with the body measurements listed on the pattern envelope. Determine if the pattern is too long or too short or if any measurements don't match up. If you need to make any alterations to the pattern, now is the time to do so—*before* you cut the fabric.

To make length adjustments, use the two parallel lines labeled "lengthen or shorten." Your teacher can show you how to do this. Be sure that you make the same changes on both the front and back pieces of the pattern.

To make width adjustments, you may need to measure the pattern pieces with the help of your teacher. Then you need to determine how much actual ease is included in the pattern. **Ease** is *the amount of fullness added to a pattern for movement and comfort*. Each part of the pattern requires a different amount of ease, depending on the stress put on that part of the garment when it is worn.

When choosing a pattern, keep in mind that a full design allows for more flexibility and requires fewer alterations. Why would one of these patterns need to closely correspond to body measurements?

How to Prepare the Fabric

You can run into problems if you don't prepare your fabric *before* you begin sewing. Just imagine how you would feel if, after you spent hours sewing a shirt, it shrank when you washed it! To avoid such problems, take the time to preshrink your fabric and check the **grain**—*the direction in which the threads run*.

506   CHAPTER 18: SEWING SKILLS

TECHNOLOGY UPDATE

Computers are increasingly used in the fashion design industry. One fashion designer uses a personal computer to design a line of women's clothing. She has created an image bank that includes figures scaled to the human body, basic designs (T-shirt, dress, skirt, pants, and so on), and files for various collars, pockets, sleeves, and prints. To create a new design, the designer selects a basic design and places it on the body. Then she tries different features on the basic design until she gets the look she wants.

**Figure 18.1
Pattern Markings**
Why do you need to understand what these pattern markings mean?

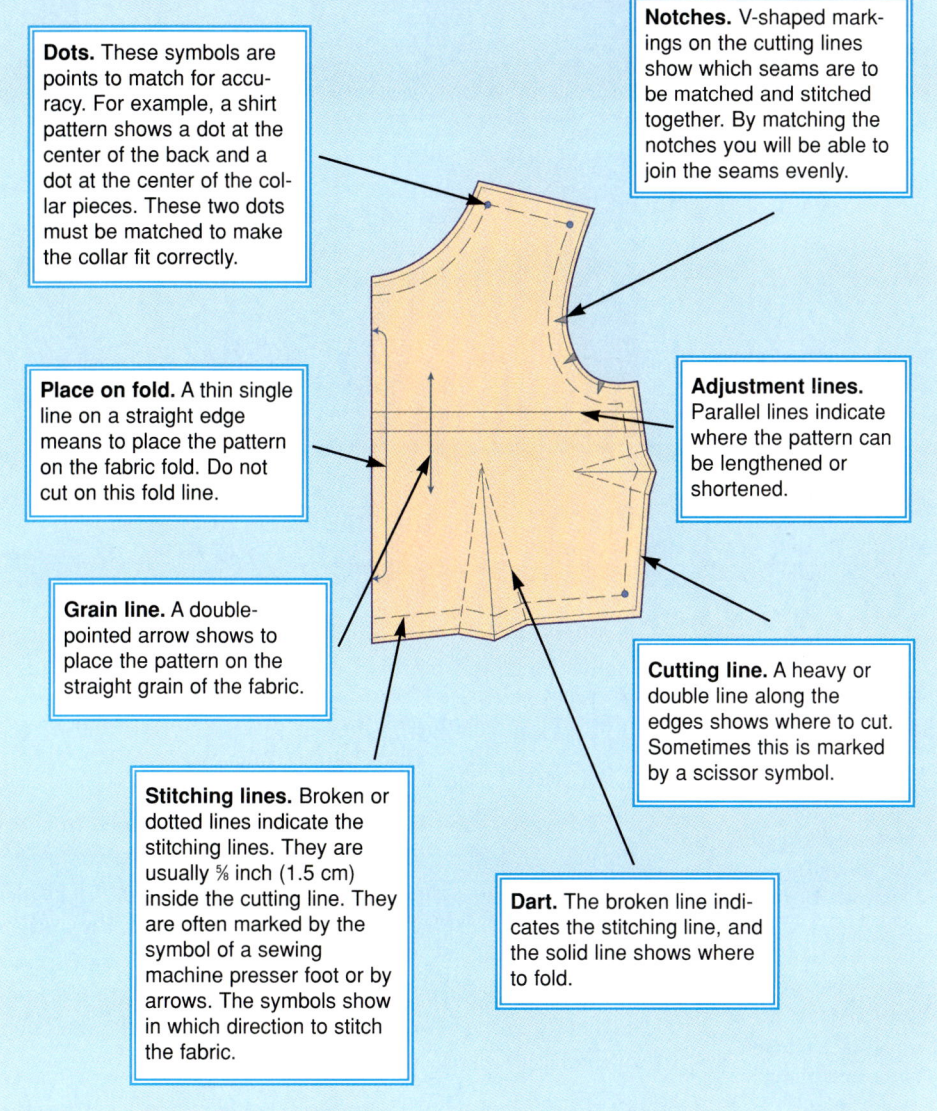

Dots. These symbols are points to match for accuracy. For example, a shirt pattern shows a dot at the center of the back and a dot at the center of the collar pieces. These two dots must be matched to make the collar fit correctly.

Place on fold. A thin single line on a straight edge means to place the pattern on the fabric fold. Do not cut on this fold line.

Grain line. A double-pointed arrow shows to place the pattern on the straight grain of the fabric.

Stitching lines. Broken or dotted lines indicate the stitching lines. They are usually ⅝ inch (1.5 cm) inside the cutting line. They are often marked by the symbol of a sewing machine presser foot or by arrows. The symbols show in which direction to stitch the fabric.

Notches. V-shaped markings on the cutting lines show which seams are to be matched and stitched together. By matching the notches you will be able to join the seams evenly.

Adjustment lines. Parallel lines indicate where the pattern can be lengthened or shortened.

Cutting line. A heavy or double line along the edges shows where to cut. Sometimes this is marked by a scissor symbol.

Dart. The broken line indicates the stitching line, and the solid line shows where to fold.

LESSON ONE: PREPARING YOUR PATTERN AND FABRIC   **507**

MORE ABOUT •••

Pattern Designs Pattern designers make sketches of their proposed designs. Once each design has been revised and improved, a finished drawing of the design, showing the various views and suggested fabric usage, is made. This finished drawing becomes the guide for making the pattern. Some designs are purchased by pattern manufacturers from famous designers, to be marketed as "designer patterns."

CHAPTER 18, LESSON 1

USING VISUALS
Refer students to Figure 18.1 and have them study the pattern markings. Then organize students into small groups to make posters of the pattern markings used in various sewing projects. They may wish to sketch pattern pieces and each type of pattern marking described in the illustration. Students should draw an arrow to show where each pattern marking is on the pattern pieces.

L1 Using Transparencies
Present Color Transparency 70, "Pattern Markings," in the TCR. Use this overhead visual to reinforce concepts from this lesson.

L2 Preparing
Suggest that students try the following sewing tips to make their projects go more quickly. Group notions and trims in a portable sewing kit. Keep the wastebasket, steam iron, and ironing board within easy reach of the sewing machine.

DID YOU KNOW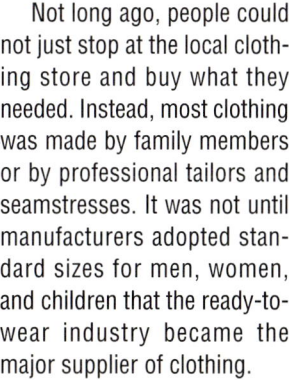
Not long ago, people could not just stop at the local clothing store and buy what they needed. Instead, most clothing was made by family members or by professional tailors and seamstresses. It was not until manufacturers adopted standard sizes for men, women, and children that the ready-to-wear industry became the major supplier of clothing.

CHAPTER 18, LESSON 1

L3 Science Research
Encourage students to find out what causes certain fabrics to shrink or wrinkle. Have them report their findings to the class.

Skills IN ACTION
Have students design a new look for a room in their home. Have them look through pattern books for styles that interest them. Ask them to determine the amount of fabric they would need to decorate their room.

L1 Student Workbook
Assign Activity 124 in the Student Workbook.

ASSESS

Evaluating the Lesson
Assign Reviewing Terms and Facts and Thinking Critically on page 509 to review the lesson; then assign the Lesson 1 Quiz in the TCR.

Reteaching
- Set up several fabric layouts throughout the room. One layout may have a pattern piece incorrectly placed; another may have fabric that has not been straightened. Have students work in groups to examine each layout and determine if it is correct. Have them discuss the changes they think should be made.
- Have students complete Reteaching Activity 18 in the TCR.

508

Preshrink fabric by following the cleaning instructions given on the bolt of fabric. Why is preshrinking important?

Skills IN ACTION

Home Decorating
Did you know that you can use your sewing skills to give your room a new look? Patterns for curtains, pillows, and other items are available. You can choose the styles and fabrics—usually at a fraction of the cost of ready-made items.

Preshrinking the Fabric

Before putting your pattern on the fabric, it is a good idea to preshrink the fabric. To do this, use the same cleaning method that you would use for the finished garment. Cleaning instructions are provided on the care label on the end of the bolt of fabric.

Checking the Grain

After you have preshrunk the fabric, you need to check the grain by looking at the fabric and locating the two selvages along the lengthwise edges. The **selvage** is *the tightly woven edge of the fabric that has no visible loose threads*. **Raw edges** are *the unfinished edges of the fabric that have loose threads*.

To test the grain, fold the fabric along the *lengthwise* grain so that the selvages are on top of one another. If the raw edges of the fabric do not line up, follow these steps:

- For woven fabrics, clip the selvage and pull a crosswise thread. Cut along the line made by the pulled thread.

508   CHAPTER 18: SEWING SKILLS

COOPERATIVE LEARNING

Science Experiment Have students experiment to learn more about fabrics and their care. Organize the class into small groups and assign one or two fabric types—such as cotton, rayon, silk, wool, polyester, and polyester blends—to each group. Have students cut their fabric into equal pieces, measure it (length and width), and record the size of each piece. Label all pieces with a laundry marker. Wash in cold or hot water and air or machine dry. Measure again. Have students make charts to compare the results. Ask them to use the charts to draw conclusions about the types of fabrics that shrink after washing. Ask each group to share their charts and conclusions.

- For knitted fabrics, cut along one crosswise row of loops to straighten the edges.

Now test the grain again by folding your fabric and matching selvages. If the crosswise ends match exactly and are at right angles to the selvage, the fabric is straight. The fold will be smooth and unwrinkled. If the edges do not match, the fabric is not straight.

You can straighten the fabric by pulling it on the true **bias**, or *diagonal*. To do that, open up the fabric and pull the two opposite corners that are too short.

You can straighten fabric by opening it up and pulling the two opposite corners. When is it necessary to straighten fabric?

LESSON ONE *Review*

Using complete sentences, answer the following questions on a separate sheet of paper.

Reviewing Terms and Facts

1. **Vocabulary** What is a *guide sheet*? What information does it contain?
2. **Identify** List five common markings on patterns.
3. **Describe** How would you adjust a pattern that is too long?
4. **Explain** Why should you preshrink fabric? How would you know what procedure to follow when preshrinking?

Thinking Critically

5. **Explain** Why is it important to read through all the directions on a pattern and to think through each step before beginning to work?
6. **Summarize** Outline the steps that you would take to prepare a pattern before beginning to sew.
7. **Contrast** Explain how to tell the difference between the selvage and the raw edge.

Applying Concepts

8. With a partner, compare the directions for two different patterns. What are the similarities and differences? Are the instructions for both clear and easy to understand? If not, how could they be improved?

LESSON ONE: PREPARING YOUR PATTERN AND FABRIC   509

MORE ABOUT • • •

Fabric Although we usually think of technology as applying to computers or other machines, technology has also improved fabrics over the years. For example, the addition of polyester to cotton has greatly reduced the need to press garments. Other improvements are washable silk and rayon. Ask students to research other improvements in fabric. Have them report their findings to the class.

CHAPTER 18, LESSON 1

Answers to Lesson 1 Review

1. Step-by-step instructions for sewing a pattern included with the pattern. It contains general information on how to use the pattern, a diagram of the pattern pieces, an explanation of pattern markings, and layouts.
2. Any five of the following: grain line, cutting line, place on fold, dart, stitching lines, dots, adjustment lines.
3. Use the two parallel lines on the pattern labeled "lengthen or shorten." Make the same changes on both the front and back pieces of the pattern.
4. To ensure that the garment will still fit after it is washed. To preshrink, follow the cleaning method described on the end of the bolt of fabric.
5. Students should mention that they will save time in the long run and reduce the risk of ruining their projects.
6. Unfolding the pattern; cutting the pieces apart; putting the unused pattern pieces back in the envelope; examining the markings; pressing the pattern pieces with a warm, dry iron; and loosely folding and stacking pattern pieces until needed.
7. Selvage is the tightly woven edge with no visible loose threads. It is the edge that does not ravel. The raw edge is the unfinished edge with loose threads.
8. Results will vary.

Enrichment

Using old pattern pieces, have students either lengthen or shorten a pair of trousers and a sleeve.

CLOSE

Encourage students to begin a "sewing checklist." Checklists should begin with steps needed to prepare pattern and fabric for sewing.

LESSON TWO
Starting to Sew

FOCUS

Lesson Objectives

After studying this lesson, students should be able to
- describe how to pin, cut, and mark fabric.
- explain how to stitch straight and curved seams and how to turn corners.
- discuss ways to finish seams.

Motivating Activity

Have students attempt to cut out a pattern piece and fabric before they have been pinned together. When they have worked for a few moments, ask: If you were an inventor, what might you invent to make this task easier? Record students' responses on the chalkboard.

Introducing the Lesson

Discuss students' responses to the Motivating Activity. Try some of the suggestions. Then give students a small pattern piece and a square of fabric. Have them pin the pattern to the fabric. Then have them cut the fabric. Point out that this method is much easier than trying to cut the fabric without pinning the pattern to it. Then tell students that in the lesson they will learn other helpful sewing techniques.

Introducing *Words to Know*

Ask students to write a definition for each of the two vocabulary words. When they have finished, have them compare their definitions with those of their classmates.

LESSON TWO
Starting to Sew

WORDS TO KNOW
backstitching
seam finishes

DISCOVER...
- how to pin, cut, and mark fabric.
- how to stitch straight and curved seams and how to turn corners.
- ways to finish seams.

Learning how to sew can be both fun and rewarding. Your sewing projects will be more successful if you practice new techniques before you begin. By carefully completing each step—from laying out the pattern pieces to hemming the finished garment—you will be able to make projects that you are proud of.

510   CHAPTER 18: SEWING SKILLS

CLASSROOM RESOURCES FOR LESSON 2

 Blackline Masters
Enrichment 20
Lesson 2 Quiz

 Transparencies
Transparency 71, "Pinning, Cutting, and Marking Your Fabric"

 Student Workbook
Activities 125, 126

Using Pattern Pieces

After you have prepared the pattern pieces and your fabric, make sure that you have all of the notions, tools, and equipment that you need for your project. If you are sewing at school, it is a good idea to write your name on your supplies.

Pinning

Look at your circled layout to see how to fold your fabric. Most layouts show the right sides folded together. Lay the pattern pieces on the fabric. The lengthwise grain markings must be parallel to the selvage. Check them with a ruler as you pin. Don't cut out any pieces until they have all been pinned in place and checked by your teacher. Follow these tips:

- First, pin the large pattern pieces that belong on the fold.

- Next, pin the pattern pieces that have a grain-line arrow. To check the grain line, place a pin at one end of the grain-line arrow. Measure from the arrow to the selvage or fabric edge. Position the pattern so that the other end of the arrow is exactly the same distance from the edge. Then pin the piece in place.

- Place the pins diagonally inside the cutting line. This keeps the fabric flat and makes it easier to cut.

- Place pins about 3 to 6 inches (7.5–15 cm) apart.

- Double-check your layout against the layout on the pattern.

Cutting

Before you begin to cut out your project, practice cutting on fabric scraps. If you cut the edges of the fabric evenly, it will be easier to sew straight seams.

Use the circled layout on the guide sheet to see how to fold the fabric and how to place pattern pieces on the fabric. How does it help you to have first circled the layout?

LESSON TWO: STARTING TO SEW **511**

CHAPTER 18, LESSON 2

TEACH

L1 Demonstrating
Show students how to pin a straight seam. Have them place pins at right angles to the seamline (about 4 inches [10 cm] apart) with the head of the pin to the outside. Ask students why it is a good idea to place pins this way. (*So that the pins can be easily removed as the fabric approaches the sewing machine needle.*) Emphasize how sewing over the pins can break the needle and cause it to shoot off at an angle. Encourage students to practice pinning and then removing the pins as they sew. Explain that they should practice until they can do this without jarring the fabric out of alignment.

L1 Using Transparencies
Present Color Transparency 71, "Pinning, Cutting, and Marking Your Fabric," in the TCR. Use this overhead visual to reinforce concepts from this lesson.

L2 Charting
Have students create illustrated flow charts showing the steps involved in pinning pattern pieces. Tell them to number the steps and write captions explaining the processes involved in the steps. Ask students to share their flow charts. Encourage them to use their flow charts as study aids when studying for the chapter test.

COOPERATIVE LEARNING

Critiquing Garment Construction Organize students into small groups. Provide each group with a garment that was not well made. Ask students to analyze the work and to identify several areas where the sewer may have made an error or neglected one or more preparatory steps. Have students write a critique of the construction of the garment, giving the sewer constructive criticism.

CHAPTER 18, LESSON 2

L1 Listing

Have students fold a piece of paper in half lengthwise and label one side "Pinning" and the other side "Cutting." Have students list five tips under each heading.

L2 Practice

Have students practice using different methods for marking fabrics, such as tailor's chalk, marking pen, tailor's tack, and dressmaker's tracing paper and tracing wheel. Have them practice each method using different types of fabrics. Have them make notes about the advantages and disadvantages of each method on each type of fabric. Ask students to share their findings with the class.

L2 Applying

Have students use a sheet of plain paper to draw circles, curves, squares, and zigzags. Let them practice stitching by following the lines on the paper as they sew. Use the sewing machine without thread for this exercise. Next, have students use lined paper to practice straight stitches. Then have them sew several straight rows of stitching on scraps of fabric.

L1 Applying

Remind students to practice sewing safety in the sewing lab. Encourage them to use a slow speed when learning how to use the sewing machine. Instruct them not to look away from the machine while it is in operation. Ask them to brainstorm other sewing safety tips to add to the guidelines. Then have them make posters of the sewing safety tips. Display the posters in the sewing lab.

Follow these guidelines:

- Place the fabric flat on the table. Use one hand to hold the fabric in place and the other hand to cut.
- Cut with long, even strokes.
- Cut in the direction of the arrows printed on the pattern seam-line markings. In this way, you will be cutting with the fabric grain, and you will not stretch the fabric.
- Cut around the outside of the notches. Cut double and triple notches together with one long edge across the top.
- Leave the pattern pieces pinned to the fabric until you are ready to stitch.

Marking

After you cut out your pattern, you need to transfer construction markings from the pattern to the fabric. Markings include darts, dots, fold lines, the center back, and buttonholes. The quickest and most accurate way to mark fabric is to use a tracing wheel and dressmaker's tracing paper. Practice until you can make a light, straight, continuous line. Seam lines don't need to be marked, because you can use the markings on the sewing machine to help you stitch a straight seam. Follow these suggestions when transferring markings:

- Use a color of tracing paper that will show up on the fabric.
- Always test the markings on a fabric scrap to make sure that they don't show through on the right side.
- Slip the tracing paper in place with the carbon next to the *wrong side* of the fabric.
- Press down lightly on the tracing wheel as you mark. You can use a ruler to guide the wheel for straight lines.
- Mark dots with an X. Mark the ends of darts with a short line.
- Mark each line or symbol so that you will know exactly where to stitch.

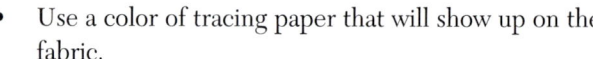

Using the proper tools can help make the task of marking fabric easier. Which color of tracing paper would you use on light-colored fabric?

512   CHAPTER 18: SEWING SKILLS

 HOME AND COMMUNITY CONNECTION

Guest Speaker Organize a visit from a local sewing store employee. Ask the speaker to demonstrate the steps involved in pinning, cutting, and marking a pattern. Have students prepare questions before the speaking engagement. Allow time for students to ask questions during the demonstrations and after. If possible, arrange to give students an opportunity to participate in the demonstrations. You may wish to have some students videotape the demonstration for reference later on.

Basic Sewing Skills

Before you can start sewing a project, you need to know how to stitch a straight seam. To sew a seam, place two pieces of fabric together with right sides facing each other. Line up the edges so that they are even. Match all markings and notches, and pin the two pieces together. The heads of the pins should be near the outside edges of the fabric. For most sewing, pins should be placed about 2 inches (5 cm) apart.

Now look at the throat plate on your sewing machine. The line markings show how far the needle is from the seam edge. Most seams are 5/8 inch (1.5 cm) wide. Find the line on the machine that is this far from the needle. If you line up the fabric edge against this mark as you sew, your seam will stay straight.

Stitching Straight Seams

To complete a project successfully, you need to stitch straight seams. Follow these steps:

1. Use the hand wheel to carry the needle down into the throat plate and up again. When it comes up, a loop of bobbin thread will come with it. **Figure 18.2** shows how to pull up the bobbin thread. Separate the threads, and pull them under the presser foot to the back.

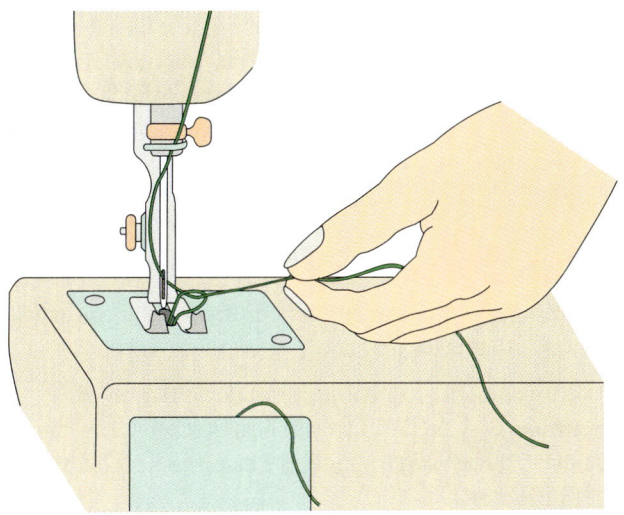

▶ **Figure 18.2 Pulling the Bobbin Thread**
Pull up the loop of bobbin thread with the thread from the needle. Where do you place the two threads?

CHAPTER 18, LESSON 2

L2 Language Arts
Have students find poems or proverbs that use the idea of stitching as a metaphor. Most will probably know "A stitch in time saves nine." Then ask the class to think about what the phrase "in stitches" means when it is used in reference to laughing. Have them ask relatives and neighbors where they think the phrase came from and what it means. Then let them use reference materials to try to identify the source of the phrase. Computers may be used for research if software is available. *(Shakespeare, Twelfth Night, Act III—"Laugh yourself into stitches.")*

L2 Experimenting
Have students work in small groups. Give each group four pieces of napped or sheen fabric. Have them stitch the pieces together so that the nap of two pieces is running in the right direction and the nap of the other two pieces is running in the wrong direction. Ask them to examine the joined pieces under different lighting conditions. Have them compare the swatches of fabric. Ask each group to determine what happens when fabric is not placed properly. (*The difference in sheen makes the joined pieces look as if they are constructed of different types of fabric.*) Have each group brainstorm what they can do to be certain their fabric is placed properly.

USING VISUALS
Have students study the diagram in Figure 18.2. Then have each student practice drawing bobbin thread through the needle head on a sewing machine.

MEETING STUDENT DIVERSITY

Cultural Perspectives Point out to students that styles of clothing vary in different countries and cultures. Therefore, clothing patterns they find in the United States may be different from the kinds of clothing patterns they would find in other countries. Have students identify the country where they would find patterns for the following clothing styles: kimono, sari, kilt, serape, sarong. Ask students to draw a view of each garment and label the name of the garment and the country in which the style developed. Display drawings on a bulletin board.

CHAPTER 18, LESSON 2

L2 Critical Thinking
Write several incorrect techniques on slips of paper, such as:
- Watch the needle instead of the fabric edges and guideline markings when sewing.
- Cut off the notches when cutting pattern pieces.
- Trim your pattern pieces to the cutting line.
- When you come to a corner, speed up the sewing machine.

Call on students to choose slips, explain the outcomes, and describe the correct procedures.

L1 Student Workbook
Assign Activities 125 and 126 in the Student Workbook.

ASSESS

Evaluating the Lesson
Assign Reviewing Terms and Facts and Thinking Critically on page 515 to review the lesson; then assign the Lesson 2 Quiz in the TCR.

Reteaching
- Have students practice their stitching techniques by having them complete a simple children's dot-to-dot using a sewing machine without the thread instead of a pencil.
- Have students complete Reteaching Activity 18 in the TCR.

Enrichment
- Give each student a strip of felt that is about 2 inches (5 cm) wide and 8 inches (20 cm) long. Have each student make a bookmark using different sewing machine stitches as decoration.
- Assign Enrichment Activity 20 in the TCR.

To practice sewing safety, keep your eye on the needle when sewing. Don't look away from the machine while sewing, and keep your fingers away from the path of the needle.

When you approach a corner, sew the last few stitches by turning the hand wheel. What should you do next?

514   CHAPTER 18: SEWING SKILLS

---

2. Place the pinned fabric pieces between the presser foot and the feed dog. Line up the outer edge of the fabric with the ⅝-inch (1.5-cm) marking on the throat plate. Position the fabric so that about ½ inch (1.3 cm) lies behind the needle. Lower the presser foot to hold the fabric.

3. Use the hand wheel to lower the needle into the fabric. Sew backward to the edge of the fabric. Then change the machine to forward, and stitch over your first stitching. This is called backstitching. **Backstitching** is *the technique of stitching over ½ inch (1.3 cm) of a seam at the beginning and end to lock the threads so that the seam won't pull out.* If your machine does not have a backstitch, you can tie the threads together after you have completed the seam.

4. As you stitch, guide the fabric with both hands, but do not push it. Keep your eyes on the fabric edges and guideline markings, and operate the machine at an even speed.

5. At the end of the seam, backstitch again. Then lift the presser foot, remove the fabric, and clip the threads close to the fabric.

Stitching Curved Seams
With curved seams, you must learn to guide the fabric with your hands so that the curves are smooth. You must also keep the stitching an even distance from the edge of the fabric. The best way to learn how to sew curved seams is to practice. Start by stitching curves drawn on a piece of paper. Then practice on scraps of fabric.

Turning Corners
Learning how to turn corners, or pivot, when you sew is another skill that takes practice. Follow these steps:

1. When you come to a corner, slow down the sewing machine. Sew the last few stitches by turning the hand wheel. The last stitch should position the needle exactly at the corner.

MORE ABOUT • • •

Sewing Equipment Using the proper equipment can make the difference between a quality garment and one that does not wear well. Before students begin working on a project, urge them to examine their supplies to make sure that the shears and pins are sharp, that the tracing wheel rolls easily, and that the sewing machine is functioning properly.

2. Lift the presser foot. Turn the fabric, with the needle still in it, so that you can stitch the next side. Put the presser foot down again.

Adding Seam Finishes

After stitching your project, you may need to add a seam finish. **Seam finishes** are *treatments used on the seam edges to prevent the fabric from raveling.* The most effective seam finish depends on the type of fabric being used. If the fabric ravels only slightly, pink the edges with pinking shears. For greater protection, stitch ¼ inch (6 mm) from each edge before pinking. If your fabric ravels easily, use a zigzag finish. Some fabrics do not ravel and, therefore, do not need seam finishes.

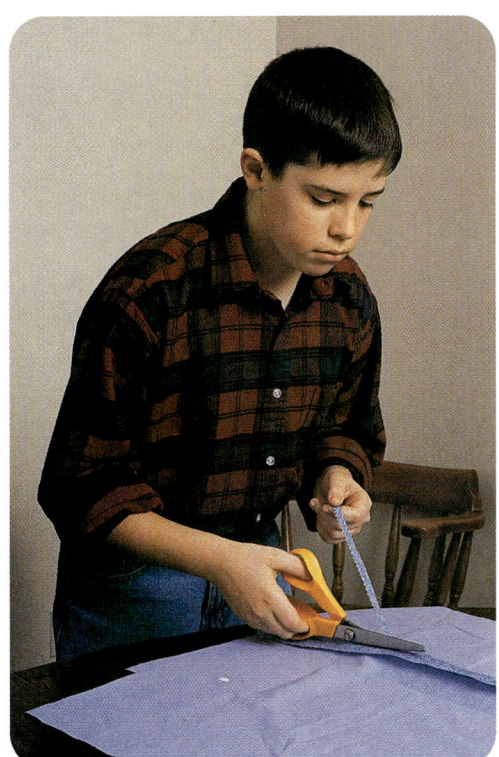

A seam finish can prevent fabric from raveling. Why are there different types of seam finishes?

LESSON TWO Review

Using complete sentences, answer the following questions on a separate sheet of paper.

Reviewing Terms and Facts
1. **Recall** List four guidelines that you can follow to learn to cut accurately.
2. **Identify** Name the tools needed to mark fabric.
3. **Vocabulary** What is *backstitching*? Why is it wise to backstitch at the beginning and end of each seam?
4. **Identify** Describe briefly three finishes that may be used on seam edges to prevent raveling.

Thinking Critically
5. **Explain** Why isn't it necessary to mark seams?
6. **Predict** What might happen if you don't practice sewing techniques before beginning a project?

Applying Concepts
7. With a partner, practice pinning, cutting, and marking a few old pattern pieces on scraps of fabric. Follow the instructions in this lesson. Compare your results, and discuss what you found easy or difficult to do.

LESSON TWO: STARTING TO SEW **515**

MORE ABOUT • • •

Seam Finishes A good way to determine how to finish a seam is to launder a piece of the fabric several times to see how much it ravels. Obtain samples of squares or rectangles of fabric. Prepare fabric ahead of time: stitch one edge; pink one edge; pink and stitch one edge; and zigzag the final edge. Launder and bring samples to class. Display the various results for students to examine. Explain to them that they may do the same with fabric before beginning their projects, and choose a seam finish based on their results.

CHAPTER 18, LESSON 2

Answers to Lesson 2 Review

1. The guidelines should include any four of the following: placing the fabric flat on the table and holding it in place; keeping shears in an upright position and cutting with long, even strokes; cutting in the direction of the arrows on the pattern seam-line markings; cutting around the outside of the notches; leaving the pattern pieces pinned to the fabric until ready to stitch.
2. Tracing wheel and dressmaker's tracing paper.
3. Backstitching is the technique of stitching over the beginning and end of a seam to lock the threads in place. It is done so that the seam won't pull out.
4. To prevent raveling, edges can be pinked with pinking shears, stitched and pinked, or zigzag stitched.
5. Seams do not need to be marked because they can be sewn with the seam guide on the sewing machine.
6. Students' responses will vary. They should include that practice will reduce errors.
7. Comparisons will vary. Students should discuss what they found easy or difficult to do.

CLOSE

If students started a sewing notebook in Lesson 1, have them transcribe their Lesson 2 notes into the notebook. Make sure they include information from this lesson. If they have not yet started a sewing notebook, have them do so now.

LESSON THREE
Using a Serger

FOCUS

Lesson Objectives
After studying this lesson, students should be able to
- identify what a serger is.
- explain the uses for a serger.
- explain how to operate a serger.

Motivating Activity
Have students read the opening paragraph of the lesson. Then have them examine the seams of some of the clothing they are wearing. Make two columns on the chalkboard and use tally marks to record the number of sewn and serged seams in students' clothing.

Introducing the Lesson
Discuss the results of the Motivating Activity. Ask students to brainstorm reasons why many manufacturers use seams made by a serger. (*Student responses might include that seams made by a serger may be cheaper, faster, or stronger.*)

Introducing *Words to Know*
Write the words *serger, cones, loopers, feed dogs,* and *stitch finger* on the chalkboard. Tell students to find the definition of each word in the textbook. Then ask students to find an example of each word in the diagram of the parts of a serger in Figure 18.3 on page 518. Ask students to explain how they think each part of the serger got its name.

LESSON THREE
Using a Serger

WORDS TO KNOW
- serger
- cones
- loopers
- feed dogs
- tail chain
- stitch finger

DISCOVER...
- what a serger is.
- the uses for a serger.
- how to operate a serger.

Take a look at the seams of the clothes you are wearing. If you made these clothes, each seam is probably a simple line of stitches. If you purchased the clothes, however, the seams probably resemble tiny tubes of fabric wrapped in thread. Seams of this kind are made by a special kind of sewing machine known as a serger.

516   CHAPTER 18: SEWING SKILLS

CLASSROOM RESOURCES FOR LESSON 3

 Blackline Masters
Lesson 3 Quiz
Peer Pressure and Decision Making 34

 Transparencies
Transparency 72, "The Parts of a Serger"

 Student Workbook
Activities 127, 128

What Is a Serger?

A **serger** is *a high-speed machine that sews, trims, and finishes a seam in one step.* Although sergers were first designed for factory use, they are now available for home sewing. A serger is a very useful piece of sewing equipment because it can save time and handle a variety of fabrics, from slippery silks to stretchy knits.

Figure 18.3 on the next page shows the parts of a serger. You can see that a serger feeds several strands of thread through guides that are placed above the machine to prevent tangling. **Cones** are *the large, rounded cylinders used to hold thread.* Sergers use cones instead of spools because sergers use more thread than sewing machines do. A cone is much larger than a spool and can hold up to five times more thread.

Sergers are known as two-thread, three-thread, four-thread, or five-thread, depending on the number of threads used to make the stitch. Each thread passes through its own tension dial. Sergers do not have bobbins. Instead, they have **loopers,** which are *rounded parts that hold the thread inside a serger.* The looper threads loop around each other and are interlocked with the needle thread or threads. Depending on the model, sergers may have one or two needles. The remaining threads are wrapped by the loopers.

TIPS for living

SERGER TERMS

Before you use a serger, it is helpful to understand these additional terms.

- **Tension dials** are like the tension control of a sewing machine. Instead of just tightening the stitch, however, you can change the pattern of the stitch by adjusting these dials.
- **Thread guides** help with the threading. To change threads, each new thread can be tied to the old one and pulled through the thread guide. Sergers need as many as eight thread guides for each strand of thread used by the machine.
- **Thread guide holders** look like antennas on the back of the machine. Each thread goes through a loop on this holder before it goes through its own set of tension dials.

LESSON THREE: USING A SERGER **517**

TECHNOLOGY UPDATE

Some manufacturers have begun to make machines that both sew and serge. Encourage your students to visit or call local sewing centers to request information on these new machines. Have them find out what the machines can do and what they cannot do. Also, compare the cost of a single sew-and-serge machine with the cost of separate sewing and serging machines. Have students make graphic organizers of their findings. Display the findings in the classroom.

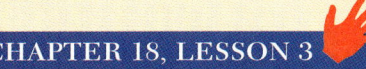

CHAPTER 18, LESSON 3

TEACH

L2 Arts and Crafts

Have students work in small groups to make craft projects and designs out of serger stitches. Let the groups choose whether to mix stitch types or to use just one type of stitch in their designs.

L2 Applying

Have students examine the clothing in their home closets to try to find an example of each type of serger stitch. Record the frequency of stitch type and in what type of garment or project each occurs. Write a brief explanation of why each stitch was used. Have students share their findings with the class.

TIPS for living

Have students locate the tension dials, thread guides, and thread guide holders on the diagram in Figure 18.3 on the next page. Have them work with partners to demonstrate how each part is used.

517

CHAPTER 18, LESSON 3

USING VISUALS

Tell students to carefully study the parts of a serger in the diagram in Figure 18.3. Then give them ten minutes to sketch and label what they remember about the serger. Have them compare their sketches with the information in the diagram. If your school has a serger, have students compare it with the one shown in Figure 18.3. Ask students to describe how the school's serger is different from the serger shown in the diagram.

L1 Using Transparencies

Present Color Transparency 72, "The Parts of a Serger," in the TCR. Use this overhead visual to reinforce concepts from this lesson.

DID YOU KNOW

Serger knives cannot be sharpened like scissors or kitchen knives. Instead, serger knives must be replaced. Avoid cutting pins, since this will dull the blades of serger knives. One or both serger blades have become dull when the trimmed edge is ragged. Serger knives have a hard steel blade and a softer blade. Usually it is the soft blade that dulls. In that case, replace only the soft blade.

Figure 18.3 Parts of a Serger
Which parts of a serger are similar to parts of a regular sewing machine?

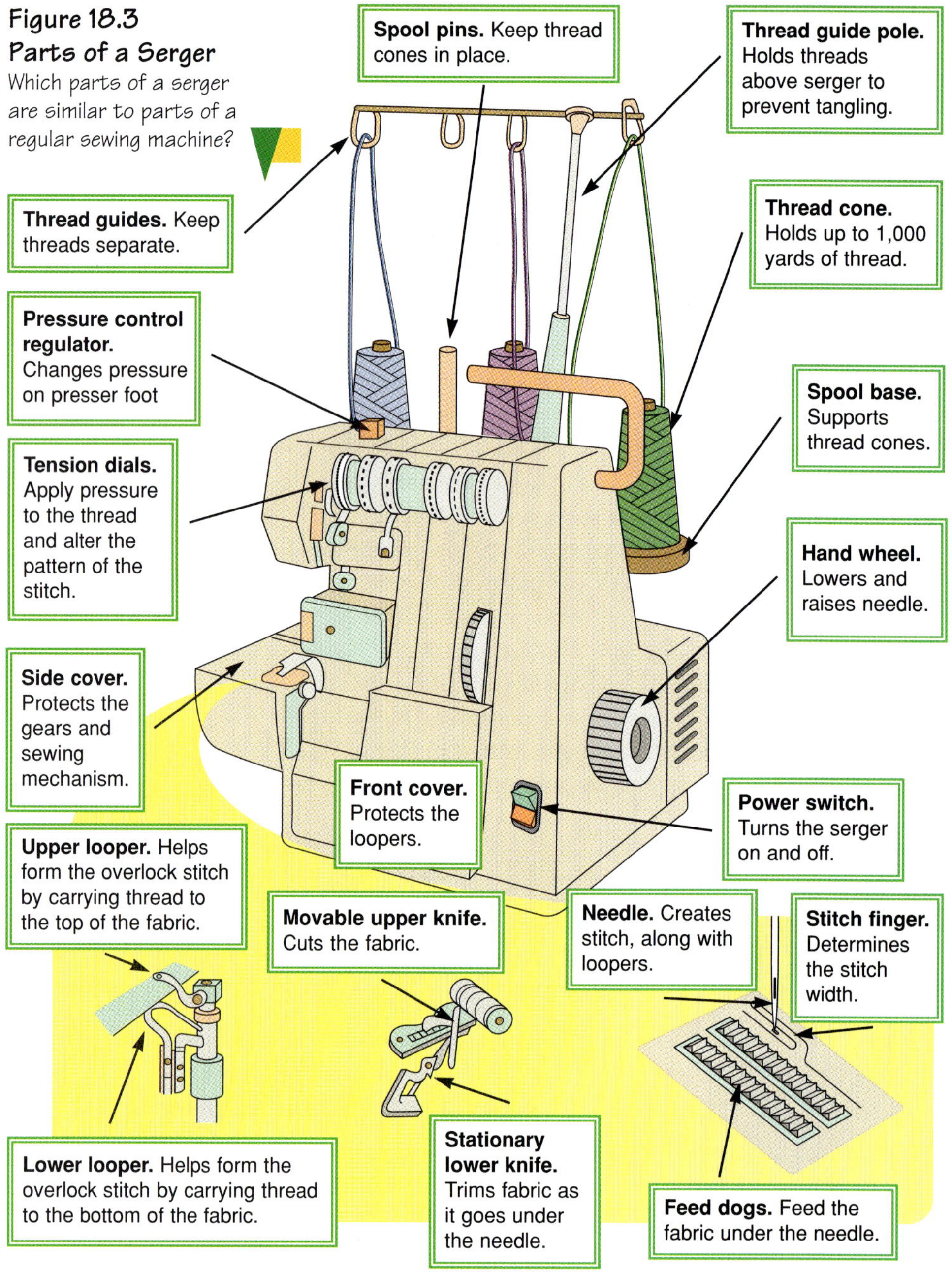

Spool pins. Keep thread cones in place.

Thread guide pole. Holds threads above serger to prevent tangling.

Thread guides. Keep threads separate.

Thread cone. Holds up to 1,000 yards of thread.

Pressure control regulator. Changes pressure on presser foot

Spool base. Supports thread cones.

Tension dials. Apply pressure to the thread and alter the pattern of the stitch.

Hand wheel. Lowers and raises needle.

Side cover. Protects the gears and sewing mechanism.

Front cover. Protects the loopers.

Power switch. Turns the serger on and off.

Upper looper. Helps form the overlock stitch by carrying thread to the top of the fabric.

Movable upper knife. Cuts the fabric.

Needle. Creates stitch, along with loopers.

Stitch finger. Determines the stitch width.

Lower looper. Helps form the overlock stitch by carrying thread to the bottom of the fabric.

Stationary lower knife. Trims fabric as it goes under the needle.

Feed dogs. Feed the fabric under the needle.

518 CHAPTER 18: SEWING SKILLS

 HOME AND COMMUNITY CONNECTION

Examining Sergers Encourage your students to visit local sewing centers to see the many different types of sergers that are on the market. Many fabric stores offer serger demonstrations or will allow customers (or potential customers) to watch in-store videos that show what the sergers can do. Ask students to report to the class about their findings.

518

Small knife blades are located inside the serger. These knives, which are positioned like the blades of scissors, trim the fabric as it passes through the machine. The result is a seam allowance that is exactly the width of the serger's stitch. As you serge, the entire seam allowance is wrapped inside the stitch.

Types of Stitches

You can produce a variety of stitches with most sergers by using different numbers of threads (from two to five) and adjusting the stitch length and tension dials. Generally, inexpensive sergers produce fewer types of stitches than expensive ones do. Some of the most common stitches are as follows:

- **Overlock stitch**—combines three threads and is most often used on stretch seams and fabrics of moderate to heavy weight. It is also used to finish seams on knits and woven fabrics.

- **Overedge stitch**—uses two threads to secure the edges of fabric and prevent raveling. On some sergers, the overedge stitch wraps around the fabric to produce a decorative finish. This stitch is sometimes used for lightweight seams.

- **Chain stitch**—uses two threads to baste fabric.

- **Safety stitch**—uses four threads to create a stable seam on lightweight woven fabrics. The extra threads help to limit how much the fabric will stretch.

You can use a serger to sew a variety of stitches. Have you seen this stitch on any of your clothes?

LESSON THREE: USING A SERGER   519

MORE ABOUT • • •

Helpful Notions for Sergers The following notions for sergers provide convenience and save time and frustration. *Compressed Air*—This helps rid serger of dust in hard-to-reach places. Lint buildup can clog knife blades and cause stitches to skip. *Magnetic Seam Guide*—This attaches to the knife cover to help guide the seam for accurate serging. *Needle and Looper Threader*—This helps thread needles and loopers. *Needle-Nose Pliers*—These help insert serger needles. *Thread Rack*—This neatly stores coned and tubed threads.

CHAPTER 18, LESSON 3

L1 Examining

Organize students into small groups. Provide each group with several examples of clothing sewn on conventional sewing machines and examples of clothing sewn on sergers. Have each group compare and contrast the quality of the sewing projects. Have each group report their findings to the class.

L3 Applying

Have interested students work in pairs to make a variety of sample serger stitches using the following directions: Start with a long stitch length and loose tension and serge a stitch on a scrap of fabric. Use a laundry marker to label the sample with the settings used. Then change the stitch length slightly and serge and label again. Repeat until students have made a range of samples showing varying stitch lengths from long to short. When the stitch length is quite short, begin adjusting the tension from loose to tight. Again, serge and label each stitch sample.

L1 Economics

Encourage students to write letters to clothing manufacturers to ask what type of equipment is being used in the production of garments or household goods. Have students ask the manufacturers to explain how the invention of the serger has affected the company's costs. Students may also wish to ask if there is any other new sewing technology that the company has begun to use. Ask students to share with the class any responses they receive from clothing manufacturers. Letters may be written using computer word processors.

CHAPTER 18, LESSON 3

L1 Demonstrate
Demonstrate for your students how to thread a serger. Then give students a chance to practice threading the serger in the classroom. Have them use the quick-method steps outlined on this page.

L2 Experimenting
Have students work with partners to experiment with the serger to see how the stitches appear. Tell them to use the following directions: Thread a serger with thread of a single color, such as black. Replace one thread with a different color, such as white. Serge a seam and observe where the white thread is visible. Replace other threads with different-colored threads to learn where they appear in the serged stitch. Ask students to describe the results of their experiment.

L2 Problem Solving
Assign Peer Pressure and Decision Making 34 in the TCR. This activity gives students the opportunity to recognize peer pressure and practice decision-making skills.

- **Flatlock stitch**—works well for flat, stretch seams with minimal bulk and for decorative stitches on knits.
- **Rolled hem stitch**—creates narrow hems and seams and is also used for decorative stitching on knit or woven lightweight fabrics.

Uses for Sergers

A serger does not replace a sewing machine because it cannot sew a single line of locked stitches. It does, however, allow you to use a greater variety of fabrics, including stretchy knits and sheers. It also allows you to take many shortcuts without reducing the quality of your sewing project.

Sergers are most commonly used to sew knits. With a serger, you can easily stitch a strong stretch seam. Sergers can also be used to sew conventional skirt or pant hems or narrow, rolled hems, such as those on cloth napkins. You can also use a serger to produce decorative stitching and reversible seams.

Learning How to Use a Serger

The most difficult part of serging is threading the machine. Your teacher can help you learn how to do this. Most sewing

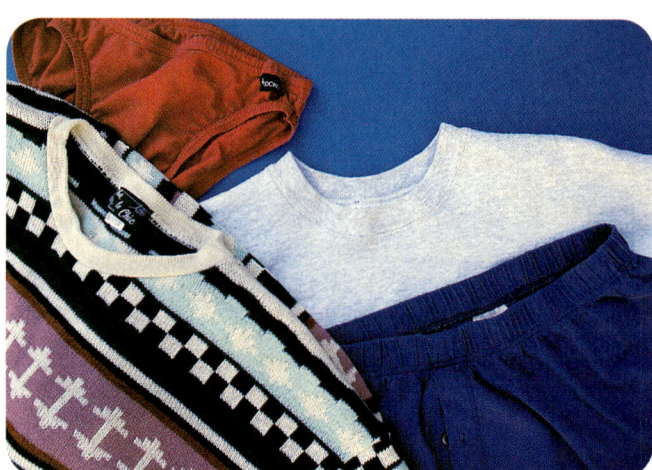

Fabrics that are usually considered difficult to handle can be sewn quickly and easily with a serger. What are some of these fabrics?

520   CHAPTER 18: SEWING SKILLS

MEETING STUDENT DIVERSITY

Physically Challenged Discuss with students—or ask physically challenged students in the class to lead a discussion on—the special needs of people with physical challenges in terms of using sewing machines, sewing equipment, and sewing sergers. For example, students who have limited use of their hands will find it difficult or impossible to thread a machine. Students who are blind or have other physical challenges may find roadblocks to using sewing machines and other sewing equipment. Have volunteers brainstorm ways students in the class can help physically challenged students with their sewing projects to ensure that the needs of physically challenged individuals are met in their sewing lab.

stores also provide demonstrations of how to thread the sergers that they sell.

Once the machine is threaded, you are ready to serge. For safety's sake, make sure that the looper cover is closed before you begin. As you work, you will see that only the needle thread enters the fabric. You will also notice that the seam is stitched where the needle enters the fabric, not where the knives cut the fabric.

Starting to Serge

When you first begin serging, try several different settings on fabric scraps. Label each scrap with the setting used to create the stitch. Then put the scraps in order to get an idea of the stitch varieties that you can make with the serger.

When you are ready to begin a project, set the stitch length and tension dials to the desired settings, and test the stitch on a scrap of fabric. For your test, make sure that you sew as you will on the final product—either with or against the grain. Keep adjusting the stitch length and tension until you achieve the result that you want.

When you sew with a serger, you should avoid using pins to keep the fabric in position. Instead, baste the fabric, or tack it with glue. Pins can seriously damage the serger's knife blades.

When you have tested the stitch and basted your fabric, you are ready to serge. Position the fabric for feeding through the machine. Unless the fabric is unusually thick, you should not need to lift the presser foot. The fabric is moved along by the feed dogs. The **feed dogs** are *the parts of the machine that position the fabric for the next stitch.*

You should begin and end each seam with a **tail chain**—*a length of thread shaped like a chain and made without fabric under the needle.* You make a tail chain by serging without passing fabric through the machine. The tail chain is created as the loopers wrap the thread around the **stitch finger,** which is *a metal prong on the needle plate or the presser foot.* The tail chain keeps the fabric from raveling and eliminates the need to backstitch or tie off the threads of the seam.

Sewing for Fun and Profit

You can sew handmade items to sell or give as gifts. Here are some ideas:
- For babies—cloth ball, baby blanket, bib
- For women—fancy hair bow, makeup bag
- For men—chef's apron, tie case
- For the home—pillows, placemats, napkins, hot pads
- For friends—locker caddy, reusable lunch bag, CD organizer

LESSON THREE: USING A SERGER

CHAPTER 18, LESSON 3

Skills IN ACTION

Have students use the ideas for sewing for fun and profit in "Skills in Action" to write a newspaper article giving reasons to take sewing lessons. Encourage students to add their own ideas to the newspaper article. Submit newspaper articles to the school newspaper for publication.

L1 **Student Workbook**
Assign Activities 127 and 128 in the Student Workbook.

ASSESS

Evaluating the Lesson
Assign Reviewing Terms and Facts and Thinking Critically on page 522 to review the lesson; then assign the Lesson 3 Quiz in the TCR.

Reteaching
- Have students outline the serger information that they feel they understand best. Then give them an opportunity to gather in small groups to compare and expand their outlines. Review completed outlines with the class.
- Have students complete Reteaching Activity 18 in the TCR.

Enrichment
Give students an opportunity to look at some very simple embroidery designs. Let them try to reproduce these designs (or others) using a serger. Have them report on what worked and what didn't work.

MORE ABOUT •••

Clothing Manufacture Have students examine their clothes to see if they can find a "Made in U.S.A." label. Explain that since 1984, the federal government has required that apparel and home fashions carry a label that clearly states where an item was made. The purpose of the labeling law was to increase jobs by promoting the sale and manufacture of garments and home fashions in the United States. Take a survey of where students' clothing was made. Make a bar graph showing how many garments were made in each country represented in the survey.

CHAPTER 18, LESSON 3

Answers to Lesson 3 Review

1. Any six: overlock stitch, overedge stitch, chain stitch, safety stitch, flatlock stitch, rolled hem stitch.
2. The tail chain is a length of thread shaped like a chain that is made when you serge without fabric under the needle. It is used to begin and end seams to keep the seams from raveling.
3. Any three: to stitch strong seams on knits; to make conventional or rolled hems; to produce decorative stitching and reversible seams; and to stitch, trim, and finish seams in one step.
4. Answers will vary, but students should mention that the sewn seam has a simple line of straight or zigzag stitches, while serged seam stitches can take a variety of shapes. Most usual are stitches that resemble tiny tubes of fabric wrapped in thread.
5. Responses will depend upon what type of machine students are using. Common responses might include: decorative stitch on sweatshirt—flatlock stitch or rolled hem stitch; secure edge of any fabric—overedge stitch; narrow hem on swimsuit—rolled hem stitch; baste a seam—chain stitch.
6. Although each student's response will differ, most should note that sergers allow people to complete professional-quality clothes in a short time.
7. Posters will differ, but must include similarities and differences between the types of sewing that can be done on a conventional sewing machine and on a serger.

CLOSE

Encourage students to reexamine the clothing in their closets. Have them identify as many types of serger-stitched clothing as possible.

522

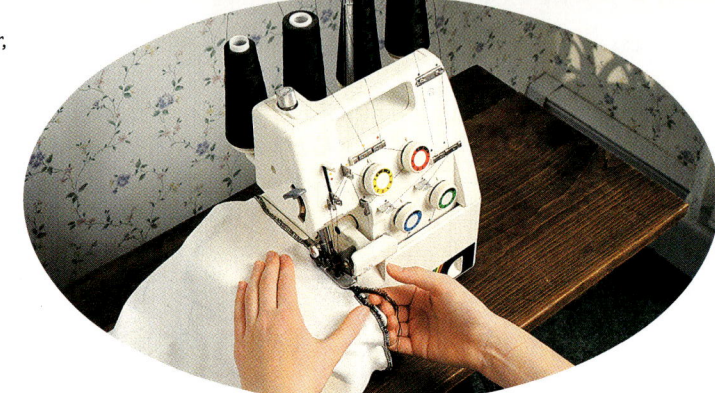

When sewing on a serger, you start and end with a thread tail chain. What does this chain replace?

The Benefits of Serging

Although sergers do not replace sewing machines, they are useful for a variety of sewing jobs. Sergers can stitch, trim, and finish the seam in one step. They are especially useful for sewing straight seams on such garments as sweatshirts. Knowing how to use a serger will help you perform many sewing tasks quickly and easily.

LESSON THREE Review

Using complete sentences, answer the following questions on a separate sheet of paper.

Reviewing Terms and Facts

1. **Identify** List the six types of stitches produced by a serger.
2. **Vocabulary** Define the term *tail chain*. What is the purpose of a tail chain?
3. **List** Name three sewing techniques that are easily done with a serger.

Thinking Critically

4. **Compare and Contrast** What is the difference between a seam stitched by a conventional sewing machine and one stitched by a serger?
5. **Apply** Which serger stitch would you use to do each of the following tasks: make a decorative stitch on a sweatshirt, secure the edge of any fabric, sew a narrow hem on a swimsuit, baste a seam.

Applying Concepts

6. Imagine that you are writing a letter to convince a local fabric store to donate a serger to your classroom. What benefits of serging would you include in the letter?
7. Make a poster showing similarities and differences between the types of sewing that can be done on a conventional sewing machine and on a serger. Display your poster in the classroom.

522   CHAPTER 18: SEWING SKILLS

MORE ABOUT •••

Sergers Sergers, also known as overlock machines, can be categorized by the number of threads they use. A two-thread overlock has one needle and one looper. With this machine, the edge is first stitched and then overlocked—a two-step operation. The three-thread machine adds one looper and an improvement: stitching and overlocking is a one-step process. As more threads are added, the sergers can make additional stitches.

LESSON FOUR
Making Your Project

DISCOVER...
- basic sewing construction techniques.
- how to finish seams.

WORDS TO KNOW
staystitching
casings
facings

Are you ready to begin sewing? Have you laid out, cut, and marked your fabric? Have you practiced sewing both straight and curved seams? Have you checked to make sure that the sewing machine is threaded correctly? If you have completed all of these steps, you are ready to make your project.

LESSON FOUR: MAKING YOUR PROJECT   523

CLASSROOM RESOURCES FOR LESSON 4

 Blackline Masters
Cross Curriculum 20
Lesson 4 Quiz
Sewing Lab Activities 1, 2, 3, 4

 Student Workbook
Activities 129, 130

LESSON FOUR
Making Your Project

FOCUS

Lesson Objectives
After studying this lesson, students should be able to
- describe basic sewing construction techniques.
- explain how to finish seams.

Motivating Activity
Drape a student volunteer with fabric pieces that have been cut out using a pattern. Ask students to write a sentence or two explaining how to get this flat piece of fabric to follow the curves of the body.

Introducing the Lesson
Have students share their responses to the Motivating Activity. (*Students might respond that they can use various tucks, folds, and gathers.*) Point out that in this lesson students will learn techniques for shaping fabric and how to shape and secure necklines and armholes.

Introducing *Words to Know*
Write the three vocabulary words on the chalkboard and have students guess at their meanings. Then have them find the definitions of the words in the lesson. Have them compare their guesses with the actual definitions.

523

CHAPTER 18, LESSON 4

TEACH

L2 Critical Thinking
Ask students to explain why staystitching is the first step of garment construction. (*Students should explain that if the seams stretch before sewing, the garment will never fit properly.*)

L3 Sewing Labs
Assign students the following activities from the *Food and Sewing Lab* booklet in the TCR.

Sewing Lab Activity 1, "Envelope Pillow." Students create an attractive pillow made with a triangular flap closure.

Sewing Lab Activity 2, "A Nylon Kite." Students make a kite that really flies, using a grid to enlarge the pattern provided.

Sewing Lab Activity 3, "A Drawstring Purse." Students use the serger to create a drawstring bag in this activity.

Sewing Lab Activity 4, "A Versatile Apron." Students choose fabrics and decorative designs to create an apron for their own use or for giving as a gift.

L2 Technology Connection
Assign Cross-Curriculum Activity 20 in the TCR. Students learn about fashion design technology in this activity.

524

Constructing Your Project

As you begin constructing your project, refer back to the guide sheet that came with your pattern. This sheet lists the steps to follow. Think through each one before you begin.

Staystitching Seams

When you make a garment, the first step is to staystitch the seams. **Staystitching** is *a row of permanent stitching made on or very near the seam line in the seam allowance.* You staystitch by using a regular machine stitch on a single thickness of fabric. This stitch follows the grain, as shown by the arrow on the pattern and guide sheet. Staystitching prevents stretching and helps in turning under edges of hems and bands.

Stitching Darts

Darts are used to help shape a flat piece of fabric to the curves of the body. They are usually found at the waistline, elbow, and back of the shoulder. For darts to create the right effect, they must have the correct width and shape. Make sure that they are accurately marked, folded, and pinned before you stitch them. When you are ready to stitch, follow these steps:

- Fold the darts so that the right sides of the fabric are together. Match the stitching lines, and pin them.

- Stitch from the wide end of the dart to the point.

- Stitch the last two or three stitches as close to the fold line as possible. This will make a sharp point without a bubble at the end. Do not backstitch.

- Tie the thread ends securely, and cut about ½ inch (1.3 cm) from the knot.

- Press the dart flat, as stitched. Press vertical darts toward the center and horizontal darts downward.

When you have finished stitching a dart, press it flat. Which way should you press vertical darts? Horizontal darts?

524 CHAPTER 18: SEWING SKILLS

TECHNOLOGY UPDATE

Using the latest technology can give a company an edge over its competitors. For example, a clothing business supplies small clothing retail stores with computer-controlled devices that take the body measurements of customers. The computer sends the measurements by modem directly to the clothing factory. There computerized lasers receive the measurements and cut the fabric to the customer's exact measurements. This process saves the customer time and money. The clothing is made much quicker and at less cost than other methods of making made-to-order garments. The factory and retailer also save time and money.

Gathering Fabric

When you need to fit a longer garment piece to a shorter one, you gather fabric. For example, you might use gathering at the tops of sleeves or at the waist of a full skirt. Gathering gives a soft, full effect. Follow these guidelines when gathering fabric:

- Set the sewing machine for a long stitch of six to eight stitches per inch. Loosen the upper tension.
- Sew two rows of stitches. Stitch one row on the seam line. Stitch a second row ¼ inch (6 mm) closer to the fabric edge. Leave long thread ends. Do not backstitch or tie knots.
- Pin the fabric edges so that the right sides are together and the notches, seams, and markings line up with each other.
- Pull up both bobbin threads from one end. Gently slide the fabric along the threads to gather half the section. Repeat at the other end until the gathered section is the proper length.
- Distribute gathers evenly, and pin about every ½ inch (1.3 cm). Gathers should not bunch up or thin out in any area.
- Stitch with a regular stitch length along the seam line, gathered side up. Make sure that the gathering stitches do not show on the right side of the garment.
- Press the seam allowances flat.

Easing Fabric

When one piece of a garment is only slightly longer than the piece to which it will be joined, easing is used. Easing creates only a slight fullness.

To ease fabric, you need to pin it before you stitch the seam. Place the right sides together, match the notches and ends, and pin every ½ inch (1.3 cm). When you stitch, put the longer seam on top and gently ease in the extra fullness. An eased seam should look smooth and unpuckered, not gathered.

Here are some ideas for storing patterns.
- Before you put the pattern pieces away, press them flat. Then fold them until they're slightly smaller than the pattern envelope.
- As your pattern collection grows, arrange the patterns by category, such as *shirts, pants, crafts.*
- Keep your patterns in a file box or cabinet.

CHAPTER 18, LESSON 4

Have students add to the ideas for storing patterns. For example, they might suggest keeping a computer file describing saved patterns, how they are categorized, and where they are located.

TEACHER TALK!

One of the most unfortunate situations in the classroom can occur when a student damages a project that represents a great deal of money and effort. Some teachers have found that sharing one of their own "disasters" can help to alleviate the situation. Others find that helping students learn to recycle hopelessly damaged projects is a good solution. For example, some garments can be redesigned for students or refashioned for a smaller sibling. Alternatively, the project could be cut down and completed as a gift for a smaller child, a baby, or even as doll clothes.

L1 Demonstrating

One of the more difficult sewing tasks for students to master is the technique of easing fabric. Show them how to push and bend the easing fabric into position as you stitch the seam. Allow students ample time to repeatedly practice this task.

MORE ABOUT • • •

Facings Have students examine the facings of a garment. Point out the added reinforcement in some clothing and ask them what they think this is. Tell them that this reinforcement is called interfacing. It is applied to the wrong side of fabric to add strength to areas that are frequently handled or that must keep their shape. Explain that in earlier times interfacings had to be carefully stitched to the facings. Now heat-sensitive interfacings that can be ironed onto the facing are frequently used. These fusible interfacings are applied to the wrong side of the facing before it is sewn onto the garment.

CHAPTER 18, LESSON 4

L1 Sequencing

List the following steps on the chalkboard: mark fabric, sew darts, lay out pattern, prepare fabric, finish seams, reduce seam bulk, cut fabric, staystitch, sew facing, and apply casings. Have students put these construction steps in the correct order. Ask students to identify important construction steps that have been left out. Add these to the ordered list.

L2 Applying

Provide each student with two pieces of fabric about 4 x 6 inches (10 x 15 cm). Have them sew the pieces together along the long edge to make a seam. Ask them to trim, grade, clip, and notch the seam allowance.

L3 Social Studies

Encourage students to explore how people in other societies and eras have fastened their clothing. To get them started, ask them to find out how wealthy women of ancient China fastened their clothes. (*embroidered loops*) Alternatively, ask them to look for examples of societies that simply knot their garments. Consider the Amish tradition of using no fasteners, only straight pins.

Teacher Talk!

Show students how to knot thread by holding it between the left thumb and forefinger and winding it once around the forefinger, about halfway along the finger pad. Position the thread between the finger pad and the thumb pad and roll the thread toward the end of the forefinger, making a loop. Turn the knot into a loop by running both the thumb and forefinger down the thread to the end.

Constructing Casings

If your garment has a pull-on waistband or sleeve band, you may need to sew casings. **Casings** are *fabric tunnels made to enclose elastic or drawstrings*. When you draw up the elastic or drawstring, a gathered appearance is created.

When you sew a casing, make sure that it is ¼ to ½ inch (6 mm–1.3 cm) wider than the elastic or drawstring it will enclose. This will allow the elastic or drawstring to move freely through the fabric tunnel. The two types of casings are fold-down and applied.

- A *fold-down casing* is often used for pull-on pants and skirts. To make a fold-down casing, fold the garment edge ¼ inch (6 mm) to the inside and then again, ¼ to ½ inch (1.3 cm) wider than the elastic. Pin it in place. Stitch close to the inner pinned edge of the casing while leaving a 2-inch (5-cm) opening for inserting the elastic.

- An *applied casing* is often used at the waistline of a dress. To make an applied casing, you need to stitch a separate strip of fabric or bias tape to the garment.

If you are inserting elastic into a casing, attach a safety pin to one end of the elastic. Pull the pin through the casing, and be careful not to twist the elastic. Leave the ends of the elastic extending several inches at the opening. Overlap the ends ½ inch (1.3 cm), and pin them. Then try on the garment to make sure that it fits, and make any necessary adjustments. Next, use the sewing machine to stitch the overlapped ends of the elastic securely. Complete the stitching needed to finish the opening.

If you are using a drawstring, you need to make an opening for pulling the ends through to either the outside or the inside of the garment. Refer to your pattern guide sheet for directions.

After constructing a casing, use a safety pin to pull the elastic through the opening. How large should the opening be?

Constructing Facings

Facings are *fabric pieces used to finish the raw edges of a garment*. Facings are sewn around the edges of necklines,

COOPERATIVE LEARNING

Changing Fashions Gathered skirts have come in and out of popularity regularly throughout history. Encourage students to look through reference materials in the library to find a history of fashion. Organize students into small groups and have each group explore an era—such as the 1860s or the 1950s—when gathered skirts were "in." Let the groups as a whole discuss the eras to determine if there appear to be any reasons behind the changing fashions.

armholes, and waistlines. You stitch them to the right side of the garment and then turn them to the inside. Follow these steps:

- Staystitch the notched edge of each facing piece.
- Stitch the facing pieces together. Trim the seams, and press them open.
- Unless you are using a knitted fabric, finish the outside edge of the facing with zigzag stitching or narrow edge stitching. Knitted fabrics do not require a finish.
- Pin the facing to the garment edge, with the right sides together and the notches and ends matching.
- Stitch the seam. Then trim and grade the seam allowances, and clip the curved areas.
- Turn the facing to the inside. Press it along the seam line, rolling the seams toward the facing side.
- Understitch the facing to help hold it in place. To understitch, open out the facing with the seam allowances toward the facing. Stitch close to the seam line from the right side of the facing through all of the seam allowances. Turn the facing back to the inside, and press it.
- Use several hand stitches to fasten the edge of the facing at each seam.

To achieve a smooth appearance, you need to trim and grade the seam allowance to reduce bulk. **Figure 18.4** on the next page describes the techniques used to reduce bulk. Pattern instructions usually indicate which technique you should use. After you remove the bulk from a facing, you may also need to clip or notch the seam allowance so that the facing can be pressed flat.

Facings can be either extensions of a piece of fabric or fitted pieces cut in the same shape as the garment area to be faced. How do you know which type of facing to use on a garment?

LESSON FOUR: MAKING YOUR PROJECT   **527**

CHAPTER 18, LESSON 4

USING VISUALS
Have students study the ways to reduce seam bulk shown in Figure 18.4 on page 528. Then have them work in small groups. Provide each group with several examples of seams that have been trimmed, graded, clipped, or notched. Have students identify and explain the procedure for each method and how each method reduces seam bulk.

L1 **Student Workbook**
Assign Activities 129 and 130 in the Student Workbook.

ASSESS

Evaluating the Lesson
Assign Reviewing Terms and Facts and Thinking Critically on page 528 to review the lesson; then assign the Lesson 4 Quiz in the TCR.

Reteaching
- Have students write an informational paragraph titled "Basic Sewing Construction Techniques."
- Have students complete Reteaching Activity 18 in the TCR.

Enrichment
Have students design a pattern for a garment. The pattern should include a guide sheet.

MORE ABOUT • • •

Construction Techniques Challenge students to apply what they have learned about hand-sewing techniques. Give each student a square piece of fabric and instruct them to try to hand sew the fabric into a ball without making any cuts in the fabric. Ask students who are successful in their attempt to make a ball to explain how they succeeded in doing this. Students should point out that by using a combination of darts and gathers, a crude ball can be made.

CHAPTER 18, LESSON 4

Answers to Lesson 4 Review

1. Staystitching is a row of permanent stitching made on or very near the seam line in the seam allowance. It prevents stretching and helps in turning under the edges of hems and bands.
2. Darts are added to a garment to shape the flat piece of fabric to the curves of the body.
3. Fold-down casings are found on pull-on pants and skirts. Applied casings are found at the waistline of a dress.
4. Trimming, grading, notching, and clipping.
5. Gathering and easing are both used to fit a longer piece of fabric to a shorter piece of fabric. Gathering gives a soft, full effect. Easing creates only a slight fullness with a smooth unpuckered look.
6. Facings are needed to finish the raw edges around curved areas such as necklines, armholes, and waistlines.
7. Students should notice that staystitching is most important on loosely woven fabrics that have a tendency to stretch.

CLOSE

If students have been keeping a sewing notebook, have them summarize the results of their sewing project in the notebook. If they have no notebook, have them set up a small display showing the pattern, the steps in the sewing process, and any problems they encountered and solved.

Figure 18.4 Reducing Seam Bulk
How do you know which technique to use to reduce seam bulk?

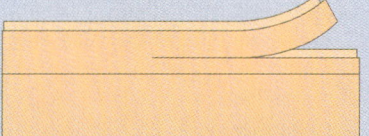
Trimming. A seam is trimmed by cutting the seam allowance to ⅜ or ¼ inch (9–6 mm). This reduces the bulk of the seam. This is usually done when the seam is enclosed in a collar, cuff, facing, waistband, or set-in sleeve.

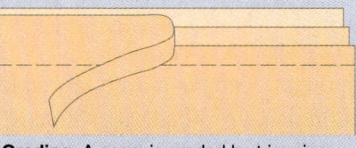
Grading. A seam is graded by trimming the seam allowances to different widths. Trim the seam allowance toward the inside of the garment narrower than the outside one. This further reduces the bulk. Grading is often done on seams for facings.

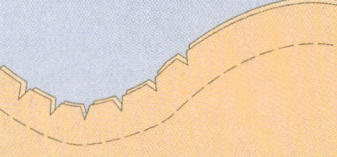
Notching. Some curved seams that have too much fabric in the seam allowance may need to be notched. Little Vs or triangles are cut out of the trimmed seam allowance.

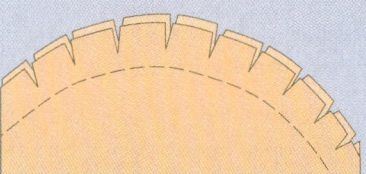
Clipping. Curved seams are clipped so that they will lie flat. Slits are cut into the trimmed seam allowance about every ¼ inch to ½ inch (6 mm–1.3 cm). Clip only to within ⅛ inch (3mm) of the seam line, being careful not to cut through the stitching.

LESSON FOUR *Review*

Using complete sentences, answer the following questions on a separate sheet of paper.

Reviewing Terms and Facts

1. Vocabulary What is *staystitching*? Why is it used?
2. Recall Why are darts added to a garment?
3. Identify Name the two types of casings, and give an example of where each could be used.
4. List What are the four techniques used to reduce seam bulk?

Thinking Critically

5. Compare and Contrast What are the similarities and differences between gathering and easing?
6. Explain Why are facings important pattern pieces?

Applying Concepts

7. With a partner, staystitch on various types of fabric scraps. Evaluate how effective the staystitching was on each type of fabric. Which fabrics benefited the most?

528   CHAPTER 18: SEWING SKILLS

MEETING STUDENT DIVERSITY

Varied Learning Styles Diversity is most obvious when students begin to compare finished projects. Remind your class that not everyone begins with the same level of sewing skills and that everyone had different challenges to overcome as they completed their project. Remind them to use constructive criticism when commenting on other students' projects. This may be an appropriate time to review how to give and accept constructive criticism. See Chapter 1 to review this topic.

LESSON FIVE
Repairing and Altering Your Clothes

DISCOVER...
- when and how to use hand-sewing techniques.
- ways to repair clothing.
- how to recycle clothing.

Although Alexa is just learning how to use a sewing machine in school, she has been hand sewing for several years. She enjoys finding creative ways to personalize her clothes, such as sewing buttons and ribbons on sweatshirts. Recently she cut up a few old pairs of jeans and turned them into a patchwork duffle bag.

WORDS TO KNOW
slip stitch
hemming stitch
shank

LESSON FIVE: REPAIRING AND ALTERING YOUR CLOTHES   529

CLASSROOM RESOURCES FOR LESSON 5

 Blackline Masters
Activity and Project Card 36, "Demonstrate Stitching Techniques"
Concept Map 28
Cooperative Learning 36
Lesson 5 Quiz
Reteaching 18
Sewing Labs 5, 6, 7, 8

 **Student Workbook**
Activity 131

LESSON FIVE
Repairing and Altering Your Clothes

FOCUS

Lesson Objectives
After studying this lesson, students should be able to
- explain when and how to use hand-sewing techniques.
- describe ways to repair clothing.
- explain how to recycle clothing.

Motivating Activity
Display the following items on a table or bulletin board: buttons, hooks and eyes, snaps, iron-on patches, decorative appliqués, needles and thread. Ask students to write an example of how each of these items could be used to make clothing repairs and alterations.

Introducing the Lesson
Ask students to share their responses to the Motivating Activity. Ask them to name other items that could be used to make clothing repairs or alterations. Then tell them that in this lesson they will learn techniques to help them get extended use out of their clothes and, at the same time, save money.

Introducing *Words to Know*
Write *slip stitch*, *hemming stitch*, and *shank* on the chalkboard and encourage the students to suggest possible meanings for these words. Then have students find the definition of each word in the lesson. Ask them to illustrate each word and write its definition next to the illustration.

529

CHAPTER 18, LESSON 5

TEACH

Try This!

You might encourage students to practice their hand-sewing skills by participating in the suggestions in "Try This." Help students by providing phone numbers of local nursing homes.

L3 Sewing Labs

Assign students the following activities from the *Food and Sewing Lab* booklet in the TCR.

Sewing Lab Activity 5, "Decorator Pillows." Students create one pillow of printed fabric and another decorated with embroidery stitches.

Sewing Lab Activity 6, "A Windsock." Students sew a colorful windsock complete with tails and ribbon.

Sewing Lab Activity 7, "A Canvas Bag." This versatile bag can be decorated and used as a book bag, a beach bag, or a gift.

Sewing Lab Activity 8, "A Quilted Book Cover." Students create this cover to personalize a photo album.

L3 Math

Tell students to estimate how much they spend on clothing each year. Then pass out clothing catalogs and let students choose a new wardrobe from the catalogs. Have them add up the total cost of the new wardrobe. Ask students to share their findings with the class. Use this as the basis of a discussion on how they can reduce the amount they must spend on clothing by repairing damaged clothing or updating old clothing.

530

Try This!

You can use your hand-sewing skills to help the elderly by sewing on buttons, mending split seams, and repairing hems. Call a nursing home to volunteer, or offer to help an elderly neighbor or relative.

When you sew a patch over a hole, use a hemming stitch. How else could you cover a hole?

Using Hand-Sewing Techniques

Some sewing jobs require hand sewing. You need to use hand sewing to baste a zipper in place, hem garments, and attach buttons, snaps, and hooks and eyes. Hand sewing gives you more control over the fabric and stitches than you would have with a sewing machine. Follow these guidelines:

- Choose a hand-sewing needle that will pass through the fabric easily.
- Select thread that matches the fabric color.
- Use a short thread—about 18 to 24 inches (46–61 cm) long—so that it won't tangle.
- Make the knot in the thread large enough to keep it from pulling through the fabric as you are sewing.

Repairing Clothing

Do you have any clothes that need to be repaired? Maybe you have a sweatshirt that has a hole in the sleeve or a pair of jeans that is missing a button. If you learn some basic hand sewing-techniques, you can easily make these repairs. **Figure 18.5** describes common hand-sewing stitches.

Fixing Small Tears and Holes

It is best to repair tears and holes while they are still small. To fix a split seam, line up the pieces of fabric and pin them in place. Then use a backstitch to sew the seam. To mend small tears, stitch back and forth across the tear to hold the torn edges together. Be sure to begin and end your stitches about ¼ inch (6 mm) above and below the tear. To cover up a hole, apply a fusible patch, or sew on a patch or appliqué.

Replacing Buttons

Replacing lost buttons is probably the most common type of clothing repair job that you will need to do.

530 CHAPTER 18: SEWING SKILLS

MEETING STUDENT DIVERSITY

Varied Learning Styles Students who lack good control of their hands and/or fingers will find hand sewing extremely difficult. Let them practice with larger materials. For example, give them a 12-inch (30-cm) square of burlap and a large needle threaded with yarn. Students can also work with needlepoint backing. Encourage students to practice and have patience until they are comfortable with the technique.

**Figure 18.5
Hand-Sewing Stitches**
How many of these stitches have you used?

Basting stitch. The basting stitch is a temporary stitch used to hold fabrics together for fittings and for matching plaids and seams. To baste, pin fabric layers together. Take even stitches about ¼ inch (6 mm) long and ¼ inch (6 mm) apart.

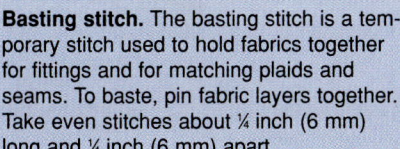

Backstitch. The backstitch is used to repair seams that are hard to reach. Bring the needle through to the upper side of the fabric. Insert the needle back at the beginning of the first stitch, and bring it out again one stitch length in front of the thread. Keep inserting the needle in the end of the last stitch and bringing it out one stitch ahead.

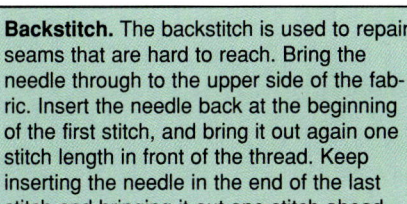

Slip stitch. The slip stitch is a hand-sewing stitch that provides an almost invisible finish. Slide the needle in one folded edge and out, picking up a thread of the under layer at this spot. Take even stitches no more than ¼ inch (6 mm) apart.

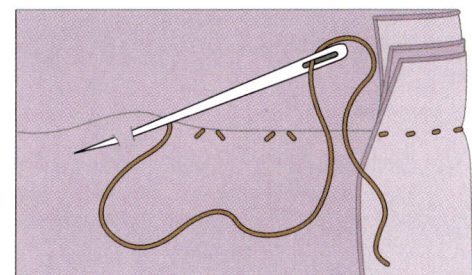

Hemming stitch. As the name indicates, a hemming stitch is a hand-sewing stitch used for hems, especially those finished with hem tape. Take a tiny stitch in the garment, then bring the needle diagonally through the hem tape on hem edge. Take all stitches in this manner, spacing them about ¼ inch (6 mm) apart.

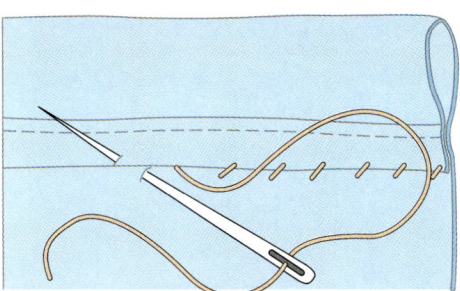

LESSON FIVE: REPAIRING AND ALTERING YOUR CLOTHES

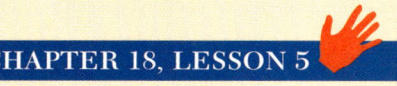

CHAPTER 18, LESSON 5

USING VISUALS
Have students study the stitching techniques illustrated in Figure 18.5. Ask them to compare these stitches with stitches made by a sewing machine and stitches made by a serger.

L2 Applying Skills
Provide each student with a 12 x 14-inch (30 x 35-cm) piece of burlap, a large needle, and yarn. Have students practice the stitches shown in the illustration in Figure 18.4. Have them make stitches large enough to emphasize the details in each stitch. Ask students to label each stitch.

L2 Activity and Project Card
Allow time for students to complete Activity and Project Card 36, "Demonstrate Stitching Techniques," in the TCR.

L2 Cooperative Learning
Assign Cooperative Learning Activity 36 in the TCR. Students work in groups to consider ways to recycle garments in this activity.

COOPERATIVE LEARNING

Recycling Garments Have each student bring an article of clothing to school that is no longer used by the family (or use garments already brought to class). Gather students into small groups and encourage them to think of new and unique ways to recycle the garments. Have each group choose one garment to actually recycle. If time permits, have them recycle every garment. Consider donating these garments to local shelters as a community service project for students.

CHAPTER 18, LESSON 5

Encourage students to apply some of the ideas they read about in the feature. Have volunteers arrange a recycled clothing display to share with the rest of the class.

L1 Applying Life Skills

Give students a pile of buttons and have them sort the buttons into shank and sew-through buttons. They will quickly see that sew-through buttons are far more common than shank buttons. As a result, learning to make a strong thread shank is a valuable skill. Have each student sew at least five sew-through buttons onto a piece of fabric. Pull, tug, and twist each button to make sure each is properly done.

DID YOU KNOW ?

Traditionally, men's button flaps are fastened from right to left, women's from left to right. Historians think that this practice started because most men are right-handed. While they were at court, traveling, or on the battlefield, the right-to-left flaps were easier for them to use. Women who were rich enough to wear buttons on their clothing usually had servants who helped them dress. The servants—most of them right-handed—also found it easier to work with a right-to-left flap. The mirror image on the women resulted in a left-to-right flap.

Recycling Your Clothes

You need only your sewing skills and a little imagination to recycle outdated clothes. Here are a few ideas:
- Turn a pair of pants into a pair of shorts.
- Make a jean vest out of an old jean jacket by cutting off the sleeves.
- Add lace, ribbon, buttons, braid, or appliqué to a sweatshirt or vest.

When you sew on a button, select a matching thread color. Double the thread with the ends knotted together for extra strength.

532 CHAPTER 18: SEWING SKILLS

There are two types of buttons: sew-through buttons and shank buttons. A sew-through button has two or four holes through it and no loop on the back. A shank button has a built-in loop on the back. When you hand sew a sew-through button, you need to add a thread **shank,** or *a stem on a button that provides room for the extra layer of fabric around the buttonhole.*

To replace sew-through buttons, follow these steps:

1. Start on the underside of the fabric, and bring the needle and thread to the right side.
2. Bring the needle and thread through a hole in the button. Place a toothpick or a pin across the top of or underneath the button to allow for a thread shank. Stitch in and out several times through the fabric and holes of the button and over the pick or pin. Finish stitching so that your needle and thread are under the button.
3. Remove the pin or toothpick. Pull the button to the top of the thread loop. Wind the thread several times around the stitches under the button to make a shank.
4. Bring the needle back to the wrong side of the fabric.
5. Secure the thread by taking several small stitches in the fabric and then knotting.

If the button you are replacing has a shank, sew it in place using five or six small stitches through the shank and into the fabric. Then fasten the thread securely.

Replacing Other Closures

Other closures commonly used for clothing are snaps and hooks and eyes. Snaps are used to hold together overlapping edges, such as those at the edge of a neckline. There are two parts of a snap—the ball half and the socket half. Follow these guidelines when replacing a snap:

- Place the ball half of the snap on the underside of the overlap, far enough from the edge so that it will not show.

TECHNOLOGY UPDATE

The zipper has come a long way since its introduction more than 100 years ago. Invented as a slide to close high boots, it replaced the long button-hooked fasteners that were popular in the 1890s. Although they were known as the "universal fastener," they were not used on clothing until 1920. One reason that they were slow to gain in popularity is that early zippers rusted and had to be removed from clothing before laundering. In fact, early zippers came with a manual describing how to operate and maintain them. Today's zippers come in plastic or teflon-coated metal and are increasingly easy to install and replace. B. F. Goodrich came up with the name "zipper" based on the zipping sound the fastener made as it was opened and closed.

- Secure the ball half by sewing five or six stitches in each hole. Carry the thread under the snap from hole to hole.
- Mark the position of the socket half. Stitch it in place.

Hooks and eyes are often used on waistbands or above zippers, where they are not visible. Attach hooks and eyes by sewing small stitches around each loop. Finish by sewing three or four stitches across the end of the hook to make sure that it lies flat.

Altering Clothes

You can get more use out of your clothes if you learn how to make some basic alterations. One common type of alteration is changing the hem of a garment. Follow these guidelines:

- Use a seam ripper to remove the thread in the old hem. Press out the hem crease.
- Put on the garment to determine the new hem length. Wear the shoes that you plan to wear with the garment. If possible, have someone mark the hem for you. Using a yardstick, place pins every 3 to 4 inches (7.5–10 cm) around the hemline. Stand still, and have the person move around you to place the pins.
- Fold the hem to the new length, and pin it in place. Double-check the length to make sure that it is even.
- Take off the garment, and place it on a table or an ironing board with the hem facing you. Using a sewing gauge or a ruler, mark the proper length of the finished hem with pins or chalk. Most hems are about 2 inches (5 cm) in depth.
- Trim away the excess fabric along the markings. Lightly press the fold of the hem.
- For most woven fabrics, you will need to use some type of hem finish to prevent raveling. The raw edge can be pinked, zigzag stitched, edge stitched, or overlapped with hem tape.

▲ Each type of hook and eye has a different purpose. A round eye is used for edges that meet, and a straight eye is used for edges that overlap. Do you know when a heavy duty eye might be used?

LESSON FIVE: REPAIRING AND ALTERING YOUR CLOTHES

COOPERATIVE LEARNING

Identifying Consequences Have students work in small groups. Assign a leader to each group to lead a discussion about the results of the following scenarios: making clothing repairs as soon as possible, using a basting stitch to sew a hem, forgetting to sew a shank on a sew-through button, refusing to repair clothing, using a double thread to stitch a hem, and removing zippers and buttons from worn-out clothing. Assign a secretary to each group to take notes about the discussion. When all the groups have finished, ask the secretaries to share their notes with the class.

CHAPTER 18, LESSON 5

L1 Applying
Have students bring garments from home that are no longer used by any family members. Identify those that have been discarded because of needed repairs and fix them. Then have the class as a whole determine how to recycle each remaining item.

L1 Student Workbook
Assign Activity 131 in the Student Workbook.

ASSESS

Evaluating the Lesson
Assign Reviewing Terms and Facts and Thinking Critically on page 534 to review the lesson; then assign the Lesson 5 Quiz in the TCR.

Reteaching
- Have students cut clothing pictures out of magazines and use those pictures to make a poster showing creative ways to recycle clothing.
- Have students complete Reteaching Activity 18 in the TCR.
- Assign Concept Map 28 in the TCR.

Enrichment
Ask students to bring to class a garment they have recycled. If this is not possible, then suggest that they take "before" and "after" pictures of the garment. Have them explain what they have done to recycle the garment.

CHAPTER 18, LESSON 5

Answers to Lesson 5 Review

1. Students may mention basting; hemming; and attaching buttons, snaps, and hooks and eyes.
2. The backstitch is a good stitch to use for hard-to-reach seams.
3. A shank is the stem on a button that provides room for the extra layer of fabric around the buttonhole. A sew-through button has two to four holes instead of a shank.
4. Measure from the floor to the garment with a yardstick. Choose an appropriate measure and place pins every 3 to 4 inches (8 to 10 cm) around the garment. The line of pins will be the line of the new hem.
5. Answers will vary. You will get more use from them, and may save money.
6. A small tear in jeans can be repaired by stitching back and forth across the tear. A larger tear can be covered with a patch or appliqué.
7. Students should describe steps listed on page 532 for replacing sew-through buttons.
8. Update, remodel, or cut them up for another use.
9. Answers will vary. Students suggest one way to repair, update, or change a garment that they no longer wear.

CLOSE

Ask students to write a few sentences explaining why hand-sewing techniques are valuable to know.

After measuring and pinning a new hem, you should look in a mirror to check the length and evenness. What might happen if you don't check carefully?

- Stitch the edge of the hem to the garment by hand, using a single thread. Be sure that the stitches do not show on the outside of the garment. Keep the stitches loose so that the hemline doesn't pucker.
- Carefully press the hem.

If you are lengthening a garment and you don't have enough fabric to form a hem allowance, you can use wide bias hem facing. Stitch one edge of the facing to the fabric edge. Then turn the facing to the inside of the garment, and stitch it in place.

Recycling Clothes

You can use many of the hand-sewing skills you have learned to recycle garments. If a garment is truly beyond repair, you can cut it into scraps and pieces to be used for other projects, such as a patchwork pillow. You can also save the fabric pieces to use as cleaning rags. Just be sure to remove any buttons or zippers that might scratch surfaces.

LESSON FIVE Review

Using complete sentences, answer the following questions on a separate sheet of paper.

Reviewing Terms and Facts

1. **Name** What types of tasks are best done by hand sewing?
2. **Identify** When is the *backstitch* a good hand stitch to use?
3. **Vocabulary** What is a *shank*? How is a shank button different from a sew-through button?
4. **Recall** How can you determine the new hem length for a garment?
5. **Identify** What are the benefits of recycling clothing?

Thinking Critically

6. **Recommend** If you had a tear in your jeans, how would you repair it?
7. **Summarize** What are the steps for sewing on a sew-through button?
8. **Apply** Identify three ways to recycle old clothes.

Applying Concepts

9. Find one garment that you own but no longer wear. Suggest ways to repair, update, or change it. Share your ideas with your classmates.

534   CHAPTER 18: SEWING SKILLS

MORE ABOUT

Buttons Button collecting is not an unusual hobby. Some archaeologists are avid button collectors because they can learn about a society by studying its buttons. The earliest buttons did not hold clothing together. They were just used for decoration. The earliest of these decorative buttons date to 2000 B.C. and were fashioned from seashells. Greeks and Romans decorated their clothing with both shell and wooden buttons. Early Europeans used buttons that were elaborately carved from ivory and bone. Some were enhanced with gems and gold leaf.

Chapter 18 Activities

Consumer Focus

On the Mend

Has the zipper in your jacket ever broken? What do you do when you get a hole in your sock? Today, many people don't mend their own clothes. They have their garments repaired or altered at sewing or dry-cleaning shops.

Try This!

Look in the yellow pages and find a shop that repairs and alters clothes. Call the shop, and find out the specific services it offers and how much they cost.

A Global View

SOMETHING BORROWED

To give their designs a new look, American textile and fabric designers often "borrow" the art of various cultures. For example, designers have used the bold geometric designs and brilliant colors found on traditional African cloth to create winter coats, ponchos, and head wraps. Designers have also decorated hats with geometric African designs.

TRY THIS!

Check your wardrobe for clothes or accessories that reflect the art of a particular culture. If possible, show these items to the class.

Technology

Smart Sewing Machines

Electronic sewing machines are now available for use in homes, and they can help make your projects easier. For example, these machines can memorize a buttonhole and then stitch the other buttonholes in exactly the same way.

Try This!

Visit a store that sells sewing machines. Find out the price of an electronic machine, and list its special features. Share your findings with the class.

SOCIAL STUDIES CONNECTION

CLOTHING CUSTOMS

Clothing styles vary from country to country because of climate, available materials, and customs. For example, people in Mexico need clothes to protect them from the heat. People in Australia, a sheep-producing country, wear many woolen clothes. In Middle Eastern countries, where modesty is valued, people wear long robes and coverings.

Follow Up

1. Find information about another country's traditional way of dressing. Try to find out why a particular clothing style developed. Give a brief oral report to the class, and show pictures of the clothing.

2. What countries come to mind when you hear the words *sari, kilt, kimono, clogs,* and *moccasins?* Compare your answers with those of a classmate. Then look in an encyclopedia or a book about clothing to see if you were correct.

CHAPTER 18 Activities

Consumer Focus

Discuss with students the possibility of returning items to the manufacturer for repair or replacement. Often specialized sportswear, name-brand clothing, and even backpacks will be replaced or repaired by the company that made the item. Ask for volunteers to contact a sporting goods manufacturer to ask about return policies.

A Global View

Discuss with students the cultural tradition of decorating clothing all over the world. Encourage students to notice this practice when visiting historical museums. Ask volunteers to research in magazines, history books, or encyclopedias to find various examples of textile design and decoration.

TECHNOLOGY

After students have read the feature and researched the features of electronic sewing machines, have them think of other ways technology is changing the clothing industry. Ask volunteers to do further research on electronic advances in sewing, knitting machines, or fabric and textile construction.

Teaching the SOCIAL STUDIES CONNECTION

Point out to students that the United States has a variety of clothing styles due to a wide range of climates and a large variety of materials available. Many of the materials are grown or manufactured in this country and other materials are imported.

Answers to Follow-Up

1. Oral reports will vary. Students should explain why a particular clothing style developed.
2. Sari—India, kilt—Scotland, kimono—Japan, clogs—Holland, moccasins—United States.

CHAPTER 18 REVIEW

Checking Comprehension

Use the Chapter Summary and the Chapter 18 Review to help students go over the most important ideas in Chapter 18.

Answers to Words to Know

1. Layouts diagram how the pattern pieces should be placed on the fabric.
2. Pattern markings are guides on the pattern pieces for making a project. The markings make it easier to lay out, cut, and sew with patterns.
3. Backstitching is the technique of stitching over ½ inch (6 mm) of a seam at the beginning and end to lock the threads so that the seam won't pull out.
4. To hold the thread.
5. To enclose elastic or drawstrings in pull-on pants and skirts.
6. Fabric pieces used to finish the raw edges of a garment.
7. It provides an almost invisible finish.

Answers to Review Questions

1. Compare your measurements with the body measurements listed on the pattern envelope.
2. Preshrink the fabric and check the grain.
3. Any three: Pin large pattern pieces that belong on the fold. Pin the pattern pieces that have a grain line arrow. Place pins diagonally inside the cutting line. Place pins 3 to 6 inches (7.5 to 15 cm) apart. Double-check your layout against the layout on the pattern.

536

CHAPTER 18 REVIEW

Chapter Summary

- Begin your sewing project by reading the pattern guide sheet, which provides a layout and step-by-step directions.
- Learn to identify and understand these pattern markings: grain line, cutting line, place on fold, dart, notches, stitching lines, dots, and adjustment lines.
- To prepare your fabrics, preshrink them and check the grain.
- Follow the correct procedures for pinning, cutting, and marking your fabric.
- To complete a sewing project, you will need to be able to stitch a straight seam and a curved seam, pivot, and finish a seam.
- A serger is a high-speed machine that sews, trims, and finishes a seam in one step.
- With a serger, you can use many types of fabric, including stretchy knits and sheers, that are difficult to sew on a regular sewing machine.
- Basic construction techniques include staystitching seams, sewing darts, gathering and easing fabric, and making casings and facings.
- After a seam is stitched, it may need further treatment to reduce the bulk and give a smooth appearance.
- Hand-sewing techniques are used to repair small tears and holes, sew on missing buttons or snaps, and change hemlines.
- With a little imagination, many garments that cannot be repaired or altered can be recycled.

Words to Know

Using complete sentences, answer the following questions on a separate sheet of paper.

1. Explain the purpose of pattern *layouts*.
2. What are pattern *markings*, and why are they important in sewing?
3. What is *backstitching*?
4. On a serger, what are the *cones* used for?
5. When would you use a *casing*?
6. Define the term *facings*.
7. Describe the advantage of a *slipstitch*.

536   CHAPTER 18: SEWING SKILLS

Review Questions

Using complete sentences, answer the following questions on a separate sheet of paper.

1. How do you determine what pattern alterations need to be made?
2. What are the two steps you should take to prepare fabric for sewing?
3. Give three tips for pinning pattern pieces to fabric.
4. What are four guidelines for transferring markings?
5. Why do sergers use cones instead of spools?

EXTRA CREDIT PROJECT

Adding to Your Portfolio Students can create a Sewing Solution Book to record methods learned in the sewing lab to deal with difficult or problematic situations. Have them review the chapter and make notes of information they wish to keep for reference. Encourage students to also record tips they learn as they work in the sewing lab. Have them write or illustrate each sewing problem on one page, and then record the solution on a facing page. Then tell students to put pages together by placing the solution upside down facing the problem which is placed right side up. This way, when the book is completed, they can read the problem, then turn the book upside down to read the solution.

CHAPTER 18 REVIEW

6. For what purpose would you use an overedge stitch? A safety stitch?
7. What is the difference between gathering and easing?
8. Briefly describe two techniques used to reduce bulk in seams.
9. Name four hand-sewing stitches.
10. How would you repair a small split in an underarm seam?

Thinking Critically

Using complete sentences, answer the following questions on a separate sheet of paper.

1. **Apply** Give three examples of sewing jobs that can be done more easily with a serger than with a regular sewing machine.
2. **Explain** What do you think is the meaning of the old proverb "A stitch in time saves nine?" How would you apply it to sewing?
3. **Analyze** What are some benefits of learning how to repair and alter your clothes?

Cooperative Learning

1. Along with several classmates, make a sewing video in which you show the steps for completing a sewing project. Work together to decide what you will include in the video, what materials you will need, and who will do each task. The video can be used to teach other students how to make a garment or a home-decorating project.
2. Working with a small group, decide on something that you could sew for your school. Some ideas include smocks for the art room, covers for the computers, or banners for the entranceway. Each person in the group should sew one part of the project.

Family & Community

1. Design a sewing area for your home. Draw a floor plan, and write a description of the room. Tell how you would organize the space and what furnishings and other materials you would include. Remember to make your space efficient, comfortable, and well-lit.
2. Have a family "sewing bee." Ask family members to gather all their clothes that have missing buttons, ripped seams, holes, broken zippers, and so on. Spend an evening together making repairs.

Building A Portfolio

1. Write a paragraph telling how you can use sewing skills in your life now and in the future. Place your paragraph in your portfolio.
2. Have someone take a photograph of you and a garment, gift, or home-decorating project that you have completed. Write a brief description of your project. Put the photo and the description in your portfolio.

CHAPTER 18 REVIEW **537**

CHAPTER 18 REVIEW

4. Any four guidelines from the list on page 512.
5. Sergers use more thread than conventional sewing machines do. A cone is larger than a spool, so a cone holds more thread than a spool.
6. To secure the edges of fabric and prevent raveling; to create a stable seam on lightweight woven fabrics.
7. Gathering gives a soft, full effect. Easing creates only a slight fullness.
8. Any two: Trimming—trim seam allowance to ⅜ or ¼ inch (1 cm or 6mm); Grading—trim seam allowances to different widths, trim seam allowance toward the inside narrower than the outside one; Notching—cut little Vs or triangles out of trimmed seam allowance; Clipping—cut slits into the trimmed seam allowance about every ¼ inch to ½ inch (6 mm to 1.3 cm), clip only to within ⅛ inch (3 mm) of the seam line, being careful not to cut through the stitching.
9. Basting stitch, backstitch, slip stitch, hemming stitch.
10. Line up the pieces of fabric and pin them in place. Use a backstitch to sew the seam.

Evaluate

Use the Chapter 18 Test in the TCR, or construct your own test using the Testmaker Software.

CLOSE

Have students apply their knowledge of the chapter's content by completing one of the alternative assessment activities listed under Family and Community or Building a Portfolio.

Answers to Thinking Critically

1. Answers will vary. Students might mention that sewing jobs using fabrics such as slippery silks, stretchy knits, and sheers can be done more easily on sergers than with a regular sewing machine.
2. Answers will vary. Students should indicate that the sooner a rip or tear is repaired, the fewer stitches are needed, and the easier the job will be.
3. Answers will vary. Students should mention that repairing and altering their own clothes can save money and reduce the amount of trash.

537

Glossary

A

accessory An interesting item added to make a space more personal; an item such as shoes, a belt, a scarf, a hat, socks, a tie, or jewelry. (8–2), (16–1)

acne A skin condition caused by overly active oil glands. (15–1)

acquaintance A person you greet or meet fairly often but do not have a close relationship with. (5–4)

acquired Learned from the people and things around you. (1–1)

addiction A person's physical or mental need for a drug or other substance. (5–5)

adolescence (a-duhl-E-suhns) The period of great growth and change between childhood and adulthood. (1–2)

advertisement A message to persuade consumers to buy. (7–1)

aerobic exercise Nonstop, repetitive, vigorous exercise that increases breathing and heartbeat rates. (11–4)

alteration A change made in a garment so that it will fit. (17–2)

amino (uh-MEE-noh) acid A chain of building blocks that make up proteins. (10–2)

appetite The desire to eat. (10–1)

appetizer A dish served before the meal. (13–1)

apprenticeship program A formal program that uses on-the-job training to teach job skills. (4–1)

aptitude test A test that predicts a person's ability to learn certain skills. (4–1)

arcing Electrical sparks that can damage a microwave oven and start a fire. (12–4)

assertive Able to explain your needs and opinions clearly while respecting the needs and opinions of others. (5–5)

attention span The length of time a person can concentrate on any one thing. (6–3)

B

backstitching The technique of stitching over ½ inch (1.3 cm) of a seam at the beginning and end to lock the threads so that the seam won't pull out. (18–2)

balanced diet A diet that is made up of a variety of foods with nutrients in the recommended amounts. (11–2)

belonging Feeling included. (5–1)

bias Diagonal to the threads in a woven fabric. (18–1)

biodegradable Able to degrade, or break down, and be absorbed by the environment. (9–2)

bobbin A small metal or plastic spool that holds the thread inside a sewing machine. (17–1)

body language The look on your face, gestures, and body stance. (2–2)

broth The liquid left when meat, poultry, fish, or vegetables have been cooked in water. (14–2)

budget A plan for using your money. (7–5)

C

calcium A mineral that helps build bones and teeth and ensures normal growth. (10–3)

calorie A unit of heat that measures the energy available in food. (10–1)

carbohydrates The starches and sugars that give the body most of its energy. (10–2)

career research The process of finding out all you can about a field of work that interests you. (4–1)

caregiver A person who takes care of a child. (6–1)

casing A fabric tunnel made to enclose elastic or a drawstring. (18–4)

casserole A combination of ingredients cooked and served in a baking dish. (14–2)

chain store One of a group of stores that bear the same name and carry the same merchandise. (7–3)

child abuse Physical or emotional mistreatment of a child. (6–1)

childproof Safe for children to play and explore in. (6–4)

cholesterol (kuh-LES-tuh-rawl) A waxlike substance the body produces and needs in small amounts. (10–2)

citizen A member of a community, such as a city, state, or country. (2–3)

classic style A style that remains in fashion for a long time. (15–2)

cleaning plan A list of daily, weekly, and occasional household jobs and of the family member or members who are responsible for each job. (8–3)

color wheel An arrangement of colors that shows the relationships of colors to each other. (15–3)

commitment Promise. (3–2)

communication The process of sending and receiving messages. (2–2)

comprehension Understanding what you read. (4–2)

compromise (KAHM-pruh-myz) An agreement in which each person gives up something in order to reach a solution that satisfies everyone. (5–6)

conduct To carry electricity. (12–2)

cone A large, rounded cylinder used to hold thread on a serger. (18–3)

conflict Any struggle, disagreement, or fight. (5–6)

conscience The internal moral code that directs people's behavior. (6–2)

consequences (CON-suh-kwen-sez) Results of a choice made or an action taken. (3–3)

conservation The saving of resources. (9–1)

considerate Thoughtful. (5–1)

consistent Reacting the same way to the same situation each time it occurs. (6–1)

constructive criticism Someone's evaluation of you that encourages you and helps you become a better person. (1–3)

consumer A person who buys goods and services. (7–1)

contamination Becoming infected with bacteria. (12–1)

convenience food Food that is already partly prepared to save time. (13–3)

conversation The sharing of ideas, thoughts, and feelings. (2–2)

cooperation Working together for the good of all. (5–1)

cooperative play Play that involves one or two other children and sharing toys. (6–3)

cope Adjust to a difficult situation. (5–3)

cost per wearing The amount of money spent for each time you wear an article of clothing. (16–3)

coworker A person an employee works with. (4–4)

credit A method of payment that lets you buy now and pay later. (7–5)

culture The ways of thinking, acting, dressing, and speaking shared by a group of people. (1–1)

curdle To separate into little particles (curds). (14–4)

customary measurement Traditional units of measure. (13–4)

D

dairy food Food made from milk. (14–4)

dart A tapered V-shaped seam used to give shape to a garment. (17–2)

debit card A card that is issued by a bank and is used to withdraw money directly from a person's bank account. (7–5)

decision A choice a person makes about what action to take. (3–3)

decompose To break down. (9–2)

default To fail to make a decision, leaving the outcome to chance. (3–3)

defrosting Thawing or unfreezing frozen food. (12–4)

dehydrated Dried so that all or most of the liquid has been taken out of a food. (14–2)

department store A store that carries a wide range of merchandise. (7–3)

dermatologist A doctor who treats skin disorders. (15–1)

design The art of combining elements in a pleasing way. (8–2)

developmental task An achievement or milestone, such as walking or talking, that can be expected of children at a certain age or stage of growth. (6–2)

diagonal On an angle. (8–2)

diet Everything you regularly eat and drink. (10–1)

Dietary Guidelines Advice on what Americans should eat to stay healthy. (11–2)

digestion The process of breaking down food into a form the body can use. (10–1)

discipline The task of teaching a child which behavior is acceptable and which is not. (6–1)

discount store A store that carries a limited selection of items at low prices. (7–3)

dough A thick mixture of flour, liquid, and other ingredients. (14–3)

dovetailing Fitting different tasks together smoothly and efficiently. (12–5)

dressing A sauce that adds flavor to a dish. (14–2)

dry-heat cooking Cooking without liquid. (14–5)

E

ease The ability to move freely in a garment; the amount of fullness added to a garment pattern for movement and comfort. (16–2), (18–1)

emotion A feeling such as happiness, fear, or love. (1–2)

empathy The ability to put yourself in another person's place. (2–1)

employee manual A book of rules that employees must follow. (4–4)

empty-calorie food A food that is high in calories but low in nutrients. (11–3)

energy efficient Made to use less energy. (9–1)

enriched Having nutrients that were lost in processing replaced in the same quantity or in greater quantity than the unprocessed food originally contained. (10–3)

entrepreneur A person who starts and runs his or her own business. (4–4)

environment All the living and nonliving things that surround you. (1–1)

evaluate To determine the value of what you have accomplished. (2–4)

exchange A trade of one item for another. (7–4)

expectation A person's idea of what should be or should happen. (5–4)

expenses The money you spend to buy goods and services. (7–5)

expire To run out. (7–4)

F

facing A fabric piece used to finish the raw edge of a garment. (18–4)

factory outlet A store that carries only one manufacturer's products. (7–3)

fad A fashion that is very popular for a short time. (15–2)

fad diet A diet that promises quick weight loss through unusual means. (11–4)

family A group of two or more people who care about each other and are committed to each other. (5–2)

fashion Style of clothing that is accepted as popular at a particular time. (15–2)

feed dogs Parts of a serger that position the fabric for the next stitch. (18–3)

fiber The tough, stringy part of raw fruits, vegetables, and grains that the body cannot digest; one of the tiny strands that make up yarns. (10–2), (16–2)

first impression An instant opinion, or image. (2–1)

fitness The ability to handle day-to-day events in a healthy way. (11–4)

fixed expenses Expenses that are always the same. (7–5)

flammable Capable of burning easily. (12–2)

flexibility The ability to adjust easily to new conditions. (4–4)

flexible expenses Expenses that vary. (7–5)

floor plan A diagram of a room arrangement. (8–2)

flossing Pulling dental floss back and forth between the teeth at the gum line to remove food particles. (15–1)

focal point Center of interest. (16–1)

food group A category of foods on the Food Guide Pyramid. (11–1)

Food Guide Pyramid A set of guidelines to help you choose what and how much to eat to get the nutrients you need. (11–1)

function Use. (8–1)

G

garnish A small amount of a food or seasoning added to decorate a food. (13–1)

generic product A product with a label listing only the product name and nutritional information. (13–2)

goal Something you want to achieve. (3–4)

goods Products made for sale. (7–1)

gossip Talking about other people and their personal lives. (2–2)

grade labeling A measurement of food quality using standards set by the government. (13–2)

graduated measuring cups Set of measuring cups in commonly used sizes. (13–4)

grain The direction in which the threads run in a fabric. (16–2), (18–1)

group play Play with several other children. (6–3)

guidance Direction. (6–1)

guide sheet A set of step-by-step instructions for sewing a pattern. (18–1)

H

habit A behavior pattern that is repeated without thinking about it. (3–3)

hard-cooked egg An egg that is left in hot water, covered, for 15 to 18 minutes. (14–5)

hazard A danger. (9–3)

hemming stitch A hand-sewing stitch used for hems. (18–5)

heredity The passing of traits or characteristics from parents to their children. (1–1)

hue The name of a color. (15–3)

hunger The physical need to eat. (10–1)

hygiene Practices that promote health. (15–1)

I

illusion A feeling that something is different from the way it really is. (8–2)

image ad An ad that connects a product or service to a lifestyle that consumers would like to have. (7–2)

impression An image you present or others present to you. (2–1)

impulse buying Making a sudden decision to buy. (7–3)

incineration Disposing of waste by burning it. (9–2)

income The amount of money you earn or receive regularly. (7–5)

independent play Play during which an infant plays alone and shows little interest in interacting with other children. Also called solitary play. (6–3)

infomercial An extended-length informational commercial that appears on television. (7–2)

information ad An ad that describes the features of a product or service and gives facts about its price and quality. (7–2)

initiative Taking action without being asked. (3–2)

insulation A material installed in the attic or walls of a building to keep it cooler in summer and warmer in winter. (9–1)

intensity The brightness or dullness of a color. (15–3)

interest A fee paid by a bank in order to use your money. (7–5)

interfacing A layer of special fabric placed between two pieces of fabric to give more shape to a garment. (17–3)

intruder Someone who uses force to get into a home. (6–4)

iron A mineral that is an essential component of blood. (10–3)

J

job applicant A person who wants a job. (4–3)

job application A form on which you supply information about yourself that will help an employer make a hiring decision. (4–3)

job interview A face-to-face meeting between an employer and a job applicant. (4–3)

job opening A job that is not filled. (4–3)

job preparation The learning required to get and keep the kind of job you want. (4–1)

K

knit fabric Fabric made by looping threads together. (16–2)

L

landfill A huge pit where waste is dumped and buried between layers of earth. (9–2)

layaway plan A scheduled payment plan in which you put a small amount of money down and make regular payments until you have paid for an item. (7–5)

layout A diagram of how pattern pieces should be placed on fabric. (18–1)

leader A person with the ability to guide and motivate others. (2–3)

leavening agent An ingredient that makes baked food rise. (13–4)

life change A major way in which your life is altered by events that you may or may not be able to control. (5–3)

logo A company's identification symbol. (15–2)

looper A rounded part that holds the thread inside a serger. (18–3)

M

major appliance A piece of large kitchen equipment. (12–3)

management Using what you have to get what you want, being organized, and planning ahead. (2–4)

marking A guide on a pattern piece for making a project. (18–1)

maturity Making wise decisions, practicing self-control, and acting responsibly. (2–1)

meal pattern Habit people follow that determines when and what they eat each day. (13–1)

meat extender A food added to meat to make a small amount of meat go farther. (14–5)

media The means of communication by which advertisers send their messages. (7–2)

mend Repair. (16–4)

menu A list of all the dishes a restaurant serves, organized by category. (11–3)

metric measurement A system of measurements based on multiples of ten. (13–4)

microwave oven An appliance that cooks by vibrating the molecules in food. (12–3)

mineral Element needed by the body in small amounts for sturdy bones and teeth, healthy blood, and regular elimination of body wastes. (10–3)

moderation Avoiding extremes. (11–2)

modesty Ideas people have about the proper way for clothing to cover the body. (15–2)

moist-heat cooking Cooking in liquid. (14–5)

N

nap A one-way texture in fabric. (17–3)

narrative format A recipe format that provides a paragraph description of the steps and ingredients in order of use. (13–3)

national-brand product A product that you see advertised on television or in newspapers or magazines. (13–2)

natural resource A material that is supplied by nature. (9–1)

need Something that you have to have in order to live. (3–1)

negotiation (ni-GOH-shee-AY-shuhn) The process of talking about a conflict and deciding how to reach a compromise. (5–6)

neutral color Black, white, beige, or gray. (15–3)

nonverbal communication Messages sent without using words. (2–2)

notion A small item that is part of the construction of a garment. (17–3)

nutrient (NOO-tree-ent) A substance in food that is important for the body's growth and maintenance. (10–1)

nutrient-dense food A food that is rich in the nutrients your body needs to stay healthy. (11–3)

nutrition (noo-TRI-shuhn) The study of nutrients and how they are used by the body. (10–1)

O

obesity A condition in which a person's weight is 20 percent or more above his or her ideal weight. (11–4)

open dating The display of a freshness date on packaged food. (13–2)

option Possible choice. (3–3)

osteoporosis A condition in which bones gradually lose their mineral content and become weak and brittle. (10–3)

P Q

parallel play Play that occurs alongside of, rather than with, another child. (6–3)

parenthood The function of being a parent. (6–1)

parenting The process of caring for children and helping them grow and learn. (6–1)

pasta A food made from flour and water and formed into shapes. (14–3)

pattern A plan for making a garment or project. (17–2)

pedestrian A person who travels on foot. (9–3)

peer A person of the same age as you. (5–4)

peer group A group of people of the same age. (5–4)

peer mediation A process by which specially trained students help other students find a solution to a problem. (5–6)

peer pressure The influence you feel to go along with the behavior and beliefs of your peers. (5–5)

perishable Likely to spoil quickly. (12–1)

personality The sum total of a person's traits, feelings, attitudes, and habits. (1–2)

personal style The kind of clothes you like best. (16–1)

pinking shears Scissors that have a zigzag edge. (17–1)

plaque (PLAK) A soft, sticky film on the teeth, created by the bacteria that live in a person's mouth. (15–1)

poison control center A medical facility with a staff trained to help in poisoning emergencies. (6–4)

pollution The changing of air, water, and land from clean and safe to dirty and unsafe. (9–1)

popularity The state of being well liked. (5–5)

potential The capacity to grow and develop. (3–1)

precaution Step taken to avoid danger. (8–3)

precycle To avoid buying products that use more packaging than necessary. (9–2)

prejudice (PRE-juh-dis) An opinion about people that is formed without facts or knowledge about those people. (5–6)

preschooler A child who is three to five years old. (6–2)

presser foot The metal piece at the end of a sewing machine needle that holds the fabric in place. (17–1)

pretreat To apply a liquid detergent or stain remover to spots before laundering a garment. (16–4)

prioritize To rank in order of importance. (2–4)

processed Changed (a food) from its raw form before it is sold. (14–1)

procrastinate To put things off. (2–4)

produce Fresh fruits and vegetables. (14–1)

promotion A move up to a better job with more responsibility. (4–4)

proofread Check for errors in grammar, punctuation, and spelling. (4–2)

protein A nutrient that is needed to build, repair, and maintain body cells and tissues. (10–2)

punishment A way of discouraging inappropriate behavior. (6–1)

R

ravel To have threads pull out of the cut edge of a fabric. (17–3)

raw edge The unfinished edge of fabric that has loose threads. (18–1)

realistic goal A goal that you can reach. (3–4)

recipe A list of ingredients and directions for preparing a specific food. (13–3)

recycling Turning waste items into products that can be used. (9–2)

redirect To turn someone's attention to something else. (6–5)

redress Action taken to correct a wrong. (7–4)

reference A person who can tell an employer about an applicant's character and quality of work. (4–3)

refund A return of money in exchange for an item purchased. (7–4)

refusal skills Ways to say no effectively. (3–1)

resource A source of information or expertise that you can use to help you meet your goals; something you need to accomplish a goal. (2–4), (3–4)

respect Consideration. (3–2)

responsibility Ability to make choices and to answer for those choices. (3–2)

risk To take a dangerous chance. (9–3)

role The way you behave when you interact with another person. (1–1)

role model A person who helps you see what is expected of you and shows you how to act in certain situations. (1–1)

rotating Turning a dish a quarter-turn or a half-turn in a microwave oven. (12–4)

S

salad A food or a combination of foods, usually served cold with a dressing. (14–2)

salmonella (SAL-muh-NELL-uh) Bacteria that are often found in raw or undercooked foods, such as meat, eggs, fish, and poultry. (12–1)

sandwich Two pieces of bread surrounding a filling, such as meat or cheese. (14–3)

sanitary Free from germs. (8–3)

saturated fat Fat found in food from animal sources. (10–2)

scald To bring food slowly to a temperature just below the boiling point. (14–4)

seam finish A treatment used on a seam edge to prevent the fabric from raveling. (18–2)

seasonal More plentiful, more readily available, and less expensive at certain times of the year. (14–1)

security Feeling safe and protected. (5–1)

self-concept A mental picture of yourself. (1–3)

self-confidence Faith in your abilities. (1–3)

self-esteem The ability to respect yourself. (1–3)

selvage The tightly woven edge of fabric that has no visible loose threads. (18–1)

serger A high-speed machine that sews, trims, and finishes a seam in one step. (18–3)

service Work performed by one person for others. (7–1)

serving A portion of food that a person would be likely to eat at one time. (11–1)

sewing gauge A 6-inch (15-cm) ruler made of metal, with an adjustable pointer. (17–1)

shank A stem on a button that provides room for the extra layer of fabric around the buttonhole. (18–5)

shape Outline. (15–3)

shoplifting Taking items from a store without paying for them. (7–3)

shopping plan A strategy for spending the money you have available to purchase the items you need or want. (16–3)

sibling A brother or sister. (5–2)

slip stitch A hand-sewing stitch that provides an almost invisible finish. (18–5)

small appliance A piece of small, electrically powered kitchen equipment. (12–3)

smoke alarm A device that sets off an alarm when smoke is present. (6–4)

snack Food eaten between meals. (11–3)

sodium A mineral that helps regulate the amount of fluids in the body. (11–2)

software A computer program or set of instructions. (4–2)

solitary play Play during which an infant plays alone and shows little interest in interacting with other children. Also called independent play. (6–3)

specialty store A store that carries only a specific type of merchandise. (7–3)

stain A soiled or discolored area. (16–4)

stamina The ability to focus on a single activity or a long time. (11–4)

standard format A recipe format that lists all the ingredients in order of use, followed by step-by-step directions for preparing the food. (13–3)

staple Food that you are likely to use often. (13–2)

status Level of importance. (15–2)

status symbol A piece of clothing or other item that gives the owner a special feeling of importance. (16–3)

staystitching A row of permanent stitching made on or very near the seam line in the seam allowance. (18–4)

stereotype An idea or image formed in advance about all members of a group. (2–1)

stitch finger A metal prong on the needle plate or presser foot of a serger. (18–3)

stitch regulator A dial or lever on a sewing machine that controls the length of the stitches. (17–1)

store-brand product Food or household item that has a store's name or another name used only by that store on the label. (13–2)

stress The body's reaction to changes around it. (5–3)

style The design of a garment. (15–2)

sunscreen A lotion that guards the skin against harmful rays of the sun. (15–1)

supervisor The person who checks an employee's work and evaluates his or her performance. (4–4)

synthetic fiber A fiber made partially or entirely from chemicals. (16–2)

T

tail chain A length of thread shaped like a chain and made on a serger without fabric under the needle. (18–3)

talent Natural ability. (2–4)

teamwork The cooperative efforts of everyone in a group to work together to reach a goal. (2–3), (4–4)

texture The way something feels or looks as if it would feel. (8–2), (13–1), (15–3)

time schedule A plan to make sure that all foods are ready to serve at the right time. (13–1)

toddler A child who is one to three years old. (6–2)

trade-off Something that you give up in order to get something more important. (3–4)

tradition A custom or belief handed down from one generation to another. (5–2)

traffic pattern The path people take to move around and in and out of a room. (8–1)

U

unique One of a kind. (1–1)

unit pricing Showing the cost of a product per unit. (13–2)

unsaturated fat Fat that comes from plants. (10–2)

utensil A kitchen tool. (12–3)

V

value The lightness and darkness of color. (15–3)

values Ideas about right and wrong and about what is important in your life. (3–1)

variable A condition that determines how long a food needs to be cooked and at what power level in a microwave oven. (12–4)

vegetarian A person who eats mainly fruits, vegetables, and grains. (11–1)

versatile Able to be worn for many occasions. (16–1)

view A version of a garment style, as shown on a pattern envelope. (17–2)

violence The use of physical force to harm someone. (9–3)

vitamin Substance needed by the body in small amounts to help regulate body functions. (10–3)

volunteer A person who donates time and energy without pay to do a service for others. (2–3)

W

want Something that you would like to have but that is not necessary for survival. (3–1)

wardrobe inventory A list of all the clothes, shoes, and accessories that you have. (16–1)

warranty A manufacturer's written promise to repair or replace a product if it does not work as claimed. (7–3)

wellness A high level of overall health. (11–2)

whole grain A food that contains all of the edible grain, including the outer layer, the bran, and the germ. (10–2)

work plan A list of jobs that need to be done and the name of the person who will do each job. (12–5)

work record A written record of how well an employee performs on the job. (4–4)

woven fabric Fabric made on a loom by interlacing lengthwise and crosswise threads at right angles. (16–2)

X Y Z

yield The number of servings a recipe will make. (13–3)

Glossary/Glosario

A

accessory/accesorio Un artículo interesante que se añade para hacer un espacio más personal; artículos tales como un cinturón, pañuelo, sombrero, corbata, zapatos, calcetines o alhajas. (8–2), (16–1)

acne/acné Una enfermedad de la piel causada por la producción excesiva de grasa por las glándulas sebáceas. (15–1)

acquaintance/conocido Una persona a quien uno conoce pero con quien no tiene amistad. (15–4)

acquired/adquirido Aprendido de las personas y las cosas que te rodean. (1–1)

addiction/adicción La necesidad física o mental que tiene una persona de una droga u otra substancia. (5–5)

adolescence/adolescencia El período de gran crecimiento y cambio entre la niñez y la adultez. (1–2)

advertisement/anuncio Un mensaje para convencer a los consumidores de que compren. (7–1)

aerobic exercise/ejercicio aeróbico Ejercicio enérgico y repetido sin parar, que aumenta la velocidad de la respiración y de los latidos del corazón. (11–4)

alteration/arreglo Un cambio hecho a una prenda de ropa para que le quede bien a una persona. (17–2)

amino acid/aminoácido Una cadena de componentes básicos de las proteínas. (10–2)

appetite/apetito El deseo de comer. (10–1)

appetizer/aperitivo Un plato que se sirve antes de la comida. (13–1)

apprenticeship program/programa de aprendizaje Un programa para aprender un arte u oficio mientras se hace el trabajo. (4–1)

aptitude test/prueba de aptitud Una prueba que predice la habilidad que tiene una persona para aprender ciertas destrezas. (4–1)

arcing/chispas Chispas eléctricas que pueden dañar un horno de microondas y provocar un incendio. (12–4)

assertive/firme Capaz de explicar con claridad las necesidades y opiniones propias, manteniendo el respeto por las necesidades y opiniones de los demás. (5–5)

attention span/capacidad de concentración La cantidad de tiempo que una persona puede mantener su atención en una cosa. (6–3)

B

backstitching/pespuntear Volver a coser ½ pulgada (1.3 cm) al principio y al fin de una costura para que no se deshile. (18–2)

balanced diet/dieta balanceada Una dieta compuesta de una variedad de alimentos, con los distintos nutrientes en las cantidades recomendadas. (11–2)

belonging/pertenecer Sentirse incluido. (5–1)

bias/biés En diagonal a los hilos de la tela. (18–1)

biodegradable/biodegradable Que se puede descomponer y ser absorbido por el medio ambiente. (9–2)

bobbin/bobina Un carretel pequeño que sujeta el hilo dentro de una máquina de coser. (17–1)

body language/lenguaje corporal La mirada, los gestos y la postura de una persona. (12–2)

broth/caldo El líquido que queda cuando se cocina carne, ave, pescado o vegetales en agua. (14–2)

budget/presupuesto Un plan para usar tu dinero. (17–5)

C

calcium/calcio Un mineral que ayuda a formar los huesos y los dientes y que asegura el crecimiento normal. (10–3)

calorie/caloría Una unidad de calor utilizada para medir la energía disponible en los alimentos. (10–1)

carbohydrate/carbohidrato La fécula y el azúcar que le dan al cuerpo la mayor parte de su energía. (10–2)

career research/investigación de carreras El proceso de averiguar todo lo posible sobre un campo de trabajo que te interese. (4–1)

caregiver/cuidador Una persona que cuida a un niño. (6–1)

casing/doblez Un tubo de tela que se usa para cubrir un elástico o cordón del que se tira. (18–4)

casserole/guisado Un conjunto de ingredientes que se cocinan en una cazuela de hornear. (14–2)

chain store/tienda de cadena Una de un grupo de tiendas que llevan el mismo nombre y la misma mercancía. (17–3)

child abuse/abuso infantil El maltrato físico o emocional de un niño. (6–1)

childproof/a prueba de niños Asegurar un sitio para que los niños puedan jugar y explorar en él. (6–4)

cholesterol/colesterol Una substancia parecida a la cera que el cuerpo produce y necesita en pequeñas cantidades. (10–2)

citizen/ciudadano Un miembro de una comunidad, tal como una ciudad, un estado o un país. (2–3)

classic style/estilo clásico Un estilo que se mantiene de moda por mucho tiempo. (15–2)

cleaning plan/plan de limpieza Una lista de los quehaceres diarios, semanales y ocasionales de la casa y de los miembros de la familia que son responsables de cada uno. (8–3)

color wheel/rueda de colores Un arreglo de colores que muestra la relación de un color a otro. (15–3)

commitment/compromiso Una promesa. (3–2)

communication/comunicación El proceso de mandar y recibir mensajes. (2–2)

comprehension/comprensión Entender lo que lees. (4–2)

compromise/acuerdo mutuo Un arreglo en el cual cada persona cede algo para llegar a una solución que satisface a todos. (5–6)

conduct/conducir Transmitir electricidad. (12–2)

cone/cono Un cilindro grande y redondeado que se usa para sostener el hilo en una remalladora. (18–3)

conflict/conflicto Cualquier lucha, desacuerdo o pelea. (5–6)

conscience/conciencia El código moral interno que dirige la conducta de las personas. (6–2)

consequences/consecuencias El resultado de una decisión o acción que se ha tomado. (3–3)

conservation/conservación El cuidado de los recursos. (9–1)

considerate/considerado Atento. (5–1)

consistent/consistente Que reacciona de la misma manera a la misma situación cada vez que sucede. (6–1)

constructive criticism/crítica constructiva Una evaluación que hace alguien de ti que te ayuda a convertirte en mejor persona. (1–3)

consumer/consumidor Una persona que compra bienes y servicios. (7–1)

contamination/contaminación Estar infectado por bacterias. (12–1)

convenience food/comida de preparación rápida Comida que ya está parcialmente preparada para ahorrar tiempo. (13–3)

conversation/conversación El intercambio de ideas, pensamientos y sentimientos. (2–2)

cooperation/cooperación Trabajar juntos para el bien de todos. (5–1)

cooperative play/juego cooperativo Juego en el que a dos o más niños comparten juguetes. (6–3)

cope/hacer frente Adaptarse a una situación difícil. (5–3)

cost per wearing/costo por uso La cantidad de dinero que se ha gastado por cada uso de una prenda de vestir. (16–3)

coworker/compañero de trabajo Una persona con quien un empleado trabaja. (4–4)

credit/crédito Un método de pago que te permite comprar ahora y pagar después. (7–5)

culture/cultura Las maneras de pensar, actuar, vestir y hablar que comparten un grupo de personas. (1–1)

curdle/cortarse Separarse en grumos. (14–4)

customary measurement/sistema de medidas estadounidense Unidades tradicionales de medida en Estados Unidos. (13–4)

D

dairy food/alimentos lácteos Comidas hechas de leche. (14–4)

dart/pinza Una costura que se estrecha en forma de "V" y que se usa para darle forma a la ropa. (17–2)

debit card/tarjeta de cobro automático Una tarjeta de banco que se usa para sacar dinero directamente de la cuenta de una persona. (7–5)

decision/decisión Una selección que hace una persona acerca de qué hacer. (3–3)

decompose/descomponerse Separarse en sus elementos básicos. (9–2)

default/a falta de directivas No tomar una decisión y dejar el resultado al azar. (3–3)

defrosting/descongelar Dejar que un alimento congelado se deshiele. (12–4)

dehydrated/deshidratado Secar un alimento hasta sacarle la mayor parte del líquido que contiene. (14–2)

department store/tienda de departamentos Una tienda que tiene una gran selección de mercancías. (7–3)

dermatologist/dermatólogo Un médico que trata las enfermedades de la piel. (15–1)

design/diseño El arte de combinar distintos elementos de una manera agradable. (8–2)

developmental task/tarea de desarrollo Un logro o hito, tal como el caminar o hablar, que se puede esperar de los niños a cierta edad o cierta etapa de su crecimiento. (6–2)

diagonal/diagonal En ángulo. (8–2)

diet/dieta Todo lo que comes y bebes con regularidad. (10–1)

Dietary Guidelines/recomendaciones dietéticas Consejos sobre lo que deben comer los estadounidenses para mantenerse sanos. (11–2)

digestion/digestión El proceso de descomponer los alimentos para que el cuerpo los pueda utilizar. (10–1)

discipline/disciplina La tarea de enseñarle a un niño cuál conducta es admisible y cuál no. (6–1)

discount store/tienda de descuentos Una tienda con una selección de mercancía limitada pero a bajos precios. (7–3)

dough/masa Una mezcla espesa de harina, líquido, y otros ingredientes. (14–3)

dovetailing/organizarse Hacer varias tareas a la vez, de manera ordenada y eficiente. (12–5)

dressing/aliño Una salsa que le da sabor a un plato. (14–2)

dry-heat cooking/cocinar en seco Cocinar sin líquido. (14–5)

E

ease/holgura La habilidad de poderse mover dentro de una prenda; la anchura que se le añade a una prenda para dar movimiento y comodidad. (16–2), (18–1)

emotion/emoción Un sentimiento, tal como la felicidad, el miedo o el cariño. (1–2)

empathy/empatía La habilidad de ponerse en el lugar de otro. (2–1)

employee manual/manual para los empleados Un libro de reglas que los empleados tienen que seguir. (4–4)

empty-calorie food/alimento chatarra Una comida con muchas calorías y pocos nutrientes. (11–3)

energy-efficient/de eficiencia energética Hecho para que use menos energía. (9–1)

enriched/enriquecido Alimento al que se le añaden las mismas o mayores cantidades de los nutrientes que se perdieron al procesarlo. (10–3)

entrepreneur/empresario Una persona que empieza o dirige su propio negocio. (4–4)

environment/medio ambiente Todas las cosas vivas o no que te rodean. (1–1)

evaluate/evaluar Determinar el valor de lo que has logrado. (2–4)

exchange/intercambiar Cambiar un artículo por otro. (7–4)

expectation/expectativa La idea de una persona de lo que debe ser o debe suceder. (5–4)

expenses/gastos El dinero que usas para comprar bienes y servicios. (7–5)

expire/vencerse Cumplirse un plazo. (7–4)

F

facing/vuelta Una pieza de tela que se usa para terminar el borde de una prenda. (18–4)

factory outlet/tienda de fábrica Una tienda que vende sólo los productos de un fabricante. (7–3)

fad/moda pasajera Una moda que es popular por muy poco tiempo. (15–2)

fad diet/régimen de adelgazamiento rápido Una dieta que promete perder de peso rápidamente por medios poco comunes. (11–4)

family/familia Un grupo de dos o más personas que se quieren y están dedicados unos a otros. (5–2)

fashion/moda Estilo de ropa que es popular durante un período de tiempo. (15–2)

feed dogs/dientes La parte de un remalladora que pone la tela en posición para el próximo punto. (18–3)

fiber/fibra La parte dura y llena de hebras de las frutas, vegetales y granos frescos que el cuerpo no puede digerir; una de las hebras pequeñas que forman el estambre. (10–2), (16–2)

first impression/primera impresión Una opinión o imagen instantánea. (2–1)

fitness/salud completa La habilidad de manejar los sucesos diarios de manera sana. (11–4)

fixed expenses/gastos fijos Los gastos que siempre son iguales. (7–5)

flammable/inflamable Que se quema con facilidad. (12–2)

flexibility/flexibilidad La habilidad de adaptarse con facilidad a nuevas condiciones. (4–4)

flexible expenses/gastos flexibles Los gastos que varían. (7–5)

floor plan/plano Un diagrama de la disposición de una habitación. (8–2)

flossing/limpiarse con hilo dental Halar el hilo dental hacia delante y hacia atrás entre los dientes y las encías para quitar los pedacitos de comida. (15–1)

focal point/centro de atención El centro de interés. (16–1)

food group/grupo alimenticio Una categoría de alimentos en la pirámide de los alimentos. (11–1)

Food Guide Pyramid/pirámide de los alimentos Una serie de recomendaciones para ayudarte a escoger los alimentos y las cantidades de ellos que debes comer para obtener los nutrientes que necesitas. (11–1)

function/función Uso. (8–1)

G

garnish/decorado Una pequeña cantidad de comida o aderezo que se usa para adornar un plato. (13–1)

generic product/producto genérico Un producto cuya etiqueta lleva sólo el nombre del producto y la información nutritiva. (13–2)

goal/meta Algo que quieres lograr. (3–4)

goods/bienes Productos hechos para vender. (7–1)

gossip/contar chismes Hablar sobre otras personas y sus vidas privadas. (2–2)

grade labeling/etiqueta de calidad Una medida de la calidad de los alimentos usando las reglas establecidas por el gobierno. (13–2)

graduated measuring cups/tazas de medir graduadas Juego de tazas de medir en los tamaños que se usan con mayor frecuencia. (13–4)

grain/hilo La dirección en que van las fibras de la tela. (16–2), (18–1)

group play/juego en grupo Jugar con varios otros niños. (6–3)

guidance/orientación Dirección o asesoramiento. (6–1)

guide sheet/hoja de instrucciones Una guía para coser un patrón paso a paso. (18–1)

H

habit/hábito Un patrón de conducta que se repite sin pensar. (3–3)

hard-cooked egg/huevo duro Un huevo que se deja en agua caliente, cubierto, de 15 a 20 minutos. (14–5)

hazard/peligro Una amenaza. (9–3)

hemming stitch/punto de dobladillo Una puntada a mano que se usa para coser los dobladillos. (18–5)

heredity/herencia La transmisión de rasgos o características de padres a hijos. (1–1)

hue/tono El nombre de un color. (15–3)

hunger/hambre La necesidad de comer. (10–1)

hygiene/higiene Las prácticas que promueven la salud. (15–1)

I

illusion/ilusión El sentido de que las cosas son distintas a como lo son en verdad. (8–2)

image ad/anuncio de imagen Un anuncio que conecta un producto o un servicio a un estilo de vida que los consumidores quisieran tener. (7–2)

impression/impresión La imagen que tú presentas o que otros te presentan a ti. (2–1)

impulse buying/compras impulsivas Decidir comprar algo súbitamente. (7–3)

incineration/incineración Quemar los desechos para deshacerse de ellos. (9–2)

income/ingresos La cantidad de dinero que ganas o recibes con regularidad. (7–5)

independent play/juego independiente Juego que el bebé hace solo, demostrando poco interés en relacionarse con otros niños. También se llama juego solitario. (6–3)

infomercial/comercial informativo Un anuncio de televisión largo que proporciona información. (7–2)

information ad/anuncio de información Un anuncio que describe las características de un producto o servicio y da información sobre su precio y calidad. (7–2)

initiative/iniciativa Actuar sin que se lo pidan a uno. (3–2)

insulation/material aislante Un material que se instala en el ático o las paredes de un edificio para mantenerlo más fresco en verano y más caliente en invierno. (9–1)

intensity/intensidad Lo brillante o fuerte que es un color. (15–3)

interest/interés Una suma que paga un banco para poder usar tu dinero. (7–5)

interfacing/entretela Una pieza de tela especial que se pone entre dos piezas de tela para darle mejor forma a una prenda. (17–3)

intruder/intruso Alguien que entra a la fuerza en una casa. (6–4)

iron/hierro Un mineral que es un componente esencial de la sangre. (10–3)

J

job applicant/candidato a un puesto Una persona que quiere un trabajo. (4–3)

job application/solicitud de trabajo Un formulario en el que un candidato escribe información sobre sí mismo que ayuda al empleador a decidir a quién dar un trabajo. (4–3)

job interview/entrevista de empleo Una reunión cara a cara entre un empleador y el candidato a un puesto. (4–3)

job opening/oportunidad de trabajo Un puesto que no se ha llenado. (4–3)

job preparation/preparación para el trabajo La enseñanza necesaria para obtener y mantener el tipo de trabajo que quieres. (4–1)

K

knit fabric/jersey Tela que se hace entrelazando hilos. (16–2)

L

landfill/relleno sanitario Un hoyo inmenso donde se echa la basura y se entierra entre capas de tierra. (9–2)

layaway plan/reservación mediante el pago de un depósito Un plan de pagos programados en el cual das un depósito pequeño y haces pagos regulares hasta terminar de pagar por un artículo. (7–5)

layout/distribución Un diagrama que muestra cómo colocar las piezas de un patrón sobre la tela. (18–1)

leader/líder Una persona que tiene la habilidad de guiar y motivar a los demás. (2–3)

leavening agent/levadura Un ingrediente que hace que crezca la masa de una comida hecha al horno. (13–4)

life change/cambio de la vida Una manera importante en que tu vida puede ser alterada por sucesos que tú no necesariamente puedes controlar. (5–3)

logo/logotipo El símbolo de identificación de una compañía. (15–2)

looper/gancho Una pieza redonda que sujeta el hilo dentro de un remalladora. (18–3)

M

major appliance/electrodomésticos Un aparato de cocina grande. (12–3)

management/manejo Utilizar lo que tienes para obtener lo que quieres, ser organizado, y planear por adelantado. (2–4)

marking/marca Una guía en la pieza de un patrón para hacer un proyecto. (18–1)

maturity/madurez Tomar decisiones inteligentes, tener control de sí mismo, y actuar responsablemente. (2–1)

meal pattern/pautas de comidas Los hábitos de las personas que determinan qué y cuándo comen cada día. (13–1)

meat extender/aumentador de carne Un alimento que se le añade a la carne para hacer que una cantidad pequeña alcance para más personas. (14–5)

media/medios de comunicación Los modos de transmitir información que usan los anunciantes para mandar sus mensajes. (7–2)

mend/remendar Reparar. (16–4)

menu/menú Una lista de todos los platos que sirve un restaurante, organizados por categoría. (11–3)

metric measurement/sistema métrico Un sistema de medidas basado en múltiplos de diez. (13–4)

microwave oven/horno de microondas Un electrodoméstico que cocina por medio de la vibración de las moléculas en las comidas. (12–3)

mineral/mineral Elemento que el cuerpo necesita en pequeñas cantidades para que los huesos y los dientes estén fuertes, para que la sangre esté saludable y para que el cuerpo elimine los desechos con regularidad. (10–3)

moderation/moderación Evitar los extremos. (11–2)

modesty/modestia Ideas que tiene la gente acerca de la manera en que la ropa debe cubrir el cuerpo. (15–2)

moist-heat cooking/cocinar en líquido Cocinar los alimentos en un líquido. (14–5)

N

nap/pelo Textura de una tela que va en una sola dirección. (17–3)

narrative format/formato narrativo La presentación de una receta en un párrafo que describe los pasos y los ingredientes en orden de uso. (13–3)

national-brand product/producto de marca nacional Un producto que ves anunciado en televisión, periódicos o revistas. (13–2)

natural resource/recurso natural Un material que proporciona la naturaleza. (9–1)

need/necesidad Algo que tienes que tener para poder vivir. (3–1)

negotiation/negociación El proceso de hablar sobre un conflicto y llegar a un acuerdo. (5–6)

neutral color/color neutral Negro, blanco, beige o gris. (15–3)

nonverbal communication/comunicación no verbal Mensajes que se mandan sin palabras. (2–2)

notion/artículo de mercería Un artículo pequeño que se usa para hacer una prenda. (17–3)

nutrient/nutriente Una substancia en los alimentos que es importante para el crecimiento y mantenimiento del cuerpo. (10–1)

nutrient-dense food/alimento cargado de nutrientes Un alimento que es rico en los nutrientes que tu cuerpo necesita para mantenerse sano. (11–3)

nutrition/nutrición El estudio de los nutrientes y de cómo los utiliza el cuerpo. (10–1)

O

obesity/obesidad Una condición en la cual el peso de una persona está un 20 por ciento o más por encima de su peso ideal. (11–4)

open dating/fecha descubierta La exposición de la fecha hasta cuando está fresca una comida empaquetada. (13–2)

option/opción Selección posible. (3–3)

osteoporosis/osteoporosis Una condición en la que los huesos gradualmente pierden su contenido mineral y se ponen débiles y frágiles. (10–3)

P Q

parallel play/juego paralelo Juego que ocurre al lado en vez de junto con otro niño. (6–3)

parenthood/paternidad y maternidad La función de un padre o una madre. (6–1)

parenting/crianza de los hijos El proceso de cuidar a los hijos y ayudarlos a que crezcan y aprendan. (6–1)

pasta/pasta Un alimento hecho de harina y agua al que se dan distintas formas. (14–3)

pattern/patrón El plan para hacer una prenda o proyecto. (17–2)

pedestrian/peatón Una persona que viaja a pie. (9–3)

peer/contemporáneo Una persona de la misma edad que tú. (5–4)

peer group/grupo de contemporáneos Un grupo de personas de la misma edad. (5–4)

peer mediation/mediación por contemporáneos Un proceso en el que estudiantes con capacitación especial ayudan a otros estudiantes a encontrar la solución a un problema. (5–6)

peer pressure/presión de contemporáneos La influencia que sientes para dejarte llevar por la conducta y las creencias de tus contemporáneos. (5–5)

perishable/perecedero Que se echa a perder con facilidad. (12–1)

personality/personalidad El conjunto total de los rasgos, sentimientos, actitudes y hábitos de una persona. (1–2)

personal style/estilo personal El tipo de ropa que más te gusta. (16–1)

pinking shears/tijeras dentadas Tijeras que tienen filo de zigzag. (17–1)

plaque/placa dental Una capa suave y pegajosa sobre los dientes causada por las bacterias que viven en la boca de una persona. (15–1)

poison control center/centro de control del envenenamiento Centro médico donde empleados entrenados ayudan con las emergencias de envenenamiento. (6–4)

pollution/contaminación del medio ambiente El cambio del aire, agua y tierra de limpio y sano a sucio y malsano. (9–1)

popularity/popularidad El estado de ser favorecido por los demás. (5–5)

potential/potencial La capacidad para crecer y desarrollarse. (3–1)

precaution/precaución Medidas que se toman para evitar el peligro. (8–3)

precycle/preciclar Evitar comprar productos que tienen más envoltura que la necesaria. (9–2)

prejudice/prejuicio Una opinión que se forma sobre otras personas sin tener datos ni conocimientos sobre ellas. (5–6)

preschooler/niño preescolar Un niño que tiene entre tres y cinco años de edad. (6–2)

presser foot/pisacostura La pieza de metal al final de la aguja de una máquina de coser que sujeta la tela en su sitio. (17–1)

pretreat/tratar de antemano Ponerle detergente líquido o quitamanchas directamente a las manchas antes de lavar una prenda. (16–4)

prioritize/priorizar Poner en orden de importancia. (2–4)

processed/procesado Que ha sido modificado (un alimento) de su forma cruda antes de venderse. (14–1)

procrastinate/dejar para luego Dejar las cosas para hacerlas más tarde. (2–4)

produce/productos de granja Frutas y vegetales frescos. (14–1)

promotion/ascenso Avance a un trabajo mejor con mayor responsabilidad. (4–4)

proofread/corregir Revisar y rectificar los errores de gramática, puntuación y ortografía. (4–2)

protein/proteína Un nutriente necesario para fabricar, reparar y mantener las células y tejidos del cuerpo. (10–2)

punishment/castigo Una manera de poner freno a la conducta poco apropiada. (6–1)

R

ravel/deshilar Salírsele los hilos al borde cortado de la tela. (17–3)

raw edge/borde cortado El borde de la tela sin terminar que tiene hilos sueltos. (18–1)

realistic goal/meta razonable Una meta que puedes alcanzar. (3–4)

recipe/receta Una lista de ingredientes e instrucciones para preparar un platillo específico. (13–3)

recycling/reciclar Convertir los desechos en productos que se pueden usar. (9–2)

redirect/desviar Hacer que alguien dirija su atención a otra cosa. (6–5)

redress/compensación Acción que se toma para corregir un error. (7–4)

reference/referencia Un informe acerca del carácter y habilidades de trabajo del candidato a un puesto. (4–3)

refund/reembolso El intercambio de dinero por un artículo que se ha devuelto. (7–4)

refusal skills/habilidades de rehusar Modos de decir que no eficazmente. (3–1)

resource/recurso Una fuente de información o experiencia que puedes utilizar para alcanzar tus metas; algo que necesitas para alcanzar una meta. (2–4), (3–4)

respect/respeto Consideración. (3–2)

responsibility/responsabilidad La habilidad de tomar decisiones y de responder por esas decisiones. (3–2)

risk/arriesgarse Correr peligros. (9–3)

role/papel La manera en que actúas cuando estás con otra persona. (1–1)

role model/modelo de conducta Una persona que te ayuda a ver lo que se espera de ti y te enseña cómo actuar en ciertas situaciones. (1–1)

rotating/dar vueltas Girar un plato un cuarto o media vuelta en un horno de microondas. (12–4)

S

salad/ensalada Un alimento o combinación de alimentos que generalmente se sirven fríos y con aliño. (14–2)

salmonella/salmonella Bacterias que se encuentran con frecuencia en alimentos crudos o no del todo cocinados tales como la carne, los huevos, el pescado y las aves. (12–1)

sandwich/sandwich Dos lascas de pan alrededor de un relleno, tal como la carne o el queso. (14–3)

sanitary/sanitario Libre de gérmenes. (8–3)

saturated fat/grasa saturada Grasa que se encuentra en alimentos que vienen de fuentes animales. (10–2)

scald/calentar sin que llegue al punto de ebullición Calentar despacio un alimento sin dejar que hierva. (14–4)

seam finish/remate Una manera de terminar el borde de una costura para que la tela no se deshilache. (18–2)

seasonal/de temporada Más abundantes, más fácil de conseguir y más baratos durante cierto tiempo del año. (14–1)

security/seguridad Sentirse tranquilo y protegido. (5–1)

self-concept/autoimagen Tu concepto de ti mismo. (1–3)

self-confidence/confianza en sí mismo Seguridad de tus propias habilidades. (1–3)

self-esteem/autoestima La habilidad de respetarte a ti mismo. (1–3)

selvage/orillo El borde de la tela que está terminado para que no se salgan los hilos. (18–1)

serger/remalladora Una máquina de alta velocidad que cose, corta y remata una costura en un solo paso. (18–3)

service/servicio Trabajo que una persona hace para otras. (7–1)

serving/ración Una porción de comida que una persona probablemente comiera en un ocasión. (11–1)

sewing gauge/regla de costura Una regla de metal de 6 pulgadas (15 cm) con un puntero que se mueve. (17–1)

shank/vástago El tallo de un botón que proporciona espacio para la capa de tela alrededor del ojal. (18–5)

shape/forma Contorno. (15–3)

shoplifting/hurto en las tiendas Llevarse artículos de una tienda sin pagar por ellos. (7–3)

shopping plan/plan de compras Una estrategia para gastar el dinero que tienes disponible para comprar los artículos que necesitas o deseas. (16–3)

sibling/hermano Hermano o hermana. (5–2)

slip stitch/punto de dobladillo Un punto a mano que luce casi invisible. (18–5)

small appliance/aparato eléctrico Un aparato eléctrico pequeño para la cocina. (12–3)

smoke alarm/alarma de humo Un aparato que hace sonar una alarma cuando hay humo. (6–4)

snack/refrigerio Alimento que se come entre comidas. (11–3)

sodium/sodio Un mineral que ayuda a regular la cantidad de líquido que hay en el cuerpo. (11–2)

software/software Un programa o unas instrucciones para computación. (4–2)

solitary play/juego solitario Juego que el bebé hace solo, demostrando poco interés en relacionarse con otros niños. También se llama juego independiente. (6–3)

specialty store/tienda especializada Una tienda que tiene sólo un tipo de mercancía en particular. (7–3)

stain/mancha Un área sucia o descolorida. (16–4)

stamina/resistencia La habilidad de concentrarse en una sola actividad por mucho tiempo. (11–4)

standard format/formato típico La presentación de una receta que enumera todos los ingredientes en orden de su uso, seguidos por instrucciones para preparar el alimento paso a paso. (13–2)

staple/alimento básico Alimento que se usa con frecuencia. (13–2)

status/prestigio Nivel de importancia. (15–2)

status symbol/símbolo de prestigio Una prenda de vestir u otro artículo que le da a su dueño un sentido especial de importancia. (16–3)

staystitching/puntadas de fijar Una línea de puntadas permanentes que se cose encima o muy cerca de la costura en el borde de la tela. (18–4)

stereotype/estereotipo Una idea o imagen formada por adelantado acerca de todos los miembros de un grupo. (2–1)

stitch finger/dedo para puntada Una punta de metal en el plato o pisacostura de una remalladora. (18–3)

GLOSSARY/GLOSARIO **555**

stitch regulator/regulador del punto Un dial o palanca en una máquina de coser que controla el largo de las puntadas. (17–1)

store-brand product/marca de la tienda Alimento o artículo doméstico que lleva en la etiqueta el nombre de una tienda o un nombre que sólo se usa en esa tienda. (13–2)

stress/estrés La reacción del cuerpo a los cambios a su alrededor. (5–3)

style/estilo El diseño de una prenda. (15–2)

sunscreen/bloqueador solar Una loción que protege la piel contra los rayos dañinos del sol. (15–1)

supervisor/supervisor La persona que revisa y evalúa el trabajo de otra. (4–4)

synthetic fiber/fibra sintética Una fibra hecha parcial o completamente de substancias químicas. (16–2)

T

tail chain/cadeneta Una cantidad de hilo en forma de cadena hecho en un remalladora sin tela debajo de la aguja. (18–3)

talent/talento Habilidad natural. (2–4)

teamwork/trabajo en conjunto Los esfuerzos cooperativos de todos los miembros de un grupo al trabajar juntos para lograr una meta. (2–3), (4–4)

texture/textura La manera en que algo se siente o luce como si se debe sentir. (8–2), (13–1), (15–3)

time schedule/programa del tiempo Un plan para asegurar que todos los platos estén listos para servir en el momento correcto. (13–1)

toddler/niño pequeño Un niño entre uno y tres años de edad. (6–2)

trade-off/intercambio El sacrificio de una cosa para obtener algo de mayor importancia. (3–4)

tradition/tradición Una costumbre o creencia que se pasa de generación a generación. (5–2)

traffic pattern/patrón de movimiento Las sendas que siguen las personas para entrar, salir y moverse alrededor de una habitación. (8–1)

U

unique/único Que sólo hay uno. (1–1)

unit pricing/dar el precio por unidad Mostrar el costo de un producto por unidad. (13–2)

unsaturated fat/grasa no saturada Grasa que viene de plantas. (10–2)

utensil/utensilio Implemento de cocina. (12–3)

V

value/opacidad Lo claro u oscuro que es un color. (15–3)

values/valores Ideas sobre el bien y el mal y sobre lo que es importante en la vida. (3–1)

variable/factor variable Una condición que determina por cuánto tiempo y a qué nivel de potencia se tiene que cocinar un alimento en un horno de microondas. (12–4)

vegetarian/vegetariano Una persona que come principalmente frutas, vegetales y granos. (11–1)

versatile/versátil Que se puede llevar puesto en muchas ocasiones distintas. (16–1)

view/modelo Una de las versiones de una prenda que se ve en el sobre de un patrón. (17–2)

violence/violencia El uso de fuerza física para hacer daño a alguien. (9–3)

vitamin/vitamina Substancia que el cuerpo necesita en pequeñas cantidades para regular sus funciones. (10–3)

volunteer/voluntario Una persona que da su tiempo y energía sin pago como servicio a otros. (2–3)

W

want/deseo Algo que quieres tener pero que no es necesario para sobrevivir. (3–1)

wardrobe inventory/inventario del vestuario Una lista de toda la ropa, los zapatos y los accesorios que tienes. (16–1)

warranty/garantía La promesa por escrito de un fabricante de arreglar o reemplazar un producto que no funciona como se afirma. (7–3)

wellness/bienestar Un alto nivel de salud total. (11–2)

whole grain/grano integral Un alimento que contiene todo lo que se puede comer del grano, incluyendo la capa exterior, el salvado y el germen. (10–2)

work plan/plan de trabajo Una lista de las tareas que hay que hacer y los nombres de las personas que van a hacer cada una. (12–5)

work record/hoja de servicio Un historial de lo bien que un empleado hace su trabajo. (4–4)

woven fabric/tela de telar Tela hecha en un telar entretejiendo los hilos que van a lo ancho con los hilos que van a lo largo, a un ángulo de 90°. (16–2)

X Y Z

yield/número de porciones El número de raciones que rinde una receta. (13–3)

Index

A

Abbreviations in recipes, 375–378
Accessories
   in room design, 233
   wardrobe, 453, 457
Accident chain, 259
Accident prevention, 172–175, 259–262, 333–336
Achieving goals, 72–73
Acne, 430
Acquaintances, 131
Acquired characteristics, 6, 7
Adolescence, 10, 13
Advertisements
   evaluating, 198–199
   influence of, 191, 192–193, 194–199, 276
Advice, 68, 69
Aerobic exercise, 320
Air pollution, 247–248
Alcohol, 138–139, 263, 309
Alterations, 493, 533–534
Amino acids, 279
Appearance
   clothing choices, 434–446
   and color, 441–444
   diet and, 273
   first impressions, 27, 438
   health and grooming, 428–433
   physical changes, 14–15
Appetite, 274–275
Appetizers, 362
Appliances, 249, 338, 342
Applicants for jobs, 95
Applications for jobs, 94–95
Applied casings, 526
Apprenticeship programs, 84
Approval, 113–114
Aptitude tests, 82

Arcing, 346
Assertiveness, 140
Attention span, 166
Attitude, positive, 28–29, 62, 73

B

Babies, 162, 166–167, 179–181
Babysitting, 176–182
Baking, 396, 400–401
Balance, 231
Balanced diet, 305
Banana milk, 408
Basic skills, 87–90
Basting stitch, 487
Beans, 417–418
Bedrooms, 229–234, 237–238
Beliefs, 142
Belonging, 113
Bias of fabrics, 509
Biodegradable products, 254
Bobbins, 486, 513
Brand names, 192, 367, 469
Bread, Cereal, Rice, and Pasta Group, 300–301, 361, 399–405
Breads, 400–402
Breakfasts, 275
Broth, 398
Budgets, 214
   clothing, 467, 469–470
   money management, 104, 212–216, 469–471, 498
   sewing projects, 498
Burns, 333–334
Businesses, 96, 103
Buttons, replacing, 530, 532
Buying. *See* Money management; Shopping
Buying clubs, 203

C

Calcium, 289
Calories, 275, 318, 320, 321

Carbohydrates, 276, 280–281
Care
   of children, 179–182
   of clothing, 468, 472–476
   hygiene, 431–433
Career research, 82–83
Careers, 78–104. *See also* Jobs
   choosing, 81–83
   developing skills, 86–91
   finding jobs, 92–97
   job preparation, 83–85
   success, 98–104
Caregivers, 152
Casings, 526
Casseroles, 396
Cereals, 403
Chain, accident, 259
Chain stitch, 519
Changes
   emotional, 13
   in families, 123–129
   in friendships, 133–135
   physical, 14–15
Charge cards, 216
Cheerfulness, 18
Cheeses, 409–410
Child abuse, 155
Childproofing, 171–172
Children
   babysitting, 176–182
   caring for, 179–182
   development of, 158–164
   parenting skills, 152–157
   play and learning, 165–170
   safety, 171–175
   with special needs, 162–163
Choices. *See also* Decisions; Shopping
   of clothing, 434–439
   consumer rights and, 207
   of food, 275–276, 313–314
   of sewing projects, 490
Cholesterol, 283, 306

Cigarettes, 138–139
Citizens, 37
Citizenship skills, 37–39
Classic styles, 436
Cleaning
   clothing, 473–476
   dishes, 329
   homes, 235–238
   hygiene, 429–422
   kitchens, 331
Cleaning plan, 236
Cleanliness, 18
Closet organization, 226, 227, 237–238
Clothing. *See also* Sewing
   accessories, 453, 457
   alterations, 493, 533–534
   budget, 467, 469–470, 498
   care and cleaning, 468, 472–476
   choices, 434–439
   cost per wearing, 470–471
   design, 440–446
   extending your wardrobe, 545–547
   fit and comfort, 462–465
   for job interviews, 96–97
   labels, 204, 468–469
   needs, 453
   purposes of, 435
   quality, 459–462
   recycling, 534
   repairing, 473, 529–533
   shopping for, 466–471
   wardrobe inventory, 453–455
Clubs, buying, 203
Coffee shake, 408
Color
   and clothing design, 440–444
   and meal planning, 363
   and room design, 231
Color schemes, 442, 443
Color wheel, 442
Comfort of clothing, 462–465, 506
Commitments, 61
Communication, 31–35
   to children, 155–157
   clothing as, 437–438
   conversation, 34–35
   listening skills, 33–34
   in relationships, 114
   resolving conflicts, 144
   verbal and nonverbal, 32–33
Communities
   resources, 45
   responsibilities, 61
   safety, 262–263
Comparison shopping, 200–205
Complaints, consumer, 210
Comprehension, 88
Compromise, 144–146
Compromising, 228
Computer skills, 90–91
Conducting electricity, 336
Cones for thread, 517
Conflicts, 141–146
Conscience, 161
Consequences, 68
Conservation, 246–251
Consideration, 29, 115–116, 227
Consistency, 155
Construction of clothing, 461–462, 524–528
Constructive criticism, 19
Consumer Reports, 199
Consumer responsibilities, 208–211
Consumer rights, 207
Consumers, 191
Contamination, 329, 330
Controlling emotions, 13–14
Convenience foods, 379
Conversation, 34–35
Cooking. *See also* Food; Meals
   breads, 400–401
   convenience foods, 379
   with dairy foods, 407, 409–410, 411
   equipment, 338–342, 382
   fruit, 392
   grains, 403–404
   measuring ingredients, 380–384
   meats and meat substitutes, 414–420
   in microwave ovens, 343–349
   school foods lab, 350–354
   terms and abbreviations, 375–378
   using recipes, 373–378
   vegetables, 395–397
Cooperation, 29, 114–115, 227
Cooperative play, 168
Coping with stress, 128, 129
Corners, sewing, 514–515
Cost per wearing, 470–471
Courtesy, 208
Coworkers, 98, 102
Credit, 216
Criticism, constructive, 19
Culture, 6–7, 275
Curdling, 407
Curved seams, 514
Custards, 411
Customary measurements, 381
Cut prevention, 335
Cutting fabric, 511–512

D

Dairy foods, 406–412
Darts, in sewing, 491, 524
Debit cards, 216
Decisions, 64–69. *See also* Choices
   importance of, 66
   influences on buying, 190–193
   responsibility, 68–69, 138–139
   steps in making, 66–67
   types of, 64–65
Decomposition, 253
Decoration
   room design, 229–234, 508
   sewing notions, 494, 497–498
Default decisions, 65
Defrosting, 344
Dehydrated soups, 398
Dental care, 432–433

Dermatologists, 430
Design
    of clothing, 440–446
        elements and principles, 230–232
    of living space, 229–234, 508
Desserts, 411–412
Developing skills, 86–91
Developmental tasks, 159–161
Diapers, changing, 180
Dictionary of Occupational Titles (DOT), 83
Diet, 272, 305, 320–322
Dietary Guidelines, 304–309
Digestion, 276
Direct mail, 197
Disabilities, 116
Discipline, 155
Discount stores, 203
Dishes
    setting table, 361
    washing, 329
Dough, 400
Dovetailing, 352
Dressing, 96–97, 436–439, 476. *See also* Appearance
Dressings for salad, 397
Drugs, 138–139, 263
Dry-heat cooking, 416
Drying clothes, 475
Dry legumes, 417–418

E

Ease in clothing, 465, 506
Easing fabric, 525
Eating out, 312–315
Eggs, 418–419
Electric shock prevention, 335–336
Electronic media, 196–197
Emotional development, 160–161
Emotional needs, 154
Emotions, 11–14, 127, 263
Empathy, 30
Emphasis, 231
Employee manuals, 100

Employment. *See* Careers; Jobs
Empty-calorie foods, 312, 318
Endorsements, 196, 198
Energy efficiency, 248–250
Energy, personal, 44
Entrepreneurs, 79, 103
Environmental concerns
    conservation, 246–251
    waste and recycling, 189, 252–257, 427, 534
Environment and heredity, 5
Equipment
    for cooking, 338–342, 345–346, 382
    for sewing, 484–485, 517–519
Etiquette and manners, 362, 368
Evaluation, 43
Exchanges, 210–211
Exercise, 129, 317–318, 320, 321
Expectations, 134–135
Expenses, 213–214
Experiences, 8, 74
Eye care, 432

F

Fabrics. *See also* Clothing; Sewing
    about, 459–461, 464
    preparing for sewing, 487, 506, 507–509, 511–512
    selecting for sewing projects, 494–497, 498
Facings, 526–527
Fad diets, 320–322
Fads in clothing, 436
Falls, accidental, 173–174, 238–239, 333
Families
    changes in, 123–129
    defined, 118
    getting along with, 120–122, 227–228
    importance of, 118–120
    influence of, 7, 275
    relationships, 117–122
    responsibility to, 60
    types of, 118
    values, 56

Fashions, 436
Fast-food meals, 314–315
Fats, 276, 281–283, 288, 306, 307
Feed dogs, 521
Feeding children, 180, 181–182
Fiber, dietary, 281
Fibers, 459
Finishes of fabrics, 461
Fire extinguishers, 334
Fire prevention, 174, 238, 334
First impressions, 27, 438
Fit in clothing, 462–464
Fitness, 317, 318, 320
Fixed expenses, 214
Flammable objects, 334
Flatlock stitch, 520
Flexibility, 100–101
Flexible expenses, 214
Floor plans, 234
Flossing, 433
Focal point, 457
Fold-down casings, 526
Food. *See also* Cooking; Meals
    choices of, 275–276, 313–314
    convenience foods, 378–379
    food groups, 297–298, 300–301, 361–362
    health and, 273–274, 276–277
    labels, 204–205, 204–206, 280, 288, 302, 307, 309, 368–370
    safety and sanitation, 328–331
    school lab, 350–354
    servings, 297, 298
    shopping, 367–370
    snacks, 311–312
    storage, 370–372
    trade-offs, 299, 302
Food Guide Pyramid, 296–302, 361–362
Food preparation. *See* Cooking
Foot care, 431
Friendliness, 29
Friends
    developing, 130–135
    diet and, 275
    peers and peer groups, 133, 136–140, 191–192, 264

responsibility to, 61
Frozen foods, 371
Fruit Group, 300–301, 362, 390–393
Fruits
    choosing, 391–392
    cooking, 392
    Dietary Guidelines, 306–307
    serving, 392–393
    storing, 371
Frying vegetables, 396
Functions, 224
Furniture, 224, 226

G

Garnishes, 363
Gathering fabric, 525
Generic products, 367
Goals, 70–74
Goods, 191
Gossip, 35, 142
Grade labeling, 368
Grain in fabrics, 460, 506, 508–509
Grains, 281, 306–307, 402–405
Grooming, 428–433
Group play, 168–169
Growth, physical, 14–15
Guidance, 155
Guide sheet for sewing, 505

H

Habits
    breaking, 28
    healthy, 296–322
    routine decisions, 65
    shopping and, 192
Hair care, 431–432
Hand care, 431
Hand sewing, 530, 531
Hard-cooked eggs, 419
Harmful substances, 138–139
Harmony, 231
Hazards, 260

Health
    characteristics of, 273–274
    Dietary Guidelines, 304–309
    fitness, 317, 318, 320
    good habits and, 296–322
    hygiene, 429–433
    importance of, 429
    laughter and, 124
    nutrition and, 276–277
    self-concept and, 19, 20
    weight and, 305, 318–319
    wellness, 303
Heredity and environment, 5
Homes
    cleaning, 235–238
    importance of, 222–223
    organization in, 223–227
    room arrangements, 225, 226
    room design, 229–234, 508
    safety precautions, 238–240, 260
    sharing space, 223, 227–229, 236–237
Honesty, 18, 209
Hooks and eyes, 533
Hues, 441
Hunger, 274–275
Hygiene, 429–433

I

Illusion, 230
Image ads, 195–196
Imagination, 163
Impressions
    first, 27, 438
    good, 26–30
Impulse buying, 201
Incineration, 253
Income, 213–214
Income management, 104
Independence, 156–157
Independent play, 166
Individuality, 4–5, 9, 496
Infants, 162, 166–167, 179–181
Infomercials, 196–197
Information ads, 195

Initiative, 62, 103
Injuries, 172–174
Insulation, 249
Intellectual development, 160
Intellectual needs, 155
Intensity of colors, 442
Interest, 215
Interfacing, 497
Interviewing for jobs, 95–97
Intruders, 172
Iron, 289
Ironing, 475–476, 487

J

Jealousy, 142
Job applicants, 95
Job applications, 94–95
Job interviews, 95–97
Job openings, 93–94
Job preparation, 83–85
Jobs. *See also* Careers
    babysitting, 176–179
    choosing, 81–83
    coworkers, 98, 102
    developing skills, 86–91
    finding, 92–97
    management skills, 92
    papers required, 93
    responsibilities, 99–101
    successful work, 98–104
    work record, 102–103

K

Kitchens
    cleaning, 331
    equipment, 338–342
    safety, 332–336
    saving time, 352
Knit fabrics, 460
Knowledge, 44

L

Labels
    on clothing, 204, 468–469

on fabrics, 496
on food, 204–205, 280, 288, 302, 307, 309, 368–370
Nutrition Facts, 369
Labs
foods, 350–354
sewing, 483–485
Landfills, 253
Laughter and health, 124
Laundry, 473–476
Layaway plan, 215
Layouts, 505
Leaders, 39
Leadership skills, 39–40
Learning. *See also* Skills
basic skills, 86–90
in children, 163–164, 170
computer skills, 90–91
Leftovers, 330
Lemon-strawberry yogurt smoothie, 408
Life changes, 123–124
Line
and clothing, 444–445
and room design, 230
Listening skills, 33–34, 90
Long-term goals, 71–72
Loopers, 517

M

Major appliances, 338, 342
Management, 42
money, 104, 212–216, 469–471, 498
resources, 43–46
skills, 43
stress, 128, 129
time, 46–48, 483–484
Manners and etiquette, 362, 368
Markings on patterns, 505–506, 507, 512
Material resources, 45
Math skills, 89
Maturity, 28, 62
Meal patterns, 362
Meals. *See also* Cooking; Food

eating out, 312–315
leftovers, 330
planning, 299, 360–365
snacks, 311–312
variety, 363
Measuring
equipment, 382
recipe ingredients, 380–384
for sewing patterns, 492–493, 506
Meat extenders, 418, 419–420
Meat, Poultry, Fish, Dry Beans, Eggs, and Nuts Group, 300–301, 362, 413–420
Media, 196–198
Mediation, peer, 145, 146
Medium cooked meats, 416–417
Mending clothes, 473, 529–533
Mentoring, 151
Menus, choosing from, 313–314
Metric measurement, 381
Microwave ovens, 343–349
about, 338, 342, 344
converting recipes, 348
safety, 346, 348–349
using, 345–347, 397
variables in cooking, 348
Milk, cooking with, 407–408
Milk, Yogurt, and Cheese Group, 300–301, 362, 406–412
Minerals, 276, 285, 287, 288–289
Misunderstandings, 142
Mix-and-match wardrobe, 456
Moderation, 307
Moist-heat cooking, 416
Money management, 104, 212–216, 469–471, 498
Moral development, 161
Movement, 231

N

Nail care, 431
Narrative format recipes, 374–375
National-brand products, 367
Natural resources, 247–251

Neatness, 18
Needs
children's, 154–155
relationships and, 112–113
special needs, 162–163
wants and, 55
wardrobe needs, 452–457
Negotiation, 145
Nonperishable foods, 371, 372
Nonverbal communication, 32–33
Notions, sewing, 494, 497–498
Nutrient-dense foods, 311
Nutrients, 272
Nutrition, 272–290
Dietary Guidelines, 304–309
Food Guide Pyramid, 296–302, 361–362
health and, 273–274, 276–277
Nutrition Facts label, 369, 403

O

Obesity, 318
Occupational Outlook Handbook, The, 83
Open dating, 370
Openings for jobs, 93–94
Opinions, 142
Options, 67, 85
Orange shake, 408
Organization. *See also* Planning
closets, 226, 227, 237–238
homes, 223–227
recipes, 374
sewing projects, 483
Ovens
convection, 338, 342
conventional, 338, 342
microwave, 338, 342, 343–349, 397
Overedge stitch, 519
Overlock stitch, 519

P

Parallel play, 168
Parenthood, 153

Parenting skills, 152–157
Parents, communicating with, 120–121
Part-time work, 85
Pasta, 404–405
Patterns, sewing, 490–493, 505–506, 507, 511–512
Paying for purchases, 215–216, 467
Pedestrians, 260
Peer groups, 133
Peer mediation, 145, 146
Peer pressure, 136–140, 264
Peers, 133, 191–192
People as resources, 45–46
Perishable foods, 329, 371
Personality, 11
Personal resources, 44–45
Personal safety, 258–264
Personal style, 453
Physical development, 160
Physical needs, 154
Pinning sewing patterns, 511
Planning
    cleaning, 236
    clothes shopping, 467
    meals, 299, 360–365
    work, 351–353
Plaque, 432
Play, 165–170
Playground safety, 173
Poison control center, 175
Poisonings, 175
Pollution, 247–248
Popularity, 138
Positive attitude, 28–29, 62, 73
Positive communication, 155–156
Positive self-concept, 17–18
Posture, 429
Potential, 55
Precycling, 254
Prejudice, 142–143, 264
Preschoolers, 162, 168–169, 181–182
Preshrinking fabrics, 508
Presser foot, 488

Pressing, 475–476, 487
Pretreating laundry, 474
Preventing
    accidents, 172–175, 259–262, 333–336
    conflicts, 143
    fires, 174, 238, 334
Price and quality, 203–204
Print media, 196
Prioritizing, 47, 73
Privacy, 115, 227
Processed food, 392
Procrastination, 48
Produce, 391
Promises, 61, 62
Promotions, 103
Proof of purchase, 205, 210
Proofreading, 89
Proportion, 231
Proteins, 276, 279
Puddings, 411
Punishment, 155

Q

Quackery, 208
Quality
    in fabrics and clothing, 459–462, 495–496
    food shopping tips, 368, 370
    and price, 203–204
Quick breads, 400
Quiet play, 170

R

Rare meats, 416–417
Raveling, 496
Raw edges of fabric, 508
Reading skills, 87–88
Realistic goals, 72
Receipts, 205
Recipes, 373–379. *See also* Cooking
    formats, 374–375
    ingredients, 378
    measuring ingredients, 380–384

    organizing, 374
    terms and abbreviations, 375–378
Recycling, 189, 255–256, 427, 534
Redirecting children, 181
Redress, 207
References for jobs, 95
Refrigerators, 342
Refunds, 210–211
Refusal skills, 57, 139
Regular stitch, 487
Reinforcement stitch, 487
Relationships. *See also* Families; Friends
    in business, 98, 100, 102
    conflict resolution, 141–146
    first impressions, 27, 438
    importance of, 112–114, 116
    peer pressure, 136–140, 264
    skills, 114–116
Reliability, 30
Religion and diet, 275
Repairing clothes, 473, 529–533
Researching careers, 82–83
Resolving conflicts, 143–146
Resourcefulness, 18
Resources, 73
    conservation, 246–251
    managing, 43–46
    planning meals, 364
Respect, 38–39, 60
Responsibility, 18, 59–63
    consumer responsibilities, 208–211
    decision-making, 68–69, 138–139
    on the job, 99–101
    parenting skills, 153–157
Restaurants, 312–315
Reusing items, 254–255
Rhythm, 231
Rice, 403
Rights of consumers, 207
Risk taking, 68, 139, 259
Role models, 8, 63
Roles, 8, 125

Rolled hem stitch, 520
Rooms
    arranging, 225, 226
    designing, 229–234, 508
Rotating food in microwaves, 347
Rules, 61–62

S

Safety
    children's, 171–175
    as consumer right, 207
    food safety and sanitation, 328–331
    home, 238–240, 260
    kitchen, 332–336
    microwave ovens, 346, 348–349
    personal, 258–264
    sewing, 483, 487, 514
Safety stitch, 519
Salads, 397
Salmonella, 329
Salt, 308
Sandwiches, 401–402
Saturated fats, 283
Savings plan, 215
Scalding, 407
Schedules. *See* Time
School foods lab, 350–354
Science skills, 89
Seams
    finishes, 515, 527–528
    stitching, 513–515, 519–522, 524
Seasonal produce, 392
Security, 113, 238
Self-concept, 16–18
Self-confidence, 19
Self-control, 13–14, 18
Self-esteem, 18
Self-expression, 437–438
Self-image, 17, 19
Selvage, 508
Sergers, 517–519
Serging, 519–522
Services, 191
Servings, 297, 298

Setting the table, 361
Sewing
    basic skills, 513–515
    choosing fabrics and notions, 494–498
    construction techniques, 524–528
    equipment, 484–485, 517–519
    hand-sewing techniques, 530, 531
    patterns for, 490–493, 505–506, 507, 511–512
    repairs and alteration, 529–534
    safety, 478, 483, 514
    school lab, 483–485
    serging, 516–522
    time management, 483–484
    using sewing machines, 485–488
Sewing machines
    about, 485
    safety, 483
    sergers, 517–519
    using, 485–488, 519–522
Shades, 441
Shakes, 407–408
Shampoo, 432
Shank of buttons, 532
Shape
    and clothing design, 444–445
    and meal planning, 363
    and room design, 230
Shared property, 39
Shared values, 56
Sharing, teaching children to, 169
Sharing space, 223, 227–229, 236–237
Shoes, 464
Shoplifting, 209
Shopping
    advertisements, 191, 192–193, 194–199
    for clothing, 466–471
    clubs, 203
    comparison shopping, 200–205
    consumer responsibilities, 208–211

    consumer rights, 207
    for fabrics, 494–497, 498
    for food, 367–370
    influences on buying decisions, 190–193
    proof of purchase, 205, 210
    refunds and exchanges, 210–211
    ways to pay, 215–216
Short-term goals, 71–72
Siblings, 119, 121–122
Simmering, 396
Size
    and meal planning, 363
    measurements for sewing, 492–493
    measuring recipe ingredients, 380–384
    servings, 297, 298
Skills, 44
    basic, 87–90
    citizenship, 37–39
    computer, 90–91
    hand-sewing techniques, 530, 531
    leadership, 39–40
    listening, 33–34
    management, 43
    parenting, 152–157
    refusal, 57
    relationship, 114–116
    sewing, 513–515, 521–522
Skin care, 430–431
Sleep for babies, 181
Slogans, 198
Small appliances, 338
Smoke alarms, 174
Smoothies, 408
Snacks, 311–312
Snaps, 532–533
Social development, 160
Social needs, 154
Sodium, 308, 309
Software, 91
Soil, 248
Solitary play, 166

Soups, 397–398
Space and room design, 230
Speaking skills, 89–90
Special-needs children, 162–163
Sports and safety, 261–262
Stains on clothes, 473, 474
Stamina, 317–318
Standard format recipes, 374–375
Staples, 367
Starches, 280
Status symbols, 435, 469
Staystitching, 524
Steaming, 396
Stereotypes, 27
Stir-frying, 396
Stitch finger, 521
Stitching. See Sewing
Stitch regulator, 487
Stitch types, 487, 519–520
Storage space, 226–227
Store-brand products, 367
Storing
    clothing, 476
    food, 370–372
Straightening fabric, 508–509
Straight seams, 513–514
Strangers, 262
Stress, 127–129
Study skills, 88
Style
    of clothing, 436–439, 453, 465, 491–492
    of room design, 232–233
Success, 74, 98–104, 353–354, 437
Sugars, 280, 281, 288, 307–308
Sunscreens, 430
Supervisors, 100
Synthetic fibers, 459

T

Table manners, 362
Table settings, 361
Tail chains, 521
Take-out food, 314–315
Talents, 44
Teamwork, 37, 40, 101, 351
Teasing, 142
Teeth, care of, 432–433
Television, 179, 195–197
Tension dials of sergers, 517
Terms in recipes, 375–378
Texture
    and clothing design, 446
    and meal planning, 363
    and room design, 230–231
Thoughtfulness, 18, 115–116
Thread guides of sergers, 517
Threading a sewing machine, 486–487
Time
    in decision-making, 68
    managing, 46–48, 483–484
    meal planning schedule, 364, 365
    open dating, 370
    as personal resource, 44
    saving in the kitchen, 352
    saving when sewing, 497
Tints, 441
Toddlers, 162, 167–168, 181–182
Tools. See Equipment
Tooth care, 432–433
Toys, 166–167, 168, 169
Trade-offs, 73
Traditions, 120
Trust, building, 115

U

Underweight, 319
Uniqueness, 4, 9, 496
Unit pricing, 370
Unsaturated fats, 283
Used goods, 205
Utensils, 338, 382

V

Values, human, 55–58, 67, 161
Values of colors, 441
Variety, 231, 363
Vegetable Group, 300–301, 362, 394–398
Vegetables
    cooking, 395–397
    Dietary Guidelines, 306–307
    salads, 397
    selecting and preparing, 395
    soups, 397–398
    storing, 371
Vegetarians, 299
Verbal communication, 32, 34–35
Versatile clothes, 453
Views of garments, 490
Violence, 263–264
Vitamins, 276, 285–288
Volunteers, 36, 39, 40

W, X

Want ads, 84
Wants, 55
Wardrobe. See Clothing
Warranties, 205, 209
Washing. See Cleaning
Waste, 252–257
Water
    conservation of, 248
    used by body, 276, 289–290
Weight
    controlling, 319–322
    healthy, 305, 318–319
Well-done meats, 416–417
Wellness, 303
Whole grains, 281
Work. See Careers; Jobs
Work plan, 351–353
Work record, 102–103
Woven fabrics, 460
Writing skills, 88–89

Y

Yeast breads, 400–401
Yield of recipes, 374
Yogurt, cooking with, 408–409

Z

Zigzag stitch, 487

Cover Art:

Front Cover—Kim Robbie/The Stock Market (photo), Diana Ong/Superstock (illustration); Back Cover—Suresh Shivdasani/Magic Photography (top), DBS Stevenson Photography (bottom)

Photographs:

Lori Adamski Peek/Tony Stone Images x, 1; Arnold & Brown Photography 197, 226, 239, 240, 257, 452, 458, 459, 464, 470; Bruce Ayers/Tony Stone Images 108, 109; Brian Bailey/Tony Stone Images 132; Billy Barnes/FPG International 431; Robert Bennett/FPG International 247; Christopher Bissell/Tony Stone Images 140; Robert Brenner/Photo Edit 168; Michelle Bridwell/Photo Edit 134, 204, 395; David Burnett/The Stock Market 99; Cary Buss/FPG International 160; Jose Carrillo/Photo Edit 193, 194, 211, 232, 249, 414; Myrleen Cate/Tony Stone Images 61; Cindy Charles/Photo Edit 172, 174; Ron Chappel/FPG International 223, 335; Stewart Cohen/Tony Stone Images 424, 425; Comstock 136, 294, 295, 326, 327; David Kelly Crow Photography 475, 476, 488, 504, 506, 508, 509, 510, 512, 514, 515, 522, 523, 524, 526, 527, 529, 533, 534; Bob Daemmrich Photography 163, 411, 429, 439, 444, 445, 446; Bob Daemmrich/Stock Boston 466, 438; Bob Daemmrich/Uniphoto 275, 281, 440, 471; Robert E. Daemmrich/Tony Stone Images 60, 84, 96, 143, 298, 400; Donna Day/Tony Stone Images 299; Mary Kate Denny/Photo Edit 4, 12, 27, 34, 37, 48, 62, 80, 103, 125, 141, 153, 156, 166, 237, 277, 284, 331, 345, 349, 350, 354, 409, 428, 465, 432, 532; Laura Dwight/Photo Edit 169; Amy C. Etra/Photo Edit 115, 145, 181, 182, 199; Jon Feingersh/The Stock Market 120; Myrleen Ferguson/Photo Edit 17, 29, 35, 116, 454; Tony Freeman/Photo Edit 15, 16, 85, 93, 114, 192, 279, 315, 328, 329, 467; Stephen Frish/Stock Boston 434; Tim Fuller Photography 43, 91, 157, 158, 171, 186–187, 188, 189, 212, 214, 215, 216, 296, 310, 338, 342, 344, 346, 351, 353, 380, 384, 392, 393, 394, 396, 403, 405, 410, 411, 418, 420, 450, 451, 480, 481, 490, 491, 493, 494, 495, 497, 498, 502, 503; Robert Ginn/Photo Edit 308; Louis Goldman/FPG International 437; Steven Gottlieb/FPG International 388, 389; Jeff Greenberg/Photo Edit 261; Howard Grey/Tony Stone Images 68; Aaron Haupt/Stock Boston 433; Michal Heron/The Stock Market 64; Index Stock 45; Bonnie Kamin/Photo Edit 236, 264; Ronnie Kaufman/The Stock Market 31; Hal Kern/International Stock 74; Steve Leonard/Tony Stone Images 191; James Levin/FPG International 56, Llewellyn/Uniphoto 319; 176; Bill Losh/FPG International 220, 221; Dick Luvia/FPG International 180; David Madison/Tony Stone Images 112, 150, 151; Felicia Martinez/Photo Edit 373; Tom McCarthy/Photo Edit 397; Fred McKinney/FPG International 165; Mug Shots/The Stock Market 52, 53, 71, 86, 412; Michael Newman/Photo Edit 9, 73, 81, 90, 130, 138, 154, 177, 260, 272, 273, 306, 307, 314, 334, 336, 363, 401, 402, 419, 455, 461, 472, 473, 505, 511, 516, 519, 520; Jonathan Nourok/Photo Edit 263; Gabe Palmer/The Stock Market 142; Jose L. Pelaez/The Stock Market 276; Photo Edit 200, 361; J. Pickerrell/FPG International 382; John Pinderhughes/The Stock Market 119; Jon Riley/Tony Stone Images 24, 25; Joel Rogers/Tony Stone Images 222; Elena Rooraid/Photo Edit 235; Andy Saks/Tony Stone Images 113; Chuck Savage/Uniphoto 312; Mark Scott/FPG International 170; Nancy Sheehan/Photo Edit 127, 152, 202, 227; Stephen Simpson/FPG International 2, 3; Steve Skjold/Photo Edit 408; Don Smetzer/Tony Stone Images 337, 406; The Stock Broker 358, 359; Superstock 8, 42, 44, 66, 70, 117, 122, 126, 146, 159, 164, 283; J. Taposchaner/FPG International 32; Ed Taylor Studio/FPG International 413; The Telegraph Colour Library/FPG International 253; Arthur Tilley/FPG International 78, 79, 137, 173, 244, 245, 251, 427; Arthur Tilley/Tony Stone Images 303; Bob Torrez/Tony Stone Images 195; John Terence Turner/FPG International 246, 278; Uniphoto 110, 111; Dana White/Photo Edit 30; Dana C. White/Dana White Productions 11 26 36, 87, 89, 97, 123, 175, 190, 206, 207, 209, 229, 259, 360, 366, 367, 368, 370, 372, 374, 379, 482, 483, 486; Dusty Willison/International Stock 19; David Young-Wolff/Photo Edit 7, 10, 18, 46, 54, 59, 83, 92, 98, 104, 131, 177, 201, 208, 224, 228, 252, 254, 255, 258, 268, 269, 274, 288, 289, 290, 302, 305, 311, 316, 317, 322, 332, 333, 343, 390, 399, 407, 489; David Young-Wolff/Tony Stone Images 38, 133, 270, 271.

Illustrations:

Shirley Bortoli 485, 507, 513, 518, 528; Anthony Cericola 282, 286–287, 304, 321, 365, 369, 375, 378, 381, 416, 454, 462, 468, 492; Sally Davies 430, 443, 456, 463; Steve Henry 256, 297; Jack Kershner 20, 33, 94, 121, 161, 225, 233, 250, 330, 391, 435, 474; Morgan Cain & Associates 442; Scott Ross 40–41, 47, 51, 101, 118, 128, 167; BB Sams 6, 178, 198, 213, 300–301; Dan Siculan 339–341, 376, 377, 383, 404, 415, 484; Margaret Sims 67